The **Rough Guide** to

Film

ROUGH GUIDES

Credits

Reference director: Andrew Lockett
Managing editor: Tracy Hopkins
Editors: Peter Buckley, Duncan Clark, Samantha Cook, Kilmeny Fane-Saunders, Sean Mahoney, Matthew Milton, Simon Smith, Joe Staines, Ruth Tidball, Patrick Davidson (consulting editor)
Picture research: Duncan Clark, Tracy Hopkins, Matthew Milton, Ruth Tidball
Layout: Dan May, Nikhil Agarwal
Proofreading: Jason Freeman
Cover: Chloë Roberts
Production: Rebecca Short

Authors: Richard Armstrong (RA), Tom Charity (TC), Lloyd Hughes (LH), Jessica Winter (JW)
Additional contributors: Roger Bardon (RB), Ronald Bergan (RBe), Michael Brooke (MB), Peter Buckley (PB), James Clarke (JC), Samantha Cook (SC), Richard Craig (RC), Eddie Dyja (ED), Mark Ellingham (ME), Erika Franklin (EF), Leslie Felperin (LF), Ali Jaafar (AJa), Alan Jones (AJ), Nick North (NN), Naman Ramachandran (NR), John Riley (JR), James Smart (JS)

Publishing information

This first edition published September 2007 by
Rough Guides Ltd, 80 Strand, London WC2R 0RL
345 Hudson St, 4th Floor, New York 10014, USA
Email: mail@roughguides.com

Distributed by the Penguin Group:
Penguin Books Ltd, 80 Strand, London WC2R 0RL
Penguin Putnam, Inc., 375 Hudson Street, NY 10014, USA
Penguin Group (Australia), 250 Camberwell Road, Camberwell, Victoria 3124, Australia
Penguin Books Canada Ltd, 90 Eglinton Avenue East, Suite 700, Toronto, Ontario, Canada, M4P 2YE
Penguin Group (New Zealand), Cnr Rosedale and Airborne Roads, Albany, Auckland, New Zealand

Printed in Italy by LegoPrint S.p.A.

The publishers and authors have done their best to ensure the accuracy and currency of all information in *The Rough Guide To Film*; however, they can accept no responsibility for any loss or inconvenience sustained by any reader as a result of its information or advice.

Typeset in Helvetica Neue and Din to an original design by Peter Buckley
672 pages; includes index

A catalogue record for this book is available from the British Library

ISBN 13: 978-1-84353-408-2
ISBN 10: 1-84353-408-8

1 3 5 7 9 8 6 4 2

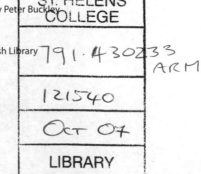

The **Rough Guide** to

Film

by
Richard Armstrong, Tom Charity,
Lloyd Hughes and Jessica Winter

ROUGH
GUIDES

Contents

Feature boxes

About the authors

Richard Armstrong

Richard Armstrong has written for *Film International*, *The Times Higher Education Supplement*, *Film Quarterly*, *Cineaste*, *Bright Lights Film Journal*, Australia's *Metro* and the online journal *Senses Of Cinema*. He is the author of *Billy Wilder* (2000) and *Understanding Realism* (2005), and a contributor to *The Encyclopedia Of The Documentary Film* (2005) and *France And The Americas: Culture, Politics, And History* (2005).

Richard would like to thank his supervisor, Dr Emma Wilson, for tolerating his lapses from the rigours of a Cambridge PhD to complete this project.

Tom Charity

Tom Charity is film critic for CNN.com and LOVEFiLM and a programming consultant for the Vancouver International Film Festival. He writes regularly for *Sight & Sound*, *Cinema Scope*, *Total Film*, *Uncut* and several British newspapers. His books include *John Cassavetes: Lifeworks* (2001) and *The Right Stuff* (1997), and he is an annual contributor to the *Time Out Film Guide*.

Tom would like to thank Fiona, Jay and Sacha for their patience, Mehilli Modi, Brad Stevens, Mark Peranson, Wai Mun Yoon, Helen Cowley, Andrew, Tracy and everyone at Rough Guides.

Lloyd Hughes

Lloyd Hughes has been reviewing films since the age of 11 for several listings magazines, the *Radio Times* and his own teenage opus *The Hughes Guide To Cinema* (sales: one copy). He has conducted interviews with hundreds of directors and stars over the last decade, and is the author of *The Rough Guide To Gangster Movies* (2005).

Lloyd would like to thank Sarah, Laura, Jane, Gareth, Edith, Liam, Sean and Aidan, as well as Tracy, Ruth and Andrew at Rough Guides.

Jessica Winter

Jessica Winter's writing appears in *Time Out London*, *The Boston Globe*, *Slate* and many other publications. She is associate editor at *Cinema Scope* and the author of *The Rough Guide To American Independent Film* (2006).

Jessica would like to thank the film department staff, past and present, at *Time Out London*: Derek Adams, Geoff Andrew, Nick Bradshaw, Dave Calhoun, Tom Charity, Gareth Evans, Wally Hammond, Trevor Johnston and Ben Walters. Thanks also to Michael Atkinson, Dennis Lim and Mark Peranson, and particularly Adrian Kinloch.

Introduction

When embarking on *The Rough Guide To Film* we had one central aim: to present the world of cinema through the lens of its leading directors. Of course, a set of nearly 840 director portraits hardly tells the whole story of the movies, which is as much an industry as an art form. In its day-to-day business of self-promotion, cinema always has more to say about its acting talent than its directorial stars, and when it comes to green-lighting and the final cut the decisions are mostly made by producers and financiers, not the man with the megaphone. But with the moneymen mostly shying away from the limelight and the big-name stars never out of it, we thought it high time that a popular guide shine a light on the directors. From professionals wielding a budget of millions to improvisers with only a DV camera and a shoestring crew, they are the people whose artistic vision is often what ultimately determines a film's value.

There is no shortage of film reviews out there – whether on the Internet or in large printed directories – but this wealth of information can actually be unhelpful to the viewer wanting to pick a film to see at the cinema or add to their DVD rental list. In *The Rough Guide To Film* we have prioritized quality over quantity, so that every film reviewed is one that is worthy of your time. That said, there are still over 2000 reviews in the book, so you will never be short of ideas for what to watch.

But there is much more to this book than reviews of individual movies: by describing each director's career, and the process by which they brought their films to the screen, this Rough Guide not only puts films in their context, but also provides an introduction to cinema itself. This ambition is reinforced by the feature boxes scattered throughout the text, in which we've covered other elements of the moviemaking business, from composers, cinematographers and actor-director partnerships to genres, film movements and national cinemas.

The book is intended to be a browser's paradise, with serendipitous juxtapositions of Hollywood big guns with arthouse miniaturists, cult horror directors with masters of classic European cinema. However, an alternative way to navigate is offered by the "Essential Films & Filmmakers" section at the beginning of the book, which includes lists of leading directors and essential films in specific genres or from different parts of the world.

Even within a book of 672 pages, we've not been able to include everything. In selecting which directors and films to include, we have tried to allow for all tastes, if not to equal degrees. The book gives priority to art over business and creativity over celebrity, preferring world cinema to mainstream ephemera that doesn't repay repeat viewing. We have aimed both to uncover new directors and to encourage readers to revisit great directors of the past. The book foregrounds the international and historical variety of the medium, from the best mainstream filmmakers of every decade to figures with their eye more on posterity than the box office. In the belief that many Hollywood blockbusters can look after themselves (or be left to gather dust), we have instead looked further afield to unearth films that will surely provide some new and welcome surprises for even the most assiduous browser of rental store shelves and online DVD catalogues.

With new DVDs being released every week and the likes of eBay offering second-hand copies of those titles that have fallen out of print, nearly all the films in the book will be available for viewing immediately (for a price) one way or another. This means our film selections have not been dictated by availability. Instead, the authors have been free to recommend whichever films they consider to be the very best of a director's work.

Of course you won't always agree with the film choices we have made, but if you write to us at mail@roughguides.com we'll be pleased to hear your views, and take them into account when preparing the next edition. We wish that even more films could have been included; feel free to let us know what you think they should have been, though it's worth checking out our other film books (see inside back cover) for specific guidance on genres from horror to chick flicks.

Sadly there are no Oscars we can hand out to the many writers and critics who have contributed to this Rough Guide, but there are many deserving cases, none more so than the four main authors, who have exercised tremendous patience and stamina for over three years while the book was being completed. If their passion for their subject gets you hooked on new directors, revives your interest in old favourites or just sends you off on a magical movie tour, then that's just what we intended the book to do.

How this book works

After the name of each director listed in this book we have supplied birth and, where appropriate, death dates. However, rather than indicate a director's nationality, we have supplied their country of birth, calling it by its current name (but indicating if it had a different name when the director was born). Details of where the director's career subsequently took them are outlined in the biographical sketch that follows.

The short reviews of a director's most important films are preceded by the film's title, its registration date, its running time, and (where applicable) whether it is in black and white (b/w). In the case of non-English-language films, we have given the name by which the film is best known in the English-speaking world, followed by either a translation of the title or the original. The key personnel involved in the making of the film are then listed: the major actors under *cast*; the cinematographer under *cin*; the composer under *m*. In the case of a documentary, participants are listed under *with*; in animation the voiceover artists are listed under *cast (voices)*.

Essential films & filmmakers

Out of the hundreds of directors listed and the thousands of films reviewed in *The Rough Guide To Film*, we have made a further selection that offers pointers and routes into the book. Arranged by genre and by country or continent, each list is further divided into five key directors, five essential classics and five less well-known films that deserve to be more widely seen. None of these lists is meant to be definitive, since discussion about which films constitute, say, the five greatest comedies or the five greatest Westerns is potentially limitless. The following represent the individual, and often highly personal, enthusiasms of our four expert authors and our other contributors, and they are designed to encourage browsing and exploration. Enjoy!

Action

5 Great Directors:
- Howard Hawks p.217
- Walter Hill p.226
- Sam Peckinpah p.418
- Raoul Walsh p.580
- John Woo p.612

5 Essential Classics:
- Children Of Men (2006) p.116
- Die Hard (1988) p.358
- Dr No (1962) p.619
- Face/Off (1997) p.613
- Raiders Of The Lost Ark (1981) p.528

5 Lesser-Known Gems
- Hatari! (1961) p.220
- House Of Flying Daggers (2004) p.625
- The Right Stuff (1983) p.267
- The Wages Of Fear (1953) p.101
- The Warriors (1979) p.227

Africa

5 Great Directors
- Nouri Bouzid p.57
- Youssef Chahine p.89
- Souleymane Cissé p.96
- Ousmane Sembène p.503
- Abderrahmane Sissako p.517

5 Essential Classics
- Cairo Station (1958) p.89
- Moolaadé (2004) p.504
- The Silences Of The Palace (1994) p.555
- Xala (1974) p.504
- Yeelen (1987) p.96

5 Lesser-Known Gems
- Abouna (2002) p.215
- Man Of Ashes (1986) p.57
- Tilaï (1990) p.404
- Waiting For Happiness (2002) p.517
- The Yacoubian Building (2006) p.xviii

American Indie

5 Great Directors
- John Cassavetes p.83
- Todd Haynes p.220
- Jim Jarmusch p.253
- Richard Linklater p.321
- John Sayles p.488

5 Essential Classics
- Bad Lieutenant (1992) p.167
- Before Sunset (2004) p.321
- Dead Man (1995) p.254

- Eraserhead (1977) p.331
- A Woman Under The Influence (1974) p.84

5 Lesser-Known Gems

- George Washington (2000) p.202
- Gummo (1997) p.286
- Heavy (1995) p.345
- Lone Star (1995) p.488
- Schizopolis (1996) p.523

Australasia

5 Great Directors

- Gillian Armstrong p.25
- Jane Campion p.76
- Baz Luhrmann p.327
- Phillip Noyce p.394
- Peter Weir p.594

5 Essential Classics

- Mad Max (1979) p.371
- The Piano (1993) p.76
- Picnic At Hanging Rock (1975) p.595
- Rabbit-Proof Fence (2002) p.395
- Strictly Ballroom (1992) p.328

5 Lesser-Known Gems

- The Chant Of Jimmie Blacksmith (1978) p.489
- Heavenly Creatures (1994) p.249
- Lantana (2001) p.301
- The Last Days Of Chez Nous (1990) p.26
- Newsfront (1978) p.395

Biopics

5 Great Directors

- Richard Attenborough p.29
- Milos Forman p.177
- Alexander Korda p.284
- Ken Russell p.481
- Martin Scorsese p.496

5 Essential Classics

- Amadeus (1984) p.179
- Gandhi (1982) p.29
- Lust For Life (1956) p.374
- Napoléon (1927) p.190
- Walk The Line (2005) p.345

5 Lesser-Known Gems

- The Chronicle Of Anna Magdalena Bach (1968) p.536
- Ed Wood (1994) p.71
- Lenny (1974) p.180
- The Private Life Of Henry VIII (1933) p.285
- Young Mr Lincoln (1939) p.176

Britain

5 Great Directors

- Terence Davies p.124
- David Lean p.303
- Michael Powell p.431
- Carol Reed p.447
- Nicolas Roeg p.467

5 Essential Classics

- Fallen Idol (1948) p.448
- The Ipcress File (1965) p.188
- Kind Hearts And Coronets (1949) p.211
- The Life And Death Of Colonel Blimp (1943) p.432
- The Red Shoes (1948) p.432

5 Lesser-Known Gems

- Career Girls (1997) p.310
- Deep End (1970) p.519
- Face (1997) p.49
- Made In Britain (1983) p.98
- Ratcatcher (1999) p.440

Canada

5 Great Directors

- Denys Arcand p.24
- David Cronenberg p.114
- Atom Egoyan p.153
- Guy Maddin p.336
- Patricia Rozema p.478

5 Essential Classics

- Archangel (1990) p.337
- I've Heard The Mermaids Singing (1987) p.478
- Jesus Of Montreal (1989) p.24
- The Sweet Hereafter (1997) p.154
- Videodrome (1982) p.115

5 Lesser-Known Gems

- Atanarjuat: The Fast Runner (2001) p.291
- The Barbarian Invasions (2003) p.24
- The Confessional (1995) p.315
- Exotica (1994) p.154
- Shivers (1975) p.115

Chick Flicks

5 Great Directors

- Frank Borzage p.56
- George Cukor p.116
- Garry Marshall p.350
- Susan Seidelman p.503
- Douglas Sirk p.514

Author favourites

Richard Armstrong

- Crimes And Misdemeanors (1989) p.8
- Man Of The West (1958) p.347
- Partie de campagne (1936) p.454
- Sullivan's Travels (1941) p.540
- Sunset Blvd (1950) p.606

Lloyd Hughes

- Les amants du Pont-neuf (1991) p.78
- Bringing Up Baby (1938) p.218
- Chinatown (1974) p.426
- Magnolia (1999) p.17
- The Passenger (1975) p.23

Tom Charity

- The Palm Beach Story (1942) p.540
- A Woman Under The Influence (1974) p.84
- The Magnificent Ambersons (1942) p.598
- In A Lonely Place (1950) p.444
- The Crime Of Monsieur Lange (1936) p.454

Jessica Winter

- Aguirre, The Wrath Of God (1972) p.224
- Chungking Express (1994) p.612
- Pierrot le fou (1965) p.199
- The Spirit Of The Beehive (1973) p.159
- Vertigo (1958) p.232

Middle East & Turkey

5 Great Directors
- Amos Gitai p.196
- Yilmaz Güney p.209
- Abbas Kiarostami p.275
- Mohsen Makhmalbaf p.338
- Jafar Panahi p.410

5 Essential Classics
- Close-Up (1989) p.277
- Gabbeh (1996) p.338
- Offside (2006) p.410
- The Wind Will Carry Us (1999) p.277
- Yol (1982) p.335

5 Lesser-Known Gems
- Blackboards (2000) p.340
- Rana's Wedding (2002) p.1
- Uzak (2002) p.86
- Wedding In Galilee (1987) p.275
- West Beirut (1998) p.144

Musicals

5 Great Directors
- Busby Berkeley p.44
- Jacques Demy p.129
- Stanley Donen p.142
- Bob Fosse p.179
- Vincente Minnelli p.372

5 Essential Classics
- Cabaret (1972) p.180
- Meet Me In St Louis (1944) p.372
- Les parapluies de Cherbourg (1964) p.130
- Singin' In The Rain (1952) p.143
- Top Hat (1935) p.484

5 Lesser-Known Gems
- Expresso Bongo (1959) p.208
- Gold Diggers Of 1935 (1935) p.45
- Love Me Tonight (1932) p.344
- Nashville (1975) p.15
- Zouzou (1934) p.6

Period Drama

5 Great Directors
- Nicholas Hytner p.242
- Anthony Minghella p.371
- Jean-Pierre Rappeneau p.440
- Tony Richardson p.458
- István Szabó p.542

5 Essential Classics
- Elizabeth (1998) p.264
- Gangs Of New York (2002) p.499
- The Go-Between (1970) p.324
- The Horseman On The Roof (1995) p.441
- The Scarlet Empress (1934) p.6

5 Lesser-Known Gems
- Blanche (1971) p.55
- The Charge Of The Light Brigade (1968) p.459
- The Draughtsman's Contract (1982) p.203

Ones to watch: directors for the future

With new directorial talent emerging all the time, there are inevitably some promising filmmakers who haven't yet produced a large enough body of work to merit an entry in this book. We'll be keeping an eye on them for the next edition of *The Rough Guide To Film*, but in the meantime here is the lowdown on some exciting and intriguing new faces, and the films which have made critics and viewers curious to see more.

Andrea Arnold UK, 1961–
Red Road, 2006, 113 min

Scottish director Andrea Arnold won the jury prize at Cannes and the plaudits of many critics with her debut *Red Road*, a naturalistic thriller with a CCTV premise. With echoes of Dogme and the Dardennes brothers, this gritty sexual revenge drama set among Glaswegian tower blocks was edgy, stylish and thought-provoking, with a strong take on female sexuality.

Judd Apatow US, 1967–
Knocked Up, 2006, 129 min

Apatow writes, directs and occasionally acts in films, but the common thread is humour: *Knocked Up* follows hard on the heels of *The 40 Year Old Virgin* (2005). A one-night stand between slacker Ben (Seth Rogen) and Alison (Katherine Heigl) leads to an unwanted pregnancy. Apatow's twenty-first-century comedy of manners is laced with intelligence and realism.

Florian Henckel von Donnersmarck
Germany, 1973–
The Lives Of Others (Das Leben der Anderen) 2006, 137 min

The perfectionist director spent several years bringing this Cold War opus to the screen, but it was time well spent. In East Germany, a state-sanctioned writer and his girlfriend are caught in the web of Stasi surveillance and state control, but one of the spies discovers his humanity whilst on watch. The film deservedly won the Oscar for best foreign-language film. Von Donnersmarck has also won prizes for his numerous shorts so his next feature is eagerly anticipated.

Oliver Hirschbiegel Germany, 1957–
Downfall (Der Untergang), 2004, 156 min

In Oliver Hirschbiegel's *Downfall*, Bruno Ganz stars as Adolf Hitler holed up in the Berlin bunker with his young secretary, Joseph Goebbels and others. Recounting Hitler's last days, the film works as both a meticulous historical reconstruction and an unnerving character drama. Along with his thoughtful prison thriller *Das Experiment* (2001), it suggests Hirschbiegel's Hollywood work, when it is released, will be worth looking out for.

Marwan Hamed Egypt, 1977–
The Yacoubian Building (Omaret yacoubean), 2006, 161 min

Adapted from the best-selling novel by Alaa Al Aswany, Hamed's multi-layered story about the inhabitants of an apartment block in Cairo was a big-budget box-office success in Egypt, daring to air controversial topics like homosexuality within its state-of-the-nation panorama. Only in his twenties when making the film, the director coaxed memorable performances from the cream of Egyptian acting talent.

Gavin Hood South Africa, 1963–
Tsotsi, 2005, 94 min

It is not that usual for a South African director to make it big, so Hood's success with *Tsotsi* is remarkable. A multi-language version of an Athol Fugard novel, it tells the story of a township gangster who finds himself in charge of a baby after a botched car-jacking. The film's heart-on-sleeve approach sometimes overreaches, but *Tsotsi* is well acted, and ultimately compelling. Hood's next feature, about the political hot potato of "rendition", looks like another big challenge.

Andrew Jarecki US, 1963–
Capturing The Friedmans, 2003, 107 min

Documentary has gone mainstream in the last few years, after decades of being written off as box-office poison. The Jarecki brothers have been at the forefront of this resurgence. Eugene's *Why We Fight* (2004) was, like most recent fare, aimed at obvious political targets, but Andrew's debut probed the more problematic terrain of a real child-molestation case. Through the use of the Friedmans' own home-video footage, the film asked whether we can really know the "truth" about lives which are so often a blend of fiction, fantasy and fact.

Kimberly Peirce US, 1967–
Boys Don't Cry, 1999, 118 min

Peirce's *Boys Don't Cry* was one of the hottest indie debuts of recent years, with its true-life story of a teenager (superbly played by the Oscar-winning Hilary Swank) who is considered a popular guy in a small Nebraskan town – until "he" is discovered to be female. The trailer-park milieu and the conviction with which the characters are drawn suggests a director destined for further great things – even if a little patience seems to be required.

Paul Andrew Williams UK, 1973–
London To Brighton, 2006, 85 min

The nasty underbelly of contemporary Britain is exposed in Williams' clever micro-budget debut feature. He uses all the tricks of guerilla filmmaking to bring the film to screen without compromising on quality. Pimps, prostitutes, low-rent criminals and general grimness permeate this unromantic slice of life, but the film is also a masterclass in carefully maintained suspense and thoughtful narrative.

Andrei Zvyagintsev Russia, 1964–
The Return (Vozvrashcheniye), 2003, 105 min

A long-absent father returns to his two teenage sons in a sleepy Russian town. Out of this simple premise Zvyagintsev crafts a multi-layered, uneasy allegory which won major prizes at the Venice Film Festival and the BBC Four World Cinema Awards. The director's cool and artful direction has raised hopes not only for his future work but also for the future of Russian art cinema.

Hany Abu-Assad

Israel, 1961–

Palestinian director Hany Abu-Assad took guerrilla filmmaking to new levels when he filmed his suicide bomber story *Paradise Now* (2005) on location in the Palestinian city of Nablus during the second intifada. One of his location managers was kidnapped by Palestinian militants, and his crew were repeatedly caught in the crossfire of gun battles between the Israeli army and Palestinian militias. That the film survived this baptism of fire – not to mention its incendiary plot – to emerge as a deeply humanistic work is testament to its director's sensitivity.

His feature debut, *Rana's Wedding* (2002), about a young Palestinian woman evading Israeli checkpoints to get to her wedding on time, was a sign of things to come. *Ford Transit*, also 2002, mixed documentary solemnity with feature-film kicks, following young Palestinian taxi driver Rajai as he treats Israeli roadblocks as his own personal assault course. Abu-Assad uses a quote from Palestinian poet Mahmud Darwish to end *Rana's Wedding*: "Under siege, life is the moment between remembrance of the first moment and forgetfulness of the last." The director himself has become the most eloquent cinematic spokesperson for life stuck in that moment. AJa

Rana's Wedding 2002, 90 min
cast Clara Khoury, Khalifa Natour, Ismael Dabbagh, Bushma Karaman *cin* Brigit Hillenius *m* Mariecke van der Linden, Bashar Abd' Rabbou

Clara Khoury plays Rana, a middle-class Palestinian woman frantically searching for her fiancé amidst the roadblocks of Jerusalem as she tries to get married before a midnight deadline. Leaving the politics in the background, Abu-Assad instead focuses on the daily trials of life under occupation, successfully depicting a region where valleys bathed in sunshine sit alongside buildings reduced to rubble.

Paradise Now 2005, 90 min
cast Kais Nashef, Ali Suliman, Lubna Azabal, Hiam Abbas, Amer Hlehel, Ashraf Barhoum *cin* Antoine Heberlé

Paradise Now depicts 48 hours in the lives of two Palestinian best friends chosen to become suicide bombers. Abu-Assad undercuts the inevitable vainglorious posturing with the all-too-human doubts that gradually envelop the two men as they grapple with the consequences of their choice. An important film for its dispassionate and at times surprisingly funny take on the tragedy of the Israeli-Palestinian conflict.

Carine Adler

Brazil, 1948–

Made when the director was in her forties, Carine Adler's *Under The Skin* (1997) was a rare examination of grief from a woman's perspective, and an adventure in style during a time of exceptional hope for British cinema.

Adler's debut, the short *Fever* (1994), was made possible by the British Film Institute's Production Fund, and was distinguished by a sensitive performance from Katrin Cartlidge. The head of the Fund told Adler that she was "great at scenes about sex", and what distinguishes her small oeuvre is the fusion of her protagonists' desire and their sense of inferiority. As in the work of Catherine Breillat, these are films about how sex feels if you are a woman.

Amongst a cluster of festival accolades, *Under The Skin* beat off competition from *Regeneration*, *The Full Monty* and *Nil By Mouth* to win Edinburgh's Michael Powell Award for best feature. While these films embody the dominant aesthetics of British filmmaking, Adler's feature has done much to carve a niche for a genuine women's cinema in Britain. RA

Under The Skin 1997, 82 min
cast Samantha Morton, Claire Rushbrook, Rita Tushingham, Christine Tremarco, Stuart Townsend *cin* Barry Ackroyd *m* Ilona Sekacz

Under The Skin traces the wounded odyssey of Iris (Samantha Morton, in her first feature film), a young woman whose mother dies suddenly of a brain tumour. Consumed with loss and in grave dispute with sister Rose (Claire Rushbrook) over the maternal legacy, Iris dons her mother's clinical wig, sunglasses and fur coat and sets out on a voyage of self-discovery in the streets and porn cinemas of Merseyside. With Iris's decentred will written into every jump cut and disconcerted camera move, this film represents a powerful new modernist impulse in British cinema.

A

Alexandre Aja

France, 1978–

The son of Algerian director Alexandre Arcady and French cinema critic Marie-Jo Jouan, Alexandre Jouan Arcady adopted the surname Aja based on his initials. His directorial debut was the black-and-white short *Over The Rainbow* (1997). After co-writing his father's *Break Of Dawn* (2002) with best friend/constant associate Gregory Levasseur, Aja scripted and directed his feature debut *Furia* (1999), a sci-fi mystery based on Julio Cortaza's novella *Graffiti*. Raised on gruesome video nasties and a fan of such survival shockers as Wes Craven's *The Last House On The Left* (1972), Aja's chosen genre was hard-core horror. *Haute tension* (*Switchblade Romance*, 2003), produced by Luc Besson, put him on the international "Splat Pack" map. Impressed, Craven let Aja loose on the remake of his 1977 classic *The Hills Have Eyes* (2006), to further acclaim. AJ

Haute tension (Switchblade Romance) 2003, 91 min

cast Cécile de France, Maïwenn Le Besco, Philippe Nahon, Franck Khalfoun, Andrei Finti *cin* Maxim Alexandre *m* François Eudes

Psycho Philippe Nahon defines the grim atmosphere of Aja's slash-fest, which is infused with the garishness of Dario Argento and the dazzle of Brian De Palma. De France follows her abducted friend Le Besco into a psychosexual creepy-crawly space that tests her ingenuity and sanity with nerve-jangling suspense, flinch-inducing blood-letting and an astonishing (some say ludicrous) final twist. A twenty-first-century primal scream.

The Hills Have Eyes 2006, 90 min

cast Aaron Stanford, Kathleen Quinlan, Emilie de Ravin, Robert Joy, Ted Levine, Vinessa Shaw *cin* Maxime Alexandre *m* tomandandy

The hills are alive with the sound of mutants! Craven's searing exploration of the extremes of contemporary American society is expertly re-tooled into an intensely savage survival shocker of the most artfully deranged kind. The graphic rape, torture and murder spree lasting twelve terrifying minutes pushes back the psyche-shaking boundaries.

Chantal Akerman

Belgium, 1950–

The *Village Voice*'s film critic J. Hoberman once boldly described Chantal Akerman as "comparable in force and originality to Godard or Fassbinder … arguably the most important European director of her generation". Far more read about than viewed, Akerman's oeuvre comprises over forty films, more than half of them feature-length works of fiction or documentary. Only a handful, mostly her weaker recent films, are available on video or DVD. And yet directors as diverse as Todd Haynes, Catherine Breillat, Claire Denis, Michael Haneke and Sally

Potter have cited her influence. Although sometimes resistant of the label "feminist", Akerman consistently examines "women's work", from domestic chores to emotional triage, and has attempted to forge a female-centric aesthetic, at odds with the linear structures of traditional, male-dominated cinematic narrative.

Akerman is the daughter of Polish Jews, both of them Holocaust survivors. In both her fiction and documentary work she often addresses their suffering and her difficult relationship with them, especially her mother. For example, in the kaleidoscopic documentary *News From Home* (1977) images of New York are cut together against a voiceover of Akerman reading her mother's letters.

At 15 years old, she was inspired to become a filmmaker while watching Jean-Luc Godard's *Pierrot le fou* (1965), and vowed to make films with a similar immediacy, "like talking to one person". She enrolled at the Brussels film school INSAS, but dropped out, eager to get on with making her own films. At just 18 she shot the short *Saute ma ville* (*Blow Up My Town*) in a night, starring in it herself as a fidgety adolescent girl who potters in her kitchen, burns a letter and then commits suicide. (One doesn't go to Akerman films for laughs.) Domestic routine and sudden violence were recurrent elements in her early work.

Restlessness, self-exposure and alienation are threaded as themes throughout Akerman's oeuvre, but any autobiographical elements are shrouded in fiction so that her films conceal as much as they expose. In *Les rendez-vous d'Anna* (1978), for example, regular actor-collaborator Aurore Clément plays a female film director with serious mother issues, who travels across northern Europe via a series of anonymous hotel rooms and train stations. In her gallery installation *Selfportrait/Autobiography: A Work In Progress*, Akerman teasingly set up her fictional realms in "conversation" with straight autobiography by running monitors showing clips from *Jeanne Dielman, 23 Quai du Commerce, 1080 Bruxelles* (1975), *Toute une nuit* (*A Whole Night*, 1982) and *Hotel Monterey* (1972) while an audio-tape played a recording of her reading from her novella-length portrait of her parents and herself, *A Family In Brussels*.

Recently, Akerman's cinematic work has become more narrative-driven. Diehard fans defended *The Captive* (2000), her adaptation of a Proust volume. But even her most zealous acolytes feel hard-pressed to love the flat, joyless comedy *Couch In New York* (1996) or the frenetic yet fizz-free *Tomorrow We Move* (2004). In many respects, Akerman was more interesting when she was "boring". LF

Je, tu, il, elle (I, You, He, She) 1974, 85 min, b/w

cast Chantal Anne Akerman, Niels Arestrup, Claire Wauthion *cin* Bénédict Delsalle, Charlotte Slovak, Renelde Dupon

Made immediately before *Jeanne Dielman*, this film is imbued with restlessness just as *Jeanne* is suffused with austerity. Akerman plays the "I" of the title who in three disjointed sections anxiously redecorates her apartment, has a tryst with a trucker, and then bickers with her female lover. Long voiceover monologues both complement and clash with the actions depicted, creating an overall sense of temporal and spiritual disjunction.

Jeanne Dielman, 23 Quai du Commerce, 1080 Bruxelles 1975, 225 min

cast Delphine Seyrig, Jan Decorte, Henri Storck, Jacques Doniol-Valcroze, Yves Bical, Chantal Akerman *cin* Babette Mangolte

Akerman's best-known film meticulously records, in medium shots, its titular character (Delphine Seyrig) preparing food, tidying her house, receiving clients for bouts of paid sex, changing her sheets and so on. An act of murder brings a blessed sense of shock after nearly three hours of hypnotic routine activities. *Jeanne Dielman* has, nevertheless, become a key text for both radical feminists and students of 1970s materialist cinema.

The Captive (La captive) 2000, 118 min

cast Stanislas Merhar, Sylvie Testud, Olivia Bonamy, Liliane Rovère, Françoise Bertin, Aurore Clément *cin* Sabine Lancelin

One of the best of Akerman's recent films, this adaptation of *The Prisoner*, the fifth volume of Proust's *Remembrance Of Things Past*, transposes the action to modern-day Brussels. Sylvie Testud (now a regular Akerman collaborator) plays Ariane, the listless love object of Simon (Stanislas Merhar). The two correspond to Proust's dysfunctional lovers Marcel and Albertine, but filtered through Hitchcock's *Vertigo* and the language games of the *nouvelle roman* movement.

Moustapha Akkad
Syria, 1930–2005

The Syrian-born Akkad will likely be remembered for two rather incongruous achievements: bringing the story of the birth of Islam to Western audiences by directing *The Message* (1976) and producing the *Halloween* series of horror films.

One of the first to see the potential – and need – for East-West dialogue, Akkad directed both English and Arabic versions of *The Message*, resulting in the unlikely sight of Anthony Quinn playing Hamza, the Prophet Mohammed's uncle. Though the film achieved only moderate box-office success, Akkad followed it up with another Quinn collaboration, *Lion Of The Desert* (1981). Reputedly financed by Libyan leader Muammar Gaddafi, it told the story of Libyan nationalist Omar Mukhtar's World War I resistance to the Italian invasion of the country. For all Akkad's directorial efforts, however, it was with his stewardship of the *Halloween* series that he made his biggest impact in Hollywood, helping set the template for horror movies with the films' modest budgets, profitable returns and diminishing artistic ambition.

Akkad died in a terrorist attack while attending a wedding in Jordan in 2005. The irony that the man who did so much to promote the positive portrayal of Arabs and Muslims in the West would die at the hands of an Islamic extremist only heightened the tragedy. AJa

The Message (Al-risalah) 1976, 220 min

cast Anthony Quinn, Irene Papas, Michael Ansara, Johnny Sekka, Michael Forest, Damien Thomas *cin* Jack Hildyard *m* Maurice Jarre

Anthony Quinn plays Hamza, the uncle of the Prophet Mohammed, in this epic retelling of the birth of Islam. The Prophet himself is never shown on screen, with characters addressing him by talking straight to camera and responding to comments we cannot hear. Akkad charts the growing influence of Mohammed and his message in seventh-century Arabia with fitting respectfulness and dramatic sweep.

Fatih Akin
Germany, 1973–

The son of Turkish immigrants to Germany, Akin made his way into the film business via Hamburg's College of Fine Arts, but it would be truer to say he graduated from the university of the city's streets. Drawing heavily on friends and relatives (including his brother Cem) for cast, crew and favours, Akin's films demonstrate a particular brand of raw, low-budget alchemy. Central to his vision are the pains and passions of the immigrant and *Gastarbeiter* experience in Germany, in particular that of his fellow Turks.

Akin caught some critics' eyes with the melodramatic *Short Sharp Shock!* (1998), in which three friends get involved in the local crime scene before Balkan passions lead Scorsese-style to a violent finale. In *Solino* (2002) an Italian couple move to Germany in the 1960s to set up a pizza parlour. *Head-On* (2004), which won the Golden Bear at the Berlin Film Festival, was his breakthrough film, its exploration of the contradictions of dual identities framed by a series of Bosphorus-set musical interludes. The documentary *Crossing The Bridge: The Sound Of Istanbul* (2005) extended the musical theme, tapping into interest in the city fostered by director Nuri Bilge Ceylan and the writer Orhan Pamuk. RC

Head-On (Gegen die Wand) 2004, 121 min

cast Birol Unel, Sibel Kekilli, Meltem Cumbul, Güven Kiraç, Catrin Striebeck *cin* Rainer Klausmann *m* Alexander Hacke, Maceo Parker

Grungy youth culture, trauma, humour and massive substance abuse signal we are in *Trainspotting* territory, Hamburg-style. And indeed the volatile characters and breakneck plot, which hurtles perilously from one obstacle to the next, make for a terrifically thrilling but heartfelt ride. Birol Unel is disturbingly convincing as Cahit, a self-destructive loner who meets the damaged Sibel (Sibel Kekilli) and agrees to marry her to enable her to escape her conservative Turkish family.

John Akomfrah
Ghana, 1957–

Of the black British filmmakers who arose in the 1980s, John Akomfrah dealt the most lyrically with the diaspora that shaped Black Britain.

The son of political activists, Akomfrah studied sociology at Portsmouth Polytechnic. After graduating in 1982, he moved to London and co-founded the Black Audio Film Collective, which became a defining force in minority filmmaking during a difficult era. His first film, *Handsworth Songs* (1986), won the John Grierson Award. Subsequent works have not lived up to its promise; this is due partly to the decline in funding for the experimental aesthetic that marks Akomfrah's strongest films. *Testament* (1988) follows a Ghanaian journalist to her country to trace a friend caught up in political unrest. Its fusion of the rational documentary she seeks to make with the lyricism of her interior journey is intriguing. Such balance is missing from *Who Needs A Heart* (1991), which charts the iconic image and corrupt reality of the British Black Power activist Michael X, while *The Last Angel Of History* (1995) employs a now-dated cyber/sci-fi template to search out literary resonances of the alienation and dislocation that marked the African migrant experience.

Akomfrah has turned increasingly to television – the British Film Institute production *Speak Like A Child* (1998) explored the search for identity through a drama involving children in an isolated institution discovering their sexuality. Even through his less successful work, Akomfrah has pushed out the boundaries of contemporary documentary. RA

Handsworth Songs 1986, 61 min
with Handsworth and Aston Welfare Association, Asian Youth Movement (Birmingham) *cin* Sebastian Shah *m* Trevor Mathison

Drawing upon the full range of expression available within the language of film, this extraordinary account of the Handsworth race riots and their political fallout brings poetic resonance to the dreams and recollections of a generation of black British immigrants.

Robert Aldrich
US, 1918–83

Robert Aldrich was the black sheep of his family, and he liked it that way. Grandson of a senator and a cousin to the Rockefellers, Aldrich could trace his ancestry back to the Mayflower. It was by choice that he started on the lowest rung of the Hollywood ladder, as a production clerk at RKO.

Aldrich quickly worked his way up to assistant director. In that capacity he served his apprenticeship to such masters as Jean Renoir (*The Southerner*, 1945), William Wellman, Lewis Milestone, Joseph Losey and even Charlie Chaplin (*Limelight*, 1952). He completed his education at the short-lived independent Enterprise, where he worked with Robert Rossen, John Garfield and Abraham Polonsky on social conscience dramas like *Body And Soul* (1947) and *Force Of Evil* (1948). (Rossen and Polonsky would both be blacklisted soon afterwards.)

Aldrich graduated to director with a couple of B-movies, then moved up a notch when Burt Lancaster hired him for the seminal "liberal" Western *Apache* (1954). The follow-up, *Vera Cruz* (1954), was very different – a slick cowboy movie pitting Lancaster against Gary Cooper in a cynical comedy of one-upmanship. It was a clear harbinger for Sergio Leone's spaghetti Westerns. (Leone, incidentally, served as assistant director on Aldrich's ill-starred *Sodom And Gomorrah*, 1962.)

Aldrich established himself as an early favourite of *Cahiers du cinéma* critics such as François Truffaut and Jacques Rivette with a remarkable run of tough, provocative pictures – *Kiss Me Deadly* (1955), *The Big Knife* (1955), *Autumn Leaves* (1956) and *Attack!* (1956). These were lauded in Europe but lambasted as violent, tasteless and excessive in the US. Rivette identified Aldrich, along with Nicholas Ray, Richard Brooks and Anthony Mann, as "the future of the cinema". For Truffaut, he was a key filmmaker of the "atomic" age.

Inevitably, there was a slump. Aldrich's subsequent output was wildly erratic in terms of quality, and indeed in its commercial reception, but consistent in other ways. He built a trusted team of collaborators, from cinematographer Joseph Biroc, who shot 22 of his 29 films, to screenwriter Lukas Heller, who wrote six of them, and even operated his own studio for a period in the late 1960s and early 1970s.

Stylistically, Aldrich's films are intense, even overwrought. The tone is often savagely satiric. Aldrich made penetrating films about male groups (*The Flight Of The Phoenix*, 1966; *The Dirty Dozen*, 1967; *The Longest Yard*, 1974) and about women (*What Ever Happened To Baby Jane?*, 1962; *The Killing Of Sister George*, 1968), but rarely about romantic love or the heterosexual couple.

Thematically, his films are characterized by their complete distrust of authority, psychologically flawed (anti-)heroes, and an existential world-view tempered with compassion and progressive democratic instincts. In an Aldrich movie, redemption may be futile, even suicidal, but self-determination is still the best you can shoot for.

While the *Cahiers* view on Aldrich's 1950s films has prevailed, the more variable 1960s work is understandably contentious, and the movies from his last – richest – decade remain severely underrated. RA

Sibling rivalry: Baby Jane Hudson (Bette Davis) and her invalid sister (Joan Crawford) in *What Ever Happened To Baby Jane?*

Kiss Me Deadly 1955, 106 min, b/w

cast Ralph Meeker, Albert Dekker, Maxine Cooper, Paul Stewart, Gaby Rodgers, Cloris Leachman, Jack Lambert *cin* Ernest Laszlo *m* Frank De Vol

The first true Aldrich movie. Buying his control by accepting a B-movie production, Aldrich took Mickey Spillane's sleazy novel and shook it upside down. Ralph Meeker's Mike Hammer becomes a brutish American thug in reckless pursuit of "the great whatsit", no matter the cost. This is *film noir* at its most apocalyptic.

What Ever Happened To Baby Jane? 1962, 134 min, b/w

cast Bette Davis, Joan Crawford, Victor Buono, Anna Lee, Maidie Norman, Marjorie Bennet *cin* Ernest Haller *m* Frank De Vol

An acerbic satire on Hollywood, with a gothic/black comic twist. Bette Davis and Joan Crawford are antiquated icons of ghoulish glamour living out their days near-enough isolated from the outside world. The script is littered with now-infamous lines, while the two leading ladies deliver memorable performances.

The Grissom Gang 1971, 128 min

cast Kim Darby, Scott Wilson, Tony Musante, Robert Lansing, Connie Stevens *cin* Joseph F. Biroc *m* Gerald Fried

Probably Aldrich's most undervalued film, this pitch-black take on the kidnap novel *No Orchids For Miss Blandish*, penned by crime-writer James Hadley Chase, is a grotesque parody of American family values and the class conflict. It's also as close as Aldrich ever got to filming a love story.

Ulzana's Raid 1972, 105 min

cast Burt Lancaster, Bruce Davison, Jorge Luke, Richard Jaeckel, Joaquin Martinez, Lloyd Bochner, Karl Swenson *cin* Joseph F. Biroc *m* Frank De Vol

Aldrich was revising Western conventions in the 1950s, but by 1972 he was free to do so without censorship or compromise. This mature masterpiece also figures as the last of his singularly bleak, challenging war movies. Burt Lancaster plays McIntosh, the scout who helps the US cavalry in their hunt for Ulzana and his followers, who have left their reservation.

Twilight's Last Gleaming 1977, 146 min

cast Burt Lancaster, Richard Widmark, Charles Durning, Melvyn Douglas, Paul Winfield, Burt Young *cin* Robert B. Hauser *m* Jerry Goldsmith

One of Hollywood's most politically minded directors, it is fitting that Aldrich made the last great conspiracy thriller of the Watergate era. This is a scarily cogent film about government corruption, nuclear brinksmanship and idealism gone insane. Charles Durning gives a sterling performance as the US president.

Marc Allégret

Switzerland, 1900–73

It is thanks to Marc Allégret that we have Brigitte Bardot, although it took Roger Vadim and then the auteurs of the post-war *nouvelle vague* to make her a household name.

Allégret assisted on author André Gide's documentary *Voyage au Congo* (1926). Briefly an assistant to French director Robert Florey, in the 1930s Allégret established himself as a key industry player. *Mam'zelle Nitouche* (1931), *Fanny* (1932), an episode in screenwriter Marcel Pagnol's Midi trilogy, *Lac aux dames* (*Ladies' Lake*, 1934), *Zouzou* (1934), the poetic realist *Gribouille* (*Heart Of Paris*, 1937) and *Orage* (*Storm*, 1938) all marked Allégret as an efficient chronicler of cinematic taste and a habitual discoverer of talent.

Although glossy post-war projects such as *Blanche Fury* (1948) and the Italian Hedy Lamarr junket *L'amante di paride* (*Loves Of Three Queens*, 1953) seem forgettable, without Allégret and these films we might never have had Simone Simon, Jean-Pierre Aumont, Michèle Morgan, Gérard Philipe and Jeanne Moreau. RA

Lac aux dames (Ladies' Lake) 1934, 94 min, b/w
cast Jean-Pierre Aumont, Simone Simon, Rosine Deréan, Illa Meery, Odette Joyeux, Vladimir Sokoloff, Paul Asselin *cin* Jules Kruger *m* Georges Auric

A continental tribute to the Hollywood star vehicle, this Tyrolean romp sees Jean-Pierre Aumont's handsome skiing instructor charm debutant Simone Simon as well as Rosine Deréan and Illa Meery. It has all the frissons of performance that you'd expect from RKO in its prime.

Zouzou 1934, 90 min, b/w
cast Josephine Baker, Jean Gabin, Pierre Larquey, Yvette Lebon *cin* Boris Kaufman, Michel Kelber, Jacques Mercanton, Louis Née *m* Boris Kaufman

Limbering up for his doomed poetic realists, here Jean Gabin remains aloof but alluring amidst a *bal musette* milieu which has all but disappeared. Josephine Baker lives up to her vivacious reputation as the laundress who longs to be on the stage and is in love with her childhood friend Gabin.

Irwin Allen

US, 1916–91

Producer-director Irwin Allen was nicknamed the "Master of Disaster". Arguably, the last word alone would have made a more accurate moniker for the filmmaker. His catastrophe-driven movies spilled over with continuity errors, inadvertent punchlines and all-around benumbing hysteria. Yet his sloppy showmanship hit paydirt with the disaster-pic fad of the mid-1970s.

In *The Story Of Mankind* (1957), Allen made a lunge towards topicality in exploiting contemporary fears about the hydrogen bomb. It, sadly, marked the last film in which all three Marx Brothers would appear, albeit not together (though Harpo does play Isaac Newton!). *The Lost World* (1960) sent Claude Rains into the Amazon to find evidence of still-living dinosaurs, before Allen managed to parlay his ridiculously convoluted *Voyage To The Bottom Of The Sea* (1961) into a successful series for television, the medium he would spend most of his career working in.

It's probably no coincidence that Allen's most coherent and financially successful film, *The Towering Inferno* (1974), had a co-director, John Guillermin (who would go on to direct the 1976 *King Kong* remake). After setting the world's tallest skyscraper alight, Allen unleashed millions of killer bees in *The Swarm* (1978), a bad-movie milestone with an epic body count and Michael Caine as a world-saving entomologist. Despite the movie's box-office failure and unquestionable awfulness, Allen was able to lure Caine into another collaboration, *Beyond The Poseidon Adventure* (1979). Indeed, given the starry casts of *Inferno* (Paul Newman, Steve McQueen, Faye Dunaway and Fred Astaire) and *Swarm* (Richard Widmark, Henry Fonda, Olivia de Havilland and José Ferrer), Irwin's most valuable gift might have been his voodoo-like ability to recruit respected actors to participate in histrionic nonsense. JW

The Towering Inferno 1974, 158 min
cast Steve McQueen, Paul Newman, William Holden, Faye Dunaway, Fred Astaire *cin* Fred J. Koenekamp, Jim Freeman *m* John Williams

With John Guillermin, the uncredited Allen co-directed this epic of panic and escape, in which the world's newly-anointed tallest building, a glass tower in San Francisco, catches fire and traps an ensemble of VIPs inside. Starring Paul Newman as the skyscraper's architect and Steve McQueen as the brave fire chief, the movie tapped the mid-1970s disaster-pic zeitgeist to massive box-office success.

Woody Allen

US, 1935–

Woody Allen is one of the most distinctive American directors of the post-war period. Having released almost a film a year for 35 years, and articulated in literate terms the ethical misgivings of his generation, Allen has staged the vicissitudes of contemporary culture with more humour and pity than any other American director.

Destined to become an actor and screenwriter as well as director, Allen Stewart Konigsberg started out as a gag writer for television, newspaper columns and stage revues. In 1961 he began performing his own material in Greenwich Village cafés, quickly making his mark on the university campus circuit. Allen traded on a now-familiar brand of self-deprecating comedy and cynical understatement suffused with knowing references to philosophy, literature, psychoanalysis and his Brooklyn Jewish upbringing. Television appearances followed, and in 1965 he wrote and starred in *What's New, Pussycat?*, a modish slapstick romp foregrounding the sexual confusion of the bespectacled, shy young Jew before a world of beautiful women.

Allen's first directed film was *Take The Money And Run* (1969), a crime spoof which set the slapstick tone for Allen's early works. In a series of parodies – *Bananas* (1971), *Everything You Always Wanted To Know About Sex, But Were Afraid To Ask* (1972), *Sleeper* (1973), *Love And Death* (1975) – Allen honed his directing skills and sought a balance between slapstick, cerebral stand-up comedy and coherent screen narrative.

Since 1975, this project has seen the director alternate between light comedy and serious drama. His finest works – *Manhattan* (1979), *Hannah And Her Sisters* (1986), *Crimes And Misdemeanors* (1989) – pull off the complex assignment of combining comedy and utter despair. Allen is an assiduously private person and a pessimist by nature, and the

but faithful liberal audience, Allen parodied his own cultural cachet in *Stardust Memories* (1980), a self-indulgent reflection on creativity which drew on a taste for Bergman and Fellini. Shot, like *Manhattan*, in crisp monochrome by Gordon Willis, *Stardust Memories* also extended an experimental bent that would become bolder in Allen's 1980s films.

Breaking with United Artists following *Stardust Memories*, Allen began an association with Orion that would result in his richest decade. The 1980s began with Bergman-lite – *A Midsummer Night's Sex Comedy* (1982) – and ended with the chamber angst of *Another Woman* (1988) and, more significantly, the ethically engaged *Crimes And Misdemeanors*. These years saw Allen chart the maturing of that generation of college graduates and Vietnam protesters who awoke to the glare of monetarism and the extreme relativity of ethical and aesthetic standards. Even the lighter *Alice* (1990) ends as a bitter repudiation of the "Greed is Good" era. As if seeking a still centre of virtue amid the contemporary buying and selling of souls, Allen's work pivoted around his then partner Mia Farrow, who did her best work ever in *Broadway Danny Rose* (1984), *Hannah And Her Sisters* and *September* (1987).

In an ambitious anecdote on the allure of classical American movie-going, *The Purple Rose Of Cairo* (1985) found Depression house-wife Cecilia (a waif-like Farrow) crossing from the audience to the movie in one of Allen's smoothest technical conceits. Allen has a love of sleight of hand and the strange permutations of fate, and few directors since Welles have so artfully toyed with cinema's apparatus. *Zelig* (1983) placed Allen's social misfit within newsreel footage of F. Scott Fitzgerald and Hitler.

When Allen and Farrow's relationship broke down in 1992 amid allegations of child abuse, his private life became tabloid scandal. Though there is little of this in the eloquent neo-expressionism of *Shadows And Fog* (1992) and the Allen-Keaton confection *Manhattan Murder Mystery* (1993), the bitter recriminations and hand-held camerawork of *Husbands And Wives* (1992) seems suffused with the crisis.

Sweet talking: Woody Allen looks up to Jessica Harper in *Stardust Memories*.

relationship between his art and his life has always been the subject of popular speculation.

While his second wife, Louise Lasser, appeared in earlier movies, his breakthrough film, *Annie Hall* (1977), closely approximated the ups and downs of Allen's long-term relationship with Diane Keaton. By now an established auteur playing to the intellectual mind-set and sexual discontents of a small

From this point, Allen's work went into slow decline. Adroitly showcasing the brightest young actors of their generation, *Bullets Over Broadway* (1994), *Mighty Aphrodite* (1995) and *Sweet And Lowdown* (1999) remain entertaining frissons. Meanwhile, *Everyone Says I Love You* (1996),

A

Celebrity (1998) and *The Curse Of The Jade Scorpion* (2002) are the work of an auteur marking time. Only *Deconstructing Harry* (1997), with its flawed writer taking stock, hinted at the gravitas of America's foremost screen moralist, while some touted *Melinda And Melinda* (2004) and *Match Point* (2005) as returns to form. Allen remains a distinctive screen presence in modern cinema. RA

Take The Money And Run 1969, 85 min

cast Woody Allen, Janet Margolin, Marcel Hillaire, Jacquelyn Hyde, Lonny Chapman, Jan Merlin *cin* Lester Shorr *m* Marvin Hamlisch

Hilariously parodying every prison picture and documentary cliché from the "sweat box" to the prison farm break, as in his stand-up comedy Woody Allen also lampoons the suburban middle-class mores of post-war America. Only someone raised under lace-curtain respectability could envisage being in solitary with an insurance salesman with this kind of dread.

Love And Death 1975, 85 min

cast Woody Allen, Diane Keaton, Olga Georges-Picot, Harold Gould, Jessica Harper, Alfred Lutter, James Tolkan *cin* Ghislain Cloquet *m* Prokofiev

Marrying the Brooklyn schlemiel's sexual befuddlement with an enduring taste for Continental philosophy and literature, *Love And Death* is slapstick for grad students. Allen and Diane Keaton's *pas de deux* set amid the turmoil of Napoleon's invasion of Russia assiduously name-drops Russian doorstops while indulging the conundrums of its title. You can feel Allen moving towards the integrity of anecdote and narrative, hope and despair of his golden years.

Annie Hall 1977, 93 min

cast Woody Allen, Diane Keaton, Tony Roberts, Carol Keane, Paul Simon, Shelley Duvall, Janet Margolin, Christopher Walken *cin* Gordon Willis

A box-office success and an Oscar winner, this "nervous romance" chronicles the turbulent relationship between neurotic New Yorkers Alvy Singer (Allen) and Annie Hall (Diane Keaton). A New Yorker famous for his affection for the city, Allen loses no opportunity to celebrate its cultural moments as well as its solipsism. The film also boasts a soundtrack ironically doused with Tin Pan Alley love songs, and it consolidated its appeal by showcasing Keaton's eccentric retro wardrobe and launching a fashion trend.

Manhattan 1979, 96 min, b/w

cast Woody Allen, Diane Keaton, Michael Murphy, Mariel Hemingway, Meryl Streep *cin* Gordon Willis *m* George Gershwin

Gauging the moral temper of a New York caught between its fabulous modernist heritage and the postmodern devaluation of human exchange, Isaac remains perhaps Allen's most obvious moral centre, around whom swirl an over-educated morass of opportunists and their marks. In the aftermath of all the buying and selling, only Manhattan, steeped in Gordon Willis's velvety cinematography and a sonorous Gershwin score, remains to anchor the lost and the lonely.

Broadway Danny Rose 1984, 84 min

cast Woody Allen, Mia Farrow, Nick Apollo Forte, Sandy Baron, Corbett Monica, Jackie Gayle *cin* Gordon Willis *m* Luigi Denza, Nick Apollo Forte

Behind the façade of the shy young Jew trying to succeed in the showbiz shallows, *Broadway Danny Rose* adds its riposte to the 1980s atmosphere of dog eat dog. By way of

tribute to his own beginnings, Allen makes a gang of old comics the chorus to the moral tale.

Hannah And Her Sisters 1986, 107 min

cast Barbara Hershey, Carrie Fisher, Michael Caine, Mia Farrow, Dianne Wiest *cin* Carlo Di Palma *m* Michael Bramon

For years, Allen was one of American cinema's finest directors of women, and this chronicle of a family over a year of small joys and disappointments finds Dianne Wiest and Barbara Hershey giving performances of rare sensitivity. Meanwhile, Allen, Michael Caine and Max von Sydow mull over the complexities of the Allen persona. Carlo Di Palma's cinematography brings class to an autumnal New York.

Crimes And Misdemeanors 1989, 104 min

cast Martin Landau, Woody Allen, Anjelica Huston, Mia Farrow, Claire Bloom *cin* Sven Nykvist

One of the most important films of its era, this tragicomedy of contemporary New York has an almost biblical gravitas. An eminent eye surgeon stands to lose everything over a sexual indiscretion. An ethical documentary filmmaker is commissioned to cover the life of a cynical opportunist. If Allen's protagonists have been stranded in a world of compromise, nothing in his oeuvre prepared us for this angry indictment of contemporary moral relativity.

Merzak Allouache

Algeria, 1944–

Torn between the generation that liberated Algeria from France and the contemporary spectres of Islam and consumerism, Merzak Allouache has chronicled a society in turmoil.

Educated at the Algerian National Film Institute and at IDHEC, the French national film school, in the late 1960s, Allouache became Cultural Adviser to the French Ministry of Culture and Information. His early films have a social realist bias. *Omar Gatlato* (1976) gained international kudos with its story of a young man's life in the "Quartier" and his responses to his experience. Reiterating a desire to break with traditional Arab storytelling, Allouache experimented with myth and irony in *Les aventures d'un héros* (*Adventures Of A Hero*, 1978) and *The Man Who Watched Windows* (1982). *Bab El-Oued City* (1994), meanwhile, returned to inner Algiers to find fundamentalism eroding its cosmopolitan flavours. The movie was shot on the run using amateur actors following the religious riots of 1988. Then followed the successful *Salut, cousin!* (*Hey, Cousin!*, 1996). Seeking to challenge First World labels of Third World cinema, *Un autre monde* (*Another World*, 2001) boldly presented an Islamic extremist as a complex character shortly after 9/11. The Alain Chabat comedy *Chouchou* (2003) was lighter in feel, its gender role-play suggesting a debt to Josiane Balasko's hit *Gazon maudit* (*French Twist*, 1995). This was followed by *Bab el web* (2004), an intriguing Third World take on the Internet. RA

Salut, cousin! (Hey, Cousin!) 1996, 102 min
cast Gad Elmaleh, Messaoud Hattau, Magaly Berdy, Ann-Gisel Glass, Jean Benguigui, Xavier Maly *cin* Pierre Aïm, Georges Diane *m* Safy Boutella

Up from Algiers, Alilo meets cousin Mok (a Parisian slicker) and, if at first he is gullible, he soon begins to see through the image and is made aware of the pain of cultural displacement. This is a key Allouache film that is full of the play with discourse that layers his best work.

Michael Almereyda
US, 1960–

At one point a name to drop in hip, downtown New York circles and later signed, perhaps disastrously so, to mini major Miramax, Harvard dropout Michael Almereyda is yet to make good on the promise shown in his early work.

After struggling as a screenwriter, collaborating on scripts with Tim Burton, David Lynch, Wim Wenders and Paul Verhoeven, Almereyda made his feature debut with the wayward *Twister* (1989), a Midwestern-set family drama with an eclectic cast. The experience wasn't a happy one, and finding it difficult to raise cash for another project he found an ingenious low-budget solution. Inspired by the work of experimental filmmaker Sadie Benning, Almereyda bought a Fisher-Price PXL-2000, the original monochrome Pixelvision camera, and shot the 56-minute featurette *Another Girl, Another Planet* (1992). The degraded, super-grainy imagery meshed beautifully with Almereyda's well-chosen soundtrack of cool indie songsters, and the director followed it up with several films in the same vein, including *Nadja* (1994).

Almereyda experimented further with Pixelvision for the documentary *At Sundance* (1995) and the engaging short *The Rocking Horse Winner* (1997) before returning to 35mm for the offbeat, shambolic mummy-movie *The Eternal* (1998, aka *Trance*). Audiences and critics were underwhelmed, but in 2000 Almereyda got sufficient backing from Miramax to make a version of Shakespeare's *Hamlet* set in contemporary New York and starring Ethan Hawke as a woolly-hatted slacker crown prince.

His follow-up, *Happy Here And Now* (2002), told an ambitious tale of cyberspace romance and fluid identities, set partly against a backdrop of New Orleans. It sported the typical Almereyda strengths – good ideas, strong visuals, great soundtrack – and the same Almereyda weaknesses – fragmentary storytelling, a tendency towards pretension. Next came the fairly straightforward documentary *This So-Called Disaster: Sam Shepard Directs The Late Henry Moss* (2003), which featured Sean Penn, Nick Nolte and Sam Shepard unfussily working out the titular play's shape through rehearsals, and the documentary portrait *William Eggleston In The Real World* (2005), which followed the eponymous

photographer around his home town with a shaky, hand-held camera. LF

Nadja 1994, 93 min, b/w
cast Suzy Amis, Galaxy Craze, Martin Donovan, Peter Fonda, Jared Harris, Elina Löwensohn *cin* Jim Denault *m* Simon Fisher Turner

Nadja is the most fully realized and likeable of Almereyda's Pixelvision pics. It replays Lambert Hillyer's *Dracula's Daughter* (1936) in Greenwich Village with Hal Hartley muse Elina Löwensohn in the title role. The grainy footage adds an atmospheric quality to this tale of modern gothic ennui.

Hamlet 2000, 112 min
cast Ethan Hawke, Kyle MacLachlan, Diane Venora, Sam Shepard, Bill Murray, Liev Schreiber *cin* John de Borman *m* Carter Burwell

This modern-day version of the Shakespearean tragedy has the gloomy Dane delivering his "To be or not to be" soliloquy in the action aisle of a Blockbuster video store. Inventively interpreted, utilizing all kinds of film and digital stocks from Pixelvision to CC cameras, the film won good reviews but experienced only patchy distribution. Bill Murray gives one of his first "serious" performances as Ophelia's pop Polonius.

Pedro Almodóvar
Spain, 1949–

There have always been significant directors who have made the transition from rank outsider to treasured institution, but perhaps no one has travelled so far along this axis as Pedro Almodóvar. A self-taught, openly gay man from the sticks, Almodóvar started out making kitsch, slapdash Super 8 shockers in the early 1970s. Since then, he has matured and refined his craft over a busy three decades to become arguably Spain's most influential, internationally respected and exportable living filmmaker.

Flamboyant plotting, lush production design and tactical use of both melodrama and black comedy have been defining characteristics of the Almodóvar style. The outrageous early films, with their soap-opera-on-acid storylines, owe an obvious debt to the schlock and exploitation cinema of the 1960s, shot through a filter of Hispanic *telenovela* drama and classic melodramas from both Spain and the US. The later films are a bit more upmarket in their inspirations, namechecking well-known weepies, and riffing on the stylized mannerisms of silent cinema and *film noir* classics like Billy Wilder's *Double Indemnity* (1944). Almodóvar's skill as a filmmaker seems to increase with every release, and his films from *The Flower Of My Secret* (1995) onwards have developed a classier veneer, even if the plots are no less over-the-top than their predecessors.

In retrospect, Almodóvar's early movies look like reactions against the Franco era, even though his first allusion to those repressive times came late, in *Live Flesh* (1997), whose lead character is born during a

Almodóvar's women

In 1999, Pedro Almodóvar dedicated his thirteenth film, *All About My Mother*, to "Bette Davis, Gena Rowlands, Romy Schneider … To all actresses who have played actresses. To all women who act. To all men who act and become women. To all people who want to be mothers. To my mother." These simple words, both touching and subversive, outline not only Almodóvar's particular vision of femininity – a precarious balance of solidarity, vitality and hope against suffering, despair and duplicity – but also his enormous affection for women and in particular women who act.

Though *Matador* (1986), *Law Of Desire* (1987) and *Live Flesh* (1997) focus on men, as do the less frenetic later works *Talk To Her* (2002) and *Bad Education* (2004), Almodóvar is more commonly associated with his women's pictures. While Carmen Maura and Victoria Abril are most usually referred to as his "muses", he has also collaborated regularly with Marisa Paredes, Penélope Cruz, Cecilia Roth, Chus Lampreave and Rossy de Palma, creating an ever-evolving corps of regulars who pop up in anything from bit parts to starring roles. In their work with Almodóvar these complex women are world-weary and hopeful, crazy and wise; they also have a luminous cinematic quality that contributes as much to the films' visual spectacle as do their saturated colours and overwrought *mise en scène*. And although tragedy is never far from the surface in an Almodóvar movie, his actresses bring to the screen a wit and verve that make their films for him less darkly doom-laden than his male melodramas.

Almodóvar met Carmen Maura in the radical ferment of 1970s Madrid. A successful stage actress, she brought a delirious, youthful energy to his first feature, the women's revenge fantasy *Pepi, Luci, Bom And All The Other Girls* (1980) – for which she also raised the funds – and clownish sweetness to *Dark Habits* (1983), about a bizarre convent of outrageous nuns. The bleakly surreal family drama *What Have I Done To Deserve This?* (1984) afforded her more nuance as the oppressed, irritable and ultimately outrageous mother, while in *Law Of Desire* (1987), Almodóvar made her into a woman who used to be a man – an intense, visceral performance that also made her a gay icon. *Women On The Verge Of A Nervous Breakdown* (1988), a visually glorious farce peopled with extraordinary-looking, grieving and distraught women, featured a characteristically deft turn from the actress as the glamorous but desperate Pepa, striving to stem the flow of chaos around her.

It was to be more than a decade before Almodóvar worked with Maura again. The next stage of his career was marked by the emergence of a new leading lady, Victoria Abril, an established Spanish screen star who made her Almodóvar debut in the sexually explicit *Tie Me Up! Tie Me Down!* (1990). While Maura brought impish comedy and sad-eyed expressiveness to the screen, Abril's performances combine overt sensuality – *Tie Me Up!* sees her play a porn actress who eventually falls for her violent kidnapper – with damaged vulnerability. The latter was especially evident in *High Heels* (1990), which also starred Marisa Paredes as the mother who neglected her. As Andrea Scarface, the dementedly ambitious TV presenter in *Kika* (1993), however, Abril got to play broad – if dark – comedy.

Other notable collaborators include the majestic Paredes, who was hilarious as a junkie nun in *Dark Habits* and wrought fine melodrama from *High Heels*, *The Flower Of My Secret* (1995), *All About My Mother* and *Talk To Her*, and Chus Lampreave – Almodóvar once called her a "female Buster Keaton" – who brought her instinctive comic clout to movies from *Dark Habits* right up to *Volver* (2006). And no account of Almodóvar's actresses can leave out Rossy de Palma, whose extraordinary physical appearance and pizzazz play no small part in the brilliance of *Women On The Verge*; she has smaller, though always key, roles in *Law of Desire*, *Tie Me Up*, *Kika* and *The Flower Of My Secret*.

In 2006, following the male-oriented *Talk To Her* and *Bad Education*, *Volver* – very literally a "return" – focused once more on the solidarity and suffering of women. The female cast, which as an ensemble won the best actress award at Cannes, is stupendous. Sensual and direct, Penélope Cruz is a revelation, as are Lola Dueñas (who plays Cruz's sister) and Yohana Cobo (her daughter). Continuity with Almodóvar's earlier work is offered by the eccentric Chus Lampreave and a triumphant comeback for Carmen Maura. It's a touching return to form for a director whose skewed but essentially optimistic universe offers endlessly rich pickings for those many magnificent women who have taken to his stage. SC

curfew in 1970. Because Franco had closed the national cinema school, Almodóvar's only option when he moved to Madrid was to teach himself about filmmaking through first-hand experience. It was in that city that he grew up, both personally and professionally: "My life and films are bound to Madrid, like the heads and tails of the same coin", he once remarked. He funded such Super 8 experiments as *Folle… folle… fólleme Tim!* (*Fuck, Fuck, Fuck Me, Tim!*, 1978) by working for the national phone company, while also

Kitchen sink melodrama: Carmen Maura (centre) plays the long-lost mother of Penélope Cruz and Lola Dueñas in *Volver*.

performing in a band, and writing comic books, novels, journalism and sometimes porn on the side. In this period he also joined the theatre company Los Golidardos, where he met eventual acting collaborators Carmen Maura and Antonio Banderas.

His first major muse, Maura co-starred in his first feature, *Pepi, Luci, Bom And All The Other Girls* (1980), a punkish story of three Madrid girls with the feel of a John Waters movie. Shot on 16mm for about $60,000, the film became an underground hit. The Alphaville theatre, where it played for nearly four years, produced Almodóvar's next, the comic melodrama *Labyrinth Of Passion* (1982), which was his first collaboration with Banderas. After the larky, robustly anti-clerical *Dark Habits* (1983) came the comedy *What Have I Done To Deserve This?* (1984), starring Maura as a cleaning lady addicted to No-Doze caffeine pills. This film marked a shift into more naturalistic territory and found niche distribution outside Spain, enhancing his reputation as the nation's newest *enfant terrible*.

Darker and more disturbing, the sex-and-death-fixated *Matador* (1986), though still shot through with black humour, demonstrated Almodóvar's skill with more serious themes – a skill shown off to even better effect in *Law Of Desire* (1987). The latter was the first film to be financed by Almodóvar's production company, El Deseo, co-run with his producer-brother Agustín Almodóvar. Although *Law Of Desire* was acclaimed by critics, the more female-centric, comfortably farcical *Women On The Verge Of A*

Nervous Breakdown (1988) proved to be the bigger financial success in Spain and abroad, particularly in the US where it broke box-office records for subtitled fare and found an audience beyond cinephiles and gay viewers.

As if to purposely sully his image after the genial *Women*'s warm reception, Almodóvar made the controversial *Tie Me Up! Tie Me Down!* (1989), an uncomfortable study of S&M in which new leading lady Victoria Abril plays a porn star kidnapped and ravished by Banderas's stalker until she falls in love with him. The film fell foul of ratings boards in several territories, and helped create the NC-17 rating in the US after it was initially awarded an X certificate. After the drag tribute *High Heels* (1990), Almodóvar took three years to make the sci-fi-tinged satire *Kika* (1993), which reaped more controversy and mixed reviews for its blithe depiction of rape.

But if the young Almodóvar loved to shock for shock's sake, the more mature artist found means of deploying extreme content to make subtler points, bringing his work more into line with the strategies of his directing heroes like perpetual provocateur Rainer Werner Fassbinder. In retrospect, *Kika* and *High Heels* seem like the final working through of the loopy impulses of Almodóvar's early career before he made a knight's move into semi-respectability with *The Flower Of My Secret* (1995). This film was a dry run for what most critics regard as his royal flush of three increasingly masterful films, *Live Flesh* (1997), *All About My Mother* (1999) and the

A

exquisite *Talk To Her* (2002). In each of these films, Almodóvar masterfully balances disturbing narrative shifts with the stabilizing effects of visual styling and nuanced performances, so that cracks that might have been cavernous in another craftsman's hands are deftly smoothed.

As the century turned, Almodóvar had secured a solid slot in the critical canon, regularly reaping rave reviews around the world. And yet he was reportedly petulant when *All About My Mother* failed to win the Palme d'Or in Cannes in 1999, though it went on to win an Oscar for best foreign-language film. He eventually "forgave" the French festival by giving it *Bad Education* as a non-competing opening film in 2004, but in between he released what many consider to be his finest film, *Talk To Her*, without the boost of a festival platform. It turned out that the film didn't really need it, as not only did it win prizes all over the world and reap considerable financial returns despite its dark corners, it also earned the director his second Academy Award, for best original screenplay, one of the extremely rare wins for a foreign-language film in that category.

Consistent in his output, Almodóvar often works on several screenplays at once and ends up making a film roughly every two years. He followed up *Bad Education* with the female-led comedy *Volver* (2006), starring Penélope Cruz. He has also produced several projects by upcoming directors, including Álex de la Iglesia's *Acción mutante* (*Mutant Action*, 1993), Guillermo del Toro's *The Devil's Backbone* (2001), Isabel Coixet's *My Life Without Me* (2003) and Lucrecia Martel's *The Holy Girl* (2004), becoming a major player in Spanish film production. LF

Law Of Desire (La ley del deseo) 1987, 100 min
cast Eusebio Poncela, Carmen Maura, Antonio Banderas, Miguel Molina, Manuela Velasco *cin* Javier Fernández

This complex, hot-to-trot love tangle touches such favourite Almodóvarian themes as jealousy, transsexuals and filmmaking. Considered one of his best early films, it also features arguably Antonio Banderas's career-best performance as a gay man so obsessed with his film-director lover (Eusebio Poncela) that he pushes a rival off a cliff. Carmen Maura plays the director's sister (formerly his brother). Also lost in the labyrinth are an assortment of preening and screaming Madrid types, including incestuous families and lovers who realize the depths of their feelings while at orgies.

The Flower Of My Secret (La flor di me secreto) 1995, 103 min
cast Marisa Paredes, Chus Lampreave, Rossy de Palma, Juan Echanove, Imanol Aria *cin* Affonso Beato *m* Alberto Iglesias

A key transitional film, this stars Marisa Paredes as a self-loathing, alcoholic romantic novelist who starts giving panning reviews to her own pseudonymously penned books. It's not hard to see an occluded if playful self-portrait at work. While Almodóvar veers towards more straight-back-and-sides storytelling here, there's still a florid lushness to the *mise en scène* even if the melodrama rings with sincerity rather than parody.

Live Flesh (Carne trémula) 1997, 103 min
cast Francesca Neri, Javier Bardem, José Sancho, Angela Molina, Liberto Rabal *cin* Affonso Beato *m* Alberto Iglesias

A rare novel adaptation (the original book was by Ruth Rendell), but one deeply transmogrified by its Madrid setting. Featuring nearly all heterosexual characters, this is in every sense Almodóvar's straightest movie. Passionate Victor (Liberto Rabal) unjustly serves time in prison for shooting a cop, David (Javier Bardem), who later becomes a paraplegic sports star. Victor learns how to become a flawless lover from battered wife Clara (Angela Molina) in order to seduce David's wife, reformed junkie Elena (Francesca Neri). Suicide pacts and conflagrations ensue.

All About My Mother (Todo sobre mi madre) 1999, 101 min
cast Cecilia Roth, Marisa Paredes, Penélope Cruz, Antonia San Juan, Candela Peña *cin* Affonso Beato *m* Alberto Iglesias

Former actress turned medical worker Manuela (Cecilia Roth) sets out for Barcelona to find her son's father after the boy's sudden death. Cross-dressing male whores, tragic lesbian stage stars and a nun with AIDS (Penélope Cruz) fill out the cast of characters. Explicit reference is made to *All About Eve* and Tennessee Williams' *A Streetcar Named Desire*. Though on paper the set-up sounds like more campy high jinks, the melodrama is actually richly resonant, enhanced by a heartbreaking performance by Roth and a glorious turn by Antonia San Juan as a trannie tart with a heart.

Talk To Her (Hable con ella) 2002, 112 min
cast Javier Cámara, Darío Grandinetti, Leonor Watling, Rosario Flores, Mariola Fuentes *cin* Javier Aguirresarobe *m* Alberto Iglesias

Possibly Almodóvar's best film, this weaves together the stories of writer Marco (Darío Grandinetti) and nurse Benigno (Javier Cámara). Both are in love with women in comas, a typical Almodóvar manoeuvre that sounds like bad taste but instead becomes the engine for a subtle essay on the nature of love and devotion. The film unfolds through a complex series of flashbacks and is bookended by striking dance numbers by Pina Bausch. It also features an hilarious and enchanting fake silent film in which a man shrinks until he can crawl inside his wife's vagina.

Bad Education (La mala educación) 2004, 109 min
cast Gael García Bernal, Fele Martínez, Daniel Giménez-Cacho, Lluís Homar, Francisco Maestre *cin* José Luis Alcaine *m* Alberto Iglesias

Touted in advance as a deeply personal project that would touch on the director's own life story, this reaped a more muted reception than usual from critics. An intricate skein of flashbacks and fictional vignettes coalesce uneasily with the central early-1980s narrative of a gay film director (Fele Martínez) who meets a young man (Gael García Bernal) claiming to be his early-adolescent lover now grown and out for fictional revenge against the priest who abused him when they were at school. But not all is as it seems in this steamy homage to *film noir* and the movies of Spanish diva Sara Montiel.

Volver 2006, 110 min
cast Penélope Cruz, Carmen Maura, Lola Dueñas, Blanca Portillo, Yohana Coba, Chus Lampreave *cin* José Luis Alcaine *m* Alberto Iglesias

Almodóvar went back to his roots with this ghost-story-cum-melodrama, which, with its strong female cast and tragicomic sensibility, plays like an older, wiser and slightly more melancholy version of *Women On The Verge*. With a career-best performance from Penélope Cruz as the tough but vulnerable young mother with a dark secret, and a more than welcome return from Maura as her own feckless mother, presumed dead, the film brought the director back to the bosom of the establishment, gaining rave reviews from around the world – and an Oscar nomination for Cruz as best actress.

Robert Altman

US, 1925–2006

Robert Altman was a maverick, a genius, an iconoclast and the grumpy old man of contemporary American cinema. It's a role he enjoyed from his 1970s heyday right up until his death in 2006.

Even though he's often mistakenly considered to be one of the 1970s movie brat generation of film school graduates – Steven Spielberg, George Lucas, Martin Scorsese, Francis Ford Coppola, et al – this World War II veteran was a good twenty years older than his contemporaries and he didn't go to film school. Altman cut his teeth in television, and that apprenticeship informs his directorial style. He often liked to use two or three cameras simultaneously, slowly zooming in and casually eavesdropping on his actors, trying to capture some chance, unscripted moment. He was a keen-eyed behaviourist who was more interested in character than plot, atmosphere than narrative, and his best films were multi-layered panoramas about intersecting lives.

Nashville (1975) is the movie that came to define "Altmanesque". It's a roaming sprawl of a film, a kaleidoscopic study of 24 characters at a country music festival, observed with a laissez-faire objectivity that shrewdly disguises its political, metaphorical and magisterial intent. *Nashville* established the blueprint for ensemble movies, such as Paul Thomas Anderson's ambitious *Magnolia* (1999), which was clearly based on the Altman model. Nominally based on short stories by Raymond Carver, Altman's *Short Cuts* (1993) was also made in this distinctive style: the lives of various inhabitants of a Californian suburb intersect and impact upon one another, caught as if by chance by a fluid camera, creating a free-flowing narrative that builds to a tumultuous climax. However, this isn't always a template for success. *A Wedding* (1978) adhered to the same formula, but lacked the satiric punch needed to counterpoint the narrative slack.

Altman's feature film career began in 1957 with *The Delinquents*, but it was thirteen years before he had his breakthrough with *M*A*S*H* (1970). The film had a low budget, no recognizable stars and little expectation, so the veteran TV director was given free rein by the studio 20th Century Fox. He effectively threw out Ring Lardner Jr's script, encouraged the actors to improvise and pioneered overlapping dialogue, for which he invented a new sound recording system. On its release, *M*A*S*H* was the most commercially successful comedy film of all time, which gave Altman a certain creative freedom for much of the decade, as other studios greedily hoped he would repeat the same financial miracle for them. He never did.

M*A*S*H was the start of Altman's campaign to systematically deconstruct film genres. Whereas Francis Ford Coppola tried to reinvigorate – and Brian De Palma tried to remake – old Hollywood formulae, Altman gleefully set out to demolish them. He successfully set his sights on the Western with *McCabe And Mrs Miller* (1971), in which frontier pioneers are revealed to be money-grabbing hucksters. *Buffalo Bill And The Indians* (1976) was another raid on the genre, with which he undermined the founding myths of the United States by exposing Buffalo Bill (Paul Newman) as a fraud. Altman intended his minor masterpiece *The Long Goodbye* (1973), adapted from Raymond Chandler's novel, to be a "long goodbye to the detective movie". *Thieves Like Us* (1974) slyly and poetically unpicked the bandit/gangster genre that had unexpectedly resurfaced after the success of *Bonnie And Clyde* (1967). *California Split* (1974) was an affably rambling take on the buddy movie, in which the friendship of inveterate gamblers Elliott Gould and George Segal disintegrates over the course of an ill-advised, drink-fuelled trip to Las Vegas.

Some critics maintain that Altman suffered from a superiority complex, a hubristic misanthropy that revealed itself in a barely disguised disdain for his characters. Altman's men were often dreamers drowning in their own bullshit, while his women were frequently on the edge of a nervous breakdown: Sandy Dennis's spinster reaching out for the comfort of a stranger in *That Cold Day In The Park* (1969); Susannah York's fractured personalities in the Bergmanesque *Images* (1972); Ronee Blakley's neurotic singer in *Nashville*; Lori Singer's cellist with a death wish in *Short Cuts*; and the dreamy and possibly demented Sissy Spacek in *3 Women* (1977). Put another way, Altman simply didn't believe in heroes or heroines.

Altman's directing method – to dispense with the script, encourage improvisation and find the film in the editing suite – was a recipe for both genius and disaster. His work was genuinely, bravely and infuriatingly experimental, and he possessed the uncanny ability to follow a masterpiece with a dud: *M*A*S*H* with the painfully wacky comedy *Brewster McCloud* (1971), *Short Cuts* with the fashion folly *Pret A Porter* (1994). There were pronounced troughs in Altman's career, especially after the new wave of American cinema ebbed away in the late 1970s and Hollywood struck back with lowest-common-denominator blockbusters. *Quintet* (1979), *A Perfect Couple* (1979) and *Health* (1980) all, rightly or wrongly, suffered from neglect. Altman was the wrong director to make a cartoon adaptation, but *Popeye* (1980) was a

13

Mavericks and Hollywood studios: a hate-hate relationship?

The role of the maverick artist forever in conflict with studio philistines is one that Robert Altman was more than happy to play, and he continually bit the hand that fed him. Part of a long and noble tradition of complaining about the boss, Altman followed in the footsteps of visionaries such as D.W. Griffith and Cecil B. DeMille who spent much of their careers trying to establish financial and creative autonomy from the moguls who regarded the studios as their own personal fiefdoms (indomitable characters like Columbia boss Harry Cohn who could tell a film wasn't working because, as he so delicately put it, "my ass begins to twitch"). Dealing with the studio heads' peccadillos has been the lot of the Hollywood hired hand for decades.

Monocled mutineer Erich Von Stroheim invented the cliché of the director as tortured genius, the man the studios loved to hate, whose misunderstood work was mutilated by the bean-counters at head office. Only two of his nine films were released at the length he'd intended, with *Greed* (1924) slashed from ten hours to just two hours and twenty minutes. Orson Welles may be the obvious candidate for über-maverick, a wild flame snuffed out by studio interference and indifference, but there are plenty of other candidates. Head-strong alpha males like Sam Fuller, Raoul Walsh, John Ford and Howard Hawks helped to define the Hollywood maverick as a hard man who stamped his personal vision on an otherwise anonymous studio product. Nonconformist John Huston, a boxing champion, notorious gambler and legendary drinker, regularly fell foul of the front office. He was given carte blanche to make the civil war pic *Red Badge Of Courage* (1951), but while he was away filming *The African Queen* (1951), MGM production chief Dore Schary brutally re-cut the film and added a cliché-riddled voiceover.

In the late 1960s and early 1970s, however, the mavericks briefly took over the asylum. *Easy Rider* (1969), a film about two renegade bikers, heralded the arrival of a new generation of Hollywood directors, idiosyncratic talents like Bob Rafelson, Robert Altman, Martin Scorsese, Brian De Palma, Hal Ashby and Francis Ford Coppola whose films bore the stamp of the individual director rather than the corporate brand. These so-called "movie brats" were given unusual levels of autonomy by the studios, but controversial director Sam Peckinpah still fought against the system. From the moment he was shut out of the editing suite of his own film, *Ride The High Country* (1962), he was locked in a near permanent war with the studios. When he saw the producer's cut of his thriller *The Getaway* (1972), Peckinpah apparently shouted "This is not my picture!" and urinated all over the screen. And when he realized that they were going to butcher his elegiac Western, *Pat Garrett And Billy The Kid* (1973), he broke into the studio at night and stole a preview print.

Ironically, it was the phenomenal success of two movies made by the "New Hollywood" generation themselves that brought the curtain down on their golden age. The box-office triumphs of Steven Spielberg's *Jaws* (1975) and George Lucas's *Star Wars* (1977) signalled the advent of the modern blockbuster, and the studio empire struck back. The last post finally sounded for the wild bunch when the infamously profligate director Michael Cimino (the true heir of Von Stroheim when it came to expense and length) brought United Artists to its knees with the box-office disaster *Heaven's Gate* (1980) and the accountants increasingly tightened their grip.

The relationship between the directors and the studio bosses hasn't always hinged upon the simple equation mavericks = good, studios = bad, however. Hollywood can impose much-needed discipline on a mercurial talent. For instance, Jules Dassin helmed some of the most deftly plotted, tautly executed and evocatively photographed *noirs* in film history, including *Thieves' Highway* (1949) and *Night And The City* (1950), while he was under contract with Fox and Universal. But as an auteur and master of his own destiny, he churned out a slew of personal projects that critic David Thomson described as "some of the most entertainingly bad movies of the sixties and seventies". Studio-imposed formulas are not necessarily a paralysing straitjacket on artistic expression, but can be a set of rules to work with and react against. And the best Hollywood movies often bristle with the tension between the two. Despite the mutual loathing, the name-calling and even the law-breaking, the studios and the mavericks undoubtedly need each other. American directors usually need the money, the clout or the distribution deals that only the Hollywood establishment can offer, and the studio bosses will always tolerate the mavericks as long as they are making them oodles of lucre. LH

genuine curio and not the unspeakable disaster it's frequently made out to be. Many of the 1970s generation – Coppola, Scorsese, Friedkin and Altman – seemed like displaced persons in the high concept, plot-driven, characterless 1980s. Altman concentrated, rather bizarrely for a director who liked to work with the largest possible canvas, on stage adaptations: *Come Back To The Five And Dime, Jimmy Dean, Jimmy Dean* (1982), *Streamers* (1983), *Secret Honor* (1984) and *Fool For Love* (1985). The nadir came in 1988 with *O.C. And Stiggs*, a teen comedy implausibly directed by a 63-year-old.

Hollywood's maverick pensioner had something of a revival in the 1990s, re-emerging with *Vincent*

And Theo (1990), gaining critical and commercial success with Hollywood satire *The Player* (1992), and discovering his métier again with *Short Cuts*. He followed this *succès d'estime* with *Pret A Porter* and a string of interesting failures: *Kansas City* (1996), *The Gingerbread Man* (1998), and two Southern-fried comedies, *Cookie's Fortune* (1999) and *Dr T And The Women* (2000).

Then came his third revival, with *Gosford Park* (2001), an Altmanesque take on the British murder mystery: another rich tapestry, another society in microcosm, the camera as much a tool of wry observation as of composition. *Gosford Park* was only let down in its final act by the director's bullish disdain for plot – the mystery limped lamely to the finishing line. After that, he again made another dud: *The Company* (2004) was to a ballet company what *Pret A Porter* was to the fashion industry.

Altman's final film, *A Prairie Home Companion* (2006), was neither ruinous nor genius, but belonged in the mildly amusing category in which too many of his later films can be found. Not quite the fitting tribute for an American hero. LH

M*A*S*H 1970, 116 min
cast Donald Sutherland, Elliott Gould, Tom Skerritt, Sally Kellermann, Robert Duvall *cin* Harold Stine *m* Johnny Mandel

An episodic, knockabout comedy apparently about the Korean conflict but patently about Vietnam, *M*A*S*H*'s anti-war, anti-authoritarian stance resonated perfectly with post-*Easy Rider* counterculture audiences. Elliott Gould and Donald Sutherland became stars thanks to their roles as a pair of unorthodox, golf-playing, Martini-making, Lothario surgeons. Altman nimbly balanced free-wheeling, anarchic – and sexist – humour with bloodily realistic scenes of emergency surgery, including the first appearance of arterial spray in a Hollywood comedy.

McCabe And Mrs Miller 1971, 120 min
cast Warren Beatty, Julie Christie, Rene Auberjonois, William Devane, John Schuck, Corey Fischer *cin* Vilmos Zsigmond *m* Leonard Cohen

Warren Beatty and Julie Christie try to live the American Dream by setting up a brothel, but soon discover that big business has unique powers of persuasion when a major corporation launches a hostile takeover. However, the real star of the film is Vilmos Zsigmond's bleached-out cinematography which adds to the sense that this is a West – and a Western – that is not yet fully developed. It is, like the town itself, being slowly constructed before our eyes.

The Long Goodbye 1973, 112 min
cast Elliott Gould, Nina Van Pallandt, Sterling Hayden, Mark Rydell, Henry Gibson, David Arkin *cin* Vilmos Zsigmond *m* John Williams

Elliott Gould's breezily dishevelled take on hard-boiled private eye Philip Marlowe is matchless in American cinema. Waking up in a world he cannot comprehend, Marlowe is a man out of time, living in a Los Angeles of self-centred neuroses, worthless friendships and topless hippies. With typical chutzpah, Altman doesn't just target the iconography of the detective movie, but carries out a philosophical assault on the genre's *idée fixe* that a lone individual can make a difference.

Nashville 1975, 159 min
cast Richard Baskin, Ronee Blakley, Karen Black, Keith Carradine, Shelley Duvall, Henry Gibson, Lily Tomlin, Gwen Welles *cin* Paul Lohmann

Nashville is the chronicle of 24 people at one music festival, including a sickly star, a shambolic BBC reporter and a deluded waitress who dreams of becoming a singing sensation. The result is sprawling without ever being self-indulgent, and is deftly held in check by an underlying narrative structure, acute political satire and overwhelming pathos. The latter is most evident in the saddest striptease ever committed to celluloid as Gwen Welles tries to please her audience by dolefully giving into requests to take her clothes off.

The Player 1992, 124 min
cast Tim Robbins, Greta Scacchi, Fred Ward, Whoopi Goldberg, Peter Gallagher, Brian James *cin* Jean Lépine *m* Thomas Newman

Despite working in the studio system all his career, Altman has always been a Hollywood outsider: witness his comments after 9/11 blaming action movies for providing a blueprint for terrorists. He was, therefore, the perfect director to helm a Hollywood satire and to formally bite the hand that feeds him. The central story about a studio exec's attempts to conceal the murder of a scriptwriter is of secondary interest compared to the joy of watching 64 star cameos and an appallingly accurate film within a film.

Gosford Park 2001, 137 min
cast Maggie Smith, Michael Gambon, Kristin Scott Thomas, Camilla Rutherford, Charles Dance, Clive Owen *cin* Andrew Dunn *m* Patrick Doyle

The upstairs/downstairs world of the British aristocracy in the 1930s was such perfect fodder for Altman that the only surprise is that it took him so long to make a film set in an English country house: the British class system in microcosm. The chaotic yet perfectly choreographed opening scenes, in which guests arriving for dinner are greeted by their hosts and their staff, are the best celluloid moments Altman had fashioned in a decade.

Allison Anders
US, 1954–

Allison Anders has brought arthouse credibility to melodrama – a traditionally "low" genre – infusing her troubled protagonists' lives with the potency of contemporary popular culture.

After a troubled childhood of family fracture, paternal abuse and gang rape at 12, Anders studied film and then, after a stream of fan letters to Wim Wenders, got the job of production assistant on *Paris, Texas* (1984). In 1987 she co-directed and co-wrote *Border Radio*, an improvised monochrome homage to the LA rock and punk scene. It was characterized by Anders' singular feeling for music, environment and subjectivity. Following the arthouse breakthrough *Gas Food Lodging* (1992), *Mi vida loca* (*My Crazy Life*, 1993) was an energetic tapestry of East LA Chicana gangs but was critically ill-perceived as little more than a "Girlz 'n the Hood" delinquency drama. Concentrating less on violence and more on emotions, Anders' film remains sonorous and poignant.

After an uncharacteristic vignette in the portmanteau film *Four Rooms* (1995) and the Scorsese-produced period feature *Grace Of My Heart* (1996), *Sugar Town* (1999) brought a succession of 1980s luminaries together for a piquant examination of LA's pop industry fringe. Ally Sheedy and Rosanna Arquette riff nicely on the tensions between their art and their own lives. Filmed on digital video and evoking Anders' own rape, *Things Behind The Sun* (2001) explored a wannabe rock chick's daily demons, yet suffered from Anders' oft-cited uncertain grasp of narrative. In 2001 she established an alert service to mobilize audiences for women's filmmaking. Her career is a reminder of what determined women bring to the mainstream. RA

Gas Food Lodging 1992, 101 min
cast Brooke Adams, Ione Skye, Fairuza Balk, James Brolin, Robert Knepper *cin* Dean Lent *m* J. Mascis

Nora (Brooke Adams) is the mother of teenage daughters Trudi (Ione Skye) and Shade (Fairuza Balk); the film charts the trio's various misadventures as a succession of men pass through their trailer-park lives. The film's triumph is its avoidance of over-sentimentality, making its final scenes all the more powerful and, more importantly, real.

Grace Of My Heart 1996, 115 min
cast Illeana Douglas, Sissy Boyd, Christina Pickles, Jill Sobule, Jennifer Leigh Warren *cin* Jean-Yves Escoffier *m* Larry Klein

Loosely based on the life of Carole King, this story follows Denise Waverly's odyssey from wannabe singer/songwriter in the era of 1960s girl groups to fame and heartache at the hands of men amid the shallows of flower power. The movie has a fine sense of history and hinges on a superb performance by Illeana Douglas.

Lindsay Anderson
India, 1923–94

Of the same generation as the French *nouvelle vague* directors, Lindsay Anderson was a British cinephile and an auteurist critic who became an auteur director himself.

The son of a major-general in the British army, Anderson went to public school in Cheltenham, England, which would later become the location for his most famous film, *If....* (1968). As a student at Oxford, he began to direct and perform in theatre and founded the film magazine *Sequence* in 1946. In *Sequence*, Anderson was a vitriolic critic of the British film establishment (documentarian Humphrey Jennings was a rare exception), and a passionate champion of the American director John Ford.

Anderson soon began practising what he preached when he moved into documentary filmmaking in the late 1940s. *O Dreamland* (1953) was an evocative study of the fairground at Brighton and his portrait of deaf-mute children, *Thursday's Children* (1954), won the Academy Award for best documentary in 1956.

As he wrote: "With a 16mm camera and minimal resources, you cannot achieve very much – in commercial terms … But you can use your eyes and ears. You can give indications. You can make poetry."

Initially better known for his theatre work at the Royal Court, Anderson formed the Free Cinema Movement with his colleagues Karel Reisz, Tony Richardson and Lorenza Mazzetti as a ploy to get their films noticed. It worked, although the movement was soon lumped into the more general, faintly disparaging description "British kitchen sink cinema", a phrase which underlines the films' social-realist attributes at the expense of the poetry Anderson held dearest.

His first fiction feature, *This Sporting Life* (1963), was a critical success but a commercial failure, and Anderson seemed unsure of which direction to take next. The two short films he made during this period are rarely screened, but he got back on track with *If....*, the first of his three intense collaborations with writer David Sherwin and actor Malcolm McDowell (who plays the lead role of Mick Travis in *If....*, *O Lucky Man!*, 1973, and *Britannia Hospital*, 1982). Taken together, the trilogy represents an ambitious, splenetic, imaginative response to a nation in terminal constitutional decline. Whether Anderson escaped that same fate is debatable. TC

This Sporting Life 1963, 134 min, b/w
cast Richard Harris, Rachel Roberts, Alan Badel, William Hartnell, Colin Blakely, Vanda Godsell, Arthur Loewe *cin* Denys Coop *m* Roberto Gerhard

Anderson's film of David Storey's novel features powerful performances from Richard Harris as a miner/rugby player and Rachel Roberts as the landlady with whom he has an affair. A box-office failure, the film was the last of the realist "kitchen sink" dramas that were prevalent in British cinema in the late 1950s and early 1960s and that also included Karel Reisz's *Saturday Night And Sunday Morning* (1960) and Tony Richardson's *A Taste Of Honey* (1961).

If.... 1968, 111 min, b/w and col
cast Malcolm McDowell, David Wood, Richard Warwick, Robert Swann, Christine Noonan, Hugh Thomas *cin* Miroslav Ondricek *m* Marc Wilkinson

Films rarely reflect their times as vividly as *If....* encapsulates the revolutionary spirit of 1968, with its story of war breaking out on the playing fields of an English public school. Originally planned as a British Western by John Ford aficionado Anderson and writer David Sherwin, this turned into something quite different: a radical shot at the hidebound British Establishment that was more in the spirit of Jean Vigo than John Ford.

Michael Anderson
UK, 1920–

Balancing technical skill with a talent for getting the best from his actors, some of Anderson's finest films are stories featuring bids for freedom.

Initially an actor, Anderson added unit production manager to his credits with Noël Coward's *In Which*

We Serve (1942), a starkly realistic wartime naval story. He wrote and directed the mildly comic *Private Angelo* (1949) with Peter Ustinov, but it was with *The Dam Busters* (1954) that he exploded into the public consciousness. Despite that film's impressive special effects, Anderson was not simply a technophile: the former actor elicited strong performances. In 1956 he turned out a finely acted version of Orwell's *Nineteen Eighty-four* and the comic spectacular *Around The World In Eighty Days*. He also turned his hand to the psychological thrillers *Chase A Crooked Shadow* (1957) and *The Naked Edge* (1961). *The Quiller Memorandum* (1966) captures the chilling rise of neo-Nazism in Cold War Berlin, while in the futuristic *Logan's Run* (1976) the state kills people at 30. Since emigrating to Canada he has worked in film and television both there and in the USA. JR

The Dam Busters 1954, 124 min

cast Michael Redgrave, Richard Todd, Ursula Jeans, Derek Farr, Patrick Barr *cin* Erwin Hillier *m* Leighton Lucas, Eric Coates

Based on reality and justly a favourite of audiences and the director himself, *The Dam Busters* is a quintessential British war movie, topped with Eric Coates' famous march – latterly an English soccer anthem. Barnes Wallis's team overcome a series of setbacks to develop "bouncing bomb" technology, enabling them to cripple German industries reliant on the Ruhr Valley. Despite the big theme, Anderson still finds time to show everyday life in bomber command.

Around The World In Eighty Days 1956, 183 min

cast David Niven, Cantiflas, Shirley Maclaine, John Gielgud *cin* Lionel Lindon *m* Victor Young

This epic picaresque comedy, painted in broad colours, showcased the impressive Todd-AO widescreen system and was rewarded with critical and popular success. As Jules Verne's hero, the unflappable Niven navigates a series of set pieces rather than a narrative, but in the end travel broadens this aristocrat's mind. Part of the fun comes from spotting the numerous star cameos, and Saul Bass animated an amusing credit sequence.

Paul Thomas Anderson

US, 1970–

Paul Thomas Anderson aspires to greatness. While that doesn't guarantee anything except, perhaps, hubris, in an era when most American movies are built to corporate specifications, Anderson stands out as an unpredictable creative force – a regenerative spirit in a stale cinematic landscape.

He grew up in the San Fernando Valley, California, where his father, Ernie Anderson, worked as a voice artist – and as the late night TV horror movie host Ghoulardi. One of seven children, Paul worked as a production assistant on TV shows such as *The Quiz Kids Challenge* from an early age.

A film school dropout, Anderson nevertheless impressed the Sundance festival with his short *Cigarettes And Coffee* (1993), and he subsequently developed the screenplay for his feature debut, *Hard Eight* (1996), under their wing.

A neo-*noir* character piece set in motel rooms, cafés and casinos, with hard-boiled performances from John C. Reilly and Philip Baker Hall (both would become Anderson staples), *Hard Eight* now looks like Anderson's most modest and unassuming film, but it was enough to get *Film Comment* magazine to nominate him as the most promising young director of the year. (Anderson himself was, however, unhappy with the studio cut.)

Boogie Nights (1997) and *Magnolia* (1999) upped the ante. Big, flamboyant, erratic ensemble epics, frescoes of southern California's suburban sprawl, they reflected the decadence of the 1970s and the emotional desperation of the late 1990s respectively. Clearly influenced by Robert Altman's work (especially *Nashville* and *Short Cuts*), Anderson has a pop-surrealist verve which blossomed in his highly eccentric take on the romantic comedy, *Punch-Drunk Love* (2002), with Adam Sandler and Emily Watson. It was an unexpected move, which kept everyone guessing about where he might head next… It turned out to be *There Will Be Blood* (2007), an adaptation of Upton Sinclair's turn-of-the-century novel *Oil*, starring Daniel Day-Lewis. TC

Boogie Nights 1997, 156 min

cast Mark Wahlberg, Burt Reynolds, Julianne Moore, Don Cheadle, Heather Graham *cin* Robert Elswit

Opening with a bravura seven-minute travelling shot (which ends, *Soy Cuba*-style, in a swimming pool), *Boogie Nights* traces the rise and fall of one Dirk Diggler (Mark Wahlberg), a prodigiously endowed performer on the 1970s porno movie scene. Exhibitionist but not prurient, nostalgic without becoming sentimental, *Boogie Nights* gets off on its own druggy, disco high – then crashes down to earth with a bump.

Magnolia 1999, 188 min

cast Tom Cruise, Julianne Moore, Jason Robards, Philip Seymour Hoffman, William H. Macy *cin* Robert Elswit *m* Jon Brion, Aimee Mann

Even more ambitious (check out that running time), Anderson's third feature is another multi-strand narrative, mapping the emotional traumas of more than half a dozen major characters as they criss-cross the San Fernando Valley in search of some kind of recognition. There is extraordinary work here from a whole slew of actors, though it's arguable Anderson pushes everything a little too far. Scored to the songs of Aimee Mann (in one audacious sequence the cast chimes in), *Magnolia* puts the operatic back into soap opera.

Punch-Drunk Love 2002, 91 min

cast Adam Sandler, Emily Watson, Luis Guzman, Philip Seymour Hoffman *cin* Robert Elswit *m* Jon Brion

Giddy and hysteric, surreal and expressionist, *Punch-Drunk Love* throws together goofball comedian Adam Sandler and arthouse princess Emily Watson, along with an experimental

A

percussive score (abstract chromatic interludes like something out of the 1960s avant-garde), novelty toilet plungers with unbreakable handles, 12,000 puddings, seven sisters and a mysterious harmonium (for good vibrations).

Wes Anderson

US, 1969–

When asked by a journalist to name "the next Martin Scorsese", Scorsese himself picked out Wes Anderson. Given Anderson's precipitous rise up the ranks, he barely needed such an endorsement. Even though his fourth film, *The Life Aquatic With Steve Zissou* (2004), proved something of an expensive flop, his whimsical, melancholy movies have spawned a fiercely loyal cult following, especially among college-educated hipsters.

Few directors' films deserve the term "character-driven" more than Anderson's. His films are also casting-, music-, mood- and even production design-driven (he works with more or less the same key production personnel every time), but whatever powers their engines, action and plot are but trace elements in the fuel. "The idea is to make this self-contained world that is the right place for the characters to live in, a place where you can accept their behaviour", Anderson has said of his approach to scriptwriting, a task he performed in collaboration with college buddy-turned-actor Owen Wilson on his first three pictures, *Bottle Rocket, Rushmore* and *The Royal Tenenbaums*. (*The Life Aquatic* was co-written with Noah Baumbach.)

The behaviour of his characters can be decidedly if deliciously odd. Full of neuroses, quirks and dreams that come to naught but still drive them on, they often inhabit slightly timeless parallel worlds that look almost like the real thing but aren't quite. See, for instance, his fantasy 1950s-style New York City in *Tenenbaums* or the patently artificial, set-constructed ship of fools in *The Life Aquatic* that seems to be floating somewhere between Italy (where the movie was filmed) and the Philippines (where its pirates come from).

The dialogue in Anderson's films offers meaty, quotable lines that have attracted big players like Bill Murray, Cate Blanchett and Gene Hackman. But part of the charm of the films is that the characters the big names play are as treasured as the walk-on parts incarnated by old friends like Kumar Pallana, a one-time convenience store clerk who's appeared in all Anderson's movies. Other trademarks include a lyrical deployment of slow motion, contrapuntal use of vintage pop (especially by 1960s Brit rockers like The Kinks and The Rolling Stones), and dazzling long takes to round off the final scenes. LF

Bottle Rocket 1995, 92 min

cast Owen C. Wilson, Luke Wilson, Robert Musgrave, Lumi Cavazos, James Caan *cin* Robert Yeoman *m* Mark Mothersbaugh

Anderson got financing for his first movie after he and Owen Wilson cobbled together a short featuring a couple of the eventual film's key scenes as a taster, but despite charmed reviews *Bottle Rocket* disappeared without a trace at the box office. This was a shame, since this effervescent story of a group of slackers (including Owen Wilson and his brother Luke) who lamely hold up a bookstore and then hide out at a desert hotel hangs together just as well as Anderson's subsequent features. James Caan adds heft as a low-level gangster.

Rushmore 1998, 93 min

cast Bill Murray, Olivia Williams, Jason Schwartzman, Seymour Cassel, Brian Cox *cin* Robert Yeoman *m* Mark Mothersbaugh

The first of Anderson's trilogy about unmoored father-figures and their oddball quasi-sons, this blithely charming story features Jason Schwartzman as geeky teenage impresario Max Fischer who, like the young Anderson, has a passion for adapting Hollywood features for the high-school stage. His other big loves include his school Rushmore and pretty teacher Rosemary (Olivia Williams). The hitch is that his best friend, wealthy middle-aged industrialist Blume (Bill Murray, in a touching performance that turned his career around), is also besotted with Rosemary. A straight-A movie.

The Royal Tenenbaums 2001, 109 min

cast Gene Hackman, Anjelica Huston, Ben Stiller, Gwyneth Paltrow, Luke Wilson, Owen Wilson *cin* Robert Yeoman *m* Mark Mothersbaugh

Inspired variously by J.D. Salinger's Glass family stories, the movies of Hal Ashby and Preston Sturges, and the eclectic mix of music that makes up the film's soundtrack, Anderson's comedy-drama centres on a family of geniuses estranged from their shifty patriarch Royal Tenenbaum (Gene Hackman). Anderson gets the balance between droll comedy, artifice and grey tristesse just right, even when depicting the potentially lurid story of two siblings (albeit one adopted) who fall in love.

The Life Aquatic With Steve Zissou 2004, 118 min

cast Bill Murray, Owen Wilson, Cate Blanchett, Anjelica Huston, Willem Dafoe, Jeff Goldblum *cin* Robert Yeoman *m* Mark Mothersbaugh

Budgeted somewhere between $25m and a rumoured $50m, this proved to be Anderson's most costly work. Although it has its ardent defenders, its story of titular sea-explorer Zissou (Murray, again) and his ragtag crew failed to click with audiences the same way *Tenenbaums* did. There are bravura shots of the Cinecittà-built set, and memorable moments from supports including Willem Dafoe, Cate Blanchett and a scene-stealing Bud Cort, but very little structure to hold the whole together.

Roy Andersson

Sweden, 1943–

When Roy Andersson's *Songs From The Second Floor* made a big splash at the Cannes Film Festival in 2000, many assumed it was his first film, as it sported the fresh, dewy inventiveness that often graces a debut. It was, in fact, his third. But his first two films had been made over 25 years before.

In 1969, Andersson made his debut with *A Swedish Love Story*, a prodigious critical and commercial success that he finally followed up six years later with *Giliap*, which went seriously over budget and over schedule. With critics vexed and the public unimpressed, the industry was unforgiving and Andersson was, in effect, handed his cards. The unemployed director could only find work making adverts. Over the next two decades he made a name for himself as the creator of – according to Ingmar Bergman – probably the best adverts in the world.

Songs From The Second Floor, which was partially self-financed, took four years to film. In interviews Andersson explained that he had been planning the film for over a decade, "collecting" faces along the way, members of the public who'd fit right in to his nightmarish world. One was discovered shopping in IKEA. The result is a melange of the grotesque and the burlesque whose theme, ironically (or appropriately) for a director of three hundred adverts, is the alienating dehumanization of consumer culture. LF

Songs From The Second Floor (Sånger från andra våningen) 2000, 98 min

cast Lars Nordh, Stefan Larsson, Hanna Eriksson, Peter Roth, Klas Gösta Ollson, Lucio Vucino *cin* István Borbás, Jesper Klevenås *m* Benny Andersson

A loose collection of sketches from the apocalypse in which spectral figures break into song on the subway, the dead come back to life and a magician accidentally saws into the body of a hapless volunteer. All these tableaux of disquiet are shot in single takes with a static camera, and are accompanied, just as surreally, by music from Abba's Benny Andersson. A film to admire if not to love.

Theo Angelopoulos
Greece, 1935–

A unique cinematic sensibility, Theo Angelopoulos's art fuses time, history and myth in a contemplative aesthetic of long takes and elegant travelling shots. Angelopoulos's early exposure to cinema was conventional enough (as a young man he liked James Cagney movies, John Ford Westerns and Stanley Donen musicals), but like all Greeks of his generation he was profoundly affected by World War II, the Greek Civil War and the dictatorships that dominated Greek life for much of the the twentieth century. When Angelopoulos was 9 years old, his father was arrested by the Communists and disappeared without a trace for months.

After his compulsory military service, Angelopoulos switched from studying law to literature, film and anthropology under Claude Levi-Strauss at the Sorbonne. He subsequently studied filmmaking in Paris at the height of the *nouvelle vague* and, on his return to Athens, worked as a film critic. His first feature, the Brechtian *Reconstruction* (1970s), recreates a real-life murder case from the point of view of the police investigating it and the TV journalists intent on reconstructing it for their cameras. Of a piece with the director's subsequent work, *Reconstruction* shows a grey, impoverished northern Greece, far from the sunny shores of Zorba, and it concertinas time. History is an immediate presence in Angelopoulos's films, with their carefully choreographed patterns of repetition and symmetry, and he establishes a continuity within the camera frame which transcends conventional dramatic causality.

Angelopoulos then embarked on what he dubbed his "History Trilogy" – *Days of '36* (1972), *The Travelling Players* (1975) and *Alexander The Great* (1980) – which merged twentieth-century Greek history with ancient myth, often within the same sequence shot. This film cycle was followed by "Trilogy Of Silence" and "Trilogy Of Borders", although, in truth, all of Angelopoulos's films bleed into each other. For example, the eponymous travelling players who wander through the years 1939–52, also crop up in *Landscape In The Mist*, which was filmed and set in 1988 (although, admittedly, the players have fallen on hard times by the later film).

With his consistent emphasis on deep focus compositions, a moving camera and takes that last for minutes, not seconds (in 230 minutes of *The Travelling Players*, there are fewer than one hundred shots), Angelopoulos demands active audience concentration. Audacious symbolism and stark, *cinéma vérité* realism co-exist within his films, which evoke both *tableaux vivants* and the long, artfully choreographed musical sequences beloved of Vincente Minnelli and Stanley Donen. Dialogue tends to be used sparingly, but his later films significantly feature the haunting music of Greek composer Eleni Karaindrou.

Fêted at home, Angelopoulos is elsewhere perhaps less widely known than he deserves to be. His cinema resists reduction to small screen formats, and it was only with *Ulysses' Gaze* (1995) that he imprinted himself on the American critical consciousness. After that film won the Grand Jury Prize at Cannes, *Eternity And A Day* (1998) went one better and collected the Palme d'Or. TC

The Travelling Players (O Thiasos) 1975, 230 min

cast Eva Kotamanidou, Aliki Georgoulis, Statos Pachis, Maris Vassiliou, Petros Zarkadis *cin* Yorgos Arvanitis *m* Loukianos Kilaidonis

Angelopoulos's most celebrated and original film tracks a theatrical troupe touring northern Greece during the turbulent war-torn period of 1939 to 1952 presenting the folk melodrama *Golpho The Shepherdess*. Epic in scale and running time, this lyrical, humanist masterpiece was the most

The travelling players on the beach: a typical example of Theo Angelopoulos's spacious, panoramic vision.

expensive Greek film of its day and the director's radical political critique somehow managed to slip through the junta's strict censorship.

Landscape In The Mist (Topo stin omichli)
1988, 126 min

cast Michalis Zeke, Tania Palaiologou, Stratos Tzortzoglou *cin* Yorgos Arvanitis *m* Eleni Karaindrou

The first of Angelopoulos's "Trilogy Of Borders" is a devastating lament for an orphaned modernity, in which two children journey across Greece towards Germany in search of their missing father. Along the way they are helped by Orestes, a stage hand from a troupe of travelling players who is facing the prospect of military service. The haunting imagery represents Angelopoulos at the height of his expressive powers.

Ulysses' Gaze (To vlemma tou Odyssea) 1995, 180 min

cast Harvey Keitel, Erland Josephson, Maia Morgenstern, Thanasis Vengos, Yorgos Michalakopoulos *cin* Yorgos Arvanitis *m* Eleni Karaindrou

The gaze is patient and unblinking, deep and challenging. Method actor Harvey Keitel takes the role of a Greek-American filmmaker who returns to his homeland to find three undeveloped reels of film made in 1905 by the first Greek filmmakers. A typically elliptical, Homeric response to both the centenary of cinema and the Balkan Wars, this film is poetic and meditative, another visionary *tour de force* that ends in the ruins of Sarajevo.

Eternity And A Day (Mia eoniotita ke mia mera) 1998, 130 min

cast Bruno Ganz, Isabelle Renauld, Achileas Skevis, Despina Bebedeili *cin* Giorgos Arvanitis *m* Eleni Karaindrou

Bruno Ganz is an ailing poet, Alexandre, who encounters an orphaned Albanian boy and decides to spend what may be his last day with him. The film exhibits Angelopoulos's typically spellbinding imagery, but this time the director's solemn concerns could be construed as solipsistic and

pretentious. Like *Ulysses' Gaze, Eternity And A Day* was co-written with the great Italian screenwriter Tonino Guerra, so it's not surprising that it won the Palme d'Or.

Kenneth Anger
US, 1927–

Though his entire filmography only adds up to about three hours of screen time, Kenneth Anger has exerted a powerful influence on filmmakers as diverse as Martin Scorsese, David Lynch, Derek Jarman and Roger Corman. Isaac Julien credited Anger's movies with "develop[ing] the vocabulary for the New Queer Cinema", and Anger arguably prescribed the grammar of MTV with the proto-music video elements of *Scorpio Rising* (1963), a pop-scored fever dream of biker boys and their toys. An oneiric haze of Dionysian hallucination or baroque nightmare suffuses all of Anger's movies, not least his first surviving piece, *Fireworks* (1947), which the 17-year-old filmmaker shot at home while his parents were away. Anger himself played "the Dreamer", who is beaten and, it's suggested, raped by a gang of sailors in the first film of his *Magick Lantern Cycle*.

Anger (né Anglemyer) was a precocious child of the dream factory: his grandmother was a wardrobe mistress, and he appeared as an 8-year-old in the 1935 film version of *A Midsummer Night's Dream*. Steeped from birth in Tinseltown lore, Anger published two volumes of *Hollywood Babylon* (and has long made noises about a third instalment), a grimly fascinating compendium of sordid celebrity lives and deaths, replete with autopsy details and crime-scene photos. From his teens onwards, Anger was also fascinated by the writings of English occultist Aleister Crowley, to whom the director dedicated *Inauguration Of The Pleasure Dome* (1954), which took its title from Coleridge's opiate befogged poem fragment "Kubla Khan".

In the late 1960s, Anger embarked on *Lucifer Rising* (1981), which took more than a decade to complete, hindered foremost by the theft of original footage and camera equipment. Featuring Marianne Faithfull and Donald Cammell as gods, and a soundtrack recorded in prison by Manson family associate Bobby Beausoleil, *Lucifer Rising* is Anger's most fast-paced film, an associative collage that accelerates to a blur. It also seems to have spun Anger off the filmmaking coil, with the exception of the extremely slight short film *The Man We Want To Hang* (2002), a straightforward and unremarkable presentation of some paintings by Aleister Crowley. JW

Fireworks 1947, 20 min, b/w
cast Kenneth Anger, Bill Seltzer, Gordon Gray

Full of phallic visual puns (including the Roman candle as male apparatus), this short film ranks as one of the most extraordinary debuts of all time, both for the precocious gifts of its teenage author and its astonishing boldness in imagining same-sex longings at a time when homosexuality was still a desire that dare not speak its name.

Scorpio Rising 1963, 30 min
cast Bruce Byron, Ernie Allo, Frank Carifi, Steve Crandell, Johnny Dodds

Winking with shiny leather and glinting chrome, this fetishist's fantasia describes the social and criminal life of smouldering biker Scorpio (Bruce Byron), a speedfreak thug whom Anger compares, with characteristic irreverence, to both Jesus Christ and Adolf Hitler. The film spurred a California obscenity trial and inspired David Lynch with its ironic use of Bobby Vinton's "Blue Velvet".

Ken Annakin
UK, 1914–

A former journalist and salesman, Annakin directed training and propaganda films during World War II. He proved equally adept at fiction, producing many entertaining yet realistic films. *Holiday Camp* (1948) introduced the Huggetts, an ordinary family wryly facing post-war life, and generated three sequels. But Annakin is best known for epics, including the comedies *Those Magnificent Men In Their Flying Machines* (1965) and its automobile equivalent *Monte Carlo Or Bust* (1969), and the war films *The Longest Day* (1962) and *The Battle Of The Bulge* (1965). *The Swiss Family Robinson* (1960) is the best of his four Disney films but the 1970s brought mostly TV work. His latest production, the historical epic *Genghis Khan*, was shot in 1992 but financial problems meant it was only released in 2005. JR

Those Magnificent Men In Their Flying Machines, Or How I Flew From London To Paris In 25 Hours 11 Minutes 1965, 138 min
cast Stuart Whitman, James Fox, Sarah Miles, Terry-Thomas, Alberto Sordi, Gert Frobe *cin* Christopher Challis *m* Ron Goodwin

The story of a 1910 London to Paris air race entertains with its comic invention and corny gags dispatched by a frankly stereotypical international cast of comedians and character actors. The title song proved popular and cartoonist Ronald Searle designed the titles. Often consigned to bank holiday afternoon TV, it works best on the big screen.

The Longest Day 1962, 180 min
cast John Wayne, Robert Mitchum, Henry Fonda, Gert Frobe, Arletty, Richard Burton *cin* Jean Bourgoin, Henri Persin *m* Maurice Jarre, Paul Anka

With co-directors Andrew Marton and Bernhard Wicki, Annakin tells the story of the Normandy landings. Though the battle scenes are impressive, there are also more intimate scenes, helping to create a set of believable characters and preventing the film becoming a mere stereotype-filled epic. The all-star cast helps to track the action, but reduces the documentary feel of the Oscar-winning photography and special effects.

Michelangelo Antonioni
Italy, 1912–2007

At Cannes in 1960, Michelangelo Antonioni's sixth feature, *L'avventura*, was screened to howls of derision, jeers and catcalls. So intense was the vilification that a group of filmmakers, writers and distributors headed by Roberto Rossellini signed a letter in support of the maligned Italian director. The Palme d'Or that year want to Federico Fellini's *La dolce vita*, but *L' avventura* was awarded the Special Jury Prize, for "the beauty of its images" and "its new language of cinema". It was a pivotal moment in the director's career – and arguably in the development of cinema itself.

A former critic who was fired during Mussolini's dictatorship for his left-wing views, Antonioni had contributed to the screenplay for Rossellini's *Un pilota ritorna* (*A Pilot Returns*, 1942) and assisted Marcel Carné on *Les visiteurs du soir* (*The Devil's Envoys*, 1942) before turning his own directorial hand to documentaries with the short film *Gente del Po* (*People Of The Po Valley*, 1947).

From *Cronaca di un amore* (*Chronicle Of A Love Affair*, 1950) – influenced by Luchino Visconti's *Ossessione* (1943) – through to the restless wanderings of *Il grido* (*The Cry*, 1959), Antonioni's first five feature films were broadly neo-realist. The stories sprang from a political engagement with the social upheavals of the post-war era, conveyed by authentic location shooting and a focus on the quotidian. To an extent, these films have since been overshadowed by the director's later work (although it could also be argued that the international recognition of his 1960s films rescued his 1950s melodramas from obscurity). Either way, it's true to say that these early films are not as widely known as they deserve to be, considering that they all demonstrate Antonioni's mastery of the medium and his expansive, fluid articulation of time and space.

Indeed, a few critics – notably David Thomson and Philip Lopate – make a persuasive case that these 1950s films represent Antonioni's finest period. Lopate writes of their "gentle, sad, understated, modest tone" and "richly layered social observation". Thomson celebrates their "tender rigour", "spontaneity of behaviour" and "precision in observation".

His first films already demonstrated the alienation and anguished eroticism that later became the director's trademarks (not for nothing was he dubbed "Antoni-ennui"), but in *L'avventura* such themes were given full expression. With that film, Antonioni moved away from conventional narrative towards a more open, ambiguous and modernist mode in which his camera was as receptive to landscape and environment as it was to character and action. Within two years of its Cannes premiere, *L'avventura* was voted the second greatest film ever made in *Sight & Sound* magazine's critics' poll.

Antonioni pressed these advances – if that's what they were – in *La notte* (*The Night*, 1961), *L'eclisse* (*The Eclipse*, 1962) and his first colour film, the expressionist *Deserto rosso* (*Red Desert*, 1964). His muse from *L'avventura*, Monica Vitti, starred in all three of these films, along with such European luminaries as Marcello Mastroianni, Jeanne Moreau, Alain Delon and Richard Harris. However, in those days of heady cinephilia Antonioni was unmistakeably the real star, sitting, regal and aloof, astride a pantheon of auteurs. As his fame spread, his films became more mannered, their architecture more baroque, but their foundations worryingly shallow. Inevitably he gravitated towards Britain and the US.

Blow-Up (1966) seemed simultaneously attracted to, and repelled by, the narcissistic fashion scene in Swinging London, in its tale of a photographer who chances upon evidence of a murder and learns a lesson in deconstructionism. Even the film's irresolution and ambivalence seemed timely, and it became an international box-office hit. But by 1970, when Antonioni grappled with the American counterculture in *Zabriskie Point*, his self-reflexive, introspective, abstracted cinema seemed too removed, too superficial, to sustain its own pretensions. Thin and incoherent, the film was only redeemed by two spectacular, hallucinatory set pieces. In one, hundreds of couples make love in the desert and, in the other, the climax, a house explodes in slow motion, a metaphorical "blow up" of all material things.

The Passenger (1975) – in which Jack Nicholson disappears in northern Africa and assumes the identity of an arms dealer – was more substantial. But for many mainstream critics Antonioni's virtuosic nihilism had become a dead end. Audiences were not interested either, and it was six years before he shot the experimental Jean Cocteau adaptation *The Oberwald Mystery* (1981) on video, and then made a long-awaited return to Italy for the masterly *Identicazione di una donna* (*Identification Of A Woman*, 1982).

Despite suffering a stroke in 1985 which paralysed him down his right side and rendered him all but mute, Antonioni continued making films, most notably the feature *Beyond The Clouds* (1995), based on his book of short stories *That Bowling Alley On The Tiber*. Still going strong in his nineties, he directed the short *Lo sguardo di Michelangelo* (*Michelangelo: Eye To Eye*, 2004) and a segment in the portmanteau film *Eros* (2004) before his death in 2007. Throughout his life, the director remained true to his vision, but his critical standing fluctuated wildly, with some revering his philosophical severity, his limitless patience and his taste for a grand aesthetic and others firmly rejecting them. More than anyone, Antonioni stood for the 1960s notion of the film director as the artist of his age – but that idea, too, has fallen out of fashion. TC

Cronaca di un amore (Chronicle Of A Love Affair) 1950, 100 min, b/w

cast Lucia Bosé, Massimo Girotti, Ferdinando Sarmi, Gino Rossi, Marika Rowsky, Franco Fabrizi *cin* Enzo Serafin *m* Giovanni Fusco

A detective is hired to investigate the past of an industrialist's wife, but the assignment rekindles an old love affair, a relationship already tainted with guilt. Reminiscent of Luchino Visconti's *Ossessione* (*Obsession*, 1943), but with a wider social spectrum, Antonioni's first feature reveals his innate compositional sense and his existential sensibility. In the same mode, Antonioni's *Le amiche* (*The Girlfriends*, 1955) and *Il grido* (*The Cry*, 1959) remain sorely underrated.

L'avventura 1960, 145 min, b/w

cast Monica Vitti, Gabriele Ferzetti, Lea Massari, Dominique Blanchar, Renzo Ricci, James Addams *cin* Aldo Scavarada *m* Giovanni Fusco

Claudia (Monica Vitti) leads the search after her best friend disappears inexplicably during a Mediterranean cruise – but she's powerless to resist the advances of her friend's lover (Gabriele Ferzetti), who is incapable of remaining faithful. "Eroticism is the disease of the age," announced Antonioni, and all other relationships and pursuits seem equally futile and corrupt. In *L'avventura*, Antonioni broke away from causal narrative structures and forged a new, modern cinematic language in which the banal and the decadent go hand in hand.

L'eclisse 1962, 118 min, b/w

cast Monica Vitti, Alain Delon, Francisco Rabal, Louis Seigner, Lilla Brignone, Rossana Rory *cin* Gianni Di Venanzo *m* Giovanni Fusco

With even less plot that his previous films, *L'Eclisse* intensifies Antonioni's identification of listless, alienated modernity as the prevailing spirit of the latter-half of the twentieth century. Humanity has allowed itself to be eclipsed – as the stunning final sequence implies. Filmed in Rome, this is one of the great city films, and perhaps the director's purest, most focused accomplishment.

Blow-Up 1966, 111 min

cast David Hemmings, Vanessa Redgrave, Sarah Miles, Peter Bowles, Jane Birkin *cin* Carlo Di Palma *m* Herbie Hancock

The combination of Swinging London, naked fashion models, a cameo appearance by the Yardbirds and the modish cinephilia of the mid-1960s turned *Blow-Up* into a must-see movie. It's a gimmicky modernist thriller, but the more abstract it becomes, the more gripping it gets. Antonioni's international hit also influenced Brian De Palma's *Blow Out* (1981) and Francis Ford Coppola's *The Conversation* (1974).

The Passenger 1975, 119 min

cast Jack Nicholson, Maria Schneider, Jenny Runacre, Ian Hendry, Steven Berkoff, Ambrose Bia *cin* Luciano Tovoli *m* Ivan Vandor

Jack Nicholson is a reporter marooned in North Africa who assumes the identity of a dead man to escape his sterile marriage and career – not knowing the corpse was a gun runner for revolutionaries. He travels to Germany and then to Barcelona, picking up a girl (Maria Schneider) en route. "What are you running from?" she asks him. "Look behind you," he tells her. A vistuoso seven-minute travelling shot at the end of the film is justly famous, as it encapsulates the detachment that is Antonioni's signature.

Michael Apted

UK, 1941–

Adept at directing actresses and ensuring authenticity, Michael Apted has had a steady workload in Hollywood.

His first industry role was as a researcher for Granada TV, where his credits included the documentary series *World In Action* and the celebrated *7-Up* (1963), which inaugurated an incremental sequence of programmes charting the experiences of a generation of Britons. His first feature was the H.E. Bates adaptation *The Triple Echo* (1973), starring Glenda Jackson as a lonely POW's wife who succours a deserter with whom she falls in love. If there is a theme to Apted, it involves strong women with the sensibilities of outsiders. Amongst a varied oeuvre are *Agatha* (1978) and *Coal Miner's Daughter* (1980), which won Sissy Spacek an Oscar for her role as the country singer Loretta Lynn making her way from backwoods Kentucky to million-selling acclaim. *Gorillas In The Mist* (1988) found Sigourney Weaver deep in Africa nurturing the wildlife as ape expert Dian Fossey.

Apted's approach owes much to BBC documentary, and his *Nell* (1994) was mocked for Jodie Foster's onomatopoeic speech, though the story's restoration of the Carolina wild child was touching and sympathetic. In *Class Action* (1990), Mary Elizabeth Mastrantonio's Maggie Ward makes a fine job of her court fight with father Gene Hackman, but the Cold War drama *Gorky Park* (1981) found Apted overawed by his all-male cast. Lacking in drama or character, other works by this dutiful director – including the Hugh Grant hospital thriller *Extreme Measures* (1996) and the Kate Winslet code-cracking drama *Enigma* (2001) – remain in the memory more for their assiduous surface detail than anything else. More intriguing was 2006's *Amazing Grace*, which focused on the parliamentary battles of eighteenth-century slavery abolitionist William Wilberforce. RA

Agatha 1978, 105 min

cast Dustin Hoffman, Vanessa Redgrave, Timothy Dalton, Helen Morse, Celia Gregory, Paul Brooke *cin* Vittorio Storaro *m* Johnny Mandel

Taking as its premise the incident in 1926 when crime-writer Agatha Christie went missing, this atmospheric reconstruction of the era remains compelling chiefly for Vanessa Redgrave's nuanced performance in the title role, recalling Celia Johnson in *Brief Encounter*.

Amazing Grace 2006, 111 min

cast Ioan Gruffudd, Albert Finney, Michael Gambon, Romola Garai, Rufus Sewell *cin* Remi Adefarasin *m* David Arnold

Ioan Gruffudd puts in a sterling performance as the outspoken and passionate William Wilberforce. Apted's direction is solid and persuasive, though the story's momentum is somewhat slowed by shoehorned flashbacks. Overall, this is one of the few costume dramas of recent years to display any real balls.

Gregg Araki

US, 1959–

A one-time music critic and USC cinema graduate, Gregg Araki is a true guerilla filmmaker. He writes, shoots, directs and edits his own low-budget movies – his debut, *Three Bewildered People In The Night* (1987), cost only $5000.

The Living End (1992) was a buzz movie for the so-called "New Queer Cinema" which emerged in the US in the early 1990s. A hustler and a movie critic – both HIV positive – take off together after the hustler shoots a cop (the echoes of Godard's *A bout de souffle* are very much intentional).

Emboldened, Araki launched his "teen apocalypse trilogy" with *Totally F***ed Up* (1993), a slacker soul-searcher with knobs on. *The Doom Generation* (1995) and *Nowhere* (1996) followed – punky, anarchic provocations which mustered a certain cachet in underground circles.

Although Araki has positioned himself outside the pieties of both mainstream and gay cinema, his pseudo-nihilist rhetorical posturing has taken on an increasingly hollow ring, and his slipshod technique is a serious handicap. After a poorly received threesome comedy, *Splendor* (1999), and an unsuccessful MTV pilot, *This Is How The World Ends* (2000), Araki went through a fallow period. He re-emerged five years later with *Mysterious Skin* (2005) – which is certainly his best film – and then the wacky pot comedy *Smiley Face* (2007). It was a comeback beyond anyone's expectations. TC

The Living End 1992, 84 min

cast Craig Gilmore, Mike Dytri, Darcy Marta, Mary Woronov, Johanna Went, Paul Bartel *cin* Gregg Araki *m* Cole Coonce

Mary Woronov has a small role here, providing a link with the alternative films made at Andy Warhol's Factory. Like Warhol, Araki is a pop iconoclast obsessed with the gaudy surface of consumer society – though Andy would have drawn the line at Araki's Marxist agit-prop (a hangover, probably, from his Godard fetish). A gay couple on the run story, *The Living End* replays a mash of *A bout de souffle* and *Pierrot le fou* with Gilmore and Dytri as two HIV-positive men (a hustler and a movie critic) taking off after the former shoots a cop. An angry, bitter AIDS movie, very much of its time.

The Doom Generation 1995, 85 min

cast James Duval, Rose McGowan, Johnathon Schaech, Cress Williams, Heidi Fleiss *cin* Jim Fealy *m* Dan Gatto

Also a couple on the run film, this time with a sexually voracious third party along for the ride, this bloodsoaked bisexual shocker is genuinely risqué, a punkier, funnier *Natural Born Killers*. With its expressionist, pop-art *mise en scène*, and playful, subversive iconography, it's Araki doing his damndest: "Welcome to Hell", reads the opening graffito, and the motif 666 recurs at every pit stop. Anarchic and erotic, the movie reserves its moral outrage for the revenge of the repressed.

Mysterious Skin 2005, 99 min

cast Chase Ellison, George Webster, Rachael Nastassja Kraft, Lisa Long, Chris Mulkey, Elisabeth Shue *cin* Steve Gainer *m* Harold Budd, Robin Guthrie

Mysterious Skin is Araki's first movie adapted from another source (a novel by Scott Heim). It is the story of two young men who were once abused by their little-league baseball coach. Neil has become a hustler, but the nerdy Brian has repressed the trauma – he believes he may have been abducted by aliens. This brave, sensitive film has no polemic up its sleeve, only a bruised curiosity about life and a trust in subjective experience. It's a challenging but strangely heartening movie.

Denys Arcand

Canada, 1941–

A history student at the University of Montreal, Denys Arcand made his first short while still at college, and went on to become Quebec's best-known filmmaker.

He learned his craft at the National Film Board making documentaries. His first feature-length film, *On est au coton* (*Cotton Mill, Treadmill*, 1970), was highly critical of abuses in the textile industry and reflected the tensions between French-speaking Quebec and English-speaking Canada. It was banned for six years for alleged political bias.

Some of this experience found its way into Arcand's third fictional feature, *Gina* (1975), about a stripper and a film crew making a documentary on the textile industry. These first narrative films were realist in vein and much concerned with the political evolution of Quebec.

That radicalism mellowed over the years. Arcand made an impact on the international scene with *The Decline Of The American Empire* (1986), but despite the grandiose title, the film was a satire about the sexual obsessions of various members of the history faculty at a French-Canadian university, and their wives and partners. Witty and erudite, like its characters, the film managed to be several degrees more caustic than, say, Lawrence Kasdan's *The Big Chill* (1983), without caricaturing its complacent intellectual targets.

Jesus Of Montreal (1989) sustained that delicate balance, this time skewering the Catholic Church in a finely wrought parable. *Love And Human Remains* (1993) and *Stardom* (2000) were both considered disappointments, but Arcand had his biggest success with *The Barbarian Invasions* (2003), which revisited the characters from *Decline* with history professor Rémy (Rémy Girard) facing death from cancer. TC

The Decline Of The American Empire (Le déclin de l'empire américain) 1986, 101 min

cast Dominique Michel, Dorothée Berryman, Louise Portal, Geneviève Rioux, Rémy Girard *cin* Guy Dufaux *m* François Dompierre

As various university colleagues assemble for dinner, Arcand cuts between the men – sharing smutty jokes and braggadocio – and the women, whose talk is equally fixated on matters sexual. For all the intellectual badinage, the film finally exposes the hypocrisy and complacency of its bourgeois mid-lifers as the rakish Rémy (Girard) is outed in front of his all-too-trusting wife. The movie was a critical hit and established Arcand on the international stage.

Jesus Of Montreal (Jésus de Montréal) 1989, 119 min

cast Lothaire Bluteau, Catherine Wilkening, Johanne-Marie Tremblay, Rémy Girard *cin* Guy Dufaux *m* Yves Laferriere

A radical historical staging of the Passion Play antagonizes the Catholic authorities who sponsored it, even as the troupe's lives mirror those of their biblical counterparts. Arcand counterpoints the teachings of Jesus with the wealth and corruption of the Church, and the venality and godlessness of society at large. Although the biblical parallels are sometimes arch, the satire has teeth, and it's a handsomely mounted film with a standout performance from Bluteau.

The Barbarian Invasions (Les invasions barbares) 2003, 99 min

cast Rémy Girard, Stéphane Rousseau, Marie-Josée Croze, Marina Hands, Dorothée Berryman *cin* Guy Dufaux *m* Pierre Aviat

Arcand checks back with the characters from *Decline Of The American Empire* eighteen years on, to find Rémy terminally ill, friends and family rallying round, even his estranged son, a financial whiz who flies back from London to take charge. Witty and rueful, *Barbarian Invasions* won two prizes at Cannes and the Oscar for best foreign language film. It's a film of considerable charm, but it's soft and sentimental beside Arcand's astringent earlier work.

Dario Argento
Italy, 1940–

"**W**ould you believe that I make movies because I want to be loved?" Dario Argento once asked. Though love is not the first word that springs to mind when considering Argento's nocturnal scream-and-slash thrillers, a childlike longing for attention and approbation is a submerged theme in his blood-drenched oeuvre. In the documentary *Dario Argento's World Of Horror* (1985), he recalls that as a boy he had to walk down a long, dark hallway each night to reach his bedroom – a primal scene revisited time and again in his patented panning and tracking shots down snaking corridors and stairways. Argento enacts an affective relationship with his audience via point-of-view Steadicam angles that position the viewer as killer or victim, while the invariably black-gloved hand that wields the knife or axe is often Argento's own. ("After all the years I have been making these films," he deadpans in *World Of Horror*, "I would probably make a pretty good murderer.") Taking his cue from Hitchcock, Argento often focuses on the stranger in a strange land who is drawn into – or even implicated – in murderous intrigue. And as in Hitchcock, or Michael Powell's *Peeping Tom* (1960), Argento's camera casts filmmaker and viewer alike as predatory voyeurs.

Son of the producer Salvatore Argento, Dario was a film critic for the Rome daily *Paese Sera*, and he worked with Bernardo Bertolucci on the screenplay for Sergio Leone's seminal spaghetti Western *Once Upon A Time In The West* (1968). He debuted as a feature director with *The Bird With The Crystal Plumage* (1970), a Morricone-scored Hitch descendant in the *giallo* style. *Giallo* was a baroque horror/mystery subgenre that found its first major proponent in Mario Bava, its name (literally meaning "yellow") derived from the colour associated with the covers of Italian pulp-fiction paperbacks. Argento made several benchmark *gialli* in the 1970s and 80s, including *Profondo rosso* (*Deep Red*, 1975) and *Tenebrae* (*Unsane*, 1982).

His films' operatic relish in highly eroticized slaughter and the mutilation of beautiful women, often via brazenly phallic weapons, has led to accusations of misogyny. Argento self-reflexively addresses the charge in *Tenebrae*, when a reporter makes the same complaint against the protagonist, a writer of murder mysteries. In the 1990s, Argento cast his daughter, Asia (now a director in her own right), in several films, including *The Stendhal Syndrome* (1996), in which her character is repeatedly raped, tortured and finally driven insane. The family connection only thickens the queasiness of Argento's delectation in female suffering, a possible stumbling block for any newcomer to his work. JW

Profondo rosso (Deep Red) 1975, 126 min
cast David Hemmings, Daria Nicolodi, Gabriele Lavia, Clara Calamai, Macha Meril *cin* Luigi Kuveiller *m* Giorgio Gaslini, Goblin

Argento's *giallo* riff on *Blow-Up* (1966) casts David Hemmings (also star of the Antonioni film) as a jazz musician turned amateur detective who's convinced that a picture missing from a murdered psychic's Rome apartment holds the key to her killer's identity. Deploying a large, demonic child-doll and no shortage of violent ends (head-bashings, scaldings and beheadings – the film's title does after all translate as "Deep Red"), the film firmly establishes many of the Argento trademarks: long panning shots, paranormal inflections and jarring shifts between carnage and awkward comedy.

Suspiria 1977, 98 min
cast Jessica Harper, Stefania Casini, Flavio Bucci, Miguel Bosé, Udo Kier, Rudolf Schöndler, Alida Valli *cin* Luciano Tovoli *m* Dario Argento, Goblin

A gruesome Grimm fairy tale painted in storybook primary colours, Argento's masterpiece pulses with *profondo rosso* – not only via artery gushings but lurid crimson backlighting and the blood-thick wine given to dance student Susie (Jessica Harper), who suspects that a coven of witches is running her Munich boarding school and killing the pupils. Argento has yet to top the featured spectacular overture of driving rain and double homicide, and the controlled cacophony of the soundtrack, by Goblin, keeps the delirium levels high.

Opera (Terror At The Opera) 1987, 107 min
cast Cristina Marsilach, Urbano Barberini, Daria Nicolodi, Ian Charleson, Coralina Catalsi Tassoni, Antonella Vitale *cin* Ronnie Taylor *m* Brian Eno

Argento secured the highest budget of his career for this account of an apparently cursed production of Verdi's *Macbeth*, whose young star Betty (Cristina Marsillach) suffers profound anxiety of influence in the form of her dead mother, who was also an opera diva. Argento's fascination with scopophilia and its discontents is crystallized when the killer outdoes *A Clockwork Orange* in forcing Betty to view his grisly handiwork, while the expressionist corridors symbolize a memory-plagued state of mind.

Gillian Armstrong
Australia, 1950–

Since coming to international attention with the Australian New Wave, Gillian Armstrong has experienced mixed fortunes, yet she has a reputation for drawing strong performances from the best young actresses of recent times.

Armstrong entered the industry as an assistant director on the strength of three shorts. At the 1976 Sydney Film Festival she won a top award for the featurette *The Singer And The Dancer*. In 1979 came *My Brilliant Career* – both a key moment in the Australian efflorescence and the film which launched actress Judy Davis.

Armstrong's best-known Hollywood ventures – *Mrs Soffel* (1984) and *Little Women* (1994) – suggested that she was being typecast as a director of costume dramas. *Mrs Soffel* focused on the relationship between Mel Gibson's common criminal and Diane Keaton's do-gooder in turn-of-the-century Pennsylvania – the project was saved by Keaton's performance. Like *My Brilliant Career*, the adaptation of Louisa May Alcott's novel *Little Women* focused on a wilful woman (Winona Ryder's Jo) trying to make it as a writer. In this charming chick flick, Susan Sarandon ministers over ingénues Kirsten Dunst and Claire Danes. The Victorian vein continued in *Oscar And Lucinda* (1997), in which eccentric English cleric Ralph Fiennes meets Cate Blanchett's liberated Australian businesswoman. Like Armstrong's best work, it drew its power from sympathetic handling of actors and a classical sense of proportion. Blanchett again made an appearance for Armstrong in 2001's *Charlotte Gray*, based on the bestselling war novel by Sebastian Faulks. RA

My Brilliant Career 1979, 100 min

cast Judy Davis, Sam Neill, Wendy Hughes, Robert Grubb, Max Cullen, Aileen Britton *cin* Donald McAlpine *m* Nathan Waks

Davis's aspirational evocation of Sybylla Melvyn's resolve to escape an outback farm for a writing career chimed with the era of screen feminism – Claudia Weill's *Girlfriends* had been released the previous year – just as the original 1901 novel chimed with the time of the suffragettes.

The Last Days Of Chez Nous 1990, 97 min

cast Lisa Harrow, Bruno Ganz, Kerry Fox, Miranda Otto, Kiri Paramore, Bill Hunter, Lex Marinos *cin* Geoffrey Simpson *m* Paul Grabowsky

Armstrong's Chekhovian exploration of a crisis summer in a Sydney suburb is built out of tiny details with staggering emotional fallout. Beth knows she's not perfect. Deep down, she knows that is why JP is leaving her. But that does not make it any easier. Bruno Ganz, Lisa Harrow and Kerry Fox gave Armstrong three of the best performances of the 1990s.

Darren Aronofsky
US, 1969–

Though none of his features to date fit the genre per se, Darren Aronofsky is in some ways a horror director at heart, given his films' fascination with deranged paranoia and physical affliction, as well as his use of subjective camera (including the "Snorricam", which is strapped to the actor's body) and exaggerated sound design to mimic jumbled, monomaniacal and sometimes even psychopathic states of mind. Another Aronofsky trademark is the repeated, rapid-fire sequence deployed like a musical refrain: the trembling hand and gulping of pills that forecasts the protagonist's crippling headaches in [*Pi*] (1998), and the accelerated montage of needles, vessels and contracting pupils that shorthand administering a heroin fix in *Requiem For A Dream* (2000).

A National Student Academy Award finalist in 1991 for his Harvard senior thesis film, Aronofsky

financed [*Pi*], his Super 16 debut feature, largely through small donations from family and friends. The film's success (Aronofsky won the director's trophy at Sundance '98) ensured a healthy budget and name actors, including Ellen Burstyn and Jennifer Connelly, for *Requiem For A Dream*. Burstyn also took a lead role in his next, much-maligned science fiction project, the thousand-year-spanning *The Fountain* (2007), alongside his wife Rachel Weisz and Hugh Jackman. JW

[Pi] 1998, 84 min, b/w

cast Sean Gullette, Mark Margolis, Ben Shenkman, Pamela Hart, Stephen Pearlman, Samia Shoaib *cin* Matthew Libatique *m* Clint Mansell

Maths genius Max Cohen (Sean Gullette) is reclusive, paranoid and plagued by horrendous migraines. It's no wonder: a shadowy consortium is hounding him for the numerical key to the stock market and a group of orthodox Jews seem convinced that Max is set to discover the name of God. Shot guerrilla-style on New York streets for an initial budget of $60,000, Aronofsky's flashy debut blurs hallucination and exterior reality to trace the contours of its antihero's addled mind.

Requiem For A Dream 2000, 101 min

cast Ellen Burstyn, Jared Leto, Jennifer Connelly, Marlon Wayans, Christopher McDonald *cin* Matthew Libatique *m* Clint Mansell

While the style assault of [*Pi*] denoted a hungry young director asserting his voice despite anonymity and budget constaints, *Requiem For A Dream* edges towards flash for flash's sake, tarting up a slick, visceral say-no-to-drugs public service announcement. Adapted from Hubert Selby Jr's novel, the movie's chemically induced mania and despair reach their nadir in one character's suppurating needle wounds and another's indignity at the wrong end of a dildo.

Dorothy Arzner
US, 1897–1979

One of Hollywood's genuine pioneers, Dorothy Arzner was the only female director to sustain a career in the early days of sound, and a lesbian proto-feminist who probably invented the boom mike. Starting out as a typist, Arzner worked her way up through the film industry, distinguishing herself as an editor before being given the opportunity to direct the light comedy *Fashion For Women* (1927). Paramount Studios were impressed enough with that film to entrust her with their first all-talkie, *The Wild Party* (1929), for which Arzner used the boom mike, by ingeniously attaching a microphone to the end of a fishing rod, to give silent star Clara Bow the freedom of movement she was used to.

Whether *The Wild Party* and Arzner's subsequent movies are proto-feminist is a matter of debate. Her stock-in-trade was "women's pictures", whose narratives were usually resolved when the heroine was put firmly back in her place – most gratuitously evident in *Christopher Strong* (1933) when Katharine

Hepburn's character dutifully commits suicide after becoming pregnant by her married lover. To detect a radical agenda in her films, you have to almost read against the grain, cherishing fleeting subversive moments and delighting in a roll call of some of Hollywood's most headstrong actresses – Hepburn, Rosalind Russell and Joan Crawford. It's not hard, however, to read a homosexual subtext in the playful shenanigans of *The Wild Party*'s all-women college, or in the slow corrosion of a loveless marriage in *Craig's Wife* (1936). Arzner's crowning, radical glory was the triumphant moment in *Dance Girl Dance* (1940) when Maureen O'Hara chastises the ogling men in a burlesque theatre for lasciviously enjoying the spectacle of female flesh, a lecture on male gaze that was to be echoed in universities decades later.

Arzner's last film, *First Comes Courage*, was made in 1943 as her career was brought to an end by a severe bout of pneumonia and a virulent strain of post-war sexism. The only directing jobs she could get after that were making commercials for Pepsi, whose chairman was married to her old friend, Joan Crawford. Arzner died in 1979, but not before her films were rediscovered and re-evaluated, and she was returned to her rightful place in the Hollywood pantheon. LH

Craig's Wife 1936, 73 min, b/w

cast Rosalind Russell, John Boles, Billie Burke, Jane Darwell, Dorothy Wilson, Alma Kruger, Thomas Mitchell *cin* Lucien Ballard *m* Morris Stoloff

Rosalind Russell plays a woman with ice in her veins who marries for money and exerts a tight, cruel grip over her rich husband. As her controlling, manipulative behaviour manages to alienate almost everyone around her, the perfect life she has worked so hard to create begins to unravel. A forensically bleak study of modern marriage and the asphyxiating paradoxes of a woman's place in the home.

Hal Ashby

US, 1929–88

Born into a Mormon household, by 21 Hal Ashby had seen his parents divorce and his father commit suicide, and had himself been married twice. By the time he burned out he had made some of the most telling film laments of his era.

In 1950 Ashby got a job mimeographing scripts at Universal. Becoming an apprentice editor, he assisted Robert Swink on projects for William Wyler and George Stevens. In 1964 he became a full editor and formed a partnership with Norman Jewison that led to an Academy Award for *In The Heat Of The Night* (1967). Jewison gave Ashby his directorial break by passing on *The Landlord* (1970). Initiating a preoccupation with outsiders amid the cultural vicissitudes of post-war America, this story of the unlikely relationship between Beau Bridges' white boy and a gaggle of Harlem tenants typified the offbeat "New

Hollywood" sensibility then emerging.

Harold And Maude (1971) essayed the love of a young patrician nonconformist for an old lady. Its mordant touch was recalled in *The Last Detail* (1973), in which sailors Jack Nicholson and Otis Young escort a young Randy Quaid to the stockade. Few American films caught the desultory post-Watergate mood so well. *Shampoo* (1975) was a Warren Beatty-produced tribute to the radical 1960s, its poignancy echoing Ashby's own melancholia. He was nominated for an Oscar for Jane Fonda's Vietnam apologia *Coming Home* (1978), but his dream of making the movie – and the director – the true star seemed forlorn amid a corporatizing Hollywood. Forced into bitter rapprochements with the studios and on a deadly spiral of drugs, negative rumours and overwork, Ashby faded after *Being There* (1979). His career epitomizes what was most powerful about the filmmaking era he lived through. RA

Harold And Maude 1971, 92 min

cast Ruth Gordon, Bud Cort, Vivian Pickles, Cyril Cusack, Charles Tyner, Ellen Geer *cin* John A. Alonzo *m* Cat Stevens

Propelled by a European streak of irony and black humour and a sonorous Cat Stevens songbook, this is one of the richest and least expected of New Hollywood's "little movies". It is a piquant tribute to the joys of life seen through the wacky perspectives of Harold, a young man who fakes suicide as a hobby, and Maude, a concentration camp survivor and funeral habitué. Vivian Pickles's staid turn as Harold's bemused mother is a joy to behold.

Being There 1979, 130 min

cast Peter Sellers, Shirley MacLaine, Melvyn Douglas, Jack Warden, Richard A. Dysart *cin* Caleb Deschanel *m* Johnny Mandel

One of the best American films of its day, *Being There* provides a richly ambivalent reading of American decline, generating huge irony out of its bemused idiot savant (Peter Sellers) caught between roles. The movie displays a compelling stillness that, to the credit of Ashby and cinematographer Caleb Deschanel, makes each scene a joy to watch.

Karimuddin Asif

India, 1924–71

Though he directed only three films in a career spanning thirty years, Karimuddin Asif will always be remembered as a man who thought on an epic scale. After directing the successful *Phool* (*The Flower*, 1945), Asif trained his sights on subcontinental history. *Mughal-E-Azam* (*The Emperor Of The Mughals*, 1960) was the most expensive Indian film of its time and took over fifteen years to complete. Progress on the film was hampered when the leading man, Chandra Mohan, died before shooting began. He was eventually replaced by Bollywood legend Dilip Kumar. After the film was released, Asif began yet another ambitious film, *Love And God*, starring Sanjeev Kumar. This time production was stalled by the director's own death. In 1986, Asif's widow patched together a version and released it. Asif has been a huge influence on his contemporaries and on Indian cinema in general, particularly on *Mughal-E-Azam* writer Kamal Amrohi who went through similar trials for his landmark *Pakeezah* (*Pure Heart*, 1971). NR

Mughal-E-Azam (The Emperor Of The Mughals) 1960, 173 min, b/w and col

cast Dilip Kumar, Madhubala, Prithviraj Kapoor, Durga Khote, Nigar Sultana, Ajit, Kumar, Jalan Agha *cin* R.D. Mathur *m* Naushad

This grand retelling of a popular subcontinental legend is justly known for its grand sets, lavish dance sequences and cast of thousands, but at its heart is a tender love story. The romance between Mughal prince Salim and the commoner dancer Anarkali is set against a backdrop of political intrigue, as the Emperor Akbar is forced to prioritize his empire above his errant son. The length doesn't in any way detract from the jaw-dropping splendour of the proceedings. The film was colourized and re-released in 2004, and was a success all over again.

Anthony Asquith

UK, 1902–68

Over a forty-year career, Asquith's early bravura technique gave way to a series of theatrical adaptations relying on his skill with actors.

The son of the Liberal prime minister (1908–16), Asquith went out to Hollywood after graduating from Oxford, and spent time with Douglas Fairbanks, Mary Pickford and their circle. He then joined the British film industry as co-writer, assistant director and stunt double for the heroine in the patriotic but unhistorical *Boadicea* (1926). His script for *Shooting Stars* (1927) satirized British cinema's aping of the American industry. Though the more experienced A.V. Bramble is credited as director, it is generally seen as Asquith's film. The imaginative camerawork in *A Cottage On Dartmoor* (1929), about an escaped prisoner bent on revenge, furthered Asquith's reputation as a virtuoso director, but he did not negotiate the move into sound cinema easily and began to be seen as lightweight.

A series of theatrical adaptations turned his career round in the late 1930s. With star Leslie Howard, he co-directed Shaw's Oscar-winning script of his own comedy of manners *Pygmalion* (1938), though two further Shaw adaptations, *The Doctor's Dilemma* (1958) and *The Millionairess* (1960), were less successful. The farce *French Without Tears* (1939) was the first of ten collaborations with writer Terence Rattigan, including the touching public-school drama *The Browning Version* (1951), but Asquith's best adaptation is Wilde's witty *The Importance Of Being Earnest* (1952).

Asquith's large wartime output included realistic dramas such as the submarinal *We Dive At Dawn* and the pro-Soviet *The Demi-Paradise* (both 1943), and climaxed with the touching air-force story *The Way To The Stars* (1945). Lighter fare included *Fanny By Gaslight* (1944), an example of the later-derided Gainsborough costume melodrama.

Annette Benson and Brian Aherne in the tragi-comic *Shooting Stars*.

Ironically two of his last films – *The VIPs* (1963), in which rich people are marooned in an airport, and *The Yellow Rolls Royce* (1964), following the fortunes of a serially owned car – are star-laden and beholden to the US in exactly the way that *Shooting Stars* had warned against. JR

Shooting Stars 1927, 72 min, b/w

cast Brian Aherne, Annette Benson, Chili Boucher, David Brooks, Donald Calthorpe *cin* Henry Harris, Stanley Rodwell

Though wittily criticizing a British film industry in thrall to America, Asquith has no qualms about using German expressionist lighting in this self-referential melodrama about love and betrayal on the set of a low-grade British Western. Asquith couples neat plot devices (the film-within-a-film opening) with melodramatic clichés (the blank bullet replaced with a real one) to create a film that is both clever and populist.

The Way To The Stars 1945, 109 min, b/w

cast John Mills, Michael Redgrave, Douglass Montgomery, Stanley Holloway, Rosamund John *cin* Derek Williams *m* Nicholas Brodzsky

Like all the best wartime films, *The Way To The Stars* is character- rather than action-driven as we follow the lives of an RAF crew and the US airmen who join them. Despite the aerodrome setting, the film doesn't leave the ground, preferring to look at Anglo-American tension and co-operation and the effects of war on John Mills's classic everyman. It was released in America under the title of the famously featured poem, *Johnny In The Clouds*.

The Importance Of Being Earnest 1952, 92 min

cast Michael Redgrave, Michael Denison, Dorothy Tutin, Joan Greenwood, Edith Evans *cin* Desmond Dickinson *m* Benjamin Frankel

The finest of Asquith's theatrical adaptations, Wilde's comedy of mistaken identity is pitched perfectly by some of the best British actors of the time, the humour counterpointed by the Edwardian candy-coloured palette and Benjamin Frankel's elegant score. Though it far outstrips any of the many adaptations of the play, it is sometimes unfairly remembered only for Edith Evans, who doesn't so much steal the scene as the entire genre with the single line "A handbag?"

Richard Attenborough

UK, 1923–

Richard Attenborough once said that the only reason he became a film director was in order to direct *Gandhi* (1982). That film perfectly exemplifies the way in which, with Attenborough, content invariably wins out over style.

Attenborough began acting at the age of 12. In 1942 he got the part of the cowardly seaman in *In Which We Serve*, a role that would see him typecast for decades –with the exception of his memorable turn as fresh-faced psychopath gangster Pinky Brown in the *noir* thriller *Brighton Rock* (1947). In 1959 he set up a production company with

director Bryan Forbes. Producing *Whistle Down The Wind* (1961) and *The L-shaped Room* (1962), Attenborough seemed to forge a link between the 1940s realism of his youth and a realist postwar new wave then in the ascendant. In 1969 he turned to directing with a mannered adaptation of Joan Littlewood's symbolist account of World War I, *Oh! What A Lovely War*. This inaugurated a preoccupation with historical moments and men that has drawn crowds of occasional filmgoers but elicited only dutiful critical plaudits. *Young Winston* (1972) was a dull portrait of Churchill's adventures in the Boer War. *A Bridge Too Far* (1977) championed British grit in the face of American bravado and Nazi might during the fateful Arnhem raid of 1944. Like the sprawling war movies of the 1960s, it sported a stellar Anglo-American cast and ranged reverently over events like a school primer. As a film, it was unambiguous and flat, failing to prepare audiences for the interesting chiller *Magic* (1978) or the triumphant success of 1982's *Gandhi*.

At a time when the contradictions of its imperial heritage were erupting in riot-torn cities across Thatcher's Britain, Attenborough's *Cry Freedom* (1987) brought liberal conviction to bear on the fate of black South African Steve Biko. Yet the focus remained on white interlocutor Donald Woods. *Chaplin* (1992) saw Robert Downey Jr faithfully rehearsing the filmmaker's life, though nothing of the madness and ambivalence that made Chaplin a genius shone through. Since *Shadowlands* (1993), Attenborough has remained a British institution: conventional and dependable. RA

Magic 1978, 107 min

cast Anthony Hopkins, Ann-Margret, Burgess Meredith, Ed Lauter, Jerry Houser, David Ogden Stiers *cin* Victor J. Kemper *m* Jerry Goldsmith

This is an underrated moment in an otherwise epic oeuvre. Adapted by William Goldman from his novel of the same name, *Magic* tells the story of the ventriloquist overcome by his dummy. Anthony Hopkins's performance provides glimpses of the ambivalent depths to come later in his career.

Gandhi 1982, 188 min

cast Ben Kingsley, Candice Bergen, Edward Fox, John Gielgud, Trevor Howard, Martin Sheen *cin* Billy Williams, Ronnie Taylor *m* Ravi Shankar

Revolving around Ben Kingsley's charismatic performance as the Indian spiritual leader, *Gandhi* is an unabashed tribute to a great twentieth-century figure. Closer to the serendipities of a David Lean epic, for once Attenborough achieves moments of genuine poetry. The opening scene of Gandhi's funeral barge captures what is exceptional about his Indian milieu.

Shadowlands 1993, 131 min

cast Anthony Hopkins, Debra Winger, Joseph Mazzello, Peter Firth, John Wood, Michael Denison *cin* Roger Pratt *m* George Fenton

A welcome burst of emotion in a sea of academic biopics, Attenborough's account of C.S. Lewis's meeting and affair with Joy Gresham is his best ever. Subtly charting the

A

growth of a man from dusty donnish celibacy to a passionate rapprochement with experience via Debra Winger's fetching vivacity, Hopkins and Attenborough gave us a film as sentimental as Attenborough himself.

Bille August
Denmark, 1948–

Until the rise of *enfant terrible* Lars von Trier, Bille August was Denmark's best-known living director. Taking a more conventional route to prominence than that of his compatriot, August is at once a confident storyteller of social period dramas in the Ingmar Bergman mould and a safe pair of hands when it comes to adapting middlebrow literary works. Strong characterization, striking cinematography and (post-Tarantino) an unfashionable willingness to treat emotions with seriousness and sentimentality have ensured that August has rarely been short of commissions.

Early work included the coming-of-age movie *Twist And Shout* (1984) and the magic realist children's film *Buster's World* (1984). *Pelle The Conqueror* (1987), still widely held to be his finest film, cemented the template for his career with its epic story of poor nineteenth-century Swedish immigrants struggling to deal with the injustices of their new lives. As with so many of August's films, it was adapted from a novel. It carried off the Palme d'Or and the Oscar for best foreign film. August maintained his high profile with *The Best Intentions* (1991), a film about Ingmar Bergman's parents' lives, entrusted to him by the legendary Swedish auteur.

Since then August has helmed a string of literary adaptations, the best known of which are Isabel Allende's *The House Of The Spirits* (1993), Peter Høeg's *Smilla's Sense Of Snow* (1997) and Victor Hugo's *Les Misérables* (1998). Universally competent, these films rarely clock in at under 140 minutes and such conventional filmmaking hasn't really excited much critical interest. Nominated for the Golden Bear award at the Berlin Film Festival in 2007, *Goodbye Bafana*, about the moral awakening of one of Nelson Mandela's prison guards, didn't break the now established pattern of August's career. It was another long, worthy but largely unexciting film. RC

Pelle The Conqueror (Pelle erobreren) 1987, 150 min
cast Max von Sydow, Astrid Vilaume, Pelle Hvenegaard *cin* Jörgen Persson *m* Stefan Nilsson

Pelle (Hvenegaard) and his father Lasse (von Sydow) struggle to deal with their arduous new life of labour on a huge farm run by rich uncaring aristocrats. As Lasse ages and Pelle grows up, their relationship is put under strain and both struggle to break free from external and internal shackles. Stirring stuff for the patient.

The Best Intentions (Den goda viljan) 1991, 181 min
cast Max von Sydow, Samuel Fröler, Pernilla August, Ghita Nørby, Lennart Hjulström, Mona Malm *cin* Jörgen Persson *m* Stefan Nilsson

Brooding, bleak and very Bergmanesque, the story of the Swedish director's parents' courtship and early marital days couldn't really have turned out any other way given the raw materials. Von Sydow is outstanding and the *mise en scène* impressively oppressive but it doesn't top Bergman's own childhood saga *Fanny And Alexander* (1982) for either verve or illumination.

John G. Avildsen
US, 1935–

John G. Avildsen's journeyman knowledge of the technical side of filmmaking would surely make a great autobiography, but great Avildsen films have been few and far between.

The son of a tool manufacturer, Avildsen worked as an advertising copywriter before assisting on a low-budget film made by a colleague. He worked his way up from assistant director on Arthur Penn's *Mickey One* (1965) to second unit on Preminger's *Hurry Sundown* (1967). He also worked on industrial films for Clairol, IBM and Shell, as well as exploitation "nudies". True to this eclectic apprenticeship, Avildsen could often be found editing his directed work.

His first feature, *Joe* (1970), was a critical breakthrough that was timely in its anatomizing of the urban hard-hat reaction to the counterculture and the liberal establishment. The recalcitrant urban male became a theme. *Cry Uncle!* (1971) peddled softcore sexual parody in Allen Garfield's repulsive private dick, while the poignant *Save The Tiger* (1973) epitomized Jack Lemmon's perennial image as the lost and fraught executive. On the other side of the masculinist Avildsen coin, *W.W. And The Dixie Dancekings* (1975) was a rambunctious Southern romp typical of mid-1970s Burt Reynolds. Then came the urban poetry of *Rocky* (1976), bringing Avildsen the Oscar for best director. *Slow Dancing In The Big City* (1978) was an oddly 1970s mix of the desultory and the mawkish.

In the 1980s, Avildsen seemed unable to envision the decade's shallow allure, becoming bogged down in the awful *Karate Kid* franchise and *Rocky V* (1990). *Lean On Me* (1989), the film that gave Morgan Freeman his break, saw a hard-hitting high-school principal offer a bunch of no-hopers a future. That this minor but gifted New Hollywood player should have directed the film makes supreme Hollywood sense. RA

Save The Tiger 1973, 100 min

cast Jack Lemmon, Jack Gilford, Laurie Heineman, Norman Burton, Patricia Smith, Thayer David *cin* James Crabe *m* Marvin Hamlisch

As Jack Lemmon's garment manufacturer faces failure and nervous breakdown, the actor keeps up a constant dialogue with a kinder era. Held together by Steve Shagan's intelligent script and Lemmon's determination to play male tragedy to the limit, this is one of the best films of its time.

Rocky 1976, 119 min

cast Sylvester Stallone, Talia Shire, Burt Young, Carl Weathers, Burgess Meredith, Thayer David, Joe Spinell *cin* James Crabe *m* Bill Conti

One of the great sleeper hits, this update of the classic boxing flick sentimentally tapped into an America depressed after Vietnam and Watergate. Big Italian hunk Sly Stallone brings humour, pathos and an immigrant grit not seen in American movies since the monochrome 1930s.

Gabriel Axel

Denmark, 1918–

Though Gabriel Axel may seem like a late-blooming one-hit wonder to audiences outside his native Denmark, the Paris-raised director in fact worked steadily away in Danish TV from the 1950s and made well-regarded films that usually didn't see much in the way of an international release. A smattering of his movies, including alluring titles such as *Det tossede paradis* (*Crazy Paradise*, 1962) and *Die Auto-Nummer – Sex auf Rädern* (*Soft Shoulders, Sharp Curves*, 1972) did receive brief US runs, and *Hagbarde and signe* (*The Red Mantle*, 1968), an austere folk epic shot in Iceland and starring Bergman regulars Gunner Björnstrand and Eva Dahlbeck, premiered at Cannes.

Axel's reputation rests almost solely on the international success of his much-loved *Babette's Feast* (1987), about a French cook who shocks and stirs her ascetic Danish milieu by crafting a rich, elaborate meal. Axel might have had another arthouse hit with *Prince Of Jutland* (1994), which interpreted the *Hamlet* story using the original Danish material, but the film fell into the hands of the often butterfingered Miramax; despite a formidable cast that included Christian Bale, Gabriel Byrne, Helen Mirren and Brian Cox, the studio sent it straight to video, misleadingly rebranded with the trashy title *Royal Deceit*. JW

Babette's Feast 1987, 103 min

cast Stéphane Audran, Jean-Philipe Lafont, Gudmar Wivesson, Jarl Kulle, Bibi Andersson, Bodil Kjer *cin* Henning Kristiansen *m* Per Norgård

Widowed and impoverished in coastal Denmark, French cook Stéphane Audran wins the lottery only to blow the loot on the ingredients (foie gras, truffles, caviar and Veuve Cliquot) for an exquisite meal. The feast amounts to a bittersweet epiphany for both the strait-laced, suspicious locals and for Babette herself in Axel's handsome, Oscar-winning adaptation of a short story by Isak Dinesen.

Hector Babenco

Argentina, 1946–

Staking out his filmmaking home on society's margins, Hector Babenco specializes in convicts, outlaws and tramps. *Pixote* (1981) provided a shocking look at the young criminal underclass of São Paulo, its *cinéma vérité* authenticity intensified by the presence of real street kids playing major roles. (In a tragic postscript, Fernando Ramos Da Silva, who played the 11-year-old title character, died from a police bullet while still in his teens.)

Born in Buenos Aires but a Brazilian citizen, Babenco rarely sentimentalizes his tough, hard-worn characters. Though his films often have a documentary immediacy, he frequently flavours social realism with fantasy sequences or flashback interludes, notably in the movie re-creations that entertain the prison inmates in *Kiss Of The Spider Woman* (1985).In the grim *Ironweed* (1987), Jack Nicholson and Meryl Streep played dosshouse drunks in upstate New York, and Babenco visualizes both his crippling bad memories and the sad figments of her addled imagination.

Babenco faltered with the bloated Amazonian epic *At Play In The Fields Of The Lord* (1991); his skills are best deployed in more intimate, even claustrophobic settings, as in *Carandiru* (2003), set inside the notorious Brazilian prison of its title, a hierarchical society unto itself that Babenco illustrates with characteristic acuity. JW

Pixote (Pixote a lei do mais fraco) 1981, 127 min
cast Marcello Mazzarella, Vincenzo Albanese, Carmelo Di Mazzarelli, Gioia Spaziani, Artuto Todaro, Biagio Barone *cin* Pasquale Mari *m* Agricantus

A homeless São Paulo kid (Fernando Ramos Da Silva) escapes from a ghastly juvenile detention centre into a slum hell of thievery, drug-dealing, prostitution and murder in which the boy is both victim and ruthless perpetrator. A descendant of Buñuel's *Los Olvidados* and a forerunner of Fernando Meirelles' *City Of God*, Babenco's unflinching, documentary-style social portrait has nerves of steel.

Kiss Of The Spider Woman 1985, 118 min
cast William Hurt, Raul Julia, Sonia Braga *cin* Rodolfo Sanchez *m* Nando Cordeiro, John Neschling

William Hurt won the best actor Oscar for his faintly Kabuki-like performance in this odd-couple melodrama. Set in a South American prison, the film pairs Raul Julia's impassioned political prisoner with Hurt's camp gay inmate, who escapes the monotony of their shared cell by narrating scenes from garish movies of a past golden age, brought to colourful life by Sonia Braga and the rich cinematography of Rodolfo Sanchez.

Clarence Badger

US, 1880–1964

Though in the 1920s he was a well-known director specializing in comedies, Badger's reputation fell with the coming of sound and now rests on just one film, *It* (1927).

Badger quickly rose from writer (on, for example, the *Lady Baffles And Detective Duck* series), to director in his own right. However, disenchanted with slapstick assignments, he moved to more sophisticated but saucy comedies – *The Danger Girl* (1916) was one of several with Gloria Swanson – and comedy Westerns starring Will Rogers. In 1926 another Badger regular, Bebe Daniels, starred in *Miss Brewster's Millions*, based on the much-adapted George Barr McCutcheon novel that Walter Hill would use in 1982. Badger and Clara Bow made *It* in 1927, and *Red Hair* and *Three Weekends* in 1928. Their collaboration epitomized the flapper age and Bow became an icon – before sound exposed her unflapperish Brooklyn accent and sex scandals ruined her. Badger too had difficulty with sound though he made several musicals including *No, No, Nanette* (1930), set on Broadway, and Rogers and Hart's *The Hot Heiress* (1933). He moved to Australia and made his last film there in 1941. JR

It 1927, 76 min

cast Clara Bow, Antonia Moreno, William Austin, Priscilla Banner, Elinor Glyn *cin* H. Kinley Martin

Ostensibly based on Elinor Glyn's novel, *It* simply takes the title and trades on the author's self-generated notoriety, even having her cameo as herself. Bow dominates the film, bringing an irresistibly vivacious sexuality to her role as a shop-girl pursuing the playboy son of the shop's owner. The now sadly debased phrase "It-Girl" was coined to describe her. An uncredited Josef von Sternberg directed some of the film and a young Gary Cooper plays a reporter.

John Badham

UK, 1939–

Journeyman John Badham is best known for the iconic *Saturday Night Fever* (1977). His career thereafter consisted of an ever slicker and emptier procession of speculative-fiction thrillers and cop movies, offering formula-fed odd couples, committee-written banter and many a stultifying car chase. He had a few hits, though – most notably the serviceable Reagan-age time-capsule piece *War Games* (1983), which rode the trend of nuclear "what if" thrillers with its blithely implausible tale of a high school computer whiz (Matthew Broderick) who inadvertently sets off the countdown to World War III. More typical of the Badham oeuvre, *Stakeout* (1987) was a by-rote buddy-cop picture with a grisly streak, and one of the unworthier sequel recipients in memory. JW

Saturday Night Fever 1977, 118 min

cast John Travolta, Karen Lynn Gorney, Barry Miller, Joseph Cali, Paul Pape, Donna Pescow, Julie Bovasso *cin* Ralf D. Bode *m* The Bee-Gees

Norman Wexler's screenplay is a gritty, often bleak portrait of a machismo-bound 19-year-old who lives with his parents and dreams of escape to Manhattan, though the film has solidified in the collective mind as a mere kitsch relic of the disco era. As Roger Ebert wrote, "There's a lot in the movie that's sad and painful, but after a few years what you remember is John Travolta on the dance floor in that classic white disco suit…"

Roy Ward Baker

UK, 1916–

Adaptable and prolific, with more than fifty movies to his name, Roy Ward Baker glided from making serviceable thrillers in the 1950s to pulpy horror for Hammer and then Amicus in the late 1960s and 70s, rounding out his wayward career with television work. *Don't Bother To Knock* (1952), featuring Anne Bancroft in her first film role, was a deftly shot but cursorily performed chamber piece hinging on the psychological breakdown of an addled babysitter, played by Marilyn Monroe in an awkward attempt to diversify her acting portfolio. Baker seemed more at ease with the goofy espionage capers of *Highly Dangerous* (1950), wherein Margaret Lockwood's entomologist journeys to the Balkans and becomes convinced she is the heroine in a radio serial while under the influence of a truth serum, and the 3D *Inferno* (1953), starring Robert Ryan as a spoiled brat stranded in the (splendidly photographed) desert. With *A Night To Remember* (1958), Baker mounted an almost documentary-style commemoration of the 1912 *Titanic* disaster, with some two hundred speaking parts and a meticulous attention to historical detail often missing from James Cameron's 1997 epic.

Baker's earliest forays into horror are considered his best, such as the alien-penetration B-movie classic *Quatermass And The Pit* (1967) and the handsomely staged, self-consciously erotic *Vampire Lovers* (1970). He didn't fare as well with the aptly titled *And Now the Screaming Starts!* (1973), while the rambunctious kung-fu pleasures of *The Legend Of The Seven Golden Vampires* (1974), with Hammer stalwart Peter Cushing as Van Helsing, can be credited not to Baker but to legendary Hong Kong co-producers the Shaw Brothers. JW

Quatermass And The Pit 1967, 97 min

cast James Donald, Andrew Keir, Barbara Shelley, Julian Glover, Duncan Lamont, Bryan Marshall, Peter Copley *cin* Arthur Grant *m* Tristram Cary

Released in the US as *Five Million Years To Earth*, Baker's first feature for the Hammer studio adapts the third of Nigel Kneale's H.G. Wells-influenced Quatermass stories, about the discovery in the London underground of an ancient Martian spacecraft which contains clues that aliens were once the architects of human history. As long-dormant energies reawaken, Baker's rough-and-ready film gains in atmospheric density.

Ralph Bakshi

Israel (formerly Palestine), 1938–

Ralph Bakshi scored a first with *Fritz The Cat* (1972), the world's original X-rated animated feature; too bad Fritz's creator, Robert Crumb, hated the movie so much that he killed off his womanizing cool cat in a subsequent comic. Raised in Brooklyn, Bakshi began his career in television cartoons, working for the Terrytoons studio (home of Mighty Mouse) and eventually striking out on his own. After *Fritz The Cat*, the impressively seedy *Heavy Traffic* (1973) mixed live action and animation in following an aspiring young comix artist, Michael, who's oppressed by his overbearing parents and by the squalid city itself – a vivid gallery of scrounging, battle-scarred downtown grotesques. *Coonskin* (1975) critiqued stereotypical images of blacks, but was itself attacked for being racist (though Spike Lee is an avowed fan). Another sweeping, often scathing overview of Americana, *American Pop* (1981), mounted nothing less than a rotoscoped history of the twentieth-century US, as seen through the prism of a Russian immigrant family, and the pop music – from vaudeville ditties to rock – that provides the soundtrack to their experiences.

Bakshi's stab at an animated film version of J.R.R. Tolkien's *The Lord Of The Rings* (1978) was left only half-completed. Having overseen a new Mighty Mouse series in the mid-1980s and directed the Rolling Stones video "Harlem Shuffle", Bakshi re-entered feature filmmaking with the live-action/animation mix *Cool World* (1992), but the results were limp and somewhat incoherent. JW

Fritz The Cat 1972, 77 min

cast (voices) Skip Hinnant, Roseta Le Noire, John McCurry, Judy Engles, Phil Seuling *cin* Gene Borghi, Ted C. Bemiller *m* Ed Bogas, Ray Shanklin

This misanthropic cartoon "for adults only" isn't for every adult – Fritz is a sleazy downtown bounder who liberally partakes of drugs and women and always seems to be getting into a scrape (the police are depicted as pigs, naturally). Its original X-rating now revised to an R, the film is episodic, meandering and relentlessly violent, and perhaps most interesting as a 1960s-hangover artefact.

The Lord Of The Rings 1978, 133 min

cast (voices) Norman Bird, Christopher Guard, John Hurt, Michael Scholes William Squire *cin* Timothy Galfas *m* Leonard Rosenman

Using a mixture of traditional animation and rotoscope (drawings laid on top of live-action footage), Bakshi did a surprisingly good, if underappreciated, job with the first half of J.R.R. Tolkien's epic fantasy. A then 18-year-old Peter Jackson is said to have watched this version and drawn on Bakshi's treatment of the ring wraiths for his own CGI-bolstered trilogy more than twenty years later. With John Hurt voicing a splendid Aragorn and the director's fluid touches, it's regrettable that Bakshi didn't get a crack at part two.

Aleksei Balabanov

Russia (formerly Soviet Union), 1959–

A leksei Balabanov began his career making arthouse adaptations of Beckett and Kafka but has metamorphosed, to the horror of some, into the Quentin Tarantino of Russian cinema.

Like his most famous hero, *Brother*'s Danila Bagrov, Balabanov was a member of the Red Army. After being discharged, he became an assistant director in the Soviet film industry and in 1990 moved to St Petersburg, which has provided the impressively imperious locations for most of his films. His adaptations of Beckett (*Happy Days*, 1992) and Kafka (*The Castle*, 1994) were critically well received but rarely seen outside the Soviet Union.

International attention came with the release of his hypnotically glacial gangster drama *Brother* (1997), about a young soldier who returns home and finds gainful employment as a hit man. Director

Nikita Mikhalkov attacked Balabanov for his obvious lack of moral stance, while critics claimed that *Brother* heralded a new character in Russian cinema: the killer as hero. If *Brother* was coldly non-judgemental of its protagonist, then *Brother 2* (2000) left no doubts about his heroic nature. Here the hit man became a folklore hero, a Russian Robin Hood taking on the Chicago Mafia and fighting for truth, which, he concludes, will always be more powerful than money.

Critics of Balabanov have spied the unwelcome influence of Tarantino in his work, and *Dead Man's Bluff* (2005) even features a dialogue between two hoodlums about the relative merits of McDonald's and Russian pancakes, blini. This comedy caper about rival gangsters and a suitcase full of heroin also invokes Tarantino's much-imitated blend of gruelling violence and hipster banter. The earlier *Of Freaks And Men* (1998) now seems like the work of a different director, although the unflinching amorality remains the same. LH

Brother (Brat) 1997, 99 min

cast Sergei Bodrov Jr, Viktor Sukhorukov, Svetlana Pismichenko, Maria Zhukova, Iurii Kuznetsov *cin* Sergei Astakhov *m* Viacheslav Butusov

Danila Bagrov can find no work when he leaves the army after the Chechen war, and finds temporary employment with his older brother as a novice hit man. The success of Balabanov's film entirely hinges upon the performance of Sergei Bodrov, whose child-like charisma maintains the audience's sympathy throughout. Everything about Bagrov is simple: he loves music, he keeps his word, he protects the weak and he kills bad people. He's a metonym of a generation on autopilot.

Of Freaks And Men (Pro ourodov i lioudiei) 1998, 93 min, b/w and col

cast Sergei Makovetsky, Dinara Drukarova, Victor Sukhorukov, Alyesha Di, Chingiz Tsydendabayev *cin* Sergei Astakhov

This study of three early-twentieth-century pornographers and the humiliation they heap upon their much-abused subjects is evocatively shot in the sepia tints of *fin-de-siècle* photographs, overlain with a patina of Lynchian surrealism and Peter Greenaway's painterly formalism. The storyline acts as a warning of the degradation that can befall a film industry with even the loftiest initial intentions, although some critics have doubted whether Balabanov has heeded that message himself.

Josiane Balasko

France, 1951–

I t is rare for a French populist director to succeed at an international level, much less a comedy director with her roots in popular satire. Josiane Balasko emerged out of the *café-théâtre* tradition of vernacular comedy in the post-May 1968 period. The exploitation and subverting of stereotypes practised at Balasko's venue, Le Splendid, became key to the director's international hit *Gazon mau-*

dit (*French Twist*, 1995). Balasko's screen career has been characterized by films which interrogate sexist French attitudes. Already a big star in France by 1995, she wrote Jean-Marie Poiré's *Les hommes préfèrent les grosses* (*Men Prefer Fat Girls*, 1981), and briefly came to international arthouse notice playing the "plain" secretarial object of businessman Gérard Depardieu's desire in Bertrand Blier's *Trop belle pour toi* (*Too Beautiful For You*, 1989). Among Balasko's directed works is *Ma vie est un enfer* (*My Life Is Hell*, 1991), in which a lonely woman falls for a demon who trips up fulfilling her wishes. Amid a riotous blend of the gross and the piquant is a particularly manic turn from Daniel Auteuil. Starring fellow *café-théâtre* denizen Thierry Lhermitte, *L'ex-femme de ma vie* (*The Ex-Wife Of My Life*, 2005) revolves around a woman trying to get her husband back in an unorthodox fashion. After a career spent writing, directing and acting in her own films, in 1995 Balasko was voted by French audiences as the second-best French director after Claude Lelouch. RA

Gazon maudit (French Twist) 1995, 107 min

cast Victoria Abril, Josiane Balasko, Alain Chabat, Ticky Holgado, Miguel Bosé, Catherine Hiegel *cin* Gérard de Battista *m* Manuel Malou

When pretty dancer-turned-housewife-and-mother Loli (Victoria Abril) answers the door to butch musician Marijo (Balasko), the scene is set for the rejuvenation of her marriage to serial adulterer Laurent (Alain Chabat) and the reassessment of modern sexual lifestyles and labels. Whilst dealing with these complex issues, this likeable movie manages to maintain a light comedy edge.

Clive Barker

UK, 1952–

A prolific horror and fantasy writer, Clive Barker first gained attention in the mid-1980s with the alarmingly graphic *Books Of Blood* series, which moved Stephen King to declare: "I have seen the future of the horror genre, and his name is Clive Barker." Appalled by the final film versions of his screenplays *Underworld* (1985) and *Rawhead Rex* (1986), Barker was compelled to make the move into filmmaking. As he said in 1987, he "decided to take the law into [his] own hands" by directing the supernatural chamber piece *Hellraiser* (1987), a veritable *Film of Blood* in which lovingly detailed acts of sadomasochism and cannibalism set a new bar for gore. *Hellraiser* spawned no fewer than six increasingly fatigued sequels, none of which were directed by Barker.

Since *Hellraiser*, Barker's filmmaking career has been sporadic: for *Nightbreed* (1990), he cast the professor of body horror himself, David Cronenberg, as an insinuating psychiatrist with a nasty secret; in *Lord Of Illusions* (1995), Scott Bakula plays a gumshoe investigating a satanic cult and a magician who

may or may not have died in a grisly accident while performing. Narrative coherence, *mise en scène* and direction of actors can't be counted among Barker's strengths as a director. But *Hellraiser* showed a flair for claustrophobic ambience and moist, decomposing textures, while splatter enthusiasts can always appreciate him as a connoisseur of gruesome make-up and generous outpourings of blood and guts. JW

Hellraiser 1987, 94 min

cast Andrew Robinson, Clare Higgins, Ashley Laurence, Sean Chapman, Oliver Smith, Robert Hines *cin* Robin Vidgeon *m* Christopher Young

A man opens a Pandora's box of demons, the Cenobites, who induct him into a heavenly hell of sadomasochistic agony and ecstasy. Deprived of a body, he enlists his ex-lover to lure home men whose flesh can reanimate his undead soul. Highly imaginative in its pile-up of repulsive set pieces, *Hellraiser* also introduces lead Cenobite Pinhead, who became the mascot of the rest of the series but appears only sparingly here.

Boris Barnet

Russia, 1902–65

Dubbed one of the "great unknowns of Soviet cinema", Barnet's often brilliant career spanned four decades and yet his work still lives in the shadow of his mentor Lev Kuleshov and Sergei Eisenstein. This is possibly because, unlike his contemporaries, he never gave his name to an abstract concept. "I am not and never was a man with theories", Barnet has said. "I have always found my material in everyday life." Or, as his estranged wife, the actress Yelena Kuzmina, poignantly remarked, he "dealt with people not statues".

Barnet was a boxer, a Red Army PT instructor and an actor (he starred in Kuleshov's *The Extraordinary Adventures Of Mr West In The Land Of The Bolsheviks*, 1924) before he turned to directing. He has been crowned the Russian king of comedy thanks to social satires such as *The Girl With The Hatbox* (1927). In this captivating rom-com about a winning lottery ticket Barnet is courageous – or foolhardy – enough to poke gentle fun at the state's New Economic Policy, which didn't play well with the authorities (this would be a constant and troubling feature of his career). *The House On Trubnaya Square* (1928), a Chaplinesque tale about the misadventures of a country girl and her duck in the big city, is considered by many to be the best silent comedy produced in the USSR. This is largely due to the daring, freewheeling dexterity of Barnet's camera, his zesty ability to convey the vertiginous experience of life in a modern city.

The director's most renowned work, however, is *Outskirts* (1933), an epic but intimate war film which received official disapproval for its equivocal, often unflattering portrayal of the Russian people. From then on, Barnet's work was bedevilled by censorship problems, with two films – *The Old Jockey* (1940) and *The Novgorodians* (1943) – being banned outright. Despite these pressures, Barnet turned out at least one more bona fide classic, *By The Bluest Of Seas* (1935), a free-form comedy about two fishermen who compete for the affections of a vivacious local beauty. Its ebullient spontaneity was a major influence on Jean-Luc Godard and provided an anarchic template for the French *nouvelle vague*. Barnet was making films until his suicide in 1965. LH

The Girl With The Hatbox (Devushka s korobkoy) 1927, 80 min, b/w

cast Anna Sten, Vladimir Mikhajlov, Vladimir Fogel, Ivan Koval-Samborsky, Serafima Birman *cin* Boris Filshin, Boris Frantsissen

Barnet's Hollywood-indebted comedy shares the innocent charm of its wide-eyed star Anna Sten who spends her time delivering hats and fending off suitors, especially after she wins the lottery. Unfortunately, the one man she does love, a homeless student, won't marry her for fear people will think he's done it for the money.

Outskirts (Okraina) 1933, 98 min, b/w

cast Aleksandr Chistyakov, Sergei Komarov, Yelena Kuzmina, Nikolai Bogolyubov *cin* Mikhail Kirillov, A. Spiridonov *m* Sergei Vasilenko

This is the poignant story of a Russian girl who falls in love with a German POW, and the effect of war on the lives of the people in her village. Critics often cite Chekhov when describing Barnet's adept skill as a miniaturist, his sly ability to observe great events through the prism of individual lives – though Chekhov never included a scene with a talking horse, as Barnet briefly and cheekily does here.

Paul Bartel
US, 1938–2000

Though other graduates of the Roger Corman factory (Coppola, Scorsese, Demme et al) used their experience there as stepping stones to more illustrious mainstream careers, Paul Bartel always felt most at home with B-grade exploitation fare. His speciality was the sex comedy, and after helming several Corman productions – *Private Parts* (1972), *Death Race 2000* (1975) and *Cannonball* (1976) – he mounted his cult classic *Eating Raoul* (1982), partly financed with the proceeds from the sale of his parents' house after Corman declined to put up the cash. Bartel later made *Lust In The Dust* (1985), a limp Wild West comedy that re-teamed *Polyester* stars Divine and Tab Hunter, and directed Jacqueline Bisset in the scattershot sex farce *Scenes From The Class Struggle In Beverly Hills* (1989). But Bartel never surpassed *Raoul*'s grimly humorous collision of sex, murder and gourmandise, and was planning a sequel, *Bland Ambition*, at the time of his death in 2000. JW

Eating Raoul 1982, 83 min

cast Paul Bartel, Mary Woronov, Robert Beltran, Susan Saiger, Ed Begley Jr, Buck Henry *cin* Gary Thieltges

The aptly surnamed Paul and Mary Bland dream of escaping hedonistic Los Angeles and opening their own country kitchen – if only they had the money. But after they kill a sex-crazed intruder and find a wad of cash in his pockets, they start luring swingers into their home to similar ends in Bartel's satirical black comedy, wherein distaste and fear towards sex manifests itself in murder and cannibalism.

Evgenii Bauer
Russia, 1865–1917

Evgenii Bauer was perhaps the most accomplished and influential Russian director of the Tsarist era, and though fewer than thirty of his films survive today, he is known to have produced over seventy between 1913 and 1917. Born into a theatrical family, he was a satirical journalist, theatrical actor, stage designer and photographer before entering the film industry as a set designer and director at the Pathé and Drankov studios. Bauer produced, directed, scripted and shot most of his films, cultivating stars such as Vera Karalli and Ivan Mozhukin.

He had a highly developed grasp of *mise en scène*, with his films characterized by an acute sense of architecture, space and light. The melodrama *Twilight Of A Woman's Soul* (1913) exhibits a feel for focus in depth that anticipates Welles, while the contemporary cultural currents of the time, such as Art Nouveau and the Symbolist preoccupation with mysticism, found expression in films such as *After Death* (1915). This was a period of Tsarist censorship, but Bauer often got around it with sardonic critiques of idle and dilettantish Russian society. *The Dying Swan* (1916) has no time for the artist struggling to present death as thousands die on the Eastern Front, but Vera Karalli gives a magnetic rendition of a soul between life and death. Bauer's life was tragically cut short by pneumonia, which he developed after breaking his legs having slipped from an embankment whilst rehearsing a limp for the character of a lame artist. RA

After Death (Posle smerti) 1915, b/w with tints, 46 min

cast Vitold Polonsky, Olga Rakhmanova, Vera Karalli, Mariya Khalatova, Tamara Gedevanova *cin* Boris Savelyev

Dwelling in memory and dream, Bauer explored the internal consequences of desire long before psychoanalysis became fashionable. In this tale of a reclusive photographer haunted by a young woman who kills herself out of love for him, Bauer confronts the audience with the wraith-like Vera Karalli in a way that reminds us of cinema's capacity to conjure apparition in darkness. The sinuous camera movement at the soirée where they meet is worthy of Ophüls.

Noah Baumbach

US, 1969–

The son of novelist Jonathan Baumbach and film critic Georgia Brown, Noah Baumbach graduated from Vassar College and began writing for *New Yorker* magazine in 1991. He made an equally precocious feature debut at 25 by writing and directing *Kicking And Screaming* (1995). Two films followed in 1997, but neither the ambitious, underrated *Mr Jealousy* nor the pseudonymously directed, subsequently disowned *Highball* found much favour, and Baumbach spent the next few years mostly writing. After co-scripting and acting in Wes Anderson's *The Life Aquatic With Steve Zissou* (2004), Baumbach realized a long-term dream with the autobiographical *The Squid And The Whale* (2005), a sleeper hit that proved his ability to intersperse wry wit with emotionally lacerating home truths remained undimmed. MB

Kicking And Screaming 1995, 96 min

cast Josh Hamilton, Eric Stoltz, Elliott Gould, Olivia d'Abo, Cara Buono, Chris Eigeman, Parker Posey *cin* Steven Bernstein *m* Will Baum, Phil Marshall

This is a bittersweet comedy about intellectually over-endowed but practically under-equipped graduates who cling limpet-like to their alma mater as though it were a security blanket against the outside world's uncertainties.

Noah Baumbach's intelligent and literate film was made when he was not much older than its protagonists, and while he's fully sympathetic to their concerns, he's never blind to the futility underlying many of their decisions.

The Squid And The Whale 2005, 81 min

cast Jeff Daniels, Jesse Eisenberg, Owen Kline, Laura Linney, William Baldwin *cin* Robert D. Yeoman *m* Dean Wareham, Britta Phillips

Noah Baumbach's Sundance hit is an unashamedly auto-biographical account of two teenagers coming to terms with their parents' separation. On top of the usual trials of adolescence – sex and peer-group acceptance – come the inflated expectations arising from the belief that literary talent must be inherited and therefore effortless. This put Baumbach back on the map after a directorial absence of eight years, and its more cringeworthy episodes have a whiff of personal demons being exorcised.

Mario Bava

Italy, 1914–1980

Mario Bava might have been content to follow in the footsteps of his father, Eugenio, as a gifted cameraman and special-effects artist. But having taken over directing duties at the last minute from a number of flaky or indisposed auteurs – twice for Riccardo Freda alone – he decided to cut out the middleman. After several such recovery mis-

"Queen of Horror" Barbara Steele about to experience *The Mask Of Satan*.

sions in the late 1950s, Bava got the chance to initiate his own directing project, and adapted Nikolai Gogol's story "The Vij" as *The Mask Of Satan* (aka *Black Sunday*, 1960), an elegant yet surprisingly graphic vampire tale. Star Barbara Steele acquired her "Queen of Horror" mantle in dual roles as the innocent Princess Katia and her fiendish ancestor, the vengeful witch Asa. Though the prolific Bava also made spaghetti Westerns, Bond spoofs and *peplum* (or mythological) films, he's best remembered for his seminal horror movies. *Blood And Black Lace* (1964), about a masked killer stalking fashion models, is widely considered the first of the great *gialli* – the Italian sub-genre that combined baroque horror with the detective thriller. Bava also pioneered the slasher flick with *A Bay Of Blood* (1971), wherein a deceased dowager's relatives whip themselves into a murderous frenzy over her inheritance.

In his final decade, Bava no longer had his pick of scripts, and often found himself relegated to Z-grade exploitation fare like the *Exorcist* rip-off *The House Of Exorcism* (1975), credited to "Mickey Lion". But Bava's signature flourishes – usually achieved on short schedules and tiny budgets – became axioms for *giallistas* such as Dario Argento, whose use of lurid colours (deep reds, purples and greens), neon backlighting and filters, stealthy dolly shots and killer's-eye camerawork all stem from Bava. It was courtesy of Argento that, very late in life, Bava's career came full circle: when the younger director fell ill with hepatitis, the consummate rescue artist helmed several scenes of *Inferno* (1980) in Argento's absence. JW

The Mask Of Satan (La maschera del demonio, aka Black Sunday) 1960, 87 min, b/w

cast Barbara Steele, John Richardson, Ivo Garrani, Andrea Cecchi, Arturo Dominici, Enrico Olivieri *cin* Mario Bava *m* Roberto Nicolosi

Undead witch Asa (Barbara Steele) attempts a vengeance mission on her nineteenth-century descendants in Bava's debut proper, set amid a foggy haunted forest and a forbidding castle. From its first scene, in which Steele is branded and has a bronze mask nailed to her face, the film is startlingly grisly for its time, but it also nimbly sidesteps most of the camp banalities that befall so many vampire flicks.

Blood And Black Lace (Sei donne per l'assassino) 1964, 88 min

cast Cameron Mitchell, Eva Bartok, Thomas Reiner, Ariana Gorini, Dante DiPaolo, Mary Arden, Franco Ressel *cin* Ubaldo Terzano *m* Carlo Rustichelli

Murder becomes a lurid art form in Bava's influential horror-thriller, wherein a mysterious assassin dispatches a series of couture models with elaborate flair in pursuit of an incriminating diary kept by the first of the victims. The movie established all the components of the nascent *giallo* sub-genre: masked killer in black gloves, convoluted plot, sensational colours, eroticized violence, a camera that identifies with the killer and a dissolute milieu where just about everyone is a suspect.

A Bay Of Blood (Reazione a catena) 1971, 90 min

cast Claudine Auger, Luigi Pistilli, Claudio Camaso, Anna Maria Rosati, Chris Avram, Leopoldo Trieste, Laura Betti *cin* Mario Brava *m* Stelvio Cipriani

A rich old lady is murdered for her estate and her assassin is killed, leaving the inheritance up for bloody grabs in the first slasher flick, the ür-text of the genre (the *Friday The 13th* series would steal several of its scenes wholesale). Bava strips away the whodunnit plot of *Blood And Black Lace* for pure gory sensation – chief witness being one spectacular geysering stump.

Jacques Becker
France, 1906–60

An assistant to Jean Renoir from 1926 to 1939, Jacques Becker went on to direct thirteen features, at least three classics among them.

The son of a wealthy industrialist, Becker studied painting and music in the Schola Cantorum, before playing piano in a jazz orchestra. The Renoirs were family friends, and when he developed an interest in cinema, it was natural that Becker should gravitate to Jean. Like Renoir, Becker was fundamentally a humanist, intent on faithfully conveying experience. His aesthetic was elegantly self-effacing, but discreetly attuned to social groupings, authenticity and character. Becker described himself as "some kind of entomologist", and you can see what he means in the devastating character revelations of *Le trou* (*The Hole*, 1959).

Becker's early films – *Goupi mains rouges* (*It Happened At The Inn*, 1943), *Antoine et Antoinette* (1947), *Rendez-vous de juillet* (*Rendez-vous In July*, 1949) – were warmly received in France, although they are little known today. But *Casque d'or* (*Golden Marie*, 1952) made Simone Signoret an international star and remains an indelible romance, and *Touchez pas au grisbi* (*Honour Among Thieves*, 1953) is one of the great French crime movies.

Unlike other old-guard French directors, Becker was admired by the new wave *Cahiers du cinéma* generation, in part because of his association with Renoir, and because he usually wrote or co-wrote his screenplays, as befitted an auteur. Nevertheless, his oeuvre was variable, as witness the undistinguished *Les aventures d'Arsène Lupin* (1956) and disappointing *Montparnasse 19* (1957), which he took over when Max Ophüls died. Becker had one more great film in him, however. Based on a real prison escape, *Le trou* would be his masterpiece. He died from a heart attack two weeks after it was completed. TC

Casque d'or (Golden Marie) 1952, 96 min, b/w

cast Simone Signoret, Serge Reggiani, Claude Dauphin, Raymond Bussières, Gaston Modot *cin* Robert Le Fèbvre *m* Georges Van Parys

A riverside café. Manda (Reggiani) can't tear his eyes away from the luminous Golden Marie (Simone Signoret), no matter that she's in the company of a band of notorious criminals. It's love at first sight, and the subsequent romantic triangle will bring one lover to the scaffold. Set in the Belle Epoque, and based on a true story, this is a rich, evocative melodrama, a thriller with a passionately romantic heart.

Touchez pas au grisbi (Honour Among Thieves) 1953, 94 min, b/w

cast Jean Gabin, René Dary, Paul Frankeur, Paul Oettly, Lino Ventura, Jeanne Moreau *cin* Pierre Montazel *m* Jean Wiener

Max and Riton have pulled off the big one, enough to retire on – but Max's girl betrays him to a rival gangster, who kidnaps Riton and wants to swap the man for the loot. The missing link between Marcel Carné's *Le jour se lève* and Jean-Pierre Melville's long line of Gallic *noir*, this key crime movie goes to prove that Jean Gabin could be stylish even in his pyjamas.

Le trou (The Hole, aka Night Watch) 1959, 83 min, b/w

cast Philippe Leroy, Marc Michel, Jean Kéraudy, Raymond Meunier, Michel Constantin *cin* Ghislain Cloquet

This meticulous re-creation of a real prison break story is one of the best two or three films in the genre: claustrophobic, intense, utterly authentic. Becker, who himself spent a year in a German POW camp, co-wrote it with one of the original prisoners, and cast it with non-professionals, including another of the cellmates. Without recourse to music or melodrama, the film builds formidable tension through its concentration of time and space, its sensitivity to sound, and the discreet accumulation of nuance.

Jean-Jacques Beineix

France, 1946–

A leading player in what critic Serge Daney termed "le cinéma du look", Beineix, with his colleagues Luc Besson and Leos Carax, dominated French cinema in the early 1980s as Godard, Truffaut et al had dominated it two decades before. But if the *nouvelle vague* was grounded in critic André Bazin's theories of realism, Roberto Rossellini and *cinéma vérité*, *le cinéma du look* was about the transcendence of image culture, postmodernism and hyper-realism.

Like Ridley Scott, Alan Parker and Adrian Lyne on the other side of the Channel, Beineix worked extensively in advertising, and every frame of his films is photographed and art directed with loving attention to the smallest detail. Style supplants substance – or, as Beineix would have it, cinema is liberated from the written word. Narrative is at best of secondary interest.

A former assistant director (to Claude Zidi, Claude Berri, Jerry Lewis and others), Beineix made his first feature in 1981. A playful thriller, *Diva* was produced relatively cheaply, but every centime was on the screen. Flamboyant and allusive, a loosely strung necklace of baroque cinematic moments, it became a cult hit in France, and then a foreign language breakthrough in Britain and the US. He hit the rocks with his second outing, *La lune dans le caniveau* (*The Moon In The Gutter*, 1983), an even more luxuriantly designed but perilously torpid adaptation of a David Goodis *noir* starring Gérard Depardieu and Nastassja Kinski. A throwback to the poetic artifice of Marcel Carné and Jean Cocteau, the film was savaged by critics and disowned by Depardieu.

The famously sexy *Betty Blue* (1986) restored his fortunes, at least commercially, but this upturn was to prove short-lived. The circus allegory *Roselyne et les lions* (*Roselyne And The Lions*, 1989) and the modern eco-fable *IP5* (1992) were both failures. Beineix spent the next decade making documentaries, but returned with the same mixture of high style and pop sensibility in the little-seen thriller *Mortel Transfert* (*Mortal Transfer*, 2001). TC

Diva 1981, 123 min

cast Frédéric Andrei, Richard Bohringer, Wilhelmenia Wiggins Fernandez, Thuy An Luu *cin* Philippe Rousselot *m* Vladimir Cosma

The film's far-fetched plot hinges on a pair of switched tape recordings (a bootleg of an opera singer, and incriminating evidence of police corruption). A series of Hitchcockian set pieces interlaced with Godardian postmodern jokes, 1980s designer chic (warehouse apartments, Athena posters), Zen, opera and Paris landmarks, *Diva* is like a long trailer for coming attractions, a pastiche entirely sufficient to itself, and nothing if not modish.

Betty Blue (37°2 le matin) 1986, 121 min

cast Béatrice Dalle, Jean-Hughes Anglade, Consuelo De Haviland, Gérard Darmon, Clementine Celarié *cin* Jean-François Robin *m* Gabriel Yared

Lashings of sex, Gabriel Yared's mournful score, and a star-making turn from Béatrice Dalle made *Betty Blue* a student favourite in its day. Playful at first, the film descends to Laingian clichés as *amour fou* takes hold, and the once formidable Betty sacrifices herself on the altar of her lover Zorg's supposed literary talent. Beineix lays it all on so thick, this is one instance where the 183-minute director's cut is too much of a good(-ish) thing.

Marco Bellocchio

Italy, 1939–

Steadily productive, but fascinatingly erratic, Marco Bellocchio couples a Buñuelian scorn for bourgeois ritual with a Wiseman-like attraction to monolithic institutions and belief systems ready for the wrecking ball. One of the youngest and more leftist sprouts in the bumper crop of new

Italian filmmakers from the first half of the 1960s (others included Pasolini, Olmi, Bertolucci and the Tavianis), Bellocchio has, in the course of some twenty movies, dynamited small-town and social-ist politics, Jesuit education (*In The Name Of The Father*, 1971), the army and the Vatican.

He lit his first and biggest fuse, however, under that most sacred foundation of Italian society: the family. His debut, *Fists In His Pocket* (1965), stirred 41 members of the centre-right Christian Democrat Party to call for the film to be banned as an offence against the Italian family. It was a charge of some irony, since the 26-year-old director made the movie with money borrowed from his own parents and shot it in mountainous Bobbio, not far from where he grew up.

Bellocchio's subsequent work, which has general-ly not been well-distributed outside of Italy, ranged from the spry pathos of 1984's *Henry IV* – starring Marcello Mastroianni as a nobleman who believes himself to be king – to 1991's *The Conviction*, a he-said-she-said account of a night spent locked in a museum that leads to semi-coerced, but ecstatic, sex. Co-scripted by Bellocchio's psychoanalyst, the latter was a philosophical argument designed as a courtroom drama, which posed cogent questions on the meaning of consent, power and pleasure.

Never complacent, Bellocchio has continued to tackle a bold range of periods, subjects and tones. Set at the turn of the twentieth century, *The Nanny* (1999) mirrors two women dealing with separation from their children: the despondent aristocrat who can't feed or bond with her newborn and the illiter-ate peasant girl who leaves her own son to nurse the rich woman's hungry boy. Although patient and affecting, *The Nanny* seems to be missing a last reel, as does *My Mother's Smile* (2002), in which a cosmopolitan painter reacts with bitter amusement and explosive rage when he learns that his mon-strous mother is up for canonization. A full-body bitch-slap to the Roman Catholic Church, the movie proved that Bellocchio's anger at institutional cor-ruption remains bright and raw. However, he muted his sometimes declamatory style for *Good Morning, Night* (2003), based on the kidnapping of former Italian prime minister Aldo Moro. JW

Fists In The Pocket (I pugni in tasca) 1965, 113 min, b/w
cast Lou Castel, Paola Pitagora, Marino Masè, Liliana Gerace, Pier Luigi Troglio, Jenny MacNeil *cin* Alberto Marrama *m* Ennio Morricone

After his older brother decides to break loose from his pro-vincial family and take a flat in town, Sandro (Lou Castel) contemplates helping his cause by getting rid of the rest of his obstreperous family. Terrifying yet banal, Sandro personifies a nation's Fascist hangover in Bellocchio's con-troversial debut, intensified by Alberto Marrama's stark black-and-white photography and the spooky thrashings of Ennio Morricone's score.

Good Morning, Night (Buongiorno, notte) 2003, 105 min
cast Luigi Lo Cascio, Maya Sansa, Roberto Herlitzka, Pier Giorgio Bellocchio, Giovanni Calcagno, Paolo Briguglia *cin* Pasquale Mari *m* Riccardo Giagni

The kidnapping and subsequent murder of former prime minister Aldo Moro by the terrorist Red Brigades in 1978 was one of the most momentous events in post-war Italian history. Bellocchio's account, seen through the eyes of increasingly doubt-stricken Brigades member Chiara (Maya Sansa), is terse, cagey and mournful; given the countercul-tural and even anarchic streaks in the director's early work, the film is a sober reckoning of ideals and ideologies past.

Shyam Benegal
India, 1934–

The nephew of legendary actor-director Guru Dutt, Benegal was an important member of India's Parallel Cinema movement, which aimed to create a thoughtful, naturalistic, arthouse alternative to the typical Bollywood fare.

After introducing the luminous Smita Patil in *Charandas chor* (*Charandas The Thief*, 1975), Benegal went on to make four films that would place him squarely in the vanguard of the Parallel Cinema movement. Made outside the commer-cial Bollywood system and featuring talent from the Film and Television Institute of India and the National School of Drama, *Ankur* (*The Seedling*, 1974), *Nishaant* (*Night's End*, 1975), *Manthan* (*The Churning*, 1976) and *Bhumika* (*The Role*, 1977) gal-vanized the Indian arthouse scene and gave rise to a new generation of independent Indian filmmakers. The following year he directed the masterly histori-cal drama *Junoon* (*A Flight Of Pigeons*). After the demise of Parallel Cinema, Benegal redefined the face of Indian television with the ambitious series *Bharat ek khoj* (1988), based on Jawaharlal Nehru's book *The Discovery Of India*. Though he never stopped making feature films, Benegal's star waned in the 1990s. He made a comeback of sorts with *Zubeidaa* (2001), featuring bankable Bollywood stars. NR

Bhumika (The Role) 1977, 142 min
cast Smita Patil, Naseeruddin Shah, Anant Nag, Swabha Deshpande, Amol Palekar, Amrish Puri *cin* Govind Nihalani *m* Vanraj Bhatia

Based on the life of actress Hansa Wadkar, *Bhumika* follows the rise of actress Urvashi (Smita Patil), whose on-screen success makes a cruel contrast to her sad personal life in which she is exploited by a series of men and is unsuccess-ful in love. The film is also a journey through the evolution of Hindi cinema, beginning in black and white and ending in glorious Technicolor.

Junoon (A Flight Of Pigeons) 1978, 141 min

cast Shashi Kapoor, Jennifer Kendal, Sanjana Kapoor, Shabana Azmi, Naseeruddin Shah *cin* Govind Nihalani *m* Vanraj Bhatia

Based on Ruskin Bond's novel *A Flight Of Pigeons*, *Junoon* is possibly the finest film to be set during the tumultuous 1857 uprising of Indian sepoys against their British rulers. A Muslim nobleman (Shashi Kapoor) hides an English family in his home to protect them from rampaging Indian soldiers, smitten as he is by the family's young daughter. This causes problems both within and outside his home, the tensions reflecting the wider chaos unfolding around them.

Zubeidaa 2001, 153 min

cast Karisma Kapoor, Manoj Bajpai, Rekha, Rajit Kapoor, Surekha Sikri, Amrish Puri *cin* Rajan Kothari *m* A.R. Rahman

In a departure from her usual raunchy dance numbers Bollywood star Karisma Kapoor plays Zubeidaa, a Muslim actress leaving her family (including her son by a previous marriage) to become the second wife of a Hindu Rajput king. When the king stands for election in newly independent India, Zubeidaa is marginalized. The film is notable for the regal performance of veteran actress Rekha as the king's first wife.

Roberto Benigni
Italy, 1952–

Before his crossover success as a director, Roberto Benigni was best known to international audiences for his performances in Jim Jarmusch's *Down By Law* (1986), as a malapropism-spouting convict, and *Night On Earth* (1991), as a ranting cab driver. Jarmusch's deadpan minimalism far better complements Benigni's yapping-terrier persona than the Italian prankster's own films, which strain to replicate the silent-era physical comedy of Charlie Chaplin and Mack Sennett. Benigni's gags are workmanlike and overwrought, his slapstick is spread thickly with treacle and his judgement is appalling, even if the abysmal Holocaust heartwarmer *Life Is Beautiful* (1997) won him stacks of accolades and the best actor Oscar.

The coarse, unfunny *Johnny Stecchino* (1991), in which Benigni plays both a dim-witted bus driver and the notorious gangster he inconveniently resembles, was Italy's biggest domestic box-office hit of its time, with Italian critics comparing the actor-director to Chaplin (meanwhile, the *Washington Post* invoked *Ernest Goes To Jail*). Non-native speakers could only assume that something had been lost in translation. Benigni's next mistaken-identity farce, *Il mostro* (*The Monster*, 1994), raised a big, bad-taste red flag: here again a little tramp is wrongly thought to be a notorious criminal, only this time it's a serial rapist and murderer who mutilates his victims. Perhaps Benigni imagined himself on a mission to prove that comedy could be mined from any setting or subject.

In *Life Is Beautiful*, the Benigni figure must yet again outrun and embarrass powerful forces – this time it's the Nazis, and even a concentration camp doesn't hinder Benigni's capacity for prank-pulling and general merriment. With the Miramax publicity motor gunning behind it, *Life Is Beautiful* was a box-office success and award-sweeper, but the studio quietly buried the dismal follow-up, *Pinocchio* (2002). Ever circumspect, the middle-aged Benigni cast himself as the puppet who wants to be a real boy, but the star suffered the indignity of being dubbed by *Road Trip*'s Breckin Meyer. JW

Life Is Beautiful (La vie è bella) 1997, 116 min

cast Roberto Benigni, Nicoletta Brachi, Giorgio Cantarini, Marisa Pareder, Horst Buchholz *cin* Tonino Delli *m* Nicola Piovani

Benigni's spunky bookseller in Fascist Italy is deported to a concentration camp, where he convinces his 5-year-old son that the entire operation is just an elaborate game. Bearing apparent similarities to Jerry Lewis's notorious and never-released *The Day The Clown Cried*, Benigni's bid to bring humour and humanity to the Holocaust is atrociously fascinating, a maudlin fiasco beyond Max Bialystock's wildest dreams.

Bruce Beresford
Australia, 1940–

Bruce Beresford's work ranges from the inspired to the insipid, the feelgood to the forgettable, but what all his best movies have in common is their reliance on a sterling cast.

From 1966 to 1971 Beresford worked at the British Film Institute Production Board, becoming head of production and overseeing features and documentaries. He was also Film Adviser to the Arts Council of Great Britain. Returning to Australia at a moment of burgeoning investment in the film industry, he directed the riotous Barry Humphries comedy vehicle *The Adventures Of Barry Mackenzie* (1972), which was critically panned but so successful it prompted a sequel.

Next came *Don's Party* (1976), which was based on the work of Australian playwright David Williamson and dissected the vanities of the masculinist Australian Left on the eve of dashed hopes in the 1969 elections. It was a key moment in the first Australian New Wave, leading to Beresford's *The Getting Of Wisdom* (1977), considered important at the time but increasingly feeling staid in its evocation of Edwardian feminine independence. In contrast, *Breaker Morant* (1980) was one of the most artistically successful of Beresford's films. Awards led to Hollywood and *Tender Mercies* (1982), a quietly powerful film following the marriage and redemption of a country singer played by Robert Duvall.

While *Driving Miss Daisy* (1989) is the movie on which Beresford's international renown rests, *King David* (1985) and *Her Alibi* (1989) were unsuited to his delicate touch or too formulaic to bear any personal stamp. *Black Robe* (1991) was an unusu-ally brutal account of white Quebecois colonization (although reliant on Brian Moore's adaptation of his own novel), while other efforts from this period largely hinged upon star performances. *Last Dance* (1995) saw Sharon Stone dressed down in a complex portrayal of a white trash Death Row inmate, while *Paradise Road* (1997) relied on strong turns by Glenn Close and Frances McDormand, and 2002's *Evelyn* was supplied much of its gusto by Pierce Brosnan. Beresford remains a key name in Australia's coming to fruition as a film-producing country. RA

Breaker Morant 1980, 107 min

cast Edward Woodward, Jack Thompson, John Waters, Bryan Brown, Charles Tingwell, Terence Donovan *cin* Donald McAlpine *m* Phil Cuneen

Based on an incident during the Boer War in which three Australian officers were executed by their British superiors to appease political sensibilities, this is an angry and compelling courtroom drama that was one of the key films in the resurgent Australian cinema of the 1970s and 80s.

Driving Miss Daisy 1989, 99 min

cast Morgan Freeman, Jessica Tandy, Dan Aykroyd, Patti Lupone, Esther Rolle, Joann Havrilla *cin* Peter James *m* Hans Zimmer

This reverent tribute to Alfred Uhry's play is saved by the performances of Jessica Tandy as the Jewish matron and Morgan Freeman as Hoke Colburn, her black chauffeur, who find a way to live together amid the turmoil of the civil rights struggle in the American deep South. The movie scored four Academy Awards and remains the picture for which Beresford will be remembered by most.

Ingmar Bergman

Sweden, 1918–2007

Ingmar Bergman's place in cinema history is unquestioned. Astonishingly productive, for stretches of the 1950s and 60s he turned out a masterpiece or two a year, and few other filmmakers can approach his exemplary craftsmanship, his innovative prowess, his influence on fellow directors or his films' intellectual and emotional potency.

For all this, however, Bergman's reputation perhaps precedes him a little too far. His massive and challenging oeuvre has deeply penetrated the cultural consciousness, and thus can be taken for granted, often reduced to a few threadbare adjectives: grim, austere, depressive and pretentious. For some, "Bergmanesque" is shorthand for all that's supposedly fusty and forbidding about the golden age of arthouse cinema. But just blow the dust off any of his old classics and one discovers cinema as ample, as pristine and as manifold in its visceral and cerebral thrills as on the day it was born.

Before beginning his film career proper, Bergman started in the theatre, as a production assistant at the Royal Theatre in Stockholm. He broke into film in the early 1940s as a screenwriter, and made his directorial debut in 1946 with *Kris* (*Cross*). Bergman directed one or two films every year for the remainder of the 1940s and early 1950s. With some notable exceptions, such as *Summer With Monika* (1953), *Sawdust And Tinsel* (1953) and *Smiles Of A Summer Night* (1955), these early efforts aren't overly significant in relation to the rest of his oeuvre, but some included signs of the great things to come.

The undertow of virtually every Bergman feature is the sometimes agonizing dilemma of living with others but without – or sometimes *despite* – God. The son of a Lutheran pastor, Bergman rejected his father's faith at an early age, but for many years his often painfully autobiographical work was informed by a probing Christian existentialism. He invested years in an onscreen exploration of what critic Philip Strick terms "the possibility of a rational belief in God" in films including medieval tales *The Seventh Seal* (1957) and *The Virgin Spring* (1959), both starring the great Max von Sydow, and the modern "God and Man" trilogy. The three films in this faith cycle were: *Through A Glass Darkly* (1961), in which God is posited as both love embodied and a household spider; *Winter Light* (1963), wherein a faithless priest has no answer for a despondent parishioner who asks, "Why do we have to go on living?"; and *The Silence* (1963), a fascinating *kammerspiel* of two diametrically opposed sisters, one a lusty mother in rude health, the other sickly and bookish.

Bergman had by and large finished positing all his theological questions by the mid-1960s, at which point his work became even more audacious. In the still astounding *Persona* (1966), the identities of a nurse (Bibi Andersson) and her mute patient (Liv Ullmann) begin to splinter and combine, climaxing in a simple yet startling trick shot in which their two faces merge into one. The gothic horror *Hour Of The Wolf* (1968) effected a similar blurring, with Ullmann as a woman whose pained empathy for her mentally disturbed husband (von Sydow) runs so deep that she begins to share his hallucinations. Ullmann and von Sydow reunited that same year for the hypnotic and strangely overlooked *Shame* (1968), in which a nameless, pointless war decimates both the Swedish countryside and a functional marriage. *Cries And Whispers* (1972), with the ever-remarkable Harriet Andersson enacting a slow and tortuous death, marked the stark apotheosis of Bergman's use of the suffering female body and the disordered female mind as the material of metaphysical inquiry.

For decades, Bergman maintained a devoted ensemble of actors (Ullmann, von Sydow, Bibi and Harriet Andersson, Gunnar Björnstrand, Erland Josephson and Ingrid Thulin), who often performed in his many stage works, as well as his films. He also regularly worked with two preferred cinematographers, Gunnar Fischer and Sven Nykvist, who

Ingmar Bergman and Max von Sydow

Thanks partly to *Bill And Ted's Bogus Journey*, the shot of a knight playing chess with Death in *The Seventh Seal* (1957) has become the iconic image from Bergman's canon. Improbable, pretentious and oddly resonant, it's the touchstone of the director's work. The part of the questing chess-player was played by Max von Sydow, in the first of eleven remarkable collaborations between the two that included classics such as *Wild Strawberries* (1958), *The Magician* (1958) and *Winter Light* (1962). Bergman was the great director of faces, the close-up king, and in von Sydow he found a granite edifice that could withstand both the torments of fate and God's indifference to them – a face to face the inevitable.

And face it von Sydow did, as the proud father who diligently whips himself with birch twigs before putting his daughter's killers to the knife in *The Virgin Spring* (1960); as the patronizing, defeated doctor in *Through A Glass Darkly* (1961), who knows his wife will lose her battle against insanity but cannot tell her; as the polite family man in *Winter Light*, whose faith has died, and who chooses to die with it; and as the island-dweller in *The Passion Of Ana* (1969), a refugee from life who oscillates between kindness and violence. It's this sense of suppressed rage beneath the stoic exterior that Bergman detected in his protégé, once saying of him: "press him somewhere so that it hurts, or so that he feels he's in a straitjacket, and he rears like a stallion." Yet director and actor rejected the idea that any of these roles were written in response to von Sydow's personality, Bergman noting that: "it's a question of acting the part of a broken man, not of being him … [a] subtle detachment often exists between Max and my madmen." Indeed, if von Sydow's roles are drawn from a single source, that source is Bergman's own personality, as the actor has suggested, arguing that the conflicted characters he has played probably represent "conflicts within Ingmar himself".

Roles in Bergman movies unexpectedly turned Sydow into Hollywood's go-to guy whenever studios needed a European with authority and a hint of a shadowy past. With the noted exception of his star turn as Jesus in *The Greatest Story Ever Told* (1965), he often played the villain, such as the sanguine assassin in *Three Days Of The Condor* (1975), James Bond's nemesis in *Never Say Never Again* (1983), and most fantastically as Ming the Merciless in *Flash Gordon* (1980). But his most famous Hollywood role wasn't as a bad guy, but as an enemy of evil, in *The Exorcist* (1973). All that work with Bergman must have come in handy for playing Father Merrin, a priest hamstrung in his struggle with a demon by that most Bergmanian of problems – a troubled conscience. LH

A stoney-faced Max von Sydow contemplates the blood on his hands in *The Virgin Spring*.

successively helped fashion the distinctive Bergman look from the 1950s to the 1970s. In addition to his six marriages, Bergman dallied with several of his actresses. Bergman's exes Ullmann and Bibi Andersson both appeared in his minimalist monument *Scenes From A Marriage* (1973), a microscopic study of a deteriorating union which Bergman updated three decades later with *Saraband* (2004), a digital-video sequel reuniting Josephson and Ullmann (the latter has herself directed two Bergman scripts). Bergman declared *Saraband* to be his last ever film, a declaration he also made at the time of the rich and fecund *Fanny And Alexander* (1982). A bittersweet tale of childhood, at once epic and confidential, the splendid *Fanny And Alexander* proved to be the crowning achievement of an extraordinary life and career. JW

Summer With Monika (Sommaren med Monika) 1953, 96 min, b/w

cast Harriet Andersson, Lars Ekborg, Johnny Harryson, George Skarstedt, Dagmar Ebbeson, Ake Fridell *cin* Gunnar Fischer *m* Erik Norgdren

A besotted pair of working-class teenagers escape clamourous Stockholm for a summer by the sea; it begins as a rapturous idyll, but by the season's end they're broke, hungry and expecting a child. A foray beyond the realms of the well-heeled bourgeoisie, this early Bergman pinnacle takes an unblinking look at young, hopeful love smothered by impoverished drudgery, powered by Harriet Andersson's fearlessly carnal turn as Monika.

The Seventh Seal (Det sjunde inseglet) 1957, 96 min, b/w

cast Max von Sydow, Gunnar Björnstrand, Bengt Ekerot, Nils Poppe, Bibi Andersson, Ake Fridell *cin* Gunnar Fischer *m* Erik Nordgren

Bergman's international breakthrough is fittingly Bergmanesque: back home from the Crusades, pensive knight Max von Sydow plays a game of chess with Death and ponders the existence of a divine creator. Even in this medieval fable, Bergman shows his gift for capturing the mood swings and cross-current emotional streams of everyday life, credibly locating the humour and humanity – even, occasionally, the fun – to be found in a godless world of bubonic plague, witch-burnings and flagellating Christians.

Wild Strawberries (Smultronstället) 1957, 88 min, b/w

cast Victor Sjöström, Bibi Andersson, Ingrid Thulin, Gunnar Björnstrand, Naima Wifstrand, Björn Bjelvenstam *cin* Gunnar Fischer *m* Erik Nordgren

Dr Isak Borg (played by legendary Swedish director Victor Sjöström) takes a long car trip to a ceremony in his honour, which becomes a quietly cathartic journey through his memories and redolent dreams, sparked by a visit to his ancient mother and encounters with other travellers. One of Bergman's more explicitly psychoanalytic works, the film covers an extraordinary spectrum of tones, from existential frostiness to bittersweet, abiding tenderness.

The Virgin Spring (Jungfrukällan) 1959, 86 min, b/w

cast Max von Sydow, Birgitta Valberg, Gunnel Lindblom, Birgitta Pettersson, Axel Düberg, Tor Isedal, Allen Edwall *cin* Sven Nykvist *m* Erik Norgren

A swinish pair of goatherds rape and murder an apple-cheeked churchgoer while her feral, pregnant half-sister looks on; and then the will of the divine scorekeeper turns the tables and tightens the screws in this adaptation of a medieval Swedish ballad. Bergman's first film with his soon-to-be indispensable cinematographer Sven Nykvist is a stark and stunned contemplation of a world in which God is very much alive, and yet everything is permitted.

Through A Glass Darkly (Såsom i en spegel) 1961, 91 min, b/w

cast Harriet Andersson, Gunnar Björnstrand, Max von Sydow, Lars Passgard *cin* Sven Nykvist *m* Johann Sebastian Bach

In the first of Bergman's "God and Man" trilogy, a young woman (Harriet Andersson in a characteristically mighty performance) loses her grip on sanity as her father, husband and brother look on in helpless anguish. Fearsomely concentrated, the film crystallizes many of Bergman's obsessive themes: generational conflict, the claustrophobic family unit, the existence and meaning of God and the self-sabotage of the mind.

Persona 1966, 85 min, b/w

cast Liv Ullman, Bibi Andersson, Margaretha Krook, Gunnar Björnstrand, Jörgen Lindström *cin* Sven Nykvist *m* Lars Johan Werle

Stage actress Elisabeth (Liv Ullmann) stops speaking following a performance of *Electra*, and goes to the seaside to convalesce with Alma (Bibi Andersson), a cheerful nurse who treats her mute patient as a confessor-priestess of sorts. As their relationship develops and then sours, the women's identities begin to mingle and merge in a tactile hallucination of surrealist imagery and dizzying dream logic, resulting in one of Bergman's most endlessly fascinating films.

Scenes From A Marriage (Scener ur ett äktenskap) 1973, 167 min

cast Liv Ullman, Erland Josephson, Bibi Andersson, Jan Malmsjö, Anita Wall, Gunnel Lindblom *cin* Sven Nykvist

Vérité-like in its raw, bracing immediacy, this six-part chamber piece, shot largely in merciless close-ups, is a virtual two-hander for the superb Bergman stalwarts Erland Josephson and Liv Ullmann, as a "ridiculously bourgeois" couple whose comfy marriage implodes when the husband deserts her for a much younger woman. Available on DVD in both its three-hour theatrical cut and a five-hour TV version, it's a stunning document of the rusted complacency, howling resentment and stubborn devotion bred by a long entanglement.

Fanny And Alexander 1982, 188 min

cast Gunn Wållgren, Jarl Kulle, Erland Josephson, Jan Malmsjö, Harriet Andersson, Bertil Guve, Allan Edwall *cin* Sven Nykvist *m* Daniel Bell

The children of a theatre company's director and leading actress thrive in the warm clasp of their family, but when their father dies and their mother marries a stern clergyman, they take refuge with a kindly antiques dealer. Bergman's final masterpiece (like *Scenes From A Marriage*, available in both its theatrical and much longer televised version) is a sweeping career recapitulation that's also unfailingly intimate and rich in specific detail.

Busby Berkeley
US, 1895–1976

"The Gang's All Here … is mainly made up of Busby Berkeley's paroxysmic production numbers, which amuse me a good deal. There is one routine with giant papier-maché bananas, cutting to thighs, then feet, then rows of toes, which deserves to survive in every case-book of blatant film surreption for the next century." That was James Agee writing in 1943 on Berkeley's first Technicolor film, impishly suggesting that one of the boldest and most inventive architects of choreographed spectacle that the cinema has produced could be capable of anything described as surreptitious. David Thomson in his *Biographical Dictionary Of Film* points out another "delicious irony" of Berkeley's career: that Hollywood began rigidly codifying onscreen morality just as the director was hitting his stride and revealing that "the cinema had a ready, lascivious disposition toward orgy".

As a "director of musical sequences" and later a fully fledged filmmaker in his own right, Berkeley made his sensational signature a massive Art Deco stage filled with scores or even hundreds of identically costumed chorus girls, their bodies – most significantly, their long, scissoring legs – in geometric alignment, fanning and falling into undulating circles and mesmerizing kaleidoscopic patterns. He often employed overhead camera shots to achieve a comprehensive view of these Machine Age wonders and his ornate production design. In Lloyd Bacon's *Footlight Parade* (1933), the de facto star of the fifteen-minute "By A Waterfall" sequence is a revolving fountain in the shape of a wedding cake. Berkeley's camera could also swoop from below, sail between creamy open thighs or close in on a chorus girl's fresh, ecstatic face. The dancers (not always precisely that in Berkeley's world, as they were often lying on their backs) move as a single entity, a *corps de ballet* – quite literally in *Dames* (1934), in which the girls dress as jigsaw pieces that unite to form a likeness of Ruby Keeler.

Given the regimentation of Berkeley's routines, it's perhaps not a surprise to discover that he started his career in the army as a director of parades and, later, United Service Organizations (USO) style shows for men in uniform. Untrained as a dancer, he worked as a choreographer for Florence Ziegfeld on Broadway. Once he arrived in Hollywood, he insisted on directing as well as choreographing the dance sequences in a cluster of "backstage musicals" that proved very profitable for Warners in 1933: Bacon's *Footlight Parade* and *42nd Street* and Mervyn LeRoy's *Gold Diggers Of 1933*, the latter with Ginger Rogers famously belting out "We're In The Money" while dressed in coins and gauze.

Of course, Depression-era audiences weren't in the money, and Berkeley's exotic extravaganzas provided ornate channels of escape during hard times while their plots often took delight in fleecing the rich, especially in *Gold Diggers Of 1935* (1935). The most satisfying of Berkeley's films are those for which he only served as director of the dance sequences; he remained mostly indifferent to non-choreographed *mise en scène*, and tended to foster broad, muggy performances.

After moving to MGM, he oversaw a series of Mickey Rooney and Judy Garland barnyards (including *Babes In Arms*, 1939), as well as *The Gang's All Here* (1943) at Fox, with "Brazilian Bombshell" Carmen Miranda as your fruit-accessorized hostess in a psychedelically coloured fantasia that hits its peak with the arrival of those aforementioned priapic bananas. Berkeley's filmmaking career closed by way of a bittersweet full circle: just seven years after directing Gene Kelly's first movie, *For Me And My Gal* (1942), Berkeley ceded choreographic duties to Kelly on the Freed Unit's *Take Me Out To The Ball Game* (1949), a swansong that bore few marks of its nominal director's iconic sensibilities. JW

Gold Diggers Of 1935 1935, 96 min, b/w

cast Dick Powell, Adolphe Mejou, Gloria Stuart, Alice Brady, Hugh Herbert, Gloria Farrell, Frank McHugh *cin* George Barnes *m* Harry Warren, Al Dubin

The idle rich and scrappy ladder-climbers play courtship games at a fancy holiday resort, but the plot is mere filler

between Berkeley's showstopping set pieces. The two big dance numbers are "The Words Are In My Heart", which cues a flotilla of dancing white baby grands, and the mini-masterpiece "The Lullaby Of Broadway", which chronicles 24 hours in the life of a nocturnal party girl who plummets to her death from a skyscraper.

Babes In Arms 1939, 96 min, b/w

cast Mickey Rooney, Judy Garland, Charles Winninger, Guy Kibbee *cin* Ray June *m* Nacio Herb Brown, Richard Rogers, Arthur Freed, Lorenz Hart

MGM's musical swami Arthur Freed headhunted Berkeley from Warner Bros to direct and choreograph this earnest, energetic version of the Rodgers and Hart stage hit, a vehicle for *Andy Hardy* sweethearts Mickey Rooney and Judy Garland. Aimed squarely at the teen demographic and mining a seam of nostalgia for bygone vaudeville days, it hit big and kicked off a franchise.

Chris Bernard
UK, 1955–

Such was the success and political accuracy of his film *Letter To Brezhnev* (1985) that Chris Bernard's phone was tapped by MI6. After filmmaking as a teenager, Bernard was involved in fringe theatre from 1976. By 1982 he was scripting the Channel 4 soap *Brookside*. *Letter To Brezhnev* was his first feature, made on an £80,000 budget raised from friends and payment deferrals. Written by Bernard's friend Frank Clarke and starring Clarke's sister, it became a surprise hit. Bernard was courted by Hollywood, and was offered *Robocop*, among other projects, but rejected the big time in favour of modest stories of ordinary people. The BBC-funded *Shadow Of The Earth* (1987), for example, was set in 1961 and revolved around three young boys mistaking the local albino for an alien. *Shooting Stars* (1991) was about a young working-class man who kidnaps an international footballer who has become his rival in love. Like *Shadow Of The Earth*, it failed to get a theatrical release, despite strong press. *A Little Bit Of Lippy* (1992) was a black comedy in which a wife discovers that her husband is a transvestite. It did little more than confirm Bernard's festival cachet. RA

Letter To Brezhnev 1985, 95 min

cast Alfred Molina, Peter Firth, Margi Clarke, Alexandra Pigg, Tracy Lea *cin* Bruce McGowan *m* Alan Gill

When working girls Teresa and Elaine bus in from Kirkby for a night on the tiles, fate leads them to a couple of Russian sailors and, for Elaine, true love. Except Sergei has to go home in the morning. Contrasting the mythical cityscape of Liverpool with the grubby details of the chicken factory and the dole queue, and redressing a long-overdue gender imbalance in British films, this was a plucky riposte to the ravages of Thatcherism and made stars of Margi Clarke and Alfred Molina.

Claude Berri
France, 1934–

In 1993 Claude Berri's *Germinal* made history by going up against Spielberg's *Jurassic Park* at the French box office, and making a fortune in the process.

Born of Polish-Romanian-Jewish parentage, this former furrier has carved out a career reminiscent of that of the classical American movie moguls. He has risen from being a jobbing actor – for Claude Chabrol and Fred Zinnemann among others – to become a producer respected by French audiences and industry. After his short *Le poulet* (*The Chicken*) won a prize at the 1963 Venice Film Festival, Berri graduated to features and a series of semi-autobiographical tragicomedies, tinged by colour from his Jewish roots. Among them were *Le vieil homme et l'enfant* (*The Two Of Us*, 1967) and *Mazel Tov ou le mariage* (*Marry Me! Marry Me!*, 1968), in which he also acted. Already a screenwriter, from 1979 Berri began to produce other directors' films as well as his own, including Roman Polanski's *Tess* (1979), Miloš Forman's *Valmont* (1989) and Jean-Jacques Annaud's *The Bear* (1989), along with films by Bertrand Blier and Maurice Pialat. In the early 1980s a number of socio-comic films – including the Catherine Deneuve vehicle *Je vous aime* (*I Love You All*, 1980), *Le maître d'école* (*The Schoolmaster*, 1981) and *Tchao Pantin* (*Bye-bye Pantin*, 1983) – saw Berri's reputation decline. Then came the huge success of *Jean de Florette* (1986) and *Manon des sources* (1986), which epitomize a "cinéma de patrimoine" (heritage cinema) aesthetic that resonates with nostalgia for a France coming to terms with the consequences of multiculturalism and urbanization.

High-budget literary adaptations followed, including *Uranus* (1990) and the aforementioned *Germinal* (1993), starring Gérard Depardieu. In 1997 *Lucie Aubrac*, starring Carole Bouquet and Daniel Auteuil, was the wartime Resistance tonic conservative audiences wanted after Michel Audiard's demolition of the post-war Resistance mystique in *Un héros très discret* (*A Self-made Hero*) the previous year. Berri has continued to act as producer on films that address a mass audience by employing a mix of high production values and populist sentiment. Those worthy of note include Annaud's *L'amant* (*The Lover*, 1991), Patrice Chéreau's *La Reine Margot* (1994) and Josiane Balasko's *Gazon maudit* (*French Twist*, 1995). RA

Jean de Florette 1986, 121 min
cast Yves Montand, Gérard Depardieu, Daniel Auteuil, Elisabeth Depardieu, Ernestine Mazurowna *cin* Bruno Nuytten *m* Jean-Claude Petit

Winning the British Film Academy's best film prize, this fetching portrait of Provençal life – in which Depardieu's city-dweller makes a dilapidated property verdant – has a rare feeling for the rhythms of rural existence and set the mood for a generation of Stella Artois ads.

Germinal 1993, 158 min
cast Gérard Depardieu, Judith Henry, Renaud, Miou-Miou, Jean Carmet, Jean-Roger Milo *cin* Yves Angelo *m* Jean-Louis Roques

One of several adaptations of Zola's 1885 novel to have made it onto the big screen over the years, this lavishly produced concoction once again boasted French cinematic stalwart Gérard Depardieu. Though this is a highly watchable movie – and undoubtedly represents a financial high point in Berri's career – fans of the original literary work may well feel a little short-changed.

Bernardo Bertolucci
Italy, 1940–

The son of Italy's most celebrated twentieth-century poet, Bernardo Bertolucci was himself considered a prodigy in his student days, and this before he swapped the pen for the camera and discovered his true calling.

Bertolucci's most famous film is *Last Tango In Paris* (1972), though it's hardly its best. Notorious for its graphic sex (and the involvement of a major American star, Marlon Brando), *Last Tango* broke cultural taboos everywhere it played. It may not look so shocking today, but you can see what all the fuss was about.

Bertolucci was only 32 at the time, but he already had five features under his belt. He was Pier Paolo Pasolini's assistant on *Accatone* (1961), and, like so many filmmakers of his generation, fell under the influence of Jean-Luc Godard – to whom he paid homage in 2003 in *The Dreamers* (an affectionate, if disappointingly depoliticized souvenir of Paris in the 1960s) and, less flatteringly, in *Last Tango*. His early films are intellectually inquiring, digressive and allusive, his cinematic exuberance balanced by social-realist concerns and Marxist leanings.

This first body of work – and Bertolucci's career can be divided up quite painlessly – is capped by the cool élan of *The Conformist* and *The Spider's Stratagem* (both 1970), brilliant adaptations of Moravia and Borges respectively. In these two films Bertolucci achieved a lucidity which was lost as he stepped onto the international stage and ceased to be a specifically Italian artist.

Last Tango In Paris gave him that international audience. It was four years before he completed another film, and when it came *1900* (1976) could not hope to match expectations – least of all those of its director, who hoped to tell the story of the Communist movement through a glossy two-part (320-minute) all-star melodrama. The operatic Oedipal drama *La luna* (1979) was equally wayward, although both films have sequences of thrilling cinema. Both benefited from Bertolucci's long-term collaboration with cinematographer Vittorio Storaro. A master colourist, Storaro's films with Bertolucci are among the most visually sumptuous ever shot.

Such luxuriance seemed to demand an epic scope, and with *The Last Emperor* (1987) Bertolucci finally found a subject befitting his style: the story of Pu Yi, the last monarch to reign over China. His most successful film commercially, it triumphed at the Oscars, winning nine Academy Awards including best picture. Produced by Jeremy Thomas, this was in some sense a British film. An "Occidental Trilogy" ensued. *The Sheltering Sky* (1990) and *Little Buddha* (1993) primarily showed that even philosophical scope can suffer from diminishing returns. Eventually even Bertolucci tired of big themes and wide horizons. *Stealing Beauty* (1995) was his first film in Italy since *The Tragedy Of A Ridiculous Man* (1981), but it was indicative of something that this was set in Chiantishire, and cast predominantly with British and American actors.

Besieged (1998) was just as slight, and again afforded an exile's view of the world, but Bertolucci's command of movement, music and colour, the dance of *mise en scène* and montage is every bit as seductive as it ever was. There is a yearning for youth in these last films which is nostalgic, yet seems to have revitalized his filmmaking. TC

The Conformist 1970, 108 min
cast Jean-Louis Trintignant, Stefania Sandrelli, Gastone Moschin, Enzo Taroscio, Pierre Clémenti *cin* Vittorio Storaro *m* Georges Delerue

Jean-Louis Trintignant is Moravia's existential antihero, a fascist cipher who betrays everything to effect a kind of numbing appeasement with society. His moral nullity is traced back to an episode of child abuse, but this Freudian explanation can't entirely account for Trintignant's rigorously disciplined banality. Every frame is densely layered, the images a flickering portfolio of the dominant modes in twentieth-century art.

The Spider's Stratagem 1970, 97 min
cast Giulio Brogi, Alida Valli, Tino Scotti, Pippo Campanini, Franco Giovanelli, Allen Midgett *cin* Vittorio Storaro

Originally made for Italian TV, this transcends that form. Adapted from a Borges story (all of three and a half pages long), it concerns a man's return to his hometown, where a statue of his father has been defaced for reasons he cannot let lie. His investigation unravels a more tangled web than he reckoned on. As elegantly as Bertolucci cuts between father and son, 1936 and 1970, the movie is ultimately too opaque for popular tastes.

Last Tango In Paris 1972, 129 min
cast Marlon Brando, Maria Schneider, Maria Michi, Cathérine Allégret, Marie-Hélène Breillat *cin* Vittorio Storaro *m* Gato Barbieri

For all his brilliant work in the 1950s, this looks increasingly like the essential Marlon Brando performance: a man lost between lust, grief, self-pity and self-loathing. Bertolucci deserves credit for pulling so much more out of him than Brando would reveal elsewhere. The movie itself is uneven and unbalanced, alternately raw and pretentious. A landmark all the same for the manner in which it put sex front and centre.

The Last Emperor 1987, 163 min
cast John Lone, Joan Chen, Peter O'Toole, Ying Ruocheng, Victor Wong, Dennis Dun *cin* Vittorio Storaro *m* Ryuichi Sakamoto

Bertolucci revived the epic form in this intelligent, visually opulent recreation of Imperial China's last representative, Pu Yi, who ruled over half the world's population at three years of age, but would grow up confined to the grounds of the Forbidden Palace, and wound up a mere gardener under the new Communist regime. It's a story pregnant with meaning, and Bertolucci delivers an astute and cinematic biopic, even if Pu Yi himself is something of a hollow man.

Luc Besson
France, 1959–

It has become a critical cliché to complain that one hotshot director or another prizes style over substance, but with the dazzlingly empty films of Luc Besson, style is the only substance. Always more popular with audiences than critics, Besson's movies are emblematic of the French *cinéma du look* of the 1980s and early 1990s with their plush, flashy aesthetic derived from advertising and music videos. Besson adores the sound and fury of machine-gun fire, explosions and overwrought women. Over-the-top is the director's first gear, especially in his late-1990s extravaganzas, *The Fifth Element* (1997), a convoluted sci-fi pastiche with the highest budget ($90 million) ever for a French-financed film, and *The Messenger: The Story Of Joan Of Arc* (1999), a vulgar, gore-splattered attempt at an epic prestige production. In an interview promoting the latter film, Besson, never lacking hubris, compared himself to Picasso.

The son of scuba divers, Besson showed his enthusiasm for the life aquatic in his first English-language production, *The Big Blue* (1988), and the undersea documentary *Atlantis* (1991). His debut feature was *The Last Combat* (1983), a post-apocalyptic survival tale that is derivative of *Mad Max* and notable for its lack of dialogue. Like many of Besson's movies, *The Last Combat* eventually takes shape as a buddy story; in later efforts, his duo of choice is the taciturn male hero paired with a younger, wild and often scantily clad female. In *The Fifth Element*, deadpan taxi driver Bruce Willis is the protective escort of flame-haired supreme being Milla Jovovich; in *Nikita* (1990), government operative Tcheky Karyo moulds smack-addled burnout Anne Parillaud into a sleek assassin. Besson's other auteurist trademarks include the POV shot through the crosshairs of a rifle and the dramatic bitch-slap.

Like *Nikita*, *Leon* (1994) centres on a poker-faced tutor and his unpredictable student. The monkish, milk-drinking hit man of the title, played by Besson perennial Jean Reno, becomes an unlikely father figure to an orphaned waif, played by Natalie Portman in her first film role. Loopy and sweet despite the high body count, *Leon* is Besson's best film, not least for the scene in which the tough killer-for-hire tries to cheer up his bereaved charge with a pig puppet.

A prolific producer, Besson once swore that he would only direct ten films. But given that he has already reached that number, with the romantic comedy *Angel-A* (2005) and the animated children's feature *Arthur And The Invisibles* (2006), it now seems increasingly unlikely that he will keep his word. JW

Subway 1985, 102 min
cast Isabelle Adjani, Christopher Lambert, Richard Bohringer, Michel Galabru, Jean-Hugues Anglade *cin* Carlo Varini *m* Eric Serra

Light-hearted, *noir*-ish notes from the underground in which Fred (Christopher Lambert), a raffish wannabe musician turned safe-breaker, flees into the Métro having stolen some valuable papers after gate-crashing the party of beautiful but bored Helena (Isabelle Adjani). Down in the depths, among the various social misfits, he must evade the clutches of both the police and Helena's husband. *Subway* still retains a stylish charm, not least because its "look" was overseen by legendary veteran designer Alexandre Trauner.

Nikita (La femme Nikita) 1990, 117 min
cast Anne Parillaud, Jean-Hughes Anglade, Tcheky Karyo, Jeanne Moreau, Jean Reno, Roland Blanche, Jean Bouise *cin* Thierry Arbogast *m* Eric Serra

Strung-out cop-killer Nikita (Anne Parillaud) comes under the wing of an unflappable French government agent (Tcheky Karyo), who renames and reprograms the feral wastrel as the glamorous assassin Josephine. But once she finishes her training and is let out into the real world, her love affair with an unwitting checkout clerk soon intrudes upon her lethal lifestyle. Slick and diverting, Besson's take on the *Pygmalion* myth lacks subtext and recognizably human characters.

Leon 1994, 136 min
cast Jean Reno, Gary Oldman, Natalie Portman, Danny Aiello, Peter Appel, Michael Badalucco *cin* Thierry Arbogast *m* Eric Serra

Leon (Jean Reno) is a "cleaner", or hit man, who becomes the de facto guardian of his 12-year-old neighbour Mathilda (Natalie Portman) after a psycho cop (Gary Oldman) blows away her entire family. The movie is stacked with cartoonish violence and the camera often lingers distastefully over young Portman's bare legs, but the two leads share a beguiling chemistry that's all the more charming, even moving, for being so unlikely.

Bigas Luna
Spain, 1946–

When General Franco died, democracy was restored and censorship laws finally repealed, and Spanish cinema experienced an intense, pressure-cooker release in which filmmakers like Bigas Luna and Pedro Almodóvar gleefully exploited their new-found freedoms with transgressive, taboo-breaking acts of defiance.

Bigas Luna entered filmmaking via 16mm porn movies, whose tropes he exuberantly adopted as part of his arsenal of shock tactics in his early career. The basic message of *Caniche* (*Poodle*, 1979) was

"bestiality is best", whereas *The Ages Of Lulu* (1990) was a carnival of rape, bondage and genital shaving. The self-referential horror movie *Anguish* (1987) had shards of wit and sophistication in a postmodern smoke-and-mirrors manner. Like Almodóvar, Bigas Luna made the journey from the margins to the mainstream without losing his ability to shock. *Jamón, jamón* (1992) and *Golden Balls* (1994) were libidinous, gluttonous satires on machismo and Spanish social mores, which for once stayed on the right side of the art/porn divide. *The Tit And The Moon* (1994) was, for Bigas Luna at least, a tender fable about a boy who becomes obsessed by the breast of a cabaret performer.

Bigas Luna refers to himself as belonging to a tradition of Spanish surrealism and the rightful heir to Luis Buñuel, but while that great iconoclast maintained a discreet, elegant distance from his outré subject matter, Bigas Luna is boorishly in your face. Despite his international success, Bigas Luna seems to have had his export licence revoked, for films like *The Chambermaid And The Titanic* (1997), *Volavérunt* (1999) and *Yo soy la Juani* (2006) have scarcely been released outside his native country. LH

Jamón, jamón 1992, 94 min
cast Penelope Cruz, Anna Galiena, Javier Bardem, Stefania Sandrelli, Juan Diego, Jodi Molla *cin* José Luis Alcaine *m* Nicola Piovani

One of the most popular Spanish films of the 1990s, *Jamón, jamón* is the project that brought actor Javier Bardem to international recognition. He plays a truck driver and would-be matador who's paid by an overweening mother to seduce her son's fiancee, Penelope Cruz, whose nipples taste of ham. An acquired taste.

Kathryn Bigelow
US, 1951–

One of few women directors in Hollywood, Kathryn Bigelow is unique for working in the traditionally masculine preserve of the action movie. After studying painting, she won a scholarship to the Whitney Museum Independent Study Program in 1971 and in the 1970s figured on the New York art scene. In her films this exposure to avant-garde practice and theory combine with a feeling for visual surfaces.

In 1978 she made the experimental short *The Set-Up*, which reflected on two men fighting in an alley, introducing themes of masculinity and voyeurism. Co-directed with Monty Montgomery, *The Loveless* (1984) came next. This biker movie evoked Edward Hopper backwaters while exploring ideas of the avenging woman and the male gaze. Following the cult success of *Near Dark* (1987), Bigelow was given a retrospective at the Museum of Modern Art. In 1989 she married industry mover James Cameron, who later collaborated on the screenplay for her most ambitious release, *Strange Days* (1995).

Like *The Loveless* and *Near Dark*, *Blue Steel* (1990) was co-written by Bigelow. This slickly shot 1980s-style thriller centring on a woman police officer played by Jamie Lee Curtis added to Bigelow's growing industry cachet, while also exploring issues of gender and dress in a way which intrigued academics. The surfing actioner *Point Break* (1991), in which Keanu Reeves' FBI agent pursued Patrick Swayze's godlike bank robber, offered little to write home about, but did see Bigelow devise an especially light Steadicam for the fleet chase sequence.

Despite such technical achievements, the commercial failure of *Strange Days* made it difficult to get other projects started. *The Weight Of Water* (2000) was a desultory tale of a photojournalist investigating a nineteenth-century murder mystery. Featuring interesting names – Sean Penn, Sarah Polley, Katrin Cartlidge – it failed to obtain UK distribution. Another star-spangled reel – this time featuring Harrison Ford and Liam Neeson – *K-19: The Widowmaker* (2002) was an effective submarine thriller dramatizing a Cold War incident in which a Russian nuclear vessel develops a lethal fault. Bigelow continued to mine male dynamics in the face-off between the two leads. She remains an adept genre mechanic, an intelligent visual stylist and a genuine maverick. RA

Near Dark 1987, 94 min

cast Adrian Pasdar, Jenny Wright, Lance Henriksen, Bill Paxton, Jenette Goldstein *cin* Adam Greenberg *m* Tangerine Dream

In this atmospheric "vampire Western" a boy in a Midwestern backwater is given a love bite by a strange and beautiful girl – a vampire who roams the highways with renegades Lance Henriksen, Bill Paxton and Jenette Goldstein in a black Winnebago. Bigelow uses the boy's predicament to explore the meaning of dysfunctional families in Reagan's America.

Strange Days 1995, 145 min

cast Ralph Fiennes, Angela Bassett, Juliette Lewis, Tom Sizemore, Michael Wincott, Vincent D'Onofrio *cin* Elwood Bredell *m* Hans J. Salter

With its rape voyeurism dividing audiences and critics, this visceral phantasmagoria tapped into both the Tarantino effect and the Rodney King backlash. In a Millennium Eve LA facing ethnic apocalypse, Ralph Fiennes' Lenny Nero fiddles with illicit "clips" of sensation recorded direct from the brains of murderers and rapists in the act. With its lost "children" and white noise spectacle of ersatz experience, here is the missing link between the dystopian *Blade Runner* and *Se7en*'s fallen realm.

Antonia Bird

UK, 1959–

Antonia Bird has demonstrated a flair for action allied to a feeling for social discontent that recalls Ken Loach. Having directed episodes of *Casualty* and *EastEnders* (during its most political era, 1985–86), Bird turned next to a drama about London's homeless, *Safe* (1993), which led to the BBC-funded *Priest* (1994). Following a gay clergyman's struggle to reconcile himself to his calling, *Priest* won festival plaudits but condemnation by America's religious Right. Scripted by Jimmy McGovern and shot on Merseyside, it showed unusual compassion for an isolated profession in a callous world.

The furore found Bird invited to Hollywood for the teen road movie *Mad Love* (1995), in which Chris O'Donnell's Matt and Drew Barrymore's Casey embark on a music-fuelled ecstasy of anti-establishment passion. Recut by a cautious Disney, *Mad Love* failed to find its audience. After her next film, *Face* (1997), Bird was again lured to Hollywood – this time by regular collaborator and *Face* star Robert Carlyle – to direct *Ravenous* (1999). In this hybrid of Western, horror and black comedy, men lost in Colorado's high country after the Alamo turn to cannibalism. Anthony Richmond's pyrotechnic cinematography oddly suited this midnight curio.

More recently, in a production partnership with Carlyle, Bird has scripted *Rebekka*, a portrait of a Playboy Playmate who contracts AIDS. With this and numerous other TV and movie projects on the boil, Bird remains one of a number of contemporary British women directors whose careers demand attention. RA

Face 1997, 105 min

cast Robert Carlyle, Ray Winstone, Phil Davis, Steven Waddington, Lena Headey *cin* Fred Tammes *m* Andy Roberts, Paul Conboy, Adrian Corker

Scripted by Ronan Bennett and shot in London, this heist thriller combines exciting set-piece action with an emotional depth reminiscent of a Michael Mann movie. Struggling to maintain some dignity in a world shorn of allegiances, Robert Carlyle's hoodlum is haunted by a pre-1980s social conscience that has no place in the modern Britain that surrounds him.

Bertrand Blier

France, 1939–

Bertrand Blier came of age as the *nouvelle vague* peaked, and his excavations of French sexual manners look back to the piquancy of Ernst Lubitsch whilst evoking the satire of Luis Buñuel.

The son of portly character actor Bernard Blier, Bertrand entered the industry in 1960 as an assistant to old-guard directors like Christian-Jaque and Jean Delannoy. Blier père's characteristic pose anticipated a number of middle-aged inadequates in his son's films, but Blier's first film – *Hitler ... connais pas?* (*Hitler – Never Heard Of Him*, 1963) – was a ciné-vérité documentary examining the experiences and attitudes of post-war French youth, offering few clues to his future direction.

After screenwriting and the short *La grimace* (1966), Blier returned to feature directing. But it was not until 1973 that the scabrous tone of *Les valseuses* (*Going Places*) attracted an international audience. Based on his own book and inspired by the populist satire of *café-théâtre*, *Les valseuses* established an irreverent perspective on middle-class French attitudes towards heterosexual love and sex that would become a running theme in Blier's films.

In the 1980s, working with Blier helped Gérard Depardieu to make it on the international stage. *Préparez vos mouchoirs* (*Get Out Your Handkerchiefs*, 1977) and *Buffet froid* (*Cold Cuts*, 1979) consolidated Blier's reputation for comedy that interrogated middle-class notions of taste. *Beau-père* (*Stepfather*, 1981) dwelt on the vicissitudes of middle-aged male desire with its story of a widower who takes his nubile stepdaughter into his bed. *My Best Friend's Girl* (1983) saw Isabelle Huppert husband-hunting in a holiday resort while her seedy older minder falls for her. *Tenue de soirée* (*Evening Dress*, 1986) was a manic evening out in which Depardieu responds to a couple's marital spat by inviting them to join him on a night of delirious burglary.

As ever, Blier's instinct for the physical attributes of his actors reinforced the assault on society. *Trop belle pour toi* (*Too Beautiful For You*, 1989) revolved around Depardieu's businessman turning from glamorous wife Carole Bouquet to pudgy secretary Josiane Balasko. In *Mon homme* (*My Man*, 1996), perhaps Blier's best for years, scruffy Gérard Lanvin is made over into prostitute Anouk Grinberg's sharp-suited pimp. Blier is one of France's best ever comedy auteurs. RA

Les valseuses (Going Places) 1973, 118 min

cast Gérard Depardieu, Patrick Dewaere, Miou-Miou, Jeanne Moreau, Jacques Chailleux, Michel Peurelon *cin* Bruno Nuytten *m* Stéphane Grapelli

Depardieu began his acting career as an antidote to his antisocial behaviour and this freewheeling tale of delinquents on the rampage resonated with his past while making his name. With the film trading in the sensations of sex in frank fashion, it isn't long before the fugitive skylarking takes on romantic connotations. Blier's film was a big commercial hit and is a classic of modern French cinema.

Préparez vos mouchoirs (Get Out Your Handkerchiefs) 1977, 109 min

cast Gérard Depardieu, Patrick Dewaere, Carole Laure, Riton, Michel Serrault, Sylvie Joly *cin* Jean Penzer *m* Georges Delerue

When Depardieu's concerned husband introduces a series of men to cheer up his depressed wife (Carole Laure), the scene is set for a broad swipe at the excesses of screen soap opera and the precious comedy of metropolitan French cinema.

Buffet froid (Cold Cuts) 1979, 93 min

cast Gérard Depardieu, Bernard Blier, Jean Carmet, Denise Gence, Marco Perrin, Jean Benguigui *cin* Jean Penzer *m* Philippe Sarde

As Depardieu's life descends into nightmare following an incident in a deserted Métro station, he falls in with a police inspector and the murderer of his wife. This absurd tribute to classical *film noir* becomes all the more alluring for being reduced to the genre's key conventions while knowingly shorn of any plot sense or motivation. The result is Blier's most Buñuelian film.

Sergei Bodrov
Russia (formerly Soviet Union), 1948–

Bodrov is responsible for one of the most remarkable films about war in the history of Russian cinema, or indeed any cinema. *Prisoner Of The Mountains* (1996) not only brought the director much-deserved international recognition, but launched its star, his son Sergei Bodrov Jr, on a short but meteoric career.

Bodrov started a course in space engineering but ended up working as a gaffer at Mosfilm, a state film studio. There he began to pen scripts, and in all he has over thirty screenplays and a novel to his credit. The title of his debut, *Non-Professionals* (1987), referred to the film's subject, a budding rock band in Kazakhstan, but could equally apply to the director's preference in actors. *Freedom Is Paradise* (1989), his award-winning breakthrough film, starred a teenage reform school inmate. Telling the poignant story of a boy who escapes from a young offenders institution to be with his incarcerated father, *Freedom* was the first film to be shot in a real gulag. *I Wanted To See Angels* (1992), a tough but tender drama about a teenager who comes to Moscow to collect a debt from a gangster, was performed by street kids whose lives depressingly resembled those of their screen counterparts.

The most famous non-professional employed by the director has been his own son, Sergei Bodrov Jr, an art history graduate who made his debut, initially against his father's better judgement, in the masterpiece *Prisoner Of The Mountains*. It was the beginning of a bright but tragically curtailed career: he went on to take the lead role in Aleksei Balabanov's *Brother*, before following his father into directing with the powerful gangster drama *Sisters* (2001). But while scouting locations for his next film in the Caucasus mountains, he was caught in a fatal avalanche and buried underneath several tonnes of snow. The title of his acting debut now seems horribly ironic. Fathers and sons – or rather the missing link between them – is a recurrent theme for Bodrov, who didn't meet his own father until he was 30 years old.

Prisoner was made after Bodrov had moved to Los Angeles ostensibly to write *Somebody To Love* (1994) for director Alexandre Rockwell. He has since directed international co-productions, but his output after *Prisoner* (which garnered huge box-office takings and five Russian Oscars) has been patchy to say the least, and the nadir was reached in 1999 with *Running Free*, a soppy melodrama about an orphan, which was narrated by a horse. LH

Prisoner Of The Mountains (Kavkazski plennik) 1996, 99 min

cast Oleg Menshikov, Sergei Bodrov Jr, Djemal Sikharulidze, Susanna Mekhralieva cin Pavel Lebeshev m Leonid Desiatnikov

Prisoner is based on a short story by Tolstoy. Bodrov Jr and Menshikov play two Russian soldiers captured by a Muslim warrior during the Chechen war. When he tries to exchange them for his imprisoned son, the Russian army renege on the deal with tragic consequences. Bodrov applies a lush autumnal palette of burnished ambers to evoke the melancholy of both captives and captor, a remarkable even-handedness that permeates the whole film.

Budd Boetticher

US, 1916–2001

The moral terrain is constantly slipping and shifting amid the rocky plains and desert nowheres-villes of Budd Boetticher's Westerns. You can taste the grit between your teeth. Executing plots driven by revenge, bereavement and psychosis, the director by and large dispensed with John Ford's moments of comic relief and Howard Hawks's redemptive tropes. Boetticher's movies had a fatalism as dry and incontestable as his barren, pitiless landscapes.

A top university athlete, Boetticher earned tough-guy credentials worthy of Hemingway by heading to Mexico after college to train as a bullfighter. His experience earned him a job as a technical adviser on Rouben Mamoulian's matador melodrama *Blood And Sand* (1941), and John Wayne later produced Boetticher's *The Bullfighter And The Lady* (1951). Boetticher kept busy through the 1940s and early 1950s cranking out tight, fleet, second-billed features. *Behind Locked Doors* (1948), set in a mental ward, was a startling precursor to Sam Fuller's *Shock Corridor* (1963).

Boetticher flourished with the septet of Westerns he made with leading man Randolph Scott, screenwriter Burt Kennedy and – with two exceptions – producer Harry Joe Brown, who was Scott's partner in the Ranown company. *Seven Men From Now* (1956), *Ride Lonesome* (1959) and *Comanche Station* (1960) were lean, saddle-sore tales of vengeance, while *The Tall T* (1957) centred on a mistaken stagecoach ambush that becomes a hostage drama. Hovering around the eighty-minute mark and shot on two-week schedules, the films are uniformly terse, slimly edited and brutally efficient; their influence on Sam Peckinpah and spaghetti Westerns would soon be evident. Having made half a dozen Westerns with André de Toth, the middle-aged Scott brought a weatherbeaten gravitas to the typical solitary man of mission, who is often in pursuit of his wife's killers or kidnappers and negotiating temporary alliances fraught with tension and cross-purposes.

Randolph Scott as the flawed hero Pat Brennan puts a protective arm around Maureen O'Sullivan in *The Tall T*.

After the stylish, ice-cold gangster picture *The Rise And Fall Of Legs Diamond* (1960), starring Ray Danton as the startlingly amoral title character, Boetticher embarked on another Mexican bullfighting odyssey – one that effectively cost him his career and much else. The making of *Arruza* (1972), a documentary on the matador Carlos Arruza, swallowed up seven years of Boetticher's life, during which time the director also suffered a divorce, a stint in jail and even a stay in a mental asylum, while Arruza himself died in a car accident in 1966. Boetticher lived for another thirty years but worked little, his Mexican misadventure perhaps confirming the dustblown pessimism of his great Westerns. JW

Seven Men From Now 1956, 78 min

cast Randolph Scott, Gail Russell, Lee Marvin, Walter Reed, John Larch, Donald Barry *cin* William H. Clothier *m* Hanry Vars

A former sheriff (Randolph Scott) prowls the desert searching for the men responsible for his wife's death, along the way encountering Lee Marvin as a fearsome outlaw with stolen gold in his sights. André Bazin described this bracing first Scott-Boetticher-Kennedy collaboration as "the least intellectual, the most subtle and least aestheticizing, the simplest and finest example of the [Western] form".

The Tall T 1957, 77 min

cast Randolph Scott, Richard Boone, Maureen O'Sullivan, Skip Homeier, Henry Silva , John Hubbard *cin* Charles Lawton Jr *m* Heinz Roemheld

Scott hitches a ride on a stagecoach that's promptly ambushed by brigands who mistake it for a bank vehicle; the plot thickens when one helpful passenger points out that all is not lost for the bandits – his wife, after all, is a wealthy heiress and would bring in a healthy ransom. A tightly coiled whorl of action and psychological drama, this is also an exacting précis of human cowardice, greed and expediency.

Ride Lonesome 1959, 73 min

cast Randolph Scott, Karen Steele, Pernell Roberts, James Coburn, James Best, Lee Van Cleef *cin* Charles Lawton Jr *m* Heinz Roemheld

Brigade (Randolph Scott) ensnares a two-bit drifter named Billy, ostensibly to deliver him to the authorities, but Brigade's real quarry is Billy's brother, Frank, for a definitive crime of years past. The film's title hints at Brigade's status: he's a lonely man with scores to settle against all odds and, as in *The Tall T*, there's a whiff of class-based resentment – the various outlaws suffer from what one might call a morbid entitlement complex.

Peter Bogdanovich

US, 1939–

Working for *Esquire* magazine in the 1960s, Bogdanovich interviewed actors and directors from the golden age of Hollywood, became their friend and even let one of them, Orson Welles, live in his spare room for a time. He made one film, *The Last Picture Show* (1971), that was worthy of his heroes, and even dubbed the *Citizen Kane* of its generation. Three decades later, Bogdanovich is better known for making cameos on the cable TV programme *The Sopranos*. As a fall from grace, it's rivalled only by that of Welles himself.

Trained as an actor, Bogdanovich came to Hollywood as a journalist, and befriended Welles, Howard Hawks and Cary Grant (all of whom he can impersonate with eerie accuracy). His first outing as a director, *Targets* (1968), was a low-budget curio starring Boris Karloff; it showed promise, but nothing to suggest the emotional and cinematic maturity of *The Last Picture Show* only three years later. *What's Up Doc?* (1972) was his breakneck homage to Hawks's screwball classic *Bringing Up Baby*, with Barbra Streisand and Ryan O'Neal as the Grant and Hepburn of their day. It broke box-office records. *Paper Moon* (1973) was an evocative re-creation of the Depression, shot through the filter of John Ford's *The Grapes Of Wrath*, with father and daughter Ryan and Tatum O'Neal surprisingly delightful as a pair of scam artists.

With depressing symmetry, Bogdanovich followed up these three aces with three woeful vanity projects for his lover Cybill Shepherd – *Daisy Miller* (1974), *Nickelodeon* (1976), and the musical *At Long Last Love* (1975), which Harry and Michael Medved listed as one of the fifty worst films ever made.

Worse was to follow when he fell in love with former Playmate Of The Year Dorothy Stratten. Just after filming had stopped on their joint venture *They All Laughed* (1981), Stratten was raped and shot dead by her ex-boyfriend. And when the studio refused to give the film the marketing push Bogdanovich believed it – and the memory of Stratten – deserved, he bought the rights to the madcap comedy himself. When it bombed at the box office, he lost an estimated $5 million and filed for bankruptcy.

Not all of Bogdanovich's subsequent work has been a disaster. *Mask* (1985) was a commercial, if anonymously directed, hit – although the headstrong director managed to lose money on it by unsuccessfully suing the studios when they cut two of his scenes. *The Cat's Meow* (2001), about old Hollywood, wasn't the glorious comeback everyone was hoping for, but had its piquant moments. Meanwhile, *They All Laughed* is acquiring a cult following led by Quentin Tarantino who knows every line of the film, and put the director up in his spare room when he was down on his luck. Tarantino has provided the most fitting epitaph for Bogdanovich: "He died for our sins." LH

The Last Picture Show 1971, 118 min, b/w

cast Timothy Bottoms, Jeff Bridges, Cybill Shepherd, Ben Johnson, Cloris Leachman *cin* Robert Surtees

An elegiac and erotic hymn to lost virginity, traditional values and an old way of life, crystallized in the closure of the local fleapit, the film focuses on the sexual adventures of the permanently vexed Timothy Bottoms and the dumbly handsome Jeff Bridges who both fall for high-school coquette Cybill Shepherd. The lustrous black-and-white photography manages to evoke the past and live in the present – to be at once mournful, lyrical and vital.

Sergei Bondarchuk
Ukraine, 1920–94

One of the Soviet Union's most celebrated actors, Bondarchuk was granted the honour of being the State Artist in 1952; two years later he gave what is for many his greatest performance, as the lead in Yulkevich's *Othello*. In 1959 he realized a secret ambition to direct. *Destiny Of Man* was about the stoicism of a Russian soldier, played by Bondarchuk himself, who is captured by the Nazis, escapes and returns home only to discover that his wife and children have been killed. The film was much vaunted for its bold evocation of warfare, something that was to become a directorial trademark.

His next film, *War And Peace* (1967), boasts the mother of all battle scenes. Four gruelling years in the making, with a reported 120,000 soldiers drafted in as extras and a budget worth the equivalent of £40 million (and this was the early 1960s), the original cut came in four parts at a total of over eight hours. Some set pieces, like the burning of Moscow, took months to prepare, but wilt in comparison to the scenes of visual and physical onslaught, filmed in the expanse of 70mm with aerial shots conveying the full shock and awe of the blood-soaked spectacle. Bondarchuk claimed that the extravagant use of helicopter shots was to gain a "Tolstoyan" perspective, but really it's nothing more (or less) than directorial bravado. This was, of course, before the days of CGI and even the smooth tracking shots of Steadicam, so for one lavish ballroom scene the director persuaded his camera operator to don a pair of rollerskates so he could glide sinuously with the actors as they danced.

Bondarchuk returned to the front line with *Waterloo* (1969), an Italian–Soviet co-production which cost $28 million and again employed the services of the Russian army, using 18,000 of them to play corpses in one astounding sequence. The 132-minute epic culminates in an hour-long battle scene, but by then the audience has already been beaten into submission by the histrionics of Rod Steiger's Napoleon and the braggadocio of Bondarchuk's camera. *Waterloo* was not a success and the director retreated to the USSR to make smaller projects, returning to the epic form with *Mexico In Flames* (1982), the Soviet take on the life of John Reed which had been immortalized the previous year by Warren Beatty's *Reds*.

In 1994, Bondarchuk died suddenly after losing a legal battle to retain the rights to *And Quiet Flows The Don*, a personal behemoth that had taken eighteen months to film but was confiscated by a bank that had foreclosed on one of his main financial backers. There was, however, a happy coda to this Russian tragedy. Eleven years after Bondarchuk's death, President Putin, no less, declared that the Russian Federation had won back the rights and that the director's last epic could finally be shown. Bondarchuk, we hope, can now rest in peace. LH

War And Peace (Voini i mir) 1967, 511 min
cast Ludmila Savelyeva, Sergei Bondarchuk, Vyacheslav Tikhonov *cin* Anatoly Petritsky, Dmitri Korzhikin *m* Vyacheslav Ovchinnikov

Everything about *War And Peace* is epic, including the script which quotes whole chunks of Tolstoy's dialogue and as a result sags like an old hammock between the truly staggering set pieces. The eight-hour Russian version was cut to six hours for the foreign market.

John Boorman
UK, 1933–

"I was born in a faceless, mindless London suburb," John Boorman writes in his engaging 2003 autobiography, *Adventures Of A Suburban Boy*. While one of his finest films, *Hope And Glory* (1987), does revisit the streets and plots of his Blitz-era boyhood, Boorman's adventures in moviemaking have been anything but provincial. His style has journeyed from fragmented *nouvelle vague noir* in *Point Blank* (1967) to darkly funny character study in the picaresque *The General* (1998), via galloping epic sweep in *Excalibur* (1981). His settings have ranged from backwoods Appalachia in *Deliverance* (1972) to Burma in the midst of civil conflict in *Beyond Rangoon* (1995) via the Brazilian rainforest in *The Emerald Forest* (1985).

Boorman's oeuvre has no particular thematic cohesion, beyond a rather ponderous mysticism and a tendency toward Nietzschean machismo. Most of his films are distinguished more by their striking visual style. *Point Blank* made bold use of variegated single-colour schemes, while the unfairly maligned *Zardoz* (1973) created a vivid, impressionist haze through super-wide apertures and diffusion filters. *Excalibur* is undoubtedly Boorman's most audacious optical experiment, a crazed efflorescence of green light and green filters on green landscapes creating a glinting emerald forest dotted with healthy bloomings of ruby-red blood.

After an inauspicious start as director of the Dave Clark vehicle *Catch Us If You Can* (1965), Boorman made two pictures with the brilliant and volatile Lee Marvin: the *nouvelle vague* offshoot *Point Blank* and *Hell In The Pacific* (1968), a two-hander with Marvin and Toshiro Mifune as two soldiers stranded on a desert island in World War II. Though he won the director's prize at Cannes for *Leo The Last* (1969), a strange would-be companion piece to *Performance* starring Marcello Mastroianni, Boorman's critical and commercial breakthrough came with, of all films, the harrowing *Deliverance*. Instead of cashing in on this success, Boorman embarked on a series of quirky and quixotic projects: a doomed *Lord Of The Rings* plan, the sci-fi curiosity *Zardoz*, the earnest but ill-fated sequel *Exorcist II: The Heretic* (1977) and *Excalibur*, a lurid, frenetic retelling of the Arthurian legend.

In later years, Boorman's judgement failed him. This was particularly evident when he ventured too far afield from the Anglo-American turf he knew: as in *Beyond Rangoon*, which miscast a drab Patricia Arquette as a bereaved doctor in Burma, and *In My Country* (2004), a woefully misguided treatise on South Africa's bloody apartheid past that somehow forgot to recruit a representative for black South Africans.

Appearing in 1987, the same year as Louis Malle's own reckoning with his wartime childhood memories (*Au revoir, les enfants*), *Hope And Glory* was a career peak, though some of Boorman's finest efforts were to follow it. He reunited with his *Deliverance* star Jon Voight for *The General*, a splendid biopic of the infamous Irish gangster Martin Cahill, and collaborated with John Le Carré for the sly, sardonic thriller *The Tailor Of Panama* (2001). JW

Point Blank 1967, 92 min
cast Lee Marvin, Angie Dickinson, Keenan Wynn, Carroll O'Connor, Lloyd Bochner, Michael Strong *cin* Philip H. Lathrop *m* Johnny Mandel

Betrayed by his wife and best friend, shot and left behind at Alcatraz, career criminal Walker (Lee Marvin) returns from the dead to get his literal and figurative payback in Boorman's lean and mean thriller. The jagged, impressionistic editing and narrative reticence create a dominant mood of ominous disorientation, while the click-clack of Walker's heels as he charges toward his quarry echoes long after the movie's end.

Deliverance 1972, 104 min
cast Jon Voight, Burt Reynolds, Ned Beatty, Ronny Cox, Billy McKinney, James Dickey *cin* Vilmos Zsigmond *m* Eric Weissberg

This adaptation of James Dickey's novel is a nerve-racking journey into the heart of darkness, as four Atlanta businessmen set off on a canoeing trip down an Appalachian river about to be dammed for a hydroelectric plant. The nearly unwatchable rape scene has inevitably overshadowed the film as a whole, which pits hubristic modern man against brute nature in a death struggle that both sides are destined to lose.

Zardoz 1973, 105 min
cast Sean Connery, Charlotte Rampling, Sara Kestleman, Sally Anne Newton, John Alderton *cin* Geoffrey Unsworth *m* David Munrow

Considered by many Boorman's fattest turkey, *Zardoz* is an unhinged class-warfare dystopia in which Sean Connery, swaddled in a red loincloth, plays a confused henchman who accidentally penetrates a sterile, sex-free brave new world called the Vortex. The film dares to envision the opiate of the masses as a levitating godhead that vomits up

guns and ammunition and intones: "The gun is good, the penis is evil!" Daft, hilarious and never boring, *Zardoz* is one of a kind – a cult classic and a credit to the director's fertile imagination.

Hope And Glory 1987, 112 min
cast Sebastian Rice Edwards, Geraldine Muir, Sarah Miles, David Hayman, Sammi Davis, Derrick O'Connor *cin* Philippe Rousselot *m* Peter Martin

A sometimes painfully intimate portrait of a family caught up in momentous times, *Hope And Glory* is a bittersweet catharsis. Boorman's memorial to his childhood in England during World War II is funny, tender and sternly unsentimental, especially in representing the wreckage of the Blitz as the landscape for a boy's own adventure.

Lizzie Borden
US, 1958–

Born Linda Borden, she changed her name to Lizzie at age 11 after hearing the children's nursery rhyme about the infamous murderess ("Lizzie Borden took an axe/and gave her mother forty whacks…"). In her films *Born In Flames* (1983) and *Working Girls* (1986), Borden took a few well-aimed whacks at a patriarchal society in which women's labour is still devalued and women's bodies objectified. Borden's cult reputation rests largely with *Born In Flames*, her low-budget dystopian speculative fiction movie of feminist insurgency, but her next film marked a big technical and artistic advance: both the production values and conventional competence of *Working Girls* are notably higher, and here Borden modulates the pointedly strident didacticism of *Flames* without softening her feminist grievances.

Borden's career then took a dismaying turn. The nasty (and strangely misogynist) schlock-thriller *Love Crimes* (1992), from a screenplay by *Pump Up The Volume* director Allan Moyle, cast Sean Young as a district attorney in pursuit of a psycho photographer who lures unsuspecting women into playing out his sadistic sexual fantasies. Borden returned to *Working Girls* territory with a survey of a telephone sex worker in the portmanteau *Erotique* (1994), but by then it seemed that her moment had passed. JW

Born In Flames 1983, 80 min, b/w
cast Honey, Adele Bertei, Jeanne Satterfield, Flo Kennedy, Pat Murphy, Kathryn Bigelow *cin* Ed Bowes *m* The Bloods, The Red Crayolas, Ibis

A decade after a bloodless revolution installs a moderate socialist government in the US, rumblings of dissatisfaction stir among the female army and radical pirate radio stations. After one of their leaders dies in prison, the disparate groups cohere into an organized rebellion that puts the media foremost in the firing line. Borden's rough-hewn feminist treatise is as relevant as ever, though its renegade energies and idealism sadly belong to another era.

Working Girls 1986, 93 min

cast Louise Smith, Deborah Banks, Liz Caldwell, Marusia Zach, Amanda Goodwin, Boomer Tibbs, Ellen McElduff *cin* Judy Irola *m* David Van Tieghem

Wryly observant and often very funny, the movie follows an Ivy League-educated photographer, Molly (Louise Smith) in her slog through a punishing double shift at a Manhattan brothel, arriving at a hard-won epiphany. With a forensic focus on workaday detail (purchase and placement of condoms, logging appointments, answering the phone), it is like an updated and transplanted *kammerspiel*, and Borden refuses to eroticize what she depicts as essentially menial work.

Walerian Borowczyk

Poland, 1923–2006

Walerian Borowczyk's name has become a byword for European porn, from the ape-meets-girl bestiality of *La bête* (*The Beast*, 1975) to the lesbian nuns of *Behind Convent Walls* (1977). Yet he was once renowned for making avant-garde fables and surreal animations that were a key influence on Terry Gilliam and the Quay brothers. He was, according to David Thomson, "arguably the finest talent that Eastern Europe has provided".

After attending art college, Borowczyk began his film career making short animations with fellow poster designer Jan Lenica. Of their many collaborations, *Dom* (*Home*, 1958) is their masterwork, with Ligia Branice (Borowczyk's future wife) the live-action component in a bizarre short about a housewife's fantasies and rituals (rituals are a constant in the director's work). The film's undoubted highlight sees a wig springing to life and greedily consuming all before it. Moving to France, Borowczyk worked with filmmaker Chris Marker on the space race satire *Les astronauts* (1959). He also created two masterpieces of stridently inventive animation: *Renaissance* (1963), in which a room full of tat magically resurrects and reconstructs itself into a series of familiar objects, and *Angels' Games* (1964), an elegiac allegory for concentration camps or gulags. Borowczyk had lived under two totalitarian regimes, Nazism and Communism, and it's not difficult to detect metaphorical and autobiographical inflections in his recurring themes of political, sexual and religious repression, and in his hermetically sealed universes that run according to their own barbaric and obscure logic.

After making his first full-length animation, *Le théâtre de Monsieur et Madame Kabal* (1963), Borowczyk segued effortlessly into live action with the dystopian fairy tale *Goto, Island Of Love* (1968) and peaked miraculously with *Blanche* (1971). In the latter, the action takes place in an impossibly flat universe; the camera making a mockery of the terms foreground and background, addressing its subjects front-on, in *tableaux* fashion. This lack of dimension extends to the characters, who are little more than marionettes defined and confined by an environment they can never truly escape.

Blanche plays on a now familiar Borowczyk theme, the destructive power of female sexuality. However, it is a charmingly chaste film, and it didn't prepare critics for what was to come from the respected, intellectual avant-garde director: *Immoral Tales* (1974), a portmanteau of four stories incorporating female masturbation, fellatio and an incestuous threesome involving the Pope. Borowczyk took advantage of the relaxation of censorship laws in France to make *La bête*, which was banned or censored in several countries. The story of an American heiress who is ravaged by a beast that she eventually kills with her wanton sexual desire, *La bête* was widely condemned as a blatant rape fantasy. However, some respected critics still consider it a masterpiece of surrealist poetry and "a truly erotic film".

After *La bête*, Borowczyk's career took a turn for the pornographic. Although some admirers claim that all his films have at least one moment of jaw-dropping iconoclasm – *Behind Convent Walls*, for instance, can be discussed in terms of Buñuelian anticlericalism – there are few defenders of *Emmanuelle V* (1985). Unfortunately, Borowczyk's pornography is now more freely available than his earlier work, which has been all but deleted from the collective memory, and a fetid smell hangs like a shroud over the erstwhile animator's career. LH

Goto, Island Of Love (Goto, l'île d'amour)
1968, 93 min, b/w and col

cast Pierre Brasseur, Ligia Branice, Jean-Pierre Andreani *cin* Guy Durban

Set in a rusting, post-industrial landscape (which, at times, seems like a blueprint for Terry Gilliam's *Brazil*) and vividly etched in dark charcoal shades, *Goto* unfolds like a Kafkaesque love triangle between Grozo, Glossia and her husband Goto III, the despot of a small isle where everyone's name begins with G. The latter is a typically surreal and delightful Borowczyk detail, as is the fiendishly intricate flytrap, which is a classic example of this ingenious director's fantastic inventions.

Blanche 1971, 90 min

cast Ligia Branice, Michel Simon, Lawrence Trimble, Jacques Perrin, Georges Wilson, Denise Peronne *cin* Guy Durban

In a fairy tale castle three lusty men are driven to destruction by the luminous innocence of the virginal Blanche (Ligia Branice), who is married to the wealthy old nobleman who owns the castle. Framed with the charming naïvety of early silent cinema and seemingly unaware of the lexicon of cinematic space, this medieval melodrama is, in turn, unsettlingly amateurish, alluringly mesmeric and strangely vertiginous.

Frank Borzage
US, 1893–1962

Love does not conquer all in the films of Frank Borzage, but it is the sole transcendent value in an ugly world, a protective but permeable bubble amid violence and penury. Amid the ravages and enforced separations of war and the hardships of poverty, Borzage's lovers find safety and redemption in each other's arms, a rapturous solace that even death can't kill. Framed in loving close-ups and swathed by soft, flat lighting, his lovers glow with a sensuous, mysterious purity that's not quite of this earth. His melodramas posit love as a secular religion, and many of his films imply a spiritual continuity between this world and the next, allowing the dead to speak in voiceover (in *The Mortal Storm*, 1940) or appear in double exposure (in *Three Comrades*, 1938). Borzage's universe also permits returning from the dead (*Seventh Heaven*, 1927), angelic visitations (*Street Angel*, 1928) and godlike transformations (*Strange Cargo*, 1940).

The man whom Andrew Sarris once praised as "an uncompromising romanticist" began as an extra for Thomas Ince, and moved on to a series of two-reelers in the 1910s which he both directed and starred in. Borzage eventually shot more than a hundred films, working frequently with leading ladies Joan Crawford, Margaret Sullavan and Janet Gaynor. With Gaynor as his female lead, Borzage won the first-ever directing Oscar for *Seventh Heaven*, a film about a Parisian sewer worker and a prostitute whose love transcends the boundaries between life and afterlife.

Though Borzage always foregrounds and idealizes romance and had little interest in realistic depictions of everyday life, his beautiful young protagonists are constantly beset: by tough economic conditions (the Depressions in inter-war Germany and America are a frequent backdrop), social upheaval, illness, the meddlings of others and, above all else, war. In both *Seventh Heaven* and the equally sublime *A Farewell To Arms* (1932), lovers discover the death of their soul mates just as the 1918 armistice is being celebrated. The struggles of working-class Germans in the 1920s and 30s provided the milieu for *Little Man, What Now?* (1934) and *Three Comrades*, while in *The Mortal Storm*, a sometimes awkward fusion of melodrama and propaganda, the Nazi rise to power divides a German family along ideological lines. (The Third Reich banned the import of Hollywood movies not long after its release.)

Borzage worked only sporadically in his later years. To this day, he remains underappreciated, even obscure, perhaps because his melodramatic sensibilities have fallen out of fashion. Although his films may seem outdated due to their immediate political and social contexts, their emotional power and visual radiance remains undimmed; these are films as timeless and eternal as the loves they honour. JW

Seventh Heaven 1927, 110 min, b/w
cast Janet Gaynor, Charles Farrell, Ben Bard, David Butler, Albert Gran, Marie Mosquini *cin* Ernest Palmer, Joseph Valentine

The title of this early Borzage silent film is derived from the seventh-floor walk-up apartment of Parisian sanitation worker Chico (Charles Farrell), who falls in love with abused prostitute Diane (Janet Gaynor) but is then called away to the battlefields of World War I. The movie placed Borzage and his impressive leading lady among the first Oscar recipients, and offers a finale bold enough to deliver a bona fide miracle.

A Farewell To Arms 1932, 85 min, b/w
cast Gary Cooper, Helen Hayes, Adolphe Menjou, Mary Philips, Jack LaRue, Blanche Frederici, Henry Armetta *cin* Charles Lang Jr *m* W. Franke Harling

World War I again tears young lovers apart in this fine adaptation of Ernest Hemingway's novel. A nurse (Helen Hayes) and an ambulance driver (Gary Cooper) revel in their newfound wartime romance until he's called back to the front, she gets pregnant and a jealous friend (Adolphe Menjou) interferes. Its feverish melodramatics finally building into visionary delirium, this film is one of Borzage's most vivid testaments to love everlasting.

John & Roy Boulting
John Boulting: UK, 1913–85
Roy Boulting: UK, 1913–2001

Socially committed, often with a libertarian left-wing slant, the twin Boulting brothers (working together as producer and director, alternating these duties on different films) never forgot to be entertaining.

After fighting with the International Brigades in the Spanish Civil War, John teamed up with his brother to make films. Their first notable effort was Roy's *Pastor Hall*. Conceived during appeasement, it was held up by the censor until 1940, when it was rushed into production as part of the war effort. Continuing their engagement with the politics of the war, the brothers symbolically set the anti-isolationist *Thunder Rock* (dir. Roy, 1942) on a lighthouse. During the war Roy and John worked for army and RAF film units respectively, making films with a documentary feel. Roy directed *Desert Victory* (1943) and *Burma Victory* (1945), while John made *Journey Together* (1945), featuring Richard Attenborough in a docu-drama about a bomber crew. Despite the brothers' left-wing philosophy, *Fame Is The Spur* (Roy, 1947) is about an increasingly rudderless Labour politician. Out of tune with post-war optimism, it was coolly received – though the equally cynical *Brighton Rock* (John, 1947), about a small-time gangster, was a box-office hit, and remains a career high. The following year's

The Guinea Pig (Roy) was less successful: the 25-year-old Attenborough is unconvincing as a work-ing-class boy facing bullying and snobbishness at an English public school.

For the 1951 Festival of Britain John directed *The Magic Box*, a stodgy biopic of cinema pioneer William Friese-Greene. The mid-1950s saw several films for American companies, but these lack the focus and commitment of the British work, and the brothers returned with a series of satires on British institutions. The army (*Private's Progress*, John, 1955), the law (*Brothers In Law*, Roy, 1957), the Foreign Office (*Carlton-Browne Of The F.O.*, Roy, 1959) and the Church of England (*Heavens Above!*, John and Roy, 1963) might be expected targets but one of the best was *I'm All Right Jack* (John, 1959), portraying a Luddite trade unionist. Character actors including Terry-Thomas and Ian Carmichael, while not moving far outside their usual personae, blossomed in these films and became part of a rep-ertory company.

Perhaps with their frustrations vented, the brothers moved on to different fare: a wedding farce, *Happy Is The Bride* (Roy, 1957), and *Suspect* (John and Roy, 1960), a thriller in which a medi-cal researcher's conscience comes into conflict with the Official Secrets Act. The painfully touching *The Family Way* (Roy, 1966), from Bill Naughton's play, shows a pair of newly-weds under family and social pressures; its success was helped by music from Paul McCartney. Despite a 33-year age differ-ence, Roy married its female lead Hayley Mills. She went on to star in his *Twisted Nerve* (1968), which was scripted by Leo Marks, and inhabits the same perverse territory as Marks's *Peeping Tom* (1960). Like that film, *Twisted Nerve* has seen its reputa-tion rise with time, helped by a score by Bernard Herrmann. JR

Pastor Hall 1940, 95 min, b/w

cast Wilfred Lawson, Nova Pilbeam, Seymour Hicks, Marius Goring, Brian Worth *cin* Mutz Greenbaum *m* Charles Brill, Hans May

Based on a true story, *Pastor Hall* is a passionate embodi-ment of the idea that for evil to triumph it needs only good men to do nothing. In a small German village in the 1930s the people have either embraced or failed to resist Nazism. But the pastor preaches against it and is sent to a concen-tration camp.

Brighton Rock 1947, 92 min, b/w

cast Richard Attenborough, Hermione Baddeley, William Hartnell, Carol Marsh, Nigel Stock *cin* Harry Waxman *m* Hans May

An amoral baby-faced gangster woos a naïve girl to pre-vent her testifying against him and is in turn pursued by an avenging angel barmaid. Attenborough dominates in the lead, but is rivalled by novelist Graham Greene's compel-ling and unusual view of redemption, the seedy seaside atmosphere and a strong supporting cast. Though it was changed from the novel, Greene very much approved of the bitterly ironic ending.

I'm All Right Jack 1959, 105 min, b/w

cast Ian Carmichael, Peter Sellers, Terry-Thomas, Richard Attenborough, Dennis Price, Irene Handl *cin* Max Greene *m* Ken Hare

A satire on pig-headed unions and corrupt management, this criticism of British labour relations retained its rel-evance for many years. Peter Sellers' performance marked him out as a real comic actor, helping him to escape Goonish silliness (though he had needed to be convinced that playing the union leader "straight" would be all the funnier). As in some other films, he took on multiple roles, also playing the lesser part of Sir John Kennaway.

Nouri Bouzid
Tunisia, 1945–

Nouri Bouzid is arguably North Africa's greatest living director. His debut feature, *Man Of Ashes* (1986), tackled questions of what it means to be a man in a modern Arab society, setting the tone for a career that would challenge audiences' assumptions about the status quo.

Man Of Ashes was followed by *Golden Horseshoes* (1989), *Bezness* (1992) and *The Gulf War… What Next* (1993), each of which revealed Bouzid's tal-ent for pawing at sore points and exposing the hypocrisies and double standards all too prevalent in Arab societies. *Clay Dolls* (2002) was the result of a particularly fruitful collaboration with rising star Hend Sabri. Playing a free-spirited woman frustrated at society's dictates, Sabri is electric, one moment performing the housework in her linge-rie, the next climbing through the bedroom win-dow to an ultimately futile escape. Four years later Bouzid returned stronger than ever with *Making Of* (2006), a typically genre-defying tale of a Tunisian breakdancer who falls in with a group of Islamic fundamentalists who try to turn him into a suicide bomber. It won the Golden Tanet at the Carthage Film Festival. AJa

Man Of Ashes (Rih essed) 1986, 109 min

cast Khadija Abaoub, Sarra Abdelhadi, Mustapha Adouani, Khaled Akrout, Yacoub Bchiri, Habib Belhadi *cin* Youssef Ben Youssef *m* Salah Mehdi

Telling the story of Hachemi as he nervously awaits his wedding day, *Man Of Ashes* touches on child abuse, pros-titution and, most crucially, notions of masculinity in Arab society. Challenging taboos and preconceptions prevalent in the Arab world, it heralded something of a renaissance in North African cinema towards the end of the 1980s.

Danny Boyle
UK, 1956–

Danny Boyle burst onto the British film scene with *Shallow Grave* in 1994. A low-budget black comic thriller about three flatmates who discover a suitcase full of money in the room of a fourth

– along with his corpse – the movie had polish and drive, and became a welcome home-grown hit. This was as nothing compared to the phenomenal success of his follow-up, *Trainspotting* (1995). Adapted from Irvine Welsh's vernacular novel about the Scottish heroin epidemic, *Trainspotting* was hardly an obvious blockbuster, but it was made with such euphoric brio that it became essential viewing, one of the most influential British films of the 1990s.

Boyle didn't quite come from nowhere. He'd been a producer at the BBC and directed the acclaimed serial *Mr Wroe's Virgins* and several episodes of *Inspector Morse*. But he is unusual in the degree to which he has refused to play the auteur, emphasizing his close association with producer Andrew Macdonald (who oversaw his first five features), screenwriter John Hodge (who wrote the first four), actor Ewan McGregor (who starred in the first three), and several key production personnel. The model here was the long-running collaboration between director Michael Powell and screenwriter Emeric Pressburger, Andrew Macdonald's grandfather. The agenda: to reproduce Hollywood entertainment values in British films, retain final cut and stay true to themselves.

Interestingly, Boyle's first four features all explored the emptiness of escapist dreams: money, drugs, America the beautiful and a desert island paradise.

Home is somewhere to get away from. Restlessly – sometimes recklessly – inventive with the camera and in the editing room, Boyle's style is dynamic and urgent but arguably superficial. His third feature, *A Life Less Ordinary* (1997), and to a lesser extent his fourth, *The Beach* (2000), were critical and financial failures, but after two experimental TV dramas shot on digital video by Dogme cameraman Anthony Dod Mantle, he bounced back with the cult zombie hit *28 Days Later...* (2002).

The charming *Millions* (2005), a fantasy about a boy who finds – and gives away – thousands of pounds, was another manipulative minor hit. Now that he's slowed down some, there remains a nagging suspicion that the shrewd and talented Danny Boyle hasn't found himself yet – all that momentum might hide a fundamental lack of direction. *Sunshine* (2007), in contrast, was a relatively expensive sci-fi spectacular, scripted by Boyle's frequent collaborator Alex Garland. Reviews were mixed and initial returns disappointing. TC

Shallow Grave 1994, 92 min
cast Kerry Fox, Christopher Eccleston, Ewan McGregor, Ken Stott, Keith Allen, Colin McCredie *cin* Brian Tufano *m* Simon Boswell

The suitcase full of money would become a habitual motif in Boyle's films. Here it falls into the laps of three flatmates who only have to dispose of the corpse of the owner and

Cillian Murphy contemplates a lonely future in an eerie, abandoned London in *28 Days Later...*

share the booty – but even that is too much stress for their friendship to stand. A claustrophobic black comedy indebted to the Coen brothers in its invigorating camera-work and bloody-minded cynicism.

Trainspotting 1995, 93 min
cast Ewan McGregor, Jonny Lee Miller, Ewen Bremner, Robert Carlyle, Kevin McKidd *cin* Brian Tufano

Ewan McGregor is Mark Renton, a heroin addict hap-lessly hooked on his no-good junkie mates (vividly played by Carlyle, Bremner et al) in this euphoric adrenalin rush through the amoral underworld of Irvine Welsh's Edinburgh. In many ways the boldest popular British film of the 1990s, this remains the high point in Boyle's career, even if you might argue its illicit brio comes through more strongly than it should.

28 Days Later... 2002, 113 min
cast Cillian Murphy, Naomie Harris, Megan Burns, Brendan Gleeson, Christopher Eccleston *cin* Anthony Dod Mantle *m* John Murphy

Boyle resurrected (and ripped off) George A. Romero's strain of zombie horror in this UK apocalypse chiller. Concocted by novelist Alex Garland, the film's all-purpose metaphor resonates with 9/11, BSE and the anthrax scares, but the movie is most memorable for its spectacularly eerie opening, with Cillian Murphy waking up from a coma to find himself alone (it seems) in a depopulated London.

Stan Brakhage
US, 1933–2003

The word "vision" is often over-used by critics, a lazy short cut to describe a stylist or mannerist, but we can talk about Stan Brakhage's vision without fear of embarrassment or cliché. For Brakhage tried to change the way we see the world. He removed cinema not only from the restraints of conven-tional narrative, but also from the rules of editing, focus and camera movement. Years before Jean-Luc Godard and the filmmakers of the *nouvelle vague*, Brakhage was hand-holding, and occasionally swinging, the camera.

Brakhage made around four hundred films, their durations ranging from nine seconds to four and a half hours, and there are three discernible, albeit overlapping, phases in his career. The first phase included early psychodramas such as *Desistfilm* (1954), set at a drunken teenage party, and his *chef d'oeuvre*, the semi-abstract *Anticipation Of The Night* (1958). Next came the home movies that courageously stripped away contemporary notions of intimacy, such as the graphic and revolutionary film of his wife giving birth, *Window Water Baby Moving* (1962). The filmmaker fastidiously docu-mented every aspect of life in the Brakhage family, from the children to the pet canary.

The director's near-neurotic devotion to fam-ily life was possibly fuelled by his own childhood. Brakhage was abandoned at birth by his mother and spent the first two weeks of his life in a Kansas City

orphanage, before being adopted. The home movie phase of Brakhage's career came to an abrupt halt when he and his wife divorced, and his new wife refused to appear before his intrusive camera. The third phase took cinema beyond representation. In *Mothlight* (1963), moths and leaves were sandwiched between two strips of celluloid and harsh white light projected through their translucent forms. In *Dog Star Man* (1964) Brakhage painted directly onto cel-luloid à la Len Lye. He finally jettisoned the lens altogether in later years, painting or scratching away at the film's surface emulsion.

"Imagine an eye unruled by manmade laws of perspective", Brakhage wrote in the seminal polemic *Metaphors On Vision* (1963). Throughout his career, he attempted to render a child's eye view of the world, to see all "the colours in a field of grass", as perceived by an infant before it acquires language and looks at that field through the narrow prism of the concept "green". In other words, his work was part of the modernist bid to escape the prison of language, narrative and codified meaning. Whether that quest is quixotic is, in some ways, irrelevant. For in the attempt to redefine vision to include dreams, memories, peripheral sightings and even the things we see with our eyes shut, Brakhage pro-duced some of the most mesmerizing, compelling and strangely familiar images in the history of film. Brakhage is not just the leading avant-garde director in the history of cinema, for some critics he is one of the greatest artists of the twentieth century. LH

Dog Star Man 1964, 74 min, b/w
cast Stan Brakhage, Jane Brakhage *cin* Stan Brakhage

A five-part experimental film, this epic was fashioned on the works of Homer and modernist poet Ezra Pound. A man ascends a mountain, comes across a dead tree, cuts it down and uses it for firewood. The narrative is mesmeri-cally cut with splurges of colour, images of solar flares and cellular structures, a shimmering miasma of scratches, internal organs and sexual daydreams, and complex super-impositions of fire, birth and a lactating breast that build rapidly to an apocalyptic crescendo.

Kenneth Branagh
UK, 1960–

Aged 23, Kenneth Branagh was the youngest actor to play Henry V in the history of the Royal Shakespeare Company. He formed his own theatre troupe not long afterwards and wrote his autobio-graphy at the age of 28. When he married Emma Thompson, the press mockingly portrayed them as theatrical royalty – Ken And Em, the überluv-vies. When the couple made *Peter's Friends* (1992) it was cruelly dubbed *Kenneth's Friends* by critics who gleefully referred to the melodrama as a poor man's version of *The Big Chill*. Sometimes it seemed that

Branagh was doing himself no favours. After being crowned the new Laurence Olivier, he chose for his directorial debut the one film that will be forever associated with Sir Larry, *Henry V* (1989).

The fact that he did it well only added to the ire. And yet it's difficult to see what he's done to be the subject of such constant ridicule. The Branagh project to make Shakespeare accessible is undeniably admirable, and successful. The box-office triumph of the Tuscan-set *Much Ado About Nothing* (1993) prepared the ground for Baz Luhrmann's *Romeo + Juliet* and John Madden's *Shakespeare In Love*. It also provided the blueprint for Branagh's future Shakespeare adaptations: unlikely stars (Keanu Reeves, Charlton Heston and Jack Lemmon, for instance) delivering the Bard in a naturalistic, non-declamatory manner in unusual settings. Only once has the formula really failed: *Love's Labour's Lost* (2000), which was re-imagined as a 1930s musical with songs by Cole Porter, Irving Berlin and George Gershwin.

Often seesawing between the brashly ingenious and the simply cheesy, Branagh at least embraces the cinematic form with gusto. *Hamlet* (1996) was one of the few recent Hollywood films to brave the wide-open spaces of 70mm. Without the theatrical context of the Bard, Branagh's work can seem unnecessarily camp: time-shift detective thriller *Dead Again* (1991) lacquered the *noir* on too thickly and *Mary Shelley's Frankenstein* (1994) met with a largely derisory response from audiences and critics alike. Only the low-key *A Midwinter's Tale* (1995) has emulated the success of his Shakespearean adaptations, but then it was about the difficulties of playing the Dane. LH

Henry V 1989, 137 min
cast Kenneth Branagh, Brian Blessed, Richard Briers, Robbie Coltrane, Judi Dench, Ian Holm, Derek Jacobi *cin* Kenneth MacMillan *m* Patrick Doyle

While Olivier's adaptation was famously experimental and metatextual, moving from a stage performance to a real battlefield during the course of the play, Branagh keeps it real, amping up the blood and mud. It's all part of his stated aim to reclaim the play from the jingoism of Olivier's wartime propaganda. His Henry is more Machiavellian and shaded than Olivier's noble prince, although his rendition of the "band of brothers" speech would rouse a pacifist to arms. In that sense, Branagh's film is both a restorative and a genuine companion piece to his predecessor's masterpiece.

Hamlet 1996, 242 min
cast Kenneth Branagh, Julie Christie, Billy Crystal, Gérard Depardieu, Charlton Heston, Richard Briers *cin* Alex Thomson *m* Patrick Doyle

Branagh transposes the play to the nineteenth century and populates it with his usual constellation of stars, plus – outshining them all – Ken Dodd as Yorick. Every scene seems to yield another minor invention, another virtuosic swoop of the camera, another narrative sleight of hand. And while it's never troubled by subtlety, it's bold, magical stuff. The only problem is that this restless bravado doesn't suit the admirable decision to use the uncut text, and into the fourth hour awe finally gives way to fatigue.

Marlon Brando
US, 1924–2004

To see Brando's *One-Eyed Jacks* (1961) back-to-back with Sidney Furie's *Southwest To Sonora* (1966) is to witness what became of the Western in the 1960s. In both films a lost Brando settles up with an errant father figure. But if the first is wilderness theatre of Oedipal proportions, the latter degenerates into a jump-cut, zoom-lensed advertisement for Western decline.

The son of a salesman and an actress in community theatre, Brando was expelled from military school. After roles in summer stock theatre, he debuted on Broadway in 1944. In 1947 his Stanley Kowalski in Tennessee Williams's *A Streetcar Named Desire* heralded the coming of Method acting and a force of aesthetic and social rebellion that would transform American screen performance.

In 1959 Brando founded Pennebaker Productions and work on *One-Eyed Jacks* began. Ejecting director Stanley Kubrick, Brando ended up as producer, director and star. Re-edited by Paramount from five to two-and-a-half hours, this watershed film nevertheless links classicism to the desultory fatalism of Sergio Leone and New Hollywood. Perhaps Paramount's tagline – "The motion picture that starts its own tradition of greatness" – foresaw the transformation. It is a pity that this is the only film Brando would ever direct. RA

One-Eyed Jacks 1961, 141 min
cast Marlon Brando, Karl Malden, Pina Pellicer, Katy Jurado, Ben Johnson, Slim Pickens, Larry Duran *cin* Charles Lang Jr *m* Hugo Freidhofer

In this smouldering revenge narrative, a terse outlaw (Brando) haunts his treacherous partner (Karl Malden), now a respected lawman. Shot by beleaguered veteran Charles Lang on the rocky California coast near Monterey, the film is imbued with the intensity of Romantic poetry. Brando's direction marshals Guy Trosper and Calder Willingham's gripping script into Panavision scenes recalling the ritual power of Anthony Mann.

Catherine Breillat
France, 1948–

Often dubbed the "bad girl of French cinema" even though she's in her late fifties, Catherine Breillat makes films that are sexual, polemical, taboo-breaking and transgressive. She is a screenwriter (Federico Fellini's *And The Ship Sails On*, 1983, and Maurice Pialat's *Police*, 1985) and an actress (her debut, fittingly, was *Last Tango In Paris*, 1972), but she started out as a novelist. Ever since writing *L'homme facile* at the age of 17, Breillat has twinned shame and desire, sexuality and indignity, regarding the tipping point for women as the moment in puberty when "you are subjected to a wave of suspicion". It's a suspicion that, according to Breillat, becomes internalized, later manifesting itself in contradictory and self-destructive sexual urges. Confronting and candidly documenting these masochistic impulses has been the driving force behind her work for the last three decades.

The director returns continually, if not compulsively, to the theme of the loss of virginity: *Une vraie jeune fille* (*A Real Young Lady*, 1976), *36 fillette* (*Virgin*, 1988) and *A ma soeur* (*Fat Girl*, 2001) are painful, brutally honest depictions of sexual awakening via degradation, culminating in the latter film's rape scene. More explicit, in every sense, Breillat's films about adult sexuality are cold, punitive studies of sadomasochism and clinical dissections of the sexual act. The most controversial of these is *Romance* (1998), the first mainstream film to show the act of penetration outside of the grind houses. Pared-down and polemical, Breillat's adult films – *Sale comme une ange* (*Dirty Like An Angel*, 1991), *Parfait amour* (*Perfect Love*, 1996), *Sex Is Comedy* (2002), *Anatomy Of Hell* (2004) – reveal a simplistic Manichean rigidity: her women are emotional, confused and fragile, her men are rapists, murderers, charmers and liars, defined entirely by their tumescence. LH

Romance 1998, 95 min

cast Caroline Ducey, Sagamore Stévenin, François Berléand, Rocco Siffredi, Reza Habouhossein *cin* Yorgos Arvanitis *m* DJ Valentin, Raphaël Tidas

Dissatisfied with her sex life, Marie (Caroline Ducey), a twentysomething school teacher, embarks on an erotic odyssey which is coldly documented, if not dissected, by Breillat's austere, unflinching lens. With its real – rather than realistic – sex scenes and inclusion of legendary porn star Rocco Siffredi among the cast, *Romance* broke one of mainstream cinema's final taboos, opening the floodgates for films such as *Intimacy*, *The Idiots* and *Baise-moi*.

Robert Bresson

France, 1907–99

Robert Bresson is one of the greatest directors in film history, yet one of the most elusive. An ascetic in an age of cinematic flourish, a spiritual person in a time without God, Bresson did not create films that lend themselves easily to audience satisfaction. As a result, his following has been limited to the most high-minded critics and, significantly, fellow filmmakers.

Educated in philosophy, painting and photography, Bresson entered the film industry in the 1930s, assisting on a range of studio vehicles including René Clair's unfinished *L'air pur* (*Pure Air*, 1939). Given Bresson's later reputation, it is surprising to find that his first directed film was a comedy, *Les affaires publiques* (*Public Affairs*, 1934), which has survived only in incomplete form. It was not until 1943 that Bresson the director seemed to spring forth fully formed in *Les anges du péché* (*Angels Of The Streets*). Announcing a characteristic preoccupation with the fate of pure souls in an impure world, Bresson focused on a secluded order of nuns and their commitment to the rehabilitation of women convicts. Based on the experience of the actual Sisters of Béthany and shot in an austere monochrome style that has come to seem quintessentially Bressonian, the film is a remarkable paean to unstinting faith.

Key to Bresson's work for commentators from Amédée Ayfre to Susan Sontag is his Jansenist Catholicism. Jansenism emphasizes original sin, the essential depravity of the human condition, the necessity for divine grace, and predestination. Humans are born bad and cannot redeem themselves without divine grace. Typically the Bressonian protagonist is a lowly figure, mired in the brutish imperatives and consequences of their earthly sojourn: in *Mouchette* (1966) the central character is a young peasant woman, while in *Au hasard, Balthazar* (*Balthazar*, 1966) it is a donkey. Paul Schrader has written of how prison crops up as a metaphor for this limited existence in key works such as *A Man Escaped* (1956), *Pickpocket* (1959) and *The Trial Of Joan Of Arc* (1962). For Bresson, imprisonment is a condition of the soul, and crime becomes a model for redemption. In *L'argent* (1983), based on a Tolstoy story, a 500 franc note is circulated as a joke, leading to the death of a family. Yet, according to the paradox of Jansenist faith, even this horror may not lead to the criminals' eventual salvation. In Bresson's films salvation is elusive and may never come. In *Pickpocket* a young man is tempted onwards from one crime to the next, the film becoming an allegory for our helplessness in the face of our everyday desires. Eventually, his story is told in diary flashbacks from his prison cell.

Bresson distanced himself from a cinema of effects, performance and glitter in all that he said and did; to watch his films is to be affected by the accumulation of mundane detail. Realism is a useful starting point for thinking about his work. *Pickpocket* was shot on location at the Gare de Lyon station in Paris. *The Trial Of Joan Of Arc* was based on the actual transcript of the court proceedings. But Bresson is far from the conventional realism of *cinéma-vérité*, the fad happening all around him in the 1960s. *The Trial Of Joan Of Arc* contrasts the savage details of her burning with almost celestial prose. As suspicious of plot as he was of all manipulation of the spectator, Bresson creates an undifferentiated surface of facts, free of connotation or significance. *A Man Escaped* is a compelling accumulation of tiny moments building to the prisoner's eventual escape. For Schrader, Bresson is one of the few modern directors who still address issues of transcendence. The subject of a film was a mere pretext. It is form, in Bresson's case a pared and precise objectivity, which touches and elevates the spectator. It is as if even the most mundane moment has significance in a higher narrative. Typically, the camera remains at the chest level of a person standing, the angle seldom changing, drastically limiting the ability to editorialize.

Bresson famously used amateur actors, stripping professionals of their studio techniques and flourishes. Roland Monod, the minister in *A Man Escaped*, described how the director repeated lines of the script over and over again to arrive at a kind of stark austerity. Other actors have recalled how the tone had to be utterly without inflection, a monotonous record designed to reiterate the everyday. Writing of *Diary Of A Country Priest* (1950), André Bazin observed: "The cast is not being asked to act out a text, not even to live it out, just to speak it." Sontag wrote of how in Bresson an action would be repeated in several different ways. In *Diary Of A Country Priest* the curé narrates in deadpan fashion how he called on the vicar of Torcy and was disappointed to find him out. Seeing the curé leaning dejectedly against the door, we then hear him tell us how he leaned against the door. Consonant with the religious ritual, and with the theme of confinement across Bresson's oeuvre, this "doubling" seems to reiterate that prison which is the Bressonian protagonist's fate.

If high Bresson held out the possibility of tiny grace notes, late Bresson seemed to be in despair. Devoid of the romantic trappings of myth, *Lancelot du lac* (1974) is a spare portrait of cruelty, pride and a desperate desire for solidarity. Without exposition or explanation, *Une femme douce* (*A Gentle Woman*, 1966) sees a young wife commit suicide, leaving her bereft husband to come to terms with his loss. Even the title of *The Devil, Probably* (1977) suggests a world in which we have foregone the promise of mercy. Arguably, Bresson's influence can be felt in realist French-language cinema from the Dardenne brothers to Sandrine Veysset. RA

Les dames du Bois de Boulogne (Ladies Of The Bois De Boulogne) 1945, 90 min, b/w
cast Maria Casarès, Elina Labourdette, Paul Bernard, Lucienne Bogaërt, Jean Marchat *cin* Philippe Agostini *m* Jean-Jacques Grünenwald

This is untypical of Bresson in its assured use of professional actors, a prowling camera and a rain-slicked vision of nocturnal Paris redolent of contemporary *film noir*, but the *mise en scène* is nevertheless characteristically tailored to a world in which the devil lurks in desire. Maria Casarès gave Bresson one of the greatest performances in French cinema as the vengeful woman who tricks the man who spurned her into marrying an ex-prostitute.

A Man Escaped (Un condamné à mort s'est échappé) 1956, 102 min, b/w
cast François Leterrier, Charles le Clainche, Jacques Ertaud, Roland Monod, Maurice Beerblock *cin* Léonce-Henri Burel *m* Wolfgang Amadeus Mozart

"This story is true. I give it as it is without embellishment." So runs Bresson's foreword to this meticulous account of a Frenchman's incarceration in a German prison camp. The

impact of this film's painstaking record of the details of incarceration can be felt as far afield as Don Siegel and *The Shawshank Redemption*.

Pickpocket 1959, 75 min, b/w
cast Martin LaSalle, Marika Green, Pierre Leymarie, Jean Pelagri, Dolly Scal, Kassagi, Pierre Etaix *cin* Léonce-Henry Burel *m* Jean-Baptiste Lully

Far from the glare of day and the tug of grace and desire, a petty thief sits in his prison cell and writes this account of his life. As a young man, he began picking pockets as a dare, but gradually the jolt of risk and the thrill of success come to define his life. He avoids his dying mother, loses his only friend and ignores the advice of the kindly police inspector who watches over him. A lean and resolutely matter-of-fact modern journey to Calvary.

The Trial Of Joan Of Arc (Procès de Jeanne d'Arc) 1962, 65 min, b/w
cast Florence Carrez, Jean-Claude Fourneau, Marc Jacquier, Roger Honorat, Jean Gillibert *cin* Léonce-Henri Burel *m* Francis Seyrig

There are fewer more powerful and heart-rending appeals to faith than Florence Carrez's suffering as Joan burns at the stake. In a time of growing alarm over the status of the political prisoner, Bresson gives us pause to consider the difficult relationship between policy and belief.

Mouchette 1966, 90 min, b/w
cast Nadine Nortier, Jean-Claude Guilbert, Marie Cardinal, Paul Hebert, Jean Vimenet, Marie Susini *cin* Ghislain Cloquet *m* Monteverdi

Nadine Nortier's portrayal of the young peasant girl Mouchette is one of the most spiritually graceful and affecting turns by a non-actor in post-war European cinema. Prey to the weaknesses and hypocrisies of rural bigots, the film's unassuming, sparely wrought protagonist becomes corrupted and undone as Bresson continues his search for grace notes in a fallen world.

Martin Brest
US, 1951–

Martin Brest is a survivor. Few industry players could overcome being fired from a Hollywood blockbuster and hit back with a box-office smash.

Brest's first film was the award-winning short *Hot Dogs For Gauguin* (1972), featuring an early turn from Danny DeVito. This led to an American Film Institute Fellowship and to Brest's first feature, *Hot Tomorrows* (1977), the tale of a New York writer obsessed with death and his aunt, which Brest wrote, directed, edited and produced. Critically praised, the monochrome film remains largely unseen. *Going In Style* (1979) was Brest's first commercial feature, a rollicking comedy in which three old men try to stick up a bank. Then came the suspense blockbuster *Wargames* (1983), but Brest fell out with the film's producers and John Badham took over as director.

Brest made his comeback with the Eddie Murphy vehicle *Beverly Hills Cop* (1984), which was produced by Don Simpson and Jerry Bruckheimer. It became one of the most successful films of the decade. His next project, *Midnight Run* (1988), was one of the best of its year. But according to a familiar pattern, four years passed before Brest directed *Scent Of A Woman* (1992), for which he was nominated for an Oscar. Reconfiguring the 1934 Mitchell Leisen comedy *Death Takes A Holiday*, *Meet Joe Black* (1998) found Brad Pitt as Death falling for a media mogul's daughter. At around 178 minutes, it fired a contemporary debate about the burgeoning length of multiplex fare. *Gigli* (2003) was an unremarkable caper comedy in which Ben Affleck's Mafia underling is laid low by Jennifer Lopez's feisty lesbian overseer. Brest's best films defined a genre, but his worst invoked critical derision. RA

Midnight Run 1988, 126 min

cast Robert De Niro, Charles Grodin, Yaphet Kotto, John Ashton, Dennis Farina, Joe Pantoliano *cin* Donald Thorin *m* Danny Elfman

Overcoming the limitations of the odd couple caper, Brest teams Robert De Niro's aging bounty hunter and Charles Grodin's Mafia bail jumper to telling effect. During the long trek to LA, to which De Niro must deliver his captive, an unexpected sense of camaraderie develops between the two men as they dodge the Mafia, FBI and fellow bounty hunters.

Scent Of A Woman 1992, 156 min

cast Al Pacino, Chris O'Donnell, James Rebhorn, Gabrielle Anwar, Philip S. Hoffman *cin* Donald Thorin *m* Thomas Newman

Overlong, overwrought; so said critics of this journey of self-discovery in which Chris O'Donnell's scholarship student spends a weekend with Al Pacino's blind and embittered Vietnam colonel. The film demands – and rewards – audience indulgence for Pacino's trademark ranting. But his tango with Gabrielle Anwar is alone worth the price of admission.

Peter Brook

UK, 1925–

Not long after he joined the newly founded Royal Shakespeare Company in the early 1960s, Peter Brook had succeeded in blowing the dust off contemporary stage interpretation of the Bard, unnerving theatre audiences with productions that privileged an austere aesthetic, metatheatrical flourishes and a strong physicality in performance. Within the RSC, Brook founded the Theatre Of Cruelty Workshop in 1963 and produced the watershed film *The Persecution And Assassination Of Jean-Paul Marat As Performed By The Inmates Of The Asylum Of Charenton Under The Direction Of The Marquis de Sade*, in which asylum patients restage the French Revolution. (*Marat/Sade* aimed, as Brook wrote, "to crack the spectator on the jaw".) Brook's riveting 1967 movie version, far from being simply an artefact of filmed theatre, added a meta-cinematic frame – the screen rendition is as much about the making of a movie as it is about the stag-

ing of a play. His severe screen adaptation of *King Lear* (1971), with Paul Scofield in the title role, is an unblinking gaze into the void that blurs the play's dividing lines between good and evil.

Of his nine films, the most well-known remains *Lord Of The Flies* (1963), in which Brook used semi-documentary techniques to capture the class-based Darwinian savagery at the bleak heart of William Golding's novel. In the 1970s, Brook founded the Paris-based International Center for Theater Creation, and he has filmed several of their stage productions, including *La Tragèdie de Carmen* (1983) and the epic Indian legend *The Mahabharata* (1989). JW

Lord Of The Flies 1963, 92 min, b/w

cast James Aubreym, Tom Chapin, Hugh Edwards, Roger Elwin, Tom Gaman *cin* Tom Hollyman *m* Raymond Leppard

Brook draws subtle parallels between the survival of the fittest and the entrenched English class system in this *vérité*-style account of schoolboys stranded on a desert island after nuclear catastrophe. Shooting on a tiny budget on an island off Puerto Rico, Brook encouraged his young actors to improvise. "Many of their off-screen relationships completely paralleled the story," he wrote, and the blurring of reality and fiction no doubt bolstered the film's chilly, discomfiting immediacy.

Mel Brooks

US, 1926–

Mel Brooks is the devout vulgarian who gave the world farting cowboys, a singing Hitler and Frankenstein's monster's monstrous erection. A former gag writer for television, Brooks discovered, with his directorial debut *The Producers* (1968), that his brand of rude exuberance was to almost everyone's taste. After the farce *The Twelve Chairs* (1970), Brooks seemed to go on a one-man mission to lampoon every conceivable movie genre. He climaxed immediately with the *Citizen Kane* of Hollywood spoofs, *Blazing Saddles* (1974), followed by *Young Frankenstein* (1974), a childish, infectious and immaculate valentine to 1930s horror movies.

Brooks's decline was, at first, gradual. *Silent Movie* (1976), the Hitchcock parody *High Anxiety* (1977) and the commercial belly-flop *A History Of The World Part 1* (1981) saw diminishing comedy returns, and Brooks was soon deserted by both the zeitgeist and his comedic talent. The director parodied *Star Wars*, Robin Hood and Dracula both lazily and tardily in *Spaceballs* (1987), *Robin Hood: Men In Tights* (1993) and *Dracula: Dead And Loving It* (1995), and his attempt at straight comedy, *Life Stinks* (1991), was equally dispiriting. But just when his directorial career was starting to plumb the woeful depths of Max Bialystock, the loser producer from his debut, Brooks engineered an unlikely come-back with a musical version of *The Producers*, which proved to be huge Broadway hit. He didn't direct the inevitable, anaemic 2005 film adaptation, but was, rather fittingly, one of the producers. LH

The Producers 1968, 88 min
cast Zero Mostel, Gene Wilder, Kenneth Mars, Dick Shawn, Renée Taylor, Estelle Winwood *cin* Joseph Coffey *m* Norman Blagman, John Morris

Theatrical entrepreneur Max Bialystock, a serial seducer of old women, and accountant Leo Bloom, a nerd marinated in his own anxieties, dream up a foolproof plan to make a bomb on Broadway by staging a play – the goose-stepping musical *Springtime For Hitler* – so badly written and acted that it will close after its opening night. The result is a barrage of frantic bad taste and zesty vulgarity.

Blazing Saddles 1974, 93 min
cast Cleavon Little, Gene Wilder, John Hillerman, Slim Pickens, Harvey Korman, Liam Dunn, Alex Karras *cin* Joseph Biroc *m* John Morris

A washed-up gunslinger (Gene Wilder) and a black sheriff (Cleavon Little) take on the railroad company, a corrupt villain (Harvey Korman) and racial stereotypes in arguably the greatest Hollywood parody ever made. Loaded with rapid, scattershot gags, this helter-skelter Western has the edge over its main rival *Airplane!* (1980) because of its unexpected political dimension. Its savvy dissection of casual and institutionalized racism clearly bears the fingerprints of scriptwriter Richard Pryor, who was originally cast in the lead role until the studio intervened.

Richard Brooks
US, 1912–92

Richard Brooks's directorial career stretched 35 years, from *Crisis* (1950) with Cary Grant, to *Fever Pitch* (1985) with Ryan O'Neal. Add to that eight years as a Hollywood screenwriter – interrupted by World War II service in the Marines – with *Brute Force* (1947) and *Key Largo* (1948) among his credits.

It was a full career. Brooks was a liberal intellectual, a former journalist, and almost all his work strained with ambition and provocation. But these qualities were usually notional; his direction tended to be stolid and flat. Perhaps because he knew the beat, newspaper drama *Deadline USA* (1952) is the pick of the early films. *Blackboard Jungle* (1955) caused more stir, and set the template for inner-city school dramas, but it hasn't aged well.

The literary adaptations *The Brothers Karamazov* (1958), *Cat On A Hot Tin Roof* (1958) and *Sweet Bird Of Youth* (1960) all fall far short of their sources, although the Tennessee Williams pair are valuable for recording the performances of Elizabeth Taylor, Burl Ives, Geraldine Page and the young Paul Newman. In his frequent battles with the censors in the 1950s, Brooks invariably came off second best.

Of his later work, *Lord Jim* (1964) was a brave stab at Conrad, with superb contributions from Peter O'Toole and James Mason, and *The Professionals* (1966) is a very good Western, although its shortcomings were soon exposed by Sam Peckinpah's *The Wild Bunch* (1969). *Looking For Mr Goodbar* (1977) proved Brooks still had an itchy need to provoke, but it felt confused and stilted. TC

Cat On A Hot Tin Roof 1958, 108 min
cast Elizabeth Taylor, Paul Newman, Burl Ives, Judith Anderson, Jack Carson, Madeline Sherwood *cin* William Daniels

Given that the Production Code prohibited any mention of the homosexuality that was at the core of Tennessee Williams's play – and the main obstacle in the marriage between Brick (Paul Newman) and Maggie the Cat (Elizabeth Taylor) – Brooks did a decent job with what was left. Even though the material doesn't make much sense in this context, the film is worth seeing for one of Taylor's best performances and, especially, to commemorate Burl Ives, who re-created his fine Broadway performance as Big Daddy.

Elmer Gantry 1960, 145 min, b/w
cast Burt Lancaster, Jean Simmons, Arthur Kennedy, Shirley Jones, Dean Jagger, Edward Andrews *cin* John Alton *m* André Previn

Burt Lancaster won an Oscar for his bravura portrayal of Sinclair Lewis's slick evangelist, who throws in with Jean Simmons's revivalist circus for questionable motives. The fiery material runs to Brooks's taste, and John Alton's photography is another bonus, though it's Lancaster's broad grin and outstretched arms which dominate. Shirley Jones won the Academy Award for best supporting actress while Brooks picked up another statuette for his screenplay – and Ms Simmons, who became his wife.

In Cold Blood 1967, 134 min, b/w
cast Robert Blake, Scott Wilson, John Forsythe, Paul Stewart, Gerald S. O'Loughlin, Jeff Corey *cin* Conrad Hall *m* Quincy Jones

This is another literary adaptation: Truman Capote's minutely reseached New Journalism account of the "senseless" murder of a Kansas farmer and his family by two would-be thieves. It's compellingly constructed, with striking, stark CinemaScope cinematography by Conrad Hall, and credible performances from Blake and Wilson as the hapless killers – but it doesn't entirely live up to its high reputation. The psychology feels contrived and the summation – making a heavyhanded case against capital punishment – feels like an afterthought.

Nick Broomfield
UK, 1948–

A sleaze-hunter willingly captured by his game, Nick Broomfield casts himself as the auxiliary subject of his shambling procedurals, and his documentaries often double as admirably transparent chronicles of their own making. While Broomfield's investigatory technique too often amounts to a frustrating pile-up of unfocused Q&As and misplaced credulity, he always stumbles upon unpredictable detours and colourful margin-dwellers on his gumshoe wanderings, and his droll, *faux-naïf* persona always smooths us over the bumpy ride.

Broomfield began as a social documentarian in the Frederick Wiseman tradition, examining the effects of new high-rise housing on working-class communities in Liverpool (*Who Cares*, 1971; and *Behind The Rent Strike*, 1974) and the attempted rehabilitation of impoverished delinquents in *Juvenile Liaison* (1975), his first project with frequent collaborator Joan Churchill. Moving to the US, Broomfield's attentions ranged from a California juvenile detention centre (*Tattooed Tears*, 1978) to a Georgia basic-training camp (*Soldier Girls*, 1980) to a Nevada brothel (*Chicken Ranch*, 1982).

In *The Leader, The Driver And The Driver's Wife* (1991), which focused on South African pro-apartheid politician Eugene Terre'Blanche, and *Tracking Down Maggie* (1994), which chased after Margaret Thatcher, a tendency that to most investigatory documentarians would have seemed a fatal flaw became a quintessentially Broomfieldian device: the utterly futile pursuit of one's slippery nominal subject. After the amusing but disappointing *Biggie And Tupac* (2002) – invaluable if only for its astonishing prison interview with fearsome hip-hop exec Suge Knight – he returned to his 1992 subject, Aileen Wuornos, for a second anguished, affecting documentary, *Aileen: Life And Death Of A Serial Killer* (2003). Broomfield then turned from documentaries to a dramatic feature based on a true story, *Ghosts* (2006), which re-enacted the tragic deaths of a group of Chinese cockle pickers at Morecombe Bay in 2004. JW

Kurt & Courtney 1998, 95 min

with Nick Broomfield, Mari Earle, Tracy Marander, Alice Wheeler, Larry Flynt, Courtney Love *cin* Joan Churchill *m* David Bergeaud, Dylan Carlson

Broomfield's guerilla methodology reaches a spectacular peak when he rushes the stage where his elusive quarry Courtney Love is accepting an award from ACLU. With Love out of his reach, Broomfield noses around some clotted gutters to unpack conspiracy theories that she might have been involved in the death of her superstar husband, Kurt Cobain, though the encounters with Love's ghastly father can only inspire sympathy for her.

Aileen: Life And Death Of A Serial Killer 2003, 93 min

with Aileen Wuornos, Nick Broomfield, Jeb Bush *cin* Joan Churchill *m* Robert Lane

Broomfield re-examines the media feeding frenzy surrounding "America's first female serial killer" and the currency is now political: Wuornos's scheduled execution is conveniently timed for the re-election of Jeb Bush, Florida's tough-on-crime governor. Broomfield pieces together a life blighted at birth: a grotesque of abandonment, incest, physical and sexual abuse, pregnancy at 13, homelessness, madness and imprisonment. By the film's end, Wuornos's fierce desire for her execution to go forward smacks of a horrible logic.

Clarence Brown
US, 1890–1987

Bridging the transition from silents to talkies, Hollywood contract director Clarence Brown combined the atmospheric cinematography of the late silents with sturdy production values and attention to stars in a way that epitomizes high Hollywood.

Brown started out in the film industry as an assistant to director Maurice Tourneur, who imparted to him the aesthetic finesse and romantic sensibility that typify Brown's "quality" product from *Flesh And The Devil* (1927) to *The Yearling* (1946).

Around 1926, Brown joined the MGM assembly line, where he made a string of moneymaking Greta Garbo vehicles. Patiently shot by William H. Daniels, these films defined Garbo's and MGM's image for decades. Adept at reflecting studio policy, in the 1930s Brown worked with Garbo, Joan Crawford, Clark Gable and Jean Harlow on films ranging from the literary adaptation *Anna Christie* (1930) to the comedy *Wife Vs Secretary* (1936) and the spectacle *The Rains Came* (1939). In the small-town drama *Ah Wilderness!* (1935), Brown showed his populism, adding patriotic gloss in the William Saroyan adaptation *The Human Comedy* (1943), starring Mickey Rooney, and *The White Cliffs Of Dover* (1944).

If Brown has been overlooked, our negligence is perhaps proportionate with Garbo's decline in critical stock. However, retrospectives and reissues do suggest that revival and re-evaluation of this arch Hollywood craftsman are underway. RA

The Eagle 1925, 91 min, b/w

cast Rudolph Valentino, Vilma Bánky, Louise Dresser, Albert Conti, James A. Marcus *cin* George Barnes

The Black Eagle (Rudolph Valentino) is simultaneously on the run from the Czarina, whose advances he has spurned, and seeking revenge against the man who has taken his father's land. Bringing Pushkin to the screen with dash and bravado, this Valentino vehicle combines set-piece action with romantic intrigue. It goes some way to explaining why women committed suicide when Valentino died in 1926.

Anna Christie 1930, 90 min, b/w

cast Greta Garbo, Charles Bickford, George F. Marion, Marie Dressler, James T. Mack *cin* William H. Daniels

As William H. Daniels evokes the foggy wharves and dank alleys of Eugene O'Neill's dockside romance, Garbo speaks her first line in a talkie and signals the shift from 1920s Hollywood decadence to 1930s social realism. She is nicely supported by Charles Bickford and Marie Dressler in this underrated treasure.

Tod Browning

US, 1882–1962

Like many a storybook hero, Tod Browning ran away to join the circus while still in his teens, and performed as a clown and a contortionist before becoming first a silent-film actor (in 1919, he played a part in D.W. Griffith's *Intolerance*) and then a director. He made a run of nine silent films in the 1920s with Lon Chaney, who was intended to star in Browning's *Dracula* (1931) before his death. After the gangster heist talkie *Outside The Law* (1930) starring Edward G. Robinson, Browning helmed *Dracula* with Bela Lugosi in the lead role. A stiff but occasionally inspired production, the film cashed in at cinemas and turned Lugosi into an icon.

The following year, however, Browning mounted the virtual career-ender *Freaks* (1932). The film revolted contemporary audiences (it was banned in Britain for thirty years) and its studio MGM (who removed their logo from the film), but eventually found lasting fame as a midnight cult item – today it's regarded as an offbeat classic. The director's career all but petered out just a few years later, although Lugosi again fulfilled bloodsucking duties

for him in *Mark Of The Vampire* (1932), a somewhat camp sound remake of the lost Browning-Chaney silent *London After Midnight*. In one of his last films, the creepy, darkly comic *The Devil-Doll* (1936), Browning cast Lionel Barrymore as a disgraced banker turned dollmaker whose charming little toys are in fact bona fide miniature humans – yet more freaks to add to the director's gallery of irregular physicality. JW

Dracula 1931, 75 min, b/w
cast Bela Lugosi, Helen Chandler, David Manners, Dwight Frye, Edward Van Sloan, Herbert Bunston *cin* Karl Freund *m* Tchaikovsky, Wagner

Photographed by the great Karl Freund, *Dracula*'s shadowy, shivery first reel or so is justly famed: Renfield's carriage journey through the foreboding Transylvanian mountains, Dracula rising from his coffin, Renfield's arrival at the Count's castle. However, the rest of the film is oddly static and lumbering; it looks more like filmed theatre when viewed alongside *Frankenstein*, James Whale's Universal horror film of the same year.

Freaks 1932, 64 min, b/w
cast Harry Earles, Olga Baclanova, Wallace Ford, Leila Hyams, Henry Victor, Daisy Earles *cin* Merrit B. Gerstad

A trapeze artist marries her circus colleague, a dwarf, planning to poison him and steal his fortune, but she doesn't bet on the solidarity among her new husband's

The fear factor in Browning's *Dracula* was largely dependent on Karl Freund's camerawork, especially in the early scenes showing Renfield's arrival at the bloodsucking Count's shadowy castle.

fellow sideshow attractions in Browning's enthralling *film maudit*. A carnival veteran himself, Browning doesn't exploit the "freaks" (microcephalics, a man without limbs, etc) but instead takes an empathetic interest in their bodies and minds, even once they decide to enact their terrible revenge.

Kevin Brownlow
UK, 1938–

Kevin Brownlow's career has been one of the most distinctive and eclectic in the post-war period. The son of artists, Brownlow grew up collecting films, a favourite being two reels from Abel Gance's 1927 epic *Napoléon*, which he later restored to great acclaim. Brownlow made his first film at 14, a 9.5mm Maupassant adaptation called *The Capture* which he financed by writing for a film magazine, and he then entered the film industry as an editing apprentice at a documentary house.

In 1956 he began making *It Happened Here* with Andrew Mollo, a hypothetical account charting the consequences of a Nazi invasion of Britain. Although completed in 1964, it was not exhibited until 1966. In 1968 Brownlow wrote of its difficult genesis in his witty book *How It Happened Here*. In the 1960s he supported himself editing and directing documentary shorts, joining Woodfall, home of the British New Wave, in 1965, where he edited Lindsay Anderson's *The White Bus* (1965) and Tony Richardson's *The Charge Of The Light Brigade* (1968). In 1975 he directed *Winstanley*, a dramatization of the radical "Digger" collective established by Gerrard Winstanley in 1649. Realist, even miserablist in tone, the film recalls Roberto Rossellini's *The Rise To Power Of Louis XIV* (1966).

Based on his respected books about the silent era *The Parade's Gone By*, *The War, The West And The Wilderness* and *Hollywood: The Pioneers*, the 1980 Thames TV series *Hollywood*, co-directed with David Gill, was a landmark of its genre. Brownlow has advised on many film-historical projects since. Following the restoration of *Napoléon*, the French government awarded him the Légion d'honneur. RA

It Happened Here 1966, 99 min
cast Pauline Murray, Sebastian Shaw, Fiona Leland, Honor Fehrson, Percy Binns, Frank Bennett *cin* Peter Suschitzky *m* Jack Beaver

These austere images of a Wehrmacht band in Regent's Park, patriots betrayed in Hampstead and rallies in Trafalgar Square flesh out the uncomfortable notion of British collaboration with the Nazis. Despite deficient sound and film stock, this curio still disturbs.

Jan Bucquoy
Belgium, 1945–

Belgium's resident bad boy, Bucqouy is a cartoonist, filmmaker, anarchist and collector of underpants. A well-known prankster, the erstwhile satirical journalist has been arrested on many occasions, once for publicly smashing a plaster bust of the King of Belgium and several times for flinging custard pies in the faces of the rich and famous. To fund his film debut, Bucquoy had to auction exhibits from his Musée De Slip Belge, a unique collection of celebrity undergarments. However, this unusual form of fundraising was entirely appropriate for a movie in which underwear features heavily. *The Sexual Life Of The Belgians* (1985) is an autobiographical tale of Bucquoy's own, often absurd and occasionally painful, sexual exploits.

The second film in the trilogy, *Camping Cosmos* (1996), found our hero running the activities at a Belgian resort, ably supported by the late Lolo Ferrari who once had the biggest breasts in the world. Part three, *Fermeture de l'usine Renault à Vilvoorde* (*Please Please Me*, 1998) possessed a more sober, political edge, focusing on the closure of a Renault car factory. With typical anarchic logic, Bucquoy didn't end his trilogy at three. In part four, *La jouissance des hystériques* (*Pleasure And Hysteria*, 2000), the director seems to abandon both script and professional principles as he is seen auditioning young hopefuls for his new film, and lasciviously trying to kiss them. Outside of this four-film trilogy, Bucquoy has made several other films, including *Friday Fishday* (1999), about a man who can only fall in love with women who smell of fish. LH

The Sexual Life Of The Belgians (La vie sexuelle des Belges) 1995, 80 min
cast Jean-Henri Compere, Noé Franq, Sophie Schneider, Isabelle Legros, Jacques Druaux, Pascale Binneri *cin* Michael Baudour *m* Francis de Smet

"My mother had nice tits." The opening line of *The Sexual Life Of The Belgians* immediately sets the tone for this spirited, attention-seeking romp through Jan Bucqouy's early sex life. There is, unsurprisingly, a devil-may-care anarchy to the narrative which detours wildly from the linear to make rueful asides about men, women and pigeons.

Tony Bui
Vietnam, 1973–

The director of the first American movie to be filmed in Communist Vietnam, Tony Bui certainly had the right credentials for the job. Bui's family were airlifted out of Saigon two weeks before the tanks rolled in, when he was only 2 years old.

Growing up in Los Angeles, Bui got his first tutorials in filmmaking by watching movies in his father's video shops. Returning to his birthplace for holidays in the early 1990s, he made the short film *Yellow Lotus* (1995) starring his uncle, Vietnamese movie star Don Duong. The award-winning short came to the attention of the Hollywood studios, which helped to secure financing for Bui's debut feature, *Three Seasons* (1999).

A lyrical portmanteau about life in Ho Chi Minh City, *Three Seasons* was made with both the official cooperation and continual interference of the Vietnamese government: the Ministry of Culture had to approve the script, a censor was present on set every day and the daily rushes were inspected by a committee. The finished product won approval in both Vietnam and America, where it became the first film to win the Grand Jury Prize and the Audience Award at the Sundance Film Festival. However, the co-production had a significance greater than the film itself. *Three Seasons* represented a new Vietnam and optimistically signalled a rapprochement between enemy nations; a cinematic and psychic healing of old wounds. The critically acclaimed movie was produced by the director's brother, Timothy Bui, and the roles were reversed two years later on *Green Dragon* (2001), an autobiographical drama about Vietnamese refugees in relocation camps in the United States. LH

Three Seasons 1999, 113 min

cast Don Duong, Nguyen Ngoc Hiep, Tran Manh Cuong, Harvey Keitel, Zoe Bui *cin* Lisa Rinzler *m* Richard Horowitz

Set over the dry, wet and growth seasons in Vietnam, this poetic, sweeping and politically airbrushed melodrama seamlessly weaves four life stories together: an American war veteran (Harvey Keitel) searches for his daughter, a cyclo driver (Don Duong) falls in love with a prostitute, a poet with leprosy discovers his muse in a lotus picker and a young street urchin sells his case of wares to passers-by.

Luis Buñuel
Spain, 1900–83

Luis Buñuel's canon is a strange and wondrous dream factory. His episodic narratives frequently break off and shift their shape, and the deranged imagery and absurdist situations follow the rigorous patterns of dream logic. Buñuel wrote "The cinema seems to have been invented to express the life of the subconscious" and his films seek to lay bare both the repressed desires

buried in the human mind and the social hypocrisies lying in plain sight that we're usually content to sleepwalk past.

Being such a committed dreamer, Buñuel was also a natural-born surrealist. His films brimmed with all the irreverence, irrationality and shock tactics that the movement espoused, most indelibly in Buñuel and Salvador Dalí's *Un chien andalou* (1928), with its infamous image of an eyeball sliced open in merciless close-up. Giving offence was a surrealist's sacred duty, and Buñuel became a devoted blasphemer enacting a fascinated ongoing rebellion against the Catholic Church that had shaped daily life in his home village of Calanda and had suffused the young Buñuel's budding sexuality. "Instinct's hard battles against chastity, occurring only in our thoughts, overwhelmed us with guilt," Buñuel wrote. "For years I lived with a sense of sin that could be delightful."

This dogma-based dichotomy of secret shame and furtive delight breaks the surface again and again in Buñuel's films, from frigid Séverine's bondage fantasies in *Belle de jour* (1967) to Conchita's puritan fixation on her own virginity in *That Obscure Object*

Luis Buñuel scrutinizes porcelain-beauty Catherine Deneuve.

Of Desire (1977), and there is a preponderance of fetish objects across his oeuvre. Another stubborn motif is desire frustrated: the amorous couple kept apart in *L'âge d'or* (1930), the guests who can't leave the room in *The Exterminating Angel* (1962) and the diners that can't eat in *The Discreet Charm Of The Bourgeoisie* (1972).

"I've always been an atheist, thank God," quipped Buñuel, whose movies racked up a lengthy rap sheet of crimes against the Church, putting the pope before a firing squad in *The Milky Way* (1968) and naming a terrorist group the Revolutionary Army of the Infant Jesus in *That Obscure Object*. The scandalous *L'âge d'or* spurred the right-wing "Young Patriots" to trash the Paris theatre where it played, leading to a ban on the film that lasted half a century. Buñuel decamped from Europe soon thereafter (following the start of the Spanish Civil War), first moving to the US (he worked for several years in the film department of the Museum of Modern Art in New York) and then Mexico. He worked steadily and often brilliantly in Mexico, producing the slum-kids tragedy *Los olvidados* (1950), a landmark of the neo-realist style that Buñuel ultimately rejected, and *The Criminal Life Of Archibaldo de la Cruz* (1955), an acrid study of the masculine ego in murderous crisis.

Franco's government welcomed Buñuel back to Spain to make *Viridiana* in 1961, and the director gleefully bit the hand that fed him, turning out a film custom-made to appal his patrons with its restaging of the Last Supper as a vulgar beggars' banquet. The movie won the Palme d'Or but was banned in Spain for two decades – a pleasing comeback for Buñuel, who was previously irritated to find he'd accidentally pleased the church he despised with *Nazarín* (1958), which chronicles a Christ-like priest's mounting despair as he suffers at the hands of those he tries to help.

The wicked parody of Leonardo's holy portrait in *Viridiana* is an especially pungent case study in Buñuel's knack for dinner-table insurrection, also demonstrated in *Discreet Charm* and *The Phantom Of Liberty* (1974), an episodic anthology of Buñuelian themes: the tyranny of decorum, the arbitrariness of convention and the practical difficulties of wild animals in the boudoir among others. Still at his peak as an artist well into his seventies, Buñuel continued tossing hand grenades at the status quo to the very end; aptly, *That Obscure Object*, his final film, ends with an explosion. JW

L'âge d'or 1930, 63 min, b/w

cast Gaston Mordot, Lya Lys, Max Ernst, Caridad De Laberdesque, Pierre Prévert, Jacques Brunius *cin* Albert Du Verger *m* Luis Buñuel

Partly due to its longer running time, *L'âge d'or* did not have the same concentrated shock effect as *Un chien andalou* (1928). Starting with a documentary about scorpions and climaxing with an orgy straight out of the Marquis de Sade's *120 Days Of Sodom*, the film follows a passionate couple who try to consummate their relationship, but are continually interrupted by forces of the church and state. Being a Buñuel film, thwarted love finds its outlet in fetishism, with the woman infamously seeking satisfaction in the marble toes of a statue.

Los olvidados (The Young And The Damned) 1950, 76 min, b/w

cast Alfonso Mejia, Roberto Cobo, Estela Inda, Miguel Inclán, Alma Delia Fuentes, Francisco Jambrina *cin* Gabriel Figueroa *m* Gustavo Pitaluga

In this early feature from Buñuel's Mexican period, a couple of thieving kids stalk the slums of Mexico City with eventual tragic repercussions. The film mostly keeps to a stark documentary mode, but also boasts a haunting dream sequence worthy of Vigo, while a stinging astringency of sentiment scrubs the film clean of liberal cant. Poverty ennobles no one here, as the kids succumb to the impotent violence born of hopeless anger.

The Criminal Life Of Archibaldo de la Cruz (Ensayo de un crimen) 1955, 91 min, b/w

cast Ernesto Alonso, Miroslava Stern, Ariadna Welter, Rita Macedeo, José Maria Linares Rivas *cin* Augusto Jiminez *m* Jorge Pérez

There are shades of Hitchcock in this lean but dense thriller, wherein a pivotal childhood event sparks a murderous obsession: the freak death of the title character's governess and its link to a supposedly magical music box begets an adult compulsion to murder women – an impulse thwarted at every turn. With bone-dry wit, Buñuel critiques masculine lust and ego, and indulges a foot fetish that would pop up in several of his other films.

Viridiana 1961, 91 min, b/w

cast Silvia Piñal, Francisco Rabal, Fernando Rey, Margarita Lozano, Victoria Zinny, Teresa Rabal *cin* José F Aguayo *m* Gustavo Pittaluga

The titular kind and pure-hearted nun hopes to help the homeless by welcoming them into her uncle's house, but her compassion only leads to abuse and humiliation. This is one of Buñuel's most despairing films, and the most calculating in its sacrilege – the vicious parody of the Last Supper, scored to Handel's *Messiah*, is perhaps less startling than the brutally pure lack of Christian charity to be found in Viridiana's tribulations.

The Exterminating Angel (El ángel exterminador) 1962, 89 min, b/w

cast Silvia Piñal, Enrique Rambal, Lucy Gallardo, Claudio Brook, Tito Junco, Bertha Moss *cin* Gabriel Figueroa *m* Raúl Lavista

An elegant dinner party spirals into sordid chaos when the guests suddenly develop a mass neurosis whereby they can't bring themselves to leave the room. "I have always chosen man against men," Buñuel once wrote, and in this delicious *commedia dell'arte* he ridicules mob mentality as expressed in the arbitrary and binding codes of "polite society", a fellowship that here degenerates into half-starved squalor.

Belle de jour 1967, 100 min

cast Catherine Deneuve, Jean Sorel, Michel Piccoli, Genevieve Page, Francisco Rabal, Pierre Clémenti, Georges Marchal *cin* Sacha Vierny

Icy, impassive housewife Séverine (porcelain-beauty Catherine Deneuve) denies her husband sex but revels in an active sadomasochistic fantasy life. She goes to work in an upscale brothel, where she entertains a variety of eccentrics and becomes entangled with a volatile young gangster. As Buñuel examines the consequences of this direct collision between dream-life and reality, he also delivers another deadpan evisceration of the *haute bourgeoisie*.

The Discreet Charm Of The Bourgeoisie (Le charme discret de la bourgeoisie) 1972, 101 min

cast Fernando Rey, Delphine Seyrig, Stéphane Audran, Bulle Ogier, Jean-Pierre Cassel, Paul Frankeur, Julien Bertheau *cin* Edmond Richard

Following on from the post-fête paralysis of *The Exterminating Angel*, this splendidly cast episodic comedy follows another stymied dinner party. Attempts to eat are continually frustrated by appetite-spoiling corpses, resident armies, understocked kitchens and long anecdotes. Woven from interlocking set pieces and dreams within dreams, *Discreet Charm* shows the surrealist in Buñuel was still alive and kicking.

That Obscure Object Of Desire (Cet obscur objet du désir) 1977, 105 min

cast Fernando Rey, Carole Bouquet, Angela Molina, Julien Bertheau, André Weber, Milena Vukotic *cin* Edmond Richard *m* Richard Wagner

On a train journey, Mathieu (Fernando Rey) tells fellow passengers the story of his tortuous affair with dancer and maid Conchita, alternately played by Carole Bouquet and Angela Molina in a yin/yang duet of desirous womanhood. As terrorist attacks rage in the background, Buñuel's final film recapitulates several of his choice themes: the consanguinity of eros and violence, and the corruptive yet inescapable influence of money upon love.

Tim Burton

US, 1958–

Tim Burton is the unlikeliest of superstar directors. His first professional credit was *Vincent*, a six-minute black-and-white animated short he made under the sponsorship of Disney (where he was one of the animators on *The Fox And The Hound*, 1981). Macabre, expressionist and funny, *Vincent* was too disturbing for the studio, and wasn't shown publicly for many years, until Burton had become one of the most powerful filmmakers in Hollywood. It remains his most autobiographical film.

Burton grew up in suburban California, but lived a gothic fantasy life suggested by Edgar Allan Poe, Roger Corman and comic books. He once threw a suit of clothes in a swimming pool and persuaded his friends that a man had evaporated inside them. Another time the carefully staged "execution" of his younger brother terrified his parents. At 12, he moved out to live with his grandmother.

Suburban banality rubs against the gothic exotic in *Beetle Juice* (1988), *Edward Scissorhands* (1990), *Ed Wood* (1994) and *Big Fish* (2003). The typical Burton hero is a misunderstood misfit who strays between these two worlds: child-man Pee-wee Herman; Edward Scissorhands, a teenager cut off from the world by his destructive/creative blade-fin-

gers; neurotic crime fighter Batman; Ed Wood, the world's least talented filmmaker; or Jack Skellington, a pumpkin king who brings Halloween horror to the festive season in *Tim Burton's The Nightmare Before Christmas* (1994 – directed by Henry Selick). These schizophrenic heroes are mostly benign, but it is their malign or anarchic alter egos to which we are magnetically attracted: agents of chaos like Betelgeuse (Michael Keaton), the Joker (Jack Nicholson in *Batman*) or the alien invaders in *Mars Attacks!* (1996).

Burton has sometimes been compared to Steven Spielberg, because of their affinity for the child's-eye view (and, perhaps, their limited engagement with the opposite sex), but the work is of a very different temperature. More intuitive, less sentimental, Burton has none of Spielberg's sense of the rightful order of things. Indeed, storytelling is not his forte. His movies get by on atmosphere and curiosity rather than narrative drive or manipulation.

If they get by, that is. *Mars Attacks!* was spoof disaster shlock directed in the manner of Ed Wood – a splenetic and subversive satire on consumer culture (including its own status as an all-star blockbuster) which was nevertheless cripplingly self-indulgent. *Sleepy Hollow* (1999) had a wispy ghoulish charm which evaporated halfway through. *Planet Of The Apes* (2001) felt like penance, a cartoonish misfire, and proved Burton's hamfisted way with action. *Big Fish* (2003) was a Gumpish slice of Southern fabulism, an indigestible apologia for escapist paternalism.

Happily, he rebounded with two pictures in 2005: Roald Dahl's *Charlie And The Chocolate Factory* was a good fit (almost too good in truth), and a further chance to explore the wackiness of being Johnny Depp. The claymation fairy tale *Corpse Bride* was quite delectable, his most romantic movie for a long time – and the first in a while that suggests he might actually like people (although preferably in a state of decomposition). With his box-office clout restored, perhaps a new creative peak is in the offing? TC

Pee-wee's Big Adventure 1985, 91 min

cast Paul Reubens, Elizabeth Daily, Mark Holton, Diane Salinger, Judd Omen, Tony Bill *cin* Victor J. Kemper *m* Danny Elfman

Personally selected by Paul Reubens (Pee-wee himself) on the basis of the unreleased short *Frankenweenie* (1984), Burton proved an inspired choice. *Bicycle Thieves* for kids, this is full of outrageous visual gags and achieves a warped child's-eye view reminiscent of the very best Jerry Lewis. Pee-wee himself is a typical Burton man-child, a mischievous innocent who treats the world as his plaything.

Edward Scissorhands 1990, 105 min

cast Johnny Depp, Winona Ryder, Dianne Wiest, Anthony Michael Hall, Kathy Baker *cin* Stefan Czapsky *m* Danny Elfman

Burton's purest candy-coloured fairy tale is an artful mix of satire, horror and romance. This was the first iconic role for frequent collaborator Johnny Depp, the monster to Vincent

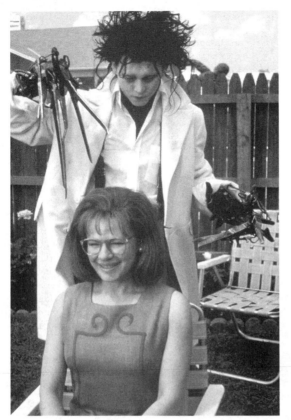

Cutting edge: Burton regular Johnny Depp in *Edward Scissorhands*.

Price's Frankenstein. An artificial boy with scissors for hands, evidently a danger to himself and others, Edward flourishes when he finds a creative outlet in topiary and hairdressing.

Batman Returns 1992, 127 min

cast Michael Keaton, Danny DeVito, Michelle Pfeiffer, Christopher Walken, Michael Gough, Michael Murphy *cin* Stefan Czapsky *m* Danny Elfman

Frustrated by the compromises inflicted on the corporate blockbuster *Batman* (1989), Burton had the clout to keep the sequel much closer to his own dark humours. This is a superhero with a *noir* sensibility, indelibly marked, like his adversary, Penguin, by childhood trauma. With Michelle Pfeiffer's Catwoman, they're quite the schizophrenic trio. Freaked, Warner Bros gave *Batman And Robin* to Joel Schumacher.

Ed Wood 1994, 127 min, b/w

cast Johnny Depp, Martin Landau, Sarah Jessica Parker, Patricia Arquette, Jeffrey Jones, Vincent D'Onofrio *cin* Stefan Czapsky *m* Howard Shore

Although it was his first box-office bomb, for many critics this is Burton's most wholly satisfying film. Z-movie auteur and angora fetishist Ed Wood may be beyond parody, but Burton and Johnny Depp bring such affection to their task that it disarms all criticism. Especially when Orson Welles is on hand to offer encouragement ("Visions are worth fighting for," he tells him. "Why spend your life making someone else's dreams?"). Even then, Martin Landau practically steals the film as the great Hungarian ham, Bela Lugosi.

Corpse Bride 2005, 76 min

cast (*voices*) Johnny Depp, Helena Bonham Carter, Emily Watson, Tracy Ullman *cin* Malcolm Hadley, Pete Kozachik *m* Danny Elfman

Burton is only the co-director (with Mike Johnson), but his stamp is all over this tale of a timid dreamer who finds himself betrothed to a corpse. Victor's *nouveau riche* parents must be the ancestors of those status-conscious suburbanites in *Edward Scissorhands*. Victoria's are such rotten examples of humanity, they might have been dreamed up by Roald Dahl. As for the journey into the underworld, it's strongly reminiscent of *Beetle Juice*. *Corpse Bride* may not mark a radical departure, but we don't read fairy tales for surprise twists or shocking revelations. We read them because they express the familiar strangeness of a world in which people marry for money not love, and the dead aren't ghouls and ghosties, but friends and loved ones.

Steve Buscemi
US, 1957–

In an interview in 2001, Buscemi named John Cassavetes as probably his biggest influence as a filmmaker. "What I learned from Cassavetes' films was that it's OK to get into trouble. Anything that you write, even if you have to start over, is valuable," he said. "So I started to write and didn't worry so much about the story, and let the story write itself through the characters."

The result was his sharply observed, richly characterized debut feature, *Trees Lounge* (1996), which marked out the Brooklyn-born Buscemi as one of the most promising actor-turned-directors of recent years. The sleepy, suburban outer-borough New York of *Trees Lounge* is a world away from the clamorous, danger-ridden prison setting of his later film *Animal Factory* (2000), but in both Buscemi focuses his keen attention less on plot mechanics than on conversational rhythms, textures of personality, local custom and the unspoken emotions concentrated in a glance or a gesture.

In between features and his many acting assignments, Buscemi directed episodes of *Homicide: Life on the Street*, *Oz* and *The Sopranos*. He returned to feature directing with *Lonesome Jim* (2005), about a depressed 27-year-old (Casey Affleck) who moves back to his parents' house. Stronger was *Interview* (2007), his tense, involving remake of Dutch filmmaker Theo van Gogh's 2003 two-hander, in which a slumming reporter (Buscemi) takes an unexpectedly complicated assignment profiling a starlet (Sienna Miller) who's far more interesting – and calculating – than she appears. JW

Trees Lounge 1996, 95 min

cast Steve Buscemi, Chloë Sevigny, Anthony LaPaglia, Elizabeth Bracco, Daniel Baldwin, Mark Boone Jr *cin* Steve Rosenzweig *m* Evan Laurie

After his boss fires him and steals his girlfriend for good measure, lonely mechanic Tommy (Buscemi) slouches towards alcoholism and his ex's restless teenage niece (Chloë Sevigny). Named after the homely bar where the protagonist spends his copious downtime, Buscemi's fine debut never solicits undue sympathy for the feckless but potentially decent Tommy; it strikes an elegant balance between wry comedy and quiet desperation, leaning toward the latter in the lingering, indelible final shot.

Animal Factory 2000, 94 min

cast Edward Furlong, Willem Dafoe, Danny Trejo, Seymour Cassel, John Heard, Tom Arnold, Mickey Rourke *cin* Phil Parmet *m* John Lurie

Ex-con Eddie Bunker's script observes a tough but sympathetic lifer (Willem Dafoe) who takes under his wing a young inmate (Edward Furlong) new to the trial-by-fire culture of hard time. Buscemi casts a near-anthropological eye on cellblock life, which here is fraught with violence and peril yet also harbours precious corners of refuge and comradeship. The movie was shot in a real prison, and many of its extras are actual prisoners, which only adds to the film's rough-and-tumble authenticity.

David Butler

US, 1894–1979

A prolific and reliable filmmaker, David Butler's best films are musicals. Although lacking any particular personal touch, they have remained popular.

Butler was born into the cinema as the son of actress Adele Belgrade and actor–director Fred J. Butler. After acting on stage in San Francisco and Los Angeles and in films by directors including John Ford, D.W. Griffith and his father, he moved behind the camera in 1927. None of his early films are mem-orable, but he has the distinction of directing one of cinema's few sci-fi musicals, *Just Imagine* (1930), set in New York in 1980. He upped his game for Mark Twain's time-travelling satire *A Connecticut Yankee* (1930), starring the comedy cowboy Will Rogers, and was Shirley Temple's regular director throughout the 1930s, on films such as *Bright Eyes* (1934) and *Little Colonel* (1935). And in 1942 he directed Bob Hope, Bing Crosby and Dorothy Lamour in *Road To Morocco*. The rest of that comedy series did not come Butler's way, but Paramount's rival studio Warners got him to try to emulate the success with Dennis Morgan and Jack Carson in *Two Guys From Milwaukee* (1946), *The Time, The Place And The Girl* (1946) and *Two Guys From Texas* (1948).

Returning to musicals proper, in 1950 he directed *Tea For Two*, the first of several Doris Day collaborations. A rare late acting appearance, as himself in Michael Curtiz's biopic *The Story Of Will Rogers* (1952), was followed by more Doris Day musicals, climaxing in his best film, *Calamity Jane* (1953). The late 1950s were taken up with television work, and in 1967 he released his last film, *C'mon, Let's Live A Little*, a limp teenage-rebel musical starring Bobby Vee. JR

Calamity Jane 1953, 101 min

cast Doris Day, Howard Keel, Allyn Ann McLerie, Philip Carey *cin* Wilfred M. Cline *m* Sammy Fain, David Buttolph, Howard Jackson

With songs like "Whip Crack Away", "The Deadwood Stage" and "Just Blew In From The Windy City", and a frothy confused-love storyline, it would be hard for this film to fail. Buckskin-wearing, tomboyish scout and sharpshooter Calam' (Doris Day) rescues a handsome lieutenant from Indians, before heading off to Chicago to find a famous actress. But she accidentally brings back the wrong woman, who becomes her rival for the affections of both the lieutenant and her best friend Wild Bill Hickock. This is now a cult gay film, partly due to the Oscar-winning song, "Secret Love".

Michael Cacoyannis
Cyprus, 1922–

Largely remembered for *Zorba The Greek*, Cacoyannis also directed adaptations of several Greek tragedies.

After studying classics, Mikhalis Kakagionis moved to London to take a degree in law, but ended up studying drama, acting and working on wartime BBC broadcasts to Greece. Deciding to move into film, he wrote *Eroica* in 1953 but, unable to find a producer, he returned to Greece where he made *Stella* (1955) and *A Girl In Black* (1956), both stories of rebellion against stifling Greek society. In 1960 he finally managed to make *Eroica*, though it hardly justified the wait, and directed a strikingly stark version of Euripides' *Elektra* two years later.

In 1964 he had his biggest international hit with *Zorba The Greek*, its success largely fuelled by Anthony Quinn's performance and Mikis Theodorakis's infectious bouzouki music. Three years later, however, the apocalyptic allegory *The Day The Fish Came Out* turned out to be a portentous mess. For his powerful if stagy version of Euripides' *The Trojan Women* (1971) he assembled an impressive international cast including Katharine Hepburn and Vanessa Redgrave, but *Iphigenia* (1977) was almost exactly opposite: home-grown actors in a tricksy film. After this his output slowed and his latest film, *The Cherry Orchard* (1999), wastes an outstanding cast in a leaden Chekhov adaptation. JR

Zorba The Greek 1964, 142 min
cast Anthony Quinn, Alan Bates, Irene Papas, Lila Kedrova, George Foundas *cin* Walter Lasally *m* Mikis Theodorakis

Zorba persuades an uptight Englishman to rediscover the meaning of life by indulging in "a bit of madness". Quinn, with an injured foot, invented his famous dance on the spur of the moment, but persuaded Cacoyannis that it was traditional. Based on the novel by Nikos Kazantzakis, whose views on religion and sensuality (as in *The Last Temptation Of Christ*) put him at odds with Catholicism and saw him excommunicated from the Greek Orthodox Church.

James Cameron
Canada, 1954–

For a decade following 1997, James Cameron didn't direct a single fiction feature and, as the years dragged on, his spectacularly misjudged Oscar acceptance speech for *Titanic* (1997) seemed more and more like a valedictory. He asked for a moment of silence for the 1500 victims of the 1912 disaster, then boomed: "I'm king of the world!"

There is certainly something totalitarian to Cameron's gargantuan budget expenditures and well-documented rampaging ego. Few of his major cast or crew members have ever worked for him more than once, with the notable exception of Arnold Schwarzenegger. But there's also no doubting his films' massive popularity, their technical innovation and bravado, or their action-thrill quotient – leaving aside, perhaps, Cameron's IMAX films *Ghosts Of The Abyss* (2003) and *Aliens Of The Deep* (2005), the latter of which *Slate* magazine's Bryan Curtis likened to "watching a megalomaniac narrate his summer-vacation video".

Coming up through the Roger Corman factory as an art director and set builder, Cameron made his debut proper with *Piranha II: The Spawning* (1982) for Corman. Though the final film seems to have been wrested away by executive producer Ovidio G. Assonitis, it presaged Cameron's career-long interest in the life aquatic. He had greater control over the surprise smash hit *The Terminator* (1984), a time-bending nightmare that remains Cameron's best achievement: dark, terse, hard, and cold. His next film, *Aliens* (1986), maintained the skyscraping levels of physical and psychological intensity, dividing itself into complementary halves: a nearly action-free, exposition-rich hour suffused with dread, and an hour of unrelenting, explosive warfare between aliens and their vastly outclassed human opponents.

Aliens coarsely italicized the feminist intonations that many viewers sensed in Ridley Scott's *Alien* and the iron-boned Ellen Ripley character

Action movies: the cinema of spectacle

"I think the spectacle got people's attention, got them to the theaters, and then the emotional, cathartic experience of watching the film is what made the film work." That's James Cameron's useful and accurate assessment of why his film *Titanic* found an audience of massive proportions in 1997. It also neatly indicates the hugely profitable (in every sense) relationship between action cinema and visual effects.

Since cinema's inception, action and film have complemented one another, like popcorn and the big screen. From the Lumière Brothers' silent short films, Buster Keaton's dazzling silent action epic *The General* (1927), *Ben Hur* (1959), *Bridge On The River Kwai* (1957) to the glorious truck chase of *Raiders Of The Lost Ark* (1981), action films have proved bankably evergreen. Often overlooked as lacking intellectual interest, action films have nevertheless provided their share of thoughtful and intelligent filmmaking. Screenwriter and director James Cameron has emerged as a major purveyor of smart and stylish action cinema which, starting with *The Terminator* (1984), brought character to the action movie. Suddenly, all the sound and fury of the genre became anchored in something emotionally real. It's why Cameron's sci-fi war film *Aliens* (1986) is such a thrill. More recently, with *The Frighteners* (1996) and his subsequent adaptation of *Lord Of The Rings,* writer-director Peter Jackson has reaffirmed the capacity for action cinema to achieve a beauty all of its own, with visual effects enhancing our sense of the latent wonders of our world.

Action films turn on the greatest tests of endurance and images of courage under fire. Step forward John McClane in *Die Hard* and everyone's favourite archaeologist, Dr Indiana Jones. But action films aren't the sole province of male characters, of course – or male directors. There's the oft-noted output of Kathryn Bigelow, for example. Her supercharged action cop movie *Point Break* (1991) and hyperkinetic science fiction *Strange Days* (1995) are genre touchstones. Nor is the action movie a purely Hollywood phenomenon of course: undisputed classics such as *The Seven Samurai* (1957) and variations on action themes, such as *Leon* (1993), have emerged from further afield.

Action cinema, with its frequently fantastical trappings, has often been the genre that best showcases visual effects, which have their own stable of star players. Just witness the work of Willis O' Brien in *King Kong* (1993), Ray Harryhausen in *Sinbad*, Phil Tippett in *Star Wars* and Dennis Muren in *Terminator 2: Judgement Day* (1991). The latter confirmed the razzle-dazzle possibilities of artfully designed computer-generated images – since the late 1980s, with *Young Sherlock Holmes* (1985), *Willow* (1988) and *The Abyss* (1989), computer-animated characters have developed in their sophistication and fascination. We're now at a moment in time in which digital stunt doubles are a standard. *The Host* (2006) and *The Polar Express* (2004) offer further evidence of the engrossing fusion of action and high-tech illusion.

But above and beyond their delight in spectacle and bodies in motion, action movies sell us on the idea of the tenacious, courageous man and woman apparently unsuited to the challenge at hand. In the dreamy, flickering glow of the movie screen, don't we all become heroes? JC

(Sigourney Weaver). Cameron has often trumpeted his own proclivity for strong, independent female characters, demonstrating his solidarity with the ladies by, for example, giving *The Abyss* a figure dubbed "the queen bitch of the universe" and, in the asinine *True Lies* (1994), contriving for Jamie Lee Curtis's character to perform a humiliating striptease. The *Terminator* films offered a more complex heroine in Sarah Conner (Linda Hamilton), the young waitress turned sinewy doomsayer, and *Terminator 2: Judgement Day* (1991), which recast Schwarzenegger as a good-guy cyborg, establishes an almost endearing family unit, with young John Connor (Edward Furlong), future freedom fighter, at its centre. Like *The Abyss*, *T2* provided a dazzling showroom of CGI innovation, but its invincible liquid-metal villain (Robert Patrick) literally lacked heft; unlike the grubby, lower-budget original, the gleaming sequel was more impressive than scary.

Having presided over many a haemorrhaging budget and troubled set (reportedly, crew members on *The Abyss* were given to gallows-humour puns like "Life's Abyss, Then You Dive"), Cameron outdid himself on *Titanic*. Two studios were required to put up all the cash – *Titanic* was Cameron's third film, after *T2* and *True Lies*, to win the distinction of most expensive movie ever made (an estimated $200 million). Renowned cinematographer Caleb Deschanel abandoned ship halfway through. Screen Actors Guild reps descended to investigate claims of maltreatment of extras. And star Kate Winslet revealed that "He has a temper like you wouldn't believe", vowing "You'd have to pay me a lot of money to work with Jim Cameron again." *Titanic* was a box-office pinnacle that will perhaps never be surpassed, lifting the all-time box-office record from *Jurassic Park* (1993) and winning a clutch of Oscars. Cameron was indeed king of the world – by diving into the fray once again, does he risk losing his crown? JW

The Terminator 1984, 107 min

cast Arnold Schwarzenegger, Michael Biehn, Linda Hamilton, Paul Winfield, Lance Henriksen, Bess Motta *cin* Adam Greenberg *m* Brad Fiedel

An apparently unkillable cyborg assassin (Arnold Schwarzenegger) returns from the future to contemporary Los Angeles to rub out one Sarah Conner (Linda Hamilton), who will eventually give birth to a formidable guerrilla leader to fight against the robot warlords. A solemn resistance soldier (Michael Biehn) also returns in the hope of saving her. Cameron's austere, pummelling thriller is single-mindedly fixated on summoning sickening dread and white-hot fear, and makes a grimy virtue of its mere $7 million budget.

Aliens 1986, 137 min

cast Sigourney Weaver, Michael Biehn, Lance Henriksen, Carrie Henn, Paul Reiser, Bill Paxton *cin* Adrian Biddle *m* James Horner

Cameron took over the directing reins from Ridley Scott for this viscous franchise's first sequel. The sole survivor of the original alien encounter, Ripley (Sigourney Weaver) awakens from hibernation after more than fifty years and soon finds herself back on the bug hunt with a rambunctious crew of marines in tow. Weaver's commanding performance explores Ripley's newly tapped maternal instincts as she becomes mama bear to Carrie Henn's big-lunged orphan amid much slimy menace and expensive weaponry.

Protective instincts: Sigourney Weaver's Ripley is put to the test in *Aliens*.

Titanic 1997, 195 min

cast Leonardo DiCaprio, Kate Winslet, Billy Zane, Kathy Bates, Frances Fisher, Jonathan Hyde, Danny Nucci *cin* Russell Carpenter *m* James Horner

Cameron's epic cost a staggering $200 million and, within the demented interior logic of Hollywood, it's money well spent in terms of technical achievement – the ship's ghastly plunge once again proves Cameron to be a singular maestro of visceral dread and terror. But his blunt-force good-or-evil characterizations and inane dialogue leave one thinking he's spent too much time among aliens and cyborgs, despite the best efforts and luminous charisma of stars Leonardo DiCaprio and Kate Winslet.

Donald Cammell
UK, 1934–96

Cult director Donald Cammell is best remembered for co-directing the iconic pop-culture classic *Performance* (1968) with Nicolas Roeg. He was an eccentric underachiever whose work was never less than provocative. Brought up in a bohemian household and initially trained as a painter, he acquired an early interest in magic and the supernatural, particularly the writings of occultist Aleister Crowley. Essentially a counter-cultural figure of the late 1960s and early 1970s, Cammell was the kind of maverick destined to both tempt and scare film-business executives with his youth-orientated sex-and-drugs unconventionality. Typically, *Performance* gathered dust before its eventual release in 1970, but went on to inspire generations of British filmmakers with its flash-forwards and flash-backwards and its seedy bravura. MGM later persuaded Cammell to helm the sci-fi thriller *Demon Seed* (1977), about a computer which impregnates a scientist's estranged wife, played by a charismatic Julie Christie. Visually impressive, the film failed to make any waves except in cult circles. Later, Cammell and his wife China Kong co-wrote the screenplay for the psycho-killer thriller *White Of The Eye* (1987), with David Keith in the disturbing lead role.

Ultimately it is hard to assess Cammell on his own terms because so few of his films were completed under his artistic control. His last major feature, *Wild Side* (1995), was recut against his wishes but restored after his death to an approximation of his original vision as *Donald Cammell's Wild Side* in 2000. In a life not short of drama, Cammell committed suicide by shooting himself in April 1996 but this too didn't go according to plan. He remained alive for a further 45 minutes during which he displayed the intellectual curiosity and self-reflection which was the hallmark of his career, by requesting a mirror to observe his own death. RC

Donald Cammell's Wild Side 2000, 115 min

cast Christopher Walken, Anne Heche, Joan Chen, Steven Bauer, Allen Garfield, Adam Novack cin Sead Mutarevic m Ryuichi Sakamoto

Christopher Walken is at his most surreally deranged as a gangster so eccentric that he even tries to rape an undercover cop to prove his love for a hooker (Anne Heche). This is a bizarre, sleazy and provocative character drama that is anything but modestly realistic or conventionally generic. Superior to the studio-released version, this posthumous "director's cut" is a true curio.

Jane Campion
New Zealand, 1954–

In Campion's fish-eye aesthetic, the protagonist is often pushed to the edge of the frame, and the world is viewed askew. It's an off-kilter perspective that the director herself attributes to growing up in New Zealand, which can often feel like living on the edge of the world.

Brought up by showbiz parents, Campion studied anthropology, an influence she recognizes in a directorial style that finds meaning in small details, like the close-up of the hole in Holly Hunter's stockings which Harvey Keitel sensually caresses in *The Piano* (1993). Another contributing factor is the art courses Campion subsequently took in Europe, which inform her painterly compositions and perfectly proportioned frames.

Moving to Australia, she enrolled in film school in Sydney, where she made *Peel* (1986), which won the short film award at the Cannes Film Festival. However, when she returned with her debut feature *Sweetie* three years later she was roundly and surprisingly booed. The story of a bullying, self-devoted show-off and her introverted sister was too rich for some critics' blood, although in retrospect it volubly articulated a key Campion trope: a self-willed woman whose bloody-mindedness, often expressed through her untrammelled sexuality, comes into conflict with an oppressive and claustrophobic community, usually her family, resulting in a form of self-destruction. The theme of the "mad woman" was extended in *An Angel At My Table* (1990), a sprawling, emotionally churning study of the New Zealand writer Janet Frame who was wrongly diagnosed with a mental illness and subjected to a series of electric shock treatments.

The Piano represents the pinnacle of the Campion oeuvre. In the stark, storm-tossed west coast of New Zealand's North Island, the director discovered a location that provided the perfect visual metonym for her themes, a small, cut-off community whose contrived domesticity collides with the primal force of nature. Campion was in her gothic element, and the nineteenth-century drama won the Palme d'Or at Cannes.

Campion's follow-up, *The Portrait Of A Lady* (1996), jettisoned the domestic chores that had been a core component of her success and was met with critical indifference. *Holy Smoke* (1999) was a return to the suburban Australian hell of *Sweetie* with the added animalistic presence of *The Piano*'s priapic Harvey Keitel as a cult de-programmer who goes to work on a wilful Kate Winslet. The result seemed self-conscious and parodic, like an artist running on memory. The thriller *In The Cut* (2003) was at least a half-successful exploration of familiar themes, but it seems that Campion has rather lost her way since leaving the southern hemisphere. LH

The Piano 1993, 121 min

cast Holly Hunter, Harvey Keitel, Sam Neill, Anna Paquin, Kerry Walker, Tungia Baker cin Stuart Dryburgh m Michael Nyman

A mute Scottish woman (Holly Hunter), sent to New Zealand with her daughter and their piano for an arranged marriage, embarks on a sensual and dangerous affair with her husband's estate manager (Harvey Keitel) that ends in truly gothic retribution. Campion masterfully orchestrates a series of counterpoints: rigid social structures versus the primal ooze of love and mud; the textures of Stuart Dryburgh's robustly sumptuous photography against Michael Nyman's minimalist score; and the raw emotions of Keitel butting up against the withheld passions of Hunter.

The Portrait Of A Lady 1996, 144 min

cast Nicole Kidman, Barbara Hershey, John Malkovich, Martin Donovan, Mary Louise Parker, Shelley Winters cin Stuart Dryburgh m Wojciech Kilar

Fragile as bone china, Kidman plays the lady of the title, who succumbs to the cruel charms of John Malkovich. Married life is fraught with melodramas, sudden deaths and revelations. Campion's unwieldy and idiosyncratic take on Henry James's novel pulls into focus the director's faults as a storyteller. But while at times the film exudes a chilly solemnity, we should welcome any mainstream film with such vaunting intellectual and cinematic ambitions, even if it doesn't quite reach the lofty heights it aspires to.

In The Cut 2003, 119 min

cast Meg Ryan, Mark Ruffalo, Jennifer Jason Leigh, Nick Damici, Sharrieff Pugh, Michael Nuccio cin Dion Beebe m Hilmar Orn Hilmarsson

An unrecognizable Meg Ryan plays a teacher who enters a liberating but possibly self-destructive bout of *amour fou* with a detective and sexual predator who could also be a serial killer. While Campion's hazy, up-close-and-personal photography conveys the myopic, sensual intensity of sexual longing, her adaptation of Susanna Moore's controversial novel falls apart with her careless handling of the generic elements and cops out with a risible climax.

Marcel Camus

France, 1912–82

In a career lasting over thirty years Camus made idealistic films that examined love, condemned war and exuded the atmosphere of exotic countries and their music. But he is best known for just one brilliant film which combines many of these traits, *Orfeu negro* (*Black Orpheus*, 1959).

Camus was an art teacher but spent World War II in a POW camp where he designed and directed plays. After his release he worked as an assistant to various directors including Jacques Becker, Luis Buñuel, Henri Decoin and Jacques Feyder. His first film was the documentary short *Renaissance du Havre* (1948) but it was not until 1957 that he was able to direct his first feature, *La mort en fraude* (*Fugitive In Saigon*, 1957). Set during the Indo-Chinese war, it was the first of several anti-war films and pronouncements from Camus. *Orfeu negro* won an Oscar, but *Os bandeirantes* (*The Pioneers*, 1960) and *L'oiseau de paradis* (*Dragon Sky*, 1962) were perceived as disappointing in comparison. *Le chant du monde* (*Song Of The World*, 1965), a pastoral Romeo and Juliet story, was seen as overly sentimental, and the wartime comedy *Le mur de l'Atlantique* (*Atlantic Wall*, 1969), though amusing, was essentially lightweight. A few more films followed before he turned to television in 1973. Ultimately, *Orfeu negro* was a brilliant one-off success. JR

Orfeu negro (Black Orpheus) 1959, 106 min

cast Breno Mello, Marpessa Dawn, Lourdes de Oliveira, Léa Garcia, Ademar da Silva *cin* Jean Bourgoin *m* Luiz Bonfá, Antonio Carlos Jobim

Orfeu negro retells the Greek myth of Orpheus and his journey to the land of the dead to recover his love Eurydice, setting it in the Rio carnival. Camus fills our eyes with intense colours and sensual dancing and our ears with samba and bossa nova, sweeping us along in a tide of emotion until the final bitter twist on the original tale.

Frank Capra

Italy, 1897–1991

Frank Capra's populism charmed Depression audiences, won industry acclaim, and impressed a generation of film historians. Even those who haven't seen his films have an inkling of what the term "Capraesque" signifies.

The son of Italian immigrants, Capra sold newspapers and played banjo in honkytonk bands as a child. In 1918 he enlisted in the army and, following World War I, he drifted rather aimlessly, although he managed to wangle his way into directing a single-reel film in San Francisco. He got a job in a film lab, and became a propman and editor before moving to the Hal Roach studio as a writer for the *Our Gang* comedies. Hired by Mack Sennett in 1925, Capra began directing Harry Langdon comedies. In 1929 he signed with Columbia, then a "Poverty Row" outfit. There, Capra went on to direct some of the most successful and best-loved comedies of the 1930s, enjoying complete creative autonomy.

The social comedy *Platinum Blonde* (1931), the atypical Shanghai melodrama *The Bitter Tea Of General Yen* (1933) and the Depression-themed *American Madness* (1932) all have their critical advocates, but it was *It Happened One Night* (1934) that set the pattern for the Capra-inspired screwball comedy. In his hands, the genre not only addressed modern sexual mores but proposed an American ethos founded on neighbourliness, fairness and common sense. The archetypal Capra scenario found an idealistic hero from the sticks triumphing over city slickers mired in cynicism, corruption and too many big words. Written by Robert Riskin with vernacular verve and a reverence for republican rhetoric, Capra's comedies proved strong vehicles for the gauche young James Stewart and Gary Cooper, and the spunky heroines of Jean Arthur and Barbara Stanwyck. Not only was the formula financially remunerative, but Capra received Oscars for *It Happened One Night* and *Mr Deeds Goes To Town* (1936), and for *You Can't Take It With You* (1938), in which Stewart's munitions heir falls for poor but daffy Jean Arthur.

His comedies were citizenship allegories for a nation in crisis: during World War II, Capra oversaw the US army's film programme and his *Why We Fight* public information documentaries proved popular – the first, *Prelude To War* (1942), won Capra another Oscar in 1942. Yet Depression morality was ill-suited to post-war times. Establishing his own production company, Capra released *It's A Wonderful Life* (1946). The fact that the movie has since become his best known – and a much-loved if overexposed staple of US and UK Christmas TV – rather belies its status as Capra's most complex and profound film.

The presidential drama *State Of The Union* (1948) is prized by some Capra fans, but he never again matched the career high that was *It's A Wonderful Life*. Capra subsequently worked on educational films for TV before releasing his last, suitably Capraesque, feature, *Pocketful Of Miracles*, in 1961. RA

It Happened One Night 1934, 105 min, b/w

cast Claudette Colbert, Clark Gable, Walter Connolly, Roscoe Karns, Jameson Thomas *cin* Joseph Walker *m* Louis Silvers

One of the most enjoyable American comedies, this collision between Clark Gable's canny reporter and Claudette Colbert's insubordinate heiress on the run celebrates homespun values while simultaneously wringing all the sexy possibilities out of its oddball antics.

Mr Deeds Goes To Town 1936, 115 min, b/w

cast Gary Cooper, Jean Arthur, George Bancroft, Lionel Stander, Raymond Walburn *cin* Joseph Walker *m* Howard Jackson

A great American fairy tale. Longfellow Deeds (Gary Cooper) wants to give away a $20 million inheritance to a bunch of dirt farmers and enchants Jean Arthur's newshound. Arthur patents a Hollywood archetype, the hotshot sob sister also seen in Capra's own *Meet John Doe* (1941) and Howard Hawks's blown kiss to the newspaper comedy *His Girl Friday*.

It's A Wonderful Life 1946, 129 min, b/w

cast James Stewart, Donna Reed, Lionel Barrymore, Henry Travers, Beulah Bondi, Gloria Grahame *cin* Joseph Walker *m* Dimitri Tiomkin

James Stewart limbers up for fraught studies of postwar masculinity as the banker at the end of his tether on Christmas Eve in a film that imbues the Capra morality tale with something of the darkness of *film noir* and the hysterics of 1950s melodrama. Sentimentality for a cynical era, this features the worst but much more importantly the best of Capra.

Leos Carax

France, 1960–

Alexandre Oscar Dupont is no name for a young Turk. So he changed it, dropping that freighted surname like a hot potato… just as Pierre (Guillaume Depardieu) in *Pola X* (1999) would drop out of his privileged upbringing to embrace the poverty, humiliation, failure – and the life – of an artist.

It's central to the ambiguity of *Pola X* – the title is an acronym for its source, Herman Melville's reviled *Pierre, ou les ambiguités*, with an X to mark the tenth draft of the screenplay – that Carax satirizes this tragic self-conception even as he mythologizes it. Insufferably pretentious or unbearably honest, *Pola X* seemed designed to fail – and in that respect, it must be considered a great success.

Carax was only 24 when he made his first film, *Boy Meets Girl* (1984), a moody, monochrome tone poem, shot by Jean-Yves Escoffier and starring Denis Lavant as Alex, which premiered at Cannes amid great excitement: might this be the next Jean-Luc Godard? Lumped in with Luc Besson, Jean-Jacques Beineix and the *cinéma du look* because of his brazen visual style and what had earlier been dubbed "l'atmosphere", Carax was more romantic and idealistic; granted that everything in his work is some kind of affectation. In the spectacular melodrama *Les amants du Pont-Neuf* (*Lovers On The Bridge*, 1991), Carax can't stop himself from throwing the Seine's homeless in our faces, even if his Paris is ultimately as authentic as a Las Vegas theme hotel.

Carax has a brilliant eye and an uncertain voice. His talents are aesthetic, not literary. *Pola X* was his first film in eight years after *Les amants du Pont-neuf* proved an exorbitant failure. It's hard to see where he can go from there. TC

Mauvais Sang (The Night Is Young, aka Bad Blood) 1986, 119 min

cast Michel Piccoli, Juliette Binoche, Denis Lavant, Hans Meyer, Julie Delpy, Carroll Brooks, Hugo Pratt, Serge Reggiani *cin* Jean-Yves Escoffier

For his second film, Carax again cast Denis Lavant as Alex, this time a young punk who becomes mixed up in a plot to steal the vaccine for an AIDS-like virus. Mixing neo-Godardian tropes with a thriller plot, a love story (as always) and a cast that bridged the classic French cinema with new wave icons and newcomers Binoche and Delpy, Carax created a truly transitional art film.

Les amants du Pont-neuf (Lovers On The Bridge) 1991, 124 min

cast Juliette Binoche, Denis Lavant, Klaus-Michael Gruber, Daniel Buain, Crichan Larson, Paulette Berthonnier *cin* Jean-Yves Escoffier

Again Lavant is Alex, now a homeless fire-eater, who falls head over heels for Juliette Binoche's Michèle, an art student who is going blind. Subsisting on the Pont-Neuf in Paris, the couple enact a blazing love story against France's bicentennial celebrations. The film's reception at the time was overshadowed by its cost (reportedly fifty times the average French budget), but it remains rhapsodic cinema, no matter what the price.

Joe Carnahan

US, 1969–

After dropping out of film school, Joe Carnahan scraped together $7300 to direct himself and some friends in the straightforwardly titled calling card *Blood, Guts, Bullets & Octane* (1999), concerning two car salesmen who take a semi-accidental dive into the criminal underworld. Its handheld-style images, hyper-wired pacing and unashamedly flaunted budget constraints drew ready comparisons with Robert Rodriguez's *El Mariachi* (1992), while its profane, pop-culture-addled dialogue and "what's in the trunk?" mystery inevitably evoked Quentin Tarantino.

Carnahan attracted named actors (Ray Liotta and Jason Patric) and, eventually, the producer's imprimatur of Tom Cruise for his second feature, the police procedural *Narc* (2002), in which the pervading influence was no longer early-1990s American indie landmarks but the grit-and-grime 1970s cop drama. He consolidated his status as an anointed up-and-comer when he was selected to direct a segment of a prestigious series of BMW commercials, though he was nudged out of the director's spot for Cruise's *Mission: Impossible 3* following "creative differences". Carnahan moved on to write and direct the Lake Tahoe-set action thriller *Smokin' Aces* (2006), but despite an impressive ensemble cast, the film proved a disappointing follow-up to *Narc*. JW

Narc 2002, 105 min

cast Jason Patric, Ray Liotta, Busta Rhymes, Chi McBride, Dan Leis, Lloyd Adams, Megan Issa, Lina Felice *cin* Alex Nepomniaschy *m* Cliff Martinez

Disgraced undercover cop Jason Patric wins a spot back on the force after he agrees to investigate the murder of another officer with the deceased's ex-partner (Ray Liotta), a loose cannon who barks in the standardized text of movie bad-cops. Shot in less than a month, *Narc* demonstrates Carnahan's agility with speed-demon action sequences and his aptitude for making the most of a resonant location (here bleakest Detroit).

Marcel Carné

France, 1909–96

For a period of seven or eight years, roughly 1938 to 1946, Marcel Carné was held in higher esteem than any other French filmmaker, even Jean Renoir.

Carné came from a family of furniture makers, and was himself an apprentice cabinet-maker before he turned to film. An assistant to Jacques Feyder and René Clair in the silent era, he turned director in 1930 with the documentary *Nogent* and made his first fictional film, *Jenny*, in 1936. *Jenny* was the beginning of a spectacularly fruitful collaboration with screenwriter Jacques Prévert – a partnership which might be compared to Powell and Pressburger on the other side of the Channel. A surrealist who revelled in puns, word play, symbolism, farce and romantic ardour, Prévert brought wit and poetry to the table.

In celebrating Prévert, critics have perhaps undervalued Carné's distinctive attributes: his refined sense of composition and light, and his ability to endow studio artifice with life. To be sure, his films of the period also owe a great deal to set designer Alexandre Trauner, composer Joseph Kosma and any number of remarkable actors, but Carné was the catalyst, the conductor at the centre of everything. That mixture

French poetic realism: style with substance

The term "poetic realism" (*réalisme poétique*) applies to a brief but important period in French cinema, from 1933 to 1939. This is not a genre instituted by moviemakers (like a comedy or a musical), but identified by critics to describe certain recurring attributes in mood and style. Consequently poetic realism is easier to recognize than it is to define – after all, almost every film is realistic to some degree, and if "poetic" implies artifice, that wouldn't narrow the field much either. The phrase was coined by literary critic Jean Paulhan to describe the mixture of symbolism and realism he found in the novels of Marcel Aymé. Pierre Chanel's 1933 adaptation of Aymé's *La rue sans nom* became the first "poetic realist" film, although it was another couple of years before the aesthetic really took root.

This was a time of political tumult in France. The Great Depression created unemployment and unrest, and the rise of fascism at home and abroad eventually inspired a counter-movement, the short-lived Popular Front that gave the country its first socialist prime minister in 1936.

In common with most of the important filmmakers of the period, Jean Renoir was a passionate advocate for the Popular Front, as witness the anarchic egalitarianism celebrated in *Le crime de Monsieur Lange* (1935), and the fervent populism of *La Marseillaise* (1938) and *La vie est à nous* (1936, a joint enterprise commissioned by the Communist Party that incorporated documentary elements). Renoir's 1934 film *Toni* stands out for its mixture of professional and non-actors re-enacting a true story on real locations, marking it as a forerunner of Italian neo-realism. But *Toni* apart, there's little in pre-war French cinema that anticipates Roberto Rossellini's *Germany, Year Zero* (1947) or Vittorio de Sica's *Bicycle Thieves* (1948). Realism in these pre-war French films boils down to a concern with the proletariat and a penchant for downbeat, pessimistic scenarios – no small thing in an industry built on escapism (then as now).

In his autobiography the director Marcel Carné recalls the reaction of his producer when he finally got around to reading Jacques Prévert's script for *Quai des brumes* (1938), the story of an army deserter's doomed love affair and the archetypal poetic realist film: "I can still see him … feverishly flipping through the screenplay, almost tearing the pages in his fury. It was dirty, everything was dirty." Yet Carné's realism is essentially a matter of style; an affect. Even the quotidian settings are meticulous studio reconstructions of working-class *quartiers* (down to the last brick, in the case of *Hôtel du Nord*, 1938) usually designed by Alexandre Trauner. And this is where the poetry comes in – as a highly cultivated *mise en scène*, a literal and metaphoric grand design which envelopes everything in a shoestring-baroque romantic fatalism. "Carné is not a realist," Orson Welles observed in 1948, recognizing an affinity: "He transfigures reality through his style." By then, even if it wasn't immediately apparent, the era of Carné, Réné Clair, Julien Duvivier and Jacques Prévert was over; in the world after the Holocaust and Hiroshima, "style" was no longer quite sufficient.

Among his peers only Renoir continued to excel, indeed his critical standing came to eclipse all the others, as if the weaknesses contemporary critics claimed to see in his 1930s work ("confusion … lack of concentration") were actually strengths. "In the cinema what counts isn't objects but human beings," he remarked in 1961, in what might have been a tacit reproach to Carné. No longer the lyrical rhetoric of high artistry, poetic realism swiftly mutated to re-emerge in the viral, subterranean form of B-movie *film noir*. TC

of working-class naturalism and romance which came to be known as a central strand of "poetic realism" was as much Carné's construct as Prévert's, and in his careful, conservative way, Carné's articulation of space surely influenced one of his assistants, the Italian Michelangelo Antonioni.

Together, Carné, Prévert and the team caught the national mood as the Popular Front lost ground, and war with Germany came to seem inevitable. In *Le quai des brumes* (*Port Of Shadows*, 1938) and *Le jour se lève* (*Daybreak*, 1939) they defined and refined poetic realism, anticipating the American *film noir* in the process. Working under the Vichy regime, they successfully camouflaged their resistance in the period allegory *Les visiteurs du soir* (*The Devil's Envoys*, 1942), a hit which proved only a dress rehearsal for the theatrical melodrama *Les enfants du paradis* (*Children Of Paradise*, 1945), often cited as the greatest of all French films.

The Prévert partnership produced only one more film, the underrated *Les portes de la nuit* (*Gates Of The Night*, 1946). Carné's work in the next ten to fifteen years is not without interest, but some of the life had gone out of it, and the radical young critics at *Cahiers du cinéma* were merciless with him. At least the triumph of *Les enfants* endured. TC

Drôle de drame (Bizarre, Bizarre) 1937, 97 min, b/w

cast Louis Jouvet, Michel Simon, Françoise Rosay, Jean-Louis Barrault, Jean-Pierre Aumont, Nadine Vogel *cin* Eugen Schüfftan *m* Maurice Jaubert

Carné's delightful second feature is an absurdist screwball farce, set in a French studio version of Edwardian London, with a wacky script by Jacques Prévert. Barrault is a psychotic vegetarian (he murders butchers), while botanist Simon abandons his mimosa after he's wrongly accused of murdering his wife by the Bishop of Bedford (Jouvet).

Le quai des brumes (Port Of Shadows) 1938, 91 min, b/w

cast Jean Gabin, Michèle Morgan, Michel Simon, Pierre Brasseur, Le Vigan, Aimos, Perez *cin* Eugen Schüfftan *m* Maurice Jaubert

Gabin is an army deserter, on the run from a murder charge, when he meets and falls in love with a trench-coated Michèle Morgan. They plan to escape, but in vain. The complete antithesis to *Drôle de drame*, this is the template for the fatalistic "poetic realism" which became Carné's stock in trade. The war clouds were gathering, the Popular Front was in disarray. Le quai des brumes articulates a national feeling of despair.

Le jour se lève (Daybreak) 1939, 85 min, b/w

cast Jean Gabin, Arletty, Jules Berry, Jacqueline Laurent, Bernard Blier *cin* Curt Courant, Philippe Agostini, André Bac *m* Maurice Jaubert

Holed up in a stand-off with police, awaiting capture or death, Jean Gabin reflects on the circumstances which

Theatre of passion: a brief moment of love between the beautiful Garances (Arletty) and the mime Baptiste (Jean-Louis Barrault) in *Les enfants du paradis*.

brought him to this fate. The doom-laden sense of existential alienation and austere, claustrophobic atmosphere clearly anticipate the mood and form of American *film noir*, just as Gabin's rough-hewn romantic predates American counterparts like John Garfield and Humphrey Bogart as an iconic working-class hero.

Les enfants du paradis (Children Of Paradise) 1945, 187 min, b/w

cast Pierre Brasseur, Arletty, Jean-Louis Barrault, Marcel Herrand, Maria Casarès, Louis Salou, Pierre Renoir *cin* Roger Hubert *m* Maurice Thiriet

Widely acknowledged as the crowning glory of classical French cinema, this sumptuous melodrama defies the Occupation stringencies under which it was made. Set in the nineteenth-century Boulevard du Crime, where popular audiences for mime shows and carnival rubbed shoulders with wealthy patrons of classical theatre, it's an extraordinarily rich tapestry, a consummate piece of film-making about unconsummated love.

Giuliano Carnimeo

Italy, 1932–

Horror and Western journeyman Giuliano Carnimeo made some twenty features, sometimes using the pseudonyms "Anthony Ascot" or "Jules Harrison", but the only entry on his résumé with a lasting reputation is *The Case Of The Bloody Iris* (1971). The film was an an example of the Italian *giallo* sub-genre of horror movies that typically featured a gloved killer, baroque plotting, lurid colours, gruesome violence and scantily clad ladies. *Bloody Iris*, released in the US under the preferable title *What Are Those Strange Drops Of Blood Doing On Jennifer's Body?*, became an influence on *giallo* master Dario Argento, who had made his debut just a year before the release of Carnimeo's film. JW

The Case Of The Bloody Iris (Perché quelle strane gocce di sangue sul corpo di Jennifer?) 1971, 94 min

cast Edwige Fenech, George Hilton, Annabella Incontrera, Paola Quattrini, Giampiero Albertini *cin* Stelvio Massi *m* Bruno Nicolai

European-horror staple Edwige Fenech plays Jennifer, a gorgeous model who unadvisedly moves into a plush apartment not long after the brutal slaying of its previous occupant. Soon enough, a gloved killer begins stalking Jennifer, her husband and landlord start acting strangely, and the body count mounts in Carnimeo's classical *giallo*, a cool-headed early variation of the sub-genre that keeps its cards remarkably close to its chest.

Niki Caro

New Zealand, 1967–

A New Zealander of European ancestry, Niki Caro has thus far looked to cultures outside her immediate experience for narrative fodder. After her short *Sure To Rise* (1994) screened at Cannes,

Caro wrote and directed her first feature, *Memory & Desire* (1997), about sexually incompatible Japanese newlyweds taking an ill-fated honeymoon in New Zealand. With her next film, *Whale Rider* (2003), Caro investigated Maori culture, broke local box-office records and swept up audience awards at the Toronto, Sundance, Rotterdam and San Francisco film festivals. The follow-up, *North Country* (2005), is the true story of a sexual harassment suit brought against a US mining company. JW

Whale Rider 2003, 101 min

cast Keisha Castle-Huges, Rawiri Paratene, Vicky Haughton, Cliff Curtis, Grant Roa, Mana Taumaunu *cin* Leon Narbey *m* Lisa Gerrard, Jeremy Sweet

In a Maori coastal village, 12-year-old Pai (the luminous Keisha Castle-Hughes, who was nominated for a best actress Oscar) is raised by her rigidly traditionalist grandfather, who blames Pai not only for her mother's death but also for the stillbirth of her male twin, who would have become their tribe's chief. Through stubbornness and subterfuge, Pai decides to take matters into her own hands in Caro's global crowd pleaser, which eludes the cloying traps inherent in its premise through a dry economy of tone and pacing.

John Carpenter

US, 1948–

In reviews of his later work, in particular, critics have dismissed John Carpenter's films as "mechanical" or "workmanlike". Yet his movies have rarely pretended to be anything more or less than straightforward action flicks (notwithstanding their elegant widescreen landscapes), with flatly drawn characters who function as cogs in his genre machine. This is never done more effectively than in *Halloween* (1978), a startlingly efficient scare-generator with which Carpenter reinvented the American strain of slasher movie (with assistance from Herschell Gordon Lewis's drive-in gorefests of the 1960s). However, Carpenter's contraptions have admittedly gone rusty and rickety in recent years.

His first feature grew out of a project he began while still a student at USC film school: the claustrophobic *Dark Star* (1974), scripted by Dan O'Bannon, coasts around with some depressed astronauts as they blow up threatening planets using self-aware smart bombs. "I got in this business wanting to make Westerns ... I made some Westerns, but they're not really Westerns, they're hidden Westerns," Carpenter once said; the deep-space Western *Dark Star* fits the bill, as does the siege Western *Assault On Precinct 13* (1976), the kidnap Western *Escape From New York* (1981) and the vampire Western *Vampires* (1998). Aliens are also an important demographic presence in the Carpenter pantheon, in the commercial failure *The Thing* (1982), the sci-fi road movie *Starman* (1984) and the underappreciated *They Live* (1988).

Whatever genre Carpenter works in, you can

usually read a social commentary between the lines. A recurrent motif is the culture in microcosm under attack, be it the pan-racial face-off in *Assault On Precinct 13* or the scientific expedition to the Antarctic in *The Thing*, wherein the titular body-snatching entity rapidly erodes any sense of trust or cohesion in the group.

Though conventional wisdom holds that Carpenter's career fell off sharply after his 1970s triumphs, perhaps his most adroit social allegory can be found in 1988's *They Live*, in which a pair of magic sunglasses reveals that aliens in corporate disguise have been keeping the proletariat docile via subliminal commands embedded in advertising. A fun, but undisciplined, anticapitalist satire featuring a wildly protracted fight between Keith David and former pro-wrestling star "Rowdy" Roddy Piper, the film prefigured the virtual-reality paranoia of *The Matrix* by more than a decade. JW

Assault On Precinct 13 1976, 91 min
cast Austin Stoker, Darwin Joston, Laurie Zimmer, Martin West, Charles Cyphers, Tony Burton, Nancy Loomis *cin* Douglas Knapp *m* John Carpenter

Understaffed and about to be shut down, a police precinct becomes the refuge of a vengeful father and then comes under siege, as a multiracial alliance of gangs descends upon the station in bloodthirsty pursuit of the grieving man inside. Laconic, sometimes nasty and thriving on a lean diet of pure fear and action, the movie is no less enjoyable for being something of a patchwork of Carpenter's favourite films.

Halloween 1978, 91 min
cast Donald Pleasence, Jamie Lee Curtis, Nancy Loomis, P.J. Soles, Charles Cyphers, Kyle Richards, Brian Andrews *cin* Dean Cundey *m* John Carpenter

Jamie Lee Curtis, daughter of original slasher-movie victim Janet Leigh, made her film debut as the teenage prey of evil incarnate Michael Myers in Carpenter's hugely successful third feature, which begins memorably with a lengthy POV prologue of the then 6-year-old psycho making his first kill. With surprisingly little blood or gore, *Halloween* made an early incision into the American horror-flick trend of the late 1970s and 80s.

The Thing 1982, 109 min
cast Kurt Russell, Wilford Brimley, T.K. Carter, David Clennon, Keith David *cin* Dean Cundey *m* Ennio Morricone

A motley crew of stock-character scientists at an Antarctic research outpost begin to succumb, one by one, to the titular shape-shifter in Carpenter's sticky, gory contribution to the library of paranoid body-snatcher movies. This *Thing* lacks the political subtext or allegorical weight of previous iterations, and is perhaps best distinguished by its delightfully disgusting special effects.

Carlos Carrera
Mexico, 1962–

The work of prolific director Carrera has not been widely seen outside his native Mexico, where he's known for black comedies that traverse the intersection of romance and revenge. He has also directed many animated, live-action and documentary shorts, winning a prize at Cannes for *El héroe* (1994). He made an international breakthrough with the controversial *El crimen del padre Amaro* (*The Crime Of Father Amaro*) in 2002, which depicts a rural parish as a creaking hotbed of avarice and fornication. The film became the highest-grossing home-grown production in Mexico's history within weeks of its release, aided by the pro bono PR efforts of the archbishop of Mexico City, who declared its viewers to be "in a state of sin". JW

El crimen del padre Amaro (The Crime Of Father Amaro) 2002, 118 min
cast Gael García Bernal, Ana Claudia Talancón, Sancho Gracia, Angélica Aragón, Luisa Huertas *cin* Guillermo Granillo *m* Rosino Serrano

Gael García Bernal plays a neophyte priest easily lured away from his vows, both by the charms of a fetching catechism teacher and the manifold perks of a holy station in a hierarchy propped up by drug-lord money. The film's tone lists somewhat in trying to balance sorrowful pathos with scalpel-sharp critique, but it amounts to a scathing pulp primer of the delusional arrogance and codified secrecy that have so damaged the Catholic Church in recent years.

John Paddy Carstairs
UK, 1910–70

Carstairs was one of four sons of the musical comedy revue star Nelson Keys but (unlike his brothers, who all worked in film too) he took his mother's maiden name to avoid charges of nepotism.

Starting as a camera assistant in 1928, he also wrote scripts, before directing the thriller *Paris Plane* in 1933 and *The Saint In London* in 1939, one of a series of films based on Leslie Charteris's novels. Though he usually worked with low budgets, he was still able to make powerfully atmospheric films such as the spy drama *Sleeping Car To Trieste* (1948). But in 1949 he directed the farce *Fools Rush In* and stuck with comedy for several years afterwards. The high point came with a series of six annual hits starring Norman Wisdom, from *Trouble In Store* (1953) to *The Square Peg* (1958), after which Wisdom continued with other directors. The hapless, childlike Norman always managed to best his "superiors" – but Wisdom denies that these were mere slapstick films, pointing to their pathos. Though the star dominated at the expense of the director, he appreciated Carstairs's efficiency.

Carstairs went on to work with character comedians such as Jimmy Edwards and Frankie Howerd before moving back to thrillers and revisiting Charteris's hero with some episodes of the 1960s

TV series *The Saint*. He was also a painter and wrote comic novels and autobiographies. JR

Trouble In Store 1953, 85 min, b/w

cast Norman Wisdom, Margaret Rutherford, Lana Morris, Joan Sims *cin* Ernest Steward *m* Mischa Spoliansky

Despite Rank Studios' low expectations, this comedy about a gormless shop assistant foiling a robbery and getting the girl touched a chord and fixed Wisdom in the British public's affection. Wisdom excelled at physical comedy and, as in all his films, the laughs come from the chaos that he unwittingly causes. He also contributed the song "Don't Laugh At Me", which became a hit single the following year.

John Cassavetes

US, 1929–89

"**M**ovies are a conspiracy", Gena Rowlands discovers in *Minnie And Moskowitz* (1971). "They set you up from the time you're a kid to believe in everything; to believe in ideals, and strength, and good guys, and romance, and of course, love. No matter how bright you are, they set you up."

John Cassavetes knew this, yet despite everything he remained a believer. He never made a film that wasn't reaching for truth. Starting with the amateur production *Shadows*, made on a shoestring from 1957 to 59, he used the new, lightweight, handheld 16mm camera to empower the actors, allowing them spontaneity and freedom of movement. The result was so fresh and vital that *Shadows* became a landmark for American independent film.

A brief, frustrating sojourn in Hollywood confirmed the filmmaker's intuitive distrust of the studios. Gathering a close-knit group of collaborators around him – including his wife Gena Rowlands, the actor Seymour Cassel and the cameraman/producer Al Ruban – Cassavetes returned to the *Shadows* model, shooting *Faces* (1968) over a six-month period in his own home, with his actor friends in front of and behind the camera, and funding the movie out of his own pocket.

Faces was such a raw and honest portrait of emotional inertia that everyone assumed it must have been improvised. In fact every word was scripted, and it's testament to the veracity of Cassavetes's dialogue that the improvisation myth stuck with him throughout his career. But this impression also owed a lot to his ground-breaking visual style, which involved shooting everything many times over in long takes, often up to ten minutes in duration, the camera following the actors in something akin to a *cinéma vérité* manner.

The success of *Faces* propelled Cassavetes to the front line in the American countercultural cinema movement which would flourish briefly in the late 1960s and early 70s. Yet *Husbands* (1970), *Minnie*

And Moskowitz and *A Woman Under The Influence* (1974) clarified the nature of Cassavetes's radicalism: he didn't despise the bourgeoisie; he wasn't interested in class, only in emotional expression. "In my opinion, these people and these small emotions are the greatest political force there is," he said. He continued making films until 1986, the most notable of his later projects being the so-called gangster movies *The Killing Of A Chinese Bookie* (1976) and *Gloria* (1980). These were anything but standard genre fare, retaining much of the fly-on-the-wall intimacy of his earlier work. *Opening Night* (1977) starred Rowlands as a theatrical actress facing up to the realities of ageing.

A contrarian in many respects, Cassavetes would recut his movies after preview screenings if the reception had been too positive. He knew that life was complicated and he believed that cinema should be too. If that meant his films were frequently troubling and abrasive, then that was the point. A marginal figure in commercial terms, since his untimely death Cassavetes has emerged as one of the most influential American filmmakers, a model and an inspiration to innumerable independent directors. TC

Shadows 1959, 81 min, b/w

cast Lelia Goldoni, Ben Carruthers, Hugh Hurd, Anthony Ray, Rupert Crosse, Tom Allen, Dennis Sallas *cin* Eric Kollmar *m* Charles Mingus

The *Citizen Kane* of American independent cinema, this opened the door for a new kind of filmmaking: young, street-savvy and self-sufficient. A semi-improvised portrait of three young bohemians in New York City, two brothers and their sister all living together in an apartment, the drama hinges on miscegenation, but the deft, subtle treatment is years ahead of its time. The movie's casual, jazzy realism marked a complete break from Hollywood norms.

Faces 1968, 129 min, b/w

cast John Marley, Gena Rowlands, Lynn Carlin, Fred Draper, Seymour Cassel, Val Avery *cin* Al Ruban *m* Jack Ackerman

Disgusted by his experience with Hollywood businessmen, Cassavetes wrote this searing critique on the spiritual malaise of the middle-aged middle classes. Taking place over the course of just one day, it plots the sudden but emphatic disintegration of a marriage, while implicating an infinitely wider social/sexual inertia. John Marley is the executive who returns from his one-night stand only to find his wife (Carlin) has responded in kind. Made for peanuts, the film was a smash and even picked up three Oscar nominations.

Minnie And Moskowitz 1971, 115 min

cast Gena Rowlands, Seymour Cassel, Val Avery, Timothy Carey, Katherine Cassavetes *cin* Arthur J. Ornitz, Alric Edens *m* Bo Harwood

Cassavetes's deliciously witty take on Hollywood romance is a modern screwball comedy, a mismatched love story between a car park attendant (Cassel, sporting a Yosemite Sam moustache) and a museum administrator (Rowlands) who believes herself to be too good for him. Cassavetes's funniest film is underpinned with an acute sense of what it means to be alone, and furnishes Gena Rowlands with her first great role.

A pensive Gena Rowlands in *A Woman Under The Influence*.

A Woman Under The Influence 1974, 155 min

cast Peter Falk, Gena Rowlands, Katherine Cassavetes, Lady Rowlands, Fred Draper *cin* Mitch Breit Bo Harwood

Gena Rowlands is extraordinary – it's one of the most devastating performances in all cinema – as housewife and mother Mabel Longhetti. Her innate nuttiness is pushed remorselessly into a full-blown breakdown by the man who professes to love her best: her husband Nick (Peter Falk), who finally can't face the embarrassment of having her around. Their reconciliation is an unforgettably painful and compassionate trial of love.

The Killing Of A Chinese Bookie 1976, 135 min

cast Ben Gazzara, Timothy Carey, Seymour Cassel, Azizi Johari, Virginia Carrington *cin* Frederick Elmes, Michael Ferris *m* Bo Harwood

Reviled on its release, and recut and re-released by Cassavetes in 1978 to equal apathy (at least in the US), *Bookie* is now rated amongst Cassavetes's best films in either version. It's a gangster thriller, but with the genre tropes left out, and the stuff of real life put back in. Gazzara gets an iconic role as Cosmo Vitelli, proud owner of the strip joint Crazy Horse West and in every sense a showman.

Love Streams 1984, 141 min

cast Gena Rowlands, John Cassavetes, Diahnne Abbott, Seymour Cassel, Margaret Abbott, Jakob Shaw *cin* Al Ruban *m* Bo Harwood

The last "true" Cassavetes film. He knew he was seriously ill when he made it, and it's impossible not to see it as a valedictory work, albeit one infused with resilience and a disarming crackpot humour. Robert (Cassavetes himself) is

a writer who lives (like Cosmo) inured to the world with a private harem of girls. His sanctuary is breached first by the arrival of the son he doesn't know, then by his doolally sister. An obstreporous, funny, bewildering, mordant film.

Michael Caton-Jones
UK, 1958–

Like many British directors in Hollywood, Michael Caton-Jones is good with actors. His first feature, the historical drama *Scandal* (1988), is probably his best. His next, *Memphis Belle* (1990), was a sterling dramatization of events covered in William Wyler's World War II documentary of the same name, in which a B17 bomber crew fly their final daylight raid over Germany. Navigating their way between Boy's Own heroics and a Hawksian bonding saga, Matthew Modine and David Strathairn acquit themselves well.

In *Doc Hollywood* (1991), one of the many early-1990s films parodying yuppie aspirations, Michael J. Fox's Beverly Hills plastic surgeon takes a detour to a small town where old-fashioned values still hold good. *This Boy's Life* (1993) was a Robert De Niro star vehicle and a rite of passage for the young Leonardo DiCaprio, in which De Niro gave vent to his psychotic side as the sweet mechanic who turns nasty after marrying Ellen Barkin. In 1994 *Rob Roy* went up against Mel Gibson's blustery *Braveheart* to more thoughtful effect, Liam Neeson bringing sensitivity and characteristic charm to the Scottish clan leader.

Caton-Jones's weak spot is high-profile projects. Remaking Fred Zinnemann's 1973 film *The Day Of The Jackal* as an all-action post-Cold War thriller (*The Jackal*, 1997), he ditched the meticulousness of the original in favour of an ersatz news story rehearsed by Bruce Willis, Richard Gere and Diane Venora with funny accents. *City By The Sea* (2001) was a pedestrian De Niro flick about an old cop's painful reconciliation with his son. Starring John Hurt as a Catholic priest mentoring the young Hugh Dancy, *Shooting Dogs* (2005) depicted the 1994 massacre of Tutsi tribespeople with compassion and a political sophistication missing from its more high-profile contemporary *Hotel Rwanda*. But the next year's Sharon Stone vehicle *Basic Instinct II* was hopelessly misconceived. RA

Scandal 1988, 115 min

cast John Hurt, Joanne Whalley-Kilmer, Bridget Fonda, Ian McKellen, Leslie Phillips, Britt Eckland *cin* Mike Molloy *m* Carl Davis

Exhuming the 1963 "Profumo Affair" in which the Conservative government was brought down by a minister's dalliance with a naïve and manipulated Christine Keeler, Caton-Jones's debut was also read as a riposte to the venality and hypocrisy of the Thatcher era. Featuring a complex performance from John Hurt as the wronged go-between Stephen Ward and nicely delineating a Britain growing out of the 1950s but not yet ready to let it all hang out, this kick-started an oeuvre that has been at its best when it had a plea to address.

Peter Cattaneo
England, 1964–

Peter Cattaneo's slender filmmaking portfolio thus far has relied on a familiar plot formula, in which plucky heroes take elaborate measures to get themselves out of a pinch. *Loved Up* (1995), a TV drama about a teenage girl encountering rave culture, showcased this human empathy and attracted enough interest to secure Cattaneo the director's chair for his first theatrical feature. In *The Full Monty* (1997), the popular local response to a Chippendales show convinces six laid-off Sheffield steelworkers to stage their own striptease for a quick buck. This massive crowd pleaser translated well abroad and became an English institution (Prince Charles re-created a scene from the film for a Prince's Trust advert), a Broadway musical and the highest-grossing British film in history. The flat-footed *Lucky Break* (2001) tried and failed to rekindle *Monty*'s success, with armed robber James Nesbitt attempting to create a diversion from his prison escape in the form of a musical tribute to Lord Nelson. JW

The Full Monty 1997, 91 min

cast Robert Carlyle, Tom Wilkinson, Mark Addy, Lesley Sharp, Emily Woof, Steve Huison, Paul Barber, Hugo Speer *cin* John de Borman *m* Anne Dudley

Cattaneo's feel-good comedy traces the genesis, training and triumphant debut of male strip act Hot Steel – comprised of six recently unemployed steelworkers – and mines laughs from the incongruity of working-class blokes of varying physiques and rhythmic competency strutting their way to cash and confidence. The script doesn't stint on laying bare the bitterness of enfeebled masculinity in post-industrial England, but the film mostly eschews the social critique of its contemporary *Brassed Off!* (1996).

Alberto Cavalcanti
Brazil, 1897–1982

Linking the realist tradition of British cinema to the continental modernist project, Alberto Cavalcanti brought zest and invention to Britain's documentary heritage.

In Paris, Cavalcanti became associated with the Surrealists. Entering the film industry in the 1920s, he decorated the sets on Marcel L'Herbier's *L'Inhumaine* (1924) with Fernand Léger. In 1926 he made his directorial debut, *Rien que les heures*, which chronicled a Parisian working day, anticipating both Walter Ruttmann's "city symphonies" and French poetic realism. In 1934 Cavalcanti was invited to work for the GPO Film Unit where, as producer, he memorably influenced the orchestration of sound and image in *Night Mail* (1936) and Humphrey Jennings' *Spare Time* (1939). Joining Ealing in 1942, Cavalcanti trained key directors and Michael Balcon credited him with forging Ealing's distinctive tenor. Such works as *Went The Day Well?* (1942), which was based on a short story by Graham Greene, the ventriloquist episode in *Dead Of Night* (1945) and the "spiv thriller" *They Made Me A Fugitive* (1947) combined topical interest with technical gloss. Returning to Brazil in 1949, Cavalcanti founded the Brazilian Film Institute, but continued to direct in Europe, moving to the US to teach film at UCLA in 1968. RA

Went The Day Well? 1942, 92 min, b/w

cast Leslie Banks, Elizabeth Allan, Frank Lawton, Basil Sydney, Valerie Taylor, Mervyn Johns, Marie Lohr *cin* Wilkie Cooper *m* William Walton

As an English village is invaded by an advance column of the German army, the people motivate themselves to deal with the breakdown of traditional social and ethical norms. Tightly directed and examining in often violent detail the collapse of the status quo, Cavalcanti's foreigner's eye brings an acuity to the prospect of the unthinkable happening in the UK.

Liliana Cavani
Italy, 1933–

In a long and patchy career, Liliana Cavani has often attempted candid, even inflammatory examinations of the fallout of fascism in her native country and beyond, as in *The Cannibals* (1969), the Mussolini-era drama of a woman's frantic search for her brother, or *La pelle* (*The Skin*, 1981), set in Italy in 1944, which cast Burt Lancaster and Marcello Mastroianni against an often shocking backdrop of everyday life under occupation, in which women and girls traded their bodies for food.

Cavani is most famous – or infamous – for *The Night Porter* (1974), in which a concentration-camp survivor (Charlotte Rampling) encounters her Nazi lover/torturer (Dirk Bogarde) in Vienna more than a decade after the end of World War II. Essentially restaging their voraciously sexual *danse macabre*, the indulgent viewer may conclude that Cavani is bravely depicting the repetition compulsion born of trauma and guilt (both the criminal's and the survivor's), but it all boils down to Nazi porno chic, the appalling bad taste reaching its nadir when the painfully thin Rampling does a shirtless-with-suspenders cabaret act. A veteran director for Italy's RAI state network, Cavani was nearing her seventies when she made what many consider to be her best film, *Ripley's Game* (2002), a faithful adaptation of Patricia Highsmith's book starring the saturnine John Malkovich. JW

Ripley's Game 2002, 110 min

cast John Malkovich, Ray Winstone, Uwe Mansshardt, Hanns Zischler, Paolo Paoloni, Maurizio Lucà, Dougray Scott *cin* Alfio Contini *m* Ennio Morricone

Wim Wenders had previously shot a somewhat loose adaptation of the titular Patricia Highsmith novel as *The American Friend* (1977). Cavani's pleasurably pulpy rendition follows the book more closely, with a perfectly cast John Malkovich as the Cheshire cat aesthete, now married and relatively settled in Tuscany but still criminally inclined enough to entice a terminally ill – and unforgivably rude – patsy to carry out his dirty work.

Nuri Bilge Ceylan

Turkey, 1959–

No one does melancholy like Nuri Bilge Ceylan. Citing Chekhov as inspiration, Ceylan insists his films are "ordinary stories of ordinary people". But there is nothing ordinary about his films, which achieve a simple power through an accumulation of aching vignettes and perfectly composed snapshots of unspoken sorrow. He creates a world in which alienation is infectious and all-pervasive, where laughter and tears are mere interludes to the main business of silence and loneliness. Ceylan's first films form a loose trilogy: *Kasaba* (*The Small Town*, 1998), *Clouds In May* (2000) and *Uzak* (*Distant*, 2002), which won the Grand Prix at Cannes. Ceylan acts as editor, writer, cinematographer and producer on all his films, which have a strong autobiographical strain. He directed himself and his wife in *Climates* (2006), a study of a break-up between a photographer and his girlfriend. AJa

Uzak 2002, 110 min

cast Muzaffer Ozdemir, Mehmet Emin Toprak, Zuhal Gencer Erkaya, Nazan Kirilmis, Feridun Koç *cin* Nuri Bilge Ceylan *m*

Mahmut, a reasonably successful but disillusioned photographer living in Istanbul, is visited by his cousin Youssef, recently made redundant from his factory job in their home village and dreaming of finding work in the big city. Eschewing major plot twists or dramatic narratives, Ceylan's masterpiece instead focuses on the fractious nature of the two men's relationship, creating an unexpectedly moving portrait of loneliness and unfulfilled dreams.

Claude Chabrol

Paris, 1930–

Along with Godard and Truffaut, Claude Chabrol is famously associated with the pioneering criticism of *Cahiers du cinéma* and the French *nouvelle vague*. But whilst his colleagues saw themselves as innovators and auteurs, Chabrol pitched himself headfirst within the industry, facing down all its conventions and compromises.

The son of a pharmacist, Chabrol was the product of precisely the bourgeois environment that he would dissect in his films. After growing up an evacuee in a remote village, following the Liberation Chabrol attended the Parisian *ciné*-clubs and began contributing pieces on Lang and Hitchcock to *Cahiers*. Both would influence Chabrol's own films, and in 1957 he co-wrote an influential book on Hitchcock with Eric Rohmer.

In the same year, Chabrol returned to Sardent to shoot his first film *Le beau Serge* (1958). Chronicling a young man's encounter with a dissolute friend, in its simple and direct mastery of story and image it is typical Chabrol. *Les cousins* (1959) was another detailed portrait of youth, suffused with the interaction of decency and flaw in an imperfect world. *Les bonnes femmes* (*The Girls*, 1960) charted the aspirations of four Parisian working girls. Human foibles coupled with ironic detachment began to become key to Chabrol's elaboration of bourgeois morality, compromise and guilt.

Arguably, Chabrol's fall from grace in the mid-1960s coincided with the fall from critical favour of a film's classical lucidity. Yet Chabrol's disciplined camerawork was nonetheless becoming a rigorous medium for the greys and off-whites of his moral universe. Built on the tension between light and dark, Chabrol has called *Les biches* (*The Does*, 1968): "the first film I made exactly as I wished." It is regarded as the moment in which Chabrol's Hitchcockian precision gives way to a geometric play of narrative space attributed to Fritz Lang's influence. Chabrol's camera would now not only stress ironic distance but add fresh conditions for his characters' destiny.

Working alongside producer André Génoves, cinematographer Jean Rabier and editor Jacques Gaillard, Chabrol's characteristic visual and moral integrity would be his contribution to European modernism. *Les biches* inaugurated a sequence of collaborations with Stéphane Audran, whom Chabrol married in 1964. In the "Hélène cycle", highlighted by *La femme infidèle* (*The Unfaithful Wife*, 1968), *Le boucher* (*The Butcher*, 1969), and *Juste avant la nuit* (*Just Before Nightfall*, 1971), Audran plays intelligent women for whom the contradictions of bourgeois respectability generate uncontainable tensions. *La rupture* (*The Break-Up*, 1970) begins as Hélène's hus-

Claude Chabrol and Isabelle Huppert

Whereas Stéphane Audran was the cool face of Claude Chabrol's work of the 1960s and 70s, Isabelle Huppert specialized in portrayals of duplicitous women. With her freckled angelic looks, quiet sexuality and talent for playing manipulative women, Huppert found her niche with Chabrol, a director who has perennially tailored his themes to showcase the right star. Their first collaboration was *Violette Nozière* (1978), a study of middle-class corruption which told the true story of a young Parisienne who shocked France by poisoning her parents in 1933. Huppert's doll-like face and a knowingness teetering on the cusp of womanhood established her blend of sexual intensity and victimized innocence. *Violette Nozière* won Huppert the best actress prize at Cannes. In *Une affaire des femmes* (*The Story Of Women*, 1988), she played Marie-Louise Giraud (renamed Latour in the film), guillotined in 1943 for performing abortions. Less concerned with the historical background of the Occupation-set story, Chabrol instead offers a slow-burning account of bourgeois mores offended by a woman driven to social transgression by character and circumstance. It is full of hysterical portent and symbolism: Marie's son wants to be an executioner; a goose has its head lopped off. And it is characteristic of Chabrol that transgression cannot but bring terrible retribution. The director dedicated the film to his actors and Huppert won the best actress award at Venice.

The dissection of bourgeois morality in Flaubert's *Madame Bovary* would seem to have been made for Chabrol's caustic eye, but his 1991 adaptation, touted by the director as the film Flaubert would have wanted, seems like stodgy generic heritage fare. Only Huppert shines, seemingly sensitive to every beat of Emma's heart and every nuance of her longing. The most Flaubertian thing in this overly respectful piece is perhaps the irony of the lush green Normandy settings recalled in the greenish bile of Emma's death scenes.

Set in Brittany, *La cérémonie* (1995) was Chabrol's adaptation of Ruth Rendell's murder story *A Judgement In Stone* and was a well-observed portrait of provincial class tension. Huppert played, with a pixie wit and delinquent rancour, a lonely village postmistress who befriends Sandrine Bonnaire's quiet mentally challenged maid, and the pair embark upon mayhem in the local manor. Bonnaire's passive turn here looks increasingly like a tribute to her colleague, playing as she does a character as disadvantaged as the mousy Pomme, Huppert's role in her debut, Claude Goretta's *The Lacemaker* (1977). After the brilliant character sketch of *La cérémonie*, came the playful exercise of Chabrol and Huppert's *Rien ne va plus* (1997). Clearly intended for export, and often resembling a television pilot, this generic tale of a pair of confidence tricksters abroad in the upmarket pistes of Switzerland found Huppert and co-star Michel Serrault emulating the easy, professional rapport between director and star. The curiosity that the Huppert/Chabrol relationship has engendered among critics is in many ways crystallized in the conundrum hovering over this film; are "Betty" and "Victor" lovers, or are "Elizabeth" and "Daddy" father and daughter? The film's highlight remains Huppert tailored in black suit and jet wig, her glossed lips a bloody red, fleecing a drunk businessman for every credit card he has. Here was surely a metaphor for all the times Huppert has trespassed against masculine middle-class France for her director mentor.

Conceived by Chabrol as an exploration of modern perversity, *Merci pour le chocolat* (*Nightcap*, 2000) displayed much of the formal design finesse for which he became renowned in the 1970s. But Chabrol's studies of the manners of the *haute bourgeoisie* have seemed fresher. Huppert plays the scheming matriarch at the centre of a family fraught by filial dissent. Then people start disappearing. Meanwhile, Huppert quietly dispenses the chocolate for which the family business is famed. *L'ivresse du pouvoir* (*The Comedy Of Power*, 2006) saw Huppert again unsettling the assumptions of the status quo. Based on the controversial "*Affaire d'Elf*", an industrial scandal which rocked the French government, this typically polished, playful film featured Huppert as the judge – Jeanne Charmant-Killman – who becomes herself corrupted as she dispatches high-ranking politicians to jail following revelations of dodgy dealing between France's leading oil company and African states. At its best, Huppert's work with Chabrol has a bite, a sexiness, and an acuity of observation which is both witty and chilling. RA

band slams their son against a wall. Determined to gain custody, Hélène is in thrall to a powerful father-in-law, a Langian Mabuse figure.

As a respectable citizen vows to kill the driver who killed his son, *Que la bête meure* (*Killer!*, 1969) continued Chabrol's exploration of the beast which lurks beneath the façade of bourgeois civilization. Combining the Langian trap with Hitchcockian confession, *Les noces rouges* (*Wedding In Blood*, 1973) was a tongue-in-cheek political thriller which satirized Gaullist aspirations in a year of national elections. Written by and starring Chabrol collaborator Paul Gégauff, *Une partie de plaisir* (*Pleasure Party*, 1974) was grounded in the break-up of Gégauff's marriage. It is one of Chabrol's most harrowing films.

In 1962, Chabrol released *Landru*, a study of the infamous poisoner of the same name. *Violette Nozière* (1978) traced the fate of a young woman who in 1933 poisoned her parents. Isabelle Huppert's fragile beauty adds to a pantheon of Chabrolian roses from Audran onwards and the film won her the best actress César. Among several Chabrols in which Huppert has appeared is *La cérémonie (A Judgement In Stone*, 1995), in which Chabrol's eye for social and psychological nuance finds ample material in the fateful liaison between a Brittany postmistress and an apparently naïve housekeeper.

The prolific director has subsequently moved between heritage, thriller and comedy modes (frequently with Huppert on the payroll), averaging a feature a year in the 1990s and being only marginally less productive in the new millennium. Although occasionally controversial – *Une affaire des femmes'* account of Vichy politics sparked public protests in 1988 – Chabrol's work has seldom generated the cinephiliac excitement attending Godard, or the devoted crowd for Truffaut. But the best Chabrols rank alongside vintage Hitchcock and Lang. RA

La femme infidèle (The Unfaithful Wife)
1968, 98 min
cast Stéphane Audran, Michel Bouquet, Maurice Ronet, Serge Bento, Michel Duchaussoy *cin* Jean Rabier *m* Pierre Jansen

Beneath Charles (Michel Bouquet) and Hélène's perfect marriage lurk secrets and longings dimly papered over by the requirements of the social sphere. As assured as Hitchcock, as claustrophobic as Lang, as stark as blood in the sink.

Les biches (The Does) **1968, 99 min**
cast Stéphane Audran, Jacqueline Sassard, Jean-Louis Trintignant, Nane Germon, Henri Attal, Dominique Verdi *cin* Jean Rabier *m* Pierre Jansen

Set in an impeccably observed off-season St Tropez, *Les biches* is one of Chabrol's most Langian conceits. The film is a vicious triangle of fiendish geometric character in which Stéphane Audran's rich benefactress watches in dismay as her young charge (Jacqueline Sassard) embarks on an affair with her own lover (Jean-Louis Trintignant).

Le boucher (The Butcher) **1969, 94 min**
cast Stéphane Audran, Jean Yanne, Antonio Passalia, Mario Beccaria, Pasquale Ferone, Roger Rudel *cin* Jean Rabier *m* Pierre Jansen

During a joyous Périgord wedding celebration, schoolteacher Hélène (Stéphane Audran) meets the local butcher Popaul (Jean Yanne). But as their relationship develops, a series of vicious murders come to light. Chabrol's film demonstrates how our best attempts at civilization are undermined by latent desires.

Juste avant la nuit (Just Before Nightfall)
1971, 107 min
cast Stéphane Audran, Michel Bouquet, François Périer, Anna Douking, Dominique Zardi, Henri Attal, Jean Carmet, *cin* Jean Rabier *m* Pierre Jansen

A witty examination of middle-class morality, this tale of a man who murders his mistress and tries to confess to family and friends finds Hélène (Audran) and Charles

(Bouquet) mired in the carefully observed and plush traps of a Chabrol at his peak.

La cérémonie (A Judgement In Stone) 1995, 112 min
cast Isabelle Huppert, Sandrine Bonnaire, Jean-Pierre Cassel, Jacqueline Bisset, Virginie Ledoyen *cin* Bernard Zitzermann *m* Matheiu Chabrol

One of the richest French films of its era, this dissection of the status quo of a bourgeois Brittany village is derived from Ruth Rendell's crime thriller *A Judgement In Stone*, but instead of mystery and suspense, its portraits – Isablle Huppert's resentful postmistress, Sandrine Bonnaire's secretive housekeeper – plumb unusual depths of social and ethical toxicity.

Gurinder Chadha
Kenya, 1960–

When critics reviewed Gurinder Chadha's debut *Bhaji On The Beach* (1992), many cooked up puns with the word *masala*, but there is some truth behind the clever wordplay. It could be said that Chadha makes *masala* movies, both in her themes, about mixing British and Asian identities, and in her approach to directing, which blends the didactic with the popular, and the personal with the universal.

Born in Kenya to Punjabi parents, she moved to Southall, London, in 1961, and after college made television documentaries including *I'm British But…*, about being a second-generation British Asian. *Bhaji On The Beach* was the first major British feature film to be directed by an Asian woman, but despite critical plaudits, she couldn't find the backing for her next script, a searing drama about Sri Lankan immigrants. When television work dried up, Chadha moved to Los Angeles to make *What's Cooking?* (2000), a comic drama about four ethnically diverse families preparing for Thanksgiving dinner. American critics in particular weren't kind, referring to "sitcom stereotypes". In response, the director decided to write "the most commercial movie I can with an Indian girl in the lead". The result, the soccer melodrama *Bend It Like Beckham* (2002), won over audiences on both sides of the Atlantic. However, the feel-good factor didn't transfer to all the critics, many of whom couldn't resist counting all the sporting clichés in *Beckham*, or "Arundhati Roy Of The Rovers" as Philip French waggishly rebranded it.

The thorny problem of making populist drama – simultaneously pleasing audiences and critics – remained unsolved in *Bride And Prejudice* (2004), which gave Jane Austen a Bollywood makeover. However, highbrow respectability seems to remain low on the list of priorities for a director who aims to make films that are "entertainment as well as informative". It seems, though, that the faint praise veiled so thinly in the epithet "crowd pleasing" will always accompany her work. LH

Bhaji On The Beach 1992, 101 min
cast Kim Vithana, Jimmi Harkishin, Sarita Khajuria, Mo Sesay, Lalita Ahmed *cin* John Kenway *m* John Altman

A coachload of women from Birmingham descend upon Blackpool to have "female fun" in a sprightly comedy which deftly fuses the deep-dish themes of interracial relations, domestic violence, the yawning gap between first- and second-generation Asians and a stirring Hindi rendition of Cliff Richard's "Summer Holiday".

Bend It Like Beckham 2002, 112 min
cast Parminder Nagra, Keira Knightley, Jonathan Rhys Meyers, Anupam Kher, Archie Panjabi *cin* Lin Jong *m* Craig Pruess

Ebullient teens Keira Knightley and Parminder Nagra share an obsession with soccer that soon creates domestic strife: Keira's mum believes her interest in soccer reveals sapphic tendencies, while Parminder's father decides a woman's place is not on the football pitch. The uplifting story only really performs when Chadha concentrates on the quiet autobiographical details of living in a Sikh household under the flight path to Heathrow airport.

Youssef Chahine
Egypt, 1926–

The unrivalled giant of Egyptian cinema, Youssef Chahine has worked in just about every genre known to movie-man: *noir*, *film à clef*, melodrama, screwball, costume drama, polemical thriller and much more, sometimes within a single work. Writing about *Destiny* (1997), Chahine's allegorical tale of a twelfth-century philosopher whose works became the target of religious fundamentalists, Jonathan Rosenbaum praised "the generous impulse that makes the movie resemble at separate times a musical, a comedy, a Western, a biopic, a biblical epic, a medieval legend and a Dumas adventure story." Always beautifully composed, bursting with energy and often structured around a love triangle, Chahine's films can accommodate wild shifts in tone. His influences are just as wide-ranging, and he wears them on his sleeve: Bollywood extravaganzas, Dreyer, Sirk, DeMille, *Citizen Kane*.

Perhaps the Italian neo-realists left the deepest impression on the director, especially in one of Chahine's best-loved films, *Cairo Station* (1958), in which the director also stars as a handicapped newspaper vendor driven to violent extremes. The ensemble-mosaic style that Chahine advanced in *Cairo Station* again provided an excellent means of expression for the socially conscious filmmaker in *People Of The Nile* (1968), a Soviet-funded production nominally on the building of the Aswan dam that enfolded a wide array of Russian and Egyptian characters.

Chahine's films challenge social and religious norms: despite its ancient setting, *Destiny* takes aim at the book-burning forces of fundamentalism – the same forces that successfully campaigned for Chahine's *The Emigrant* (1994), about the biblical Joseph, to be banned in Egypt. The director has also controversially depicted interfaith relationships and bisexual desire. In *Alexandria Again And Forever* (1989), the last instalment in his autobiographical "Alexandria trilogy", Chahine plays his own alter ego, Yehia, a filmmaker who mourns the end of his romance with a young actor (their affair is memorialized in a Gene Kelly-style dance number) but also finds himself attracted to a beautiful actress. Never one to look askance at a musical number, Chahine turned out one of his most boisterous productions yet in 2001 with the mischievous pastiche *Silence… We're Rolling* (2001). A tale of a lonely singer-actress seduced by an avaricious cad with designs on her money, the film is, like so many of Chahine's films, a colourful valentine to the movies. JW

Cairo Station (Bab el hadid) 1958, 75 min
cast Farid Chawqi, Hind Rostom, Youssef Chahine, Hassan El Baroudi, Abdel Aziz Khalil, Naima Wasfy, Said Khalil *cin* Alvise *m* Fouad El Zahiri

In his genre-straddling breakthrough, Chahine plays a limping newspaper seller who is hopelessly enthralled with a beautiful and rather cruel young woman; she hawks drinks at the station and is betrothed to a porter who's trying to start a union. Clearly influenced by Italian neo-realist cinema, the film is also quintessential Chahine in its embrace of seemingly dissonant tones and styles, holding comedy, tragedy and the musical in its breathless embrace.

Alexandria… Why? (Iskanderija… lih?) 1978, 133 min
cast Ahmed Zaki, Naglaa Fathy, Farid Shawqi, Mahmoud El-Meliguy, Ezzat El Alaili, Mohsen Mohiedine *cin* Mohsen Nasr *m* Fouad El-Zahry

Chahine pioneered the idea of film autobiography in Egypt with his "Alexandria trilogy" (rounded out by *An Egyptian Story*, 1982, and *Alexandria Again And Forever*). Set during World War II, this first instalment in the series views an epoch of national history through the life of Chahine's young alter ego, Yehia Mustafa. But his story is just one among many in a colourful, entertainingly jumbled medley of characters and subplots.

Charlie Chaplin
UK, 1889–1977

Charlie, or "the little fellow", or "the tramp", or "Charlot", is the best-known comic figure in the history of the cinema. His Victorian slum upbringing, his consummate mastery of mime and his understanding of a mass audience's affection for proletarian pluck, made Chaplin a millionaire and a household name.

The son of music-hall entertainers, Chaplin had a rather traumatic childhood: his father died when he was young and his mother suffered from mental illness, meaning that Charlie spent many of his formative years in the workhouse. Performing on the stage by the age of 8, Chaplin joined Fred Karno's theatrical troupe in 1906, where he learned several of the comic skills he incorporated into his screen persona. On an American tour in 1913 Chaplin was spotted by Mack Sennett and signed to a contract with Keystone Studios. *Kid Auto Races At Venice* (1914) saw the actor improvise the battered bowler, baggy trousers, moustache and cane that would become his trademark. Further early films saw him supporting Fatty Arbuckle and Mabel Normand, but *Caught In The Rain* (1914) saw Chaplin directing himself and extending control over his creation. In 1916 Chaplin famously said: "All I need to make a comedy is a park, a policeman and a pretty girl."

an art as complete as cinema has ever been. From 1915, Chaplin was with Essanay Studios, where his slapstick timing, irreverence towards authority and faux aristocratic airs – coupled with a quaint nineteenth-century sentimentalism – endeared him to audiences the world over. This graceful everyman came into his own in *The Tramp* (1915).

At Mutual Studios from 1916, Chaplin's contract gave him overall control of his work and such Mutuals as *The Rink* (1916), *The Immigrant* (1917) and *The Cure* (1917) remain brilliant examples of silent comedy. Arguably, Chaplin did his best work in the short form. *The Rink* was adapted from a Karno ice-skating routine, and Chaplin combined graceful choreography with clumsy pratfalls. In *The Immigrant* Chaplin confronted the tragicomic implications of arrival in teeming Ellis Island. *The Cure* showed the skill with which Chaplin was able to invent and integrate the sketch and narrative.

In 1918 Chaplin signed with First National to do eight two-reelers for $1 million. The hilarious war comedy *Shoulder Arms* appeared in 1918, and Chaplin's first full-length feature *The Kid* (1921) was almost as successful as Griffith's *The Birth Of A Nation* (1915). In 1919 Chaplin formed United Artists with Griffith, Mary Pickford and Douglas Fairbanks. *A Woman Of Paris* (1923) was a subtly observed study of manners resembling Lubitsch. Although not a commercial success, *The Gold Rush* (1925) is widely reckoned to be Chaplin's masterpiece. At the first Oscar ceremony in 1928, Chaplin was awarded a special statuette for writing, directing, producing and acting in *The Circus* (1928).

Like many of his generation, he resisted the talkies' incursion. Nominally silent, *City Lights* (1931) nonetheless had sound effects and a score composed by Chaplin. It was a hit, despite adverse predictions. *The Great Dictator* (1940) was a satire in which Chaplin doubled as Axis tyrant Adenoid Hynkel and a Jewish barber. It marked the final appearance of the tramp and the beginning of Chaplin's decline. His subsequent work became increasingly patchy and passé. *Monsieur Verdoux* (1947) details the exploits of a latter-day Bluebeard, its misogyny the bitter flipside of the tramp's exaggerated respect

The tears of a clown: Charlie Chaplin in *Limelight*.

Cinematically, Chaplin's directing style was unadventurous. Using a simple aesthetic – long shots for comedy, close-ups for sentiment – he nevertheless integrated direction, acting, props and editing into

for women. Set on the streets of London around 1914, *Limelight* (1952) charted a clown's decline in prescient and sentimental fashion. Chaplin's career had long been dogged by moral and political scandals, culminating in 1947 with a subpoena from the House Un-American Activities Committee. In 1952 Chaplin was denied an American visa. *A King In New York* (1957) was a series of cheap jibes at the American way of life but, like *A Countess From Hong Kong* (1966), was hopelessly out of touch with the times.

Chaplin settled in Switzerland, but returned to America and a rapturous welcome to receive an honorary Oscar in 1972. Few other directors have had such a feeling for screen comedy and its contract with the audience. RA

The Kid 1921, 68 min, b/w

cast Charles Chaplin, Edna Purviance, Jackie Coogan, Carl Miller, Tom Wilson, Henry Bergman *cin* Roland Totheroh

Chaplin's first feature saw him reaching out to the integrated comedy of later work but, like the early Essanays and Mutuals, balances the humour and pathos to more satisfying effect. Here, the tramp takes an orphan under his wing against the full flood of cops and public officialdom. Chaplin and Jackie Coogan bring grace and charm to an oppressive Victorian world.

The Gold Rush 1925, 96 min, b/w

cast Charles Chaplin, Mack Swain, Tom Murray, Henry Bergman, Malcolm Waite *cin* Roland Totheroh *m* Charles Chaplin

A masterful showcase for Chaplin's visual invention – witness the Thanksgiving dinner of an old boot and "spaghetti" laces – this spoof of the Klondike Gold Rush can be mawkish, yet it remains a vivid and amusing evocation of humility amid insatiable mania.

City Lights 1931, 87 min, b/w

cast Charles Chaplin, Virginia Cherrill, Florence Lee, Harry Myers, Allan Garcia, Hank Mann *cin* Roland Totheroh, Gordon Pollock *m* Charles Chaplin

In *City Lights* the little tramp falls for a blind flower seller and a series of misadventures silly and sentimental follow. Contrived to make the most of Chaplin's facility for physical tragicomedy, and featuring a nuanced performance by Virginia Cherrill, this masterpiece of mime arrived just as the silent era vanished forever.

Modern Times 1936, 85 min, b/w

cast Charles Chaplin, Paulette Godard, Henry Bergman, Chester Conklin, Allan Garcia *cin* Roland Totheroh *m* Charles Chaplin

Released during the depths of the Depression but lacking the political savvy of even Frank Capra, Chaplin's portrait of a society striving for contentment in a fractious over-mechanized world carries overlooked resonances for these modern times.

Etienne Chatiliez

China, 1952– ← *France, 1952–*

Chatiliez made three hugely popular movies in the 1980s and 90s that weren't just comedies, but social experiments that arguably presaged the phenomenal success of reality television, ingenuously centred, as they were, on a simple concept or device. "Child Swap" could easily have been the subtitle for Chatiliez's film debut, *Life Is A Long Quiet River* (1988), the first of three cuckoo-in-the-nest scenarios he devised with co-writer Florence Quentin. Here, an uptight, middle-class family discover that their 12-year-old daughter was swapped at birth with the son of a family of lowlifes. The resulting class conflict is a poisoned cocktail of Luis Buñuel's bourgeois-baiting and Bertrand Blier's gross bad taste. The slobs and snobs are equally grotesque, and no character is spared the director's mordant wit, making it almost impossible to identify with any of them. Chatiliez eschews the visual opulence of, say Alan Parker, for a defiant naturalism, resulting in one of the highest grossing films at the French box office in the 1980s.

Chatiliez continued in the same acerbically successful vein with *Tatie Danielle* (1990), in which a curmudgeonly aunt causes mischievous chaos when she moves in with her nephew's family, and *Le bonheur est dans le pré* (*Happiness Is In the Field*, 1995), or "Husband Swap", as it could easily be re-titled. The director has since made two more bourgeois-probing comedies, both without writer Florence Quentin or, it has to be said, much critical success. LH

Le bonheur est dans le pré (Happiness Is In The Field) 1995, 106 min

cast Michel Serrault, Eddy Mitchell, Sabine Azéma, Carmen Maura, François Morel, Jean Bosquet *cin* Philippe Welt *m* Pascal Andreacchio

Francis (a permanently vexed Michel Serrault), the much put-upon owner of a toilet seat factory, discovers that he's the double of a man who went missing 26 years earlier and gamely tries for another shot of happiness with the man's comely wife. Despite the presence of ex-footballer Eric Cantona in a cameo role, this isn't just a film for Manchester United fans. Gently winding, *Le bonheur* ripples with undercurrents of mordant satire and charming malevolence.

Chen Kaige

China, 1952–

The son of veteran filmmaker Chen Huai'ai, Chen Kaige was sent to the country for re-education for three years during the Cultural Revolution, and ended up denouncing his own father. The climax of his film *Farewell My Concubine* (1993) is probably the most vivid celluloid account of that terrible time.

Conscripted into the army, and at one point a Red Guard, Chen returned to Beijing only in 1975, when he found work in a film laboratory. In 1978 he was among the first students at the reopened Beijing Film Academy. His first feature, *Yellow*

Earth (1984), announced a political sophistication which wasn't necessarily welcomed by the Party. Set in 1939, it tells the story of an uneasy encounter between the Communists and China's peasants. It's a simple tale, but Chen's emphatic use of music and song, ethnographic elements, and striking landscape photography by Zhang Yimou synthesized in a powerful folkloric *mise en scène*. His subsequent features confirmed the arrival of an important new filmmaker.

With the international success of *Farewell My Concubine* in 1993 (it shared the Palme d'Or with *The Piano*), Chen's filmmaking took on a less personal, more Western feel. Elliptical allegories gave way to opulent melodramas. There was more emphasis on psychology, and sex, but less coherence and conviction. Meanwhile his former cameraman, Zhang Yimou, had gone on to greater fame and fortune as a director in his own right. To confirm how badly Chen had lost his way, his first English-language film, the ludicrous "erotic thriller" *Killing Me Softly* (2002), proved an embarrassment for all concerned. He kept up the chase for an international audience with *Together* (2003), a clichéd but relatively successful middlebrow gloss on earlier themes, and *The Promise* (2005), a disastrously garish and incoherent stab at replicating Zhang Yimou's *Hero* (2002).

Incidentally, Chen has acted in a few films, quite impressively in his own historical epic *The Emperor And The Assassin* (1999). He also played the Captain of the Imperial Guards in Bertolucci's *The Last Emperor* (1987). TC

Yellow Earth (Huang tudi) 1984, 89 min
cast Xue Bai, Wang Xueqi, Tan Tuo, Liu Qiang *cin* Zhang Yimou *m* Zhao Jiping

Chen's debut stands as a landmark in Chinese filmmaking, the first notable feature from the "Fifth Generation" of Chinese directors. A Communist soldier is sent to a northern village to collect the local folk songs (the lines will be rewritten for military morale boosters). The Communists are set on reforming the peasants' traditions of tithe marriage and feudalism, but the soldier's experiences reveal the difficulty of imposing progress from outside.

King Of The Children (Haizi wang) 1987, 106 min
cast Xie Yuan, Yang Xuewen, Chen Shaohua, Zhang Caimei, Xu Guoqing, Gu Changwei *cin* Gu Changwei *m* Qu Xiaosong

Barely educated himself, a young man is sent to teach illiterate pupils in a village school. As his confidence picks up, he begins to depart from Mao's prescriptions, a blasphemy for which he incurs the anger of the authorities. Again, a simple story is imbued with political resonance and a visionary feel for time and place (the stunning province of Yunnan). For some, Chen's third film is his masterpiece.

Life On A String (Bian zou bian chang) 1991, 108 min
cast Liu Zhongyuan, Huang Lei, Xu Qing, Zhang Zhengyuan, Ma Ling, Zhang Jinzhan *cin* Gu Changwei *m* Qu Xiaosong

A blind musician roams the villages of a desert terrain, waiting for the day his old master's prophecy will be fulfilled: that after he has broken the thousandth string on his instrument, he will find a prescription to restore his sight. Chen's philosophical allegory is his least conventional film, a meditation on blindness and vision, song and silence. Adjust to the slow pace and opaque, episodic structure and let your senses guide you through passages of immense power.

Farewell My Concubine (Ba wang bie ji) 1993, 156 min
cast Leslie Cheung, Zhang Fengyi, Gong Li, Lu Qi, Ying Da, Ge You, Li Chun, Lei Han *cin* Gu Changwei *m* Zhao Jiping

Using international movie stars for the first time (Gong Li and Leslie Cheung), Chen's epic attempts to frame more than fifty years of Chinese twentieth-century history through the story of two friends in the Peking Opera. As the country enters its Maoist phase, their jealousies come to seem trivial indeed. A more accessible film, with gorgeous Technicolor photography and a surfeit of melodrama, it is for many the high point in Chen's career to date.

Patrice Chéreau
France, 1944–

Chéreau is an award-winning director of plays, operas and films whose internationally acclaimed career spans four decades – yet he's probably best known for one taboo-breaking scene of fellatio.

A theatre and opera director since 1964 (including a legendary production of Wagner's *Ring* cycle in Bayreuth), Chéreau added a new entry to his CV in 1974 with *La chair de l'orchidée*, an adroit film adaptation of the James Hadley Chase thriller *Flesh Of The Orchid*. His subsequent career has encompassed the award-winning gay love story *L'homme blessé* (*The Wounded Man*, 1983) and *Son frère* (*His Brother*, 2003), an unblinking examination of the devastating effect a blood disorder has on a young man and the unforeseen consequences it has for his relationship with his estranged brother.

There are, however, three films for which Chéreau is rightly celebrated. *La reine Margot* (1994), starring a luminous Isabelle Adjani, was an operatically sumptuous and vigorous historical epic about the power play in the court of Catherine De Medici. *Those Who Love Me Can Take The Train* (1998) was about a different kind of power play altogether: the ebb and flow of relationships between friends on their way to a funeral. With *Intimacy* (2001) Chéreau broke a record and a taboo: it was the first major English-language movie to show unsimulated sex, an act of fellatio between actors Mark Rylance and Kerry Fox. The British censors' decision to release the film uncut became front-page news, but Chéreau seemed genuinely surprised that the press were only interested in the sex scenes – he wanted to talk about his film in relation to Ingmar Bergman.

Intimacy remained the touchstone for Chéreau's subsequent work in both *Son frère*'s poignant tale of two estranged brothers and the slow-burning chamber piece *Gabrielle* (2005), which placed a loveless marriage under a forensic microscope. LH

La reine Margot 1994, 162 min
cast Isabelle Adjani, Vincent Perez, Daniel Auteuil, Jean-Hugues Anglade *cin* Phillippe Rousselot, Goran Bregovic

Chéreau's adaptation of Alexandre Dumas' sixteenth-century historical romp is a camply compelling delight. At the court of deranged King Charles IX, Catholics (wolfish and incestuous in silk) and Protestants (strapping and stern in black) gather for the wedding of Margot, Charles's Catholic sister, to Henri de Navarre, King of the Protestants. Intended to quell religious strife, the marriage instead kicks off an orgy of sectarian murder – but against this grisly background, unlikely alliances begin to form, starting with Margot and Henri themselves.

Those Who Love Me Can Take The Train (Ceux qui m'aiment prendront le train) 1998, 120 min
cast Pascal Greggory, Valéria Bruni-Tedeschi, Charles Berling, Jean-Louis Trintignant *cin* Eric Gautier

As the last request of a wealthy painter, his friends and relatives take a long, uncomfortable train journey to his funeral. Most of their lives seem to be in melodramatic flux, and Chéreau's mobile camera adroitly emphasizes the claustrophobic tensions that bubble under the polite surface of this artificially close community. At the subsequent wake, antipathy leads inevitably to arguments, revelations and ultimately violence in this melancholic, grandiloquent and abstruse examination of human remains.

Intimacy (Intimité) 2001, 119 min
cast Mark Rylance, Kerry Fox, Timothy Spall, Alastair Galbraith, Philippe Calvario *cin* Eric Gautier *m* Eric Neveux

Based on Hanif Kureishi's novella about a man and woman who have weekly sex in his flat. The most shocking thing about this depressing drama is not the sordid rutting but the shabby state of his squalid lodgings. A film to put you off sex for life – or at least watching other people have sex. It's quite possible that this was the director's subversive, detumescent intent.

Ching Siu-Tung
Hong Kong, 1953–

Film runs in the blood for Ching Siu-Tung, whose father Gang Cheng directed a number of Shaw Brothers classics, among them *The Magnificent Swordsman* (1968). Ably following in his father's footsteps, Ching has also made a reputation for himself as a director of martial arts movies, including his debut *Duel To The Death* (1982) and the *Swordsman* trilogy (1990–92). In between, he made the classic *A*

Chinese Ghost Story (1987) and *A Terracotta Warrior* (1990), which featured a rare appearance by director Zhang Yimou as a leading man. Ching's highest-profile movie of recent years is perhaps the trashy *Naked Weapon* (2002), but his best work of late has arguably been as an action director and choreographer, a position he took on Stephen Chow's *Shaolin Soccer* (2001) as well as all three of Zhang Yimou's martial arts epics to date. NN

A Chinese Ghost Story (Qiannü Youhun) 1987, 98 min
cast Leslie Cheung, Joey Wong, Wu Ma, Wang Zuxian *cin* Huang Yongheng, Tom Lau, Sander Lee, Li Jiaogao, Liu Putang *m* Romeo Díaz, James Wong

A lowly travelling tax collector (Leslie Cheung) stays the night at a haunted temple, only to discover a beautiful woman there (Joey Wong) who may be too good to be true. Cantonese pop tunes, rough-and-tumble humour and a supernatural love story create an irresistible 1980s Hong Kong pop classic, and Ching Siu-Tung's best-loved movie. In true Hong Kong style, two sequels duly appeared (in 1990 and 1991), both directed by Ching, but both predictably adding little to the original.

Sylvain Chomet
France, 1963–

With only one full-length feature film, Chomet has announced himself as a singular talent in animation who has supplied a much-needed antidote to Disney whimsy. A French comic-book artist, Chomet moved to London, saw Nick Park's masterpiece *Creature Comforts* (1989) and was inspired to write and direct his own film. Unfortunately it took him ten years to make. Chomet almost quit the business when the subject of his labours, *The Old Lady And The Pigeons* (1998), was rejected by the Ottawa International Animation Festival.

However, the film subsequently gained an Oscar nomination for best animated short, and the artist began work on *Belleville Rendez-vous* (2002), which was inspired by the deeply unpleasant stories that he had heard about the Tour de France. Five years in the making, *Belleville* seemed like a nostalgic riposte to Pixar, who used 3-D realism to represent the world of insects and fish through the anthropomorphic prism of human societies. In contrast, *Belleville* used 3-D technology to bring the imagined world fully and vibrantly to life – a virtual surreality, in other words. LH

Belleville Rendez-vous (Les triplettes de Belleville) 2002, 81 min
cast (voices) Jean-Claude Donda, Dirk Denoyelle, Monica Viegas, Graziella de Vila, Michel Robin *m* Benoît Charest

An old woman with a club foot and her barking mad hound Bruno set off to rescue her cycling grandson after he's kidnapped from the Tour de France by the French Mafia and bundled off to the Manhattan-like metropolis of Belleville. The cartoon is a stew of influences: the jazz age of Josephine Baker and Django Reinhardt, the Heath Robinson inventiveness of Nick Park, and the wordless symphonies of workaday noises created by Jacques Tati.

Aditya Chopra
India, 1971–

Son of revered producer/director Yash Chopra, Aditya Chopra burst onto the Bollywood scene with his debut feature *Dilwale dulhania le jayenge* (*The Big-Hearted Will Win The Bride*, 1995). Shrewdly pitched at the non-resident Indian market, the film broke all records and overtook Ramesh Sippy's *Sholay* (1975) as the longest-running Indian film ever, playing for over 600 weeks at the Maratha Mandir cinema in Mumbai. More importantly for Chopra, the film entered the UK and US mainstream charts. His star-studded follow-up, *Mohabbatein* (*Love Stories*, 2000), did not fare so well, but was still a box-office success. Since then, Chopra has reinvented himself as one of India's most successful producers, farming a series of hits including a number of his father's films. Something of a recluse, known for sneaking into cinemas incognito and taking copious notes on audience reactions, Chopra has transformed his family company Yash Raj Films into one of Asia's most successful production houses, modelled on the tightly controlled family-run studios of the past. NR

Dilwale dulhania le jayenge (The Big-Hearted Will Win The Bride) 1995, 189 min
cast Shah Rukh Khan, Kajol, Amrish Puri, Anupam Kher, Farida Jalal, Satish Shah *cin* Manmohan Singh *m* Jatin, Lalit

When Londoner Simran (Kajol) is taken to her family's native Punjab to get married to a local lad, her boyfriend, fellow Londoner Raj (Khan), follows, determined to win over her stern father. Carefully designed to stir feelings of nostalgia amongst moneyed South Asian audiences worldwide, the film successfully played up traditional Indian values. It established Khan as the top romantic lead of his generation and created a succession of similarly themed films that cashed in on the diaspora market with varying degrees of success.

Baldev Raj Chopra
India, 1914–

The writer/producer/director B.R. Chopra started out as a film journalist before turning his hand to directing. He is best known for films that tackle social issues. *Naya daur* (*The New Age*, 1957) explored the conflict between modernization and the traditional way of life, *Insaaf ka tarazu* (*The Scales Of Justice*, 1980) dealt with rape and its aftermath, while *Nikaah* (*Marriage*, 1985) was an examination of Muslim marriage. *Kanoon* (*The Law*, 1960) was a rarity in Hindi cinema – a courtroom drama without any song sequences.

Chopra also nurtured the career of his brother Yash,

giving him his directorial break with *Dhool ka phool* (*Flowers Of The Dust*, 1959). Apart from his contribution to cinema, B.R. Chopra will be remembered for his epic television series *Mahabharat* (1988–90), based on the Indian epic. Commanding a 96 percent viewership in India, it was no less than a cultural phenomenon. In 1998, Chopra was accorded India's highest film prize, the Dadasaheb Phalke award. NR

Naya daur (The New Age) 1957, 173 min, b/w
cast Dilip Kumar, Ajit, Vyjayantimala, Chand Usmani, Jeevan, Nasir Hussein, Manmohan Krishna *cin* M.N. Malhotra *m* O.P. Nayyar

Shankar (Kumar) is a horse-cart driver in a village. When the local landlord's son decides to introduce a bus service, it threatens to put him and his fellow carters out of business. Shankar is challenged to a race between horse-cart and bus, which he must win to keep the village alive. *Naya daur* works because it believes in its own Utopian fantasy. In newly independent, Nehruvian-socialist India where rapidly encroaching mechanization was seen as a threat, the film was a huge hit among the masses.

Yash Chopra
India, 1932 –

If your perfect Bollywood movie features warbling heroines swathed in acres of diaphanous chiffon, lovers being inexplicably transported to the snow-capped mountains and verdant meadows of Switzerland just as they burst into song, and a prevailing air of charming amateurism and serious camp, then Yash Chopra is the director for you.

It's probably fair to say, however, that Chopra isn't viewed in this cynical way in India, where he is a major player. Not only one of the Bollywood film industry's longest serving directors, he is also a mogul with his own studio and distribution network, a man dubbed the "King Of Romance" by the country's newspapers. According to his biographer Rachel Dwyer, Chopra hasn't just left his mark on Indian cinema, but on Indian culture itself, where the phrase "a Yash Chopra wedding" is common parlance.

Working for his brother's production company, B.R. Films, Chopra directed his feature debut *Dool Ka Phool* (*Blossom Of Dust*, 1959), a kitchen sink musical about an arranged marriage and an abandoned child. Of his early films *Waqt* (*Time*, 1965) is generally considered to be the most important, the start of Yash Chopra's love affair with conspicuous consumption. In the 1970s, the director turned mogul and started his own production company, Yash Raj Films, for which the love triangle melodrama *Daag* (1973) rang cash registers all across the subcontinent. The director then turned his hand to action movies such as *Deewar* (*The Wall*, 1975), an immensely popular synthesis of gangsters, gunplay and catchy musical numbers, and the two-fisted melodrama *Trishul* (*The Trident*, 1978).

This bullets and ballads formula didn't continue

to work its magic at the box office in the 1980s, as Indian cinemas started to echo with the sound of love songs and hearts beating as one, so Chopra changed direction with *Faasle* (*Distances*, 1985) and *Chandni* (1989). The former was the first of Chopra's films to use Switzerland as an improbable backdrop, while the latter set the romantic template for his subsequent movies, including the star-crossed drama *Lamhe* (*Moments*, 1991) and the stalker flick *Darr* (*Fear*, 1993). In 1997, Chopra took seven years off directing to concentrate on his business empire and produce movies by his son Aditya Chopra, but he made a triumphant return in 2004 with *Veer-Zaara*. LH

Waqt (Time) 1965, 206 min

cast Sunil Dutt, Sadhana Shivdasani, Raaj Kumar, Shashi Kapoor, Sharmila Tagore, Balraj Sahni *cin* Dharam Chopra *m* Ravi

A classic variation on Chopra's favourite theme of star-crossed lovers, *Waqt* tells the convoluted tale of a family split apart after an earthquake destroys their home. The children go their separate ways, but two of the brothers later become rivals for the affections of the same woman. Chopra demonstrates his unerring knack for tragic irony and even more tragic kitsch, especially in the earthquake scene whose shameless use of toy buildings and back projection would even give Ed Wood second thoughts.

Deewaar (The Wall) 1975, 174 min

cast Shashi Kapoor, Amitabh Bachchan, Neetu Singh, Nirupa Roy, Parveen Babi, Madan Puri *cin* Kay Gee *m* R.D. Burman

Credited as creating a new kind of antihero in Bollywood cinema – the angry young man – *Deewaar* launched actor Amitabh Bachchan's career into the stratosphere. Here, he plays the black sheep of the family, the head of a smuggling ring corrupted by a toxic mixture of penthouse suites and louche women. Despite the fact that Chopra leaves no cliché unturned, especially in his flagrant use of thunder and lightning to up the melodramatic ante, this film is oddly compelling.

Chandni 1989, 186 min

cast Sridevi, Rishi Kapoor, Vinod Khanna, Waheeda Rehman *cin* Manmohan Singh *m* Hariprasad Chaurasia, Shiv Kumar Sharma

Wide-eyed ingénue Chandni is set to marry her photographer boyfriend until his family and India's strict caste system intervene. Chopra imbues his romance with an infectious glee, which is largely generated by the perky charisma of actress Sridevi as the eponymous heroine. She spends much of the film kitted out in chiffon and singing in the rain, which has the result of turning the movie into a wet sari competition.

Pavel Chukhrai
Russia (formerly Soviet Union), 1946–

The son of Grigory Chukhrai, the legendary director of *Ballad Of A Soldier* (1959), Pavel Chukhrai worked his way up through the domestic film industry as an assistant director and cinematographer before making his directorial debut with *People In The Ocean* (1980). However, it was with his fourth feature film, *The Thief* (1997) – a finely calibrated amalgamation of domestic drama and political allegory – that Pavel blazed brilliantly, but briefly, onto the international scene. Wining three awards at the Venice Film Festival and earning an Oscar nomination for best foreign film, *The Thief* was a significant feature in the short-lived renaissance of Russian cinema in the mid-1990s that included Sergei Bodrov's *Prisoner Of The Mountain*, Aleksei Balabanov's *Brother* and Nikita Mikhalkov's *Burnt By The Sun*. Chukhrai, however, seems to have lost the impetus generated by his phenomenal international success, taking seven long years to make his next feature film, the disappointing KGB drama, *A Driver For Vera* (2004). LH

The Thief (Vor) 1997, 97 min

cast Vladimir Mashkov, Yekaterina Rednikova, Misha Philipchuk, Amaliya Mordvinova *cin* Vladimir Klimov *m* Vladimir Dashkevich

Seen through the eyes of 6-year-old Sania, *The Thief* tells the story of how the boy's mother, Katia, is seduced by a bullying con man, who effortlessly charms communities before robbing them. This sensitively acted heart-wringer is nine parts personal drama to one part political allegory. The con man can be seen as Stalin (the clue is a tattoo of the dictator proudly inked on his chest), Katia is Mother Russia and Sania the Soviet people. Thankfully *The Thief* wears its metaphors lightly.

Michael Cimino
US, 1939–

A student of architecture who dreamed (still dreams, who knows?) of remaking Ayn Rand's *The Fountainhead*, Michael Cimino is a perplexing American artist.

His most famous movie is the notorious *Heaven's Gate* (1980), a $44 million Western which has been blamed for the demise of that genre; the death of United Artists, the studio which backed it; and even the end of that brief era in Hollywood history when the filmmakers enjoyed creative freedom. Savaged by American critics, withdrawn and cut from 219 to 150 minutes, *Heaven's Gate* recouped only $1.5 million at the box office, and became a by-word for artistic self-indulgence. (Steven Bach's bestselling production history, *Final Cut*, laid the blame squarely on the director.)

Something similar befell Orson Welles and *The Magnificent Ambersons* (1942). When a new studio head came in, he established the motto "Showbusiness not genius" as a direct rebuke to Welles. *Ambersons*, even in its studio-cut form, is now regarded as a masterpiece, and there is a small but growing minority who hold that *Heaven's Gate* was rejected because its radical story stratagems subverted Hollywood convention.

Cimino's second feature as director, *The Deer Hunter* (1978), was already on that course. It celebrates working-class bonds through atmosphere, ceremony,

THE ROUGH GUIDE TO FILM

ritual – time – at the expense of dramatic incident. One of the first Hollywood films to acknowledge that Vietnam had become a national nightmare, it was a big hit, and won five Oscars. Before that, he had done only a quirky buddy movie, *Thunderbolt And Lightfoot* (1974), with Clint Eastwood, Jeff Bridges and (almost) no pretensions.

Since *Heaven's Gate*, Cimino's work has been infrequent but invariably overblown. The unrealized projects have so much more poetry than the ones that got made: adaptations of *Crime And Punishment*, *The Fountainhead* and André Malraux's *Man's Fate*, a Dostoyevsky biopic, and a film about the Tour de France (*The Yellow Jersey*). TC

The Deer Hunter 1978, 182 min

cast Robert De Niro, John Cazale, John Savage, Christopher Walken, Meryl Streep, George Dzundza *cin* Vilmos Zsigmond *m* Stanley Myers

Even in the 1970s, there was nothing to prepare you for the immersive first half of *The Deer Hunter*: in particular a wedding party that runs for nearly an hour and cements everything we need to feel for its Pennsylvania millworkers going off to war. The Vietnamese section is more problematic, reverting to metaphors and contrived heroics, but still, Cimino dug into a central trauma in contemporary American lives.

Heaven's Gate 1980, 219 min

cast Kris Kristofferson, Christopher Walken, John Hurt, Sam Waterston, Brad Dourif, Isabelle Huppert *cin* Vilmos Zsigmond *m* David Mansfield

Rarely has a film divided critics and audiences so sharply as this reviled masterpiece. The 1890 Johnson County War was a bitter bloody dispute between wealthy Wyoming cattle barons and the poor immigrant homesteaders who rustled their stock. Cimino goes to great lengths to explicate the class issues, arguably romanticizing the immigrants in the process. A movie about the capitalist carve-up of the "land of the free", *Heaven's Gate* envelops you in regret for ideals corrupted, loves lost, lives wasted – or, some would say, time spent.

Souleymane Cissé

Mali (formerly French Sudan), 1940–

Trained in Moscow during the Soviet era, Cissé became one of the most important of the second generation of African filmmakers. When his masterpiece *Yeelen* (*Brightness*, 1987) won the Jury Prize at Cannes, hopes were raised for a new wave of Francophone African cinema that would make big waves in the West. These aspirations were dashed as the continent's troubles piled up but Cissé's work remains one of the most challenging and ambitious portfolios Africa has produced.

Cissé's first feature was *Cinq jours d'une vie* (*Five Days In A Life*, 1973), about an unemployed young man who resorts to petty theft. But it was with *Den muso* (*The Girl*, 1975) that the director seemed to gain some real momentum. The film told the harrowing story of a mute Malian girl whose family disown

her when she becomes pregnant after being raped. Next came *Baara* (*Work*, 1978), which tackled issues of corruption and personal integrity. *Finyé* (*Wind*, 1982), Cissé's other stand-out film, was a more ambitious and highly topical story of a university protest movement fighting for democracy against a military dictatorship. After *Yeelen* was released, Cissé didn't direct another film for eight years; *Waati* (*Time*, 1995) explored the evils of apartheid and the role of women across the whole of Africa and once again showed the range and power of his work. RC

Yeelen (Brightness) 1987, 105 min

cast Aoua Sangaré, Issiaka Kané, Niamanto Sanogo, Balla Moussa Keita *cin* Jean-Noël Ferragut *m* Michel Portal, Salif Keita

Visually astounding, the story follows in dream-like fashion the attempts of Nianankora (Kané) to thwart the efforts of his shaman father to kill him through magic. Cissé's screenplay leans heavily on traditional Bambara storytelling tropes; the result is a unique mixture of the timeless and the modern with a strong claim to being Africa's best-ever film. World music maestro Salif Keita contributed to the film's evocative soundscape.

René Clair

France, 1898–1981

A highly respected artist in the 1920s and 30s, René Clair's career declined in the post-war period and his reputation has diminished over time. Even his best-known comedies now look somewhat mannered and over-designed, his social criticism a little fey and complacent. Nevertheless, even if he doesn't belong to the first rank, Clair was a whimsical innovator who brought charm and wit to everything he touched.

Of the generation who fought in the Great War, Clair was a poet and a journalist (he wrote many articles about film throughout the 1920s and 30s) who found his métier when he acted in two Louis Feuillade serials. Aligned with the Dadaists, Clair made his second short film, *Entr'acte*, as a diversion, a surreal jape to be shown during the intermission of Francis Picabia's ballet *Relâche* (1924). It was based on a one-page treatment by Picabia, and Erik Satie wrote the score. Nevertheless, as *Paris qui dort* (*The Crazy Ray*, 1923), *Le voyage imaginaire* (*The Imaginary Voyage*, 1925) and *Un chapeau de paille d'Italie* (*The Italian Straw Hat*, 1927) make clear, his cinematic allegiances lie with the fantastic trick films of Georges Méliès and the slapstick comedy of Charlie Chaplin, Buster Keaton and Mack Sennett.

Clair was initially sceptical about sound films, but his ingenious interpolation of sound effects and music in his early-1930s movies, including *Sous les toits de Paris* (*Under The Roofs Of Paris*, 1930) and *A nous la liberté* (*Liberty For Us*, 1931), proved both wildly popular and influential. Although Clair was not fond of location-shooting, his meticulously designed sets and stock characters shaped a cheery and vivacious image of Paris. Away from home, he was less comfortable. Moving first to England and then to Hollywood, Clair's imaginative drive faltered, and he never recovered the standing he enjoyed in the early 1930s. But he was still more than capable of producing deft, delectable entertainments – such as *Les belles de nuit* (*Beauties Of The Night*, 1952) and *Les grandes manoeuvres* (*Summer Manoeuvres*, 1955). TC

Un chapeau de paille d'Italie (The Italian Straw Hat) 1927, 114 min, b/w
cast Jim Gérald, Marise Maia, Paul Ollivier, Albert Préjean, Valentine Tessier, Alice Tissot *cin* Maurice Desfassiaux, Nicolas Roudakoff

Charting the disastrous consequences of the encounter between a hungry horse and some tasty millinery, Clair's adept adaptation of a Labiche play mocks the bourgeois hypocrisies of la Belle Epoque. Substituting sight gags for verbal wit, it ticks along nicely, and the climax at a wedding is a fine piece of slapstick.

Le million 1931, 89 min, b/w
cast René Lefèvre, Annabella, Louis Allibert, Vanda Gréville, Paul Ollivier, Odette Talazac, Raymond Cordy *cin* Georges Périnal *m* Georges Van Parys

Clair's second sound film, after the slight but hugely popular *Sous les toits de Paris* (*Under The Roofs Of Paris*, 1930), is a ground-breaking musical comedy about a man who wins the lottery but loses the ticket to prove it. A lively, typically elegant farce, it again shows Clair's creative response to the possibilities of sound (asynchronous though it was). The poor chap ends up on the stage at the Paris opera.

A nous la liberté (Liberty For Us) 1931, 104 min, b/w
cast Raymond Cordy, Henri Marchand, Rolla France, Germaine Aussey, Paul Ollivier *cin* Georges Périnal *m* Georges Auric

Two convicts escape from prison. One is captured, the other becomes a business tycoon in the gramophone business – but his factory is itself a kind of prison. Clair's satire on the industrial age is cleverly conceived (with regular musical interludes) but also slow and stilted. A direct influence on Chaplin's *Modern Times* (1936).

I Married A Witch 1942, 76 min, b/w
cast Veronica Lake, Fredric March, Cecil Kellaway, Robert Benchley, Susan Hayward, Elizabeth Patterson *cin* Ted Tetzlaff *m* Roy Webb

The best of Clair's Hollywood films begins in seventeenth-century New England and then fast-forwards 250 years, when a witch's spirit is freed to emerge as Veronica Lake. She sets about avenging herself on the descendant of her nemesis, a self-righteous politician (March), but falls in love with him. Lake was rarely better used, and Cecil Kellaway is also delightful as the malicious spirit's father.

Bob Clark
US, 1941–2007

Bob Clark's eclectic career encompasses everything from teen farce (*Porky's*, 1981) and family capers (*A Christmas Story*, 1983, *Baby Geniuses*, 1999) to romance (*Now And Forever*, 2002). He has attracted acclaim and derision in equal measure – the Broadway adaptation *Tribute* (1980) was nominated for a Berlin Golden Bear, while *Rhinestone* (1984), in which Sly Stallone becomes a country singer, was nominated for a Razzie Award. If Clark has a signature genre, it is the horror movie: early successes in this line include *Children Shouldn't Play With Dead Things* (1972), *Deathdream* (aka *Dead Of Night*, 1973) and *Black Christmas* (1974). Also noteworthy is *Murder By Decree* (1979), in which Sherlock Holmes investigates Jack the Ripper. AJ

Deathdream (aka Dead Of Night) 1973, 88 min
cast John Marley, Lynn Carlin, Henderson Forsythe, Richard Backus, Anya Ormsby *cin* Jack McGowan *m* Carl Zittrer

The Monkey's Paw meets Vietnam allegory in this creepy cult classic. A dead soldier is wished back to life as a walking corpse by his grief-stricken mother, his confused bloodthirstiness seen as shellshock by those he encounters. The scriptwriter was Alan Ormsby, who was also responsible for the special-effects make-up and was the leading man in other early Clark films.

Black Christmas 1974, 98 min
cast Olivia Hussey, Margot Kidder, Kier Dullea, Andrea Martin, John Saxon, Marian Waldman *cin* Reginald Morris *m* Carl Zittrer

This seminal psycho-in-the-sorority-house-attic shocker anticipated the vogue for slasher movies hinged on a particular calendar date. It was promoted with the classic tagline: "If this film doesn't make your skin crawl, then it's on too tight."

Larry Clark
US, 1943–

In his twenties, Clark became famous for photographing the lithe bodies of naked teenagers. Whether he should be doing the same in his sixties is a matter of some controversy.

A former speed addict, Clark spent much of the 1960s photographing his junkie friends, often with needles in their arms and occasionally with guns in their hands. The results were compiled into the notorious photo essay *Tulsa* (1971), which he followed up twelve years later with *Teenage Lust*, a title which just about sums up Clark's entire oeuvre. In between times, Clark ingested sulphates and was jailed for nineteen months for shooting a man in the arm during a card game.

In an interview with *The New York Times* Clark claimed that he decided to become a filmmaker after watching Gus Van Sant's paean to louchely beautiful junkies, *Drugstore Cowboy* (1989), which Van Sant has since admitted owed a stylistic debt to *Tulsa*. Clark was not impressed and decided that "now was the time for me to show them how to do it". Hanging out with skateboarders in Manhattan's Washington Park (typically, Clark saw nothing wrong with a 52-year-old donning low-slung hipsters and learning

THE ROUGH GUIDE TO FILM

how to skate), the photographer came across 19-year-old wunderkind Harmony Korine, who wrote a script for Clark based on his own teenage life. With some of Korine's friends virtually playing themselves, *Kids* (1995) was a controversial document of addled teens, in which Clark's camera yet again dwelt on young bodies.

Another Day In Paradise (1998) was a less controversial but equally gruelling road movie about a surrogate family of junkies and thieves. *Bully* (2001) was a return to teenage kicks and created yet more controversy as Clark placed his camera between the thighs of Bijou Phillips, who was wearing only the scantiest of hotpants. The little-seen sci-fi satire *Teenage Cavemen* (2002) is probably the most revealing of all Clark's movies; shorn of the patina (or indeed excuse) of zeitgeist realism, it unspools like the soft-porn fantasies of a dirty old man. LH

Kids 1995, 91 min
cast Leo Fitzpatrick, Justin Pierce, Chloe Sevigny, Yakira Peguero *cin* Eric Edwards *m* Lou Barlow, John Davis

One day and night in the lives of skaters who drink, take drugs, party and screw, including the self-styled Virgin Surgeon, Telly, and one of his conquests, Jennie, who's discovered she is HIV-positive. Using non-professional actors and filmed in a seemingly non-judgemental documentary style, *Kids* has a quiet moralism, a subdued horror at a generation on autopilot. Though Clark would never admit it, *Kids* is closer than you'd think to the sermonizing likes of *Reefer Madness* (1936).

Bully 2001, 113 min
cast Brad Renfro, Bijou Phillips, Rachel Miner, Michael Pitt, Kelli Garner, Daniel Franzese, Leo Fitzpatrick *cin* Steve Gainer

Based on the real-life case of a young man called Bobby Kent, the bully of the title, who was gruesomely murdered by his best friends, the film shows Clark less at home with the violence than the sex. Asked about the infamous close-up of Bijou Phillips's crotch, Clark laughed that his girlfriend threatened to leave him if he kept that shot in the film. He did and she didn't.

Alan Clarke
UK, 1935–90

Although he worked almost exclusively for the small screen, Clarke's stock has risen many times over since his untimely death from cancer. Writing in 1999, critic Richard Kelly called him "the most important British filmmaker to have emerged in the last thirty years – the most productive, the most prodigious, the most restlessly innovative, the most impulsively radical, the most redoubtable".

Clarke directed some two dozen plays for television between 1969 and 1989, and three variable films for the cinema. Most of this work is unobtainable. By necessity, his reputation rests largely on *Scum* (which the BBC banned in 1977 and Clarke

remade for the cinema in 1979), the teleplay *Made In Britain* (1983) and *The Firm* (1988), set in a borstal, a young offenders centre, and the world of football hooliganism, and featuring scorching performances from the young Ray Winstone, Tim Roth and Gary Oldman respectively. Clarke's angry young men were younger, and much, much angrier than the working-class heroes ennobled by John Osborne and Karel Reisz in the 1950s and 60s.

An intuitive anarchist, Clarke honed his filmmaking to a point where dramaturgy was no longer relevant. In the teleplay *Elephant* (1989) – which was an influence on Gus Van Sant's film of the same name – he pushes towards a pure Steadicam aesthetic of volition and violation. In this, he seems a more truly cinematic figure than contemporaries Mike Leigh and Ken Loach. TC

Made In Britain 1983, 73 min
cast Tim Roth, Eric Richard, Geoffrey Hutchings, Terry Richards, Sean Chapman, Bill Stewart *cin* Chris Menges

One of three collaborations with writer David Leland, this is a typically uncompromising portrait of Trevor, a young skinhead battering his brains against all authority. The film doesn't caricature the liberal social worker who tries to help, but this pathological anarchist is an impossible case: a highly intelligent, articulate sociopath. Clarke discovered 19-year-old Tim Roth and unleashed the seething aggression within – it's an indelible performance, and it set the actor on his way.

Rita, Sue And Bob Too 1986, 89 min
cast Siobhan Finneran, Michelle Holmes, George Costigan, Lesley Sharp, Willie Ross, Patti Nicholls *cin* Ivan Strasburg *m* Michael Kamen

Rude, unpatronizing comedy about a middle-class man carrying on with two teenage babysitters from a sink estate. Written by Andrea Dunbar (who came from a similar background), this is one of Clarke's few films made for the cinema, but it's not one of his strongest. Nevertheless, the direct, unpretentious populism is intriguing. It's like a *Confessions…* comedy directed by a social realist.

Elephant 1989, 39 min
cast Gary Walker, Bill Hamilton, Michael Foyle, Danny Small, Robert Taylor *cin* Philip Dawson, John Ward

A montage of eighteen sectarian murders, one after another, with no context or characterization, *Elephant* is a unique and powerful response to Northern Ireland's Troubles. Clarke's final film is his most radical artistic statement, and quite unlike anything being made in television or mainstream cinema at the time. The assassins' grim and ruthless purpose is a bleak commentary on tit-for-tat violence, and forces us to say "Enough is enough".

Jack Clayton
UK, 1921–95

Specializing in literary adaptations that often carried a pungent gothic aroma (his second short was a version of Gogol's "The Overcoat"), Jack Clayton rode the first crest of the British New Wave with his debut feature, the gritty, realistic and sexually explicit drama *Room At The Top* (1958), taken from John Braine's novel of the same name. Clayton's first film with horror elements also proved to be his best: *The Innocents* (1961), starring Deborah Kerr as a new governess trying to keep her Victorian cool in a haunted, isolated mansion. In another ghost story of sorts, *Our Mother's House* (1967), a dead woman's seven children bury her in the garden of their gothic pile and try to conceal her death. The director's shallow, miscast adaptation of *The Great Gatsby* (1974) was coolly received, as was *Something Wicked This Way Comes* (1982), a dark, overwrought rendition of the Ray Bradbury novel. However, his final theatrical feature, *The Lonely Passion Of Judith Hearne* (1987), about a lonely, alcohol-dependent piano teacher, presented Maggie Smith with one of her finest roles. JW

Room At The Top 1958, 117 min, b/w

cast Laurence Harvey, Simone Signoret, Heather Sears, Donald Wolfit, Donald Huston *cin* Freddie Francis *m* Mario Nascimbene

One of the first British "kitchen sink" dramas of the 1950s, *Room At The Top* tackles the class system in its tale of a young civil servant (Laurence Harvey) in a bleak northern town who has to choose between a path up the social ladder and true love with an older Frenchwoman (Simone Signoret). The movie is striking for both its focus on the lives of regional working-class people and its love scenes, which were explicit for the time and resulted in the film's initial X-rating.

The Innocents 1961, 100 min, b/w

cast Deborah Kerr, Martin Stephens, Pamela Franklin, Megs Jenkins, Michael Redgrave, Peter Wyngarde *cin* Freddie Francis *m* Georges Auric

A governess (Deborah Kerr) responsible for a pair of rich orphans becomes convinced that vengeful ghosts are using the children as vessels in this chilling gothic tale adapted from the Henry James story "The Turn Of The Screw". With silvery, shadowy black-and-white cinematography by the great Freddie Francis and a screenplay co-written by Truman Capote, the movie is wickedly funny, psychologically astute and, all these decades later, still genuinely scary.

René Clément
France, 1913–96

Derided by the French *nouvelle vague*, yet the very model of industry professionalism, René Clément provides the link between the pre-war "Tradition of Quality" and the post-war French *cinema d'auteurs*.

Clément entered the industry in 1934 as a cameraman and assistant director. Making shorts and documentaries prepared him for *La bataille du rail* (1946), a revival of pre-war realism and a powerful tribute to the wartime resistance that featured non-professional actors. The same year, acting as technical consultant on Cocteau's fantasy *La belle et la bête* (*Beauty And The Beast*), Clément stipulated his creed: "I want to explore all genres and in each of my films I look for a new tone, a different style." Considered *mise en scène* and a careful way with scripts made Clément a dependable industry craftsman and he was recognized by the Academy for both *Au delà des grilles* (*Beyond The Gates*, 1949) and *Jeux interdits* (*Forbidden Games*, 1952).

The Knave Of Hearts (1954) found post-war heartthrob Gérard Philipe as an inconstant lover amidst an unusually realist London backdrop. Aside from *Plein soleil* (*Purple Noon*, 1960), and the lumbering, if enjoyable, international co-production *Is Paris Burning?* (1966), later work seemed increasingly anonymous, bearing out Clément's reputation as a competent hack. RA

Jeux interdits (Forbidden Games) 1952, 90 min, b/w

cast Brigitte Fossey, Georges Poujouly, Lucian Hubert, Suzanne Courtal, Jacques Marin, Laurence Badin *cin* Robert Juillard *m* Narciso Yepes

An allegory of adult folly, seen through the eyes of innocents, this tale of children who play in an animal cemetery contrasts the treachery and violence of the grown-up world with something of the passion of childhood. The scene in which the little girl's parents are caught in a hail of machine-gun fire is still a singularly brutal anti-war image.

Plein soleil (Purple Noon) 1960, 119 min

cast Alain Delon, Marie Laforêt, Maurice Ronet, Elvire Popesco, Erno Crisa, Frank Latimore, Bill Kearns *cin* Henri Decaë *m* Nino Rota

Amidst the jump cuts and earnest trendiness of the *nouvelle vague*, it was easy to forget what plain craftsmanship was worth. This classical adaptation of Patricia Highsmith's *The Talented Mr Ripley* pivots around a chilly performance by Alain Delon as the amoral Ripley and the great cool greens and blues of Henri Decaë's underwater cinematography.

George Clooney
US, 1961–

George Clooney is no ordinary movie star. A struggling actor who found fame relatively late in life as the twinkling Dr Ross in *ER*, Clooney's promotion to film idol was in no way guaranteed. After a series of commercial belly flops, serious doubts were raised about Clooney's box-office potential until Steven Soderbergh's Elmore Leonard adaptation *Out Of Sight* (1998). By no means a financial success, the slinky crime thriller convinced critics that the debonair TV star could transfer his charisma to the big screen.

More importantly, Clooney seemed to find a kindred spirit in Soderbergh and together they set up the company Section Eight. Their first production, *Ocean's 11* (2001), was a massive international hit, and from the windfall they were able to bankroll such non-mainstream fare as Todd Haynes's *Far From Heaven* (2002), John Maybury's *The Jacket* (2005) and Clooney's directorial debut *Confessions Of A Dangerous Mind* (2002), about a game show host who claimed to have been an assassin for the CIA. Clooney's filmmaking style owed a lot to Soderbergh's yen for colour-coding: the game show sequences are shot in a splash of primary pop art colours, while the spy scenes evoke the chilly greys of 1960s espionage movies.

The film had an autobiographical dimension, as Clooney's father was a local TV celebrity and news anchorman. The star's next offering was about his dad's hero: broadcast journalist Edward R. Murrow, who fearlessly stood up to Senator Joe McCarthy's communist witch-hunt. Shot in handsome, high-contrast monochrome, *Good Night, And Good Luck* (2005) is a consummate work of assured maturity and Clooney deservedly won an award for his screenplay at the 2005 Venice Film Festival. It's hard to think of a recent Hollywood star who has continued to plough his own furrow irrespective of commercial demands, and put his money where his mouth is. George Clooney is definitely no ordinary movie star. LH

Confessions Of A Dangerous Mind 2002, 113 min

cast Sam Rockwell, Drew Barrymore, George Clooney, Julia Roberts, Rutger Hauer, Maggie Gyllenhaal *cin* Newton Thomas Sigel *m* Alex Wurman

Based on game show producer Chuck Barris's "unauthorized autobiography", Clooney's debut is slick, hip entertainment which plays like a series of cool jazz riffs. Although the film is a joy to watch, it sorely lacks the capriciously byzantine elements that usually accompany a script by Charlie Kaufman, the writer of *Being John Malkovich*. Kaufman later explained that changes were made to his script that he wasn't entirely happy with.

Good Night, And Good Luck 2005, 93 min, b/w

cast David Strathairn, George Clooney, Robert Downey Jr, Jeff Daniels, Patricia Clarkson *cin* Robert Elswit

David Strathairn rightfully walked off with the best actor award at the Venice Film Festival for his steely performance as Edward R. Morrow, the decent and quietly defiant news anchorman who stood up to Senator McCarthy and the "reds under the beds" witch-hunt in 1950s America. Every frame exudes a sense of supreme directorial control – the measured pacing, the stunning monochrome photography, the note-perfect acting – and we're clearly in the hands of a filmmaker who knows how to call the shots.

Robert Clouse

US, 1928–97

Clouse is the oft-maligned director of martial arts film *Enter The Dragon* (1973) who contributed both greatly and dubiously to the cult of Bruce Lee. After an early career in American television, Clouse won a Golden Globe for his short *The Legend Of Jimmy Blue Eyes* (1964) and moved into feature films at the behest of director Fred Zinnemann. A dependable craftsman of solid, if unspectacular, action movies, Clouse would have disappeared into journeyman obscurity if Bruce Lee hadn't seen *Darker Than Amber* (1970). After watching the forgettable detective thriller, Lee somehow concluded that Clouse was the right man to helm *Enter The Dragon*. A historic collaboration between Hong Kong and Hollywood, the film took on a much greater significance when Lee died suddenly three weeks before its release, leading to decades of Triad rumours and conspiracy theories.

The cult of Bruce Lee soon flourished, with a little help from Clouse who penned a biography of the star and a coffee-table book about the making of the movie. Clouse's other contribution to the Bruce Lee archives is less respectable. *Game Of Death* (1978) credits the dead star as lead actor, screenwriter and co-martial arts director, but actually contains less than forty minutes of genuine footage of Lee, culled from his last unfinished film. The rest of the movie is shamelessly padded out with lookalikes. Despite the fact that Clouse's plodding direction was considered one of the weakest elements of *Enter The Dragon*, the director continued to mine the chop-socky seam with *Blackbelt Jones* (1974), a 1970s hybrid of blaxploitation and kung fu, *The Big Brawl* (1980), Jackie Chan's first American movie, and *Gymkata* (1985), one of the lowest blows in martial arts' cinematic history, a kung-fu endorsement of Ronald Reagan's "Star Wars" defence policy. LH

Enter The Dragon 1973, 98 min

cast Bruce Lee, John Saxon, Shih Kien, Jim Kelly, Bob Wall, Yang Sze, Ahna Capri, Angela Mao *cin* Gil Hubbs *m* Lalo Schifrin

Bruce Lee is enlisted by a British agent to infiltrate a martial arts tournament and end the traffic in opium and female flesh run by a James Bond-style baddie, who even has his own island lair. Indisputably a cult hit, this is the film that kick-started the kung-fu craze in Hollywood. But aside from the feats – and the feet – of the legendary Lee, *Enter The Dragon* offers few pleasures, not even knowing, ironic ones.

Henri-Georges Clouzot

France, 1907–77

"J'ai l'oeil américain", one character announces in *Le corbeau* (*The Raven*, 1943): "I see everything." The French Hitchcock, Clouzot was a beady misanthrope and an exacting craftsman who excelled in the suspense genre and developed a tyrannical reputation. Nothing escaped him.

Clouzot began his career directing the French-language versions of German films in early-1930s Berlin. He was then confined to a sanatorium for four years as he recovered from a tuberculosis-related illness. (Health problems plagued his life.)

Ménage à trois: Vera Clouzot, the wife, watches Simone Signoret, the mistress, with her husband in *Les diaboliques*.

Perhaps these experiences account in part for the disenchantment rife in his work. Few films of the 1940s or any other decade evince quite as much cynicism about human weakness as the poison-pen thriller *Le corbeau*, Clouzot's second feature as a director in his own right. Banned first by the Vichy government and then again, after the war, as a slur on the national character, *Le corbeau* led to a four-year hiatus before he could resume his career.

His two most famous films, *The Wages Of Fear* (1953) and *Les diaboliques* (1954), are fiendish contraptions designed to wring fear and anxiety from the audience at every opportunity. They were very popular in their day, in France and across Britain and the US, and have withstood the test of time; indeed, American remakes – Jeremiah Chechik's *Diabolique* (1996) and William Friedkin's *The Sorceror* (1977) – have only underlined the superiority of the originals. *Les diaboliques*, in particular, has been influential on the development of the shocker – Hitchcock allegedly made *Psycho* as a riposte to the French contender for his "master of suspense" tag.

Never very prolific (11 features in 27 years), Clouzot revealed another side to his character in the documentaries he made in the latter phase of his career, *Le mystère Picasso* (1956) and a series of rehearsal films with conductor Herbert von Karajan. In the former, you can hear him urging the greatest artist of the twentieth century to hurry up, and complete his work before the reel runs out. TC

Le corbeau (The Raven) 1943, 93 min, b/w

cast Pierre Fresnay, Pierre Larquey, Micheline Francey, Ginette Leclerc, Louis Seigner *cin* Nicolas Hayer *m* Tony Aubin

More than a serviceable whodunnit (though it is that), this bleak thriller exposes a town to the contagion of rumour and innuendo when poison-pen letters set neighbours against each other. Probably the most honest film to come out of Vichy France, it made for very uncomfortable viewing. Guilt and paranoia are so pervasive here that everyone is susceptible to infection. Clouzot spares no one.

Quai des orfèvres (Goldsmiths' Embankment) 1947, 102 min, b/w

cast Louis Jouvet, Suzy Delair, Bernard Blier, Simone Renant, Charles Dullin, Pierre Larquey *cin* Armand Thirard *m* Francis Lopez

A woman believes she has killed a lascivious old man, and conceals it from her husband, never knowing that he meant to kill him himself. Complications ensue. This fine police thriller restored Clouzot's good standing in France, although it's populated with prostitutes, lesbians and pornographers. At least there's Louis Jouvet's police investigator to affect some sense of decency.

The Wages Of Fear (Le salaire de la peur) 1953, 144 min, b/w

cast Yves Montand, Charles Vanel, Peter Ven Eyck, Folco Lulli, Véra Clouzot, Dario Moreno *cin* Armand Thirard *m* Georges Auric

Nail-biting tension as mercenary truck drivers take a highly explosive cargo across South American dirt roads. One of the most famous French films of its era, *The Wages Of Fear* holds up despite its heavy use of back projection and unconvincing location work (it was shot in the South of France). Upfront, with the drivers, everything feels all too real. It was named best film at both the Cannes and Berlin festivals that year.

Les diaboliques 1954, 114 min, b/w

cast Simone Signoret, Véra Clouzot, Paul Meurisse, Charles Vanel, Pierre Larquey *cin* Armand Thirard *m* Georges Van Parys

Prime horror considered the most frightening chiller of its day, *Les diaboliques* did the same for the bath that Alfred Hitchcock's *Psycho* did for the shower six years later. A wife (Véra Clouzot) and mistress (Simone Signoret) plan to murder the man they share, the tyrannical headmaster of a boarding school, by drowning him in the bath – only the dead won't lie.

Jean Cocteau
France, 1889–1963

A poet first and foremost, Cocteau saw "le cinématographe" – his preferred term – as an extension of his writing and painting. Or rather, each creative medium was inextricably linked to the others, to the poetic imagination from which all stems. It is sometimes forgotten, for example, that *Orphée* was a play nearly twenty years before Cocteau made it into a film.

In film industry terms, Cocteau was less than an amateur, a complete novice, when the surrealist patron le Vicomte de Noailles gave him carte blanche and a million francs to make *Le sang d'un poète* (*The Blood Of A Poet*) in 1930 "without material, artistic or moral constraints". When he returned to filmmaking in the late 1940s, Cocteau sought to stay true to the innocence of that first adventure. He saw cinema as a medium of enchantment and hypnosis, a dream realm where classical mythology permeates the modern consciousness.

At his worst, Cocteau's work could be pretentious, airless and arch, but his films have a playful, inventive quality which mitigates the solipsism – they are avant-garde, to be sure, but they can also be seen as fantasy films. Cocteau's effects may be simple – reverse motion, or stepping through mirrors to pass to the underworld – but they are also truly special. TC

La belle et la bête (Beauty And The Beast)
1946, 96 min, b/w

cast Jean Marais, Josette Day, Marcel André, Mila Parély, Michel Auclair, Nane Germon *cin* Henri Alekan *m* Georges Auric

Before there was Disney there was poetry. Cocteau's second "first" film begins with a plea for "childlike simplicity". And who could resist such an exquisite fairy tale, a medieval tableau brought to life? Superbly shot in limpid monochrome by Henri Alekan, it's a tender, romantic film with living statuary (the baroque castle is courtesy of designer Christian Bérard) and an elegant – yet cuddly – beast (the director's lover and muse, Jean Marais). It's every bit as enchanting as Cocteau intended.

Orphée (Orpheus) 1950, 112 min, b/w

cast Jean Marais, Maria Casarès, François Périer, Marie Déa, Edouard Dermithe, Juliette Gréco *cin* Nicolas Hayer *m* Georges Auric

"It is the privilege of legends to be timeless", notes our narrator at the outset. And so it has proved for this infinitely strange and beguiling allegory which is also a kind of coded autobiography. Orphée (played by Cocteau's lover, Jean Marais) is an acclaimed poet who has fallen out of fashion. After a despised rival is knocked over by two uniformed motorcyclists, he becomes fascinated with the Princess Death (Casarès), but when his neglected wife Eurydice (Déa) dies, Orphée follows her into the underworld to reclaim her. It is a mythology Cocteau returned to in his valedictory *Le testament d'Orphée* (1960).

The Coen Brothers
Joel Coen: US, 1954–
Ethan Coen: US, 1957–

The two Coen brothers are quite singular in contemporary Hollywood. They are the doyens of American independent cinema, creating movies, indeed worlds, that are uniquely and identifiably theirs. The Coens are consummate puppet masters, dexterously pulling the strings of their characters, who are usually at least one sandwich short of a picnic. Their world is a pick'n'mix universe of the hardboiled and screwball, where Evelle Snoats, Bernie Bernbaum and Ulysses Everett McGill are common names and even the dimmest person cracks wise.

Although Joel officially sits in the director's chair and Ethan the producer's, their movies are true collaborations – they are known as "the two-headed director" for good reason. While Ethan studied philosophy, Joel studied film, and one of his first jobs was as assistant editor on Sam Raimi's *The Evil Dead* (1981). The brothers scraped together the money to fund their own debut, *Blood Simple* (1984), which is, in many ways, grimly atypical of their oeuvre. Tracing a bar owner's failed attempt to bump off his unfaithful wife and the resulting spiral of murders and misunderstandings, this Southern gothic *film noir* has an abrasive, untidy energy that was smoothed out in their later films. *Raising Arizona* (1987), starring Nicolas Cage and Holly Hunter as childless hicks who steal a baby from a local furniture magnate, was their first move into screwball territory. The film serves as a useful barometer: whether you find the slapstick farce deliriously inventive or coldly calculating is a good indicator of how you'll feel about the rest of their work.

Miller's Crossing (1990) is a labyrinthine 1920s *noir* in which the loyalties of gambler Gabriel Byrne are tested by the demands of gangland kingpin Albert Finney and his rival Jon Polito. However, the film's real strength lies in its style, as it pays homage to classic gangster films with Tommy guns, toughguy slang and, above all, hats. The brothers suffered from periodic writer's block while writing *Miller's Crossing* and used the experience to create the Palme d'Or-winning *Barton Fink* (1991). Coen-regular John Turturro plays self-important playwright Fink who is constantly plagued by his salesman neighbour John Goodman, who could be either a serial killer or a figment of his fevered imagination.

The Coens' next effort, *The Hudsucker Proxy* (1994), co-written by Sam Raimi, was a misguided attempt to move into the Hollywood mainstream with a bigger budget, star actor (Paul Newman) and powerhouse producer (Joel Silver). A film about the invention of the hula hoop, it was a broad, misfiring satire on big business and a meditation on all things circular. *Fargo* (1996), however, was their most intimate, endearing and complete project to date. Its success was largely due to the one thing notably lacking from their previous work – human warmth; supplied, in this case, by the sympathetic and realistic character of Marge (Joel's wife, Frances McDormand). Sadly, "The Dude", the larger-than-life central character of *The Big Lebowski* (1998), was another of the Coens' cartoon characters. The brothers remained in kooky mode for the eclectic, if not entirely cohesive, *O Brother Where Art Thou?* (2000), which starred George Clooney as one of three convicts on the run in the Deep South.

Flanked by cinematographer Roger Deakins's luminous black-and-white photography, *The Man Who Wasn't There* (2001) saw Billy Bob Thornton as a cuckolded barber who kills his wife's lover and becomes obsessed with teenager Scarlett Johansson – oh, and he's visited by aliens. The latter sub-plot is the typical curve ball the Coens like to throw at audiences. Or rather liked: their two follow-ups – *Intolerable Cruelty* (2003) and *The Ladykillers* (2004) – are free of the Coens' trademark and philosophical window dressings. *Intolerable Cruelty* is a straight rendition of a Preston Sturges-style battle-of-wits romantic comedy, but at least it's funny. Their remake of Ealing comedy *The Ladykillers*, on the other hand, is a gurning, barrel-scraping exercise in racial stereotypes and jokes about irritable bowel syndrome, which raised serious doubts about where the brothers are going next. However, to judge by their next project, *No Country For Old Men* (2007), based on the Cormac McCarthy novel, they are heading southwards and into thriller country.

As with Hitchcock and Kubrick, everything in a Coen brothers film is pre-planned to the utmost detail. The result is a highly stylized, hermetically sealed world, peppered with in-jokes and references to their own films. The quirkier details in their movies have encouraged many critics to look for hidden meanings in their work, but the Coens have insisted that they don't deal in symbolism. Perhaps we should take them at their word and enjoy their films for what they are – sublimely playful and masterfully capricious. LH

Blood Simple 1984, 99 min

cast Frances McDormand, John Getz, Dan Hedaya, M. Emmet Walsh, Samm-Art Williams *cin* Barry Sonnenfeld *m* Carter Burwell

A bar owner (Dan Hedaya) hires a memorably corrupt and sweaty private eye (M. Emmet Walsh) to kill his wife (Frances McDormand). The Coens' debut includes signs of great things to come, especially in the virtuoso camera movements and the standout scene in which bolts of light punch through a wall peppered with gun shots. However, there's little of the knowing humour that characterizes their later work: this is a movie of grim, unblinking and intolerable cruelty.

Fargo 1996, 98 min

cast Frances McDormand, Steve Buscemi, Peter Stormare, William H. Macy, Harve Presnell, Kristin Rudrüd *cin* Roger Deakins *m* Carter Burwell

Frances McDormand's winningly low-key performance as pregnant police officer Marge Gunderson has an emotional weight that grounds the whole film in credible reality. Her role acts as a domestic counterpoint to the *noir*-tinged story of a car salesman, William H. Macy, who hires two violent

Escaped convict George Clooney and the rest of the Soggy Bottom Boys recording their bluegrass hit in *O Brother Where Art Thou?*

losers, Steve Buscemi and Peter Stormare, to kidnap his wife so they can share the ransom from her rich parents.

The Big Lebowski 1998, 117 min

cast Jeff Bridges, John Goodman, Julianne Moore, Steve Buscemi, David Huddleston, Philip Seymour Hoffman *cin* Roger Deakins *m* Carter Burwell

One Coen talent is to unite apparently random elements from different cultural forms and make them work as a whole. Cheech and Chong stoner humour, tenpin bowling and Raymond Chandler novels are combined in this unique entity that critics have dubbed "bowling *noir*". Jeff Bridges plays genial dope-smoking bowler Jeff "The Dude" Lebowski, who turns detective and gets embroiled in a kidnapping after mobsters mistake him for another, richer Lebowski and soil his precious rug.

O Brother Where Art Thou? 2000, 106 min

cast George Clooney, John Turturro, Tim Blake Nelson, Holly Hunter, John Goodman, Chris Thomas King *cin* Roger Deakins *m* T. Bone Burnett

A road movie with references to Homer's epic *The Odyssey* (which the Coens claim never to have read), *O Brother Where Art Thou?* tells the tale of escaped cons George Clooney, Tim Blake Nelson and John Turturro who break free from a chain gang and survive a series of comic adventures – and cut a bluegrass record – during the Great Depression. The title comes from the worthy, social-conscience film a director plans to make about the Depression in Preston Sturges's *Sullivan's Travels* (1941).

Intolerable Cruelty 2003, 103 min

cast George Clooney, Catherine Zeta-Jones, Geoffrey Rush, Cedric the Entertainer, Edward Herrmann *cin* Roger Deakins *m* Carter Burwell

The first of the Coens' films to be based on someone else's script, this screwball comedy lacks all the loopy tangents that fans have come to expect. However, it's one of the few recent Hollywood rom-coms that actually work. It's genuinely equal to Preston Sturges at his acerbic best and boasts a performance by George Clooney that's reminiscent (if a tad self-consciously) of Cary Grant at his most imperious.

Nigel Cole
UK, 1959–

After cutting his teeth in television (directing episodes of *Cold Feet* among other shows), Nigel Cole has produced relatively benign examples of a particular strain of readily exportable Britflick, in which English roses *d'un certain âge* transgress social boundaries for a worthy cause. *Saving Grace* (2000) tickled the funny bone via the incongruity of a very proper matron skinning up. As the recent widow who starts cultivating marijuana to pay off her late husband's debts, Brenda Blethyn took far too much quasi-naughty delight in getting high (and the film is timidly careful in making sure she gains no material benefit from her illegal hemp adventures). *Calendar Girls* (2003) giggled at proper matrons stripping off, with a Women's Institute chapter deciding to pose nude for their fundraising calendar. Helen Mirren and Julie Walters provided an astringent comic presence that kept things rea-

sonably clear of Anglo-whimsy. Cole switched his allegiance to the American twentysomething demographic with *A Lot Like Love* (2005), a bland but likeable thwarted-romance comedy. JW

Calendar Girls 2003, 108 min

cast Helen Mirren, Julie Walters, John Alderton, Linda Bassett, Annette Crosbie, Celia Imrie *cin* Oliver Curtis, Ashley Rowe *m* Patrick Doyle

The first hour or so of Cole's ingratiating comedy, a distaff *Full Monty*, establishes with light, deft strokes the various complications and contradictions of a late-blooming pin-up career. The soufflé caves in once jealousy and talk-show hosts enter the soft-focus picture, but the film remains a genial lesson in how to honour yet subvert womanly expectations.

Chris Columbus
US, 1958–

A graduate of the New York University film school, Chris Columbus sold his fourth screenplay to Steven Spielberg: *Gremlins* (1984) was a horror-style satire of Frank Capra's Christmas perennial *It's A Wonderful Life* (1946). Darker in the original conception (the family dog was eaten, the mom decapitated, and loveable Mogwai transformed into hateful Stripe), the movie developed into something safer... but it's still the one Columbus movie to have some teeth. Maybe because it was directed by Joe Dante.

Screenplays for *The Goonies* and *Young Sherlock Holmes* (both 1985) established Columbus as a popular purveyor of kiddie entertainment, and he was allowed to turn director with *Adventures In Babysitting* (1987). It was only natural for teen movie mogul John Hughes, tiring of directing chores, to pass the reins over to Columbus – though no one could have predicted what a huge hit *Home Alone* (1990) would be.

A series of sentimental comedies followed (*Only The Lonely*, 1991; *Mrs Doubtfire*, 1993; *Stepmom*, 1998; *Bicentennial Man*, 1999), some popular, some not. Then Spielberg passed on *Harry Potter*, and author J.K. Rowling gave Columbus her blessing, as long as certain conditions were met. A mainstreamer with no real style or recognizable voice of his own, Columbus may have been the perfect candidate for the franchise – although Terry Gilliam acidly remarked that *Harry Potter And The Philosopher's Stone* (2001) "looked like it had been made by a committee without a head". Columbus's belated version of Jonathan Larson's 1996 rock musical *Rent* (2005) felt dated and failed to win over new fans, but his fortunes revived somewhat with his producer credit on the hit family comedy *Night At The Museum* (2006). TC

Home Alone 1990, 103 min

cast Macaulay Culkin, Joe Pesci, Daniel Stern, John Heard, Roberts Blossom, Catherine O'Hara *cin* Julio Macat *m* John Williams

When the rest of the family embark on a transatlantic flight for Paris, 8-year-old Kevin (Macaulay Culkin) is accidentally left to fend for himself at home for Christmas. At first he thinks it's a dream come true, gorging on the contents of the fridge, but two bungling burglars arrive to keep him busy. *Tom and Jerry*-style slapstick gags mix uneasily with saccharine sentiment – but this was a family film everybody got. It made big bucks at the box office and made Culkin a star.

Harry Potter And The Philosopher's Stone (aka Harry Potter And The Sorceror's Stone) 2001, 152 min

cast Daniel Radcliffe, Rupert Grint, Emma Watson, John Cleese, Robbie Coltrane, Richard Griffiths *cin* John Seale *m* John Williams

The first chapter in the long-running *Potter* series is an introduction to Hogwarts School and its magical curriculum. Assiduously faithful to J.K. Rowling's bestseller (hence that running time), this was a typically cautious and self-effacing enterprise, and very popular it proved to be. Columbus allowed himself to have a bit more fun with *The Chamber Of Secrets* (2002), then stepped back to produce the third, directed by Alfonso Cuarón.

Bill Condon
US, 1955–

After paying his dues at length with television work and, improbably, as for-hire director of a perfunctory horror sequel called *Candyman: Farewell To The Flesh* (1995), Bill Condon's film career proper began with *Gods And Monsters* (1998). Winner of an unexpected Oscar for best adapted screenplay, the film speculated on the final days of James Whale, who directed Boris Karloff in *Frankenstein* (1931) and died in mysterious circumstances in 1957.

After writing the screenplay for the messy 2002 film version of John Kandre and Fred Ebb's musical *Chicago*, Condon took on another famous name for his next directorial outing, *Kinsey* (2004). The film was a fully fledged biopic of Alfred Kinsey, the American professor of entomology and zoology whose bestselling 1948 study *Sexual Behavior In The Human Male* lit the first sparks of the sexual revolution. By contrast, Condon's splashy next project, the Motown-inspired musical *Dreamgirls* (2006), was a surprisingly rushed and shallow affair. Despite the heavy-hitting roster (Beyoncé Knowles, Eddie Murphy, Oscar-winning newcomer Jennifer Hudson), the film was less grand than grandstanding and unable to produce even a single hummable song. jw

Gods And Monsters 1998, 105 min, b/w and col

cast Ian McKellen, Brendan Fraser, Lynn Redgrave, Lolita Davidovich, Kevin J. O'Connor, David Dukes *cin* Stephen M. Katz *m* Carter Burwell

Condon explores the last days in the life of ageing Hollywood director James Whale (Ian McKellen) and his wistful longing for his strapping, simple gardener (Brendan Fraser). McKellen's *tour de force* performance flits between dandyish charm, anger, shame and terror – late in life, Whale suffered a stroke that played havoc with his mind and memory, which adds weight and pathos to the film's use of flashbacks.

Kinsey 2004, 118 min

cast Liam Neeson, Laura Linney, Chris O'Donnell, Peter Sarsgaard, Timothy Hutton, John Lithgow, Tim Curry *cin* Frederick Elmes *m* Carter Burwell

With graceful economy and ample humour, Condon and a superlative cast illustrate how Alfred Kinsey – the son of a zealously Methodist family, and a man who did not lose his virginity until well into his twenties – became the founder of the Institute for Sex Research. As in *Gods And Monsters*, writer-director Condon maintains a disciplined formal conceit: the film uses Kinsey's own sexual case history as its structure.

Cooper & Schoedsack
Merian C. Cooper: US, 1893–1973
Ernest B. Schoedsack: US, 1893–1979

Merian C. Cooper was one of American cinema's great primitives. After an intrepid career as an explorer, fighter pilot, National Guardsman and journalist, he met Ernest B. Schoedsack in the Ukraine in 1920, where they were both agitating against the Bolsheviks. Cooper wanted to make films; Schoedsack had been a cameraman in the Signal Corps during the Great War and worked at Keystone Studios. Natural adventurers and kindred spirits, they teamed up a few years later for two ethnographic films, *Grass* (1925) and *Chang* (1927).

Grass (1925) was a spectacular account of the hardships endured by 50,000 Bakhtiari tribesmen – and their half-million livestock – during their annual forty-day migration into northern Iran. *Chang*, a fictionalized documentary shot in northern Thailand, recorded a tribal family's travails against rampaging wildlife using the contemporary image-modification technology Magnascope. Footage from this enormously influential film would crop up in adventure movies for decades. The two men shared the director's credit on these two films, though Schoedsack manned the camera while the larger-than-life Cooper gravitated towards a producer's role.

Shot partly in the Sudan and Tanzania, Cooper and Schoedsack's first fiction feature, co-directed with Lothar Mendes, was the Victorian imperialist adventure *The Four Feathers* (1929), one of the last lavish silent productions. *King Kong* (1933) completed the shift from ethnography to dramatization, becoming a classic adventure movie and a huge box-office success. Cooper went on to become production head at RKO, where he oversaw the launch of the Astaire-Rogers musical cycle and many of John Ford's post-war Westerns. He pressed Schoedsack into service on everything from fantasy adventure films to drawing-room comedies. Of these later movies, the most interesting is *Dr Cyclops* (1940), a miniaturized people flick which utilized an early form of 3-strip Technicolor. *Mighty Joe Young* (1949) was a remake of *Kong* in everything but name, and typified Schoedsack and Cooper's unpretentious brand of showmanship. RA & TC

King Kong 1933, 100 min, b/w

cast Fay Wray, Robert Armstrong, Bruce Cabot, Frank Reicher, Sam Hardy, Noble Johnson *cin* Eddie Linden, Vernon Walker, J.O. Taylor *m* Max Steiner

For many, still the greatest fantasy film of them all, *King Kong* has a primitive, mythic power and at least two iconic images: the winsome, screaming Fay Wray in the paw of the giant gorilla, and the monster swatting off biplanes atop New York City's Empire State building. This was Cooper's baby – he claimed the story came to him in a dream – and impresario Carl Danham (Armstrong) is obviously based on Cooper himself. Kong was the sublime handiwork of special effects maestro Willis O'Brien. Schoedsack and Cooper took bit parts as the aviators who shoot down the beast.

Francis Ford Coppola
US, 1939–

Francis Ford Coppola towered over American cinema in the 1970s. One of the last of its visionary creators, Coppola stands at the heart of that efflorescence of American auteur cinema which became known as New Hollywood.

The son of Carmine Coppola, sometime flautist with Toscanini, and the Italian actress Italia Pennino, Francis made his first 8mm film while convalescing from polio at the age of 10. After graduating in drama from Hofstra College, he studied filmmaking at UCLA. There he made the softcore 'nudie' *Tonight For Sure* (1961) and won the Samuel Goldwyn Award in 1962 for the screenplay *Pilma Pilma*. He was then apprenticed to the Roger Corman exploitation movie factory, trying his hand as a soundman, script doctor, editor, dialogue director and associate producer. Eventually, Corman invited him to direct a gothic chiller, *Dementia 13* (1963). But it was *You're A Big Boy Now* (1967) that earned Coppola his stripes, a tale of a young man's bid for independence that was a jump-cut celebration of Godardian aesthetics. Then came the opportunity to enter the industry with the fantasy musical *Finian's Rainbow* (1968), featur-

ing Fred Astaire. Its failure was largely due to the Hollywood establishment's inability to connect with the post-war baby boomer audience. More timely was *The Rain People* (1969), a road movie with something to say to the countercultural urge to drop out. Despite low returns, in 1969 Coppola was financed by Warner Bros to establish American Zoetrope, a San Francisco production facility dedicated to a new generation of filmmakers.

Coppola remained active on the industry fringes, and in 1970 he earned an Academy Award for his *Patton* screenplay (co-written with Edmund North). But he would score his greatest success with *The Godfather* (1972), which he co-wrote and directed. As a reward for its fabulous box-office returns, Paramount financed Coppola's art project *The Conversation* (1974). Produced, directed and written by Coppola, the film foregrounded Walter Murch's sound design, highlighting a technology which would become essential to the emergent multiplex cinema-going experience. *The Godfather, Part II* (1974) extended and deepened *The Godfather*'s critique of the post-war American status quo. With *The Godfather, Part III* (1990), Coppola's trilogy is the most sustained directorial achievement in modern American cinema. Much trumpeted, *Apocalypse Now* (1979) was a bold, massively expensive and logistically disastrous attempt to come to terms with the Vietnam War which almost bankrupted Coppola. His wife Eleanor's journal remains one of the most revelatory publications on modern cinema; Fax Bahr and George Hickenlooper's 1991 documentary, *Hearts Of Darkness*, is a compelling record that demonstrates that draconian ambition can occasionally triumph over the fiscal imperative in American cinema.

Apocalypse Now added to the auteur's list of Oscars, winning the Palme d'Or at Cannes, and eventually turned a profit. But the 1980s saw Coppola saddled with debts and committed to limited budgets. The musical *One From The Heart* (1982) was self-indulgent and a box-office disaster. *The Outsiders* and *Rumble Fish* (both 1983) were teen movies consolidating the Brat Pack stars of the era. Fraught with problems, the period gangster epic *The Cotton Club* (1984) pushed Coppola further into debt. The time-travel romance *Peggy Sue Got Married* (1986), starring Kathleen Turner, was a thoughtful antidote to the *Back To The Future* razzamatazz and has gained a cult reputation. Something of a metaphor for Coppola's own history, *Tucker: The Man And His Dream* (1988) told the story of the post-war automobile entrepreneur who challenged the monopoly of the US majors.

It is almost tragic that a director renowned for his breathtaking vision and historical acuity is now so subsumed in the industry that he is probably better known at large for star vehicles like Robin Williams's

Jack (1996) and Matt Damon's *The Rainmaker* (1997). Coppola's last good film was *Bram Stoker's Dracula* (1992), a bravura potpourri of visuals and camerawork. One hopes that *Megalopolis*, a mooted project concerning a futuristic city that is already decades in the pipeline, will be as Coppolaesque as its title suggests. RA

The Godfather 1972, 175 min
cast Marlon Brando, Al Pacino, James Caan, Richard Castellano, Robert Duvall, Sterling Hayden, Diane Keaton *cin* Gordon Willis *m* Nino Rota

Much more than a dynastic Mafia romance, *The Godfather* is an epic exploration of the structures of power that animated America in the post-war period. It revolves around stupendous performances from Marlon Brando as the patriarch Vito Corleone and Al Pacino as the reluctant rising son – with this film New Hollywood really arrived and finally delivered.

The Godfather, Part II 1974, 200 min
cast Al Pacino, Robert Duvall, Diane Keaton, Robert De Niro, John Cazale, Talia Shire *cin* Gordon Willis *m* Nino Rota

Coppola's sequel explores Vito Corleone's Sicilian roots and his rise to power in New York at the start of the twentieth century, as well as the Mafia's entry into post-war politics under the leadership of his son Michael. Shot with a European sensitivity, this film charts the falling out of love between America and the Mob – and what that does to the soul of Michael Corleone.

The Conversation 1974, 113 min
cast Gene Hackman, John Cazale, Cindy Williams, Allen Garfield, Frederic Forrest, Teri Garr, Robert Duvall *cin* Bill Butler *m* David Shire

Anticipating the Watergate affair, Coppola's character study of a repressed surveillance expert (Gene Hackman) and his progress through a dangerously ambiguous world remains quintessential New Hollywood in its feeling for character and sublime sense of place.

Apocalypse Now 1979, 153 min
cast Martin Sheen, Robert Duvall, Marlon Brando, Frederic Forrest, Dennis Hopper, Larry Fishburne *cin* Vittorio Storaro *m* Carmine & Francis Coppola

In this phantasmagoric journey into the Vietnam War, Coppola dramatized the collision between a powerful but naïve technocracy and an ancient civilization undergoing bloody transformation. One of the best ever portraits of Americans transfigured by their experiences in the old world.

Sofia Coppola
US, 1971–

There is family and then there is *family*. Sofia Coppola has *family*. In fact her first screen appearance was as the Corleone baby christened at the climax of *The Godfather* (1972). She went on to appear (sometimes under the stage name Domino) in many of her father's films including *The Outsiders* (1983), *Rumble Fish* (1983) and, notoriously, *The Godfather, Part III* (1990), where she inherited the role vacated by an exhausted Winona Ryder.

All of which might be immaterial, except that it's worth noting that the first American woman to be nominated for the Academy Award for best director had a head start, and that all three films signed by Coppola *fille* to date have expressed a certain listlessness not unknown among the offspring of the rich and famous.

A friend gave her Jeffrey Eugenides' novel *The Virgin Suicides* when she was at art school, toying with fashion and photography, but unsure which way to go. Even though she heard a studio had picked up the rights to the book, against everyone's advice she wrote her own adaptation and was eventually allowed to make it independently, albeit with

A young Vito Corleone (Robert De Niro) with his friend Clemenza (Bruno Kirby Jr) in New York's Little Italy at the turn of the century in *The Godfather, Part II*.

her father producing. A wistful mood piece about the longing and loss of adolescent ardour, the endless mystery of the opposite sex, it was an unusual, tantalizing first film, very difficult to categorize – but distinguished by Coppola's sure compositional sense and excellent ear for music (the ambient score was by Air).

She trumped it with *Lost In Translation* (2003). This was a Sofia original, a May-December romance between a middle-aged movie star and the neglected young bride of a fashion photographer (any resemblance to Coppola's soon to be ex-husband Spike Jonze was presumably coincidental). Oscar glory followed (but she won for her writing, not direction). *Marie Antoinette* (2006) reunited her with Kirsten Dunst from *The Virgin Suicides*, and met with a mixed response at its Cannes premiere. By and large the French critics adored its wittily modern portrait of a high-society party girl, while British and American reviews complained about its superficial apoliticism. TC

The Virgin Suicides 1999, 97 min

cast James Woods, Kathleen Turner, Kirsten Dunst, Josh Hartnett, A.J. Cook, Hanna Hall, Leslie Hayman *cin* Edward Lachman *m* Air

This is the story of the Lisbon girls, five teenage sisters growing up in a strict Catholic household in suburban Michigan in the mid-1970s. When 13-year-old Cecilia tries to kill herself, the sisters become an object of curiosity and wonder to the local boys. When she eventually succeeds, the girls seem to pass into another realm entirely, untouchable, romantic figures in a mythic sense. Coppola's evocative, dreamy debut is very good on mood, but evaporates in the cold light of day.

Lost In Translation 2003, 97 min

cast Bill Murray, Scarlett Johansson, Giovanni Ribisi, Anna Faris, Akiko Takeshita, Fumihiro Hayashi *cin* Lance Acord *m* Kevin Shields

Jaded middle-aged movie star Murray flirts with a lonely young American bride (Johansson) in the alien environment of the Hyatt hotel, Tokyo, in this breakthrough (sort of) indie hit. Combining culture-clash comedy (some of it very broad) with acute character observation, the film takes its own sweet time to allow jet-lagged estrangement to drift towards human connection.

Roger Corman

US, 1926–

Roger Corman called his autobiography *How I Made A Hundred Movies In Hollywood And Never Lost A Dime*. It was an exaggeration on at least two counts, but a typically strong pitch from the veteran huckster.

As a director, anyway, Corman has just over fifty credits to his name. Had he not retired from the fray in the early 1970s, he might easily have made that a hundred. After all, this is the man who made *The Little Shop Of Horrors* (1960) in just two days.

As a producer, he's credited on something like 350 exploitation movies, of which the last 150 – anything since the mid-1980s – are unmitigated dross. Very few of these films had any commercial presence at all, but Corman's production methods are nothing if not cost-efficient. In Hollywood, they joked that he could set up a movie on a payphone, shoot it there in the booth and finance it with the money in the change slot.

Seemingly intent on following in his father's footsteps, Corman had studied engineering at Stanford, but soon brought his considerable intelligence to focus on the likes of *Swamp Women* (1955), *Attack Of The Crab Monsters* (1957) and *Teenage Cave Man* (1958). He became house director at American International Pictures, churning out half a dozen B-movies a year, on ten-day schedules (or less) and three-line screenplays. Horror was a mainstay of Corman's years at AIP, and among his best works were his eight Edgar Allen Poe adaptations, including *The Pit And The Pendulum* (1961), *The Raven* (1963), *The Masque Of The Red Death* (1964) and *The Tomb Of Ligeia* (1964). The lessons Corman learned were speed, economy, sex and violence (cheap thrills, in other words), and these were the values he inculcated in the novices who came to work for him over the next four decades – a period in which, as he has noted, the studios gradually co-opted his brand of exploitation pictures and made them over as expensive blockbusters.

Many Corman protégés became important figures in their own right. On *The Terror* (1963), for example, a piece of gothic schlock tossed off to take advantage of the castle set built for the same year's *The Raven*, Francis Coppola, Monte Hellman, Jack Hill and Jack Nicholson all lent a hand in the directing department. When Corman decided to concentrate on producing for the drive-in trade, he gave Peter Bogdanovich, Joe Dante, John Sayles, Jonathan Demme, Jonathan Kaplan, Gale Anne Hurd, James Cameron, Paul Bartel, Ron Howard and George Armitage their first breaks. He brought Martin Scorsese to Hollywood for *Boxcar Bertha* (1972).

If Corman's own films have been overshadowed, it's partly because his attitude towards them was inherently dismissive. Although many of the AIP pictures are amusing – Corman brought a level of irony to even the least promising assignment – few of them muster any emotional or intellectual engagement, or any connection with the world outside the drive-in. A comparison between Corman's terse but resolutely minor *The St Valentine's Day Massacre* (1967) and Coppola's *The Godfather* (1972) exposes a great gap in ambition and accomplishment.

A pity, because in some of the more surreal moments of the popular, relatively up-market Poe cycle and in *The Intruder* (1962) and even *Bloody Mama* (1970), Corman shows what a fine filmmaker he could be, when he chose. TC

A Bucket Of Blood 1959, 66 min, b/w

cast Dick Miller, Barboura Morris, Anthony Carbone, Julian Burton, Ed Nelson, John Brinkley *cin* Jacques R. Marquette *m* Fred Katz

The first of Corman's black comedies – an even cheaper companion piece to *The Little Shop Of Horrors* – is played relatively straight. It's treasurable for cult actor Dick Miller's lead performance as Walter Paisley, a busboy at a wickedly satirized beatnik café, whose artistic leanings get the better of him… Walter's grisly sculptures are uncannily lifelike. Or perhaps "deathlike" would be a better description.

The Intruder 1962, 80 min, b/w

cast William Shatner, Frank Maxwell, Beverley Lunsford, Robert Emhardt, Jeanne Cooper *cin* Taylor Byars *m* Herman Stein

Corman injected liberal politics even into New World's cheapo *Nurses…* series, but this was his only out-and-out "message movie". Still, it's bolder than Stanley Kramer would have countenanced. William Shatner is a charismatic white supremacist who stirs up a lynch mob in a small Southern town. A box-office flop, it soured Corman on serious drama, but for such a topical movie it holds up very well.

The Masque Of The Red Death 1964, 84 min

cast Vincent Price, Hazel Court, Jane Asher, Skip Martin, David Weston, Patrick Magee *cin* Nicolas Roeg *m* David Lee

With the following year's necrophile *The Tomb Of Ligeia*, this is Corman's best Poe adaptation. Vincent Price is in his element as the fiendish twelfth-century Prince Prospero, who devises satanic entertainments for his "guests" while the plague rages beyond his castle walls. Nic Roeg's cinematography is audaciously inventive, and gives the movie a somewhat incongruous psychedelic spin.

Bloody Mama 1970, 90 min

cast Shelley Winters, Pat Hingle, Don Stroud, Bruce Dern, Diane Varsi, Robert De Niro, Robert Walden *cin* John A. Alonzo *m* Don Randi

Corman made more polished films than this *Bonnie And Clyde* cash-in, but nothing sleazier. Drenched in Freud, the Barker clan comprise a sadist, a homosexual, a junkie (Robert De Niro sniffing glue) and a lady-killer, and they all take turns in Ma's bed (Shelley Winters on overdrive). Not subtle, certainly, but an antidote to the strain of family sentimentality you find in *The Public Enemy* (1931) and its sort.

Henry Cornelius
South Africa, 1913–58

After much experience as an editor and then a producer, Cornelius directed only five films before illness intervened – yet two, *Passport To Pimlico* (1949) and *Genevieve* (1953), are classics.

Cornelius studied theatre with Max Reinhardt in Berlin but with the rise of the Nazis he moved to Paris where he became a film editor. Moving on to London, he worked with Alexander Korda before returning to South Africa to make propaganda shorts. Back in Britain he produced several Ealing films, before Michael Balcon assigned him to direct *Passport To Pimlico*, in which an area of south London declares independence. Despite its success, Balcon refused to pay Cornelius more and the director quit to set up his own company. His first production was the obviously Ealing-inspired *The Galloping Major* (1951), about an officer-turned-racehorse-owner. It was only mildly successful so Cornelius offered his next project – *Genevieve* (1953), about two men in a veteran car race – to Ealing. But Balcon turned it down and as a result this classic comedy was produced by the Rank Organization. Ironically, Rank hated the finished film and it was only Cornelius's persistence that eventually persuaded them to release what went on to become one of their most profitable films.

Cornelius seemed finally to be set as a director but, increasingly ill, he directed only two more films. *I Am A Camera* was adapted from Christopher Isherwood's memoirs via John Van Druten's play, but in 1955 it could hardly hope to do justice to the lurid atmosphere of pre-war Berlin, more successfully shown in Bob Fosse's *Cabaret* (1972). It was a critical disaster. In 1958 Cornelius directed the light, feel-good comedy *Next To No Time*, about a man on a transatlantic crossing who gains in confidence as he travels further west, but he died before its release. JR

Passport To Pimlico 1949, 85 min, b/w

cast Stanley Holloway, Barbara Murray, Raymond Huntley, Paul Dupuis, Hermione Baddeley *cin* Lionel Banes, Cecil Cooney *m* Georges Auric

A wartime bomb in south London unearths buried treasure and documents showing that Pimlico is still part of Burgundy. Taking the chance to escape post-war greyness, local residents claim the booty, suspend rationing, set up border controls and a local government and embrace continental drinking hours and pavement cafés. A typically quirky Ealing comedy, filled with character actors who gently satirize British spirit and the sometimes hard-to-spot spoils of wartime victory.

Genevieve 1953, 86 min

cast John Gregson, Dinah Sheridan, Kenneth More, Kay Kendall *cin* Christopher Challis *m* Larry Adler

How Rank missed the potential of this ever-popular comedy is a mystery. The story of two men in a London-to-Brighton vintage car race with their increasingly frustrated partners provides an opportunity to take a wry look at the British character and male rivalry. Harmonica player Larry Adler wrote the infectious score and claimed to live on the royalties for the rest of his life.

Catherine Corsini
France, 1956–

Catherine Corsini has gained a reputation for provocative portraits of contemporary womanhood featuring France's best actresses. After studying drama with a view to becoming an actress, Corsini opted to write and direct films. Various shorts finally led to *Poker* (1987), in which Caroline Cellier plays a poker compulsive who must come up with big money quickly.

Then, following the disappointing Provençal-set drama *Les amoureux* (*The Lovers*, 1993), Corsini reached an international audience with the Karin Viard vehicle *La nouvelle Ève* (*The New Eve*, 1998). *La répétition* (*Replay*, 2001), featuring Emmanuelle Béart and Pascale Bussières, revisits the relationship between an actress and her girlhood friend and keeps true to the autobiographical streak established by *La nouvelle Ève*. *Mariés mais pas trop* (*The Very Merry Widows*, 2003) finds Jane Birkin and Emilie Dequenne in the comedic vein suggested by *La nouvelle Ève*, but comedy notoriously does not travel and Corsini has yet to follow up her incursion into the Anglo arthouse. RA

La nouvelle Eve (The New Eve) 1998, 94 min

cast Karin Viard, Pierre-Loup Rajot, Catherine Frot, Sergi López, Laurent Lucas, Mireille Roussel *cin* Agnès Godard

Revolving around a magnetic performance by Viard, this funny yet powerful portrait of liberated and aggressive modern womanhood unblinkingly stares at the contradictions faced by women torn between the comfort of intimacy and the longing for identity.

Costa-Gavras

Greece, 1933–

For a while, Costa-Gavras made it seem as though political filmmaking could really change the world. Born of Russian-Greek parentage, Costa-Gavras had a Greek Orthodox education, but owing to his father's suspected communism, was denied entrance to university. Moving to Paris, where he took French citizenship in 1956, he attended the Sorbonne and the national film school IDHEC. Following work under the wings of Yves Allégret, René Clair and Jacques Demy, Costa-Gavras made his debut with *The Sleeping Car Murders* (1965), an efficient whodunnit featuring Simone Signoret and Costa-Gavras regular Yves Montand.

He won international acclaim, and the Oscar for best foreign film, with the political thriller *Z* (1969). *L'aveu* (*The Confession*, 1970) starred Yves Montand as the victim of a Czech government witch-hunt. *State Of Siege* (1972) reduced Uruguayan geopolitics to a staple US-versus-terrorist format. Combining star performance, newsworthy confrontations, and *cinéma vérité* aesthetics, 1970s Costa-Gavras links the high-art commitment of Jean-Luc Godard and Francesco Rosi with the commercial conspiracy thriller. In 1982 *Missing* won the Palme d'Or at Cannes, but the thrillers *Betrayed* (1988) and *Music Box* (1989) found 1970s conviction cowed by 80s conservatism. The hostage thriller *Mad City* (1997) was a fine John Travolta vehicle, but Billy Wilder's *Ace In The Hole* remains a finer exposé of the workings of the media. RA

Z 1969, 125 min

cast Yves Montand, Jean-Louis Trintignant, Jacques Perrin, François Périer, Irene Papas, Georges Géret *cin* Raoul Coutard *m* Mikis Theodorakis

Shot in Algeria to avoid suppression in Greece, this dramatization of the investigation into the 1965 assassination of Gregory Lambrakis brings all the pace and allure of Hollywood storytelling to its political exposé, and it remains a landmark political thriller.

Missing 1982, 122 min

cast Jack Lemmon, Sissy Spacek, Melanie Mayron, John Shea, Charles Cioffi, David Clennon, Jerry Hardin *cin* Ricardo Aronovich *m* Vangelis

This atmospheric evocation of Chile's brutal regime under General Pinochet captures the blatant contradictions of US foreign policy via the progress of Jack Lemmon's Middle-American innocent investigating his son's disappearance.

Kevin Costner

US, 1955–

Costner had been a star for just three years (since *The Untouchables* and *No Way Out*, both in 1987) when he persuaded Orion to put up $15 million so that he could direct and star in a Western.

At a time when that genre was moribund, *Dances With Wolves* (1990) would be three hours long, with forty percent of its meagre dialogue in the Lakota dialect (subtitled). Orion initially released the film on just fourteen prints, but the reviews were raves – Costner was compared to everybody from John Ford to Akira Kurosawa – and the movie went on to play for nearly a year, becoming one of the most commercially successful Westerns ever made, and beating out Martin Scorsese's *GoodFellas* for the best picture and best director Academy Awards.

That movie now looks like a flash in the pan. Costner's directorial career has suffered from the actor's slide from grace, first with the post-apocalyptic bomb *Waterworld* (1995), which Costner ended up directing himself, uncredited, after falling out with Kevin Reynolds, then with the misconceived and rather too similar *The Postman* (1997). A return to the Western with *Open Range* (2003) was warmly received, but that film's pleasure in landscape and companionship was marred by a hackneyed story and Costner's sentimental streak. TC

Dances With Wolves 1990, 180 min

cast Kevin Costner, Mary McDonnell, Graham Greene, Rodney A. Grant, Floyd Red Crow Westerman *cin* Dean Semler *m* John Barry

Sent from the Civil War to man an army outpost on the Western frontier, Lieutenant Dunbar (Costner) finds himself left to his own devices – until he begins to strike up a relationship with the Native American tribe who are his only neighbours. Costner's "regular guy epic" brings a populist touch to unfashionable material. It's ponderous and sentimental in places, but very handsomely shot, and the patient development of the friendship between Dunbar and the authentically observed Lakota natives pays emotional dividends.

Alex Cox

UK, 1954–

An anarchist in the film business, Alex Cox hasn't had an easy ride. How could it be otherwise?

After abandoning his law studies at Oxford, and studying film at Bristol and UCLA, Cox found himself on the fringes of Hollywood. It was here that he managed to put together his first feature, *Repo Man* (1984), a punk black comedy which quickly established a cult following. Returning to the UK, Cox made *Sid And Nancy* (1986), about Sex Pistol Sid Vicious (played by Gary Oldman), his love affair with Nancy Spungen (Chloe Webb), and their descent into junk hell. This is as close as Cox has strayed towards the mainstream.

Turning down the offer to direct Chevy Chase, Martin Short and Steve Martin in *¡Three Amigos!*, Cox made his own spoof spaghetti, *Straight To Hell* (1986) instead. A wild mix of film buffoonery and punk rock pretension, the film was written in three days and shot in three weeks. It was a failure on every level and sullied the filmmaker's reputation, perhaps permanently. *Walker* (1987) was a more focused attempt to resurrect the energy and subversion of the Marxist spaghetti Western. But reviews at the time were unsympathetic, and the film was barely distributed.

Since then, Cox has cut an increasingly beleaguered figure. He made an authentic Mexican film, *El patrullero* (*Highway Patrolman*, 1991, one of his best, most sober efforts), TV documentaries about Akira Kurosawa and the *Emmanuelle* porn series, and an episode of a Japanese detective show, *Hama Mike*. He refused a director's credit on *The Winner* (1995) after the producers recut it. And he came close to making *Fear And Loathing In Las Vegas* – a perfect project – but after another falling out it went to Terry Gilliam, a maverick with a less political sensibility. *Revengers Tragedy* (2002) sought to update Thomas Middleton's Jacobean play to contemporary Liverpool, but erratic performances and the relentlessly lurid, hectoring style confounded most viewers. TC

Repo Man 1984, 92 min

cast Harry Dean Stanton, Emilio Estevez, Tracey Walter, Olivia Barash, Sy Richardson *cin* Robby Müller *m* Tito Larriva, Steven Hufsteter

Delinquent punk Otto (Emilio Estevez) gets mixed up in the car repossession trade when he's conned into helping the first of what turns into a memorable parade of cynical crackpots. Still Cox's funniest and most entertaining effort, it has a kind of Roger Corman drive-in feel, but with an anarchic edge. The plot motor (a much sought-after 64 Chevy) is straight out of *Kiss Me Deadly*, and later turned up in *Pulp Fiction*.

Sid And Nancy 1986, 114 min

cast Gary Oldman, Chloe Webb, David Hayman, Debby Bishop, Andrew Schofield *cin* Roger Deakins *m* Joe Strummer, Pogues, Pray For Rain

Cox conceived of this Sex Pistols saga as a love story, focusing on the damaged, and damaging, relationship between "guitarist" Sid Vicious (played with savage and tender conviction by Oldman) and heroin addict Nancy Spungeon (Webb). It's a harrowing (if ultimately redemptive) ride, but not entirely humourless, and shot through with a sometimes surreal lyricism. Look for Courtney Love in her first screen role.

Walker 1987, 94 min

cast Ed Harris, Richard Masur, René Auberjonois, Keith Szarabajka, Sy Richardson *cin* David Bridges *m* Joe Strummer

Cox takes up the anti-imperialist cause with all guns blazing in this underrated blast of satire, allegory and surrealism. Based on the true story of William Walker, an evangelical soldier of fortune who briefly conquered Nicaragua, this was a timely assault on American colonialism – and it never lets you forget it. The anachronisms (like having tanks and machine guns prop up the puppet state) are very much the point, but don't detract from the tragic dimension Harris brings to Walker himself.

Paul Cox

Netherlands, 1940–

Few modern directors have tackled the metaphysics of identity and passion as evocatively as Paul Cox. The son of a film producer, Cox studied photography at art school, before an exchange trip to Australia eventually led to him emigrating in 1965, and becoming a successful photographer.

Cox's early film shorts dwelt in moods of isolation and alienation, and his 1980s features, such as *Lonely Hearts* (1982), *Man Of Flowers* (1983), *Cactus* (1986) and *Vincent: The Life And Death Of Vincent Van Gogh* (1987), focused in limpid fashion on damaged characters becoming spiritually cut-off from the world around them. *My First Wife* (1984) was an anguished account of the breakdown of Cox's own marriage, but in a decade preoccupied with the material world, this Bressonian vision gained little more than festival plaudits. Cox has since amassed an impressive body of work. *Innocence* (2000) and *Human Touch* (2004) were both critically acclaimed and, while hardly box-office smashes, won several international awards. RA

Man Of Flowers 1983, 91 min

cast Norman Kaye, Alyson Best, Chris Haywood, Sarah Walker, Julia Blake, Bob Ellis *cin* Yuri Sokol

An art collector pays a model to strip for him, and their lives begin to intertwine. Sensitive to the play of feelings and memory, Cox's control of performance, and the extraordinary Australian light, confers a genuine dignity upon this account of solitary desire.

111

Vincent: The Life And Death Of Vincent Van Gogh 1987, 99 min
cast John Hurt, Gabi Trsek, Marika Rivera *cin* Paul Cox *m* Jean François Rogeon, Philip Faiers, Norman Kaye

Inspired by the correspondence between the artist and his brother, Theo, this remains the most complex account of Vincent Van Gogh's life. Narrated by John Hurt, *Vincent* is a moving portrait of the painter redolent with the joy of colour and passion that is Cox's trademark.

Wes Craven
US, 1939–

Onward from his still-startling solo directing debut, *Last House On The Left* (1972), Wes Craven has remained a definitive purveyor of horror filmmaking, setting trends and enjoying great commercial success for more than three decades. The visceral mayhem of his 1970s work broke the generally acknowledged boundaries for onscreen violence and gore while seeking to allegorize the violent social and moral disintegration of post-Vietnam America. In the 1980s he introduced the decade's most enduring bogeyman, pizza-faced Freddy Krueger from *A Nightmare On Elm Street* (1984) and its many successors. In the 1990s, Craven perfected the postmodern horror movie with the self-reflexive *Scream* (1996) and its two sequels, which at once followed and deconstructed the mechanics of the genre (while launching an avalanche of jokey slasher-flick imitators).

Craven began dabbling in 16mm filmmaking while still teaching in the humanities department at Clarkson College in upstate New York, an unlikely prologue to his movie career. *Last House On The Left*, a sleaze-horror revamping of Ingmar Bergman's *The Virgin Spring* (1960), was banned outright in Britain and Australia, and established what would become a Craven motif: the family hearth and home as the forum for the final battle royale between villains and would-be victims. *The Hills Have Eyes* (1977) pits a vacationing middle-class family against a clan of feral cannibals in a desert showdown that Craven's adherents have interpreted as an appropriately grisly allegory of the American war in Vietnam. Despite the redoubling campness of its sequels, the original *A Nightmare On Elm Street* is a potent screamer that, like many of Craven's movies, posits that the realization of our worst fears comes from within our own minds, homes and neighbourhoods.

Though Craven's résumé includes the loveable schlock flick *Swamp Thing* (1982; adapted from the DC Comics series), the leaden Haitian-voodoo thriller *The Serpent And The Rainbow* (1988) and the syrup-stained inspirational *Music Of The Heart* (1999), his name remains synonymous with the American horror film. The dark class-conflict satire

The People Under The Stairs (1991) cast *Twin Peaks* supporting players Everett McGill and Wendy Robie as incestuous weirdos harbouring cannibals in their basement, and *Scream* marked a career resurgence for Craven while offering an auto-critique of the genre that he has been so instrumental in defining. The whiffs of sexual puritanism evident in *A Nightmare On Elm Street* and in John Carpenter's *Halloween* (1978), with their virginal heroines and intimations of teen sex as capital offence, come under particularly close scrutiny in *Scream*. After predictably diminishing returns for the *Scream* sequels, Craven scored a sleeper hit with the tightly constructed *Red Eye* (2005), a claustrophobic mile-high thriller for the War on Terror age. JW

Last House On The Left 1972, 85 min
cast David Hess, Lucy Grantham, Sandra Cassel, Marc Sheffier, Jeramie Rain, Fred Lincoln *cin* Victor Hurwitz *m* David Alexander Hess

Kidnapped by a gang of psycho sadists, teenager Mari (Sandra Cassel) and her friend Phyllis (Lucy Grantham) are humiliated, tortured, raped and murdered – and all not far from Mari's secluded home in the woods, where the killers coincidentally take shelter with her parents for the night. Setting an almost unwatchable ordeal in an incongruously pastoral setting, *Last House* is a merciless exploitation flick turned surprisingly classical revenge drama.

A Nightmare On Elm Street 1984, 91 min
cast John Saxon, Ronee Blakley, Heather Langenkamp, Amanda Wyss, Nick Corri, Johnny Depp, Robert Englund *cin* Jacques Haitkin *m* Charles Bernstein

If the viewer can forget Freddy Krueger's later ascension to comedy-mascot icon, this oneirophrenic frightener remains powerful. A group of high-schoolers – led by plucky virgin Nancy (Heather Langenkamp) – fight to stay awake in order to elude a serial killer who strikes in his victims' dreams. With its scares hinging heavily on the disorientation and derangement caused by severe sleep deprivation, the film skilfully blurs the line between dream and reality.

Scream 1996, 111 min
cast Drew Barrymore, Neve Campbell, David Arquette, Courtney Cox, Rose McGowan, Skeet Ulrich, Jamie Kennedy *cin* Mark Irwin *m* Marco Beltrami

A serial killer in a Münch-esque mask and black cloak terrorizes a small town whose inhabitants all seem equally steeped in the bloodier aspects of pop culture – indeed, you'd think they all imagined themselves as characters in a horror movie. Craven's clever, hugely successful postmodern riff on scary movies is both acutely self-aware and genuinely jolting, and revived both the slasher genre and Craven's directorial profile.

Charles Crichton
UK, 1910–99

After being one of the mainstays of British film comedy during the post-war years, Charles Crichton performed the rare feat of re-entering the limelight with one of the biggest British comedies in decades.

Crichton entered the industry as an assistant editor at Alexander Korda's London Films in 1935. He worked on some of the most prestigious releases of the era, including *Sanders Of The River* (1935), *Things To Come* (1936), and *The Thief of Bagdad* (1940). Following a short – *The Young Veterans* (1941) – Crichton joined Ealing Studios as a director and his work came to reflect the studio's realist house style with which he made his reputation.

He was at his filmmaking peak from the late-1940s to the mid-50s. *Hue And Cry* (1947) was an agile story of East End boys who solve a crime, the details of which they detect in a comic strip. Shot on East End streets and bomb sites, the film evoked the British "spiv crime" cycle of the period, as well as conjuring the parochial populism that was Ealing's hallmark. *The Lavender Hill Mob* (1951) built on this tradition, but by the time of *The Titfield Thunderbolt*'s plea for preserving the branch line before the nationalizing zeal of British Rail in 1953, Ealing looked passé.

Less praised nowadays are the early Crichtons, which drew upon Britain's documentary heritage yet evoked the specifics of post-war life. *Painted Boats* (1945) was the first of a projected series of docudramas: set on Britain's canals, it chronicled a threatened way of life. Starring Britain's blonde bombshell Diana Dors, *Dance Hall* (1950) turned a spotlight on the lives of working-class women. But 1950s Crichton became increasingly middle-of-the-road (1954's topical weepie *The Divided Heart*) and faddish (1959's *The Battle of the Sexes*). Crichton accepted an invitation to Hollywood but after a dispute with Burt Lancaster while directing *Birdman Of Alcatraz* in 1962, Crichton turned to churning out TV shows (although they included *Danger Man* and *The Avengers*). It was only after working in training films with John Cleese that he was offered *A Fish Called Wanda* (1988), the biggest hit of his career. RA

The Lavender Hill Mob 1951, 78 min, b/w

cast Alec Guinness, Stanley Holloway, Sidney James, Alfie Bass, Marjorie Fielding, John Gregson *cin* Doulas Slocombe *m* Georges Auric

Starring Alec Guinness as the timid bank teller involved in a gold bullion robbery and Stanley Holloway as his seedy mentor, this sublime film best epitomizes the parodic talents of Ealing comedy, chronicling a native English politesse desperately trying to come to terms with an increasingly unpredictable world. The car chase scene remains priceless.

A Fish Called Wanda 1988, 108 min

cast John Cleese, Jamie Lee Curtis, Kevin Kline, Michael Palin, Maria Aitken *cin* Alan Hume *m* John Du Prez

Earning Crichton an Oscar nomination, this unlikely caper – in which John Cleese plays a London barrister defending a mobster – bears all the eccentric hallmarks of Ealing updated for a meaner, more frenetic era. The result never lets up.

Michael Crichton
US, 1942–

Michael Crichton has turned his scientific background into profitable entertainments. After studying at Harvard Medical School, he had a spell in a hospital emergency department, all the while writing thrillers calling upon his medical training. Crichton's first bestseller, *The Andromeda Strain*, became a hit film in 1971, and his books have formed the basis for successful movies ever since, most famously 1993's *Jurassic Park*. In 1972 Crichton made his directing debut with the Ben Gazzara TV movie *Binary* (aka *Pursuit*), in which a terrorist threatens to release nerve gas at a political convention.

If 1970s Hollywood thrillers were typically paranoid about the status quo, Crichton's work gave paranoia an increasingly technological twist, most effectively in *Westworld* (1973) and *Coma* (1978). An exception was 1978's *The First Great Train Robbery*, in which Sean Connery and Donald Sutherland's nineteenth-century gentleman thieves meticulously plan a bullion robbery. Routine projects such as 1981's *Looker* (plastic surgery patients murdered by a mysterious corporation) and 1984's *Runaway* (Tom Selleck's future cop stops killer robots) bore out the nutshell concepts of corporate American cinema. The so-so nailbiter *Physical Evidence* (1989) and Crichton's subsequent credits, such as *Disclosure* (1996, co-producer) and *Twister* (1996, co-screenplay, co-producer), proved that his penchant for superficially intelligent, morally simplistic storytelling was much in demand at committee level. RA

Westworld 1973, 89 min

cast Yul Brynner, Richard Benjamin, James Brolin, Norman Bartold, Alan Oppenheimer, Victoria Shaw *cin* Gene Polito *m* Fred Karlin

Taking a hackneyed idea – machines turn against men – this fantasy finds guileless consumers Richard Benjamin and James Brolin buying into a vacation wonderland where mechanized cowboys and android bar floozies fulfil your every need. That is, until everything goes horribly wrong and Yul Brynner's robot gunslinger starts to malfunction… Shot with deliberately little visual flair, the bland images almost collude with the sense that this is a fantasy about to be subverted.

John Cromwell
US, 1888–1979

Directing many of the finest Hollywood stars of his day, John Cromwell's "women's pictures" provided a template for the flowering of the form in the post-war melodramas of Douglas Sirk. His consummate studio craftsmanship was also reflected in the other genres he tackled, such as the swashbuckler *The Prisoner Of Zenda* (1937) and the biopic *Abe Lincoln In Illinois* (1940).

Bringing with him a Broadway reputation as actor, director and producer, Cromwell's talents suited an industry newly wiring for sound and dialogue. Soon evolving as a storyteller, Cromwell directed Bette Davis in *Of Human Bondage* (1934). *Ann Vickers* (1933) saw Irene Dunne's social worker exposing prison injustices, foreseeing Cromwell's superb *Caged* (1950). *Made For Each Other* (1939), uniquely measured the reality of marriage against romantic fiction.

With the exception of *Since You Went Away* (1944), a moving drama of home-front pluck starring Claudette Colbert, Jennifer Jones and Shirley Temple, Cromwell's work of the 1940s declined in quality – opportunities lost following his blacklisting by the House Un-American Activities Committee. *Dead Reckoning* (1947) remains an underrated Bogart *noir* detailing a war veteran's investigation of a best buddy's murder. Consonant with the gritty post-war tenor, *Caged* found Eleanor Parker's first offender in a tough world characterized, like Cromwell's *The Racket* (1951), by atmospheric camerawork. Scripted by Paddy Chayefsky, *The Goddess* (1958) was an exposé of Hollywood containing something of Cromwell's own love-hate relationship with the industry. Still a much underrated director, Cromwell rewards serious attention. RA

Of Human Bondage 1934, 83 min, b/w

cast Leslie Howard, Bette Davis, Frances Dee, Kay Johnson, Reginald Denny, Alan Hale *cin* Henry W. Gerrard *m* Max Steiner

Making the most of RKO's budget restrictions and limited settings, Cromwell's version of W. Somerset Maugham's story deploys camera movement to capture the feints and lunges of Bette Davis's shallow waitress as she ensnares Leslie Howard's club-footed suitor. Cromwell's punchy emotions remain a model for what the "women's picture" would become.

David Cronenberg
Canada, 1943–

Discussing his film *Spider* (2002) upon its release, David Cronenberg equated the film's many expressionist variations of dingy, mouldy wallpaper to its schizophrenic protagonist's "cerebral lining" – a phrase that captures the director's rich meldings of the visceral and the contemplative, the physical and the metaphysical. "For me, the human body is the first fact of human existence," Cronenberg has said, and his films accordingly suture the mind–body split. Indeed, the phrase most often attached to his movies is "body horror", a catch-all description that variously evokes Marilyn Chambers' armpit phallus in *Rabid* (1976), Geneviève Bujold sinking her teeth deep into pulpy conjoined skin in *Dead*

Ringers (1988) and the chilly auto-erotica of *Crash* (1996), in which a car-accident victim's leg wound becomes an erogenous orifice. As the revolutionaries of *Videodrome* (1982) would cry: "Long live the new flesh!" While the body-horror label risks trapping a stunningly dense and accomplished oeuvre in the ghetto of genre, it also implies the excitement and astonishment that Cronenberg's transgressive projects so often inspire.

Cronenberg's icy first featurettes show a young director already sure of his fecund thematic territory, investigating the convergence of fringe medicine and outlaw sexuality in *Stereo* (1969), wherein subjects at a sex-research institute undergo brain surgery to acquire telepathic powers, and *Crimes Of The Future* (1970), which arranges a bizarre interface of dermatology and paedophilia. In Cronenberg's "venereal" first two features, *Shivers* (1975) and *Rabid* (1976), a radical form of medical treatment begets a contagion that in turn leads to mass zombie havoc. This is the classic Cronenberg scenario: a scientist – perhaps not mad, exactly, but fervently committed – makes a revolutionary advance in his field of expertise, with spectacularly unintended consequences. In *The Brood* (1979), Samantha Eggar undergoes "psychoplasmic" therapy – whereby mental and emotional trauma takes physical form – and produces scores of deformed, murderous children who prey upon her young (human) daughter. Made after a difficult custody battle between Cronenberg and his former wife, *The Brood* is perhaps the director's most cathartic and autobiographical film.

Following the atypical drag-racing movie *Fast Company* (1979), Cronenberg scored his first solid hit with *Scanners* (1980), an action-driven telepathic thriller with an exploding head as its *pièce de résistance*. In the quintessentially Cronenbergian *Videodrome*, porn-cable station boss Max Renn (James Woods) discovers his television screen is permeable and acquires a gooey, programmable VCR in his abdomen; the film's labyrinthine conspiracy soon gives way entirely to Max's hallucinations. Frenzied by its ideas, its narrative boldly splintered, *Videodrome* marked a creative watermark for the director, who would not make another film from his own original material for seventeen years.

Yet Cronenberg's movies always carried his imprimatur. *The Dead Zone* (1983), in which Christopher Walken wakes from a long coma with newfound psychic powers, was one of the best in a contemporary glut of Stephen King adaptations, and *The Fly* (1986), a loose remake of the 1958 Vincent Price classic, managed to be at once a gruesome shocker (boasting state-of-the-art special effects) and a tender love story. Despite, or because of, its uncompromising horror quotient and philosophical rigour, *The Fly* remains far and away Cronenberg's biggest commercial hit, though its success hardly nudged the director towards profitable complacency.

Financing for *Dead Ringers* (1988) proved difficult, given its tragic, lurid narrative of drug-addicted, co-dependent twin gynaecologists (played by Jeremy Irons in an astonishing double performance), and Cronenberg faced predictable moral opprobrium for his graphic adaptations of epochal "obscene" books: William S. Burroughs' *Naked Lunch* (1991) and J.G. Ballard's *Crash* (1996). In between was his flawed but underrated *M. Butterfly* (1993), adapted from David Henry Hwang's gender-bending hit play.

Cronenberg returned, however briefly, to original-screenplay work with the crafty virtual-reality adventure *eXistenZ* (1999), which glistened with spinal bioports and sticky-icky "game pods". Released around the same time as *The Matrix*, the movie appeared as the smarter, scrappier arthouse cousin to the self-important blockbuster. *Spider* dared to immerse itself in skewed subjective reality, here in service of an empathic, daringly unsentimental depiction of mental illness. Cronenberg won rapturous reviews for his studio-funded neo-Western *A History Of Violence* (2005), continuing a twenty-year roll that's perhaps unrivalled among English-language directors for challenge and consistency. JW

Shivers 1975, 87 min
cast Paul Hampton, Joe Silver, Lynn Lowry, Allan Migicovsky, Susan Petrie, Barbara Steele *cin* Robert Saad *m* Fred Mollin

In Cronenberg's smart and superbly unsettling debut feature (released in the US as *They Came From Within* and also known as *The Parasite Murders*), a faecal-looking parasite wreaks zombie chaos on a Ballardian island apartment complex – the results of a crazed doctor's attempt to create "a combination of aphrodisiac and venereal disease that will hopefully turn the world into one beautiful, mindless orgy".

Videodrome 1982, 87 min
cast James Woods, Sonja Smits, Deborah Harry, Peter Dvorsky, Les Carlson, Jack Creley, Lynne Gorman *cin* Mark Irwin *m* Howard Shore

Seeking new material for his trashy cable station, Max Renn (James Woods) discovers *Videodrome*, a sadomasochistic snuff-movie show that turns out to be a subliminal pirate signal being transmitted as part of a fearsome conspiracy. Expanding Cronenberg's perennial interest in viral transmission and the body as a social and biological battleground, this is his most ingeniously choreographed collision of the provocations of horror and the consolations of philosophy (and vice versa).

The Fly 1986, 92 min
cast Jeff Goldblum, Geena Davis, John Getz, Joy Boushel, Les Carlson, George Chuvalo, David Cronenberg *cin* Mark Irwin *m* Howard Shore

Scientist Seth Brundle (Jeff Goldblum) is on the verge of perfecting his revolutionary "teleportation" technique, but after a fly buzzes into his teleportation pod during a demonstration, he begins transforming into the monstrous Brundlefly, while his anguished girlfriend (Geena Davis) looks on helplessly. This surprise smash hit, aided by Chris Walas's astounding special effects, is an unflinching confrontation of mortality, laying bare the pain of loving someone with a disease that disfigures body and mind.

Crash 1996, 100 min
cast James Spader, Holly Hunter, Elias Kotesa, Deborah Kara Unger, Rosanna Arquette *cin* Peter Suschitzky *m* Howard Shore

After surviving a car accident, ad director James Ballard (James Spader) finds himself drawn to a group of crash-fetishists whose sex drives and death wishes are satisfied at the point of impact, seeking, as their ringleader (Elias Koteas) explains, the "benevolent psychopathology that beckons towards us". This controversial masterpiece is a faithful adaptation of J.G. Ballard's 1973 novel, but it's also vintage Cronenberg, intently tracing the patterns of scars left by the dual impact of technology and sexuality.

Spider 2002, 98 min
cast Ralph Fiennes, Miranda Richardson, Gabriel Byrne, Lynn Redgrave, John Neville, Bradley Hall *cin* Peter Suschitzky *m* Howard Shore

Released from an asylum to a grimy East End halfway house, schizophrenic Spider (Ralph Fiennes) begins sifting his murky memories of a decades-old crime involving his saintly mother (Miranda Richardson), nasty-drunk father (Gabriel Byrne) and Dad's tarty mistress (also played by Richardson). Cronenberg's first-person cinema miraculously externalizes Patrick McGrath's diary of a madman through sight and sound alone, without resorting to a word of bookish voiceover.

A History Of Violence 2005, 96 min
cast Viggo Mortenson, Maria Bello, William Hurt, Ed Harris, Ashton Holmes *cin* Peter Suschitzky *m* Howard Shore

Completely atypical for Cronenberg in its exemplary restraint, this taut thriller-cum-rural *noir* grips from beginning to end. Tom Stall (Viggo Mortenson) is an unlikely local hero who thwarts a robbery in a quiet Indiana diner. But more violence ensues and his small-town American dream is assaulted by mobsters led by a disfigured Carl Fogarty (Ed Harris) intent on proving that bloodshed underpins the idyllic façade. Easily the director's most accessible film for non-aficionados.

Cameron Crowe
US, 1957–

Cameron Crowe's story illustrates the truth that fortune favours the young. While still in his mid-teens, he found a mentor in gonzo rock journalist Lester Bangs and became a reporter for *Rolling Stone* (decades later he recreated his precocious adventures in 2000's autobiographical *Almost Famous*). When Crowe was just 25, his first movie script became the teen-film landmark *Fast Times At Ridgemont High* (1982), and he stuck with high school for his lovable first directing effort, *Say Anything...* (1989), which gave us a romantic hero for the ages in the form of droll kickboxer Lloyd Dobler, the nice guy who gets the girl.

Crowe faltered only when he moved up an age bracket to twentysomethings for the lightweight *Singles* (1992), an episodic, instantly dated portrait of two couples in grunge-era Seattle. Thereafter his films acquired an unpalatable Hollywood-slick coating: *Jerry Maguire* (1996) was a cynical corporate fairy tale (replete with apt catch phrase "Show me the money!"); *Almost Famous* sanitized and sentimentalized decadent 1970s rockers; *Vanilla Sky* (2001), a faithful but incoherent remake of Alejandro Amenábar's *Abre los ojos* (*Open Your Eyes*, 1997), amounted to little more than a worshipful star vehicle for Tom Cruise; *Elizabethtown* (2005) was a romantic comedy set at a Southern wedding. JW

Say Anything... 1989, 100 min

cast John Cusack, Ione Skye, John Mahoney, Joan Cusack, Lili Taylor, Amy Brooks, Pamela Segall, Eric Stoltz, Lois Chiles *cin* Lazlo Kovacs

Recent high-school graduate Lloyd Dobler (John Cusack), a prototype for the early-1990s principled slacker, initiates a romance with a beautiful academic superstar (Ione Skye), causing rifts in her adoring relationship with her ethically compromised father (John Mahoney). Crowe's debut was sweetly optimistic and bitingly funny, and peppered with expertly sketched minor characters.

Alfonso Cuarón
Mexico, 1961–

Many auteurs abandon their home countries – and their better instincts – once they hear the siren call of Hollywood, but Alfonso Cuarón has shifted easily between his native Mexico and the US while maintaining his artistic integrity on both sides of the border. Even when taking over the big-budget franchise of a worldwide blockbuster, his directorial stamp is unmistakable.

Cuarón's raucous Mexico City-set sex comedy *Sólo con tu pareja* (*Love In The Time Of Hysteria*, 1991) was a huge domestic hit and caught the attention of the big American studios. They signed up the young director for two gorgeously photographed adaptations: *A Little Princess* (1995), which won critical acclaim and Oscar recognition but couldn't find a sizable audience, and *Great Expectations* (1998), a chic, faithful update of the Charles Dickens novel.

Returning to Mexico, he collaborated with his brother Carlos (who also wrote *Love In The Time Of Hysteria*) on the screenplay for *Y tu mamá también* (*And Your Mother Too*, 2001), which *Village Voice* critic J. Hoberman memorably described as *Beavis And Butt-head* meets *Jules And Jim*. Cuarón then returned to the US when Warner Bros offered him *Harry Potter And The Prisoner Of Azkaban* (2004). The director freely admitted he hadn't read any of the books or seen the previous films, but his take quickened the pace and added pubescent hormonal frissons to the previously workmanlike franchise. Cuarón received further critical acclaim for *Children Of Men* (2006), a dystopian British sci-fi thriller set in a near future plagued by global human infertility and based on P.D. James's novel of the same name. JW

Y tu mamá también (And Your Mother Too) 2001, 105 min

cast Maribel Verdú, Gael García Bérnal, Diego Luna, Marta Aura, Diana Bracho, Ana López Mercado *cin* Emmanuel Lubezki *m* Liza Richardson

A pair of randy teenagers, wealthy Tenoch (Diego Luna) and working-class Juan (Gael García Bérnal), lure the older, unhappily married Luisa (Maribel Verdú) on a trip to a fabled beach that may or may not exist in Cuarón's horny hothouse of a road movie. The mordant Godardian voiceover provides a socioeconomic context for the hilarious "Mexican Pie" shenanigans, and the poignant last reel reveals that the stakes have been much higher than anticipated.

Children Of Men 2006, 109 min

cast Clive Owen, Michael Caine, Julianne Moore, Claire-Hope Ashitey, Pam Ferris, Danny Huston *cin* Emmanuel Lubezki *m* John Tavener

Probably the best-reviewed mainstream movie of 2006, Cuarón's thrilling, splendidly grubby dystopia is at heart a platonic couple-on-the-run film. Clive Owen's grief-benumbed office drone becomes reanimated when he's called upon to usher the future of mankind – a pregnant woman – to safety through the lawless, war-torn moonscape that England has become. Michael Caine adds heart and humour as a genteel survivalist and pot dealer, but it's the flabbergasting single-take set pieces that make *Children* a singular experience, from a sickening slow-motion escape from a country estate at dawn to the climactic charge through rubble and gunfire. Amazing.

George Cukor
US, 1899–1983

George Cukor was known in his time as a "women's director", a tag that stuck. A quick skim over some of his many films' titles – *Little Women* (1933), *The Women* (1939), *A Woman's Face*, *Two-Faced Woman* (both 1941), *The Actress* (1953), *Les Girls* (1957) – does reveal a filmography with a high oestrogen count. But the label was less a reference to the gender of his protagonists than snide condescension: Cukor specialized in fizzy romantic comedies, with a sideline in tear-jerkers and costume drama; he had a reputation in Hollywood for his acid tongue; and he was gay.

A Broadway director who decided to try his luck in movies during the advent of talkies in the late 1920s, Cukor built his celluloid career largely upon stage and literary adaptations (*Little Women*, *David Copperfield*, 1935, and *Romeo And Juliet*, 1936). His early films employed lengthy medium shots using a stationary or lightly mobile camera, the frames evoking an invisible proscenium (as many early talkies did). He later moved on to more complex tracking and panning shots, including the ninety-degree rotation that became his signature, but he remained essentially cautious in his approach to film grammar and *mise en scène*.

Cukor's witty oeuvre bubbles over with class-conscious satire – most biting in *Dinner At Eight* (1933),

Close colleagues: George Cukor and Katharine Hepburn

Katharine Hepburn fascinated George Cukor. He was openly gay but always discreet, intrigued by the emotional clash between masquerade and reality; she was an androgynous beauty and something of a maverick, both fiercely private and wilfully outspoken. His famed light touch with actresses was never more apparent than in his work with her. While respecting the quirkiness that marked out this old-money nonconformist from other Hollywood stars, the "women's director" also toned down her more stagy affectations, encouraging her to develop nuances that produced some of her finest movie performances.

When he first met Hepburn, trying out for *A Bill Of Divorcement* (1932), the director described the skinny hopeful as a "boa constrictor on a fast". He did, however, recognize her edgy elegance, and used numerous lingering shots of her face to convince audiences that she was beautiful. The result, a striking screen debut, sparked off a relationship that was to last fifty years and encompass ten pictures.

Cukor's *Little Women* (1933), the definitive movie version of Louisa May Alcott's story, gave Hepburn the role she was born to play in the form of tomboy Jo. A volatile friendship developed between actress and director as the movie progressed. Sharing a liberal sensibility and a taste for the subversive, they had high hopes for their next joint venture, the curious *Sylvia Scarlett* (1935), in which Hepburn's character disguises herself as a ragamuffin boy, arousing unsettling sexual desire from the men (including a young Cary Grant) and women around her. The film, though it has since won gay and feminist fans, proved too much for audiences at the time, and was a spectacular flop. Cukor remained relatively unscathed, but Hepburn spent the next few years trying to shake off the label of "box-office poison".

The director brought her some rehabilitation with *Holiday* (1938), in which Hepburn and Grant play kindred spirits who yearn to escape the stuffed-shirt claustrophobia of money-obsessed high society. It's one of Hepburn's subtlest turns, funny, spirited and vulnerable, but it took *The Philadelphia Story* (1940), another sparkling comedy with Cary Grant, to finally win audiences round. Her performance here, while mannered, offers the distinctive combination of sharp and sweet that Cukor found so appealing.

In 1941 Hepburn started an intense, 25-year-long affair with the gruff (married) actor Spencer Tracy, who also became friends with Cukor. The three worked together several times. After the failure of the earnest political melodrama *Keeper Of The Flame* (1942), which led to accusations of communist sympathies, they struck gold with two opposites-attract comedies in the vein of the couple's hit for George Stevens, *Woman Of The Year* (1942). *Adam's Rib* (1949), an articulate battle-of-the-sexes romp about sparring husband-and-wife lawyers, benefits not only from the actors' intimacy and their easy closeness with Cukor, but also from their friendship with the film's scriptwriters Ruth Gordon and Garson Kanin: actors, writers and director were thick as thieves, and it shows. It's tempting to believe we are seeing the real Kate and Spence up there on screen, a fantasy that would have delighted Cukor. *Pat And Mike* (1952), produced by the same dream team, transports the witty repartee and sexual chemistry to the world of sports.

In the 1970s, as earlier films like *Sylvia Scarlett* and Howard Hawks's *Bringing Up Baby* (1938) were re-emerging on the arthouse circuit, Cukor and Hepburn created a gently subversive comment on ageing and gender politics with the Edwardian period piece *Love Among The Ruins* (1975), which also starred Laurence Olivier. It was to be their last great film together. sc

The Women and *The Philadelphia Story* (1940) – and battle-of-the-sexes rounds – the Spencer Tracy and Katharine Hepburn face-offs in *Adam's Rib* (1949) and *Pat And Mike* (1952). A major theme that emerges from his fifty-plus films is the clash or blurring between the private self and its public performance, which is explored in his two spins on the Pygmalion tale – *Born Yesterday* (1950) and *My Fair Lady* (1964). This theme was also visited in *A Double Life* (1947), wherein Ronald Colman plays an actor whose Othello begins to infect his own personality, and in the gender-bending *Sylvia Scarlett* (1935), in which Katharine Hepburn's title character is not the only person transformed when she begins posing as a boy.

Cukor directed the peerless Katharine Hepburn in ten films (including her debut, 1932's *A Bill Of Divorcement*); few other directors so instinctively grasped her tomboy allure, flinty vulnerability and wry, sophisticated wistfulness. Though Cukor once called her an amateur, the pair became formidable allies. Labelled "box-office poison" and having been rejected for the role she coveted most, Scarlett O'Hara, Hepburn joined forces with Cukor, who'd been fired as director of *Gone With The Wind* (1939), to create *The Philadelphia Story*, a glittering consolation prize and one of the best-loved Hollywood movies of any era.

With a pitch-perfect ear for both comic timing and luxuriant pathos, Cukor also guided dozens of other actors – men as well as women – to slews of Oscar nominations and career-best performances, including John and Lionel Barrymore, Judy Garland, Cary Grant, Judy Holliday, James Mason and James Stewart. Greta Garbo named Cukor's *Camille* (1936) her favourite of all her films. Cukor was a pivotal force in MGM's first golden age, but if he must be summed up by a sobriquet, it is surely "*actor's* director". JW

Dinner At Eight 1933, 107 min, b/w
cast Marie Dessler, John Barrymore, Wallace Beery, Jean Harlow, Lionel Barrymore, Billie Burke, Lee Tracy *cin* William Daniels *m* William Axt

Essentially a series of interconnected character vignettes, this snappy Depression-era comedy centres upon a social climber (Billie Burke) who arranges a dinner party for a haughty visiting English couple, but also introduces us to her bankrupt shipping-magnate husband (Lionel Barrymore), their lovelorn daughter and her older lover, a trashy trophy wife and an over-the-hill actress. Deceptively light in tone, it's an equal-opportunities class satire with deep shades of yearning and even tragedy.

Camille 1936, 108 min, b/w
cast Greta Garbo, Robert Taylor, Lionel Barrymore, Elizabeth Allen, Henry Daniell *cin* William H. Daniels *m* Herbert Storhart

Adapted from Alexander Dumas' tragic novel *La dame aux camélias* (1848), *Camille* stars Greta Garbo as a sickly Parisian courtesan torn between two men. With the support of Cedric Gibbons' luxurious sets, costume designer Adrian's gorgeous gowns and a fine supporting cast, Cukor displays his talent for skilfully guiding his leading ladies through their greatest performances in this classic MGM tear-jerker.

The Women 1939, 132 min, b/w
cast Joan Crawford, Norma Shearer, Rosalind Russell, Mary Boland, Joan Fontaine, Paulette Goddard *cin* Oliver T. Marsh *m* Edward Ward, David Snell

Steadfast Mary (Norma Shearer) discovers her wealthy husband is having an affair with social-climbing shop girl Crystal (Joan Crawford), leading to the dubious privilege of her admittance to the poisonous inner circle of backbiting that is the first-wives' club of upper-crust Manhattan. Cukor, the consummate "women's director", helms a peppery script by two women, adapted from a play written by a woman, with a sprightly all-female cast; even the dogs and horses were female, apparently.

The Philadelphia Story 1940, 108 min, b/w
cast Katharine Hepburn, Cary Grant, James Stewart, Ruth Hussey, Roland Young, John Howard *cin* Joseph Ruttenberg *m* Franz Waxman

Imperious high-society princess Tracy (Katharine Hepburn) is due to marry a bit of a bore, but then her scheming ex-husband (Cary Grant) appears on the scene and, after marinating in champagne, Tracy and magazine hack Mike (James Stewart) begin making eyes at each other. Sly, sexy and brimming with frothy dialogue, this is a soulful comedy of remarriage – of second chances, self-recognition and subtle inner transformation; it's both pragmatic and romantic at heart.

A Star Is Born 1954, 169 min
cast Judy Garland, James Mason, Jack Carson, Charles Bickford, Tommy Noonan, Lucy Marlow *cin* Sam Leavitt *m* Harold Arlen

In Cukor's first musical and first colour film, an ambitious ingénue (Judy Garland) marries the alcoholic, over-the-hill actor (James Mason) who facilitated her big Hollywood break, and soon her star is rising in inverse proportion to his embarrassing decline. The troubled Garland, then 32 and looking more than her age, is fruitfully miscast as the fresh-faced newcomer, adding a layer of pathos and desperation to this flawed but fascinating study of mutual self-sacrifice.

Michael Curtiz
Hungary (formerly Austro-Hungarian Empire), 1886–1962

Michael Curtiz (born Mihaly Kertesz) directed films for six decades, starting in 1912 – he had some sixty to his name before he arrived in Hollywood in 1926. Although most of this early work has been lost or forgotten, he was not only prolific but probably Hungary's most respected filmmaker of the period.

Contracted to Warner Bros for most of his career, Curtiz became the studio's most important director. A martinet who paraded around in white breeches and riding boots brandishing a fly whisk, Curtiz was unpopular with actors and crew, who bore the brunt of his mangled English, most famously the injunction on *The Charge Of The Light Brigade* (1936) to "Bring on the empty horses".

Curtiz frequently ran into trouble with studio executives for going over schedule or shooting excessive coverage, but these things are relative: Warner Bros' assembly line was often the quickest among the big studios, overheads were scrupulously monitored and most Curtiz movies were shot in under forty days. Warner Bros recognized that when he went over schedule or budget, it was to build up stronger sequences. In any event, the clipped storytelling that the studio encouraged suited him perfectly.

Curtiz was predisposed towards action more than art. "There is no mind-reader on the lot that can keep ahead of Mike when you turn him loose with machine guns, revolvers, bullets and gas bombs. I think he would rather play cops and robbers than eat", read one internal memo from 1938. When William Keighley fell worryingly behind schedule on *The Adventures Of Robin Hood* (1938), it was to Curtiz that the studio turned. He delivered a massive hit.

Nothing if not versatile, Curtiz ranged freely across melodramas, gangster films, musicals, war pictures, comedies, horror movies and historical dramas. Anyone who loves the Hollywood movies of the Golden Age will harbour fond memories of his work, for instance, James Cagney screaming blue murder as he walked to the electric chair in *Angels With Dirty Faces* (1938) or hoofing his way to an Oscar in the George M. Cohan biopic *Yankee Doodle Dandy* (1942).

Nevertheless, his pragmatism and versatility excluded Curtiz from serious critical study: he was a gifted artisan, not an auteur. There was no dominant theme to his work and with only a couple of notable exceptions – the Elvis Presley vehicle *King Creole* (1958) and the John Wayne Western *The Comancheros* (1961) – the movies he made outside his Warner Bros heyday were undistinguished.

Yet Curtiz was arguably the first of the great action directors – especially in his twelve films with Errol Flynn. His movies felt bigger than their budgets, they had scope and movement. Curtiz was a clean storyteller, with a knack for punching up key dramatic scenes with appropriate expressionist flourishes (see, for example, the use of shadows in Robin Hood's climactic duel with Guy of Gisbourne).

It is entirely appropriate that Curtiz will always be remembered for the quintessential studio film *Casablanca* (1942), with its peculiar mystique as the film classic that fell together almost by accident. If producer Hal B. Wallis called most of the creative shots that really counted, there's no doubt that "casting" Curtiz as director was critical to the film's success (even though William Wyler had been Wallis's first choice). TC

Angels With Dirty Faces 1938, 97 min, b/w

cast James Cagney, Pat O'Brien, Humphrey Bogart, Ann Sheridan, George Bancroft, The Dead End Kids *cin* Sol Polito *m* Max Steiner

Two kids from the slums. One grows up to be a gangster (Cagney); the other a priest (O'Brien). The boys in the old neighbourhood idolize the former, but maybe the Father can persuade his old friend to do something to help? One of five films Curtiz directed in 1938, this classic gangster thriller features an electric performance from James Cagney, nearly subverting the movie's socially responsible message.

The Adventures Of Robin Hood 1938, 111 min

cast Errol Flynn, Olivia de Havilland, Basil Rathbone, Claude Rains, Eugene Pallette *cin* Tony Gaudio *m* Erich Wolfgang Korngold

Curtiz took over the impeccable Hollywood treatment of England's legendary outlaw after William Keighley went over budget. Douglas Fairbanks had set the template back in the 1920s, and Disney and Kevin Costner have had stabs at it since, but this is the version everyone remembers. It's a rousing, bravura entertainment, in gorgeous Technicolor and with a splendid Korngold score. Cagney had been originally cast, but Robin became an aristocrat when Flynn inherited the role, thus neutering any subversive intent.

Casablanca 1942, 102 min, b/w

cast Humphrey Bogart, Ingrid Bergman, Claude Rains, Paul Henreid, Sydney Greenstreet *cin* Arthur Edeson *m* Max Steiner

A chaotic production for which no one harboured any great hopes, this wartime allegory turned out to be a great love story and, for many, the most fondly remembered souvenir of Hollywood's Golden Age. Bogart is Rick Blaine, a committed neutral in Vichy-controlled Morocco; the movie tests the limits of his cynicism by putting the fate of lost love Ilsa (Bergman) and her heroic husband (Henreid) in his lap.

Mildred Pierce 1945, 113 min, b/w

cast Joan Crawford, Jack Carson, Zachary Scott, Eve Arden, Ann Blyth, Bruce Bennett, George Tobias *cin* Ernest Haller *m* Max Steiner

Based on a James M. Cain novel, this is a fascinating fusion of the "women's picture" and *film noir*. In what stands as her greatest role, Joan Crawford is a career woman who pulls herself up through hard work and sheer determination from waitress to restaurateur, but whose drive is also her undoing. Blyth is her Achilles' heel, the spoiled daughter who steals her man. The only surprise is that Rainer Werner Fassbinder never got around to a remake.

D

John Dahl
US, 1956–

Duplicity is the driving force behind John Dahl's dark, cynical films, which at their best buzz along on the jumpy energy of a lie or a con that might just stick. The drifter mistaken for a hit man in *Red Rock West* (1992) keeps his mouth shut, takes the money and runs (or tries to); the *femme fatale* in *The Last Seduction* (1994) does the same with her husband's drug score. (Both of these baroque neo-*noirs* found their audiences on cable before winning a place in cinemas, a release pattern that denied Linda Fiorentino her shoo-in Oscar nomination for *The Last Seduction*.) In *Rounders* (1998), card shark Matt Damon makes a living by marking suckers in poker games; in *Joy Ride* (aka *Roadkill*, 2001), two guys ask for trouble when they prank-call a trucker via CB radio, inviting him to a hotel using a fake coquettish falsetto. Dahl then turned his hand to a World War II POW drama, *The Great Raid* (2005), and a story about a hit man trying to go straight, *You Kill Me* (2007). JW

The Last Seduction 110 min, 1994
cast Linda Fiorentino, Peter Berg, Bill Pullman, J.T. Walsh, Bill Nunn, Herb Mitchell *cin* Jeffrey Jur *m* Joseph Vitarelli

After her sleazy husband (Bill Pullman) scores $700,000 in a drugs sale, scheming bitch Bridget (Linda Fiorentino) steals the money and hides out in a dead-end town. Bridget is as ruthless as a hungry panther, and one of the film's pleasures comes from just how conspicuous this girl on the run makes herself, whether hooking her stilettos into a chain-link fence for al fresco sex or calling out at the bar: "Who do I have to fuck in this town to get a Manhattan?"

Stephen Daldry
UK, 1961–

An award-winning London theatre director, Stephen Daldry made his film debut with *Billy Elliot* (2000), about an 11-year-old boy (Jamie Bell) who gives up boxing lessons in favour of ballet and discovers, with the aid of his disillusioned but encouraging teacher (Julie Walters), that he has real talent. Transcending many of the clichés its plot summary might suggest, *Billy Elliot* enjoyed both critical and commercial success, helping Daldry to earn the director's chair for *The Hours* (2002), an adaptation of Michael Cunningham's Pulitzer Prize-winning novel. The movie won Nicole Kidman the best actress Oscar despite the indignity of a poorly designed prosthetic nose that left her looking even less like Virginia Woolf. *The Hours* evidently marked out Daldry as a page-to-screen man, as he then signed up for the prestigious literary adaptation of Michael Chabon's *The Amazing Adventures Of Kavelier And Clay* (2007). JW

Billy Elliot 2000, 110 min
cast Jamie Bell, Julie Walters, Gary Lewis, Jamie Draven, Jean Heywood, Adam Cooper, Stuart Wells *cin* Brian Tufano *m* Stephen Warbeck

Set against the bleak, hardscrabble background of northeast England during the 1984 miners' strike, *Billy Elliot* (from a semi-autobiographical script by Lee Hall) follows the lead of *Brassed Off!* (1996) and *The Full Monty* (1997) in depicting performance as a viable escape from post-industrial blight and oppressive macho norms. The film hinges on Jamie Bell's feisty, vulnerable turn as Billy, whose fledgling love for ballet puts him at odds with his on-strike miner dad.

The Hours 2002, 115 min
cast Nicole Kidman, Julianne Moore, Meryl Streep, Stephen Dillane, Miranda Richardson, George Loftus *cin* Seamus McGarvey *m* Philip Glass

Decisive days in the lives of three women: in 1923, Virginia Woolf (Nicole Kidman) embarks on writing *Mrs Dalloway*; a stifled 1950s housewife (Julianne Moore) makes her husband's birthday cake; and a present-day New Yorker (Meryl Streep) plans a fête for her AIDS-stricken friend. The streamlining of Michael Cunningham's homage to Woolf is elegant and well performed, but literal-minded and pitched at the level of melodrama, sacrificing the novel's subtleties of characterization for outsize feminine cliché.

Frank Darabont
France, 1959–

Frank Darabont may plunder generic clichés, but he does so to intense effect. Beginning as production assistant on the cheap shocker *Hell Night* (1981), he decorated the sets on Ken Russell's *Crimes Of Passion* (1984), pitching scripts all the while. He was called in to rewrite *Nightmare On Elm Street 3: Dream Warriors* (1984), co-wrote the screenplay for Kenneth Branagh's *Mary Shelley's Frankenstein* (1994) and became an in-demand script doctor, working on films such as *Saving Private Ryan* (1998). Darabont's genre activities paid off in his directorial debut *The Shawshank Redemption* (1994), adapted from the Stephen King novel of the same name.

It is significant that his first film fared less well at the US box office than it has on home entertainment formats. *The Green Mile* (1999) and *The Majestic* (2001), neither falling below 140 minutes, remain well suited to television, having the staying power of afternoon matinées. His movies faithfully deploy the archetypes of the past. Indeed, Darabont has likened pitching to Hollywood executives to being a punch-drunk fighter in a classic boxing picture. Turning from Warner Bros to Preston Sturges's Paramount Pictures for *The Majestic* (2001), Darabont's movie cast Jim Carrey as a blacklisted screenwriter who shows up in an apple-pie Californian suburb and is mistaken for a local war hero. In 2007, he filmed his fourth Stephen King adaptation, *The Mist*, in which a small town is besieged by carnivorous creatures following a freak storm.

Perhaps Hollywood's most watchable nostalgist, Frank Darabont has established a brand of back-to-basics populism that has won over audiences and the Academy alike – he was the first director to be nominated for a best picture Oscar for his first two films. RA

The Shawshank Redemption 1994, 142 min
cast Tim Robbins, Morgan Freeman, Bob Gunton, William Sadler, Clancy Brown, Gil Bellows *cin* Roger Deakins *m* Thomas Newman

Based on Stephen King's modern tale of good and evil, this account of Tim Robbins' quiet man accused of murder combines gruelling incarceration scenes with nostalgia for the "quality" picture of Hollywood's past. Darabont revels in genre iconography – from Rita Hayworth to the old-timer's pet mouse.

The Green Mile 1999, 189 min
cast Tom Hanks, David Morse, Bonnie Hunt, James Cromwell, Michael Clarke Duncan *cin* David Tattershall *m* Thomas Newman

Owing as much to a James Cagney flick as to the metaphysics of Stephen King's source novel, *The Green Mile* stars Tom Hanks as a prison warden who reminisces about the time he spent overseeing a gentle giant (Michael Clark Duncan) on death row in 1935. Only Fred and Ginger can alleviate Duncan's eternal suffering.

The Dardenne Brothers
Jean-Pierre Dardenne: Belgium, 1951–
Luc Dardenne: Belgium, 1954–

The universe of the Dardennes brothers – one of austerity, poverty and crime – is a world away from the mussels and beer stereotypes of theme-bar Belgium. Brought up in the dilapidated steel town of Seraing which provides the brutal, post-industrial backdrop to most of their dramas, the working-class brothers took up documentary-making in the late 1970s, before moving into fiction in 1986 with

Tim Robbins ponders his next move with fellow inmate Morgan Freeman in "quality" picture *The Shawshank Redemption*.

121

Falsch (*False*). Their third feature film, *La promesse* (*The Promise*, 1996), hoisted the siblings onto the world stage, and they have since won the Palme d'Or twice.

The Dardennes' films are characterized by a certain raw energy and by similar themes, settings and visual idioms. Their characters exist on the margins of society – black marketeers, illegal immigrants, minimum-wage earners – and are locked into painful, unresolved issues with either their parents or their children. *La promesse* refers to the promise a teenager makes to the widow of an African worker that sets him on a collision course with his father, a sleazy trafficker in human trade. *Rosetta* (1999), the brothers' first Cannes winner, follows a spunky, damaged young girl trying to deal with her alcoholic, trailer-trash mother. In *Le fils* (*The Son*, 2002) a father reluctantly teaches carpentry to the boy who murdered his son, while in *L'enfant* (*The Child*, 2005) a small-time hood nonchalantly sells his own baby on the black market.

Frequently wordless, the characters in these films regularly communicate in gestures or rapid movements. The camera operator in *Rosetta* and *Le fils* often has to sprint to catch up with them, and this perpetual motion becomes improbably hypnotic, like Robert Bresson on the run. As a result, the audience becomes just as familiar with the napes of characters' necks or the back of their heads as with their faces. Yet the Dardennes still elicit a strong empathy from their audience; so much so, in fact, that the Belgian government passed the "Rosetta Plan" in 1999 to protect young people on the minimum wage, following publicity generated by the film, *Rosetta*. LH

Rosetta 1999, 95 min

cast Emilie Dequenne, Fabrizio Rongione, Anne Yerrnaux, Olivier Gourmet *cin* Alain Marcoen *m* Jean-Pierre Cocco

The surprise winner of the Palme d'Or at the 1999 Cannes Film Festival, *Rosetta* introduced the Dardennes brothers' uncompromising style to a wider audience. The camera stays resolutely on the back of a 17-year-old tearaway as she deals with the rank squalor that is her day-to-day existence, hoping to find a job that will give her a normal life. Impetuous and stoic, her task becomes painfully Sisyphean at times, but the audience is with her every step of the way.

Le fils (The Son) 2002, 104 min

cast Olivier Gourmet, Morgan Marinne, Isabella Soupart, Nassim Hassaïni, Kevin Leroy, Félicien Pitsaer, Rémy Renaud *cin* Alain Marcoen

Opening, in typical Dardennes mode, on the back of the protagonist's head, the camera stays loyally by his side for the next 104 minutes. This unusual point of view means that we know more about the character's bald spot than his state of mind and can only hazard a guess at his motivations for befriending his son's killer, which in turn seem paternal, sexual and vengeful. This *faux-naïf* method artlessly builds to an edge-of-your-seat level of suspense worthy of Hitchcock.

Julie Dash
US, 1952–

One of just a handful of black women directors working in the American film industry, New York-born Julie Dash studied filmmaking on both American coasts, under William Friedkin among others. Her signature film, the exotic *Daughters Of The Dust* (1991), was the first full-length film directed by an African-American woman to get a general theatrical release in the US. That fact alone has guaranteed Dash a place in the history books, but much of her work has been worthy, competent and sadly forgettable.

Dash's résumé prior to making *Daughters* reflects a typical struggling filmmaker's eclectic mix of personal projects and jobs for hire. Her student film, *Diary Of An African Nun* (1971), offered a visually striking, monochrome adaptation of a short story by novelist Alice Waters. The director's outlook grew out of a very 1970s and 80s women's studies mindset, and both this first film and her subsequent work seem to connect with or celebrate black female icons, such as the black actresses of her AFI graduation film *Illusions* (1982). Her 1975 dance film *Four Women* was inspired by the Nina Simone song of the same name, *Phyllis Wheatly* (1989) was a short film about a nineteenth-century writer, and the TV drama *The Rosa Parks Story* (2002) was about the famous civil rights activist who fought against racial segregation. Given her determination to retain complete artistic control of her films, Dash has continued to struggle to find funding for her works and her recent career has yet to match the heights of *Daughters Of The Dust*. LF

Daughters Of The Dust 1991, 112 min

cast Cora Lee Day, Alva Rogers, Barbara-O, Trula Hossier, Umar Abdurrahamn *cin* A. Jaffa Fielder *m* John Barnes

Dash's best and most distinctive work is a labour of love years in the making that paradoxically takes place over one day. The film is set on one of the Gullah islands off the Georgia and South Carolina coast, circa 1902, and an unborn child acts as narrator as a group of African-American women prepare for a family celebration. Although a narrative fiction, *Daughters* has an ethnographic quality, capturing the islanders' unique way of life and distinct patois, poised culturally somewhere between Africa, Europe and the US.

Jules Dassin
US, 1911–

He was called the first American neo-realist, though in truth Dassin worked best within the framework of the thriller. It was a genre he inflected with location shooting and a social conscience, before his career was derailed by the House Un-American Activities Committee witch-hunts. Nevertheless, Dassin was able to pick up the pieces in Europe, where he would make his home in France and Greece.

With a string of mediocre B-movies to his name, Dassin hit his stride only after the revelation of Roberto Rossellini's *Rome, Open City* (1945) and a propitious meeting with producer Mark Hellinger, an influential New York newspaper columnist whose friends included Al Capone, Bugsy Siegel and Dutch Schultz. Hellinger had produced *High Sierra* (1941) and *The Killers* (1946), among others, and he and Dassin hit it off immediately.

Their first collaboration was *Brute Force* (1947), a hard-hitting prison movie written by Richard Brooks. A police thriller, *The Naked City* (1948), came next. Sadly, the heavy-drinking Hellinger died of a heart attack before the film's release. He was 44 years old. According to Dassin, the studio excised sequences emphasizing the poverty gap in the city – the screenwriter Albert Maltz was one of the Hollywood Ten, and Dassin himself was under suspicion as a potential Communist sympathizer. He made one more movie in Hollywood – *Thieves' Highway* (1949) – before being named before HUAC by director Edward Dmytryk in 1952 and forced into exile. He went first to Britain (where he made *Night And The City*, 1950), then France, before finally settling in Greece and marrying actress Melina Mercouri. He did, however, return to the US to make the civil rights ghetto thriller *Upright!* (1968).

By his own estimation, Dassin was "lucky". He was only out of work for five years. Invited to adapt a sordid crime novel by Auguste Le Breton, Dassin transformed it into what François Truffaut called "the best *film noir* I have ever seen". That may be hyperbole, but *Rififi* (1955) remains a classic heist movie, not least for the brilliantly staged 28-minute near-silent robbery sequence at its heart. The film was a tremendous success, and Dassin would make another dozen European films, mostly in Greece. Only a few of the later films have been widely seen: the brassy *Never On A Sunday*, starring his wife, Mercouri (1960); and another flashy caper movie, *Topkapi* (1964). Looking back, however, it's easy to feel that Dassin forfeited his most creative years to the blacklist. TC

The Naked City 1948, 96 min, b/w

cast Barry Fitzgerald, Howard Duff, Dorothy Hart, Don Taylor, Frank Conroy, Ted de Corsia *cin* William H. Daniels *m* Miklós Rósza, Frank Skinner

Producer Mark Hellinger persuaded Universal that they had to shoot this semi-documentary-style policier on the streets of New York. It was a seminal move, and guaranteed what now looks like a fairly routine thriller its place as a footnote in the history of American filmmaking. (According to Dassin, Hellinger lost several battles that would have made the film more political.) Fitzgerald is the police detective on a manhunt for a murderer. A well-known TV series followed belatedly.

Thieves' Highway 1949, 94 min, b/w

cast Richard Conte, Valentina Cortese, Lee J. Cobb, Barbara Lawrence, Jack Oakie *cin* Norbert Brodine *m* Alfred Newman

This unjustly neglected *film noir* got a boost recently when Criterion issued it on DVD. Based on a semi-autobiographical novel by Al Bezzerides (*Kiss Me Deadly*), who also scripted, it tells the story of Nico (Conte), a war veteran, who returns home to find his father has been crippled by a racketeer in the California fruit trade (Cobb). Nico goes into the trucking trade himself to exact his revenge. Certainly Dassin's best American film.

Night And The City 1950, 100 min, b/w

cast Richard Widmark, Gene Tierney, Googie Withers, Francis L. Sullivan, Herbert Lom *cin* Max Greene *m* Benjamin Frankel, Franz Waxman

Dassin transformed London into an expressionist *noir* mantrap in this compelling thriller. It has a great central character in Richard Widmark's relentless hustler Harry Fabian, whose constant wheeling and dealing catches up with him when his attempts to muscle in on the wrestling circuit backfire. Even if the baroque style feels over-determined, it represents some sort of a notional link between the worlds of Charles Dickens and Raymond Chandler.

Rififi (Du rififi chez les hommes) 1955, 117 min, b/w

cast Jean Servais, Carl Möhner, Robert Manuel, Perlo Vita, Magali Noël *cin* Philippe Agostini *m* Georges Auric

Relocated to Paris, Dassin took on a sordid heist novel as an assignment and crafted this expert and highly influential thriller. Famous for the superbly choreographed safe-breaking sequence, the film is more concerned with the fallout from the job as the plan falls apart. (*The Asphalt Jungle* must have been an influence here.) Dassin also appears as expert safe-cracker Cesar le Milanais (under the pseudonym Perlo Vita).

Delmer Daves
US,1904–77

Although writer-director Delmer Daves turned his hand to almost everything, only one or two films of his have passed into the canon. Graduating from Stanford University with a law degree, Daves fitted in a stint as a prop boy on Cruze's *The Covered Wagon* (1923). Following acting chores and advising on college settings, he collaborated on stories and screenplays, including Humphrey Bogart's breakthrough *The Petrified Forest* (1936). With the submarine drama *Destination Tokyo* (1943), he became a director, although he also wrote, produced and directed for studios as disparate as Warner Bros, Fox and MGM.

A feeling for people suffuses the 1945 propaganda piece *Pride Of The Marines*, in which John Garfield played a blind war hero. *Dark Passage* (1947) was an under-appreciated Bogart and Bacall *film noir* in tune with the post-war fad for authentic settings and fraught psychology. *The Red House* (1947) is perhaps Daves's most complex film, a melodrama bubbling with intimations of incest, necrophilia and violence. It is dominated by Edward G. Robinson's performance.

Daves is best known for a string of 1950s Westerns. *3:10 To Yuma* (1957) was arguably his best film. *Broken Arrow* (1950) was pioneering in its sympathetic presentation of Native Americans. *The Last Wagon* (1956) revolved around Richard Widmark's vengeful trapper on a journey increasingly evoking those of the Mann-Stewart Westerns of the period. Advertised as "Authentic Greatness", the Jack Lemmon vehicle *Cowboy* (1958) found a hotel clerk broken in on a cattle drive with a grizzled Glenn Ford. Delmer Daves's high points generally reflected industry fashion. With hindsight, he epitomizes the classical Hollywood workhorse pro. RA

The Red House 1947, 100 min, b/w
cast Edward G. Robinson, Lon McCallister, Allen Roberts, Judith Anderson, Rory Calhoun, Julie London *cin* Bert Glennon *m* Miklós Rózsa

One of the most psychoanalytically fraught films of its era. In this melange of incest, necrophilia and rampant possessiveness, Edward G. Robinson plays a paraplegic old man desperate to keep his daughter's young man from touching her, while outside something lurks in the woods. Overwrought – and all the better for it.

3:10 To Yuma 1957, 92 min, b/w
cast Glenn Ford, Van Heflin, Felicia Farr, Leora Dana, Henry Jones, Richard Jaeckel, Robert Emhardt *cin* Charles Lawton Jr *m* George Duning

In this intense drama, Daves effortlessly juggles claustrophobic interiors with the drama of parched soil and close-ups with crane shots. Van Heflin is the dirt farmer in financial strife who is paid to escort a murderous outlaw (Glenn Ford) on the train to the state penitentiary at Yuma.

Terence Davies
UK, 1945–

Arguably the most important British filmmaker of his generation, Terence Davies is a poet of the cinema, at once austere and passionate. Despite (or because of) this, he has struggled to find support for his work, especially since the production arm of the British Film Institute closed down in the early 1990s.

Born into a Catholic, working-class family in Liverpool, Davies was abused by his violent father (who died when he was 6), and bullied at school for his homosexuality. He found succour in a close relationship with his mother, and in escaping to the movies, especially Hollywood musicals and melodramas of the 1950s. These formative experiences remain the prevailing influences in his own, very personal films. Davies was in his early thirties when he made the first in what became the autobiographical "Terence Davies Trilogy", comprising *Children* (1976), *Madonna And Child* (1980) and *Death And Transfiguration* (1983), which were released as a single 85-minute feature in 1984.

Davies developed a process dependent on meticulously designed shots, tableau-like evocations of memory linked by emotional (and musical) association more than narrative chronology. These might be elaborate crane shots, or apparently simple close-ups, like a shot of the light falling across a piece of carpet, held for minutes in *The Long Day Closes* (1992). Although the 1950s childhood evoked in both *Distant Voices, Still Lives* (itself a diptych, 1988) and *The Long Day Closes* is in many ways painful and even harrowing, the films transcend social realism and self-pity in their distilled stylization, their loving recreation of time and space, and moments of intense communal joy (often involving song, cinema, or even slapstick comedy). Their combination of art-film style and reverence for working-class popular culture is unique in British cinema.

When he adapted John Kennedy Toole's Southern Baptist memoir *The Neon Bible* in 1995 there was a suspicion he was revisiting familiar themes once too often (despite the obvious cultural difference). But his Edith Wharton adaptation, *The House Of Mirth* (2000), was a triumph, recreating nineteenth-century New York's "polite society" on Edinburgh locations, and casting *X Files* star Gillian Anderson on the strength of her resemblance to the paintings of John Singer Sargent. TC

Distant Voices, Still Lives 1988, 84 min
cast Peter Postlethwaite, Freda Dowie, Angela Walsh, Dean Williams, Lorraine Ashbourne, Sally Davies *cin* William Diver, Patrick Duval *m* Sammy Fain

The first of two autobiographical features recreating Davies' childhood in Liverpool in the 1940s and 50s. A genre unto themselves, they unfold as memory in a series of stylized vignettes, both rigorously ascetic and profoundly humanist. *Distant Voices* is dominated by the violently abusive father figure (Peter Postlethwaite) who lords it over the household. Wives and daughters – and Davies' own surrogate – find respite and communion in sing-alongs at the pub.

The House Of Mirth 2000, 140 min
cast Gillian Anderson, Eric Stoltz, Dan Aykroyd, Eleanor Bron, Laura Linney, Anthony LaPaglia, Johdi May *cin* Remi Adefarasin

Every inch a match for Scorsese's *Age Of Innocence* (1993), Davies' Edith Wharton adaptation is a subtle but devastating critique of social exclusion and hypocrisy. Working on a bigger scale, with a starry cast, Davies retained the emotional intensity of his earlier films while delivering a more linear narrative. In her best big-screen role, Anderson is the New York socialite who is ostracized on the basis of rumours and innuendo – and because of her own strength of character.

Robert Day
UK, 1922–

Having worked in TV from 1956, Robert Day debuted with *The Green Man* (1956), drawn from a script by the British writing, producing and directing team of Frank Launder and Sidney Gilliat (adapting their own play, *Meet A Body*). This delicious black comedy, in the vein of the previous year's *The Ladykillers*, finds watchmaker and sometime assassin Hawkins (Alistair Sim) struggling to complete his assignment to blow up a pompous politician.

Day was at ease in any genre, be it Ealing-style comedy, horror flick, mythological epic (1965's *She*, based on an H. Rider Haggard story), prison-escape farce (1960's *Two Way Stretch* with Peter Sellers) or Tarzan movie (five of which he made in the 1960s). His most fruitful collaboration may have been with Boris Karloff, with whom he made two frighteners set in Victorian London: *The Grip Of The Strangler* (1958), with Karloff as a socially conscious novelist investigating the Haymarket Strangler, and *Corridors Of Blood* (1962), with Karloff as a doctor who becomes addicted to the anaesthetic gas he's invented and subsequently becomes enmeshed with a gang of murderers. Intriguingly, Day also worked with comedian Tony Hancock on *The Rebel* (1961), and made *The Man With Bogart's Face* (1980) as his quirky swansong. JW

Corridors Of Blood (The Doctor Of Seven Dials) 1962, 86 min, b/w

cast Boris Karloff, Betta St John, Finlay Currie, Francis Matthews, Adrienne Corri, Christopher Lee, Francis de Wolff *cin* Geoffrey Faithfull *m* Buxton Orr

Humanitarian Dr Thomas Bolton (Boris Karloff) loses his research notes to a macabre ring of killers-for-profit, who blackmail the doctor into helping them sell corpses to the local hospital. Day conjures a brooding, repressive ambience, aided by then-ascendant Hammer Films star Christopher Lee in a small but indelible turn as the villainous Resurrection Joe.

Basil Dearden
UK, 1911–71

Dearden has come to represent all the verities of classical British cinema. If the much-vaunted "social problem" aesthetic of his films now looks rather creaky, at the time it seemed tough-minded and assertive.

After West End theatre, Dearden went to the Ealing studios of his producer/mentor Basil Dean, where he began co-directing comedies with star Will Hay – including his finest, *My Learned Friend* (1943). After his solo directorial debut, *The Bells Go Down* (1943), Dearden began a long association with producer/screenwriter Michael Relph. This led to a bold attempt to use mainstream aesthetics to treat "difficult" issues. Films like *Frieda* (1947), looking at a community's response to a "good German", *The Blue Lamp* (1950), examining juvenile gun crime and *Victim* (1961) are most provocative when the rigid narrative strains to contain its ideological contradictions.

Some time before the "Angry Young Men" of the late 1950s and early 60s tackled social realism, Dearden's films touched upon issues such as the probation service (*I Believe In You*, 1951), delinquency (*Violent Playground*, 1958) and race (*Sapphire*, 1959). The director also demonstrated a sure hand with comedy (*The Smallest Show On Earth*, 1957) and the crime caper (*The League Of Gentlemen*, 1960), but his Hollywood epic *Khartoum* (1965), starring Charlton Heston, showed more assurance than flair. Arguably, many of Dearden's best films laid the groundwork for the television realism of the 1960s. RA

My Learned Friend 1943, 76 min, b/w

cast Will Hay, Claude Hulbert, Mervyn Johns, Ernest Thesiger, Charles Victor, Hy Hazell, Lloyd Pearson *cin* Wilkie Cooper *m* Ernest Irving

Frantic and inspired, Will Hay's last movie (which he co-directed) finds his incompetent barrister trying to save himself and a group of witnesses from insane murderer Grimshaw (Mervyn Johns), who is determined to eliminate all those responsible for putting him behind bars. The final scene on top of Big Ben makes a suitably demented climax.

Victim 1961, 100 min, b/w

cast Dirk Bogarde, Sylvia Syms, John Barrie, Peter McEnery, Anthony Nicholls, Dennis Price *cin* Otto Heller *m* Philip Green

The most notorious of the Dearden/Relph "social problem" films, this story of a London barrister compromised by a past homosexual indiscretion scratches beneath the refined surfaces of post-war Britain. (Homosexuality was illegal in the UK until 1967.) Dirk Bogarde bravely risked his pin-up status by portraying the solicitor torn between marital respectability and the lure of the underworld.

Alex de la Iglesia
Spain, 1965–

Genre flame-thrower Alex de la Iglesia has launched his combustible brand of slapstick ultraviolence and black-comic mayhem into the realms of the superhero adventure, the Satanic procedural, the spaghetti Western and more, deranging and mutating each genre into a shape that's unmistakably Iglesian. His first short film won the esteem of Pedro and Agustín Almodóvar, who produced his debut feature, *Acción mutante* (*Mutant Action*, 1991), about physically and mentally handicapped terrorists who wage a guerrilla war against the thin, gorgeous and healthy. Iglesia turned the tired priest-versus-Satan thriller on its head with the unrelentingly brutal *The Day Of The Beast* (1995), a big critical and commercial success in Spain that belatedly won an American release in 1999.

Plot outlines only give a hint of the chaos, carnage and emotional sadism of an Iglesia film – though 2002's spaghetti Western riff *800 Bullets* did show the director's sentimental side, and all of his movies sparkle with a certain poptastic charm. In *Perdita durango* (*Dance With The Devil*, 1997), tough chick

Perdita (Rosie Perez) and her malevolent foetus-trafficking mate Romeo (Javier Bardem) drive from borderland Mexico to Las Vegas after kidnapping a young couple for use in a human sacrifice. In the chamber piece *La comunidad* (*Common Wealth*, 2000), Carmen Maura plays a real estate agent who discovers a fortune in a dead man's house and comes into macabre conflict with the man's neighbours. In *Crimen ferpecto* (*The Perfect Crime* , 2004), a homely wage slave seizes on a department store murder as a blackmail opportunity.

La comunidad and *The Perfect Crime* wear Hitchcock's influence on their tattered sleeves; indeed, all of Iglesia's work is as frantic with references to other films as a blood-soaked Quentin Tarantino pastiche. His evident love of cinema and his meta-movie tropes, combined with his singularly unhinged bravado, have attracted the attention of cult-flick mavens, but they've also earned establishment stamps of approval: *The Day Of The Beast* won six Goya Awards (the Spanish equivalent of the Oscars) and in 2002, the Film Society of Lincoln Center in New York gave Iglesia a retrospective. JW

The Day Of The Beast (El dia de la bestia) 1995, 104 min

cast Alex Angulo, Armando De Razza, Santiago Segura, Terele Pávez, Nathalie Seseña, Jaime Blanch *cin* Flavio Martinez Labiano *m* Battista Lena

Iglesia's breakthrough hit in his native Spain pits the naïve but determined Father Angel (Alex Angulo) against the forces of evil after he concludes that the Antichrist will be born in Madrid on Christmas Day. Fighting fire with fire, the Padre steals, brawls and seeks the blood of a virgin in his race against time. Hypercharged with concussive violence and film references, the movie is at heart a hilarious slapstick comedy.

Jean Delannoy
France, 1908–

When exponents of the *nouvelle vague* railed against the old guard, they had Jean Delannoy in mind. The brother of silent actress Henriette Delannoy, he entered films in the 1920s as an actor before working his way up via editor and maker of shorts to his first feature, *Paris-Deauville* (1935). In the mid-1940s he hit his stride with *L'éternel retour* (*Love Eternal*, 1943) and *La symphonie pastorale* (1946), which remain elegant paradigms for the mainstream marriage of image and sentiment. The latter, an intensely correct analysis of the consequences of pastor Pierre Blanchar's love for blind ward Michèle Morgan, won the Grand Prix at Cannes. Delannoy's 1950 critique of organized religion, *Dieu a besoin des hommes* (*God Needs Men*), shared the International Prize at Venice, but his other post-war work – *Les jeux sont faits* (*The Chips*

Are Down, 1947), *La minute de vérité* (*The Moment Of Truth*, 1952) – seemed starry but tired. Closely involved throughout his career with screenwriters such as Jean Aurenche and Pierre Bost – the bane of François Truffaut and associates – the official line on Delannoy accuses him of emotional frigidity. But after the ragged excesses of early Godard, his restraint can be a tonic. RA

L'éternel retour (Love Eternal) 1943, 123 min, b/w

cast Madeleine Sologne, Jean Marais, Jean Murat, Junie Astor, Pierre Piéral, Yvonne de Bray, Jane Marken *cin* Roger Hubert *m* Georges Auric

Written by Jean Cocteau, this tale of the love between two people united even in death has a mythic charge, deriving as much from its brooding *mise en scène* in a castle overlooking the sea as from the performances of Jean Marais and the impossibly beautiful Madeleine Sologne. These blond creatures drift wraith-like through their passion, and the film was accused of collaborationist politics after World War II. Today, however, its energies seem more redolent of a sublime metaphysics.

Guillermo del Toro
Mexico, 1964–

Approaching fanboy genre fare with all the jokey seriousness of a Marvel-comic scribe, Guillermo del Toro marries science fiction to horror while adding auteurist motifs – his inner entomologist and zealous Catholic upbringing surface again and again in his imagery and symbolism. He has tried with increasing success to alternate mainstream crowd pleasers with more arthouse pursuits: he followed *Cronos* (1993), a densely atmospheric retinkering of the vampire myth, with the schlocky bugs-amok thriller *Mimic* (1997), his sole unhappy venture with the ever-meddlesome Miramax studio. After *The Devil's Backbone* (2001), a gripping historical ghost story with intonations of Victor Erice's great *The Spirit Of The Beehive* (1973), del Toro embarked on a series of high-grossing comic-book adaptations, and returned to the arthouse for the ambitious, Oscar-winning phantasmagoria *Pan's Labyrinth* (2006).

Fittingly for a director who has pursued a somewhat recombinant career, del Toro's films tend to focus on hybrid, human-ish creatures caught between species or worlds: the undead seller of antique clocks in *Cronos*, the nasty superbreed of insect that can impersonate an average New York commuter in *Mimic*, the vengeance-seeking spirit of a child in *The Devil's Backbone*, the half-vampire hero of *Blade II* (2002), the mythological menagerie of *Pan's Labyrinth*, and the demonic superhero of *Hellboy* (2004), a bright-red beast who's a franchise in the making and is evidently close to del Toro's pulpy heart. JW

The Devil's Backbone (El espinazo del diablo) 2001, 106 min

cast Marisa Paredes, Eduardo Noriega, Federico Luppi, Fernando Tielve, Iñigo Garcés, Irene Visedo cin Guillermo Navarro m Javier Navarrete

Towards the bitter end of the Spanish Civil War, the orphan Carlos (Fernando Tielve) arrives at an isolated boys school, where myriad menaces include an anguished bully, encroaching Fascism and the ghost of a pupil who died during the air raid that the school and its personnel survived untouched. Its air thick with foreboding, the violence of this mournful film crescendoes to become a veiled elegy for the Spanish Republic.

Hellboy 2004, 122 min

cast Ron Perlman, John Hurt, Selma Blair, Rupert Evans, Karel Roden, Jeffrey Tambor, Doug Jones cin Guillermo Navarro m Marco Beltrami

Fire-engine red with horns, a tail and a boulder-sized right hand, Hellboy (del Toro regular Ron Perlman) is a 60-year-old adolescent originally summoned from the infernal depths by the Nazis but raised as a force for good. The film's CGI wizardry often overwhelms the story's scrappy outsider charm, but *Hellboy* is certainly one of the more idiosyncratic among the pantheon of mutant superhero movies.

Strange meeting: Ivana Baquero as Ofelia gets her instructions from the faun Pan

Pan's Labyrinth (El laberinto del fauno) 2006, 119 min

cast Ivana Baquero, Maribel Verdú, Sergi López, Doug Jones cin Guillermo Navarro m Javier Navarrete

The Spanish Civil War provides the backdrop for this frightening child's-eye fairy tale, shot through with strains of *Alice In Wonderland*. After her mother marries an intimidating military man, grave-faced Ofelia wanders from their creepy, creaky new home into an elaborate underground lair, where the titular faun assigns the young girl three dangerous quests – which double as opportunities for del Toro

to unleash all the metamorphizing powers of his imagination. The film is all the more disturbing and enchanting for its refusal to draw a line between reality and nightmare.

Cecil B. DeMille
US, 1881–1959

Depending on your point of view, master vulgarian Cecil B. DeMille is either a calculating cynic or an eager-to-please showman. Banking on cinema audiences' bottomless appetites for sex and lavish spectacle, he won big over and over again, nabbing his best-picture Oscar for the circus epic, *The Greatest Show On Earth* (1952), a title just grandiose enough to befit the trash balladeer's career.

DeMille was a literal Hollywood pioneer, shooting the first feature-length Western, *The Squaw Man* (1914), in what was then just another rural California town. Within a few years, DeMille was a specialist in leering sex comedies that burst with conspicuous consumption and intemperate passion, revelling in greed and lust before wagging the finger of condemnation at both (or, as film historian Philip Kemp puts it, "preaching virtue, while giving audiences a good long look at vice"). He could even work one of his patented bathtub scenes into an eighteenth-century Western like *Unconquered* (1947), one of several bloated "oaters" and outdoor expeditions he made with Gary Cooper.

Especially in later films, such as the sudsy biblical fandango *Samson And Delilah* (1949), the primacy of spectacle – gigantic sets, swarms of extras, ponderous declamation instead of dialogue – snuffs out most of the spontaneous signs of life. *The Ten Commandments* (1956) remade his 1923 silent of the same name and added a decidedly impudent publicity blitz (across America, DeMille unveiled thousands of granite monuments inscribed with the Ten Commandments). The director himself dubbed the film's golden calf set piece "an orgy Sunday-school children can watch" – perfectly encapsulating the brazen DeMille mix of the pious and the tawdry. JW

The rise and fall of the ancient epic

Every time old Hollywood made an epic, it was holding up a mirror to itself. It's not difficult to see why an empire run on the whims of tyrants and built upon violence, excess and ruthless conquest would appeal to studio moguls. But, in charting the rise and fall of potentates and empires, the studios planted the seeds of their own destruction.

Although the Roman superspectacle epic had its origins in Italy, with films such as the silent classic *Cabiria* (1914), Cecil B. DeMille spearheaded the genre in Hollywood with *The Ten Commandments* (1923) and *King Of Kings* (1927). DeMille was the director who most fluently articulated the paradoxes of the Roman epic by both piously castigating and blatantly emulating the worst of the Roman Empire's excesses. Following in his footsteps, Fred Niblo directed *Ben-Hur: A Tale Of The Christ* (1925), which was heralded as the most expensive film ever made with its $4 million budget and a cast apparently numbering 125,000. Thousands of extras (later known as "DeMillions") were a *sine qua non* of the genre, along with a disingenuous blend of sex, violence and righteous sermonizing. The standard-bearer of all this profitable hypocrisy was DeMille's *Sign Of The Cross* (1932), which was full to its sanctimonious brim with nudity, orgies, lesbians, torture, Christian-eating lions and Charles Laughton in all his louche glory as Nero.

The genre rumbled along in the 1930s with *The Last Days Of Pompeii* (1935), but by the 1940s, ancient epics seemed to have gone the way of the Romans. However, DeMille once again proved to be a miracle worker, bringing the epic back from the dead with *Samson And Delilah* (1949), which made more filthy lucre than any other movie that year. And the floodgates opened. The 1950s and early 1960s were the golden age of flamboyance and antiquity. The studios now had an economic reason for their extravagance, as they were pitched in desperate combat with the television set. They tried to strike a fatal blow to their enemy with their new weapons, CinemaScope and VistaVision (not to mention colour), and the religious epic *The Robe* (1953) was the first movie to be filmed in the wide, open spaces of CinemaScope. The studio moguls believed that epic movies could give the public something that TV could not: the spectacle of miraculous special effects, jaw-dropping panoramas and awe-inspiring set pieces, not to mention the sly eroticism of all those togas, orgies and diaphanous dresses. The widescreen blockbusters didn't kill off the threat of television, but the grandiose likes of *Quo Vadis* (1951), *The Ten Commandments* (1956), *Ben-Hur* (1959) and *Spartacus* (1960) at least appeared to be cinema's triumphant saviour.

It's an irony almost worthy of a Greek tragedy that the genre that had done so much to save Hollywood, almost destroyed it. But by the mid-1960s, the epic had even begun to eclipse the outlandish excesses of the old empire. Caligula would surely have blushed at the vast expense of the 65 lavish costumes specially made for Elizabeth Taylor in *Cleopatra* (1963), whose budget spiralled violently and infamously out of control. The most expensive movie of its time, and the byword for Hollywood self-indulgence, *Cleopatra* dealt a serious blow to the historical spectacle, but the genre was finally toppled by *The Fall Of The Roman Empire* (1964). Given the thumbs down by critics and public alike, this box-office disaster, together with extravagant commercial failures like *The Greatest Story Ever Told* (1965) and *The Bible: In The Beginning* (1966) (and big-canvas dramas like *Star!*, 1968) brought the old Hollywood studio empire to its knees, allowing the barbarians (in the form of the new, maverick directors) briefly past the gates.

At the beginning of the new millennium, Ridley Scott's *Gladiator* (2000) heralded the epic's third coming. Its resurrection made perfect filmic and economic sense in a digital age when computer-generated imagery means that studios no longer have to employ vast crowds or build gigantic sets. The genre returned in various incarnations, including biblical epics (2004's *The Passion Of The Christ*) and Greek myths (2004's *Troy*). However, despite the cost-cutting advantages of CGI, the new epics somehow managed to match the old ones for huge expense on a biblical scale. *Troy* cost an estimated $200 million, and equally extravagant contemporaries such as *Alexander* (2004) and the crusader epic *Kingdom Of Heaven* (2005) were notable flops, despite all the marketing hype. Once again, Hollywood seems to have failed to heed the lessons of history. LH

Samson And Delilah 1949, 128 min

cast Victor Mature, Hedy Lamarr, George Sanders, Angela Lansbury, Henry Wilcoxon, Olive Derring, Fay Holden *cin* George Barnes *m* Victor Young

Guilty pleasures abound in this hackneyed and gaudy Old Testament melodrama, with a hilariously wooden Victor Mature as the hero whose powers reside in his hair, and an equally stilted Hedy Lamarr as the *femme fatale*. The ornate sets and preposterous dialogue distinguish the affair as a DeMille original, while Angela Lansbury and George Sanders camp it up in delicious supporting roles.

The Ten Commandments 1956, 220 min

cast Charlton Heston, Yul Brynner, Anne Baxter, Edward G. Robinson, John Derek, Yvonne De Carlo, Vincent Price *cin* Loyal Griggs *m* Elmer Bernstein

Charlton Heston parts the Red Sea in DeMille's final film, an aptly monumental blowout for a career built on twin pillars of shameless sensationalism and moral righteousness. Endless and blathery, its big set pieces – the orgy scenes, the Israelites' exodus from Egypt, the receiving of the tablets of stone – still pack a stupendous punch, and Yul Brynner as Rameses makes a lively foil to Heston's ponderous Moses. Biblical kitsch never got any better.

Jonathan Demme

US, 1944–

Jonathan Demme's is one of the most interesting oeuvres of the last 25 years. As well as taking on several roles in the filmmaking process, Demme has made films ranging from screwball comedy to documentary. Writing film reviews at the University of Florida led to drafting press releases and writing for *Film Daily*. After a stint directing television commercials, Demme became a publicist for Roger Corman before graduating to producing and writing. In 1974 he directed *Caged Heat*, a women-in-prison flick which, whilst conforming to Corman's exploitation aesthetics, sensitively explored relationships among women oppressed by the system. *Crazy Mama* (1975) was a rollicking gangster movie revolving around women on the road. Demme's *Something Wild* (1986) and *Married To The Mob* (1988) famously revived these themes.

Citizens Band (aka *Handle With Care*, 1977) was an Altmanesque fresco of lives interlaced by the shortwave radio culture of the era. Demme is at his best when celebrating the heterogeneity of American life, and works such as *Citizens Band*, *Something Wild* and *Married To The Mob* revel in the society and *mise en scène* of America's highways and suburbs. Following the assured and Hitchcockian *The Last Embrace* (1979), *Melvin And Howard* (1980) related the tabloid bizarrerie of a blue-collar worker claiming to be Howard Hughes's beneficiary. It marked Demme's international breakthrough.

The deservedly Oscar-winning *The Silence Of The Lambs* (1990) conjured up a real feel for backwoods life and elicited a fine performance from Jodie Foster as a hard-nosed FBI professional. Despite bringing AIDS to the attention of mainstream audiences and earning Tom Hanks an Oscar for best actor, *Philadelphia* (1993) was disappointing. So too were the Toni Morrison adaptation *Beloved* (1998) and *The Truth About Charlie* (2002), a reworking of the 1964 Audrey Hepburn comedy-thriller *Charade*. Demme's remake of *The Manchurian Candidate* (2004), transposed the basic plot to a topical Gulf War setting.

It is rare for a mainstream American director to double as a documentary maker. While he spent his days shooting the lacklustre Goldie Hawn vehicle *Swing Shift* (1984), Demme spent his nights on the Talking Heads concert film *Stop Making Sense* (1984). His record of humorist Spalding Gray – *Swimming To Cambodia* (1987) – was an understated but riveting watch. *Cousin Bobby* (1992) followed a relative of Demme's, a minister in Harlem. *Storefront Hitchcock* (1998) caught something of vernacular street life in its portrait of musician Robyn Hitchcock. Consonant with a lifelong interest in Haiti, *The Agronomist* (2003) charted the life of human rights activist Jean Dominique. Altogether,

Demme's output amounts to a body of work that is nothing if not eclectic and original. RA

Stop Making Sense 1984, 88 min
with David Byrne, Tina Weymouth, Chris Frantz, Jerry Harrison *cin* Jordan Cronenweth *m* Talking Heads

One of the most successful concert movies ever, this documentary of the Talking Heads in action makes no concessions to showbiz, simply capturing David Byrne's idiosyncratic sensibility as it spoke to Demme's feeling for the American underground.

Something Wild 1986, 114 min
cast Jeff Daniels, Melanie Griffith, Ray Liotta, Margaret Colin, Tracey Walter, Dana Preu, Jack Gilpin *cin* Tak Fujimoto *m* John Cale, Laurie Anderson

Blending screwball comedy and *film noir* with postmodern glee, this key 1980s film finds a mild-mannered Jeff Daniels caught up with Melanie Griffith's whirlwind-in-a-Louise-Brooks-bob and taken over the rainbow to the dark side of the American dream.

The Silence Of The Lambs 1990, 118 min
cast Jodie Foster, Anthony Hopkins, Scott Glenn, Ted Levine, Anthony Heald, Diane Baker, Brooke Smith *cin* Tak Fujimoto *m* Howard Shore

With the subversive suggestion that serial cannibal Hannibal Lecter (Anthony Hopkins) is in some crucial sense civilized, and the unlikely, uneasy bond he establishes with FBI girl Clarice Starling (Jodie Foster), Demme brought a profundity to this project that the horror genre rarely achieves.

The Manchurian Candidate 2004, 130 min
cast Denzel Washington, Meryl Streep, Liev Schreiber, Jon Voight, Kimberley Elise, Jeffrey Wright, Ted Levine *cin* Tak Fujimoto *m* Rachel Portman

A rare remake that exceeds the original, *The Manchurian Candidate* transposes the post-Korea Cold War intrigues of the 1962 film to a modern late-capitalist post-Cold War Washington. Demme creates a finely acted – Denzel Washington, Meryl Streep – and filmically bold essay in cold ambition and brutal geopolitics.

Jacques Demy

France, 1931–90

A happy working-class boy who grew up in the Atlantic port of Nantes, Jacques Demy began making animated short films in his bedroom when he was still a child, creating models and puppets, a world unto himself. He would stay true to that project throughout his career.

The Demy-monde is a place of romance, song, grace and sometimes sorrow. Often, as one French critic said of *Les parapluies de Cherbourg* (*The Umbrellas Of Cherbourg*, 1964), it is "even better than heaven". A contemporary of the *nouvelle vague* (he married the first New Wave filmmaker, Agnès Varda, in 1962), Demy shared his generation's adoration for cinema and leftist politics – but politics rarely encroached on his Utopian fantasies except in the most general sense. "Yes, there is trouble everywhere", sighs the café proprietress (Danielle Darrieux) whenever she picks up a newspaper in *Les demoiselles de Rochefort* (*The Young Girls Of Rochefort*, 1967).

Demy cited Bresson, Ophüls, Cocteau and Donen as his influences – and there are echoes of Carné and Prévert too. Cocteau and Donen in particular are inescapable in everything after his first two films: the poetic but constricted *Lola* (1960) and the atypical *La baie des anges* (*Bay Of Angels*, 1962).

It was only with his third film that Demy realized his dream of an all-sung musical, and it is on *Les parapluies de Cherbourg* and its sister film, *Les demoiselles de Rochefort*, that his international reputation was established – and still stands. Lusciously scored by Michel Legrand, and wholeheartedly embracing an effervescent pastel palette (Demy repainted interiors and entire streets according to his colour design), these irresistible confections pour the elation and exuberance of the Hollywood musical into quotidian settings to arrive at an emotional pitch which is pure and direct. At his best Demy was nothing short of sublime.

The critical and commercial success of these musicals took Demy to Hollywood, but *Lola In LA*, better known as *Model Shop* (1968), didn't click (Demy dubbed it "Model Flop"). On his return to France, the Cocteau-esque *Peau d'âne* (*Donkey Skin*, 1970) didn't fare any better, and after the British-produced *The Pied Piper* (1971) Demy tried his hand at non-musical comedy with *A Slightly Pregnant Man* (1973). A six-year hiatus ended with the bizarre, little-seen *Lady Oscar* (1980), a Japanese film set in the French Revolution and cast with British unknowns.

In his last decade Demy managed to make three more musicals, none of them widely seen outside France. But his critical reputation has fluctuated with the political fashions of the times: these later films may yet prove ripe for reassessment. In the meantime, his widow Agnès Varda has honoured his memory in *Jacquot de Nantes* (1991) and the documentaries *L'univers de Jacques Demy* and *Les demoiselles ont eu 25 ans* (*The Young Girls Are 25 Years Older*), and by overseeing the restoration of *Les demoiselles de Rochefort*. TC

Lola 1960, 91 min, b/w

cast Anouk Aimée, Marc Michel, Jacques Harden, Elina Labourdette, Margo Lion, Alan Scott *cin* Raoul Coutard *m* Michel Legrand

Demy planned this as a full-blown musical but, presented with a tenth of the budget he needed, he had to curtail his ambitions – though he still managed to shoot it in CinemaScope. As the beloved eponymous cabaret artiste, Anouk Aimée announces that "to want happiness is to already have a bit of it". Godard praised the film to the skies, and quoted from it in *Une femme est une femme* (1961) and *Bande à part* (1964).

La baie des anges (Bay Of Angels) 1962, 85 min, b/w

cast Jeanne Moreau, Claude Mann, Paul Guers, Henri Nassiet *cin* Jean Rabier *m* Michel Legrand

This is the anomaly in the Demy oeuvre, a crisp, focused three-way love affair between a young bank clerk (Mann), a reckless blonde (Moreau) and the casinos of Nice and Monte Carlo, with nary a song in sight. It's a film about compulsion. Mann's ruinous infatuation mirrors Moreau's own gambling addiction, and the high life that goes with it. Love as a game of chance, and the stakes are damnation and redemption.

Les parapluies de Cherbourg (The Umbrellas Of Cherbourg) 1964, 92 min

cast Catherine Deneuve, Nino Castelnuovo, Anne Vernon, Ellen Farner, Marc Michel, Mireille Perrey *cin* Jean Rabier *m* Michel Legrand

Demy's first fully fledged musical is a simple love story in which a shop girl (Catherine Deneuve, in her first major role) pledges herself to a mechanic, but marries another after he goes off to the Algerian war, leaving her pregnant. The scenario is mundane and the dialogue entirely sung – you could even call it a soap opera. And like the best opera, it's absolutely overwhelming.

Les demoiselles de Rochefort (The Young Girls Of Rochefort) 1967, 126 min

cast Catherine Deneuve, Françoise Dorléac, George Chakiris, Grover Dale, Danielle Darrieux, Gene Kelly *cin* Ghislain Cloquet *m* Michel Legrand

Deneuve and her sister Françoise Dorléac co-star in this companion piece to *Les parapluies*, which is in a lighter, joyful vein. Gene Kelly and George Chakiris point up American influences, but *Demoiselles* is no imitation; it exists in its own romantic universe. Somehow, Demy contrives to keep his lovers at arm's length until the very last frames. Poetic, romantic and playful, it's designed to entrance and delight – and can hardly fail to do so.

Claire Denis
France, 1948–

A white liberal director who spent her formative years living in colonial Africa, Claire Denis is one of the most original and daring directors to emerge from France. What she seems to be attempting, and frequently achieving, is a phenomenological, almost existential, cinema. Her ambition is, in her words, "to capture moments … pieces of time". There is an almost anthropological interest in minutiae – gestures, faces, surfaces – as her camera zeroes in and lingers long on pinpoint details. Denis self-deprecatingly puts her meditative style down to the fact that she is "a bit slow".

Brought up in colonial Africa where her father worked for the French civil service, she drew upon her childhood experiences for her first, highly acclaimed feature, *Chocolat* (1988). Recounting the story of the family of a French governor in Cameroon whose world falls apart when they take in the survivors of a plane crash, it was a typically heady Denis concoction of allegory and reverie. It's a style that seems to have evolved out of her experiences working as assistant to Jim Jarmusch, Wim Wenders and Jacques Rivette, three directors more interested in fleeting moments than grand narratives. But whereas those auteurs maintain a glacial distance from their subject matter, the work of Denis often radiates a sensual warmth.

After five feature films, which included both African and French urban settings, this semi-abstract approach found its fullest expression in *Beau travail* (1999), universally regarded as her *chef-d'oeuvre*. Focusing on the simmering, homoerotic tensions in the French Foreign Legion (enclosed male worlds are a Denis speciality), it was an elliptical collection of small details, a mosaic of textures and memories. Her next film, *Trouble Every Day* (2001), caused a storm of controversy in Cannes over its cannibalistic sex scenes. Once the storm had passed, the lasting impression was not disgust but disappointment that Denis hadn't carried on the good work of *Beau travail. Vendredi soir* (2002), set over the course of one intoxicating Friday night, focused on a man and a woman who meet by chance in a Parisian traffic jam. Denis filmed her native Paris like a curious outsider, again constructing a narrative, and a meaning, by piecing together significant, and insignificant, details. It is probably the only film that will ever feature a shot of anchovies dancing on a pizza.

Of all her films, *L'intrus* (*The Intruder*, 2004) feels most like the natural successor to *Beau travail.* Not because of its colonial setting, or the reappearance of actor Michel Subor, or the hazy intensity of cinematographer Agnès Godard's imagery, but because it registers no formal difference between the dream sequences and reality. This sense of diurnal reverie is emphasized by scenes that drift in and out of inky blackness as if we're experiencing the world of a man who is slowly, woozily losing consciousness. LH

Beau travail 1999, 93 min

cast Denis Lavant, Michel Subor, Grégoire Colin, Richard Courcet, Nicolas Duvauchelle *cin* Agnès Godard *m* Charles Henri de Pierrefeu

Denis Lavant is threatened by a new recruit in the Foreign Legion and allows his anger to simmer in the North African sun. Conceived as both a free adaptation of Herman Melville's *Billy Budd* and a sequel to Jean-Luc Godard's *Le petit soldat* (1963), *Beau travail* is like a kind of ballet without music. Denis constructs unlikely moments of synchronized elegance, such as the men doing their ironing with the grace and choreographed precision of a homoerotic dance piece.

Ruggero Deodato
Italy, 1939–

Ruggero Deodato started out as assistant to Roberto Rossellini and second unit director for Joseph Losey and Sergio Corbucci before making his uncredited feature debut when Antonio Margheriti walked off the set of *Ursus, il terrore dei kirghisi* (*Hercules, Prisoner Of Evil*, 1964). Branded a misanthrope for his angry and cynical work, Deodato epitomizes the golden age of Italy's exploitation cinema. *Ultimo mondo cannibale* (*Cannibal*, 1976) and *Cannibal Holocaust* (1980) rank amongst the most contentious horrors ever for their inclusion of actual animal butchery, the latter becoming a reviled video nasty. *La casa sperduta nel parco* (*The House On The Edge Of The Park*, 1980) attracted further controversy for its scenes of sexual abuse and gory torture. AJ

Cannibal Holocaust 1980, 95 min

cast Robert Kerman, Francesca Ciardi, Perry Pirkanen, Luca Barbareschi, Salvatore Basile, Ricardo Fuentes *cin* Sergio d'Offizi *m* Riz Ortolani

A documentary crew disappears in Colombia. When their film is found it contains graphic footage of them being eaten alive. Banned in 33 countries, the defining film in Deodato's oeuvre sent him into Italian courts to prove it wasn't a "snuff" film. Arguably the most shocking movie ever made.

Brian De Palma
US, 1940–

Brian De Palma is the most controversial director to have emerged from the movie brat generation of film school graduates. A misogynist, a genius, a copycat, a cine-literate aesthete, an emotionless technician, all of these epithets have been thrown his way – and they all have some validity. The director's variable career has ambled from peak to trough, success to flop, controversy to obscurity. Although he's best known for films with a high body count, he began his career making comedies – *Greetings* (1968), *The Wedding Party* (1969) and *Hi, Mom!* (1970) – and later reinvented the horror film by dreaming the just-when-you-think-it's-over coda in *Carrie* (1976).

De Palma is the closest mainstream American cinema has come to a hip-hop artist; he is a cultural magpie who samples riffs, or rips off samples, from other directors, borrowing plotlines, shots and sequences. The climax of *The Untouchables* (1987), in which a pram and its infant passenger trip perilously down a set of stone steps amidst a volley of gunfire, is a virtual shot-for-shot remake of the famous Odessa steps sequence from Sergei Eisenstein's *Battleship Potemkin* (1925). One of De Palma's most fully conceived films, *Blow Out* (1981), starring John Travolta as a sound engineer convinced he has recorded evidence of a politician's murder, is Michelangelo Antonioni's *Blow-Up* (1966) reworked as a paranoid conspiracy thriller. Alfred Hitchcock's imposing shadow also looms large over the director's ouevre. De Palma's *Obsession* (1976),

Scarface and the reinvention of the gangster movie

In the 1980s and early 1990s, the American gangster genre returned to the scene of the original crime movies, the Prohibition era of the 1920s that had inspired the classic films of the 1930s. Taking their stylistic and nostalgic cues from *Once Upon A Time In America* (1984), movies like *The Cotton Club*, *Johnny Dangerously* (both 1984), *The Untouchables* (1987), *Miller's Crossing* (1990), *Billy Bathgate*, *Bugsy* and *Mobsters* (all 1991) wheeled out a stately procession of jalopies, Tommy guns and speakeasies. But while these films respectfully doffed their fedoras to the classic gangster period, *Scarface* (1983) was the only one to return to the original source material. And, significantly, this remake wasn't a period piece, updating the story to the 1980s. (It is, however, something of a period piece now, a florid monument to that decade's conspicuous consumption and coke-addled, self-interested decadence.) Howard Hawks's 1932 original was one of three early masterpieces (the others were *Little Caesar*, 1930, and *The Public Enemy*, 1931) that laid down the template for the mobster movie, setting the rules for iconography, dress codes, narratives, themes and morality. All three set their Machiavellian protagonists on a steep rise-and-fall trajectory, the classic tragic narrative of the man who would be king: a loyal lieutenant usurps the boss and kills his father figure, blazes brightly and briefly as king of the city, until a fatal flaw undoes all his bad work. In Hawks's *Scarface*, dubbed "the Borgias living in Chicago" by its writer Ben Hecht, Tony Camonte is trapped by the love of two women, ice maiden Polly and his own sister Ceska. When Ceska marries his best friend, incestuous feelings that have been buried (albeit in a shallow grave) rise to the surface and the gangster kills his old mate.

De Palma's story was surprisingly faithful to the original, but the director supersized every element – the violence, the intimations of incest and the protagonist's dubious taste in shirts. Above all, he cranked up the visual style to dangerous levels of hyper-realism that were matched only by Al Pacino's volcanic, almost parodic approach to the role of Tony Montana. While Hawks was a no-nonsense director, keeping most shots at eye-level ease, De Palma and writer Oliver Stone are both famously allergic to nuance. De Palma seems to see plot as merely a handy device for linking set pieces. And Stone provided him with many opportunities for directorial showboating. The *pièce de résistance*, Montana's defiant last stand against the swarming hordes of a drug baron's army, was orchestrated with operatic contempt for subtlety, and finally untied *Scarface* from the moorings of realism, with Stone's diligent research into the *modus operandi* of the narcotics trade deliriously abandoned in an orgy of sweeping auteur flourishes and actorly grandstanding.

While it barely made money on its initial release, *Scarface*'s influence is clear. Opulent, excessive and emphasizing the constituent parts over the narrative whole, *Scarface* plunged the gangster movie into its baroque phase. There are three high-water marks of this style-first era. Abel Ferrara's sumptuous elegy for a dead gangster walking, *The King Of New York* (1990), hummed with spectral melancholy and self-conscious artistry, with Christopher Walken ratcheting up the thespian intensity as the lonely crime czar with political ambitions. In *Menace II Society* (1993), avowed *Scarface* obsessives the Hughes brothers lacquered a patina of ghetto realism onto their MTV stylings. But the supreme movie of the new baroque was, undoubtedly, *GoodFellas* (1990). Although ostensibly a biopic, the film's true subjects were gangster movies, rather than gangsters themselves, and the camera was undoubtedly the true star. Classic narrative cohesion and traditional character development were telescoped into spectacular set pieces. Martin Scorsese's camera consistently stole scenes from his actors, famously following Ray Liotta and Lorraine Bracco in one long, sinuous take from their VIP entrance at the back of a nightclub, through the kitchen, all the way to the front of the stage. And with its urgent, kinetic energy and jump-cut frenzy, the last-day-of-the-wise-guy montage brought the film to a suitably combustible zenith.

The dictum that every action has a reaction applies to film as it does to the rest of the universe. The pendulum started to swing after the release of Quentin Tarantino's *Reservoir Dogs* (1992). Here, the camera rarely announced itself, and its long, static takes were almost televisual in the deferential way they served Tarantino's hipster dialogue. The film references were no longer the exclusive preserve of the filmmaker, but the mundane subject of the characters' conversations. More recently, a curious and amoral Scorsese/Tarantino hybrid has emerged. Self-aware, visually strident, drawn in bold, attention-seeking strokes, movies such as the South Korean shocker *Oldboy* (2003) only ever place a value upon realism in their unflinching and gruelling scenes of violence and torture. Funny that. LH

in which a businessman becomes obsessed with a doppelgänger of his dead wife, is essentially a *Vertigo* redux. *Body Double* (1984) is *Rear Window* meets *Vertigo*, and *Dressed To Kill* (1980) adds *Psycho* to the mix, even opening with a mischievous homage to the film's infamous shower scene.

The problem with excavating raw material entirely from the vaults of cinematic history is that the resulting work can be ahistorical, amoral and airless. De Palma seems to shrug off any social responsibility, viewing the repeated acts of violence against women in his thrillers in purely technical terms.

He was condemned as a misogynist following *Body Double* and *Dressed To Kill*, and feminist groups picketed cinemas angry about what they saw as the peephole pleasures of watching women being cut up for entertainment. De Palma has yet to solve the puzzle of how to make a film about voyeurism without making a voyeuristic film, although whether he actually sees that as a problem is another matter. Indeed, he seems to have got some mischievous pleasure out of making the perversely outré *Body Double*, in which the hero is unapologetically a voyeur and a young, sexually liberated woman is graphically penetrated by a drill.

Even his detractors, however, have to agree that there is a virtuosic élan to every Brian De Palma picture. No matter how uneven the film – and they have been precariously erratic of late – there will always be one redeeming feature, whether it's Tom Cruise perilously dangling from a wire in *Mission: Impossible* (1996), the 12-minute tracking shot that audaciously opened *Snake Eyes* (1998) or the Kubrickian space sequences in *Mission To Mars* (2000). His bloody masterpiece *Scarface* (1983) was one glorious set piece after another, ratcheting up the baroque until it became a machine-gun opera. *Carlito's Way* (1993) offered him an alternative direction – character-based, low-key, with only the odd welcome flash of bombast – but, sadly, he seems to have declined it.

The accusations of misogyny and vulgar plagiarism have tended to overshadow the director's avant-garde credentials. However, throughout his career, De Palma has played deft, intellectual games with the linearity of time and the fallibility of human perception. In *Sisters* (1973), a Bergmanesque thriller about doubles, De Palma's split screen became an astute technical analogue of the protagonist's state of mind. *Casualties Of War* (1989) pulled the rug out from underneath the audience in the very last shot, *Raising Cain* (1992) toyed capriciously with time's arrow, and *Femme Fatale* (2002), packaged as an erotic thriller, owed more to avant-garde writer Jorge Luis Borges than Sharon Stone.

In 2006, critics at the Venice Film Festival loudly trumpeted De Palma's return to form with *The Black Dahlia* (2006). But when the hype died down, other reviewers saw it for what it was, an underpowered James Ellroy adaptation with a few dazzling set pieces (including, a career highlight, the discovery of a dead woman's body) and the most ridiculous, jaw-dropping denouement in recent mainstream American cinema. LH

Carrie 1976, 98 min

cast Sissy Spacek, Piper Laurie, Amy Irving, William Katt, Betty Buckley, John Travolta, Nancy Allen *cin* Mario Tosi *m* Pino Donaggio

At the heart of this grisly horror movie is a sympathetic character study of a neurotic young outsider. Sissy Spacek's brittle Carrie is bullied at school and at home until she uses her telekinetic powers to exact a terrifying revenge. The slaughter at the prom is De Palma at his pyrotechnical best, but it only really resonates because of the care the filmmaker has taken to build an emotional core – a fact that his detractors, and the director himself, would do well to remember.

Scarface 1983, 170 min

cast Al Pacino, Steven Bauer, Michelle Pfeiffer, Robert Loggia, Mary Elizabeth Mastrantonio *cin* John A. Alonzo *m* Giorgio Moroder

This deliriously excessive blood-splattering remake of Howard Hawks's 1932 gangster classic plays like a game of dare between the director, writer and actor to see who can go the most over-the-top the fastest: Al Pacino with his barking performance as Cuban criminal Tony Montana, Oliver Stone and his epigram-strewn script ("I don't break my word or my balls for nobody") or De Palma with his violent, opulent and operatic set pieces.

Body Double 1984, 114 min

cast Craig Wasson, Melanie Griffith, Gregg Henry, Deborah Shelton *cin* Stephen H. Burum *m* Pino Donaggio

Body Double begins like a porno version of *Rear Window*, but soon turns into something else: a porno version of *Vertigo*. Actor Craig Wasson rents a luxury apartment from a friend, where he spies on the naked antics of an exhibitionist neighbour, but when she is killed, the voyeur soon becomes morbidly obsessed with porn actress Melanie Griffith. Tacky, ingenious, clichéd, dazzling and morally dubious, with flourishes of technical chutzpah and garish genius, this is quintessential De Palma.

The Untouchables 1987, 120 min

cast Kevin Costner, Sean Connery, Robert De Niro, Andy Garcia, Charles Martin Smith, Richard Bradford *cin* Stephen H. Burum *m* Ennio Morricone

De Palma's epic, David Mamet-scripted take on the 1960s TV series of the same name stars a virtuous Kevin Costner as Elliot Ness, the Treasury department official who brought down Al Capone. Robert De Niro wore the same style of silk underwear as the famous gangster, but disappointingly, Sean Connery did not immerse himself as deeply in his role of a genial Irish cop, bullishly retaining his Scottish accent. Stylish and pacey.

Carlito's Way 1993, 145 min

cast Al Pacino, Sean Penn, Penelope Ann Miller, John Leguizamo, Ingrid Rogers, Luis Guzman *cin* Stephen H. Burum *m* Patrick Doyle

Al Pacino is surprisingly low-key as a hood who leaves jail and tries to go straight, but is fatally compromised by the scheming of his coke-fuelled lawyer. Sean Penn is unrecognizable in a Harpo Marx-style curly wig as the shyster with big plans for himself and his client, and he steals the film right out from under Pacino's nose. Of the many crimes on display, that is surely the most daring.

Vittorio De Sica
Italy, 1901–74

Vittorio De Sica's film career spanned over fifty years, during which he ranged from matinée idol to arthouse auteur and commercial jobbing director. He grew up in a lower middle-class district of Naples

Italian neo-realism and its legacy

Although, by the late-1970s, Vittorio De Sica's reputation had been overshadowed by his neo-realist peer Roberto Rossellini, De Sica's influence can still be felt whenever a director takes to the streets and employs non-professional actors from where the film is actually being shot. For David Thomson, De Sica is the "pioneer sponsor of the non-professional actor", his portraits of urban working-class people in *Sciuscià* (*Shoeshine*, 1946) and *Bicycle Thieves* (1948) setting a fresh standard for spontaneous and naturalistic performance in European cinema. Recruiting his actors where he found them, De Sica saw them as key to the integrity of a new realist cinema: "against the absence of human solidarity, they are a word in favour of the poor and the unhappy."

Non-establishment acting is not without its precedents. In De Sica's casting of individuals who personify the social types and values he sought to show, there is something of the technique of "typage" employed by the Russian directors Eisenstein and Pudovkin in the 1920s. The passage of time in a quotidian Rome in *Bicycle Thieves* anticipated something of the formal splendour of Antonioni's modernist environments in works like *L'eclisse* (1962) and *Red Desert* (1964). However, it is perhaps a measure of the late twentieth century's decline of traditional values that, whereas De Sica's characters belong to their environments, the post-war arthouse cinema presented characters progressively alienated from their worlds. In the late-1940s, neo-realism's influence spread to Hollywood: real locations, long takes and deep focus brought verisimilitude and urgency to American thrillers and the social conscience genre, whether studio-made or independent, in films such as *The Lost Weekend* (Billy Wilder, 1945) and *The Naked City* (Jules Dassin, 1948). *The Best Years Of Our Lives* (William Wyler, 1946) featured Harold Russell among its actors, a paraplegic ex-navy veteran, who brought veracity to the film's account of post-war readjustment. Further afield the likes of Satyajit Ray in India, Akira Kurosawa in Japan, the German directors who briefly created the new sub-genre of the *Trümmerfilm* (rubble film), and filmmakers in Spain, Scandinavia and Eastern Europe all took note.

While these decades saw crises in studio filmmaking around the world, whenever filmmakers sought to escape studio acting and arthouse artifice to return to real life, they were responding to the influence of neo-realism. The minimalist meditations on experience in Bresson's *A Man Escaped* (1956) and *Mouchette* (1966) remind us of Lamberto Maggiorani's intensity as the bereft father of *Bicycle Thieves*. Consonant with a movement marginal to the Italian industry, neo-realism's legacy has tended to be felt less in canonic establishment cinema and more in improvisatory experimental trends typified in America by John Cassavetes – *Shadows* (1959), for example – and developed in *Faces* (1968), *A Woman Under The Influence* (1974), and in Shirley Clarke's *The Connection* (1961).

Neo-realism was an aesthetic which tapped into a particular transition in Italian life. In Britain's New Wave cinema, which also drew on its own native documentary tradition, *Saturday Night And Sunday Morning* (1959) and *Billy Liar* (1963) poignantly recorded an industrial revolution giving way to the jukebox inner cities of postmodernity. Ken Loach's films, such as *Poor Cow* (1967) and *Kes* (1969), regularly employed unknown actors from the environments in which the drama took place. Although sometimes criticized for his actors' mannerisms, Mike Leigh extended the representation of British types while proffering a desultory portrait of the urban scene following the ravages of Thatcherite economic reform in *High Hopes* (1988), *Naked* (1993) and *Secrets And Lies* (1995).

The 1990s saw a renewed interest in filmmaking which uncovered underrepresented pockets of experience. While the Danish Dogme "manifesto" decried traditional acting, this era also witnessed filmmakers such as Larry Clark and Harmony Korine experimenting with non-professional actors in, respectively, *Kids* (1995) and *Gummo* (1997). Independent American features like *Heavy* (1995), *Trees Lounge* (1996) and *Sling Blade* (1996) found drama in the everyday tribulations of the American social undergrowth. *The Blair Witch Project* (1999) brought together actors who had never acted before and who have scarcely been heard from since, while *United 93* (2006) used non-professionals to depict the ordinary citizens who downed hijacked United Airways flight 93 on September 11, 2001. The 1990s also saw a renaissance in Iranian cinema, in which directors like Abbas Kiarostami (*And Life Goes On…*, 1992) and Samira Makhmalbaf (*The Apple*, 1998) drew upon quirky experiences and non-professional actors to chronicle the everyday vicissitudes of life under Islamic law. RA

before going on the stage. In the 1920s he enjoyed a flourishing stage career as the archetypal petit-bourgeois nice guy. Light romantic film roles followed, most notably in Mario Commencini's *Gli uomini … che mascalzoni* (*What Rascals Men Are*, 1932).

In 1940 De Sica made his directorial debut with *Rose scarlatter* (*Two Dozen Red Roses*), initiating a series of romantic comedies which became increasingly socially aware, typically finding their female protagonists in orphanages and boarding schools. The introduction of wider social preoccupations reflected the burgeoning spirit of neo-realism, a current then challenging the consensual entertainment values of Italian cinema in the Fascist era.

Sciuscià (*Shoeshine*, 1946) put De Sica at the heart of neo-realist innovation. Scripted by the neo-realism theorist Cesare Zavattini, this account of the shoeshine boys of the post-war Italian streets was shot on location using non-professional actors. Also scripted by Zavattini, De Sica's *Bicycle Thieves* (1948) remains a key moment in the neo-realist movement. As André Bazin, filmmaker and writer for *Cahiers du cinéma*, pointed out: rather than restraining or interpreting the reality of what the camera showed, De Sica spoke to reality and reality spoke to De Sica, introducing a phenomenological sense of real experience missing from the studio-based genre palliatives of the previous era. The brute realism of the 1940s evolved into an anarchist fantasy in *Miracolo in Milano* (*Miracle In Milan*, 1951), in which the denizens of a shantytown are rescued from eviction by divine intervention. De Sica's *Umberto D.* (1952) closed the high neo-realist era.

Always in thrall to the industry in his attempt to raise filmmaking capital, De Sica was prevailed upon to cast producer David O. Selznick's wife Jennifer Jones in *Indiscretion Of An American Wife* (1953), intended as a modest romantic drama but upgraded and then abandoned to its box-office fate by Selznick. Already the neo-realists were reaching towards the compromises of the mainstream. De Sica returned to proletarian themes in *Two Women* (1961), an Alberto Moravia adaptation set in a ravaged post-war Italy. Its star – Sophia Loren – would appear opposite heartthrob Marcello Mastroianni in De Sica's rose-tinted comedies *Ieri, oggi, domani* (*Yesterday, Today And Tomorrow*, 1963) and *Matrimonio all'italiana* (*Marriage, Italian Style*, 1964). In 1971 came *The Garden Of The Finzi-Continis*, an ambitious international production charting the decline of a Ferrarese Jewish dynasty amid the racism of Mussolini's Italy. The name of Vittorio De Sica will forever be associated with the neo-realist movement and its dusty compassion. RA

Bicycle Thieves 1948, 96 min, b/w

cast Lamberto Maggiorani, Enzo Staiola, Lianella Carell, Gino Saltamerenda *cin* Carlo Montuori *m* Alessandro Cicognini

A workman must have a bicycle for a job; his bicycle is stolen; so he loses the job. This economic syllogism is the basis for one of the most heart-searching accounts of everyday life in film history. Producer David O. Selznick, so the story goes, was only prepared to commit if De Sica cast Cary Grant in the lead role instead of the ordinary citizen Lamberto Maggiorani, whose performance is so understatedly moving.

Umberto D. 1952, 89 min, b/w

cast Carlo Battisti, Maria Pia Casilio, Lina Gennari, Memmo Carotenuto *cin* G.R. Aldo *m* Alessandro Cicognini

Charting the fortunes of an old man who has lost everything but his little dog, the film's failure at the box office undermined De Sica's career and the future

of neo-realism itself. The film is sentimental yet compassionate; Zavattini described it as having reached a state of "terminal purity".

Virginie Despentes
France, 1969–

With her first feature, Virginie Despentes rode the crest of the wave of violence that broke over French cinema in the early-2000s. Before becoming a novelist, Despentes sang in a punk band and was an assistant in a peepshow. Her work clearly derives from a respected incendiary impulse in French cinema. *Baise-moi* (2000) was based on her own controversial 1995 novel, with a screenplay she adapted herself, and which she co-directed with porn star Coralie Trinh Thi. It raised a storm in the French press and elsewhere, eliciting protest from Catherine Breillat, Claire Denis, Jean-Luc Godard and other industry figures when it was given an X-rated certificate. Citing as her influence Maurice Pialat's bleak examination of the French social undergrowth, Despentes co-wrote the screenplay for Gilles Paquet-Brenner's *Les jolies choses* (2001) – another movie adapted from one of Despentes's uncompromising novels. RA

Street scene: the touching authenticity of De Sica's *Bicycle Thieves*.

Baise-moi 2000, 77 min

cast Karen Bach, Raffaëla Anderson, Delphine McCarty, Gabor Rassov *cin* Benoît Chamaillard *m* Varou Jan

Shot in grubby (digital) style and unremitting in its portrayal of sex and violence, this punchy visceral film follows a pair of angry young women, played by two former porn actresses, whose killing spree disconcerts us by forcing viewers to recognize the cinema-goer's compulsive need for violent fantasy. Yet it also, somehow, manages to remind us of the contingent pleasures of cinema itself: *Baise-moi* is as smart and funny as its antiheroines are cunning and sassy.

Arnaud Desplechin
France, 1960–

Novelistic, cine-literate, psychological, philosophical, theological, Arnaud Desplechin's films deftly flit from genre to genre and can be as exuberantly and exasperatingly flighty as his indecisive protagonists. He has audaciously borrowed formulae from various genres for each of his Frankensteinian experiments: *La sentinelle* (1992) grafts elements of the horror movie onto the espionage thriller in its tale of an awkward student who finds solace in a mysterious shrunken head; *Ma vie sexuelle* (1996) places the melodrama on the analyst's couch; the English-language curio *Esther Kahn* (2000) elides costume drama with social realism (but not always comfortably); and his *chef-d'oeuvre Kings And Queen* (2004) is everything Desplechin has ever done writ exuberantly large.

In making *Kings And Queen*, the director seems to have been guided by François Truffaut's maxim for *L'enfant sauvage* (*The Wild Child*, 1970) to include four ideas every minute. The result is not just a compendium of Desplechin's own films, but of seemingly every film he has ever enjoyed: a cinematic hodgepodge of Freud, ancient myth, theology, dream sequences and hip-hop, all cut together with the over-caffeinated, inventive edginess of the *nouvelle vague*. Only Paul Thomas Anderson's similarly mythic and unashamedly soapy *Magnolia* (1999) comes close to its metaphysical and meta-textual pleasures. LH

Ma vie sexuelle (My Sex Life) 1996, 178 min

cast Mathieu Amalric, Emmanuelle Devos, Emmanuel Salinger, Marianne Denicourt, Thibalt de Montalembert *cin* Eric Gautier *m* Krishna Lévy

Desplechin's most intellectually and emotionally stImulating film before *Kings And Queen*, with whom it shares two of its leading actors (Emmanuelle Devos and Mathieu Almaric), follows an impish university professor flitting indecisively between three women. This domestic epic brims with *joie de vivre*, psychoanalysis, dream imagery, philosophy and matter-of-fact eroticism, although, as often with the dexterously gifted, some directorial self-discipline wouldn't have gone amiss.

Kings And Queen (Rois et reine) 2004, 153 min

cast Mathieu Amalric, Nathalie Boutefeu, Catherine Deneuve, Emmanuelle Devos, Maurice Garrel *cin* Eric Gautier *m* Grégoire Hetzel

This head-spinning, sensory-overloading family saga documents the parallel lives of a single mum whose father is dying of cancer and her ex-boyfriend who's been sectioned to a local mental hospital. Absorbingly surreal, *Kings And Queen* is stuffed to the brim with polymorphous pleasures and emotional intelligence, but is somehow rendered compellingly believable by the humanity of its opaque and contradictory characters.

André de Toth
Hungary (formerly Austro-Hungarian Empire), 1912–2002

André de Toth seems destined to be remembered as the one-eyed director who made the best 3-D movie ever (*House Of Wax*, 1953). That would be a grave injustice to a tough, vigorous professional who brought an unsentimental intelligence to everything he made.

Educated for the law in Budapest, de Toth was a young, unproduced playwright when he came under the patronage of the writer Ferenc Molnár (*Liliom*). Interested in movies, he graduated from camera assistant to director in double-quick time, and directed five films in the years 1939–40, before fleeing Vienna for Hollywood, via England and Alexander Korda. (De Toth was not Jewish, but despised fascism.)

Like fellow European émigrés Fritz Lang and Robert Siodmak, de Toth brought a grim, harsh, even brutal sensibility to the studio material he was given. He gravitated naturally to *film noir* (*Pitfall*, 1948, and *Crime Wave*, 1954, are probably his strongest), and that *noir* perspective also comes through in his numerous vividly staged Westerns, including *Ramrod* (1947), *The Indian Fighter* (1955), *Day Of The Outlaw* (1959), and six Randolph Scott vehicles. De Toth looked back on a life lived to the full (actress Veronica Lake was one of his seven wives) in his autobiography, *Fragments* (1995), and in the instructive *De Toth On De Toth* (1997). TC

None Shall Escape 1944, 86 min, b/w

cast Alexander Knox, Marsha Hunt, Henry Travers, Richard Crane, Dorothy Morris, Trevor Bardette *cin* Lee Garmes *m* Ernst Toch

Knox is Wilhelm Grimm, who lost a leg and his pride in World War I, and who rose to oversee the genocide of the Jews in Western Poland. His day of judgement before the International War Crimes Commission anticipates the Nuremberg Trials (even with the war still raging). De Toth's prophetic and insightful second Hollywood film probes the psychology of Nazism with fierce conviction. Written by Lester Cole, one of the "Hollywood Ten".

Day Of The Outlaw 1959, 96 min, b/w

cast Robert Ryan, Burl Ives, Tina Louise, Nehemiah Persoff, Jack Lambert, Alan Marshal *cin* Russell Harlan *m* Alexander Courage

This violent, ice-cold Western with Robert Ryan and Burl Ives is probably de Toth's finest accomplishment. Making much of the snowbound township setting, the film pits Ryan against his fate, and against a renegade cavalry unit who show up in the wrong place at the wrong time. Bleak, atmospheric, and packing a mean punch, this deserves to be better known. Bertrand Tavernier reckoned it was "as original and ahead of its time as *Johnny Guitar*".

Michel Deville

France, 1931–

One of the more conventional contemporaries of the French *nouvelle vague*, Michel Deville has a varied oeuvre that is all too often overlooked. Deville entered the industry as an assistant to director Henri Decoin in 1951. Directing from 1958, Deville established himself as an exponent of a literary, light-comic mode informed by his brief experience with France's state theatre company, the Comédie Française. Among his hits were *Ce soir ou jamais* (*Tonight Or Never*, 1960) with Anna Karina, *Adorable menteuse* (*Adorable Liar*, 1962) with Marina Vlady and *L'ours et la poupée* (*The Bear And The Doll*, 1970) with Brigitte Bardot.

In contrast to the solipsistic focus of the *nouvelle vague*, Deville typically takes in the group context surrounding his protagonists. Deville also dealt in thrillers: *Lucky Jo* (1964) was a tale of small-time crooks, led by Eddie Constantine; *La dossier 51* (1978) had more political undercurrents, charting its protagonist's surveillance by the government. There were even erotic costume dramas from Deville, often co-written with Nina Companéez, such as *Raphaël ou le débauchée* (1970). In the 1980s Deville's work briefly gained Anglo-American distribution. *Death In A French Garden* (1985) was an intricate and adulterous thriller. *Le paltoquet* (1986), with Daniel Auteuil and Fanny Ardant, was a César-winning drama with a distanced look and a spare barroom setting. *Un monde presque paisible* (*Almost Peaceful*, 2002) was a rambling tale of French Jews adapting to Parisian life after the war. Conventional he may have (superficially) been, but Deville works with an enviably delicate touch. RA

La lectrice 1988, 98 min

cast Miou-Miou, Régis Royer, Christian Ruché, Marianne Denicourt, Charlotte Farran, Maria Casarés *cin* Dominique Le Rigoleur *m* Beethoven

Miou-Miou plays Constance, a young woman whose habit of reading to her boyfriend in bed leads to a sequence of erotic encounters both subversive, delicious and problematic. The film engagingly animates a very French philosophical intercourse between language, narratives and sexuality.

Danny DeVito

US, 1944–

The would-be master of nasty, Danny DeVito has pursued a middling line in cynical black comedies in addition to his steady work as a character actor. Few of his identifying marks as a film-maker work to his credit: his favoured flashback structures are clumsily deployed (especially in the meandering 1992 biopic *Hoffa*), his use of low and oblique camera angles fussy and distracting, and his flat-footed direction results in obvious set-ups and strange gaps in the comic timing, as if he intended to dub a laughter track onto *Throw Momma From The Train* (1987) or *Death To Smoochy* (2002). *The War Of The Roses* (1989) perhaps best harnessed DeVito's predilection for vicious mirth – with much of the credit going to its game stars Michael Douglas and Kathleen Turner, just as Ben Stiller and Drew Barrymore enlivened the real-estate farce *Duplex* (aka *Our House*, 2003). JW

The War Of The Roses 1989, 116 min

cast Michael Douglas, Kathleen Turner, Danny DeVito, G.D. Spradlin, Marianne Sägebrecht, Peter Donat *cin* Stephen H. Burum *m* David Newman

Director DeVito also plays the divorce lawyer in this autopsy of a marriage, which unfolds in flashback as the perfect coexistence of smug marrieds Michael Douglas and Kathleen Turner falls apart and the bickering couple proceed to tear down their house in a burst of nihilistic frenzy. Cruel, misanthropic and finally even violent, the film goes too far, and fully intends to.

Kirby Dick

US, 1952–

Although he is not as well known as his much-laurelled fellow documentarists Michael Moore and Errol Morris, Kirby Dick has quietly become one of the more interesting non-fiction filmmakers working in America today. Despite ostensibly lurid titles such as *Private Practices: The Story of A Sex Surrogate* (1986) and *Sick: The Life And Death Of Bob Flanagan, Super-Masochist* (1997), his films' evident empathy and abundant insight go hand in hand. Dick's technique often entails fostering collaborative relationships with his subjects – as he did for *Sick*, with Flanagan and his partner-dominatrix, Sheree Rose – or even handing over the filming equipment altogether, as in *Chain Camera* (2001), for which Dick edited together raw footage shot by high school students.

In the playful portrait *Derrida* (2002), which he co-directed with Amy Ziering Kofman, the French deconstructionist proved to be decidedly less forthcoming than some of Dick's other subjects. The Oscar-nominated *Twist Of Faith* (2004) follows a churchgoing fireman after he discovers that he lives down the street from the priest who molested him as a boy. The film once again proved Dick's scrupulous hand with material that elsewhere typically receives only a hysterical tabloid treatment. And Dick's investigative prowess shone brightly in *This Film Is Not Yet Rated* (2006), a fascinating look inside the secretive and, it would seem, severely compromised American movie-rating system. JW

Sick: The Life and Death Of Bob Flanagan, Super-Masochist 1997, 89 min
with Bob Flanagan, Sheree Rose, Cathy Flanagan, Bob Flanagan Sr, Tim Flanagan, Sara Douchette *cin* Jonathan Dayton *m* Blake Leyh

Debilitated by cystic fibrosis, performance artist Bob Flanagan used self-inflicted pain to protest and counter-act his own body's betrayals. Enormously moving, this amazing documentary neither flinches from Flanagan's voluntary self-tortures (he hammers his penis to a board and then extracts the nail, all in extreme close-up) nor turns politely away when the disease finally takes the upper hand.

Thorold Dickinson
UK, 1903–84

Dickinson directed only nine features but his screenwriting, criticism and teaching added to his importance. Ironically his two best films, *Gaslight* (1940) and *The Queen Of Spades* (1949), share a dark atmosphere but were works for hire, while his more upbeat personal projects were less successful.

When Dickinson was expelled from Oxford for preferring film and theatre to study, he became a scriptwriter and editor and, alive to European and Soviet cinema, showed classic films to a small but influential group of cinephiles at the London Film Society. In 1934, when director J. Walter Ruben fell ill, he completed *Java Head*, a historical romance set in his home town of Bristol, though his first credit was the stylish if slightly overwrought World War I drama *The High Command* (1937).

Dickinson worked on a number of propaganda films as war loomed. He helped Ivor Montagu make Spanish pro-Republic films, and extolled job training in the zesty information short *Yesterday Is Over Your Shoulder* (1940). His next feature, *The Arsenal Stadium Mystery* (1939), was hardly a masterpiece but enjoyable enough, especially for devotees of the football club whose players feature. The contrast with the following year's morbid melodrama *Gaslight* could hardly be greater. The Disraeli biopic *The Prime Minister* (1941) did little to energize the sometimes recalcitrant genre. But Dickinson sprang back with *Next Of Kin* (1942), which embodied the wartime maxim "Be like Dad – keep Mum".

Men Of Two Worlds (1946) gave voice to Dickinson's social conscience and post-war hopes, but the story of a Europeanized African's return home to tribal superstition did not come off. Conversely he stepped in at the last minute for the supernatural *The Queen Of Spades*, and it turned out to be one of his best and most successful films. *The Secret People* (1952), a study of a group of anarchists, was another personal project, but whether for artistic or political reasons it did not prove popular and was his last British feature. After a couple of Israeli films he ran UNESCO's film unit and then went into teaching, pioneering film studies in Britain. JR

Gaslight 1940, 84 min, b/w
cast Anton Walbrook, Diana Wynyard, Frank Pettingell, Cathleen Cordell, Robert Newton *cin* Bernard Knowles *m* John Addison

Despite the melodramatic plotting and lurid atmosphere typical of Patrick Hamilton's stories, Dickinson keeps the lid on tight, intensifying the film's power. The conceit of a woman calculatedly being driven insane by her husband is not unique, but this is a particularly effective version. Preparing for George Cukor's 1944 remake, MGM destroyed the negative of Dickinson's film and it only survived through covert preservation.

The Queen Of Spades 1949, 95 min, b/w
cast Anton Walbrook, Edith Evans, Yvonne Mitchell, Ronald Howard, Mary Jerrold *cin* Otto Heller *m* Georges Auric

With labyrinthine sets, fluid camerawork and expressionistic lighting, *The Queen Of Spades* perfectly captures the eerie atmosphere of Pushkin's story. A St Petersburg army officer is so desperate to learn a countess's secret of winning at cards that he seduces her daughter to get close to her, but accidentally scares the old lady to death. Respectively obsessive and implacable, Walbrook and Evans play terrifyingly off each other.

William Dieterle
Germany, 1893–1972

Despite earlier commercial success, William Dieterle may be one of Hollywood's greatest lost romantics.

He began acting in the Berlin theatre, joining Max Reinhardt's company in 1918. He also appeared in many films, including Paul Leni's *Waxworks* (1924) and F.W. Murnau's *Faust* (1926). In 1923 he began directing and a very young Marlene Dietrich appeared in his first film, *Der Mensch am Wege* (*Man By The Wayside*). From 1930 Dieterle was in Hollywood, becoming a dependable craftsman at Warner Bros. His early work was promising – *The Last Flight* (1931), *Her Majesty Love* (1931) – but after the striking *A Midsummer Night's Dream* (1935), co-directed with Reinhardt, Dieterle became the studio's man for stodgy biopics starring Paul Muni: *The Story Of Louis Pasteur* (1936), *The Life Of Emile Zola* (1937) and *Juarez* (1939), the latter saved by Bette Davis's rich histrionics.

Moving to RKO in 1939 resulted in some of

Dieterle's finest work, including the Charles Laughton version of *The Hunchback Of Notre Dame* (1939) and *All That Money Can Buy* (1941). Under the influence of David O. Selznick for the Paramount Jennifer Jones projects *Love Letters* (1945) and *Portrait Of Jennie* (1948), Dieterle's romantic sensibility flourished, prompting the notion that he could have excelled with the lush spectacles favoured by 1950s Hollywood as an antidote to television. But involvement in liberal politics – Dieterle was instrumental with Fritz Lang in getting Bertolt Brecht and Kurt Weill out of Germany – led to McCarthyist censure in 1947. Directing assignments became less interesting and Dieterle's career went into terminal decline. RA

The Hunchback Of Notre Dame 1939, 116 min, b/w

cast Charles Laughton, Maureen O'Hara, Cedric Hardwicke, Thomas Mitchell, Edmond O'Brien *cin* Joseph August *m* Alfred Newman

A deserved highlight of Hollywood's *annus mirabilis*, although slightly overshadowed at the time by the other classic films of 1939, the first sound version of Victor Hugo's gothic tale features Charles Laughton giving one of his most layered, moving performances as the deformed bell-ringer, tragically in love with fiery gypsy Maureen O'Hara. Dieterle brings all of his skill as an industry craftsman in orchestrating sweeping, spectacular scenes and hordes of extras, while musical director Alfred Newman was nominated for an Oscar.

Portrait Of Jennie 1948, 86 min, b/w and col

cast Jennifer Jones, Joseph Cotten, Ethel Barrymore, Lillian Gish, Cecil Kellaway, David Wayne *cin* Joseph August *m* Dimitri Tiomkin

Luis Buñuel admired this story of the love between Joseph Cotten's struggling artist and Jennifer Jones's ethereal spirit, whom he spots one day in New York's Central Park. Inspiring the young man to paint from his heart, the girl – bedecked in oddly Victorian fashion in the late 1940s – matures to almost diaphanous womanhood in successive encounters, and is played by Jennifer Jones more as wraith than with substance. Few Hollywood films toy with cinema's capacity for absence and presence with such lingering, happy melancholy.

Edward Dmytryk

Canada, 1908–99

If it hadn't been for the House Un-American Activities Committee hearings, Edward Dmytryk could have been a contender.

Joining Paramount as a messenger boy at 15, by 1930 Dmytryk had worked his way up to editor, cutting a slew of pictures including Leo McCarey's 1935 comedy hit *Ruggles Of Red Gap*. Officially a director from 1939, Dmytryk cut his teeth on Columbia and RKO B-pictures such as the enjoyable fillers *The Devil Commands* (1941) and the Ginger Rogers war weepie *Tender Comrade* (1943).

Dmytryk's 1943 programmer *Captive Wild Woman*, in which John Carradine implants human glands in a gorilla and comes up with a beautiful young woman, was clearly a reference point for Woody Allen's Carradine episode in *Everything You Always Wanted To Know About Sex...* (1972). Murky thrillers *Murder, My Sweet* (aka *Farewell My Lovely*, 1944) and *Cornered* (1945) made Dmytryk fit for the A-list and gave 1930s musical star Dick Powell a new lease of life. Critical plaudits followed for the 1947 *noir* exposé of anti-Semitism *Crossfire*, but Dmytryk's communist affiliations led to his investigation by HUAC as one of the "Hollywood Ten", and he spent a year in jail. Exile in England followed.

Returning to America in 1951, Dmytryk testified and was reinstated in the industry. As if in divine retribution, he made few good films thereafter. There was *The Sniper* (1952), a tense throwback to

Dick Powell as Philip Marlowe keeps a steady hand when dealing with Claire Trevor in *Murder, My Sweet*, Dmytryk's accomplished *film noir*.

Walt Disney: the only real filmmaker in America

For some cultural commentators, Disney has become a byword for homogenization, globalization and commercialization. This bland corporate image seems at odds with the company's founder, who was a risk-taker, loss-maker and genuine innovator, the man who Sergei Eisenstein, an unlikely fan, once dubbed the only real filmmaker in America. Walt Disney was more than just a producer and studio head – he was the chief creative force behind many of the films made by the studio during his lifetime. Particularly in the case of the animations, his influence was more important than that of the films' individual directors, and it is for that reason that these films are reviewed under his name in this book.

Walt was born in Chicago in 1901. He started a course at the Kansas City Art Institute but dropped out at the age of 16 to volunteer as a Red Cross ambulance driver in World War I. On his return, he worked as a commercial artist in Kansas, and together with one of his colleagues, Ub Iwerks, founded the first Disney company, Laugh-O-Gram Films, in 1922. The company, which specialized in short animations, went bankrupt in 1923 and Ub and Walt moved to Los Angeles where they tried again, this time with Walt's financier brother, Roy. After success with a series of cartoons based on Lewis Carroll's *Alice In Wonderland*, the Disney brothers formed their own studio, with the creative input of Ub. Their next character, Oswald the Lucky Rabbit, proved to be anything but: Walt didn't own the rights to Oswald (a mistake he'd never make again) and when a deal fell through with the distribution company, they took Oswald and almost all of his animators away from the Disney brothers to form their own studio. It's part of the Disney legend that on the train ride back from that fateful meeting Walt invented a character called Mortimer Mouse. His wife preferred the name Mickey.

It was Ub, rather than the less dexterously gifted Walt, who drew Mickey, but it was Disney who insisted upon the innovation that saved the company and changed animation history – Mickey's cartoon debut, *Steamboat Willie* (1928), was the first cartoon to use synchronized sound (including Walt as the voice of Mickey). Two years later, Roy made an equally important contribution to the history of the Disney corporation, signing a licensing deal to manufacture Mickey Mouse products. During the 1930s Mickey was joined by a whole host of other cartoon characters, including Pluto, Goofy and Donald Duck. In addition, Walt continued to push for technical improvements in the studio's work, introducing the use of Technicolor as well as the "multiplane" technique (invented by Ub) which added depth and dimension to the animations. But the major breakthrough came in 1937 with *Snow White And The Seven Dwarfs*, America's first ever feature-length animation, and for Eisenstein the single greatest film ever made. Impossible as it is to believe now, before the film was released cynics concurred that the public had no interest in watching a cartoon that lasted longer than seven minutes or so, and when the budget ballooned to over $1.5 million and the company went into serious debt, *Snow White* was dubbed "Disney's Folly". On its release, it made a staggering $8 million and enabled Walt to make his most experimental film, *Fantasia* (1940), two hours of ambitious, often abstract animation set to the music of composers including Bach, Tchaikovsky, Stravinsky, Beethoven and Schubert.

Walt sincerely believed that *Fantasia* represented the future of animation, but his prophetic enthusiasm wasn't shared by hostile critics or an apathetic public. Designed to place cartoons in the echelons of high art, *Fantasia* was attacked as tasteless, kitsch and an insult to classical music. The embarrassing failure of Disney's pet project has been cited by biographers as the moment that he started to fall out of love with the medium. By the outbreak of World War II, the finances of the Disney company were in a parlous state. The war had closed the lucrative European markets that had accounted for over forty percent of revenue. What's more, the strained relationship between the authoritative Disney and his overworked and underappreciated animators reached breaking point in 1941 when they downed pencils and went on strike. Of the next two major projects, *Dumbo* and *Bambi* (both 1942), only the former turned a slight profit.

After the war, the company's balance sheets weren't any healthier and *Cinderella* (1950) was released as a money-making exercise. From then on, Walt seemed to lose interest in the animated films, concentrating on television, whose virtues he'd been prophetically extolling since the 1930s (cannily ensuring the corporation retained TV rights on all its work). In 1954 he hosted the *Disneyland* series, and the happy man with the thin moustache

the lean thrillers of the past, but Dmytryk's postwar work – *The Caine Mutiny* (1953), *Broken Lance* (1954), *Raintree County* (1957) – suffered for being little more than vehicles for ageing stars Spencer Tracy and Humphrey Bogart. The melodrama *Walk On The Wild Side* (1962) could have been good, boasting a cast that included Barbara Stanwyck, Anne Baxter, Jane Fonda and Capucine, but was too impressed by its mod sexiness. From the late 1970s, Dmytryk taught, becoming professor of film at the University of Southern California and writing *On Directing*, a key film studies textbook. With more pluck, he might have been as lionized as Nicholas Ray. RA became the nation's favourite uncle (and a prominent supporter of the notorious anti-communist committee, HUAC). A year later, on July 17, 1955, he opened the corporation's first theme park, Disneyland, in California.

By then the corporation had moved into live-action movies, with *Treasure Island* in 1950. *Mary Poppins* (1965) mixed live action and animation to charming effect, and its star, Julie Andrews, became the first actor in a Disney film to win an Oscar. Although *Mary Poppins* was directed by studio stalwart Robert Stevenson, it was a very personal project for Walt and it was hailed by many as his greatest achievement. Walt died the year that Andrews picked up her gong, although rumours persist that he was cryogenically frozen and is still waiting to be thawed when they discover a cure for cancer. Since his death the global influence of the corporation he founded has steadily increased but the studio has stayed true to Walt's original vision, of bringing a touch of fantasy into people's lives. A series of classic animations in the early 1990s – *Beauty And The Beast* (1991), *Aladdin* (1992) and *The Lion King* (1994) – boosted the company's fortunes, and a collaboration with Pixar brought Disney into the age of CGI with *Toy Story* (1995), *Monsters, Inc.* (2001) and *Finding Nemo* (2003). LH

Snow White And The Seven Dwarfs
1937, 83 min
dir David Hand *cast (voices)* Adriana Caselotti, Harry Stockwell, Lucile La Verne, Moroni Olsen *m* Frank Churchill, Leigh Harline, Paul Smith

While the titular heroes are obviously the main attraction, the real star is the multiplane method, which brings weight and depth to the animation, thus making it a wholly immersive experience. Rendered in the terrifying chiaroscuro of German expressionism, the evil queen learns from her magic mirror that she is not the fairest in the land. The unknowing owner of that title, Snow White, is condemned to death. The regal minions, however, let Snow White escape into the woods, where she comes across some scene-stealing dwarves.

Pinocchio 1940, 88 min
dir Ben Sharpsteen, Hamilton Luske *cast (voices)* Dickie Jones, Christian Rub, Cliff Edwards, Evelyn Venable *m* Leigh Harline, Paul J. Smith

Only ever wanting to be a good little boy, the animated puppet Pinocchio is a sideshow freak who is kidnapped and sent to Pleasure Island to be turned into a donkey. Once again Disney proves to be the tormentor of children's imaginations and sleep patterns. Despite the comic relief of Jimmy Cricket, it's the disturbingly resonant image of the donkey-boys that weighs like a nightmare on the brains of the living.

Fantasia 1940, 120 min
dir Ben Sharpsteen *presenter* Deems Taylor *m* Bach, Tchaikovsky, Dukas, Stravinsky, Beethoven, Ponchielli, Mussorgsky, Schubert

Set to music conducted by the ever-flamboyant Leopold Stowkowski, *Fantasia* is Walt's idiosyncratic version of heaven and hell, the creation of the planets, and abstract expressionism. Highlights include Mickey Mouse as the sorcerer's apprentice and a group of dancing hippos. A curious synthesis of the bold and the cute.

Bambi 1942, 70 min
dir David Hand *cast (voices)* Donnie Dunagan, Peter Behn, Bobby Stewart *cin* Chuck Wheeler *m* Edward Plumb, Frank Churchill

While Disney is synonymous with the cute, the anthropomorphic and the wholesome, he subverted his own good intentions by traumatizing generations of children with the death of Bambi's mother, which was many young film-goers' first encounter with the concept of mortality. *Bambi* became a terrifying epiphany shared by millions around the globe.

Dumbo 1942, 64 min
dir Ben Sharpsteen *cast (voices)* Edward Brophy, Herman Bing, Sterling Holloway *cin* Chuck Wheeler *m* Oliver Wallace, Frank Churchill

When circus elephant Mrs Jumbo's baby arrives, he soon becomes a figure of fun because of his huge ears. But, with the help of his friend Timothy Mouse, Dumbo uses his ears to fly and becomes a star. Almost rivalling *Bambi* in the trauma department (a side effect of World War II?), *Dumbo* also boasts the most surreal set piece outside of *Fantasia* with the "pink elephants on parade" fantasy sequence. The star was modelled on live elephants who were regularly brought into the Disney studios.

The Jungle Book 1967, 78 min
dir Wolfgang Reitherman *cast (voices)* Phil Harris, Sebastian Cabot, Louis Prima, George Sanders, Sterling Holloway *m* George Bruns

A young boy, Mowgli, is raised by wolves in the Indian jungle, but when they hear that scary tiger Shere Khan is near, they pack him off to the humans. However, Khan, voiced by George Sanders, soon gets to hear about the boy. The film that Walt was working on when he died is one of his greatest triumphs, blessed with Disney's best music in the form of Louis Armstrong's jaunty "I Want To Be Like You", a song that has gloriously transcended its filmic origins.

Murder, My Sweet (aka Farewell My Lovely)
1944, 95 min, b/w
cast Dick Powell, Claire Trevor, Anne Shirley, Otto Kruger, Mike Mazurki, Miles Mander, Douglas Walton *cin* Harry J. Wild *m* Roy Webb

When private detective Philip Marlowe (Dick Powell) is approached by big lug Moose Malloy (Mike Mazurki) to track down his missing girlfriend, he doesn't expect to find smooth-talking beauty Helen Grayle (Claire Trevor) at the end of the road. One of the most underrated but accomplished *films noirs* of the classical era, this trawl through the social swamp of Raymond Chandler's Los Angeles – complete with a hallucinatory dream sequence when Marlowe is slugged – is shadowed in a dirty light cast over slick performances from Powell and a venomous, disappointed Trevor.

141

Crossfire 1947, 85 min, b/w
cast Robert Ryan, Robert Mitchum, Robert Young, Gloria Grahame, Sam
Levene, Paul Kelly *cin* J. Roy Hunt *m* Roy Webb

One of the most daring thrillers of the 1940s, this exposé of
anti-Semitism and weak-kneed liberalism is held together
by a cunning performance from the terrific Robert Ryan
as repressed, softly spoken psychopath Montgomery.
Dmytryck's portrait of post-war America is as dank and
wayward as a drugged nightmare.

Jacques Doillon
France, 1944–

Even within French cinema, which has an established and respected tradition of addressing
the often turbulent emotional lives of children
and young adults, Jacques Doillon's work is
brave and unique. He entered the film industry
in 1966, making his way as an editor. Directing
from 1969, he came to critical attention with *Les
doigts dans le tête* (*Touched In The Head*, 1974),
which revolved around the problems of a young
baker's apprentice. Generational conflicts, particularly between fathers and daughters, remain
a perennial theme of his. He tends to focus on
female characters, especially so in *Ponette* (1996),
a spare, minimalist drama of violent emotions. In
La drôlesse (*The Hussy*, 1979), a repressed young
man locks a teenage girl in an attic, beginning
a bizarre, quasi-Oedipal relationship of blurred
roles and power games. Informed by Goethe's tale
of blighted adolescence, *Le jeune Werther* (1992)
explored the Romantic sensibility against the
contemporary backdrop of Parisian classrooms
and streets, training youth parlance upon sophisticated emotional landscapes. Drawing upon his
own experiences, screenwriting and improvising
to encourage identification between actor and
role, Doillon's hermetic worlds recall a tradition
of subjective realism that can be traced from John
Cassavetes to Mike Leigh. RA

Ponette 1996, 97 min
cast Victoire Thivisol, Matiaz Bureau Caton, Delphine Schiltz, Léopoldine
Serre, Xavier Beauvois *cin* Caroline Champetier *m* Philippe Sarde

Doillon had a psychiatrist on hand to watch over Victoire
Thivisol, the little girl who plays Ponette, whose mother
has just died in a car accident. The film follows a 4-year-old
negotiating the various beliefs and myths her friends and
the adults around her use to deal with grief. Contrasting
close-ups of Thivisol with the bare village milieu, Caroline
Champetier's camera fills the film with Ponette's unutterably moving struggle to understand.

Roger Donaldson
Australia, 1945–

Roger Donaldson has made a number of slickly
produced genre films, several of which endure
as very effective pieces. Born in Australia, he moved
to New Zealand at the age of 19, and soon emerged
on the crest of a wave of successful antipodean filmmakers which would later include Jane Campion,
Vincent Ward and Peter Jackson.

Donaldson's earliest films, such as the action
thriller *Sleeping Dogs* (1977) and the gangster
comedy *Nutcase* (1980), demonstrated an affinity
for genre. His first American studio film was *The
Bounty* (1984), a new account of Captain Bligh starring Anthony Hopkins and Mel Gibson. Donaldson
has been most comfortable in the thriller genre; *No
Way Out* (1986) was one of the best neo-*noirs* of the
decade. But he moved in quite a different direction
with his next film, the Tom Cruise vehicle *Cocktail*
(1988), about the professional and personal winning streak of a cocky young barman. In the comedy *Cadillac Man* (1990) a car salesman (Robin
Williams) is held hostage in his showroom by an
unhinged Tim Robbins.

After a series of poorly received thrillers in the
1990s, *Thirteen Days* (2000) was a welcome return
to form, focusing on John F. Kennedy's negotiation
of the Cuban Missile Crisis. It was followed by *The
Recruit* (2003), a solid CIA action movie, and *The
World's Fastest Indian* (2005), based on the true story
of an elderly Kiwi who broke a land speed record on
his ancient Indian motorcycle. JC

No Way Out 1986, 114 min
cast Kevin Costner, Gene Hackman, Sean Young, Will Patton, Howard Duff,
George Dzundza *cin* John Alcott *m* Maurice Jarre

In this twisty and kinetic thriller, a Pentagon staff member
(Costner) is enlisted to investigate the murder of his boss's
mistress. He suspects his boss (Hackman) may be the culprit, but when his own affair with the woman is uncovered
he himself becomes a suspect. Featuring top-flight performances from the two leads, *No Way Out* has a perfectly
judged mood and pace.

Stanley Donen
US, 1924–

Responsible for some of the greatest Hollywood
musicals ever, Donen has been unjustifiably
neglected, possibly because he did some of his finest
work as a co-director. A dancer since he was a small
boy, Donen made his Broadway debut aged 16 in *Pal
Joey*, the start of his lifelong friendship with Gene
Kelly. The two worked together as choreographers
on *Anchors Aweigh* (1945) and *Take Me Out To The
Ball Game* (1949), and made their auspicious directo-

rial debuts together. Under the guidance of legendary MGM producer Arthur Freed, they divided their duties in *On The Town* (1949) and gave the musical a radical refit. The decision to film on the streets of New York, rather than on a traditional sound stage, was genuinely revolutionary, audaciously removing the musical from its rarefied world. Donen remained in the open air for *Funny Face* (1957) and *The Pajama Game* (1957) but even in his studio work, his choreography and camerawork were characterized by a virtuosic aplomb. It's in dazzling evidence in *Seven Brides For Seven Brothers* (1954), *Funny Face*, *Singin' In The Rain* (1952) and *Royal Wedding* (1951), in which Fred Astaire elegantly defies gravity by dancing on the ceiling.

Donen left musicals just as they were about to go into terminable decline in the 1960s, and moved into light comedy with *Arabesque* (1966) and the underrated, intricately crafted *Two For The Road* (1967) which charts the breakdown of a marriage over several trips around France, relayed in a series of flashbacks and flash-forwards which literally overtake one another. The need for continual invention seemed to get the better of Donen in the painfully modish *Bedazzled* (1968), while the old man's fantasy *Blame It On Rio* (1984) was a sad conclusion to a sparkling career.

This inconsistency has led some mealy-mouthed critics to claim that the director did his best work in tandem: with Gene Kelly in *On The Town*, *Singin' In The Rain* and *It's Always Fair Weather* (1955), and with George Abbott on *The Pajama Game* and *Damn Yankees* (1958). The dexterous handling of time shifts in *Two For The Road* should be enough to silence the doubters, but if more proof were really needed, you only have to look at the fine thriller *Charade* (1963). Its panache and narrative nous is perhaps best summed up in the wry, elegant charm of Cary Grant and Audrey Hepburn playing "who's who?" amongst a small regiment of thieves in Paris. LH

On The Town 1949, 98 min

cast Gene Kelly, Frank Sinatra, Jules Munshin, Betty Garrett, Ann Miller, Vera-Ellen, Florence Bates *cin* Harold Rosson *m* Leonard Bernstein

Three sailors get a 24-hour leave pass in New York and go in search of women – Gene Kelly (who also co-directs) gets the hots for "Miss Turnstiles", Frank Sinatra is swept away by a female cab driver and Jules Munshin becomes matey with an anthropologist. Given the freedom of the city, *On The Town* bristles with energy and brio, even if it does slack a little on the narrative.

Singin' In The Rain 1952, 102 min

cast Gene Kelly, Donald O'Connor, Debbie Reynolds, Jean Hagen, Cyd Charisse *cin* Harold Rosson *m* Nacio Herb Brown, Arthur Freed

With the advent of sound, an aspiring actress (Debbie Reynolds) has to provide the voice for a vocally challenged silent star (Jean Hagen) and falls in love with the leading man (co-director Gene Kelly). This buoyant satire contains the most famous dance number and some of the finest ditties

in the history of film musicals. It also has the zingiest patter this side of a Preston Sturges comedy. But it can also be read as a sly allegory about blacklisted writers who surreptitiously used other scribes as fronts during the McCarthy era.

Funny Face 1957, 103 min

cast Fred Astaire, Audrey Hepburn, Kay Thompson, Michel Auclair *cin* Ray June *m* George Gershwin, Ira Gershwin

A zesty celebration and astute send-up of Parisian boho chic. Scoring no points for sexual politics, Audrey Hepburn stops being a bookworm in favour of the hedonistic lifestyle of a fashion clothes horse and falls head over expensive heels for the wrinkly charms of snapper Fred Astaire, 30 years her senior. It is, however, a "design classic".

The Pajama Game 1957, 101 min

cast Doris Day, John Raitt, Carol Haney, Eddie Foy Jr, Barbara Nichols, Reta Shaw, Mary Stanton *cin* Harry Stradling *m* Richard Adler, Jerry Ross

Union firebrand Doris Day is caught in a tug of love between her head and her heart as she falls for new management apprentice, John Raitt. This blue-collar musical, which was co-directed with George Abbott, does include some key Donen moments, not least the ground-breaking use of a genuine municipal park in the celebrated workers' picnic scene.

Richard Donner
US, 1930–

In his *Biographical Dictionary Of Film*, David Thomson dismisses Richard Donner with an entry that's brief and to the point. It reads "Mr. Donner has made several of the most successful and least interesting films of his age. And one doubts it's over yet." With few exceptions, Donner's filmography is a slog through slick, sickly formulae; hollow and meretricious, his movies are a case study in soulless blockbuster bloat, frequently distinguished by the rancid sentimentality of their endings (the denouement of his 1988 Dickens update *Scrooged* may provide the most ghastly example).

Matters weren't always so dire. After a decades-long apprenticeship in television (he directed episodes of *The Twilight Zone*, *The Man from U.N.C.L.E.*, *Kojak*, even *Gilligan's Island*), Donner established his box-office clout with epochal back-to-back hits: many a 1970s childhood is indelibly marked with any number of chilling set pieces from his solid *Exorcist* cash-in *The Omen* (1976), wherein Gregory Peck and Lee Remick slowly discover that their adopted child carries the brand of the beast, and *Superman* (1978) is a deft and properly respectful celluloid treatment of the comic-book franchise. Removed from the *Superman* sequel, Donner began scraping the bottoms of some very expensive barrels: *The Toy* (1982) was the nadir of Richard Pryor's big-screen emasculation, while kiddie treasure hunt *The Goonies* (1985) and the hugely popular *Lethal Weapon* action tetralogy viciously attacked eardrums and brain cells. The early stages of *Conspiracy*

Theory (1997), featuring Mel Gibson as a babbling cabbie kidnapped and tortured by shadowy villains, promised a bold paranoia thriller (French arthouse director Olivier Assayas, of all people, has spoken positively of the first few reels). But the film was undone by touchy-feely gloop, ludicrous plot contortions and a staggeringly stupid finale. JW

The Omen 1976, 111 min
cast Gregory Peck, Lee Remick, David Warner, Billie Whitelaw, Harvey Stephens, Leo McKern *cin* Gilbert Taylor *m* Jerry Goldsmith

Belatedly piggybacking on the success of Satan-spawn features such as *Rosemary's Baby* and *The Exorcist*, Donner's thriller managed to win a cult following with its tale of an American diplomat and his wife who slowly realize that their moody kid might have the mark of the devil. The film is creepy and schlocky in equal doses, although its most significant legacy may have been to guarantee many years' worth of dumb jokes directed at boys named Damien.

Superman 1978, 143 min
cast Christopher Reeve, Margot Kidder, Gene Hackman, Marlon Brando, Valerie Perrine, Ned Beatty *cin* Geoffrey Unsworth *m* John Williams

Years in the planning and released just a year after *Star Wars* set a new bar for massively profitable action spectacle, this big-screen introduction to the "Man of Steel" traces Superman's alien origins on planet Krypton (with dad Marlon Brando), his childhood in the American heartland and his adult sojourn to the corrupt city of Metropolis. Christopher Reeve was perfectly cast in the lead role, equally at ease with light comedy and sober heroism.

Mark Donskoi
Ukraine (formerly Russian Empire), 1901–81

Though always sensitive to the politics of the day, Donskoi was by no means a dull propagandist. He is best known for his classic trilogy based on Gorky's autobiography.

Born in the creative hotbed of Odessa, Donskoi wrote poetry and fiction, studied both medicine and law, and was imprisoned by the Whites during the Russian Civil War before deciding to move into film in 1926. After editing, scripting and acting he moved into directing with the politically conformist *In The Big City* (1928). In the early 1930s he began to consider adapting Maxim Gorky's autobiographical trilogy but the author dissuaded him. When *The Childhood Of Maxim Gorky* finally appeared in 1938, Gorky was dead. Donskoi followed it with *My Apprenticeship* (1939) and *My Universities* (1940), which marked the climax of his career. Other fine films followed, including *The Rainbow* (1944) and *The Village Teacher* (1946), which was distinguished by stunning photography from Sergei Urusevsky. Donskoi's Gorky connection continued with reverential adaptations of *Mother* (1956) and *Foma Gordeyev* (1959), and his last two films (*The Heart Of A Mother*, 1966, and *A Mother's Devotion*, 1968)

continued the move towards stultification in their hagiography of Lenin's mother. JR

The Childhood Of Maxim Gorky (Detstvo Gorkovo) 1938, 98 min, b/w
cast Aleksei Lyarsky, Varvara Masalitinova, Mikhail Troyanovsky, Elizaveta Alekseyeva *cin* Piotr Yermolov *m* Lev Schwartz

Gorky eschewed self-pity for his autobiographical account of a childhood of grinding poverty and Donskoi expertly creates a similarly compelling story of the author's struggle. Unfortunately the increasingly dominant and often mendacious state-sanctioned artistic credo of socialist realism means that the standard drops a little through the other two films of the trilogy, which follow Gorky into his late teens.

Ziad Doueiri
Lebanon, 1963–

For a man who has directed only a couple of features to date, Lebanese filmmaker Ziad Doueiri certainly punches above his weight in terms of reputation and following. After an apprenticeship as Quentin Tarantino's assistant director, Doueiri triumphantly announced his arrival with his debut feature, *West Beirut* (1998). Recounting the city's split into sectarian halves with the outbreak of the 1975 Lebanese Civil War, it was a work of undeniable sensitivity and humour. It was perhaps inevitable that his second feature, *Lila Says* (2004), would be a comparative disappointment. For all its flaws, however, the film did include one of the most memorable comments on the Arab-Israeli conflict yet committed to film: "If I had to choose between pussy and a free Palestine", muses its teenage protagonist Chimo, "I'd choose pussy!" AJa

West Beirut (West Beyrouth) 1998, 105 min
cast Rami Doueiri, Mohammad Chamas, Rola al Amin, Carmen Loubbos, Joseph Bou Nassar *cin* Richard Jacques Gale *m* Stuart Copeland

This semi-autobiographical look at the outbreak of the Lebanese Civil War in 1975 – which would see the capital city Beirut split into a predominantly Muslim west and Christian east – put Doueiri on the world cinema map. Effortlessly mixing pathos, adolescent hijinks and moments of tragedy, Doueiri's film perfectly captures the surreal spectacle of neighbours turning their guns on each other and families being torn apart by warfare.

Gordon Douglas
US, 1907–93

Douglas was a prolific director. Despite the ordinariness of some of his films (which he himself recognized) he still managed an impressive strike rate in a variety of genres.

After working as a child actor, Douglas wrote gags for Hal Roach before moving into directing.

His early films ranged from *Saps At Sea* (1940), starring Laurel and Hardy, to the bizarre Bela Lugosi horror *Zombies On Broadway* (1945), but nothing in these films particularly marked Douglas out. He had greater success with a few Westerns and detective films and in 1954 directed *Them!*, which rose above its B-movie sci-fi origins to become a classic of the genre. In the same year he directed the musical romance *Young At Heart* starring Frank Sinatra and Doris Day. Sinatra found Douglas pliant enough to be worth engaging four more times: in the Rat Pack comedy musical *Robin And The Seven Hoods* (1964), and three detective films, *Tony Rome* (1967), *The Detective* (1968) and *The Lady In Cement* (1968). Meanwhile the spy spoof *In Like Flint* (1967) managed to enjoyably mock the already wry James Bond. JR

Them! 1954, 94 min, b/w

cast James Whitmore, Edmund Gwenn, Joan Weldon, James Arness, Onslow Stevens *cin* Sid Hickox *m* Bronislau Kaper

A classic of the 1950s "nuclear mutation" genre, graced with Oscar-nominated special effects. Following nuclear tests in New Mexico, giant ants threaten to take over America, leaving no option but to try to find the queens and destroy them. One of a slew of movies that reflect fears about the Cold War and technological advances, *Them!* also benefits from sensitive photography and performances less wooden than usual in such films.

Alexander Dovzhenko

Ukraine (formerly Russian Empire), 1894–1956

Dovzhenko was the poet of Ukrainian cinema, the creator of bucolic, folkloric, exuberant hymns to the nation's landscape and its people. Serving in the Red Army during the Civil War, he went to Germany in the early 1920s and learnt about the avant-garde, returning home as a painter and political cartoonist. Despite having no previous interest in the cinema, Dovzhenko then rolled up to the Odessa film studios in 1926 in the hope of gaining employment. There is little of historical interest in his earliest efforts, but his fourth film is regarded as a triumph of delirious idiosyncrasy. *Zvenigora* (1928) covers centuries of sprawling Ukrainian history, vividly expressed in a series of inchoate images which the director referred to as "a catalogue of all my creative possibilities". The film made little sense to the Soviet film bureaucrats, who sought Sergei Eisenstein's approval before releasing it. Legend has it that the great Soviet director didn't know what to make of *Zvenigora* either, but instinctively knew it was the work of a considerable talent.

Zvenigora is, amongst many other things, a symbolic folk tale about a 1000-year-old grandfather and his two grandsons, the capitalist Paul (bad seed) and the brave soldier Timosh (good seed). The latter character reappeared in *Arsenal* (1928), an elliptical tale of trench warfare and a revolt at a Kiev arsenal, in which Dovzhenko took film montage to new poetic levels, jettisoning the prosaic concerns of conventional narrative, cross-cutting between time periods and allowing the audience to fill in the blanks. Although it eschewed the expressionistic symbolism of *Zvenigora* for a newly discovered romanticism, *Arsenal* famously ends with Timosh defiantly facing enemy fire with his shirt torn open – the bullets bouncing off his indestructible body.

Earth (1930) took Dovzhenko's romanticism to new, giddy, reckless heights in its lyrical, passionate and ebullient paean to the union of man, nature and tractor. Making an avant-garde symphony to the pastoral traditions of the Ukraine was a dangerous thing to do in the Soviet Union in the 1930s, as both formalism and nationalism fell under suspicion, and many of Dovzhenko's associates became victims of Stalin's purges. However, despite these considerable pressures, Dovzhenko stubbornly made one more notable film, *Ivan* (1931), about the building of the Dnieper River dam, before succumbing to the dictates of socialist realism. Stalin took a personal interest in *Shchors* (1939), a biography of the Bolshevik leader Nikolai Shchors, and the director's last film, *Muchurin* (1949) was an anaemic exercise in propaganda, extolling the life of a Soviet biologist. Even if Dovzhenko himself wasn't a victim of Stalin, his idiosyncratic artistry certainly was. LH

Arsenal 1928, 70 min, b/w

cast Semyon Svashenko, Amvrosi Buchma, Georgi Khorkov, Dmitri Erdman, Sergei Petrov, M. Mikhajlovsky *cin* Daniil Demutsky *m* Igor Belza

Etched in inky monochrome, Dozhenko's training as a caricaturist comes clearly to the fore in this film's series of discontinuous, striking images, such as that of a gas victim laughing himself to death. However, understanding the complex narrative of this story of a rebellion at a munitions factory is frustratingly contingent upon knowledge of historical figures, events and even dress codes, so the DVD commentary is a blessed necessity.

Earth (Zemlya) 1930, 73 min, b/w

cast Semyon Svashenko, Stepan Shkurat, Mikola Nademsky, Yelena Maximova, Yulia Solntzeva *cin* Daniil Demutsky *m* Vyacheslav Ovchinnikov

From the opening scene's rapt close-ups of sunflowers, pears and oxen, the fecund imagery of *Earth* is filled with meaning. This pantheistic ode can be overripe at times, as in the farmers' orgasmic reactions to the coming of the glistening new tractor, but the rhapsodic scenes of nature are poignantly contrasted with the hard, gleaming edge of machinery; the natural balance irreversibly affected when the blades inflict deep wounds into Mother Nature in a montage of fast, rhythmic cuts.

Srdjan Dragojevic
Serbia (formerly Yugoslavia), 1963–

Dragojevic is the director of one of the most important, controversial, harrowing and funny movies about the Balkan conflict: *Pretty Village, Pretty Flame* (1996). He used the same broad comic approach on this film, based on a true story about a Serb unit besieged inside a tunnel by Bosnian soldiers for ten days, that had previously served him so well in *We're No Angels* (1992), a sex farce about a philanderer who's tamed into marriage by his pregnant girlfriend.

Pretty Village, Pretty Flame is one of a clutch of films made about the Balkan conflict in the mid-1990s, including Michael Winterbottom's *Welcome To Sarajevo* (1997) and Emir Kusturica's *Underground* (1995). Dragojevic's film was closer to the latter, not just in its farcical, Felliniesque take on the theatre of war, but also in the international controversy it inspired. *Pretty Village, Pretty Flame*'s protagonists were Serbs, and not entirely unsympathetic Serbs at that, which prompted accusations that the movie was thinly veiled propaganda or, as one film festival director put it, "a work of fascism". Ironically, in his own country (where the film broke box-office records) the director was accused of being anti-Serbian, largely thanks to early scenes of boorish soldiers shamelessly burning Muslim villages.

While the Karadzic government was cool about *Pretty Village, Pretty Flame,* it was distinctly chilly about Dragojevic's next project, *Wounds* (1998), even prohibiting advertising for this nihilistic portrait of Serb teenagers seduced by the easy money and glamorous lifestyle of Balkan gangsters after being irrevocably damaged by the war. Both films now seem like a detour for Dragojevic who, in 2005, came full circle with *We're No Angels 2*, a hyperactive sex comedy. LH

Pretty Village, Pretty Flame (Lepa sela lepo gore) 1996, 129 min
cast Dragan Bjelogrlic, Nikola Kojo, Zoran Cvijanovic, Dragan Maksimovic, Velimir Bata Zivojinovic *cin* Dusan Joksimovic *m* Aleksandar Sasa Habid

The real-life standoff between besieged Serbs and a troop of Bosnian soldiers acts as the centrepiece for this tragicomedy about two friends, Milan and Halil, a Serb and a Muslim respectively, who find themselves on opposing sides of the Brotherhood and Unity tunnel. From the first scene of a hapless Communist official opening the tunnel who cuts his own thumb, instead of the ribbon, Dragojevic sets the tone for a film that shifts violently in time and timbre: brutal, farcical, funny and vulgar.

Carl Theodor Dreyer
Denmark, 1889–1968

Though his work is associated with emotional austerity and slow, stately pacing, Carl Theodor Dreyer made films that glisten with blood, sweat and tears; the Scandinavian winter wind may forever howl outside the door, but inside it's a hothouse of conflicting desires and orthodoxies. He took female suffering as his great theme: in *The Passion Of Joan Of Arc* (1927) and *Day Of Wrath* (1943) women are persecuted by the murderous patriarchal authority of the church; in *Ordet* (*The Word*, 1955) they are oppressed by domineering fathers or betrayed by their own bodies; in *Gertrud* (1964) the weary title character endures her own profound existential disappointment. Dreyer's early silent, *Master Of The House* (1925), neatly sums up his interest in domestic despotism.

The subject matter resonates with Dreyer's own life: he was born out of wedlock to a Swedish houseservant who gave him up for adoption and died horribly just eighteen months later, after attempting a self-induced abortion (a tragedy implicitly revisited in *Ordet*). Ironically, for an artist so attuned to male oppression in his work, he wasn't entirely unacquainted with a little light tyranny himself: Dreyer made Maria Falconetti kneel painfully on stones for some of her close-ups in *Joan Of Arc* (it was to be her only film), and during the shooting of *Day Of Wrath*, he left the elderly Anna Svierkier tied to a ladder while the rest of the cast and crew took their lunch break, apparently so that Svierkier would appear more palpably distressed when her character is burned at the stake for witchcraft.

Dreyer began in the silent era, dominated by the aesthetics of D.W. Griffith. *Leaves From Satan's Book* (1919) is an *Intolerance*-style four-part historical epic covering Palestine in the time of Jesus Christ, the Spanish Inquisition, the French Revolution and contemporary Finland. With *The Passion Of Joan Of Arc*, Dreyer made radical innovations in film grammar, eschewing establishing shots in favour of close-ups and deploying oblique angles, skewed framing and disjointed cutting that disrupts the viewer's sense of the spatial relations between Joan (who is filmed in soft charcoal shades) and her relentless examiners (who are shot in harsh contrasts).

Dreyer's first sound film, *Vampyr* (1931), intensified this discombobulation, completely effacing the boundaries between reality and dream as experienced by Allan Grey, a devoted student of vampirism and devil worship. The film was a critical and commercial failure; Dreyer suffered a nervous breakdown not long after its completion, and made just four more features before his death in 1968.

The director used gentle, gliding camera movements to prowl the corridors of the crumbling Parisian château in which *Vampyr* was shot. The technique became a Dreyer trademark in *Day Of Wrath* and *Ordet*, both of which examine religious orthodoxy as a source of fear, enforced ignorance and inter-family strife. Dreyer once said that he aimed for "realized mysticism", and, true to mysticism's emphasis on subjective experience, his films achieve a powerful mystery – an unknowability that was never more magical than in *Ordet*, which depicts a supernatural occurrence, a literal rising from the dead, with extraordinary matter-of-factness. *Day Of Wrath*, set in the witch-trial era of seventeenth-century Denmark, also takes place under a shroud of mystery. The young, wayward wife Anne (smoky-eyed Lisbeth Movin) is certainly not in the devil's employ, and yet, as Mark Le Fanu writes, "Anne dramatizes (most beautifully and subtly) a defiance of convention that can only be called bewitching or witchlike. In some profound, moving and tragic way she is a witch."

The eponymous heroine of Dreyer's valedictory film, *Gertrud*, also defies convention, her impossibly idealized conception of love destined to leave both her and the men in her life unhappy. At the film's Cannes premiere, the stationary tableaux of the near-neurasthenic heroine and her disappointing suitors drove the audience to catcalls and walkouts. Dreyer was never properly appreciated – or, more to the point, funded – in his own time, but perhaps his exquisite canon seems all the more precious for being so small. JW

The Passion Of Joan Of Arc 1927, 90 min, b/w
cast Maria Falconetti, Eugène Silvain, Maurice Schutz, Michel Simon *cin* Rudolph Maté, Goestula Kottula, Ole Schmidt

Contradicting those who might label Dreyer as "slow", David Bordwell has counted more than 1500 cuts in this pioneering silent masterpiece, which draws heavily from transcripts of the actual trial. Working almost solely in close-ups, Dreyer makes a canvas of Maria Falconetti's face, which registers terror, pain and visionary fervour with naked abandon.

Day Of Wrath (Vredens dag) 1943, 97 min, b/w
cast Thorkild Roose, Lisbeth Movin, Sigrid Neiiendam, Preben Lerdorff Rye, Anna Svierkier, Albert Hoeberg *cin* Carl Andersson *m* Poul Schierbeck

Anne, the young, restless wife of an ageing parson, falls in love with her new stepson in seventeenth-century Denmark, where witch-burning fever has infected the parishes. Filmed during the Nazi occupation of Dreyer's native country, *Day Of Wrath* is a powerful account of lethal ideological lunacy, anchored by a brilliantly multifaceted performance from Lisbeth Movin as Anne, who is by turns plaintive, nasty, sultry and tragic.

Ordet (The Word) 1955, 125 min, b/w
cast Henrik Malberg, Emil Hass Christensen, Preben Lerordd Rye, Cay Kristainsen, Birgitte Federspiel *cin* Henning Bendtsen *m* Poul Schierbeck

A farmer and his three sons live on a prosperous Danish farm. One son falls in love with a girl whose devoutly Christian father doesn't approve; a second believes himself to be the earthly representative of Jesus Christ; and the agnostic third son loses his wife in childbirth. Adapted from Kaj Munk's play, Dreyer's hypnotic chamber piece is bold enough to present us with a miracle, in one of the most wondrous finales in cinema history.

Gertrud 1964, 116 min
cast Nina Pens Rode, Bendt Rothe, Ebbe Rode, Baard Owe, Axel Strobye, Anna Malberg *cin* Henning Bendtsen *m* Jorgen Jersild

As uncompromising as its eponymous heroine, Dreyer's last film alienated audiences with its long, static shots of numb, lethargic conversation. But as always with this director, patience reaps rewards, and *Gertrud* slowly comes into focus as a portrait of a woman who stubbornly searches for a nonexistent perfect love, running away from all of its flawed real-life manifestations.

Slatan Dudow
Bulgaria, 1903–63

To call Slatan Dudow a mere propagandist is to miss his lyricism and humanity. After participating in Moscow-sponsored unrest in Sofia, Dudow fled to Berlin in 1922 where he studied stage directing and organized a workers' theatre. While researching a thesis on revolutionary theatre in Moscow in 1929, he made his first film, *Wie der Berliner Arbeiter wohnt* (*How The Berlin Worker Lives*). Dudow's didactic tone would become tempered with a realism about human affairs that was lacking in the fascist documentaries of the era.

Kuhle Wampe (*To Whom Does The World Belong?*, 1932), his most famous film, remains a searching depiction of socioeconomic conditions in the Weimar Republic. Banned by the Nazis, it resulted in Dudow's exile, first to France, then to Switzerland, where he remained throughout World War II. Returning to East Germany after the war, he made propaganda films for the Communists but his empathy for the people surfaces through his lectures in the impressively edited *Frauenschicksale* (1952), in which four women fall prey to a West Berlin Lothario but survive and grow through experience.

Dudow received the state filmmaking award three times and was honoured in 1974, when his final film, the unfinished *Christine* (1963), was re-released in the West, its director having died in a car accident. Dudow's works link the naturalism of 1930s documentary with the personal heroism of New German Cinema. RA

Kuhle Wampe (To Whom Does The World Belong?) 1932, 73 min, b/w
cast Hertha Thiele, Ernst Busch, Martha Wolter, Adolf Fischer, Lili Schönborn, Max Sablotzki *cin* Gunther Krampf *m* Hanns Eisler

Co-scripted by Bertolt Brecht and banned for "insulting Hindenberg and religion", Slatan Dudow's poem to the

Berlin proletariat rises above its partisan purposes to become a tough-minded but intelligent plea for political Utopia in the face of stifling old German "respectability". A young woman, dismayed by the apathy of inmates in an internment camp, turns to a young idealist for inspiration, while we are invited to keep an open mind...

John Duigan
UK, 1949-

British-born Duigan emigrated to Australia in 1961 and became part of the Australian cinema renaissance. His films, often about youth and life's turning points, are touched with eroticism. *Mouth To Mouth* (1978), a drama about unemployed hustlers, and the outback wedding comedy-drama *Dimboola* (1979) were followed by *Winter Of Our Dreams* (1981), about a prostitute and a bookshop owner. In *One Night Stand* (1984) four teenagers hear a New Year's Eve announcement of nuclear war. *Vietnam* (1987), one of several TV mini-series, tells of Australians in the war, while *Romero* (1989) is a biopic of the assassinated bishop of El Salvador. But his international breakthrough came with *The Year My Voice Broke* (1987), a semi-autobiographical coming-of-age drama about disappointed love, which was followed by the adolescent story *Flirting* (1990). The *Jane Eyre* prequel *Wide Sargasso Sea* (1993) brought no particular credit but the erotic comedy *Sirens* (1994) was well received. *The Parole Officer* (2001) was an unexpected move into broad comedy. JR

The Year My Voice Broke 1987, 105 min
cast Noah Taylor, Leone Carmen, Ben Mendelsohn, Graeme Blundell, Lynette Curran *cin* Geoff Burton *m* Christine Woodruff

Teenager Freya (Leone Carmen) is coveted by her sensitive, gawky childhood friend Danny (Noah Taylor), but is herself attracted to the local rugby hero, Trevor (Ben Mendelsohn), an all-round lad with an eye for trouble. Sometimes labelled as the Australian *Stand By Me* (1986), Duigan's evocative film deftly interweaves a tale of adolescent longing with a keen sense of place: a New South Wales backwater town where the universal and the particular melt into each other.

Sirens 1994, 95 min
cast Hugh Grant, Tara Fitzgerald, Sam Neill, Elle Macpherson, Portia de Rossi, Kate Fisher *cin* Geoff Burton *m* Rachel Portman

An apparently undemanding comedy, *Sirens* touches on class, religion, love, sex and Anglo-Australian relations. An uptight English vicar tries to redeem an earthy Australian painter of blasphemous nudes, while his wife undergoes a sexual awakening. Supermodel Elle Macpherson turns in a good performance but doesn't neglect to display her more expected talents. Based (very loosely) on the painter Norman Lindsay, also the subject of Michael Powell's *The Age Of Consent* (1969).

Marguerite Duras
Vietnam (formerly French Indochina), 1914–96

Marguerite Duras was an intellectual giant of the French literary world, and her films were, arguably, as seismically significant for experimental cinema. She became known for her elliptical, autobiographical antinovels (*nouveaux romans*), which obsessively and ferociously detailed the self-destructive powers of love. Her most famous contribution to cinema is as the screenwriter for Alain Resnais's *Hiroshima mon amour* (1959), in which a French actress embarks on an intense affair with a Japanese businessman while making a film about the A-bomb. Many of Duras's novels have been adapted for the screen by auteur directors: *Barrage contre le Pacifique* (*This Angry Age*, 1958) by René Clément, *The Sailor From Gibraltar* (1967) by Tony Richardson and *The Lover* (1992) by Jean-Jacques Annaud. The outspoken novelist wasn't fond of any of the adaptations, and particularly Annaud's, and once claimed that was the reason she became a film director.

Duras directed nineteen films in all, most of them variations on the themes of loss and memory. All her films are characterized by their allusive/ elusive qualities: narrative cohesion and coherence splinter, and meaning, slippery at the best of times, ultimately resides with the spectator rather than the work. Or as critic Vincent Canby once wrote, "I've yet to see a film of hers that didn't seem a carefully thought-out, overly intellectualized mistake". Her films certainly split the critics. *Le camion* (*The Lorry*, 1977) – a conversation piece between the director and Gérard Depardieu punctuated by images of a lorry from an imagined film – was roundly booed at the Cannes Film Festival. However, *Nathalie Granger* (1972), *India Song* (1975) and *Les mains negatives* (1978) are the subject of impassioned critical eulogies, such as this from critic Amy Taubin: "no other woman has produced a body of work approaching the obsessive and erotic power of Marguerite Duras." LH

India Song 1975, 120 min
cast Delphine Seyrig, Michel Lonsdale, Mathieu Carrière, Claude Mann, Vernon Dobtcheff, Didier Flamand *cin* Bruno Nuytten *m* Carlos d'Alessio

With sound and image divorced and every voice we hear offstage and unaccounted for, *India Song* unfolds a halting narrative of thwarted love and longing between the sexually liberated wife of a French ambassador (Delphine Seyrig) and the ex-vice consul (Michel Lonsdale), who desperately wants to be added to her long list of lovers. Hypnotic, sensual and opaque, *India Song* is a coquettish text that playfully teases the viewer at will.

Julien Duvivier

France, 1896–1967

Often dismissed as a studio workhorse, Julien Duvivier made some of the most iconic and successful French films of all time in a career spanning the history of French cinema from the silents to the *nouvelle vague*.

Duvivier first pursued an acting career, then became an assistant to the theatrical innovator and film director André Antoine. Antoine encouraged him towards filmmaking and in 1918 Duvivier became an assistant to Feuillade and L'Herbier. He directed his first film in 1919, *Le prix du sang* (*The Price Of Blood*) and was prolific throughout the 1920s and 30s, averaging two films a year. The 1930s saw him become one of the top French directors alongside Clair, Renoir, Carné and Feyder. The fragmented French industry enabled Duvivier to flourish, producing, scripting, and forging creative partnerships with such talents as screenwriters Charles Spaak and Henri Jeanson, set designer Jacques Krauss, and stars Harry Baur and Jean Gabin. Duvivier was responsible for the great Gabin trilogy of *La bandera* (*Escape From Yesterday*, 1935), *La belle équipe* (*They Were Five*, 1936) and *Pépé le Moko* (1937). Duvivier's trademark camera movement combined with long takes contributed to the atmospheric *mise en scène* of these tales of proletarian despair that became known as poetic realism. In 1937 he also directed *Un carnet de bal* (1937), a sentimental film made up of vignettes revolving around a widow (Marie Bell) who tracks down the former dance partners listed on an old dance card from her teenage years.

In 1938 Duvivier was invited to Hollywood to direct Fernand Gravet and Luise Rainer in MGM's life of Johann Strauss. *The Great Waltz* was a big hit and in 1940 Duvivier returned to Hollywood where he made *Tales Of Manhattan* (1942). Featuring Charles Boyer, Rita Hayworth, Ginger Rogers and Henry Fonda, the narrative is centred upon a tailcoat that brings bad luck to whoever wears it. *Flesh And Fantasy* (1943), another all-star portmanteau, followed before Duvivier returned to France. There he had great success with *The Little World Of Don Camillo* (1951), which won a prize at Cannes. Duvivier went on to direct some of France's biggest post-war stars, including Danielle Darrieux, Françoise Arnoul and Micheline Presle. Ever-versatile, Duvivier even crossed the Channel to make *Anna Karenina* (1948) for British producer Alexander Korda. The sheer number of films Duvivier made has meant much of his good work has been obscured: he is a director ripe for re-evaluation. RA

La belle équipe (They Were Five) 1936, 94 min, b/w

cast Jean Gabin, Viviane Romance, Raymond Aimos, Charles Vanel, Jacques Baumer, Charles Dorat *cin* Jules Kruger *m* Maruice Yvain

A vivid snapshot of the Popular Front years, in which a bunch of reprobates who win a sweepstake decide to resurrect a café-concert. Nicely observed and full of communitarian generosity and the humour of human foible, *La belle équipe* is reminiscent of Jean Renoir at his best.

Pépé le Moko 1937, 93 min, b/w

cast Jean Gabin, Mireille Blin, Gabriel Bagrio, Lucas Gridoux, Gilbert-Gil *cin* Robert Hakim, Raymond Hakim *m* Vincent Scotto, Mohamed Ygerbouchen

A seminal moment in film history, *Pépé le Moko* is the original French *film noir*. The iconic screen presence of Jean Gabin and the fatalistic existentialism of pre-war France converge in the unlikely – perhaps – setting of the *souks* and alleys of the Algiers casbah.

Clint Eastwood
US, 1930–

It might seem perverse to say that Clint Eastwood has worked under the cultural radar. After all, as a star, he's been a box-office champ for five decades – a record only John Wayne could match. The man is an American icon. People all over the world know him by his first name. Presidents quote his one-liners. Yet it comes as a shock to see how prolific he's been as a director. He's made 27 features since *Play Misty For Me* in 1971 – more than Martin Scorsese, Francis Ford Coppola or Steven Spielberg.

Born in the Depression era, Eastwood worked as a lumberjack and an army swimming instructor before he landed a contract with Universal in the 1950s. He tasted a measure of success in the TV show *Rawhide*, and that might have been it, if it wasn't for Sergio Leone taking him to Europe and making him the last big-screen cowboy star in *A Fistful Of Dollars* (1964), *For A Few Dollars More* (1965) and *The Good, The Bad And The Ugly* (1966). Leone and Don Siegel, who directed him in five films (most famously *Dirty Harry*, 1971), were such a profound influence on him as a director that Eastwood dedicated *Unforgiven* (1992) to them both. Eastwood has occasionally borrowed from Leone's baroque style, with sweeping crane shots and sometimes grotesque wide-angle compositions, but ex-editor Siegel's pragmatic, economical, self-effacing approach and lean, clean sensibility is nearer to the mark.

Quick to capitalize on his box-office clout and take control of his own career, Eastwood formed his Malpaso company in 1970 and forged a long, stable relationship with Warner Bros, who distributed all his films from 1975. Using a tight-knit team of trusted collaborators (including cinematographers Bruce Surtees and Jack N. Green, composer Lennie Niehaus and editor Joel Cox), keeping overheads low and shooting with legendary speed, Eastwood was a model producer. It has bought him a degree of autonomy. Whether by arrangement or innate caution, over the last three decades he has alternated overtly commercial vehicles, especially police thrillers in the *Dirty Harry* mould, with more personal projects.

Judged by the thrillers alone, Eastwood might be considered a competent hack. At their worst, with their absolutist morality and fetish for handguns, these films pander to right-wing vigilante fantasies. Indulgent critics have been quick to point to redeeming qualities: a penchant for casting "strong" women, and the star's readiness to play with his own image, to act his age, for example. But too often, particularly in the latter half of his career (*The Rookie*, 1990; *Absolute Power*, 1997; *True Crime*, 1999; *Blood Work*, 2002), the calculation is cynical and the execution slipshod or simply tired.

On the other hand, the personal films are very different from what you might expect. *Breezy* (1973) and *The Bridges Of Madison County* (1995) are delicately handled romances, both transcending their potentially sentimental scenarios. *Bronco Billy* (1980) and *Honkytonk Man* (1982) are idiosyncratic, laid-back, underrated character pieces laced with a certain wry appreciation for Americana. The latter allowed Eastwood to sing – adding another string to his bow (a composer in his own right, he wrote the score for *Mystic River*, and has contributed songs to a number of his films). *White Hunter, Black Heart* (1990) is another underrated, eccentric film, a fictionalized portrait of director John Huston during the making of *The African Queen* which gave Eastwood the chance to essay a cavalier, expansive, charming, but in some ways monstrous, personality.

It's a diverse, curious collection. And we haven't yet covered his major works: *The Outlaw Josey Wales* (1976), *Unforgiven*, *A Perfect World* (1993) and *Mystic River* (2003). Eastwood has made many violent movies in his career, but these four films take violence as their subject. In each, his (anti)heroes pass between degrees of atonement, redemption, punishment and perdition. While fingering both psychological and sociopolitical causes, it's clear that Eastwood (no less than Michael Moore) sees violence as a peculiarly American phenomenon. Witness, for example, the Stars and Stripes in the background at the climax of both *Unforgiven* and *Mystic River*. In these pieces, he points to a facility for death instilled deep in the psyche of the American male.

Eastwood came into his own in his seventies – it's hard to think of any other American filmmaker who has been so productive at this age. The American Film Institute named his recent output as "the greatest cinematic work of the twenty-first century". But what's most interesting about these later movies is that they make no bones about being an old man's films. That isn't always a compliment; some of his movies can seem lazy and complacent. There are even repetitive and redundant stretches in the war drama *Flags Of Our Fathers* (2006), a moving account of the Battle of Iwo Jima and the famous photograph of the planting of the American flag on Mount Suribachi. However, there is nothing tired about tackling the bloodiest battle of World War II from both sides – from the American perspective in *Flags* and from the Japanese perspective in *Letters From Iwo Jima* (also 2006). The director resolved to take on this dual-perspective challenge after visiting the island of Iwo Jima in preparation for *Flags*. It was a massive undertaking not just in terms of logistics, but also in terms of imagination.

If we take the two films together – as one four-hour epic in two parts – *Iwo Jima* is an old man's movie in the best possible sense. The full weight of a lifetime's experience has been brought to bear in the unobtrusive staging, near monochrome imagery

and delicate score, and in the thoughtful, honest account of the violence societies inflict upon their citizens, be it in the name of democracy and freedom or king and country. We witness a great deal of courage on both sides, but also hypocrisy, racism, bullying, cowardice and blind loyalty, and often these are two sides of the same coin. Few movie stars have interrogated the nature of heroism as doggedly as Eastwood over the years, but whatever else he may have to say on the subject, *Letters From Iwo Jima* could prove to be his masterpiece. TC

The Outlaw Josey Wales 1976, 134 min

cast Clint Eastwood, Chief Dan George, Sondra Locke, Bill McKinney, John Vernon, Paula Trueman *cin* Bruce Surtees *m* Jerry Fielding

Bent on revenge after his family, and then his Confederate comrades, are massacred, Josey Wales (Eastwood himself) is rehabilitated as he reluctantly assumes responsibility for the odd group of pioneer stragglers who coalesce around him. With a fine idiomatic, picaresque script by Philip Kaufman, and a lyrical appreciation for the wilderness, this stands as a redemptive response to Vietnam, and is arguably Eastwood's finest Western.

Unforgiven 1992, 131 min

cast Clint Eastwood, Gene Hackman, Morgan Freeman, Richard Harris, Jaimz Woolvett, Saul Rubinek *cin* Jack N. Green *m* Lennie Niehaus

Working from an examplary screenplay by David Webb Peoples, Eastwood fashioned one of the indelible revision-

Director Clint Eastwood shows how it should be done on the set of *The Outlaw Josey Wales*.

ist Westerns. Handsomely shot and superbly cast, the film presents an American frontier irreparably scarred. It's a sorry tale, in which one injustice spirals into many; mercenary values and multiple misunderstandings culminate in a mythic shoot-out underpinned with a tragic sense of loss and regret.

Mystic River 2003, 137 min

cast Sean Penn, Tim Robbins, Kevin Bacon, Laurence Fishburne, Marcia Gay Harden, Laura Linney *cin* Tom Stern *m* Clint Eastwood

Eastwood earned some of the best reviews of his career for this dark, brooding thriller, adapted from Dennis Lehane's novel. As with *Unforgiven*, he assembled an extraordinary ensemble cast to probe the ramifications of a young girl's murder. Grieving father Penn and homicide detective Bacon suspect their childhood friend Robbins, who was himself abused as a child.

Million Dollar Baby 2004, 132 min

cast Clint Eastwood, Hilary Swank, Morgan Freeman, Jay Baruchel, Mike Colter *cin* Tom Stern *m* Clint Eastwood, David Potaux-Razel

Swank is the determined working-class wannabe boxer who persuades Eastwood's reluctant trainer to stand in her corner. Trumping Martin Scorsese's *The Aviator* at the Oscars (Eastwood came away with best picture and best director, while Hilary Swank was best actress), this conservative boxing melodrama is almost as old-fashioned as its title, but satisfying and well observed for all that – and the controversial final act would never have been countenanced in the old days.

Letters From Iwo Jima 2006, 141 min

cast Kazunari Ninomiya, Watanabe Ken, Ihara Tsuyoshi, Kase Ryo *cin* Tom Stern *m* Kyle Eastwood, Michael Stevens

Beginning where he left off in the American-focused *Flags Of Our Fathers*, Eastwood now shows us the reverse angle of the World War II Battle of Iwo Jima. This Japanese-language companion piece resonates with the same themes as the earlier film, deepening and darkening our understanding of young men being wantonly sacrificed in the name of their countries. Eastwood's spare, fluid, eloquent moviemaking shows atrocities on both sides, squarely attributes the worst of these to Japan's military-imperial dictatorship, and then gently sifts the black sands of Iwo Jima for moments of solace, grace and mercy.

Uli Edel
Germany, 1947–

In a career spanning three decades, Uli Edel has only made a handful of feature films, but they have included one of the most punishing, controversial and critically lauded German movies of recent years, a realization of a dream project and one of the most ridiculed erotic thrillers in Hollywood history.

Ever since he first read Hubert Selby Jr's *Last Exit To Brooklyn*, Edel wanted to adapt the oft-banned novel for the big screen. Initially unable to secure the rights to Selby's tales of Brooklyn addicts, transvestites and prostitutes, Edel turned his attention to a not dissimilar milieu: the true story of a 13-year-old German junkie. Unflinching in its raw details of an addict's life, *Christiane F.* (1981) acquired international notoriety, cult status and critical acclaim. Eventually securing the rights to his pet project in the mid-1980s, Edel found a way to streamline Selby's fractured stories and monologues into one seamless narrative. The unrelentingly bleak *Last Exit To Brooklyn* (1989) divided the critics, especially American scribes who claimed not to recognize their own country in Edel's sleazy recreation of 1950s New York.

Edel made his next film, *Body Of Evidence* (1992), at the moment when erotic thrillers were the *genre du jour* in Hollywood (thanks to the phenomenal success of *Basic Instinct*) and when leading lady Madonna released the album *Erotica* and a popular coffee-table book of her fantasies. However, the film was poorly received by critics and cinema-goers alike – "a laughable parody of the genre, best buried" and "excruciatingly incompetent" were typical reviews – and Udel's reputation suffered immeasurably. Since then he's made a mediocre boy-meets-ghoul children's flick called *The Little Vampire* (2000), which is a saccharine world away from the creatures of the night that peopled *Christiane F.* and *Last Exit To Brooklyn*. LH

Christiane F. (Christiane F. Wir Kinder vom Bahnhof Zoo) 1981, 131min

cast Natja Brunckhorst, Thomas Haustein, Jens Kuphal, Rainer Wölk, Jan George Effer *cin* Justus Pankau, Jürgen Jürges *m* Jürgen Knieper

Christiane F is based on the true story of a young German girl whose revelations of her life as a teenage junkie made national headlines. Edel's camera doesn't shy away from the squalor; from his protagonist's first fix after a David Bowie concert to the private hell of going cold turkey, the director even seems to be a little addicted to the sordid debaucheries he unflinchingly depicts.

Last Exit To Brooklyn (Letzte Ausfahrt Brooklyn) 1989, 98 min

cast Stephen Lang, Jennifer Jason Leigh, Burt Young, Peter Dobson, Jerry Orbach, Alexis Arquette *cin* Stefan Czapsky *m* Mark Knopfler

Edel selected a few narrative strands from Hubert Selby Jr's infamous novel for his film, including that of a hooker who is gang-raped and a union official who falls for a transvestite, while adding his own redemptive character, Big Joe. Despite his painstaking evocation of 1950s Brooklyn, Edel's direction is, at times, airless, stilted and mechanical, and *Last Exit To Brooklyn* becomes a melodrama that is both overwrought and over-thought.

Blake Edwards
US, 1922–

Despite a variable career, Blake Edwards has directed some of the most successful comedies in Hollywood's history. Born into a family with Hollywood connections – his grandfather directed silent star Theda Bara – Edwards broke into the industry as an actor, appearing in *The Best Years Of Our Lives* (1946), amongst others. In 1948 he co-produced and co-scripted two Lesley Selander Westerns for Allied Artists, while successfully writing for radio and television. He then worked for Columbia as a screenwriter on Richard Quine comedies like *My Sister Eileen* (1955) and *Operation Mad Ball* (1957), earning a reputation for effervescent dialogue and plaudits in *Cahiers du cinéma*.

The early 1960s saw him established as a director, with a diverse series of glamorous, big-budget features. *Operation Petticoat* (1959) was a spoof submarine movie starring Cary Grant and Tony Curtis. *Breakfast At Tiffany's* (1961) is a comedy institution. *Experiment In Terror* (1962) was an assured thriller in which Glenn Ford's killer stalks Lee Remick, its play with viewpoint foreseeing the work of Brian De Palma and John Carpenter. The pessimistic alcoholism drama *Days Of Wine And Roses* (1963) saw Jack Lemmon on terrific non-comic form. The *Pink Panther* cycle, with Peter Sellers as the befuddled Inspector Clouseau, demonstrated Edwards' penchant for slapstick, integral to his interrogation of post-war masculinity.

Relations between the studios and the independently minded Edwards grew tense when the ambitious silent comedy tribute *The Great Race* (1965) and *What Did You Do In The War, Daddy?* (1966) flopped. After the failure of the costly musical *Darling Lili* (1970), starring his new wife Julie Andrews, Edwards left for Britain and a reprise of the Pink Panther. He cast Andrews in a number of subsequent movies, including the Dudley Moore midlife crisis comedy *10* (1979) and *Victor/Victoria* (1982), a bold essay on sexual allure featuring Andrews as a cross-dressing nightclub performer. But while those two films reaped big bucks at the box office, *S.O.B.* (1981) and *Sunset* (1988) betrayed Edwards' dissatisfaction with Hollywood. Much-fêted, he is now a respected industry elder. RA

Breakfast At Tiffany's 1961, 115 min

cast Audrey Hepburn, George Peppard, Patricia Neal, Buddy Ebsen, Mickey Rooney, John McGiver *cin* Franz Planer *m* Henry Mancini

The best-known yet the most atypical of Edwards' films, this tribute to Audrey Hepburn's charm and hauteur has had generations believing, in spite of themselves, that she could play the daughter of a Texan dirt farmer relocated to 1960s Manhattan. The fruit of Edwards' perennial rapport with composer Henry Mancini, "Moon River" went a long way to persuading the cynical.

The Party 1968, 98 min

cast Peter Sellers, Claudine Longet, Marge Champion, J. Edward McKinley, Fay McKenzie *cin* Lucien Ballard *m* Henry Mancini

True to Edwards' satirical outsider's view of Hollywood, this trendy tale of a producer's soirée gate-crashed by Peter Sellers' hapless Indian actor remains one of the most hysterical curios of its day. Sellers, demonstrating his mastery of physical comedy, is of course the star of the show.

Atom Egoyan
Egypt, 1960–

Fixated on quasi-therapeutic rituals of sorrow and processes of denial, the films of Atom Egoyan observe people who are forever held at one remove from themselves, and those closest to them, by the recorded image. In *Family Viewing* (1987), a young man's strained relationship with his father reaches breaking point when he discovers that videos of his childhood have been taped over by his dad's homemade pornography. In *Speaking Parts* (1989), one woman obsesses over a movie bit-player via video while another compulsively watches footage of her dead brother. The photographer in *Calendar* (1993) replays video footage of his ex-wife and her lover as a mourning rite for his marriage. Egoyan maintains a cool, appraising distance that renders his films' half-submerged emotions (and subterranean deadpan humour) all the more potent, while his characters wander in the hall of eternal return, lined with screens and two-way mirrors, filled with receding ghosts.

Born in Cairo to Armenian parents (the family moved to Canada when Egoyan was 3), he debuted with the hour-long *Next Of Kin* (1984), in which a young man undergoing video-assisted family therapy decides to tell an Armenian couple, falsely, that he is their long-lost son. The film established what would become two major Egoyan themes: family dysfunction mediated and exacerbated by images, and willed self-delusion as a mechanism to defer grief. After *Family Viewing* and *Speaking Parts*, *The Adjuster* (1991) centred on an insurance-company employee with something of a guru-therapist complex, intimately involving himself in the lives of clients who have lost their homes to fire or other disaster. *The Adjuster* saw Egoyan inching towards an unfocused sprawl, but his next film, *Calendar*, was a concentrated marvel, a slow-motion replay of a relationship in its death throes. The operatic *Exotica* (1994) marked an apex of Egoyan's penchant for jigsaw-puzzle narratives, in which time is fragmented and characters' motivations and relationships reveal themselves incrementally, through the striptease of editing.

Distributed by Miramax, *Exotica* earned a wider audience for Egoyan, and he won an Oscar nomination for *The Sweet Hereafter* (1997), a wrenching adaptation of the Russell Banks novel about a bus accident that devastates a wintry small town. *Felicia's Journey* (1999), adapted from the William Trevor novel, had choppy thriller undercurrents but faltered due to Bob Hoskins' over-the-top lead performance. The avowedly self-conscious *Ararat* (2002) staged a movie-within-a-movie to address both the 1915 Armenian genocide in Turkey and the moral and aesthetic questions raised by such a project. Egoyan's next film, the disappointing and atypical investigative jigsaw *Where The Truth Lies*, premiered at Cannes in 2005. He followed this with a very personal documentary project, *Citadel* (2006), which recorded, on a handheld DV camera, his wife and close collaborator Arsinée's Khanjian's first visit to Lebanon in 28 years. JW

Calendar 1993, 75 min
cast Atom Egoyan, Arsinée Khanjian, Ashot Adamian, Michelle Bellerose, Natalia Jasen *cin* John F. Seitz *m* Victor Young

A photographer (Egoyan) shoots Armenian churches for a heritage calendar without realizing that his wife (Egoyan's real-life spouse Arsinée Khanjian) and their guide are beginning an affair; after the break-up, the photographer watches video of the lovers and hires women to re-enact the marriage's dying moments. A potent distillation of grief and regret, the film tracks a series of repetitive-compulsive ceremonies in which videotape is a torturous fetish object, a balm that holds the wound open.

Exotica 1994, 103 min
cast Don McKellar, Mia Kirschner, Arsinée Khanjian, Elias Koteas, Bruce Greenwood, Sarah Polley *cin* Paul Sarossy *m* Mychael Danna

This engrossing roundelay gathers interlocking stories set around an exotic dance club, where bereaved client Bruce Greenwood and dancer Mia Kirschner seem to be entangled in a therapeutic *pas de deux* that they rehearse night after night. Staffer Elias Koteas begins to meddle in their relationship, eventually entangling several other characters, all with their own secrets and shames. The narrative fragments assemble themselves with slow-burn precision, culminating in the illuminative flash of the startling ending.

The Sweet Hereafter 1997, 110 min
cast Ian Holm, Sarah Polley, Caerthan Banks, Tom McCamus, Arsinée Khanjian, Alberta Watson *cin* Paul Sarossy *m* Mychael Danna

Unlike much of Egoyan's work, the concept of loss resonates poignantly on both an emotional and intellectual level in this study of a small community who have to come to terms with the death of all but one of their children in a bus crash. The film is shot in a melancholic, wintry light, and a haunting incandescence seeps hypnotically through each perfectly proportioned frame.

Sergei Eisenstein
Latvia (formerly Russian Empire), 1898–1948

For many critics, Sergei Eisenstein is the most important director in Soviet, if not world, cinema. He invented a form of film grammar that seemed like the cinematic equivalent of Einstein's $e = mc^2$: thesis + antithesis = synthesis. This equation was at the centre of his theory of the "montage of attractions", the revolutionary hypothesis that meaning in cinema is constructed by the juxtaposition of opposites. As he puts it in the main book outlining his theories, *The Film Sense* (1942): "two

film pieces of any kind, placed together, inevitably combine into a new concept, a new quality, arising out of that juxtaposition."

After serving in the Red Army, Eisenstein worked for the Proletkult Workers Theatre Group in Moscow, and he was to maintain a career in the theatre throughout his working life. He made his first short, a spoof on American thrillers called *Glumov's Diary* (1923), for the stage production *Enough Simplicity For Every Wise Man*. He quickly moved from the theatre to the cinema, and built his reputation with his first three features, *Strike* (1924), *Battleship Potemkin* (1925) and *October* (1927), which represent, in turn, the initial application, sophisticated cultivation and avant-garde augmentation of his cinematic equation.

The first full-length articulation of his theories of montage and "typage" (using non-professionals with clear physical traits in representative roles), *Strike* is about a factory strike brutally quelled by police. Eisenstein replaced the bourgeois fallacy of a single protagonist with the concept of a collective as the hero, and orchestrated the cast into an expressionist choreography of mass protest, cutting everything together in a fury of juxtaposed editing. In *Battleship Potemkin*, a fictionalized account of an episode in the failed Russian revolution of 1905, Eisenstein finely calibrated his cutting and compositional techniques to assemble one of the most celebrated sequences in celluloid history: the Odessa steps scene. However, the film failed as Communist propaganda, never attaining the phenomenal reputation and exposure in its own country that it achieved in the rest of the world. *October* was commissioned to celebrate the tenth anniversary of the 1917 revolution, and took montage to new, and often impenetrable, extremes. The film was condemned in some quarters for being too abstract (or "formalist", to use the language of the Soviet critics), a portent of the criticisms that would dog the director for the rest of his life.

For the next decade, Eisenstein's career lurched fitfully from expectation to frustration to humiliation. *The General Line* (1929), an ode to the revolutionary benefits of rural modernization, had to be re-edited when Stalin's policy on collectivization changed. By the time the melodrama (renamed *Old And New*) was released in Soviet cinemas, the director was already in the US, meeting Walt Disney and making plans for a Hollywood movie based on Theodore Dreiser's 1925 novel *An American Tragedy*. When those plans came to nought, Eisenstein travelled to Mexico to make the first of his *film maudits*, *Que Viva Mexico!*, a lush, extended hymn to Latin American culture, which he abandoned in 1932 after a bitter dispute with his financial backer Upton Sinclair.

Returning home, Eisenstein toiled under the official Stalinist doctrine of socialist realism. In 1937, *Bezhin Meadow* was banned before it was completed, and he was forced to make a humiliating public *mea*

A classical sound: Eisenstein and Prokofiev

The major Hollywood studios have generally fought shy of working with big-name composers who have already established their reputations in the concert hall. The Soviet film industry had no such qualms, and the two great-est composers of the Soviet era, Sergei Prokofiev and Dmitri Shostakovich, both had important, if erratic, cinema careers. Prokofiev worked on fewer films than his younger colleague – a total of eight – but his scores are better known, partly because the two he wrote for Eisenstein are largely acknowledged as masterpieces.

In 1918, with the Kremlin's blessing, Prokofiev left Russia to tour the world – primarily as a virtuoso pianist but also with a growing reputation as a cutting-edge composer. On various trips to America he discussed projects with Gloria Swanson and Walt Disney, but these came to nothing, and it was not until 1933 that he composed his first film score, *Poruchik Kizhe* (*Lieutenant Kizhe*, 1934), for director Aleksandr Faintzimmer. A wonderfully witty satire on the idiocy of officialdom and bureaucracy, set in the eighteenth century, it tells of how a clerk accidently adds a name to a list of officers that he is copying out. The nonexistent Lieutenant Kizhe goes on to have a "career" which ends in imprisonment and death. The film is perfectly matched by Prokofiev's music whose precise synchronization with the action is almost balletic. It begins with a lone cornet solo (signalling Kizhe's birth) leading into the lightest of military marches to accompany a parade-ground drill sequence. The famous "Troika" piece, with its jingling sleigh bells, is so associated with Russia that it has often been used in other films (including Woody Allen's *Love And Death*, 1975) as a kind of shorthand for all things Russian.

Prokofiev's most celebrated cinematic relationship, with Sergei Eisenstein, got off to a shaky start. He turned down the invitation to score the multi-part epic film *The Year 1905* on the twentieth anniversary of the 1905 Revolution – although in the end only Eisenstein's *Battleship Potemkin* (1925) ever got made. There were discus-sions about him working on Eisenstein's doomed collectivization story *Bezhin Meadow* but it was not until 1937 that the two men actually completed a project together. This was the medieval epic *Alexander Nevsky*, Eisenstein's first completed sound film and an overtly propagandist work about the thirteenth-century Russian prince who saved his country from Swedish and German invaders. The film climaxes in the famous "Battle on the Ice" for which Prokofiev wrote music from Eisenstein's storyboard, and the sequence was then filmed to fit in with the idea of the music. The result is a thrilling synthesis of sound and vision, in which a gradual momentum builds to a brilliant climax as the ice breaks and the Teutonic knights are drowned.

During World War II, Prokofiev worked on a number of films which remain largely unknown outside Russia. These were essentially propaganda works: *Tonya* (1942) about a heroic telephonist, *Partisans Of The Ukrainian Steppe* (1942), *Kotovsky* (1943) – for which the composer was reunited with Faintimmer – and *Lermontov* (1944), a biopic of the early nineteenth-century poet. Of these, only *Tonya* has a score of any real substance.

For Eisenstein's next historical epic, the two-part *Ivan The Terrible* (1944, 1946), Prokofiev provided music that was less simply illustrative music than he had for *Nevsky*, with a greater emphasis on the psychological development of character. The American critic James Agee has described the film as "a visual opera, with all of opera's proper disregard of prose-level reality". Once again, there's a powerful accord between sound and vision, beginning with the strident brass and strings that complement the dramatic storm clouds of the opening. Other powerful set pieces include the percussion-heavy music for the burning of Moscow and the brilliantly sustained tension which leads to the kill-ing of one of Ivan's rivals in the cathedral. Eisenstein's death in 1948 robbed Prokofiev of the only director with whom he wanted to work and, increasingly ill, he wrote no more film scores. JR

culpa: "In recent years I have become self-absorbed. I have retreated into my shell." After apologizing for his previous "theoretical conceptions", Eisenstein produced his most accessible and popular film, *Alexander Nevsky* (1938), which was as blunt a rebut-tal of his avant-garde aesthetic as his previous state-ment. A dubious slice of historical propaganda about a thirteenth-century prince who fights off a Teutonic invasion, *Nevsky* was clearly a warning about the rise of Germany under Hitler. It was subsequently banned for the duration of the Nazi-Soviet pact.

In the following years, Eisenstein had many more projects officially rejected. When he was finally allowed back behind a camera, it was to make a film about Stalin's hero: *Ivan The Terrible* (1944). In Part I, Ivan was unequivocally heroic, and Eisenstein was duly honoured with the Stalin Prize. However, the Ivan presented in the second instalment (1946) was a vengeful megalomaniac, and parallels were clear-ly drawn between Ivan's private army and Stalin's secret police. The dictator wasn't impressed, and he invited Eisenstein to the Kremlin in 1947 to give him a history lesson. Work on Part III was aban-doned and the footage destroyed, but the director never instigated the Part II re-shoots that Stalin demanded. The second instalment was eventually released in 1958, several years after both Eisenstein and Stalin's deaths.

Once the revolutionary, Eisenstein has now become a dusty icon, a statue ripe for toppling. The assault on his reputation has been led by critic David Thomson who argues that "it is no longer possible to view Eisenstein as the man who laid down the theoretical basis for the medium". Eisenstein's techniques have been pillaged and quoted by other directors, but they have not become the building blocks of the cinematic narrative. The director even dispensed with them himself in his later historical epics. On its re-release in the late 1990s, *Battleship Potemkin* was garlanded with less praise than at any time in its history, and certainly far less than in the heady days of 1958, when it was voted the greatest film ever made. Eistenstein's works don't elicit a passionate response, but instead evince a cool, academic admiration. LH

Strike (Stachka) 1924, 82 min, b/w
cast Maxim Straukh, Grigori Alexandrov, Mikhail Gomorov, Aleksandr Antonov, Yudif Glizer, I. Ivanov *cin* Eduard Tissé

This stirring and riotously abstract representation of a workers' strike and its brutal suppression contains one of the earliest and most celebrated articulations of Eisenstein's theories of montage and typage. A gang (all non-professionals chosen for their physical appearance) are introduced by their nicknames and, as they move together in mass protest, their images dissolve into those of the animals they unerringly resemble.

Battleship Potemkin (Bronenosets Potyomkin) 1925, 75 min, b/w
cast Alexander Anotonov, Vladimir Barsky, Grigori Alexandrov, Mikhail Gomorov, Beatrice Vitoldi, Aleksandr I. Levchin *cin* Eduard Tissé

A shot across the bows of conventional cinema, Eisenstein's masterpiece is avant-garde cinema at its most intellectual, iconoclastic and visceral, if not a little homoerotic (all those loving shots of buff sailors in tight tops). Even though the Odessa steps massacre only took place in the director's febrile imagination, it has now become a part of twentieth-century history, endlessly analyzed and reproduced, whether in De Palma's *The Untouchables* or painter Francis Bacon's screaming popes. Its place in the pantheon is deserved.

October (Oktyabr) 1927, 103 min, b/w
cast Vasili Nkinandrov, Nikolai Popov, Layaschenko, Boris Livanov, Eduard Tissé, Niolai Podvoisky *cin* Eduard Tissé

October contains one of the most celebrated juxtapositions in Eisenstein's filmography: the authority of the leader of the emergency government is mocked and undermined by shots of a mechanical peacock flapping its metal wings.

Defiant mother: a moment from the famous Odessa steps sequence in Eisenstein's *Battleship Potemkin*.

The film is just as infamous for the scenes it doesn't include; it was re-edited to excise Trotsky's role in the revolution because Stalin wanted his rival removed from history.

Alexander Nevsky 1938, 112 min, b/w

cast Nikolai Cherkasov, Nikolai Okhlopov, Andrei Abrikosov, Vera Ivashova, Dmitri Orlov, Vasili Novikov *cin* Eduard Tissé *m* Sergei Prokofiev

This story of the thirteenth-century prince who repulsed the Teutonic knights paralleled contemporary events but was shelved during the Nazi-Soviet pact and only re-released when the Nazis invaded in 1941. An extremely nationalistic work, it deliberately contrasts lyrical landscape shots of Nevsky at home with the ruthless violence of the robotic, baby-killing Teutonic knights. Prokofiev and Eisenstein worked very closely on the score and it shows. The great set piece Battle on the Ice was parodied in Ken Russell's *Billion Dollar Brain* (1967).

Ivan The Terrible, Part I (Ivan Grozny I) 1944, 99 min, b/w

cast Nikolai Cherkasov, Lyudmila Tselikovskaya, Serafima Birman, Mikhail Nazvanov, Mikhail Zharov *cin* Eduard Tissé *m* Sergei Prokofiev

In this moody, idolizing biography, Stalin's role model and favourite demagogue is depicted as a hero valiantly uniting the Russians against the Tartars and Boyars. A sense of bourgeois opulence seeps through every frame: in the ornate sets, shimmering costumes, Eisenstein's operatic sweep and the opening scene in which Ivan is showered in gold coins as part of his ostentatious coronation.

Stephan Elliott

Australia, 1963–

Stephan Elliott had an unlikely international feel-good hit in 1994 with *The Adventures Of Priscilla, Queen Of The Desert*, and has been doing his best to live it down ever since.

Elliott began at the bottom, as a runner (on *Silver City*, 1984) and third assistant director (on Dusan Makaveyev's *The Coca Cola Kid*, 1985), before drawing attention with two short films as writer-director in 1991. His first feature, *Frauds* (1993), was a surreal black comedy with pop star Phil Collins as a dicey insurance claims investigator. Stylish and malicious, it was invited to show at Cannes – although Elliott subsequently disowned the producers' cut.

Priscilla came next, a road movie following two drag queens and an ageing transsexual (Terence Stamp) on a two-week bus ride through the outback to a possible comeback gig in Alice Springs. Camp and outrageous, with some broad comic swipes at homophobia and a sentimental coda, it was a crossover hit everywhere it played. It's also Elliott's only overtly gay film to date. "I set out to be completely offensive, but somehow that's been overlooked", Elliott noted. "Maybe because we rewrote the ending and made the last 20 pages very sugary … It just struck a chord. I still scratch my head and wonder why."

Although he was courted by Hollywood on the back of *Priscilla*'s success, Elliott chose to follow up with another Australian film, *Welcome To Woop Woop* (1997). It was a genuinely biting, if still very broad, satire at the expense of several Australian sacred cows, star Rod Taylor among them. The film was almost unanimously reviled (one Australian critic called it a national embarrassment), and international distribution was piecemeal at best. Elliott again complained that he'd been made to tone down the satire by his producers, but *Woop Woop* is probably his most intriguing and underrated effort.

Eye Of The Beholder (1999) was his first American film, although after the financing fell through it was shot in Canada on an independent budget. It starred Ewan McGregor as a surveillance operative who falls in love with the serial killer (Ashley Judd) he is supposed to be trailing. Again, the reviews were vicious, but if the movie is trash, at least it's bravura trash, with some extraordinary third-generation Hitchcockian set pieces as elaborate as anything by De Palma or Argento. It even topped the US box-office charts for a week or two. TC

The Adventures Of Priscilla, Queen Of The Desert 1994, 102 min

cast Terence Stamp, Hugo Weaving, Guy Pearce, Bill Hunter, Sarah Chadwick, Mark Holmes *cin* Brian Breheny *m* Guy Gross

Priscilla is a tour bus. The queens are within: ageing Bernadette, bitchy Felicia and sensitive Mitzi (though in truth, they all have their moments). This brash camp comedy put Terence Stamp in a dress and its writer-director on the map, wowing audiences of every persuasion. Elliott makes much of the surreal disconnect between disco glam and desert outback, but underneath its exuberant surface this is a more conventional melodrama than it looks.

Welcome To Woop Woop 1997, 96 min

cast Johnathon Schaech, Rod Taylor, Noah Taylor, Paul Mercurio, Susie Porter, Dee Smart *cin* Mike Molloy *m* Guy Gross

Schaech is lured into the desert town of Woop Woop, where Rod Taylor presides over a kind of Ur-Australian enclave. It's 'roo meat for dinner and *The Sound Of Music* is the only entertainment in sight. A furious satirical broadside directed against the Aussie national character, this wasn't the safe way to follow Priscilla (no gay characters for a start), and it blew up in Elliott's face. Gruelling though it may be, *Woop Woop* does have a vicious integrity – a bit like an outback *Britannia Hospital*.

Maurice Elvey

UK, 1887–1967

Elvey is the most prolific director of feature-length British films ever. However, much of his large output is lost or forgotten, leaving him unfairly overlooked, although the recent rediscovery of his biography of Lloyd George has led to something of a reassessment. Absconding to London as a child, Elvey fell into acting and then cinema. His films are notable for location work and design, especially *Maria Marten: Or The Murder In The Red Barn* (1913), *The Life Story Of David Lloyd George* (1918) and his two versions of *Hindle Wakes* (1918 and 1927). An idea of his range can be gained by comparing his last silent film, the historical epic *Balaclava* (1928), and his first sound film, the futuristic *High Treason* (1928). His many sound films include vehicles for the singer Gracie Fields (for example, *Sally In Our Alley*, 1931) and the wartime nursing drama *The Lamp Still Burns* (1943). In 1957 failing sight forced him to retire. JR

The Life Story Of David Lloyd George 1918, 152 min, b/w

cast Norman Page, Alma Reville, Ernest Thesiger, Douglas Munro, Thomas Canning *cin* Maurice Elvey

Elvey thought this his best film, but following its suppression for political reasons it was lost until 1996, when it had its belated premiere. Page's impersonation of Lloyd George is uncanny and the settings add to the realism. This gives the romanticized story a documentary quality that may have contributed to its political problems. Alma Reville, who plays Lloyd George's daughter, went on to become Mrs Alfred Hitchcock.

Cy Endfield
US, 1914–95

Hounded out of Hollywood when the House Un-American Activities Committee (HUAC) identified him as a Communist in 1951, Cy Endfield moved to Britain, where he would live and work for the remainder of his life. Endfield never quite transcended the B-movie trappings of genre cinema, but within those confines he was a genuine auteur, usually writing as well as directing (and sometimes producing) his own films, and imprinting them with his hard-boiled, unsentimental world view and a progressive class consciousness.

Endfield joined the Young Communist League at Yale University, and was involved in progressive theatre groups in the 1930s. A gifted magician, he so impressed Orson Welles that he was invited to join the Mercury company as an apprentice.

His first films were World War II propaganda shorts. In the first, *Inflation* (1942), Hitler and the Devil inveigle the American public to spend thoughtlessly – until President Roosevelt puts a stop to it by explaining the dangers of inflation. The US Chamber of Commerce deemed all this to be anticapitalist, and the film was shelved.

Endfield made his feature debut in 1946. All his American films were B-movies, but *The Sound Of Fury* and *The Underworld Story* (both 1950) are excellent *noir* thrillers fired with the director's anger at the witch-hunts and blacklisting.

In Britain, Endfield worked prolifically, making films for television and more B-movies (ini-

tially borrowing the name of his friend, Charles de Latour). The best of these is *Hell Drivers* (1957), a tough action melodrama about the dangerous world of… road haulage. Borderline ridiculous, the film exudes a steely vigour which is hard to resist – and assembles a remarkable cast (Stanley Baker, Patrick McGoohan, Sean Connery, Peggy Cummins, William Hartnell, Sid James). In Baker, Endfield found his perfect leading man – grim, strong, resolute – and they made seven films together. Most famous, of course, was *Zulu* (1963), a rare opportunity to work on an "A" production.

Endfield made just three more films, all of them troubled by production difficulties, and retired from the fray after the improvisatory *Universal Soldier* (1971, with George Lazenby and Germaine Greer), returning only to script the belated sequel *Zulu Dawn* (1979). In his retirement, he invented a pocketsized computer notetaker which he called a "microwriter". TC

Zulu 1963, 135 min

cast Stanley Baker, Jack Hawkins, Michael Caine, Ulla Jacobsson, James Booth, Nigel Green *cin* Stephen Dade *m* John Barry

Rorke's Drift, 1879: 139 British infantry hold off a Zulu force more than 4000 strong. Although Endfield's only epic is sometimes tarred as imperialist, it's actually a very judicious account of the military tactics which saved the day for the Welsh Guard. Although the troops' heroism is stirring, there's no triumphalism here. Indeed, it more than holds its own against Ridley Scott's *Black Hawk Down*.

Jean Epstein
Poland (formerly Russian Empire), 1897–1953

Jean Epstein was a leading figure in the French avant-garde. He found his way to Paris in 1921, where he fell under the influence of theorist Louis Delluc, and began writing about the cinema. In their writings, Epstein and his colleagues argued that cinema's strength did not lie in straight narrative, and celebrated the medium's potential for impressionism. Epstein put these ideas into practice in a series of melodramas for Pathé, including *Coeur fidèle* (*The Faithful Heart*, 1923), which featured rapid editing and unusual close-ups (he once wrote that the close-up was the "soul of cinema"). Something of cinema's impressionistic quality, or "photogénie", as Epstein dubbed it, can also be felt in his *La chute de la maison Usher* (*The Fall Of The House Of Usher*, 1928).

La glace à trois faces (*The Three-Sided Mirror*, 1927) had a complex narrative which foresaw the temporal dislocations of Alain Resnais and was one of the first films made for the new "art" cinema circuits. *Finis terrae* (*The End Of The Earth*, 1929) was one of a cycle of films shot in Brittany, their naturalism anticipating Italian neo-realism. However,

Epstein's later films lacked the mysterious invention of his avant-garde period, the legacy of which can be felt in post-war experimenters from Maya Deren to David Lynch. Few directors have so extended the cinema's capacity for suggestion. RA

La chute de la maison Usher (The Fall Of The House Of Usher) 1928, 65 min, b/w and col

cast Marguerite Gance, Jean Debucourt, Charles Lamy, Fournez-Goffard, Halma *cin* Georges Lucas, Jean Lucas

One of most captivating horror films of all time, this Edgar Allan Poe adaptation has all the unconscious resonance of Poe's own mindset and the gothic tradition of which he was a part. Seldom has film been used to evoke the other side with such pain and clarity.

Victor Erice
Spain, 1940–

The sole complaint one can make against Victor Erice is actually a high compliment: the man simply doesn't work often enough. From his epochal start more than thirty years ago, Erice has made a grand total of three features, each a pensive, richly suggestive masterpiece. His feature debut, *The Spirit Of The Beehive* (1973), is perhaps the most beloved, a gorgeously unsettling tale of a displaced Spanish childhood under the shadow of ascendant Fascism but illuminated by the dream-light of the cinema. Set circa 1940, the year Erice was born, and released in the dying days of the Franco regime, *Beehive* has become a model example of how to embed political critique beneath surface story – notably among the Iranian New Wave auteurs (its tale of a child's stubborn quest resonated loudly for Abbas Kiarostami, one of Erice's greatest admirers).

The South (1983) shared many affinities with *Beehive*: both films observe family members alienated from their home and from each other; both measure the fallout of the Spanish Civil War through a girl's eyes; and both weave references to classic movies into their childhood (in *Beehive* it's James Whale's *Frankenstein*; in *The South*, both Spanish melodrama and Hitchcock's *Shadow Of A Doubt* prove fecund inspiration). Spare on dialogue, Erice's films prize contemplation, a meditative watchfulness that often dissolves into reverie.

Given the painterly influences that suffuse his work – most obviously those of Caravaggio and Vermeer – it was only fitting that Erice would eventually make a film about a painter. In the quasi-documentary *The Quince Tree Sun* (aka *The Dream Of Light*, 1992), Antonio López García struggles with, and finally gives up on, a painting of a quince tree during the autumn of 1990. A patient and tender account of the artistic process (we watch him build his easel, assemble his palette, even measure by millimetres how the branches lower under the weight of the ripening fruit), *Dream Of Light* reveals López García to be a painstaking perfectionist – and given the protracted intervals between his rich, luminous films, perhaps Erice is too. JW

A child's-eye view: Ana Torrent in the hypnotic *The Spirit Of The Beehive*.

The Spirit Of The Beehive (El espíritu de la colmena) 1973, 97 min

cast Fernando Fernan Gómez, Terésa Gimpera, Ana Torrent, Isabel Telleria, Laly Soldevilla, José Villasante *cin* Luis Cuadrado *m* Luis de Pablo

Forced to flee their home during the Spanish Civil War, a family relocates to a remote village on the Castilian plateau, where little daughter Ana (Ana Torrent) becomes determined to summon the spirit of Frankenstein's monster after seeing the 1931 film. Erice's seminal, hypnotic debut is at once a universal story of the fears and mysteries of childhood and a political allegory of the barrenness and haunted sorrows of Franco's Spain.

The Quince Tree Sun (El sol del membrillo, aka The Dream Of Light) 1992, 132 min
cast Antonio López García, Maria Moreno, Enrique Gran, José Carretero *cin* Javier Aguirresarobe *m* Pascal Gaigne

A major influence on the Iranian New Wave, this semi-staged documentary observes the painter Antonio López García at work on a painting of a quince tree he planted himself. Seasons change, the fruit ripens and falls and as the artist pursues his increasingly quixotic project, one begins to question the very possibilities of representational art – of which this film is a splendid example.

Jean Eustache
France, 1938–81

Outside France, Jean Eustache is the least known of the great filmmakers. Even in France, at the time of writing, none of his films, not even his acknowledged masterpiece *The Mother And The Whore* (1973) is available on DVD. Yet to many of the later post-*nouvelle vague* French directors – Arnaud Desplechin, Catherine Breillat, Claire Denis and Olivier Assayas, for example – Eustache is at least as important as Godard or Truffaut. He was the most honest, the most lacerating of artists.

Eustache was born into a working-class family in Pessac, a small town in the South of France. He would later mine his early adolescent yearnings for the autobiographical *Mes petites amoureuses* (*My Little Loves*, 1975), in which 13-year-old Daniel is a lonely, awkward child, confused and fascinated by the opposite sex. Pessac also featured in two documentaries, both entitled *La rosière de Pessac* (*The Virgin Of Pessac*, 1968 and 1979), studies of community, tradition and change based around an annual ceremony in which a local young woman is chosen as the town's most virtuous.

Eustache made a number of short documentaries throughout his career, notably *Le cochon* (*The Pig*, 1970), a careful record of the slaughtering and dismemberment of a pig, and *Une sale histoire* (*A Dirty Story*, 1977), in which a voyeuristic anecdote is recounted twice, once by the actor Michel Lonsdale, then again, in its original telling, by Eustache's friend Jean-Noël Picq. Picq also figured in the director's last film, *Le jardin des delices de Jerome Bosch* (*The Garden Of Delights Of Hieronymous Bosch*, 1979). Experimental and provocative, Eustache's documentaries nevertheless exhibit a generosity of spirit which is not always obvious in the narrative films.

His first fictional films were shorts: *Les mauvaises fréquentations* (*Bad Company*, 1963) and *Le père noël a les yeux bleus* (*Santa Claus Has Blue Eyes*, 1966). Both centred on the male pursuit of the opposite sex, and both were heavily marked by the new freedoms established by the *nouvelle vague*. But Eustache's treatment was even more caustic than

Godard's; indeed his work can be seen as a veiled critique of Godard and Truffaut's misogynistic tendencies. The movie-mad, charming, narcissistic, pretentious, despicable, chauvinist Alexandre (Jean-Pierre Léaud) in *The Mother And The Whore* could stand for either of these auteurs, although he is also, obviously, an unflinching self-portrait.

Despite the support of the French critical establishment and the minor commercial success of *The Mother And The Whore*, Eustache remained a marginal figure in the industry. His suicide in 1981 undoubtedly reflected his professional frustrations. It might also be taken as confirmation of an anguished humanism, profoundly troubled by codes of masculinity and the spiritual impoverishment of the modern permissive society. TC

The Mother And The Whore (La maman et la putain) 1973, 219 min, b/w
cast Jean-Pierre Léaud, Françoise Lebrun, Bernadette Lafont, Isabelle Weingarten *cin* Pierre Lhomme, Jacques Renard, Michel Cenet

Nearly four hours in length, this psychosexual marathon is not for the faint-hearted, but well worth tackling. Léaud is Alexandre, a compulsive womanizer and intellectual who lives with one woman (Lafont), proposes to another (Weingarten) and, rebuffed, talks a third (Lebrun) into a wretched *ménage à trois*. Shot in Eustache's own apartment in long, documentary-style takes, it feels raw and unmediated. In fact every word was scripted, and the camera's gradual distancing from Alexandre's point of view is artfully done.

Marc Evans
UK, 1959–

A veteran Welsh television director, Marc Evans followed up his Welsh-language feature debut with the English-language *House Of America* (1996), wherein a Welsh family abandoned by their patriarch scrabble for crumbs of the American dream. Evans's debt to Ken Loach was less evident in the flashier *Resurrection Man* (1997), an adaptation of Eoin McNamee's novel based on the Shankhill Butcher's killing spree in Belfast in 1975. Like many freely fictionalized treatments of real-life events, the film smacked of pointless opportunism: *Natural Born Killers* flavoured by the Troubles. *Resurrection Man* shared its ugly estimation of human nature with *My Little Eye* (2001), a haunted-house screamer that doubled as a poisoned satire of the then-peaking reality TV craze. The morbid, maudlin psycho-thriller *Trauma* (2004) was notable if only for roughing up Colin Firth's usual veneer of sphinx-like stoic charm, while *Snow Cake* (2006) was a snowbound drama about a grieving Englishman's friendship with an autistic Canadian woman (Sigourney Weaver). JW

My Little Eye 2001, 95 min
cast Sean C.W. Johnson, Kris Lemche, Stephen O'Reilly, Laura Regan, Jennifer Sky *cin* Hubert Taczanowski *m* Flood, Alan Moulder, Rob Kirwan

Evans appeared on a 2002 cover of *Sight & Sound* magazine with Mike Leigh and Lynne Ramsay on the strength of this knowingly noxious reality-TV parody, in which the insufferable young inmates of a *Big Brother*-type programme discover they're in fact trapped inside a particularly macabre spin on *Survivor*. Evans spies on these fishes in a barrel through the bleary surveillance cameras posted throughout their house, which adds a Haneke-style mustering of forced audience complicity.

Richard Eyre

UK, 1943–

Richard Eyre is one of the many directors who flit between theatre and film. Some, such as Mike Leigh or Julie Taymor, harbour a distinctive style or set of thematic concerns that they carry with them from the stage to the screen, but Eyre has no such defining style. His stage productions in the early 1970s were often contemporary and controversial, but his recent theatre work has been defined by its eclecticism (*King Lear* to *Mary Poppins*), so it's not surprising that there isn't a unifying force in his film career.

After cutting his teeth on the BBC's *Play For Today* television programme, Eyre made his movie debut with *The Ploughman's Lunch* (1983), a collaboration with writer Ian McEwan. The political drama was notable for one *coup de cinéma*: Eyre slipped actor Jonathan Pryce into the Conservative party conference, and filmed him mingling with the unsuspecting politicians. After the long-forgotten comedy *Laughterhouse* (1984), Eyre didn't make another cinema feature for seventeen years. Then came *Iris* (2001), an intimate, intelligent and meticulously crafted drama tracing the life of novelist Iris Murdoch from her youth as a vibrant young Oxford student to her later battle with Alzheimer's disease. A personal project for Eyre whose mother struggled with the debilitating illness, *Iris* boasted finely wrought performances by Judi Dench and Kate Winslet, but was visually anaemic.

Eyre's next film, *Stage Beauty* (2004) bawdily chronicled a young actress's struggle to break the male monopoly of women's roles on the Elizabethan stage. The director clearly hoped the film would repeat the capricious charm and box-office success of John Madden's *Shakespeare In Love* (1998), but it failed on both counts. And just when the critics had Eyre pegged as a director who's more at home on stage than screen, he surprised them with the psychological thriller *Notes On A Scandal* (2006), in which he finally came to terms with the visual demands of the medium. LH

The Ploughman's Lunch 1983, 107 min
cast Jonathan Pryce, Tim Curry, Rosemary Harris, Frank Finlay, Charlie Dore, David De Keyser, Bill Paterson *cin* Clive Tickner *m* Dominic Muldowney

Against the backdrop of the Falklands War and the 1982 Conservative party conference, opportunistic journalist James Penfield (Jonathan Pryce) writes a book about the Suez Crisis which spins another lie, that one of Britain's greatest foreign policy disasters was actually a famous victory. Serving as both a time capsule and a political drama, Eyre's debut is a sobering, urgent, yet uneven essay on the enduring Faustian allure of power.

Notes On A Scandal 2006, 92 min
cast Judi Dench, Cate Blanchett, Bill Nighy, Andrew Simpson, Juno Temple, Max Lewis *cin* Chris Menges *m* Philip Glass

Based on Zoë Heller's bestseller, *Notes On A Scandal* stars Judi Dench, both impish and demonic, as a teacher nursing a painful crush on a naïve colleague (Cate Blanchett), who is conducting an illicit affair with a young pupil. Ultimately, Patrick Marber's dark-hued script doesn't quite deliver on all its promises, but the film remains Eyre's finest cinematic achievement, aided greatly by Chris Menges' vibrant cinematography.

The Farrelly Brothers

Peter Farrelly: US, 1956–
Bobby Farrelly: US, 1958–

Gross-out humanists Peter and Bobby Farrelly could almost be seen as the low-comedy counterparts to body-horror maestro David Cronenberg. Tackling themes as diverse as schizophrenia, disability, conjoined twins and the subjective nature of reality, they prompt visceral laughter and glean surprising pathos from the myriad ways our bodies can shock, embarrass and betray us. Though they've never bothered honing their rudimentary technical skills (dingy cinematography is a given), the brothers have perfected the rude art of the wildly distended gag – no one rivals the Farrellys for taking a joke too far.

They rode the first wave of Jim Carrey's megastardom with their debut, *Dumb And Dumber* (1995), which established both their fearless gifts for filthy hilarity (as in the justly renowned explosive diarrhoea scene) and equal-opportunity ribbing (there's a priceless parakeet-related joke at the expense of a blind boy). In their nastiest creation, the underrated *Kingpin* (1996), former star bowler Woody Harrelson, his hand amputated by angry opponents, mentors Amish prodigy Randy Quaid against sleazy comb-over casualty Bill Murray (in a deliriously brilliant, ad-libbed performance). The sleeper hit of summer 1998, *There's Something About Mary*, returned to the trusty *Dumb And Dumber* plot of two hapless guys chasing after the same gorgeous girl – as did *Me, Myself & Irene* (2000) in its own way, with Carrey playing both Jekyll and Hyde – and, in the film's signature set piece, provided an uproarious lesson in the mechanical defects of the postcoital urethra.

Beginning with *Shallow Hal* (2001), wherein a hypnotized Jack Black falls for an obese woman who somehow looks just like willowy Gwyneth Paltrow, the Farrellys began swimming in gentler, more salu-brious streams, as in the conjoined-twin comedy *Stuck On You* (2003) and in their most temperate offering yet, *Fever Pitch* (aka *The Perfect Catch*, 2005). A sprightly adaptation of the Nick Hornby novel that exchanges football fandom for baseball frenzy, the movie yet again proved the brothers' loose-limbed dexterity within the usually sterile and treacle-sweet confines of the romantic comedy. JW

There's Something About Mary 1998, 119 min
cast Cameron Diaz, Matt Dillon, Ben Stiller, Lee Evans, Chris Elliott, Lin Shaye, Jeffrey Tambor, Markie Post, Keith David, W. Earl Brown *cin* Mark Irvin

Ben Stiller still pines for his teen-years dream girl (Cameron Diaz) a decade after their date to the senior prom hit a profound snag in the form of a reproductive organ caught in a zipper. The directors deliver this carnage in extreme close-up, going on to provide Diaz punked out in semen-based hair gel, a guy with a nervous skin rash of biblical proportions, a dog being given mouth-to-mouth resuscitation and much more – the movie's all-out assault of indignities amounts to an unhinged form of generosity.

Stuck On You 2003, 118 min
cast Matt Damon, Greg Kinnear, Eva Mendes, Wen Yann Shih, Pat Crawford Brown *cin* Daniel Mindel *m* Michael Andrews, Billy Godrum, Tom Wolfe

Matt Damon and Greg Kinnear are conjoined twins: suave Kinnear is bent on an acting career in Hollywood, bashful Damon is just along for the ride. The movie boasts several genius gags but invests more energy in loopy, empathetic characterization. For the first time, the Farrellys create three-dimensional protagonists. It's perhaps no coincidence that their most affecting film to date is a study of the "can't live with you, can't live without you" pangs of sibling symbiosis.

John Farrow

Australia, 1904–63

A colourful character who never quite made it into the auteurs' pantheon, John Farrow could be relied on to bring conviction and imagination to even the stalest studio assignments.

Educated in Australia and England, Farrow went to sea as a young man, and served in the Royal Navy, the Royal Canadian Navy, the US Marine Corps and the Merchant Service. (He was made a CBE, a Knight of Malta, and a Knight of the Grand Cross of the Holy Sepulchre, and won numerous decorations.) He was also a prolific writer, producing verse, short stories, plays, a novel, a Tahitian–English dictionary, and a number of well-received biographies – many of them on religious themes (he converted to Catholicism after World War II).

Farrow came to Hollywood in the late 1920s, initially to advise on sea pictures, and was soon writing scripts. He made his directorial debut with MGM's musical short *The Spectacle Maker* (1934), and the following year was one of four uncredited directors who tried to salvage the troubled *Tarzan Escapes* (1936). While on set, he met his second wife, Maureen O'Hara, who played Tarzan's Jane. Among their seven children were actresses Mia and Tisa Farrow.

Wounded during his service in World War II, Farrow returned to filmmaking, and was nominated for an Oscar for the propaganda movie *Wake Island* (1942). He brought a sober authenticity to *Two Years Before The Mast* (1946) and made a fine Western, *Hondo* (1953), but, like many other studio directors, his most exciting work was in *noir* thrillers, such as *The Big Clock* (1948), *Night Has A Thousand Eyes* (1948), *Alias Nick Beal* (1949), *Where Danger Lives* (1950) and *His Kind Of Woman* (1951). TC

The Big Clock 1948, 95 min, b/w

cast Ray Milland, Charles Laughton, Maureen O'Sullivan, George Macready, Rita Johnson, Elsa Lanchester *cin* John F. Seitz *m* Victor Young

The clock is running when Milland (who would play devil's advocate for Farrow in *Alias Nick Beal*) is put in charge of a manhunt in which the chief suspect is... himself. An ingenious, witty *film noir* with Charles Laughton as a murderous media magnate (Milland's boss), and Laughton's wife Lanchester as an artist/witness. Screenwriter Jonathan Latimer was another regular Farrow collaborator. Remade by Roger Donaldson as *No Way Out* (1986).

Rainer Werner Fassbinder

Germany, 1945–82

Fassbinder was the most prolific and prodigious figure in the New German Cinema of the 1970s. In a film career which lasted only from 1968 to 1981, he directed 41 full-length films for cinema and television, including the fifteen-and-a-half-hour *Berlin Alexanderplatz* (1980).

Born in Bavaria just weeks after the end of World War II, Fassbinder was the son of a doctor, but when his parents divorced five years later he was brought up by his mother. A translator, she was one of the models for that redoubtable self-made businesswoman, Maria Braun (*The Marriage Of Maria Braun*, 1978). She also acted in more than twenty of his films under her maiden name, Lilo Pempeit.

A movie nut from childhood, Fassbinder tried and failed to get into film school. Bisexual and rebellious, he dropped out of drama school to participate in Munich's underground theatre scene, quickly establishing himself as a playwright and director, and building up a close-knit "family" of actors, including Hanna Schygulla, Kurt Raabe, Ingrid Caven (who was his wife for a time), Ulli Lommel and others. It was a volatile but dynamic group, at the forefront of the radical left-wing politics and bohemian alternative lifestyles of the period.

Fassbinder's first films were experiments, made very cheaply, and influenced equally by Godard, Straub, Brecht and American genre cinema. Most notable among his early work are his gangster movies, the last and the best of which was *The American Soldier* (1970), and he even made a Western, *Whity*, in 1971. If these were conceived as a kind of critical "anti-cinema", Fassbinder came to embrace the full emotional amplification of Hollywood melodrama, taking inspiration from the ironic and expressionist aesthetics of Douglas Sirk and Nicholas Ray. *Fear Eats The Soul* (1974) was modelled on Sirk's *All That Heaven Allows*, albeit thoroughly transmuted to 1970s Germany. Together with *Love Is Colder Than Death* (1969) and *I Only Want You To Love Me* (1976), it spells out Fassbinder's raw, brutally intense emotional pitch.

A domineering figure professionally, he was fascinated by power relationships and submissives – like the title characters in *Martha* (1973), *The Bitter Tears Of Petra Von Kant* (1971) and *Effi Briest* (1974). Such preoccupations led to accusations of misogyny, and a four-year split from his most famous muse, Hanna Schygulla, but while Fassbinder's heroines are often trapped in suffocating social roles, many of them operate with admirable enterprise, wit and resourcefulness. He was a progressive and a pessimist.

In common with the other leading lights of the New German Cinema – Werner Herzog, Wim Wenders, Volker Schlöndorff, Margarethe von Trotta – Fassbinder was haunted by the legacy of fascism and deeply antipathetic towards the materialism and economic exploitation endemic to capitalist West Germany. Often, as in *The Merchant Of The Four Seasons* (1972), *Fear Eats The Soul* and *Why Does Herr R. Run Amok* (1970), Fassbinder focuses on working-class characters excluded by and alienated from Germany's "economic miracle". In *Fox And His Friends* (1975), Fassbinder himself is a carnival worker who wins a fortune on the lottery – and then allows his new, bourgeois boyfriend to spend it all. In the end, even his corpse will be stripped of his last few marks.

Fassbinder's career is so rich, it is difficult to pick out only a handful of titles to highlight. But it wasn't until *The Marriage Of Maria Braun* at the end of the 1970s that international critics and art-house audiences really embraced him. With *Lola* (1981) and *Veronika Voss* (1982), this formed the "Bundesrepublik Deutschland trilogy", in which Fassbinder presented a personal history of post-war Germany styled in the manner of the movies of the period. To this project the TV mini-series *Berlin Alexanderplatz*, an adaptation of Döblin's classic 1929 novel of the same name, serves as something more substantial than a prologue. Fassbinder died from a massive drug overdose two years later at the age of 37, a devastating loss to the New German Cinema. TC

Fear Eats The Soul (Angst essen Seele auf)
1974, 93 min
cast Brigitte Mira, El Hedi Ben Salem, Barbara Valentin, Irm Hermann, Rainer Werner Fassbinder *cin* Jürgen Jürges

Douglas Sirk gets a German social realist makeover. Shot in a two-week gap between other projects, this melodrama focuses on a love story between an ageing German cleaning lady (Mira) and a younger Arab immigrant worker (Ben Salem). Their romance meets with hostility and suspicion at every turn, not least from her avaricious, racist family. Fassbinder himself appears as Mira's deeply unpleasant son-in-law.

Effi Briest 1974, 140 min, b/w
cast Hanna Schygulla, Wolfgang Schenck, Ulli Lommel, Karl-Heinz Böhm, Ursula Strätz *cin* Jürgen Jürges, Dietrich Lohmann *m* Camille Saint-Saëns

Fassbinder's fascinating, highly respectful approach to Theodor Fontane's nineteenth-century novel is a rigorous study in repression. Hanna Schygulla stars as the 17-year-old bride of an ageing aristocrat, her vivacity sapped by the stifling social conventions of the time – and her own moral timidity. The actress became Fassbinder's muse in several of his most popular films. Shot in shimmering monochrome, with antiquated dissolves and titles.

Fox And His Friends (Faustrecht der Freiheit)
1975, 123 min
cast Rainer Werner Fassbinder, Peter Chatel, Karl-Heinz Böhm, Harry Bär, Adrian Hoven, Ulla Jacobsen *cin* Michael Ballhaus *m* Peer Raben

Fassbinder took the lead role here, as an out-of-work carnival worker who strikes it rich on the lottery, and becomes besotted with a snobbish young bourgeois who helps him spend his money furnishing a new apartment with antiques from his lover's boutique. As so often in his work, desire and exploitation go hand in hand, and the film's *nouveau riche* hero ends up all the poorer for it.

The Marriage Of Maria Braun (Die Ehe der Maria Braun) 1978, 119 min
cast Hanna Schygulla, Klaus Löwitsch, Ivan Desny, Gisela Uhlen, Elisabeth Trissenaar *cin* Michael Ballhaus *m* Peer Raben

The most acclaimed of Fassbinder's achievements, the Bundesrepublik Deutschland (BRD) trilogy constitutes a sour, tragicomic chronicle of the Konrad Adenauer era of reconstruction and the economic miracle. In this first instalment, Maria (Hanna Schygulla) is a war widow whose husband returns from the grave, but only to be incarcerated for the next decade. Maria dedicates herself to preparing a perfect home for his release, applying both her brain and her body to become a successful businesswoman. It's a tragically misguided enterprise.

Veronika Voss (Die Sehnsucht der Veronika Voss) 1982, 104 min, b/w
cast Rosel Zech, Hilmar Thate, Cornelia Froboess, Annemarie Düringer, Doris Schade *cin* Xaver Schwarzenberger *m* Peer Raben

Each of the films in the BRD trilogy is built around a tragic heroine, in this case the eponymous Veronika Voss (played by Rosel Zech). This is the story of a starlet at the UFA film studios: rumoured to be a mistress of Goebbels, she falls into drug addiction after the war. Shot in icy black and white, the film's look is reminiscent of Billy Wilder's *Sunset Boulevard* (1950).

Berlin Alexanderplatz 1980, 931 min
cast Günter Lamprecht, Hanna Schygulla, Barbara Sukowa, Karin Baal, Helmut Griem, Ivan Desny *cin* Xaver Schwarzenberger *m* Peer Raben

Alfred Döblin's novel was a favourite of Fassbinder's; his character in *Fox And His Friends* is also known as Franz Biberkopf, the name of Döblin's antihero. Made for television (like most of Fassbinder's films), but as a fourteen-part mini-series, this amounts to one of the most extraordinary films ever made. Set in Germany in the 1920s and 30s, it's the chronicle of a country stumbling towards fascism.

Federico Fellini
Italy, 1920–93

In an era when Italian cinema means the easy consolations of Roberto Benigni's *Life Is Beautiful*, the aesthetic and moral challenges posed by Federico Fellini seem at once important and exotic.

The son of a commercial traveller, Fellini ran away to the circus as a child, an experience which marked him and his work. Moving to Rome in 1939, he became a cartoonist and illustrator, working in The Funny-Face Shop after the war drawing caricatures of visiting GIs. Befriended by veteran actor Aldo Fabrizi, he began writing theatre sketches. This led to him working for Roberto Rossellini, contributing to the scripts of both *Rome, Open City* (1945) and *Paisà* (1946). Fellini's first directed film was *Luci del varietà* (*Lights Of Variety*, 1950), co-directed with Alberto Lattuada. Following the fortunes of a girl who joins a troupe of travelling players, the film drew upon Fellini's love of the greasepaint and tack of the theatre, a world to which he would return in later films.

Fellini's first solo direction was *Lo sceicco bianco* (*The White Sheik*, 1952), during the production of which he forged important relationships with playwright Tullio Pinelli, scriptwriter Ennio Flaiano and composer Nino Rota. Steeped in the post-war culture of the "fumetti" – photo-based comic strips popular among the Italian lower middle classes – it was a satiric tale of a housewife who becomes enamoured with a character in a comic strip. The film also included a cameo role for Fellini's wife, actress Giulietta Masina, as a prostitute. Fellini and Masina

Federico Fellini and Giulietta Masina

Sad and hopeful, innocent and otherworldly – whether Giulietta Masina embodies Fellini's vision, or whether his vision was honed through his association with her, is debatable. What is undeniable, however, is that at least two of the seven films they made together are masterpieces of world cinema, and that their power rests largely on Masina's unique performances.

A popular radio actress, famous in Italy for her leading role in the Fellini-scripted soap *Terzoglio* (1942), Masina married Fellini in 1943. Following their first movie together, *Luci del varietà* (*Lights Of Variety*, 1950), she had a small role as a kindhearted prostitute in *La sceicco bianco* (*The White Sheik*, 1952). The two sealed their creative collaboration, however, with *La strada* (1954), a fable about love, brutality and redemption that he wrote especially for her. As with all the characters in *La strada*, Masina plays an archetype, a stylized rendition of innocence. A plucky waif with black button eyes (for all the world like a cartoon character), Masina is sad clown and wounded cur. Often compared with Chaplin, she resembles his Little Tramp "with the face of an artichoke", as *La strada*'s Fool puts it, and while her circus make-up may be a mask of sorts, her elastic features and phenomenal physical presence express volumes. Though it reveals the seamy underbelly of society in all its brutalism, the vision of *La strada* is poetic rather than documentary, and it has been accused of betraying the tenets of neo-realism and of exploitative sentimentality. Masina's virtuosity as a performer brooks no reproach, however, and the film won the Oscar for best foreign film.

Her next major role was in *Nights Of Cabiria* (1957), Fellini's affectionate, if ambivalent, portrayal of Rome's underclass. Here, playing the beleaguered prostitute who survives on her dreams, Masina brings the same tragicomic intensity as she does to *La strada*, but this time she's pugnacious and more rebellious, victimized, but never entirely a victim. It's a remarkably fine balance – and one that Shirley MacLaine, who has been compared with Masina, and who reprises the Cabiria role in Bob Fosse's 1968 musical *Sweet Charity*, never quite achieves. A bustling little powerhouse of a woman, tough and earthy, her child-like face punctuated by startling black eyebrows, Masina embodies human hope and resilience.

Actress and director next worked together in the histrionic *Juliet Of The Spirits* (1965), Fellini's first colour film, in which Masina's rendition of a woman driven to the point of insanity by her husband was rumoured to be drawn from experience. The film may be excessive and self-indulgent, but Masina, displaying her characteristic hope and toughness, remains compelling.

Juliet wasn't well received, and Masina moved into radio and television. Some twenty years later she made a welcome return as the ageing dancer reunited with her old partner (Marcello Mastroianni) in the elegiac *Ginger And Fred* (1985). The bittersweet scene when they dance together again, a brief recapturing of the past, could, if one was feeling sentimental, be read as a metaphor for her creative reunion with her husband. Giulietta Masina and Federico Fellini died within months of each other in 1993, their fiftieth year of marriage. SC

had married in 1943, and the actress's gamine innocence, described by Tom Charity as the missing link between Charlie Chaplin and Shirley MacLaine, would become Fellini's feminine conscience in a sad and beautiful world.

Fellini's early work shows a fascination with humanity's weakness for illusion, increasingly pronounced in a world without faith or apparent moral bearings. Set in the seaside town of Rimini where Fellini grew up, *I vitelloni* (1953) was a semi-autobiographical study of shiftless young men with money to spare but no direction, but it was *La strada* (1954) which brought him to international attention. This film was the first in Fellini's acclaimed "trilogy of loneliness", all three of which starred Giulietta Masina. Responding to left-wing criticism that *La strada*'s shift towards the subjective betrayed the objective spirit of Italian neo-realism, *Il bidone* (*The Swindlers*, 1955), second in the trilogy, was a bitter story of con men posing as priests to swindle

peasant farmers. Evoking in matter-of-fact style the details of urban squalor, the third in the trilogy, *Nights Of Cabiria* (1957), gave Masina her greatest role as the prostitute whose simple faith in things beguiles those around her.

La dolce vita (1960) was one of the keynotes of the post-war European art cinema efflorescence on which Fellini's textbook reputation rests. *8½* (1963) was so called because it was the director's eighth-and-a-half film to date, and it is a vibrant example of the modernist impulse that made 1960s cinema so distinctive. Both of these films starred Marcello Mastroianni, whose urbane but troubled persona can be seen as a projection of the director's own self-image. *Juliet Of The Spirits* (1965), a tribute to Masina, dwelled in the fantasies and neuroses of a woman who thinks her husband is betraying her. Heavily criticized at the time, *Fellini-Satyricon* (1969) evoked the carnival spirit of Roman author Petronius, exploring human sexuality in all its forms.

After the characteristically Felliniesque *The Clowns*, (1970), a documentary in which Fellini celebrates the great clowns of history, *Fellini's Roma* (1972) was a cornucopia of the director's rollicking impressions of the Italian capital. That was followed by *Amarcord* (1973), a comic blend of soap opera and humour set in the director's home town.

After a fresh tide of experiment in *Fellini's Casanova* (1976), *City Of Women* (1980) starred Mastroianni as the director's ageing disappointed alter ego mired in the contemporary wave of militant feminism, but by now the Fellini carnival seemed passé. *Ginger And Fred* (1985) nostalgically revelled in the vulgarity of television in an age when spectacle and illusion are all we have. In 1993 the director received an Academy Award for lifetime achievement. He is one of the cinema's greatest artists. RA

La strada 1954, 104 min, b/w

cast Giulietta Masina, Anthony Quinn, Richard Basehart, Aldo Silvani, Marcella Rovena *cin* Otello Martelli *m* Nino Rota

One of the masterpieces of European cinema, Fellini's odyssey through the tragicomic existence of Masina's

waif-like Gelsomina, the clown to Anthony Quinn's brutish strongman, is as sad and hilarious as the dark little towns through which they pass. Few directors have chronicled man's fall as truthfully.

La dolce vita 1960, 176 min, b/w

cast Marcello Mastroianni, Yvonne Furneaux, Anouk Aimée, Anita Ekberg, Alain Cuny, Annibale Ninchi *cin* Otello Martelli *m* Nino Rota

As the 1960s begin, a helicopter carries a statue of Christ out of Rome. The cinema has few more poignant images of moral disenchantment than this opening shot in Fellini's excursion into Roman high life, an existence simultaneously disgusting and attractive to Marcello Mastroianni's journalist as he chronicles these vapid lives. This film is both Fellini's most eloquent statement on life's carnival and the pop classic that made paparazzi an indelible feature of the modern world.

8½ (Otto e mezzo) 1963, 138 min, b/w

cast Marcello Mastroianni, Claudia Cardinale, Anouk Aimée, Sandra Milo, Rossella Falk, Barbara Steele *cin* Gianni Di Venanzo *m* Nino Rota

It may not have weathered as well as *La dolce vita*, but Fellini's account of a modern filmmaker (Marcello Mastroianni) with creative block has many a brilliant moment. Although it now seems self-indulgent, the film remains visually impressive and resonates throughout Woody Allen's oeuvre, including his 1980 film tribute *Stardust Memories*.

Juliet Of The Spirits (Giulietta degli spiriti) 1965, 145 min

cast Giulietta Masina, Mario Pisu, Sandra Milo, Valentina Cortese, Caterina Boratto *cin* Gianni Di Venanzo *m* Nino Rota

A veritable cavalcade of oddball characters and even odder events make this oneiric feast one of Fellini's most characteristic and piquant works. Using his wife, Giulietta Masina, as the vector of fraught bourgeois sensibility, Fellini gives us either a persuasive essay on modern existential dismay or another adoring auteur's take on beautiful womanhood.

Fellini's Roma 1972, 128 min

cast Peter Gonzales, Fiona Florence, Marne Maitland, Britta Barnes, Anna Magnani *cin* Giuseppe Rotunno *m* Nino Rota

No less inventive than Fellini's early works, this almost narrative-less jaunt through his favourite city is full of the extravagantly drawn character types and crazy imagery that have made the director one of the richest chroniclers of human foible and fantasy.

Amarcord 1973, 123 min

cast Puppela Maggio, Magalia Noël, Armando Brancia, Ciccio Ingrassia, Nando Orfei *cin* Giuseppe Rotunno *m* Nino Rota

Fellini turned his anarchic gaze back to his seaside home town for this accessible Oscar-winning portrait of provincial Italian life during the Fascist era. This charming excavation of human desire never stints on the funny characters, scatological conceits and generosity of his best work.

Anita Ekberg beguiles Marcello Mastroianni in Rome's Trevi Fountain in *La dolce vita*.

Abel Ferrara

US, 1951–

The films of Abel Ferrara belong to the proud tradition of exploitation filmmaking, in which the visceral bursts of blood and sex only punctuate deeper social and soulful concerns. His downtown New York City teems with pushers, junkies, tramps, hoodlums and bad cops, all similarly disfigured by their ravenous cravings; Ferrara most overtly embodied the bloodsucking human condition via the vampire-philosopher played by Lili Taylor in *The Addiction* (1995). Much of Ferrara's work enacts the profound solipsism and physical debasement associated with the throes of religious ecstasy, and he often engages with Catholic imagery and dogma, most infamously in *Bad Lieutenant* (1992), wherein a nun is raped and tortured on an altar.

Ferrara's first film was the epistolary porno *Nine Lives Of A Wet Pussy* (1976), which he directed under the pseudonym Jimmy Boy L. He took the lead role in his first proper feature, which bore the self-explanatory title *The Driller Killer* (1979), from a script by his longtime writer-collaborator Nicolas St. John. Released in 1979, this "video nasty" straddled the last days of the sex-'n'-horror drive-in market and the first stirrings of the American independent renaissance, as did Ferrara's rape-revenge quickie *Ms 45* (1981). Ferrara won a critical breakthrough with the icy, brutal *King Of New York* in 1990, which prowled crime scenes, drug dens and orgies with Christopher Walken's impassive ganglord.

After the controversial *Bad Lieutenant* came the meta-movie *Dangerous Game* (1993) featuring Harvey Keitel and Madonna. The director described it as "*The Player* meets *Contempt*" and the leading lady called the director a "scumbag". Ferrara secured his highest budget ever, $20 million, for the spottily distributed remake *Body Snatchers* (1993). He then tried his hand at period melodrama with the histrionic, near-nihilist *The Funeral* (1996), set among a mob-ruled union racket in Depression-era New York, and stumbled with his attempt at a *Rashomon*-like narrative in *New Rose Hotel* (1998). But the unexpectedly poignant (and little-seen) *'R Xmas* (2001), about an aspirational husband-and-wife team of heroin distributors, won a slot on *Cahiers du cinéma*'s Top 10 of 2001. Given that *Go Go Tales* (2007) is a comedy about the proprietor of a lap-dancing club and *Mary* (2005) a drama about an actress who becomes fixated on Mary Magdalene, it's clear that Ferrara's not done with his obsessions yet, and nor are they with him. JW

Ms 45 1981, 81 min
cast Zoë Tamerlis, Bogey, Albert Sinkys, Darlene Stuto, Helen McGara, Nike Zachmanoglou, Peter Yellen *cin* James Momèl *m* Joe Delia

Thana (Zoë Tamerlis), a mute garment-district employee, is raped on her way home from work, and then raped again – at which point she concludes that enough is enough. Ferrara's potent low-budget revenge fantasy seethes with pointed feminist anger and made a cult heroine out of star Tamerlis, just 17 at the time of filming; she went on to co-write Ferrara's *Bad Lieutenant*.

King Of New York 1990, 111 min
cast Christopher Walken, David Caruso, Laurence Fishburne, Victor Argo, Wesley Snipes, Janet Julian *cin* Bojan Bazelli *m* Joe Delia

The focal point of Ferrara's stark yet enigmatic journey through the underworld is Christopher Walken's multifaceted performance as a crime boss with equal parts good and evil spinning like a gyre inside of him: he commands ruthless troops of pushers and thugs, yet wants to give all his ill-gotten gains to a local hospital. Full of twists and elisions, the film only gains in mysterious power for being so discombobulated, with Walken's scary, serene gaze holding it all together.

Bad Lieutenant 1992, 98 min
cast Harvel Keitel, Victor Argo, Anthony Ruggiero, Robin Burrows, Victoria Burrows, Frankie Thorn, Victoria Bastel *cin* Ken Kelsch *m* Joe Delia

This dark night of the soul tracks a drug-gobbling New York cop (Harvey Keitel): he terrorizes and steals from the citizens he's bound to protect, he's up to his eyeballs in debt to some fearsome bookies and he's increasingly tortured by the quiet fortitude of a nun who refuses to name the two men who raped her. An unflinching confrontation with spiritual degradation and the limits of forgiveness, Ferrara's best-known film cedes the stage to Keitel's naked (sometimes in every sense) performance.

Marco Ferreri

Italy, 1928–97

J. Hoberman once asked Wong Kar-Wai which was his favourite recent Hollywood film, and the Hong Kong director replied with the question: "Could any film by Marco Ferreri be called a Hollywood film?" Though his films consistently attracted international stars (regulars included Marcello Mastroianni, Gérard Depardieu and Michel Piccoli), Ferreri could never have been mistaken for a Hollywood aspirant. Often teeming with graphic sex, nihilism, violence and perversion, his movies are profoundly ambivalent: exhibiting a simultaneous compulsion and revulsion for sex, food and other essential pleasures; at once attacking bourgeois values (marriage, family, fidelity) and lamenting their demise; both observing and internalizing the resentful misogyny of emasculated man in the age of feminism. Upon Ferreri's death in 1997, Cannes artistic director Gilles Jacob said by way of tribute, "No one was more demanding nor more allegorical than he in showing the state of crisis of contemporary man."

His early films often attacked the institution of marriage: in *The Conjugal Bed* (1963), marital sex kills; in *The Ape Woman* (1963), a man turns his furry wife into a lucrative earner; in the chillingly calm and austere *Dillinger Is Dead* (1969), starring Piccoli, a man's overpowering alienation culminates in the murder of his wife. The 1970s saw Ferreri's project become more and more wildly outré: characters resolve to eat themselves to death in *Blow-Out* (1972); *Don't Touch The White Woman* (1974) re-enacts Custer's Last Stand (literally) on a Paris construction site as a protest against the then-waning war in Vietnam; and a poor sod cuts off his own penis in *The Last Woman* (1976). The latter film was a sustained (and perhaps inadvertently comic) wail of sexual self-disgust and ineffectual machismo that was sustained in the Bukowski adaptation *Tales Of Ordinary Madness* (1981), starring Ben Gazzara. As Ferreri grew older, so did his subversives: *House Of Smiles* (1990) explored geriatric sex and tyrannical repression at an old-age home.

Reading the cast list and synopsis of a Ferreri movie is sometimes preferable to watching it; for example, *The Future Is Woman* (1984) cannot live up to the promise of its dream-casting duo of Ornella Muti and Hanna Schygulla. The films exert a punitive effect by containing all the grossness, disgust and despair of the contemporary world as Ferreri saw it. JW

Blow-Out (La grande bouffe) 1973, 133 min

cast Marcello Mastroianni, Ugo Tognazzi, Michel Piccoli, Philippe Noiret, Andrea Ferreol, Monique Chaumette *cin* Mario Vulpiani *m* Philippe Sarde

Four men retire to a villa and take up a self-annihilating eating regimen in Ferreri's most famous film, which opened the Cannes Film Festival in 1973 and divided critics: some thought it a devastating critique of excessive modern appetites, others a toxic – and literally flatulent – juvenile stunt. Either way, at well over two hours it's a long, exhaustively itemized last supper.

Tales Of Ordinary Madness (Storie di ordinaria follia) 1981, 108 min

cast Ben Gazzara, Ornella Muti, Susan Tyrrell, Tanya Lopert, Roy Brocksmith, Katia Berget *cin* Torino Delli Colli *m* Philippe Sarde

One provocateur adapts another in Ferreri's take on gutter poet Charles Bukowski, whose alter ego is here played by an astutely cast Ben Gazzara as a drink-soaked poet stumbling fecklessly through a rotation of bars and women. The alcohol-smeared fatalism is thickly convincing, though the English dialogue can sometimes be stilted.

Todd Field

US, 1964–

With roles such as the mysterious pianist in *Eyes Wide Shut*, Ashley Judd's love interest in *Ruby In Paradise* and Anne Heche's fiancé in *Walking And Talking*, Todd Field had solidly established himself as a working actor, if not quite a star, before his superb first feature, *In The Bedroom* (2001), quietly announced the arrival of a stunning new filmmaking talent. (Field has expressed his gratitude to the late Stanley Kubrick, who let Field observe him behind the camera during the actor's ample downtime on the set of *Eyes Wide Shut*.) As an oft-absent student at the American Film Institute, Field made several shorts, including his thesis film *Nonnie & Alex* (1995), a Special Jury Award winner at Sundance about a young boy grieving for the loss of his mother to cancer.

Following the Oscar-nominated *In The Bedroom*, Field collaborated with Tom Perrotta on an adaptation of Perrotta's novel *Little Children* (2006). A well-performed chronicle of suburban lust and dissatisfaction, *Little Children* was noteworthy for giving child star Jackie Earle Haley a meaty comeback role as a convicted paedophile whose return from prison disturbs the neighbourhood's equilibrium. JW

In The Bedroom 2001, 130 min

cast Sissy Spacek, Tom Wilkinson, Nick Stahl, William Mapother, William Wise, Celia Weston, Marisa Tomei *cin* Antonio Calvache *m* Thomas Newman

Based on the short story *Killings* by the late Andre Dubus (to whom the film is dedicated), Field's assured debut feature, set in coastal Maine, observes a husband and wife (Sissy Spacek and Tom Wilkinson, both extraordinary) in mourning following the violent death of their only child (Nick Stahl). With exquisite patience, grace and attention to telling detail, Field dissects the couple's implacable sorrow and anger, until the rage they've heretofore bottled behind closed doors is finally turned outward.

Mike Figgis

UK, 1948–

Of all British directors in Hollywood, few have wended their way as dexterously between Art and Mammon as Mike Figgis. After spending part of his childhood in Kenya, Figgis dabbled in jazz around Newcastle, joining The People Show, an experimental performance group in which he played, wrote, directed, acted, composed and did the sound. Turned down by the National Film School in 1976, he made a 16mm short, persuading Channel 4 to finance a TV feature, *The House*, in 1984.

Figgis then wrote, directed and scored *Stormy Monday* (1987) and Hollywood beckoned. *Internal Affairs* (1990) was an angry examination of police corruption in a morally decentred Los Angeles, and one of Richard Gere's best films. Focusing on the renovation of a department store with a grisly past, cult favourite *Liebestraum* (1991) reworked the psychological currents underpinning *film noir*. If the Terence Rattigan adaptation *The Browning Version* (1994) felt over-reverent, *Leaving Las Vegas* (1995) and *One Night Stand* (1997) were richly observed watersheds in the lives of their protagonists. Figgis is unusual for scoring his own films, and in *One Night Stand* his musical themes resonate poetically with the interaction between lovers Wesley Snipes and Nastassja Kinski.

The End Of Sexual Innocence (1998), *Miss Julie* (1999) and *Timecode* (2000) were audacious experiments in performance and aesthetics. *Timecode* was an experimental Hollywood soap in which four continuous, 93-minute shots filmed simultaneously in LA play in parallel on a screen split in quarters. In *Hotel* (2001), Figgis self-reflexively alternated between staged scenes and a spontaneity reminiscent of the Dogme aesthetic. Returning to the mainstream with the Sharon Stone vehicle *Cold Creek Manor* (2003), Figgis remains one of the most watchable of Hollywood's British filmmakers. RA

Stormy Monday 1987, 93 min

cast Melanie Griffith, Tommy Lee Jones, Sting, Sean Bean, James Cosmo, Mark Long *cin* Roger Deakins *m* Mike Figgis

An underrated gem, Figgis's debut is an atmospheric thriller set in *Get Carter*'s stomping ground of Newcastle. Sean Bean plays a young Irishman who takes a job working for shady jazz club owner Finney (Sting, in his best role) and soon comes up against Tommy Lee Jones's corrupt US businessman who's forcing the local businesses out. Figgis garners uniformly excellent work from his cast, and his jazz score is fabulous.

Liebestraum 1991, 113 min

cast Kevin Anderson, Kim Novak, Pamela Gidley, Bill Pullman, Graham Beckel *cin* Juan Ruiz Anchia *m* Mike Figgis

An architectural journalist (Kevin Anderson) visiting his dying mother (Kim Novak, in her final film) takes an interest in the destruction of a local department store which was the location of a brutal double murder in the 1950s. Toiling dangerously between memory, dream and a baleful present, this modern *film noir* caught something of the regret that permeates the best examples of the genre.

Leaving Las Vegas 1995, 112 min

cast Nicolas Cage, Elisabeth Shue, Julian Sands, Richard Lewis, Steven Weber, Valeria Golino *cin* Declan Quinn *m* Mike Figgis

Nicolas Cage's suicidal screenwriter and Elisabeth Shue's prostitute became the most poignant love story of 1995. Shot for $3.5 million on 16mm, Figgis's Hollywood art movie had a modernist patina and an emotional truth rare in 1990s American cinema, riffing on regret with an assurance worthy of Miles Davis.

David Fincher

US, 1962–

David Fincher is one of the most technically gifted filmmakers of his generation. His films to date have been erratic, veering from the inspired millennial satire *Fight Club* (1999) to the efficient but relatively anonymous *Panic Room* (2002). He started playing around with movie cameras at 8 years old. George Lucas was a neighbour, and apparently the 11-year-old Fincher used to see him picking up his newspaper in his dressing gown each morning. It demythologized film directors for him. He went on to work at Lucas's special effects company Industrial Light and Magic, and has credits on *Indiana Jones And The Temple Of Doom* (1984) and *Return Of The Jedi* (1983). Fincher's command of computer-enhanced imagery is second to none.

In his twenties he began shooting commercials. His first was an anti-smoking warning which showed an unborn foetus smoking in the womb, and he went on to make ads for Nike, Levi's, Pepsi and Coke. He also made pop videos, notably for Madonna's "Express Yourself" and "Vogue", which were both highly praised for their sleek, striking allure.

His first feature, *Alien*[3] (1992), was an unhappy experience, and he disowned it after studio interference. There were rumours that the studio, in turn, were less than thrilled that their expensive and elaborate sets were all but indistinguishable in the stygian gloom. Failing to follow through on the action impetus of James Cameron's *Aliens*, *Alien*[3] aims to be a more philosophical horror film – it's set on a prison planet where a religious cult has flourished. Many of its flaws were alleviated in a belatedly released "assembly cut", running 28 minutes longer, which featured on a Collectors' Edition DVD in 2004.

Se7en (1995) was the film that established Fincher's commercial and artistic credentials. Audaciously bleak and, again, literally dark, it was emphatic enough to become an against-the-grain hit. *The Game* (1997) was less successful, a lighter conceit about a millionaire trapped in a black joke of a role-playing game which strips him of wealth and status. In order to find himself, the hero must lose everything, "hit bottom" – an idea which anticipates the philosophy of Tyler Durden in *Fight Club*, Fincher's best film.

After the safer *Panic Room*, Fincher was linked with a good number of projects, including a *Mission: Impossible* sequel and an adaptation of James Ellroy's *Black Dahlia*, both of which ended up with other directors. Eventually he settled on *Zodiac* (2007), another film about a serial killer, this time the man who terrorized San Francisco at the height of the hippie era. Although not a commercial success, *Zodiac* was widely admired for its methodical portrait of an obsessive personality (amateur detective and author Robert Graysmith).

There is an unresolved tension in Fincher between the slick stylist who fashions advertisements for the highest bidder and the angry nihilist who forces challenging, subversive films like *Se7en* and *Fight Club* through the system. It could be argued that this dual personality both helped and hindered *Fight Club*, as problematic and provocative a film as Hollywood produced in the 1990s. TC

Come and get it: Brad Pitt takes on all comers as the anarchic Tyler Durden in *Fight Club*.

Se7en 1995, 127 min

cast Brad Pitt, Morgan Freeman, Gwyneth Paltrow, Richard Roundtree, R. Lee Ermey, Kevin Spacey *cin* Darius Khondji *m* Howard Shore

In this nihilistic thriller about a multiple murderer who stages his crimes as illustrations of the Seven Deadly Sins, Fincher powerfully communicates a vision of the modern city as a Babylonian den of iniquity, in which good men fight a losing battle against evil. *Se7en* engulfs you in its uncompromisingly bleak outlook. To the extent that this is a stylistic affectation, the film is faintly risible. Nevertheless, within the Hollywood context, it's a singular work, boldly conceived and executed.

Fight Club 1999, 139 min

cast Brad Pitt, Edward Norton, Helena Bonham Carter, Meat Loaf Aday, Jared Leto, Zach Grenier *cin* Jeff Cronenweth *m* The Dust Brothers

Working from a cold, subversive, super-ironic script by Jim Uhls, Fincher hit on a convulsive stream-of-unconsciousness style rendered in subliminal images, freeze-frames and fantasy gags. Call it "American Ugly". Edward Norton is the unnamed yuppie who gets in touch with his pain after his apartment blows up, Brad Pitt his anarchic alter ego Tyler Durden. Together they thrash things out in a dilapidated brownstone on the dark edge of town.

Zodiac 2007, 158 min

cast Jake Gyllenhaal, Robert Downey Jr, Mark Ruffalo, Anthony Edwards, Brian Cox *cin* Harris Savides *m* David Shire

Fincher's meticulous, restrained account of the Zodiac killings turns on our fascination with unsolved crimes. Rather than a film about a serial killer, this is a film about three investigators who become obsessed with the case: the cop (Mark Ruffalo), the crime reporter (Robert Downey Jr) and the author (Jake Gyllenhaal). *Zodiac* is a fascinating procedural precisely because Fincher leaves room for doubt – his concern is not with establishing guilt, but with the way in which not knowing drives and cripples these three men.

Terence Fisher
UK, 1904–80

Of the directors primarily associated with the heyday of Hammer Films, Terence Fisher has the strongest claim for auteur status. A late bloomer who trained as an editor and was well into his forties before he made his first feature, Fisher was 52 when he directed Hammer's hugely successful *The Curse Of Frankenstein* (1957), shot in lurid Eastmancolor with soon-to-be paragons of British horror, Christopher Lee and Peter Cushing, in their first onscreen pairing.

Curse is a period costume drama that no doubt looks tame to contemporary audiences, but it was startlingly dark and graphic for its time: Cushing's Dr Frankenstein wipes a palmful of blood on his jacket, collects eyes from the local charnel house and pushes a man down the stairs. The movie enraged critics (the *Telegraph* deemed it "for sadists only", and the *Observer*'s C.A. Lejeune reckoned it "among the half-dozen most repulsive films I have encountered") and catapulted both a studio and a moribund genre into a bloody renaissance.

Fisher set the Hammer standard for gothic gore and stately psychotronica, especially with his first Frankenstein sequel, *The Revenge Of Frankenstein* (1958), with the coolly aristocratic Cushing as the cerebral, amoral Baron. Fisher scored a second success for Hammer via another metaphor-rich Victorian monster in *Dracula* (1958, retitled *Horror Of Dracula* for its US release).

Despite being a versatile director, Fisher remained identified with horror: he helmed *The Stranglers Of Bombay* (1959), a shocking account of grisly cult worship in 1820s India, and dared to depict somewhat sympathetic monsters in *Curse Of The Werewolf* (1962) and *The Phantom Of The Opera* (1962). Hammer's most expensive production to date, *Phantom* failed at the box office, and the unhappy studio sidelined Fisher for two years. Their relationship resumed in 1964 with *The Gorgon*, featuring the redoubtable Cushing/Lee team and Fisher's first female monster (played by Barbara Shelley). Fisher returned to old stomping grounds with *Dracula Prince Of Darkness* (1965) – for which the script was so bad that Fisher and Lee decided the Dracula role should be played silently – as well as a sometimes ropey Frankenstein cycle in the late 1960s and early 1970s. He returned to form with his version of Dennis Wheatley's black magic thriller *The Devil Rides Out* (aka *The Devil's Bride*, 1968), which has developed something of a cult status among horror aficionados. JW

The Revenge Of Frankenstein 1958, 94 min

cast Peter Cushing, Michael Gwynn, Francis Matthews, Eunice Gayson, John Welsh, George Woodbridge *cin* Jack Asher *m* Leonard Salzedo

The richest of Fisher's Frankenstein movies sidelines the monster in favour of Peter Cushing's Baron, who shows his gratitude to the crippled hangman who helped him escape the gallows by offering to build him a new body, crafted from material easily obtained at the local poor hospital. Cushing chillingly inhabits this self-deluded homicidal samaritan, while the film's expertly staged climax explosively literalizes a grievous class divide.

Horror Of Dracula 1958, 82 min

cast Peter Cushing, Christopher Lee, Michael Gough, Melissa Stribling, Carol Marsh, Valerie Gaunt *cin* Jack Asher *m* James Bernard

With its sensational Technicolor photogaphy, spry camerawork and frank sexuality, Fisher's second Hammer hit loosely adapts Bram Stoker's novel and provides a startling contrast to Tod Browning's iconic 1931 black-and-white version of the tale. Fisher's film manages to add intriguing erotic dimensions to the title character, while also carefully limiting the befanged Christopher Lee's screen time as the demonic count.

The Devil Rides Out 1968, 95 min

cast Christopher Lee, Charles Gray, Nike Arrighi, Leon Greene, Patrick Mower, Gwen Ffrancon-Davies *cin* Arthur Grant *m* James Bernard

A relatively restrained effort from Fisher who establishes a wonderfully oppressive atmosphere in which the two leads – Christopher Lee as the noble Duc de Richleau and the suavely camp Charles Gray as the devil-worshipping Mocata – vie for supremacy. In the most notable scene Lee and his three companions spend the night within a sacred circle drawn on the floor. From here they are able to resist Mocata's satanic powers, which are manifested in the form of hallucinatory cinematic effects, including the appearance of a giant tarantula.

Robert Flaherty
US, 1884–1951

Before the ground-breaking work of Robert Flaherty the term "documentary" didn't even exist. An explorer and surveyor, Flaherty turned director in order to document the lives of his friends, the Hudson Bay Eskimos. The resultant film, *Nanook Of The North* (1922), pioneered the controversial methods that the director adopted throughout his career, which took him to Samoa to film *Moana* (1926) and Ireland for *Man Of Aran* (1934). Flaherty's real-life subjects became actors in the stories he wanted to tell, and his films were cut and cast like Hollywood movies. The narratives were invariably constructed around a series of battles against the elements, in which Hollywood photographic nous and editing techniques were craftily employed to build tension into every scene. "You have to distort a thing to catch its true spirit" was Flaherty's response to accusations of inauthenticity. Other charges against him include the fact that the director's stories were consciously anachronistic. He persuaded the Eskimos to return to the dangerous practice of harpooning walruses, when they had long used guns, and the people of Aran hunted basking sharks for his cameras for the first time in fifty years.

After the phenomenal success of *Nanook*, the public were less interested in Flaherty's subsequent films. Notoriously difficult, he fell out with several members of the film industry, and had to leave part way through filming *Tabu* (1931) because of conflicts with co-director F.W. Murnau. He found work in Britain with John Grierson, who first coined the term "documentary" to describe Flaherty's pioneering approach, and was hired by producer Michael Balcon to make *Man Of Aran*. His mix of fact and fiction found its logical conclusion in *Elephant Boy* (1937), in which his anthropological material was cut into Zoltan Korda's flawed adaptation of Rudyard Kipling's tale. *The Land* (1942) was sponsored, but ultimately suppressed, by the American government, while the Standard Oil Company coughed up for his last film, *Louisiana Story* (1948). The latter is regarded by many as his finest film, although its idealistic picture of the oil industry now seems terribly naïve. Despite the fact that it now looks oldfashioned, Flaherty's work has had a profound influence not just on documentary makers, but also on directors like Harry Watt, Humphrey Jennings and Werner Herzog, who operate in the space between fiction and ethnography. LH

Nanook Of The North 1922, 79 min, b/w

with Nanook, Nyla, Cunayou, Allee, Allegoo *cin* Robert Flaherty

Flaherty canoed two hundred miles with two movie cameras, plus processing and projecting equipment, to capture the lives of the Inuits. This wondrously photographed confluence of ethnography and action movie is the least controversial of all his re-enactments because his subjects were friends whose spirit and rituals he arguably got to know. Nanook himself became a brief sensation in America, but soon returned to Hudson Bay, where he died of starvation.

Louisiana Story 1948, 77 min, b/w

with Joseph Boudreaux, Lionel LeBlanc, E. Bienvenu, Frank Hardy, C.T. Guedry *cin* Richard Leacock *m* Virgil Thomson

The story of an oil-strike in the Louisiana bayou is told from the perspective of a 13-year-old boy and filmed with the director's customary poeticizing vision, enhanced by Virgil Thomson's rich but restrained score. The subsequent development of the oilfield is presented as a heroic struggle between man and nature, and the whole film comes across as a hymn to the machine age and an expression of an altogether more optimistic era.

Richard Fleischer
US, 1916–2006

In a Hollywood career that lasted over forty years and produced in excess of fifty movies in different genres, Richard Fleischer never really succeeded in imposing a recognizable signature on his work. A solid and highly professional director, he made a handful of distinguished films, an equal amount of duds and wrote an entertaining autobiography *Just Tell Me When To Cry* (1993).

The son of animator Max Fleischer, Richard started out in the film industry cutting newsreels at RKO-Pathé's New York office from 1942. After directing segments of RKO's *This Is America* documentary cycle and originating the *Flicker Flashbacks* silent movie anthology, Fleischer directed his first feature, the early custody drama *Child Of Divorce* (1946). There followed a series of small-scale realist studio pictures which were attuned to the growing pains of post-war America. In *So This Is New York* (1948) a rural man goes to stay with affluent relatives in the big city. *Armored Car Robbery* (1950) was a heist thriller shot by Guy Roe on high-contrast stock on the streets of Los Angeles. In the *noir*ish *His Kind Of Woman* (1951), Robert Mitchum's gambler is coerced into securing border passage for a mobster. Its happy-go-lucky shift from thriller to parody – see, for example, Mitchum's banter with Jane Russell – was the result of production difficulties, and the film is actually credited to John Farrow. *The Narrow Margin* (1952) was a taut thriller following a crucial witness on her train journey to a murder trial. Shot in New Mexico border country, *Violent Saturday* (1956) was the story of a small town besieged by a gang of thugs led by Lee Marvin. *The Girl In The Red Velvet Swing* (1956) was a factual account of the murder of a New York architect. Featuring a fine turn from Orson Welles as Clarence Darrow, *Compulsion* (1958) dramatized the Leopold-Loeb murder case of the 1920s.

In the 1960s and 70s Fleischer roved among lumbering projects from the medieval (*The Vikings*, 1958) to science fiction (*The Fantastic Voyage*, 1966) and war (*Tora! Tora! Tora!*, 1970). He recaptured some of his old narrative drive in *The Boston Strangler* (1968), a retelling of the Albert DeSalvo case, *10 Rillington Place* (1970), and the futuristic nightmare of an overpopulated New York, *Soylent Green* (1973). His slavery movie *Mandingo* (1975) divides opinion – between those who regard it as a hard-hitting antidote to the cosy world of *Gone With The Wind*, and those who see merely a camp and exploitative slice of American gothic. The 1980s saw the good projects drying up and films like *The Jazz Singer* (1980), *Amityville 3-D* (1983), *Conan the Destroyer* (1984) and *Red Sonja* (1985) did Fleischer's reputation no good at all. RA

10 Rillington Place 1970, 111 min, b/w

cast Richard Attenborough, Judy Geeson, John Hurt, Pat Heywood, Isobel Black, Phyllis MacMahon *cin* Denys Coop *m* John Dankworth

Reconstructing the events at 10 Rillington Place, where serial killer Reginald Christie murdered Beryl Evans in 1949 but left her husband to go to the gallows, Fleischer opts for a sombre evocation of an austerity Britain sexually repressed beneath the lace curtains. Playing Christie with all the meek ineffectuality at his command, Richard Attenborough turns in a spooky performance opposite John Hurt's mentally challenged Timothy Evans. It remains a baroque twist on the kitchen-sink drama at the tail end of the Swinging Sixties.

Victor Fleming
US, 1889–1949

Fleming is a puzzle: involved in two of the greatest and most popular Hollywood films of all time, he was equally able to make undistinguished fare; and despite a reputation for action he produced a string of romantic films featuring outstanding performances.

A former racing driver, Fleming entered the film industry as a stuntman, working his way up to cinematographer. He worked regularly with Douglas Fairbanks who went on to star in Fleming's first film (co-directed with Theodore Reed), *When The Clouds Roll By* (1919), a life-affirming comedy about suicide. The versatile Fleming made everything from Anita Loos comedies (*Woman's Place*, 1921, and *Red Hot Romance*, 1922) to Conrad (*Lord Jim*, 1925), working well with actors. The saucy comedy *Man Trap* (1926) starred Clara Bow (they had an affair); Emil Jannings won an Oscar for the now-lost *The Way Of All Flesh* (1927); and *The Virginian* (1929) made a star of Gary Cooper (another one of Bow's beaux).

From 1932 on, Fleming was contracted to MGM. Jean Harlow starred in the steamy *Red Dust* (1932) with Clark Gable, and then in the uproarious Hollywood satire *Bombshell* (1933). He also proved a steady hand on classy literary adaptations, such as *Treasure Island* (1934) and *Captains Courageous* (1937), and the aeronautical dramas *Test Pilot* (1938) and *A Guy Named Joe* (1943). Fleming also directed scenes on several films with director troubles, and 1939 saw the release of two particularly problematic productions. Though you might not guess from watching it, *The Wizard Of Oz* was struggling before Fleming brought it to heel. Meanwhile on *Gone With The Wind*, Clark Gable thought director George Cukor was spending too much time directing Vivien Leigh, so Fleming took over. Perhaps not surprisingly, juggling both projects led to a nervous breakdown and Fleming was replaced on the latter film by Sam Wood, although Fleming got sole directorial credit and picked up the Oscar.

While his stock was riding high, his career continued as unevenly as ever. 1941 saw an effective (if overlong) adaptation of *Dr Jekyll And Mr Hyde*, starring Spencer Tracy and Ingrid Bergman, but the ambitious *Joan Of Arc* (1948) – also starring Bergman – was a critical and box-office failure. This was a shattering blow for Fleming and he died just a few months after the film's release. JR

Bombshell 1933, 95 min, b/w

cast Jean Harlow, Lee Tracy, Frank Morgan, Franchot Tone, Una Merkel *cin* Harold Rosson *m* Hoagy Carmichael

Hollywood has an occasional habit of self-laceration with stinging satires on its own stupidity and venality, and few are stronger than *Bombshell*. Like Harlow herself, Lola Barnes is a star at the mercy of an unscrupulous PR man E.J. Hanlon (Lee Tracy) and a parasitic family. When she wants out, Hanlon does all in his power to get her back. Based on Fleming's old girlfriend Clara Bow, Lola's career is illustrated with clips from Harlow's own films.

The Wizard Of Oz 1939, 101 min

cast Judy Garland, Frank Morgan, Ray Bolger, Bert Lahr, Jack Haley, Billie Burke *cin* Harold Rosson *m* Harold Arlen, E.Y. Harburg

A hurricane whisks schoolgirl Dorothy (Judy Garland) and her dog Toto from sepia Kansas to a Technicolor magical kingdom. Accompanied by a cowardly lion, a tin man with no heart and a scarecrow without a brain, she braves a wicked witch and flying monkeys only to discover that the titular wizard is a sham and that, really, "there's no place like home". The mythic story, psychedelic imagery and catchy tunes have entranced audiences since day one though, astonishingly, the Oscar-winning song "Over The Rainbow" was very nearly cut.

Gone With The Wind 1939, 222 min

cast Vivien Leigh, Clark Gable, Hatty McDaniel, Leslie Howard, Olivia de Havilland *cin* Ernest Haller, Ray Rennahan, Wilfred M. Cline *m* Max Steiner

The prospect of Margaret Mitchell's bestselling Civil War novel coming to the screen (and who would play Scarlett O'Hara) left America on tenterhooks for months, while production difficulties became the stuff of legend. With its opening scenes set on an antebellum Southern estate, the film has been criticized for its idealized depiction of "good" slave owners. In fact the two leads, Scarlett O'Hara (Vivien Leigh) and Rhett Butler (Clark Gable), are selfish, driven, often unsympathetic, occasionally tiresome and yet, some-

how, completely compelling. In the end, the film's sheer sweep and bravura, and Max Steiner's brilliant main theme, carries the day.

Bryan Forbes
UK, 1926–

Actor, screenwriter, director, producer and studio head Bryan Forbes's career tracked the fortunes of British cinema from the 1940s to the 1980s. Before the onslaught of multiplexes and special effects, Forbes stood for a very British brand of repression and drizzly dismay.

Forbes was primarily an actors' director, acting himself from 1949 following a stint at RADA and fetching up in such worthy war films as *The Small Back Room* (1949), *The Wooden Horse* (1950), *The Colditz Story* (1955). Writing for *Picturegoer* magazine extended his industry savvy and in 1959 he formed the production company Beaver Films with Richard Attenborough. Among the best of his screenwriting credits are the union-bashing *The Angry Silence* (1959) and the lively caper movie *The League Of Gentlemen* (1960).

Forbes made his directing debut in 1961 with the haunting *Whistle Down The Wind*, based on the novel by Mary Hayley Bell. He then directed, scripted and produced another literary adaptation, *The L-Shaped Room* (1962), a quietly powerful story of a French girl's experience in a seedy English boarding house peopled by a colourful roster of British actresses including Avis Bunnage, Patricia Phoenix and Cicely Courtneidge. Desultory and beautifully observed, it caught the mood of a Britain on the cusp of moral renewal. *Seance On A Wet Afternoon* (1964) and *The Whisperers* (1966), respectively a claustrophobic story of a demented medium played by Kim Stanley and a poignant portrayal of old age starring Edith Evans, were actors' pieces and Forbes indulged his leading ladies to the full. *King Rat* (1965) was a grimly realistic war film set in a Japanese POW camp in Singapore, an ensemble piece which boasted particularly strong performances from George Segal and James Fox.

In 1969 Forbes was appointed head of production at Associated British (EMI), but initial success with other people's projects – *The Railway Children* (1970), *The Go-Between* (1970) – did not compensate for his inability to reconcile the perennial difficulties of the industry with a risky creative sense. Forbes resigned in 1971.

Among later works, *The Madwoman Of Chaillot* (1969) is ponderously verbose, but *The Stepford Wives* (1975) is an interesting polemic involving the suppression of feminist instincts in an American suburb. The cast of venerable luvvies seemed endless in 1976's *The Slipper And The Rose*, an overblown staging of *Cinderella*, while *International*

173

Velvet (1978) was a shamelessly sentimental update of *National Velvet* (1944) with Tatum O'Neal taking the Elizabeth Taylor role as the plucky horse-loving youngster. RA

Whistle Down The Wind 1961, 99 min, b/w

cast Hayley Mills, Bernard Lee, Alan Bates, Norman Bird, Diane Holgate, Elsie Wagstaff, Alan Barnes *cin* Arthur Ibbetson *m* Malcolm Arnold

Set on a stark Lancashire farm, Bryan Forbes's film is a poem to childhood, detailing the longing of three children, led by a luminous Hayley Mills, who discover a killer in the barn (a louche Alan Bates) and decide that Jesus has come to stay with them. Sheltering him as the police close in, the children apply cherished Anglican values in a dour but hopeful Eden.

The Stepford Wives 1975, 115 min

cast Katharine Ross, Paula Prentiss, Peter Masterson, Nanette Newman, Tina Louise *cin* Owen Roizman *m* Michael Small

Paula Prentiss finally found something her congenial kook-iness could fight in this adaptation of novelist Ira Levin's quietly menacing tale of hysterical suburban politesse. Prentiss and Katharine Ross star as new arrivals to an creepily idealized Connecticut suburb filled with exemplars of the perfect submissive American housewife. Gradually they start to uncover the terrible truth behind why all the other women are so perfect. Truer and more pointed than the 2004 remake.

John Ford
US, 1894–1973

Asked about his cinematic influences, Orson Welles cited "John Ford, John Ford, and John Ford". In a directing career that stretched through six decades, Ford established himself as the pre-eminent American filmmaker before the talkies were out of their infancy. He won the Academy Award for best director four times – more than any other director. Ford may have bucked against the studio system, but he was also a product of that system, and one of its consummate practitioners.

Although born and bred in America, Ford was fiercely proud of his Irish heritage (even though he never used his family name of O'Fearna). If he became famous for his Westerns, perhaps that is because in the Western he could re-envisage the promise and romance of his parents' immigrant dream. To Ford, as to Frank Capra, America was a precious ideal, to which the country and its citizens must be accountable. Ford, the youngest of eleven children, opted to follow his brother Francis out West (the frontier was not long settled then), to California. Twelve years his senior, and a leading star and director in his own right, Francis had assumed the professional name Ford, and Sean – or "Jack", or "John" – followed suit. Biographers suggest the younger brother laboured under an inferiority complex, and would later take satisfaction in cast-ing Francis (whose directing career tapered out in the late 1920s) in unflattering bit parts as drunks and blowhards.

It should be a Hollywood myth, but John Ford really did ride as a klansman in D.W. Griffith's *Birth Of A Nation* (1915), as well as appearing in a string of lesser two-reelers. Ambitious and a quick learner, he started directing in 1917 under the patronage of cowboy star Harry Carey. Together, they made 25 popular Westerns – and although they later had a falling out, Ford always acknowledged how Carey's laid-back, quietly dignified acting style influenced his ideas about performance. Nine years after Griffith, Ford laid his own foundation myth, *The Iron Horse* (1924), about the transcontinental railway. Though it's an unpretentious, folksy epic, it lacks the warmth and light touch that he brought to many more routine assignments in those early days. Even so, the film was a big hit, and Ford's reputation continued to rise. He was one of the top directors on the Fox lot when he first worked with a young prop man called Marion Morrison (John Wayne) in 1928.

While Francis Ford's directing career was derailed by his artistic pretensions, John Ford was canny enough to balance out prestige pictures with commercial entertainments, and generally treated both with equal care, a philosophy he stuck to throughout his career. Thus, less than eighteen months after his first outstanding critical success, *The Informer* (1935), he was directing Shirley Temple in *Wee Willie Winkie* (1937). A lumbering piece of expressionism, *The Informer* has not dated well, despite being hailed as one of the great masterpieces of the medium at the time. Nor have its companion pieces, *The Long Voyage Home* (1941) and *The Fugitive* (1947). All three films are conceived as visual poems, and seem heavily influenced by Sergei Eisenstein's theories of symbolism and montage. One suspects that if he had enjoyed complete freedom – or perhaps a state sponsor – Ford would have specialized in turgid exercises such as these. It's when his self-consciously "poetic" pictorialism is offset by dramatic narrative and "lower-class" subject matter – such as Westerns – that Ford really comes into his own. And he had the wit to realize it. At a celebrated meeting of the Screen Directors Guild in 1950, Ford introduced himself this way: "My name is John Ford. I am a director of Westerns."

Although even his greatest films are marred by broad slapstick humour and sentimental interludes, Ford nevertheless elevated the popular idiom to express his own complex, ambivalent, sometimes tragic sense of the tensions between tradition and progress, personal liberty and social justice, duty and desire. Ford was a stylist who moved the camera unobtrusively, and came to prefer simple, eye-level set-ups. Yet his unerring eye for composition and light – as well as the graceful, patient tempo he insisted upon – could infuse a seemingly straightforward scene with great delicacy and feeling. The mature

The Western: destiny to demise

It may kick up a little dust every now and then, but to all intents and purposes the Western has been moribund for a quarter of a century or more. Some say *Heaven's Gate* killed off the genre in 1980, but in truth Michael Cimino's monumental epic was just the last nail in a coffin that John Ford began sizing up in 1962's *The Man Who Shot Liberty Valance*. From the late 1960s onwards, the Western had only one true subject, and that was its own demise.

Where did this death wish come from? Before we answer that, it is worth remembering that the Western's artistic heyday was shorter than we sometimes imagine. Although it was a popular form in silent cinema, it was overwhelmingly B-movie fodder for most of the 1930s – until John Ford made *Stagecoach* and *Drums Along The Mohawk* in 1939. Even that might be considered something of a false dawn. It would be seven years before Ford made another, *My Darling Clementine* (1946), and that was when he really fell in love with the West, along with the rest of the world.

Ford made six more indelible Westerns over the next decade. Howard Hawks made *Red River* (1948), *The Big Sky* (1952) and *Rio Bravo* (1959). Anthony Mann shot ten Westerns between 1950 and 1960, and Bud Boetticher managed a dozen in the same time frame. In 1959 there were 48 Western TV series on the air, yet by 1975 that figure was down to four.

If the genre's popular appeal spiked in the 1950s, that surely relates to the moral authority the US enjoyed post-World War II. More than any other genre, the Western speaks to America's sense of nationhood, the foundation myth enshrined in that ringing phrase "Manifest Destiny". First voiced by expansionist politicians in the 1840s, this was the principle that "Americans" had a divine duty to spread freedom and democracy across the land (and to hell with the savages who stood in their way).

In the image of the nineteenth-century cowboy, a man doing what a man's gotta do, Hollywood found a hero and an iconography fit for the twentieth century – the American Century. You didn't have to be American to buy into it either. Sergio Leone and the Italians weren't the only non-Americans to make Westerns – so did the Germans and the Eastern Europeans, among others. When Soviet premier Nikita Krushchev visited the US in 1959 at the height of the Cold War, he made two special requests: he wanted to visit Disneyland, and he wanted to meet John Wayne.

By the late 1960s the notion of Manifest Destiny no longer inspired faith at home or abroad; rather it lay exposed as a cover for a genocidal capitalist landgrab. Nor were the parallels between Native American tribes and Vietnamese peasants lost on audiences or filmmakers, as revisionist Westerns like Robert Aldrich's *Ulzana's Raid* (1972) clearly demonstrate. Even the patriarchal prerogative no longer held good: in this new breed of Western, sons stood up to their fathers, and their wives divorced them.

It's no accident that George "Dead or Alive" Bush sought to resurrect such a potent mythology in his post-9/11 rhetoric, just as he's always played up his spurious Texan credentials. But outside Texas, it just doesn't wash. You can't turn back the cultural clock, and the Western will never have the pop-cultural currency it did in the past. However, that's not to say that individual filmmakers won't make resonant, relevant Westerns. HBO's series *Deadwood* brought the Western thundering back to the small screen in 2004, and the following year saw four Westerns in the cinema: *Brokeback Mountain*, *The Three Burials Of Melquiades Estrada*, *The Proposition* and *The New World*. If there's one thing all these have in common, it's that they subvert the conservative ideology attributed to the genre. The American Century is over. But American history is far from spent. TC

Ford style can be dated to the banner year 1939, when he made his first sound Western, *Stagecoach*; his first colour film, *Drums Along The Mohawk*; and the masterly *Young Mr Lincoln*. (*Stagecoach* also marked his discovery of Monument Valley, with its ancient sandstone buttes.) He followed these with *The Grapes Of Wrath* (1940) and *How Green Was My Valley* (1941), two very fine literary adaptations made for Darryl Zanuck at Fox which are on a par with his best Westerns, and which were also praised to the skies at the time.

A mass of contradictions, Ford was a perfectionist who filmed such meagre coverage that the studio editors had no choice but to follow his shot pattern, but he shied away from any plaudits and refused to discuss his work in anything but the most pragmatic terms. Like many directors from the silent era, he was a tyrant on the set. He liked nothing better than to abuse and humiliate his collaborators, and brooked no insubordination. Yet he commanded intense loyalty from his team, and worked with many of the same cast and crew for decades; they became known as the "John Ford Stock Company". The most famous of these players was of course John Wayne, who starred in fourteen of his films and whose persona – resolute, rational, stoical – was a Fordian ideal that came to stand for the national character. Henry Fonda was another important Ford actor, his more thoughtful and civilized demeanour in marked contrast to the ruggedness of Wayne.

A natural conservative, a military history buff and a patriot justifiably proud of his naval intelligence work in World War II (for which he was promoted to rear admiral), Ford was also a progressive Democrat who spoke out against the McCarthy blacklist and ridiculed Wayne's reactionary Republican politics.

The ambivalence in Ford's historical films and, centrally, his Westerns is one reason why he has fallen out of the high esteem he enjoyed in his lifetime. While his popular cavalry trilogy (*Fort Apache*, 1948; *She Wore A Yellow Ribbon*, 1949; *Rio Grande*, 1950) significantly toned down the reactionary bigotry of James Warner Bellah's source stories, there's no mistaking the director's belief in America's Manifest Destiny, nor his admiration for the military as an institution, patriarchy and all.

Nevertheless, ambivalence cuts both ways. If Ford is drawn to the mythic romance of America the brave, he is not blind to the pathology wrapped up in it. In a very famous line from *The Man Who Shot Liberty Valance* (1962), a newspaper editor assures politician Ransom Stoddart (James Stewart) that he will suppress facts which have emerged about his past: "This is the West, sir. When the legend becomes fact, print the legend." Ford's critics take this to be his creed. Yet if *Valance* is about anything, it's about exposing the falsity of the legend, just as surely as *Fort Apache* reveals the bigotry and egoism of Henry Fonda's Colonel Owen Thursday – and valorizes the memory of the men who died under him. For this reason *The Searchers* (1956) remains Ford's most vital work, the film which most clearly confronts the latent racist anxieties and historical suppressions which agitate John Wayne's persona and cloud the Western myth. TC

Stagecoach 1939, 96 min, b/w
cast John Wayne, Claire Trevor, Thomas Mitchell, George Bancroft, John Carradine, Andy Devine, Louise Platt *cin* Bert Glennon *m* Boris Morros

This elegantly simple Western puts half a dozen stock social types on a stagecoach and throws John Wayne's outlaw, the Ringo Kid, and Geronimo into the mix to shake things up.

Ford satirizes the hypocrisy of outwardly respectable characters and reveals the innate goodness of lower-class types like Ringo, and the prostitute Dallas (Trevor). Balancing exciting action sequences (ground-breaking stunt work by Yakima Canutt) with delicately directed scenes of human intimacy, *Stagecoach* was a model Western, and helped rehabilitate the genre.

Young Mr Lincoln 1939, 101 min, b/w
cast Henry Fonda, Alice Brady, Marjorie Weaver, Arleen Whelan, Richard Cromwell, Ward Bond *cin* Bert Glennon *m* Alfred Newman

So confident was he in the Great Man of History, Ford persuaded Henry Fonda to play "honest Abe" as a starchy, wily, small-town lawyer with the hand of Destiny on his shoulder. This is the sort of Americana Ford excelled at, combining lyricism, sentimentality, humour and nostalgia. Eisenstein was an admirer.

Harsh realities: the Joad family reach rock bottom in the stark, documentary-like Great Depression classic *The Grapes Of Wrath*.

The Grapes Of Wrath 1940, 129 min, b/w
cast Henry Fonda, Jane Darwell, John Carradine, Russell Simpson, Charley Grapewin, Dorris Bowden *cin* Gregg Toland *m* Alfred Newman

Among the most eloquent social conscience pictures to emanate from a Hollywood studio, this version of John Steinbeck's then-controversial Dust Bowl novel takes its expressive, angry lyricism from Gregg Toland's stark, documentary-like cinematography. Ford connected with the hardships and suffering of Steinbeck's rural refugees – Oakies who head West to California to escape the Great Depression – so much that some have said this is "his most Irish film".

How Green Was My Valley 1941, 118 min, b/w
cast Walter Pidgeon, Maureen O'Hara, Roddy McDowall, Donald Crisp, John Loder, Anna Lee *cin* Arthur Miller *m* Alfred Newman

The film that beat *Citizen Kane* to best picture in 1941 is often caricatured as a sentimental wallow in poverty – but it's hard to imagine that Welles himself wasn't influenced by it, judging by the markedly similar literary *tristesse* which infuses his *The Magnificent Ambersons* (1942). The film's downbeat elucidation of crippling domestic and social tradition and its endorsement of unionism make it one of Ford's least complacent and most misunderstood works.

They Were Expendable 1945, 135 min, b/w

cast Robert Montgomery, John Wayne, Donna Reed, Ward Bond, Jack Holt, Marshall Thompson *cin* Joseph H. August *m* Herbert Stothart

One of the most emotionally nuanced, least bombastic of contemporary World War II movies, this was a story about a real-life officer in the Pacific campaign, John Bulkeley, whom Ford knew personally, and whose torpedo boat unit had covered the navy's retreat in the wake of Pearl Harbor. An elegiac, compassionate portrait of self-sacrifice, it illustrates what critic and director Peter Bogdanovich identifies as the key Fordian theme of "glory in defeat".

My Darling Clementine 1946, 97 min, b/w

cast Henry Fonda, Victor Mature, Linda Darnell, Walter Brennan, Cathy Downs, Tim Holt, Ward Bond *cin* Joseph P. MacDonald *m* Cyril J. Mockridge

Ford's first post-war movie romanticized the real Wyatt Earp (Fonda), turning history into a noble morality tale about the civilizing of the wilderness, with Earp taking the marshal's badge in Tombstone after the murder of his brother James. If it's myth, the filmmaking has the purity and poetry to make it resonate – like the seemingly trivial bit of business Fonda improvised balancing back in his chair on the porch.

Fort Apache 1948, 127 min, b/w

cast Henry Fonda, John Wayne, Shirley Temple, Pedro Armendariz, John Agar, George O'Brien *cin* Archie J. Stout *m* Richard Hageman

The first of Ford's famous "cavalry trilogy", based on short stories by James Warner Bellah. The cavalry Westerns are distinguished by Ford's scrupulous attention to historical detail, as well as his sophisticated grasp of the wider historical picture. Bellah's attitude is personified by Fonda's Lt Colonel Thursday, a Custer-like martinet whose blinkered sense of duty leads his regiment to disaster. Ford's own philosophy is represented by second-in-command Captain Kirby York (Wayne), whose more relaxed approach to the rule book allows him to grasp ambiguity and paradox, and to act accordingly.

Wagon Master 1950, 86 min, b/w

cast Ben Johnson, Joanne Dru, Harry Carey Jr, Ward Bond, Alan Mowbray, Jane Darwell *cin* Bert Glennon *m* Richard Hageman

This is one of Ford's simplest, but most affecting and enduring films, even if it's curious to see a group of Mormon pilgrims (being led West by Ward Bond, Harry Carey Jr and Ben Johnson) presented without editorial comment. The democratic inclusiveness extends to a group of theatricals and a tribe of Navajos. Ford often used music and dance to celebrate community and kinship (in front of and behind the camera), but never more expansively than here.

The Quiet Man 1952, 129 min

cast John Wayne, Maureen O'Hara, Victor McLaglen, Barry Fitzgerald, Mildred Natwick, Arthur Shields *cin* Winton C. Hoch *m* Victor Young

One of Ford's most heartfelt pictures, *The Quiet Man* is the story of an Irish-American ex-boxer, Sean Thornton (Wayne), who returns to his home village of Innisfree, courts the feisty Mary Kate (O'Hara), and ends up fighting his brother-in-law (McLaglen) because he refuses to pay her dowry. Ford took a charming love story and greatly expanded the sense of community surrounding it with humour and warm affection – casting family and friends across the board.

The Searchers 1956, 119 min

cast John Wayne, Jeffrey Hunter, Vera Miles, Ward Bond, Natalie Wood, Hank Worden *cin* Winton C. Hoch *m* Max Steiner

John Wayne is Ethan Edwards, searching for the Indian renegades who kidnapped his niece and murdered his brother's family. Riven with anguish and conflict, *The Searchers* is a psychological Western but Ford imbues it with the classical virtues of his earlier, more innocent visions – it's both his most terrible and his most beautiful work. It's also probably his most influential: Martin Scorsese, Paul Schrader, John Milius, George Lucas and Wim Wenders have all been moved to revisit themes and images from this film.

The Man Who Shot Liberty Valance 1962, 121 min, b/w

cast John Wayne, James Stewart, Vera Miles, Lee Marvin, Edmond O'Brien, Andy Devine, John Carradine *cin* William H. Clothier *m* Cyril J. Mockridge

Ford made a couple more films before he retired from the fray three years later, but to all intents and purposes this was his last testament, certainly his last great film. James Stewart is a US senator who journeys back to attend a pauper's burial in Shinbone, and there reveals the true story of how law and order came to the West. A tragedy, a lament for lost youth, the freedom of the frontier and the ideals which civilized it, this is an old man's film in the best sense: wise, meditative and tender.

Milos Forman

Czech Republic (formerly Czechoslovakia), 1932–

Orphaned by the Holocaust (his father was Jewish, his mother Protestant; both died in the concentration camps), Milos Forman was 16 when Czechoslovakia became Communist, and 36 when the Soviet tanks reasserted Kremlin repression in Prague in 1968, forcing him to pursue his filmmaking career in the West. For all that, Forman describes himself as basically nonpolitical. His early films are humanist comedies with an edge of satire, but in his subsequent Hollywood career he has gravitated towards weightier biopics, albeit with a strong libertarian streak. These later films have met with popular mainstream acclaim, although critics generally prefer his first four, supposedly more personal, movies.

Forman was a graduate of the prestigious FAMU screenwriting course in Prague, funding his studies by moonlighting as a TV announcer and presenter. In the 1950s he worked as a writer, and when the authorities opened the doors of the Barrandov Studios to a younger generation of filmmakers, including his contemporaries Jirí Menzel and Ivan Passer, Forman made the transition to directing by way of a couple of short documentaries. By the early 1960s this new generation was taking advantage of a slight political thawing to make films that are characterized by a fresher and more irreverent approach. Forman was a key member of the Czech New Wave (or Czech film miracle as it was also called).

His first feature, the autobiographical *Cerný Petr* (*Black Peter*, 1963), won a prize at the Locarno Film Festival, and *A Blonde In Love* (1965) was nominated for the Academy Award for best foreign film, international recognition which helped him with the authorities at home. Nevertheless, the more caustic *The Firemen's Ball* (1967) was banned in Czechoslovakia for twenty years, and only released in the West when François Truffaut and Claude Berri bought out the equally unimpressed Italian producer, Carlo Ponti.

Forman spent 1968 dodging riots and demonstrations, initially in the US, where he was planning his first American film, *Taking Off*, with screenwriter Jean-Claude Carrière, then in Paris and Cannes (where he withdrew *Firemen's Ball* from competition in solidarity with the student protestors, despite his own very different experience of Communism). When the Prague Spring came to an abrupt end, Forman decided to stay in the West. *Taking Off* (1971) retained the lightness of touch, the quirky, comical spin on *cinéma vérité* which distinguished his Czech movies, and offered a fresh, undogmatic take on the counterculture. It was critically praised, but a box-office flop.

He was a director for hire on *One Flew Over The Cuckoo's Nest* (1975), a Michael Douglas production adapted from Ken Kesey's bestseller. But it was a natural fit. Forman knew all about institutionalized madness, and he carried off a remarkably forceful movie, fluctuating between antic liberation and harrowing repression, with a stunning Jack Nicholson performance at its core. *Cuckoo's Nest* became the first film since *It Happened One Night* in 1935 to win a clean sweep of the five major Academy Awards.

The 1960s musical *Hair* (1979) was a misstep, and suggested Forman was out of synch with the times. His next three features were also period films, and all literary adaptations. A disappointment, *Ragtime* (1981) lacked the energy of E.L. Doctorow's kaleidoscopic novel; and *Valmont* (1989) was also underpowered, as well as overshadowed by Stephen Frears's *Dangerous Liaisons* (1988). But *Amadeus* (1984) was another big success, with Tom Hulce as a braying Mozart destroyed by his mediocre rival Salieri (F. Murray Abraham). It bagged eight Oscars from eleven nominations, including best picture and best director.

Forman made two accomplished biopics centred on provocative, eccentric individualists from late-twentieth-century American life. *The People Vs. Larry Flynt* (1996) is a lively chronicle celebrating the iconoclastic publisher of *Hustler* magazine

(played by Woody Harrelson) as a champion of the First Amendment, although some felt it soft-pedalled the debasing pornography which made him a millionaire. *Man In The Moon* (1999) focuses on the enigmatic cult comedian Andy Kaufman (Jim Carrey), whose postmodern fondness for fooling his audience amounted to an angry critique of show-business sham. Both are entertaining pictures which revel in paradox but fail to nail their subjects. *Goya's Ghosts* (2006), with Stellan Skarsgard as the artist and Javier Bardem as a witch-hunting monk, inevitably recalled his biggest triumph, *Amadeus*. TC

A Blonde In Love (Lásky jedné plavovlásky)
1965, 83 min, b/w

cast Hana Brejchová, Vladimír Pucholt, Vladimír Mensík, Antonin Blazejovsky, Milada Jezkova *cin* Miroslav Ondricek *m* Evcen Hilin

An amateur jazz piano player seduces a young factory girl in a provincial town, only for her to show up later on his doorstep (he's still living with his parents). He's embarrassed. She's humiliated. They're appalled. An affectionate, naturalistic comedy, co-written by future director Ivan Passer on the basis of improvised rehearsals with the nonprofessional cast, this was immediately recognized as a key film in the Czech New Wave.

The Firemen's Ball (Horí, má panenko) 1967,
73 min, b/w

cast Jan Vostrcil, Josef Kolb, Josef Svet, Frantisek Debelka, Josef Sebánek *cin* Miroslav Ondricek *m* Karel Mares

A volunteer firefighters' committee presides over a mildly disastrous beauty contest in another small Czech town. Before the night is through, all the prizes will be stolen and a house will burn down. Quirky, building on observational comedy (using nonprofessional actors and real locations) but also accommodating slapstick and a melancholy farce, *The Firemen's Ball* was seen as ideologically unsound – even a satire on the Politburo itself – and banned in Czechoslovakia. Internationally, however, it proved very popular.

Taking Off 1971, 92 min

cast Lynn Carlin, Buck Henry, Linnea Heacock, Georgia Engel, Tony Harvey, Audra Lindley, Allen Garfield *cin* Miroslav Ondricek

Forman collaborated with Jean-Claude Carrière, John Guare and Jon Klein on the screenplay for his first American film, a deft, droll, nonjudgemental comedy on the generation gap which counterpoints scenes of a runaway daughter embracing the hippie lifestyle and her bourgeois parents doing their painful best to get hip. Something of a rarity, it's probably Forman's most underrated movie.

One Flew Over The Cuckoo's Nest 1975,
134 min

cast Jack Nicholson, Louise Fletcher, William Redfield, Will Sampson, Brad Dourif *cin* Haskell Wexler, Bill Butler, William A. Fraker *m* Jack Nitzsche

Jack Nicholson gives an indelible performance as congenital rebel Randle P. McMurphy in Forman's most explicit anti-authoritarian statement. Alternately wildly funny – when McMurphy takes his fellow asylum inmates for some recreation, for example – and harrowing (when Louise Fletcher's Nurse Ratchett reasserts her control), the film puts you through an emotional wringer, and doesn't sweeten any pills.

Amadeus 1984, 180 min

cast F. Murray Abraham, Tom Hulce, Elizabeth Berridge, Simon Callow, Roy Dotrice *cin* Miroslav Ondricek *m* Wolfgang Amadeus Mozart

Peter Shaffer's play about the rivalry between Mozart and Salieri makes very broad points about the nature of genius, but Forman's lavish film is compelling and spectacular, with a tremendous score driving the pace. It may be close to kitsch, but unlike *Ragtime*, it hits all its dramatic peaks. Filmed in Prague, this Oscar triumph marked Forman's return to Czechoslovakia after sixteen years in exile.

Bill Forsyth

UK, 1946–

"There must be more to life than suicide", an unemployed teenager muses in Bill Forsyth's first feature film, *That Sinking Feeling* (1981). Commenting on the mordant humour of his native Glasgow, Forsyth observed, "At the bottom of every joke is despair, you can't produce a laugh without it." The most interesting comic filmmaker of his generation, Forsyth is a study in melancholy and disappointment.

The son of a plumber-turned-grocer, he left school at 16 and entered the film industry by chance, answering an ad to become an assistant at an industrial film company. He quit the National Film and Television School after just three months, preferring to make films in the real world. His first directorial credits are short experimental films, *Language* (1969), and *Waterloo* (1970), a "psychological monologue" which emptied the cinema when it screened at the Edinburgh Film Festival. ("That was the first time I felt like a filmmaker because I had actually moved an audience – if not emotionally, I had actually moved them out of their seats.")

In 1977 Forsyth began working with the Glasgow Youth Theatre, and he wrote the original screenplay for *Gregory's Girl* as a vehicle for them. But it wasn't until they shot *That Sinking Feeling* (about desperate unemployed kids planning the theft of a shipment of kitchen sinks) in three weeks on just £6000 that they found a backer for *Gregory*. These first two films were released in London within weeks of each other in 1981, and the critics hailed an exciting new talent. The charming adolescent angst of *Gregory's Girl* proved especially popular, translating into a box-office hit in Britain and the US (where the Glasgow dialect had to be subtitled).

On a bigger scale, *Local Hero* (1983) had an American studio and star (Burt Lancaster) attached. Again, Forsyth balanced whimsy and subversion, inverting stereotypes (a highland village welcomes the oil business with open arms) and mixing idiosyncratic comic touches with underlying pathos. Critics were reminded of Ealing Studios' *Whisky Galore*; Forsyth himself felt it was close in spirit to Michael Powell's *I Know Where I'm Going*, and said he

was "trying to present a cosmic viewpoint to people, but through the most ordinary things". The ironically titled *Comfort And Joy* (1984), about a turf war between Glasgow's leading ice-cream makers, struck a less confident balance, though it paved the way for Forsyth's best film, the tragicomic coming of age memoir *Housekeeping* (1987). This was Forsyth's first American film, produced under the auspices of David Puttnam at Columbia. Less happy (though underrated) was *Breaking In* (1989), a low-key character piece starring Burt Reynolds and written by John Sayles.

Puttnam also produced Forsyth's most ambitious film, the $20 million *Being Human* (1993). Comprising five stories spanning 6000 years, each featuring Robin Williams as the hapless Hector, *Being Human* was a philosophical comedy about the human condition, fear, anxiety, superstition and masculinity. Warner Bros didn't know what to make of it, and the director's original 160-minute cut was virtually halved. Commercially, it was a nonstarter. A flawed but fascinating compromise version went straight to video in Britain, running for 125 minutes. It was five years before Forsyth made another film. *Gregory's Two Girls* (1999) was not so much a sequel as a catch-up with the filmmaker's most popular character, still played by John Gordon Sinclair, eighteen years on. Unfortunately Forsyth's earnest attempts to weave in a wider political consciousness aren't entirely integrated, and the more sombre mood left audiences cold. TC

Gregory's Girl 1981, 91 min

cast John Gordon Sinclair, Dee Hepburn, Jake D'Arcy, Claire Grogan, Robert Buchanan, William Greenlees *cin* Michael Coulter *m* Colin Tully

One of the most astute and engaging comedies about adolescence, Forsyth's breakthrough movie is his funniest film. Gregory (Sinclair) is a hopelessly timid sixth-former whose gawky immaturity is contrasted with the sense and self-possession of the girls in his school, and in particular the glamorous Dorothy (Hepburn), star of the school football team. It's a different universe from the slick teen movies Hollywood churns out.

Housekeeping 1987, 116 min

cast Christine Lahti, Sara Walker, Andrea Burchill, Anne Pitoniak, Barbara Reese, Margot Pinvidic, Bill Smillie *cin* Michael Coulter *m* Michael Gibbs

Closely based on Marilynne Robinson's novel about two sisters growing up in Idaho under the care of an eccentric aunt (luminously played by Christine Lahti), *Housekeeping* is a haunting film about individuality, convention, maturity and love. It treats these and other familiar Forsythian themes – the discrepancy between private and public worlds, for example – with great depth and tenderness.

Bob Fosse

US, 1927–87

There have been few directors in the history of cinema who have visualized their own deaths on screen, but Bob Fosse did just that in the auto-biographical and uncannily prophetic *All That Jazz* (1979). Roy Scheider's noxious, chain-smoking perfectionist with a weak heart was a thinly veiled portrait of Fosse himself, the hoofer turned choreographer turned filmmaker.

The son of a vaudeville entertainer, Fosse entered burlesque at an early age (and never really left), eventually working on Broadway and in Hollywood as a dancer. He immediately stamped his own style – angular, inelegant and energetic – on the Broadway musical with his 1954 choreographic debut *The Pajama Game*. He was soon directing Tony Award-winning musicals with a distinctive and dynamic signature style that bristled with tightly coiled energy and thinly veiled sexuality. His work in Hollywood as a choreographer included such films as *My Sister Eileen* (1955), *The Pajama Game* (1957) and *Damn Yankees* (1958).

As a film director his career was a series of high kicks and low blows. *Sweet Charity* (1969) garnered no awards and little praise, but *Cabaret* (1972), won eight Oscars, including best director, beating *The Godfather*'s Francis Ford Coppola. *Cabaret* was an unusually realistic musical, with production numbers that never stepped beyond the Kit Kat Club, and Fosse was equally sure-footed with the dramatic sections. He also demonstrated this dexterous ability in the straight drama *Lenny* (1974). Shot in musky monochrome, this biopic of comedian and firebrand Lenny Bruce is an evocatively melancholic and seriously underrated masterpiece.

Fosse returned to Broadway in the mid-1970s to make *Chicago*, whose troubled production he later documented in *All That Jazz*. A work of breathless invention and utter self-absorption, the outlandish folly was to all intents and purposes Fosse's last will and testament. However, his film career ended not with a bang, but with a cinematic whimper. His final film was the underwhelming retelling of the life and death of Peter Bogdanovich's murdered girlfriend Dorothy Stratten, *Star 80* (1983). In 1987, Fosse died, just like his *All That Jazz* alter ego, from a massive but wholly expected heart attack. LH

Cabaret 1972, 124 min

cast Liza Minnelli, Michael York, Helmut Griem, Joel Grey, Fritz Wepper, Marisa Berenson *cin* Geoffrey Unsworth *m* John Kander, Fred Ebb

Based on the stage musical (itself adapted from a play based on Christopher Isherwood's 1939 *The Berlin Stories*), this is the film that brought Liza Minnelli out of her mother's shadow in the role of an American singer performing in a Berlin nightclub during the Nazis' rise to power. It helped to establish, or at least reiterate, the cinematic image of rouged decadence: smoky nightclubs, mascara-heavy lashes, sultry, androgynous women in fishnets and waistcoats, and the Fosse touch – the bowler hat tilted at a rakish angle over one eye.

Lenny 1974, 111 min

cast Dustin Hoffman, Valerie Perrine, Jan Miner, Stanley Beck, Gary Morton, Rashel Novikoff *cin* Bruce Surtees *m* Ralph Burns

Dustin Hoffman, blister raw and at his chameleonic best, loses himself in the role of notorious comedian Lenny Bruce, who was hounded to his death after a series of prosecutions for obscenity (such as using the word "cocksucker" in a public place). Criminally underrated, Fosse's first non-musical is note-perfect and Bruce Surtees' luminous black-and-white photography enhances this unapologetic elegy to a foul-mouthed martyr.

Marc Forster
Germany, 1969–

Despite being based in the States, Marc Forster is a German-born Swiss citizen. After a TV documentary apprenticeship, his first feature *Loungers* (1995) – a black comedy about four aspiring lounge singers – won the Slamdance Film Festival's audience award. It took five years and intervening family tragedies for his second to emerge, but *Everything Put Together* (2000) showed increasing maturity in its study of the emotional and social disintegration of a woman following her baby son's unexpected death. In 2001, *Monster's Ball* won Halle Berry an Oscar and Forster a far bigger budget for his next venture, *Finding Neverland* (2004). Visually rich but dramatically confusing, *Stay* (2005) explored the relationship between a young man and his equally troubled psychiatrist. This departure for Forster led to the playful postmodernism of *Stranger Than Fiction* (2006), in which Will Ferrell's tax inspector discovers that he's a character in novelist Emma Thompson's current project. MB

Monster's Ball 2001, 112 min

cast Billy Bob Thornton, Halle Berry, Heath Ledger, Peter Boyle, Sean Combs, Mos Def *cin* Roberto Schaefer *m* Asche and Spencer

Marc Forster's international breakthrough came with this Georgia-set drama about a black woman (Halle Berry) getting involved with a racist Death Row prison guard (Billy Bob Thornton), unaware that he was instrumental in the execution of her long-incarcerated husband. Forster's understated direction, seemingly at odds with the emotionally, sexually and racially charged material, infuses their scenes with a riveting intensity, helped immeasurably by the entire cast's nuanced depictions of deeply damaged individuals.

Finding Neverland 2004, 101 min

cast Johnny Depp, Kate Winslet, Julie Christie, Radha Mitchell, Dustin Hoffman, Freddie Highmore *cin* Roberto Schaefer *m* Jan A.P. Kaczmarek

Far more genteel than *Monster's Ball*, but no less psychologically penetrating, this trip to Edwardian London looks at the life and preoccupations of the writer J.M. Barrie (Johnny Depp). Trapped in a loveless marriage and smitten with a lonely widow (Kate Winslet) and her four sons, Barrie finds himself inspired to write *Peter Pan*, thereby securing his immortality. It's a delicately poised study of genuine innocence in the face of popular prurience.

Freddie Francis

UK, 1917–2007

Freddie Francis had already won a cinematography Oscar (for 1960's *Sons And Lovers*) when he became a director for Brit-horror factory Hammer Films. He's generally viewed as an inferior successor to Hammer mainstay Terence Fisher, who was sidelined at the studio for two years around the time that Francis hit his stride there with straightforward titles such as *Paranoiac* (1962), starring Oliver Reed as the insane heir to an addled family's fortune, *Nightmare* (1963) and *Hysteria* (1964). Moving to rival studio Amicus, Francis helmed their first two bids for a piece of Hammer's terror market: the portmanteau *Dr Terror's House Of Horrors* (1964) and *The Skull* (1965). Both films featured Hammer nobility Christopher Lee and Peter Cushing, who also teamed up for Francis's most intriguing film, *The Creeping Flesh* (1972). After the anthology *Tales From The Crypt* (1972) and a few horror flicks for his son Kevin's Tyburn Films, Francis returned to cinematography, shooting *Cape Fear* (1991) for Martin Scorsese and several films for David Lynch including the visually stunning *The Elephant Man* (1980), and winning a second cinematography Oscar for the American Civil War film *Glory* (1989). JW

The Creeping Flesh 1972, 94 min

cast Christopher Lee, Peter Cushing, Lorna Heilbron, George Benson, Kenneth J. Warren, Duncan Lamont *cin* Norman Warwick *m* Paul Ferris

Hammer's quintessential mad scientist, Peter Cushing, here discovers an ancient skeleton and, peering into his microscope, declares he has found the antidote to the evil that lurks within all men, much to the interest of asylum warden Christopher Lee. The crystalline cinematography illuminates a bulging textbook of classic gothic tropes, and revisits the discomfiting theme of unchecked female eroticism touched upon by Terence Fisher's Dracula movies.

Jesús Franco

Spain, 1930–

Insanely prolific, Jesús Franco has perhaps 180 movies to his name – or rather, to any of his fifteen or more pseudonyms, which include Clifford Brown, Wolfgang Frank and Betty Carter. By the late 1960s Franco was averaging five or six features per year; his only present-day rival in sheer output is Japanese splatter king Takashi Miike. Unfortunately, what Franco gained in speed he lost in terms of *mise en scène*, narrative momentum and other cinematic niceties, though he could always spare plenty of time for supple, gauzily clad female flesh and the well-aimed splash of gore.

He made Westerns, spy thrillers and the odd Zorro film, but Franco is most closely identified with leisurely paced horror schlock made on the cheap, often derived from well-known previous sources and increasingly steeped in soft-porn titillation. *The Awful Dr Orlof* (1961) riffed on Georges Franju's then-recent *Eyes Without A Face* (*Les yeux sans visage*, 1959), and *Miss Muerte* (1965), with a script by Jean-Claude Carrière, rejigged Cornell Woolrich's novel *The Bride Wore Black* (1940). With its gothic horror tropes and skin-flick come-ons, *Miss Muerte* is a vivid early template for the Franco project: a woman seeking revenge for the death of her mad-scientist father, who suffered a heart attack after a scathing review of his mind-control experiments, presses into service an exotic dancer called "Miss Death" who sports a see-through spider costume and long, poisoned fingernails.

Franco attempted an ill-fated Dracula film, *El Conde Dracula* (1969), with Hammer veteran Christopher Lee as the Count and Klaus Kinski as Renfield, but enjoyed more luck mounting horny distaff variations on Stoker's story. These included *Vampyros lesbos* (1970), which relied equally on dramatic zooming shots and black-and-red lingerie for its sensational frisson, and *Female Vampires* (1973), starring Lina Romay (Franco's future wife) as the mute, sexually insatiable bloodsucker. Deeper into the 1970s, Franco specialized in offbeat porn (perhaps he always had) and, in 1982, helmed an instalment of the *Emmanuelle* series, *Las orgias inconfesables de Emmanuelle* (*Emmanuelle Exposed*). JW

Vampyros lesbos 1970, 89 min

cast Ewa Strömberg, Soledad Miranda, Andrés Monales, Dennis Price, Paul Muller *cin* Manuel Merino *m* Jesús Franco, Manfred Hübler, Sigi Schwab

A voluptuous blond estate lawyer travels on business to a small island off the Turkish coast, where she falls for a sultry temptress with a taste for blood. The movie boasts some remarkably tender lesbian love scenes (charmingly interspliced with shots of scorpions, bugs and kites), but the real star of the movie is the lysergic hodgepodge of a soundtrack by Manfred Hübler and Sigi Schwab – teeming with synths, sitars, jazz drumming and babbling vocals, it's a veritable "head movie" symphony.

Georges Franju

France, 1912–87

Georges Franju once said that the scariest movie he ever saw was a medical film called *Trepanation For Epileptic Seizures*, which recorded the drilling of a semiconscious patient's skull. Perhaps it's no surprise, then, that Franju's best-known film, *Eyes Without A Face* (*Les yeux sans visage*, 1959), induced fainting spells in audiences with its unblinking depiction of the surgical removal of a woman's face.

A devoted film archivist, Franju founded the Cinémathèque Française in 1936 with Henri

Langlois, who was also co-director on Franju's first documentary short, *Le Métro* (1934). As a solo director, Franju made *Le grand Méliès* (1952), a half-hour biopic of the pioneering French silent director George Méliès, and many documentary shorts that suggested a debt to surrealism. One of these shorts was a horror film of sorts, *Blood Of The Beasts* (1949), which looked deep inside a series of slaughterhouses on the outskirts of Paris and is at once resolutely nonchalant and almost unwatchably graphic. No less unflinching was *Hôtel des invalides* (1951), a documentary in which disfigured war veterans are depicted against the backdrop of the national army museum housing Napoleon's tomb.

Franju was in his mid-forties before he made his first fiction feature, and aside from *Eyes Without A Face*, his oeuvre has been strangely neglected outside of France. This despite the fact that it includes such gems as the asylum-breakout thriller *La tête contre les murs* (*The Keepers/Head Against The Wall*, 1959), the Agatha Christie-style murder intrigues of *Spotlight On A Murderer* (1960) and the gorgeous throwback *Judex* (1963), an inspired homage to the crime-fighting creation of early French director Louis Feuillade. JW

Eyes Without A Face (Les yeux sans visage)
1959, 90 min, b/w

cast Pierre Brasseur, Alida Valli, Edith Scob, Juliete Mayniel, François Guérin, Béatrice Altariba *cin* Eugen Schüfftan *m* Maurice Jarre

A mad doctor is murderously obsessed with giving his mutilated daughter – the delicately ethereal Edith Scob – a new visage in Franju's clinically detached horror story. Scripted by the dynamic duo Boileau and Narcejac and shot by ace cinematographer Eugen Schüfftan (whose credits include films for Lang, Murnau and Pabst), this indelible movie is all the more unsettling for its matter-of-fact tone, notwithstanding Maurice Jarre's circus-from-hell score.

John Frankenheimer
US, 1930–2002

In the 1960s, John Frankenheimer was touted as one of the most exciting new filmmakers of those tumultuous times, an American auteur in the making. Yet over the next two decades he looked more like a journeyman, an anonymous professional with a pragmatic approach to indifferent material. Both these versions hold some truth. It's also the case that much of Frankenheimer's best work was for television – where he cut his teeth directing live drama in the 1950s, and to which he returned to make his last worthwhile films in the 1990s.

Tall and athletic, Frankenheimer chose acting over a career in tennis. Conscripted during the Korean War, he served in the air force, becoming a cameraman in a photographic unit. He parlayed that experience into a gig as an assistant director at CBS, and soon moved up. Between 1954 and 1960 he directed 152 live television dramas, working with stars such as Ingrid Bergman, John Gielgud and Jason Robards. He was probably the most flamboyant visual director to come out of the medium. Live television gave Frankenheimer a taste for deep focus, wide-angle lenses and long, fluid takes – a Wellesian style which was only slightly modified over the course of his long career.

His first feature film, *The Young Stranger* (1957), was a Hollywood version of a TV play he'd directed, and proved an unhappy experience. It was four years later – when the live TV era was at an end – that he returned to moviemaking, hitting his stride with the seminal true-life prison drama *Birdman Of Alcatraz* in 1962. It was one of four collaborations with actor-producer Burt Lancaster. The period from 1962 to 1966 was Frankenheimer's golden era. He helmed two prescient political thrillers, both of them classics of Cold War cinema: *The Manchurian Candidate* (1962) and *Seven Days In May* (1964). *The Train* (1964) was a spectacular World War II allegory, which he took over from Arthur Penn at Lancaster's invitation. And *Seconds* (1966) is a virtuoso piece of sci-fi philosophy which has proved an enduring cult item.

Frankenheimer might have thrived in the studio era, but his eclectic tastes make it hard to pinpoint a strong thematic signature in a body of work which swings from the racing movie *Grand Prix* (1966) to literary adaptation *The Fixer* (1968), from skydiving action in *The Gypsy Moths* (1969) to all-star comic shenanigans in *The Extraordinary Seaman* (1969). It's easier to point to limitations: he was weak (or uninterested) when working with female characters, and preferred action to reflection, in his career and in his heroes.

A friend of the Kennedys, he drove Robert Kennedy to LA's Ambassador hotel on June 5, 1968 – the day the Senator was assassinated. Coincidentally, perhaps, Frankenheimer's artistic decline can be dated from that time. He had a facility for thrillers, and most of his later work was in that genre, but although there were sometimes flashes of his former panache – his *French Connection II* (1975) is arguably superior to Friedkin's original – the features after *Black Sunday* (1977), and the five-year drinking binge which followed that film's commercial failure, were not worthy of his reputation.

Unexpectedly, he rallied, winning three Emmy awards in three years for his HBO dramas *Against The Wall* (1994), *The Burning Season* (1994) and *Andersonville* (1996). For cable TV, Frankenheimer was able to recapture the political resonance which invigorated his best 1960s films. It says something about the state of the movie business that his theatrical features of this time include the dire *The Island Of Dr Moreau* (1996) and *Reindeer Games* (2000). TC

Birdman Of Alcatraz 1962, 147 min, b/w

cast Burt Lancaster, Karl Malden, Neville Brand, Thelma Ritter, Telly Savalas, Edmond O'Brien *cin* Burnett Guffey *m* Elmer Bernstein

Burt Lancaster won kudos and an Oscar nomination for his restrained performance as Robert Stroud, a barely educated double murderer who revealed himself to be an extraordinary polymath (including his ground-breaking ornithological research) during decades of imprisonment, often in solitary confinement, at Alcatraz. Working for the most part in the narrow confines of Stroud's cell, Frankenheimer nevertheless creates a compelling portrait of a man's better nature awakening under the least promising circumstances.

Seven Days In May 1964, 118 min, b/w

cast Burt Lancaster, Kirk Douglas, Fredric March, Ava Gardner, Edmond O'Brien, Martin Balsam *cin* Ellsworth Fredricks *m* Jerry Goldsmith

Another paranoia classic, this time with Burt Lancaster leading the military chiefs of staff in a coup against a "soft" president. This is gripping filmmaking, prescient and influential in its stress on modern surveillance technology, with a fine, terse script by *Twilight Zone* creator Rod Serling and an outstanding ensemble cast. Lancaster would have another go at the White House ten years later in Robert Aldrich's *Twilight's Last Gleaming*.

Seconds 1966, 105 min, b/w

cast Rock Hudson, Salome Jens, John Randolph, Will Geer, Jeff Corey, Richard Anderson *cin* James Wong Howe *m* Jerry Goldsmith

Ageing banker John Randolph is almost unwittingly sucked into a secret society which stages his death, puts him under the surgeon's knife, and then reintroduces him to Californian society as artist Rock Hudson. The movie loses its way in the middle section, but it's another vividly rendered American nightmare from a filmmaker intent on pushing past the comfort zone.

Stephen Frears
UK, 1941–

Stephen Frears is one of the finest craftsmen of modern British cinema, and like many artisans he subsumes his personal style to the demands of the material. Whether he's making a contemporary thriller like *Dirty Pretty Things* (2002) or a period drama like *Dangerous Liaisons* (1988), he cuts his cinematic cloth to suit the genre. *The Grifters* (1990) brims with uncharacteristic directorial flourishes, as Frears's fluid camera emphasizes the conspiratorial web-weaving of his damned protagonists; whereas, in the socially realistic *The Van* (1996), his camera is at its most demure and self-deprecating as it observes his working-class Irish heroes.

A brainwashed Laurence Harvey is watched by his mother (Angela Lansbury) in Frankenheimer's Cold War thriller *The Manchurian Candidate*.

The Manchurian Candidate 1962, 126 min, b/w

cast Frank Sinatra, Laurence Harvey, Janet Leigh, Angela Lansbury, Henry Silva, James Gregory, Khigh Dhiegh *cin* Lionel Lindon *m* David Amram

A nail-biting conspiracy thriller based on Richard Condon's black comedy about a returning Korean War hero (Harvey) and his platoon – all of whom have been brainwashed by the Communists. Frankenheimer's extravagant visual style matches the outrageous, shocking script, and Lansbury, Sinatra and Dhiegh give indelible performances. Sinatra, who was also a producer, apparently requested that the film be withdrawn after John F. Kennedy's assassination. It was intelligently remade in 2004 by Jonathan Demme.

At London's radical Royal Court Theatre, he worked with directors Karel Reisz and Lindsay Anderson, going on to assist Reisz on *Morgan – A Suitable Case For Treatment* (1966) and Anderson on *If...* (1968). His own directorial debut was with the hard-boiled parody *Gumshoe* (1971), a quixotic hybrid of *Billy Liar* and *The Maltese Falcon*. He spent the next thirteen years patiently learning his craft in television before returning in 1984

183

with *The Hit*, a beguiling synthesis of mobsters and metaphysics. The unexpected success of his next film, *My Beautiful Laundrette* (1985) brought Frears uncomfortably into the limelight, garnering awards and critical hyperbole in equal measure. Then, with the handsome Joe Orton biopic *Prick Up Your Ears* (1987), he continued his successful television partnership with playwright Alan Bennett.

Frears's work seesaws in quality. On the upside: the *noir*-inflected panache of *The Grifters*, the underrated slow-burning horse opera *The Hi-Lo Country* (1998), the buoyantly charming Nick Hornby adaptation *High Fidelity* (2000) and *The Queen* (2006), penned by one of Britain's most exciting writers, Peter Morgan. On the downside: the stereotypical British mix of pluck and nudity in *Mrs Henderson Presents* (2005) and the Capra-esque box-office dud, *Accidental Hero* (1992). And then there are the unmitigated disasters: *Sammy And Rosie Get Laid* (1987), courtesy of *Laundrette* screenwriter Hanif Kureishi, was a self-indulgent fiasco, and *Mary Reilly* (1996), courtesy of *Dangerous Liaisons* screenwriter Christopher Hampton, was a box-office disaster. This neatly sums up the strengths and weaknesses of Frears's approach. In making himself as director secondary to the writer, there are no saving graces if the script is lacklustre or poor; Frears has no signature style to lift the film or provide temporary relief. His collaborations with talented writers are among his best films, and among his worst. LH

My Beautiful Laundrette 1985, 97 min
cast Gordon Warnecke, Daniel Day-Lewis, Saeed Jaffrey, Roshan Seth, Derrick Branche, Shirley Anne Field *cin* Oliver Stapleton *m* Ludus Tonalis

Originally made for television, this symbolic, sensual and iconoclastic drama was released in cinemas after it enraptured critics at the Edinburgh Film Festival. It's hard to think of a better example of 1980s zeitgeist: multiculturalism, racism, Thatcherism, class and sexual politics are all explored through the prism of a tender love story as an Asian entrepreneur (Gordon Warnecke) and his punky white lover (Daniel Day-Lewis) open a laundrette together.

Dangerous Liaisons 1988, 119 min
cast Glenn Close, John Malkovich, Michelle Pfeiffer, Uma Thurman, Keanu Reeves, Swoosie Kurtz *cin* Philippe Rousselot *m* George Fenton

John Malkovich and Glenn Close have never been better than as a pair of lascivious, game-playing eighteenth-century aristocrats who plot to steal the innocence of Uma Thurman and seduce the virtuous and married Michelle Pfeiffer. The wit and dexterity of Christopher Hampton's script (adapted from Pierre Choderlos de Laclos's classic French novel) find their sparkling visual equivalent in the director's sinuous and seductive camerawork.

The Grifters 1990, 110 min
cast Anjelica Huston, John Cusack, Annette Bening, Pat Hingle, Henry Jones, Michael Laskin *cin* Oliver Stapleton *m* Elmer Bernstein

When his mother (Anjelica Huston) doesn't get on with his new belle (Annette Bening), a nimble-fingered con man with an Oedipus complex (John Cusack) finds that his house of cards falls apart spectacularly. The collusion

between craftsman Frears and auteur Martin Scorsese (as producer) resulted in virtuosic camerawork reminiscent of *GoodFellas*. Scorsese's big set pieces can sometimes overwhelm the story, but Frears, the consummate storyteller, integrates them seamlessly into the narrative.

The Queen 2006, 97 min
cast Helen Mirren, Michael Sheen, James Cromwell, Sylvia Syms, Alex Jennings, Helen McCrory *cin* Affonso Beatto *m* Alexandre Desplat

Peter Morgan has carved a niche for himself as a writer who can take factual material and spin it into fictional gold. Here, he and Frears speculate on the personal and political machinations that went on behind the scenes at Balmoral and Number 10 Downing Street in the week following Princess Diana's death. The director's strengths and weaknesses are exposed once again: he elicits an Oscarwinning performance from Helen Mirren in the title role, but when it comes to the cinematography, his television roots show through.

Charles Frend
UK, 1909–77

Frend's directorial career rose and fell with Ealing Studios, where he made his two best films, extolling British grit in the face of adversity. After editing four films for Hitchcock he directed *The Big Blockade* (1940), about anti-German sanctions, but his first big success was *The Foreman Went To France* (1942), in which the factory foreman hero stops the Nazis from obtaining vital machinery. War stories suited him but he fell ill while shooting *San Demetrio, London* (1943), about a stricken oil tanker and the heroic attempts to steer it home, and an uncredited Robert Hamer completed it. Both films were part of a trend at Ealing – initiated by the arrival of leading documentarists to the studio – towards a greater degree of realism in action pictures. The historical rural romance *The Loves Of Joanna Godden* (1947) was an atypical minor success, but Frend's best films are *Scott Of The Antarctic* (1948) and *The Cruel Sea* (1953). After Ealing closed in the mid-1950s, Frend rather lost his way. There were stints in television (including several episodes of *Danger Man* in the 1960s) and he also worked as assistant director on David Lean's overblown *Ryan's Daughter* (1970). JR

Scott Of The Antarctic 1948, 111 min
cast John Mills, Derek Bond, Kenneth More, James Robertson Justice, Diana Churchill *cin* Jack Cardiff, Osmond Borradaile *m* Ralph Vaughan Williams

Heroic failure has always been honoured in England but Scott's doomed quest for the South Pole was an unusual choice of subject. From his initial attempts to raise interest and money through to the team's realization that they have failed, Scott is portrayed as a flawed, under-prepared leader, overreaching himself and making it inevitable that Amundsen would win the race. It is beautifully photographed and Vaughan Williams wrote a highly atmospheric score which he later recast as his seventh symphony.

The Cruel Sea 1953, 126 min, b/w

cast Jack Hawkins, Donald Sinden, Denholm Elliott, Stanley Baker, Virginia McKenna *cin* Gordon Dines *m* Alan Rawsthorne, Gerard Schurmann

Frend brought a gritty authenticity to Eric Ambler's Oscar-nominated adaptation of Nicholas Monserrat's bestseller. As a captain of a Royal Navy corvette, Jack Hawkins (in one of his best roles) leads an inexperienced crew, symbolically recruited from all walks of civvy street, into the Atlantic. Encountering storms and enemy action, they learn to pull together, but at the climax the captain faces an enormous moral dilemma.

Karl Freund

Czech Republic (formerly Austro-Hungarian Empire), 1890–1969

As much as any single director, Karl Freund defined the visual aesthetics of the German cinema renaissance that followed World War I as cinematographer on Wegener's *The Golem* (1920), Murnau's *The Last Laugh* (1924), Lang's *Metropolis* (1927) and other landmarks. Freund was also a technical innovator and a resourceful crewman, helping to develop a new type of light-sensitive film for Walter Ruttmann's *Berlin: Symphony Of A Great City* (1927) and strapping the camera to his chest to achieve expressive movement for *The Last Laugh*. After relocating to Hollywood, Freund shot Tod Browning's *Dracula* (1932) and was largely responsible for the film's eerily sinister atmosphere. Promoted to the directing ranks, he made a brief series of movies, of which his first, the Universal horror flick *The Mummy* (1932), and the last, the Peter Lorre frightener *Mad Love* (1935), are his best. He then returned to cinematography, winning an Oscar for 1937's *The Good Earth*. Freund later worked in television, where he continued to introduce innovations. In the 1950s he was director of photography on *I Love Lucy*, one of the first TV shows to be shot and edited on 35mm film and the first to use the three-camera setup that is standard for sitcoms to this day. JW

The Mummy 1932, 73 min, b/w

cast Boris Karloff, Zita Johann, David Manners, Edward van Sloan, Arthur Byron, Noble Johnson, Leonard Mudie *cin* Charles Stumar *m* Tchaikovsky

A year after *Frankenstein* made him a star, Boris Karloff plays the ancient priest Im-ho-tep, who is inadvertently resurrected by a young archaeologist and, now calling himself Ardath Bey, searches for the reincarnation of his princess sweetheart. Deliberately paced and edged with suggestions of sexual blasphemy, the film rests on Karloff's deep reserves of ominous charisma (he appears in full mummy make-up only briefly, and spends most of the film in fez and robes).

Mad Love (The Hands Of Orlac) 1935, 68 min, b/w

cast Peter Lorre, Frances Drake, Colin Clive, Isabel Jewell, Ted Healy, Sara Haden, Edward Brophy *cin* Chester Lyons, Gregg Toland *m* Dimitri Tiomkin

Peter Lorre plays the demented Dr Gogol, who's obsessed with an actress at the Théâtre du Grand Guignol. After her concert-pianist husband injures his hands, the surgeon replaces them with those of a dead killer, and suddenly the musician discovers a new talent for throwing knives… With echoes of *Pygmalion* and *The Phantom Of The Opera*, this droll and gleefully deranged gothic tale was both Freund's valedictory as a director and Lorre's Hollywood debut.

William Friedkin

US, 1935–

In the early 1970s William Friedkin directed a pair of massive critical and commercial successes, regarded by some commentators as exemplars of their respective genres: *The French Connection* (1971), a down-and-dirty New York police thriller, and *The Exorcist* (1973), a high-voltage frightener about demonic possession. Despite the lofty claims made for it (notably by Mark Kermode in his BFI monograph), today *The Exorcist* looks like no more than a rancid slab of horror-porn, with Linda Blair's pea-green projectile vomit only the most famous money shot among its endless ejaculations of shock and calculated sacrilege.

The French Connection, however, still has a lot going for it, including the redoubtable Gene Hackman as maverick cop Popeye Doyle and some expertly helmed and edited action sequences. The film does leave a nasty aftertaste in its reactionary politics; released the same year as Don Siegel's *Dirty Harry*, it exploits similar anxieties of America's "silent majority" during tumultuous and uncertain times via the adventures of a mad-as-hell working man who reins in foreign (French) drug peddlars and who is introduced beating up a black suspect.

Friedkin buffed *Connection*'s hard carapace to a 1980s sheen with *To Live And Die In LA* (1985). A Conradian tale of a forger (Willem Dafoe) and the two cops trying to nail him, the film was told in a painstakingly forensic fashion, and you could be forgiven for mistaking it for a Michael Mann movie. All the Mann hallmarks were present and correct: searingly bright colours, monomaniacal male protagonists, a fascination with process and procedure, an overwhelming aura of moral cynicism and a pompous synthesizer soundtrack.

Other than these, Friedkin's films mainly hold interest as grisly train wrecks and badly dated cultural artefacts. Friedkin has unadvisedly made two "gay films": *The Boys In The Band* (1970), a bitchfest of self-loathing, slang-slinging friends, and *Cruising* (1980), featuring Al Pacino as a bewildered cop descending into a leathery S&M underworld. *Sorcerer* (1977) was a disastrous remake of Clouzot's *The Wages Of Fear* (1953), while the crudely misogynistic thriller *Jade* (1995) is arguably the worst film ever made from a Joe Eszterhas script; given the schlockmeister scribe's track record, that's some kind of achievement. JW

The French Connection 1971, 99 min

cast Gene Hackman, Fernando Rey, Roy Scheider, Tony Lo Bianco, Marcel Bozzuffi, Frédéric de Pasquale *cin* Owen Roizman *m* Don Ellis

Winner of five Oscars including best picture, director and actor, this grimy cop movie is short on characterization and long on law-and-order fervour. Its chief satisfactions lie in a few handsome set pieces: a suspenseful, funny two-step of evasion and pursuit between Popeye Doyle (Gene Hackman) and his poker-faced quarry (Buñuel regular Fernando Rey) on the New York subway, and the famous chase scene pitting Doyle's knackered stolen car against an elevated train.

The Exorcist 1973, 122 min

cast Ellen Burstyn, Max von Sydow, Lee J. Cobb, Kitty Winn, Jason Miller, Jack MacGowran, Linda Blair *cin* Bill Malley *m* Jack Nitzsche

A concerned mother (Ellen Burstyn) turns to a pair of Catholic priests (Jason Miller and Max Von Sydow) to evict Satan from her child's body in this well-acted but deeply cynical exploitarama, which reaches a nadir when the possessed girl bloodily masturbates with a crucifix. The 2000 re-release version added subliminal demon imagery and the famous but fleeting "spider-walk".

To Live And Die In LA 1985, 116 min

cast William L. Petersen, Willem Dafoe, John Pankow, John Turturro, Dean Stockwell, Robert Downey *cin* Robby Müller *m* Wang Chung

With its glossy good looks – courtesy of Robby Müller – this movie is untypical of Friedkin. It's a fastidiously framed investigation of the sliding scale of authenticity and corruption, but it can't quite sustain its pretensions and it becomes increasingly overwrought. The film is, however, consistent in the things that count: its shot-by-shot beauty and its attention to detail.

Kinji Fukasaku

Japan, 1930–2003

The irreverent genre fire starter Kinji Fukasaku is the godfather of the *yakuza* (Japanese Mafia) film and a founding influence on younger Japanese pulp artisans such as Takeshi Kitano and Takashi Miike, as well as Western trash cinephiles like Quentin Tarantino. Steeped in gore and handheld chaos, Fukasaku's ultraviolent, high-decibel gangster operas shoved aside the more decorous Japanese crime movies popular in the 1960s and deromanticized the underworld as cinema-goers knew it. The seminal *Battles Without Honour And Humanity* (1973) and *Graveyard Of Honour* (1975), both loosely based on actual events, blasted open clamorous slaughterhouses where bloody, brutal self-interest is the only law that holds.

Beginning as a prolific crime-flick specialist for the Toei studio, Fukasaku took an early interest in the disaffected and disenfranchised youth of post-war and boom-era Japan. He centred on young hoods who fall foul of local *yakuza* in the jumpy *Blackmail Is My Life* (1968) and on a group of undereducated friends denied access to the nation's economic renaissance in *If You Were Young: Rage* (1970). Acrid social commentary underpins most of Fukasaku's major films: *Battles Without Honour And Humanity* begins in 1946, as the *yakuza* menace rises out of the devastation of Hiroshima. Fukasaku allegorizes a society disabled and dehumanized in mind and soul by the ravages of war, as *Battles* and its four sequels cover scores of characters over four cities and a quarter of a century.

Of course, Fukasaku didn't just make *yakuza* films; his résumé includes the camp yet sinister and deliciously sick-minded *Black Lizard* (1968), starring female impersonator nonpareil Akihiro Maruyama as a connoisseur of stolen jewels and preserved bodies, and the grimly affecting *Under The Fluttering Military Flag* (1972), in which a war widow hears contradictory stories of her husband's death. The director also contributed the Japanese sequences to the Pearl Harbor drama *Tora! Tora! Tora!* (1970). Fukasaku had a wicked sense of humour, and his last completed feature, *Battle Royale* (2000), is also his funniest. A pitch-black satire that sometimes plays like a Paul Verhoeven reimagining of TV's *Survivor*, the movie gave ample evidence that the 70-year-old director had lost none of his taste for graphic confrontation. JW

Battles Without Honour And Humanity (Jingi naki tatakai) 1973, 99 min

cast Bunta Sugawara, Hiroki Matsukata, Tatsuo Umeniya, Nobou Kaneko, Toshie Kimura, Junie Tanaka *cin* Sadaji Yoshida *m* Toshiaki Tshushima

In decimated post-war Hiroshima, thugs form alliances to fill the power vacuum, and young tough Shozo Hirono (Bunta Sugawara) begins his bloody, detour-riddled ascent through the *yakuza* ranks. The first and best of a five-film series (available as the DVD box set *The Yakuza Papers: Battles Without Honour And Humanity*), this quintessential Fukasaku thrashing is a sacred text for action cultists and an enraged commentary on the violence and inhumanity of post-war Japan.

Battle Royale (Batoru rowaiaru) 2000, 114 min

cast Takashi Kitano, Tatsuya Fujiwara, Aki Maeda, Taro Yamamoto, Masanobu Ando, Ko Shibasaki *cin* Katsumi Yanagijima *m* Masamichi Amano

In the near future, the Japanese government, reacting to escalating youth anarchy, starts choosing high-school classes at random for exile to a desert island. Each student is given one weapon (ranging from a large saucepan lid to a machine gun); the game ends when only a single contestant is left alive. Blood-soaked and consistently hysterical, Fukasaku's satire also offers a priceless bit of casting: Takeshi Kitano as a hapless teacher turned track-suited tyrant.

Samuel Fuller

US, 1911–97

In a cameo in Godard's *Pierrot le fou* (1965), Fuller famously defines cinema as: "Love, hate, action, violence, death. In one word: emotion." Regaling his audiences with snappy tabloid-style B-dramas combining gutsy realism, a raw political instinct and intensely physical filmmaking, Fuller had (at least in the early days) no time for critics or official taste. Yet the French came to regard his unselfconscious style as essential to modern cinema.

Fuller started in journalism, as a *New York Journal* copyboy and crime reporter. During the Depression, he drifted across America on freight trains. He started writing fiction in the mid-1930s. Pulpy and action-filled, his novels presaged his later work as a screenwriter and director: his films express struggle and clash through unaffected dialogue and vivid camerawork, and their titles – *Run Of The Arrow*, *The Crimson Kimono*, *The Naked Kiss* – would not look out of place on cheap paperback covers.

Initial screenwriting chores bore the frenetic stamp of urban lives: *Gangs Of New York* (1938), *Bowery Boy* (1940), *The Power Of The Press* (1943), *Shockproof* (1948). In World War II, Fuller served with the 1st Infantry Division from North Africa to Normandy, his experience as a common rifleman crucially shaping his outlook. His directing debut was *I Shot Jesse James* (1949), which studied the psychological consequences of the outlaw's assassination. Subsequent films – *The Steel Helmet* (1950), *Fixed Bayonets* (1951), *Park Row* (1952), *Pickup On South Street* (1953), *House Of Bamboo* (1955), *Forty Guns* (1957) – are miniature epics of war, big-city journalism, Cold War friction and the underworld.

Fuller wrote and produced many of his films himself, often on the fringes of the studio system. This way of working had its problems, but it afforded him the latitude to address difficult topics during a time of political consensus. *Run Of The Arrow* (1957) saw Rod Steiger as a Civil War Confederate so embittered by the South's defeat that he joins the Sioux nation. It predicted the racial divisions of the 1960s. Focusing on the rivalry between a Japanese-born LA detective (James Shigeta) and his Caucasian buddy (Glenn Corbett), *The Crimson Kimono* (1959) tackled the tragedy of racism head on. *Underworld USA* (1961) continued the war movie theme, presenting the shift from Prohibition gangsterism to corporate theft as an ongoing war seen through the prism of one man's revenge. *Merrill's Marauders* (1962) explored the moral and physical distress of an infantry patrol in the Burma jungle, the mobile camera apostrophizing the savage absurdity of battle. Fuller saw it as a dry run for his cherished project *The Big Red One*, while it also carries the whiff of America's Vietnam adventure. *Shock Corridor* (1963) is Fuller's most complete statement of the madness and division of post-war America. Appearing in the year of *Kiss Me, Stupid*, Billy Wilder's similarly frenetic riposte to sexual hypocrisy, *The Naked Kiss*

(1964) hinges on a compelling performance from Constance Towers as a former prostitute exposing small-town mores.

Always politically independent despite being claimed by both Right and Left, Fuller reiterated humanity in an age of excess. Constance Towers, Gene Evans, Richard Widmark… all did fine work for Fuller. After television Westerns, aborted projects and small roles in films by Godard, Dennis Hopper (*The Last Movie*, 1971) and Wim Wenders (*The American Friend*, 1977) Fuller directed his magnum opus, *The Big Red One*, in 1980. He remains one of American cinema's most passionate, problematic spirits. RA

Pickup On South Street 1953, 80 min, b/w
cast Richard Widmark, Jean Peters, Thelma Ritter, Richard Kiley, Murvyn Vye, Willis Bouchey *cin* Joseph MacDonald *m* Leigh Harline

"Don't wave the flag at me", sneers Richard Widmark's cheap pickpocket when he is accused of Communist espionage in this gritty portrait of the New York underworld. The scene in which Widmark lifts a purse on the subway only to find it contains microfilm is tense observant storytelling at its best. Accused by some of McCarthyite sympathies, by others of being commie-loving, this is a superb example of Fuller's ambivalent, supremely moral cinema.

House Of Bamboo 1955, 102 min
cast Robert Ryan, Robert Stack, Shirley Yamaguchi, Cameron Mitchell, Sessue Hayakawa *cin* Joseph MacDonald *m* Leigh Harline

Shot in CinemaScope in Japan, this was apparently Godard's favourite of Fuller's films. A remake of William Keighley's *Street With No Name*, it stars Robert Stack as a military policeman who infiltrates a gang run by a former GI played by Robert Ryan. It can be read as an American take on a post-war Japanese underworld peopled by cartoon gooks and craggy hoods, or as rigorous reportage from the underbelly of the *Pax Americana*. Incendiary, whichever way you look at it.

Shock Corridor 1963, 101 min, b/w and col
cast Peter Breck, Constance Towers, Gene Evans, James Best, Hari Rhodes, Larry Tucker, William Zuckert *cin* Stanley Cortez *m* Paul Dunlap

A reporter (Peter Breck) bent on the scoop of the century gets himself admitted to an insane asylum to expose the murderer of a patient. Amid the sickness of post-war America – a black man shouting Ku Klux Klan slogans, a raving nuclear scientist – he starts to really lose his mind. Strikingly shot by Stanley Cortez using harsh single-source light, the film relentlessly tracks Breck's descent into the abyss.

The Big Red One 1980, 113 min
cast Lee Marvin, Mark Hamill, Robert Carradine, Bobby DiCicco, Kelly Ward, Stéphane Audran *cin* Adam Greenberg *m* Dana Kaproff

Fuller always wanted to work with Lee Marvin and over the decades while he tried to get his war movie made they regularly dreamed the dream. The result is a brisk account of the 1st Infantry Division's odyssey from hitting the North African beaches to liberating Falkenau death camp. No heroics, no set pieces, no bullshit… this is a story of love, hate, action, violence, death and grace under fire.

Sidney J. Furie

Canada, 1933–

Sidney Furie's most successful films, made in the 1960s, captured something of the youth sensibility and New Wave modernism of that period. His feature debut, *A Dangerous Age* (1958), made in his native Canada, announced a feel for the vicissitudes of youth in its tale of a teenage elopement. *A Cool Sound From Hell* (1959) mixed jazz, teenage rebellion and beat poetry with striking cinematography. Furie moved to Britain in 1960, where he directed *The Boys* (1962), which revolved around East End youths accused of murder amid grainy naturalistic locations, and two musical vehicles for Cliff Richard and The Shadows, *The Young Ones* (1961) and *Wonderful Life* (1964). *The Leather Boys* (1964) responded to the alarmism of Basil Dearden's *Victim* (1961) with a more nuanced treatment of homosexuality. *The Ipcress File* (1965) led to Hollywood, where he directed the mannerist Marlon Brando Western *The Appaloosa* (1966) and *Little Fauss And Big Halsy* (1970), an attempt to exploit the countercultural dynamics of *Easy Rider* (1969). Mid-career works include the Billie Holiday biopic *Lady Sings The Blues* (1972) and a surprisingly hard-hitting and grimly humorous Vietnam War film, *The Boys In Company C* (1978). *Superman IV: The Quest For Peace* (1987) proved the most lacklustre of the four Superman films, since when Furie has largely churned out straight-to-video action fodder that does him little credit. These include *Iron Eagle* (1987), a gung-ho air-force movie starring Louis Gossett Jr, which has spawned three spin-offs. RA

The Ipcress File 1965, 109 min

cast Michael Caine, Nigel Green, Guy Doleman, Sue Lloyd, Gordon Jackson, Aubrey Richards, Frank Gatliff *cin* Otto Heller *m* John Barry

Michael Caine's Cockney spy Harry Palmer brought an irreverent attitude and lippy charm to the British secret agent – a "swinging London" antidote to James Bond overkill. Len Deighton's complex plot – disappearing scientists and a mysterious tape – is handled well. Darkly and flashily shot by Otto Heller, including a sequence in which Palmer is brainwashed by being shown what seem to be avant-garde art movies, this is the best of the three Harry Palmer thrillers.

Vincent Gallo
US, 1962–

Renaissance man Vincent Gallo has created a persona that melds self-obsession with self-loathing, domination with martyrdom. His extreme multitasking on his second feature film, *The Brown Bunny* (2003) – he toiled as lead actor, director, writer, producer, editor and cinematographer – suggests both a narcissistic control freak and a compulsive loner, exhausted by his solitude. Like a ragged stray cat, the onscreen Gallo always seems to be in desperate need of love and attention even as he hisses warnings at sympathetic onlookers to stay clear.

Gallo set out for New York City at age 16, and quickly established himself as a downtown jack-of-all-trades: a painter, breakdancer, motorcycle racer and bandmate of a pre-fame Jean-Michel Basquiat. Later a reliable character actor and Calvin Klein model, Gallo the filmmaker debuted with the low-budget *Buffalo '66* (1998), in which his beleaguered protagonist Billy Brown is unaccountably alluring to the buxom tap-dance pupil he kidnaps. In the road movie *The Brown Bunny* (2003), motorcycle racer Bud Clay likewise proves irresistible to seemingly every woman he meets. Anyone sensing a pattern here need not be reminded that *Bunny* famously reaches its zenith during a three-minute sequence in which Chloë Sevigny performs apparently unsimulated fellatio on her director. JW

Buffalo '66 1998, 105 min
cast Vincent Gallo, Christina Ricci, Anjelica Huston, Ben Gazzara, Rosanna Arquette, Mickey Rourke *cin* Lance Accord *m* Vincent Gallo

Petulant, pathologically touchy and just sprung from jail in bleak Buffalo, New York, Gallo's Billy Brown kidnaps an incongruously willing dance student (Christina Ricci) and brings her home to his frightful parents (Anjelica Huston and Ben Gazzara), whom he detests but longs to impress. Ragged around the edges and raw as a fresh wound, this is a blackly comic two-fingered salute to Gallo's decayed home town.

Abel Gance
France, 1889–1981

One of early cinema's most fearless innovators, Abel Gance originated a propulsive, breathtaking film rhythm and grammar that influenced the great Soviet filmmakers of the silent era. (More recently, Canadian director Guy Maddin has reanimated Gance's editing style in his own films, notably *The Heart Of The World*, 2000.) Fittingly for a practitioner of a newborn medium, Gance was an incurable experimenter in his silent epoch, beginning with his short films of the 1910s. In *La folie du Docteur Tube* (*The Madness Of Doctor Tube*, 1915), about a cocaine-sniffing mad scientist, Gance employed funhouse-mirror imagery and other distorting optical effects to represent the doctor's addled brain state.

Gance developed what would become his signature rapid-fire cutting technique in the anti-war tract *J'accuse!* (1919) and in *La roue* (*The Wheel*, 1922), with some shots lasting for merely a single frame. *La roue* made a crucial early impression on the young Akira Kurosawa – with its inserts, flashbacks and parallel action – while *J'accuse!* displayed a macabre, perhaps exploitative irony in casting real-life soldiers – some of whom would die in battle shortly after filming – as accusatory "ghosts of the dead". Gance one-upped this casting stunt in the 1938 sound version of *J'accuse!*, which featured facially scarred and disfigured World War I veterans.

Perhaps oddly in light of the anti-war *J'accuse!*, Gance achieved his greatest filmmaking triumph via an epic tribute to a French war hero: *Napoléon* (1927) is a grand, emotive chronicle of the man's life from childhood through to his triumphant early career. The film's hagiographic approach only mildly counteracts its boundless energies and pioneering technical bravado – the film anticipates widescreen vistas in its use of Polyvision, in which three images are screened simultaneously, side by side. Gance's extraordinary ambition in these films is illustrated most dramatically by their length: *Napoléon* and *La roué* both last well over four and a half hours.

After the coming of sound, Gance wasn't able to sustain his career on the same grand scale, with *La fin du monde* (*End Of The World*, 1930) being a diverting forerunner of Hollywood disaster flicks about a comet headed for earth. His later efforts included the sentimental *Paradise perdu* (*Paradise Lost*, 1939), which studied a man lamenting his wife's death and the ravages of World War I; the flaccid swashbuckler *Le Capitaine Fracasse* (1942); and the bloated, star-studded epic *Austerlitz* (1960). Gance did enjoy a last-act comeback, however, living to see the premiere of Kevin Brownlow's magnificent five-hour restoration of *Napoléon* at the Telluride Film Festival in 1979. JW

Napoléon 1927, 330 mins, b/w

cast Albert Dieudonné, Abel Gance, Gina Manés, Antonin Artaud, Nicolas Koline *cin* Léonce-Henry Burel, Jules Kruger, Jean-Paul Mindwiller

Starring Albert Dieudonné as Napoleon and Gance himself as Saint-Just, this frankly uncritical biopic (the first of what the director intended as a six-part epic) spans Napoleon's boyhood through to his early military campaigns. The film makes thrilling use of Gance's technical ingenuity, which encompassed hand-holding the camera, swinging it from the ceiling and strapping it to a horse; it's small wonder that the film gallops along at such an exhilarating pace.

Tay Garnett
US, 1894–1977

One of Hollywood's first writer-directors, Tay Garnett was among those unfortunates who weren't in line when the critics of *Cahiers du cinéma* were handing out auteur medals in the 1950s. Yet he had the sort of macho, derring-do life that the likes of Jean-Luc Godard coveted. Garnett was originally a navy flight instructor, but his career came dramatically down to earth when he crashed his plane and was left with a distinctive limp and a walking stick. However, if it weren't for the Naval Air Service, he may never have moved into film – he started his career as a stunt flyer.

When he was discharged from the navy, Garnett became a gag man for Hal Roach, and then a scriptwriter specializing in manly melodramas, before finally turning to directing with the prizefighting yarn *Celebrity* (1928). Although he is best known for a 1946 adaptation of James M. Cain's *The Postman Always Rings Twice*, the lustiest of *films noirs*, there are other treasures to be unearthed: *Her Man* (1930), the director's personal favourite, which played in Paris for three years; the tear-jerking *One Way Passage* (1932); and the rousing, romantic *China Seas* (1935). Spending his later years as a TV director, Garnett was finally rediscovered in 1977, only months before his death – and arguably twenty years too late – by the French. LH

China Seas 1935, 87 min, b/w

cast Clark Gable, Jean Harlow, Rosalind Russell, Wallace Beery, Lewis Stone, Robert Benchley *cin* Ray June *m* Herbert Stothart

This rollicking adventure has everything you'd expect from an old-fashioned seafaring tale: derring-do, pirates, a typhoon and a love triangle. On a ship bound from Hong Kong to Singapore, the captain (Gable) is caught up in a tempestuous relationship with a nightclub singer (Harlow). But more stormy weather lies ahead when Gable's ex, a recently bereaved society beauty (Russell), boards his vessel. Garnett's ripping yarn is awash with stirring action sequences, scintillating wit and improbable storylines.

The Postman Always Rings Twice 1946, 113 min, b/w

cast Lana Turner, John Garfield, Cecil Kellaway, Hume Cronyn, Audrey Totter, Leon Ames, Alan Reed *cin* Sidney Wagner *m* George Bassman

John Garfield plays a drifter who finds work at an isolated road-side diner and falls in lust with the owner's frustrated young wife, Lana Turner, in her myriad white outfits. The couple's hot-blooded thoughts soon turn to murder, but their schemes don't quite go to plan. If Garnett's *noir* stylings are a little on the pallid side, his narrative moves at a considerable pace, eliciting the same pared-to-the-bone vitality as James M. Cain's pugnacious novel.

Tony Gatlif
Algeria, 1948–

Many filmmakers have been wrongly described as unique, but Tony Gatlif genuinely fits that often lazy adjective. Born to a gypsy family in Algeria, Gatlif is, to date, the only director to have made a film about the Romany people from within that community. The director spent his youth as a homeless delinquent on the streets of Paris, but his life was turned around when he met his hero, the actor Michel Simon, who advised him to attend drama school.

Since debuting in 1975 with *La tête en ruines* (*Head In Ruins*), a powerful evocation of his vagrant past, Gatlif has released a new film every few years, including the flamenco drama *Vengo* (*I Come*, 2000) and *Exils* (2004), for which he won the directing award at Cannes. He is best known for his gypsy triptych, which began with *Les princes* (1983), a bleak survey of a small community in the Parisian suburbs. The second instalment, Gatlif's masterpiece *Latcho drom* (*Safe Journey*, 1993), peerlessly excavates the history of the gypsy nation in an impressionistic odyssey spanning both time and continents. In the final film of the trilogy, *Gadjo dilo* (*The Crazy Stranger*, 1997), Gatlif's devotion to documentary *vérité* extended to placing actor Romain Duris in a gypsy community and filming the results. When Duris unexpectedly fell in love with a young gypsy woman, Gatlif changed the script to suit, thus confirming his commitment to an emotional and ethnographic truth. This commitment characterizes the director's impressive and wonderfully musical body of work and it was continued in *Transylvania* in 2006. LH

Latcho drom (Safe Journey) 1993, 103 min
cin Eric Guichard *m* traditional

Taking customs, rituals and ancient beliefs in its narrative sweep, *Latcho* segues seamlessly from India to Spain, via Egypt, Turkey, Hungary and Romania, from one intoxicating number to the next. All rhyme and little conventional reason, this mesmerizing travelogue does away with dialogue to tell its story exclusively in song and dance. Never has a tale of global persecution and institutionalized racism been so exhilarating.

Gadjo dilo (The Crazy Stranger) 1997, 100 min
cast Romain Duris, Rona Hartner, Izidor Serban, Florin Moldovan, Ovidiu Balan, Dan Astileanu *cin* Eric Guichard *m* Tony Gatlif

Looking for the gypsy singer who was a favourite of his father, a young Parisian joins a community of fiery, passionate and foul-mouthed gypsies. The "crazy outsider" is taken in by their leader, the boorish Izidor, as a surrogate son and by the dancer Sabina, who has other, more libidinous, plans for him. Strong on atmosphere but weak on narrative, *Gadjo dilo* is an emotional, bawdy and joyous testimony to a cinematically overlooked people.

Jean Genet
France, 1910–86

According to Jean-Paul Sartre, Genet was "a liar, thief, pervert, saint and martyr". Genet only directed one film, which lasted all of 26 minutes, but it has been crowned the most important gay short in the history of cinema. After a difficult childhood and a notorious youth spent drifting through Europe as a beggar, thief and prostitute, Genet was committed to life imprisonment in 1947. However, during his various sojourns in jail, he had become a highly regarded novelist, writing his debut, *Our Lady Of The Flowers*, on brown-paper bags. As a free man, Genet wrote *The Thief's Journal* and numerous other novels, as well as award-winning plays such as *The Maids* and *The Balcony*. For the cinema, he wrote the stories for Tony Richardson's *Mademoiselle* (1966) and, most notably, Rainer Werner Fassbinder's *Querelle* (1982). However, his single greatest contribution to cinema was the silent porn poem *Un chant d'amour* (*A Song Of Love*, 1950), which was banned for decades around the world. The film's invocation of the lyrical and the marginal became the sensual model for queer cinema and for directors such as Derek Jarman, Todd Haynes, John Maybury and Richard Kwietnowski; it set the gold standard for homoerotic imagery. LH

Un chant d'amour (A Song Of Love) 1950, 26 min, b/w
cast Java, André Reybaz, Coco Le Martiniquais, Lucien Sénémaud *cin* Jean Cocteau *m* Gavin Bryars

Starring an assortment of pimps and dancers, Genet's lyrical ode to machismo details the unfettered fantasies of an Algerian prisoner, a preening young buck and a sexually tormented prison officer. Despite the displays of genitalia, both flaccid and tumescent, the most erotic element in this film – some would claim in the entire history of cinema – is the billowing of cigarette smoke, passed lovingly, symbolically and enchantingly from one prisoner to another, through a small chink in a cell wall.

Ritwik Ghatak
India, 1925–76

Ritwik Ghatak was 22 years old when the Partition separated Pakistan from the newly independent India and divided the states of Bengal and Punjab along religious lines, causing the deaths of half a million people and the dislocation of some ten million more. It was the defining trauma of Ghatak's life, the powder keg for his vehement, incendiary art.

A writer and a Marxist, Ghatak became involved in the radical Indian People's Theatre Association (IPTA) in Calcutta, acting and writing plays, determined to rouse the conscience of the audience. He turned to film to expand that reach. "I wanted to use the cinema as a weapon", he wrote. "What has seemed to me a most urgent need, is to present to the Bengali people this miserable, impoverished face of divided Bengal, to make them conscious of their own existence, their past and their future."

Ghatak's first feature was *Nagarik* (*The Citizen*, 1953), about an idealistic young man's fruitless search for a job, and the poverty and misery which consume his family. Too hard-hitting for the time, it was released only posthumously, in 1977. The great Indian filmmaker Satyajit Ray mused that, had it been released at the time, *Nagarik* might have defined Bengali cinema. Instead, it was Ray's *Pather Panchali* (*Song Of The Road*, 1955) which received accolades at home and abroad.

The two men admired each other's work, and there is no need to pit them against each other, but given Ray's pre-eminence in the critical canon, and Ghatak's relative obscurity, it is worth quoting Jacob Levich on their differences: "Ray is the suitable boy of Indian film, presentable, career-oriented, and reliably tasteful. Ghatak, by contrast, is an undesirable guest: he lacks respect, has 'views', makes a mess, disdains decorum. Worst of all, he talks politics."

After a short sojourn in Bombay (where he scripted Bimal Roy's hit *Madhumati*, 1958), Ghatak returned to Calcutta and had a success with the poignant comedy *Ajantrik* (*Pathetic Fallacy*, 1957), about a taxi driver's relationship with his battered old cab. A children's film, *Baru theke paliy* (*Runaway*, 1959), followed. But it was his next film, *The Cloud-Capped Star* (1960), which crystallized his style and made his reputation. A searing melodrama about a refugee family in Calcutta, it's the story of Nita, the oldest daughter, whose self-sacrifices fail to forestall tragedy. Melding popular idioms (Bollywood melodrama, song, myth and folk tale) with an expressionist, modernist aesthetic – particularly in his use of non-naturalistic sound – Ghatak forged a cinema that was unique and unsettling, critically engaged with socioeconomic and historical realities but never in thrall to realism. Most commentators consider this to be Ghatak's masterpiece. He himself preferred *E-Flat* (1961), an ambitiously structured autobiographical film recreating his experiences of IPTA. But it was savagely attacked by the Communist press and derided by the audience. Ghatak's alcoholism dates back to this failure.

The third in his de facto "partition trilogy", *Subarnarekha* (*Golden River*) was filmed in 1962 but not released until three years later. Arguably an even greater accomplishment than *The Cloud-Capped Star*, *Subarnarekha* was rejected at the time for its reliance on melodrama and coincidence. Yet these criticisms seem trite beside the power and intensity of the film – few directors can match Ghatak's ability to express utter, unadulterated anguish. As the young writer Abhi comes to realize in the film, people do not want to hear about suffering. *Subarnarekha* was another commercial failure, and Ghatak did not make another feature until *A River Called Titash* in 1973, by which time he was fighting tuberculosis and alcoholism. In between, he did direct several documentaries, wrote quite extensively on cinema, and spent two fulfilling years teaching at the Film and Television Institute of India in Pune, where he was a significant influence on Adoor Gopalakrishnan, Kumar Sahani, Mani Kaul and Ketan Mehta, among others.

Reflecting the difficulties of its production, *A River Called Titash* is a sprawling, ragged and frustrating film, yet shot through with moments of brilliance. Two years later, his last film, *Reason, Argument And Story* (1975), featured Ghatak himself as a "broken" intellectual, an author on the rocks, consumed by alcohol and impotence, winding his way through Bengal towards his own death. The film is but semi-coherent and finds its maker for once on the brink of self-pity, but still pressing for justice, rich in longing, and searching for radical solutions not just to cinema, but to the world at large. Ghatak died in 1976 at the age of 50. TC

The Cloud-Capped Star (Meghe dhaka tara)
1960, 127 min, b/w

cast Supriya Choudhury, Anil Chatterjee, Bijon Bhattacharya, Guita De, Gita Ghatak *cin* Dinen Gupta *m* Jyotirindra Moitra

Ghatak's best-known film is a brilliantly structured melodrama about the terrible demands of poverty and family on the prospects of a young woman (Supriya Choudhury). Her tragic flaw, the sin of omission: she fails to protest at injustice to herself and her dreams, and at the hands of those she loves most dearly.

Subarnarekha (Golden River) 1965, 143 min, b/w

cast Abhi Bhattacharya, Madhabi Mukherjee, Satindra Bhattacharya, Bijon Bhattacharya, Gita De *cin* Dilipranjan Mukherjee *m* Bahadur Khan

More explicitly political than *Cloud-Capped Star*, *Subarnarekha* begins with scenes of abandonment and separation in the wake of Partition. A young orphan boy, Abhi, is adopted by the educated Bengali refugee Ishwar and his younger sister, Sita. Ishwar almost immediately quits the refugee colony where he was to teach to take up a provincial clerical post. Putting his own family's security above his people's future, Ishwar sets himself up for a terrible fall. The extraordinary climax quotes from Tagore, T.S. Eliot's *The Waste Land* and, musically, Fellini's *La dolce vita*.

Alexei Gherman
Russia (formerly Soviet Union), 1938–

Alexei Gherman had his first three films banned by the Soviet authorities. With his fourth, made in the post-*glasnost* era, he discovered an uncomfortable truth about the freedom of speech: that in their own way, critics can be as brutal as censors. Gherman's solo debut *Trial On The Road* (1971), based on the writings of his novelist father Yuri Gherman, was banned as "an ideological error" because it took a sympathetic view of Soviet POWs when they were still officially considered traitors. *Twenty Days Without War* (1976) followed a war correspondent travelling home to see his ex-wife acting in a turgid piece of Soviet propaganda. The protagonist's caustic remarks about the film-within-a-film were enough to warrant a ban.

Gherman made his third film and his one acknowledged classic, *My Friend Ivan Lapshin*, in 1982. Based on his father's stories, the film painted small-town Russia as teeming with crime and rank with squalor. After seeing the overcrowded flat in which the detective hero lives, the censor asked "Why is the apartment so poor?" and the film was shelved until 1986. Four years later, it was voted the best Soviet film of all time by national critics. Despite this success and his new post-*glasnost* freedom, the director didn't make another film for over a decade, instead dedicating his time to working with young filmmakers.

Taking seven years from script to screen, his next film *Khrustalyov, My Car* (1998) prompted mass walkouts when it was eventually shown at Cannes.

A Felliniesque tale of a denounced Red Army surgeon brought out of his gulag to save Stalin's life, the film was modernist and mesmerizing to some, but inchoate and self-indulgent to the baffled majority. Eight years later, Gherman finally ventured behind the camera again to make the sci-fi opus *Hard To Be A God* (2006). LH

Twenty Days Without War (Dvadtsat dnei bez voini) 1976, 100 min, b/w
cast Yuri Nikulin, Liudmila Gurchenko, Aleksei Petrenko, Angelina Stepanova, R. Sadykov, Mikhail Kononov *cin* Valeri Fedosov *m* Viktor Lavrov

A writer and war correspondent leaves the front line at Stalingrad during World War II and embarks on a mini-odyssey as he travels by train to a film shoot where one of his books is being adapted. The people he meets and the Russia he sees en route paint a devastating portrait of a country in the grip of a deepening malaise.

My Friend Ivan Lapshin (Moi drug Ivan Lapshin) 1986, 99 min, b/w and col
cast Andrei Boltnev, Nina Ruslanova, Andrei Mironov, Aleksei Zharkov, Zinaida Adamovich *cin* Valery Fedosov *m* Arkady Gagulashvili

Gherman's fluid camera focuses on Chief Inspector Ivan Lapshin as he pursues both the Soloviev gang and his inamorata, Natasha, while his provincial town slowly going to hell. Set in 1935, on the eve of Stalin's most terrifying purges, the film is thick with atmosphere, memorable minor details and keen observations of everyday life. Elegantly shot in sepia with splashes of colour, *Lapshin* is deliciously ripe with foreboding.

Bahman Ghobadi
Iran, 1968–

Bahman Ghobadi is the first Iranian Kurdish film director, the first to shoot an Iranian film in his native Kurdish language and the director of the first feature film to be shot in Iraq following the fall of Saddam Hussein, 2004's *Turtles Can Fly*. In between stints as assistant director to Abbas Kiarostami on *The Wind Will Carry Us* (2000) and as an actor in Samira Makhmalbaf's *Blackboards* (2000), he debuted as a writer-director with *A Time For Drunken Horses*, which shared the Camera d'Or at Cannes in 2000. *A Time For Drunken Horses* and *Turtles Can Fly* belong to a fecund Iranian cinema tradition, in which the experiences of children double as allegories or microcosms of the society at large. Both films observed a determined band of orphaned or refugee kids eking out a skeletal living at an Iraqi border, but eschewed the mawkish treatment of children discernible in the films of Majid Majidi.

In between *Horses* and *Turtles*, Ghobadi made *Marooned In Iraq* (2002), an improbably jaunty but ultimately harrowing road movie wherein an elderly man seeks out his estranged wife across the Iran–Iraq border in the aftermath of the first Gulf War. In 2006, Ghobadi made another road movie, *Half Moon*, which dealt with similar themes in its story of an elderly Kurdish musician travelling to Iraqi-Kurdistan for a final concert. JW

Turtles Can Fly (Lakposhtha hâm parvaz mikonand) 2004, 98 min
cast Shahab Ebrahimi, Faegh Mohamadi, Allah-Morad Rashtian, Rojan Hosseini, Saeed Mohammadi, Iran Ghobadi *cin* Saed Nikzat

Set in a refugee camp just before Operation Iraqi Freedom, Ghobadi's film begins with a girl jumping off a cliff to her death, and the rest of the movie leaves no doubt that the region's future is as much of a void as that which she leaps into. Observing a boy named Satellite who acts as a father figure and foreman to his fellow refugee children, Ghobadi rarely lingers on a single scene; like Satellite, the film is always charging on to the next pressing situation.

Mel Gibson
US, 1956–

The compact directorial career of megastar Mel Gibson has placed a startling dramatic emphasis on physical torment and disfigurement. In all of his films to date, Gibson has put grievous suffering centre stage, most spectacularly in his controversial *The Passion Of The Christ* (2004), an unrelentingly savage depiction of the twelve hours leading to Jesus Christ's crucifixion. (Gibson is a devout traditionalist Catholic.) In his debut feature, the mawkish if well-meaning *The Man Without A Face* (1993), Gibson starred as a kindly loner with terrible facial burns who is suspected of paedophilia. At the time, his decision to play the scarred protagonist appeared to be a pointed renunciation of his handsome leading-man features in a bid to be taken seriously as a filmmaker.

Gibson's next effort, *Braveheart* (1995), a grisly yet sentimental ode to Scots folk hero William Wallace, proved a crowd pleaser and an Oscar winner. The film closes with Wallace's excruciating death (he is hung until barely conscious, put on the rack, disembowelled on a cross and at last decapitated), a Stations of the Cross spectacle that provided a warm-up for the barbarities of Gibson's appalling 127-minute biblical snuff movie *The Passion Of The Christ*, which Quentin Tarantino compared, not unwarrantedly, to the work of Japanese shock radical Takashi Miike. The accusations of anti-Semitism which followed the film's release have persisted, and overshadowed the 2006 release of *Apocalypto*, a technically accomplished and supremely gruesome epic that portrays the last days of the Mayan civilization. JW

Braveheart 1995, 177 min
cast Mel Gibson, Sophie Marceau, Patrick McGoohan, Catherine McCormack, Alun Armstrong, Ian Bannen *cin* John Toll *m* James Horner

Winner of Academy Awards for best picture and best director, Gibson's epic second film is the gruesome creation-mythos of medieval Scottish freedom fighter William Wallace, heroically embodied by the director himself. Despite two dewy love interests (Scottish maiden Catherine McCormack and French queen Sophie Marceau), *Braveheart's* cameras focus overwhelmingly upon mortified flesh: impalings, throat-slicings, spearings and hatchetings abound.

The Passion Of The Christ 2004, 127 min

cast James Caviezel, Monica Bellucci, Maïa Morgenstern, Hristo Jivkov, Francesco De Vito, Claudia Gerini *cin* Caleb Deschanel *m* John Debney

As numerous critics have happily pointed out, Mel Gibson's brutal biblical epic focusing on the last hours before Jesus's crucifixion plays out like a gore-hungry horror movie. It includes small roles for demons and the walking dead, scenes of vicious, interminable torture that the camera never flinches from and, of course, there's the small matter of the crucifixion. Only Pier Paolo Pasolini's hugely controversial *Salo* (1975) matches it for incessant, airless sadism.

Lewis Gilbert

UK, 1920–

Throughout his long career, Gilbert has produced a wide range of films examining morality, often of a decidedly traditional variety. He graduated from child actor to assistant director, working on Hitchcock's *Jamaica Inn* (1939). After directing wartime shorts and documentaries, his first notable feature was the medical drama *Emergency Call* (1952). In 1954 he made the crime drama *Cosh Boy* and the claustrophobic wartime lifeboat story *The Sea Shall Not Have Them*. After the murder melodrama *Night Must Fall* (1955) he returned to war with *Reach For The Sky* (1956) and *Carve Her Name With Pride* (1958). *The Greengage Summer* (1961) dexterously negotiates the issue of lesbianism, and sexuality is also the theme of *Alfie* (1966), a dark fable of laddishness. Another male fantasy followed with three Bond films: *You Only Live Twice* (1967), *The Spy Who Loved Me* (1977) and *Moonraker* (1979). Offsetting these were the films sometimes dubbed Gilbert's "housewife" trilogy, *Educating Rita* (1983), *Shirley Valentine* (1989) and *Stepping Out* (1991). The first two were about women re-evaluating their lives (Julie Walters and Pauline Collins, respectively),

while the latter starred Liza Minnelli as a New York dance teacher. Gilbert's work-rate unsurprisingly slowed after that, but the gentle comedy *Before You Go* appeared in 2002. JR

Reach For The Sky 1956, 135 min

cast Kenneth More, Muriel Pavlow, Lyndon Brook, Dorothy Alison, Lee Patterson *cin* Jack Asher *m* John Addison

More plays the pilot Douglas Bader who, despite losing both legs in a flying accident, returned to become a Battle of Britain ace. But unlike some war films, this eschews schoolboy heroics. Following Bader through the accident, surgery and physiotherapy, it includes various setbacks and shows that the courage and determination that enabled him to make a comeback also made him, on occasion, a difficult character.

Alfie 1966, 114 min

cast Michael Caine, Jane Asher, Shelley Winters, Denholm Elliott, Eleanor Bron *cin* Otto Heller *m* Sonny Rollins

"My name is…" Directly addressing the audience, Caine grabbed the film and made himself a star in this downbeat story of the dream of sexual freedom turning sour with venereal disease and abortion. Apparently out of joint with the time, it was nevertheless a success and has lasted better than many "hipper" films that embraced the concept. The sequel *Alfie Darling* (1975) and remake (2004) trail in the dust.

Domestic bliss: a laddish Michael Caine addresses the audience as the eponymous Cockney philanderer in *Alfie*.

Terry Gilliam
US, 1940

Exuberant and indefatigable, Terry Gilliam has one of the most flamboyant and individual visual signatures in contemporary cinema. So much so that one can picture some of the projects that got away almost as vividly as the films he did pull off. He is a rampant fantasist and his unpredictable, subversive sense of humour keeps pulling the magic carpet out from under your feet.

From 1969, he was the sixth member of the Monty Python team, the unseen hand whose iconoclastic cutout animated sequences did so much to imprint the Python brand of surreal, absurdist humour on the public imagination. He co-directed the Pythons' first narrative film with Terry Jones. *Monty Python And The Holy Grail* (1974) was a bargain-basement medieval epic, an irreverent take on the myth of King Arthur. As filmmaking it was crude, but the comedy (Gilliam and the team co-wrote the screenplay) was savage, taboo-breaking, and wildly funny. He went solo for his next project, an adaptation of Lewis Carroll's nonsense poem *Jabberwocky* (1977) steeped in murk and mire. It wasn't quite Python, but it wasn't anything else either. If the Python influence was still evident in *Time Bandits* (1981), Gilliam was nevertheless emerging as his own man. The wildly inventive fantasy film was about a young boy yanked from suburbia by a gang of time-travelling dwarves. *Brazil* (1985) is probably Gilliam's masterpiece. Inspired by George Orwell's totalitarian allegory *1984* (and made in that very year), but inflected with the absurdity of Kafka, the film's Big Brother is bureaucracy run amok, snuffing out even the merest spark of individuality. The film was distributed by 20th Century Fox everywhere except the US, where Universal held the rights, and where studio boss Sidney Scheinberg prepared his own version, with a happy ending.

With the filmmakers and the studio at loggerheads, Gilliam took out a full-page advertisement in *Variety* magazine reading: "Dear Sid Scheinberg: when are you going to release my movie *Brazil*?" Although the compromise 132-minute version failed to take off at the box office, *Brazil*'s reputation and cult following has continued to grow, even as Gilliam's adventurously ramshackle career has been blighted with misfortune.

He was unfairly blamed when the budget doubled during production of *The Adventures Of Baron Munchausen* (1988) and though the reviews were mostly good, it was never properly distributed. You might also argue that Gilliam's unrestrained imagination could be an exhausting place to visit. His gifts for picture-making are not matched by any discipline of narrative structure. But he bounced back with *The Fisher King* (1991), his most conventional film, and the ingenious eco sci-fi *12 Monkeys* (1995). A deranged Steadicam trip, *Fear And Loathing In Las Vegas* (1998) was less successful. Then a cherished project to film *Don Quixote* fell apart after a series of natural disasters culminated in star Jean Rochefort falling ill. The whole farrago was caught on camera in Keith Fulton and Louis Pepe's tragicomic documentary *Lost In La Mancha* (2002). An expensive Miramax production, *The Brothers Grimm* (2005) was another troubled production, the director losing his cinematographer mid-shoot at the insistence of his producers. It didn't have a fairy-tale ending. While post-production wrangling held up that project, Gilliam went straight into a smaller film, *Tideland* (2005), a very dark piece that was like a Jan Svankmajer picture without the animation. The critics hated it in the US, and it was not widely seen.

One of cinema's dreamers, Gilliam has always been ready to butt his head against the system. Fascinated by history, legend and myth, he often seems out of step with Hollywood moviemaking. None of his films engages with what is commonly known as the real world except as a metaphorical prison – or literal insane asylum. His madcap escapades are among the most memorable movies of recent times. TC

Brazil 1985, 143 min
cast Jonathan Pryce, Robert De Niro, Katherine Helmond, Ian Holm, Bob Hoskins, Michael Palin, Kim Greist *cin* Roger Pratt *m* Michael Kamen

Sam Lowry (Pryce) is a clerk in a nightmarish police state who generally keeps his head down until he catches a glimpse of his dream girl (Greist). The film's true "hero" is a guerilla plumber named Tuttle (De Niro). As a piece of visionary cinema, it's Gilliam's richest and most coherent work: an astonishing amalgam of surrealism, black comedy, and what the director accurately dubbed retro-futurist design.

12 Monkeys 1995, 129 min
cast Bruce Willis, Madeleine Stowe, Brad Pitt, Christopher Plummer, Joseph Melito, John Seda *cin* Roger Pratt *m* Paul Buckmaster

An apocalyptic fantasy flick for the millennium, this vertiginous time-travelling thriller is a weird, wild ride that takes in everything from eco-angst to Hitchcock, and is loosely inspired by Chris Marker's famous 20-minute short *La jetée* (1962). As is usual with Gilliam, it's all over the place, but on this occasion the creativity is energizing, not enervating.

Tideland 2005 117 min
cast Jodelle Ferland, Jeff Bridges, Brendan Fletcher, Janet McTeer *cin* Nicola Pecorini *m* Mychael Danna

This is arguably Gilliam's boldest and darkest picture. It follows a little girl (10-year-old Ferland) who gets lost in her imagination as her junkie parents go on permanent vacation. Her only contact is with a bizarre witchy neighbour (McTeer), her lobotomized brother (Fletcher), four doll heads who are her only friends, and a talking squirrel who may or may not want the best for her. The Lewis Carroll overtones are entirely deliberate, though Flannery O'Connor is closer to the twisted spirit of the piece.

François Girard

Canada, 1963–

"**M**aking films is making music", François Girard has said. If we were to make a distinction between a director and a film artist, Girard would fall into the second category. He has made just three feature films in a twenty-year career. The first, *Cargo* (1990), has not been seen outside Quebec. But *Thirty Two Short Films About Glenn Gould* (1993) was an international hit, and picked up thirteen Genie Awards (the Canadian Oscars). Another collaboration with writer Don McKellar, *The Red Violin* (1998) was also widely praised, and scored eight Genies, as well as the Oscar for best soundtrack.

While it may be coincidental that both his best-known films have musical themes, it's significant that they are so adventurous in form. *The Red Violin* spans five centuries and continents to tell the biography of the titular instrument, and *Thirty Two Short Films About Glenn Gould* is exactly what it says it is. Girard's other projects have included an hour-long film with cellist Yo-Yo Ma playing Bach, and a concert film of Peter Gabriel's Secret World tour (where the stage director was Robert LePage). In 2005, he directed Wagner's opera *Siegfried* with the Canadian Opera Company in Toronto, and in 2007 he finally returned to the screen with an exotic historical romance, *Silk*, starring Keira Knightley and Michael Pitt. TC

Thirty Two Short Films About Glenn Gould
1993, 93 min
cast Colm Feore, Derek Keurvorst, Katya Ladan, Devon Anderson, Joshua Greenblatt *cin* Alain Dostie *m* Bach, Beethoven

The great, eccentric Canadian pianist Glenn Gould (who died in 1982) is most famous for his interpretation of the *Goldberg Variations*. Taking their cue from Bach, Girard and writer Don McKellar structure their portrait as 32 fragments or vignettes, each revealing another side to this phenomenal talent. Mixing documentary, dramatization and abstraction (including a segment from Norman McLaren's *Spheres*, 1969), the film is quite miraculous.

Amos Gitai

Israel, 1950–

Israeli cinema's premier iconoclast, Amos Gitai has made a career out of taking aim at sacred cows. Gitai first tried his hand at filmmaking while serving as a reservist during the 1973 Yom Kippur War. Working as part of a helicopter rescue team, he used an 8mm camera given to him by his mother to capture the war going on around him. He narrowly avoided death when his helicopter was shot down on his 23rd birthday. The incident would prove a formative moment: he channelled his experiences into a 1993 documentary, *Kippur: War Memories*, and later a fictional dramatization, *Kippur* (2000).

Gitai first came to prominence with *House* (1980), a documentary which traced the story of a house in West Jerusalem and its Palestinian and Israeli owners from 1948 onwards. The film was originally commissioned by the Israeli Broadcasting Authority, but was rejected on completion for its treatment of the politically sensitive issue of land rights between Israelis and Palestinians. That the film remains in circulation at all is down to the fact that Gitai rescued a sole VHS tape, from which he was able to make copies that have been shown at festivals around the world. Gitai continued the story in 1998 with *A House In Jerusalem* and again in 2006 with *News From Home*.

After another documentary was rejected by the Israeli authorities – *Field Diary* (1983), a critical examination of the Lebanon War – Gitai decamped to France with his family. He would remain there for a decade, until the beginning of the Oslo peace process between the Israelis and Palestinians seemed to herald cause for optimism. Nothing if not prolific, while in France Gitai directed a series of controversial fictional features seemingly designed to incur the wrath of conservatives back home. *Esther* (1986), *Kadosh* (1999) and particularly *Kedma* (2002) – which questioned the very existence of Israel with its dyspeptic look at the creation of the country in 1948 – all kept Gitai's name in the headlines at home and abroad. While his later films have tended towards didacticism, he has become a stalwart of the international film festival circuit, rarely making films which don't at least provide talking points. *Free Zone* (2005), for instance, cast Natalie Portman as an American Jewish girl caught between two endlessly quarrelling women, an Israeli taxi driver (Hana Laszlo) and a Palestinian woman (Hiam Abbass). Laszlo's performance won her the best actress prize at that year's Cannes Film Festival. AJa

House 1980
cin Emanuel Aldema

In *House*, Amos Gitai documents the changing inhabitants – both Israeli and Palestinian – of a West Jerusalem house from the 1948 Arab-Israeli War onwards. Undeniably moving in its depiction of the intractability of the conflict, the film successfully integrates politics and human drama.

Jonathan Glazer

UK, 1966–

Despite earning a degree in theatre design and direction and beginning his career on the stage, it was the pop videos that he made for Radiohead, Massive Attack, Jamiroquai and Blur that established

Jonathan Glazer as one of the most visually inventive young directors in the business. In the 1990s and 2000s, he also directed a number of innovative advertisements, including award-winning campaigns for Guinness and Stella Artois. Unlike the prototypical promo-director, Glazer brought intellectual depth, a feeling for character, emotion and drama, and a surrealist's delight in psychological mischief to his first two highly acclaimed features, the radically different *Sexy Beast* (2000) and *Birth* (2004). TC

Sexy Beast 2000, 88 min
cast Ray Winstone, Ben Kingsley, Ian McShane, Amanda Redman, Cavan Kendall, Julianne White *cin* Ivan Bird *m* Roque Baños

Although it came after a barrage of contemporary British gangster films, many of them featuring Ray Winstone, this one stood out for its Pinteresque script (by Louis Mellis and David Scinto) and a clutch of high-calibre performances led by a terrifying, cast-against-type (and Oscar-nominated) Ben Kingsley. To be sure, it has plenty of visual flash too, not least an underwater bank heist, but the third act doesn't quite sustain the earlier tension.

Birth 2004, 100 min
cast Nicole Kidman, Cameron Bright, Danny Huston, Lauren Bacall, Alison Elliott, Arliss Howard *cin* Harris Savides *m* Alexandre Desplat

An intrepid second effort, to put it mildly, this collaboration with Luis Buñuel's former writer Jean-Claude Carrière casts a surreal eye on the sophisticated Upper West Side set. Widow Nicole Kidman is stung by an improbable case of *amour fou* when a 10-year-old boy shows up claiming to be her husband, reincarnated. Presenting love as an enchantment – or a curse – this modern fairy tale is an extraordinarily perverse film to come out of the mainstream.

John Glen
UK, 1932–

Starting in the film industry in the 1950s, John Glen came late to feature directing. However, he started at the top with a Bond film and went on to direct four more movies in the series. He had directed action sequences for 1969's *On Her Majesty's Secret Service* but his first solo effort, *For Your Eyes Only* (1981), avoided some of the previous excesses. *Octopussy* (1983) and *A View To A Kill* (1985) were disappointing and *The Living Daylights* (1987) and *Licence To Kill* (1989), though attempting to reinvigorate the series, lacked panache. Two unexceptional films followed: the motor-racing drama *The Chequered Flag* (1990) and the actioner *Aces: Iron Eagle III* (1992). That year Glen took over *Christopher Columbus: The Discovery*, a film as bloated as Marlon Brando's fee, when Ridley Scott departed for his own rival Columbus project. The 2001 thriller *The Point Men*, which starred Christopher Lambert, was closer to home territory, but still largely disappointing. JR

The Living Daylights 1987, 130 min
cast Timothy Dalton, Maryam d'Abo, Art Malik, Desmond Llewellyn, Jeroen Krabbé *cin* Alec Mills *m* John Barry

New Bond Timothy Dalton distanced himself from Roger Moore's tongue-in-cheekisms, producing a darker character, closer to Fleming's conception. Meanwhile the post-Cold War story was more contemporary and the villains a change from the old-style megalomaniacs. The attempt to redefine a franchise that some saw as approaching its sell-by date worked on that level, but the stunts, such as tobogganing on Maryam d'Abo's cello case, sat uneasily with the newly minted realistic character.

Jean-Luc Godard
France, 1930–

Writing about *Hot Blood*, of all things, in 1957, Godard said that: "If cinema no longer existed, Nicholas Ray alone gives the impression of being able to reinvent it, and what is more, of wanting to." Later, he would refine the remark, declaring, "The cinema is Nicholas Ray". Discussing the impact of Alain Resnais in 1959, he claimed, "You can describe *Hiroshima mon amour* as Faulkner plus Stravinsky", and then went on to liken the director to Picasso. You can sense the filmmaker's creative fire in the critic's hyperbole. If cinema has a Stravinsky or a Picasso, it's surely Godard himself. Has anyone come closer to reinventing the form and dragging it into the modern age than this prodigious talent? There is a scholarly website devoted to his work. Its name: Cinema=Jean-Luc Godard=Cinema.

This indivisible association with his art is a Godardian hallmark (he appears as himself, or as a sometimes cranky, clownish variation thereof, in more than half a dozen recent films), so much so that his extraordinary *Histoire(s) du cinéma* project (1989–98), ostensibly a chronicle of the medium, emerges instead as a history of the twentieth century through the prism of Godard's autovideography. This videography comprises not only the seventy-plus films, videos and TV programmes he has authored, but the thousands of movies he made his own simply by watching them – starting with the competing German and Allied newsreels he saw in Switzerland as a child during World War II: the same pictures, but with different soundtracks ("the same fight, but different victors", as he put it).

Godard began his career as a critic, and in a sense, he still is one. What emerges from the *Histoire(s)* is a profound apprehension that cinema has failed – failed to keep pace with the twentieth century, failed to adequately reflect its horrors. War – World War II and the Holocaust, the Arab-Israeli conflct, Vietnam, Algeria and the Balkans – is a constant moral touchstone for Godard.

197

G

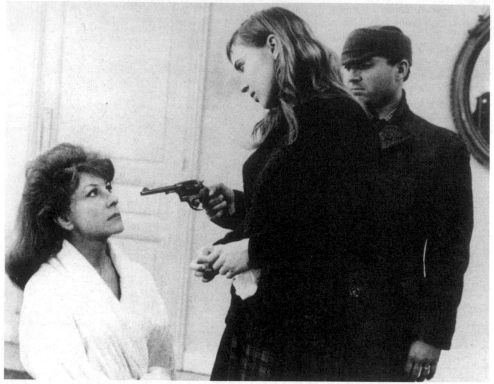

"All you need to make a movie is a girl and a gun": Godard follows his own advice in the crime thriller *Bande à part*.

Godard's critical engagement with form is another constant in his oeuvre, which has remained more radical and experimental than that of any of his *nouvelle vague* peers. That crucial disjunction between picture and sound (he and partner Anne-Marie Miéville formed a production company called "Sonimage" in the 1970s) is every bit as central to his films as his politics (which famously swung towards Maoism in the late 1960s), or such recurring themes as prostitution and imperialism. This is a body of work dense with meaning, but even at his most didactic Godard is preoccupied with Brecht and the construction of meaning. "If you understand me then I have not been clear", he says in *Notre musique* (2004), echoing an earlier remark: "To participate in the established forms [of communication] is to lose what is particular to your experience."

In these comments, far more revealing than his popular aphorisms from the early 1960s ("All you need to make a movie is a girl and a gun"; "Cinema is truth 24 times a second"; "Tracking shots are a question of morality"; "You need a beginning, a middle and an end – but not necessarily in that order"), we can begin to understand Godard's love/hate relationship with Hollywood, and why he has kept even the French film industry at arm's length. That tension is inscribed in all his witty deconstructions of genre – the thriller in *Bande à part* (Band

Of Outsiders, 1964), and the "neo-realist musical" ("that is, a contradiction in terms") in *Une femme est une femme* (*A Woman Is A Woman*, 1961). And it is itself an explicit theme in *Le mépris* (*Contempt*, 1963), his only US co-production.

Even at his most fashionable, during the boom years of the *nouvelle vague*, audiences in France were thin on the ground. It was his speed and economy – combined with profitable foreign sales – which facilitated his astonishing productivity: fifteen features and seven "sketches" (contributions to portmanteau films) between 1960 and 1967. *Les carabiniers* (*The Riflemen*, 1963) recorded fewer than 3000 ticket sales in its opening two-week run in Paris. Godard's passion, radicalism and independence made him a filmmakers' filmmaker – the invention and sheer "joie de cinéma" of the *nouvelle vague* period (1959–67) were an inspiration to (for example) Bernardo Bertolucci in Italy, Glauber Rocha in Brazil, Jerzy Skolimowski in Poland, Dušan Makavejev in Yugoslavia, Alexander Kluge in Germany and Nagisa Oshima in Japan, and were later embraced for similar reasons (but stripped of politics) by a new generation of American independents: Quentin Tarantino, Hal Hartley and Gregg Araki among them.

The *nouvelle vague* period culminated with *Weekend* (1967), the "End of Cinema", as the closing title declared. "Cinema is capitalism in its purest form … There is only one solution, and that is to turn one's back on the American cinema", he said at the time. For many it was the end of Godard. The Maoist period which followed remains his most obscure (Godard himself disparages it), and by the time of his move to video in the mid-1970s in collaboration with Anne-Marie Miéville many had been definitively alienated.

The standing of his work post-1979, when he returned to narrative feature films, remains hotly contested. Often dismissed by distributors and reviewers at the time, these more contemplative, lyrical, but still challenging and oppositional films are now ranked alongside his *nouvelle vague* period by many critics. Yet even if Godard's career breaks down into these three or four acts, it's worth remembering that his second feature, *Le petit soldat* (*The Little Soldier*, 1960), was already subversive enough to be banned for three years. *First Name: Carmen* (*Prénom Carmen*, 1983) is as romantic as anything from the 1960s. And *Histoire(s) du cinéma* takes us right back to the wildly free-associative cinephilia of Godard's journalism in the 1950s.

There are common characteristics which run through these films like DNA: a magpie fetish for quotation, pastiche and allusion, both literary and cinematic; veneration and debasement of women; the music of Beethoven; and that restlessly inquisitive modernist dialectic which counterpoints, for example, the primary Technicolor scope of Raoul Coutard's cinematography in *Le mépris* with the director's characteristically asymmetrical compositional sense. As *Passion* (1982) definitively demonstrates, Godard is a classicist who lives firmly in the present. Few filmmakers are more historically minded, or less indebted to convention. TC

A bout de souffle (Breathless) 1959, 90 min, b/w

cast Jean-Paul Belmondo, Jean Seberg, Daniel Boulanger, Jean-Pierre Melville *cin* Raoul Coutard *m* Martial Solal

Godard's first feature bursts with energy. It is radical for its bebop-style montage (including the pragmatic use of jump-cuts), its mixture of neo-realism thriller elements, and an almost anthropological fascination with its young lovers. Belmondo is a pugnacious petty criminal, Seberg the American in Paris who falls for him – but ultimately earns his contempt when she shops him for murdering a cop.

Une femme est une femme (A Woman Is A Woman) 1961, 84 min

cast Anna Karina, Jean-Paul Belmondo, Jean-Claude Brialy, Marie Dubois, Nicole Paquin, Marion Sarraut *cin* Raoul Coutard *m* Michel Legrand

A notional musical (but not really), shot in colour and in the widescreen CinemaScope format, this replays the sour romanticism of *A bout de souffle* in a lighter register. Exuberant and showy, it's a playful formal experi-

ment underscored with typical emotional rigour. Karina is Angela, who announces she wants to be with child in the next 24 hours. Her beau (Brialy) demurs, and she turns to his pal Alfred Lubitsch (Belmondo) instead.

Le mépris (Contempt) 1963, 103 min

cast Brigitte Bardot, Michel Piccoli, Jack Palance, Fritz Lang, Giorgia Moll, Jean-Luc Godard *cin* Raoul Coutard *m* Georges Delerue, Piero Piccioni

Godard's take on Alberto Moravia's *Contempt* – with Fritz Lang directing a film of *The Odyssey*, and Michel Piccoli as a screenwriter whose marriage to Brigitte Bardot is on the rocks – is a signpost in film history. Defiantly classicist in content, radically innovative in form, it represents the uneasy marriage of the sensual and the cerebral which is the essence of Godard's cinema. "You love me?" Bardot asks Piccoli. "Totally, tenderly, tragically", he replies.

Alphaville 1965, 99 min, b/w

cast Eddie Constantine, Anna Karina, Howard Vernon, Akim Tamiroff, Laszlo Szabo, Michel Delahaye *cin* Raoul Coutard *m* Paul Misraki

This is one of Godard's most fascinating hybrids: a *noir* sci-fi allegory, shot entirely in contemporary Paris, with Eddie Constantine's trench-coated Lemmy Caution trying to make sense of a surreal world where women are barcoded, dictionaries are bibles, but certain words are being written out: "conscience", "tenderness", "why"… Godard originally wanted to call it *Tarzan vs. IBM*, which sums up the dominant theme quite succinctly.

Pierrot le fou (Crazy Pete) 1965, 110 min

cast Jean-Paul Belmondo, Anna Karina, Dirk Sanders, Raymond Devos, Graziella Galvani *cin* Raoul Coutard *m* Antoine Duhamel

Perhaps the consummate Godard film of the period, this has Ferdinand (Belmondo) taking off on a spontaneous road trip with the babysitter when she turns out to be an ex-lover, Marianne (Karina). By this stage, Godard treated narrative as a thread on which to peg his myriad ideas about politics, society, women, poetry, and so on, but the larky comic playfulness and rich artistic command make it one of his most accessible ventures.

Weekend 1967, 103 min

cast Mireille Darc, Jean Yanne, Jean-Pierre Kalfon, Yves Beneyton, Jean-Pierre Léaud *cin* Raoul Coutard *m* Antoine Duhamel, Mozart

Godard's most vicious and vitriolic assault on bourgeois consumerism is an absurdist Buñuelian conceit fuelled with revolutionary ire. It begins with an unhappily married couple setting off to persuade her mother to part with her money, and ends in massacre, cannibalism and the premonition "Fin du cinéma". The centrepiece is a virtuoso eight-minute travelling shot of a traffic jam. From here there was no turning back.

Tout va bien (All Is Well) 1972, 95 min

cast Yves Montand, Jane Fonda, Vittorio Caprioli, Jean Pagnol, Pierre Oudry *cin* Armand Marco

From Godard's most polemical period, this employs Jane Fonda (!) and Yves Montand as a media couple (she's a reporter, he's a commercial filmmaker) caught up in a wildcat strike in a sausage factory. Brechtian devices serve to demonstrate and underline capitalist structures at work in the industrialized world. Co-directed by Jean-Pierre Gorin, it's a demanding theoretical discourse, more interesting to look back on than to watch.

Sauve qui peut – la vie (Slow Motion/Every Man For Himself) 1980, 89 min

cast Isabelle Huppert, Jacques Dutronc, Nathalie Baye, Roland Amstutz *cin* William Lubtchansky, Renato Berta, Jean-Bernard Menoud *m* Gabriel Yared

This was Godard's return to feature film-making after a long exile in video. He called it his "second first film", and after the theoretical works of the 1970s it's a return to basics. While political commitment remains a key concern, sexuality and art are as integral to this mature, interrogative phase in Godard's work. Here Jacques Dutronc plays one Paul Godard, an embittered or at least embattled filmmaker, and henceforth Godard's art would often take a quasi-autobiographical, first-person angle.

Passion 1982, 88 min

cast Isabelle Huppert, Hanna Schygulla, Jerzy Radziwilowicz, Michel Piccoli *cin* Raoul Coutard *m* Ravel, Fauré, Beethoven, Dvorak, Mozart

A Polish film director's attempts to recreate classical paintings for the movie camera make for one of Godard's most visually breathtaking films (even as the financiers complain there is no story). The sublime images are counterpointed with the agitation involved in (re-)creating them, while Huppert plays a stuttering factory worker trying to find some dignity in work. It's a meditation on labour, craftsmanship, aesthetics and transcendence, and marked Godard's first collaboration with cinematographer Raoul Coutard in sixteen years.

First Name: Carmen (Prénom Carmen) 1983, 84 min

cast Maruschka Detmers, Jacques Bonnaffé, Myriem Roussel, Jean-Luc Godard, Hyppolite Giradot *cin* Raoul Coutard *m* Ludwig van Beethoven

Lightly riffing on Bizet and the lovers-on-the-run crime film, this has all the best Godardian staples: lyrical sequences devoted to Beethoven; absurdist satire featuring Godard himself as crazy Uncle Jean; jump-cuts, overlapping sound and shock sound cuts; dialogue consisting of quotations and appropriations; sexual antagonism and passion.

Histoire(s) du cinéma 1989–98, 267 min

Twenty years in conception, Godard's eight-part, five-hour video essay is a magical mystery tour through the medium of cinema conducted by Godard himself. Densely allusive, with overlapping text and imagery constantly battling for our attention, it is also an autobiographical memoir, and an epitaph for cinema from one of its most ardent believers. Critics have likened it to *Finnegans Wake*, in both its scope and form, and its importance.

Michel Gondry
France, 1963–

Born in Versailles, Michel Gondry came from a strongly musical background, and began his career playing drums for the band Oui Oui. He also directed their promo videos, which were spotted by Björk. The eccentric Icelandic performer gave Gondry's prodigiously inventive ideas a global platform – starting with "Human Behaviour" in 1993 – and he would spend the next decade creating similarly mind-bending promos and television

commercials. Following in fellow videomeister Spike Jonze's footsteps (*Being John Malkovich, Adaptation*), Gondry's first two cinema features were written by Charlie Kaufman. Despite the apparently perfect match, *Human Nature* (2001), though crammed with memorable moments, was an ambitious misfire, but *Eternal Sunshine Of The Spotless Mind* (2004) achieved a near-perfect blend of form and content. After a documentary detour via the effervescent *Dave Chappelle's Block Party* (2005), Gondry returned to France for *The Science Of Sleep* (2006), a romantic fantasy starring Gael García Bernal and Charlotte Gainsbourg. MB

Eternal Sunshine Of The Spotless Mind 2004, 108 min

cast Jim Carrey, Kate Winslet, Kirsten Dunst, Mark Ruffalo, Elijah Wood, Tom Wilkinson, Jane Adams *cin* Ellen Kuras *m* Jon Brion

Michel Gondry's second feature finally proved that he could make a feature-length film as consistently innovative as any of his three-minute masterpieces. He fused a sweet-natured romantic comedy with an essay on memory as intricate as anything by Alain Resnais. Jim Carrey and Kate Winslet are wholly convincing as the former lovers who decide to wipe each other from their memories for the sake of emotional convenience, only to realize the downside the hard way.

The Science Of Sleep (La science des rêves) 2006, 106 min

cast Gael García Bernal, Charlotte Gainsbourg, Alain Chabat, Miou-Miou, Emma de Caunes *cin* Jean-Louis Bompoint *m* Jean-Michel Bernard

Gondry's first self-written feature lacks the structural cohesion of his earlier Charlie Kaufman-scripted efforts, but as a showcase for his outlandish imagination it does just fine. Gael García Bernal returns to his childhood bedroom, and his vivid, endearingly ramshackle dreams play an increasingly vital role in commenting on his life, not least when he takes an interest in his new neighbour (Charlotte Gainsbourg) and has to get to grips with maturity.

Stuart Gordon
US, 1947–

The director of three cult horror classics that expertly grafted jaw-dropping invention onto blood-soaked splatter, gore-meister Stuart Gordon got his career going in the 1970s, having founded Chicago's renowned Organic Theatre Company in 1969. His first feature was *Re-Animator* (1985), based on H.P. Lovecraft's short story "Herbert West – Reanimator", and he successfully resurrected the writer's work again the following year with *From Beyond*. He had his third hit with *Dolls* (1987), which played on the latent spookiness of children's toys, but since then, Gordon has never really managed to break out of the straight-to-video ghetto. His one opportunity to cross over into the Hollywood mainstream was scuppered after creative differences with Disney on *Honey, I Shrunk The Kids* (1989), which he was due to write and direct. However, Gordon did manage to give critics and horror cognoscenti a genuine shock in 2005 when he returned to his theatrical roots by directing a well-received film adaptation of David Mamet's combative play *Edmond*. LH

Re-Animator 1985, 95 min
cast Jeffrey Combs, Bruce Abbott, Barbara Crampton, David Gale, Robert Sampson, Gerry Black *cin* Mac Ahlberg *m* Richard Band

One of the masterpieces of 1980s horror, *Re-Animator* boasts an unbeatable synthesis of wit, invention, gory spectacle, the grandest of Guignol, the highest of camp and a severed head. Jeffrey Combs plays an archetypal mad scientist who brings the dead back to life with his magic serum. His Frankensteinian ambitions are thwarted by his professor, who covets the fluorescent elixir of life and doesn't stop, even when his head has been removed from his shoulders, until the film climaxes with a delirious zombie holocaust.

Claude Goretta
Switzerland, 1929–

If it wasn't for Claude Goretta and Alain Tanner, Swiss cinema would never get a mention in the textbooks. The son of Italian immigrants, Goretta studied law at the University of Geneva before turning to filmmaking at the British Film Institute. His name first registered in the public consciousness for the vibrant documentary short about Piccadilly night life, *Nice Time* (1957), which was co-written and co-directed with Tanner and was part of the British Free Cinema movement. Goretta then worked in television, before distinguishing himself with a series of intimate portraits of subjectivity viewed from the outside. *Le fou* (*The Madman*, 1970) charts its protagonist's growing insanity, while *L'invitation* (1973), which recalls the humanism of Renoir and was nominated for an Oscar, is an insightful comedy about an office party that goes awry. The eloquent, sensitive drama *The Lacemaker* (1977), starring Isabelle Huppert, briefly made Goretta an arthouse name, and the similarly themed *La provinciale* (*A Girl From Lorraine*, 1981) featured Nathalie Baye as a young woman from the provinces negotiating the emotional tumult of Paris. *Si le soleil ne revenait pas* (*If The Sun Never Returns*, 1987) was an atmospherically shot allegory concerning village life, superstition and the conflict between the individual and the crowd. Goretta is still active as a director, although he now works mostly for television. RA

The Lacemaker (La dentellière) 1977, 107 min
cast Isabelle Huppert, Yves Beneyton, Florence Giorgetti, Anne Marie Düringer, Renata Schroeter *cin* Jean Boeffety *m* Pierre Jansen

In what is perhaps her most complex role, as well as the one that made her name, Isabelle Huppert plays a quiet beautician, Béatrice, who falls in love with a sophisti-

cated intellectual. Few films manage to convey the silent dynamics of people attempting to relate quite as *The Lacemaker* does, making this social dilemma irreducible to pat political definitions. Béatrice is as unprepossessing yet multi-layered as Félicité, the peasant heroine of Flaubert's *A Simple Tale*.

Edmund Goulding
UK, 1891–1959

Bette Davies called him "one of the great Hollywood directors" and, after William Wyler, her personal favourite. A former actor and singer himself, and a writer and playwright before he came to Hollywood in the aftermath of World War I, Goulding was first and foremost an actors' director. At a time when the studio production line was at its height, Goulding was famous for devoting entire mornings to rehearsal. His private life was marked by hedonism: heavy drinking, drug addiction and promiscuous bisexuality. Nevertheless, he was an intelligent, cultured man, as sensitive as he was sensual.

He wrote many of his scripts in his early days at MGM, where he made breakthrough pictures with Joan Crawford (*Sally, Mary And Irene*, 1925), Greta Garbo (*Love*, 1927) and Gloria Swanson (*The Trespasser*, 1929). Not surprisingly, he was entrusted with sundry Barrymores, Garbo, Crawford and Wally Beery for the decidedly up-market, Oscar-winning, but not very good, *Grand Hotel* (1932). Switching to Warner Bros a couple of years later, he became associated with "women's pictures" such as the definitive Bette Davis melodramas *Dark Victory*, *The Old Maid* (both 1939) and *The Great Lie* (1941). Goulding's career waned along with the decline of the studio system. After switching to 20th Century Fox he made three more notable dramas, Somerset Maugham's *Of Human Bondage* and *The Razor's Edge* (both 1946), and the astonishing *Nightmare Alley* (1947). TC

Dark Victory 1939, 106 min, b/w
cast Bette Davis, George Brent, Humphrey Bogart, Geraldine Fitzgerald, Ronald Reagan, Cora Witherspoon *cin* Ernest Haller *m* Max Steiner

Bette Davis suffered mightily in four masochistic melodramas helmed by Goulding. This is the best of them, with a screenplay by Casey Robinson. She is quite magnificent as a socialite with a fatal brain tumour who falls in love with her doctor (Brent). It's an emotional blowout handled with Goulding's typically assured brisk delicacy. The final fading of the light constitutes one of Bette's most memorable moments.

Nightmare Alley 1947, 111 min, b/w
cast Tyrone Power, Joan Blondell, Colleen Gray, Helen Walker, Mike Mazurki, Taylor Holmes *cin* Lee Garmes *m* Cyril J. Mockridge

The odd one out in Goulding's filmography has a well-warranted cult reputation. Tyrone Power (with whom Goulding had made *The Razor's Edge*) gets his best ever role as a slick charlatan who talks his way up from fairground huckster to society spiritualist, but crashes back to become the lowest of the low, a carnival geek. The *noir* photography is by Lee Garmes. Jules Furthman's script is based on an even darker novel by William Lindsay Gresham.

Ashutosh Gowariker
India, 1968–

After playing supporting roles in Indian film and television for over ten years, Gowariker finally took the plunge into directing in 1993 with the mediocre thriller *Pehla Nasha*. The cops and terrorists tale *Baazi* (1995) was only marginally better. But after this faltering start Gowariker stepped back, took stock of his situation and decided to follow his heart. After a long period of struggle, he convinced his friend and *Baazi* leading man, Bollywood superstar Aamir Khan, to act in his dream project *Lagaan* (*Land Tax*, 2001). Khan also produced the film. The heady blend of cricket and colonialism was a box-office smash in India and became only the third Indian film to be nominated for the Oscar for best foreign-language film. It was followed by the critically acclaimed *Swades* (*Our Country*, 2004), which contrasted a young scientist's hi-tech environment at NASA with the simple village life to which he returns in a bid to get his childhood nanny to join him in the US. NR

Lagaan (Land Tax) 2001, 224 min
cast Aamir Khan, Gracy Singh, Rachel Shelley, Paul Blackthorne, Suhasini Mulay *cin* Anil Mehta *m* A.R. Rahman

In the late 1890s, Bhuvan, an upright villager, takes up the challenge of beating the local British rulers at their own game – cricket – in exchange for getting land taxes waived for the next three years. A loss would mean the village paying double the tax. The film cleverly combines India's passion for Bollywood with its love of cricket and is ultimately an inspirational tale about the triumph of the underdog in the best traditions of sport-themed cinema.

David Gordon Green
US, 1975–

Emerging in a period when American independent cinema has by and large been subsumed by the mainstream, David Gordon Green stands out like the proverbial sore thumb. His first feature, *George Washington* (2000), was no calling card to Hollywood. A poetic-realist reverie, it evoked the dreams and innocence of childhood in an impoverished (if sun-burnished) corner of the American South. For want of anything else to compare it to, critics cited Harmony Korine's *Gummo* (1997) and Terrence Malick's *Days Of Heaven* (1978), films radically different from each other, but which share Green's elliptical aversion to narrative and attraction to the wrong side of the tracks. Imperfect as the anal-

ogy may have been, it did Green no harm. Malick was sufficiently impressed that he produced and supplied the story for Green's third film, *Undertow* (2004).

Studying filmmaking at the North Carolina School of the Arts, Green got his first taste of the movie business working for 20th Century Fox in his summer break. Then, in 2000, with $46,000 in the bank, he wrote a screenplay, and persuaded his college friends to work on the film for free and equipment companies to lend them cameras, lights and lenses. For a film made so cheaply and so quickly (nineteen days), *George Washington* is beautiful and luxuriously slow. Like Malick, Green and his close collaborator, cinematographer Tim Orr, would shoot in the magic hour of twilight, and allow their compositions to linger.

All The Real Girls (2003) was in the same vein, mixing actors and nonprofessionals in a partly improvised, loosely strung love story. Occasionally awkward or overly cute, the film is graced with scenes of emotional insight and poetry. Nevertheless, it raised the question of where and how Green might develop his peculiar sensibility.

Undertow (2004) was an inconclusive step towards the mainstream – at least, it was his most narrative-driven film to date. Set in the poor Deep South, Malick's story was reminiscent of Davis Grubb's gothic fable *The Night Of The Hunter*, with a murderous stepfather chasing two boys down river in pursuit of a stash of gold coins. Green brings gusto to the melodrama, but his zooms, freeze-frames and jump-cuts seem to belong to another era: a Roger Corman drive-in from the mid-1970s. The result was strange, intriguing, but only half convincing.

Snow Angels (2007) found Green working across a broader canvas, adapting a small-town novel by Stewart O'Nan, and again tying his emotional epiphanies to a melodramatic form. But *Pineapple Express* (2007) was completely unexpected, a stoner buddy comedy with rising stars Seth Rogen and James Franco. TC

George Washington 2000, 89 min
cast Candace Evanoiski, Donald Holden, Damien Jewan Lee, Curtis Cotton III *cin* Tim Orr *m* Michael Linnen, David Wingo

This lyrical, burnished mood piece dogs along with a handful of kids (mostly African-American) on the wrong side of the tracks in some North Carolina backwater. A melancholy, strangely beautiful evocation of children's hopes and fears in a landscape of rusty car-wrecks and broken buildings, *George Washington* is one of those rare, memorable movies which opens up America a little bit.

Peter Greenaway
UK, 1942–

Peter Greenaway loves systems, symmetries, nomenclature, lists. But above all he loves numbers, and the number 92 in particular. He is first and foremost a painter, not just because of his Baroque sensibilities and Vermeer-like compositions, but because he prioritizes the image over the word, wanting to destroy the "tyranny of the text", the stranglehold the nineteenth-century novel still has over conventional cinema. All of Greenaway's films wilfully eschew emotion, and feeling is often exclusively supplied by his composer, who is most frequently Michael Nyman.

Working as a film editor at the Central Office of Information, Greenaway developed his interest, if not obsession, with arcane knowledge, and started making his own short films. These included *Windows* (1975), a study of people in one area who died falling from windows. In 1980 he completed his first full-length film, *The Falls*, a fictional three-hour documentary about 92 people whose surnames all begin with Fall which also enumerated 92 ways to make a film, 92 facts about bird law, and so on. Persuaded to apply a narrative formula to his preferred systematic approach, Greenaway constructed *The Draughtsman's Contract* (1982), a mischievously cerebral murder mystery which also provided information about colour symbolism and the organization of the English landscape in the late seventeenth century.

Decay and symmetry were the primary themes of *A Zed And Two Noughts* (1985), the eye-opening apotheosis of which was a threesome involving a pair of separated Siamese twins and a legless woman (who had her good leg amputated for reasons of symmetry). The naked body is a recurring image in Greenaway's work. The weakness of the flesh is often the undoing of his characters, whether due to fatalistic desire in *The Cook, The Thief, His Wife And Her Lover* (1989) or stomach cancer in *Belly Of An Architect* (1987). His films also often include an element of game-playing, which is expressed most capriciously in *Drowning By Numbers* (1988), wherein the audience is invited to spot the numbers playfully embedded into every scene. As intellectually stimulating as this countdown is, whether it actually adds up to anything is questionable.

Greenaway's fascination with games and hidden systems can also be seen in the seven colours of the rainbow motif in *The Cook, The Thief, His Wife And Her Lover*, one of the few subtleties (courtesy of his regular star cinematographer Sacha Vierny) in a film that gorges on scatology, nudity and over-ripe allegory. *The Cook* revealed a misanthropy that the director has never denied, but most audiences were prepared to forgive, in the name of political satire. However, there came a point in *The Baby Of Macon* (1993), when the lead character is systematically raped by 113 people, that Greenaway lost the goodwill of most of his viewers. Audience numbers have dwindled ever since; a crude catalogue of male sexual fantasies, *8½ Women* (1999) attracted almost no sustained interest from the public or the critics.

In recent years, Greenaway has embraced digital technology, with projects such as *Prospero's Books* (1991) and *The Pillow Book* (1996) overlaying and overloading masses of information and doing full justice to the director's magpie mind. With these films, audiences could finally experience the full eclectic intelligence of a man once described by critic Pauline Kael as "a cultural omnivore who eats with his mouth open". Attempting to destroy "the tyranny of the single image", Greenaway then created *The Tulse Luper Suitcases* (2003–04), a multimedia magnum opus that includes three feature films, as well as CD-ROMs, books, DVDs and a website. The project focuses on 92 suitcases, which are themselves Chinese boxes full of narratives. All of the *Tulse Luper* films struggled to find distribution; it looks as though his own films have become the first casualties of the death of cinema that he himself predicted. Sadly, it's now possible to think of Greenaway as Prospero, alone on an island of his own magnificent, fecund imagination. LH

The Draughtsman's Contract 1982, 103 min

cast Anthony Higgins, Janet Suzman, Anne Louise Lambert, Hugh Fraser, Neil Cunningham, Dave Hill *cin* Curtis Clark *m* Michael Nyman

In 1694 an artist is commissioned to paint views of a rich woman's country estate in exchange for sex, but his paintings soon start to yield clues that suggest her husband has been murdered. *The Draughtsman's Contract* is elegant, erotic and playful, and it's almost impossible not to be dazzled by Greenaway's brilliant erudition, fiendish game playing and fabulous way with a pun. The director is clearly very pleased with himself, too.

Drowning By Numbers 1988, 118 min

cast Joan Plowright, Juliet Stevenson, Joely Richardson, Bernard Hill, Jason Edwards, Bryan Pringle *cin* Sacha Vierny *m* Michael Nyman

By far Greenaway's most pleasurable work, if only to spot the numbers that are discreetly (and occasionally blatantly) embedded in each scene. The numerals progress from 1 to 100 in traditional order as a tale of murder, lust and water unfolds. Three women, all called Cissie Colpitts (a favourite Greenaway name), drown their husbands while the local coroner turns a blind eye. Michael Nyman's music is stunning, the cinematography by long-time collaborator Sacha Vierny is sumptuous, and the tableaux are at their most painterly. This is Greenaway squared.

The Cook, The Thief, His Wife And Her Lover 1989, 124 min

cast Richard Bohringer, Michael Gambon, Helen Mirren, Alan Howard, Tim Roth, Ciaran Hinds, Gary Olsen *cin* Sacha Vierny *m* Michael Nyman

An ornate, unsubtle allegory about gangsterism and free-market capitalism, Greenaway's best-known film takes the 1980s mantra that greed is good to its logical and literal conclusion. Michael Gambon stars as a gluttonous mobster who gorges himself on a series of feasts which are the epicurean epitome of conspicuous consumption, unaware that his wife, Helen Mirren, is devouring bookish Alan Howard in the back of his restaurant.

Prospero's Books 1991, 129 min

cast John Gielgud, Michael Clark, Michel Blanc, Isabelle Pasco, Erland Josephson, Tom Bell *cin* Sacha Vierny *m* Michael Nyman

The acres of genitals are not the only eye-popping things on display in this feast of sensual and intellectual overload. Made at a time when the CD-ROM seemed to represent the future of technology, Greenaway grasped the form with two excitable hands, overlaying text and images to dizzying effect, as pages of Prospero's beloved books are superimposed upon the screen. Less Bill Shakespeare and more Bill Gates, this is an erudite, opulent and erotic take on *The Tempest*.

Paul Greengrass
UK, 1955–

Paul Greengrass has benefited from a combination of historical events and a 1990s taste for realism. After serving his apprenticeship on hard-hitting television documentary series, he made *Resurrected* (1989), a TV-funded film about a British soldier returning from the Falklands War after years believed missing. Angry about the hypocrisy and small-mindedness of army and civilian communities alike, the film's interrogation of masculinity in modern Britain echoed the British New Wave of the 1960s. A decade later, his television documentary *The Murder Of Stephen Lawrence* (1999) won a BAFTA award for its gripping, realist depiction of the contentious case of a murdered black youth.

Earning a name for himself as a chronicler of issues vexing the British national conscience, Greengrass directed *Bloody Sunday* (2002), a docudrama about the infamous 1972 Londonderry civil rights march which ended in the shooting of marchers, political outcry and decades of legal debate. He changed direction somewhat with his first Hollywood feature, the expertly orchestrated chase thriller *The Bourne Supremacy* (2004) and its sequel, *The Bourne Ultimatum* (2007), but returned to his realist, docudrama approach – and became a hot media property in America – when he made *United 93* (2006), one of the first features to tackle the tragic events of 9/11. RA

The Bourne Supremacy 2004, 125 min

cast Matt Damon, Franka Potente, Brian Cox, Julia Stiles, Joan Allen, Gabriel Mann, Karl Urban, *cin* Oliver Wood *m* John Powell

Paul Greengrass brings the busy hand-held camera and staccato cutting of his television work to the Bourne action thriller franchise, making the aesthetic seem less like fashionable concession and more necessary to the fatal reflexes of Matt Damon's taciturn protagonist. Framed by the CIA and driven out of hiding to square himself with the suits, amnesiac Jason Bourne embarks on a nonstop chase through vivid Continental locations to the film's icebound Moscow conclusion.

United 93 2006, 111 min

cast Christian Clemenson, Gary Commock, J.J. Johnson, Polly Adams, Trish Gates, Cheyenne Jackson *cin* Barry Ackroyd *m* John Powell

A real-time account of the fate of hijacked United Airlines Flight 93, which was brought down by its passengers on September 11, 2001. The courage of those who fought back against the hijackers has been much touted as a symbol of popular resilience in the face of terrorism, but Greengrass handles his subject sensitively, without sensationalism or political moralizing. *United 93* is a powerful memorial to the victims of 9/11.

John Grierson
UK, 1898–1972

John Grierson's impact on documentary, and on the tone and reputation of British cinema, has been far-reaching. Investigating the role of the media in America in the 1920s, he began writing film criticism for the *New York Sun*, and it was in that role that he became the first person to use the term "documentary", in a review of Robert Flaherty's *Moana* (1926). Three years later, he released his own documentary film and sole directorial credit, *Drifters*, about British herring fishermen. Having founded the film unit of the British Empire Marketing Board, Grierson then spent much of the 1930s cultivating a whole generation of documentarists and overseeing such films as *Housing Problems* (1935) and *Night Mail* (1936) for the GPO Film Unit where he had bigger budgets and greater latitude.

In 1939, Grierson established the National Film Board of Canada, which is still a major force in the country's film industry. After a spell in the US, he returned to the UK where his TV show, *The Wonderful World*, showcased documentaries from around the world. His book *Grierson On Documentary* also confirmed him as a significant theorist. A tireless propagandist for the public information film, Grierson's name became synonymous with the heyday of British documentary-making, even if his purist assumptions are now increasingly challenged. His influence could be felt in the postwar British New Wave, in television documentary and in the films of Ken Loach. Grierson once wrote "I regard cinema as a pulpit". His conception of an edifying patrician realism may belong to another world, but he, nevertheless, opened up a world of experience to the eye of the camera. RA

Drifters 1929, 49 min, b/w

cin Basil Emmott

Informed by the films of Sergei Eisenstein and premiering alongside *Battleship Potemkin* (1925) at the London Film Society, this account of North Sea herring fishermen is steeped in Grierson's zeal for documentary's educational vocation. Earnest and often dynamic in its orchestration of man battling the elements, *Drifters* foreshadowed an extraordinary era of state-sponsored filmmaking.

D.W. Griffith

US, 1875–1948

Moving cinema forward from its roots in melodrama and the peepshow, D.W. Griffith refined the language of American fiction film and became the father of classical Hollywood cinema.

Born into an impoverished Southern family, the son of a Confederate Civil War hero, Griffith was a failed actor and struggling writer when he approached pioneer Thomas Edison looking for work in 1907. Edison gave Griffith a lead acting role in the short film *Rescued From An Eagle's Nest* (1907), but it was at the motion picture company Biograph that Griffith established himself as a director. He directed his first film, *The Adventures Of Dollie*, in 1908, and over the next five years, he made over 450 short films for Biograph. Nurtured in theatrical, novelistic and painterly conventions, Griffith worked to translate literary emotions and attitudes into filmic form.

Using close-ups, masks and iris shots, he broke through the proscenium arch that had restricted primitive cinema to the conventions of the theatre and established a genuinely cinematic *mise en scène*. Whether or not Griffith was the first director to actually use a close-up, his Biograph films refined the techniques of American narrative cinema. He recognized that scenes did not have to be shot in static fashion as they unfolded, but could be broken down into constituent pieces of action and then reassembled to support a particular dramatic narrative. And he and his innovative cameraman G.W. "Billy" Bitzer used storytelling control to manipulate time on screen.

Griffith coached a roster of talented stars, including Mary Pickford, Lillian and Dorothy Gish, Wallace Reid and Harry Carey, who all regularly appeared in his Biograph pictures. He also significantly extended the scope of cinema's canon, making adaptations of works by Robert Browning and Edgar Allan Poe, and filming philosophical essays like *Man's Genesis* (1912) and social problem pictures like *The Musketeers Of Pig Alley* (1912). By graduating from the standard single or two-reels to the multi-reel *Enoch Arden* in 1911, the pioneering director also helped to evolve the feature-length film in the US.

Griffith left Biograph in 1913 to focus on full-length features and made his best-known film, *The Birth Of A Nation*, two years later. Although the Civil War epic made a fortune at the box office, its racist depiction of blacks drew widespread condemnation and strong protests from the NAACP (National Association for the Advancement of Colored People). Taken aback by the response, Griffith poured his energies into his next feature, *Intolerance* (1916). The film was a plea for human compassion that threaded together stories, both lavish and intimate,

from four different historical epochs, but it appeared too complex for contemporary audiences and it was a commercial disappointment (despite its influence on directors such as Sergei Eisenstein and Fritz Lang).

Whether for their politics or their alienating scale, Griffith's epics do not now seem as engaging as his intimate dramas (the majority of which starred Lillian Gish). *True Heart Susie* (1919) found Gish's characteristically Griffithian heroine suffering amid nicely realized American settings. *Hearts Of The World* (1918) and *Broken Blossoms* (1919) were emblematic of the actress's waif-like appeal and bore a sentimental intensity that easily matched the Hollywood "women's pictures" of the 1940s and 50s. *Way Down East* (1920) was saved from moralizing by the director's facility with melodramatic narrative and Gish's committed portrayal of a woman's journey from innocence to experience, as was 1921's *Orphans Of The Storm*.

In the 1920s, Griffith became increasingly unable to connect with the decade's appetite for exotic sex and rollicking optimism, and his relationship with the studios grew more fraught. His later works also lacked the innovations of his early features, although *Isn't Life Wonderful?* (1924) arguably foresaw Italian neo-realism. Despite brief success with the talkie *Abraham Lincoln* (1930), Griffith proved incapable of making the transition to the industry of the 1930s and spent his remaining years in obscurity. However, he still deserves to be recognized as a key figure in the evolution of not just American film, but of all cinema. RA

The Birth Of A Nation 1915, 180 min, b/w

cast Lillian Gish, Mae Marsh, Henry Walthall, Miriam Cooper, Mary Alden, Ralph Lewis *cin* G.W. Bitzer *m* Joseph Carl Breil

This epic restaging of the American Civil War, based on a novel by Thomas Dixon called *The Clansman*, was a huge commercial success. Its scale, orchestration and dramatic intensity took American cinema to new levels of invention. However, its blatant racism and its veneration of the Ku Klux Klan caused widespread controversy upon its release and has continued to complicate its historical reputation.

Intolerance 1916, 163 min, b/w

cast Lillian Gish, Mae Marsh, Robert Harron, Constance Talmadge, Miriam Cooper, Alfred Paget *cin* Billy Bitzer *m* Joseph Carl Breil

A vivid and sometimes shocking tapestry of man's inhumanity through the ages, this ancient masterwork retains real power. If its sentiments are often antiquated and naïvely didactic, nevertheless Griffith's orchestration of crowd scenes in Biblical Judea is monumental, while the art direction of Babylon is a gargantuan prototype for the trumperies of 1920s DeMille. Paradoxically for the prudish Griffith, the pre-Hays Code eroticism gets pretty hot too.

Broken Blossoms 1919, 90 min, b/w

cast Lillian Gish, Richard Barthelmess, Donald Crisp, Arthur Howard, Edward Peil, George Beranger, Norman Selby *cin* Billy Bitzer

Evoking a nineteenth-century London of fogbound mews and dingy alleys, Griffith conjured an archetypal cinematic

D.W. Griffith and Lillian Gish

Lillian Gish once lobbied to have D.W. Griffith's face appear on an American stamp. The title of the silent movie star's 1969 memoir – *The Movies, Mr Griffith And Me* – indicated just how significant their experience together was to her, and the book is full of devotional prose. At the end of her life, Gish left money to the Museum of Modern Art's film library for the preservation of Griffith's work.

Gish was born into a broken home in Springfield, Ohio in 1893. She took to the stage as a child actor, together with her sister Dorothy. Something of the pathos of these early experiences found its way into Gish's trademark screen waif. Introduced to Griffith by Mary Pickford, Lillian made her first film – *The Unseen Enemy* – in 1912. Griffith would go on to mould Gish's screen style and image at the time when many of the director's protégées were making the transition from histrionic acting to a more realistic approach. As historian Eric Rhode wrote: "no one has equalled his ability to draw performances of such quicksilver grace and spontaneity out of young women."

Between 1912 and 1913, Gish and Griffith made twenty two-reelers together before *Judith Of Bethulia* (1913) gave Gish her first important role. In 1915 Gish played the key role of Elsie Stoneman in *The Birth Of A Nation*. The star's characteristic image of grace, kindness, intelligence and pluck was perfected between *Intolerance* (1916), in which hers is the hand rocking the cradle of human compassion, and *Orphans Of The Storm* (1921). While steeped in nineteenth-century melodrama, Griffith's allegiance to realism led him to draw naturalistically on the experiences of his players. On one occasion he allegedly planned a scenario based upon Gish's horror of hurting animals. She was Griffith's devotional ideal of femininity, an angel in a morally ambivalent world.

But while Griffith's sentimentality was often mawkish – as titles such as *The Great Love* (1918), *The Greatest Thing In Life* (1919) and *A Romance Of Happy Valley* (1919) suggest – *Broken Blossoms* (1919) saw Lillian Gish reaching for a clarity which belies our prejudices about the schmaltzy tenor of silent cinema. Granted, this creaky melodrama featured a gentle Chinaman giving refuge to a helpless girl victimized by her drunken father, and was entirely unprogressive in its acceptance of contemporary fears about miscegenation. But Gish's portrayal of a frightened soul gives us a being teetering on the edge of joy and self-knowledge, her pained delicate features lighting up in moments of childlike pleasure. As David Thomson put it: "she drew equally upon veins of hysteria and transcendence, abandon and purity".

True Heart Susie (1919) was a rustic conceit in which Gish played a gingham-clad girl opposite the callow youth played by Robert Harron. By contrast with the high Victorian Pollyanna ideal then being exploited by Griffith protégée Mary Pickford, Gish brought to such roles a spiritual and physical integrity that suggested she was giving her all for her art. Her poignant acting in *Way Down East* (1920) transcends its quaint views on illegitimacy and maternity. Famously climaxing on a fast-moving ice floe, the film resulted in the actor losing the sensation in her wrist, following prolonged exposure to the freezing water. Despite Griffith's Victorian sensibilities, Gish's combination of gravitas and playful intelligence has informed modern performers, from Isabelle Huppert to Emily Watson. The strong sensitive woman battling a politically and physically brutal world remains a compelling screen scenario, while the spiritual vein of melodrama that Griffith and Gish mined persisted in Janet Gaynor's work with F.W. Murnau and Frank Borzage.

The jagged, assertive poses of 1920s American cinema could not have been further removed from Gish's performances, her tiny features concisely articulating tense and inward experiences. The scene in *Orphans Of The Storm* (1921), in which she tentatively acknowledges the voice of her long-lost sister (played by Dorothy Gish) in the Paris streets, is a miracle of economy and pent-up longing. Gish was now a major star and able to command higher fees than the declining Griffith could afford, and the two amicably parted company. In King Vidor's *La Bohème* (1925) and Victor Sjöström's *The Wind* (1928) Lillian went on to deliver two of the defining performances of the silents' late flowering. This haunting and brilliant talent belonged to a gracious woman with none of the affectation or innuendo of the "Roaring 20s". While the America that emerged from World War I clamoured for sensation and superficial gesture, Griffith and Gish had committed themselves to tracing the soul's bitter passage through an imperfect world. RA

setting for moral desecration. Lillian Gish inhabits the role of a brutalized, innocent Victorian-style waif in an unprecedented and deeply moving fashion, but it's telling that Griffith rejects even the slightest hint of inter-racial romance between her character, Lucy Burrows, and Richard Barthelmess's kindly Chinese benefactor.

Way Down East 1920, 123 min, b/w
cast Lillian Gish, Richard Barthelmess, Lowell Sherman, Burr McIntosh, Edgar Nelson *cin* Billy Bitzer

A genuine case of the triumph of aesthetics over politics, this creaky plea for monogamy succeeds chiefly through Griffith's feeling for suspense – the ice-floe climax – and Gish's histrionic intensity and invention. If you can get

Victorian waif: the delicate Lillian Gish gave one of her greatest performances in Griffith's fogbound melodrama *Broken Blossoms*.

past the Sunday-school propaganda, this is an often epic backwoods morality tale held together by a mesmerizing performer.

Orphans Of The Storm 1921, 143 min, b/w

cast Lillian Gish, Dorothy Gish, Creighton Hale, Joseph Schildkraut, Frrank Losee, Catherine Emmett, Morgan Wallace *cin* D.W. Griffith

Sisters Lillian and Dorothy Gish bring earnest conviction to this historial epic in their roles of two young orphans tragically separated and thrown into the turmoil of Paris during the French Revolution. Griffith revels in the storming of the Bastille and milks every opportunity for human pathos for all it could possibly be worth.

Robert Guédiguian

France, 1953–

Robert Guédiguian once said that "tracking shots are a moral matter", a statement recalling Jean-Luc Godard's assertively political cineaste's aesthetics. His work prompted one critic to describe him as "the French Ken Loach"; few contemporary directors have such a feeling for ordinary French life.

Guédiguian is the son of an Armenian dockworker, born in the Marseilles suburb of L'Estaque – to which his films frequently return. While studying sociology in Paris, he became interested in film and radical politics. His first movie – *Dernier été* (*Last Summer*, 1980) – focused on a young unemployed man trying to break out of the poverty-stricken L'Estaque, but dying in a bungled robbery. The film's success enabled Guédiguian to finance other young directors' work. Breaking with the glossy surfaces of the *cinéma du look* that dominated 1980s French filmmaking, early Guédiguians such as *Rouge midi* (*Red Noon*, 1983) and *Dieu vomit les tièdes* (1989) explored real issues like immigration, exploitation and redundancy. *L'argent fait le bonheur* (*Money Brings Happiness*, 1992) found local women combating gangland violence and racism in their community. The solidarity between ordinary people mired in difficult circumstances recurs throughout Guédiguian's oeuvre, a mood echoed in his family of staple actors, including Ariane Ascaride (Guédiguian's wife), Jean-Pierre Darroussin, Gérard Meylan, screenwriter Jean-Louis Milesi and cinematographer Bernard Cavalié.

In 1997 Guédiguian signed a petition against France's illiberal immigration policy alongside 59 other directors. The commitment to grass-roots, as opposed to party, politics is typical of Guédiguian. His humanism has been compared to Renoir's. *L'argent fait le bonheur* even features the bridge from which the hero jumps in Renoir's Midi-set 1934 film, *Toni*. Guédiguian blends a feeling for the realities of 'les petites gens', the working class, with a nostalgic melancholy for the passing of the class-defined status quo. Unusually for a modern filmmaker, he often symbolizes this vanishing experience using the silent iris shot.

Following the popular success of the love story *Marius et Jeannette* (1997), *À la place du coeur* (*Where The Heart Is*, 1998) transplanted a James Baldwin novel to explore the impact of racial prejudice on a young woman and her black lover. *À l'attaque* (*Charge!*, 2000) was a rollicking critique of globalization. Reminiscent of Altman's *Short Cuts*, the layered *La ville est tranquille* (*The Town Is Quiet*, 2000) got behind the official version of recent Marseillaise prosperity to explore the real vicissitudes of people's lives. *Marie-Jo et ses deux amours* (*Marie-Jo And Her Two Lovers*, 2002) finds Ascaride playing a woman having to choose between a husband she loves and the harbour pilot she adores. *Mon père est ingenieur* (*My Father Is An Engineer*, 2004) reworked the nativity of Jesus Christ in Marseilles, while *The Last Mitterand* (*Le promeneur du champ de mars*, 2005) charts the final years of France's Socialist President François Mitterrand. RA

Marius et Jeannette 1997, 102 min
cast Ariane Ascaride, Gérard Meylan, Pascale Roberts, Jacques Boudet, Frédérique Bonnal *cin* Bernard Cavalié

Aside from winning Ariane Ascaride the best actress César of that year, this funny and fresh tale of an affair between a careworn supermarket cashier and a security guard (Gétard Meylan) rivalled *La haine* (1995) at the French box office, attracting 2.6 million admissions.

The Last Mitterand (Le promeneur du champ de mars) 2005, 116 min
cast Michel Bouquet, Jalil Lespert, Philippe Fretun, Anne Cantineau, Sarah Grappin *cin* Renato Berta

Away from Guédiguian's usual Marseille stomping ground and ensemble plotting and casting, this portrait of the late French president's final days still resonates with all of the director's usual humanity – despite focusing primarily on one patrician leader. Michel Bouquet earned all the plaudits for his portrayal of the president, which was both affecting and subtle, whether he was gorging on tiny birds at a kind of last supper, lecturing miners at a run-down colliery or musing on the transience of power.

Val Guest
UK, 1911–2006

The best films in Val Guest's long and varied career represent in microcosm many of the most significant strands of post-war British cinema. A canny reader of the national mood, Guest was in the right place at the right time several times over: directing Ealing-style comedy (*Miss Pilgrim's Progress*, 1949), pioneering science fiction (*The Quatermass Xperiment*, 1955), at the heart of trends using documentary approaches to drama (*The Day The Earth Caught Fire*, 1961), and at the front of the stage when British films about rock music began to change the media landscape of the 1960s (*Expresso Bongo*, 1959). He was even at the helm of *Confessions Of A Window Cleaner* (1974) – a film that epitomized the cheeky soft-porn style that flourished briefly in the 1970s – and also co-directed a James Bond movie (albeit a spoof), *Casino Royale* (1967), starring David Niven, Ursula Andress, Woody Allen and Orson Welles.

Guest was energetic and prolific, especially in the 1950s, and often notched up several films a year. At heart a popular filmmaker with a strong sense of humour, he also worked hard at integrating location filming, hand-held camerawork and a documentary-style feel into other genres, including the war film (*The Camp On Blood Island*, 1959) and the crime thriller (*Hell Is A City*, 1960). More of an audience pleaser than a critics' favourite, Guest suffered

a career nose-dive in the 1970s, hitting the bottom of the barrel with Cannon and Ball's police comedy *The Boys In Blue* in 1983. RC

Expresso Bongo 1959, 111 min
cast Laurence Harvey, Sylvia Syms, Cliff Richard, Yolande Donlan, Meier Tzelniker, Susan Hampshire *cin* JohnWilcock *m* Robert Farnon

Laurence Harvey as hustling agent Johnny Jackson steals the show from Cliff Richard's fresh-faced talent Bongo Herbert in this engaging satire on England's Tin Pan Alley. The film was adapted by Wolf Mankowitz from his hit West End musical. There's an intriguingly varied cast but what really engages is Guest's energetic picture of a Soho of spivs, strip joints and wannabes on the make as the rock generation seized control of the music business.

The Day The Earth Caught Fire 1961, 98 min
cast Janet Munroe, Leo McKern, Edward Judd, Michael Goodliffe, Bernard Braden, Reginald Beckwith *cin* Harry Waxman

With a BAFTA-winning screenplay written by Guest and Wolf Mankowitz, this low-tech Cold War thriller sees nuclear tests send the Earth off its axis towards meltdown. Londoners struggle to cope with water shortages, riots and protests as apocalypse looms. Guest's deliberately documentary feel – there is no score – cranks up the tension beautifully. This is a landmark in British sci-fi, which may acquire some additional kudos in the era of climate change.

John Guillermin
UK, 1925–

Best suited to macho subjects, after leaving the RAF Guillermin worked his way up from French documentaries to British low-budget films and TV, though the mystery *Town On Trial* (1957) was the first to rise above the ordinary. *I Was Monty's Double* (1958), the story of a decoy soldier, was an improvement, and *Tarzan's Greatest Adventure* (1959) is the most serious of the series, though *Tarzan Goes To India* (1962) returned to type. *Guns At Batasi* (1964) and *The Blue Max* (1966) marked a return to war but his later career saw several disaster movies: *Skyjacked* (1972), *The Towering Inferno* (1974) and, courting accusations of hubris, a remake of the classic *King Kong* (1976). The all-star *Death On The Nile* (1978) is among the best Agatha Christie adaptations but Guillermin then embarked on a sequel to the disastrous *King Kong* (*King Kong Lives*, 1986) which only avoided being reviled by being largely ignored. JR

The Blue Max 1966, 156 min
cast George Peppard, James Mason, Ursula Andress, Jeremy Kemp, Karl Michael Vogler *cin* Douglas Slocombe *m* Jerry Goldsmith

Guillermin's wartime flying experience made him a natural for this story of a German World War I ace whose renegade tactics infuriate his superiors, though the romantic machinations sit less easily. Unsurprisingly the aerial sequences are the most impressive part (during the shoot Guillermin would relax by taking a plane up) and Jerry Goldsmith's score is among his best.

G

Yilmaz Güney

Turkey, 1937–84

Turkey's *enfant terrible* Yilmaz Güney deserves to have his own life made into a film. Born into a Kurdish family, Güney frequently fell foul of the Turkish authorities for his political activities, and was imprisoned on a number of occasions.

Once described by American critic J. Hoberman as "Clint Eastwood, James Dean and Che Guevara combined", Güney began his career as a hugely popular action star in the 1960s during the golden age of Yeşilçam, Turkey's premier film studio. Güney was also a prominent actor in the New Turkish Cinema that emerged in that decade, as blood-soaked genre features gave way to a more contemplative, introspective cinema. His first jail sentence came in 1961 after he was found guilty of writing "subversive content" in a short story he had composed while still a student. His release after an eighteen-month sentence helped earn him a reputation as an anti-establishment figure.

Tiring of only appearing before the camera, Güney set up his own production company, Güney Filmcilik, in the mid-1960s and began directing heartfelt features about the plight of Kurds in Turkey, most notably *Umut* (*Hope*, 1970), *Aci* (*Pain*, 1971), *Umutsuzlar* (*The Hopeless Ones*, 1971) and *Agit* (*Elegy*, 1972). During this artistically creative period, Güney's run-ins with the Turkish authorities continued unabated. Arrested in March 1972 for harbouring anarchist refugees accused of a political assassination, he was released under a general amnesty in 1974 only to be re-arrested in September that year for allegedly killing a judge during a drunken brawl while filming *Endise* (*Anxiety*, 1974).

While his supporters maintained that he had been wrongfully convicted, Güney spent much of the rest of the decade behind bars. Not that it stopped him from working – he directed *Sürü* (*The Herd*, 1978), *Düsman* (*The Enemy*, 1979) and most famously *Yol* (*The Road*, 1982) from his prison cell, via precise handwritten notes to his assistant Serif Gören. It was *Yol*, a breathtakingly ambitious film that captured a Turkey still reeling from the effects of the September 1980 military coup, that finally brought him international acclaim. Güney escaped from prison in 1981 and fled to France. He died in Paris in 1984, shortly after completing his final film, *Duvar* (*The Wall*, 1983), a devastating look at life in a Turkish prison. AJa

Yol (The Road) 1982, 114 min

cast Tarik Akan, Serif Sezer, Halil Ergün, Necmettin Cobanoglu *cin* Erdogan Engin *m* Sebastian Argol, Kendal

A milestone in Turkish cinema, *Yol* shared the 1982 Palme d'Or with Costa-Gavras's *Missing*. An excoriating look at Turkish authoritarianism, the film follows five prisoners as they prepare for a week-long furlough. As the five men head off warily to cross the blue remembered hills beyond which their former lives remain, Güney paints a powerful portrait of the hardships inflicted on Turkey's diverse population by the succession of military coups in 1960, 1972 and 1980.

G

Philip Haas
US, 1944–

After getting his start as a maker of documentaries in Britain (his subjects included artists Gilbert and George), Philip Haas went on to show a proclivity for stately, occasionally quirky literary adaptations, approaching the likes of W. Somerset Maugham, A.S. Byatt and Paul Auster with respect, intelligence and an often stifling decorum. *The Music Of Chance* (1993), in which a defeated poker player and his benefactor end up conscripted to build a wall in the winner's backyard, sustained a deadpan restraint, but his later films became more overwrought. *Angels And Insects* (1995) whipped up an enjoyably ludicrous Victorian lather of entomology, class conflict and incest, but the sexually charged *The Blood Oranges* (1997) went straight to video. *Up At The Villa* (1999), with Kristin Scott Thomas as a widow ensconced at a Tuscan estate weighing her tangled romantic options, suffered from discordant acting styles, as the performers oscillated between glum passivity and eager scenery-chewing. But Haas changed gears with bracing results for *The Situation* (2006), an independently financed drama that captured the real-life horrors faced by Iraqis during wartime. JW

Angels And Insects 1995, 117 min
cast Mark Rylance, Patsy Kensit, Saskia Wickham, Kristin Scott Thomas, Annette Basland *cin* Bernard Zitzermann *m* Alexander Balanescu

Brilliant but penniless entomologist Adamson (Mark Rylance) returns from the Amazon to the Alabaster estate, where he charms the patriarch with his Darwinian erudition and wins his daughter's hand in marriage, which enrages her snobbish brother. Meanwhile, a fellow bug enthusiast (Kristin Scott Thomas) harbours thwarted feelings for Adamson… This A.S. Byatt adaptation puts base instincts – sex, violence, and copious breeding – under the microscope, while the shock revelation wriggles wetly just beneath the film's plush surfaces.

The Situation 2006, 106 min
cast Connie Nielsen, Damian Lewis, Mido Hamada, Said Amadis *cin* Sean Bobbitt *m* Jeff Beal

From a script by one-time Iraq correspondent Wendell Steavenson, this propulsive thriller was one of the earliest fictional films to be set amid the second Iraq war, and though the protagonist is a romantically confused American reporter (Nielsen), the movie is most interested in the fates of the political factions that the war created. From the ripped-from-the-headlines opening scene (based on the drowning of an Iraqi at the hands of American soldiers), the filmmakers discover much brutality and stupidity in the chaos of battle, and little in the way of hope.

Lasse Hallström
Sweden, 1946–

A gentle, humanist filmmaker who is sometimes a little too easy on the palate, Lasse Hallström is probably the most famous Swedish director aside from Ingmar Bergman – although his first success came with a very different local export. *ABBA: The Movie* (1977) was a relaxed vehicle for the famous supergroup loosely modelled on Richard Lester's freewheeling Beatles films.

Prior to the ABBA experience, Hallström had spent nearly a decade as a producer, writer and director in Swedish TV. Among his early films, the most notable are his first feature, *A Girl And A Guy* (1975), and the short *Shall We Go To My Place Or Your Place Or Each Go Home Alone?* (1973), which is included on Criterion's Region 1 DVD of his breakthrough movie, *My Life As A Dog* (1985). It was this charming, bittersweet comedy about a lonely, imaginative 12-year-old farmed out to relatives by his sickly mother which established Hallström's taste for domestic trials and tribulations, dysfunctional families, and resilient and resourceful kids – as well as his deft feel for this precarious emotional terrain and sensitivity with actors of all ages.

It earned him two Oscar nominations (as director and co-writer) and, inevitably, a one-way ticket to Hollywood, although it would be another six years before he got an American movie made. First there was a two-year commitment to bring Astrid Lindgren's *The Children Of Bullerby Village* to the screen, in two features and a TV series. Then there was a false start in America, when he was fired from the Cher/Winona Ryder vehicle *Mermaids* (1990).

Once Around (1991), which followed, suggested why he might have had problems. On the face of it this was a conventional romantic comedy starring Richard Dreyfuss and Holly Hunter, but Hallström deliberately unbalanced the material by rendering Dreyfuss's character grating and obnoxious. It bewildered audiences, and Hallström hasn't attempted anything quite as adventurous since.

The quirks in *What's Eating Gilbert Grape* (1993) were altogether cosier, and the film found a warm welcome. Since then, locked in the embrace of Harvey Weinstein, Hallström has become a reliable (or predictable) purveyor of polished middlebrow Miramax mellow-dramas. They include the underrated *Something To Talk About* (1995), the polished John Irving adaptation *The Cider House Rules* (1999), 2000's *Chocolat* (starring Juliette Binoche and Johnny Depp) and the Newfoundland-set adaptation of E. Annie Proulx's *The Shipping News* (2001). None of Hallström's latest films – *An Unfinished Life* (2004), *Casanova* (2005), *The Hoax* (2006) – really broke this well-established mould. TC

My Life As A Dog (Mitt liv som hund) 1985, 101 min

cast Anton Glanzelius, Manfred Serner, Anki Lidén, Tomas von Brömssen, Melinda Kinnaman, Kicki Rundgren *cin* Jörgen Persson *m* Björn Isfalt

Steering clear of sentimentality, this affecting memoir of a lonely child retreating into a fantasy life earned comparisons with François Truffaut's seminal *Les quatre cents coups* (*The 400 Blows*). The title is a reference to stoical young Ingemar's identification of himself with the hound Laika, the first animal sent into orbit by the Russians. One of the most successful foreign-language films of the 1980s.

What's Eating Gilbert Grape 1993, 118 min

cast Johnny Depp, Juliette Lewis, Mary Steenburgen, Leonardo DiCaprio, John C. Reilly *cin* Sven Nykvist *m* Alan Parker

Trapped in Endora, Iowa, and itching to escape his crushing (if beloved) family, Gilbert meets Becky, a runaway teen with a different perspective on things. Hallström demonstrated his shrewd eye for talent by casting the then 19-year-old Leonardo DiCaprio as Johnny Depp's mentally impaired brother in this winsome mixture of eccentricity and the mundane. It's a delicate, poignant film if you don't object to the calculation.

The Hoax 2006, 115 min

cast Richard Gere, Alfred Molina, Hope Davis, Marcia Gay Harden, Stanley Tucci *cin* Oliver Stapleton *m* Carter Burwell

Hallström and screenwriter William Wheeler fashion a smart, spry escapade out of this true story about a fake. Richard Gere plays Clifford Irving, a frustrated novelist who informs his publisher that his next book will be the authorized biography of reclusive billionaire Howard Hughes. It's such a crazy claim that everyone chooses to believe it. Channelling Hughes, even Irving convinces himself he can play this game and win.

Robert Hamer
UK, 1911–63

For a few years in the mid-1940s, it seemed as though Robert Hamer might turn out to be one of Britain's finest directors of the post-war period. The son of the character actor Gerald Hamer, he joined London Films as a clapper boy in 1934. In 1935 he graduated to editor, working on Hitchcock's *Jamaica Inn* (1939) before moving to Ealing in 1941 where he cut *The Foreman Went To France* (1942) and helped complete the screenplay for *San Demetrio, London* (1943), amongst other credits.

In 1945 he completed his first directing job, "The Haunted Mirror", an episode in the portmanteau film *Dead Of Night*. As Ealing scholar Charles Barr has noted, mirror worlds recur throughout Hamer's best work, becoming a metaphor for the repression of sexual desire amid the class- and convention-bound atmosphere of austerity Britain. In "The Haunted Mirror" a man is possessed by the spirit of his ancestor, a murderous Regency aristocrat. In *Pink String And Sealing Wax* (1945), the world of the bourgeois dinner table is countered by the libidinous energies of a Brighton tavern. In the London underworld of *It Always Rains On Sunday* (1947) it seems as though the populist quietism of the Ealing style itself is undermined by the instincts of a criminal netherworld. Star Googie Withers' assertive sexuality dominates these three films, challenging the conservatism of the post-war status quo.

Following his masterpiece *Kind Hearts And Coronets* (1949), Hamer was disappointing, suffering from the progressive alcoholism which would cut short his career. *The Long Memory* (1952) was a competent revenge thriller set amid the mud-swept flats of the Thames Estuary, starring John Mills as an embittered convict. *Father Brown* (1954) saw Alec Guinness playing G.K. Chesterton's sleuth in an intermittently effective if now creaky throwback to an earlier England. Hamer's best work continues to inspire retrospectives. RA

Kind Hearts And Coronets 1949, 106 min, b/w

cast Dennis Price, Alec Guinness, Joan Greenwood, Valerie Hobson, Audrey Fildes, Miles Malleson *cin* Douglas Slocombe *m* W.A. Mozart

The saga of an embittered heir apparent's murderous succession to the family fortune is dominated by Dennis Price as Louis D'Ascoyne and Alec Guinness in a bravura compendium of performances as his assorted victims. Steeped in the blackest humour, this is one of the most gleefully amoral films ever made.

Guy Hamilton

France, 1922–

The director of four classic Bond movies and two best-of-British war movies, Guy Hamilton's own life story has been something of an action-adventure. Born in Paris to British parents, Hamilton joined the industry aged 17 as an apprentice to a film studio in Nice. However, with the onset of World War II, he had to escape the Nazis by secretly boarding a boat to North Africa. Serving with the British forces, he later found himself back in France and lost behind enemy lines. Rescued by the Resistance, he ended up in a nervy game of cat and mouse with German soldiers searching the Breton countryside for his unit. His own war story was the same mixture of derring-do, nerve-jangling excitement and British pluck that characterized his war movies: *The Colditz Story* (1955), *Battle Of Britain* (1969) and *Force 10 From Navarone* (1978).

After the war, Hamilton worked as a sought-after assistant director, most notably on two legendary films, Carol Reed's *The Third Man* (1949) and John Huston's *The African Queen* (1951). As a director, he made the functional J.B. Priestley adaptation *An Inspector Calls* (1954) and a succession of B-movies in the early 1950s, before making his reputation with *The Colditz Story*. He could corral large casts and big budgets, and deftly manoeuvre between spectacular set pieces, pin-drop moments of heightened tension and scenes of unlikely gallows humour – the essential recipe for the James Bond franchise.

Hamilton directed the authoritative early Bond movie, *Goldfinger* (1964), with a narrative economy and believability that became his directorial hallmarks. The Bond producers turned to the action veteran when they needed someone to steady the ship on *Diamonds Are Forever* (1971) after George Lazenby unexpectedly quit and Sean Connery was drafted back in. Hamilton was also entrusted with the transition from Connery to Roger Moore on *Live And Let Die* (1973) and *The Man With The Golden Gun* (1974), successfully curbing the actor's camp excesses which later sailed the series dangerously close to the shores of parody. Whether working on Bond movies, classic war films, spy thrillers like *Funeral In Berlin* (1966) or Agatha Christie adaptations *The Mirror Crack'd* (1980) and *Evil Under The Sun* (1982), Hamilton has always been a safe pair of hands. LH

Goldfinger 1964, 112 min

cast Sean Connery, Honor Blackman, Gert Froebe, Shirley Eaton, Harold Sakata, Bernard Lee *cin* Ted Moore *m* John Barry, Monty Norman

Although it's the third film in the series, this is genuine Bond. *Goldfinger* sets the gold standard, as it were, for cool gadgets, cars with unique extras (the Aston Martin with ejector seat and missile launcher), evil henchmen (the bowler-hat-wearing Odd Job), set pieces (the Fort Knox heist), bad puns (Pussy Galore) and unbelievable sex (Bond amorously converting a lesbian to heterosexuality).

Battle Of Britain 1969, 131 min

cast Laurence Olivier, Michael Caine, Robert Shaw, Christopher Plummer, Susannah York *cin* Freddie Young *m* Ron Goodwin, William Walton

Laurence Olivier, Michael Caine and Christopher Plummer head an all-star ensemble cast of RAF heroes pitting their Spitfires and Hurricanes against German Messerschmitts in the skies above Britain during World War II. The plucky Brits have to fight against knackered old clichés, as well as the Hun, in this uncomfortably retro slice of patriotic breast beating – but the impressive pre-CGI dogfights are a testosterone-fuelled treat for action lovers.

Diamonds Are Forever 1971, 120 min

cast Sean Connery, Jill St John, Charles Gray, Lana Wood, Jimmy Dean, Bruce Cabot, Joseph Furst *cin* Ted Moore *m* John Barry, Monty Norman

After the reflective melancholy of Peter Hunt's *On Her Majesty's Secret Service* (1969), this film was effectively a statement of intent, a back-to-basics Bond movie of two-wheeled car chases and scantily clad ladies. Appropriately set in the bright, gaudy lights of Las Vegas and complete with thinly veiled references to Howard Hughes in the shape of the villainous hermit, *Diamonds Are Forever* saw the welcome return of both Hamilton and Sean Connery.

Michael Haneke

Germany, 1942–

A stern, imposing figure, Austrian Michael Haneke was the dominant filmmaker to emerge to prominence in Europe in the 1990s, probably more influential even than the universally admired Krzysztof Kieślowski. His films are rigorous and cerebral modernist texts, but they're also often provocative and controversial in their unsparing depiction of the modern condition – "a slap in the face", as he puts it.

Haneke studied philosophy at Vienna University prior to a career in the theatre and television. His first three features constitute a trilogy on emotional glaciation ("emotionale Vergletscherung") which brought him a coterie of admirers in critical circles, although they remain less well known than his later work. *The Seventh Continent* (1989), *Benny's Video* (1992) and *71 Fragments In A Chronology Of Chance* (1994) all take place in contemporary Austria, and analyse aspects of alienation in an affluent bourgeois society.

In *The Seventh Continent* a seemingly typical Viennese family go about their daily routine until they form a suicide pact. It is an action without explanation, without meaning… and as such, an appropriate response to the meaninglessness of their lives. In *Benny's Video*, a teenager takes an electric cattle prod to a friend and videotapes her death pangs, his numb amorality the product of media desensitization and emotionally absent parenting.

And in *71 Fragments* – a dress rehearsal for his masterpiece, *Code Unknown* (2000) – Haneke fashions a cubist social panorama around another violent rupture. At least one of these films is inspired by an actual news story, but in their stark, neutral, affectless style they're all symptomatic of a great moral, philosophical void. It's a world view with scant consolations.

To the extent that Haneke blames the media for this condition, and arguably privileges high culture over low, his work can seem unduly reductive and even reactionary, a charge that might be levelled at *Funny Games* (1997), whose tale of the torture and murder of a bourgeois family brought him an international audience. In 2007, he chose to extend that audience by filming a shot-for-shot English-language remake starring Tim Roth and Naomi Watts.

Haneke's stature had by now outgrown the limitations of the Austrian film industry (although his influence there is etched across many young directors), and, like Kieślowski before him, he relocated to Paris. *Code Unknown* was the inspired response to his new circumstances. Modelled on the disjointed structure of *71 Fragments*, but on an even wider scale, *Code Unknown* found a cross section of multicultural Europe rubbing shoulders but failing to connect in one Parisian avenue (or in a bravura ten-minute travelling shot).

The Piano Teacher (2001) was a lurid psychosexual scourge, based on Elfriede Jelinek's novel, and featuring an extraordinary performance from Isabelle Huppert as the perverted virtuoso. It won three major prizes at Cannes. Huppert also starred in the apocalyptic fable *Time Of The Wolf* (2003), which falls into disappointingly familiar tropes after an intensely atmospheric opening. A long-nurtured project, *Caché* (*Hidden*, 2005) found him back at his best, bearing down on the hypocrisies and repressions of the bourgeois intelligentsia who are his fondest audience. TC

Funny Games 1997, 108 min
cast Susanne Lothar, Ulrich Mühe, Frank Giering, Arno Frisch, Stefan Clapczynski, Doris Kunstmann *cin* Jürgen Jürges

It was with this self-reflexive violent entertainment (or anti-entertainment), that Haneke reached an international audience. Two home invaders torture and kill another bourgeois Austrian family, with a complicit postmodern nod and a wink to audience sensibilities. Vicious and repellent, *Funny Games* demands that viewers share the victims' pain and suffering, while chastizing their prurience and sadism in watching.

Code Unknown (Code inconnu) 2000, 118 min
cast Juliette Binoche, Thierry Neuvic, Sepp Bierbichler, Alexandre Hamidi, Ona Lu Yenke *cin* Jürgen Jürges *m* Giba Gonçalves

Subtitled "incomplete journeys to various destinations", and shot in a series of long, single takes, *Code Unknown* is Haneke's most arresting film to date, a formally adventurous, fascinating portrait of society in flux, with national borders disintegrating but economic boundaries ever more firmly entrenched. Flipping from Kosovo to child abuse, agricultural policy to racism, the film transcends its index of issues and social discontents to insist on human connections the characters themselves cannot make.

Caché (Hidden) 2005, 117 min
cast Daniel Auteuil, Juliette Binoche, Annie Girardot, Maurice Bénichou, Bernard Le Coq, Walid Afkir *cin* Christian Berger *m* Ralph Rieckermann

TV intellectual Daniel Auteuil is comfortably married to Juliette Binoche, but their cosy existence is drastically undermined when they start receiving anonymous video surveillance tapes of their home. At first they assume it's a prank, then, a threat, and then a childish drawing triggers Auteuil's conscience: he harbours a guilty secret. *Caché* is a suspense story that transcends genre archetypes; its allusions to French colonial guilt don't preclude wider understandings of racial and class divides. But the biggest schism in the film is between the face Auteuil puts on for the world and the one he can't look at in the mirror.

Curtis Hanson
US, 1945–

To get his membership of the Directors Guild of America in the mid-1980s, Curtis Hanson needed the endorsement of three members. He went to John Cassavetes ("the maverick independent"), Don Siegel ("the consummate studio director") and Sam Fuller ("who worked in both worlds").

The anecdote reveals the extent to which Hanson was already a Hollywood insider, steeped in and shaped by the auteurism of the 1960s. A photographer and film journalist, and later an assistant to Robert Towne, like so many others he turned filmmaker under the auspices of Roger Corman, co-writing *The Dunwich Horror* (1970), then writing and directing *Sweet Kill* (1971, aka *The Arousers*), an exploitation thriller with Hitchcockian elements and Tab Hunter as an impotent psycho killer.

Some years later, *The Silent Partner* (1978), which he wrote and produced but did not direct, was a considerable improvement, an ingenious heist thriller which garnered praise from Hitchcock himself. Hanson also wrote *White Dog* for Sam Fuller (1982). As a director, though, his work remained well under the radar (*The Little Dragons*, 1980; *Losin' It*, 1983), until he found his feet with a string of smartly crafted, tightly constructed suspense pictures: *The Bedroom Window* (1987), *Bad Influence* (1990), *The Hand That Rocks The Cradle* (1992) and *The River Wild* (1994), which saw Meryl Streep tackling villains on a family river-rafting holiday.

At this stage Hanson might have been regarded as a studio pro in the tradition of Don Siegel. Clever in their own way, these thrillers wouldn't hold up outside their generic conventions. *LA Confidential* (1997) is an altogether more ambitious attempt to expand on those conventions, building on the most useful elements of *film noir* to expose the social (racial, sexual) hypocrisies of Hollywood in the 1950s. That the film came only a couple of years after the Rodney King riots suggests its portrait of endemic police brutality and corruption was still very relevant. No doubt novelist James Ellroy and screenwriter Brian Helgeland deserve considerable credit, but it had been assumed that Ellroy was too intimidating, too hard-boiled for Hollywood; Hanson proved otherwise. The movie picked up nine Oscar nominations (winning two of them) and was widely recognized as the best *noir* thriller since *Chinatown* (1974).

Finally in a position to pick and choose, Hanson has pursued a commendably eclectic course. *Wonder Boys* (2000) was the sort of movie Hollywood studios don't make any more, a literate, adult dramatic comedy based on Michael Chabon's novel, and reviews were strong. *8 Mile* (2002), Eminem's fictionalized autobiography, was a complete change of pace, as were the chick flick *In Her Shoes* (2005) and the poker fable, *Lucky You* (2007). At this stage of his career, Hanson seems ready for anything. An excellent craftsman, good with actors, he seems closer to a William Wyler figure than the mavericks he admires so much. He's worked the system and come out on top. TC

LA Confidential 1997, 138 min
cast Kevin Spacey, Russell Crowe, Guy Pearce, James Cromwell, Kim Basinger, Danny DeVito *cin* Dante Spinotti *m* Jerry Goldsmith

Although they hardly know the why and the wherefore, three very different cops combine to uncover a tapestry of corruption and sleaze in 1950s Los Angeles. Featuring career-turning performances from a shrewdly picked cast, Hanson's intelligent condensation of James Ellroy's complex crime novel is a landmark in 1990s Hollywood cinema, a neo-*noir* digging into the parallax between reality and appearance in the city of dreams.

Wonder Boys 2000, 111 min
cast Michael Douglas, Tobey Maguire, Frances McDormand, Robert Downey Jr, Katie Holmes, Rip Torn *cin* Dante Spinotti *m* Christopher Young

The wonder boys of the title are an acclaimed but hopelessly lost novelist and his deliquent protégé (played by Michael Douglas and Tobey Maguire, respectively). They're unlikely heroes for a big-budget studio movie, and Hanson's engaging shaggy dog story is a rare departure from genre. Unpredictable, warm and funny, it's a rich character piece and probably his most personal film.

8 Mile 2002, 110 min
cast Eminem, Kim Basinger, Mekhi Phifer, Brittany Murphy, Evan Jones, Omar Benson Miller *cin* Rodrigo Prieto *m* Eminem, Luis Resto

An underdog story set in the Detroit rap culture, this was a star vehicle for Eminem, who acquits himself well enough as a trailer park factory worker with a gift for rhyme. A slice of blue-collar populism as irresistible as *Rocky*, the movie

updated musical traditions with some semblance of social realism (the film acknowledges poverty and deprivation, but not drugs). It was a gamble that paid off.

Robin Hardy
UK, 1939–

One-hit wonder Robin Hardy directed one of the strangest and most fervently admired British horror movies of all time, *The Wicker Man* (1973), and hardly a whisper has been heard from him since. Sending a devout cop to an isolated Scottish isle to pursue a missing-child case, *The Wicker Man* arranges an eventually combustive meeting of uptight Christian piety and lusty pagan rites, featuring an ass-slapping seduction song-and-dance by a dubbed and luscious Britt Ekland, a graveyard orgy and "fertility lessons" in which naked girls jump over fire, among other unhinged set pieces. Thirteen years later, Hardy helmed the deeply disappointing *The Fantasist* (1986), about a sexually conflicted Dublin woman whose neighbour may or may not be the local serial killer. In 2006 Hardy demanded that his name be left off promotional materials for Neil LaBute's *The Wicker Man* remake, but his own remake/follow-up, provisionally titled *Cowboys For Christ*, has been in the works for some time. JW

The Wicker Man 1973, 102 min
cast Edward Woodward, Britt Ekland, Diane Cilento, Ingrid Pitt, Christopher Lee, Lesley Mackie, Walter Carr *cin* Harry Waxman *m* Paul Giovanni

Arriving in a Scottish island community to investigate the disappearance of a young girl, a chaste, churchgoing mainland policeman (Edward Woodward) discovers a strange

Strange happenings: a fertility ritual unfolding in *The Wicker Man*.

brew of sex-soaked paganism, benevolently overseen by tweedy Lord Summerisle (Christopher Lee). Crowned by an unforgettable fiery finale, the film is an unpredictable mix of genres and tones, at once funny, chilling and thrillingly bizarre; there's been nothing like it before or since.

Mahamat-Saleh Haroun
Chad, 1961–

Wounded in the Chadian Civil War, Haroun escaped from his home country in a wheelbarrow and became an exile in France. There he studied film and journalism, and spent five years working as a reporter in Bordeaux. He directed his first short film in 1994 and his debut feature, *Bye Bye Africa*, in 1999. *Bye Bye Africa* was part-fact and part-fiction, a drama within a documentary in which the director himself played a filmmaker by the name of Haroun. It won a couple of prizes at the Venice Film Festival.

His follow-up, *Abouna* (*Our Father*, 2002), was equally sophisticated, albeit in a minimalist style. Haroun has cited directors Abbas Kiarostami, Hou Hsiao-Hsien and Takeshi Kitano as his personal favourites, and the former would certainly seem to have influenced this film. *Daratt* (*Dry Season*, 2006), a sparse but hopeful fable about a young man sent out to avenge the death of his father, was one of just seven films commissioned by theatre director Peter Sellars for his prestigious New Crowned Hope project in Vienna. TC

Abouna (Our Father) 2002, 84 min
cast Ahidjo Mahamat Moussa, Hamza Moctar Aguid, Zara Haroun, Mounira Khalil *cin* Abraham Haile Biru *m* Diego Moutapha Ngarade, Ali Farke Touré

Set in Chad, Haroun's poignant second feature is the story of two sons trying to make sense of the sudden unexplained departure of their father – who, it turns out, hasn't visited his place of work for the past two years. Their bewilderment isn't complete until they watch a movie and come away half-convinced they have spotted him on the screen. The director's spare, elliptical style is leavened with humour, music and a rich, vibrant palette.

Mary Harron
Canada, 1956–

The director of several solid, smart, if sometimes slightly stolid, features, Mary Harron is now recognized as one of the more engaging talents to have emerged from the Sundance talent pool of the 1990s. After moving from Canada to the UK in her teens, Harron co-founded *Punk* magazine and wrote for the music press and British broadsheets before beginning her film and television career at the BBC.

She cut her filmmaking teeth making segments for the up-market magazine programme *The Late Show*, short films such as "How To Make An Oliver Stone Film", and the documentary *Winds Of Change* (1994) about South Africa in the 1950s.

Harron broke into feature filmmaking in 1996 with *I Shot Andy Warhol*, which she also co-wrote. Her debut was an impressively cast indie flick based on the shooting of Andy Warhol in 1968. In this film and in her 2000 adaptation of Bret Easton Ellis's notorious slasher novel *American Psycho*, Harron demonstrated a knack for depicting the frictions between distinct social milieux and competing subcultures. She also displayed a documentarian's eye for period detail and a BBC-trained director's ability to tell a story simply, but well.

Returning to the biopic, Harron delved deeper into the past with *The Notorious Bettie Page* (2005). This lavish, charming, but slight film traces the early life of America's first bondage pin-up, a sweet-natured, God-fearing girl from Nashville who became a notorious sex icon in the 1950s and part of a Senate pornography investigation. LF

I Shot Andy Warhol 1996, 100 min
cast Lili Taylor, Jared Harris, Martha Plimpton, Stephen Dorff, Lothaire Bluteau, Danny Morgenstern *cin* Ellen Kuras *m* John Cale

This typically mid-1990s offbeat, indie pic casts a half-nostalgic, half-cynical eye back to the 1960s. The "I" of the title is the radical, man-hating feminist and author of *The S.C.U.M. Manifesto* Valerie Solanas (intensely portrayed by the ever-excellent Lili Taylor), who really did earn her fifteen minutes of fame by shooting Andy Warhol (Jared Harris) at his Factory studio in 1968.

American Psycho 2000, 101 min
cast Christian Bale, Justin Theroux, Josh Lucas, Samantha Mathis, Chloë Sevigny, Reese Witherspoon, Bill Sage *cin* Andrzej Sekula *m* John Cale

This adaptation of Bret Easton Ellis's famously brutal and gruelling novel divided viewers neatly between those who felt the book had been castrated and those who felt Harron had improved on the text by jettisoning the ultraviolence in favour of social satire and ambiguity. Featuring a snarling, splendidly creepy performance by Christian Bale, who turns the main character's monologues about MOR rock stars into masterful soliloquies of banality, *Psycho* remains droll yet troubling viewing that dissects rather than celebrates Ellis's misogynistic book.

Hal Hartley
US, 1959–

Esoteric and experimental, yet drawn to fictional narrative and comedy, Hal Hartley is inevitably a marginal figure. One of the few doggedly independent filmmakers to emerge in the US in the 1990s, Hartley enjoyed a measure of success with his ironic comedies *The Unbelievable Truth* (1989), *Trust* (1990) and *Simple Men* (1992), but fell out of favour as the decade progressed and his work took on a more academic feel.

The son of an ironworker, Hartley set his first three features in suburban Long Island, where he grew up. Despite this strong sense of place, and their limited means (his feature debut, *The Unbelievable Truth*, was shot in eleven days for just $75,000), his films are not naturalistic.

Strongly influenced by Jean-Luc Godard (Hartley has also cited that supreme farceur, Preston Sturges, and the rigorous moralists Bresson and Dreyer), he developed an instantly identifiable style based on laconic, yet highly polished, repartee delivered in a disaffected, deadpan monotone by a repertory company of fashion-plate bohemians including Martin Donovan, Bill Sage, Robert Burke, Parker Posey and his first muse, Adrienne Shelly.

Likely reflecting his own experience as a working-class artist and intellectual, Hartley gets comic mileage out of the contrast between quotidian settings, melodramatic plot twists, and his characters' bent for intense philosophizing, as well as their matter-of-fact approach to vaguely taboo topics such as abortion, pornography, rebellion and nonconformity. This paradoxical disconnection extends to his penchant for tragicomic farce, and to his eccentric, schizoid characters. In *The Unbelievable Truth*, the enigmatic Josh (Robert Burke) is variously rumoured to be both a priest and a murderer (in fact he's neither). In *Amateur* (1994), Isabelle (Isabelle Huppert) is an ex-nun turned pornographer and, she says, a virgin nymphomaniac.

From the first, the nonconformist Hartley has regularly applied himself to short films, where he is even more free to doodle and experiment. In *Flirt* (1993) he even shot the same script in three different ways, with three different casts in three different countries. Yet despite this desire to innovate, there is a suspicion that his formalism has become mannered. With the exception of the impressive *Henry Fool* (1997), since *Amateur* Hartley's films have become less engaging, and more conceptual, with typically idiosyncratic genre scenarios: horror in *No Such Thing* (2001), sci-fi in *The Girl From Monday* (2005). Still a prolific director in the twenty-first century (recent projects have included 2006's *Fay Grim*, an espionage-themed sequel to *Henry Fool*), he has retained his independence and established his own digital distribution company, Possible Pictures. Since *Simple Men*, he has also composed his own scores, sometimes under the alias Ned Rifle. TC

Trust 1990, 106 min

cast Adrienne Shelly, Martin Donovan, Merritt Nelson, John MacKay, Edie Falco, Gary Sauer *cin* Michael Spiller

When high-school dropout Maria announces she's pregnant, her father drops dead on the spot – and her mother blames Maria. It's only when she meets the strong, intense, dangerously sincere Matthew that Maria begins to really

think about her life – but can she trust a man who despises television? A terse, furious, funny picture, written to within an inch of its life.

Simple Men 1992, 105 min

cast Robert Burke, William Sage, Karen Sillas, Elina Löwensohn, Martin Donovan, Mark Chandler Bailey *cin* Michael Spiller *m* Ned Rifle

Two brothers – a criminal and a bookworm – search for their father, a 1960s anarchist on the run, in upstate New York, finding few answers, but more trouble and desire. Hartley's most conspicuously Godardian film plays with convention to exuberant effect (there's even a dance sequence à la *Bande à part*). The fashion-plate philosophizing is very watchable, even if Hartley's methods are already beginning to show diminishing returns.

Henry Fool 1997, 137 min

cast Thomas Jay Ryan, James Urbaniak, Parker Posey, Maria Porter, Kevin Corrigan *cin* Michael Spiller *m* Hal Hartley

An emotional, socially attuned statement, *Henry Fool* is a scabrous portrait of a marginal artist/hustler and his influence on the Grim family, notably the shy Simon and his promiscuous sister Fay. Dense, complex, erratic, hilarious, tragic and disgusting, it remains Hartley's most ambitious work to date, the one picture where he truly seems to be challenging himself, not just playing with formal conceits.

Anthony Harvey
UK, 1931–

Harvey's filmography is not large, or consistent in theme or quality, yet a couple of his films stand out, marked by the performances he draws from the actors.

His facility with actors is perhaps the result of his RADA training. The adopted son of actor Morris Harvey, Anthony played the young Ptolemy in *Caesar And Cleopatra* (1945) before moving into editing, working with the Boulting Brothers and Kubrick, among others. In 1967 he shot the racial drama *Dutchman* in six days for £20,000 and on the strength of it was offered *The Lion In Winter* (1968). Harvey was unfazed by the very literary historical drama and star casting, and gained an Oscar nomination. He followed this with *They Might Be Giants* (1971), a quirky yet touching film about a man who believes he is Sherlock Holmes. Katharine Hepburn, whom Harvey had first worked with on *The Lion In Winter*, starred in his fine TV version of Tennessee Williams's *The Glass Menagerie* (1973). *Eagle's Wing* (1978) was an effective British Western with an international cast, but *Players* (1979), a tennis/love story set at Wimbledon and featuring famous players of the time, was a misfire. After *Richard's Things* (1980), a quietly effective look at the fallout when a widow discovers that her husband was having an affair, Harvey ended his features career with the quirky comedy *Grace Quigley* (1985), again starring Katharine Hepburn. JR

The Lion In Winter 1968, 137 min

cast Peter O'Toole, Katharine Hepburn, Anthony Hopkins, John Castle, Nigel Terry *cin* Douglas Slocombe *m* John Barry

It is Christmas 1183 and the riven families of the French and English courts jockey for position as the dying Henry II prepares to name his successor. Filmed on location, the chilly mood is decidedly unfestive. James Goldman subtly expands his original stage play but the film is mostly notable for a set of powerhouse performances and one of John Barry's finest scores, evoking period music without aping it.

Henry Hathaway

US, 1898–1985

Henry Hathaway has many classics to his credit. The son of theatrical folk, he entered the film industry as a child actor in Allan Dwan Westerns. After military service in World War I, he became an assistant to directors Frank Lloyd, Josef von Sternberg and Victor Fleming.

Hathaway began directing Randolph Scott Westerns in 1932, gaining a reputation for efficiently rendered, sterling action in films such as *The Lives Of A Bengal Lancer* (1935). *Peter Ibbetson* (1935) followed Gary Cooper's passion for Ann Harding beyond the grave, allegedly impressing the surrealists. In the 1940s Hathaway worked with producer Louis de Rochemont at 20th Century Fox on the semi-documentaries *The House On 92nd Street* (1945), *13 Rue Madeleine* (1946), *Call Northside 777* (1948). These established a semi-realist cycle of post-war crime pictures with a far greater emphasis on location shooting. The best (and the weirdest) of Hathaway's crime movies is undoubtedly *Kiss Of Death* (1947) with Richard Widmark, in his debut role, creating one of *film noir*'s most chillingly extreme psychopaths. The scene in which he terrorizes a fellow criminal's wheelchair-bound mother before pushing her down stairs still packs an unnerving punch.

In the 1960s Hathaway was the studios' action director of choice. He directed three-fifths of the super-Western *How The West Was Won* (1962), and was chosen by John Wayne to helm his vanity horse opera *True Grit* (1969). But Hathaway waded through a lot of chaff in the course of his career and close inspection of his oeuvre suggests fewer director's choices than miracles of collaboration. RA

The Lives Of A Bengal Lancer 1935, 109 min, b/w

cast Gary Cooper, Franchot Tone, Richard Cromwell, Guy Standing, C. Aubrey Smith, Kathleen Burke *cin* Charles Lang *m* Herman Hand, Rudolph G. Kopp

In this rousing action movie set on British India's northwest frontier Gary Cooper plays Lieutenant Alan McGregor, torn by conflicting allegiances to self and regiment as he and his comrades protect the border against the threatening Afghan prince Mohammed Khan. Good clean fun.

The House On 92nd Street 1945, 88 min, b/w

cast William Eythe, Lloyd Nolan, Signe Hasso, Gene Lockhart, Leo G. Carroll, Lydia St Clair, Harry Bellaver *cin* Norbert Brodine *m* David Buttolph

Made with the cooperation of the FBI and introduced by J. Edgar Hoover himself, this low-key account of government agents going after Nazi spies foregoes the use of big-name stars in favour of naturalistic performance and tireless attention to procedure.

Kiss Of Death 1947, 98 min, b/w

cast Victor Mature, Richard Widmark, Brian Donlevy, Coleen Gray *cin* Norbert Brodine *m* David Buttolph

When the wife of jailed robber Nick (Victor Mature) commits suicide, he decides to give evidence about his accomplices in order to secure his release. Unfortunately, at the subsequent trial the psychotic Tommy Udo (Richard Widmark) is found not guilty. Shot in New York and Sing Sing, this is a surprisingly disturbing film that sets a sentimental view of family life against grittily depicted and extremely violent crime.

Howard Hawks

US, 1896–1977

Howard Hawks was the ultimate Hollywood pro, and the leading independent director of his day. In a directorial career stretching from 1926 to 1970, he made over forty features, but never more than two with the same studio. He was his own producer, and never allowed himself to be trapped by long-term contracts. He worked in every major genre, and produced classics in each of them.

The French auteurist critics put him in the highest pantheon, alongside Alfred Hitchcock and Orson Welles. Yet Hawks was the least pretentious of great filmmakers. His style is transparent and unobtrusive; he didn't want the aesthetics to distract from the characters. He once told John Wayne, "Duke, if you can make three good scenes in this picture and don't annoy the audience the rest of the time, you'll be good. And if I make five good scenes, and don't annoy the audience, I think I'll be good."

Nor did Hawks take credit as a screenwriter, although it's clear from the recurring themes and motifs in his movies how closely he worked with first-rate writers such as Jules Furthman, William Faulkner, Ben Hecht, Charles Lederer, Nunnally Johnson, Dudley Nichols and Leigh Brackett. Early in his career Hawks developed certain storytelling stratagems to which he remained faithful. He didn't like to play emotions straight, but would present them obliquely. He'd skew a tragic scene towards comedy. He believed in stories, but shied away from cliché. He would always look for the new twist, an unexpected wrinkle, "to have some fun", as he put it. It's an instinct which gives pictures made sixty years ago a fresh, modern spin.

Hawks studied engineering as a young man, and in many respects that's how he approached storytelling. Yet it was the revelation of character which really excited him. He liked understatement, found virtue in stoicism ("Who's Joe?" asks Cary Grant when one of his closest friends dies in the line of duty in *Only Angels Have Wings*, 1939). But Hawks was also among the first directors of the sound era to shake his actors out of polite theatricality. He loved overlapping speech, and what he called "three-cushion" dialogue (after pool). Cross-purposes make for strong dramatic situations and comic misunderstanding. In *His Girl Friday* (1939) Cary Grant and Rosalind Russell rattle through their lines so fast they set a new record (240 words a minute).

Although he made screwball comedies (*Bringing Up Baby*, 1938), musicals (*Gentlemen Prefer Blondes*, 1953), and assisted on a horror movie (*The Thing From Another World*, 1951), Hawks most often specialized in what today we would call "action films", featuring gangsters, cowboys, detectives, aviators and racing drivers. Yet for all his Hemingwayesque mythomania, as a director Hawks was uninterested in action per se, and invariably despatched his second unit director to film those sequences. By today's standards his movies (save for the screwballs) feel decidedly leisurely. The real action takes place indoors, in the exchange of looks and words, the studied (yet relaxed and intuitive) evaluation of character. Few filmmakers were as sensitive to group dynamics, or as preoccupied with male friendship, often spanning the generations.

Hawks espoused (and identified with) an idealized, ritualized masculinity which undoubtedly spoke to the adulatory young auteurist critics who grew up on the very genres Hawks ennobled. Its characteristics were professionalism, courage and grace under pressure, camaraderie, resourcefulness, self-reliance, (self-) respect. Hawks worked repeatedly with such men's men as Gary Cooper, Humphrey Bogart and John Wayne, but tempered their heroic status by emphasizing their responsibility to the group, mentoring younger men – Montgomery Clift in *Red River* (1948), Ricky Nelson in *Rio Bravo* (1959) – and looking after the old – Walter Brennan in *To Have And Have Not* (1945) and many others.

He has been championed by feminists for the forthright, independent-minded women in his films, and he showcased a long line of admirable actresses, including Louise Brooks, Frances Farmer, Katharine Hepburn, Jean Arthur, Rosalind Russell, Barbara Stanwyck and Angie Dickinson. He more or less invented Lauren Bacall and gave Rita Hayworth her first break. That said, these women are virtually interchangeable faces of the Hawksian Woman, and her quality is usually vouchsafed by earning parity with the Hawksian hero on his terms. That is, by subjugating her womanly emotionalism to become "one of the boys".

As critic Robin Wood has pointed out, the comedies provide the flip side to this essentially conservative, patriarchal paradigm. Time and again, in *Bringing Up Baby, I Was A Male War Bride* (1949)

and *Monkey Business* (1952), Cary Grant is cruelly mocked and humiliated, stripped of his clothes and his dignity, the deadpan butt of an irrational cosmic joke. Thus, it can be said that the comedies apologize for the dramas.

Yet as Hawks matured, the comedy and drama strands came together; definitively so in his masterpiece, *Rio Bravo*, a leisurely, affectionate Western as funny and as serious as anything he ever made. The film was, according to Jean-Luc Godard, "a work of extraordinary psychological insight and aesthetic perception", but Hawks made it in such a way that his psychological insights could pass unnoticed. As Godard clarified, Hawks "succeeded in fitting all that he holds most dear into a well-worn subject". Hawks himself liked *Rio Bravo* so much that he essentially spent his final decade of filmmaking replaying the same characters, themes and motifs over and over again, in *Hatari!* (1961), *El Dorado* (1966) and his final film, *Rio Lobo* (1970). TC

Scarface 1932, 90 min, b/w
cast Paul Muni, Ann Dvorak, Karen Morley, Osgood Perkins, Boris Karloff, C. Henry Gordon *cin* Lee Garmes, L. William O'Connell *m* Adolph Tandler

A fateful "X" motif marks the spot in Hawks's seminal gangster film, an un-fond portrait of Al Capone, played as a primitive thug by Paul Muni. Unlike several Cagney movies from the period, there is no grudging respect for the criminal here; Hawks and screenwriter Ben Hecht draw parallels with the Borgias, even insinuating an incest theme. Remade and updated by Brian De Palma fifty years later, but more faithfully than you might suppose.

Twentieth Century 1934, 91 min, b/w
cast John Barrymore, Carole Lombard, Walter Connolly, Roscoe Karns, Etienne Giradot, Ralph Forbes *cin* Joseph August

This screwball classic is a spirited satire of self-dramatizing theatrical types, with Barrymore in his element as self-styled genius Oscar Jaffe, a Broadway impresario with an ego as big as the Great White Way. Hawks let Carole Lombard cut loose as Jaffe's greatest protégée, Lily Garland, and between them they helped establish the genre's breakneck pace. The dialogue is by crack team Ben Hecht and Charles MacArthur.

Bringing Up Baby 1938, 102 min, b/w
cast Cary Grant, Katharine Hepburn, Charles Ruggles, May Robson, Barry Fitzgerald, Walter Catlett, Fritz Feld *cin* Russell Metty *m* Roy Webb

"The love impulse in man often reveals itself in terms of conflict", pronounces psychiatrist Dr Lehman (Feld). Certainly that's true in the cinema of Howard Hawks. This is another expertly plotted screwball farce, with madcap Katharine Hepburn locating the beast in Cary Grant's much abused paleontologist, who only wants to recover his intercostal clavical. Baby is a leopard. Remade in 1972 by Peter Bogdanovich as *What's Up, Doc?*

Only Angels Have Wings 1939, 121 min, b/w
cast Cary Grant, Jean Arthur, Richard Barthelmess, Rita Hayworth, Thomas Mitchell, Allyn Joslyn *cin* Joseph Walker *m* Dimitri Tiomkin

A pilot himself, Hawks made a number of credible dramas about flyers. Scripted by Jules Furthmann, this was

H

the richest of the lot, with Cary Grant heading a small aviation company charged with delivering the mail over the Andes. The romance between the aloof Grant and headstrong Jean Arthur set the template for Bogart and Bacall and many of Hawks's subsequent screen lovers; indeed in many ways this is the template for his later glories.

His Girl Friday 1939, 92 min, b/w

cast Cary Grant, Rosalind Russell, Ralph Bellamy, Gene Lockhart, Porter Hall, Helen Mack *cin* Joseph Walker *m* Morris W. Stoloff

Hawks had the inspired idea to take Hecht and MacArthur's newsroom comedy play *The Front Page* and transform star reporter Hildy Johnson into a woman (Rosalind Russell), thus injecting a sexual dynamic into the proceedings. Cary Grant, again, is her ex-husband and editor, Walter Burns, and Bellamy is wickedly typecast as a stuffed shirt, Hildy's new fiancé. You could break your neck just trying to keep up with their repartee.

To Have And Have Not 1945, 100 min, b/w

cast Humphrey Bogart, Lauren Bacall, Walter Brennan, Hoagy Carmichael, Dan Seymour, Marcel Dalio *cin* Sid Hickox *song* Hoagy Carmichael

Legend has it that Hawks made a wager with Ernest Hemingway that he could make a film of any of his novels, even this one. In the end, he retained little more than the broadest outline and the title, preferring to fashion his own, superior version of 1942's *Casablanca*, with Humphrey Bogart and Lauren Bacall "fishing" off Martinique. Sparks fly, and the chemistry is palpable: "You know how to whistle, don't you Steve? Just put your lips together and blow."

The Big Sleep 1946, 114 min, b/w

cast Humphrey Bogart, Lauren Bacall, John Ridgely, Martha Vickers, Dorothy Malone *cin* Sid Hickox *m* Max Steiner

This classic Raymond Chandler adaptation is all about style and atmosphere. Less neurotic than the best *films noirs* (Hawks was probably too well-adjusted for the genre), it's much more interested in the Bogie and Bacall rematch than in anything so mundane as a plot. By now they were an item and the movie was fashioned around them as a kind of courtship comedy with corpses. Hawks reportedly lost track of who killed who in the meantime.

Red River 1948, 133 min, b/w

cast John Wayne, Montgomery Clift, Walter Brennan, Joanne Dru, John Ireland, Noah Beery Jr *cin* Russell Harlan *m* Dimitri Tiomkin

This is *Mutiny On The Bounty* on the cattle trail. Even John Ford acknowledged that it was Hawks who drew out John Wayne's first great performance as tyrannical cattledriver Tom Dunson. Method man Montgomery Clift represents a different, softer generation, but stands his ground as Dunson's adopted son Matt Garth. It's another essential study in self-respect and responsibility, and universally acknowledged as one of the finest Westerns ever made.

Rio Bravo 1959, 141 min

cast John Wayne, Dean Martin, Angie Dickinson, Walter Brennan, Ricky Nelson, Ward Bond *cin* Russell Harlan *m* Dimitri Tiomkin

Another essential Western and the director's definitive masterpiece. Hawks was unhappy with the sight of town sheriff Gary Cooper begging citizens for help in *High Noon*. In *Rio Bravo*, John Wayne relies on his deputies: a cripple, a drunk and a young gunfighter. This was Hawks's first film after a three-year sabbatical in Europe, and you can sense his pleasure at being back among friends.

Among friends: John Wayne's deputies, Walter Brennan, Dean Martin and Ricky Nelson, enjoy a sing-along in *Rio Bravo*.

Hatari! 1961, 157 min

cast John Wayne, Elsa Martinelli, Hardy Kruger, Red Buttons, Gérard Blain, Michèle Girardon *cin* Russell Harlan *m* Henry Mancini

Hawks and his favourite screenwriter, Leigh Brackett, recycle many of their favourite scenes and set-ups in this congenial entertainment set in the world of African big game hunting. Although the title is Swahili for "danger!" and the stars performed many of their own stunts, the only real tension here is sexual, and even that is played for laughs. Wayne again stars, this time with Red Buttons, Elsa Martinelli and a pet leopard. If it ain't broke, don't fix it.

El Dorado 1966, 127 min

cast John Wayne, Robert Mitchum, James Caan, Charlene Holt, Michele Carey, Arthur Hunnicutt *cin* Harold Rosson *m* Nelson Riddle

A remake of *Rio Bravo*, to be sure, but with a less claustrophobic ambience and a poignant autumnal feel. John Wayne is back, this time with Mitchum as "a tin star with a drunk pinned on" (the Dean Martin role) and James Caan as the young buck Mississippi (a variation on Ricky Nelson's Colorado). The gentle, comic sensibility suggests the kind of Western Yasujiro Ozu might have made.

Todd Haynes
US, 1961–

One of the leading lights of the New Queer Cinema movement in the early-1990s, Haynes is also, in many ways, a feminist director perennially fascinated by the structures that define a woman's place in society. He was, for a while, one of America's most controversial filmmakers, loathed by the religious right and The Carpenters.

Aged just 9, Haynes made his first short film, a version of *Romeo And Juliet*, on Super 8 and played both lovers himself. He continued this independent small-scale approach in college and had his first brush with controversy with *Superstar: The Karen Carpenter Story* (1987). Re-enacting the singer's doomed battle with anorexia using a cast of Barbie dolls and handcrafted cardboard sets, the film was withdrawn after Richard Carpenter obtained a "cease and desist" order (Haynes had used the duo's songs without permission). The controversy surrounding his next film, *Poison* (1991), went all the way to Washington when the American Family Association wished hellfire and damnation upon the National Endowment for the Arts for giving public money to a movie containing "explicit porno scenes of homosexuals involved in anal sex".

Despite the fact that *Poison* became a liberal *cause célèbre* and won the Grand Jury Prize at Sundance, it took Haynes four long years to find funding for his next project, the extended AIDS metaphor *Safe* (1995). Critics, even admiring ones, were perplexed by the filmmaker's story of a suburbanite (Julianne Moore) who becomes allergic to the twentieth century and seeks help from a New Age guru. Some suggested that Haynes should have been more clinical in his diagnosis

of her disease and the efficacy of alternative medicines, but most regarded *Safe* as a mesmerizing and cerebral take on how illness informs identity. *Velvet Goldmine* (1998) played like a multicoloured, amped-up antidote to the white, antiseptic stillness of *Safe*. The strutting peacock world of 1970s glam rock was inventively and exuberantly celebrated as a Utopia of cross-dressing and sexual experimentation, and Haynes abandoned his previous strict directorial control in favour of a hedonistic flurry of self-indulgence.

For *Far From Heaven* (2002), Haynes thankfully gathered in the reins once again. A painstaking pastiche of the "women's pictures" of Douglas Sirk, the film forged the same themes, narratives and super-saturated look that had defined the German director as an auteur in the 1950s. Haynes and cinematographer Edward Lachman fastidiously studied every frame of *All That Heaven Allows* (1955) to faithfully recreate Sirk's lush, autumnal palette. *Far From Heaven* is a sumptuous homage to one of the two directors who have informed Haynes's political and directorial sensibilities. It also satisfyingly completes the connection to the other great influence on Haynes's work, Rainer Werner Fassbinder, who had already doffed *his* cap to *All That Heaven Allows* in *Fear Eats The Soul* (1974).

In 2007, Haynes completed a long-cherished project, a biopic of Bob Dylan, *I'm Not There*, in which several actors play various incarnations of his Bobness, including the distinctly female Cate Blanchett. No one can ever accuse Haynes of lacking ambition, or indeed imagination. LH

Poison 1991, 85 min

cast Edith Meeks, Larry Maxwell, Susan Norman, Scott Renderer, James Lyons, John R. Lombardi *cin* Maryse Alberti *m* James Bennett

Haynes switches constantly and inventively between three stories in *Poison*: "Hero" is a teen flick about a troubled youth who kills his father and flies out of the window; "Horror", a 1950s B-movie pastiche about a scientist who discovers the human sex drive in liquid form, drinks it and turns into a monster; and "Homo", which provoked the wrath of America's religious Right, is a harrowing, Jean Genet-inspired tale of prison life and male rape.

Velvet Goldmine 1998, 124 min

cast John Rhys Myers, Ewan McGregor, Christian Bale, Toni Collette, Eddie Izzard, Emily Woof *cin* Maryse Alberti *m* Carter Burwell

By his own admission, Haynes's problem is that he wants to put too much into his movies. Here, he bolts a *Citizen Kane* structure and an homage to Oscar Wilde onto the unwieldy story of a David Bowie-like rock star (Jonathan Rhys Meyers) who fakes his own death to escape the trappings of fame. While Rhys Meyers fits the part, Ewan McGregor as an Iggy Pop clone is far too blokey to be androgynous and comes across like a camp brickie.

Far From Heaven 2002, 107 min

cast Julianne Moore, Dennis Quaid, Dennis Haysbert, Patricia Clarkson, Viola Davis, James Rebhorn *cin* Edward Lachman *m* Elmer Bernstein

Suburban 1950s housewife Julianne Moore uncovers her husband's homosexuality and begins a chaste relationship with her black gardener. Confounding expectations, Haynes concentrates on the latter relationship, a theme Douglas Sirk had tackled five decades earlier in race-relations drama *Imitation Of Life* (1959). This leaves frustratingly little space for the one story Sirk could never have explored explicitly: gay love. Beyond the delights of the film's visual splendour, Haynes adds little to a sub-genre already brimming with subtext.

Amy Heckerling

US, 1954–

In an otherwise chequered career, Bronx-born Amy Heckerling has gifted audiences with two standard-bearers of the teen movie: the ribald and bittersweet ensemble comedy *Fast Times At Ridgemont High* (1982) and the California tonic *Clueless* (1995), which reimagined the good-hearted meddler of Jane Austen's novel *Emma* as a shopaholic high-schooler. However, Heckerling also helmed the quippy, tiresome gangster farce *Johnny Dangerously* (1984), made a half-hearted attempt to recapture the magic teen demographic with the university-set *Loser* (2000) and steered two instalments of the ventriloquized-infant *Look Who's Talking* franchise, though she wisely jumped ship once gabby animals began edging out the gabby babies. JW

Fast Times At Ridgemont High 1982, 92 min

cast Sean Penn, Jennifer Jason Leigh, Judge Reinhold, Phoebe Cates, Brian Backer, Ray Walston, Nicolas Cage, Forest Whitaker *cin* Matthew F. Leonetti

Scripted by 25-year-old Cameron Crowe, Heckerling's first feature remains remarkable even in the post-*American Pie* era for an offhand sexual frankness that's neither moralistic nor self-consciously outrageous. It also provided an early glimpse of many a future star: Jennifer Jason Leigh, Nicolas Cage, Forest Whitaker and, of course, Sean Penn as the mischievous yet oddly beatific surfer dude Spicoli, whose stoner greeting "Aloha Mr Hand" became an enduringly popular T-shirt slogan.

Clueless 1995, 98 min

cast Alicia Silverstone, Stacey Dash, Brittany Murphy, Paul Rudd, Donald Faison, Elisa Donovan, Wallace Shawn *cin* Bill Pope *m* David Kitay

Centred on an effervescent performance from Alicia Silverstone (formerly known only as the babe from the Aerosmith videos), Heckerling's savvy Jane Austen update pokes affectionate fun at its spoiled but sweet heroine, arranges her mild and edifying comeuppance, compiles a glossary of nouveau teen slang and blithely delivers a benevolent moral. All this plus a taboo-busting stepsibling romance!

Monte Hellman

US, 1932–

A cult figure for European cinephiles but sadly neglected in his own country, Monte Hellman was the existentialist of the exploitation circuit.

When both philosophies fell out of fashion in the 1980s Hellman's career petered out, and save for a brief association with Quentin Tarantino during the development of *Reservoir Dogs* (1992), he's remained tied to the achievements of the late 1960s and early 70s.

Almost inevitably, it was Roger Corman who gave him his shot. An investor in Hellman's theatre company, Corman told him the writing was on the wall when the building was torn down to make way for a cinema in the late 1950s. Hellman made his directorial debut with *Beast From Haunted Cave* in 1959, laboured alongside Francis Coppola, Jack Hill and others on *The Terror* (1963), then took off for the Philippines with Jack Nicholson to shoot *Back Door To Hell* and *Flight To Fury* (both 1964, the latter scripted by Nicholson from a Hellman story idea).

Whenever possible Corman liked to squeeze a second film out of his productions, so, having agreed to let Hellman and Nicholson make a Western, *Ride In The Whirlwind* (1965), on location in Utah, he persuaded them to go straight into *The Shooting*, with eighteen days apiece and a week of prep in between. Along with a third Western, the spaghetti-flavoured *China 9, Liberty 37* (1978), these stark, nihilistic, ambiguous B-movies remain Hellman's most fruitful attempts to wrestle meaning – or rather, meaninglessness – out of American genre cinema. *The Shooting* was also the first of four films with actor Warren Oates – a collaboration which brought out the best in each of them.

On the back of his critical reputation in Europe and the opening of the gates to young filmmakers after *Easy Rider*, Hellman was invited to make *Two-Lane Blacktop* (1971) for Universal. Announced as "the movie of the year" by *Esquire* and "an instant classic" by *Rolling Stone* even before it opened, this wilfully inconclusive car race movie crashed at the box office and only developed its strong cult following years later.

Hellman hasn't made another film with a Hollywood major since, although in typically piecemeal fashion he did edit Peckinpah's *Killer Elite* (1975), step in to finish *The Greatest* (1977) and *Avalanche Express* (1979) when their original directors died, shoot second unit on *Robocop* (1997) and executive produce *Reservoir Dogs*.

Silent Night, Deadly Night 3 (1989) was hardly a fitting last hurrah, but the previous year's *Iguana* was an altogether more intriguing effort, a bizarre cross between *The Tempest* and *Phantom Of The Opera*. Sadly it too was hampered by production difficulties and went virtually unseen. TC

Ride In The Whirlwind 1965, 82 min

cast Cameron Mitchell, Millie Perkins, Jack Nicholson, Katherine Squire, George Mitchell *cin* Gregory Sandor *m* Robert Jackson Drasnin

The first of two legendary, laconic "existentialist" Westerns directed by Hellman for Roger Corman back to back, this was written by its star, Jack Nicholson. It's the bleak tale of three cowpokes who are mistaken for outlaws by a bloodthirsty posse and reduced to criminality to survive. *The Shooting*, which followed, was even less conventional, an enigmatic, confusing picture written by Carole Eastman, and closer to Antonioni than to John Ford.

Two-Lane Blacktop 1971, 101 min

cast James Taylor, Warren Oates, Laurie Bird, Dennis Wilson, David Drake, Rudoph Wurlitzer *cin* Jack Deerson *m* Billy James

The road (to nowhere) movie was a quintessential 1970s trip, and this is about as stripped down as it gets. Singer James Taylor and Beach Boys drummer Dennis Wilson are The Driver and The Mechanic respectively, taking all comers in their souped-up 55 Chevy. Their automated cool is contrasted with Warren Oates's gabby desperation as GTO, a pompous square and a loser, but a loser capable of carrying the movie to enduring cult status.

Cockfighter 1974, 83 min

cast Warren Oates, Richard B. Shull, Harry Dean Stanton, Ed Begley Jr, Laurie Bird, Troy Donahue *cin* Nestor Almendros *m* Michael Franks

The subject matter may be near the knuckle – the fights are for real – but this Corman exploitation curio is fascinating, and ultimately quite moral. Contrary to what you might expect, it's also often funny, with a light touch that can probably be ascribed to Charles Willeford (*Miami Blues*), who adapted his own novel for the film. Warren Oates is great as the obsessive Mansfield, who lives for the sport and has taken a vow of silence, but the film has a strong documentary aspect too.

Frank Henenlotter

US, 1950–

Writer, director and editor Frank Henenlotter's cult horrors are like the man himself – brash, irrepressible, manic and irreverent. Raised on trashy B-movies in Manhattan grind houses, he began making them himself after finding "producers dumb enough to back my personal sleazy obsessions". The warped cartoon *Basket Case* (1982) announced the indie auteur's arrival, and won him the hearts of gore-hounds around the world. *Basket Case 2* (1990) and *Basket Case 3: The Progeny* (1992) replaced the original's mean-streets atmosphere with a freakier backdrop and extreme comedy overkill. His second feature *Brain Damage* (1987) is his best, and the self-explanatory *Frankenhooker* (1990) is similarly offensive fun. His latest mission is rescuing favourite exploitation and sexploitation obscurities and releasing them on his "Sexy Shockers From The Underground" DVD label. AJ

Basket Case 1982, 89 min

cast Kevin Van Hentenryck, Terri Susan Smith, Beverly Bonner, Robert Vogel, Diana Browne *cin* Bruce Torbet *m* Gus Russo

Mutant Siamese twin Belial is carried about in a basket by his normal brother Duane. He is determined to take sick revenge on the doctors who separated them. This is a

thoroughly entertaining, gruesome and nasty no-budget creature discomfort.

Brain Damage 1987, 89 min

cast Rick Herbst, Gordon MacDonald, Jennifer Lowry, Theo Barnes, Lucille Saint-Peter, Vicki Darnell *cin* Bruce Torbet *m* Gus Russo, Clutch Reiser

In this psycho-delic tale, a boy is preyed upon by a parasitic being that injects him with an addictive hallucinogen in return for food in the form of human brains. *Brain Damage* succeeds as a meditation on drug culture, a visceral shocker and a mind-blowing, pitch-black comedy.

Mark Herman

UK, 1954–

Notwithstanding a terrible late Dudley Moore vehicle called *Blame It On The Bellboy* (1992), Mark Herman is best known for a pair of films in which musical performance becomes a redemptive instrument for beleaguered working-class characters. In *Brassed Off* (1996) – which many heralded as a grittier precursor to *The Full Monty* (1997) – a miners' brass band practices for a big competition at the same time that their colliery is under threat of closure, while in *Little Voice* (1998) a painfully shy young woman (Jane Horrocks) undergoes a stunning transformation whenever she opens her mouth to sing. (The latter film is adapted from Jim Cartwright's play *The Rise And Fall Of Little Voice*, which catered to Horrocks' astonishing gifts for vocal mimicry.) Unfortunately, both movies combine clichéd caricature with heavy-handed moralizing, and Herman as a writer-director is far too fond of the cloying close-up and the contrived melodramatic showdown. The football-themed *Purely Belter* (2000) entertained a few British punters upon its release, but probably didn't create any new converts to Herman's partly gritty, partly feel-good social realist strain of filmmaking. JW

Little Voice 1998, 97 min

cast Jane Horrocks, Michael Caine, Ewan McGregor, Jim Broadbent, Brenda Blethyn *cin* Andy Collins *m* John Altman

The eponymous L.V. (Jane Horrocks) is a meek, mousy introvert, except when she's singing along to her dear departed dad's old records, when she belts out uncannily accurate impersonations of Judy Garland, Marlene Dietrich and Shirley Bassey. Her blowsy gargoyle of a mother (Brenda Blethyn) and a low-rent talent scout (Michael Caine, oozing sleaze from every pore) decide to cash in on L.V.'s talents in Herman's broad, mawkish comedy, which only sizzles when Horrocks takes the stage.

Werner Herzog

Germany, 1942–

"Filmmaking is athletics over aesthetics", says the indefatigable Werner Herzog, whose

A dangerous mixture: Werner Herzog and Klaus Kinski

If the relationship between a star and director can be like a marriage, then Herzog and Kinski were undoubtedly the Burton and Taylor of their day. They didn't just make movies together, the duo seemed to be involved in their own private competition – the lunatic Olympics – to see who could out-mad the other. Combustible, often inseparable, Herzog later described their union as being like "two critical masses that result in a dangerous mixture when they come into contact". Herzog threatened to shoot Kinski on the set of *Aguirre, Wrath Of God* (1972) and years later seriously planned to fire-bomb his home. He would have succeeded, if hadn't been for Kinski's pet dog. Klaus, in return, regularly ranted at the director and thrust a sabre at Werner's neck on the set of *Cobra Verde* (1987). In his autobiography he accused Herzog of treachery, sadism, dim-wittedness, megalomania and, most hurtful of all, a lack of talent. The director, in return, began his documentary of his favourite actor, *My Best Fiend* (1999), with extended footage of the thesp breaking off a stage performance to roundly and protractedly abuse the audience. If their tempestuous relationship has since overshadowed their work, then they only had themselves to blame.

They first met when Herzog was a teenager, terrified like the rest of the residents of a Munich boarding house when the actor moved in for a few months. The sight of Kinski foaming at the mouth, destroying the bathroom and assorted furniture must have remained in the director's mind when casting his fourth movie, *Aguirre, Wrath Of God*. For Herzog, Kinski represented the human being at his most atavistic, not just uncivilized but untamed, more than once referring to him as "the beast". He cast him as a vampire in *Nosferatu The Vampyre* (1979) and a man driven to madness in *Woyzeck* (1979), but it was really in the middle of wild nature that the flaxen-haired, wild-eyed actor seemed most at home. In *Aguirre*, he was both primal and primate, almost as authentically simian as the monkeys who desert his raft. In *Fitzcarraldo* (1982) he was the classic Herzog leading man, quixotic, obsessive and not unlike Herzog himself. In *Cobra Verde* both director and star seemed like a couple revisiting the good times to keep them together, going on a second honeymoon by repeating the glories of *Aguirre*. It didn't succeed. The troubled shoot sparked irreconcilable differences and they never worked together again.

Despite the shouting matches and the death threats, there was a bizarre form of mutual dependence. Herzog has since said that their roles often merged. Kinski claimed that he literally called the shots: "every scene, every angle, every shot is predetermined by me". And yet without Herzog, there is nothing in Kinski's bulging CV that comes as close to greatness as the leads in *Aguirre* and *Fitzcarraldo*. Right up until his death of a heart attack in 1991, his regular employers were the makers of low-grade schlock like *Asylum Erotica* (1971) and *Crawlspace* (1986). Herzog might have been the only director to see the genuine warmth in the actor, rather than the overheating fury. LH

astonishing body of work is evidence of a director with the physical and psychological fortitude of an iron-man triathlon runner. Herzog's is a cinema of extremes: of climate, circumstance and human endurance. He knows a thing or two about outer limits. Born in Munich in the midst of World War II, Herzog grew up in Sachrang, a remote village on the mountainous border with Austria. Often freezing and always hungry, and living with no running water, plumbing or even mattresses, Herzog experienced a childhood that an outside observer might see as miserable, but he recalled it ecstatically to Paul Cronin in *Herzog On Herzog*. "Everyone I know who spent their early childhood in the ruins of post-war Germany raves about that time", he said. "It was anarchy in the best sense of the word. There were no ruling fathers around and no rules to follow. We had to invent everything from scratch."

To a great extent Herzog also invented his filmmaking career from scratch. With no formal training and very little money, he set up Werner Herzog Filmproduktion to produce his first short, *Herakles* (1962), and all his subsequent films. Being only 19 at the time, Herzog was significantly younger than his New German Cinema contemporaries, who included Rainer Werner Fassbinder, Wim Wenders and Volker Schlöndorff.

Herzog's films have always been fascinated by the cruelties of man and nature, and by trauma, hardship and chaos. Over the course of his many documentaries, he has chased mirages in the Sahara for *Fata Morgana* (1970), journeyed to a volcanic Caribbean island on the brink of exploding for *La Soufrière* (1977) and, in *Little Dieter Needs To Fly* (1997), he took former pilot and Vietnam POW Dieter Dengler back to the Laotian jungle from which he had made a harrowing, miraculous escape. Dramatic landscapes like these become as much part of the psychology of Herzog's films as the interaction between the characters, which has contributed to the director's well-developed image as the romantic visionary of

New German Cinema.

The director's fiction films are marked by his experiences of documentary making, and employ the rigour of a Method actor in realizing a vision. Herzog placed all bar one of his cast under hypnosis for *Heart Of Glass* (1976); he cast Bruno S., a man who had spent most of his young life in mental institutions, as the teenager introduced into society after years of total isolation in *The Enigma Of Kaspar Hauser* (1974); and he recruited hundreds of indigenous Indians to assist his crew in dragging a steamboat over a mountain in the Amazon for *Fitzcarraldo* (1982). Perhaps the greatest testament to Herzog's inflexible will, however, is the fact that he managed to make five films with the highly irascible egomaniac Klaus Kinski. The actor's frenzies, both on and off-camera, electrify Herzog's documentary about their turbulent relationship, *My Best Fiend* (1999), wherein Herzog confirms the famous tale that he threatened to shoot Kinski if he walked out on the unfinished *Aguirre, The Wrath Of God* (1972), but quashes the legend that he actually directed Kinski from behind the barrel of a gun. "Every grey hair on my head I call Kinski", the director averred.

Herzog has called the German New Wave directors of the post-war era "orphans who had no teachers", but he acknowledged his German forefathers in making *Nosferatu The Vampyre* (1979), an update of F.W. Murnau's silent masterpiece. He also gave Kinski seventeen minutes of nefarious screen time as the befanged title character. His final collaboration with Kinski was on the epic but somewhat disjointed African adventure *Cobra Verde* (1987).

Since *Cobra Verde*, Herzog has focused almost exclusively on a fascinating documentary career, with the exception of the disappointing drama, *Invincible* (2002), about a Jewish strongman in 1930s Berlin. His documentaries include the apocalyptic *Lessons Of Darkness* (1992), shot in the Kuwaiti desert after the first Gulf War, and *Grizzly Man* (2004), shaped from the eighty hours of video footage left behind by the late Timothy Treadwill, a quintessentially Herzogian figure who lived and died among grizzlies in Alaska. JW

Aguirre, The Wrath Of God (Aguirre, der Zorn Gottes) 1972, 93 min

cast Klaus Kinski, Cecilia Rivera, Ruy Guerra, Helena Rojo, Del Negro, Peter Berling *cin* Thomas Mauch *m* Popol Vuh

In his first fractious collaboration with Herzog, wild-eyed Klaus Kinski plays a power-mad sixteenth-century explorer, a megalomaniac in search of the fabled city of El Dorado who is slowly undone by fever, tribal incursions and his delusions of grandeur. From its stunning first shot of ant-like human voyagers descending the Andes to its final hallucinatory rain of monkeys, the film is an indelible journey into the heart of darkness; it is Herzog's richest achievement.

The Enigma Of Kaspar Hauser (Jeder für sich und Gott gegen alle) 1974, 110 min

cast Bruno S., Walter Ladengast, Brigitte Mira, Willy Semmelrogge, Gloria Dör, Volker Prechtel, Ennos Patlas *cin* Jörg Schmidt-Reitwein

Based on a true story, *Enigma* is about a mysterious young man who appeared in Nuremburg one morning, unable to speak but in possession of a note that claimed he had spent his life imprisoned in a cellar. In Herzog's devastating fable, Kaspar Hauser, played by the mesmerizing Bruno S., proves a puzzle to the nineteenth-century scientists, doctors and rational minds who try to analyze him, but eventually end up making entertainment out of him.

Stroszek 1976, 108 min

cast Bruno S., Eva Mattes, Clemens Scheitz, Buckhard Driest, Pitt Bedewutz, Wilhelm von Homburg *cin* Ed Lachman *m* Chet Atkins, Sonny Terry

Herzog's affinities with Fassbinder are clearest in the toughness and empathic pessimism of this shaggy dog story, in which an eccentric trio – including alcoholic street performer Bruno and battered prostitute Eva – trade a violent Berlin for the bleak, barren Railroad Flats of Wisconsin. The film's last act is a miniature masterpiece of absurdist despair that manages to pull off an unlikely stroke of visual symbolism – locating twin black holes of existential dread in the eyes of a dancing chicken.

Nosferatu The Vampyre (Nosferatu: Phantom Der Nacht) 1979, 103 min

cast Klaus Kinski, Isabelle Adjani, Bruno Ganz, Roland Topor, Walter Ladengast, Dan Van Husen *cin* Jörg Schmidt-Reitwein *m* Popol Vuh

Herzog famously unleashed thousands of painted rats into the town square of Delft in Holland for this sinuous, gorgeously photographed homage to F.W. Murnau. It is a recognizable scion of the original but is nonetheless sui generis. Klaus Kinski's brief but indelible turn as the vampire is justly famed, while Bruno Ganz's Jonathan Harker is a pitifully pale and clammy index of corrupted flesh and spirit.

Klaus Kinski: a crazed obsessive up the Amazon in *Fitzcarraldo*.

Fitzcarraldo 1982, 137 min

cast Klaus Kinski, Claudia Cardinale, José Lewgoy, Miguel Angel Fuentes, Paul Hitscher, Grande Otélo *cin* Thomas Mauch *m* Popol Vuh

In a role first intended for Jason Robards (with Mick Jagger originally cast as his "retarded actor sidekick", according to Herzog), Kinski plays a crazed yet often endearing Irish adventurer. Brian Fitzgerald is a rabid Enrico Caruso fan who is determined to build an opera house in the middle of the Amazon jungle. The film's spectacularly arduous shoot was captured in Les Blank's *Burden Of Dreams* (1982), the definitive making-of documentary.

Peter Hewitt

UK, 1965–

P eter Hewitt's film career has been neither an excellent adventure nor a bogus journey, but like most of his movies, resides somewhere in the middle. After winning a BAFTA for his short film, *The Candy Show* (1990), he brought a zesty visual imagination to the teen comedy sequel *Bill & Ted's Bogus Journey* (1991). Although this infectiously silly comedy is clearly no *Citizen Kane*, it is matchless in a career that has specialized in adapting children's favourites, from the iffy *Tom And Huck* (1995) to the totally heinous *Garfield* (2004) (to borrow some *Bill & Ted* speak).

At least Hewitt inflected *The Borrowers* (1997) – a whimsical story about little people who live under the floorboards and steal all the everyday things that mysteriously go missing – with the same charm and chutzpah as his most excellent debut feature. The comedy *Whatever Happened To Harold Smith?* (1999) briefly became tabloid fodder because of a scene in which a naked Stephen Fry pedantically instructs his 8-year-old daughter in the ways of the birds and the bees. *Harold Smith's* humour was a little broad for most critics, but it seemed like a beacon of subtlety in comparison to *Thunderpants* (2002), a noxious stinker of a movie about a schoolboy whose fart-power is harnessed by NASA to save a stranded space rocket. Hewitt followed up the fart-fest with the woeful *Garfield* and the lame superhero lark *Zoom* (2006). Totally bogus. LH

Bill & Ted's Bogus Journey 1991, 93 min

cast Alex Winter, Keanu Reeves, George Carlin, William Sadler, Joss Ackland, William Sadler, Pam Grier *cin* Oliver Wood *m* David Newman

One of the few sequels that's better than the original, this astutely stupid romp is also one of the few Hollywood teen comedies to make a prolonged reference to Ingmar Bergman's *The Seventh Seal*. Once the dudes have defeated the Grim Reaper at Twister and other parlour games, he helps them smite their archenemies, their robotic doubles, and performs with their band, the Wyld Stallyns, at the San Dimas Battle of the Bands competition.

Scott Hicks

Uganda, 1953–

C utting his teeth on the Australian films *Down The Wind* (1975) and *Freedom* (1982) and the occasional INXS video, Scott Hicks became a Hollywood player after directing the arthouse hit *Shine* (1996), a flashy, self-consciously tough biopic of the disturbed pianist David Helfgott. *Shine* won an Oscar for Geoffrey Rush and established the style that *Salon* magazine's Andrew O'Hehir summed up perfectly: "Add weeping violins and sprightly woodwinds to Yasujiro Ozu's *Tokyo Story* or Robert Bresson's *Mouchette*, so the audience knows what to think and feel at every moment, and you get Hicks." The director cashed in his *Shine* success with two adaptations of bestsellers: *Snow Falling On Cedars* (1999), from David Guterson's metaphor-choked courtroom thriller, and the Stephen King-derived *Hearts In Atlantis* (2001), a nostalgia-dappled, ostentatiously ominous tale of a young boy's friendship with an old neighbour (Anthony Hopkins). JW

Shine 1996, 106 min

cast Armin Mueller-Stahl, Noah Taylor, Geoffrey Rush, Lynn Redgrave, John Gielgud, Googie Withers *cin* Geoffrey Simpson *m* David Hirschfelder

Son of a domineering Polish emigrant to Australia, pianist David Helfgott struggles to surmount Rachmaninoff's mountainous *Piano Concerto No. 3*, suffers a spectacular breakdown and begins a slow climb towards novelty stardom. Hicks's biopic is wondrously performed – Noah Taylor embodies Helfgott the pre-breakdown introvert, Geoffrey Rush the older, jabbering exhibitionist – though its blame-dad account of Helfgott's illness is simplistic and its inspirational pretensions are mawkish and borderline exploitative.

George Roy Hill

US, 1922–2002

F or a while in the late 1960s George Roy Hill's films displayed a fashionable pop sensibility. His directing career had begun late, following Yale music studies and service in World War II and Korea. In 1957 he began writing for television and directing Broadway plays. Following reverent screen adaptations of Tennessee Williams (*Period Of Adjustment*, 1962) and Lillian Hellman (*Toys In The Attic*, 1963), he made the Peter Sellers vehicle *The World Of Henry Orient* (1964), displaying that breezy 1960s way with comedy that would characterize his best work. Buoyed by a soundtrack bringing together period standards and new numbers, 1967's *Thoroughly Modern Millie* parodied the Roaring Twenties.

Wedded to recollections of the chart hit "Raindrops Keep Fallin' On My Head", *Butch Cassidy And The Sundance Kid*'s 1969 paean to the frontier days trod

225

a cute path between *The Wild Bunch* (1969) and *Jules et Jim* (1961). The film remains a tribute to Paul Newman and Robert Redford's screen chemistry, and the formula was successfully repeated in 1973's *The Sting*. If Hill's commercial persona was tested by the Kurt Vonnegut adaptation *Slaughterhouse-Five* (1972), the barnstorming epic *The Great Waldo Pepper* (1975) had unexpected things to say about masculine bonding and Hollywood high adventure. *The World According To Garp* (1982), however, did little more than demonstrate Robin Williams's capacity for fatuous whimsy. RA

Butch Cassidy And The Sundance Kid 1969, 110 min
cast Paul Newman, Robert Redford, Katharine Ross, Strother Martin, Henry Jones, Jeff Corey *cin* Conrad Hall *m* Burt Bacharach

Despite the presence of Katharine Ross as Sundance's girl Etta, this is, as Paul Newman has insisted, "a love affair between two men": Newman's gang-leader Butch Cassidy and Robert Redford's unstable gunman Sundance. The classic buddy movie, the film benefits from a witty script by William Goldman. After the whimsy, charm and lively set pieces of the first half, the mood sours as the pair are pursued by a posse to the inevitable tragic conclusion and famous freeze-frame finale.

The Sting 1973, 129 min
cast Paul Newman, Robert Redford, Robert Shaw, Charles Durning, Ray Walston *cin* Robert Surtees *m* Scott Joplin, Marvin Hamlisch

Setting a gambling scam in a richly realized Depression-era Chicago, this modern gangster movie bounced along to Marvin Hamlisch's sonorous arrangements of Scott Joplin. Its pairing of Paul Newman and Robert Redford epitomized the buddy dynamics of the 1970s and embellished Redford's boyish blond image.

Jack Hill
US, 1933–

An outwardly very straight, mild-mannered white gentleman who studied musical composition at UCLA and grew up in the film business, Jack Hill is responsible for some of the sleaziest, most depraved, lurid B-movies of the 1960s and 70s. He was one of the key players in the blaxploitation boom, and is often credited with inventing the popular "women in prison" sub-genre. Stranger still, a quarter of a century later, Hill's films were re-released and critically rehabiliated under the patronage of Quentin Tarantino, and Mr Hill was respectable at last.

The son of an art director for Warner Bros and Disney, Hill was on the same UCLA film postgraduate course as Francis Coppola. As a general fixer for Roger Corman, he wrote and directed additional scenes on Coppola's *Dementia 13* (1963). His first solo outing was the macabre black comedy *Spider Baby, Or The Maddest Story Ever Told*, shot in 1964 with Lon Chaney Jr, but not released until 1968.

Hill describes his second film, the little-seen *Pit Stop* (shot in 1967, released 1969), as "really an art film race car movie". In this period he also undertook to write and direct four movies starring Boris Karloff (including the dire Edgar Allan Poe-inspired *House Of Evil*, 1968) for a Mexican producer, to be shot back to back in Hollywood and Mexico – the catch being that Karloff wouldn't leave Hollywood. Hill shot all four Hollywood sections in four weeks, and left Juan Ibáñez to direct the remainder.

He had more success with *The Big Doll House* (1971), a campy women-in-chains picture which spawned a sequel and many imitators, and was the first of four films he made with the formidable actress Pam Grier. *Coffy* (1973) and *Foxy Brown* (1974) are seminal blaxploitation revenge thrillers, both scripted by Hill in the revolutionary patois of the time. Like Hill's last cult item, *Switchblade Sisters* (1975), they can be enjoyed both as rudimentary period kitsch, and as semi-feminist/semi-pornographic genre films. TC

Coffy 1973, 91 min
cast Pam Grier, Booker Bradshaw, Robert DoQui, William Elliott, Sid Haig, Allan Arbus *cin* Paul Lohman *m* Roy Ayers

Revenge is a dish called Coffy in this blaxploitation hit. A nurse by day, Coffy (Pam Grier) dedicates her nights to tracking down the drug dealers who introduced her 11-year-old sister to smack. Any radical feminist credentials are heavily compromised by *Coffy's* prurient sex and violence – this is a jaw-droppingly lurid film at times – but Grier is magnificent and in her prime.

Switchblade Sisters 1975, 91 min
cast Robbie Lee, Joanne Nail, Monica Gayle, Asher Brauner, Chase Newhart, Marlene Clark *cin* Stephen Katz *m* Medusa

The sisters are doing it for themselves in this girl-gang B-movie. Maggie (Nail) is inducted into the Jezebels when leader Lace (Lee) takes a shine to her, but one-eyed Patch (Gayle) spots a way to get rid of her rival. Crudely made, it dresses up its sex and violence in the rhetoric of radical feminism and then puts the whole thing on roller skates.

Walter Hill
US, 1942–

Nobody – not even George Lucas – invested more in the Melvillian ideal of a pure, mythic cinema than Walter Hill. He goes back far enough to have scripted films for Sam Peckinpah and John Huston, and maybe their taste for distilled machismo rubbed off. In his first film as director, *Hard Times* (1975), he cast Charles Bronson as a fighter surviving the Depression by his bare knuckles. In his second, *The Driver* (1978), the characters didn't have names, just designations: the driver, the girl, the detective. He is a writer with no patience for words, and as a director he immediately hit upon the dynamic principles that action/reaction is the natural conduit for the cinematic revelation of story, and that men are most themselves when they're in trouble.

"Movies aren't life-like", Hill has said. "They're a very abstract code, a dance we've been cultured to." His early films aspire to the elemental simplicity of myth: *The Driver*, a Zen thriller, cool and quizzical as Isabelle Adjani's stare; the pulsing gang odyssey of *The Warriors* (1979); *The Long Riders* (1980), with the Carradine clan lining up alongside the Keachs and the Quaids; *Southern Comfort* (1981), replaying Vietnam in the Louisiana swamps…

He had a big hit with the relatively conventional Eddie Murphy cop comedy *48 Hrs* (1982) and then a big flop with a pet project, *Streets Of Fire* (1984). He lost his way. His intuition deserted him on the likes of *Brewster's Millions* (1985) and *Crossroads* (1986). Even apparently more personal projects like *Extreme Prejudice* (1987) and *Trespass* (1992) didn't pass muster. The graceful lyricism of his best work was drowned out in mechanical overkill. His movies didn't look stark anymore – they looked barren. He has worked steadily, but only thrived on those too-rare occasions when he's been allowed to return to his favourite genre, the Western, in *Geronimo: An American Legend* (1994), *Wild Bill* (1995) and the HBO series *Deadwood* (2004). TC

The Warriors 1979, 94 min
cast Michael Beck, James Remar, Thomas Waites, Dorsey Wright, Brian Tyler, David Harris *cin* Andrew Laszlo *m* Barry DeVorzon

"Warriors. Come out to play-e-ay…" Explicitly modelled on Xenophon's *Anabasis*, *The Warriors* exists in a midnight-movie New York where tribal gangs dress like the Village People and no beating hurts worse than wounded pride. After a meeting of the tribes ends in bloodshed, the Warriors are erroneously fingered for breaking the truce and have to fight their way along the subway line all the way back to Coney Island. It's a lot of fun.

The Long Riders 1980, 99 min
cast David, Keith and Robert Carradine, James and Stacy Keach, Dennis and Randy Quaid, Nicholas and Christopher Guest *cin* Ric Waite *m* Ry Cooder

Hill cast four sets of brothers as… four sets of brothers. This conceit has overshadowed one of the last great classical Westerns, a work of rare beauty and simplicity retelling the oft-filmed Jesse James–Cole Younger story as a piece of cinematic folklore. It marked the beginning of what proved to be a fruitful long-term collaboration with composer Ry Cooder and a one-off with Scottish screenwriter Bill Bryden.

Southern Comfort 1981, 105 min
cast Keith Carradine, Powers Boothe, Fred Ward, Franklyn Seales, T.K. Carter, Lewis Smith *cin* Andrew Laszlo *m* Ry Cooder

A war movie without a war. Hill puts a unit of National Guardsmen in the Louisiana bayou and watches them blunder into a bloody confrontation with local Cajuns. It could be a metaphor for Vietnam, or it might just be an ingenious spin on John Boorman's *Deliverance* (1972). Either way, there isn't a wasted word. Boothe and Carradine would both reappear in Hill's work as late as his 2004 HBO Western *Deadwood*.

Geronimo: An American Legend 1994, 115 min
cast Jason Patric, Gene Hackman, Robert Duvall, Wes Studi, Matt Damon, Rodney A. Grant *cin* Lloyd Ahern *m* Ry Cooder

An underrated late Western, scripted by John Milius and Larry Gross. This authentically bloody chronicle of the last Apache warrior presents an unromantic picture of white expansionism, the clash between incompatible cultures and the apparently inexorable "progress" of civilization. Screen time is effectively shared between Geronimo himself (Studi), Southern cavalry officer Gatewood (Patric), General Crook (Hackman) and chief scout Al Sieber (Duvall).

Arthur Hiller
Canada, 1923–

In 1997 Arthur Hiller directed the comedy turkey *An Alan Smithee Film: Burn Hollywood Burn*, which played on the fact that when a Hollywood director wants to remove his name from a film it is replaced by the pseudonym Alan Smithee. Ironically, Hiller had his own name removed from the film following a dispute over the editing. Yet the name Arthur Hiller itself does not stand for a distinctive vision, despite his having directed some memorable films.

Hiller directed television in the 1950s, most notably the NBC series *Playhouse 90*, *Alfred Hitchcock Presents* and *Gunsmoke*. In 1957 he directed his first feature, the elopement drama *The Careless Years*. There followed a mishmash of films that were glossy, sometimes successful and occasionally interesting. If the Julie Andrews vehicle *The Americanization Of Emily* (1964) was symptomatic of a Hollywood losing its bearings, the Rock Hudson desert war flick *Tobruk* (1967) displayed an adroit feel for action. A brief collaboration with screenwriter Neil Simon yielded *The Out-Of-Towners* (1969), an odyssey of corporate frustration in which Jack Lemmon and wife Sandy Dennis venture to New York for a doomed job interview. This was followed by the romantic drama *Love Story* (1970).

Scripted by Paddy Chayefsky, *The Hospital* (1971) used its institutional setting as a metaphor for an inefficient America and a mismanaged Vietnam War. In the 1980s, comedies like *Author, Author!* (1982) and *The Lonely Guy* (1984) proved that Hiller responded best to strong performers – in these cases Al Pacino and Steve Martin – and smart scripts. These days, his status flickers in time to graveyard-shift reruns of certain titles. RA

The Out-Of-Towners 1969, 97 min
cast Jack Lemmon, Sandy Dennis, Anne Meara, Ann Prentiss, Ron Carey, Sandy Baron *cin* Andrew Laszlo *m* Quincy Jones

Perhaps the nth degree for the neurotic menopausal New York comedy which Jack Lemmon made his own, this catalogue of modern urban horror starts as Lemmon's executive fetches up in the Big Apple with his Iowa wife Sandy Dennis for a crucial interview and doesn't let up until Cuban revolutionaries hijack their plane at the end. In between, there are Central Park muggings, fouled-up hotel reservations, transit strikes and a blizzard.

Love Story 1970, 100 min

cast Ali MacGraw, Ryan O'Neal, John Marley, Ray Milland, Russell Nype, Katherine Balfour *cin* Dick Kratina *m* Francis Lai

Ignoring the advent of New Hollywood, not to mention free love and the pill, Hiller's simplistic story of love and leukaemia nevertheless made box offices jingle from Bangor to San Diego. Ali MacGraw is the lost love remembered by Ryan O'Neal.

Alfred Hitchcock
UK, 1899–1980

Alfred Hitchcock is as well known among popular audiences as among cinephiles, his name uniquely associated with the thriller. In turn, his meditations on human fallibility and cinema's apparatus have made him an object of fascination for generations of critics and theorists.

Alfred Hitchcock and the modern thriller

Alfred Hitchcock has become a model and a metaphor for every director with ambitions to extend the modern thriller. Every time a character is accused of a crime they didn't commit, the touchstone is Hitchcock. Every time a director trades in sudden shocks, critics call it "Hitchcockian". Whenever the chase matters more than the outcome, we remember Hitchcock.

He was a showman, a moralist, a mechanic, a manipulator, a romantic. For the multiplex generation, his greatest legacy remains *Psycho* (1960); when Marion Crane was unexpectedly stabbed to death in a shower, the slasher cycle was born. With its eye on the manipulative potential of Hitchcockian editing combined with the ritual cutting of female flesh, it was John Carpenter's *Halloween* (1979) that first exploited this strand in a low-budget horror. The element of punishment brought down on young women for their sexual proclivities in the slasher cycle is a translation of the Catholic retribution which, for French commentators and critics since, informed Hitchcock's studies of guilt. But however adept at manipulating audiences Brian De Palma and Wes Craven have been, the cycle seems empty alongside the moral resonances and wit of the best Hitchcocks. Belonging to a New Hollywood generation steeped in classical cinephilia, De Palma was the "movie brat" most enamoured of the "Master of Suspense". This could be felt from the blatant lifting of Hitchcockian style in *Sisters* (1973) to the overwrought *Vertigo* romanticism of *Obsession* (1976). Equally, Craven's *Nightmare On Elm Street* and *Scream* franchises of the 1980s and 90s reiterated Hitchcock's most mechanistic tendencies, but lacked his urbane eye for the absurdity of the universe.

It was in France in the 1960s that the "Hitchcock industry" of critical analysis got into full swing. Hitchcock's influence can be felt across the oeuvres of François Truffaut and, especially, Claude Chabrol. Truffaut's *The Bride Wore Black* (1967) is full of resonances, while the presence of extreme violence in Chabrolian small towns owes more than a little to Hitchcock's very English horror. From Hitchcock, Chabrol also derived a sense of irony, the relationship between guilt and the individual (*Le boucher*, 1969) and the prospect of murder. In *La décade prodigieuse* (*Ten Days Wonder*, 1972) Hitchcock's celebrated God-like omniscience can be felt in Orson Welles's paterfamilias, while Anthony Perkins (the mother-fixated Norman Bates in *Psycho*), here plays the young man with lustful feelings towards his mother. Ever since *The 39 Steps* (1935), Hitchcock's influence could be felt all over the modern political thriller. Just as satirical, regarding political aspirations, Chabrol's *Les noces rouges* (*Blood Wedding*, 1973) drew upon Hitchcock's confessional mode, while his *Landru* (1962), *Violette Nozière* (1978) and *La cérémonie* (1995) all essay murder behind closed curtains – the classic Hitchcockian eruption of savagery out of bourgeois respectability.

Other directors have been sensitive to the characteristically Hitchcockian fate of the individual. Billy Wilder was congratulated by Hitchcock himself on the release of *Double Indemnity* (1944), a claustrophobic examination of guilt and an ordinary protagonist's temptation to murder for money and sex. This popular fascination amongst post-Hitchcock directors with ordinary characters pushed beyond everyday innocuousness by rogue circumstance also manifested itself in *The Bedroom Window* (Curtis Hanson, 1987), *The Narrow Margin* (Peter Hyams, 1990) and *A Simple Plan* (Sam Raimi, 1998); while Roman Polanski's *Frantic* (1988) and Jonathan Mostow's *Breakdown* (1997) traded on the missing woman conceit Hitchcock initiated in *The Lady Vanishes* (1938).

Finally, one must not forget another characteristic of Hitchcock's thrillers – his penchant for romantic comedy; directors from Stanley Donen (*Charade*, 1963) to Woody Allen (*Manhattan Murder Mystery*, 1993) have fallen under that particular influence.

With so many examples to hand, it is clear that Hitchcock has done much to shape the modern thriller; yet guilt, pursuit and fate are but a few of the characteristics found in his films that can equally be spotted in every genre of modern cinema, in turn highlighting the epic scope of this one director's influence. RA

Hitchcock was born a Catholic and attended Jesuit school, a background that would have far-reaching implications. In 1920 he entered the film industry, designing intertitles (the screens that punctuate silent movies explaining the narrative and providing dialogue) for the London branch of Famous Players-Lasky (later Paramount). Hitchcock quickly became head of department, gaining directing experience in the meantime. It was here that he met his wife, Alma Reville. A talented screenwriter with a good ear for dialogue, she collaborated on the scripts of many of Hitchcock's films. When Famous Players was taken over by Michael Balcon in 1922, Hitchcock was retained as an assistant director, turning his hand to art direction and screenwriting. Early experience in a range of crafts fed into his predilection for meticulous preparation and enabled him to achieve his unique position as a director who combined the qualities of an auteur with an understanding of every aspect of the industry.

His first directed film, *The Pleasure Garden* (1925), was shot in Munich and influenced by the Soviet montage school and the German expressionists – Hitchcock liked to quote Fritz Lang's *Der müde Tod* (*Destiny*, 1921) as his favourite movie. In *The Lodger* (1926), about a landlady who suspects her tenant of being Jack the Ripper, Hitchcock imported the modernism of Lang and Sergei Eisenstein into British studio filmmaking via foggy sets and dynamic cutting. He also explored what would become familiar themes – for example, the ordinary individual tripped into guilt by circumstance and mistaken identity. *The Lodger* marks the first instance of the director himself appearing in the early scenes of his films, a trait which would become a trademark like the appearance of Lang's hand in his films.

Moving to a larger studio, British International Pictures (BIP), in 1927, Hitchcock made four more silents (*The Ring*, *The Farmer's Wife*, *Champagne* and *The Manxman*) before embarking on his first talkie, *Blackmail* (1929). Initially a brisk policier, it develops into a disturbing tale of rape and domestic trauma. Technically, *Blackmail* was ahead of its time – particularly in the way sound was used to contribute to the mounting tension. A notable example is the way the heroine's trauma at having killed a man is emphasized by the amplification of the word "knife" in a banal, everyday conversation. The film illustrated Hitchcock's astute understanding of cinema. He once said: "If it's a good movie, the sound could go off and the audience would still have a perfectly clear idea of what was going on." Equally innovative was the film's use of the German Schüfftan process (first used in Lang's *Metropolis*, 1927), a precursor of the blue screen process whereby actors are inserted into painted or modelled backgrounds. Here it is employed to great effect in the chase over the top of the British Museum.

Hitchcock's international reputation began to grow following the release of *The Man Who Knew Too Much* (1934), made after rejoining Michael Balcon at British-Gaumont. His first transatlantic hit, this effective little film revolves around a British couple holidaying in Switzerland who become embroiled in an international intrigue. Deploying sudden shocks and a sinister mood amid an apparently serene romantic interlude, Hitchcock established a pattern of combining thrills and romantic comedy. Of the films that followed, *The 39 Steps* (1935), *The Secret Agent* (1936) and *The Lady Vanishes* (1938) are widely regarded as Hitchcock's best British work. Adapted from John Buchan and Somerset Maugham respectively, *The 39 Steps* and *The Secret Agent* remain fleet and highly cinematic films.

After *The Lady Vanishes* won the New York Critics' best director award, Hitchcock was signed by David O. Selznick and went to Hollywood. Exposed to the resources of the American studios, Hitchcock entered a hugely productive period, making some of the greatest films in the history of the cinema. If *Rebecca* (1940) seemed bookish after the pyrotechnics of his British films, Hitchcock was reminded by the literary-minded Selznick of the need for solid characterization and narrative complexity. He learned fast, turning the Daphne du Maurier adaptation into a fluently shot and powerful psychodrama, and setting a trend for "paranoid wives" movies that would last the decade. *Rebecca* won the Oscar that year for best picture. Hitchcock followed it with *Suspicion* (1941), in which Joan Fontaine again played a young wife, this time convinced that her husband is trying to kill her.

Suspicion marked the first appearance in a Hitchcock film of Cary Grant who, with James Stewart, became the archetypal Hitchcockian leading man: flawed, bewildered, at odds with denatured reality. Another actor prepared to play against type for Hitchcock was Joseph Cotten, who portrayed a sadistic murderer in *Shadow Of A Doubt* (1943), a film which created suspense through the interplay of character and atmosphere, and was the director's personal favourite of all his films. Few of Hitchcock's movies relate so well to the small-town milieu in which most Americans lived as *Shadow Of A Doubt*, which subverts the era's picket-fence world from within. But Hitchcock's genius derived from his ability to invest the everyday with a horror of experience imparted by his Catholic upbringing. The religious aspect of Hitchcock's work appealed most strongly to the French critics who lionized him in the decades after World War II.

Hitchcock continued to experiment in the mid-1940s. The single-set war drama *Lifeboat* (1944) was followed by *Spellbound* (1945), a psychoanalytical thriller famed for its Salvador Dalì dream sequence, *Notorious* (1946), a lavish romantic thriller, and

H

Hands-on direction: Hitchcock coaching one of his signature blondes, Kim Novak, on the set of *Vertigo*.

Rope (1948), an adaptation of a Patrick Hamilton play inspired by the murder of a young boy by the college students Nathan Leopold and Richard Loeb. In *Notorious* Ingrid Bergman plays a woman recruited by the FBI to infiltrate a Nazi group in South America who falls in love with her FBI contact Cary Grant. As in so many Hitchcocks, the plot is merely a vehicle for deeper concerns, a "Macguffin" used to provide motivation: the true subject of *Notorious* is the pathological tangle of feelings generated by Grant's manipulation of Bergman. Bergman was a "Hitchcock blonde", the latest in a tradition extending from *Blackmail*'s Anny Ondra via *Rear Window*'s Grace Kelly and *Vertigo*'s Kim Novak to *Marnie*'s Tippi Hedren. Beautiful but icy, sexy but aloof, the signature blonde became the vulnerable but ambiguous centre of the Hitchcock thriller. Open to extreme violence, capable of grave duplicity, she was the victim of the worst Hitchcock could bring to bear.

Hitchcock's work flowered in the 1950s. *Strangers On A Train* (1951) was an adroit adaptation of

Patricia Highsmith's novel in which a pair of bored strangers meet and contract to murder each other's worst bugbear. The sinister, suggestive dynamic between Robert Walker and Farley Granger veils depths of unspoken desire considered positively perverse in a mainstream film at that time. Unsettling smug post-war preconceptions about American masculinity, Hitchcock's 1950s heroes contain more than a little of the pathological antihero. *Rear Window* (1954) and *Vertigo* (1958) severely unbalanced James Stewart after decades of upstanding integrity. In *The Wrong Man* (1956) another national icon, Henry Fonda, played a musician mistaken for a murderer in a bleak urban world. It was one of François Truffaut's favourite films and recalled Lang's drab *mise en scène* in *You Only Live Once* (1937). *North By Northwest* (1959) played the unseating of Cary Grant's advertising executive against a glossy magazine backdrop of Mount Rushmore and the Midwestern wheatlands. The scene in which Grant is told to catch the next bus

Alfred Hitchcock and Bernard Herrmann

Composer Bernard Herrmann has said that "cinema is music". The screeching slicing strings of Herrmann's score during Hitchcock's infamous shower montage in *Psycho* (1960), remain the cinephile's model for the melding of music and moving images. Born in 1911 in New York, Herrmann studied at the prestigious Juilliard School and was heading his own orchestra by the age of 20. After tenures at CBS Radio and as guest conductor at the New York Philharmonic, Herrmann, by now a composer, began scoring for feature films. He had already worked with Orson Welles on Mercury Theatre productions for CBS and in 1941 the young director asked him to write the score for his first film *Citizen Kane*. The film earned Herrmann an Academy Award nomination but he actually received his one and only Oscar for an entirely different film made the same year – William Dieterle's *The Devil And Daniel Webster*.

Herrmann collaborated once more with Welles on *The Magnificent Ambersons* (1942) but arguably his best work was for Alfred Hitchcock for whom he scored a total of eight films, beginning in 1955 with *The Trouble With Harry*. Set in a very proper, autumnal Vermont, and revolving around the perturbed townsfolk's consternation over what to do with a dead man, *The Trouble With Harry*'s tone of cool irony was perfectly complemented by the pixie wit of Herrmann's music. The composer described movie music as "a kind of binding veneer that holds a film together". From *The Man Who Knew Too Much* (1956) to *Marnie* (1964), Hitchcock's US work now seems unthinkable without Herrmann's singular orchestrations, with their atmospheric shifts from chamber delicacy to dissonant brass and percussion, their emphatic use of strings and their characteristic employment of ostinatos (insistently repeated patterns of notes).

Accompanying a simple man's dark night of the soul, Herrmann's score for *The Wrong Man* (1956), with its downbeat colours, nicely underwrote the movie's documentary-like account of the mental deterioration that afflicts Henry Fonda's jazz musician following his wrongful arrest for armed robbery. *Vertigo* (1958) was one of the finest scores of the 1950s. James Stewart's obsessive love for Kim Novak is abetted by lush glowing orchestral colours that teeter into vibrant fantasy as the Hollywood soundtrack's traditional allegiance to the Romantic composers is pushed into a kind of luxurious hysteria. The opening sequence of the chase thriller *North By Northwest* (1959) features Saul Bass's modernist credits marshalling themselves horizontally in tandem to the strident horns of Herrmann's score. They provide an apt fanfare to the movie's bravura combination of Cold War plotting and romantic comedy.

But no Hitchcock score is as celebrated as the one for *Psycho*. At first, Hitchcock baulked at having any music during the shower sequence, but when he heard Herrmann's slashing glissandos with their horrible intimations of lacerated flesh and startled terror, he admitted how "improper" his intuition had been. So many sequences of *Psycho* derive their mood and character from the music. The loneliness of the rain-swept expanse of the Arizona highway, along which Janet Leigh's thief drives, is suggested by the soundtrack's wandering ostinatos. Later, the Bates Motel is rendered portentous by teetering strings – a thin wail at the edge of despair. As Marion dresses in her cabin, the violas seem anxious. As the detective Arbogast climbs the stairs, faint tremolos and harmonics subtly build suspense. As Hitchcock told François Truffaut, "I was directing the viewers. You might say I was playing them, like an organ."

By the time of *The Birds* (1963), Herrmann was Hitchcock's sound consultant, and the soundtrack – consisting of simulated bird sounds produced on an electronic instrument called a Trautonium – became integral to the film's entire design. The composer's relationship with the director only came to an (abrupt) end when Herrmann's darkly effective music for the Cold War thriller *Torn Curtain* (1966) was rejected by Hitchcock on the grounds that the studio wanted something more 'pop', which Herrmann refused to provide. The two men never spoke again and one of Hollywood's most fruitful collaborations was at an end. Ironically by the late 1960s the emergence of a 'Hitchcock industry' meant that such homages as Truffaut's *The Bride Wore Black* (1967) benefited hugely from Herrmann's evocative scoring. Then in the 1970s, New Hollywood movie tyro Brian De Palma hired Herrmann to provide the atmosphere for both the slick suspense flick *Sisters* (1973) and the *Vertigo* homage *Obsession* (1976). Herrmann also provided a beautifully langorous and world-weary score for Martin Scorsese's *Taxi Driver* (1976) and was due to compose the music for De Palma's *Carrie* but died in 1975 before starting work on it. RA

on a deserted Illinois highway used the widescreen frame to emphasize isolation and to crank up the suspense. The dissolution of the post-war American ego reached its murky climax in *Psycho* (1960).

Hitchcock was often accused of seeing actors as pawns in a fastidious *mise en scène*; most notoriously, actress Tippi Hedren has often described the filming of *The Birds* (1963) as a deeply traumatic experience.

Capitalizing on the "creature feature" trend of the time, *The Birds* focuses on a complacent American status quo as nature turns against humanity.

As clever at manipulating his public image as at manipulating audiences, the rotund "Master of Suspense" with the lugubrious English tone and dark wit became the star of his own television shows, *Alfred Hitchcock Presents* (1955–62) and *The Alfred Hitchcock Show* (1962–65). His later movies – *Marnie* (1964), *Torn Curtain* (1966), *Topaz* (1969), *Frenzy* (1972) and *Family Plot* (1976) – show sharply declining powers. But as his touch weakened so his critical cachet grew. The writers at *Cahiers du cinéma* and at Britain's *Movie* magazine thought Hitchcock the epitome of cinema's unique genius. Books by Robin Wood, Peter Bogdanovich and Claude Chabrol and Eric Rohmer celebrated Hitchcock's preoccupations and methods. Truffaut's 1969 book of interviews remains a key work. "Hitchcockian" has become a stamp of approval for new thrillers, while Hitchcock's influence can be felt in subsequent generations from the late-1960s films of Claude Chabrol and Brian De Palma's homages of the 1970s to the brazen fright mechanics of John Carpenter and Wes Craven. RA

Blackmail 1929, 82 min, b/w
cast Anny Ondra, John Longden, Sara Allgood, Donald Calthrop, Cyril Ritchard *cin* Jack Cox *m* James Campbell, Reg Connelly

As dawn breaks over London a bedraggled young woman climbs into bed. Outside, they have found a body and it looks like murder. Hitchcock's first sound feature was an efficient documentary-like policier underscored by a murky story of molestation and murder.

The 39 Steps 1935, 86 min, b/w
cast Robert Donat, Madeleine Carroll, Godfrey Tearle, Lucie Mannheim, Peggy Ashcroft *cin* Bernard Knowles *m* Hubert Bath, Jack Beaver

Short, sharp and to the point, this spirited blend of political thriller and rom-com pulses with suspense and piquant sexual wit. Seeing Robert Donat and Madeleine Carroll together, you could be watching a British Clark Gable and Carole Lombard.

Sabotage 1936, 76 min, b/w
cast Oscar Homolka, Sylvia Sidney, John Loder, Desmond Tester, Joyce Barbour, Martita Hunt, Peter Bull *cin* Bernard Knowles

British Hitchcock is a treat, and this Joseph Conrad tale of European anarchists in London builds to a gripping climax. Bringing her Depression waif persona to the streets of late-Victorian Holborn, American Sylvia Sidney imparts just the right level of desperation as her little brother falls victim to Oscar Homolka's swarthy ogre.

The Lady Vanishes 1938, 96 min, b/w
cast Margaret Lockwood, Michael Redgrave, Paul Lukas, Cecil Parker, Dame May Whitty, Linden Travers *cin* Jack Cox *m* Cecil Milner

Replete with the appeasement politics of the 1930s but stuffed with British pluck and common sense, the conundrum of the little old lady who disappears on a train journey never loses steam. Bringing out the best in Margaret Lockwood and

Michael Redgrave and a sterling cast of domestic stalwarts, *The Lady Vanishes* looks forward to Hollywood.

Rebecca 1940, 130 min, b/w
cast Laurence Olivier, Joan Fontaine, George Sanders, Judith Anderson, Nigel Bruce, Gladys Cooper *cin* George Barnes *m* Franz Waxman

Hitchcock's first American film is a bravura essay in sexual entrapment as Joan Fontaine's naïve young wife is drawn into marriage by Laurence Olivier's troubled widower only to be driven mad by his horrible past. Stealthily binding his trembling, almost prepubescent heroine with a series of seductive camera moves, Hitchcock makes Manderley a metaphor for marriage as emotional rape, while Judith Anderson's poisonous chatelaine Mrs Danvers longs for her former mistress.

Notorious 1946, 102 min, b/w
cast Cary Grant, Ingrid Bergman, Claude Rains, Louis Calhern, Leopoldine Konstantin *cin* Ted Tetzlaff *m* Roy Webb

One of Hitchcock's most deceptive surfaces, on the face of it this war espionage thriller seems fairly ordinary, but Hitchcock makes the triangle of US agent Devlin (Cary Grant), his chic blonde prey (Ingrid Bergman) and her repressed Nazi husband (Claude Rains) into a claustrophobic tangle of allegiances and sexual longing. The wine-cellar episode is a *tour de force*.

Strangers On A Train 1951, 101 min, b/w
cast Farley Granger, Robert Walker, Ruth Roman, Leo G. Carroll, Patricia Hitchcock, Laura Elliott *cin* Robert Burks *m* Dimitri Tiomkin

Playing on the simultaneous anticipation and apprehension of the random travelling encounter, *Strangers On A Train* finds Farley Granger's troubled tennis hotshot trapped in a bleak contract with Robert Walker's smooth but psychotic co-passenger. From the clever mental conceit of Patricia Highsmith's novel, Hitchcock's film descends into a murky, delirious and finally lacerating merry-go-round.

Rear Window 1954, 112 min
cast James Stewart, Grace Kelly, Wendell Corey, Thelma Ritter, Raymond Burr, Judith Evelyn *cin* Robert Burks *m* Franz Waxman

Revelling in the possibilities of film, Hitchcock was one of the prophets of Film Studies, and James Stewart's invalid watching his neighbours without them knowing has become seminal to the theory of spectatorship. Saving its thrills to the end, this is also a terrific battle-of-the-sexes comedy. The prize: that most svelte of Hitchcock blondes, Grace Kelly.

Vertigo 1958, 128 min
cast James Stewart, Kim Novak, Barbara Bel Geddes, Tom Helmore, Henry Jones, Ellen Corby *cin* Robert Burks *m* Bernard Hermann

One of the most powerful examinations of male desire in the history of the cinema, this chronicle of a detective's mania for a dead woman finds James Stewart at his most unbalanced and Hitchcock at his most assured. Perversely, the film that disturbs the very roots of Hollywood romanticism was shot in hazy pastels on bright San Francisco afternoons.

Psycho 1960, 109 min, b/w
cast Anthony Perkins, Janet Leigh, Vera Miles, John Gavin, Martin Balsam, John McIntyre *cin* John L. Russell *m* Bernard Herrmann

A Hitchcock fan since the 1930s, critic C.A. Lejeune was so flummoxed by *Psycho* that she retired. Coming at the very start of the 1960s, as Hollywood braced itself for the teen audience, *Psycho* pushed the thriller in the direction of blood lust and obsessive mother love.

The Birds 1963, 119 min
cast Tippi Hedren, Rod Taylor, Suzanne Pleshette, Jessica Tandy, Ruth McDevitt, Veronica Cartwright *cin* Robert Burks *m* Bernard Herrmann

Hitchcock's riposte to the burgeoning drive-in schlock market, this quite harrowing account of a small Californian town besieged by the bird population is laden with Freudian symbolism. Famously subjecting his leading lady, blonde ex-model Tippi Hedren, to an avian onslaught of ferocious laceration for art, Hitchcock's orchestration of quotidian horror and black humour is consummate.

Mike Hodges
UK, 1932–

Mike Hodges' *Get Carter* (1971) was one of the most accomplished, note-perfect debuts by any British director. How he ended up as a director for hire on *Morons From Outer Space* fourteen years later is one of the inexplicable tragedies of British cinema. Having directed the current affairs TV series *World In Action*, Hodges brought a long-lens documentary approach to *Get Carter*, his own adaptation of Ted Lewis's 1970 pulp novel *Jack's Return Home*. He then formed a production company with the film's star, Michael Caine, and producer, Michael Klinger, and made *Pulp* (1972), an indulgently modish comedy about a novelist who gets caught up in a murder. It hasn't aged well.

Hodges' problems began on *The Terminal Man* (1974), an adaptation of a Michael Crichton novel about a computer scientist who implants a microchip in his own brain. When Terrence Malick saw the film, he wrote to the director, exclaiming "you achieve moods that I've never experienced before … Your images make me understand what an image is." Unfortunately, Malick was one of few people who saw the film; it wasn't released in the UK. Hodges went from one problematic project to the next in the 1980s, and his filmmaking CV went considerably awry; only the jokey sci-fi epic *Flash Gordon* (1980) gave him a rare commercial success. *A Prayer For The Dying* (1987) was a preposterous melodrama starring Mickey Rourke as an IRA gunman with a conscience. When Hodges finally got to make a personal project, the supernatural thriller *Black Rainbow* (1989), it was denied proper distribution.

At the age of 68, Hodges' career was resurrected with the arch, cerebral thriller *Croupier* (1998). Dismissed by British critics and the public, the film found new life in the US, where it became the sleeper hit of 2000. Hodges shelved plans for his retirement and started work on a new film. The result, *I'll Sleep When I'm Dead* (2004), was a slow-burning, austere thriller starring *Croupier*'s Clive Owen as a former gangster who returns to his South London roots to investigate his

brother's suicide. With echoes of *Get Carter*, it brought Hodges' career satisfyingly full circle. LH

Get Carter 1971, 112 min
cast Michael Caine, Britt Ekland, John Osborne, Ian Hendry, Bryan Mosley, Geraldine Moffatt, Dorothy White *cin* Wolfgang Suschitzky *m* Roy Budd

Lauded by the Britflick geezer generation for all the wrong reasons (*Loaded* magazine even had a *Get Carter* comic strip), Hodges' debut is a finely judged, beautifully observed and ultimately disapproving study of British machismo. Michael Caine has rarely been better than as the Kray-like mobster who returns to his home town of Newcastle to avenge his brother's murder. *Get Carter* is rivalled only by *Performance* (1970) as the greatest gangster film ever made in Britain.

Croupier 1998, 94 min
cast Clive Owen, Kate Hardie, Alex Kingston, Gina McKee, Nicholas Ball, Nick Reding, Alexander Morton *cin* Mike Garfath *m* Simon Fisher Turner

Scripted by Paul Mayersberg, the writer of *The Man Who Fell To Earth* (1976), *Croupier* is stimulating, intellectual fare. With an arch, *noir*-ish voiceover, novelist Clive Owen recounts how he took a job as a croupier and robbed his own casino after being ensnared by a *femme fatale* (Alex Kingston). Multi-layered and metaphorical, *Croupier* works as both a richly atmospheric thriller and an extensively researched insight into the twilight world of British casinos.

Agnieszka Holland
Poland, 1948–

In a diverse and sometimes frustrated career that spans several countries and languages, Agnieszka Holland has never shied away from faith, identity, war or other daunting subjects in her films.

It's possible that her sometimes tumultuous life has conditioned her for bold choices: the murder of her father, a leftist journalist, when she was 13; film school in Prague followed by arrest and solitary confinement without charge in 1970; eight months of separation from her daughter after the anti-Solidarity imposition of martial law in her native Poland in 1981–82. "It helps in directing, when you know what suffering, separation, fear mean", she once said. Holland has focused several times on individuals' responses to the Nazi menace during World War II: in her screenplay for *Korczak* (1990), directed by her mentor Andrzej Wajda, and in her own films *Angry Harvest* (1986), a bizarre quasi-romance between a Polish farmer and a Jewish refugee, and the internationally successful *Europa, Europa* (1990), a German-French co-production based on the true story of a German Jew who survived the Holocaust by concealing his identity.

Holland followed *Europa, Europa* with the eerie French production *Olivier, Olivier* (1992), in which a young boy goes missing and then, six years later, reappears to his family – or does he? The story's supernatural infusions were revisited in *The Third Miracle*

(1999), featuring Ed Harris as a sexually tempted priest investigating a candidate for sainthood, and *Julie Walking Home* (2002) about a miracle healer.

After *Olivier, Olivier*, Holland made her first American film, *The Secret Garden* (1993), but she has proven slightly tone-deaf in a few of her other English-language films, including the woeful *To Kill A Priest* (1988), which pitted an idealistic man of the cloth against the Polish government agent who wants him dead, and *Total Eclipse* (1995), a shrill, somewhat louche account of the love affair between French poets Rimbaud and Verlaine. Holland continued to plough the biopic territory in 2006 with *Copying Beethoven*, which was concerned with the final years of the composer's life. JW

Europa, Europa 1990, 112 min
cast Marco Hofschneider, Julie Delpy, Hanns Zischler, André Wilms, Andrzej Mastalerz, Delphine Forest *cin* Jacek Petrycki *m* Zbigniew Preisner

Based on true events, *Europa, Europa* tells the story of Solomon Perel (Marco Hofschneider), a German Jew who survives the Holocaust through improvisatory performance, first blending into a Communist orphanage in Poland, and then donning a Nazi uniform. Mining many bitter ironies and casting survival in terms of resourceful creativity and sheer luck, Holland's film is arguably an extreme metaphor of assimilation; it's both droll and, at times, almost unbearably tense.

Nicole Holofcener
US, 1960–

Nicole Holofcener has a feeling for the unspoken stuff of female friendship that is rare in a cinema so traditionally sold on heterosexual love. Her name showing up more than once among Woody Allen crews in the 1980s and evoking something of Allen's feeling for the interpersonal, Holofcener's work has been lazily compared to his New York comedies.

Well received at the Sundance Film Festival, *Walking And Talking* (1996) feeds on the feminist legacy of films such as Claudia Weill's *Girlfriends* (1978) and Allen's concern with cultural assimilation. As stints on the TV show *Sex In The City* (1998) showed, Holofcener is adept at capturing the warp and weft of the everyday. Her features display a burgeoning confidence with metaphor and the unexpressed depths of personal dynamics. And with successes such as *Lovely And Amazing* (2001) and *Friends With Money* (2006) under her belt, Holofcener's remains a career to watch. RA

Walking And Talking 1996, 85 min
cast Catherine Keener, Anne Heche, Todd Field, Liev Schreiber, Kevin Corrigan, Randall Batinkoff *cin* Michael Stuhler *m* Billy Bragg

Amelia (Catherine Keener) and Laura (Anne Heche) have been friends since they were kids. Preparing for Laura's wedding to Frank (Todd Field) is giving them both doubts

about the future. Trading in post-*Friends* self-examination but leavened with a feeling for the grubbier precincts of American culture – Z-movies, porn, Frank's mole – *Walking And Talking* signalled the arrival of a brilliant raconteur for the carrot cake constituency.

Lovely And Amazing 2001, 91 min
cast Catherine Keener, Brenda Blethyn, Emily Mortimer, Raven Goodwin, Aunjanue Ellis, Jake Gyllenhaal *cin* Harlan Bosmajian *m* Craig Richey

Gently teasing the culture of cosmetic surgery and self-improvement, *Lovely And Amazing* chronicles the liposuction trauma of menopausal mother Jane (Brenda Blethyn). Meanwhile, her daughters totter beneath self-image burdens which endear and exasperate. Holofcener's bite-sized flow never leaves us short-changed.

Tobe Hooper
US, 1943–

Perhaps it's appropriate that the inspiration for the *ne plus ultra* of slasher flicks came to its creator when he was trapped in a packed department store during high holiday season: Tobe Hooper remembers finding himself in front of a chainsaw display and thinking, as he put it, "I know how I could get out of this place fast." *The Texas Chainsaw Massacre* (1974) was a feast of ripped and ravaged flesh, scraped together with a negligible budget and a cast and crew made up largely of local friends and acquaintances. The film has been claimed as transgressive art, but while it has been hugely influential, it is also rancid and hollow.

The massive profitability of *Massacre* (which was, incidentally, distributed in the US by a wing of the Peraino crime family, who had previously scored big with the 1972 porn film *Deep Throat*) led to Hooper's larger budgets for the frighteners *Death Trap* (1976) and *Salem's Lot* (1979), the latter a Stephen King adaptation starring David Soul. Hooper was fired from the directorial chair of *Venom* (1982) in favour of horror journeyman Piers Haggard, and though he is credited as its director, the hit *Poltergeist* (1982) is thought to have relied heavily on its producer, Steven Spielberg. Hooper helmed a jokey sequel to *Massacre* in 1986, starring Dennis Hopper, and has since worked consistently in television, contributing episodes to *Tales From The Crypt* and the *Nightmare On Elm Street* spin-off *Freddy's Nightmares*. With more than thirty years gone by since Leatherface's coming-out party, Hooper remains something of a one-hit wonder. JW

The Texas Chainsaw Massacre 1974, 83 min
cast Marilyn Burns, Gunnar Hansen, Allen Danziger, Edwin Neal, Paul A. Partain, William Vail *cin* Daniel Pearl *m* Tobe Hooper, Wayne Bell

A comely gang of dumb kids make all the wrong moves on a road trip, one by one meeting grisly ends in a farmhouse inhabited by the inbred family from hell. Despite the meagre budget, Hooper managed some particularly macabre set design chez Leatherface (check out the fine outsider-art collection of skin tapestries and bone-based sculpture), but the prolonged bloody torments eventually become less shocking than stultifying.

Dennis Hopper
US, 1936–

Dennis Hopper is one of the great iconoclasts of American cinema. As an actor in the 1950s, he fetched up in *Rebel Without A Cause* (1955) and *Giant* (1956) and was traumatized by James Dean's death in 1955. He also gained an early reputation for being difficult to work with. By the late 1960s he had turned to directing and 1969's *Easy Rider* became an *Urtext* of countercultural revolt made for $375,000 but making $19 million in North America alone. Catapulted to the New Hollywood epicentre as the studios tried to court the youth market, and narcotic and aesthetic experiment became the new production standard, Hopper embarked on *The Last Movie* (1971). Shooting a Western in the Andes, Hopper's stuntman becomes drawn into a maelstrom of tribal ritual and primitive filmmaking. Steeped in Hollywood lore, yet adrift amid an exotic wilderness both geo-cultural and film-cultural, Hopper's movie toys with an arsenal of ideas from film and the plastic arts. It was a critical and commercial disaster. Hopper retreated into drink and drugs before famously "recovering" in the 1980s, when acting appearances, notably for David Lynch in *Blue Velvet* (1986), seemed to signal the return of the maverick in an age of corporate caution and conformity.

Hopper's Canadian film *Out Of The Blue* (1980) suggested the rebirth of an auteur. Taken over from writer-director Leonard Yakir after a few weeks shooting, the film is a vivid punk hymnal, an uncompromising screed in which Linda Manz's forsaken angel plays out the lacerating consequences of having a junkie mother and an incestuous paedophile father (Hopper). Subsequent works – *The Hot Spot* (1990), *Chasers* (1994) – were second-rate studio projects. An exception is 1988's *Colors*, which translates the virile experimentalism of *Easy Rider* to Los Angeles gangland, and sheds that plea for studio kudos in favour of his trademark nihilism. One of Hollywood's unhinged geniuses, Hopper remains a model for true independence in American filmmaking. RA

Easy Rider 1969, 95 min
cast Peter Fonda, Dennis Hopper, Jack Nicholson, Phil Spector, Antonio Mendoza, Warren Finnerty, Tita Colorado, Karen Black *cin* Laszlo Kovacs

Just as Simon and Garfunkel crooned about hitting the road in America, two men ride their motorcycles from California to New Orleans, in search of the United States and some great coke. After *Bonnie And Clyde* and *The Graduate*, *Easy Rider* completed the trinity of films that saw off the Production Code and forced Hollywood studios to sit up and take notice of a burgeoning American New Wave. Hopper's movie is a phantasmagoria of cacti, solar flair and gleaming choppers, finished with a *vérité* hallucination of genuine avant-gardism.

James W. Horne
US, 1880–1942

The history of American silent comedy is impossible to imagine without James W. Horne. After stage experience, he entered the Kalem studio in 1911. Directing from 1915 to 1942, he worked with many of the best comedians of their day – Buster Keaton, Charlie Chase and Laurel and Hardy – while his career embraced features, serials and two-reelers. He is responsible for a number of definitive Laurel and Hardy short films, including *Beau Hunks* (1931), *Laughing Gravy* (1931) and *Way Out West* (1937), and the Keaton classic *College* (1927). He also made a significant contribution to the Saturday serials of the late 1930s and early 40s with such films as *The Shadow* (1940), *The Iron Claw* (1941), *Holt Of The Secret Service* (1941) and *Captain Midnight* (1942). In a different decade, you wonder what he could have done with the likes of Bob Hope and Jerry Lewis. RA

College 1927, 63 min, b/w
cast Buster Keaton, Ann Cornwall, Flora Bramley, Harold Goodwin, Snitz Edwards *cin* Dev Jennings, Bert Haines *m* William Perry

Riffing on the nerd-versus-jock scenario exploited in Harold Lloyd's *The Freshman*, Buster Keaton marshals all his athletic grace and pluck to win Ann Cornwall, the girl he loves, away from a strutting college he-man. The "Great Stone Face" is marvellously dexterous as he mimics a soda jerk, while another hilarious highlight occurs when, instead of hurling the hammer, it hurls him! This remains one of Keaton's finest moments on screen and – as sound came in – one of the last great silent comedies.

Way Out West 1937, 65 min, b/w
cast Stan Laurel, Oliver Hardy, Sharon Lynn, James Finlayson, Rosina Lawrence, Stanley Fields *cin* Art Lloyd, Walter Lundin *m* Marvin Hatley

Having promised to deliver the title deed of a gold mine to the daughter of a prospector, Stan and Ollie head off to Brushwood Gulch where they immediately fall out with the evil owner of the saloon Mickey Finn (James Finlayson). A spoof Western and the best of the comic duo's features, outstanding moments include their desperate attempts to get the deed back, a hilarious soft-shoe dance routine and, of course, their immortal rendition of "Trail Of The Lonesome Pine".

Hou Hsiao-Hsien
China, 1947–

Critic J. Hoberman called him "the world's greatest active narrative filmmaker" – a description which belies Hou Hsiao-Hsien's apparent lack of interest in narrative. Despite negligible distribution in the English-speaking world throughout most of his career, the Taiwanese director is a revered figure among serious critics and cinephiles.

Having studied at the National Taiwan Arts Academy, Hou began his movie career as an assistant director and scriptwriter. Hou's first film as a director was the largely formulaic *Cute Girls* (*Jiushi liuliu de ta*, 1980) but by the time of *The Boys From Fengkuei* (*Fengkuei-lai-te jen*, 1983) a personal signature was beginning to emerge.

Hou is essentially a minimalist who has become the master of the master-shot – that is, he favours long takes with very little cutting. In *Flowers Of Shanghai* (1998), each scene is played out in just a single take, with transitions signalled by a fade to black. (A solitary point-of-view shot is a crucial exception.) His initially static style has incorporated more movement over the years in the form of simple, unobtrusive panning shots or the occasional travelling shot like the one which starts his transitional *Millennium Mambo* (2001), but this scarcely compromises his level detachment from the action. Such an aesthetic is far from the Western mainstream tradition of cutting-room editorializing. Coupled with his oblique way with narrative, which works by implication and nuance leaving much drama off screen, it means Hou requires an engaged, active viewer.

Yet for all his essentially modern formalist rigour, Hou is a humanist dedicated to character observation in a naturalistic setting, even sentimentally so. He is repeatedly drawn to autobiography and nostalgia in his numerous period films, although these also reflect still-pressing questions about Taiwanese identity. *Three Times* (2005) serves as a neat summation of his abiding concerns and aesthetic modulations, telling three thwarted love stories in three specific periods, and in three distinct styles. In his pursuit of cinema-as-contemplation Ozu has always been an emotional touchstone, and Hou paid tribute to the Japanese master in *Café Lumière* (2003). Like Ozu, Hou seems to focus on very little – mundane conversations, banal details – and maintains a constant equilibrium throughout, yet somehow cuts deep into the human heart. TC

A Summer At Grandpa's (Dongdong de jiaqi) 1984, 98 min

cast Wang Qiguang, Gu Jun, Mei Fang, Lin Xiuling *cin* Chen Kunhou *m* Edward Yang, Du Duzhi

Typical of Hou's early work, this simply immerses you in a child's-eye view of the world. Eleven-year-old Tung-Tung and his 4-year-old sister Ting-Ting may not appreciate the matters of life and death encroaching on their experience as they while away the holidays with their grandparents, but Hou captures them so vividly that the film has the feel of autobiography. Until recently this was Hou's most widely seen film in the West.

The Time To Live And The Time To Die (Tongnian wangshi) 1985, 137 min

cast You Anshun, Tian Feng, Mei Fang, Tang Ruyun, Xiao Ai *cin* Li Ping-Bin *m* Wu Chuchu

Progressing from *A Summer At Grandpa's*, this applies similar strategies to a more complex (but still autobiographical) situation and a longer time frame, with a mainland family adjusting to life in Taiwan in the 1950s. Through the accumulation of everyday moments naturalistically observed as a series of recurring patterns, Hou distils a serene yet deeply moving sense of the passage of time.

A City Of Sadness (Beiqing chengshi) 1989, 157 min

cast Tony Leung Chiu-Wai, Xin Shu-fen, Li T'ien-lu, Kao Chieh, Ikuyo Nakamura *cin* Chien Huai-en *m* Chang Hung-yi

Hou's most ambitious film to date is again intimate in focus, following the fortunes of a family through four brothers and their wives, but resonating with the tumultuous political events of the years after the defeat of the Japanese in 1947 and the arrival of the Chiang Kai-Shek nationalists. Some measure of the film's nuance and reach: it features dialogue in Taiwanese, Cantonese, Mandarin, Japanese and Shanghainese. It won the Golden Lion at the Venice Film Festival.

Flowers Of Shanghai (Hai shang hua) 1998, 125 min

cast Tony Leung Chiu-Wai, Michelle Reis, Jack Gao, Carina Lau *cin* Lee Ping-ben *m* Yoshiro Hanno

The flowers of the title are kept women in what were called "flower houses", the brothels of the late nineteenth century. At his most formalist here, Hou shoots every scene in a single shot, panning between the women and their gentleman callers. Entirely set in parlours (there is no sexual contact), it's beautifully photographed, with enormous ructions and emotional turbulence taking place underneath its immaculately composed surface.

Ron Howard
US, 1954–

Ronny Howard made his first acting appearance at eighteen months in a movie called *Frontier Woman* (1956). He was Opie on TV's *The Andy Griffith Show* (1960–68), and a perpetual whitebread teenager as Richie Cunningham in the sitcom *Happy Days* (1974–80), a spin-off from the George Lucas teen movie *American Graffiti* (1973). His most noteworthy film performance was opposite John Wayne in the Duke's last film, *The Shootist* (1976). The following year he made his debut as a director with *Grand Theft Auto*, a juvenile car-wrecking extravaganza made for Roger Corman.

If his child actor image still overshadows Howard's profile as a director, that's in part because there's something of the nice, clean-cut, all-American Richie Cunningham in the competent, workmanlike light comedies, like *Splash* (1984) and *Parenthood* (1989), with which he cut his teeth and the bland sentimental dramas with which he earns plaudits, like the Irish costume drama *Far And Away* (1992). If there's a common thread in his work (which is versatile enough) then it would be family values. His more interesting suspense movies, *Ransom* (1996) and *The Missing* (2003), find an element of neurosis in close family ties, but more typical is the drearily conservative boxing biopic *Cinderella Man* (2005), a prestige movie that bombed. Still, despite his patchy commercial record, Howard was entrusted with the adaptation of Dan Brown's *The Da Vinci Code* (2006). Critics crucified him, but the audience flocked.

One of Hollywood's favourite sons, Howard picked up the Academy Award for best director for *A Beautiful Mind* in 2001, defeating David Lynch, Robert Altman, Ridley Scott and Peter Jackson. TC

A Beautiful Mind 2001, 135 min

cast Russell Crowe, Ed Harris, Jennifer Connelly, Paul Bettany, Adam Goldberg, Judd Hirsch, Josh Lucas *cin* Roger Deakins *m* James Horner

This creative biopic of mathematician John Nash (Russell Crowe) played fast and loose with the facts, but vividly illustrates an unstable imaginative intelligence in the process. A seemingly demented second act is the most unexpected passage in Howard's otherwise well-behaved career, but the movie reverts to sentimental type in the end. The big Oscar winner of the year, despite complaints that it had glossed over Nash's bisexuality.

The Missing 2003, 137 min

cast Tommy Lee Jones, Cate Blanchett, Eric Schweig, Rachel Evan Wood, Jenna Boyd, Steve Reevis *cin* Salvatore Totino *m* James Horner

Cate Blanchett gives a bravura performance in this underrated, strikingly shot Western, a box-office bomb which puts a female twist on the oft-told story of *The Searchers*. (Blanchett reunites with her father, Tommy Lee Jones, to track down her abducted daughter.) If it doesn't resonate with nearly the same depth, at least in has the guts to recognize something terrifying and powerful in the Native American Other. Very handsomely shot too.

King Hu
China, 1931–97

Anyone curious as to the roots of Ang Lee's *Crouching Tiger, Hidden Dragon* (2000) and Zhang Yimou's *House Of Flying Daggers* (2004) should read on. The appropriately named King Hu was the master of *wuxia* (swordplay) epics in the 1960s, and is perhaps the best-known director to emerge from the legendary Shaw Brothers studios.

Born in Beijing, Hu made his way to Hong Kong as a teenager and found work at Shaw, first as an actor and writer during the 1950s, then as a director. His first major credit as writer-director was *Sons Of The Good Earth* (1965), the story of Chinese World War II resistance fighters battling against the Japanese, in which he also played the

lead. His talents established, it was not long before he set about making the definitive *wuxia* works: his last Shaw movie *Come Drink With Me* (1966, currently the subject of Tarantino remake rumours), and the acknowledged classics *Dragon Inn* (1966) and *A Touch Of Zen* (1969). These last two films both appeared in the Top 10 of the Hong Kong Film Awards Best 100 Chinese Motion Pictures, announced to celebrate a century of movies in Hong Kong. No other director matched this feat.

Hu moved away from full-blown *wuxia* epics after *A Touch Of Zen* but continued to direct acclaimed features in a similar mould, such as the Yuen Biao vehicle *The Valiant Ones* (1975) and the underrated *Raining In The Mountain* (1979). His last film, after a lengthy hiatus in the 1980s, was the horror *Painted Skin* (1993). NN

A Touch Of Zen (Xia nü) 1969, 200 min

cast Hong Qiao, Chun Shih, Han Hsue, Han Yin-Chieh, Hsu Feng, Bai Ying *cin* Chou Yeh-Hsing, Hua Hui-Ying *m* Ng Tai Kong, Wu Dajiang

An artist hears strange noises in the supposedly haunted fort near his home. Investigating, he comes across a beautiful woman, who is revealed to be on the run from imperial agents who have killed her family, and he becomes drawn into her adventure. Incorporating similar plot elements to its predecessor *Dragon Inn*, the epic *A Touch Of Zen* builds on the earlier movie with spectacular set pieces, including a battle in a bamboo forest that would influence countless martial arts movies to come.

Hugh Hudson
UK, 1936–

Hudson has never built on the success of his first film, *Chariots Of Fire* (1981). As an Eton schoolboy Hudson made films, including a short about Oliver Cromwell, before entering advertising and chalking up over 1500 TV ads. *Chariots Of Fire* was a phenomenal success, scriptwriter Colin Welland famously declaring to the Oscars audience "the British are coming!" Hudson's career now seemed set, and while *Greystoke: The Legend Of Tarzan, Lord Of The Apes* (1984) could not hope to top *Chariots*, it was still reasonably successful. However, his next film, *Revolution* (1985), about the American War of Independence, was a legendary disaster, half-heartedly supported by the failing Goldcrest Company, and blighted by pre-release rumour and Al Pacino's wayward accent.

A 1987 Labour Party political broadcast, wryly nicknamed "Kinnock: The Movie", was a small-scale success but *Lost Angels* (1989), about a juvenile delinquent, was not released in Britain until 1991 (under the title *The Road Home*), and things got worse when his commission to direct the official 1992 Olympic film was withdrawn. *My Life So Far* (1999), Sir Denis Forman's memoir of family

Martial arts films

Martial arts movies have been a staple of Chinese cinema for almost a century and are currently enjoying a surge of new-found enthusiasm in Europe and North America. Long regarded as ultra-lowbrow, such movies owe their new popularity in part to recent high-profile directors – Quentin Tarantino, Ang Lee and Zhang Yimou – who have made the most of the visual energy inherent in the form. *Crouching Tiger, Hidden Dragon* (2000), *Hero* (2002), *Kill Bill* (2003), *House Of Flying Daggers* (2004) and *Curse Of The Golden Flower* (2006) have all been major arthouse hits.

The Chinese call their martial arts movies *wuxia pian*, which literally means chivalrous combat film. *Wuxia* stories, which have been part of China's literary culture since ancient times, experienced a popular revival in the nineteenth century and were regularly serialized in newspapers. They were also a staple ingredient of the highly stylized and acrobatic form of theatre known as Peking Opera. Though centring on the activities of heroic knights, adept in the art of swordplay, there is more to the *wuxia* tradition than just hyper-energetic displays of mindless violence. A bigger idea is at work, one based on self-expression, transformation and national identity. In the 1920s there was a strongly felt sense that cinema could be used as a means of recording and reinforcing traditional Chinese culture at a time when the influence of the West seemed to be growing stronger. The first significant martial arts film, *The Burning Of The Red Lotus Monastery* (1928), was made as a serial; it was followed by *Swordswoman Of Huangjiang* (1930), a film which illustrates just how important female warriors were from the very start of *wuxia* films.

When China became a Communist state in 1949, *wuxia* movies were disapproved of and their production was transferred to Hong Kong and Taiwan but with a market within the Chinese diaspora. The same year saw the start of a long and very popular series of films based on the life of Wong Fei Hong, a famous healer and martial artist, who was for many years portrayed by Kwan Tak Hing. In a neat twist of fate, Hong's enemy in these films was portrayed by Shek Kihn who went on to play Bruce Lee's nemesis in *Enter The Dragon* (1973). Other actors who have played Hong include Jackie Chan in *Drunken Master* (1978) and Jet Li in *Once Upon A Time In China* (1991).

After opening studios in Hong Kong in 1961, the legendary Chinese film producers the Shaw Brothers became the main producers of *wuxia* movies, helping to raise standards by the introduction of more sophisticated cinematography and increasingly prolonged action sequences. One of the best Shaw Brothers' directors was King Hu who made one of the studio's most memorable films of the 1960s, *Come Drink With Me* (1966), starring Cheng Pei-Pei as a valiant swordswoman on a mission to save her captured brother. The film used trampolines to allow performers to launch dramatically into their moves, establishing a trait that endures. In the 1970s sword-based martial arts films were largely replaced by films in which unarmed combat dominated. The intense Bruce Lee, and later Jackie Chan, became the principal icons of this style, with Lee blazing a trail with *Fist Of Fury* (1972) and *Way Of The Dragon* (1972). The success of these two films led to Hollywood backing for the hugely popular *Enter The Dragon*, a film which for many Westerners came to epitomize the martial arts genre.

In a similar way Ang Lee's *Crouching Tiger, Hidden Dragon* has kick-started the recent international enthusiasm for the genre. The armed and unarmed combat showcased in the film was based around Wudan, a form of martial arts centring on spiritual, rather than physical, strength. For its director the idea was to counter the genre's dependence on revenge stories. He wanted a story that "negated" violence. The martial arts film had once again transformed itself and the subsequent success of movies like *House Of Flying Daggers* suggests that its popularity is here to stay. JC

turmoil, was something of a return to form, but *I Dreamed Of Africa* (2000), starring Kim Basinger as a wealthy Italian woman who becomes a conservationist in Africa, was a disappointment. JR

Chariots Of Fire 1981, 123 min

cast Ben Cross, Ian Charleson, Nicolas Farrell, Nigel Havers, Cheryl Campbell *cin* David Watkin *m* Vangelis

Based on the true story of two British runners in the 1924 Olympics. The dour Scot Eric Liddell and the Jewish Harold Abrahams face prejudice, are pulled between friendship and rivalry, and struggle with the clash between their consciences and the quest for glory. Vangelis's Oscar-winning throbbing electronic score accompanied slow-motion scenes of early-morning training on the beach in an iconic (and much-parodied) moment.

John Hughes
US, 1950–

Chicago-area loyalist John Hughes became a major convenor of the Brat Pack – the group of largely underwhelming young stars whose overlapping movie résumés and dating patterns made them the tabloid darlings of the 1980s – with the high-school kvetchfest *The Breakfast Club* (1985). It was a high-school companion piece to the post-university *St Elmo's Fire*, directed by Joel Schumacher, which was released the same year and shared several of its lead actors. Hughes had previously written a couple of *National Lampoon* farces and had his directorial debut with *Sixteen Candles* (1984), a charming if facile day-in-the-life of an overlooked middle child, which anointed the flame-haired beauty Molly Ringwald as a movieplex princess.

Hughes worked flat out for the next seven years, on *The Breakfast Club* as well as the lighter teen romps *Weird Science* (1985) and *Ferris Bueller's Day Off* (1986), before trying his hand at marginally more adult fare with *She's Having A Baby* (1988). Somehow, however, the strain of going grown-up coarsened the jokes and thickened the air with cloying sentiment, despite the jocular everyman presence of John Candy in *Planes, Trains & Automobiles* (1987) and *Uncle Buck* (1989).

A prolific writer and producer, Hughes has often provided strong scripts for other directors – notably the teen movies *Pretty In Pink* (1986) and *Some Kind Of Wonderful* (1987) for Howard Deutsch and the comedies *Home Alone* (1990) and *Home Alone 2* (1992) for Chris Columbus. His own directorial CV is relatively short, and at the moment ends with 1991's *Curly Sue* (1991), a clumsy *Paper Moon* redux. JW

The Breakfast Club 1985, 97 min

cast Emilio Estevez, Paul Gleason, Anthony Michael Hall, John Kapelos, Judd Nelson, Molly Ringwald, Ally Sheedy *cin* Thomas Del Ruth *m* Keith Forsey

Nothing if not schematic, Hughes's generation-in-a-can drama assembles a cross section of high-school archetypes – jock Emilio Estevez, bad boy Judd Nelson, misfit Ally Sheedy, geek Anthony Michael Hall and prom queen Molly Ringwald – for all-day detention and watches the feathers fly. Trite and claustrophobic, the movie is nonetheless a useful time-capsule artefact, and the gifted Ringwald rises above the fray.

Ferris Bueller's Day Off 1986, 102 min

cast Matthew Broderick, Alan Ruck, Mia Sara, Jeffrey Jones, Jennifer Grey, Cindy Pickett *cin* Tak Fujimoto *m* Ira Newborn

Bratty high-school truant Ferris (Matthew Broderick) decides to risk one last absence and recruits two buddies for the romp. Broderick infuses a potentially insufferable character with offhand charm and sincere insincerity and, until its mawkish finale, the movie is light on its feet and endlessly quotable.

Ken Hughes
UK, 1922–2001

Ken Hughes won an amateur filmmaking prize at the age of 14 and later went on to work as a sound effects assistant for the BBC. After his feature debut, *Wide Boy* (1952), Hughes spent a large part of his early career making dark dramas and thrillers for both film and television, many of which he also wrote, including the Shakespeare update *Joe Macbeth* (1955), *The Long Haul* (1957) and *The Small World Of Sammy Lee* (1963). The 1960s brought bigger budgets and his controversial masterpiece, *The Trials Of Oscar Wilde* (1960). However, he also became embroiled in *Of Human Bondage* (1964) – replacing Bryan Forbes, who had himself replaced Henry Hathaway – and was one of the many directors of the James Bond spoof *Casino Royale* (1967).

Although he dismissed it, Hughes's most profitable film was the family musical fantasy *Chitty Chitty Bang Bang* (1968), based on the novel by Ian Fleming. The impressive set pieces of his self-scripted historical document *Cromwell* (1970) were offset by considerable longueurs. Bankruptcy in 1975 stalled Hughes's career and, despite his moving to the US and filming the likes of the Mae West mess *Sextette* (1978) and the slasher *Night School* (1981), it never really recovered. JR

The Trials Of Oscar Wilde 1960, 123 min

cast Peter Finch, Yvonne Mitchell, James Mason, Nigel Patrick, Lionel Jeffries, John Fraser *cin* Ted Moore *m* Ron Goodwin

Peter Finch's magisterial, BAFTA-winning performance as the titular Irish playwright dominates this highlight of Ken Hughes's varied career and gave *Trials* the upper hand over Gregory Ratoff's Wilde biopic of the same year. This offers a provocatively sympathetic view of Wilde's homosexuality and the slander trial that he self-destructively initiated.

Hunsinger & Hunter
Tom Hunsinger: US, 1952–
Neil Hunter: UK, 1964

Writer-directors Neil Hunter and Tom Hunsinger essay complex characters with a moral sense akin to that of Eric Rohmer and an emotional fluidity reminiscent of Mike Leigh. Their partnership began when Hunsinger responded to Hunter's ad in trade paper *The Stage* for actors to appear in his 16mm short *Tell Me No Lies* (1992). But instead of performing, Hunsinger produced the film, which charted the vicissitudes of identity amongst a trio of gay students.

The duo then co-wrote and co-directed their first feature, *Boyfriends* (1995), which found three men's relationships in crisis during a weekend break. After slots at assorted gay and lesbian festivals, *Boyfriends* was shown at London's Institute of Contemporary Arts, and the filmmakers soon found themselves at the vanguard of British art cinema. They again shared writing and directorial duties on *Lawless Heart* (2001), which also focused on the trials of three men and was that rarity – a "French" film made in Britain – and on *Sparkle* (2007), a comedy starring Stockard Channing and Bob Hoskins about a young Liverpudlian who moves to London. RA

Lawless Heart 2001, 100 min

cast Bill Nighy, Douglas Henshall, Tom Hollander, Clémentine Célarié, Ellie Haddington, Sukie Smith *cin* Sean Bobbit *m* Adrian Johnston

With *Lawless Heart*, Hunter and Hunsinger have produced one of the most striking British films of the 2000s. This exploration of the lives of a tight-knit community dealing with sudden death interwove character, dialogue and *mise en scène* with impressive truth and assurance. Juxtaposing sad, funny and scurrilous registers, the film charts three men coming to terms with their lives in the dour wake of loss amid the haunting mud flats of Essex.

John Huston
US, 1906–87

A muscular storyteller with literate tastes and a cynical vision, John Huston established himself with a number of genre classics at the tail end of the studio era, lost his way somewhat in the 1960s, but kept working, hitting several career highs in his last two decades.

The son of the successful stage and screen actor Walter Huston (whom he directed in *The Treasure Of The Sierra Madre*, 1948), John gave up his studies to become a professional boxer, enrolled in the Mexican cavalry, before embarking on a career in the movies, initially as an actor then as a screenwriter. A brief stint in London was followed by a year in Paris studying painting before his return to Hollywood where he returned to scriptwriting – mostly for Warner Bros – on a wide range of films including the one that reignited Humphrey Bogart's career, *High Sierra* (1941).

It wasn't until he was in his sixties that Huston entirely shook off his image as a talented dilettante, perhaps because of his wide range of interests outside of the movies but also because of a reputation for working against rather than with the studio system. He was also known as a man's man, a hard-drinking character in the Hemingway mould who could easily lose interest in a project. Very few of his films feature women in anything but marginal roles, and, even when sympathetically depicted, are often seen as a disruptive element in a male world.

Several of his best movies were very faithful adaptations of literary sources – including his first film, the classic Sam Spade detective thriller *The Maltese Falcon* (1941), *The Treasure Of The Sierra Madre*, *Key Largo* (1948) and *The African Queen* (1951). The auteurist critics found him wanting: "The worst Hawks film is better than Huston's best", François Truffaut declared (an untenable opinion which he recanted after becoming a director himself).

In *Picture*, Lillian Ross's fascinating account of the making of *The Red Badge Of Courage* (1951), Huston seems on the verge of a masterpiece until the studio reins him in. He capitulates with a bored shrug, tak-

ing off for the safer commercial waters of *The African Queen* (where Peter Viertel's thinly veiled memoir *White Hunter, Black Heart* has him more interested in bagging an elephant than knuckling down to the movie). His more audacious artistic ventures often fall to vulgarity or overemphasis: *Moulin Rouge* (1952), *Moby Dick* (1956), *The Night Of The Iguana* (1964), *Reflections In A Golden Eye* (1967)… and these are by no means his worst films. Yet Huston's intellectual curiosity, his cavalier taste for adventure and mordant humour frequently pay off too. Few of his generation even attempted so much.

"The trick is in the casting", he used to say, and he regularly brought the best out of a star, indelibly so in the case of Humphrey Bogart. A larger-than-life actor himself, Huston made memorable appearances in *Chinatown* (1974) and *Winter Kills* (1979) and played the lead in Orson Welles's unfinished *The Other Side Of The Wind* (1972). He also steered both his father and his daughter, Anjelica, to Oscar wins – the former in *The Treasure Of The Sierra Madre*, the latter in *Prizzi's Honor* (1985).

Work never dried up but after an impressive start with the melancholy Western *The Misfits* (1961), the 1960s proved a decade in which Huston seemed to lose his touch. *The Night Of The Iguana* and *Reflections In A Golden Eye* qualify as honourable failures, *The Bible* (1966) – in which the director played Noah – and *Casino Royale* (1967) proved out-and-out duds. So it's little short of miraculous that in his sixties and seventies Huston made such valiant and varied triumphs as *Fat City* (1972), *The Man Who Would Be King* (1975), *Wise Blood* (1979) and *The Dead* (1987), inspired by Leonard Gardner, Rudyard Kipling, Flannery O'Connor and James Joyce, respectively. And it's characteristic of this wildly erratic, carelessly prolific director that they should have been interspersed with such abject failures as *The Mackintosh Man* (1973), *Phobia* (1980) and *Escape To Victory* (1981). TC

The Maltese Falcon 1941, 100 min, b/w

cast Humphrey Bogart, Mary Astor, Sydney Greenstreet, Peter Lorre, Elisha Cook Jr, Barton MacLane, Lee Patrick *cin* Arthur Edeson *m* Adolph Deutsch

The third and definitive screen version of Dashiell Hammett's detective novel is scrupulously faithful to the writer's tough, cynical vision, and musters an iconic gallery of Dickensian villains in Mary Astor, Sydney Greenstreet, Peter Lorre and Elisha Cook Jr. It remains one of the most accomplished directorial debuts on record and helped transform Bogart from heavy to hard-boiled hero. The actor and director proved lasting friends and collaborators..

The Treasure Of The Sierra Madre 1948, 126 min, b/w

cast Humphrey Bogart, Walter Huston, Tim Holt, Bruce Bennett, Barton MacLane, Alfonso Bedoya *cin* Ted McCord *m* Max Steiner

Humphrey Bogart, Walter Huston and Tim Holt star in a sardonic adventure story based on B. Traven's novel, a

The odd couple: Katharine Hepburn and Humphrey Bogart sweat it out in *The African Queen*.

fable about gold prospectors striking it lucky south of the border – or so they think. Shot on location and eschewing Hollywood glamour, it was ahead of its time in many ways, and again extended Bogart's range as he convincingly succumbs to gold fever. This is one adventure yarn that really hasn't dated.

The Asphalt Jungle 1950, 112 min, b/w

cast Sterling Hayden, Louis Calhern, Jean Hagen, Sam Jaffe, James Whitmore, John McIntire *cin* Harold Rosson *m* Miklós Rózsa

Another flawless adaptation, this time from an underworld novel by W.R. Burnett. It's the remorseless story of a gang of thieves falling apart after pulling off a robbery. Probably the most influential heist movie of them all, shot in a crisp semi-documentary style with virtually no music, it anticipates Dassin's *Rififi* (1954) and Kubrick's *The Killing* (1956) and has been remade no less than three times. Look for one of Marilyn Monroe's better early roles too.

The African Queen 1951, 103 min

cast Katharine Hepburn, Humphrey Bogart, Robert Morley, Peter Bull, Theodore Bikel, Walter Gotell *cin* Jack Cardiff *m* Allan Gray

Bogart and Katharine Hepburn enact a battle-of-the-sexes romance under the guise of an exotic action adventure yarn. She's the prim English missionary left high and dry in German East Africa when her brother dies; he's Charlie Allnut, a broken-down steamboat skipper and unlikely knight in shining armour. Together they fend off leeches and a marauding German gunboat. Huston knew this was a sure thing and he wasn't wrong.

Fat City 1972, 96 min

cast Stacy Keach, Jeff Bridges, Susan Tyrrell, Candy Clark, Nicholas Colasanto, Art Aragon *cin* Conrad Hall *m* Marvin Hamlisch

An unremittingly downbeat – but tremendously moving – portrait of the bottom rung of the boxing circuit, where perennial losers slug it out for chump change in small-town arenas. Stacy Keach is Tully, over the hill but still plodding on; Jeff Bridges is his discovery, the not-so-great white hope, Ernie. Evocatively photographed by Conrad Hall in a succession of sun-blasted California backstreets and bars, it's arguably Huston's finest film.

The Man Who Would Be King 1975, 129 min
cast Sean Connery, Michael Caine, Saeed Jaffrey, Christopher Plummer, Karroum Ben Bouih, Jack May *cin* Oswald Morris *m* Maurice Jarre

First mooted for Gable and Bogart in the 1940s, this splendid Kipling satire on British imperialism has Sean Connery and Michael Caine as two unscrupulous ex-infantrymen turned adventurers conning their way to the crown in tribal Kafiristan (now divided between Afghanistan and Pakistan). The sparring, macho relationship between Connery and Caine is perfectly judged and Huston's storytelling skill gets its perfect vehicle.

Wise Blood 1979, 108 min
cast Brad Dourif, Ned Beatty, Harry Dean Stanton, Daniel Shor, Amy Wright, Mary Nell Santacroce *cin* Gerry Fisher *m* Alex North

An extraordinary Southern satire with Brad Dourif's Hazel Motes evangelizing the Church of Truth Without Christ, "where the blind don't see and the lame don't walk and what's dead stays that way". Except that he meets his match in Harry Dean Stanton's blind seer. Based on Flannery O'Connor's Southern Gothic novel, it's grotesque yet astringent, and the sort of movie you can't imagine getting made these days.

Prizzi's Honor 1985, 129 min
cast Jack Nicholson, Kathleen Turner, Robert Loggia, John Randolph, William Hickey, Angelica Huston *cin* Andrzej Bartkowiak *m* Alex North

Huston's penultimate film was a return to form after a prolonged wayward spell. It's an elegant black comedy about two professional killers who fall in love: Jack Nicholson's slow-witted Mafioso and Turner's WASP assassin. Their love affair gets in the way of business protocol, with tragic results. The film features a standout performance from Huston's daughter Anjelica. Based on a novel by Richard Condon.

The Dead 1987, 83 min
cast Anjelica Huston, Donal McCann, Helena Carroll, Cathleen Delany, Ingrid Craigie *cin* Fred Murphy *m* Alex North

Huston was dying when he shot this beautiful adaptation of James Joyce's short story, and it makes a poignant swan song to his long career – a reverie for lost love, Ireland, and family set (mostly) at a Twelfth Night party in an affluent Dublin household. There are strong performances from the largely Irish cast, but Anjelica Huston takes the honours with a perfectly pitched monologue at the film's end in which she reminisces about the boy who got away, shattering her fond husband's illusions at a stroke.

Nicholas Hytner
UK, 1956–

Given that he's an award-winning London theatre director, it's no surprise that Nicholas Hytner plumped for stage-to-screen adaptations to mark his transition into movies. He debuted with *The Madness Of King George* (1994), based upon the Alan Bennett play that Hytner had previously directed on stage (the filmmakers slightly tweaked Bennett's original title, *The Madness Of George III*, so that American audiences wouldn't mistake it for a sequel), and followed with *The Crucible* (1996), adapted by Arthur Miller from his 1953 stage allegory of McCarthyism.

Having worked with two powerhouse casts (including Nigel Hawthorne, Helen Mirren and Ian Holm in *Madness* and Daniel Day-Lewis, Joan Allen and Paul Scofield in *Crucible*), Hytner next mounted the modest domestic comedy *The Object Of My Affection* (1998), the gawky but charming story of a gay man (Paul Rudd) and a straight woman (Jennifer Aniston) experimenting with cohabitation. Hytner returned to the proscenium arch for the hackneyed *Center Stage* (2000), yet another case study of cinema's uncomfortable relationship with ballet. He reunited with Bennett for a faithful but flat adaptation of their stage collaboration *The History Boys* (2006), about an unconventional teacher guiding a scrupulously diverse group of wisecracking schoolboys. JW

The Madness Of King George 1994, 110 min
cast Nigel Hawthorne, Helen Mirren, Amanda Donohoe, Rupert Everett, Ian Holm, Rupert Graves, Julian Wadham *cin* Andrew Dunn *m* George Fenton

The magnificent Nigel Hawthorne reprises the role he honed on the London and New York stage as George III, the metabolically imbalanced royal whose mounting mania and delusions threw his inner circle into disarray. Set in the late eighteenth century, the film deftly weaves the backroom political intrigues kicked up by his illness, and succeeds in inspiring sympathy and affection for the man while candidly acknowledging him to be an ineffectual tyrant.

The Crucible 1996, 123 min
cast Daniel Day-Lewis, Winona Ryder, Paul Scofield, Joan Allen, Bruce Davison, Rob Campbell, Jeffrey Jones *cin* Andrew Dunn *m* George Fenton

Long beloved of high-school drama clubs all across the US, Arthur Miller's 1953 melodrama of the infamous seventeenth-century Salem witch trials generates ferocious speed and near-hysterical momentum, in keeping with its story of a pious, devil-fearing community in thrall to the wild tales of a few teenage girls. As John Proctor, the man in the eye of the storm, Daniel Day-Lewis (the late Miller's son-in-law) cuts as commanding and poetic a figure as always.

Kon Ichikawa

Japan, 1915–

The prolific Kon Ichikawa's bold range of subject matter and stylistic versatility would be superb assets for any socially engaged filmmaker born into Japan's tumultuous twentieth century. He has tried his hand at the youth-in-crisis movie (*Punishment Room*, 1956), brutal war films (*The Burmese Harp*, 1956, *Fires On The Plain*, 1959), thrillers (*The Pit*, 1957, *The Inugamis*, 1976), domestic black satire (*Odd Obsession*, 1959, *The Makioka Sisters*, 1983), period costume drama (*An Actor's Revenge*, 1962), documentary (*Tokyo Olympiad*, 1965), samurai drama (*The Wanderers*, 1973) and more. His very eclecticism, however, has perhaps slowed his entry into the undisputed canon of great Japanese auteurs, though a travelling retrospective in 2001 (curated by the Cinémathèque Ontario's James Quandt, one of the director's most perceptive admirers) introduced many to his oeuvre.

Ichikawa was trained as an animator (US occupation forces seized his 1946 debut, an animated bunraku-puppet movie), and storyboards remained a crucial component in the pre-production of his live-action films; though he preferred sets to locations, his widescreen images often show a fine attunement to landscape and seasonal change. His wife, Natto Wada, scripted the literary adaptations that powered the 1950s–60s high tide of his career: *Punishment Room* drew on the controversial novel by youth-cult star Shintarô Ishihara; *Conflagration* (1958) was based on the book by patriot and famous *seppuku* casualty Yukio Mishima and inspired by the true story of a troubled monk who burned down Kyoto's Golden Pavilion to preserve it from tourist hordes and moral degeneracy. Degradation in all its forms fascinated Ichikawa, be it the desperate measures taken by starving Japanese soldiers in *Fires On The Plain* (they resort to cannibalism and coprophagy) or the withering physical faculties and deadened conscience of *Odd Obsession*'s vain protagonist, who discovers that he's only aroused when jealous, and thus engineers an affair between his wife and son-in-law.

"I don't have any unifying theme", Ichikawa once said, adding that he simply made the films that he liked and the films that his studio assigned him. Yet his work returns again and again to insuperable generation gaps and the bestial, even nihilistic, nature of man, while the high mortality rate of fathers and father figures in his work casts social unrest and generational conflict in terms of an everlasting Oedipal complex. JW

The Burmese Harp (Biruma no tategoto)
1956, 116 min, b/w
cast Shoji Yasui, Rentaro Mikuni, Tatsuya Mihashi, Tanie Kitabayashi, Yunosuke Ito *cin* Minoru Yokoyama *m* Akira Ifukube

At the end of World War II, soldier-harpist Mizushima (Shoji Yasui) fails to convince a ragtag regiment of Japanese troops to surrender to the British before they're slaughtered. Going in search of his own regiment, he dons the robes of a Buddhist monk and resolves to bury his comrades himself. Ichikawa's international breakthrough strikes a delicate balance, depicting the brute horrors of war and its aftermath with infusions of gentle sentiment.

An Actor's Revenge (Yukinojo henge) 1962, 110 min
cast Kazuo Hasegawa, Fujiko Yamamoto, Ayako Wakao, Ganjiti Nakamura, Raizo Ichikawa *cin* Setsuo Kobayashi *m* Yasushi Akutagawa

Veteran Japanese star Kazuo Hasegawa pulls astonishing double duty as the thief Yamitaro and the kabuki female impersonator Yukinojo, whose effeminate appearance and hoarse, trembling voice masks a fierce resolve for vengeance against the people who caused his parents' death. Mixing comedy and melodrama, and nineteenth-century Japanese music and modern jazz, the movie is as eclectic in its assemblage as Ichikawa's oeuvre is in its entirety.

Shohei Imamura

Japan, 1926–2006

Imamura began in film as Yasujiro Ozu's assistant, working most notably on *Tokyo Story* (1953), before directing his own films which were the anarchic, rough-hewn antithesis of his master's stately gentility. Imamura's early films pulsated with a nervy, untidy energy. He debuted with *Stolen Desire* (1958), but it was his fifth film, *Pigs And Battleships* (1961), that ushered in the first important phase of his career. *The Insect Woman* (1963), *Intentions Of Murder* (1964), *The Pornographers* (1966) and *Profound Desire Of The Gods* (1968) all controversially examined both the physical human underbelly and the underbelly of Japanese society. As Imamura put it, "I am interested in the relationship of the lower part of the human body and the lower part of the social structure." Imamura was something of an iconoclast, consciously rebelling against Japanese studio strictures and the style of Ozu and becoming, along with Nagisa Oshima and Masahiro Shinoda, a key member of the Japanese New Wave.

After retiring in 1970 to make television documentaries, Imamura made a triumphant return to film with *Vengeance Is Mine* (1979), and continued to mature and improve with age. *Ballad Of Narayama* (1983), *Black Rain* (1989), *The Eel* (1997) and *Warm Water Under A Red Bridge* (2001) exuded not just maturity, but often an old man's sense of mischief. If his style mellowed towards the end of his life, his preoccupations with sex, animals and lowlife did not.

Imamura tried to show the real Japan, including the unfashionable provinces, which are populated in *Pigs And Battleships* by feral gangsters, whores and hustlers who greedily swarm around a US naval base. He has been dubbed the cultural anthropologist of Japanese cinema, but could easily be dubbed its entomologist or zoologist. As titles such as *The Insect Woman* and *The Eel* suggest, animal and insect imagery abounds: a carp thrashes around in its tank whenever its mistress does wrong in *The Pornographers*, and frisky frogs, snakes and birds parallel the human protagonists with their own squelchy lovemaking in *Ballad Of Narayama*.

His films are also drenched in sex. As with the naïve country girl who becomes a call girl and then a ruthless madam in *The Insect Woman*, women often come out on top. Lusty and single-minded, they defy demure Japanese stereotypes; the rape victim in *Intentions Of Murder* does not follow tradition and kill herself in shame, but instead makes herself a comforting meal. Not just strong characters, Imamura's women can be transcendentally mystical: in *Warm Water Under A Red Bridge*, Saeko's orgasms replenish the local river and give succour to the fish. This idiosyncratic form of atavism was at the core of Imamura's ideology, and whether they're killers, prostitutes or earthly goddesses, his characters act as reminders of our uncivilized, primitive selves. LH

Vengeance Is Mine (Fukushu sura wa ware ne ari) 1979, 140 min
cast Ken Ogata, Rentaro Mikuni, Mitsuko Baisho, Chocho Miyajo, Mayumi Ogawa, Nijiko Kiyokasawa *cin* Shinsaku Himeda *m* Shinichiro Ikebe

A killer on the road finds solace with a madam of a bordello, though this human bond doesn't affect his barbaric habits, even after the odd couple get engaged. While making love to his fiancée, he whispers sweet nothings into her ear: "I killed another man in Tokyo today." Dispassionate and callous in its unflinching and unerring objectivity, this is Imamura at his most violently atavistic and fantastically depressing.

Ballad Of Narayama (Nayayama bushiko) 1983, 130 min
cast Ken Ogata, Sumiko Sakamoto, Tonpei Hidari, Takejo Aki, Shoichi Ozawa *cin* Masao Tochiizawa *m* Shinichiro Ikebe

In a mythical, remote province there is so little food that anyone over the age of 70 has to be taken to the top of a mountain and left to the elements. Sixty-nine-year-old Orin is prepared to go, but not until she finds a wife for her widowed son and finally settles all her unresolved issues. This Palme d'Or winner – a remake of Keisuke Kinoshita's 1958 kabuki film – is funny, shocking and oddly serene.

The Eel (Unagi) 1997, 121 min
cast Koji Yakusho, Misa Shimizu, Fujio Tsuneta, Mitsuko Baisho, Akira Emoto, Sho Aikawa *cin* Shingeru Komatsubara *m* Shinichiro Ikebe

After serving time for killing his adulterous wife, Takuro Yamashita sets up his own barber's shop. At first he only has an eel – his pet and his confidant – for company, but his shop slowly becomes the centre for a community of oddballs. Book-ended by scenes of jolting violence, *The Eel* is a tranquil, lyrical and occasionally magical essay on nature, human and otherwise.

Hiroshi Inagaki
Japan, 1905–80

Immersed in the movies his whole life, Hiroshi Inagaki began his long film career as a child actor in silent movies in the 1920s. He directed his first movie in 1928, the start of a filmography that was to total over seventy directorial credits as well as over forty writing credits.

In the 1930s and 40s Inagaki directed a number of period films that helped develop the samurai genre in Japanese cinema, long before Akira Kurosawa started making his celebrated samurai works. But Inagaki's most acclaimed films roughly coincide with Kurosawa: the *Samurai* trilogy (1954–56), often held to be one of the pinnacles of the genre, and 1969's *Samurai Banners*.

The Rickshaw Man (1958) drove to the heart of class divisions with its story of a humble rickshaw driver who is taken in by a wealthy family after rescuing their son, only to begin a relationship with the mother after her husband dies. The film won the Golden Lion at the 1958 Venice Film Festival, and its lead Toshirô Mifune received the best actor award. It was followed by a string of films, most notably 1962's shogun epic *Chushingura* (*The Loyal 47 Ronin*). Mifune also starred in Inagaki's last film, *Ambush At Blood Pass* (1970), after which Inagaki struggled to find work and sadly descended into alcoholism, which would eventually kill him in 1980. NN

Samurai (Musashi Miyamoto) 1954, 93 min
cast Toshirô Mifune, Rentaro Mikuni, Kuroemon Onoe, Kaoru Yachigusa, Mariko Okada, Mitsuko Mito *cin* Jun Yasumoto *m* Ikuma Dan

Long-time Inagaki collaborator Toshirô Mifune stars as Takezo, a peasant who is forced to train as a samurai after a series of unfortunate adventures leave him in fear of his life. The film is as much about the search for identity as it is about the way of the samurai. A remake of an earlier Inagaki film from the 1940s, this was the first film in his *Samurai* trilogy.

Samurai Banners (Furin kazan) 1969, 165 min
cast Toshirô Mifune, Yoshiko Sakuma, Kinnosuke Nakamura, Yūjirô Ishihara, Katsuo Nakamura, Kankuro Nakamura *cin* Kazuo Yamada *m* Masaru Satô

Toshirô Mifune is Kansuke Yamamoto, a samurai so desperate to see the unification of sixteenth-century Japan under one rule that he is willing to stoop pretty low to achieve that aim. The banner he chooses to support is that of Lord Takeda, whose rise to power and relentless defeat of his rivals is aided by the conniving Yamamoto's underhand dealings and betrayals.

Alejandro González Iñárritu
Mexico, 1963–

There was a revolution in Mexican film at the start of the twenty-first century and Alejandro González Iñárritu was its leader. After working as a DJ on Mexico City's leading radio station WFM, he made radio and television commercials, and formed his own production company. He then teamed up with novelist Guillermo Arriago to make eleven short films, which soon melded into three stories and, over the course of 36 drafts, became one movie – *Amores perros* (*Love's A Bitch*, 2000). Beginning mid-action with two panicked youths and a heavily bleeding dog slumped in a speeding car, this visceral, cerebral and emotional wallop of a movie shuttles back and forth in time. It rewinds to the action replay of an accident in which various strata of Mexican society collide: the working-class tearaways who profit from dog fighting, a *haute bourgeoisie* model and an ex-revolutionary who now earns a living as a hit man.

The film's criminal elements and triptych structure drew false comparisons with *Pulp Fiction* (1994), but whereas Quentin Tarantino has little interest in the world outside the cinema, Iñárritu has a modernist, almost gauche belief that film has a social, moral and spiritual component. *Amores per-*

ros was hailed as the start of a new Mexican revolution that included Guillermo Del Toro's *The Devil's Backbone* (2001) and Alfonso Cuarón's *Y tu mama tambien* (2001). This wasn't simply supposition, the three directors worked closely together – Iñárritu introduced Cuarón to actor Gael García Bernal, who then starred in *Y tu mama tambien*, and Del Toro was editing consultant on the sprawling original cut of *Amores perros*.

After a couple of heady years, the invigorating promise of Mexican cinema seemed to dissipate, not least because the three amigos moved on: Del Toro went back to Hollywood to make *Blade 2* (2002), Cuarón helmed *Harry Potter And The Prisoner Of Azkaban* (2004) and Iñárritu made *21 Grams* (2003) in the US. Unlike many directors who have a stunning debut and then jettison the team that made their success possible, Iñárritu retained the services of his production designer (Brigitte Broch), cinematographer (Rodrigo Prieto) and, most importantly, his writer (Guillermo Arriaga). While critics pointed out the superficial similarities between the two films – three sets of lives intersect thanks to a car accident – *21 Grams* was more byzantinely brilliant than its predecessor, its puzzle-plot structurally analogous to the quantum mathematical theory that Sean Penn's professor expounds in a key scene. *21 Grams* announced Iñárritu not just as major Mexican director, but as a genuine American auteur. Whether he confirmed that promise with *Babel* (2006) is a matter of heated critical debate. For some, this star-studded global enterprise, in which interlocking narratives ambitiously span different continents and adopt various languages, was his most towering achievement yet. However, cynics voiced vastly different opinions on a sprawling opus they regarded as baggy, indulgent and dangerously close to self-parody. LH

Amores perros (Love's A Bitch) 2000, 154 min
cast Emilio Echevarria, Gael García, Goya Toledo, Alvaro Guerrero, Vanessa Bauche, Jorge Salinas *cin* Rodrigo Prieto *m* Gustavo Santaolalla

Critics often claim that only two of the three stories work: they praise the kinetic energy of the down-and-dirty tales of dog fights and paid assassins, but spurn the sedate story of the media couple whose dog disappears beneath the floorboards of their love nest. In fact, it is this section with its tonal and stylistic shift which reveals Iñárritu at his most accomplished and dexterous, reminiscent of Luis Buñuel at his bourgeois-satirizing best.

21 Grams 2003, 124 min
cast Sean Penn, Benicio Del Toro, Naomi Watts, Charlotte Gainsbourg, Melissa Leo, Clea DuVall *cin* Rodrigo Prieto *m* Gustavo Santaolalla

Less acclaimed than its predecessor, *21 Grams* (which refers to the amount of weight that reportedly leaves a human body when it dies) is not only more cerebrally challenging than *Amores perros*, it's also more emotionally involving. If crying on cue is the litmus test of great acting, Clea DuVall choking back the tears in hospital is a small example of transcendent genius.

Juzo Itami
Japan, 1933–97

Ultimately the victim of Japan's celebrity culture, Itami was the country's pre-eminent satirist who took on the yakuza (Japanese Mafia) and suffered the consequences. The son of leading director Mansaka Itami, Juzo was an actor, writer, commercials director and chat-show host, before finally becoming a filmmaker at the age of 51. His award-winning debut, *The Funeral* (1984), had all the essential Itamo ingredients. With a strong female character at its centre in the form of his wife Nobuko Miyamoto (a constantly luminous presence throughout his work), the film was a buoyant and acerbic Buñuelian satire on social rituals. In this case, Itami trained his sardonic lens on the traditionally correct way to bury one's father, but subsequently dished out the same treatment to Japanese attitudes towards food, crime, sex, death and taxes.

Tampopo (*Dandelion*, 1985), styled as "Japan's first noodle Western", was a phenomenally successful international export, although it was something of a flop in its home country, where his next two films fared far better. *A Taxing Woman* (1987) and *A Taxing Woman's Return* (1988) were about a demure tax inspector who doggedly brings organized crime to account. Itami returned to the subject of gangsters with *Minbo no onna* (*The Gentle Art Of Japanese Extortion*, 1992), which painted the yakuza as buffoons and dishonourable cowards. Shortly after the film's release, Itami was attacked outside his home by five hoodlums who slashed him across the face, neck and arms. Almost as an act of defiance, the director used his subsequent hospitalization and placement on the witness protection scheme as comedy material for *The Last Dance* (1993) and *Women Of The Police Protection Programme* (1997). Two days before a celebrity magazine was due to print claims of an alleged affair, Itami threw himself off the roof of an eight-storey building, apparently leaving a suicide note claiming that "only through death can I prove my innocence". LH

Tampopo (Dandelion) 1985, 114 min
cast Tsutomu Yamazaki, Noboku Miyamoto, Koji Yakusho, Ken Watanabe, Rikiya Yasuoka cin Masaki Tamura m Kunihiko Murai

A truck driver rides into town and helps a widowed restaurant owner make the best noodles in Tokyo. This *Rio Bravo*-inspired plot is only the main course in a gleefully anarchic comedy that was originally conceived as consisting of thirty anecdotes about food, and it is these asides – such as the art of slurping and an erotic moment between a gangster, his moll and an egg yolk – that are the real *amuses bouches*.

Minbo no onna (The Gentle Art Of Japanese Extortion) 1992, 125 min
cast Nobuko Miyamoto, Akir Takaranda, Takehiro Murata, Yasuo Daichi cin Yonezo Maeda m Toshiyuki Honda

Itami's sixth film is an immaculately researched comedy about the tactics and dirty tricks of the yakuza. In true Western fashion, a no-nonsense lawyer (Nobuko Miyamoto) takes on gangsters who have requisitioned a hotel for their own unsavoury purposes. However, comedy soon gives way to violence, just as it did in Itami's own ill-fated life.

Joris Ivens
Netherlands, 1898–1989

Documentarist Joris Ivens filmed in many of the most newsworthy locations in the world between the 1930s and 80s. After serving in World War I, he studied photochemistry in Berlin, where he became involved in student politics, and his radicalization continued while he was working in Dresden and Jena. In 1926, he became the manager of the Amsterdam branch of his family's photography business, and the following year, he co-founded the film society Filmliga, which became a major influence on Dutch film culture.

The symphonic character of Ivens' early documentaries owed much to the avant-garde movements of the time. *The Bridge* (1928) was a rhythmic essay on the structure and function of a Rotterdam drawbridge, and it is considered a landmark in Dutch cinema. After lecturing in the Soviet Union in 1929 at the invitation of Vsevolod Pudovkin, Ivens shot the documentary *Komsomol* (*Song Of Heroes*, 1932), which celebrated the Soviet experiment as a modernist vision of industrial progress. The film marked a shift in Ivens' work from the aestheticization of experience to the more committed rendition of sociopolitical realities. Of his subsequent films, *Borinage* (1933) profiled the harsh realities of life in a Belgian mining community, *New Earth* (1934) detailed the Dutch effort to hold back the water of the Zuider Zee and reclaim the land, and *The Spanish Earth* (1937) looked at the plight of civilians caught up in the Spanish Civil War, becoming one of the first films to highlight the atrocities of the Franco regime.

Benefiting from the financial backing of the Roosevelt administration in the US, Ivens then produced some of his most powerful films, including *The 400 Million* (1938), which charted the misery of the Chinese people after the Japanese invasion. *The Power And The Land* (1940), which was made for the US Department of Agriculture, glorified the electrification of American farms. Ivens was offered the post of Film Commissioner for the Netherlands East Indies in 1944, and initially took the job. However, his sympathy for the Indonesian liberation struggle resulted in his resignation, and the anti-colonial film *Indonesia Calling* (1946).

In 1951, Ivens was identified as a Communist by the House Un-American Activities Committee, and never worked in the US again. He then spent four decades making documentaries in areas where left-wing movements challenged international capital. One of these films, *Song Of The Rivers* (1954), utilized footage shot in 32 different countries and was seen by an amazing 250 million people worldwide. After a period in Prague, he established a permanent base in Paris and made *La Seine a rencontré Paris* (*The Seine Meets Paris*, 1957), a poetic tribute to the role of the river in the lives of Parisians. A decade later, he contributed to *Loin du Vietnam* (*Far From Vietnam*), a film sympathetic to the North Vietnamese cause, on which Jean-Luc Godard, Agnès Varda and Claude Lelouch also worked. This was one of the many films Ivens made about the Communist world in this period.

The release of his memoirs and an archive at the Dutch Film Museum coincided with the Dutch government apologizing to the acclaimed "Flying Dutchman", and he received a Golden Lion for lifetime achievement at Venice in 1988. For his influential use of montage and his committed internationalism, modern documentary filmmaking owes Ivens a considerable debt. RA

The Spanish Earth 1937, 52 min, b/w

with Manuel Azaña, José Díaz, Dolores Ibárruri, Enrique Lister, Martinez de Aragón *cin* John Fernhout, Joris Ivens

Unashamedly taking the Republican part, this film follows the everyday struggle for survival of villagers caught up in the Spanish Civil War. With English-language narration by Ernest Hemingway and John Dos Passos, it is considered one of the most important documentaries on the conflict, and is a vivid example of the camera being used on the front line of a conflict.

James Ivory

US, 1928–

The relationship between producers and directors has been significant throughout British film history, but rarely has a filmmaking partnership been as important as that of James Ivory and Ismail Merchant. Over the last four decades, Ivory's directorial style has become readily identifiable as the English-heritage marque of the Merchant-Ivory filmmaking brand.

Originally intending to be a set designer, Ivory studied architecture and fine arts before being drawn to direction at the University of Southern California. Beginning his career in documentaries, he made *Venice: Themes And Variations* (1957) and *The Sword And The Flute* (1960). The latter film was about Indian art, and prompted the Asia Society to commission Ivory to shoot a film in India. It was there that he met producer Ismail Merchant and screenwriter and author Ruth Prawer Jhabvala and formed one of the most enduring filmmaking teams of recent decades.

Merchant-Ivory's first international success was *Shakespeare Wallah* (1965), an exploration of the vanishing British way of life in post-colonial India. It signalled a preoccupation with cultural clash and displacement that has since remained central to the Merchant-Ivory tradition. However, the subsequent failures of *The Guru* (1968) and *Bombay Talkie* (1970), a tribute to the Indian film industry that was suffused with cultural misunderstandings and a self-reflexive edge, led to the team leaving India.

In America, Ivory continued looking for his niche with a retelling of the 1921 Fatty Arbuckle scandal. The result, *The Wild Party* (1975), was a brittle exposé of the moral bankruptcy behind the riotous veneer of pre-Production Code Hollywood. *Autobiography Of A Princess* (1975) found Ivory back in Europe filming a tea party at which a displaced maharaja's daughter recalled her past. The film's record of "Old World" manners proved key to the Merchant-Ivory vision. However, he returned to the US for *Roseland* (1977), a portmanteau film set in New York's Roseland ballroom that was distinguished by characteristically sincere turns from Teresa Wright and Lou Jacobi.

In 1979, an adaptation of Henry James's *The Europeans* inaugurated a cycle of Edwardian literary tributes, including *The Bostonians* (1984), that finally established the Merchant-Ivory name. Attentive to the tensions of sensibility and place in stories of Anglo-Americans confronted with morally unabashed Continentals, these excavations of repression came to resemble a critique of contemporary Britain's return to Victorian values under successive Tory governments. One of their biggest successes, *A Room With A View* (1985), traced the sexual awakening of E.M. Forster's English heroine (Helena Bonham Carter) in an atmospheric turn-of-the-century Florence. Another Forster adaptation, *Maurice* (1987), resonated with a diversifying 1980s Britain as it stealthily broached the issue of homosexuality in the punts of Edwardian Cambridge. The appeal for tolerance in *Howards End* (1992) also chimed with a country looking for a new direction, and the film did terrific business, while *Remains Of The Day* (1993), based on a novel by Kazuo Ishiguro, apotheosized the dynamics of Britain's class heritage.

Ivory briefly broke his series of literary adaptations in 1995 with *Jefferson In Paris* (1995), but the film erred towards stodge. However, he returned to form with *A Soldier's Daughter Never Cries* (1998), from a novel by Kaylie Jones, which was lightened by Leelee Sobieski's understated performance as a young American eagerly throwing herself into 1960s Paris. Based on an Ishiguro screenplay, *The White Countess*

Tuscan outing: Helena Bonham Carter and Judi Dench go for a ride in Merchant-Ivory's adaptation of E.M. Forster's novel *A Room With A View*.

A Room With A View 1985, 117 min

cast Maggie Smith, Helena Bonham Carter, Denholm Elliott, Daniel Day Lewis, Simon Callow, Judi Dench *cin* Tony Pierce-Roberts *m* Richard Robbins

With its sterling cast – including Helena Bonham Carter as the "transfigured" Lucy Honeychurch and Maggie Smith as her spinster chaperone – this Florentine excursion is as sprightly as the Baedeker travel guides it reviled. The tempering of Ivory's stylish depiction of English Home Counties values with the liberating effects of romantic Tuscany ensured that the film became a key landmark in the British film renaissance of the 1980s.

Howards End 1992, 142 min

cast Anthony Hopkins, Emma Thompson, Helena Bonham Carter, Vanessa Redgrave, James Wilby, Samuel West *cin* Tony Pierce-Roberts *m* Richard Robbins

This involved tale of changing class relations in Edwardian England is one of the Merchant-Ivory team's most challenging adaptations, with double plot lines and indecorous conflict above and beyond the usual issue of settling suitable marriage partners for the protagonists. Emma Thompson ran off with the Academy Award for best actress in what is undoubtedly "her" film, notwithstanding other solid performances from the British thespian aristocracy.

The Remains Of The Day 1993, 134 min

cast Anthony Hopkins, Emma Thompson, Peter Vaughan, James Fox, Ben Chaplin, Christopher Reeve, Hugh Grant, Michael Lonsdale *cin* Tony Pierce-Roberts *m* Richard Robbins

Anthony Hopkins gives an award-winning performance as the traditional pre-war English butler in this adaptation of Kazuo Ishiguro's fine novel. His character's stiff upper lip is at once a metaphor for the meticulous Merchant-Ivory reinvention of the past and a cautionary critique of the social displacements to which the British are prone.

(2005) was a romantic drama set in 1930s Shanghai that revolved around diplomat Ralph Fiennes' relationship with displaced Russian aristocrat Natasha Richardson. It didn't live up to earlier career highlights, but confirmed Merchant-Ivory's reputation as a potent arthouse crowd puller. It was the last film on which Ismail Merchant would be producer; he died the year the film was released. RA

Peter Jackson
New Zealand, 1961–

Back when he was cooking up latex models in his mum's oven and casting his friends in his home-made horror-comedy *Bad Taste* (1987), Peter Jackson would have been surprised as anyone to find out that, a decade later, he'd be handed the reins of an epic movie trilogy based on a beloved – and supposedly unfilmable – fantasy tome. All three parts of Jackson's CGI-enabled adaptation of J.R.R. Tolkien's trilogy *The Lord Of The Rings* (2001–03) – which clocked in at some nine hours in total – were phenomenal commercial and critical successes. John Boorman, who once attempted to helm his own *Rings* cycle, praised Jackson's work as an achievement "of such scope and magnitude that it can only be compared to the building of the great Gothic cathedrals". The hosannas culminated in a sweep of Oscars for the final segment, *The Return Of The King* (2003). However, this wholehearted endorsement of Jackson by the mainstream was not entirely at the expense of his fondness for gross-out thrills. The lead orc in *Return Of The King*, whose physiognomy evokes a pig in the last stages of syphilis, could have stepped straight out of *Bad Taste*, while the film's early close-up of the rotting Gollum biting into a juicy, writhing fish is a testament to Jackson's high valuation of the ickiness factor.

Jackson coined the term "splatstick" to describe his early features. *Meet The Feebles* (1989) was an unhinged mutation of *The Muppet Show*, its deft puppetry telling a backbiting tale of drug abuse, extortion, robbery and murder. Cult favourite *Bad Taste* hinged on an alien fast-food franchise that descends on New Zealand to farm human meat, and in the impressive *Braindead* (1992), Jackson conducts a blood-squirting, flesh-rotting symphony of zombie havoc that certainly gives his hero George Romero a run for his money.

The director's gifts for lurid black comedy were never more evident than in his best film, *Heavenly Creatures* (1994), a recounting of a real-life 1950s murder in which teenage friends Pauline Parker and Juliet Hulme bludgeoned Parker's mother to death. *Heavenly Creatures* used some of the locations of the real-life events to add a documentary-style authenticity, while daring to envision the girls' labyrinthine imaginary world. The film evokes a fever dream worthy of Terry Gilliam in conjuring up the make-believe kingdom of Borovnia, a bawdy and violent fantasia populated by life-size plasticine figures.

Following the sleeper success of *Heavenly Creatures*, which launched Kate Winslet's big-screen career, Jackson directed the odd supernatural thriller comedy *The Frighteners* (1997), but his mind was already on hobbit-related matters. In an unprecedented production decision by New Line, the three instalments of *The Lord Of The Rings* were shot back-to-back before the first one was even released – to tremendous acclaim – in 2001. The films' many battlefield scenes and the story's epic conflict between the forces of good and evil gained an added resonance in the midst of terrorist attacks and the wars in Afghanistan and Iraq. Basking in *Rings*' golden glow, Jackson won the added honour of the highest upfront salary ever paid to a director: $20 million to helm *King Kong* (2005). A remake of one of his favourite films, *King Kong*'s story draws from a typically Jacksonian combination of fantasy, horror and buried romance. JW

Heavenly Creatures 1994, 98 min
cast Melanie Lynskey, Kate Winslet, Sarah Peirse, Diana Kent, Clive Merrison, Simon O'Conner *cin* Alun Bollinger *m* Peter Dasent

In 1950s New Zealand, sullen introvert Pauline Parker (Melanie Lynskey) meets transplanted Brit Juliet Hulme (Kate Winslet), a sickly drama queen with an overactive imagination. As the girls delve ever deeper into a fantasy world of pop-culture icons and violent retribution, Jackson's perfectly calibrated nightmare carefully sustains a breathless pace and an unnerving pitch of hermetic hysteria, barrelling headlong towards a conclusion that's no less horrifying for being inevitable.

The Lord Of The Rings: The Return Of The King 2003, 201 min

cast Elijah Wood, Ian McKellen, Liv Tyler, Viggo Mortensen, Sean Astin, Cate Blanchett, Christopher Lee, Andy Serkis *cin* Andrew Lesnie *m* Howard Shore

How do you summarize the Oscar-winning final entry in Jackson's monumental celluloid transcription of J.R.R. Tolkien's secular scripture? A Manichean battle between innocence (as embodied by Elijah Wood's saucer-eyed Frodo) and corruption (the slimy and sibilant Gollum), perhaps. The latter is the trilogy's real star, his charisma being equal parts state-of-the-art CGI animation and deft characterization from Andy Serkis, the actor who "modelled" him. Essentially a series of eye-popping, cross-cut set pieces sutured with stilted exposition and dreamy romantic interludes, Jackson's *chef-d'oeuvre* is undeniably impressive.

King Kong 2005, 187 min

cast Naomi Watts, Jack Black, Adrien Brody, Thomas Kretschmann, Andy Serkis *cin* Andrew Lesnie *m* James Newton Howard

Jackson's remake of the 1933 classic is much faster, yet far longer, than the original. Starry-eyed actress Ann Darrow (Naomi Watts) and rapacious movie producer Carl Denham (Jack Black) embark on a speculative adventure to Skull Island, where Ann becomes first enticement and then love interest to the titular beast. Jackson retains several key members of his ace *Lord Of The Rings* team: Andrew Lesnie again provides the eye-popping cinematography and Andy "Gollum" Serkis delivers a protean CGI-assisted performance as the hairy hero. But it's Watts who's the true special effect – has anyone ever delivered a more moving performance opposite a blue screen?

Henry Jaglom
UK, 1941–

Actor, producer, director, screenwriter, editor, Henry Jaglom remains an unsung model for independence in modern American cinema. He trained at the Actors Studio before landing roles off-Broadway and in television. In 1967 he shot an unreleased documentary in Israel on the Six Day War. A player in the New Hollywood efflorescence, he appeared in Richard Rush's *Psych-Out* (1968), Jack Nicholson's *Drive, He Said* (1971) and Dennis Hopper's *The Last Movie* (1971). He was also an editorial consultant on *Easy Rider* (1969).

His first feature – *A Safe Place* (1971) – was an experimental lament for cinema's past that revolved around an emotionally vulnerable Tuesday Weld. Orson Welles, a perennial influence on Jaglom, appeared as a magician. Female subjectivity coloured several Jaglom films, although *Tracks* (1976) explored America's Vietnam trauma, while *Sitting Ducks* (1978) was a wacky road movie that sprung ready-made from the chemistry between Michael Emil and Zack Norman's eternal optimists.

Jaglom didn't quite manage to sustain this impetus, and his subsequent efforts were marked by a big heart but intermittent inspiration. *Always* (1985) was a California confessional in which Jaglom and his ex-wife Patrice Townsend virtually played themselves

as they pondered where their marriage went wrong. *Someone To Love* (1987) saw Jaglom and his buddies pondering post-marital solitude while Orson Welles (in his last screen role) tried to stay objective. *New Year's Day* (1989) pursued the rumination on Jaglom's midlife crisis in a New York apartment where he confronted a bevy of women with problems of their own. Welles, Emil, Andrea Marcovicci: Jaglom's actors really shone in *Someone To Love*, but by the late 1980s the scripts and the sensibility seemed late-1970s.

An autobiographer in many ways second only to Woody Allen, Jaglom exposed a catalogue of his weaknesses in 1995's *Last Summer In The Hamptons*. However, his *Festival In Cannes* (2001) found him in a Croisette habitat, cavorting with celebrities as Greta Scacchi tries to finance her own project. His best work views a man's world through the adroitly drawn gaze of women protagonists. RA

Tracks 1976, 92 min

cast Dennis Hopper, Taryn Power, Dean Stockwell, Topo Swope, Michael Emil, Zack Norman, Alfred Ryder, Barbara Flood *cin* Paul Glickman

One of the most successful of Henry Jaglom's attempts to do American art cinema, this account of a Vietnam vet's journey as he accompanies his dead buddy's coffin across the country audaciously measures the decline of traditional movie narrative against the inner disintegration of Dennis Hopper's traumatized serviceman. Patently taking its cue from *Easy Rider*'s cornucopia of the road, Jaglom's film could be seen as a genuine eulogy for New Hollywood and a particular moment in America's dream life.

Steve James
US, 1954–

Chicago-based director Steve James made his name with the basketball documentary *Hoop Dreams* (1994). Since then he has made forays into dramatic filmmaking, though his documentaries remain his best work.

A touching and inspiring exploration of the pursuit of the American Dream, *Hoop Dreams* interweaves the personal and the public, following two African-American teenagers who dream of basketball glory. Incredibly, the film was not nominated for best documentary at the Oscars but it otherwise proved a slam dunk all round. James's next film, *Prefontaine* (1997), was less captivating, a standard-issue sports biopic about the American athlete Steve Prefontaine who died aged 24. James returned to the documentary format with *Stevie* (2002), about an abused young man living in a series of Illinois foster homes. JC

Hoop Dreams 1994, 170 min

with William Gates, Arthur Agee, Emma Gates, Ken Curtis, Sheila Agee, Arthur Agee *cin* Peter Gilbert *m* Ben Sidran

Steve James condensed 250 hours of footage – the result of seven years of filmmaking – into three glorious hours on the screen. Initially intended to be a short film about

Chicago's playground courts, the project expanded with the discovery of its teen heroes William Gates and Arthur Agee. A modern American classic.

Miklós Jancsó
Hungary, 1921–

If you ever believed that arthouse cinema was haughtily above the whims of fashion, you only have to look at the career of Miklós Jancsó. A leading light of the Hungarian New Wave in the 1960s and 70s, at the peak of his international success, he was generally considered a worthy equal to the likes of Michelangelo Antonioni and Ingmar Bergman. But today, Jancsó is in danger of becoming one of the forgotten men of world cinema – his films are now rarely seen outside his native country.

Jancsó started his career making newsreels, before graduating to features with *The Bells Have Gone To Rome* in 1958, but he became an internationally recognizable name with *The Round-Up* (1965). His reputation grew further with the release of *The Red And The White* (1967), *Silence And Cry* (1967) and *The Confrontation* (1969). Each of his films from the 1960s and 70s, whether they were set in the nineteenth or twentieth centuries, contained sly parallels to contemporary, Communist Hungary through the symbols and metaphors he designed to befuddle the censors. Jancsó's trademark is the sequence shot in which his camera hypnotically glides, zooms and weaves around his characters in takes lasting up to ten minutes. *Red Psalm* (1972) was composed of only 28 immaculately choreographed shots, *Elektreia* (1974) only eight. His characters loom in and out of frame and often communicate through actions rather than words, reduced to the status of pawns, metonyms or figures in the landscape (often the wide, open, unforgiving Hungarian plains). They are all part of Jancsó's allegorical ballets, his inscrutable Kafkaesque studies of the mechanics of power and the responsibilities of individuals in a repressive regime or revolution.

Whether Jancsó's career represented a refinement or repetition of style was a bone of contention in the 1970s. Critical opinion veered between admiration for his contemplative restraint and accusations of dehumanization and mechanization. He was even suspected of being a mannerist descending into self-parody, which was apotheosized by an early shot in *Agnus Dei* (1970) in which the camera ambles slowly across a familiar plain and comes to rest on a young woman emerging naked from the river. (Nudity was another Jancsó trope, which in his later films came to represent liberation of the spirit and rebellion.) However, repetition is often the vice of the visionary, and at worst, Jancsó was responsible for creating his own strangely mesmerizing genre. Since his international fame ebbed away in the late 1970s, Jancsó has directed over 25 films, mostly satires and comedies for Hungarian audiences that have only rarely been screened abroad. LH

The Round-Up (Szegénylegények) 1965, 90 min, b/w
cast János Görbe, Tibor Molnár, András Kozák, Gábor Agárdy, Zoltán Latinovits *cin* Tamás Somlo

All the peasants from one village are arrested by police in the hope of weeding out supporters of a revolutionary outlaw. Although set in Hungary in 1860, there are clear echoes of the retaliations that followed the failed anti-Soviet uprising of 1956. Abstract, opaque, spectacular and curiously unmoving, this is Jancsó's masterpiece, and it is stubbornly unlike the work of any other director.

The Red And The White (Csillagosok, katonák) 1967, 90 min, b/w
cast Jószef Madaras, András Kozák, Tibor Molnár, Jácint Juhász, Antoli Yabbarov *cin* Tamás Somlo

Jancsó was commissioned by the Soviet government to celebrate the fiftieth anniversary of the Bolshevik revolution of 1917 and the defeat of the Whites by the Reds. However, his abstract disregard for individuals and simple psychology meant there were no clear-eyed Communist heroes or obvious villains, just a series of executions and battles in superbly rendered panoramas with groups of fated men entering and leaving the frame. It was immediately withdrawn from distribution in the Soviet Union.

Elektreia (Szerelmem, Elektra) 1974, 70 min
cast Mari Töröcsik, Jozsef Madaras, György Cserhalmi, Mária Bajcsay, Lajos Balázsovits, Gabi Jobba *cin* János Kende *m* Tamás Cseh

In the mid-1970s, Jancsó filmed in Italy and made, in the words of one critic, "bitter erotica". However, he did have one last masterpiece in him. Based on the Elektra myth, this is the most Jancsósian of dramas: symbolic, balletic and oddly captivating. He keeps the number of scenes to a bare minimum while retaining the delirious folk musical element he had introduced in *The Confrontation* (1969).

Agnès Jaoui
France, 1964–

Agnès Jaoui is a rare species of filmmaker that the French seem to specialize in. Like Josiane Balasko, Valeria Bruni-Tedeschi and Nicole Garcia, she is an actress-writer-director. Jaoui also belongs to the select subset of the husband-and-wife partnership. She's been writing and starring with spouse Jean-Pierre Bacri ever since they met in a theatre production in 1987 and agreed that they didn't like the sorts of roles they were being offered. They entered the film world in 1993 by writing the screen adaption of their first play *Kitchen With Apartment*, and followed with *Smoking/No Smoking* (1993) and *On connaît la chanson* (*Same Old Song*, 1997) for legendary auteur Alain Resnais.

The two comedies directed by Jaoui were built on the same ensemble model, and inhabit a social milieu where characters crisscross arbitrarily around the axis of a disagreeable character played by Bacri. In *Le goût des autres* (*The Taste Of Others*, 2000), he plays a gauche businessman whose toilet humour is not to the taste of the actress he is ineptly wooing. In *Look At Me* (*Comme une image*, 2004) he is a tyrannical wreck, a famous author surrounded by a gaggle of sycophants and a daughter who hopelessly craves his attention. Both films display a wry humour and sly charm, and rival the best of mid-period Woody Allen for their piquant observations about human relationships. LH

Le goût des autres (The Taste Of Others)
2000, 112 min

cast Anne Alvaro, Jean-Pierre Bacri, Alain Chabat, Agnès Jaoui, Gérard Lanvin, Christiane Millet, Wladimir Yordanoff *cin* Laurent Dailland

A subtle, compelling comedy whose appeal sneaks up on the audience like the improbable charm of Jean-Pierre Bacri's taste-free businessman. By the end of the film we're even rooting for a character who only an hour earlier had made everyone in the cinema – characters and audience – cringe with the embarrassment of the socially superior. A small triumph for good taste.

Derek Jarman
UK, 1942–94

There will never be another filmmaker like Derek Jarman. His work was a sparkling collision of influences: cinematic, theoretical, painterly, political and poetic. He was a gay, avant-garde provocateur like his hero Pier Paolo Pasolini and just as importantly Jarman was a constant gardener, a eulogist for rural Britain like his other heroes, the equally adventurous Powell and Pressburger.

Jarman's childhood, as seen in home movies in *The Last Of England* (1988), spanned continents as his RAF officer father moved his family from England to Italy to India. As an art student in the 1960s, Jarman befriended David Hockney, amongst others, before breaking into cinema as a set designer on Ken Russell's *The Devils* (1971) and *Savage Messiah* (1972). His artistic training is obvious not just in *Caravaggio* (1986), which is composed as a series of tableaux in the inimitable chiaroscuro style of the eponymous artist, but also in the minimalist compositions of *Edward II* (1993). Jarman's very sparing use of design wasn't entirely down to his famously low budgets; stark theatricality was a key component of the director's aesthetic, as was his daring use of anachronisms – phones and typewriters in *Caravaggio*, 1930s gangsters and modern riot police in *Edward II*.

A gay activist both in and out of the cinema, Jarman aimed to reclaim the previously closeted or suppressed, such as the philosopher *Wittgenstein* (1993) or the crucified saint *Sebastiane* (1976). The latter, a sunbaked homoerotic odyssey in Latin, made stark parallels between religious and homosexual persecution (as did many of his later films). It got Channel 4 into serious trouble when it was transmitted in the UK in 1985 (Jarman claimed that he managed to sneak the first erect penis into British cinema via a cunning trick with aspect ratio). Jarman didn't just reclaim, he also re-contextualized, making *The Tempest* (1979) a metaphor for homosexuality. He cheekily pursued the same theme in *The Angelic Conversation* (1985), in which Judi Dench read Shakespearean sonnets about studly young men; the inference about Britain's greatest playwright was obvious.

However, there was another side to the radical filmmaker: conservatism. While *Jubilee* (1977) is celebrated as Britain's first punk movie, it is seen through the ultimately disapproving eyes of Queen Elizabeth I, and Jarman arguably shares her disdain. Concluding not with a three-minute gob of musical spite, but an ode to the British landscape, *Jubilee* is, in hindsight, comfortingly pantheistic rather than dangerously anarchistic. In interviews, the director waxed nostalgic for the dear Old Blighty celebrated in The Smiths song "The Queen Is Dead", for which he made a dazzling, Kenneth Anger-esque video. *The Garden* (1990), set in Jarman's own backyard, was a very peculiar English pastoral, made with the same celebratory intent as Powell and Pressburger's eccentric paean, *A Canterbury Tale* (1944).

Jarman had been diagnosed as HIV positive in the mid-1980s, and confronted his illness head-on in 1993 with *Blue*. The extraordinary film was composed of a blue screen throughout, and a soundtrack dominated by Jarman's own, often truculent voice recounting his life with the disease, interspersed with the voices of John Quentin, Nigel Terry and Tilda Swinton. When he finally succumbed to AIDS, Jarman left behind a unique body of work, but just as importantly he left a tradition – that lives on in the work of John Maybury, Isaac Julien and Sally Potter – of a British cinema that is painterly, sexual and political. LH

Jubilee 1977, 100 min

cast Jenny Runacre, Nell Campbell, Toyah Willcox, Jordan, Hermine Demoriane, Ian Charleson, Orlando *cin* Peter Middleton *m* Brian Eno

With his short Super 8 films, Jarman had embraced punk's do-it-yourself aesthetic years before the anarchic revolution of 1977, and *Jubilee* bristles with the amateurish energy of the subculture. Queen Elizabeth I and her mystic John Dee travel to a post-apocalyptic Britain where Bod and her gang of young nihilists run riot.

The Tempest 1979, 95 min

cast Heathcote Williams, Karl Johnson, Toyah Willcox, Peter Bull, Richard Warwick, Elisabeth Welch, Jack Birkett *cin* Peter Middleton *m* Wavemaker

Jarman loitered around the edges of self-indulgence and, with his mates starring in his films, his work can sometimes feel like a club the audience does not belong to. This does occasionally seem like a home movie in which some giddy friends have raided the dressing-up box, but it is, nevertheless, a uniquely lusty and unfaithful adaptation of the Bard, topped off by a rudely exuberant Hollywood-style song-and-dance number.

Caravaggio 1986, 93 min

cast Nigel Terry, Sean Bean, Tilda Swinton, Nigel Davenport, Robbie Coltrane, Michael Gough *cin* Gabriel Beristain *m* Simon Fisher-Turner

A synchronous mix of Jarman's low-budget aesthetic and the sixteenth-century painter's own pared-down vision results in a series of ravishingly elemental tableaux. The director adopts the theatrical artifice of employing one set for many different locations while using anachronisms to underline the timelessness of his themes, making explicit the connection between the two maverick artists divided by centuries.

Jim Jarmusch

US, 1953–

Of all the directors to emerge from the burgeoning US independent scene of the late 1980s, few have made so much out of being abroad in America.

Having studied at the Cinémathèque Française in Paris and been the teaching assistant of legendary director Nicholas Ray at the Tisch School of the Arts in New York, Jim Jarmusch made his first film in 1981. Shot on 16mm, *Permanent Vacation* chronicled a sense of urban dislocation and predicted a central theme of his future work. His first feature, *Stranger Than Paradise* (1984), was derived from a short entitled *New World*, and won the Caméra d'Or at Cannes. However, Jarmusch's true breakthrough came with *Down By Law* (1986), a comic tale about three Louisiana jailbirds, which was a key moment in the new American cinema. His follow-up, *Mystery Train* (1989), was a meditation on storytelling itself, with three encounters in Memphis hotel rooms being used to reflect on how we supply narrative to make sense of the world around us. Featuring Japanese Elvis fans and casting blues singer Screamin' Jay Hawkins as an argumentative receptionist, *Mystery Train* made pop culture integral to the American indie sensibility.

If some critics have pronounced Jarmusch adept at episodes but weak on whole narratives, others have been more alive to the poetic and musical currents in his work. Focusing on a series of oddball taxi rides in LA, New York, Paris, Rome and Helsinki, *Night On Earth* (1991) turned apparently dead moments into premonitions of eternity. Scripted and improvised dialogue were combined with beautifully monochrome, stationary long takes to highlight the apparently inconsequential in normal human experience.

Jarmusch's take on the Western, *Dead Man* (1995), featured a soundtrack by Neil Young, and the 1997 documentary *Year Of The Horse* followed the Canadian musician on tour. *Horse* was a workmanlike glimpse of Young's act, but Jarmusch generated

A melancholy Bill Murray on a quest to find the mother of his newly discovered son in the droll *Broken Flowers*.

an atmospheric sense of presence by mixing film stock and videotape. Following the hit-man thriller *Ghost Dog: The Way Of The Samurai* (1999), *Coffee And Cigarettes* (2003) was a series of short dialogues filmed in black-and-white over two decades in which a string of recognizable faces – including Jarmusch regulars Roberto Benigni and Steve Buscemi, as well as Cate Blanchett, Bill Murray and Iggy Pop – reflect on a variety of everyday themes.

Two years later, Jarmusch returned to form with *Broken Flowers*. A gift for Bill Murray, who plays a jaded figure driven to a cross-country odyssey in search of the ex-girlfriend who bore his son, the film includes all the Jarmuschian humour and geographical ennui of the director's best work. Jarmusch remains one of America's most idiosyncratic auteurs. RA

Stranger Than Paradise 1984, 89 min, b/w

cast John Lurie, Eszter Balint, Richard Edson, Cecillia Stark, Danny Rosen *cin* Tom DiCillo *m* John Lurie

Willie, a Hungarian expatriate in New York, is initially irritated when his less-Americanized cousin Eva comes to visit, but eventually grows to like her. After she moves to Ohio to stay with an aunt, Willie and his friend Eddie embark on a road trip to find her. Observed with wry humour and featuring a soundtrack that combines original music by John Lurie with recordings by Screamin' Jay Hawkins and Bartok, this is a gem of exilic cinema.

Down By Law 1986, 107 min, b/w

cast Tom Waits, John Lurie, Roberto Benigni, Nicoletta Braschi, Ellen Barkin, Billie Neal *cin* Robby Müller *m* John Lurie, Tom Waits

Three petty criminals – John Lurie, Tom Waits and Roberto Benigni – are flung together by Jarmuschian fate in this comedic, but similarly themed, follow-up to *Stranger Than Paradise*, which is memorable for Benigni's assertion that "It's a sad and beautiful world". Few road movies since Frank Capra's *It Happened One Night* (1934) have so successfully celebrated this kind of simple, riotous camaraderie.

Dead Man 1995, 120 min, b/w

cast Johnny Depp, Gary Farmer, Robert Mitchum, Lance Henriksen, Gabriel Byrne, John Hurt, Alfred Molina *cin* Robby Müller *m* Neil Young

Wounded and dying, Johnny Depp's unassuming clerk – William Blake – heads out into the wilderness. He hooks up with a Native American who believes him to be the visionary poet of the same name, and whose responses take Jarmuschian dialogue to fresh heights of the gnomic. With a haunting score by Neil Young, this is one of the most controversial and elusive Westerns ever made.

Ghost Dog: The Way Of The Samurai 1999, 116 min

cast Forest Whitaker, John Tormey, Cliff Gorman, Henry Silva, Isaach de Bankolé *cin* Robby Müller *m* RZA

Jarmusch's most commercial project to date, this reworking of the hit-man thriller sub-genre centres on a grave performance by Forest Whitaker as the eponymous assassin who is turned on by the Mob bosses he had been working for. Ghost Dog's strict adherence to the Bushidō samurai code brings some existential gravitas to the ironic show-stopping dialogue.

Humphrey Jennings
UK, 1907–50

Humphrey Jennings made some of the most poetic films in the history of British cinema. He brought an eye for the unusual and a vernacular sensibility to the depiction of the British experience.

Originally a painter and critic, Jennings joined the UK's GPO Film Unit in 1934 as a designer, editor and actor. He also co-organized the International Surrealist Exhibition in 1936 and co-founded the public-research project Mass Observation in 1937, which documented the everyday lives of the British people. Jennings's first solo film as director was *Spare Time* (1939), a portrait of the British at play that introduced a new iconography of popular leisure to British cinema and influenced the post-war Free Cinema movement.

Jennings's modernist leanings, coupled with a palpable feeling for his fellow countrymen, bore fruit in his wartime documentaries, including the celebrated *Fires Were Started* (1943). *Listen To Britain* (1941) evoked the British experience through the noise of transport and industry: men singing on a troop train, entertainers in a factory canteen, the clatter of everyday life and pianist Myra Hess performing a lunchtime recital at the National Gallery. *Words For Battle* (1941) used contemporary imagery to interpret fine poetry, while *A Diary For Timothy* (1945) looked at what the post-war world might hold for a baby born in 1944. There was a Blakean mysticism about Jennings's view of Britain that depicted the oddity of the everyday, but this failed to translate to post-war success. Jennings died while scouting locations for a new project, but his specific sensibility lives on in the work of Lindsay Anderson (who was an admirer) and later directors such as Mike Leigh and Patrick Keiller. RA

Fires Were Started 1943, 74 min, b/w

cast George Gravett, Philip Dickson, Fred Griffiths, Loris Rey, Johnny Houghton, William Sansom *cin* C. Pennington-Richards *m* William Alwyn

Following a day's work for the men of the Auxiliary Fire Service in London's docklands, Jennings treats the 1940–41 Blitz as a modern purgatory rained down upon Londoners from the air. A drama-documentary with a sense of the bizarre – for example, walls are shown ripped out, exposing the clutter of everyday life – *Fires Were Started* is a tribute to a stoic generation.

Jean-Pierre Jeunet
France, 1955–

Jean-Pierre Jeunet is the most commercially successful French director of all time, but was recently engaged in a war of attrition with both national critics and the local industry, and even lost the right to call one of his films, *A Very Long*

Engagement (2004), French.

Jeunet first came to international prominence with *Delicatessen* (1991) and *City Of Lost Children* (1995), two films he co-directed with artist and comic-book designer Marc Caro. The duo had previously made several award-winning animated shorts together, and continued in the same vein for their features. Both films were live-action "cartoons", with disturbingly quirky, hermetic universes that were simultaneously retro and futuristic, dictated by a delirious logic and captured by a fish-eye lens and MTV aesthetic. With a fastidious eye for ingenious detail, Jeunet and Caro were the gods of small things. They created a distinctive brand of Grand Guignol fairy tales, graced by Jacques Tati-esque inventiveness and populated by a company of Federico Felliniesque grotesques.

Just when the team had firmly established themselves as the rightful heirs to Georges Méliès and Jules Verne, they split up. Only Jeunet responded to an offer from Hollywood to helm the fourth *Alien* film; Caro refused to be part of the studio system and worked from his computer at home as the film's design supervisor. It was assumed that Caro would do better after the split, being the visionary element of the duo, and the ultimately anodyne *Alien: Resurrection* (1997) only seemed to confirm these suspicions. However, it was Jeunet who improbably went on to greater international success.

Jeunet's first solo feature, *Amélie* (2001), represented one of the greatest about-turns in recent cinema history. Just when critics thought they had got the measure of the director as an engineer of surreal dystopias, he produced one of the sunniest, most whimsical pieces of French confection since Jacques Demy's *The Umbrellas Of Cherbourg* (1964). *Amélie* became the most commercially successful French film of all time, but led to a running battle between the director and some Parisian critics who condemned his chocolate-box beautification of the perennially seedy Montmartre district.

"*Amélie On The Front*" or "*Amélie Goes To War*" is how some critics dubbed *A Very Long Engagement*, chiefly because it shared both the same star, the doe-eyed Audrey Tautou, and the same breathless, hectic invention, Jeunet's peculiar synthesis of hyperreality and hyperactivity. Taking six months to shoot, with thousands of extras and a reported budget of $60 million, the World War I epic was then the most expensive French film ever made. However, it can no longer be officially described as French, following a bitter legal dispute over the fact that the production company, 2003 Productions, was part-owned by American giant Warner Bros. LH

Delicatessen 1991, 99 min

cast Dominique Pinon, Marie-Laure Dougnac, Jean-Claude Dreyfus, Karin Viard, Ticky Holgado *cin* Darius Khondji *m* Carlos D'Alessio

Delicatessen takes place in a future where meat is scarce, so a carnivorous landlord murders handymen and turns them into cutlets for his tenants. However, the plot is secondary to incidental delights, such as the famous, oft-imitated scene in which a man pumping up his bicycle tyre, an old woman beating a carpet, a clown painting a ceiling and a girl playing a cello all rhythmically accompany the springs of an old bed as the butcher and his wife make noisy love.

City Of Lost Children (La cité des enfants perdus) 1995, 112 min

cast Ron Perlman, Daniel Emilfork, Judith Vittet, Dominique Pinon, Jean-Claude Dreyfus, Marc Caro *cin* Darius Khondji *m* Angelo Badalamenti

Once again the plot – this time about a mad scientist who steals the dreams of children – is peripheral to a catalogue of oddball pleasures, such as a brain in a tank, sinister Santas and a race of blind people with one artificial eye each. Four years in the making, Jean-Pierre Jeunet and Marc Caro's delirious fantasy employs more special effects than any other film in the history of French cinema.

Amélie (Le fabuleux destin d'Amélie Poulain) 2001, 122 min

cast Audrey Tautou, Mathieu Kassovitz, Rufus, Yolande Moreau, Flora Guiet *cin* Bruno Delbonnel *m* Yann Tiersen

The gamine Audrey Tautou stars as an innocent Montmartre waitress who carries out random acts of kindness, righting wrongs for other people while leading a lonely, melancholy existence until she happens upon Nino (Mathieu Kassovitz). Yet again, it's the incidental that's most pleasing in this bright, whimsical film, but instead of cannibals and cyclopses, it's the magic of *crème brûlée*.

A Very Long Engagement (Un long dimanche de fiançailles) 2004, 133 min

cast Audrey Tautou, Gaspard Ulliel, Jean-Pierre Becker, Dominique Battenfeld, Clovis Cornilliac *cin* Bruno Delbonnel *m* Angelo Badalamenti

One of the few films to be made about the French involvement in World War I since Stanley Kubrick's *Paths Of Glory* (1957), this is filmed in the sepia of old photographs with a stylistic nod to the poet and screenwriter Jacques Prévert. Audrey Tautou plays a young widow who tracks down her husband in the stubborn belief that he has not really been executed by a firing squad. The plot is a thin Maginot Line on which Jeunet hangs a series of visually staggering set pieces.

Norman Jewison
Canada, 1926–

Norman Jewison and Sidney Lumet once represented the face of liberal concern in Hollywood. After acting and writing for the BBC, Jewison joined CBS in America and directed a series of musical spectaculars. In 1963 he broke into features with such comedy vehicles as *Forty Pounds Of Trouble* (1963), featuring Tony Curtis, and *Send Me No Flowers* (1964), with Doris Day. His training in television was evident in his handling of narrative in films such as *The Cincinatti Kid* (1965), a tense poker game starring Steve McQueen.

Jewison finally made his name with the comedy *The Russians Are Coming! The Russians Are Coming!*

(1966) and *In The Heat Of The Night* (1967), a race-relations drama based on a novel by John Ball. But he then changed direction with *The Thomas Crown Affair* (1968), a caper movie with slick 1960s split-screen appeal, and *Gaily, Gaily* (1969), an amiable ramble through author Ben Hecht's memories of Chicago in 1910. Disgusted with the conservatism of Nixon's America, Jewison left for foreign locations in the early 1970s, and filmed the blowsy *Fiddler On The Roof* (1971) and *Jesus Christ Superstar* (1973). On his return the controversialist in Jewison agitated conservatives with the futuristic violence of *Rollerball* (1975) and the labour politics of the Teamster-union-inspired *F.I.S.T.* (1978). Featuring a characteristically compelling Al Pacino as an embattled attorney, *...And Justice For All* (1979) struck another blow for liberalism.

In the 1980s, Jewison addressed the issue of race more subtly in the cross-racial romantic comedy *Moonstruck* (1987), which proved to be one of the most charming films of its era and an Oscar-winner for lead actress Cher. The director also continued his self-styled "race trilogy" (begun with *In The Heat Of The Night*) with *A Soldier's Story* (1984), a whodunnit about the murder of a black army officer in the Deep South. However, the third instalment, *The Hurricane* (1999), about the wrongful imprisonment of an African-American boxer, betrayed the director as a liberal out of his time. Jewison had also been slated to direct a biography of the militant civil rights leader Malcolm X, but he stepped aside for black director Spike Lee. RA

The Cincinatti Kid 1965, 113 min
cast Steve McQueen, Edward G. Robinson, Karl Malden, Ann-Margret, Tuesday Weld, Rip Torn, Joan Blondell *cin* Philip H. Lanthrop *m* Kaki Schifrin

Graduating from Doris Day fluff to a suspenseful gambling drama based on a novel by Richard Jessup, Norman Jewison directed his first prestige studio picture. This Depression-era poker standoff between Steve McQueen and Edward G. Robinson remains an adroitly written character study and the grandaddy of the poker genre.

In The Heat Of The Night 1967, 109 min
cast Sidney Poitier, Rod Steiger, Warren Oates, Quentin Dean, James Patterson, Lee Grant, Scott Wilson *cin* Haskell Wexler *m* Quincy Jones

The culmination of Hollywood's liberal issues cycle of the time, this examination of American race relations revolves around the interplay between Rod Steiger's irascible and bigoted Southern small-town police chief and Sidney Poitier's smart young forensics expert from Philadelphia. Forced to work together on a murder inquiry, the two begin to lift the blinkers of mistrust and slowly manage to find a degree of mutual respect.

The Thomas Crown Affair 1968, 102 min
cast Steve McQueen, Faye Dunaway, Paul Bruke, Jack Weston, Todd Martin, Yaphet Kotto *cin* Haskell Wexler *m* Michel Legrand

A magnificent curio of its time, this sexy, stylish cat-and-mouse game in which Faye Dunaway's insurance investigator tries to apprehend Steve McQueen's bored financial wizard was a slick studio riposte to the European arthouse movies invading the downtown US grind houses in the mid-1960s. It was remade by John McTiernan in 1999, with Rene Russo and Pierce Brosnan taking over the lead roles.

Jia Zhang-Ke
China, 1970–

The leading light of China's "no future" generation, Jia wrote a novel when in his early twenties, studied painting and then entered the Beijing Film Academy, where he became one of the so-called Sixth Generation of filmmakers. Their films, some shot illegally, were both difficult to make and almost impossible to see in their home country. Emerging in the hothouse atmosphere of the 1990s, these socially committed filmmakers unapologetically addressed issues of political unrest, economic expansion and continuing censorship. However, this urgency didn't necessarily translate to the style of the films themselves – certainly not in Jia's case. With a patience-testing, highly deliberate tempo, he cultivated a long-take style and narrative austerity worthy of his hero Robert Bresson. Carefully scrutinizing the state of the nation, he examined cultural changes as the economy moved from state Communism to a peculiar strain of capitalism.

According to Jia, beneath the surface sheen of conspicuous consumption, brand names and communication technology, little has fundamentally changed in Chinese society. With an almost ascetic astringency, the director has chronicled a generation living in limbo: in *Pickpocket* (1997), a raw, abrasive study of a petty thief; in the sprawling *Platform* (2000), about a Maoist theatre troupe who have to face the sour realities of the free market; and in his masterpiece *Unknown Pleasures* (2002). Similar themes were explored in his first officially sanctioned movie, *The World* (2004). Here, a Beijing theme park provides an almost too perfect metaphor for globalization: in a global village containing miniaturized attractions from around the planet, Jia zeroes in on the park workers whose only real experience of the world outside China is this fantasy land.

Some critics sensed a new maturity in his next offering, the appropriately titled *Still Life* (2006), which won the Golden Lion at the Venice Film Festival. Following parallel stories of two people searching for old loves in a town that's being demolished to make way for a dam project, the drama was arguably more lyrical and nuanced than its predecessors, although the languor remained the same. LH

Unknown Pleasures (Ren xiao yao) 2002, 113 min

cast Wei Wei Zhao, Qiong Wu, Qing Feng Zhou, Hong Wei Wang, Ru Bai, Xi An Liu, Shou Lin Xu, Ren Ai Jun, Dao Xiao, Zi Ying *cin* Nelson Yu Lik-wai

Bin Bin yearns for the star of the local Mongolian Liquor King Troupe while he hangs out in bars and clubs with his friend Xiao Ji, surrounded by the latest consumer durables. Global and national events play out on TV like electronic wallpaper, a constant yet near invisible presence. Jia deftly weaves a tapestry of listless ennui, while the mobile camera seems unwilling to spend much time with the protagonists, sporadically tracking new characters, as if to demonstrate the futility of trying to find any action.

Jaromil Jireš

Slovakia (formerly Czechoslovakia), 1935–2001

A Czech New Wave director who blended observational realism with stream-of-consciousness fantasy, Jaromil Jireš was born in Bratislava and educated at the FAMU film school in Prague. He worked in multimedia theatre before making his feature debut, *The Cry* (1962), a sensitive study of a young couple awaiting the birth of their first child. Over the next five years, Jireš's scripts were continually rejected by the government-sponsored film industry, which perhaps made him the ideal director of the politically motivated drama *The Joke* (1968). Adapted from Milan Kundera's caustic novel, *The Joke* was a moving tale of a young man's disillusionment with socialism after a throwaway comment is used as "evidence" of subversion. The film ran into political difficulties and largely went unseen until after the Velvet Revolution in 1989.

Despite the cultural chill that followed the Soviet invasion in 1968, Jireš made his most formally adventurous film, *Valerie And Her Week Of Wonders*, in 1970. *Valerie* was followed by the fatalistic World War II drama *...And Give My Love To The Swallows* (1972), which saw a Resistance heroine awaiting execution reassess her life via dislocating flashbacks. Jireš then worked mostly in television and documentary, although his 1991 feature *Labyrinth* was a partial return to earlier form. Sadly, a car crash prematurely ended his career. MB

Valerie And Her Week Of Wonders (Valerie a týden diva) 1970, 77 min

cast Jaroslava Schallerová, Helena Anýžová, Petr Kopřiva, Jiří Prýmek, Jan Klusák *cin* Jan Čuřík *m* Luboš Fišer

This adaptation of a novel by the Czechoslovak Surrealist Group co-founder Vítězslav Nezval is both a coming-of-age story and a stylized, sensual horror film, whose bleached-out dream-like ambience is easier to grasp than its wayward narrative. As 13-year-old Valerie starts menstruating, she encounters vampires, witches, weasels and the unwanted attention of sinister men, and is protected only by her magical earrings.

Alejandro Jodorowsky

Chile, 1929–

Born to Russian-Jewish parents in Chile and basing his filmmaking career in Mexico, Alejandro Jodorowsky became, for a brief moment in 1970–71, the darling of the New York countercultural cognoscenti with *El Topo* (*The Mole*, 1970). He wrote, directed, scored and starred in the movie, which is equal parts Sergio Leone-style Western, grisly biblical rewrite and Federico Felliniesque freak show. Jodorowsky's surrealist-influenced phantasmagoria became a must-see midnight sensation at downtown New York's Elgin Theater, where the thick haze of pot smoke only enhanced the film's trippy ambience – it featured castration, bandits raping monks, a crucifixion by shotgun, self-immolation and the perhaps unique sight of an armless man carrying a legless man.

The film was as visceral as its creator's background was colourful. A one-time circus clown and puppeteer, Jodorowsky studied mime with Marcel Marceau, founded a surrealist journal in Paris and directed avant-garde theatre in Paris and Mexico City. *El Topo* was preceded by the equally surreal but lesser-known *Fando y Lis* (1968). After *El Topo* won the passionate advocacy of John Lennon and, as a result, an ABKCO distribution deal, Jodorowsky followed up with *The Holy Mountain* (1973), another dizzying succession of surreally gruesome imagery (flayed sheep, birds flying from open wounds, etc) starring Jodorowsky as the Alchemist, who can turn shit into gold.

The Holy Mountain did not meet with the underground acclaim that *El Topo* did, and Jodorowsky's filmmaking fortunes slumped, though he remained a prolific writer of books and comics. His attempt to adapt Frank Herbert's *Dune* fell apart (the participation of Orson Welles, Salvador Dali and Pink Floyd had been planned), and *Tusk* (1978), a film about the friendship between a girl and an elephant, never received a release. Jodorowsky staged a comeback in 1989 with *Santa Sangre* (*Holy Blood*) about an asylum patient who is reunited with his armless mother and embarks on a murder spree at her behest. The film is typical Jodorowsky in its deranged violence and nightmare imagery. Jodorowsky has disowned the only other feature he has directed in recent years – the messianic fantasy *The Rainbow Thief* (1990). He has recently been lining up a new project involving rock star Marilyn Manson called *King Shot*. JW

One man show: Jodorowsky scripted, directed, wrote the music for and starred in the surreal cult classic *El Topo*.

El Topo (The Mole) 1970, 125 min

cast Alejandro Jodorowsky, Brontis Jodorowsky, Mara Lorenzio, David Silva, Paul Romo *cin* Rafael Cordiki *m* Alejandro Jodorowsky

A leather-clad mystery man on a horse (Jodorowsky) and his naked kid (the director's son, Brontis) ride into a corpse-littered town, which was lately the scene of some outrage. After abandoning his child, the man seeks to prove his devotion to his new lover by hunting down and killing a famed quartet of desert sharpshooters. Jodorowsky's rendition of both Old and New Testaments makes up in sheer dumbfounding bravado whatever it may lack in coherence.

Roland Joffé

UK, 1945–

The meteoric rise and fall of Roland Joffé is one of the most salutary tales in recent British cinema. The first and, so far, only director of the British soap *Coronation Street* to win a Palme d'Or, Joffé blazed brightly in theatre before moving into television, and then film. His reputation for making some of the most important and controversial drama on British television led directly to David Puttnam employing him as director on *The Killing Fields* (1984). The fine, sprawling Cambodian War film garnered three Oscars, but was outshone by Joffé's next film, *The Mission* (1986), which beat off stiff competition from

Andrei Tarkovsky's *The Sacrifice* to take the Palme d'Or at Cannes. After only two films, Joffé had established an enviable reputation as a director who could seamlessly integrate visual splendour with a social conscience, and peerlessly unite the diverse British traditions of David Lean and Ken Loach.

The unexpected commercial failure of his next film, *Fat Man And Little Boy* (1989), the true story of the development of the atomic bomb, seems to have set Joffé's career back so far that it has never quite recovered. A specialist in filming in dangerous locations, the director met his match when his cameras rolled on the streets of Calcutta for consciousness-raising drama *City Of Joy* (1992). The crew endured home-made bombs and teeming mobs unhappy with the portrayal of their city as corrupt, venal and leper-strewn. As with the later film *Vatel* (2000), the warm critical praise didn't translate into box-office success. However, the lowest point of his career has to be the Demi Moore vehicle, *The Scarlet Letter* (1995) in which Joffé infamously gave Nathaniel Hawthorne's classic tragedy a happy ending. LH

The Killing Fields 1984, 142 min

cast Sam Waterston, Haing S. Ngor, John Malkovich, Julian Sands, Craig T. Nelson, Spalding Gray, Bill Paterson *cin* Chris Menges *m* Mike Oldfield

In this harrowing true story, journalist Sydney Schanberg (Sam Waterston) befriends his Cambodian aide Dith Pran

(Haing S. Ngor) while living dangerously in war-torn Pnomh Penh, but has to leave him behind after the return of the savage and pitiless Khmer Rouge. The film is thick with atmosphere and charged with righteous anger, and Joffé's hypnotic hold never once loses its grip.

The Mission 1986, 125 min

cast Robert De Niro, Jeremy Irons, Ray McAnally, Aidan Quinn, Cherie Lunghi, Ronald Pickup *cin* Chris Menges *m* Ennio Morricone

A powerful exploration of duty and compassion in which a Jesuit priest (Jeremy Irons) and a slave trader (Robert De Niro) join forces to protect a tribe of Amazonian Indians from Portuguese and Spanish marauders. Chris Menges' sweeping, epic photography is stunning, particularly in the spectacular waterfall sequence, but it does occasionally err on the side of postcard pictorialism.

Karan Johar

India, 1972–

Son of the well-known producer Yash Johar, Karan Johar is a director, screenwriter and producer, as well as the host of a popular TV chat show. With only a handful of directorial credits under his belt, he is already one of the most successful filmmakers India has ever produced.

After a minor acting role in Aditya Chopra's *Dilwale dulhania le jayenge* (*The Big-Hearted Will Win The Bride*, 1995), Johar made his debut as a writer/director with the Archie-comics-inspired candyfloss romance *Kuch kuch hota hai* (*Something Happens*, 1998). The film was phenomenally successful amongst Indians globally and broke into the UK Top 10. It was followed by the family melodrama *Kabhi khushi kabhie gham* (*Happiness And Tears*, 2001), which debuted at number three in the UK charts. Johar continued his golden run, this time as a producer, with *Kal ho naa ho* (*Tomorrow May Never Come*, 2003) and *Kaal* (*Time*, 2005). Returning to directing, he polarized Indian audiences with his take on modern marriage in *Kabhi alvida naa kehna* (*Never Say Farewell*, 2006). Johar is one of the pioneers of the Non-Resident Indian (NRI) genre that espouses traditional Indian values for the benefit of Indian audiences worldwide. NR

Kabhi khushi kabhie gham (Happiness And Tears) 2001, 210 min

cast Amitabh Bachchan, Shah Rukh Khan, Hrithik Roshan, Kajol, Rani Mukherjee *cin* Kiran Deohans *m* Sandesh Shandilya, Babloo Chakravorthy

The youngest son of a family tries to reunite his estranged elder brother with their stern father. Shrewdly mixing family values and jingoism with song and dance and melodrama, the film is populated by a virtual who's who of Bollywood. Set mostly in national heritage locations in the UK, it is a multi-generational, multi-hankie spectacle that appeals to the eyes as well as the heart.

Terry Jones

UK, 1942–

Terry Jones has always found it difficult to shrug off his association with the Monty Python phenomenon. He originally worked in repertory theatre, but began writing ground-breaking satire for the BBC in 1965, pitching up in *Monty Python's Flying Circus* when it first aired in 1969.

After the Pythons' first big-screen effort, the sketch-show-formatted *And Now For Something Completely Different* (1971), Jones took on the directorial duties for several Monty Python films, which all displayed narrative coherence and a feeling for historical detail. Co-directed by Terry Gilliam, *Monty Python And The Holy Grail* (1974) followed a quest structure that fed on the clichés of Arthurian legend and wallowed gleefully in the grime of the medieval world. After the success and scandal of the religious satire *Monty Python's Life Of Brian* (1979), *Monty Python's The Meaning Of Life* (1983) returned to the sketch format, but the film's preoccupation with sex, death and bodily functions suggested a Python tradition desperately trying to stay alive.

Attempting to shed the Python skin, Jones made *Personal Services* (1987) based on the experiences of notorious London madam Cynthia Payne, and proved himself adept at depicting the sexual cornucopia beneath the staid English veneer. The comic fantasy *Erik The Viking* (1989) drew upon schoolboy perceptions of Norse mythology, and revelled in using ridiculous names set against a backdrop of gruesome reality. Jones's 1996 take on the Kenneth Grahame classic *The Wind In The Willows* was cartoonish, but its rampaging developers and fascistic weasels suggested liberal outrage at Britain's Thatcherite status quo. Despite a few misses, Jones's work has always managed to exceed the apparently ephemeral. RA

Monty Python And The Holy Grail 1974, 90 min

cast Graham Chapman, John Cleese, Terry Gilliam, Eric Idle, Terry Jones, Michael Palin, Connie Booth, Carol Cleveland *cin* Terry Bedford *m* Neil Innes

Revelling in the absurd possibilities of the Dark Ages, this riposte to academic medievalism (which Jones co-directed with Terry Gilliam) gave us a fresh set of clichés to rehearse down the pub, including the squire who follows his master with clapping coconut shells to emulate his horse, the joust reread as a Sam Peckinpah bloodbath and, who could forget, the Knights who say Ni.

Monty Python's Life Of Brian 1979, 93 min

cast Graham Chapman, John Cleese, Terry Gilliam, Eric Idle, Terry Jones, Michael Palin, Carol Cleveland *cin* Peter Biziou *m* Geoffrey Burgon

Shot on Tunisian sets left over from Franco Zefferelli's *Jesus Of Nazareth* (1977) and mired in the vernacular English humour of the underdog, this assault on religious myth and hypocrisy upset the religious establishment and was banned in some parts of the UK and the US. However, *Brian* prevailed, and in doing so gave rise to more barroom imitations than any British comedy in decades.

Spike Jonze
US, 1969–

Despite an acting role in a big Hollywood movie (*Three Kings*, 1999), a high-profile (if short-lived) marriage to Sofia Coppola, and a side-career as a superstar director of pop videos, Spike Jonze remains an elusive figure. His two features to date – both highly original comedies – have been closely identified with screenwriter Charlie Kaufman, who even gives his name to the lead character in the second film. Evasive or just plain monosyllabic in interviews, Jonze seems intent on preserving the enigma.

We do know that he came up through the skate-boarding scene, taking photographs, contributing to magazines and making short films… which led to pop promos. Unlike the overproduced, slick, fast-cutting MTV cliché, Jonze's videos tend to be low-fi, almost amateurish in their use of real locations, natural light and hand-held camera. They're high-concept and postmodern, in that they're often predicated on a surreal or theatrical twist. Thus for "DaFunk" Jonze simply puts a man in a dog suit and follows him around New York. For the Beastie Boys' "Sabotage" he dresses the band in joke wigs and false moustaches and recreates a *Starsky And Hutch*-style scenario in four minutes. Often the line between self-parody, pastiche and sincerity is blurry. (Jonze videos are available as a DVD collection.)

As a director, Jonze tends to transparency. There are outlandish, surreal moments in both his films, but scarcely a shot which calls attention to itself. Indeed, for all the vaunted strangeness of Kaufman's scripts, Jonze plays them quite straight. While *Being John Malkovich* (1999) involves a wildly fantastic turn of events – a puppeteer accesses a portal into the actor John Malkovich's brain – Jonze concentrates on the story's emotional through-line: a man who falls in love with a woman who is not his wife. Similarly, while *Adaptation* (2002) explicitly distances itself from conventional Hollywood storytelling in its tangential approach to Susan Orlean's book *The Orchid Thief*, it's no less explicit in its preoccupation with the themes of passion, ardour and mutability. It's worth noting too that, for all the sly trickery in these films, they are distinguished by a whole host of unexpectedly touching performances. TC

Being John Malkovich 1999, 113 min
cast John Cusack, Cameron Diaz, Catherine Keener, Orson Bean, Mary Kay Place, Charlie Sheen, John Malkovich *cin* Lance Acord *m* Carter Burwell

A puppeteer on the verge of a midlife crisis takes a job as a filing clerk on the seventh-and-a-half floor, and happens across an entry point into the mind of the actor John Malkovich. The commercial possibilities are not lost on him, though he gets more than he bargained for. There's real yearning in this bizarre, mind-bending comedy about voyeurism, sex and the human desire to play God. You can't get much further out of the box than this.

Adaptation 2002, 115 min
cast Nicolas Cage, Meryl Streep, Chris Cooper, Tilda Swinton, Cara Seymour, Brian Cox, Judy Greer *cin* Lance Acord *m* Carter Burwell

Charlie Kaufman writes himself into the script as a screenwriter trying to adapt a non-fiction book about orchids into a movie – and even invents a twin brother (both parts are played by Nic Cage) to illustrate his mixed feelings about the work. All of which is sort of true. Discursive, unpredictable, and very funny, *Adaptation* is as brilliantly original as an adaptation can be. It has everything except an ending.

Neil Jordan
Republic of Ireland, 1950–

A restless, intriguing talent whose best work wrestles with layers of national and sexual identity, Neil Jordan is the pre-eminent Irish filmmaker – a son of the Troubles, you might say – but too provocative and political to be entirely trusted in Hollywood.

Born into an artistic Catholic family (his grandfather and mother are painters), Neil Jordan won acclaim for his collection of short stories *A Night In Tunisia* before turning his attention to cinema at the age of 30. John Boorman hired him as a script consultant on *Excalibur* (1981) and helped him get started. He wrote the screenplay for Joe Comerford's *Traveller* (1981), then directed his first feature, *Angel* (1982), an atmospheric nocturne with Stephen Rea as a saxophonist who witnesses a sectarian killing. Morose and introspective, Rea would become Jordan's signature actor.

Angel begins and ends in a dancehall called "Dreamland", and Jordan has stayed remarkably open to fantasy and dream imagery throughout his career (he even made a thriller called *In Dreams*, 1999). This interest in psychology and myth flourished in his second film, an ornate expressionist horror fable based on Angela Carter's writing, *The Company Of Wolves* (1984). *Mona Lisa* (1986), his first international success, was an urban realist thriller with a vivid sense of London's seedy sex trade, seen through the eyes of an unusually innocent Bob Hoskins.

Hollywood called, and Jordan's next two pictures – *High Spirits* (1998) and *We're No Angels* (1989) – are case studies in the pitfalls of that place. He headed to Britain, reasserting his own literary voice with charm and wit in *The Miracle* (1991), although as is sometimes the case with this ambitious filmmaker, that film's narrative ultimately seemed forced. The same might be said of *The Crying Game* (1992), but this IRA thriller had so many wheels turning that it entranced critics and audiences alike, becoming a huge hit in the US for Miramax and propelling Jordan to the blockbuster heights of *Interview With The Vampire* (1994), a tricky assignment which he handled confidently enough.

Its success allowed Jordan to make his long-cherished Michael Collins biopic (1996), a cogent, compelling portrait of the Republican leader which might be compared to Spike Lee's *Malcolm X* in its educational purpose. An impressive achievement, the film didn't have the impact it deserved. Nor did Jordan's inspired take on Patrick McCabe's novel *The Butcher Boy* (1997), a magical realist black comic tragedy which stands as his most audacious film to date. TC

Mona Lisa 1986, 104 min
cast Bob Hoskins, Cathy Tyson, Michael Caine, Robbie Coltrane, Clarke Peters, Kate Hardie *cin* Roger Pratt *m* Michael Kamen

Bob Hoskins is an innocent in the underworld, a driver who falls for high-class prostitute Cathy Tyson in this strangely engaging mixture of *noir* thriller, whimsy, and improbable love story. She asks him to help her find a friend who has disappeared into London's sleazy underbelly. Besotted, he plunges on regardless of the risk. Jordan's first international hit consolidated his early promise.

The Crying Game 1992, 112 min
cast Forest Whitaker, Miranda Richardson, Stephen Rea, Adrian Dunbar, Jaye Davidson, Breffini McKenna *cin* Ian Wilson *m* Anne Dudley

IRA man Rea journeys to London to make his peace with the lover of the black British soldier he kidnapped and came to feel he knew. Notwithstanding its famous twist, this romantic thriller has plenty to say about Irish politics, love, violence and desire. Jordan won the Oscar for best original screenplay, one of six nominations for this surprise Miramax hit – though the success came too late to save backers Palace Pictures from filing for bankruptcy.

Michael Collins 1996, 132 min
cast Liam Neeson, Julia Roberts, Stephen Rea, Alan Rickman, Aidan Quinn, Ian Hart, John Kenny *cin* Chris Menges *m* Elliot Goldenthal

While Jordan's admiring account of Michael Collins's career is up for debate, there's no question that this biopic is a powerful and coherent exploration of a seismic period in Irish history. Without sacrificing its credibility, Jordan gives the story some of the panache – and moral complexity – of a gangster saga. Powerful performances, too, from Neeson in the title role and Rickman as Eamonn De Valera.

The Butcher Boy 1997, 110 min
cast Stephen Rea, Fiona Shaw, Eamonn Owens, Alan Boyle, Niall Buggy, Brendan Gleeson, Gerard McSorley *cin* Adrian Biddle *m* Elliot Goldenthal

A black comedy about an urchin at war with his tormentors in small-town Ireland, circa 1960, this steadily turns into something more disturbing and provocative. Francie Brady (Eamonn Owens) has a rich fantasy life to compensate for his straitened circumstances, but the odds are always against him in this land of repression. Based on the novel

by Patrick McCabe, who also wrote Jordan's later, tailor-made *Breakfast On Pluto* (2005).

Breakfast On Pluto 2005, 135 min
cast Cillian Murphy, Liam Neeson, Stephen Rea, Brendan Gleeson, Ian Hart, Ruth Negga, Gavin Friday *cin* Declan Quinn *m* Anna Jordan

Raised by a devout but unloving foster mother in a small Irish town, all Kitten (Murphy) knows about his real ma is that she looks like 1950s starlet Mitzi Gaynor. Setting out to track her down, he entrances a series of colourful men along the way. Kitten is reminiscent of two previous Jordan heroes: like Francie Brady in *The Butcher Boy*, he seeks refuge from a cruel and hypocritical society in a vivid fantasy life; like Dil in *The Crying Game* he rejects violence and embraces his own femininity. It is a form of poetic passive resistance addressed specifically (but not exclusively) towards the IRA, sectarianism and the forces of repression.

Rupert Julian
New Zealand, 1879–1943

Cinema history has not been kind to Rupert Julian. Although he was a prolific figure in silent-era Hollywood – directing at least sixty films and acting in nearly a hundred – his reputation is based on just one film, *The Phantom Of The Opera* (1925).

A stage actor in his native New Zealand, Julian arrived in the US in 1913 and was soon commanding attention as a character actor. He played Scrooge in the Dickens adaptation *The Right To Be Happy* (1916) and was a notable Kaiser Wilhelm in *The Kaiser, The Beast Of Berlin* (1918), which also featured Lon Chaney. Julian directed both films, but his big break as a director came in 1923 when Irving Thalberg fired an overspending Erich von Stroheim from *Merry-Go-Round* and Julian took over. The resulting lavish Viennese romance owed much to von Stroheim's vision and rather flattered Julian's own abilities.

For *The Phantom Of The Opera* Julian was reunited with Lon Chaney. Unfortunately Julian had become an irascible and difficult man and he and Chaney (by now a big star) argued incessantly. Despite this, the film is a highly successful adaptation of Gaston Leroux's lurid 1910 novel. From then on, however, Julian's career went into a marked decline. With the advent of sound he lost whatever touch he had, and his career fizzled out after just two talkies. RB

The Phantom Of The Opera 1925, 93 min, b/w
cast Lon Chaney, Mary Philbin, Norman Kerry, Snitz Edwards, Gibson Gowland *cin* Milton Bridenbecker, Charles van Enger, Virgil Miller

The Paris Opéra is built above a labyrinth of murky vaults where lurks a mysterious masked man – the phantom (Lon Chaney). Having made his vocal protégée Christine (Mary Philbin) a star, he now wants her love and abducts her to his underground home complete with luxurious bedroom and organ. Beautifully designed but slackly paced, the film is transformed by Chaney's mesmerizing performance – particularly spine-tingling is the moment when Christine tears the mask from his face and his horror seems almost greater than hers.

K

Cédric Kahn
France, 1966–

Cédric Kahn is a young gun, a darling of film critics, if not the French police. Inspired by the films of Maurice Pialat, Kahn worked as his mentor's assistant before continuing his neo-documentary tradition in his own work. His first two films, *Bar des rails* (*Railway Bar*, 1991) and *Trop de bonheur* (*Too Much Happiness*, 1994) have rarely been seen outside France, but his third, *L'ennui* (1998), has been talked about by many, if seen by relatively few. It was briefly considered to be one of the most sexually explicit mainstream films ever made, but was, however, soon cast into the shadows by a barrage of movies made at the end of the century – such as *Baise-moi* and Catherine Breillat's *Romance* – that, unlike Kahn's film, went the whole pornographic hog and contained acts of real, unsimulated sex. *L'ennui* was the first of three films by Kahn that studied men whose obsessions lead them to the brink of mental illness, and who have a disabling, emotional disconnection with women. In this case, a balding philosophy professor is driven crazy by his teenage lover's apparent lack of feeling or intellect.

While *L'ennui* shocked the bourgeoisie, *Roberto Succo* (2001) managed to shock the police. Visitors to the 2001 Cannes Film Festival witnessed the unusual sight of the police themselves noisily picketing an event. They were protesting about the film's perceived glamorization of a French serial killer who had murdered two of their colleagues in cold blood. With *Red Lights* (2004), Kahn only offended hard-core Georges Simenon fans with his idiosyncratic take on the crime writer's novel, in which a wife becomes alarmed by her husband's erratic, and possibly murderous, behaviour. More recently, the acutely observed *L'avion* (2005) was a meditative story of a boy grieving for his father. LH

L'ennui 1998, 122 min
cast Charles Berling, Sophie Guillemin, Arielle Dombasle, Robert Kramer, Alice Grey, Maurice Antoni *cin* Pascal Marti *m* Richard Wagner

A married lecturer has regular, grunting sex with an artist's model but becomes increasingly obsessed with her when she continually refuses to analyse or romanticize their habitual rutting. Based on the Alberto Moravio novel, *L'ennui* follows a tradition that is peculiar, if not exclusive, to male French directors of depicting women as either sirens or ciphers.

Roberto Succo 2001, 125 min
cast Stefano Cassetti, Isild Le Besco, Patrick Dell'Isola, Vincent Dénériaz, Aymeric Chauffert, Viviana Aliberti *cin* Pascal Marti *m* Julien Civange

While Kahn is definitely not guilty of glamorizing the serial killer who raped and murdered at random after escaping from a mental home, he also neither condemns nor comments upon his behaviour. Kahn follows the Maurice Pialat tradition of exploring a genre through the prism of neo-realism. He succeeds when placing his camera in front of the haunted and hypnotic Succo, but is less sure when following the dictates of a police procedural.

Kang Je-gyu
South Korea, 1962–

Undisputed South Korean box-office champion Kang Je-gyu broke domestic takings records with *Gingko Bed* (1996), in which an academic tangles with the ghost of a general who feeds on the living of Seoul. He followed that up with *Shiri* (1999), a gun-crazy Armageddon tale that bested *Titanic* at the South Korean ticket offices. When *Shiri* debuted, nuclear-fortified North Korea was still frontier territory for thrillers produced just below the 38th parallel. The film follows a pair of South Korean intelligence agents on the bloody trail of a lynx-eyed female assassin who kills for an NK terrorist group trying to incite a war of reunification. For his next film, Kang looked back to the actual Korean conflict in *Tae Guk Gi: The Brotherhood Of War* (2004), which drew on *Saving Private Ryan* (1998) for its framing device and upped the ante with unrelenting gore and hammering sound design. Though it took its name from the South Korean flag, *Tae Guk Gi* was hardly patriotic – here war was a paroxysm of pointless brutality that coarsens and disfigures the soul. JW

Shiri (Swiri) 1999, 125 min

cast Hang Suk-Kyu, Kim Yu-Jin, Choi Min-Sik, Song Kang-Ho *cin* Kim Sung-Bok *m* Lee Dong-Jun

Terrorists plot to detonate a bomb at a North versus South football match in Kang's countdown to apocalypse, named after a fish native to streams of both the Korean nations. The writer-director is better at action than he is with actors, but he does manage a sustained hum of anxiety and dread amid the endless, deafening shoot-outs and he maps the film's – and the countries' – fault lines along the fissures of one character's split identity.

Garson Kanin

US, 1912–99

Although better known as a screenwriter, as a director Garson Kanin remains one of the treasures of 1930s Hollywood dialogue comedy.

During the Depression Kanin dropped out of high school to assist the family finances by working as a vaudeville comedian. After studying at the American Academy of Dramatic Art, he made his Broadway debut in 1933. Four years later, he directed his first play and, in 1938, he headed to Hollywood. There he directed a series of comedies that, with hindsight, seem startlingly modern in their exploration of sexual mores. In *Bachelor Mother* (1939) Ginger Rogers' shop girl fosters an abandoned child. One of the snappiest films of the era, its interrogation of a woman's traditional place is a foretaste of the more emancipated wartime temper. Following *My Favorite Wife* (1940), *Tom, Dick And Harry* (1941) saw Rogers' independent heroine measuring her worth against the competing attributes of her suitors.

During World War II, Kanin produced and directed documentaries for the US government. These included *The True Glory* (1945), a tribute to the Allied war effort in the final year of the campaign, which he made in collaboration with Carol Reed and the British Ministry of Information. Screenplays co-written with his wife Ruth Gordon – *Adam's Rib* (1949), *Pat And Mike* (1952) – wittily essayed post-war sexual dynamics, but Kanin didn't direct another feature until the unsuccessful, zany beard-themed comedy *Some Kind Of Nut* in 1969. He is, however, a key name in pre-war Hollywood comedy. RA

My Favorite Wife 1940, 88 min, b/w

cast Cary Grant, Irene Dunne, Gail Patrick, Randolph Scott, Ann Shoemaker, Donald MacBride *cin* Rudolph Maté *m* Roy Webb

Challenging Hollywood's romantic mythology from within, this Cary Grant comedy postulates the seemingly unthinkable: what if your beloved died, you married again and your beloved returned? If its well-appointed society milieu suggests Depression escapism, the idea that love accommodates itself to circumstances is a foretaste of the kind of films that became popular during the war years.

Jonathan Kaplan

France, 1947–

A sensitive director who has been unable to generate material worthy of his talent, Jonathan Kaplan is a Roger Corman exploitation veteran who seemed on the verge of a major career in the mid-1980s, but has generally found television more receptive to his nonstop work ethic.

The Parisian-born son of blacklisted American composer Sol Kaplan, Jonathan was a child actor who made his Broadway debut in William Inge's *The Dark At The Top Of The Stairs*, directed by Elia Kazan. He attended film school at New York University, then – at the recommendation of lecturer Martin Scorsese – learned his trade with Corman on the likes of *Night Call Nurses* (1972), *The Student Teachers* (1973) and *White Line Fever* (1975). Passably witty, Kaplan's exploitation pictures don't have much else going for them. But given a proper script (by Tim Hunter and Charles S. Haas), he delivered the goods with *Over The Edge* (1979), one of the best films about teenage rebellion.

Kaplan directed three TV movies before his next theatrical feature, *Heart Like A Wheel* (1983), which garnered favourable reviews at the New York Film Festival for its forthright portrayal of female racer Shirley Muldowney (played by Bonnie Bedelia). It was enough to get Kaplan the job of directing Jodie Foster and Kelly McGillis in the rape drama *The Accused* (1988), his most widely seen movie, which was controversial for its provocative depiction of the crime.

Is Kaplan a sensitive director of low-key human stories with a feminist streak, or a sensationalist hack still tarred by his exploitation roots? The case could be made either way. In the early 1990s, he veered from the salacious thriller *Unlawful Entry* to the bittersweet period piece *Love Field* (both 1992) and the camp TV film *Reform School Girl* (1994), before taking up a long residency on the TV show *ER*. His latest film for the big screen, *Brokedown Palace* (1999), which nimbly told the story of two young women imprisoned for drug smuggling in Bangkok, still hasn't settled the argument. The truth may be that Kaplan's rarely better than the material he's given. TC

Over The Edge 1979, 94 min

cast Michael Kramer, Matt Dillon, Pamela Ludwig, Vincent Spano, Tom Fergus, Harry Northrup, Andy Romano *cin* Andrew Davis *m* Sol Kaplan

Kaplan tells it like it is in this grim portrait of teen delinquents bored and ignored in a desolate Colorado planned community. Influential (though not a hit), the film introduced Matt Dillon to the world, and anticipated both *River's Edge* (1986) and *Elephant* (2003). Kurt Cobain even wrote about it in his diaries.

K

The Accused 1988, 111 min

cast Kelly McGillis, Jodie Foster, Bernie Coulson, Leo Rossi, Ann Hearn, Carmen Argenziano, Steve Antin *cin* Ralf D. Bode *m* Brad Fiedel

Based on a real incident of gang rape, this controversial drama has the male onlookers indicted for complicity in the crime, but doesn't shy away from extending that dubious privilege to the audience. Jodie Foster won the Academy Award for her (actually quite mannered) trailer-trash performance, though what makes the film work is putting her up next to the tall, classy lawyer Kelly McGillis.

Raj Kapoor

India, 1924–88

Son of the well-known stage and film actor Prithviraj Kapoor, Raj Kapoor was a man of many talents. He was not simply a popular actor, but was also an editor, producer and very successful director who had a keen ear for music. Famous for living life to the full, he was known as the showman of Hindi cinema. After a few small parts, Kapoor made his debut as a leading man in Kidar Sharma's *Neel Kamal* (1947). The following year he formed the RK production company and directed himself in *Aag*, in which a young man gives up studying law and pursues a career in the arts, all the while looking for an elusive childhood sweetheart. The film began Kapoor's electric onscreen pairing with leading lady Nargis. In *Awaara* (1951) Kapoor adopted a Chaplinesque tramp persona, while *Shree 420* (1955) decried the corrupting influences of big cities. By now Kapoor was firmly established as a superstar. While continuing to explore social issues, he also increasingly concentrated on more personal, human interest stories – and, it must be said, the female form – in films such as *Sangam* (1964) and the ambitious *Mera Naam Joker* (1970). NR

Awaara 1951, 193 min, b/w

cast Raj Kapoor, Nargis, Prithviraj Kapoor, K.N. Singh *cin* Radhu Karmakar *m* Shankar-Jaikishan

A bandit kidnaps a judge's wife but lets her go unharmed when he learns she is pregnant. Suspecting the child's paternity, the judge throws her out and the child becomes a thieving street urchin. Kapoor brought in a Chaplinesque persona and elements of *noir* and neo-realism, combining them with the musical melodrama of Hindi cinema and some grand dream sequences to create an enduring classic.

Mera Naam Joker 1970, 224 min

cast Raj Kapoor, Manoj Kumar, Padmini, Simi Garewal, Rajendra Kumar *cin* Radhu Karmakar *m* Shankar-Jaikishan

Raj Kapoor's most indulgent, epic film was box-office poison when first released. But it has since been reappraised, and is now considered by many to be a masterpiece. Borrowing partly from his own life, Kapoor narrates the life story of a circus clown from boarding school through to his last ever show over several chapters, capturing the tears behind the greasepaint.

Shekhar Kapur

Pakistan (formerly India), 1945–

When the British production company Working Title was looking to stir up the costume drama with a fresh, relevant take on the story of Queen Elizabeth I they turned to the Lahore-born, British-educated Shekhar Kapur.

A registered chartered accountant in the UK, Kapur took off for Bollywood to make films in his mid-twenties and wound up an actor. He eventually realized his directing ambitions with two well-received but conventional entertainments, his debut *Masoom* (1983) and, most notably, the popular *Mr India* (1987). He made his name with the controversial *Bandit Queen* (1994) – a searing, taboo-breaking biopic of Phoolan Devi (who branded the film "disgusting" from her prison cell) somewhat evocative of a feminist Peckinpah movie.

In a mission statement he attached to his copy of Michael Hirst's screenplay for *Elizabeth* (1998) Kapur cited *The Godfather* and *Trainspotting* as his models: the former for its sense of all-enveloping intrigue, the latter for its vigorous shooting style. *Elizabeth* had a florid, flamboyant look, a wildly eclectic cast (including Vincent Cassel, Sir John Gielgud and former Manchester United footballer Eric Cantona) and energy to spare. The film was nominated for seven Academy Awards, including best picture and best actress (Cate Blanchett).

This triumph should have propelled Kapur into the front ranks of Hollywood directors. However, his follow-up, *The Four Feathers* (2002) proved an unhappy venture, an expensive remake of the British (anti-)colonial epic backed by Miramax, plagued by production difficulties and hamstrung by miscasting and mixed motives (it was re-edited post-9/11, to the director's discomfort). For one reason or another, Kapur has since struggled to get his projects off the ground, including a mooted Nelson Mandela biopic. Nearly a decade after his biggest success, he returned to the life of Elizabeth I with *The Golden Age* (2007), again with Cate Blanchett in the lead role. TC

Elizabeth 1998, 124 min

cast Cate Blanchett, Geoffrey Rush, Christopher Eccleston, Joseph Fiennes, Richard Attenborough *cin* Remi Adefarasin *m* David Hirschfelder

Kapur's first English-language film is a bold, intuitive costume drama that plays fast and loose with history in the service of sweeping melodrama and a vivid sense of high-stakes machinations. *Elizabeth* is the story of the young Tudor queen (Cate Blanchett) surviving plot and counterplot, but at the cost of renouncing her love for Robert Dudley (Joseph Fiennes).

K

Phil Karlson
US, 1908–85

Best remembered for his hard-hitting, tabloid-style crime stories of the 1950s, in particular *Kansas City Confidential* (1952), Phil Karlson was a minor B-movie director whose taut, terse style clicked with the *film noir* idiom. As Bertrand Tavernier and Jean-Pierre Coursodon put it in their *50 ans de cinéma américain*, "in the urban jungle he was like a fish in water". In less realist genres, he "seemed lost". A one-time law student, Karlson started as a prop guy at Universal Studios, and worked his way up through second-unit directing for Abbott and Costello and then directing B-pictures at Monogram. He hit his stride in the early 1950s, especially in a handful of semi-documentary *noir* films starring John Payne. Of these, *Kansas City Confidential* is probably the best known, but *99 River Street* (1953) is actually more interesting. The reactionary *Phenix City Story (1955)* had a muckraking zeal worthy of Sam Fuller, whose novel became the source for Karlson's newspaper thriller *Scandal Sheet* (1952). Subsequent films in the director's prolific career were considerably more varied, ranging from Elvis Presley as a boxer in *Kid Galahad (1962)* to the Civil War drama *A Time For Killing* (1967). Karlson scored a surprise box-office hit late in life with the redneck vigilante movie *Walking Tall* (1973), based on the story of Sheriff Buford Pusser. TC

99 River Street 1953, 83 min, b/w
cast John Payne, Evelyn Keyes, Brad Dexter, Frank Faylen, Peggie Castle, Jay Adler *cin* Franz Planer *m* Arthur Lange, Emil Newman

A tense, satisfying *film noir* with perennial everyman figure John Payne as a washed-up boxer trying to pull himself out of the frame for his wife's murder. It's a brutal, cynical story about the underside of the supposedly booming Eisenhower era – and the unusual climax is a real highlight.

Lawrence Kasdan
US, 1949–

Working as an advertising copywriter while striving to crack Hollywood, Lawrence Kasdan eventually proved himself to be vital to the American blockbuster by working on the scripts of *The Empire Strikes Back* (1980), *Raiders Of The Lost Ark* (1981) and *Return Of The Jedi* (1983). Breaking into directing, he established his reputation with his debut *Body Heat* (1981), a sultry, contemporary *film noir* in the spirit of Billy Wilder's *Double Indemnity* (1944). Next came *The Big Chill* (1983), a comedy-drama about the reunion of a group of college friends, which became a baby boomer classic.

Kasdan's visually understated films often dramatize issues around community, regret and responsi-bility. He has also built a repertory of enduring star actors that includes Kevin Kline and Kevin Costner, who starred together in Kasdan's energetic ensemble Western *Silverado* (1985). The director followed that up with the sombre romantic drama *The Accidental Tourist* (1988). A meditative piece in which William Hurt and Kathleen Turner grieve for their dead son, it featured an impressive Oscar-winning turn by Geena Davis as a kooky dog trainer.

The director's love of genre fuelled the Western *Wyatt Earp* (1994), in which Kevin Costner's lawman makes a stately journey from innocence to experience in the vast American West. Later films, such as the ensemble farce *I Love You To Death* (1990), *Grand Canyon* (1991), which tapped into zeitgeist angst about urban life, the romantic comedy *French Kiss* (1995) and the small-town drama *Mumford* (1999), have proved less successful, and in 2003 Kasdan played it safe by directing *Dreamcatcher*, an adaptation of a Stephen King novel. JC

Body Heat 1981, 113 min
cast William Hurt, Kathleen Turner, Richard Crenna, Ted Danson, J.A. Preston, Mickey Rourke *cin* Richard H. Kline *m* John Barry

Revisiting classic 1940s *film noir* territory in the 1980s, *Body Heat* sees Kathleen Turner in smouldering *femme fatale* mode as she dupes doomed Florida lawyer William Hurt into murdering her wealthy husband with verbal games and steamy sex. Introducing a new baroque *noir* style courtesy of cinematographer Richard H. Kline, this startlingly effective film still features the time-honoured visual tropes of dark shadows, Venetian blinds and foggy nights.

The Big Chill 1983, 105 min
cast Kevin Kline, Tom Berenger, William Hurt, JoBeth Williams, Glenn Close, Mary Kay Place, Jeff Goldblum, Meg Tilly *cin* John Bailey

The impressive ensemble cast play a group of thirtysome-things who gather for the funeral of an old college friend who has committed suicide. As the funeral turns into a weekend reunion, the friends reminisce about their school days and begin to reconsider their lives to a soundtrack of classic 1960s hits by the likes of Marvin Gaye, Aretha Franklin and The Temptations.

Mathieu Kassovitz
France, 1967–

The director of one of the most explosive studies of simmering racial tensions in Paris, 1995's *La haine (Hate)*, Mathieu Kassovitz is now arguably better known for acting in one of the sweetest and most sanitized portrayals of the same city.

He began his career as an actor, appearing in his father Peter Kassovitz's *Au bout du bout du banc (Make Room For Tomorrow*, 1979) at the age of 11, before moving into directing. His first two features explored race relations in Paris to very different ends. *Métisse* (1993), a Gallic variation of Spike Lee's *She's Gotta Have It* (1986), centred on the comic tra-

Fear and loathing in the Parisian suburbs: Saïd (centre) and his friends Vinz (left) and Hubert in *La haine*.

vails of a pregnant West Indian woman and her two lovers, a black Muslim and a white man. The anti-police movie, *La haine*, was an incandescent and incendiary essay on crime and punishment in the seething aftermath of a riot in a Parisian suburb. There were similar outbreaks of street fighting in the capital when the film was released, and some commentators tried to establish a causal link.

Kassovitz seemed to offer a vital new approach to French film, a zeitgeist cinema that was political, realistic and cinematic. Yet he has never lived up to the rich promise of *La haine*, possibly because he dispensed with the social components and righteous indignation that made it such a controversial, bristling success. *Assassin(s)* (1997), about an old hit man and his young apprentice, was critically reviled and roundly ignored, and the director's career took a turn for the preposterous with the grisly murder mystery *Crimson Rivers* (2000) and the imbecilic Hollywood thriller *Gothika* (2003). Kassovitz admits he made the latter for the money, but although it netted him millions, it lost him much more in kudos.

There is an unfortunate symmetry to his twin careers as director and actor: when one has taken a dive, the other has taken off. With his model looks, Kassovitz gave a typically charismatic performance in Jacques Audiard's *Regarder les hommes tomber* (*See How They Fall*, 1994). However, he is most widely recognized for his role as Audrey Tautou's enigmatic object of affection in Jean-Pierre Jeunet's Parisian fairy tale, *Amélie* (2001), which depicted a city free of racial tensions, or indeed other races. LH

La haine (Hate) 1995, 98 min
cast Vincent Cassel, Hubert Koundé, Saïd Taghmaoui, Abdel Ahmed Ghili, Edouard Montoute, François Levantal *cin* Pierre Aim *m* Assassin

Opening with a riot in a Parisian suburb, this monochrome masterpiece follows a day in the life of three friends, Hubert, an African, Saïd, an Arab, and Vinz, a Jew, whose friend Abdel was beaten up in police custody. Hot-headed Vinz gets hold of a policeman's gun and promises to kill a cop if Abdel dies. Humming with a nervy, angry energy, *La haine* is liberally strewn with references to Martin Scorsese in both the script and in Kassovitz's electrifying stylistics.

Philip Kaufman
US, 1936–

Philip Kaufman has followed an erratic filmmaking path that has rarely been lacking in interest or unpredictability. Beginning his directorial career as a superb craftsman of B-movies, Kaufman later became a specialist in sexy literary adaptations. During the 1970s, Kaufman helmed low-budget treats such as *The Great Northfield Minnesota Raid* (1972), with Robert Duvall as the iconic outlaw Jesse James, and *The White Dawn* (1974), a fact-based tale of three sailors stranded in the Arctic. He also wrote *The Outlaw Josey Wales* (1976), but he clashed with star Clint Eastwood, who replaced him in the director's chair. Kaufman came into his own with a sly, hypnotic 1978 remake of *Invasion Of The Body Snatchers* and the vivid Bronx-gang ensemble piece *The Wanderers* (1979), which was somewhat confusingly released the same year as Walter Hill's gangland epic *The Warriors*.

The Right Stuff (1983) looked like a candidate for being Kaufman's *chef-d'oeuvre*, but his respectful yet cheeky three-hour-plus history of the American space programme bombed upon its release. The director made his next two films in Europe. Both of them concerned love triangles and were preoccupied with sexuality and the Yin-Yang of gender relations. *The Unbearable Lightness Of Being* (1988) deftly rendered the substance of Milan Kundera's novel while smoothing out the chronology, but the soft-core romping of *Henry & June* (1990), taken from Anaïs Nin's writings, had a whiff of self-congratulation about it. The latter movie was overshadowed by controversy. The US ratings board invented a new branding for mainstream adult films, NC-17, to replace the ignominious X in the movie's honour, but many newspapers still refused to run ads for the film.

Kaufman's career has bounced around rather aimlessly since then: *Rising Sun* (1993) was a dull Michael Crichton adaptation, *Twisted* (2004) a terrible serial-killer schlockfest and *Quills* (2000) a rousing, bawdy treatise on the convergence of sex, creativity and madness that went too far in making a martyr out of its asylum-bound antihero, the certifiably loathsome Marquis de Sade. JW

The Right Stuff 1983, 193 min
cast Sam Shepard, Scott Glenn, Ed Harris, Dennis Quaid, Fred Ward, Barbara Hershey, Kim Stanley, Veronica Cartwright *cin* Caleb Deschanel *m* Bill Conti

Adapted from Tom Wolfe's swaggering book, Kaufman's epic of gung-ho Americana has its cake and eats it too. It chuckles at the absurdities and inanities of the American space programme while reserving starry-eyed wonder for the personnel and their forays into the wild blue yonder; it contrasts the laconic, gum-cracking machismo of sound-barrier breaker Chuck Yeager with the telegenic boyishness of the Magnificent Seven astronauts, and decides to cheer them both.

The Unbearable Lightness Of Being 1988, 171 min
cast Daniel Day-Lewis, Juliette Binoche, Lena Olin, Derek de Lint, Erland Josephson, Pavel Landovsky *cin* Sven Nykvist *m* Mark Adler

Milan Kundera's novel, set before and after the 1968 Soviet invasion of Prague, is perhaps too cerebral to translate easily to the screen. However, Kaufman makes an honourable attempt, helped no end by his fantastic lead actors. The film is that rare historical romance that neither beatifies its protagonists nor trivializes the events at hand; it also pays intelligent attention – rare in an American filmmaker – to female sexual desire.

Aki Kaurismäki
Finland, 1957–

Aki Kaurismäki is Finland's most famous director, and together with his older brother Mika, he once accounted for a third of the country's film output. His films are characterized by laconic humour, detached irony and smoking – he could be considered the Nordic cousin of Jim Jarmusch.

He started making his own distinctive brand of cinema in the early 1980s; his films so recognizable because of his regular team – cinematographer Timo Salminen, actors Kati Outinen and Matti Pellonpää – and his typical dispassionate visual style. The director coolly elicits a dry sense of ironic detachment through his camera lens that is as passively undemonstrative as his protagonists who glumly eke out a living on the margins of society (and are often accompanied by a dog). Frequently defined by their blighted landscapes, Kaurismäki's characters suffer from emotional atrophy for specifically political, rather than hazily existential reasons.

His narratives tend to come in clusters. *Crime And Punishment* (1983), *Hamlet Goes Business* (1987) and *La vie de bohème* (*Bohemian Life*, 1992) were literary adaptations with a contemporary twist. *Shadows In Paradise* (1986), *Ariel* (1998) and the masterly *Match Factory Girl* (1990) all featured blue-collar heroes, and *Drifting Clouds* (1996), *The Man Without A Past* (2002) and *Lights In The Dusk* (2006) form a trilogy about the socially deprived.

Kaurismäki's road movies represent an escape from the workaday world. *Calmari Union* (1985) is about seventeen men called Frank who try to make it to the other side of the Helsinki tracks, a distant utopia that many will never reach. *Leningrad Cowboys Go America* (1989), his break-out hit, is about "the worst rock'n'roll band in the world" who aimlessly tour the armpit of America. (Another feature starring the band, 1994's *Leningrad Cowboys Meet Moses*, and a concert film followed.) The film clearly displays the anticapitalist director's queasy relationship with the United States. In his work, Americanization is routinely equated with homogenization, but American popular culture, in the shape of rock'n'roll, jukeboxes and Cadillacs, offers the possibility of escape, however temporary.

Directors who rigorously pursue the same themes through the same visual idioms can often become parodies of their former selves, but Kaurismäki (despite a few false notes like 1990's *I Hired A Contract Killer*), has been honing his instinct and finessing his palette. He has made some classics, like *Match Factory Girl*, *Ariel* and *Leningrad Cowboys Go America*, but it was the deadpan and soulful *The Man Without A Past* that epitomized classic Kaurismäki with its ambient melancholy, impressive low-key acting, and spirited and quirky use of music. LH

Leningrad Cowboys Go America 1989, 79 min
cast Matti Pellonpää, Nicky Tesco, Kari Väänänen, Jim Jarmusch, Sakke Järvenpää, Heikki Keskinen *cin* Timo Salminen *m* Mauri Sumén

With their inimitable tunes and magnificent quiffs, Finnish folk group Leningrad Cowboys head out onto the highways of America's Deep South, inflicting their unique interpretation of popular music onto unsuspecting and unimpressed locals. A bad joke that became a very tangible reality (like Spinal Tap the success of the film made a success of the band), and which was made with one bleary eye on the cult market, this unique road movie is beguilingly droll, absurdly laconic and, unlike the band themselves, genuinely lyrical.

Match Factory Girl (Tulitkkutehtaan tytto) 1990, 69 min

cast Kati Outinen, Elina Salo, Esko Nikkari, Vesa Vierikko, Reijo Taipale, Silu Seppälä, Outi Mäenpää, Marja Packalén *cin* Timo Salminen

A painfully austere combination of socialism, minimalism and pessimism in which Kaurismäki charts the gloomy existence of shy factory worker Iris (Kati Outinen). Given a cheque and ordered to get rid of her baby by her lover, the pregnant Iris blithely takes revenge not just on him, but on almost every man she meets. In a typical Kaurismäki touch, she doesn't say a word for the first twelve minutes of the film, and only then breaks her silence to order a beer.

The Man Without A Past (Mies vailla menneisyyttä) 2002, 97 min

cast Markku Peltola, Kati Outinen, Juhani Niemelä, Kaija Pakarinen, Sakari Kuosmanen, Annikki Tähti *cin* Timo Salminen

All the characteristic Kaurismäki tropes are present – laconic humour, snail's pace, jukeboxes – and the story is familiarly slight: a man is beaten so badly that he loses his memory; seeking refuge with the Helsinki homeless he strikes up a quirky relationship with a Salvation Army officer. Despite its lack of originality, this is not unlike the sort of autumnal classic that Ozu produced: disciplined, poignant and charming, ostensibly the product of a director in charge of the elements.

Yoshiaki Kawajiri

Japan, 1950–

Numbering among the few filmmakers to have attracted attention beyond the niche of Japanese anime, Yoshiaki Kawajiri is regarded as one of the most influential in his field, standing alongside Katsuhiro Otomo (*Akira*, 1988), Satoshi Kon (*Perfect Blue*, 1997, and *Millennium Actress*, 2001) and Mamoru Oshii (*Ghost In The Shell*, 1995). Having worked in animation for years, Kawajiri finally made his splash with *Wicked City* (1987), an inventive sci-fi feature in which agents must thwart a breakaway group hellbent on shattering a peace treaty between our world and a parallel dimension. This was followed by *Goku Midnight Eye* (1989), in which a private dick makes use of special powers he acquires from an eye implant. Kawajiri's most famous work, *Ninja Scroll*, followed in 1993. More recently, *Vampire Hunter D: Bloodlust* (2000) carried on his brand of stylish and beautifully choreographed mayhem, with a story of a half-human, half-vampire bounty hunter who sets out to rescue a girl kidnapped by vampires. Like *Wicked City*, the movie was based on the novels of Hideyuki Kikuchi. NN

Ninja Scroll (Jûbei ninpûchô) 1993, 94 min

cast (English voices) Richard Barnes, Sonny Byrkett, Richard Cansino, Dean Elliott, Richard Epcar *cin* Hitoshi Yamaguchi *m* Kaoru Wada

A landmark work in modern anime, *Ninja Scroll* perhaps doesn't quite match the intellectual pretensions of *Akira* or *Ghost In The Shell*, but it more than makes up for it in dazzling visuals and sheer entertainment, as we root for a ninja who takes on an enemy with a troupe of demons at his command.

Elia Kazan

Turkey, 1909–2003

For a decade midway through the twentieth century Elia Kazan was the leading director in America. On Broadway he was nominated for seven Tony awards between 1947 (when he won for Arthur Miller's *Death Of A Salesman*) and 1960 (Tennessee Williams's *Sweet Bird Of Youth*). In Hollywood, he was nominated for the best director Oscar five times between 1948 (when he won for *Gentleman's Agreement*) and 1964 (*America, America*, for which he was also nominated for best screenplay).

Kazan's family were Greeks from Anatolia. He was born in Constantinople, but his parents emigrated to the US when he was 9 years old. (*America, America* is based on his uncle's story.) He went into the Yale Drama School on a scholarship, then into the Group Theatre under Lee Strasberg. There he acted in productions of Clifford Odets' *Golden Boy* and *Waiting For Lefty*, flirted with communism (becoming a member of the party from 1934 to 1936), and appeared in minor movie roles for Anatole Litvak in *City For Conquest* (1940) and *Blues In The Night* (1941) before finding his true vocation.

Collaborating with such extraordinary new playwrights as Williams and Miller, Kazan took the impetus from Group Theatre to advance social themes and greater psychological realism. His production of *A Streetcar Named Desire* with Marlon Brando electrified Broadway in 1947. The subsequent 1951 film version – for all its merits – is essentially of importance as a record of this landmark stage production and, in particular, of Brando's mesmerizing performance (an Oscar-winning Vivien Leigh replaced Jessica Tandy as the female lead, Blanche DuBois). Crucially, Kazan fought the Production Code tooth and nail to preserve the integrity of Williams's then-shocking text.

Kazan himself was mostly dismissive of his early films, although the sentimental *A Tree Grows In Brooklyn* (1945) and the thriller *Boomerang!* (1947) are respectable, well-acted examples of their type. Praised in its day for tackling anti-Semitism, *Gentleman's Agreement* (1947) now looks timid and obvious. An atmospheric thriller about the search for a killer carrying pneumonic plague, *Panic In The Streets* (1950) marks the first time Kazan really

THE ROUGH GUIDE TO FILM

The Method: Elia Kazan and Marlon Brando

Marlon Brando and Elia Kazan only made three movies together. Yet their collaborations have exerted more influence on the art and craft of acting than any other modern film or play. Kazan and Brando were the greatest exponents of the Method, the school of psychological realism pioneered by the Russian tutor Constantine Stanislavsky. Not only have heavy-duty thesps such as James Dean, Dustin Hoffman and Robert De Niro benefited from their experiments, but everyone who has appeared before a camera since the late 1950s has been influenced – whether consciously or unconsciously – by their work. Before the Method, the dominant mode of screen acting was starchy, perfectly enunciated and very proper. Encouraging improvisation, hesitation and introspection (and let's not forget a certain amount of mumbling), Brando and Kazan helped to turn acting inside out. The breakthrough came in 1947. This was the year that Kazan co-founded the Actors Studio, which practised the teachings of Stanislavsky, and put the results on stage in the first Broadway production of *A Streetcar Named Desire*. Brando famously brooded across the stage in his vest, exuding a sweaty sexuality and cold ferocity. His performance became a bona fide piece of stage history. Even in the tamer film adaptation, Brando still succeeded in projecting a uniquely feral potency onto the screen.

In the pair's next venture, *Viva Zapata!* (1952), the actor totally inhabited the role of the titular Mexican revolutionary, with a self-righteous anger (and, of course, moustache). Yet their masterpiece was undoubtedly *On The Waterfront* (1954). As Terry Malloy, an ex-boxer fighting his own kindness, Brando transformed the screenplay's "I could have been a contender" speech into one of the most fabled in cinema history. The monologue was a performance poised delicately between vulnerability and brutality. (It was famously re-enacted by another formidable double act, De Niro and Scorsese, in *Raging Bull*.) However, there were worrying signs of flab in Brando's 1960s work: expensive junk such as Charlie Chaplin's *The Countess From Hong Kong* (1967) and Christian Marquand's *Candy* (1968). He did, however, redeem himself in the 1970s. His Kleenex-enhanced, yet stately and moving performance as Don Vito Corleone in *The Godfather* (1972) has passed into legend. The actor seemed at the time to be going handsomely, even enviably, to seed. In *Last Tango In Paris* (1972), Bernardo Bertolucci poignantly documented the end of Brando's insolent beauty. In *Apocalypse Now* (1979) he was bald, bulbous and properly mythic. But by the end of his life he had become sideshow spectacle, more famous for his eccentric behaviour – his ice-cream binges and his regular dispensing with his trousers on the set of *The Score* (2001) – than for his performances. There was a last twinkling in *Don Juan De Marcos* (1994), but he was killing time, trading on former glories. He died in 2004, a year after the death of the director with whom he had made his best work. The pair had given popular culture some of its most enduringly iconic drama. LH

stretched his muscles with the camera, tapping into the growing appetite for realism and *noir* aesthetics. He himself reckoned that *Viva Zapata!* (1952), with Brando as the Mexican revolutionary leader, was the first time he "used a visual style to speak thematically".

It was in 1952 that Kazan testified before the House Un-American Activities Committee (HUAC) as a friendly witness, naming known Communists. Without a doubt this was the central drama of Kazan's life, and for many of his colleagues it was a defining moment in which he was found sadly wanting. Unlike the persecuted alleged Communists, Kazan kept working.

Perhaps fuelled by the conflicting emotions and painful self-analysis of this deeply divisive period, he went on to make his most intense, turbulent movies: *On The Waterfront* (1954), a thinly veiled justification for the stance Kazan and screenwriter Budd Schulberg had taken; *East Of Eden* (1955), with James Dean tearing up the screen; Tennessee Williams's provocative erotic comedy *Baby Doll* (1956); the astute political satire *A Face In The Crowd* (1957); the lyrical, anguished love stories *Wild River* (1960) and *Splendor In The Grass* (1961); and finally the cathartic personal epic, Kazan's greatest single achievement, *America, America* (1963).

In these films he transcended the stagy artificiality which was still the Hollywood norm. To be sure he wasn't the only director leaving the sound stages behind, but the typically Kazanian powerhouse combination of challenging subject matter, dynamic location shooting, and the heightened, even overwrought naturalism of blistering Method performances helped change the face of American cinema. Kazan introduced Brando and James Dean to the screen, and directed (among others) Lee J. Cobb, Rod Steiger, Karl Malden, Carroll Baker, Eva Marie Saint, Montgomery Clift, Lee Remick and Natalie Wood in indelible performances – their influence would extend to such 1970s stars as Robert De Niro (the lead in Kazan's final film, *The Last Tycoon*, 1976) and beyond.

His reputation clouded by his HUAC testimony, Elia Kazan remained a controversial figure until his death at the age of 94. He directed only three more films after *America, America*. *The Arrangement* (1969) was based on his own, very personal novel but was considered a disappointment, not least by its director. *The Visitors* (1972), a rarity, was based on his son Chris Kazan's script. Shot independently, it's closer in spirit to his second wife Barbara Loden's seminal *Wanda* (1971). TC

A Streetcar Named Desire 1951, 122 min, b/w

cast Vivien Leigh, Marlon Brando, Kim Hunter, Karl Malden, Randy Bond *cin* Harry Stradling *m* Alex North

By bringing Tennessee Williams's carnal drama to the screen more or less intact, Kazan chipped away at the strictures of the Production Code. It's a filmed play (he had also directed the stage version), but Kazan gives it a strong sense of New Orleans. All four lead actors were nominated for Oscars. Ironically, Marlon Brando was the only loser among them, though his performance remains the definitive Stanley Kowalski.

Viva Zapata! 1952, 113 min, b/w

cast Marlon Brando, Jean Peters, Anthony Quinn, Joseph Wiseman, Margo, Frank Silvera, Mildred Dunnock *cin* Joseph MacDonald *m* Alex North

Written by John Steinbeck, this portrait of the Mexican revolutionary leader Emiliano Zapata (Marlon Brando) turns into a disenchanted allegory about the corrupting influence of power. It's an absorbing film with striking performances.

On The Waterfront 1954, 108 min, b/w

cast Marlon Brando, Eva Marie Saint, Karl Malden, Lee J. Cobb, Rod Steiger, Pat Henning, Leif Erickson *cin* Boris Kaufman *m* Leonard Bernstein

As a rationale for naming names, this Kazan–Budd Schulberg classic is suspiciously self-serving. But on its own terms, the story of a longshoreman standing up to mob-union corruption is never less than riveting. This movie represents the pinnacle of 1950s Method acting on screen, with Brando at the height of his powers and inspiring, powerful work from Steiger, Malden et al. Again, the use of real locations pays dividends. It won eight Oscars from twelve nominations.

East Of Eden 1955, 115 min

cast James Dean, Raymond Massey, Julie Harris, Richard Davalos, Jo Van Fleet, Burl Ives *cin* Ted McCord *m* Leonard Rosenman

An overwrought domestic drama set in Salinas, 1917, and based on John Steinbeck's novel. Cal Trask's forlorn attempts to win the affection of his self-righteous father (Massey) represented James Dean's first leading role in the cinema, and his emotionally raw performance ennobled misunderstood youth everywhere. Julie Harris was top-billed as Abra, the girl who comes between Cal and his brother. This was Kazan's first colour film – though he continued to work in black and white on a regular basis.

Unspoken desire: Marlon Brando exudes sweaty sexuality and cold ferocity in *A Streetcar Named Desire*.

Wild River 1960, 109 min, b/w
cast Montgomery Clift, Lee Remick, Jo Van Fleet, Jay C. Flippen, Albert Salmi, Barbara Loden *cin* Ellsworth J. Fredricks *m* Kenyon Hopkins

Although it's less well known, this is one of Kazan's finest films. Montgomery Clift is a civil servant sent to persuade an obstinate old woman to abandon her family home before the valley is flooded to make way for a dam. There's a delicately observed love story between Clift and Lee Remick (the woman's widowed granddaughter), and a complex, sophisticated take on the price of progress.

Splendor in The Grass 1961, 124 min
cast Natalie Wood, Warren Beatty, Pat Hingle, Barbara Loden, Sandy Dennis, Audrey Christie *cin* Boris Kaufman *m* David Amram

Kazan tries to invest William Inge's troubled teenage love story with a critique of Middle-American values, but the results are not entirely convincing. Natalie Wood was Oscar-nominated for her performance as a vulnerable Midwestern girl who is pushed over the edge by unrequited love for the son of a local bigwig (Beatty in his first film). Loden, as Wood's promiscuous sister, went on to become Kazan's wife.

America, America 1963, 177 min, b/w
cast Stathis Giallelis, Frank Wolff, Harry Davis, Elena Karam, Estelle Hemsley, Lou Antonio *cin* Haskell Wexler *m* Manos Hadjidakis

Often overlooked, Kazan's masterpiece is his most personal film, an immigrants' saga based on his uncle's epic odyssey from Anatolia to Ellis Island. Stark, vivid imagery combines with an almost biblical sense of foundational myth. Every step feels hard-earned and momentous. The script was Kazan's first – it also became his first novel, a form to which he devoted more time over the latter years of his life.

Buster Keaton
US, 1895–1966

According to showbiz legend it was Harry Houdini who dubbed 6-month-old Joe Keaton Jr "Buster" after he emerged intact from a fall down a flight of stairs. Such death-defying pratfalls would become Buster's stock in trade before he was 5 years old. The youngest member of The Three Keatons, he was flung hither and thither about the stage by his parents in a hair-raising vaudeville act, "the roughest act there ever was". This unconventional upbringing would prove the perfect background for a slapstick comedy genius, one of the handful of silent movie stars whose fame has endured into the new century.

Artistically, he was not regarded as Charlie Chaplin's equal by audiences of the day, although the pendulum of popular taste has now swung the other way. Rooted in mime, Chaplin's poetic sensibility harked back to Victorian melodrama, while Keaton's stoic, indomitable struggle against a booby-trapped universe still feels modern – not least because the pragmatic, strategic, rationalist Buster is often implicated in the mess. If he wasn't the architect of his own misfortunes he was usually the contractor.

Yet whatever the odds, he never gave up. He took the fall, dusted himself off and went right back to the job at hand.

Keaton appeared in his first two-reelers as a sidekick to Fatty Arbuckle in the period 1917–19. When Fatty signed to Paramount to make features, Keaton in effect assumed complete artistic control over Joseph Schenck's Comique studio. (In 1921 Keaton married Schenck's sister-in-law, the actress Norma Talmadge.) The next decade represented an astonishing burst of creative endeavour, starting with the nineteen short films Keaton shot before his feature directorial debut, *Three Ages* (1923). Many of these shorts are co-credited to Keaton and Eddie Cline, who also co-directed three of the features, but Cline was the first to concede that the lion's share of the invention came from Keaton. The hilarious *One Week* (1920), the first of the films to be released, shows the Keaton persona already fully formed, as Buster haplessly constructs a prefabricated box house.

Keaton was fascinated by machines off screen too (taking apart and reassembling a motion picture camera to learn how it worked, for example), but his brand of physical slapstick depended on inch-perfect design and split-second timing. He quickly developed a cinematic style to express his comic vision: he favoured location shooting (finding more inspiration in the real world than in a studio setting), a mobile camera, and a sparse cutting style with few close-ups. ("Tragedy is a close-up," he said, "comedy, a long shot.")

Graduating to features by way of the cheeky tripartite *Intolerance* parody *Three Ages*, Keaton was soon applying the lessons from the two-reelers to more elaborate situations and expansive stories: recreating the American Civil War with assiduous care in *The General* (1926), availing himself of a magnificent prop in the form of an ocean liner for *The Navigator* (1924), and staging a cyclone for the climax of *Steamboat Bill, Jr* (1928). His sophisticated grasp of cinema technique is most obvious in the Pirandellian whimsy of *Sherlock Jr* (1924), in which Buster's projectionist dreams his way into the action on screen – but Keaton's mastery is more typically revealed in the organic bedding of his gags within narrative, and the eloquent transparency of his images, which strive for authenticity in visual and emotional effect.

Although they now look like comic masterworks of the very highest order, both *The General* and *Steamboat Bill, Jr* were box-office failures, and Schenck persuaded Keaton to abandon his independence to sign with MGM. It proved an unhappy marriage, and Keaton failed to adapt to the sound era. Despite succumbing to the alcoholism that had cut short his father's vaudeville success, Keaton continued to act in other people's films – most notably, Chaplin's *Limelight* (1952) – for the remainder of his career. It wasn't until a retrospective at the Cinémathèque Française in the 1960s that audiences rediscovered Keaton's deadpan melancholia and daredevil dexterity, his genius for slapstick and miraculous, implacable perseverance. TC

Three Ages 1923, 63 min, b/w
cast Buster Keaton, Wallace Beery, Margaret Leahy, Joe Roberts, Lillian Lawrence *cin* William McGann

Adopting a three-part structure so that the film could be broken down into two-reelers if it flopped, Keaton parodied D.W. Griffith's *Intolerance* (1916) by setting stories in the prehistoric era, the Roman age and the present day. In each period Buster is an underdog vying for a girl against a stronger rival. Other motifs also recur (a conceit taken up by Bill Forsyth's *Being Human* in 1994).

Our Hospitality 1923, 74 min, b/w
cast Buster Keaton, Natalie Talmadge, Joe Roberts, Joseph Keaton, Leonard Chapman, Craig Ward *cin* Elgin Lessley, Gordon Jennings

Buster innocently steps into the middle of a blood feud when he starts courting the daughter of his family's mortal enemies – who, nevertheless, can't lay a finger on him while he's their guest. A satire at the expense of old Southern values, this is a big step forward from *Three Ages*, though it was made straight afterwards, and it finds Keaton structuring narrative and embedding gags in character and situation.

Sherlock Jr 1924, 44 min, b/w
cast Buster Keaton, Kathryn McGuire, Joseph Keaton, Ward Crane, Jane Connelly *cin* Elgin Lessley, Byron Houck

Anticipating Woody Allen's *The Purple Rose Of Cairo* (1985) by seven decades, this film is a work of genius. Keaton daydreams his way onto the movie screen, where he's the only constant in a breathtaking montage of slapstick stunts. The dazzling formal mastery here places Keaton several generations ahead of the postmodern avant-garde. It ends on an astounding chase sequence with Buster careering down the highway perched obliviously on the handlebars of a driverless motorbike.

The Navigator 1924, 59 min, b/w
cast Buster Keaton, Kathryn McGuire, Frederick Vroom, Noble Johnson, Clarence Burton *cin* Elgin Lessley, Byron Houck

Buster's all at sea, manfully struggling to keep a deserted ocean liner afloat – and blissfully unaware that his fiancée is also on board. Keaton spent $25,000 on the film's giant floating prop and he wrings every last laugh out of it, easily getting his money's worth (it was one of his biggest box-office hits). It may lack the emotional and narrative sophistication of some of his films, but this certainly is one of his funniest.

Seven Chances 1925, 56 min, b/w
cast Buster Keaton, Ruth Dwyer, Ray Barnes, Snitz Edwards *cin* Elgin Lessley, Byron Houck

Bankrupt stockbroker Buster will inherit a fortune if he marries by 7pm. His girl is insulted by his mercenary haste, but hordes of women have no such scruple, resulting in one of the more memorable chase scenes in the movies – including the famous set piece in which he causes, then outruns, a rock fall. Eagle-eyed viewers may spot Jean Arthur in an early role.

The General 1926, 75 min, b/w
cast Buster Keaton, Marian Mack, Glen Cavender, Jim Farley, Frederick Vroom *cin* Dev Jennings, Bert Haines

Probably Keaton's most highly regarded film today, *The General* is a superbly mounted action picture set against the backdrop of the American Civil War. In the first half, Buster chases after a stolen railway engine. In the second he tries to return it safely to the South. The symmetry is pure Keaton. Both ways, he's one man against insurmountable odds. It's a perfectly realized movie, and a comic masterpiece.

Steamboat Bill, Jr 1928, 71 min, b/w
cast Buster Keaton, Ernest Torrence, Marion Byron, Tom McGuire, Tom Lewis, Joseph Keaton *cin* J. Devereux Jennings, Bert Haines

Junior is a city-educated fop and a grave disappointment to his riverboat captain pop. But it's all hands on deck when the family livelihood is threatened. Another masterpiece, this features one of the most dangerous stunts ever performed, in which Keaton stands stock still as a housefront falls around him. It also includes the sequence where Buster is marched to a milliner by his father and tries on a variety of inexplicably hilarious hats, topped off by the famous boater.

The Cameraman 1928, 69 min, b/w
cast Buster Keaton, Marceline Day, Harry Gribbon, Harold Goodwin, Sidney Bracy *cin* Elgin Lessley, Basil Wrangell

Although credited to Edward Sedgwick, Keaton's first film for MGM and his last worthy vehicle has enough insightful asides on the business of moviemaking to make it a valid addendum to an astonishing creative run. He plays a still photographer anxious to shoot motion-picture newsreels for the studios (MGM in fact). Looking for something newsworthy to shoot is something of a challenge, but Buster rises to the occasion.

William Keighley
US, 1889–1984

William Keighley's gangster movie *Each Dawn I Die* (1939) was reputedly Joseph Stalin's favourite film. Keighley started out as an actor, then directed on Broadway from 1928. Entering Hollywood as an assistant and dialogue director, he racked up credits with William Dieterle (*Jewel Robbery*, 1932) and Michael Curtiz (*The Cabin In The Cotton*, 1932, and *The Adventures Of Robin Hood*, 1939). A director from 1932, Keighley oversaw a raft of Warner Bros second features and prestige releases through the 1930s and 40s, although he excelled in gangster movies. *"G" Men* (1935), *Bullets Or Ballots* (1936) and *Each Dawn I Die* remain classics in the fast-talking tabloid crime cycle that sustained Warners through the Depression.

Although Keighley was not as adept at comedy, his 1942 film *The Man Who Came To Dinner* was a humorous showcase for the cantankerous Monty Woolley. *Torrid Zone* (1940) transferred the stock James Cagney prison flick dynamic to a Central American plantation from which Cagney's resentful foreman longs to flee. Ann Sheridan ably decorated *The Fighting 69th* (1940), in which Warner Bros regulars Pat O'Brien, Alan Hale and Frank McHugh went to the Western Front for a lesson in wartime recruitment. During the war, Keighley headed the motion picture division of the Army Air Corps, directing the feature documentary *Target For Today* (1944) in Britain. For the most part, his post-war work was weak – with the exception of the intelligent docu-*noir* starring Richard Widmark, *The Street With No Name* (1948) – but the director exploited his sonorous voice as a radio host before drifting to Paris and a second career photographing architecture. His output is integral to the history of Warner Bros during its finest decade. RA

Each Dawn I Die 1939, 89 min, b/w

cast James Cagney, George Raft, Jane Bryan, George Bancroft, Maxie Rosenbloom, Stanley Ridges *cin* Arthur Edeson *m* Max Steiner

One of the darkest of the Warner Bros crime programmers of the 1930s, this is a powerful indictment of political corruption and prison abuses. James Cagney evolves from bitter crusading reporter to hardened jailbird, betrayed by the system and his buddy George Raft (better than usual). Charting Cagney's progression from idealist to psychotic social victim, Keighley's measured film is a foretaste of the Depression gangster flick's evolution into its alter ego, *film noir*.

Patrick Keiller

UK, 1950–

Patrick Keiller is one of the several film essayists who emerged in Britain in the mid-1990s. The idea for his feature debut, *London* (1994), came to him while he was commuting from north to south London to work as a teacher. He committed his vision to celluloid only after going back to college and making short films under the aegis of the London Film Cooperative.

London demonstrates the style that came to define Keiller's work: a montage of workaday scenes dispassionately recorded by a camera that remains stubbornly static while the world passes blithely by. Over these images intones a nameless and unseen narrator (played by Paul Scofield) who tells us about his similarly invisible friend, Robinson. The film claims to be a record of their perambulations around London, as they follow the literary ley lines of the capital by tracing the steps of H.G. Wells, Charles Baudelaire and Daniel Defoe. However, *London* is as much about the political landscape as the capital's topography, and Scofield's narration is an informed, impassioned rant against John Major's Tory government.

The sequel, *Robinson In Space* (1997), is a whistle-stop tour of England, from Reading to Doncaster, and many places in between, including the semi-mythical "Toyota" (the road sign for the car factory has become an iconic still from the film). While *London*

was a rounded essay, *Robinson* is a miscellany of arcane trivia and polemics, but the film's revelations, especially about defence contracts, are worryingly illuminating. More conventional was the made-for-TV documentary, *The Dilapidated Dwelling* (2000), which asked interesting questions about the state of Britain's housing stock and property market. LH

London 1994, 85 min

with Paul Scofield *cin* Patrick Keiller

For Keiller's austerely meditative approach to work, every single shot has to be visually arresting as we're invited to gaze at random snatches of banality for significant lengths of time. Thankfully the director possesses a canny eye for the off kilter, which makes the world seem both familiar and strange. Keiller focuses on a Britain saddled with an unpopular government and a London in the grip of a terrorist campaign. *Plus ça change…*

Richard Kelly

US, 1975–

Richard Kelly counts among his favourite movies *The Empire Strikes Back* (1980) and *Back To The Future* (1985). While his debut feature has a few superficial things in common with the latter blockbuster (being a high-school, time-travel comedy), *Donnie Darko* (2001) is also a beautifully warped, suggestively darkened refraction of his 1980s megahit influences.

Kelly grew up in a well-to-do Virginia suburb, not unlike the community depicted in *Donnie Darko*, and he completed the movie's script shortly after graduating from the University of Southern California's film school in 1997. Within a couple of years, the screenplay caught the attention of Drew Barrymore, who became the movie's executive producer and had a small acting role in it. Kelly was just 25 when the film premiered at Sundance in 2001. Its theatrical release didn't make much impact, but *Donnie Darko* gradually blossomed into a tremendous cult hit on video and DVD, sparking obsessive websites and eventually a theatrically released director's cut. Kelly's follow-up, *Southland Tales*, premiered at Cannes in 2006, but faced a re-edit and a long delay before its theatrical release. An MTV-generation sci-fi musical comedy set on a sweltering Fourth of July, it seems unlikely to generate the same kind of following as its predecessor. JW

Donnie Darko 2001, 113 min

cast Jake Gyllenhaal, Holmes Osborne, Mary McDonnell, Jena Malone, James Duval, Maggie Gyllenhaal *cin* Steven Poster *m* Michael Andrews

Unfolding in the Halloween-haunted weeks before the 1988 presidential election, Kelly's inspired first feature follows a smart, restless, possibly disturbed kid (Jake Gyllenhaal) with a superhero moniker who may have found a wormhole in the time-space continuum. The film contains all the emotional violence, perversity and anguish that adolescence can unleash. Shaded in autumnal tones of dread and muted grief and scored to a lovingly compiled 1980s pop soundtrack, it's one of the most impressive American debuts in a generation.

Erle C. Kenton
US, 1896–1980

Erle Kenton was a competent studio hack mostly specializing in comedy and horror pictures. He learned his trade with Mack Sennett, starting in front of the camera but directing his first two-reeler in 1919 – an apprenticeship he would put to good use calling the shots for Abbott and Costello in more than half a dozen pictures for Universal. Today, his horror films are more highly prized, especially *House Of Frankenstein* (1944). But only one of his hundred-plus credits has attained the stature of a classic… TC

Island Of Lost Souls 1932, 72 min, b/w
cast Charles Laughton, Richard Arlen, Leila Hyams, Kathleen Burke, Bela Lugosi, Stanley Fields *cin* Karl Struss

Banned in Britain and several Midwestern states for thirty years, this adaptation of H.G. Wells's *The Island Of Doctor Moreau* remains genuinely creepy. Charles Laughton is the crazed Frankenstein-like scientist, lording it over the natives and indeed evolution itself, and he's joined by Bela Lugosi as "the sayer of the law", and Kathleen Burke as an exotic "panther girl". Superbly photographed by Karl Struss, it ends in the spine-chilling "House of Pain".

Lodge Kerrigan
US, 1964–

An underrated auteur of the US independent scene of the 1990s, Lodge Kerrigan is unique among American directors for his design sense and bold investigation of inner states. He seemed to appear from nowhere, having attended New York University before his first feature *Clean, Shaven* (1995) established his profile at international film festivals. A bleak, almost plot-free tale in which a schizophrenic suspected of murder is pursued through a bleak uncaring landscape, Kerrigan's debut was made all the starker by its haunting images and an expressionistic approach to the sound design, bearing a decidedly "European" questioning of narrative and character. *Claire Dolan* (1998), featuring a masterly performance from Katrin Cartlidge, was nominated for a slew of festival awards.

Returning to Kerrigan's earlier theme – a disturbed character's negotiation of a world out of kilter – *Keane* (2004) started from the premise of a man (Damian Lewis) searching for his daughter, who he claims was abducted at the New York Port Authority building. But as his odyssey progresses, questions arise as to the man's sanity, his intentions towards a young woman and her daughter, and what actually happened to his own child. Kerrigan combines the decentred objectivity of high *film noir* with an attitude to narrative that borders on abstraction. RA

Claire Dolan 1998, 95 min
cast Katrin Cartlidge, Vincent D'Onofrio, Colm Meaney, John Doman, Maryann Plunkett *cin* Sharon Lomofsky *m* Ahrin Mishan, Simon Fisher-Turner

Centring upon a stonily terse performance from the late great Katrin Cartlidge, Kerrigan's tense abstracted account of an up-market call girl's attempt to leave it all behind lends European arthouse style mature intimations of the Hollywood women's picture. Moving through the aseptic corporate interiors of her midtown Manhattan patch with the dexterity of a cat and the wardrobe of a modern Joan Crawford, Cartlidge brings a wealth of submerged longing to Claire's need for authentic connection.

Irvin Kershner
US, 1923–

If Hollywood hadn't seduced him, Irvin Kershner could have been a 1970s-style movie brat. Following army service he attended film courses at the University of Southern California. Kershner marked time with TV work, having made documentaries for the US Information Service. His 1958 feature debut was *Stakeout On Dope Street*, a low-budget thriller from the Roger Corman stable. At its best, Kershner's work is marked by documentary rawness and a feeling for urban humanity. His 1961 drama *The Hoodlum Priest* won the Catholic Film Office Award at Cannes. With its effectively evoked wintry Montreal setting, *The Luck Of Ginger Coffey* (1964) – an affecting tale of an Irish immigrant (Robert Shaw) – evinced Kershner's feeling for the small details of urban lives. *The Flim-Flam Man* (1967) was a predictable morality yarn revolving around George C. Scott's con man and Michael Sarrazin's fey young charge, but 1970's *Loving* was made of rarer stuff.

Subsequent Kershner projects plot his decline: the witless Barbra Streisand vehicle *Up The Sandbox* (1974), through the awful *Raid On Entebbe* (1976), to big-budget corporate chores such as *The Empire Strikes Back* (1980) and Sean Connery's James Bond comeback *Never Say Never Again* (1990). Only the 1978 Faye Dunaway-Tommy Lee Jones thriller *Eyes Of Laura Mars* – its feeling for street chic foreseeing the 1980s – bore a personal stamp. Kershner's best films chart the dismay of the artist caught in the machine. RA

Loving 1970, 89 min
cast George Segal, Eva Marie Saint, Sterling Hayden, Keenan Wynn, Nancie Phillips, Janis Young, David Doyle *cin* Gordon Willis *m* Bernardo Segall

In a poignantly observed story, George Segal's commercial illustrator rages at a world that forsakes the artist in him. Irvin Kershner's film remains one of the undiscovered moments from an era in American cinema when lumbering studio flops, executive confusion and rising film schools happily contrived to make great little movies. Bringing together rich supporting turns from Eva Marie Saint and Sterling Hayden, this is a finely balanced amalgam of screwball antics, moral satire and lonely passion.

Eyes Of Laura Mars 1978, 104 min
cast Faye Dunaway, Tommy Lee Jones, Brad Dourif, Raúl Julia, Rene Auberjonois, Frank Adonis *cin* Victor J. Kemper *m* Artie Kane

In *Eyes Of Laura Mars*, co-scripted by John Carpenter, the B-movie slasher is given the disco glitzy treatment. Chic New York fashion photographer Laura Mars (Faye Dunaway), famous for her S&M layouts, turns clairvoyant when she starts looking through the eyes of the sick psycho who has been murdering her friends.

Mehboob Khan
India, 1907–64

Regarded as one of India's greatest ever film-makers, Mehboob Khan will always be known as the champion of the underdog, highlighting themes of social oppression and the fight against it in film after film. Born Ramzan Khan in rural Gujarat, he ran away to sample the glitter of Bombay's film world. Some supporting acting work later, Khan finally debuted as a director in 1935 with *Al Hilal* (*Judgement Of Allah*). The De Mille-esque epic, in which ill-equipped Arabs defeat the might of the Roman army, has an eerie resonance to today's times. *Aurat* (1940) documents the travails of a peasant woman whose life is a long fight against the elements and sleazy landowners. Khan revealed his left-leaning ways (his production company logo was a hammer and sickle) with *Roti* (1942), a scathing attack on the capitalist way of life. He changed tack with the love-triangle drama of *Andaaz* (1949), in which superstars Raj Kapoor and Dilip Kumar sought the beautiful Nargis's favours. Khan will, however, be always remembered for his remake of *Aurat*, the celebrated *Mother India* (1957) which, in addition to winning the best actress award for Nargis at the Karlovy Vary festival, was nominated for the best foreign film Academy Award. NR

Mother India (Bharat Mata) 1957, 172 min
cast Nargis, Sunil Dutt, Rajendra Kumar, Raaj Kumar, Kanhaiyalal *cin* Faredoon A. Irani *m* Naushad

This sprawling epic depicts the struggles of Radha, who has to farm a tiny piece of land and bring up two young sons in conditions of extreme poverty after her husband leaves them. In addition, she has to fend off the sexual advances of the local landlord, to whom the family is in debt. One of her sons eventually becomes a bandit and Radha has to choose between maternal love and justice. This hugely influential film raised the role of the mother in popular Indian cinema to almost divine heights.

Michel Khleifi
Israel, 1950–

Michel Khleifi is in many eyes the godfather of Palestinian cinema. His first fictional feature, *Wedding In Galilee* (1987), was a milestone film, at last giving cinematic voice to a people who had until then been entirely defined by their political quest for statehood. Khleifi had begun his career as a documentary maker. His debut film was the feature-length documentary *A Fertile Memory* (1980), a mosaic of shared remembrances by Palestinians of life before and after the 1948 partition of Palestine. Following *Wedding In Galilee*, Khleifi continued to work intermittently in fiction filmmaking. But it was with another documentary, *Route 181: Fragments Of A Journey In Palestine-Israel* (2004), that he scored his greatest triumph. AJa

Wedding In Galilee (Noce en Galilée) 1987, 100 min
cast Mohamad Ali El Akili, Bushra Karaman, Makram Khoury, Yussuf Abu-Warda, Anna Achdian *cin* Walther van de Ende *m* Jean-Marie Sénia

A Palestinian father attempts to negotiate with the Israeli authorities to waive the dusk-till-dawn curfew so that his son can get married. His request is initially rejected, but finally accepted. Tensions simmer as opponents on both sides seek to make political capital out of the supposed celebrations. Steeped in the pastoral traditions of Palestinian family life and social customs, this is a landmark in Palestinian cinema and a fascinating, if overly leisurely, insight into Palestinian society.

Route 181: Fragments Of A Journey In Palestine-Israel 2004, 270 min
with Michel Khleifi, Eyal Sivan *cin* Philippe Bellaiche

Clocking in at an epic four and a half hours, *Route 181* follows the border originally envisaged by United Nations Resolution 181 in 1947, which first mooted the partition of Palestine and the creation of the state of Israel. Co-directed with Israeli filmmaker Eyal Sivan, the film is a riveting account of the seemingly insurmountable obstacles that divide the two peoples, as well as the tantalizingly common ties that link them.

Abbas Kiarostami
Iran, 1940–

A poet, painter and photographer, Abbas Kiarostami is a minimalist master, the finest filmmaker to emerge from the specific cultural conditions prevalent in Iran at the end of the twentieth century and arguably the most formally adventurous director of his generation. At first blush, it's easy to underestimate his slow, subtle cinema, predicated as it is on long fixed-camera shots, minimal cutting, naturalistic *mise en scène*, and a syntax of repetition and elision. Influenced by both neo-realism

New Iranian Cinema

"The greatest films of the world today are being made in Iran." Werner Herzog, 1995

Throughout its history Iranian art cinema, with its humanistic emphasis on ordinary people, expressive storytelling and philosophical reflection, has been formed in relation to, rather than in spite of, limited resources and labyrinthine restrictions. And despite the particular social conditions in which it was born, the current flowering of the so-called "New Iranian Cinema" – as represented by auteurs like Abbas Kiarostami, Mohsen and Samira Makhmalbaf, Marziyeh Meshkini, Majid Majidi and Jafar Panahi – is, in fact, a natural progression from Iran's first "New Wave". In the volatile political climate of the 1960s – when the monarchy, keen to modernize and Westernize, and with strong links to the US, was under threat from Islamicist revolutionaries – filmmakers like Faroogh Farrokzad and Ebrahim Golestan took inspiration from Persian poetry, Czech and French New Wave cinemas and Italian neo-realism to create formally – and thus also politically – radical films on a shoestring. One such, Dariush Mehrjui's *The Cow* (1969) – banned in Iran for its emphasis on abject rural poverty and deep-set traditionalism – was smuggled out of the country to the Venice Film Festival, where it sparked a groundswell of foreign interest in Iranian cinema.

The tension between traditionalists and modernizers in Iran has never been straightforward, and nowhere is this precarious balance writ larger than in the movies. Contradictions are rife. While the filmmakers of the first Iranian New Wave faced censorship under the monarchy, restrictions on what could be shown on screen became even more rigorous following the Islamic Revolution of 1979, during which many cinemas in Tehran were burned. However, eager to encourage quality home-grown cinema – and to create richly profitable cultural exports – the Ayatollah Khomeini increased funding for filmmakers while calling on them to reject the corrupting influence of the West. Many directors fled into exile; those who stayed elaborated the cinematic language first uttered by their 1960s forebears. Not permitted even to hint at romance, sexual desire or violence, they turned increasingly to allegory, often placing children at the centre of visually arresting and philosophical fables. These were the films that caused Herzog to wax so lyrical; meanwhile, the vast bulk of the country's output was – and remains – commercial, comprised of popular action movies, thrillers, melodramas and comedies that are rarely seen abroad.

While they never speak out directly against the authorities, many of Iran's art movies are slyly subversive, and banned for domestic consumption. At the same time, key directors, among them Kiarostami, Panahi and Mohsen Makhmalbaf, are encouraged by the authorities to enter international film festivals, where their prestige brings Iran much-needed visibility and cultural status. Ironically, the films' concentration on rural poverty – with the exception perhaps of Panahi's work, which has a more urban thrust – undercuts the modernity suggested by their formal sophistication, and their emphasis on the experience of women challenges not only the status of women under Islamic regimes, but also Western assumptions about their subjugation and compliance.

Iran possesses an impressive number of female directors for any country, but of course their story is hardly straightforward. In 2001 the feminist Tahmineh Milani was imprisoned and threatened with execution for *The Hidden Half* – about a woman with a radical political past – before Iran's reformist president Mohammad Khatami (1997–2005) intervened on her behalf. Hana Makhmalbaf's *Joy Of Madness* (2003), a digital documentary which followed her sister Samira casting her bleakly lyrical film about post-Taliban Afghanistan, *At Five In The Afternoon* (2003), was banned in Iran partly because Samira's headscarf was perceived to be too revealing.

In 2007, the release of the Cannes Jury Prize-winner *Persepolis* – based on Marjane Satrapi's phenomenally successful graphic novel about a feisty Tehrani girl growing up pre- and post-Revolution – raised yet another set of challenges, not only for the Iranian authorities, sensitive to Islamophobia, but also for Western arthouse audiences more familiar with the abstract poetics of the Iranian auteurs. SC

and postmodernism, Kiarostami is an anomaly in contemporary cinema and virtually unknown to the majority of mainstream audiences, yet he is enormously respected in Europe and elsewhere (his influence on Chinese filmmaker Zhang Yimou and the Turk Nuri Bilge Ceylan is obvious) and he has mentored a number of Iranian filmmakers, most notably Jafar Panahi.

After working as a commercial artist in the 1960s, Kiarostami helped set up a film department at the Institute for the Intellectual Development of Children and Young Adults in Tehran. He ran the department from 1969 to 1974, and it was there that he made his first short, *Bread And Alley*, in 1970. As with the Italian neo-realists, children figure prominently in Kiarostami's cinema, as protagonists (*The Traveller*, 1974, *Where Is The Friend's House?*, 1987), subjects (*Homework*, 1989, *ABC Africa*, 2001), and even antagonists (*Ten*, 2002). By focusing on children, Kiarostami not only disarms government censors, but also achieves a frank and unaffected realism. The goal, as he explains it in the manifesto film *10 On Ten* (2004), is "absolute truth" (although, as he also acknowledges, this is an illusory and unobtainable quest).

Kiarostami's aesthetic goes further than the neo-realist model because it doesn't simply consist of real people enacting stories in actual locations; he all but dispenses with plot to privilege "real time". That is, the audience experiences time in pace with the characters on screen (repetition and narrative ellipsis may be the correlatives of such a strategy). In *10 On Ten*, he talks about the necessity of liberating the cinema from the tyranny of technology; of creation by subtraction. He uses a minimal crew and mostly eschews a score. So persuasive is the illusion of reality that often viewers erroneously assume (watching *Ten*, for example) that they are watching a documentary.

A number of Kiarostami's films are nonfiction (*Homework*, for example). The others combine documentary and dramatic fiction in varying measures, not to camouflage artifice but to explore the limitations of any truth to which filmmakers – and the rest of us – lay claim. In the nonfiction narrative feature *Close-Up* (1989) an Iranian who passed himself off as the famous local director Mohsen Makhmalbaf plays himself in reconstructions of his fraud and in documentary-like courtroom scenes. In the end, he even meets the real Makhmalbaf for the first time – although even this "reality" is potentially scripted. In *And Life Goes On...* (1991), an actor playing Kiarostami journeys to the Koker region where he made *Where Is The Friend's House?* after a calamitous (real) earthquake to make sure that his erstwhile collaborators have survived. Filmmakers also appear in *Through The Olive Trees* (1994, the third part of the so-called "Koker Trilogy", ostensibly dealing with offscreen events from *And Life Goes On...*) and *The Wind Will Carry Us* (1999), while Kiarostami appears on (or sometimes off) screen as himself in *Homework*, *ABC Africa* and *10 On Ten*.

It may be apparent by now that Kiarostami's oeuvre is an ongoing project in which each film is a reflection on what has gone before. This is most obvious in the Koker trilogy, but also clear in the shift towards minimalism over the last decade, a paring down which culminates in the Zen landscape pieces of *Five* (2003). Describing *Five*, Kiarostami's sometime collaborator and acolyte Mania Akbari said, "*Five* is the look of an artist who came on a scene one day and took off his coat and threw it away. And then took off the rest of his clothes and threw them away. And then took off a leg, and threw that away too. And the other leg. And one by one, he took off everything and threw it away from the scene, until just one finger was left, and then all that was left was the scene." TC

Close-Up (Namayeh nazdik) 1989, 97 min

cast Hossain Sabzian, Mohsen Makhmalbaf, Hossain Farazmand, Abdolfazl Ahankhah, Mehrdad Ahankhah *cin* Ali Reza Zarrin-Dast

Although Kiarostami's realism is not overtly political, the culture clash between educated, relatively wealthy Tehranis and the country's impoverished majority is an abiding interest. Here that dramatic contrast is delineated in the true story of Sabzian, an illiterate film buff who impersonated director Mohsen Mahkmalbaf, even "casting" a middle-class family for his next film. During his trial (shot in *vérité* style), Sabzian claims his fraud was not malicious, that he was in some sense delusional.

Through The Olive Trees (Zir-e darakhtan-e zeyton) 1994, 103 min

cast Mohammad Ali Keshavarz, Farhad Kheradmand, Hossein Rezai, Zarifeh Shiva, Tahereh Ladanian *cin* Hossein Djafarian, Farhad Saba

The third instalment of the Koker trilogy is ostensibly the recreation of a behind-the-scenes love story Kiarostami observed during the filming of *And Life Goes On...* between two peasant actors who played a couple in that film. The young man believes he should marry his leading lady for real. The film reveals its grace notes to patient observers who will savour a final ten-minute shot of ineffable beauty (which is sadly reduced on the small screen).

A Taste Of Cherry (Ta'ame-gilas) 1997, 95 min

cast Homayoon Irshadi, Abdol Hossain Bagheri, Afshin Khorshid Bakhtiari, Safar Ali Moradi *cin* Homayoon Payvar

Kiarostami's Palme d'Or winner is a road movie which goes round in circles in the foothills outside Tehran, as a Mr Badii picks up a series of men with a singular request: to bury him after he has killed himself. The camera scarcely leaves the confines of Badii's vehicle, and rarely indulges even in a two-shot of driver and passenger together. Another conversation film, often visually tedious, it nevertheless achieves a rare and precious epiphany before it's done.

The Wind Will Carry Us (Bad mara khahad bourd) 1999, 118 min

cast Behzad Dourani, Farzad Sohrabi, Shahpour Ghobadi, Masood Mansouri, Masoameh Salimi *cin* Mahmoud Kalari

Here Kiarostami refines earlier themes, this time in a bone-dry comic vein reminiscent of Samuel Beckett's absurdist abstract dramas. Yet this too is ostensibly a realist film, a straightforward account of three Tehranis arriving in a dirt-poor Kurdish village. It's highly elliptical, though: we only ever see one of the three, an engineer, who is another of the director's alter egos. For all its mazy formalism, this is a deeply humane and perfectly simple film about cultural incomprehension. Funny too.

Ten 2002, 94 min

cast/ crew Mania Akbari, Roya Arabshahi, Katayoun Taleidzadeh, Mandana Sharbaf, Amene Moradi, Amin Maher, Kamran Adl

Ten single shots, of around ten minutes each, trained on either the driver (a sophisticated divorcée, played by Mania Akbari) or her (mostly female) passengers: an old woman, her sister, a prostitute, etc. In narrative terms *Ten* tells us next to nothing. Yet it speaks volumes about the status of women in Iran today. It is also another audaciously self-abnegating formal experiment. Using a static digital video camera, non-actors, no formal script and removing himself from the scene, Kiarostami somehow contrives to make the ultimate Kiarostami film.

К

Krzysztof Kieślowski

Poland, 1941–96

Of all European directors of recent decades, Krzysztof Kieślowski is the most obvious legatee of the high seriousness that we associate with Ingmar Bergman and Andrei Tarkovsky. He pushed traditional European art cinema in the face of Hollywood dominance and the burgeoning auteur cinemas from other parts of the world.

Kieślowski made his first film in 1969, but it would be another ten years before he attracted international attention with *Camera Buff* (1979), a satire on Polish film censorship. Other late-1970s work, such as *The Night Porter's Point Of View* (1978), explored tensions between the personal and the political. Kieślowski was a key figure in Poland's "cinema of moral unrest", along with Andrzej Wajda, Feliks Falk and Krzysztof Zanussi. Their films contained far-reaching criticism of the status quo in Poland under Communism, and were characterized by a direct and raw realism and a strong moral sensibility. These qualities can be seen in Kieślowski's *No End* (1984), which was a typically subtle exploration of moral choices and political restrictions in Polish daily life.

In showing three different outcomes to one story, *Blind Chance* (1982) offered three solutions to the Polish situation, and was suppressed under martial law. Its structure presaged the ten-part television production *Dekalog* (1988), a series of hour-long stories of Polish life inspired by the Ten Commandments. *Dekalog* made Kieślowski's name, and provided the material that led to *A Short Film About Killing* (1987) and *A Short Film About Love* (1988). In these films Kieślowski began to elaborate a theme of interconnectedness that would be key to his oeuvre. If his narrative reticence and obscure images have generated criticism, they have equally been praised for the thematic ambiguity and density they bring to his work.

Layered with its own coincidences and asides, *The Double Life Of Véronique* (1991) was Kieślowski's first international co-production and his first major success. A pair of identical girls who don't know of one another – Véronique in France and Veronika in Poland, both portrayed by Irène Jacob – share a number of strengths and weaknesses, including musical talent. When Veronika collapses during a recital, Véronique feels a change come over her. Always touched by their mutual sympathy, the women embody an affinity that, Kieślowski suggests, enables each to learn from the other, and may be seen as symbolic of our best hope amid a fragmenting collective experience.

This timely notion, explored in an era of progressive European integration, most rigorously informs Kieślowski's masterwork, the *Three Colours* trilogy of 1993–94. Using the values embodied in the French tricolour, *Blue* (1993), *White* (1994) and *Red* (1994) each explore elements of Liberty, Equality and Fraternity through the prisms of individual lives. *Blue* is a melancholy examination of the experience of a grieving woman after the death of her composer husband and their daughter in a car accident. It contains some of the most beautiful camerawork in modern cinema, the light and colour confounding the customary critical method of evaluating cinematography and content separately when discussing arthouse filmmaking.

While *Blue* tended to foreground sight and *Red* hearing, *White* represented touch or ownership. Charting expatriate Polish hairdresser Karol's rejuvenation following divorce from his French wife, *White* is the most political of the three films. Returning to Poland and making a killing on a land scam, Karol comes to seem like the embodiment of the overheated post-Communist economies. Resembling a Slav Bob Hoskins, Zbigniew Zamachowski eventually wins Julie Delpy's limpid, ambivalent Dominique, but at tremendous cost. Sombre after the azure sheen of *Blue*, *White* casts a sardonic eye on what Europe became in the 1990s.

Red, about an encounter between a young model and a retired judge, remains the most accessible of the trilogy. The opening sequence, in which Piotr Sobocinski's camera literally follows a phone call under the Channel from the Continent to England, remains one of the most startling and audacious openings in recent film history, stating the preoccupation with the aural as it suggests a society anxious to connect.

Fleetingly interconnected as Julie, Karol and Valentine's paths cross, perfectly realized in its ideas about cinema and experience, Kieślowski's trilogy, like his work generally, is the most convincing apologia for the metaphysical since Bresson. RA

A Short Film About Killing (Krótki film o zabijaniu) 1987, 85 min

cast Miroslaw Baka, Krzysztof Globisz, Jan Tesarz, Zbigniew Zapasiewicz
cin Slawomir Idziak *m* Zbigniew Preisner

Taking as its starting point the Commandment "Thou shalt not kill", *A Short Film About Killing* follows the random murder of a cab driver by a young man who is in turn executed for the crime. Dissolving the distinction we think exists between murder and judicial execution, the yellow wash and muddy edges of the cinematography show everything through the killer's myopic gaze, making for a shocking watch.

A Short Film About Love (Krótki film o milosci) 1988, 87 min

cast Grazyna Szapolowska, Olaf Lubaszenko, Stefania Iwinska, Piotr Machalica *cin* Witold Adamek *m* Zbigniew Preisner

"Thou shalt not commit adultery": a young postal worker spies on and falls obsessively in love with his neighbour, an older woman. Humorous and emotionally revealing by turns, and played with tender conviction by Grazyna Szapolowska and Olaf Lubaszenko, this remains one of the most moving statements on love in decades.

Three Colours: Blue (Trois couleurs: bleu) 1993, 98 min

cast Juliette Binoche, Benoît Régent, Hélène Vincent, Florence Pernel, Emmanuelle Riva *cin* Slawomir Idziak *m* Zbigniew Preisner

So damaged is Julie (Binoche) by the death of her composer husband and their daughter that she backs away from all ties and contacts. In attempting to complete her husband's score, *A Symphony For Europe*, she gradually rediscovers who her husband was and what her life can be. With its stunning compositions by Slawomir Idziak and script by regular Kieślowski collaborator Krzysztof Pieszewicz, this was the film that made Binoche a star, and she rises to the occasion with staggering sensitivity.

Three Colours: Red (Trois couleurs: rouge) 1994, 99 min

cast Irène Jacob, Jean-Louis Trintignant, Frédérique Feder, Jean-Pierre Lorit, Samuel Lebihan *cin* Piotr Sobocinski *m* Zbigniew Preisner

Recalling Ingrid Bergman in her beauty and intelligence, Irène Jacob plays Valentine, a Genevan model incongruously brought into contact with a reclusive judge (Jean-Louis Trintignant) by a traffic accident. Eavesdropping on other lives by monitoring his neighbours' phone calls, the judge becomes a godlike voyeur who is gradually tempered by Valentine's compassion, watching over a pained world just as the model's chewing-gum billboard advertisement watches over the traffic.

Henry King
US, 1886–1982

Few Hollywood directors have portrayed love with such sensitivity and feeling as Henry King. He excelled in the sincere depiction of human fellowship against a backdrop of rustic Americana.

Raised on the family plantation in Virginia, King worked in railroad offices, acted in touring road shows across the American South and directed and acted in vaudeville, burlesque and regular theatre before entering the film industry as an actor in 1912. By 1915 he was directing, having his first success with the army comedy *23½ Hours' Leave* (1919). In 1921 King established Inspiration Pictures. *Tol'able David* (1921), a tale of the Appalachian backwoods in which a young man proves himself, displays a feeling for the people and the rural American experience in an era of rapid modernization that remains key to King's oeuvre.

The 1930s and 40s were King's richest years and saw him generate, with John Ford and Howard Hawks, the template for American movies that continues to define Americans' relationship to their national cinema. In *State Fair* (1933), a Midwestern family travel to the regional produce show and realize various aspirations, agricultural, culinary and romantic. Twilight is often significant in King's work, and the setting sun behind the trees underscores daughter Margie's contentment. Margie would be Jeanne Crain's character in the 1945 remake and again in King's own *Margie* (1947), which recalled the heroine's 1920s schooldays in a small town in Ohio.

Spending much of his career at 20th Century Fox, King's work defined that studio's homespun pre-war image. Steeped in Nunnally Johnson's vernacular dialogue, *Jesse James* (1939) was a vigorous tribute to American backwoods sensibilities. Other notable films

Bursting the bubble: Irène Jacob poses for Samuel Lebihan in *Three Colours: Red*.

of the time were *In Old Chicago* (1938), *Chad Hanna* (1940), *Maryland* (1940) and that prestigious tribute to President Wilson, *Wilson* (1944), which saw King doing patriotic duty at a time of national solidarity.

King was an old-style storyteller, as he ably demonstrated in the African adventure *Stanley And Livingstone* (1939), the notable Gregory Peck Western *The Gunfighter* (1950) and his Ernest Hemingway adaptations *The Snows Of Kilimanjaro* (1952) and *The Sun Also Rises* (1957). His leisurely films focused on medium shots and minimal camerawork. Typically, he would open with a close-up, then pull back slowly to locate his characters. He also had a feeling for star portraiture that earned him a reliable reputation in the front office. In a career lasting until 1962, he coached some of Hollywood's biggest names, including Lillian Gish, Vilma Banky, Henry Fonda, Tyrone Power, Alice Faye, William Holden, Gregory Peck and Ava Gardner.

King was Jennifer Jones's director of choice, and the saintly tribute *The Song Of Bernadette* (1943) and the lush Oriental romance *Love Is A Many-Splendored Thing* (1955) were major hits. But, aside from the acclaimed Gregory Peck war movie *Twelve O'Clock High* (1949), the charming *I'd Climb The Highest Mountain* (1951) and *Carousel* (1956), King's post-war work became increasingly homogenized as big budgets, wide screens and exotic locations overcame his picket-fence naturalism. He remains, however, an American humanist of distinction. RA

In Old Chicago 1938, 111 min, b/w

cast Tyrone Power, Alice Faye, Don Ameche, Alice Brady, Andy Devine, Brian Donlevy, Phyllis Brooks *cin* J. Peverell Marley *m* Louis Silvers

Filmed in response to MGM's 1936 recreation of the 1906 San Francisco earthquake, this early disaster movie is a fiery pre-CGI evocation of the devastating 1871 Great Fire of Chicago (which was apparently started by a cow kicking over a lantern in a barn). The film – and the city – goes out with a bang, while Alice Faye sings her heart out.

Wilson 1944, 154 min

cast Alexander Knox, Charles Coburn, Geraldine Fitzgerald, Cedric Hardwicke, Thomas Mitchell *cin* Leon Shamroy *m* Alfred Newman

One of the very few Hollywood prestige projects of the classical era that still works, this lush Technicolor tribute to President Woodrow Wilson (Alexander Knox), the great Progressive and founder of the League of Nations, oozes with the liberal optimism of the war years. Like its subject, the film is elegant and stoic.

Carousel 1956, 128 min

cast Gordon MacRae, Shirley Jones, Cameron Mitchell, Barbara Ruick *cin* Charles G. Clarke *m* Richard Rodgers, Oscar Hammerstein II

Taking Ferenc Molnar's play *Liliom* and setting the action in a Maine fishing village, perhaps King got the balance between glossy Fox production values and down-home sincerity just right as Gordon MacRae's departed carny is allowed a day on earth to visit his beloved Shirley Jones. Sporting some emotive Rodgers and Hammerstein tunes and all the schmaltz of a bygone era, this was King's answer to the overheated *mise en scène* of 1950s melodrama.

Dmitri Kirsanoff
Estonia (formerly Russia), 1899–1957

Dmitri Kirsanoff was an intensely self-critical filmmaker whose early metaphorical, poetic films gave way to more conventional commercial assignments.

He arrived in Paris in 1919, where he supported his cello studies by acting and playing in an orchestra. His first film, *L'ironie du destin* (*The Irony Of Fate*, 1923), is lost. Thinking himself technically deficient, he employed a cameraman for the *ménage à trois* melodrama *Ménilmontant* (1924) but, unhappy with the resultant tripod-bound work, ended up shooting the film himself hand-holding the camera. Kirsanoff regarded himself as part of neither the French avant-garde nor the Russian émigré community, but this isolation helped him develop a visual and technical style that anticipated much later avant-garde cinema. *Brumes d'automne* (*Autumn Mists*, 1926) was overtly poetic with its musical structure and seen-through-tears landscapes. *Rapt* (1933), based on C.F. Ramuz's novel *La séparation des races*, deals with the fallout from an abduction, and is the first Swiss sound film (featuring a score by Arthur Honegger).

Kirsanoff dismissed many of his post-*Rapt* films, as either of uneven quality or compromised by outside forces. The thriller *Le crâneur* (*The Show-Off*, 1950) was one of several films calculatedly made for commercial success. Three shorts that he did like were *Deux amis* (*Two Friends*, 1946), *Arrière-saison* (*End Of Autumn*, 1950) and *Une chasse à courre* (*Death Of A Stag*, 1951), a satirical look at the "noble sport" of deer hunting. His second marriage was to editor Monique Kirsanoff. JR

Ménilmontant 1924, 38 min, b/w

cast Nadia Sibirskaia, Yolande Beaulieu, Guy Belmont, Jean Pasquier *cin* Dmitri Kirsanoff

Kirsanoff's poetic camerawork and editing capture the wintry, desolate atmosphere of Ménilmontant, a poor, working-class district on the eastern edge of Paris. Together with Sibirskaia's central performance, it is enough to turn what could be a hackneyed melodrama (a man serially sleeps with two sisters before being murdered by a mystery attacker) into something altogether different.

Takeshi Kitano
Japan, 1947–

The single most arresting filmmaker working in Japan today, Takeshi Kitano is one of the most original and idiosyncratic artists in world cinema. Oscillating between extreme, hard-boiled yakuza thrillers, wild knockabout comedy and plaintive, frankly sentimental, love stories, Kitano likes to mix things up. Indeed, his anarchic fondness for counter-

K

point is a defining characteristic; violence and comedy are closely related in his work, sometimes to unsettling effect. He has a penchant for departing from the script to improvise situations as the environment inspires him, and prefers deadpan performances, a still, detached camera and deliberate, off-the-beat editing. In this respect, his closest cinematic forebear may be Buster Keaton – although his only out-and-out comedy, *Getting Any?* (1995), was his biggest failure.

Kitano was the youngest of four sons in a working-class family whose father, Kikujiro, was violent and abusive (Takeshi speculates that he may have been in a yakuza gang). Takeshi studied engineering but dropped out of college and gravitated to Tokyo's seedy entertainment district, Asakusa. There he met Kiyoshi Kaneko, and they formed a "manzai" stand-up comedy double act called "The Two Beats". (As an actor, Kitano is still often credited as "Beat" Takeshi.) Ironically, given his later taciturn onscreen persona, Beat Takeshi was the motor-mouth of the duo, a quick-fire improviser with Kaneko as the straight man. Perhaps it's from this form of comedy that Kitano developed his taste for counterpoint. He certainly reproduced this style of exchange as a director: very often his dialogue scenes are essentially monologues, with one character speaking and playing off the silence of another (usually Kitano himself).

The Two Beats broke up in the early 1980s, by which time Kitano had made his mark as an actor, notably as Sergeant Hara in Nagisa Oshima's *Merry Christmas, Mr Lawrence* (1983). A fellow iconoclast, Oshima was an important early influence. Kitano also had significant roles in Takashi Ishii's *Gonin* (1995) and, less happily, Robert Longo's *Johnny Mnemonic* (1995). Something of a cultural polymath, Kitano is also a constant presence on Japanese TV (for a long time appearing in seven different shows a week), a painter of distinction, a composer, an author and a columnist… all of which frees him from the financial constraints imposed on most genre filmmakers.

Originally only slated to star in the film, he turned director on *Violent Cop* (1989) when Kinji Fukasaku dropped out. Although the material is formulaic, Kitano's use of long, static shots, his minimalist performance and the soft jazz score are anything but. The next year's *Boiling Point* – which he also wrote – is the first true Kitano film, and one of his best. While he appears as a spectacularly sociopathic rogue yakuza, the film's real hero is a slacker mechanic who may even be daydreaming the whole movie. (There are two similarly unprepossessing yet sympathetic protagonists in the sober, quasi-autobiographical *Kids Return*, 1996).

A Scene At The Sea (1991) was even stranger: it's about a deaf garbage man teaching himself to surf – and virtually a silent movie. But Kitano really hit his stride with *Sonatine* (1993), an existential yakuza thriller which morphs into something quite unexpected in the second half – and which features prob-

ably the most iconic Kitano performance. Kitano said, "A sonatine is the kind of piece you play when you're learning to play piano. I figured I was at about that stage in my directing career, so it seemed like an appropriate title."

More conventional (at least by his own standards), *Hana-Bi*, or *Fireworks*, won the Golden Lion at the Venice Film Festival in 1997, thus marking Kitano's official acceptance on the world stage. Kitano himself played a taciturn cop who turns bank robber to give his sick wife a second honeymoon before she dies. True to form, he followed it with *Kikujiro* (1999), a largely improvised sentimental comedy about a lonely child's misadventures with a lowly yakuza. *Brother* (2000) is basically *Sonatine* in America, a pulpy gangster flick with no excess fat, but little of the resonance or surprise of the earlier film.

Dolls (2002), on the other hand, was a bravura aesthetic experiment, a triptych of love stories inspired by bunraku puppet theatre. In outline it's close to kitsch esoterica, but the visuals are spellbinding, with swathes of sumptuous colour and bold symbolism. A similar aesthetic confidence informs the style of *Zatoichi* (2003), a quirky remake of the long-running blind samurai series, and his biggest commercial hit to date. More recently, *Takeshis'* (2005) and *Kantoku – Banzai!* (2007) are both, in different ways, riffs on the director's Beat Takeshi persona. TC

Boiling Point (3-4x Jugatsu) 1990, 96 min

cast Masahiko Ono, Yuriko Ishida, Takahito Iguchi, Minoru Iizuka, Takeshi Kitano, Makoto Ashikawa, Hisash Igawa *cin* Katsumi Yanagishima

A slacker comic fantasy of sorts, Kitano's second film is a very curious fish, mixing absurdist humour with shocking sadism (mostly deriving from the sociopathic yakuza played by the filmmaker himself). Many elements of this film later became regular Kitano motifs, while its unconventional *mise en scène* and haphazard continuity left many critics perplexed: was the director a naïf or a genius?

Sonatine 1993, 94 min

cast Takeshi Kitano, Aya Kokumai, Tetsu Watanabe, Masanobu Katsumura, Susumu Terajima *cin* Katsumi Yanagishima *m* Joe Hisaishi

Perhaps the strangest yakuza movie since Seijun Suzuki's heyday in the late 1960s, *Sonatine* begins by delineating (in highly abbreviated form) the temporary exile of Kitano's mob lieutenant Murakawa with a cadre of his men. But safely arrived on their deserted island retreat, the yakuza lose their discipline, falling to the innocent pleasures of beach games (the men) and existential ennui (Murakawa).

Hana-Bi (Fireworks) 1997, 103 min

cast "Beat" Takeshi, Kayoko Kishimoto, Ren Osugi, Susumu Terajima, Tetsu Watanabe *cin* Hideo Yamamoto *m* Joe Hisaishi

This Venice prize-winner addresses Kitano's near-fatal motorcycle accident of 1995, but tangentially, through the character of Horibe (Ren Osugi), a cop abandoned by his family after he's paralysed from the waist down, who comes back from despair by taking up painting (Kitano's own stunning artwork). Meanwhile Nishi, his old partner (played by Kitano), is also alienated after his wife is stricken by leukaemia – but his response is more violent, romantic and nihilistic.

281

Zatoichi 2003, 115 min
cast "Beat" Takeshi, Tadanobu Asano, Michiyo Ohgusu, Yui Natsukawa, Guadalcanal Taka cin Katsumi Yanagishima m Keiichi Suzuki

Yes, it's a remake: the story of a blind but deadly swordsman spawned several dozen sequels from the 1960s onwards. And yes it features the requisite slapstick comedy and fountains of blood, but like Gus Van Sant's *Psycho* or Brian De Palma's myriad Hitchcock variations, *Zatoichi*'s interest resides in form not content – in colour, movement, rhythm. It's an art film in the purist sense.

Cédric Klapisch
France, 1961–

Screenwriter-director Cédric Klapisch has a preoccupation with community that is increasingly poignant in a corporatized world. His big 1996 hit *When The Cat's Away* seemed to reaffirm the value of both grass-roots experience and European auteur cinema in the year of *Mission: Impossible*.

After graduating from New York University in 1985, Klapisch worked as a camera operator on shorts before returning to France to direct industrial and documentary segments for television. His experience in shorts fed into the examination of miniature lives. *Rien du tout* (*Little Nothings*, 1992), Klapisch's feature debut, saw a Parisian shopkeeper trying to introduce American-style methods. A surprise hit, it was followed by *Le péril jeune* (*Good Old Daze*, 1994), another comedy in which a group of old schoolfriends gather for the birth of a baby fathered by one of their number, since deceased. Its wry and affectionate tribute to the political demonstrations and squats of the early 1970s exemplified Klapisch's interest in the collision of past and present.

Un air de famille (*Family Resemblances*, 1996) does not hide its theatricality. Based on the play written by Jean-Pierre Bacri and Agnès Jaoui, who also starred in the film, it hilariously details familial resentments on the occasion of a family get-together. Out of the social, cultural and romantic complications of a Barcelona flat-share, *L'auberge espagnole* (*Pot Luck*, 2002) coaxed nuanced performances from a stellar cast, which led to the release of a sequel, *Les poupées russes* (*Russian Dolls*) in 2005. But while such names as Audrey Tautou and Judith Godrèche now figure in his cast lists, Klapisch has yet to revive the happy multicultural accident of Garance Clavel's odyssey in *When The Cat's Away*. RA

When The Cat's Away (Chacun cherche son chat) 1996, 90 min
cast Garance Clavel, Renée Lecalm, Zinedine Soualem, Olivier Py cin Benoît Delhomme

Bouncing by on a stop-go rhythm, this charming miniature, in which Chloé loses her cat but finds love against the noisy clash of Bastille gentrification, combined a *nouvelle vague* shoot with intimate social observation. This is a film that dates in the best sense, since Popincourt, the area of Paris in which it was filmed and which it documents so well, will never be the same again.

Randal Kleiser
US, 1946–

Randal Kleiser's graduation film *Peege* (1972) was about the prospect of death, a theme he returned to in several films including the TV movies *The Gathering* (1977) and *The Boy In The Plastic Bubble* (1976), in which John Travolta plays a teenager without an immune system. Travolta then starred in the smash-hit musical *Grease* (1978). There was more teen love in the island fantasy *Blue Lagoon* (1980), which generated accusations of exploitation, and in the holiday romance *Summer Lovers* (1982). For younger audiences, Kleiser directed the UFO fantasy *The Flight Of The Navigator* (1986), the Disney sequel *Honey, I Blew Up The Kid* (1992) and the 3-D Disney attraction *Honey, I Shrunk The Audience* (1995). Adult fare included Jack London's *White Fang* (1991) and *It's My Party* (1996), about an AIDS patient's farewell bash. The technophiliac Kleiser's trailer for the modern-day Arthurian tale *Royal Standard* (1999) was made to be broadcast over the Internet and the musical *Red Riding Hood* (2004) was shot on virtual sets. *Lovewrecked* (2005) returned to *Blue Lagoon* territory, as a teenage girl is marooned on a beach with the rock star of her dreams. JR

Grease 1978, 110 min
cast John Travolta, Olivia Newton-John, Stockard Channing, Jeff Conaway, Barry Pearl cin Bill Butler m Jim Jacobs, Warren Casey

Mixing newly commissioned songs with favourites from the stage musical and a few 1950s classics on the soundtrack, *Grease* became a juggernaut musical. Two high school seniors – a goody-two-shoes and a greaser – have a rocky relationship: should she become more tarty to keep him? Should he become a one-woman man? It's not going to be an easy ride through school pep rallies, dance competitions, drive-in dates and drag races to graduation and the surreal carnival ending.

Elem Klimov
Russia (formerly Soviet Union), 1933–2003

Elem Klimov was unfortunate enough to suffer the differing fates of working under Communism and under a free-market economy: he couldn't get his films *released* in the former and couldn't get them *made* in the latter. He directed five features in the pre-glasnost years, but they were all shelved for one reason or another by the State Committee for Cinematography.

Welcome (1964), a satire about an authoritarian summer camp for young communists, was banned on the curious grounds that the protagonist's granny looked like Khrushchev, and her funeral was officially interpreted as being a fantasy about the demise of the Soviet leader. *Adventure Of A Dentist* (1965), in which a maverick dentist's successful methods incur the wrath of his less talented peers, was an intentional allegory about the plight of the gifted individual in Soviet society, and was never released. Klimov's edgy *nouvelle vague* self-consciousness ran heretically counter to the state's demands for socialist realism. With *Agony* (1975), which retold the Rasputin legend, the director made the mistake of humanizing rather than caricaturing the deposed tsar, and the film was shelved for ten years.

In 1979, Klimov's wife, director Larissa Shepitko, was killed in a car accident just as she was about to start shooting the melodrama *Farewell* (1983). Two days later, Klimov took over filming the story of a Siberian village drowned to make way for a hydro-electric dam. It was banned for being reactionary. After completing his epic masterpiece, *Come And See* (1985), Klimov was the founding First Secretary of the Union of Soviet Filmmakers and set about releasing the three hundred films that had been shelved by the censors. The terrible irony of his new career is that Klimov did not benefit from the new freedom himself, and never made another film. LH

Come And See (Idi i smotri) 1985, 142 min

cast Alexei Kravchenko, Olga Mironova, Luiubomiras Laucevicius, Vladas Bagdonas, Victoor Lorents *cin* Alexei Rodionov *m* Oleg Yanchenko

A hallucinatory odyssey about a young partisan who witnesses the brutal destruction of some of the 638 Belarusian villages that were systematically and savagely ransacked by the Nazis during World War II. Both lyrical and brutal, the haunting qualities of this mournful epic were no doubt inspired by the director's own painful memories of the Battle of Stalingrad, which he somehow managed to escape on a home-made raft.

Alexander Kluge
Germany, 1932–

Alexander Kluge was one of the key filmmakers and theorists of the New German Cinema. A lawyer, novelist and political writer, he became Fritz Lang's assistant in 1958. Making shorts from 1960, Kluge became the spokesman for a new generation of West German filmmakers coalescing around the Oberhausen Manifesto, a statement of intent drafted at the International Short Film Festival in 1962. It protested the lack of artistic ambition in the post-war film industry, and called for an *Autorenkino*, a cinema of authorship. Kluge and his colleagues also stressed the need for filmmakers to acquaint themselves with all aspects of production, a reflection of Kluge's involvement with the Ulm Film Institute.

Kluge's first feature – *Yesterday Girl* (1966) – was a pivotal moment in this experimental phase. His film won the Special Jury Prize at the Venice Film Festival, bringing much-needed international recognition to West German filmmaking. Kluge became an influential figure in the movement, and Rainer Werner Fassbinder dedicated *Lola* (1981) to him. In the 1970s and 80s, the New German cineastes' work was part of a wider cultural project designed to confront the legacy of the Nazi period and the divisions wrought by the Cold War. This need to "work on our history" embraced political activism, fiction, television documentary and sociological research, finding expression in Kluge's films *Der Kandidat* (1980), *Krieg und Frieden* (*War And Peace*, 1983), and the collective project *Deutschland im Herbst* (*Germany in Autumn*, 1978).

Kluge, who wrote many of his own scripts, used the metaphors of "frictions" and "fractions", in which verbal and audiovisual communication is used to distance the spectator. Despite their belief that cinema belonged crucially to the spectator, the New German Cinema failed to attract West German audiences and made the most impact internationally. Kluge also won the Venice Golden Lion for *Die Artisten in der Zirkuskuppel: ratlos* (*Artists At The Top Of The Big Top: Disoriented*, 1968), and the critics prizes at Cannes and Venice respectively for *Der starke Ferdinand* (*Strongman Ferdinand*, 1976) and *Die Macht der Gefühle* (*The Power Of Emotion*, 1983). In Kluge's writings and films, West German cinema negotiates its way out of a difficult past. RA

Yesterday Girl (Abschied von Gestern) 1966, 90 min, b/w

cast Alexandra Kluge, Günter Mack, Eva Maria Meineke, Hans Korte, Edith Kuntze-Pellogio, Peter Staimmer *cin* Edgar Reitz, Thomas Mauch

Based on one of Alexander Kluge's own stories, this recounts the journey of a Jewish fugitive who makes her way into West Germany only to experience exploitation and cynicism in the land of the "Economic Miracle". It's a visually inventive film that uses direct address, intertitles, voiceover, accelerated motion, surrealistic episodes and a non-synchronous Brechtian soundtrack to demonstrate the inseparability of individuals from history. As in many of Kluge's films, the engaging female protagonist – played by his sister Alexandra – forces us to confront the consequences of historical apathy.

Masaki Kobayashi
Japan, 1916–96

One of the leading Japanese filmmakers of his generation, Masaki Kobayashi perhaps failed to attract greater international attention simply because he had such talented peers, Akira Kurosawa, Kenji Mizoguchi and Yasujiro Ozu among them. But Kobayashi's finest works deserve to be considered in such company, and his contribution to the samurai genre was significant. Making his directorial debut in 1952, Kobayashi had his first major triumph with "The Human Condition" trilogy – *No Greater Love*, *Road To Eternity* (both 1959) and *A Soldier's Prayer* (1961) – a series of impassioned pacifist films which reflected the director's own experiences during World War II. The slow-burning samurai drama *Harakiri* (1962) won the Special Jury Prize at Cannes. Kobayashi's next film was *Kwaidan* (1964), a spellbinding compendium of four horror stories. *Samurai Rebellion* (1967) starred Toshirô Mifune as a samurai battling with divided loyalties. NN

Harakiri (Seppuku) 1962, 135 min, b/w

cast Tatsuya Nakadai, Rentaro Mikuni, Shima Iwashita, Akira Ishihama *cin* Yoshio Miyajima *m* Tôru Takemitsu

As peace descends on seventeenth-century Japan, samurai find themselves out of work and often living in poverty. An older warrior opts to commit hara-kiri, the honourable way for samurai to die, and goes to a local nobleman's house to perform the deed. However, he is stunned to find out what happened to his son-in-law in that same house and, with his life given new purpose, he sets out for revenge.

Kwaidan (Kaidan) 1964, 183 min

cast Rentaro Mikuni, Tatsuya Nakadai, Katsuo Nakamura, Kanemon Nakamura *cin* Yoshio Miyajima *m* Tôru Takemitsu

An Oscar-winning film featuring four separate ghost stories, *Kwaidan* is quite a different beast from Kobayashi's other films. With a running time of over three hours, it's a supremely atmospheric, visually dazzling work, and remains one of the best portmanteau films ever made.

Andrei Konchalovsky
Russia (formerly Soviet Union), 1937–

Studying cinema at the state film school, VGIK, Andrei Konchalovsky befriended Andrei Tarkovsky and collaborated on three of his screenplays, including his masterpiece *Andrei Rublev* (1966). Konchalovsky's own early directing projects, *The First Teacher* (1965), *Asya's Happiness* (1967), *Nest Of Gentry* (1969) and *Uncle Vanya* (1971) all struck a chord in the USSR, but it was the epic *Siberiade* (1979) that brought him international acclaim. It also brought him an offer to relocate to Hollywood from actor Jon Voight, a huge admirer of the film. Although he was not offered any immediate work, Konchalovsky made the move to America. While *Maria's Lovers* (1984), *Duet For One* (1986) and *Shy People* (1987) bore his signature, being atmospheric, understated character studies, something was lost in the transition from East to West. Worse was to follow: he somehow became a director of action movies, successfully with *Runaway Train* (1985) and woefully and anonymously with *Tango And Cash* (1989).

Konchalovsky returned to Russia in 1991 to make *The Inner Circle*, which made history by being the first movie filmed inside the Kremlin and KGB headquarters. However, the true story of Stalin's projectionist was severely hampered by the uncomfortable presence of British and American actors in the starring roles, an unfortunate compromise that has begun to define the director in recent years. His career has since been eclipsed by that of his younger brother, Nikita Mikhalkov, who apparently learnt about filmmaking while acting in *Nest Of Gentry* and *Uncle Vanya*. However, Konchalovsky has returned to Russian subjects in more recent films and, perhaps as a consequence, 2002's *House Of Fools* (*Dom durakov*) showed a surer touch. LH

Asya's Happiness (Istoriya asi klyachinoy, kotoraya lyubila, da ne vshla zamuzh) 1967, 99 min, b/w

cast Iya Savvina, Lyubov Sokolova, Alexandre Surin, Gennady Yergorychev, Ivan Petrov *cin* Georgi Rerberg

Banned by the authorities because of its characters' loose talk about gulags, *Asya's Happiness* is a bucolic charmer about life on a remote collective farm. When plucky heroine Asya becomes impregnated by her roguish lover, who subsequently refuses to marry her, she stubbornly declines to care and considers her options.

Runaway Train 1985, 111 min

cast Jon Voight, Eric Roberts, Rebecca De Mornay, Kyle T. Heffner, T.K. Carter, John P. Ryan *cin* Alan Hume *m* Trevor Jones

Based on an original script by Akira Kurosawa and adapted by novelist Edward Bunker, *Runaway Train* stars Jon Voight and Eric Roberts as escaped convicts who board the titular locomotive and whose raw humanity is painfully revealed as they're forced to make life or death decisions. Aided by Konchalovsky's cerebral and muscular direction, this is that rare beast in contemporary Hollywood – an existential action movie.

Alexander Korda
Hungary (formerly Austro-Hungarian Empire), 1893–1956

It is debatable whether Alexander Korda should be best remembered as a director or a producer, but in both roles (sometimes simultaneously) he made some outstanding films, pushed the British industry in new directions and created a springboard for its future.

From 1914 on, Korda directed and later produced over thirty films in Budapest, Vienna and Berlin. Three unhappy years in Hollywood saw films including *The Private Life Of Helen Of Troy* (1927) – Korda liked "Private Lives" – and *The Princess And The Plumber* (1930). Dissatisfied, he moved to France, where he directed *Marius* (1931) as part of the classic Marcel Pagnol trilogy. Continuing on to Britain, he produced films which belied their low budgets as he looked beyond the home market. *The Private Life Of Henry VIII* (1933) broke America, earning Charles Laughton an Oscar. Some years later it would prove to be Korda's ticket back to Hollywood on his own terms. He built a studio in Denham, near London, and his future films were made by his own production companies. *The Private Life Of Don Juan* (1934) felt like a retread but he hit his stride again with *Rembrandt* (1936), though it was not commercially successful; its misanthropic hero was not as charming as the ebullient Henry.

Korda turned to producing, where he would ultimately wield his greatest influence, before returning to the director's chair with the historical biopic *Lady Hamilton* (aka *That Hamilton Woman*, 1941), about Nelson's mistress. In 1942 he was knighted, but for his war work rather than his cinematic achievements: it seems his US production activities had in part been a front for British intelligence. His last two films were *Perfect Strangers* (1945), in which a married couple reassess their lives after the war, and an adaptation of Wilde's comedy of manners *An Ideal Husband* (1948). Thereafter he returned to producing, sometimes working with his brothers, director Zoltan and designer Victor, and helped a new generation of British filmmakers. JR

The Private Life Of Henry VIII 1933, 97 min, b/w
cast Charles Laughton, Robert Donat, Franklin Dyall, Miles Mander, Laurence Hanray *cin* Georges Périnal *m* Kurt Schroeder

Between them, Hans Holbein's portrait and Charles Laughton's performance define the much-married monarch in the public mind. In a masterly semi-comic performance, Laughton belches and throws half-eaten chicken legs over his shoulder as he progresses through his last five wives, yet never loses our sympathy. But this has overshadowed some excellent acting from the rest of the cast, and the work of Korda's art-director brother Victor and French cinematographer Georges Périnal.

Zoltan Korda
Hungary (formerly Austro-Hungarian Empire), 1895–1961

Although he was overshadowed by his elder brother and frequent collaborator Alexander, Zoltan Korda directed a series of colonial films that portrayed African and Indian "natives" as more human than was usual at the time. Nevertheless, he sometimes struggled to balance his message with the expected exciting set pieces and grand vistas.

After Hungary and Hollywood, the brothers arrived in Britain in the early 1930s. Two years in the making, Zoltan's African drama *Sanders Of The River* (1935) overcame an uneasy mix of studio and location through a series of powerful performances, and was a commercial success. Similar problems bedevilled *Elephant Boy* (1937), which

he co-directed with Robert Flaherty, but again the acting – by newly found star Sabu – saved it. The Sabu vehicle *The Drum* (1938) was better balanced, although the low budget is apparent. The Rudyard Kipling adaptation *Jungle Book* (1942) is the best of the Sabu films.

Considered by many to be his finest film, *The Four Feathers* (1939) found a balance between impressive visuals and the story of a cowardly guardsman's redemption, but it is dazzlingly politically incorrect. Korda made a handful of war films in the early 1940s, of which *Sahara* (1943), starring Humphrey Bogart, is the standout. Two literary adaptations followed: Ernest Hemingway's *The Macomber Affair* (1947) was set on a safari, while Aldous Huxley's murder thriller *A Woman's Vengeance* (1948) was a rare excursion away from the colonies. In 1951, Korda directed *Cry, The Beloved Country*, an excellent drama about racial division in South Africa. Co-directed with Terence Young, *Storm Over The Nile* (1955) was a remake of *The Four Feathers* that resorted to reusing some of the older film's footage – it was a disappointing last film for Korda. JR

Cry, The Beloved Country 1951, 103 min
cast Canada Lee, Charles Carson, Sidney Poitier, Joyce Carey, Geoffrey Keen, Michael Goodliffe *cin* Robert Krasker *m* Raymond Gallois-Montbrun

This story of South African racial politics is excellently translated for the screen by Alan Paton from his own novel. Searching for his lost son, a black preacher encounters a bigoted white landowner and their different experiences and clashing ideologies are explored. The dignified performances mix anger with sorrow, avoiding a merely hectoring tone. Remade in 1995, the story was also the basis of Kurt Weill's musical *Lost In The Stars* (filmed in 1974).

Hirokazu Koreeda
Japan, 1962–

Hirokazu Koreeda's meetings between experience and recall, documentary and fiction, are rare in modern cinema. Joining TV Man Union in the late 1980s, a production company known for innovation and collective ownership, Koreeda made his name in documentaries. *Lessons From A Calf* (1991) chronicled the rearing of a calf by a group of schoolchildren.

His subsequent work has reflected on loss, bereavement and recollection with documentary veracity. Rejecting fly-on-the-wall objectivity, Koreeda finds realism in close-ups, long takes and studied attention to human interaction. The documentary *August Without Him* (1994) focused on a man dying of AIDS. The following year, Koreeda's first fiction feature, *Maborosi* (1995), concerned a woman, trying to cope with loneliness, who remarries after her husband inexplicably commits suicide – the director dwells on the reconciliation of the inner and outer worlds with mystical grace. Returning to documentaries, Koreeda made *Without Memory* (1996), about a victim of medical malpractice who is unable to form new memories. Memory is also the key to the hereafter in the impressive *After Life* (1998).

In their own ways, *Distance* (2001) and *Nobody Knows* (2004) both deal with characters coming to terms with loss, the latter winning Yanagi Yuya the best actor award at Cannes. More recently, *More Than A Flower* (2006) was the story of a samurai who avenges his father's death. In these digital times, Koreeda remains faithful to the memory of the real. RA

After Life (Wandâfaru raifu) 1998, 118 min
cast Arata, Erika Oda, Taketoshi Naito, Sadao Abe, Kotaro Shiga, Yusuke Iseya *cin* Yukuru Sato, Shigeki Nakamura, Yutaka Yamakazi

The Japanese religion of Shinto emphasizes not the hereafter but finding happiness in the here and now. Caught in a limbo between life and death, the bureaucrats of the afterlife coax the recently deceased to recall their happiest memory, which is then put onto film. Using non-professional actors and depicting an amusing account of low-budget filmmaking, Koreeda reflects upon the cinema's role in our search for love.

Harmony Korine
US, 1973–

Whatever else Harmony Korine does with his life and career – it was eight years between his second and third features – he will be remembered for giving vivid expression to the amoral, promiscuous, drug-addled, battered-and-bruised-and-thoroughly-confused generation of teenagers who came of age in the early 1990s.

Korine was only 18 when he met photographer Larry Clark and sold him the screenplay for *Kids* (1995), a shocking *vérité*-style portrait of teen torpor and turmoil, with an HIV-injected gangbang for a finale. Korine and Clark fell out, but not before Clark had bought another script in a similar vein, *Ken Park*, eventually filmed in 2002.

The son of a documentary filmmaker, Korine had cinema in his blood. So he claimed anyway – in interviews he's a fabulist and mythomaniac. But the passion is there for all to see, and somehow Korine persuaded producer Cary Woods to back *Gummo* (1997), a provocative free-form portrait of a blighted Midwestern suburb peopled predominantly by teen misfits, retards and runaways. Some critics condemned it as a freak show, but Korine evidently feels at home here (in fact most of it was shot in the outskirts of Nashville, where he grew up). Perceptive viewers found echoes of John Cassavetes, Alan Clarke and Werner Herzog: hard truths and tough love. *Julien Donkey-Boy* (1999) had a narrower focus

– a severely dysfunctional family including pater familias Werner Herzog, Chloë Sevigny, and Ewen Bremner as the eponymous schizophrenic son – but featured a similar mixture of improvisation, "real people" and actors. It was shot on dozens of mini digital cameras, and followed the diktats of Dogme 95's Vows of Chastity.

Then, silence. Korine took a lot of drugs, dabbled in art videos and photography (he even has an absurdist novel to his name), and finally re-emerged in 2003 with *Above The Below*, a modest documentary of his friend David Blaine starving himself above the River Thames. It says something that he's almost as well known for an unseen and incomplete film – the legendary *Fight Harm*, a candid-camera project in which Korine picks and loses fights with a string of bystanders – as for the movies he's actually pulled off. Yet there's something heartening about his refusal to play the Hollywood game, and there remains the persistent hope that he'll pull something special out of the hat and surprise us all.

As to that third feature, *Mister Lonely* premiered well at Cannes 2007 (out of competition). The film earned an extremely mixed reception, as might be expected for a project featuring Hispanic star Diego Luna as a Michael Jackson impersonator who is invited to a Scottish commune by Marilyn Monroe-lookalike Samantha Morton. In another story strand, Werner Herzog plays a priest who accidentally drops a nun out of the cargo doors of a plane along with more conventional aid packages. TC

Gummo 1997, 89 min
cast Jacob Sewell, Nick Sutton, Lara Tosh, Jacob Reynolds, Darby Dougherty, Chloë Sevigny *cin* Jean-Yves Escoffier *m* Randy Poster

Set in Xenia, Ohio, the site of America's worst-ever tornado, this is an impressionistic, absurdist, punk collage of teenage enervation. Korine takes off with the tornado idea to twist from *cinéma vérité* to improvisation to pre-scripted material, throwing punk rock, Bach, Buddy Holly and mumbled, confessional doggerel into the mix. The result is breathtaking, provocative, and often repellent, but somehow vivid and vital in a way few movies manage.

Henry Koster
Germany, 1905–88

Scripting the anti-abortion *Kinderseelen klagen euch an* (*Children's Souls Accuse You*, 1927) led the Jewish Henry Koster to meet the future Pope Pius XII, and religion was a recurrent theme in his work. Nazism forced him to move to America in the 1930s, where he helped to save Universal Studios from bankruptcy with *Three Smart Girls* (1936) and five further Deanna Durbin musical collaborations with producer Joe Paternak. Koster took over *The Bishop's Wife* in 1947, turning a sure-fire disaster into a wry triumph. Gogol's story of mistaken identity, *The Inspector General* (1949), was hampered by star Danny Kaye's interference with the directing, but the enchanting James Stewart comedy *Harvey* (1950) was Koster's masterpiece. Stewart and Koster worked together on several other films, including, most notably, the air crash thriller *No Highway* (1951). The biblical epic *The Robe* (1953) was the first film to use the widescreen CinemaScope format but, as *D-Day, The 6th Of June* (1956) showed, Koster was not an "epic" director. Returning to religion, he made *The Story Of Ruth* (1960) and *The Singing Nun* (1966). JR

Harvey 1950, 104 min, b/w

cast James Stewart, Josephine Hull, Peggy Dow, Charles Drake, Cecil Kellaway *cin* William Daniels *m* Frank Skinner

The story of an alcoholic's friendship with the eponymous invisible six-foot-three-and-a-half-inch rabbit could be either dark or whimsical, but Koster manages to have it both ways. Ultimately this is a story of redemption, in which the rabbit's existence is proved and James Stewart's amiable hero's "delusions" are indulged.

Grigori Kozintsev
Ukraine (formerly Russia), 1905–73

When F. Scott Fitzgerald said, "There are no second acts in American lives", he could easily have been talking about the careers of film directors, who tend to blaze brightly but briefly before burning out or selling out. Grigori Kozintsev is, like Luis Buñuel, an exception to that rule. He formed, with Leonid Trauberg, the Factory of the Eccentric Actor (FEKS), an iconoclastic theatre company that incorporated vaudeville, slapstick, circus tricks and Dada into their ambitious productions. Much of that anarchic invention was on view in the duo's film debut, *The Adventures Of Oktyabrina* (1924), and in their subsequent collaborations. Russian writer Nikolai Gogol was also an influence in the duo's early years, as is evidenced by *The Overcoat* (1926), their adaptation of his famous short story. Their dazzling apex from the silent period, *The New Babylon* (1929), is a tableau of startling imagery which celebrates the Paris uprising of 1871. A worthy equal to *Battleship Potemkin* (1925) in the annals of revolutionary cinema, *The New Babylon* marked the first of Kozintsev's fabled collaborations with composer Dmitri Shostakovich.

During the sound era, the directors continued to struggle against the restraints of socialist realism with their lively interpretation of the events of the October revolution seen through the eyes of a typical worker – the Maxim trilogy: *The Youth Of Maxim* (1935), *The Return Of Maxim* (1937) and *The Vyborg Side* (1939). Not long afterwards, their work inevitably succumbed to state censorship. The duo parted ways after World War II, and

while Trauberg has fallen into obscurity, Kozintsev became internationally renowned for three classic adaptations. Freighted with political significance, these films irreverently cut the original texts to the bone and re-calibrated them with sensually opulent imagery. *Don Quixote* (1957) evinces a panoramic magic and majesty, while *Hamlet* (1964) is for many critics the greatest Dane in cinema history, and *King Lear* (1970) was revered by Laurence Olivier for its "stark brilliance". LH

The New Babylon (Nonyi vavilon) 1929, 120 min, b/w

cast Yelena Kuzmina, Pyotr Soblovesky, Dmitri Gutman, Sophie Magarill *cin* Andrei Moskvin, Yevgeni Mikhailov *m* Dmitri Shostakovich

Grigori Kozintsev and Leonid Trauberg use stunningly strident montages, lustrous black-and-white photography and iridescent lighting to recreate the Paris uprising of 1871. They locate their revolution in The New Babylon, a department store in which the rich consume conspicuously, and choose a plucky shop girl to valiantly lead the doomed rebellion.

Hamlet 1964, 150 min, b/w

cast Innokenti Smoktunovsky, Mikhail Nazvarnov, Elza Radzin-Szolkonis, Yuri Tolubeyev *cin* Jonas Gritsius *m* Dmitri Shostakovich

Kozintsev had Elsinore Castle painstakingly constructed on a rocky outcrop next to the sea and the waves crashing against the rocks and the dark, foreboding cliffs provide the perfect foil to Shakespeare's turbulent drama. This is a lean, mean *Hamlet*, energized by a vigorous epic sweep, and augmented by Dmitri Shostakovich's pulsating score.

King Lear (Korol Lir) 1970, 139 min, b/w

cast Yuri Yarvet, Elsa Radzinya, Galina Volchek, Valentina Shendirkova, Karl Sebris, Regimantis Adomaitis *cin* Jonas Gritsius *m* Dmitri Shostakovich

In a major departure from Shakespeare's text, Kozintsev keeps the Fool alive and the character's skinny, emaciated frame is a deliberate simulacrum of a concentration camp survivor – the emphasis here is as much on the suffering of the people as it is on the psychology of the king. As for the reason why he kept the Fool alive, Kozintsev claimed it was because he liked him so much.

Stanley Kubrick
US, 1928–99

Often portrayed in the press as a control freak, a genius, a recluse and a perfectionist who would personally check if cinemas were projecting his films correctly, Stanley Kubrick's reputation amongst film critics is equally contrary. For many, he stands as one of twentieth-century cinema's unique visionaries and innovators, eschewing orthodox psychology to examine the myriad ways in which human beings are stripped of both their humanity and their will by forces larger than themselves. For others, he became an overrated, misanthropic purveyor of coldly mechanical, self-important technical exercises.

Kubrick's father ignited the two defining passions in his life: photography and chess. The young Kubrick turned his first amateur obsession into a job when he became a photographer for *Look* magazine at the age of 17. While the influence of this career is palpable in his filmmaking, his enthusiasm for chess is less obvious, but equally important. Many colleagues have remarked that every move Kubrick made as a director was given the full, fastidious contemplation of a chess player, while a sense of control permeates every frame of his work, as if nothing has been left to chance and his characters are pawns in his hands. Fittingly, it was the money he made as a chess champion that partly financed his first feature, *Fear And Desire* (1953), which he also wrote, produced, photographed and edited.

His second film, *Killer's Kiss* (1955), concerned another of his passions, boxing. An abrasive *film noir* charting a doomed romance between a down-on-his luck pugilist and a nightclub dancer, it strikingly evokes the moody chiaroscuro of his earlier photographs. Heist movie *The Killing* (1956) was his first minor classic and the first film in which he connected with his inner chess player: his characters, who exhibit all the free will of rooks and pawns, are skilfully manoeuvred through the vagaries of fate and systematically taken out of the game one by one. *Paths Of Glory* (1957) centres on a trial during World War I in which trumped-up charges of cowardice are levelled at three soldiers whose fate is sealed by pragmatic generals using them to instil discipline into the other men. The film is an uncharacteristically rousing polemic from a director whose work often has a chilly, haughty demeanour. *Paths Of Glory*'s star, Kirk Douglas, then employed Kubrick to direct his next production, *Spartacus* (1960), after sacking Anthony Mann. Although *Spartacus* is the least typical of the director's films, especially in its display of human sentiment, it is the most impressive of the late-1950s and early-1960s Roman spectaculars.

Kubrick was a director for hire on *Spartacus*, employed by a leading man with similar control issues, which inevitably led to epic battles for dominance. It was a mistake Kubrick would never make again. To ensure complete artistic freedom, he took the unprecedented step of moving from Hollywood to England in 1961. Borehamwood duly stood in for Middle America in his adaptation of Vladimir Nabakov's controversial *Lolita* (1962), starring a splendidly unctuous James Mason as a European émigré academic obsessed with a lollipop-sucking nymphet. Unfortunately, the comedy of disquiet was alarmingly unbalanced by Peter Sellers' decision to play his character with all the nuanced subtleties of a Looney Tunes cartoon. However, Kubrick's next project, *Dr Strangelove: Or, How I Learned To Stop Worrying And Love The Bomb* (1964), seemed tailored to suit Sellers' broad comic approach, and he was given full rein to showcase his mercurial talents by playing three different characters. The superbly scabrous *Strangelove*

originally ended with a custard-pie fight in which the president is struck down, but was hurriedly changed after John F. Kennedy's assassination and replaced with the far more resonant finale of an H-bomb being dropped from a plane to the incongruous strains of Vera Lynn's "We'll Meet Again".

Even though *Dr Strangelove* is the notorious perfectionist's most fully conceived film, nothing prepared film-goers for the quantum leap that was *2001: A Space Odyssey* (1968). Co-written by Kubrick and novelist Arthur C. Clarke, the film is an ambitious, mysterious and portentous exploration of human history and a post-human future. A vital element of the entire sensual, kinetic experience is the stunning use of classical music: the spaceship famously docks to the sprightly rhythms of *The Blue Danube* and the Earth, the sun and the moon magically align to the solemn tempo of *Also Sprach Zarathustra*. This iconoclastic appropriation of existing orchestral music became an essential component of his idiom, whether it was the primal scream of Penderecki's strings in *The Shining* (1980), or Beethoven becoming part of the ultra-violence in *A Clockwork Orange* (1971).

Next, Kubrick made the film that, in many ways, changed his life. His adaptation of Anthony Burgess's *A Clockwork Orange* became a *cause célèbre* with its unflinching and incessant scenes of violence. Kubrick's films had always evinced a pitiless anti-humanism, but this unforgiving misanthropy found its most disturbing expression in a rape scene in which his probing camera effectively became one of the assailants, as Malcolm MacDowell warbles "Singin' In The Rain" while cutting off Adrienne Corri's clothes. Kubrick's fabled sense of control seemed to slip in the one scene that absolutely necessitated calm detachment. The director initially weathered the storm of complaints, but after receiving death threats and reading reports of copycat violence, he removed the film from British cinemas. The self-imposed ban was only rescinded after his death, in accordance with his will.

Moving into less controversial territory, Kubrick filmed an adaptation of William Makepeace Thackeray's novel *Barry Lyndon* (1975), a rake's progress through eighteenth-century society. The ravishingly languorous period drama is justly celebrated for its interior scenes shot exclusively in the dim, hazy glow of candlelight, for which Kubrick helped to invent a new kind of photographic lens. This obsession with new technology was also evident, possibly too evident, in *The Shining*, which had the first extensive use of Steadicam in cinema history. The result was one of the most celebrated sequences in the Kubrickian canon – a young boy pedalling his tricycle along the labyrinthine corridors of the Overlook Hotel while the camera sinuously follows behind.

Although he had a unique and enviable contract with Warner Bros which essentially gave him full artistic licence and a full-time salary, Kubrick didn't make another film for seven years. Then came *Full Metal Jacket* (1987), which followed a platoon of US Marines through military training and into bloody conflict. The director had set himself the challenge of making a Vietnam War film that was neither pro- nor anti-war, and that refused to experience the battle from the soldier's point of view. To some, Kubrick succeeded in inventing a war movie that denied the viewer the powerful narcotics of cheap emotion and vicarious thrills, and produced a clear-headed, objective account of what war does to human beings. However, compared to the total immersion models of *The Deer Hunter* (1978) and *Apocalypse Now* (1979), *Full Metal Jacket* seemed too detached, schematic and empty to the majority of critics. Kubrick's overpowering sense of control seeped through every frame, stagnating into a form of clinical minimalism. *Full Metal Jacket* also suffered from Kubrick's bloody-minded insistence on filming in Britain: dismantled gasworks in East London were a poor substitute for Vietnam.

By the early 1990s Kubrick was more than a director, he was a myth and a chimera, a grandee and a hermit. However, when he employed Hollywood's royal couple, Tom Cruise and Nicole Kidman, on *Eyes Wide Shut* (1999), the director unwittingly became tabloid fodder. The fact that the film went over schedule encouraged scurrilous reports about the explicit nature of the sex scenes between Cruise and Kidman, and fuelled innuendo about the real reason why Harvey Keitel left the project prema-

turely. It took fifteen painstaking months to shoot, with the director sometimes insisting on more than fifty takes for many scenes, even for an apparently simple shot of Cruise walking through a door. Kubrick died only days after showing the completed film to relieved executives, and his untimely death only added to the sense of overheated anticipation.

When the film was finally released, there was a distinct feeling of anticlimax, for *Eyes Wide Shut* turned out to be a rather pompous and occasionally ludicrous melodrama. The domestic scenes between Cruise and Kidman were extraordinarily acted and photographed, but Cruise's descent into sexual depravity was clearly the work of a director who didn't get out much and the sex orgy was unfortunately reminiscent of an ersatz Hammer production, even down to the spooky mansion. A more fitting epitaph was Steven Spielberg's completion of a project that he had been working on intermittently with Kubrick, the vastly underrated *A.I. Artificial Intelligence* (2001), which balanced the sentimentality of Spielberg and the anti-humanism of Kubrick to near-perfect Yin and Yang effect. LH

The Killing 1956, 85 min, b/w

cast Sterling Hayden, Coleen Gray, Vince Edwards, Jay C. Flippen, Marie Windsor, Elisha Cook Jr *cin* Lucien Ballard *m* Fangoria

The Killing's racetrack heist set piece was a clear sign of Stanley Kubrick's emerging brilliance. It is edited like a puzzle, with the robbery told from the perspective of each gang member as it shuttles back and forth through time. This breaking down of narrative and withholding of infor-

The ultra-cool look and authentic feel of *2001: A Space Odyssey* was the work of a brilliant design team, including Harry Lange, a former NASA designer.

mation was a direct influence on Quentin Tarantino, who employed similarly byzantine methods in *Reservoir Dogs* (1991) and *Jackie Brown* (1997).

Spartacus 1960, 198 min
cast Kirk Douglas, Jean Simmons, Laurence Olivier, Charles Laughton, Peter Ustinov, Tony Curtis *cin* Rusell Metty *m* Alex North

The best of the Roman epics that conquered Hollywood in the 1950s and early 60s. Spectacular, allegorical, sweeping and intimate, the stirring tale of a gladiator who sparks a slave rebellion is driven by a raging sense of injustice (it was penned by left-wing writer and martyr Dalton Trumbo who'd been blacklisted by Hollywood for two decades). The vision and the anger clearly belong to producer and political activist Kirk Douglas and not to Kubrick, whose preferred modus operandi was to maintain a chilly and controlling distance from the proceedings.

Dr Strangelove: Or, How I Learned To Stop Worrying And Love The Bomb 1964, 93 min, b/w
cast Peter Sellers, George C. Scott, Sterling Hayden, Keenan Wynn, Slim Pickens, Peter Bull *cin* Gilbert Taylor *m* Laurie Johnson

The film's subtitle suggests the sort of modishly wacky comedy this might have become. The fact that it remains a poignantly brilliant satire is due, in part, to the fact that Kubrick filmed the comedy like the paranoid conspiracy thriller it was originally intended to be, with angular monochrome photography and Ken Adam's shadowy, claustrophobic sets acting as the perfect foil to the childish slapstick.

2001: A Space Odyssey 1968, 156 min
cast Keir Dullea, Gary Lockwood, William Sylvester, Daniel Richter, Leonard Rossiter, Margaret Tyzack *cin* Geoffrey Unsworth *m* Richard Strauss

With *2001*, Kubrick jettisoned the anchor of conventional narrative and constructed an audiovisual spectacle of pure cinema which wondrously reaches sensory overload with the psychedelic light show known as the "Stargate sequence". In many ways, this film is the *Sgt Pepper* of cinema: ground-breaking in its day, a milestone in revealing the possibilities of the medium, it now seems very much a product of its time, an antique curio.

A Clockwork Orange 1971, 136 min
cast Malcolm McDowell, Patrick Magee, Michael Bates, Warren Clarke, John Clive, Adrienne Corri, Steven Berkoff, David Prowse *cin* John Alcott

Shorn of the illicit thrill of watching a smudgy fifth-generation videotape that was the only way of seeing the film in the UK for over two decades, the faults of *A Clockwork Orange* become all too apparent. The film plays like a series of brilliantly amoral set pieces strung together by a slack narrative whose pacing is as questionable as its dubious sexual politics.

Barry Lyndon 1975, 184 min
cast Ryan O'Neal, Marisa Berenson, Hardy Krüger, Patrick Magee, Steven Berkoff, Gay Hamilton *cin* John Alcott *m* Leonard Rosenman

Kubrick's rollicking and, at times, rambling adaptation of William Makepeace Thackeray's novel about a rogue's odyssey through the battlefields and bedrooms of eighteenth-century Europe is exceptionally beautiful. Yet not even the bucolic splendour, the painterly compositions or the revolutionary lighting can disguise the fact that all-American Ryan O'Neal is tragically miscast as the quintessentially British antihero.

The Shining 1980, 146 min
cast Jack Nicholson, Shelley Duvall, Danny Lloyd, Scatman Crothers, Barry Nelson, Philip Stone, Joseph Turkel *cin* John Alcott *m* Wendy Carlos

For many, this is the greatest horror movie ever made. Others, unimpressed by the slight story and Jack Nicholson's cartoon lunacy, dubbed *The Shining* an extended advert for Steadicam, while Stephen King was distinctly unamused by the changes to his novel. And the critics do have a point, because despite some bravura and near-miraculous set pieces, the whole is, ultimately, less than the sum of its iconic parts.

Lev Kuleshov
Russia, 1899–1970

Dubbed the "father of Soviet cinema", Lev Kuleshov is one of the great theorists of narrative cinema, whose ideas have arguably been more influential than those of his contemporary Sergei Eisenstein. Impressively, he first formulated these ground-breaking hypotheses without the aid of celluloid, creating instead "films without film" in his workshop at the State Film School.

His main axiom, the "Kuleshov effect", states that a viewer's interpretation of an individual shot is dictated by its context. His theories of acting demanded that performances should not come from an expression of false emotion or with the aid of props, but through physical gestures and minimal movements of the body. The director demonstrated both of these theories in his debut feature, *The Extraordinary Adventure Of Mr West In The Land Of The Bolsheviks* (1924), in which an American visitor finally sees the true worth of the Soviet Union and its people. The film wasn't a sterile application of abstract formulae, but a zesty farce, brimful of slapstick, chase sequences and *joie de cinéma*. However, it raised the socialist realist hackles of hardline Bolsheviks who complained about the unhealthy influence of Hollywood.

Although his Communist credentials were never in question, Kuleshov didn't hide his internationalism, and this influence was visible in his two other classics. The psychological thriller *By The Law* (1926) was adapted from a novel by Lenin's favourite author, Jack London, and set in the Yukon during the gold rush, while his first sound film, *The Great Consoler* (1933), was based on a series of essays by the American writer O. Henry. However, it wasn't the Americana that the authorities objected to, but his perceived formalism, his preference for aesthetics over ideology. Kuleshov was denounced by the state in 1935 and forced to admit his cultural crimes. His directorial career ended in 1944, but he continued teaching until his death in 1970. Kuleshov has since been somewhat unfairly overlooked outside of the academic world, but his contribution to developing the syntax of film has lived on. LH

The Extraordinary Adventures Of Mr West In The Land Of The Bolsheviks (Neobychainye priklyucheniya mistera Vesta v strane bolshevikov) 1924, 80 min, b/w

cast Boris Barnet, Vsevolod Pudovkin, Sergei Komarov, Alexandra Khokhlova *cin* Alexander Levitzky *m* Benedict Mason

The American president of the YMCA, Mr West, visits the Soviet Union with his cowboy buddy Jeddy (played by future director Boris Barnet) and becomes the target for reprobates and a fake countess played by Kuleshov's wife Alexandra Khokhlova. With its knockabout comedy, *Mr West* plays like some kind of perverse tribute to Hollywood, helped by the fact that the eponymous hero is a dead ringer for Harold Lloyd.

By The Law (Po zakonu) 1926, 80 min, b/w

cast Alexandra Khokhlova, Sergei Komarov, Vladimir Fogel, Pyotr Galadzhez *cin* Konstantin Kuznetsov

During the gold rush, a prospector kills two of his companions but is captured by a man and his wife who hold him prisoner in their hut over the winter, intending to hand him over to the authorities in the spring. This harrowingly tense psychodrama (one of the Soviet Union's first psychological thrillers) plays out as the trio's relationships change subtly over the course of the lonely winter months.

Harry Kümel

Belgium, 1940–

A screenwriter and director of film, opera, theatre and commercials, Harry Kümel began making award-winning short films in his teens, including *Anna la bonne* (1958), which was based on a Jean Cocteau poem. Moving into television, he made *De Grafbewaker* in 1965, which featured the writings of Franz Kafka. Heavily influenced by Josef von Sternberg, about whom he made a documentary in 1969, Kümel made his feature debut with the extraordinary transvestite tragedy *Monsieur Hawarden* (1969). His most internationally famous movie is the contemporary erotic vampire masterpiece *Daughters Of Darkness* (1971). The truly bizarre *Malpertuis* (1972), based on the novel by Belgian gothic fantasy writer Jean Ray, stars Orson Welles keeping control over a houseful of forgotten Greek gods sewn into human skins. AJ

Daughters Of Darkness (Les lèvres rouges) 1971, 87 min

cast Delphine Seyrig, Danièle Ouimet, John Karlen, Andréa Rau, Paul Esser, Georges Jamin *cin* Edward van der Enden *m* François de Roubaix

The Countess Elizabeth Báthory legend gets a lyrical lesbian makeover as glamorous bloodsucker Delphine Seyrig imposes her ancient evil self on a naïve couple honeymooning in a deserted seaside hotel in Ostend. Stylish violence, perverse humour, explicit sexuality and a refined surreal atmosphere make this cocktail of undead revisionism (shower water is deadly to these vampires) a cult classic.

Zacharias Kunuk

Canada, c. 1958–

The first Inuit to make a feature film, Zacharias Kunuk represents a link with the ancient past. He was brought up in the same survivalist traditions dramatized in *Atanarjuat: The Fast Runner* (2001): he slept in a single-room sod hut or igloo alongside his six siblings, and the men in the family hunted with dog sleds. At nine, he was taken away from his family to attend school in Igloolik, where he learned English and was taught Christianity. That was also where he was exposed to movies – Saturday morning pictures at the community centre.

A sculptor, he earned enough to buy a video camera and started shooting in the early 1980s, eventually spending eight years with the Inuit Broadcasting Corporation, interviewing elders about the old ways. Along with screenwriter Paul Apak, cameraman Norman Cohn and producer Pauloosie Qulitalik, he formed an independent production company in the 1990s with a view to making dramatic films. Shot on digi-Beta widescreen, *Atanarjuat* was hailed as one of the most important films ever made in Canada, and was distributed around the world. In the spring of 2005, Kunuk and Cohn collaborated on a second film, *The Journals Of Knud Rasmussen* (2006). Set in the early twentieth century, when the Inuit way of life was changing under the impact of Christian colonialism, the film featured an unusual and potent mix of sound, image and Inuit oral tradition. TC

Atanarjuat: The Fast Runner 2001, 168 min

cast Natar Ungalaaq, Sylvia Ivalu, Peter Henry Arnatsiaq, Lucy Tulugarjuk, Madeline Ivalu *cin* Norman Cohn *m* Chris Crilly

Based on an Inuit legend passed down orally over centuries, this tells a story of passion, jealousy and murder redolent of Greek myth. At its centre is the extraordinary ten-minute chase sequence in which the naked Atanarjuat runs across the ice floes. For all the drama of the story, the film's importance lies in its depiction of a way of life that persisted for thousands of years, but is now largely gone.

Akira Kurosawa

Japan, 1910–98

The first Japanese filmmaker to make an impact in the West, Akira Kurosawa was considered one of the masters of cinema for most of his long and distinguished career. His reputation has fallen off somewhat in recent years, yet he remains a touchstone for many filmmakers in Japan and the US. His muscular yet nuanced approach to filming action and conflict is particularly admired, but so too is the probing humanism and philosophical seriousness that underscore his work.

291

Toshirô Mifune: Kurosawa's leading man

Very few directors can authentically claim to have discovered their star, but Akira Kurosawa did just that. When Toshirô Mifune applied to Toho Studios to become a cameraman, he somehow ended up auditioning as an actor in the "new faces" section. Kurosawa was working on set at the time and heard about an extraordinary event taking place nearby – a man in the midst of a violent frenzy so convincing that no one really knew if he was playing a part or having a fit. Clearly impressed by what he'd just seen, Kurosawa persuaded a reluctant studio to award the madman a contract. Of the seventeen films that Kurosawa made between 1948 and 1965, Mifune starred in all but one.

Their first collaboration *Drunken Angel* (1948) was well received at home, as was *Stray Dog* (1949), but it was only when Mifune donned a sword and samurai garb in *Rashomon* (1950) that the world took notice, of star, director and even the Japanese film industry. Kurosawa once said of his leading man: "The speed of his movements was such that he said in a single action what it took ordinary actors three separate movements to express." And that versatility is no more evident than in *Rashomon*, where Mifune plays four different interpretations of the same character. In one scene alone, he flits between lustful, feral and pitiful in the space of a few seconds. After winning an Oscar for best foreign-language film, they proceeded to make two more outstanding features, *Seven Samurai* (1954) and *Yojimbo* (1961). Both movies were reconfigured as horse operas (*The Magnificent Seven*, 1960, and *A Fistful Of Dollars*, 1964), with Mifune's character in *Yojimbo* laying down the blueprint for a new Western antihero – aloof, amoral and in need of a good wash. In the former he was less knight errant than whirling dervish, Kurosawa's own Tasmanian Devil. Between *Seven Samurai* and *Yojimbo*, director and star turned out the odd classic, such as *Throne Of Blood* (1957) and *The Hidden Fortress* (1958). And then, in 1965, their creative marriage hit the rocks.

During the making of *Red Beard* (1965) the pair fell out so badly that they never worked together again. In a bid for independence, Mifune had formed his own production company and made his first and and only film as a director, *The Legacy Of The 500,000* (1963). Despite appearing in over a hundred films and becoming the most famous Japanese actor in the world, he never emulated his achievements with Kurosawa, often starring in international co-productions like John Boorman's *Hell In The Pacific* (1968) – opposite that other doyen of sensitive machismo, Lee Marvin – the World War II drama *Midway* (1976) and the television epic *Shogun* (1980), playing a Japanese warlord. Kurosawa slowed down without Mifune, completing only six films in his last 28 years, but managed two masterpieces without his protégé – *Kagemusha* (1980) and *Ran* (1985). Fittingly, though, they died within a year of each other – Mifune in 1997 and Kurosawa in 1998. LH

The Kurosawa family had been samurai for several generations. His father was the director of a military-affiliated physical education institute, but he was a progressive man who taught athletics, baseball and swimming alongside martial arts and sword fighting. Akira Kurosawa was encouraged to read Western literature and he studied Western painting at art school. The three seminal events in his childhood were the death of his older sister, the devastating Great Kanto Earthquake of 1923 in which more than 100,000 people died and the suicide of his beloved brother Heigo.

Kurosawa's film career dates back to 1936, when he began his apprenticeship as a third assistant director. Ambitious, confident and unusually tall, Kurosawa rose through the directorial ranks quickly, while also making a name for himself as a screenwriter. His first solo feature as director was *Sugata Sanshiro* (1943), in which a young man learns about life through judo. Although it was relatively well received, the military censors complained the film was "too British-American", a critique that followed Kurosawa throughout his career. Of all the great Japanese filmmakers, he was the most closely attuned to Western tastes, with his transpositions of Shakespeare (*Macbeth*, *King Lear* and *Hamlet* became *Throne Of Blood*, 1957, *Ran*, 1985, and *The Bad Sleep Well*, 1960) and his taste for Dostoyevsky (*The Idiot*, 1951), Westerns and John Ford (most evident in the samurai films *Rashomon*, 1950, *Seven Samurai*, 1954, and *Yojimbo*, 1961). In *The Quiet Duel* and *Stray Dog* (both 1949), Kurosawa incorporated such diverse elements as Japanese Noh drama, Western art, silent cinema, Soviet montage and the classical Hollywood narrative into his approach.

In turn, American and European filmmakers have remade Kurosawa pictures in their own idiom: *Seven Samurai* became *The Magnificent Seven* (1960) and inspired *Battle Beyond The Stars* (1960) and *A Bug's Life* (1998); *Yojimbo* became Sergio Leone's *A Fistful Of Dollars* (1964); *Rashomon* became Martin Ritt's *The Outrage* (1964); and *The Hidden Fortress* (1958) supplied George Lucas with the plot line for *Star Wars* (1977). Kurosawa even tried his hand at a Hollywood film when he was invited to direct the Japanese side of the Pearl Harbor epic, *Tora! Tora! Tora!* (1970). But he was fired from that ill-fated project after suffering what appeared to be a nervous breakdown. Later, it was only through the support of George Lucas and Francis Ford Coppola that Kurosawa was able to make *Kagemusha* (1980) and *Ran*.

All of this cross-cultural traffic helps to explain Kurosawa's eminence in the West, but it also fuelled a critical backlash – in some quarters, he just isn't Japanese enough. However, it is more relevant to point out that Kurosawa's didacticism seemed indebted to nineteenth-century literature in ways that weren't true of fellow directors Yasujiro Ozu, Kenji Mizoguchi and Mikio Naruse, whose films have arguably better withstood the test of time. Even Kurosawa's most admired works are strident; he preferred to underline an irony rather than risk it going unremarked and he often encouraged his actors to pitch their performances perilously close to hysteria.

Nevertheless, Kurosawa usually pulled off even his boldest conceits, like filming Shakespeare without the verse or pushing *Seven Samurai* to what was then considered an unthinkable length (160 minutes). He inspired his loyal collaborators to do extraordinary work, none more so than actor Toshirô Mifune, who was a towering and volcanic presence in sixteen of his films, from *Drunken Angel* in 1948 to *Red Beard* in 1965. Mifune exemplified the director's intensely dramatic, yet deeply intimate, sense of life and death in the balance. Few filmmakers sought out meaning with such tenacity, and the philosophical rigour in Kurosawa's films is always compelling.

On a technical level, Kurosawa was a master of composition and a perfectionist who commanded the respect of his crew. He had a keen eye for the elements, and when he was introduced to John Ford in 1957, Ford said: "I have seen your films. You love the rain." A delighted Kurosawa replied: "You really have seen my films." In the 1950s, Kurosawa was probably the most kinetic action director in the world, especially after he first used TohoScope cinematography for *The Hidden Fortress*. Surprisingly he didn't embrace colour for the duration of an entire film until 1970 (with *Dodes'kaden*), but there is a rhapsodic pageantry in later movies like *Ran*, in which he marshalled colour-coded armies with supreme artistry and created some of the most vivid and nightmarish battle scenes ever filmed. Although there is no denying the creeping self-consciousness in Kurosawa's later work, his penultimate film, *Rhapsody In August* (1990), which dealt with the atomic bombing of Nagasaki, was a simple, touching movie about making peace with the past. TC

Rashomon 1950, 88 min, b/w
cast Toshirô Mifune, Machiko Kyo, Masayuki Mori, Takashi Shimura, Minoru Chiaki *cin* Kazuo Miyagawa *m* Fumio Hayasaka

One of the most famous foreign-language titles in film history, *Rashomon* was the first Japanese film to be invited to the Venice Film Festival, where it won the Golden Lion.

Credited with opening up Western audiences for Japanese filmmakers, it uses contradictory, subjective flashbacks pertaining to an alleged murder and rape to query the nature of truth.

Ikiru (Living) 1952, 143 min, b/w
cast Takashi Shimura, Shinichi Himori, Haruo Tanaka, Minori Chiaki, Miki Odagiri, Bokuzen Hidari *cin* Asakazu Nakai *m* Fumio Hayasaka

Takashi Shimura plays a city bureaucrat, a widower with a married son, who scrambles desperately for some meaning to his existence when he is diagnosed with cancer and given only months to live. This is the flip side to Kurosawa's samurai films, an introspective, naturalistic contemporary drama combining progressive social criticism with a universal humanist message.

Seven Samurai (Shichinin no samurai) 1954, 160 min, b/w
cast Takashi Shimura, Toshirô Mifune, Yoshio Inaba, Seiji Miyaguchi, Minoru Chiaki, Daisuke Kato, Isao Kimura *cin* Asakazu Nakai *m* Fumio Hayasaka

Beset with bandits, a farming village enlists the aid of seven ronin – masterless samurai – to protect them. They fortify the village and teach the peasants how to fight, but will the cost of the battle prove too great? Kurosawa makes us wait nearly an hour and a half before the first samurai-bandit confrontation, yet the film feels lean and tight. The action scenes were staged with deliberation, discipline and compassion, and the characters so sharply delineated that we feel for them when the violence begins. Kurosawa's masterpiece was the longest and most expensive Japanese film of its time, but it was also the most acclaimed.

Throne Of Blood (Kumonosu jo) 1957, 110 min, b/w
cast Toshirô Mifune, Isuzu Yamada, Takashi Shimura, Akira Kubo, Hiroshi Tachikawa, Minoru Chiaki *cin* Asakazu Nakai *m* Masaru Sato

Kurosawa's take on *Macbeth* is a period drama in which Toshiro Mifune stars as a samurai usurper who comes to a grisly end in Cobweb Castle, his body memorably pierced by volley after volley of incoming arrows. The stylized, expressionist *mise en scène* is influenced by traditional Japanese Noh theatre. The poetry, of course, is all in the picture-making.

The Hidden Fortress (Kakushi-toride no san-akumin) 1958, 123 min, b/w
cast Toshirô Mifune, Misa Uehara, Minoru Chiaki, Kamatari Fujiwara, Takashi Shimura, Susumu Fujita *cin* Ichio Yamazaki *m* Masaru Sato

Set during Japan's sixteenth-century civil wars, *The Hidden Fortress* sees a general escort a princess (and her comedy-relief peasant consorts) incognito through enemy terrain. After the gruelling Maxim Gorky adaptation *The Lower Depths* (1957), Kurosawa declared that this film would be "100 percent entertainment" and it remains his most purely thrilling film, in part because he so enjoyed framing in the widescreen TohoScope format for the first time.

Sanjuro 1962, 96 min, b/w
cast Toshirô Mifune, Tetsuya Nakadai, Yuzo Kayama, Takashi Shimura, Seizabuor Kawazu *cin* Fukuzo Koizumi, Kozo Saito *m* Masaru Sato

A rare example of a sequel that improves on the original – not that *Yojimbo* (1961) is any slouch – this follow-up is an altogether wittier exercise. Toshirô Mifune reprises his role as the eponymous samurai mercenary, this time look-

Toshirô Mifune as the titular warrior in *Sanjuro* wonders what to do with his nine incompetent accomplices.

ing on in disbelief as his eager young allies struggle to free their uncle from the clutches of a corrupt politician. The final duel is justly famous.

Red Beard (Akahige) 1965, 185 min, b/w
cast Toshirô Mifune, Yuzo Kayama, Reiko Dan, Miyuki Kuwano, Kyoko Kagawa, Tatsuyoshi Ehara *cin* Asakazu Nakai, Takao Saito *m* Masuri Sato

Although by no means Kurosawa's best-known film in the West, *Red Beard* is one of his finest. Set in the nineteenth century, it's the episodic story of an arrogant young doctor learning from an experienced colleague. Potentially sentimental, the film benefited from the immense care and imagination Kurosawa lavished upon it. It was also his last collaboration with Toshirô Mifune – playing the authority role here – and arguably his final masterpiece.

Dersu Uzala 1975, 141 min
cast Maksim Munzuk, Yuri Solomin, Svetlana Danilchenko, Dmitri Korshikov *cin* Fyodor Dobrovravov, Yuri Gantman, Asakazu Nakai *m* Isaak Shvarts

Unable to find funding in Japan after the radically experimental *Dodes'kaden* (1970), Kurosawa turned to the Soviet Union and took voluntary exile in Siberia to make this historical film about a Russian explorer's relationship with his guide, a nomadic tribesman. Although it was criticized upon its release for its supposedly shallow pictorialism, this epic's ecological message delivered through stunning 70mm imagery, now seems more prescient.

Ran 1985, 160 min
cast Tatsuya Nakadai, Akira Terao, Jinpachi Nezu, Daisuke Ryu, Mieko Harada *cin* Asakazu Nakai, Takao Saito, Masaharu Ueda *m* Toru Takemitsu

Kurosawa tackles Shakespeare's *King Lear* with the same gusto he brought to *Macbeth* a quarter of a century earlier, in this tale of a great warlord who blindly plunges his country into civil war when he divides it between his three sons.

If there are parallels with his own troubled career, it's clear that the filmmaker saw this film as a universal statement on the human condition: "Man is born crying, and when he dies, enough, he dies."

Diane Kurys
France, 1948–

An actress turned writer and director, Diane Kurys mined her childhood and adolescence to good effect in a series of modest autobiographical works. These films – including *Diabolo menthe* (*Peppermint Soda*, 1977), *Cocktail Molotov* (1980) and *La Baule-les-Pins* (*C'est la vie*, 1990) – were small-scale, domestic dramas enriched with affection and insight; in their honesty and lightness they might be likened to François Truffaut's Antoine Doinel films, albeit from the other side of the bed. Like Truffaut's, Kurys's later work lost some of its focus. Despite working with most of the major French actresses of her time – Isabelle Huppert (*Aprés l'amour*, 1992), Béatrice Dalle and Anne Parillaud (*A la folie*, 1994), Juliette Binoche (*Les enfants du siècle*, 1999) and Sophie Marceau (*Je reste!*, 2003) – Kurys's low-key liberal humanism looks sentimental and complacent beside the more rigorous and challenging feminist films of her exact contemporary, Catherine Breillat. Attempts to inject some "edge" – in *A la folie* for example – have felt forced and unconvincing. TC

Coup de foudre (At First Sight) 1983, 110 min

cast Miou-Miou, Isabelle Huppert, Guy Marchand, Jean-Pierre Bacri, Robin Renucci, Patrick Bauchau *cin* Bernard Lutic *m* Luis Enriquez Bacalov

Kurys's most widely acclaimed film is a tender love story between two women – a Jewish housewife (Isabelle Huppert) who married to save herself from deportation in 1942 and a sophisticated artist (Miou-Miou) – set during World War II and in the early 1950s. It is inspired by the story of the filmmaker's own mother and, while not explicit, is notable as one of the first non-judgemental movies about lesbianism.

La Baule-les-Pins (C'est la vie) 1990, 96 min

cast Nathalie Baye, Richard Berry, Zabou, Jean-Pierre Bacri, Vincent Lindon, Valéria Bruni-Tedeschi *cin* Giuseppe Lanci *m* Philippe Sarde

This bittersweet recollection of summer at the seaside in 1958 devotes most of its time to sisters Frédérique (13) and Sophie (6). But in the background Kurys recounts the ramifications of a family split in countless small but telling details. As usual, she elicits a fine performance from a leading French actress, in this case Nathalie Baye, and the evocation of time and place is unerringly exact.

Emir Kusturica

Bosnia-Herzegovina (formerly Yugoslavia), 1955–

In his study *The Cinema Of Emir Kusturica*, critic Goran Gocic writes that the director's work abounds with contradictions, and "potentially strongest among them is the merging of the socially marginal position with an ecstatic experience of life". Long, loud, tumultuous, proudly vulgar and flamboyantly miserablist, Emir Kusturica's oeuvre bears out Gocic's assessment with its inextricable linkage of passion and pain, optimism and cynicism, celebration and squalor.

Born into a middle-class family in Sarajevo (his father worked for the Ministry of Information), Kusturica associated with petty criminals in his youth, but at 18 he left to study at Prague's FAMU Film Academy, the alma mater of many Czech New Wave luminaries. Returning to his home town, Kusturica debuted with the wry, touching *Do You Remember Dolly Bell?* (1981), a coming-of-age tale that unfolded in a working-class Sarajevo neighbourhood in the 1950s.

His next film, *When Father Was Away On Business* (1985) was also a period piece about the perks and perils of growing up, set in the years when prison camps were used to crack down on any hint of internal dissent. Bittersweet and understated, the film received an Oscar nomination and won the Palme d'Or – a first for a Yugoslav director. (Kusturica won the prize again a decade later for *Underground*.) With *Time Of The Gypsies* (1988) Kusturica told yet another rites-of-passage story, but this time depicted a Gypsy community and added touches of magical realism.

As Yugoslavia began to disintegrate in the early 1990s, Kusturica relocated to Paris and chose the US as the setting for his first film abroad. *Arizona Dream* (1993) is a disjointed comedy starring Johnny Depp as a fish-counter for New York's Department of Game and Fish who is tricked into attending his uncle's wedding. But it's admirable for assembling an energetic and eclectic cast that includes Jerry Lewis, Faye Dunaway and a spot-on Vincent Gallo as a narcissistic actor.

Kusturica returned to the epic subject of his homeland for *Underground* (1995), an outrageous binge-and-purge of half a century of Yugoslav history. The film earned terrific reviews, but also scathing attacks for being pro-Serb, or at least, insufficiently anti-Serb. (He is by ancestry a Bosnian Muslim, but he never publicly condemned the Serb aggression.) Kusturica has never shied away from a fight (in 1993, he challenged extreme-right Serbian politician Vojislav Seselj to a duel; Seselj declined), but following the *Underground* controversy, he announced that he was quiting filmmaking.

Kusturica's retirement proved to be short-lived, but he steered away from full-frontal politics in his next films. *Black Cat, White Cat* (1998) – which topped *Underground* for comic grotesquerie – returned to the milieu of *Time Of The Gypsies*, while *Super 8 Stories* (2001) was a fan's document of the band No Smoking. The director returned to the Bosnian conflict in 2004 for *Life Is A Miracle*, but maintained a troublingly apolitical perspective on Yugoslavia's violent collapse, while his penchant for sprawling set pieces and broad farce only achieved diminishing returns. The rural slapstick picaresque *Promise Me This* (2007) was poorly received at Cannes. JW

When Father Was Away On Business (Otac na sluzbenom putu) 1985, 136 min

cast Mreno de Bartoli, Miki Manojlovic, Mirjana Karanovic, Mustafa Nadarevic *cin* Vilko Filac *m* Zoran Simjanovic

Set during the years of 1950–52 when Tito's Yugoslavia broke away from the Soviet Union and suspected supporters of Stalin were denounced, this film is told from the perspective of a young boy who is told that his imprisoned father is "away on business". In fact, his philandering father was reported to the authorities by a wronged girfriend and sent to a labour camp. Poignant, droll and Czech-inflected, this is Kusturica in a minor key.

Time Of The Gypsies (Dom za vesanje) 1988, 142 min

cast Davor Dujmovic, Bora Todrovic, Ljubica Adzovic, Husnija Hasmovic *cin* Vilko Filac *m* Goran Bregovic

The archetype that Kusturica returned to time and again in his early career was the coming-of-age tale. Here Perhan (Davor Dujmovic), a Gypsy boy with telekinetic powers and a heart of gold, seeks both a remedy for his sister's deformed leg and marriage to his sweetheart, despite her mother's contemptuous disapproval. Alternately hopeful and despairing, the movie glimmers with magic-realist grace notes, and Kusturica works wonders with his cast of largely nonprofessionals.

Underground (Podzemlje: Bila jedom jedra zemlja) 1995, 160 min

cast Miki Manojlovic, Lazar Ristovski, Mirjana Jokovic, Slavko Stimac *cin* Vilko Filac *m* Goran Bregovich

"Once upon a time, there was a country…" So begins Kusturica's apocalyptic tragicomedy, which is, loosely speaking, a love triangle composed of two crooks and an actress. The film uses the previous fifty years of Yugoslav history, particularly the nation's then-ongoing implosion, as fodder for a cacophonous carnival picaresque, stuffed to bursting with bawdy burlesque and scatological japes. For better or worse, the film treats war in terms of preordained self-destruction rather than political cause and effect.

Stanley Kwan
Hong Kong, 1957–

Hong Kong's leading arthouse director prior to Wong Kar-Wai, Stanley Kwan has specialized in emotionally nuanced, formally inventive films revealing a particular sensitivity to women and an interest in social constraints past and present. In 1996 he became the most prominent director in Hong Kong to come out as a gay man.

The eldest son of a Chinese émigré to Hong Kong, Kwan studied communications, then joined the TVB television station as a trainee actor. He quickly switched to production, and worked as an assistant director to several of the "New Wave" Hong Kong directors: Ann Hui, Patrick Tam and Yim Ho. Following them into feature production, he made his first film, *Women*, in 1985.

Kwan established his international credentials with his third feature, *Rouge* (1987), a "supernatural love story" which paved the way for Maggie Cheung to win the Silver Bear at the Berlin Film Festival for her performance as Ruan Ling-Yu (the "Chinese Garbo") in his most complex film, *Actress*, in 1991. *Red Rose, White Rose* (1994) was a deft, sumptuously photographed adaptation of a well-known historical novella by Eileen Chang that deserved a wider audience, but his first gay feature, *Lan Yu* (2001) was gratifyingly well received in Hong Kong and on the festival circuit. While he remains an engaging and adventurous talent, Kwan has lost some of the excitement and assurance that looked set to propel him to the front ranks. TC

Rouge (Yanzhi kou) 1987, 96 min

cast Anita Mui, Leslie Cheung, Emily Chu, Man Tsz-Leung *cin* Bill Wong *m* Michael Lai

Anita Mui is the heartbroken ghost who returns to Hong Kong fifty years after committing suicide to find out why her lover (Leslie Cheung) has yet to join her in the afterlife. *Rouge* is a funny, sad story beautifully told. Kwan captures

the changing face of this booming metropolis and ties it to a glamorous love story from a bygone era, contrasting the tragic passion of yesteryear with the relationship of a rather colourless and conventional modern couple.

Actress (Ruan Ling-Yu) 1991, 167 min

cast Maggie Cheung, Tony Leung, Shin Hong, Carina Lau, Lawrence Ng, Cheung Chung *cin* Poon Hang-Sang *m* Siu Chung

One of the best movies about movies, *Actress* employs a sophisticated flashback structure to conjure the life and times of iconic Chinese screen star Ruan Ling-Yu (played here with rare grace by Maggie Cheung). "Behind-the-scenes" sequences show Kwan and Cheung interviewing Ruan's contemporaries and exploring the social mores which this tragic feminist heroine defied in her life and work.

Richard Kwietniowski
UK, 1957–

Like John Maybury, Richard Kwietniowski is a gay British director who made a big splash with his award-winning debut, but struggled for years to find financing for his second film. Before making his first feature, Kwietniowski worked in various areas of the film industry while making acclaimed shorts such as a modern update of *The Ballad Of Reading Gaol* (1988) with Quentin Crisp. He claims that he never intended to make a feature film until he read *Love And Death On Long Island* (1990), Gilbert Adair's wry reworking of *Death In Venice*. The director's wickedly funny adaptation was a hit in Cannes in 1997, winning numerous awards upon its release and earning Kwietniowski the BAFTA for most promising newcomer in 1999. However, all this counted for nought when he tried to get support for his second feature. After three projects fell through, Kwietniowski finally made *Owning Mahowny* (2003) six frustrating years after his glittering debut. Also about obsession, the sombre drama starred a typically impressive Philip Seymour Hoffman as a bank employee who embezzles money to fuel his gambling habit, but it suffered from limited distribution. LH

Love And Death On Long Island 1997, 93 min

cast John Hurt, Jason Priestley, Fiona Loewi, Sheila Hancock, Maury Chaykin *cin* Oliver Curtis *m* The Insects, Richard Grassby-Lewis

A superbly nuanced John Hurt plays Giles De'ath, a closeted and cloistered novelist who becomes magnificently obsessed with attractive young actor Ronnie Bostock (Jason Priestley) after accidentally catching his performance in *Hot Pants College II*. After fantasizing about answering questions about Ronnie on *Mastermind*, the old intellectual tracks down the object of his affection and inveigles his way into his life.

Neil LaBute
US, 1963–

N eil LaBute's work has often explored territory at odds with the prevailing political correctness of the times. Under the influence of David Mamet, LaBute's plays, such as *Filthy Talk For Troubled Times* and *Sanguinarians And Sycophants*, dealt with male discontent, and he was not afraid to have his characters say things that might offend.

Though sometimes patchy, at their best LaBute's interactions of character and camera in confined spaces reflect a ferocious social and psychological intelligence. His first film, *In The Company Of Men* (1997), initially shocked with its story of two men attempting to strike a blow for male pride, and then made a tidy profit. *Your Friends And Neighbors* (1998), continued his unflattering critique of human behaviour, though his best screenplay prize at Cannes for the Renée Zellweger-Morgan Freeman caper *Nurse Betty* (2000) felt like a belated nod for the edginess of his earlier work.

Tracing the burgeoning affair between Gwyneth Paltrow and LaBute regular Aaron Eckhart's literary researchers, *Possession* (2002) pleased neither arthouse followers nor stern devotees of A.S. Byatt's source novel. His scapel cut deeper in *The Shape Of Things* (2003), based on LaBute's own play, in which Rachel Weisz's manipulating iconoclast makes a project of Paul Rudd's nerdy student to everybody's hurt and dismay. Another substandard effort followed in the shape of a remake of horror classic *The Wicker Man* (2006), which saw Nicolas Cage stranded on a island where the locals are heavily involved in witchcraft. RA

In The Company Of Men 1997, 93 min
cast Aaron Eckhart, Matt Malloy, Stacy Edwards, Emily Cline, Jason Dixie *cin* Tom Hettinger *m* Ken Williams

Two executives (Aaron Eckhart and Matt Malloy) decide to assuage their hurt male pride by courting, then dumping, a vulnerable young deaf woman from the typing pool. Savage and accurate in its appreciation of American prep-school mores and workplace manners, this was office politics for the Tarantino era, lent depth by Stacy Edwards' turn as the innocent Christine and the sting in the film's ending. Made for $25,000, LaBute's debut won copious awards.

Your Friends And Neighbors 1998, 100 min
cast Amy Brenneman, Aaron Eckhart, Catherine Keener, Nastassja Kinski, Jason Patric, Ben Stiller *cin* Nancy Schreiber

LaBute took six modern types and let them play out their insecurities and cruelties against studied metropolitan back-drops – dinner, coffee shops, bookstores – revealing the cracks and fissures in the ethical veneers of a generation. Less successful at the box office than *In The Company Of Men*, perhaps it was the airless *mise en scène* that made this seem more difficult to face than even LaBute's debut – or perhaps it mirrors too accurately the games we play with one another.

Gregory La Cava
US, 1892–1952

G regory La Cava is one of the most underrated of American comedy directors. Educated at the School of the Art Institute of Chicago and at the Art Students League of New York, La Cava became a political cartoonist before entering the film industry as an animator, working on a number of movies featuring legendary characters Mutt and Jeff and the Katzenjammer Kids. After a stint as editor-in-chief of Hearst International Comic Films, La Cava began writing and directing live-action two-reelers, among them W.C. Fields vehicles at Paramount, before graduating to features.

Through the 1930s he established a lasting reputation for deftly controlled, well-acted social comedies, such as the political fantasy *Gabriel Over The White House* (1933), the Claudette Colbert vehicle *She Married Her Boss* (1935) and the rare historical comedy *Affairs Of Cellini* (1934). He coaxed complementary performances from Katharine Hepburn, Ginger Rogers and Andrea Leeds in *Stage Door* (1937), and his *Fifth Avenue Girl* (1939) and *The Primrose Path* (1941) displayed a unique sensitivity to American class divisions. This ability was demonstrated in the lasting favourite *My Man Godfrey* (1936), which earned the director his reputation as a master of screwball comedy. Frequently in dispute with the studios, La Cava's career ended after a clash over the script for *One Touch Of Venus* (1948) eleven days into the shooting, and he is not credited for his work on the film. RA

My Man Godfrey 1936, 96 min, b/w

cast William Powell, Carole Lombard, Gail Patrick, Eugene Pallette, Alice Brady, Mischa Auer *cin* Ted Tetzlaff *m* Charles Previn, Rudy Schrager

This is a wonderful Depression satire, in which Carole Lombard's society circle drag William Powell's tramp in off the streets, and he unexpectedly civilizes their madcap ways. Shot with sober detachment by Ted Tetzlaff, and scripted by the Marx Brothers' scenarist Morrie Ryskind, the comedy remains a little to the left of outright bonkers.

Ringo Lam
Hong Kong, 1954–

Stylish, kinetic action and intense, visceral dramatic confrontations are the strongest notes in the combustible cinema of Ringo Lam, a mainstream thriller specialist whose career straddles Hong Kong and Hollywood.

Like many Hong Kong directors, Lam served his apprenticeship at the TVB television studio, where he briefly studied acting before switching to production. Unhappy with his circumstances there, he studied film at York University in Toronto and became a Canadian citizen before returning to Hong Kong in 1981. His first four movies were popular comedies, but as soon as he was granted the freedom to write his own material he turned to the thriller genre with the intense *City On Fire* (1987). It was a breakthrough movie, not only for Lam but also for his friend the actor Chow Yun-Fat – not to mention one Quentin Tarantino, who "borrowed" the setup (an undercover cop infiltrates a gang of jewel thieves) and the climax (after the robbery recriminations and bullets fly) for *Reservoir Dogs*.

School On Fire (1988) was a more realistic take on how triads impinge even on the schoolyard, but the film was heavily censored and banned in some territories. And the previous year's *Prison On Fire* was a gripping prison drama powered by compelling performances from Chow and Tony Leung Ka Fai. Subsequent efforts have been workmanlike, but more generic. Following John Woo to the US, Lam failed to graduate beyond the Jean-Claude Van Damme B-picture level (they have made three films together, the first being 2001's *The Replicant*) and he has kept one foot firmly in the Hong Kong film industry. TC

City On Fire (Longhu fengyun) 1987, 110 min

cast Chow Yun-Fat, Danny Lee, Sun Yueh, Roy Cheung *cin* Andrew Lau *m* Teddy Robin Kwan

Lam's first crime thriller is still his best-known film, if only because Quentin Tarantino borrowed the framework for *Reservoir Dogs*. Chow Yun-Fat stars as an undercover cop

who infiltrates a gang of jewel thieves and is left in a sticky situation when a climactic heist unravels. The high velocity camerawork and rapid-fire editing are typical of Lam's shoot first, ask questions later style.

John Landis
US, 1950–

Merchant of broad, noisy, generally profitable farce, John Landis makes movies that are rather less than the sum of their big-budget set pieces and special effects – take away Rick Baker's still-impressive wolf make-up from *An American Werewolf In London* (1981), for instance, and you're not left with much of a film. *The Kentucky Fried Movie* (1977) is a hit-or-miss hodgepodge of skits parodying various films and TV shows, and *National Lampoon's Animal House* (1978) remains a cornerstone of the college-hijinks genre.

Landis's films became less palatable as they grew more ambitious: the obnoxious, budget-busting *The Blues Brothers* (1980) lodges in the memory as an interminable car chase occasionally relieved by musical interludes (Aretha Franklin, James Brown, Ray Charles and Cab Calloway all put in appearances, alongside stars Dan Aykroyd and John Belushi), and Landis contributed an unbearably mawkish pro-tolerance segment to the omnibus *Twilight Zone: The Movie* (1983). The film has cast a permanent shadow over Landis's career, due to the deaths of star Vic Morrow and two child actors in a helicopter crash on set.

Landis's best and probably most widely seen film is his long-form video for Michael Jackson's "Thriller", in which Baker's make-up effects are again the indispensable co-stars. Otherwise, the director cranked out a frayed string of forgettable 1980s comedies, including *Spies Like Us* (1985) and *Three Amigos!* (1986) with Chevy Chase, and *Trading Places* (1983), *Coming To America* (1988) and *Beverly Hills Cop III* (1994) with Eddie Murphy. Landis has since gravitated more towards television work, but still makes the occasional comedy feature, such as the poorly received *Blues Brothers 2000* (1998). JW

National Lampoon's Animal House 1978, 109 min

cast John Belushi, Tim Matheson, John Vernon, Verna Bloom, Tom Hulce, Cesare Danova, Peter Riegert, Mary Lewis Weller *cin* Charles Correll

Villainous Vernon Wormer, dean of Faber College, recruits a waspy fraternity to help him get rid of Delta House, the beer-guzzling, toga-partying, academically disinclined heroes of Landis's campus lark, featuring force of nature John Belushi as John "Bluto" Blutarsky, whose finest moment comes when he imitates a freshly popped zit.

Fritz Lang
Austria (formerly Austro-Hungarian Empire), 1890–1976

As one of the greatest directors in the history of the cinema, Fritz Lang's best films are a fluent marriage of philosophical gravitas, visual allure and sophisticated design.

Rather than fulfill has parents' wish and become an architect, Lang spent the period between 1910 and 1914 hawking hand-painted postcards around Europe and training as a painter in Paris. At the outbreak of World War I he returned to Vienna and joined the Austrian army, only to be honorably discharged in 1916 after giving up an eye to the cause. Writing screenplays while convalescing, Lang entered the film industry as a scriptwriter for German producer Joe May. In 1917 he joined the film company Decla-Bioscop as a director and went on to make some of the most acclaimed German films of the 1920s, among them *Dr Mabuse, der Spieler* (*Dr Mabuse, The Gambler*, 1922), *Destiny* (1921), *Die Nibelungen* (1924), *Metropolis* (1927) and *M* (1931). Epic in conception and execution, these films showcased aesthetic instincts well-formed in Lang even at his directorial beginnings.

Responding to post-World War I pessimism and the expressionist impulse in modern art, Lang created sensational scenarios that explored the dynamics of a Germany in a state of moral meltdown. As the 1920s turned into the 1930s he adopted a more naturalistic approach, anticipating the dark cities of his later American productions with the Berlin intrigue *Spione* (*The Spy*, 1928) and the sinister murder mystery *M*. Following *Das Testament des Dr Mabuse* (1933), in which Lang put the rhetoric of Nazism into the mouths of criminals, Hitler's propaganda minister Josef Goebbels unexpectedly invited Lang to take charge of the German film industry, so the story goes. Lang left for France, where he worked briefly, directing the fairground melodrama *Liliom* (1934) starring Charles Boyer.

Also in 1934 Lang was invited to Hollywood. However compromised he was by the studio system, his American work is what many modern viewers tend to remember best. His thrillers of the 1940s and 50s seem to epitomize modernity as a condition both faithless and painful. His first Hollywood project, the allegorical *Fury* (1936) was the portrait of an ordinary citizen degraded by an obtuse and vicious status quo. Starring Spencer Tracy in one of his finest roles, the film remains an angry warning against the lure of mob rule.

Though frustrated by studio interference – Lang worked at many of the majors as well as independently – he made impressive contributions to many genres. *You Only Live Once* (1937) starred Henry Fonda and Sylvia Sidney as waifs tossed by the mean Depression temper. In *The Return Of Frank James* (1940) and *Western Union* (1941), Lang mastered a peculiarly American genre, the Western, during a golden era in its evolution; he later charted its baroque decline in *Rancho Notorious* (1952).

His work in the 1940s darkened with the wartime mood. He demonstrated astute management of urban space as a metaphor for the vicissitudes of psychology in *Man Hunt* (1941), in one episode pitting Hitler's would-be assassin against Gestapo thugs in the blind corridors of the London Underground. Then, following the gripping *Hangmen Also Die* (1943), came the classic *films noirs The Woman In The Window* (1944) and *Scarlet Street* (1945) – two examinations of how accidental encounters can send an individual's life into turmoil.

If *Ministry Of Fear* (1944) and *Cloak And Dagger* (1946) reread the European war as an unusually pessimistic whodunnit, the richly patterned *Secret Beyond The Door...* (1948), *The Big Heat* (1953), *While The City Sleeps* (1956) and *Beyond A Reasonable Doubt* (1956) chart a vicious and sexually wanton post-war world of greed and shocking violence. (The moment in which Lee Marvin hurls scalding coffee in Gloria Grahame's face in *The Big Heat* is one of the most devastating scenes in the history of the American thriller.)

Lang had been considered a difficult director to work with for a number of years, and this reputation had worsened by the 1950s. In 1956 he travelled to India where he directed *Der Tiger von Eschnapur* (*The Tiger Of Eschnapur*, 1958) and its sequel *Das Indische Grabmal* (*The Indian Tomb*, 1960), based on his and his ex-wife Thea von Harbou's scripts. He returned to Germany for his final film, *Die Tausend Augen des Dr Mabuse* (*The 1000 Eyes Of Dr Mabuse*, 1960), a sequel that evoked the paranoia and invention of the original Mabuse films. In 1963 Jean-Luc Godard paid tribute to the director by casting Lang as himself in *Le mépris* (*Contempt*), while Lang's purity of conception can be felt in the 1960s thrillers of Claude Chabrol. In 1969 Marcel Hillaire paid tribute by appearing as "Fritz" in Woody Allen's *Take The Money And Run*. Lang remains the archetypal classical auteur as troubled perfectionist. RA

Dr Mabuse, der Spieler (Dr Mabuse, The Gambler) 1922, 270 min, b/w
cast Rudolf Klein-Rogge, Alfred Abel, Aud Egede Nissen, Gertrude Welcker, Bernhard Goetzke *cin* Carl Hoffmann *m* Konrad Elfers

More than simply a tale of a criminal mastermind defeated by a vigilant detective, *Dr Mabuse, der Spieler* ranges across Berlin in search of the causes and nature of human corruption. Taking advantage of the chaos of inflation and patrician decadence to control the status quo, Mabuse becomes an invisible but immanent tyrant amid a fluid *mise en scène* of desire and display, so reflecting the looming social collapse of Germany under the Weimar Republic.

Metropolis 1927, 83 min, b/w

cast Alfred Abel, Gustav Fröhlich, Brigitte Helm, Rudolf Klein-Rogge *cin* Karl Freund, Günther Rittau *m* Gottfried Huppertz

The influence of Lang's vision of a mechanized future of blank conformity and incipient violence can be felt in everything from the work of George Orwell to *Blade Runner*, while its message speaks to our own experience of identity tags, passwords, public surveillance and ubiquitous bureaucracy.

M 1931, 118 min, b/w

cast Peter Lorre, Otto Wernicke, Ellen Widmann, Inge Landgut, Gustav Gründgens, Theodor Loos *cin* Fritz Arno Wagner

Showing the narrative control that would distinguish his American films, Lang's tale of a city petrified by reports of a serial killer used an infamous Düsseldorf child murderer as inspiration for an examination of municipal politics. Caught between the blundering mechanisms of the city fathers and the spite of the underworld, Peter Lorre's pop-eyed deviant becomes the very principle of desire in a world without pity.

Fury 1936, 94 min, b/w

cast Spencer Tracy, Sylvia Sidney, Walter Abel, Bruce Cabot, Edward Ellis, Walter Brennan *cin* Milton Krasner *m* Arthur Lange

Lang got off to a blinding start with his first US film, despite massive studio interference. Spencer Tracy plays Joe, who is arrested as a suspected kidnapper and then narrowly escapes a lynching as a frenzied mob burns down the jail. Believing Joe to be dead, the DA charges several of the townspeople with murder and, in a brilliant touch, Lang intercuts newsreel footage of the crowd as individual "alibis" are read out.

The Woman In The Window 1944, 99 min, b/w

cast Edward G. Robinson, Joan Bennett, Dan Duryea, Raymond Massey, Edmund Breon *cin* Milton Krasner *m* Arthur Lange

One of *film noir*'s most brilliant conceits. As mild professor Edward G. Robinson leaves his club and lingers a little too long before the painting of beautiful Joan Bennett, he is drawn into a nightmare of deep darkness and unsparing violence.

Scarlet Street 1945, 103 min, b/w

cast Edward G. Robinson, Joan Bennett, Dan Duryea, Jess Barker, Margaret Lindsay, Rosalind Ivan, Samuel S. Hinds *cin* Milton Krasner *m* Hans J. Salter

When Edward G. Robinson's lonely cashier catches sight of Joan Bennett's Kitty in a see-through coat late one night, he thinks he is dreaming. After saving her from assault, he finds himself caught up in a world completely beyond his experience. Reading city streets as corridors of the soul and sexual longing as the fate of modern man, this *noir* classic stood on the cusp of Langian urban allegory and the moral downfall of the post-war world.

Rancho Notorious 1952, 89 min

cast Marlene Dietrich, Arthur Kennedy, Mel Ferrer, Lloyd Gough, Gloria Henry, Jack Elam, William Frawley, Dan Seymour *cin* Hal Mohr *m* Emil Newman

Later Lang films continued to mine the excesses of obsession, and this Western explores the nature of guilt through the story of a man driven to hunt his fiancée's killers until he has become as evil as his prey. Suffused with halftones and irony, this melancholy movie features Marlene Dietrich as a fading bar-room singer, and makes use of a musical refrain to signal the changing of America's innocence into veiled dismay.

The Big Heat 1953, 90 min, b/w

cast Glenn Ford, Gloria Grahame, Jocelyn Brando, Lee Marvin, Carolyn Jones *cin* Charles Lang Jr *m* Daniele Amfitheatrof

Few American thrillers have characterized US municipal politics in such venal and vicious colours. As Glenn Ford's embittered cop seeks the killers of his wife, the corruption fairly oozes from the screen. Gloria Grahame gives a performance of sweet and sour vivacity.

Beyond A Reasonable Doubt 1956, 80 min, b/w

cast Dana Andrews, Joan Fontaine, Sidney Blackmer, Barbara Nichols, Philip Bourneuf, Shepperd Strudwick *cin* William Snyder *m* Herschel Burke Gilbert

When Dana Andrews' writer deliberately implicates himself in a murder in order to demonstrate the fallibility of capital punishment, the only witness to the scam is accidentally killed. The crusading hero is faced with the awful and arbitrary nature of modern fate. This is perhaps Lang's most geometric play of theme and *mise en scène*.

Walter Lang
US, 1896–1972

Best known for musicals and comedies, Walter Lang was more a craftsman than an auteur, but he thrived in the studio system. After ten years as a moderately successful director, he joined 20th Century Fox in the mid-1930s. *The Mighty Barnum* (1934) was an enjoyable (if highly fictional) biopic of the impresario Phineas T. Barnum. In 1938 he directed a couple of light satires, *The Baroness And The Butler* and *I'll Give A Million*, but his ambitious adaptation of Maurice Maeterlinck's *The Blue Bird* (1940) was lost on audiences. Of his many 1940s musicals, the best is the dazzling Technicolor *Moon Over Miami* (1941). Following less successful forays into other genres, his later musicals included the first Richard Rodgers and Oscar Hammerstein musical to make it to the screen, *State Fair* (1946), and the multiple Oscar-winning *The King And I* (1956). After *Snow White And The Three Stooges* (1961) he was offered *The Sound Of Music* (1965) but he chose to retire instead. JR

The King And I 1956, 133 min

cast Deborah Kerr, Yul Brynner, Rita Moreno, Martin Benson, Terry Saunders *cin* Leon Shamroy *m* Richard Rodgers, Oscar Hammerstein II

Yul Brynner, who came to this film after first taking the role of the impetuous king of Siam on Broadway, stars opposite Deborah Kerr who plays the English governess employed to look after his many children. Their relationship is initially spiky, but Anna and the king gradually grow to respect and even love each other. This visually stunning film includes Rodgers and Hammerstein's standout songs "Getting To Know You", "Hello Young Lovers" and "Shall We Dance?", with the versatile Marni Nixon dubbing Deborah Kerr's singing.

Claude Lanzmann
France, 1925–

A decorated Resistance figure, friend to Jean-Paul Sartre, director of a prominent cultural journal and a controversial filmmaker, Claude Lanzmann is a leading figure in post-war French life. After World War II he was awarded the Resistance Medal with Rosette and the Légion d'honneur. Following philosophy studies at Tübingen University and the Free University of Berlin, Lanzmann became associated with the circle around Sartre and Simone de Beauvoir, and today still publishes *Les temps modernes*, the journal they founded together.

Lanzmann's first film was *Pourquoi Israel?* (*Israel, Why*, 1973), a documentary on the birth of Israel told through the "subjective reportage" of those who experienced the events first-hand. The film established Lanzmann's style of in-depth interviews interspersed with the camera's objective contemplation of historical sites. Steeped in the assumption that the individual is responsible for his or her actions, Lanzmann's histories record a heroic but tragic modernity. Following the epic Holocaust history *Shoah* (1985), the controversial *Tsahal* (1994) offered testimonies from Israeli soldiers and civilians on events since the Yom Kippur War of 1973. In *Sobibor, October 14, 1943, 4pm* (2001) Lanzmann traced the stories of the inmates who escaped the Nazi concentration camp. Lanzmann is one of the most lacerating chroniclers of horror in the modern world. RA

Shoah 1985, 566 min
cin Dominique Chapuis, Jimmy Glasberg, William Luptchansky

Comprising footage extracted from over 350 hours of interviews with people who both lived and worked in the Nazi death camps at Auschwitz, Belzec, Chelmno, Sobibor and Treblinka – including former inmates, German military personnel and civilian workers – *Shoah* explores the individual effects of the Nazi destruction of European Jewry. The result is one of the most compelling films in documentary history.

Charles Laughton
UK, 1899–1962

It is one of the tragedies of American film history that Charles Laughton directed only one film. Larger than life in his performances as well as in his physique, Laughton's *The Night Of The Hunter* (1955) combines grossness with passages of pure poetry. Following service in World War I, Laughton found his way into amateur dramatics, going on the London stage as a graduate of RADA before making his film debut in 1928. Pursuing a distinguished, if uneven, acting career in Britain and America,

Laughton has come to embody the very image of the archetypal genius constrained by the necessity of churning out performances to sustain his screen presence. His single directorial credit is a complex mixture of balmy riverside days and German-expressionist nights, each image rent by the misery visited upon us by money and desire. RA

The Night Of The Hunter 1955, 92 min, b/w
cast Robert Mitchum, Lillian Gish, Shelley Winters, Billy Chapin, James Gleason, Sally Ann Bruce, Peter Graves *cin* Stanley Cortez *m* Walter Schumann

A modern Appalachian allegory of good versus evil, in which Laughton evokes compassion for children caught between the apathy of adults and the machinations of religious hysteria. The pastoralism of James Agee's script, the gothicism of Stanley Cortez's cinematography and terrific performances from Lillian Gish and Robert Mitchum make this an unforgettable film.

Ray Lawrence
UK, 1948–

Ray Lawrence has brought a moral intelligence to his work that is unique in modern Australian cinema. Born in the UK but moving to Australia as a child, Lawrence pursued a television career as an adult and became a leading director of commercials. In 1985 he wrote and directed *Bliss*, based on the Peter Carey novel of the same name. This surreal and comic midlife-crisis saga cleverly sidestepped the temptation to become standard fare, examining the consequences of an executive's clinical death on the operating table and subsequent re-evaluation of his life and the lives of those around him. The film was well received and it revealed a director keen to make films on his own terms. Significantly, Lawrence has found it difficult to raise funding for the projects that interest him, making releases irregular. The detective story-cum-character study *Lantana* (2001) played the Toronto Film Festival in the days following the 9/11 attacks in the US, and in interviews at the time Lawrence questioned cinema's commitment to portraying violence. His next film, *Jindabyne* (2006), told the story of how three fishermen's lives are changed when they find the body of a murdered woman. RA

Lantana 2001, 121 min
cast Anthony LaPaglia, Geoffrey Rush, Barbara Hershey, Kerry Armstrong, Rachael Blake *cin* Mandy Walker *m* Paul Kelly, Shane O'Mara, Steve Hadley

Tagged "a mystery for grown-ups", *Lantana* is based on Lawrence's play *Speaking In Tongues*. After a body is discovered in the brush, Anthony LaPaglia's detective embarks on a multistranded investigation into the intertwined sexual relationships in a Sydney suburb. Following the narrative from a number of different but interconnected perspectives, this is as penetrating as Robert Altman's *Short Cuts* (1993) or Paul Thomas Anderson's *Magnolia* (1999).

One-hit wonders

In directing *The Kentuckian* (1955) and co-directing *The Midnight Man* (1974), Burt Lancaster is one of the few people in the world to have directed one and a half movies. There are plenty, however, who have warmed the director's chair only once. Many of them, like Lancaster, are actors. And plenty of them take the walk to the other side of the camera in their stride. Frank Sinatra, for instance, handled his World War II movie *None But The Brave* (1965) with deft efficiency, while Gary Oldman garnered numerous awards for the abrasive drama *Nil By Mouth* (1997). His script and direction received ecstatic reviews, with critics hailing him as Britain's answer to John Cassavetes. Which makes the lack of an Oldman follow-up all the more puzzling. It's much less mystifying when the reviews are terrible, however. Johnny Depp even pulled his directorial debut, *The Brave* (1997), from cinematic release after its withering reviews at the Cannes Film Festival. Maybe his decision was due to a fit of pique. Or could it be that when he looked at his work again, he saw what the critics saw: a film with loving shots of its star (one Johnny Depp) looking impossibly beautiful and buff in a funereally paced melodrama that took laconic narcissism to new levels of indolence. Perhaps Depp's drubbing was unnecessarily strong: most thespians' greenhorn efforts tend to be met with the kind of congenial indifference that accompanied James Cagney's *Short Cut To Hell* (1957) or Bill Murray's *Quick Change* (1990).

Bad reviews and bruised egos must surely take their toll. Imagine what Eddie Murphy's reaction must have been after having written, directed, produced and starred in *Harlem Nights* (1989) only to receive this brutally concise review of his pet project: "Written and directed by Eddie Murphy – these are words that will for evermore strike fear in the hearts of movie-goers everywhere." One well-worn theory is that actors can't really afford the time to direct a film properly. Acting in a movie usually begins and ends on set, which can take a couple of months at most, whereas directing can take at least a laborious year of their lives from pre- to post-production – as Marlon Brando discovered on the Western *One-Eyed Jacks* (1961). Initially hired as an actor, the star of *On The Waterfront* flexed his celebrity muscle to sack writer Sam Peckinpah and force director Stanley Kubrick to leave "by mutual consent". Picking up the megaphone himself, the Method actor proved to be a fiendishly methodical director. Brando insisted on being in charge of all the minutiae of production, with the result that the budget went from $1.6 million to $5.6 million, and the shooting from sixty days to six months. Having used six times more film stock than the norm, the neophyte's initial cut lasted four and a half hours. At which point the studio took control, applied the scissors, and released the film at a viewer-friendly 141 minutes. Critics agreed that *One-Eyed Jacks* was the typically eccentric product of a mercurial talent – and they only saw the *producers*' version.

The finest example of the one-off, and perhaps the most frustrating case of thwarted genius, is undoubtedly Charles Laughton's febrile, visionary *The Night Of The Hunter* (1955). Now regarded as a classic – a baroque, expressionistic and pantheistic fairy tale for adults – it was greeted by indifferent, baffled reviews and sudden death at the box office on its release. Laughton's plans for his next movie, an adaptation of Norman Mailer's *The Naked And The Dead,* which the larger-than-life thespian had written himself, were swiftly put on the back burner, where they sadly remained. After Laughton's death in 1962, esteemed French critic Robert Benayoun penned this elegy to the one-hit wonder: "To make only one film, but to make it a work of genius: isn't that, in the context of a journeyman profession, the shining example that Laughton has given us?"

Laughton belongs to a small but illustrious group of people who made one bona fide classic but then never bothered the Directors Guild again. For instance, one question most people ask after watching the disturbing serial-killers-in-love story *The Honeymoon Killers* (1970) is: who exactly is Leonard Kastle? When the film's original director Martin Scorsese decided to film everything in master shots, he faced the severe displeasure of the producers who didn't approve of his arty techniques. They sacked him, employed Donald Volkman, then sacked him and finally plumped for the movie's writer, Leonard Kastle. The novice later vanished from the face of the moviemaking earth, without a single other directorial credit to his name – his sudden disappearance only adding another layer of grungy enigma to the movie's cultish lustre. The mundane truth is that Kastle returned to his day job of composer, and eventually became a professor of composition and music history at the New York State University at Albany. The music world beckoned another highly promising film director, James William Guercio. Director of that curate's egg of a police procedural *Electra Glide In Blue* (1973), he retired from film-making to become manager of a rock band – those masters of the power ballad, Chicago. Which means that, in his case, cinema's loss was music's loss too. LH

Jindabyne 2006, 123 min

cast Laura Linney, Gabriel Byrne, Chris Haywood, Deborra-Lee Furness, John Howard *cin* David Williamson *m* Paul Kelly, Dan Luscombe

When fishermen find the body of a murdered woman the event changes everything for everyone. Like a stone flung into a still pool, the ripples from this powerfully executed exposition of violence and the community will haunt you. Laura Linney's Claire is one of her richest creations.

David Lean

UK, 1908–91

Alfred Hitchcock, Michael Powell and David Lean: the three great British filmmakers of their generation were born within a radius of fifty miles and just nine years apart. Each of them served an apprenticeship in the silent era, learned their craft from the bottom up, proved their mettle in their thirties, and hit a creative peak in middle age. Of the three, it was Lean who commanded the greatest respect among critics and his peers – he was nominated for the Academy Award for best director seven times, and won twice. And although he only made one feature in the last twenty years of his life, *A Passage To India* (1984) was received with a gratifying (and unjustified) warmth.

Lean was first and foremost a superb craftsman. In the pre-war years he developed a reputation as the best editor in the country; his films are distinguished by their control of rhythm and shrewd use of counterpoint. Lean's camera is more self-effacing

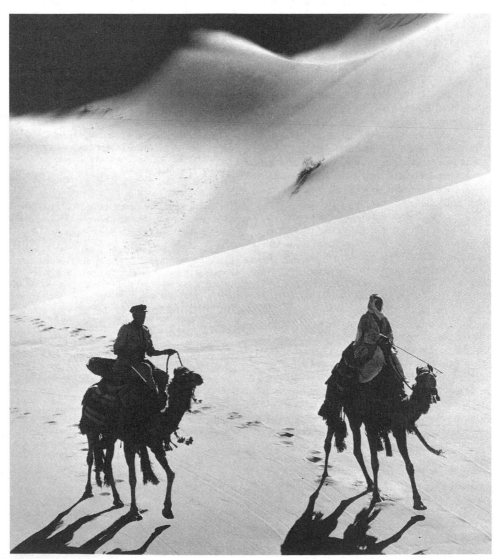

David Lean made the most of Jordan's spectacular Wadi Rum desert, where much of *Lawrence Of Arabia* was filmed.

than Hitchcock's or Powell's, and although he was famed for his perfectionist compositional sense, his eye was more conventional. It's in the cutting that you feel both the romantic ardour and the repression that create the central tension in his work.

His first films as director, *In Which We Serve* (1942), *This Happy Breed* (1944) and *Blithe Spirit* (1945), were collaborations of one kind or another with the writer Noel Coward, and Coward's is the stronger voice. They now seem unutterably patronizing, but remain fascinating time capsules. By *Brief Encounter* (1945) Lean was asserting his own cinematic prowess with greater confidence, and although he remained on some level a "literary" director, the adaptations on which his reputation rests have been thoroughly reconfigured into spectacle.

When Hitchcock was anointed an auteur in the late 1950s, Anglo-Saxon critics fought a quixotic rearguard action on behalf of his pre-Hollywood, 1930s British thrillers. You can make a similar – and stronger – case for the British studio films David Lean made in the late 1940s and early 50s: hardly parochial, his two Dickens adaptations, *Great Expectations* and *Oliver Twist* (1946 and 1948), remain definitive, and capitalize on the best resources of the busy post-World War II British film industry. Less well known are *The Passionate Friends* (1949) and *Madeleine* (1950), which were vehicles for his third wife, Ann Todd. Rather fine melodramas, they are recognizably the work of the Englishman who made *Brief Encounter*. The comedy *Hobson's Choice* (1954) is unavoidably theatrical, but charming in its own right.

Then came *Summertime* (aka *Summer Madness*, 1955), Lean's first colour film, his first with an American movie star (Katharine Hepburn), and his first to be shot on foreign location (Venice). When he went to scout locations, producer Alexander Korda told him: "Don't be afraid of the obvious places, David, go for the big effects." It was advice Lean took to heart. His horizons stretched, the movies grew in scale, scope and length, and some of the humanity went out of them. Even so, and granted that its politics are confused, it would be hard to argue that *Lawrence Of Arabia* (1962) is less than the masterpiece Lean decreed it must be. For the last time in his work, scale and substance were in accord – perhaps because this apparently reserved and practical director identified so closely with his flawed, flamboyantly conflicted hero.

Thereafter Lean's vision tended to veer consistently towards the bombastic. His 1965 adaptation of Boris Pasternak's novel, *Doctor Zhivago*, singularly failed to integrate the poignant love story at its centre within the epic, background events of the Russian Revolution. Despite several thrilling set pieces, characterization was too frequently sketched in and largely unconvincing. *Ryan's Daughter* (1970), set against the Irish rebellion of 1916, was even more overblown and not helped by its starry but incongruous casting. *A Passage To India* was a par-

tial return to form, but the director fudged the anti-colonial sentiments of E.M. Forster's original novel and while Judy Davis provided a nuanced performance as Miss Quested, Alec Guinness's "goodness, gracious me" turn as the Indian professor Godbhole was frankly laughable. TC

Brief Encounter 1945, 86 min, b/w
cast Celia Johnson, Trevor Howard, Stanley Holloway, Joyce Carey, Cyril Raymond, Valentine Dyall *cin* Robert Krasker *m* Sergei Rachmaninov

Celia Johnson and Trevor Howard meet by chance at a railway station. Both are married and neither will stoop to impropriety. Yet there is an immediate attraction and a series of stolen lunch dates develops into one of cinema's most affecting love affairs. It was Lean who hit on the flashback structure which takes Noel Coward's play out of the station, and this is where the filmmaker's romantic inclinations blossom (Rachmaninov's *Piano Concerto No. 2* does the rest).

Great Expectations 1946, 118 min, b/w
cast John Mills, Anthony Wager, Valerie Hobson, Jean Simmons, Bernard Miles, Alec Guinness *cin* Guy Green *m* Walter Goehr

Breaking away from Coward, Lean graduated to Charles Dickens and produced two authentic classics. The first, *Great Expectations*, is steeped in florid, inky atmospherics and splendidly cast (Alec Guinness is particularly memorable as Herbert Pocket, and even 38-year-old John Mills as Pip works quite well). It loses a little of its lustre after the boldly appalling childhood scenes, but it's a very adroit piece of compression. Two years later, *Oliver Twist*, like the novel, was more melodramatic and sentimental, but Lean's linear storytelling is a model of clarity.

The Bridge On The River Kwai 1957, 160 min
cast William Holden, Alec Guinness, Jack Hawkins, Sessue Hayakawa, James Donald, Andre Morell *cin* Jack Hildyard *m* Malcolm Arnold

Set in a prisoner-of-war camp in Burma, 1943, Lean's first big Hollywood film seasons boy's-own heroics with a heavy dose of irony to satisfying, if faintly facile, effect. Alec Guinness is marvellous as Colonel Nicholson, who at first declines to have his men build a bridge for the Japanese, then resolves to build them a better one than they could ever make. *Kwai* won seven Oscars, including best picture, best actor and best director.

Lawrence Of Arabia 1962, 228 min
cast Peter O'Toole, Alec Guinness, Anthony Quinn, Jack Hawkins, Omar Sharif, Jose Ferrer, Anthony Quayle *cin* Freddie Young *m* Maurice Jarre

Buoyed by the success of *Kwai*, Lean persuaded Sam Spiegel to bankroll this four-hour, 70mm desert epic about the eccentric English cartographer and scholar who united the Arab tribes to fight the Turks during World War I – and cast the virtually unknown Peter O'Toole in the lead. The result is a triumph for actor and director, a film of tremendous sweep and stunning vistas that never loses sight of the complexities and contradictions that agitated Lawrence.

Doctor Zhivago 1965, 200 min
cast Omar Sharif, Julie Christie, Geraldine Chaplin, Rod Steiger, Alec Guinness, Tom Courtenay *cin* Freddie Young *m* Maurice Jarre

Attempting to best himself, Lean turned to Boris Pasternak's 1957 novel, and again enlisted the aid of screenwriter Robert Bolt and composer Maurice Jarre. This time, though, the film's central romance (between Omar Sharif and Julie Christie) is allowed to dominate the Russian Revolution going on in the background. Flimsy characterization and visual grandiloquence combine to occasionally powerful effect. This popular film proved a great box-office success, but is essentially very hollow.

Patrice Leconte

France, 1947–

Since the 1980s, Patrice Leconte has stood in many people's minds for sophisticated French export cinema. Sexy, witty – but with enough intellectual grist to make the viewer feel smug – the Leconte release has become an arthouse staple.

He fell for movies as the *nouvelle vague* broke in the 1960s, signing up at the national film school IDHEC (now FEMIS), and making cartoons and shorts on the side. His directing debut came in 1975, and his American breakthrough in 1978 – translated as *French Fried Vacation*, *Les bronzés* was a sex romp set in a holiday camp on the Ivory Coast. It was the fruit of Leconte's involvement with L'Equipe Splendid, a *café-théâtre* troupe comprised of Josiane Balasko, Michel Blanc and Thierry Lhermitte.

In 1989 Blanc played the voyeur in Leconte's Georges Simenon adaptation *Monsieur Hire*, a success at the box office outside France, though untypical of Leconte's work. Closer to his territory were *The Hairdresser's Husband* (1990) and *Tango* (1993), in the latter of which Lhermitte, Richard Bohringer and Philippe Noiret callously discuss their relationships with women as they pursue Lhermitte's errant wife (Miou-Miou) across the Midi. Its swooping aerial photography and glaring primary colours revived Leconte's cartoonish sensibility.

Although usually his own screenwriter, Leconte did not script *Ridicule* (1996), a literate and absorbing dissection of pre-Revolution politics in the French court which became a modest international hit. The Alain Delon-Jean-Paul Belmondo spy spoof *Une chance sur deux* (1998), the fanciful *The Girl On The Bridge* (1999), and the dull Juliette Binoche vehicle *La veuve de Saint-Pierre* (*The Widow Of Saint-Pierre*, 2000) reiterated Leconte's crowd-pleasing, César-winning stature. Starring another Leconte regular, Sandrine Bonnaire, *Confidences trop intimes* (*Intimate Strangers*, 2004) found a distraught woman entering the wrong door and confessing her marital problems to a financial adviser rather than to a psychologist. As usual, its piquant interrogation of our sexual prejudices played profitably to French and foreign audiences alike. *My Best Friend* (2006) was a delightful comedy of manners in which a businesswoman challenges Daniel Auteuil's ambivalent François to demonstrate that someone somewhere likes him. RA

Monsieur Hire 1989, 79 min

cast Michel Blanc, Sandrine Bonnaire, Luc Thullier, André Wilms, Eric Berenger, Marielle Berthon *cin* Denis Lenoir *m* Michael Nyman

A lonely middle-aged tailor – who is also the prime suspect in the murder of a young girl – spies on the woman in the apartment opposite. Economically constructed out of elliptical scenes thriving on Michel Blanc's understated performance and the subtle treatment of the relationship that develops between the two main characters, Leconte's Simenon adaptation is a classic in the cinema of loneliness and sexual longing.

The Hairdresser's Husband (Le mari de la coiffeuse) 1990, 80 min

cast Jean Rochefort, Anna Galiena, Roland Bertin, Maurice Chevit, Philippe Clévenot, Jacques Mathou *cin* Eduardo Serra *m* Michael Nyman

This tale of male sexual bliss revolves around the fulfilment of a man snatched from solitary longing by an ample woman. As a 12-year-old Antoine is initiated sexually by his voluptuous hairdresser; in middle age he falls for another coiffeuse, and they marry. Treating its subject with chauvinistic wit and a hint of melancholy, this is an elegantly shot celebration of the female form.

L'homme du train (The Man On The Train) 2002, 90 min

cast Jean Rochefort, Johnny Hallyday, Jean-François Stévenin, Charlie Nelson, Pascal Parmentier *cin* Jean-Marie Dreujou *m* Pascal Estève

Bank robber Milan (Hallyday) goes to a provincial French town to case the local bank. With no place to stay, he accepts the offer of a bed from retired schoolteacher Manesquier (Rochefort). Like a metaphor for cinema itself, this tale of exchanged identities centres on the two characters' realizing that they are tempted by one another's lifestyles and how much more satisfying their lives might have been had they each had the other's past.

Ang Lee

Taiwan, 1954–

Ang Lee is a consummate professional; his films are handsomely mounted, well acted, crisply photographed and a little cold to the touch. With his longtime filmmaking partner James Schamus – who has, at the time of writing, been a producer of every one of Lee's films and screenwriter of all but two – Lee evinces a particular interest in cultural and generational conflicts as they play out within and between individuals. This preoccupation began with his first feature, *Pushing Hands* (1992), in which an ageing Chinese tai chi master relocates to upstate New York to live with his son's family. (Lee himself was born and raised in Taiwan and moved abroad after college to study film at New York University.)

A pair of gay lovers stages a heterosexual marriage ceremony for the benefit of one partner's traditional Taiwanese parents in Lee's second film, *The Wedding Banquet* (1993), which continued the culture-clash theme while introducing another Lee motif: the all-too-frequent incompatibility between emotional instinct and social convention. Lee has also taken a recurrent interest – first seen in the mouthwatering *Eat Drink Man Woman* (1994) – in young women who struggle to identify and assert their own will in a patriarchal society, from the dispossessed Dashwood sisters in *Sense And Sensibility* (1995) to Zhang Ziyi's spoilt-princess-turned-bandit-queen in *Crouching Tiger, Hidden Dragon* (2000). (Lee has half-jokingly called *Crouching Tiger* "*Sense And Sensibility* with martial arts".)

While it's easy to admire Lee's elegant work, until recent years it's often been difficult to love or embrace it (especially his flatfooted attempt at an American Civil War epic, 1999's *Ride With The Devil*). His cool, distant, even decorous approach sometimes keeps his characters at arm's length and his dramatic action securely under glass. This is partly due to his muted, unerringly tasteful style, but is perhaps inevitable given his calm, even serene, fascination with repression, be it self-willed or socially enforced. Repression torments the abused-child-turned-explosive-CGI-freak in *Hulk* (2003), the secretive hedonists of 1970s American suburbia in *The Ice Storm* (1997) and the clandestine cowboy sweethearts of *Brokeback Mountain* (2005).

In *Crouching Tiger*, mere lingering gazes between the wistful would-be lovers (played by Chow Yun-Fat and Michelle Yeoh) insinuate the everlasting passion of soul mates. A loving homage to the kinetic delirium of the Chinese martial-arts epic in its Shaw Brothers heyday, *Crouching Tiger* won a rapturous response from audiences and critics alike, becoming the highest-grossing foreign-language film in Hollywood history. It was the first Ang Lee film to aspire beyond intelligent social satire and rueful reconciliation towards something like ecstasy, while *Brokeback Mountain* (for which Lee won his second best-director Oscar) is perhaps his warmest, most emotionally involving film to date – a weepie that comes by those tears honestly. JW

The Wedding Banquet (Xiyan) 1993, 106 min
cast Winston Gao, May Chin, Mitchell Lichtenstein, Sihung Lung, Ah-Leh Gua *cin* Jong Lin *m* Mader

Wai-Tung (Winston Gao), a gay Taiwanese transplant to Manhattan, tries to make his traditional mother happy from afar by marrying a Chinese immigrant (May Chin), but things get more complicated when his parents decide to fly in for the ceremony. Although a pivotal sexual indiscretion on the wedding night stretches viewer credulity slightly, this smooth situation comedy of well-meaning deception found an adoring audience and achieved the most profitable earnings-to-budget ratio of its year.

The Ice Storm 1997, 112 min
cast Kevin Kline, Sigourney Weaver, Joan Allen, Jamey Sheridan, Christina Ricci, Elijah Wood *cin* Frederick Elmes *m* Mychael Danna

Paying meticulous attention to 1970s costumery and interior design, Lee's adaptation of Rick Moody's novel unfolds over Thanksgiving weekend, 1973, in suburban Connecticut, where the well-off locals variously fill their days with adultery, kleptomania, wife-swapping and heavy petting in a rubber Nixon mask. With its fine calibration of the novel's shift from droll satire to gaping tragedy, the film conjures up a suitably chilly air of congenital alienation.

Crouching Tiger, Hidden Dragon (Wo hu zang long) 2000, 120 min
cast Chow Yun-Fat, Michelle Yeoh, Zang Ziyi, Chang Chen, Lung Sihung, Cheng Pei-Pei *cin* Peter Pau *m* Tan Dun

Based on the novel by Wang Du Lu, Lee's stately, beautifully performed recasting of the *wu xia pian* (chivalrous combat film) for the global blockbuster market hinges on the disappearance of the Green Destiny sword and the moral destiny of its thief, royal hellcat Jen (Zhang Ziyi). Although its narrative is slightly disjointed, the film triumphs in its thrilling yet ethereal fight sequences, borne aloft on invisible wires and overseen by master martial arts choreographer Yuen Wo-Ping.

Brokeback Mountain 2005, 134 min
cast Heath Ledger, Jake Gyllenhaal, Michelle Williams, Anne Hathaway, Randy Quaid, Linda Cardellini *cin* Rodrigo Prieto *m* Gustavo Santaolalla

Adapted from E. Annie Proulx's short story about two cowboys whose passion for each other extends across decades, marriages, kids, divorces, fearsome social censure and hundreds of miles, Lee's romantic epic is multi-layered, achingly subtle and stunningly photographed – in short, his finest film to date. Jake Gyllenhaal is touching as the puppyish Jack Twist, and Michelle Williams and Anne Hathaway are superb as the wives who look the other way, but it is Heath Ledger's clenched, wrenching performance as the taciturn Ennis Del Mar that's the soul of the film. A peerless heartbreaker, an instant classic and one of the best American films of the 2000s.

Jack Lee
UK, 1913–2002

Jack Lee directed a couple of classic wartime stories but the rest of his slender output is more ordinary. His early life was described in brother Laurie's classic *Cider With Rosie*. Jack joined the GPO Film Unit and edited Humphrey Jennings's *London Can Take It* (1940). Jennings's influence is evident in the realism that marks Lee's speedway story *Once A Jolly Swagman* (1948) and his POW film *The Wooden Horse* (1950). While *Turn The Key Softly* (1953) was a realistic exploration of the difficulties faced by women rehabilitating after serving prison sentences, Lee also made the melodrama *The Woman In The Hall* (1947) and *A Town Like Alice* (1956), a companion piece to *The Wooden Horse* in which a group of women POWs trek through the Asian jungle. But this was his last success. His final film, the wartime intelligence story *A Circle Of Deception* (1960), was marked by bitterness. Disillusioned, Lee emigrated and led the South Australian Film Board, helping to nurture that country's cinema. JR

The Wooden Horse 1950, 101 min

cast Leo Genn, David Tomlinson, Anthony Steel, David Greene, Peter Burton *cin* C. Pennington-Richards *m* Clifton Parker, Eric Rogers

The real-life story of a group of British POWs escaping from Stalag Luft III by tunnelling under an exercise horse. Eschewing big stars, Lee creates an ensemble piece, concentrating on the men's personalities rather than the action (there is very little overt drama, but there are plenty of tense situations). This understatement adds to the film's power and sense of reality, helping it define the genre of the British POW film.

Spike Lee

US, 1957–

Spike. Never has a director's name seemed so apt. Spiky is an adjective that describes not just the thorny issues that the director so regularly and controversially confronts, but the abrasive, bristling form that his narratives often take. And, as many journalists have discovered to their cost, spiky just about sums up Lee's prickly public persona too. No wonder he changed his name from Shelton. Studying film at New York University, he was almost expelled after cutting all the racist moments from D.W. Griffith's *The Birth Of A Nation* (1915) into a twenty-minute short, *The Answer*. However, he did graduate and garnered awards for his 1983 graduation short *Joe's Bed-Stuy Barbershop: We Cut Heads*. Oscillating between the twin poles of controversy and acclaim, Lee set a pattern at film school that he would doggedly follow throughout his filmmaking career.

Lee's low-budget debut feature, *She's Gotta Have It* (1986), is a sassy monochrome comedy about one woman and her three boyfriends. Its smart urbanity took black cinema out of the ghetto of blaxploitation and away from the cussing of male stars like Eddie Murphy. In many ways, *She's Gotta Have It* is atypical of the director's work, but *Do The Right Thing* (1989) is vintage Lee – provocative, virtuosic, incendiary and burning with rage and invention. Chronicling the events that lead up to a riot on a hot night in Brooklyn, Lee deliberately overturns melting-pot pieties. In a key scene, Mookie, the erstwhile peacekeeper, defiantly hurls a trash can through the window of his white employer's pizzeria, and ignites a race riot. The fact that Mookie was played by the director prompted some commentators to claim that he was inciting racial hatred, suggesting that his direction is unbalanced and one-sided. In fact, Lee is never in less than two minds. The raw energy of his work comes from the friction of opposing forces: pragmatic compromise and militant separatism, the teachings of Martin Luther King and the teachings of Malcolm X.

Spike Lee is undoubtedly the most famous African-American director in the world, and this may well have given him some messianic qualities. In addition to his feature films, he has raised consciousness about black history in a series of documentaries, the best of which, *4 Little Girls* (1997), was a forceful enquiry into a church bombing that killed four young black girls in Alabama in 1963. He also seems to have elected himself spokesperson for African-American culture; for example, publicly berating Quentin Tarantino for the excessive use of the word "nigga" in *Jackie Brown* (1997). However, the boot has occasionally been on the other foot. *Mo' Better Blues* (1990) drew bitter accusations of anti-Semitism for the stereotypical depiction of Jewish nightclub owners as grasping and exploitative.

Race relations always top Lee's agenda. *Get On The Bus* (1996) followed twenty black men on a coach trip to the Million Man March, and they all contribute to a typical cacophony of high-octane opinions. The scabrous *Jungle Fever* (1991) asked if interracial romance was truly possible – the answer came back in the negative. However, his greatest achievement may have been to get Hollywood to stump up the cash – the biggest budget given to a black director – to make a 1992 biopic about Malcolm X, a man still demonized by much of America. It was the picture Lee said he was born to make.

Lee's films are often remembered for their dazzling riffs and freestyle noodlings, such as the breathless monologue of hate in *25th Hour* (2002) or the disorienting change of lens in *Crooklyn* (1994), which gave his characters an elongated, hall-of-mirrors appearance. However, too much virtuosity can be a vice. A review of the TV satire *Bamboozled* (2000) about a blackface minstrel revival crystallizes critical opinion about much of the director's work: "it balances between brilliance and incoherence". However, working within the narrow confines of a strict genre for the heist movie *Inside Man* (2006) finally gave the ageing *enfant terrible* some much-needed discipline. The result was, arguably, one of the most satisfying movies Lee has ever made. Too many ideas and too much mercurial verve can often weigh a narrative down – as in the slack *Summer Of Sam* (1999), a scattershot mosaic of Brooklyn life in 1977 – and Lee's energies can sometimes be misdirected. His second feature, the frat comedy *School Daze* (1998) was described as an "arrogant, humourless, sexist mess", the sex worker comedy *Girl 6* (1996) was dubbed "simply muddled" and *She Hate Me* (2004), a satire about a black man who sires children for lesbians who start to fall for his masculine charms, was roundly condemned by gay activists as a sad male fantasy.

Not just a chronicler of race relations, Lee is also a formidable archivist of New York stories: the autobiographical *Crooklyn*; the plaintive crime thriller *Clockers* (1995) about drug dealing and black-on-black violence; and *25th Hour*, the first major film to engage with the events of 9/11. Lee again became involved in the political action in 2005 when Hurricane Katrina devastated New Orleans. Incensed by the government's slow response to the disaster, he made the TV mini-series *When The Levees Broke: A Requiem In Four Acts* (2006). LH

She's Gotta Have It 1986, 84 min
cast Tracy Camilla Jones, John Canada Terrell, Tommy Redmond Hicks, Spike Lee, Ray Dowell, Joie Lee *cin* Ernest Dickerson *m* Bill Lee

Like mid-career Woody Allen with added sex and sass, Lee energetically probes the hectic love life of New Yorker Nola Darling (the luminous Tracy Camilla Jones) who skilfully juggles three lovers at a time: Greer (John Canada Terrell), Jamie (Tommy Redmond Hicks) and Mars (Lee himself). A little rough around its low-budget edges, this remains the best of the director's often ill-advised, bullish forays into the delicate world of male-female relationships.

Do The Right Thing 1989, 120 min
cast Danny Aiello, Ossie Davis, Ruby Dee, Giancarlo Esposito, Spike Lee, Bill Nunn, John Turturro *cin* Ernest Dickerson *m* Bill Lee

Set over one hot day in a rundown area of Brooklyn, New York, *Do The Right Thing* sees an argument between a white pizzeria owner and his black customers gradually build into a catastrophic race riot. The film bristles with anger and bravura, but Lee dexterously and unexpectedly leavens the mix with humour, while the constraints of geography and chronology allow him to focus his energies in ways that he's never quite managed since.

Jungle Fever 1991, 132 min
cast Wesley Snipes, Anabella Sciorra, Spike Lee, Ossie Davis, Ruby Dee, Samuel L. Jackson *cin* Wynn Thomas *m* Stevie Wonder, Terence Blanchard

A wealthy, married architect (Wesley Snipes) and an office temp (Anabella Sciorra) feel the heat – or do they? In the gospel according to Lee, attraction between races is not physical but mythical, with white women buying into

the concept of the big black dick. Looking for Freudian significance, some critics have pointed to Lee's own family history and the fact that after his mother died, his father married a white woman.

Malcolm X 1992, 202 min
cast Denzel Washington, Angela Bassett, Albert Hall, Al Freeman Jr, Delroy Lindo, Spike Lee *cin* Ernest Dickerson, David Golia *m* Terence Blanchard

Denzel Washington humanizes but never sanctifies Malcolm X, the pimp who found religion in prison and became the charismatic leader of the Black Power movement. Beginning with footage of Rodney King's beating at the hands of Los Angeles police, the ensuing three and a half hours take the form of an old-fashioned biopic, which proved too straight for some critics. Despite these caveats, *Malcolm X* is a genuine epic with an impressive scope, sweep and cinematic élan.

25th Hour 2002, 135 min
cast Edward Norton, Philip Seymour Hoffman, Barry Pepper, Rosario Dawson, Anna Paquin *cin* Rodrigo Prieto *m* Terence Blanchard

Ostensibly about a drug dealer's last day of freedom before he goes to prison, this sprawling character study includes an extraordinary scene in a New York apartment overlooking the site of Ground Zero. The shot of the remaining rubble from the Twin Towers is both unearthly and banal, and Lee captures it in a mournful, crepuscular light.

Inside Man 2006, 129 min
cast Denzel Washington, Clive Owen, Christopher Plummer, Jodie Foster, Willem Dafoe *cin* Matthew Libatique *m* Terence Blanchard

Denzel Washington is archetypal cool cop Keith Frazier. With his career dented by a corruption charge and an engagement ring to buy, Frazier is only just resisting the urge to sweat when robbers hold up a Manhattan bank and take hostages. Caught between the demands of gentleman thief Dalton Russell (Clive Owen) and the machinations of Manhattan's amoral power brokers (Christopher

Tracking back: director Spike Lee and star Denzel Washington discuss a shot on the set of *Inside Man*.

Plummer and Jodie Foster), Frazier battles to save the hostages and his own career – without selling his soul. Lee could teach Steven "Ocean's 11" Soderbergh a thing or two about making a decent heist movie.

J. Lee Thompson
UK, 1914–2002

Science fiction, historical epic, slasher movie, light comedy, spy film, musical, Western, you name it – there doesn't seem to be a genre that J. Lee Thompson didn't dabble in. He was the sort of dependable, professional and solid craftsman – like Ronald Neame and Guy Hamilton – who was the workmanlike backbone of the British, and then American, film industry.

Lee Thompson's early career seemed to promise much more than journeyman anonymity. A West End playwright by the time he was just 20, and a scriptwriter before and after World War II, his first decade of films as a director were littered with international accolades. The Berlin Film Festival awarded him the FIPRESCI prize for *Woman In A Dressing Gown* (1957) and *Ice Cold In Alex* (1958), and gave a special prize to young actress Hayley Mills for *Tiger Bay* (1959). Starring Diana Dors in a career-best role as a killer on death row, *Yield To The Night* (1956) was nominated for the Palme d'Or at the Cannes Film Festival. As with his best work of the 1950s, Lee Thompson dexterously elided suspense with social realism.

These minor-key crime movies were ultimately overshadowed by the box-office glory of his war movies *Ice Cold In Alex* and *The Guns Of Navarone* (1961). After the success of *Navarone*, he moved to America to make *Cape Fear* (1962). Unfortunately, this intense revenge drama turned out to be the high point of his Hollywood career by some distance. With the exception of the underrated *Planet Of The Apes* sequels, it was a sad case of diminishing critical returns. These dipped exponentially with the nine films he made with Charles Bronson where, as with *10 To Midnight* (1984), the *Death Wish* star would sleepwalk through his role as a maverick cop or craggy vigilante. LH

Ice Cold In Alex 1958, 138 min, b/w
cast John Mills, Sylvia Syms, Anthony Quayle, Harry Andrews, Liam Redmond, Peter Arne, Diane Clare *cin* Gilbert Taylor *m* Leighton Lucas

After the fall of Tobruk, John Mills, Harry Andrews, Sylvia Sims and Diane Clare make a perilous journey by ambulance across the Libyan desert teeming with Nazi tanks, picking up South African officer Anthony Quayle along the way. Even though this is a tautly executed war movie, its scale is small and claustrophobic, its characterization delicately nuanced, and its pleasures minor key. Arguably, it's closer to the domestic spirit of the kitchen-sink genre than to a big-budget, explosive action movie.

The Guns Of Navarone 1961, 158 min
cast Gregory Peck, David Niven, Anthony Quinn, Stanley Baker, Anthony Quayle, James Darren, Irene Papas *cin* Oswald Morris *m* Dimitri Tiomkin

J. Lee Thompson replaced Alexander Mackendrick, who was sacked for working too slowly on this Alastair MacLean adaptation. While it would have been fascinating to see what a maverick like Mackendrick would have made of the gung-ho heroics, Lee Thompson seems more suited to the material's derring-do and righteous pluck. Gregory Peck, Stanley Baker and David Niven form part of a crack team of saboteurs who embark on a dangerous mission to destroy the titular guns on a Greek island. The result is big and bold, but not without the moments of doubt and ethical tension that characterized the very best of early Lee Thompson films.

Cape Fear 1962, 99 min, b/w
cast Gregory Peck, Robert Mitchum, Polly Bergen, Lori Martin, Martin Balsam, Jack Kruschen *cin* Samuel Leavitt *m* Bernard Herrmann

When Martin Scorsese remade *Cape Fear* in 1991, he muddied the waters of good and evil, but the original psychodrama is black and white, in both the moral and aesthetic sense. Robert Mitchum is genuinely unsettling as the psychotic ex-convict out for revenge on the decent lawyer (Gregory Peck) who put him away. This was arguably the last film to utilize effectively Lee Thompson's ability to build tension through atmosphere rather than pyrotechnics – precious qualities which evaporated later in a miasma of big budgets and dumb action.

Mike Leigh
UK, 1943–

More than any other post-war British filmmaker, Mike Leigh has nurtured Britain's hallowed tradition of television directors helming feature films of exceptional humour and insight.

The son of a Russian-Jewish doctor, Leigh was raised in a working-class suburb of Manchester. Becoming disillusioned with RADA's hidebound atmosphere, he joined the London Film and Television School. In 1973 he began writing and directing a series of dramas for the BBC, excavating the dynamics of a society weathering the social and psychological consequences of post-war consumerism. "Buttock-clenching" would become a critical commonplace in descriptions of Leigh's singular analysis of British manners and mores. His first feature, based on his own play and funded by actor Albert Finney, was *Bleak Moments* (1971), a portrait of social dysfunction in which a woman left alone with a mentally retarded sister attempts to work through her own repression. *Bleak Moments* foresaw the characteristic fate of Leigh protagonists sundered from themselves and others.

Leigh's improvisational method places characters and actors at the heart of the work. Descending from the revolution engendered by John Cassavetes, the *nouvelle vague*, public "happenings" and the Living Theatre, Leigh generates performances partly from the script but more significantly from the stuff of his actors' own experiences, instincts and intuitions. Working alone with Leigh, actors do not even discuss their roles with the other cast members before group work begins. The result is organic, resonating with the colours and textures of personal history, interpersonal dynamics and sociohistorical vibration. During the making of *Secrets And Lies* (1996) Leigh did not let any actor know more than their character would know, thereby building the film's cathartic birthday party out of completely individual perspectives. His films appear to be unfolding before our eyes.

After establishing his name with observant television plays such as *Nuts In May* (1976) and *Abigail's Party* (1977), *High Hopes* (1988), Leigh's first feature since *Bleak Moments*, made a positive impact at the New York Film Festival and contributed to his growing international reputation. The film marked the passage of quality drama, and the BBC audience that sustained it, to the arthouse where Leigh would become a major draw.

Following the lighter *Life Is Sweet* (1990), *Naked* (1993), Leigh's angriest riposte to British social decline, was a vision of England derived from *film noir*. David Thewlis's Manchester rapist's odyssey to London depicted wholesale disaffection in the splenetic wordplay and striking otherness of everyday Britons. By comparison, the Oscar- and Palme d'Or-winning *Secrets And Lies*, despite its funereal tone, had an affection for its familial potpourri that belied regular critical charges of condescension. Following a black woman's search for her birth mother in a London of grave post-Thatcherite antagonisms, *Secrets And Lies'* plea for social cohesion was released in the year before Princess Diana's death saw unprecedented public grieving and Britons endorsed a "New Labour" consensus in Tony Blair's landslide election victory.

After *Career Girls* (1997), *Topsy-Turvy* (1999) used the Merchant-Ivory costume tradition in a tribute to Gilbert and Sullivan that shifted Leigh's trademark preoccupation with revealing dynamics to a Victorian setting. Jim Broadbent, who portrayed Gilbert, also appeared in *Vera Drake* (2004), a powerful account of a woman in 1950s London who, unbeknown to her family, moonlights as an abortionist. Along with 2002's award-winning *All Or Nothing*, *Vera Drake* gained Leigh and star Imelda Staunton accolades and notices that once again confirmed Leigh's status as Britain's best chronicler of moral decline. RA

High Hopes 1988, 112 min
cast Philip Davis, Ruth Sheen, Edna Doré, Philip Jackson, Heather Tobias, Lesley Manville *cin* Roger Pratt *m* Andrew Dickson

Featuring Leigh regulars Philip Davis, Ruth Sheen and Lesley Manville, this thought-provoking, but apparently shapeless, portrait of life in London's King's Cross – an area ripe for gentrification in the 1980s, but still home to denizens with dialectical materialist complaints about the new order – demonstrated the director's ability to put his finger on Britain's sociopolitical pulse.

Life Is Sweet 1990, 103 min
cast Alison Steadman, Jim Broadbent, Claire Skinner, Jane Horrocks, Stephen Rea, Timothy Spall, David Thewlis *cin* Dick Pope *m* Rachel Portman

While Spall's clueless Aubrey seeks to bring *nouvelle cuisine* to north London, Broadbent's Andy renovates a dilapidated mobile snack bar. Meanwhile, Andy's daughters, a tomboy and an angry anorexic, try to cope with their suburban existence. With its relentlessly sunny optimism – embodied by Leigh's then-wife Steadman's housewife Wendy – Leigh measured the dream of Thatcherite enterprise against the grass-roots reality.

Secrets And Lies 1996, 142 min
cast Timothy Spall, Brenda Blethyn, Phyllis Logan, Marianne Jean-Baptiste, Claire Rushbrook, Elizabeth Berrington *cin* Dick Pope *m* Andrew Dickson

Like so many Mike Leigh creations before her, nervy middle-aged mother Cynthia (Brenda Blethyn) treads the thin line between pathos and cartoon caricature. The revelatory moment in a greasy spoon café in which she discovers that she has a grown-up daughter (Marianne Jean-Baptiste), who just happens to be black is one of the most genuinely affecting moments in Leigh's career.

Career Girls 1997, 87 min
cast Katrin Cartlidge, Lynda Steadman, Mark Benton, Kate Byers, Andy Serkis, Joe Tucker, Margo Stanley *cin* Dick Pope *m* Marianne Jean-Baptiste

Catching that 1990s British moment as university passed from being the province of the young to an option for the mature, this vignette, in which a pair of graduates reminisce about university life, laid bare the hopes and expectations of a generation. Played with warmth and acuity by Lynda Steadman and Leigh regular Katrin Cartlidge, it remains one of the undiscovered serendipities of recent British cinema.

All Or Nothing 2002, 128 min
cast Timothy Spall, Lesley Manville, Ruth Sheen, Marion Bailey, Timothy Bateson, Alison Garland, Edna Doré *cin* Dick Pope *m* Andrew Dickson

Timothy Spall's Phil is a London cab driver eking out a living and in a loveless marriage with Lesley Manville's supermarket cashier Penny. Elsewhere on the council estate where they live, single mum Maureen (Ruth Sheen) discovers that daughter Donna is pregnant by her abusive boyfriend. If Leigh's social surrealism felt more like a work in progress, *All Or Nothing* builds into melodrama of grave sociological acuity.

Vera Drake 2004, 125 min
cast Imelda Staunton, Phil Davis, Peter Wright, Alex Kelly, Daniel Mays, Adrian Scarborough, Heather Craney *cin* Dick Pope *m* Andrew Dickson

Offering a measured performance by Imelda Staunton and a carefully observed portrait of its time, this account of a well-meaning 1950s abortionist's progress from quiet pilgrim to social pariah powerfully evokes the middle-class post-war consensus which Leigh and his generation did their best to expose.

Mitchell Leisen

US, 1898–1972

If Mitchell Leisen has received too little critical attention it is the fault of the auteur theory – deftly orchestrating the svelte flow of pre-war studio comedies, he made Paramount pictures not Leisen movies, and his lasting reputation has suffered for his efforts.

Architectural training led Leisen to designing advertising art at the *Chicago Tribune*. He entered the film industry in 1919 as a costume designer, then art director, working with Cecil B. DeMille, Allan Dwan and Raoul Walsh at Paramount. In 1933 he made director, and the journeyman rapidly became known for methodical professionalism and a reputation for sympathetic direction of actresses second only to George Cukor's. *Death Takes A Holiday* (1934) was sardonic and scrupulous, as Fredric March's Death falls for Evelyn Venable's morbid Grazia amid Italianate gardens and melancholy pools. Less obviously Paramount-DeMille in style was *Hands Across The Table* (1935), in which Carole Lombard's manicurist spars with Fred MacMurray's impoverished playboy.

Billy Wilder was dissatisfied with Leisen's cavalier attitude towards his scripts for the marvellous *Midnight* (1939) and the Claudette Colbert newsgal yarn *Arise, My Love* (1940), considering Leisen's work to be more concerned with style than content. *Swing High, Swing Low* (1937) is an essay in orchestration, Leisen breezily accommodating the interaction of MacMurray's feckless musician and Lombard's impeccable comic timing. Leisen shepherded Barbara Stanwyck from screwball comedy to fashionable melodrama in *Remember The Night* (1941) and *No Man Of Her Own* (1950) with the ease of one never given to unnecessary flab nor flourish. It seems appropriate that, with the studios' post-war decline and his brand of elegant comedy going out of style, Leisen's career gracefully devolved to television. RA

Easy Living 1937, 91 min, b/w

cast Jean Arthur, Edward Arnold, Ray Milland, Franklin Pangborn, William Demarest, Luis Alberni *cin* Ted Tetzlaff *m* Boris Morros

In this Depression-era fairy tale a fur coat lands on working girl Jean Arthur's head, and she winds up a kept woman in a fabulous hotel suite. But just so she doesn't lose her sense of honour, she meets Ray Milland's penniless Arthur... Written with Preston Sturges's feeling for slapstick in mind, but directed with Leisen's characteristic feeling for *mise en scène* and sumptuous interiors, this is a classic of its kind.

Midnight 1939, 94 min, b/w

cast Claudette Colbert, Don Ameche, John Barrymore, Mary Astor, Francis Lederer, Hedda Hopper *cin* Charles Lang Jr *m* Frederick Hollander

If there is anything in critic Jonathan Rosenbaum's notion of global synchronicity, Leisen offers further evidence. Appearing the same year as Jean Renoir's *La règle du jeu*, and bearing an uncanny resemblance to that depiction of the pre-war social set on the brink, Leisen's tale of Colbert's gold-digger prowling for a fortune amid Parisian counts and faux cab drivers perhaps lacks the vision of the Renoir film but has all the manners and mores.

Claude Lelouch

France, 1937–

Claude Lelouch introduced the world to French cinema with the Sunday-supplement gloss of *Un homme et une femme* (*A Man And A Woman*, 1966), and won an Oscar for the screenplay.

The son of a Jewish confectioner of Algerian *pied-noir* stock, Lelouch fell in love with film at an early age. At 13 he won a prize at the Cannes Amateur Film Festival with his short *Le mal du siècle* (1950). In 1956 he entered the industry, making shorts and commercials. Between 1957 and 1960 he made shorts for the French army. His first feature – *Le propre de l'homme* (*The Right Of Man*, 1960) – was financed by his family, but it was *Un homme et une femme* that made Lelouch a household name.

Quickly becoming associated with a genre of star-laden contemporary romanticism, symbolized by telephoto flattening and watery Muzak, Lelouch drew as much criticism for degrading emotional experience as acclaim for his modern sensibility. Starring Annie Girardot and Yves Montand, *Vivre pour vivre* (*Live For Life*, 1968) capitalized on this style, as did *La vie, l'amour, la mort* (*Life, Love, Death*, 1969). *La bonne année* (*Happy New Year*, 1973) was a thriller set on the Côte d'Azur starring Lino Ventura. By revisiting the two characters from his first international success in *Un homme et une femme: Vingt ans déjà* (*A Man And A Woman: Twenty Years Later*, 1986) he fed the perception outside of France of his being a one-hit wonder.

The Jean-Paul Belmondo comeback *Les misérables* (1995) made a structural virtue of nostalgia and contributed to the improving international image of this arch-arthouse-for-export filmmaker. In his home country, he has long been respected and remains prolific, and his more recent preoccupation with chance and coincidence has been evident in films such as *Hasards ou coïncidences* (*Chance Or Coincidence*, 1998) and *And Now... Ladies And Gentlemen* (2002), which both starred his partner Alessandra Martines. Lelouch also contributed episodes to the "France" section of the portmanteau project *11'09"01* (2002). RA

Un homme et une femme (A Man And A Woman) 1966, 102 min

cast Anouk Aimée, Jean-Louis Trintignant, Pierre Barouh, Valérie Lagrange, Simone Paris, Paul le Person *cin* Claude Lelouch *m* Francis Lai

Anouk Aimée and Jean-Louis Trintignant conduct an intense, roller-coaster love affair against the backdrop of a sumptuous Paris, all accompanied by a prodigious amount of modernist movie trickery. The amorous abandon, coated in Francis Lai's irresistible theme, influenced many films of the period, from Bo Widerberg's *Elvira Madigan* to George Roy Hill's *Butch Cassidy And The Sundance Kid*.

Kasi Lemmons

US, 1964–

Kasi Lemmons served three years on the long-running soap *As The World Turns* in the late 1980s. She was Jodie Foster's best friend in *The Silence Of The Lambs* (1991) and blown to bits in John Woo's *Hard Target* (1993). But movie roles for African-American women were thin on the ground. She had been to film school, and in the early 1990s wrote a screenplay. The script was well received, but studios weren't falling over themselves to make an all-African-American arthouse film, and it took her four years to find the backing that enabled her to direct it too. When *Eve's Bayou* finally hit the screen in 1997 it became one of the most successful indie releases of the year.

It was, however, four years before Lemmons was able to make another film. *The Caveman's Valentine* (aka *The Sign Of The Killer*, 2001) was an unexpected follow-up, although it reunited her with actor Samuel L. Jackson, this time playing a paranoid New York hermit/pianist/detective, Romulus Ledbetter – a larger-than-life character stranded in a disappointingly ho-hum whodunnit. Her third feature, *Talk To Me* (2007), is a funky portrait of radical 1960s DJ "Petey" Greene. TC

Eve's Bayou 1997, 108 min

cast Samuel L. Jackson, Lynn Whitfield, Jurnee Smollett, Meagan Good, Debbi Morgan *cin* Amy Vincent *m* Terence Blanchard

A deceptively languid coming-of-age story set in Louisiana back in the 1950s, the film is a family melodrama with some of Tennessee Williams's fragrantly tragic sensibility: 10-year-old Eve (Smollett) vies with her older sister Cisely (Good) and their mother Roz (Whitfield) for the perfect love of her father Louis Batiste (Jackson), but Louis' careless charm keeps leading him astray. The movie echoes with the resonance of the past. Memories fold into the present tense, some true, some false.

Paul Leni

Germany, 1885–1929

Despite being crowned by an expert in German expressionism, Siegfried Kracauer, as "one of the outstanding film directors of the post-World War I era", Paul Leni's status as a master of psychological horror remains sadly obscured.

From Robert Wiene's *The Cabinet Of Dr Caligari* (1919) onwards, set design was a key, defining component of German expressionism, so it's not surprising that a set designer such as Leni (who trained with Max Reinhardt's theatre company) would become one of the leading lights of the movement. Leni explicitly understood the psychological impact of scenery, that decor was not merely decoration but acted as a mental landscape for both characters and audience. In the gospel according to Leni, the camera was an X-ray machine, expressing "the reality of an inner event". Although his debut was *Backstairs* (1921), *Waxworks* (1924) is, in effect, the first Paul Leni movie proper. It proved so globally successful that he was headhunted by Universal Studios.

Leni opened his Hollywood account with a *locus classicus* of horror iconoclasm, *The Cat And The Canary* (1927). He followed this archetypal haunted-house movie with three more films that skilfully elided Hollywood genre and European arthouse: *The Chinese Parrot* (1927), the classic Victor Hugo adaptation *The Man Who Laughs* (1928) and *The Last Warning* (1929). Even though the latter was punctuated by bursts of speech, we'll never know how this most visual of directors would have fared in the early years of the talkies, when sound prevailed over vision. For, like his compatriot and fellow master of the visual arts F.W. Murnau, Leni died far too young. LH

Waxworks (Das Wachsfigurenkabinett) 1924, 83 min, b/w

cast William Dieterle, Emil Jannings, Conrad Veidt, Werner Krauss, Olga Belajeff *cin* Helmar Lersky

A portmanteau movie in which a writer is hired to tell the stories of three stars of a waxwork museum – Jack the Ripper, Harun al Raschid and Ivan the Terrible. The breathtaking set designs – especially in the Arabian section – are the real attraction. They are genuinely surreal in their Gaudi-like decor, and not dissimilar to the dream sequences in Hitchcock's *Spellbound* made twenty years later.

Sergio Leone

Italy, 1929–89

"I was born in the cinema", Sergio Leone used to say – a rhetorical flourish which wasn't to be understood as literal truth, but as Fordian legend. His father was a filmmaker and his mother an actress from the silent era which was about to vanish with Sergio's arrival. The young Sergio was a regular visitor at the Cinecittà film studios, and worked his way from runner to assistant director (working on such Hollywood biblical epics as *Quo Vadis?*, 1951, *Ben-Hur*, 1959, and *Sodom And Gomorrah*, 1963,

Ennio Morricone: a fistful of music

Probably the most prolific cinema composer ever, Morricone has scored some 500 films and television programmes as well as writing numerous works of classical music, such as *Voci di silenzio*, his response to 9/11. His music is marked by a dizzying range of styles, a fondness for unusual instruments and an ingenious use of manipulated natural sounds informed by *musique concrète*.

Morricone completed a four-year conservatory harmony course in six months while working as a professional trumpeter before going on to work as a pop producer, for which he used a pseudonym. (Occasionally credited as Dan Savio or Leo Nichols, Morricone is not, as some have claimed, Bruno Nicolai and Nicolai Piovani, who are composer/conductors in their own right.) His many songs include "Here's To You", taken from the movie *Sacco And Vanzete* (1971), which became a hit for Joan Baez. Having started his film career as an arranger-conductor and uncredited co-writer for Mario Nascimbene, his first solo credit was for Luciano Salce's *The Fascist* (1961). His international break came with Sergio Leone's *A Fistful Of Dollars* (1964), and he continued to work with Leone until his last film, *Once Upon A Time In America* (1983), the score for which is often surprisingly gentle, given its setting among the New York Mafiosi. However, this association has meant that he will probably always be associated with spaghetti Westerns – a term he considers derogatory – and he has often expressed annoyance that these scores have overshadowed the rest of his work.

It's an understandable complaint, notwithstanding the power of his scores for Leone. For instance, Morricone demonstrated a real affinity for the work of Giuseppe Tornatore in his beautifully complementary scores for *Cinema Paradiso* (1989) and *Malèna* (2000), a gentle coming-of-age drama. He also worked with politically committed directors such as Bernardo Bertolucci – on *Before The Revolution* (1964) and *The Tragedy Of A Ridiculous Man* (1981) – and Pier Paolo Pasolini (*Theorem*, 1966). For the controversial *The Battle Of Algiers* (1965), Morricone composed a percussive score of startling violence and adapted a gently falling theme whistled by the film's director, Gillo Pontecorvo.

In the lurid Italian *giallo* movies (named after the yellow covers of Italian translations of pulp fiction novels) Morricone enjoyed living up to the outrageousness of the visuals with his music. Discordant nursery music or psychedelic Hammond organs may now seem clichéd but in such *Grand Guignol* films as Dario Argento's *The Bird With The Crystal Plumage* (1970) and *Four Flies On Grey Velvet* (1971) the music still stands up. Argento's relationship with Morricone was an artistically profitable one, and was revived 35 years later for the movies *The Stendhal Syndrome* (1996) and *The Phantom Of The Opera* (1998). Morricone is also an admirer of the movies and film scores of John Carpenter; rather perversely, the score Morricone wrote for their only collaboration, *The Thing* (1982), sounds like one of Carpenter's own.

Despite initial wariness, Morricone worked increasingly in Hollywood and wrote impressive scores for Roland Joffé's *The Mission* (1986), Roman Polanski's *Frantic* (1988), Franco Zeffirelli's *Hamlet* (1990) and Brian De Palma's *The Untouchables* (1987), *Casualties Of War* (1988) and *Mission To Mars* (2000). He has been Oscar-nominated five times, and finally received a lifetime achievement statuette in 2007. But it is not just the movie industry that owes him a debt. He was in many ways one of the most influential composers of the twentieth century, for his sound-world and epic motifs have inspired jazz musicians, hip-hop and techno producers and classical composers alike. JR

---

which were all shot in Rome). Leone thus epitomizes second-generation cinema – in a sense, he was the first of the movie brats (or, as Jean Baudrillard preferred, "the first postmodernist filmmaker") because his films were primarily "about" other films.

Leone probably fancied himself as more of a classicist: he was an admirer of John Ford and David Lean (his intellectual pretensions were indeed pretence). He believed his movies to be in the great tradition of the Hollywood stories he grew up with. A Roman, he instinctively understood these films in mythic terms that contemporary America had yet to wake up to. His first film, *The Colossus Of Rhodes* (1961), was an undistinguished sword-and-sandals epic starring Rory Calhoun. With the Italian film industry in the doldrums, Leone latched on to the trend for what the Americans dubbed "spaghetti

Westerns" – cheap European cowboy movies shot in Spain primarily for domestic consumption.

It is unfortunate that *Variety* had already coined the term "horse opera", because that's a more apposite description of what Leone was up to. Crude in comparison with his later work, *A Fistful Of Dollars* (1964) nevertheless served notice of a prodigious talent capable of reinventing a genre grown stale from overfamiliarity. In the US, Westerns had been thoroughly domesticated by the small screen. Leone imported a US TV star (Clint Eastwood, from *Rawhide*) but brought a brazen cynicism to a story lifted wholesale from Akira Kurosawa's samurai classic *Yojimbo* (1961): a mercenary gunfighter plays rival clans against each other and stands back as the town destroys itself. A smash hit across Europe, *A Fistful Of Dollars* immediately spawned a sequel,

Spaghetti madness: the bad Lee Van Cleef has the ugly Eli Wallach in his sights, while the good Clint Eastwood looks on.

For A Few Dollars More (1965). Clint Eastwood is in essentially the same role (though he is not "the man with no name", as the marketing myth suggests), and Lee Van Cleef and Gian Maria Volonté essay character types Leone would explore more completely in his next film, *The Good, The Bad And The Ugly* (1966).

By now the flamboyant Leone style was exerting itself, although each film marks a step up in ambition and scale, and the tempo becomes ever more stately. A master of widescreen Techniscope composition, he brought depth and movement to his landscapes with elegant crane shots and brazen pans; he also evinced a startling propensity for juxtaposing wide shots with ultra-tight close-ups. Ennio Morricone's eclectic and innovative scores were also integral to the films' impact – flippant and ironic, but with an undertow of nostalgia and regret. As his budgets grew, Leone came to commission Morricone's scores first, and choreographed his actors to the music. Since Leone used a technique of post-synchronized sound, he was able to play Morricone's score on the set of *Once Upon A Time In The West* (1968) to fix the mood.

Much derided by contemporary US critics for their supposed "violence" (Pauline Kael branded them "fascist"), the Leone Westerns show little love for the land (which is mostly desert scrub) and have no faith in human decency. His conception of the laconic and all but invulnerable antihero propagated legions of action supermen from Dirty Harry through to the Terminator. His interest in women was negligible. Yet, for all that, Leone's cynicism is clearly meant as a corrective to the naïve pioneer romanticism espoused by Hollywood; his frontiersmen may be grubby mercenaries, but they are not without moral shading, and there is a bon viveur's delight in Eli Wallach's resourceful rogue Tuco in *The Good, The Bad And The Ugly*. Far from fascist, the politics in the *Once Upon A Time* films (and the flawed but fascinating *A Fistful Of Dynamite*, 1971, really belongs with them) are quasi-Marxist; the profit motive spurs the plots, but provides little solace in the long run.

Cut by twenty minutes on its US release, *Once Upon A Time In The West* under-performed at the box office – although it now stands as one of the key films in the genre – and Leone appeared to lose his confidence. But when it finally emerged after more than a decade of prevarication, *Once Upon A Time In America* (1983) proved worth the wait. Again, it was misunderstood in the country that inspired the film, and the studio butchered it. But in its unabridged form this is a magnificent film, the director's masterpiece. TC

The Good, The Bad And The Ugly (Il buono, il brutto, il cattivo) 1966, 180 min
cast Clint Eastwood, Eli Wallach, Lee Van Cleef, Aldo Giuffrè, Mario Brega, Luigi Pistilli *cin* Tonino Delli Colli *m* Ennio Morricone

The third and best of the so-called "Dollars" trilogy Leone made with Clint Eastwood expands on and amplifies character types, themes and situations from the earlier pictures. The American Civil War setting throws the mercenaries' self-interest into sharp relief, the film's rambunctious black comedy notwithstanding. Structured as a series of sly reversals, it raises one-upmanship to an art form, culminating in the stunning ten-minute three-way duel in the middle of a huge cemetery designed to look like a Greek amphitheatre.

Once Upon A Time In The West (C'era una volta il West) 1968, 165 min
cast Henry Fonda, Claudia Cardinale, Jason Robards, Charles Bronson, Frank Wolff, Gabriele Ferzetti *cin* Tonino Delli Colli *m* Ennio Morricone

Casting iconic blue-eyed boy Henry Fonda as the bad guy, Leone simultaneously pays homage to a fistful of Westerns and subverts them. With story credits for Bernardo Bertolucci and Dario Argento, both young turks at the time, this is a foundation myth writ large, one of the most imposing CinemaScope films ever made. It's also a real slow burn: Leone lays it out and bides his time, yet it's not a minute too long.

A Fistful Of Dynamite (Giù la testa) 1971, 157 min
cast Rod Steiger, James Coburn, Romolo Valli, Maria Monti, Rik Battaglia *cin* Giuseppe Ruzzolini *m* Ennio Morricone

Also known as *Duck, You Sucker!* and *Once Upon A Time… The Revolution*, this rubs an incendiary IRA romantic, John (James Coburn), up against a pragmatic Mexican peasant, Juan (Rod Steiger), and stands back as sparks fly. Leone initially didn't want to direct it himself (Peckinpah and Bogdanovich were talked about) but evidently threw himself into the project, which he co-wrote with Sergio Donati and Luciano Vincenzoni. It's a grand swamp of a movie, over-the-top but also unexpectedly plangent.

Once Upon A Time In America 1983, 229 min
cast Robert De Niro, James Woods, Elizabeth McGovern, Treat Williams, Tuesday Weld, Burt Young *cin* Tonino Delli Colli *m* Ennio Morricone

It's hard to think of a more barbarous studio hatchet job than the chronological 139-minute US cut, so intrinsic are the flashbacks to Leone's meditation on time, memory and identity. Spanning 45 years, from the Roaring Twenties to 1968, the film chronicles the friendship of two gangsters, Noodles (Robert De Niro) and Max (James Woods). Mature and melancholy, it is a story of disillusionment and the American Dream: rags to untold riches… ending up in the back of a garbage truck.

Robert Lepage
Canada, 1957–

Film fans first got a glimpse of Robert Lepage as one of the actors staging a revisionist interpretation of a Passion play in Denys Arcand's *Jesus Of Montreal* (1989). The casting was appropriate. Lepage was a rising star on the Montreal theatre scene, and over the next decade he became internationally famous for his avant-garde mixed-media productions, which he devised, wrote, directed and (often) starred in. The dazzling invention and ingenuity of the stage work is still there in Lepage's films (five to date, starting with *The Confessional* in 1995), but it sometimes feels less organic and more contrived. His later films included the thriller *The Polygraph* (1996), the Japanese-set Québécois separatist satire *Nô* (1998) and *Possible Worlds* (2000), a cerebral film touching on the idea of parallel lives. Like his alter ego Philippe in *The Far Side Of The Moon* (2003) Lepage has "original technique and unusual ideas", but the dense layering of philosophical conceit – combined with his penchant for visual sleight of hand – can come across as tricksy and pretentious. Even so, one fancies that if Lepage hailed from a more fashionable cinematic hotspot (East Asia for example) his critical standing would be a good deal higher. TC

The Confessional 1995, 100 min
cast Lothaire Bluteau, Patrick Goyette, Jean-Louis Millette, Kristin Scott Thomas, Ron Burrage *cin* Alain Dostie *m* Sacha Puttnam

Marc and his brother Pierre (Bluteau and Goyette) meet in Quebec City, 1989, on the occasion of their father's funeral, and start digging into the past to resolve nagging questions about their mother and their true identity. Lepage's highly assured first feature is arguably his most satisfying. A clever flashback structure revolves around (and incorporates) Alfred Hitchcock's 1953 movie *I Confess*, which was shot in the same city.

Mervyn LeRoy
US, 1900–87

During his long tenure at Warner Bros (interrupted by a few years at MGM coinciding with World War II) Mervyn LeRoy turned his hand to most of the popular genres, and churned out plenty of moneymakers too. Jack Warner reckoned he was "a great director with a small 'g'", but others (Bertrand Tavernier and J.P. Coursodon in their book *50 ans de cinéma américain*) have characterized his style as "uniformly anonymous". For his part, LeRoy liked to say "good stories make good movies" and left it at that.

After his family was impoverished by the San Francisco earthquake of 1906, LeRoy entered vaudeville at a young age. He followed his cousin Jesse L. Lasky to Hollywood, and worked his way up to director just as the silent era was coming to an end. The gangster movie *Little Caesar* (1931) is historically important as its success spawned a wave of imitators, but aside from Edward G. Robinson's still venomous performance the film has dated badly (compare, for instance, William Wellman's *The Public Enemy*, 1931, and Howard Hawks's *Scarface*, 1932).

It is debatable how much credit LeRoy deserves for the astringent social criticism which distinguishes his best films, *I Am A Fugitive From A Chain Gang* (1932) and *They Won't Forget* (1937), as the "social conscience" picture was something of an in-house speciality, but there is no question that these are two of the most influential examples, and among the most progressive Hollywood films of the Golden Age. At the other end of the spectrum, LeRoy directed the influential musical *Gold Diggers Of 1933* (1933), which introduced social conscience elements to Busby Berkeley routines.

During his MGM period LeRoy oversaw the production of *The Wizard Of Oz* (1939), but went back to directing in part because that film failed to meet commercial expectations. He did three melodramas with Greer Garson (including the very popular *Random Harvest*, 1942), the wartime romance *Waterloo Bridge* (1940) with Vivien Leigh, and *Little Women* (1949) with June Allyson, Elizabeth Taylor, Janet Leigh and Margaret O'Brien. As the studio system went into decline, LeRoy continued to diversify, albeit sticking to literary and stage adaptations, helming the widescreen epic *Quo Vadis?* (1951), the prepubescent horror *The Bad Seed* (1956) and the musical *Gypsy* (1962) among many others. TC

Little Caesar 1931, 79 min, b/w

cast Edward G. Robinson, Douglas Fairbanks Jr, Glenda Farrell, Stanley Fields, Sidney Blackmer *cin* Tony Gaudio

"Mudder of Mercy – is this the end of Rico?" This seminal gangster movie was really just the beginning. It made Robinson a star and established a hard-hitting vernacular style of contemporary crime drama which became synonymous with Warner Bros. Adapted from a novel by W.R. Burnett, the film is loosely based on the life of Al Capone. It is dated by its reliance on static set-ups, an imposition of the early sound recording techniques.

I Am A Fugitive From A Chain Gang 1932, 90 min, b/w

cast Paul Muni, Glenda Farrell, Helen Vinson, Preston Foster, Edward Ellis, Allen Jenkins *cin* Sol Polito *m* Leo F. Forbstein

Based on Robert E. Burns's autobiography, this stark, lean film remains a shocking indictment of penal servitude in the deep South, where life on the chain gang consisted of slave labour augmented with physical and mental torture. The film also comments on the relationship between unemployment and crime, recidivism, political corruption, the shabby treatment of returning World War I veterans, and the north/south divide. The pessimistic conclusion is particularly memorable, although it's mitigated somewhat by the film's own reformist zeal.

Richard Lester

US, 1932–

Arriving in Britain in his early twenties, Richard Lester had the good fortune to catch the eye of Peter Sellers, who was looking for a collaborator to bring the manic radio hit *The Goon Show* to television.

The result, *A Show Called Fred* (1956) united Lester with Peter Sellers and Spike Milligan. It was followed by *The Running, Jumping And Standing Still Film* (1959), an eleven-minute slapstick short which now looks like the missing link between Buster Keaton and Monty Python, and likely landed him *A Hard Day's Night* (1964) at the fever pitch of Beatlemania.

The Knack… And How To Get It and *Help!* (both 1965) made Lester synonymous with Swinging London. Although he quickly abandoned modish New Wave "lite" camera trickery (jump cuts, rapid zooms and hand-held camera), he remained associated with Spike Milligan and the anarchic British humour of the period, most notably with the grimly absurdist post-apocalypse of *The Bed-Sitting Room* (1969).

Like his only contemporary US film of the period, *Petulia* (1968), *The Bed-Sitting Room* was a commercial failure, and it was four years before Lester made another feature. He never seemed as *au courant* thereafter. In the 1970s he brought an earthy, unsentimental humour to a series of entertaining historical escapades, including *The Three Musketeers* (1973), its companion piece *The Four Musketeers* (1974), *Royal Flash* (1975), and the autumnal *Robin And Marian* (1976). Taking over *Superman II* (1980) from Richard Donner, Lester injected a welcome sense of fun and even a dash of romance.

If everything he made up to that point is worth a look, the same cannot be said of his last three narrative features. He pretty much retired from filmmaking after his friend Roy Kinnear died falling from a horse during the shooting of *The Return Of The Musketeers* in 1989. Director Steven Soderbergh published a book of interviews with Lester, *Getting Away With It*, in 1999. TC

A Hard Day's Night 1964, 87 min, b/w

cast The Beatles, Wilfred Brambell, Norman Rossington, John Junkin, Victor Spinetti, Anna Quayle *cin* Gilbert Taylor *m* John Lennon, Paul McCartney

The New Wave goes pop in Lester's irresistibly optimistic Beatles movie (their first and his third feature). Cranking up "a day in the life" hand-held *vérité* with slapstick surrealism, Marx Brothers-style wordplay, and of course the band's liberating rock'n'roll, Lester captures the giddy excitement, the now-ness of the moment. Enormously influential if not entirely original, the film's jump-cut aesthetic anticipated MTV by two decades.

Petulia 1968, 105 min

cast Julie Christie, George C. Scott, Richard Chamberlain, Arthur Hill, Shirley Knight, Pippa Scott *cin* Nicolas Roeg *m* John Barry

Too little seen, Lester's artiest picture is a fascinating outsider's view of late-1960s America. Julie Christie is the kooky socialite with an abusive husband and her sights set on divorced surgeon George C. Scott – who has problems of his own. The cut-up storytelling technique is strikingly similar to Roeg's subsequent work, though he's only credited as cinematographer here. For those lucky enough to see it, *Petulia* endures, not simply as a time capsule, but as a vivid creative response to those times.

Rock'n'roll at the movies

The history of rock'n'roll at the movies begins in 1955. As Bill Haley sang "Rock Around the Clock" over the opening titles of *Blackboard Jungle*, fans everywhere pulled out pocket knives and began slashing cinema seats. It's been a love-hate relationship ever since. The following year, Frank Tashlin shoehorned performances by Little Richard, Gene Vincent, The Platters, Fats Domino, and Eddie Cochran into his Jayne Mansfield send-up, *The Girl Can't Help It*, and Elvis Presley made his screen debut as Clint Reno in *Love Me Tender*. The Elvis movies became a regular money-spinner, but there are many Presley fans who remain unimpressed by Hollywood's watering down of Presley's dynamic raw sex appeal in the series of anodyne light comedies they yoked to him.

It wasn't until Richard Lester got his turn behind the camera that the movies truly caught up with pop music's spirit of youthful rebellion. Inspired by the *nouvelle vague* and the anarchic comedy of The Goons, the ex-pat American Lester first pepped up the British jazz scene in *It's Trad, Dad!* (1962), which featured cameos by Chubby Checker, Gene Vincent and Gary U.S. Bonds among the 25 numbers it crammed into 73 minutes. But that was just a dress rehearsal for *A Hard's Day's Night* (1964), a portrait of the Fab Four shot when Beatlemania was just reaching its pitch. With its slapstick surrealism and general air of off-the-cuff larkiness, the movie was absolutely in sync with its stars, and set a benchmark against which all future band movies would be judged. Not surprisingly, Lester was also persuaded to direct the Beatles' second, less convivial effort, *Help!* (1965).

As the rock'n'roll generation came of age there was increased traffic between pop and cinema. Movies got hipper, or tried to, and hooking on to rock was a preferred route for reaching the youth. D.A. Pennebaker was in the right place at the right time to catch Dylan going electric in the seminal documentary *Don't Look Back* (1967), and the Maysles brothers were in the right place at the wrong time to watch the end of peace and love at Altamont in the Rolling Stones' documentary *Gimme Shelter* (1970).

Incidentally, the same year Mick Jagger became one of the first rock stars to enhance his street cred with a movie when he starred in Donald Cammell and Nicolas Roeg's psychedelic gangster flick *Performance* (1970). David Bowie followed in his footsteps, playing an alien – entirely convincingly – in Roeg's *The Man Who Fell to Earth* (1976). The year 1970 also saw the release of the definitive concert movie, *Woodstock*, featuring Jimi Hendrix, The Who, Janis Joplin and others. Among its team of editors was the fledgling director Martin Scorsese, who was also arguably the first filmmaker to really tie rock music to the narrative rhythm of his movies. That marriage produced some landmark movies in the late 1960s and throughout the 1970s: *Easy Rider* (Dennis Hopper, 1969); *Mean Streets* (Scorsese, 1973); *American Graffiti* (George Lucas, 1973); and *Apocalypse Now* (Francis Ford Coppola, 1979). In the 1980s, a more corporate ethos dominated, and after the success of *Saturday Night Fever* (John Badham, 1977) and *Grease* (Randal Kleiser, 1978) pop soundtracks became an integral part of the financial equation for most youth-oriented films, to increasingly bland effect. Even so, the rock musical per se never took off as a genre, despite such isolated commercial successes as *Fame* (Alan Parker, 1980) and, more recently, *Moulin Rouge!* (Baz Luhrmann, 2001).

By the early 1980s rock had its own visual language and its own medium, Music Television (MTV), which is often blamed for the abbreviated shot-lengths of contemporary American cinema. But MTV did eventually produce its own crop of visionaries, among them Spike Jonze (*Being John Malkovich*, 1999), Michel Gondry (*The Science Of Sleep*, 2006) and Jonathan Glazer (*Birth*, 2004). Meanwhile gifted filmmakers continue to riff off the emotional epiphanies imparted in song to take their pictures to another level. Rock and pop songs are as fundamental to the films of Wes Anderson, Wong Kar-Wai and Paul Thomas Anderson as symphonic scores were to an earlier generation. Quentin Tarantino has taken the whole concept to another level with his mix score for the *Kill Bill* films (2003 and 2004), which even self-consciously used pop music already used in other films; and it's rare indeed to find a movie actor who doesn't secretly aspire to be a rock'n'roll star. TC

Barry Levinson
US, 1942–

There are at least two Barry Levinsons. One is a prolific, slick but highly erratic studio hack who made it onto the A-list with back-to-back hits *Good Morning, Vietnam* (1987) and *Rain Man* (1988); the other is a personal filmmaker who has chronicled his family's experience of America in the twentieth century over the course of four warm, witty pictures, all set in his hometown, Baltimore.

Levinson was the son of a businessman who started the city's first discount warehouse (he drew on this for the first-generation epic *Avalon*, 1990). A child in the 1950s (*Liberty Heights*, 1999), he reached maturity in the early 1960s (*Diner*, 1982) and paid his way through college by door-to-door selling (*Tin*

Men, 1987) and working at a car dealership (*Tin Men* – like *Rain Man* – begins in a car showroom). There's an ongoing historical project here, summed up in the sentiments of the grandfather at the end of *Avalon*: "If I knew things would no longer be, I would have tried to remember better."

The Baltimore films, which will likely prove his legacy, are characterized by affectionate period detailing, sympathetic performances, comic exasperation at the oncoming rush of girls and cars, and an underlying sadness at the impermanence of things. TV is a Levinson *bête noir* – although, ironically, he has produced some outstanding TV shows (notably the Baltimore cop show *Homicide: Life On The Street*, 1993), and got his break as a TV comedy writer for Carol Burnett and Marty Feldman. Of his more recent film projects, which have largely leaned towards comedy, *Wag The Dog* (1997) is probably the pick over *Man Of The Year* (2006), but both dealt satirically with presidential politics and the US media. TC

Diner 1982, 110 min

cast Steve Guttenberg, Daniel Stern, Mickey Rourke, Kevin Bacon, Timothy Daly, Ellen Barkin *cin* Peter Sova *m* Bruce Brody, Ival Kral

After a decade as a successful screenwriter Levinson turned director with this very funny, poignant autobiographical picture about a young man's bewilderment with the opposite sex. The fresh-faced cast all went on to bigger (not necessarily better) things. And the dialogue is great: hilariously pedantic, rich, overlapping riffs which anticipate Tarantino in their obsession with pop culture and macho one-upmanship ("What's that John Wayne movie called? The one with the stagecoach?").

Rain Man 1988, 133 min

cast Dustin Hoffman, Tom Cruise, Valeria Golina, Jerry Molen, Jack Murdock, Michael D. Roberts *cin* John Seale *m* Hans Zimmer

A self-confident yuppie car salesman, Charlie Babbit (Cruise) is outraged when he discovers his old man has bequeathed the bulk of his fortune to Raymond (Hoffman), a brother he didn't know he had, an autistic savant who has spent most of his life in a residential home. Charlie kidnaps him and they embark on a long road trip together with predictable results; Raymond even proves a whiz at blackjack. *Rain Man* has more than enough syrup to smooth over its oddly hollow centre.

Bugsy 1991, 136 min

cast Warren Beatty, Annette Bening, Harvey Keitel, Ben Kingsley, Elliott Gould, Joe Mantegna *cin* Allen Daviau *m* Ennio Morricone

Of all Levinson's high-profile "director-for-hire" projects, this portrait of mobster Benjamin "Bugsy" Siegel is the one that seems the least compromised by outside forces, and the one which most fully engages his imagination. *Bugsy* plays like a gangster movie of the period, but with more explicit sex and violence. Anticipating *Casino*, it is a film about thuggish romantics, the American dreamers who built Las Vegas.

Albert Lewin
US, 1894–1968

Too educated to make films aimed at "the people", Albert Lewin was nevertheless entrusted with creative control over increasingly ambitious projects. The result: lumbering failures and interesting curios.

Educated at New York University and Harvard, Lewin taught English at the University Of Missouri before becoming drama and film critic at the *Jewish Tribune*. He entered Hollywood as a reader for Samuel Goldwyn, then script clerk for King Vidor; in 1924 he became a screenwriter at MGM. Producer Irving Thalberg had faith, and eventually Lewin became a producer himself. He had a hand in the production of such successes as the Greta Garbo vehicle *The Kiss* (1929), the Harlow shocker *Red-Headed Woman* (1932), the Oscar-winning *Mutiny On The Bounty* (1935) and *The Good Earth* (1937).

At Paramount, Lewin began his directing career with *The Moon And Sixpence* (1942), a compromised Somerset Maugham adaptation with a strong George Sanders in the lead role. However, Lewin's reputation rests on his successful adaptation of *The Picture Of Dorian Gray* (1945). Reduced to a vehicle for Sanders' trademark devilishness, *The Private Affairs Of Bel Ami* (1947) did Maupassant's original no favours. Producing and writing as well as directing, Lewin's work had a reverence for actorly performances and the written word that could make for starchy films. But for an overripe sensibility that foresaw 1950s melodrama – see *Pandora And The Flying Dutchman* (1950), for example – his best work exceeded the literary in search of something more. Lewin finished his career working on screenplays for other directors and for television. RA

The Picture Of Dorian Gray 1945, 110 min, b/w and col

cast Hurd Hatfield, George Sanders, Angela Lansbury, Peter Lawford, Donna Reed, Lowell Gilmore, Richard Fraser *cin* Harry Stradling *m* Herbert Stothart

In what was Hurd Hatfield's finest performance, Oscar Wilde's *Dorian Gray* becomes an essay in a humanity compromised by Sanders' modern vision of evil as the hedonistic Lord Henry Wotton. This Faustian tale of a young man who sells his soul to keep his youth while his portrait ages instead holds true to Wilde's wit and is steeped in a decadent *fin-de-siècle* mood.

Pandora And The Flying Dutchman 1950, 122 min

cast James Mason, Ava Gardner, Nigel Patrick, Sheila Sim, Harold Warrender, Mario Cabré, Marius Goring *cin* Jack Cardiff *m* Alan Rawsthorne

Jack Cardiff's lush cinematography is a thing of loveliness in this retelling of the myth of the sailor condemned to the seas in search of a woman's devotion. Lewin set the action in Spain in the 1930s, and James Mason (the mysterious sailor) and Ava Gardner (an American who is the object of fierce competition by a number of potential suitors) act like there's no tomorrow.

Herschell Gordon Lewis
US, 1926–

Hailed as the "Godfather of Gore" and insanely prolific (he made nine films in 1968 alone), Herschell Gordon Lewis tried his hand at soft-core flicks, nudist camp movies, hillbilly comedies and even blaxploitation films in search of a quick buck (he had previously been an unlikely professor of literature at the University of Mississippi). But he soon carved out his own crimson-stained niche with his horror movies, made on the cheap in Florida for the drive-in market of the 1960s: *Blood Feast* (1963), *Two Thousand Maniacs!* (1964) and *Color Me Blood Red* (1965) comprised his informal "Blood trilogy".

Why did he work in the horror genre? "It was simply a business decision", Lewis once told an interviewer; it certainly wasn't an artistic decision, given the narrative incoherence, inept camerawork and atrocious acting that characterizes much of his work. Nonetheless, Lewis has a devoted cult of admirers: *Two Thousand Maniacs!* inspired the names of both John Waters' *Multiple Maniacs* (1971) and the folk-rock band 10,000 Maniacs, and *Blood Feast* is, if nothing else, one of a kind. As the critic Andrew Grossman wrote, the film's "ridiculous nadirs of execution meld, trancelike, with sublime heights of fearless intent". Unarguably an innovator, Lewis set new heights for onscreen violence, with *Blood Feast* one-upping the infamous shower scene from *Psycho* (1960) in its opening moments.

With occasional exceptions, such as the biker-chick flick *She-Devils On Wheels* (1968), the sci-fi romp *Monster A Go-Go* (1965) and the kids' film *Santa Visits The Magic Land Of Mother Goose* (1966), Lewis soldiered on within the gore format until the early 1970s. He churned out *A Taste Of Blood* (1967), in which a man becomes possessed by Dracula; *The Gruesome Twosome* (1967), about wig makers who employ hideous means to get their pelts; and his final film for thirty years, *The Gore Gore Girls* (1972), a somewhat *giallo*-like tale of a serial killer targeting a strip joint. (The film's signature image was mangled breasts that bleed both white and chocolate milk.) Lewis has since become a marketing guru, writing several bestsellers on advertising and public relations and setting up his own direct marketing company. He returned to moviemaking in 2002 with the straight-to-DVD release *Blood Feast 2: All U Can Eat*. JW

Blood Feast 1963, 67 min
cast William Kerwin, Mal Arnold, Connie Mason, Lyn Bolton, Scott H. Hall, Toni Calvert *cin* Herschell Gordon Lewis *m* Herschell Gordon Lewis

Shot in just a week, this blockbuster of the drive-in circuit concerns a caterer who collects female body parts for a rite to honour the goddess Ishtar. Astonishingly for a film made in 1963, video sales of *Blood Feast* were banned in Germany until as late as 2004 – an indicator of the movie's go-for-broke approach to grisly violence, which begins with a memorable amputation in a bathtub.

Two Thousand Maniacs! 1964, 87 min
cast William Kerwin, Connie Mason, Jeffrey Allen, Ben Moore, Jerome Eden, Gary Bakeman *cin* Herschell Gordon Lewis *m* Larry Wellington

Lewis aficionados often cite this as his finest hour, a horror riff on *Brigadoon* relocated to Pleasant Valley, a town decimated in the American Civil War. The town only comes to life again once every century, when its inhabitants ensnare unsuspecting northerners for ghastly (and inventive) revenge killings. The film is significantly more proficient than *Blood Feast*, but didn't make as much money – perhaps an instructive lesson for its decidedly slapdash director.

Joseph H. Lewis
US, 1907–2000

Possibly the best picture-maker in B-movies, Joseph Lewis is admired with intense devotion by film aficionados – but only a handful of his forty plus features are readily available. From the evidence, it would be wrong to assume that the others are without interest, although Lewis himself is said to have counted the *noir* mystery *My Name Is Julia Ross* (1945) as the "real" beginning of his career.

A former editor, he apparently persuaded Universal to let him direct by asking for no more than his editor's salary. He promptly alienated the crew with his complex set-ups; his penchant for shooting through the wheels of wagons had him nicknamed "Wagon Wheel Joe". He made ten Westerns in the years 1937–40, earning about $250 a shot, directed the East End Kids and Bela Lugosi in films for Monogram, and made a couple more "oaters" with actor Johnny Mack Brown. Then *film noir* freed him from the constraints of the cowboy code – if a man who staged a duel with a harpoon (in *Terror In A Texas Town*, 1958) can be said to have been constrained. In later years, Lewis worked exclusively in television, on shows such as *The Investigators* and *Gunsmoke*.

Lewis was the perfect *noir* director: he was by instinct a visual expressionist with a subversive disregard for respectable society and a taste for sex and violence. Driven to find the unusual angle, the creative solution, and utterly impatient with the conventional way of doing things, he was an imaginative outlaw who identified passionately with the beautiful sharp-shooting sociopath Annie Laurie Starr (Peggy Cummins) in his best-known film, *Gun Crazy* (1949). Lewis was saddled with mediocre scripts throughout his career, but by force of his own will he transformed the material into something distinctive. This was equally true whether the film in question was a

Western like *Seventh Cavalry* (1956), a crime thriller like *The Undercover Man* (1949) or an early *noir* like *So Dark The Night* (1946). "He was an alchemist-director", wrote Charles Tesson in *Cahiers du cinéma*, "a forger of genius. Pine always looked like oak in his work, thanks to the polish of his style." TC

Gun Crazy 1949, 87 min, b/w

cast Peggy Cummins, John Dall, Berry Kroeger, Harry Lewis, Russ Tamblyn *cin* Russell Harlan *m* Victor Young

A genuinely subversive Bonnie and Clyde couple-on-the-run story, *Gun Crazy* celebrates and sexualizes the *amour fou* of carnival gunslingers Bart Tare (John Dall) and Annie Laurie Starr (Peggy Cummins). Annie wants to live without working for it. Bart guesses where it will all end, but figures she's worth it. Among many notable sequences, a bank robbery filmed in an unbroken take from the back seat of the getaway car conveys all the risk and exhilaration of the moment.

The Big Combo 1955, 89 min, b/w

cast Cornel Wilde, Richard Conte, Jean Wallace, Brian Donlevy, Robert Middleton, Lee Van Cleef, Earl Holliman *cin* John Alton *m* David Raksin

Police detective Diamond (Cornel Wilde) carries on an obsessive vendetta against Mob boss Mr Brown (Richard Conte), hinging on his classy girlfriend Susan (Jean Wallace). This gangster film is pitched into *noir* abstraction by the rampant chiaroscuro of cinematographer John Alton, who transforms bare stages into suggestive pools of light and shadow.

Marcel L'Herbier

France, 1888–1979

Marcel L'Herbier is a key figure in French silent cinema, crucial to French modernism. A writer in the symbolist vein, L'Herbier came to film via the cinematographic unit of the French army during World War I. His first film, the short *Phantasmes* (1917), is notable for its use of soft focus, which presaged an era of French impressionism often overlooked in favour of German and Russian cinema of the 1920s. The melodrama *Eldorado* (1922) alternates between smoky realism and gargantuan modernist architecture, featuring superimposition, tinting and an extraordinary use of space. And the interaction of cubist sets by Fernand Léger and Alberto Cavalcanti and original music by Darius Milhaud in *L'inhumaine* (1923) epitomizes the aesthetic boldness of that era, while its emotional understatement looks forward to the work of Alain Resnais.

Setting up a production facility in 1923, L'Herbier's mobile camerawork, modernist settings and non-linear editing continued to distinguish in *L'argent* (1928). In the 1930s, melodramas such as *Le bonheur* (1935) and *Adrienne Lecouvreur* (1938) were fine star vehicles, and with *La nuit fantastique* (*Fantastic Night*, 1942) he paid respect to movie pioneer Georges Méliès. In 1943 L'Herbier co-founded L'Institut Des Hautes Etudes Cinématographiques, the French national film school, and was an influential writer on film aesthetics, promoting a uniquely French eclecticism within film culture. RA

L'argent 1927, 195 min, b/w

cast Pierre Alcover, Alfred Abel, Brigitte Helm, Mary Glory, Raymond Rouleau, Antonin Artaud, Jules Berry, Yvette Guilbert *cin* Jules Kruger

L'Herbier's masterpiece, this tale of financial collapse at the stock exchange is told with an endlessly expressive camera that guides us through the corridors and rooms of Emile Zola's complex source novel. The cinematography delineates a world in which desire and the pursuit of power is played out against a modernist backdrop of splendid anomie.

Doug Liman

US, 1962–

Doug Liman might have only a handful of films under his belt but this small output has kept his batting average high. He first attracted attention with the indie male-bonding comedy *Swingers* (1996). This was followed by the even edgier *Go* (1999), which successfully replicated the shock value, pacy narrative and dark humour of Quentin Tarantino's *Pulp Fiction* (1994) with its triptych tale of drug-dealing misadventure on the fringes of 1990s rave culture. An incongruously involved car chase in what was otherwise a resolutely grungy film suggested Liman could do big-budget pyrotechnics and might want to prove it. He soon got his chance with the Matt Damon CIA thriller *The Bourne Identity* (2002), his capable direction helping to kick-start a highly successful franchise.

In the following years Liman worked increasingly as a producer, for both film and TV, including executive producing episodes of cult youth smash *The O.C.* in 2003–04. By the time of *Mr & Mrs Smith* (2005), Liman seemed to have left his indie roots far behind. Starring Brad Pitt and Angelina Jolie as husband and wife assassins who discover their employers have asked them to kill each other, it was Liman's biggest hit to date. But for all the obvious thrills and Hollywood royalty on show it was sobering to see that his former indie naturalism and Steadicam verve – Liman was his own cinematographer on *Swingers* – had all but evaporated. RC

Swingers 1996, 96 min

cast Jon Favreau, Vince Vaughn, Ron Livingston, Alex Desert, Heather Graham, Patrick van Horn *cin* Doug Liman *m* Justin Reinhardt

Friends on the bottom rung of the Hollywood ladder try to help lovelorn Mike (Jon Favreau) get over his ex-girlfriend, who stayed in New York when he came west to pursue his acting dream. Cue male dating rituals and high jinks set in the parties and bars of Las Vegas and LA as Mike struggles to let go. Scripted by Favreau, the movie is anchored by strong performances from him and Vince Vaughn, and Liman marshals the action with vigour and panache.

The Bourne Identity 2002, 119 min
cast Matt Damon, Franka Potente, Chris Cooper, Clive Owen, Brian Cox, Adwale Akinnuoye-Agbaje *cin* Oliver Wood *m* Moby, John Powell

Matt Damon plays the forgetful assassin who slowly comes to the realization that he is a killer his former employers no longer want to have alive. Robert Ludlum's espionage thriller is given a subdued but big-budget treatment by Liman, whose unfussy direction – including one great Parisian car chase – avoids the obvious traps of Bond pastiche or ultra violence. But for all the acclaimed "realism" the result is a little flat and though Damon looks good in his role, it is only Chris Cooper as a cynical CIA chief who really makes anything out of the script's limited characterization.

Richard Linklater
US, 1960–

Despite his unassuming, easy-going disposition, the man who pinned the label "slacker" to his own generation is one of the more prolific and intriguing filmmakers around. Richard Linklater has successfully combined a mildly anti-authoritarian Hollywood career with his own conceptually adventurous, left-field independent projects, hitting a double home run in 2004 with the release of *School Of Rock* and *Before Sunset*.

Linklater's films speak to a young, sophisticated, bohemian audience who believe themselves to be on the fringes of society. His heroes are generally too passive to be called "rebels" or "outlaws" (with the exception of 1998's disappointing studio venture *The Newton Boys*); instead they are artists, dropouts, or simply young people still feeling their way in the world.

Often staging his films in real time, Linklater is a people-watcher, not a visual stylist – which is not to say that there aren't grace notes, especially when he's fully engaged by a project (as in *Before Sunset*). That engagement can be fleeting, not least because he seems boundlessly curious about life. It's hard to imagine any other filmmaker who would go from the anti-sports black comedy *Bad News Bears* (2005) to the animated Philip K. Dick science fiction *A Scanner Darkly* (2006) and a free adaptation of Eric Schlosser's nonfiction bestseller *Fast Food Nation* (2006). TC

Slacker 1991, 97 min
cast Richard Linklater, Rudy Basquez, Jean Caffeine, Jan Hockey, Mark James *cin* Lee Daniel

A conversational relay in which the camera shadows a character for a few minutes in real time and then sidles off with someone else, *Slacker* is a radically off-centre doodle of a movie, sketching personalities and random observations from the Austin, Texas scene. Plotless and pointedly pointless, the movie both indulges and satirizes the hundred eccentric, aimless souls who ramble through it: people identified in the credits as "Dostoyevsky Wannabe", "Ultimate Loser" and "Wants To Leave Country".

Dazed And Confused 1993, 101 min
cast Jason London, Rory Cochrane, Wiley Wiggins, Parker Posey, Matthew McConaughey, Milla Jovovich, Ben Affleck *cin* Lee Daniel

Asked to nominate his favourite American film of the 1990s, Quentin Tarantino chose this spot-on recreation of the last day of high school in May 1976. Seniors talk politics while next term's freshmen are subjected to brutal initiation rites. Scanning some two dozen youngsters (unknowns at the time), Linklater again mixes satire and sympathy with an ironic but unmistakably countercultural intelligence.

Waking Life 2001, 101 min
cast Wiley Wiggins, Lorelei Linklater, Ethan Hawke, Julie Delpy, Steven Soderbergh *cin* Richard Linklater, Tommy Pallota *m* Glover Gill

Adopting a near-plotless, freewheeling structure similar to *Slacker*, *Waking Life* follows a dreaming Wiley Wiggins on a string of curious encounters with philosophically minded friends and acquaintances. Linklater hit on the inspired notion of "painting over" his digital video footage with computer animation (Bob Sabiston's rotoscope technique), which imparts a woozy, throbbing pulse to the images. Linklater would return to this technique for 2006's *A Scanner Darkly*.

Before Sunset 2004, 77 mins
cast Ethan Hawke, Julie Delpy *cin* Lee Daniel *m* Julie Delpy, Glover Gill

This may be the perfect sequel, but it's better described as a companion piece – to 1995's *Before Sunrise*, of course. In the earlier film, an American backpacker (Ethan Hawke) met a French girl (Julie Delpy) on a train to Vienna. They talked the night away, agreed to meet again in a few months and went their separate ways. Nine years later, their paths cross in Paris. He is a novelist (and has written about that night), married, unhappy. She is a political activist, single, frustrated. They talk all evening. And they fall in love for the second time. Bliss.

A Scanner Darkly 2006, 100 min
cast Keanu Reeves, Robert Downey Jr, Woody Harrelson, Winona Ryder, Rory Cochrane *cin* Shane F. Kelly *m* Graham Reynolds

Another wildly ambitious project, a rotoscoped version of Philip K. Dick's novel of drug-addled paranoia. Reeves is Bob Arctor, an undercover police agent who wears a "scramble suit" to protect his identity – not that he knows who he is anymore. Don't expect a thriller. With its slow-burning and frequently aimless conversational overload it's more like a psychedelic *Big Brother*, albeit unusually absurdist in tone. It's not just the suits that get scrambled.

Ken Loach
UK, 1936–

There is a persistent myth about Ken Loach. It's that his TV play *Cathy Come Home* (1966) changed the law on homelessness and was responsible for the creation of the charity Shelter. As Loach is the first to admit, Shelter was already in existence and the television drama only brought the issues into the public arena. Although this may seem like a small point, it's crucial to an understanding of Loach's work because the socialist director doesn't believe that one film can make an iota of difference. This may seem surprising, almost self-defeating, as the director appears to be on a one-man mission to raise political consciousness.

Loach began his career as a trainee director at the BBC, where he formed one of the most important partnerships in his career. Working with producer Tony Garnett, Loach made, among others, *Up The Junction* (1965), which controversially tackled the subject of abortion, and *Cathy Come Home*. The star of that TV play, Carol White, also elicited her 1960s brand of charisma in Loach's first feature film, the austere, miserabilist *Poor Cow* (1967) about the travails of a young, married woman whose bad boy hubby is residing at Her Majesty's Pleasure. Two years later, Loach made the feature for which he is still best known in the UK, his locus classicus, *Kes* (1969), based on a novel by Barry Hines and produced and co-written by Garnett. Returning to television, Loach only made a handful of features in the 1970s and 80s, including *Family Life* (1971), the earnestly indulgent and semi-improvised drama *Looks And Smiles* (1981) and the genuine curio *Fatherland* (1986), about a folk singer who leaves East Germany for the West. However, he enjoyed an unlikely renaissance in the 1990s.

Loach hates the expression "political film-maker" as he believes all films are political, or at least ideological, and regards the term as a sly way of marginalizing left-wing directors. However, it's undeniable that some of his films tackle political issues head-on: the shoot-to-kill policy in Northern Ireland in *Hidden Agenda* (1990); the dissolution of the Left during the Spanish Civil War in *Land And Freedom* (1995); the Nicaraguan conflict in *Carla's Song* (1996); and the human rights of poorly paid Latin American cleaners in *Bread And Roses* (2000), his only North American film to date.

During a career lasting over four decades, the working classes have unerringly been Loach's subject, and this hasn't changed in recent years. Without succumbing entirely to salt-of-the-earth stereotypes, his workers are flawed, headstrong and often hopeless: the scheming construction workers on a London building site in the boisterous *Riff-Raff* (1990); the unemployed father trying to find the money for his daughter's communion dress in the grimly humorous *Raining Stones* (1993); the single mum who is the scourge of social services in the unsubtly polemical *Ladybird, Ladybird* (1994); the alcoholic who moonlights while on the dole in *My Name Is Joe* (1998); and the teenage drug dealer in *Sweet Sixteen* (2002).

When discussing Loach's aesthetic, critics can't avoid using words like gritty and realistic. Loach exhibits a personal modesty which is translated into his directorial style, a self-effacing *cinéma vérité* approach. However, there are some distinctive char-

acteristics in his work, such as his concerns with the family unit and his ability to capture the flavour and timbre of previously undocumented lives and communities (including authentic accents and dialects that need to be subtitled for the American market). If the director eschews a distinct personal style, it's because he puts himself at the service of his writers, from his long association with firebrand playwright Jim Allen (writer of his early TV plays and *Hidden Agenda*, *Raining Stones* and *Land And Freedom*) to his fruitful partnership with Paul Laverty (writer of *Carla's Song* and the Scottish films *My Name Is Joe*, *Sweet Sixteen* and 2004's *Ae Fond Kiss*).

Loach's scripts are often the result of months of research, but they are not usually shown in their entirety to the actors, who never quite know what will happen next. In a standout moment in *Riff-Raff*, a builder played by Ricky Tomlinson is having a sneaky bath in a show home when he's surprised by three Muslim women who are being escorted around the premises. The look of shocked amazement on Tomlinson's face was genuine, as the actor was simply instructed to "have a bath", and had no idea of the director's cruel intentions. These disingenuous methods are Loach's means to a naturalistic end. His quest for authenticity extends to employing nonprofessional actors in supporting or occasionally starring roles, most notably Martin Compston (who was an apprentice footballer) in *Sweet Sixteen*, comedienne Crissy Rock in *Ladybird, Ladybird* and, most famously, David Bradley in *Kes*, whose emotionally devastating performance is singed into the retina of anyone who's ever seen the film.

In 2006, Loach received the top prize at Cannes for *The Wind That Shakes The Barley* (2006). Most critics agreed that this potent drama about the aftermath of the Irish uprising was by no means the director's finest work, and that the prize was, in all but name, a lifetime achievement award. And few would disagree that his career has deserved such an honour. LH

Kes 1969, 113 min
cast David Bradley, Lynne Perrie, Freddie Fletcher, Colin Welland, Brian Glover, Bob Bowes, Robert Naylor *cin* Chris Menges *m* John Cameron

Newcomer David Bradley plays a weedy schoolboy who finds meaning in his deprived life by caring for a young kestrel. Bradley is almost overshadowed by Brian Glover's barnstorming performance as an ultra-competitive games teacher. Almost but not quite, because Bradley, like the film, evinces an aching poignancy. This is Loach's most affecting and effective attempt at uniting the universal and the particular.

Land And Freedom 1995, 110 min
cast Ian Hart, Rosana Pastor, Iciar Bollain, Tom Gilroy, Eoin McCarthy, Frédéric Pierrot *cin* Barry Ackroyd *m* George Fenton

Idealistic young Scouser David Carr (Ian Hart) joins the International Brigade during the Spanish Civil War, only to watch the opposition to Generalissimo Franco fracture.

Peter Mullan wreaks havoc on the car of an overzealous official in *My Name Is Joe*.

Amidst the impressive battle scenes, Loach bravely, or foolhardily, stops the action to stage a lengthy discussion about the ideological pros and cons of land collectivization. Intellectual cinema at its most rousing.

Carla's Song 1996, 125 min

cast Robert Carlyle, Oyanka Cabezas, Scott Glenn, Salvador Espinoza, Louise Goodall, Richard Loza, Gary Lewis *cin* Barry Ackroyd *m* George Fenton

At the height of the civil war, a young Nicaraguan woman (Oyanka Cabezas) takes home her Scottish bus driver boyfriend (Robert Carlyle), who has his eyes opened by American involvement in the country's affairs. This is a film of two halves: romantic and political, and it's only the first half that works. Loach is at his most boldly romantic, especially when Carlyle cheekily takes Cabezas to Loch Lomond on a double-decker. But when the love story takes a back seat in the second half, Carlyle becomes a passenger in a narrative that doesn't quite seem to know where it's going.

My Name Is Joe 1998, 105 min

cast Peter Mullan, Louise Goodall, David McKay, Anne Marie Kennedy, Gary Lewis, David Hayman *cin* Barry Ackroyd *m* George Fenton

A recovering alcoholic and football coach (Peter Mullan) falls in love with a community health worker, expecting his addictions to tear them apart. The script verges close to the mad/bad stereotypes that afflict most addicts in Hollywood feelgood movies, especially when Mullan gleefully splashes paint all over a Department of Health and Social Security official's car. However, these generic tendencies are reined in by Loach's natural pessimism and Mullan's tender, bristling performance.

Sweet Sixteen 2002, 106 min

cast Martin Compston, William Ruane, Annmarie Fulton, Michelle Abercromby, Gary McCormack *cin* Barry Ackroyd *m* George Fenton

Martin Compston exudes a scruffy charisma as the teenager who deals drugs to buy his mum a caravan. *Sweet*

Sixteen is edgy, grim and unexpectedly jaunty in places. Loach is perhaps too charmed by his lead character, sketching him as a loveable rogue rather than a parasitical drug dealer. Local politicians weren't too chuffed by the squalid portrayal of the fine parish of Greenock – and it's hard to blame them.

The Wind That Shakes The Barley 2006, 127 min

cast Cillian Murphy, Padraic Delaney, Liam Cunningham, Gerard Kearney, William Ruane *cin* Barry Ackroyd *m* George Fenton

Loach's one-sided take on the Irish Uprising starts off as a war movie between the militantly idealistic IRA and the savage and unprincipled British army. In the second half, polemic gives way to subtlety as the republican fighters are split between those who support the compromised Free State, which has sworn allegiance to the Crown, and those who will never give up their arms until Ireland is totally free. This is bold, incendiary filmmaking dressed up as period epic, only let down by its flabby middle section which turns the movie into a debating chamber.

Joseph Losey
US, 1909–84

Driven from the US by political prejudice, taking refuge in Britain where he made films under assumed identities and fêted as a European auteur, Joseph Losey epitomized 1960s examinations of the relationship between individuals and politics.

In the 1930s Losey became involved in radical theatre, a decision with serious implications for his career. After attending Sergei Eisenstein's film classes in Moscow, in 1936 he worked on the

Living Newspaper, a celebrated series of stage productions that drew upon the work of Bertolt Brecht, with whom Losey also later collaborated. In 1938 he supervised numerous documentary shorts for the Rockefeller Foundation, and his directing debut, an industrial film called *Pete Roleum And His Cousins*, previewed at the 1939 New York World's Fair.

After war service, Losey signed with RKO, earning a reputation for rapidly produced, socially aware thrillers. His debut, *The Boy With Green Hair* (1948), was an unusual allegory on racism in which a war orphan is ostracized for being different. *The Lawless* (1950) examined a southern California town beset with racial and sexual tensions, while Evelyn Keyes excelled as the suburban housewife worried by *The Prowler* (1951) who falls prey to Van Heflin's venal cop. *M* (1951) continued the trend, wherein contemporary Los Angeles unfolds as a spiritual wasteland, catching something of the castigatory mood of Fritz Lang's original. In tight, clean style, Losey showed his facility for disseminating human dynamics across the image and essaying individual guilt as a corollary of social dysfunction.

Named as a communist during the House Un-American Activities hearings, Losey was blacklisted in Hollywood and sought exile in Britain. There he consolidated a preoccupation with human frailty and spiritual corruption in such films as the anti-capital-punishment thriller *Time Without Pity* (1957) and the impressive British heist movie *The Concrete Jungle* (aka *The Criminal*, 1960). There followed three works bringing genuine insight to the British class system, each scripted by British playwright Harold Pinter. *The Servant* (1963), which uncovered the hidden antagonisms of a London playboy's residence; *Accident* (1967), in which the status quo in a summery, donnish Oxford unravels after a random event; and the L.P. Hartley adaptation *The Go-Between* (1970).

The 1960s also saw Losey go hip with the spy spoof *Modesty Blaise* (1966) and the 1968 Elizabeth Taylor vehicles *Boom!* and *Secret Ceremony*, which were both sophisticated, but misfiring, dramas. Taylor was one of the many big-name actors to cross Losey's path throughout his career, others included Stanley Baker, Dirk Bogarde and Jeanne Moreau. In 1976, Losey moved to France and, therefore, only made one further English-language film, the posthumously released *Streaming* (1985). Aside from *Monsieur Klein* (1976), his later work suggested a director whose critical plaudits by *Cahiers du cinéma* had overtaken his inspiration. However, the bulk of the work he left behind shows him to have been one of cinema's best-developed political consciences. RA

The Prowler 1951, 92 min, b/w

cast Van Heflin, Evelyn Keyes, John Maxwell, Katherine Warren, Emerson Treacy, Madge Blake *cin* Arthur Miller *m* Lyn Murray

With a taut script by blacklisted Dalton Trumbo (writing under a pseudonym), this edgy *noir* explores themes that recur throughout Losey's work: class difference, duplicity and the gap between how things look and how they are. Van Heflin plays a cop investigating a prowler at the home of lonely housewife Evelyn Keyes. Soon he is preying on her himself, "accidentally" killing her husband and then marrying her. When they need to hide out in a ghost town in the Mojave desert, their mutual illusions begin to unravel, eventually leading to the bleakest of denouments.

Accident 1967, 105 min

cast Dirk Bogarde, Stanley Baker, Jacqueline Sassard, Michael York, Vivien Merchant, Delphine Seyrig *cin* Gerry Fisher *m* John Dankworth

Another exercise in sexual tension and repressed pain, this time set within the calm of a summer's day in Oxford. Dirk Bogarde is outstanding as an uptight professor obsessed with a student, the beautiful Anna (Jacqueline Sassard), whom he retrieves from a car accident in which her boyfriend is killed. Harold Pinter's script – a masterpiece of obliqueness and understatement – is perfectly complemented by Losey's elliptical direction in which flashbacks gradually reveal the emotional agony beneath the protagonists' coolly civilized behaviour.

The Go-Between 1970, 116 min

cast Julie Christie, Alan Bates, Dominic Guard, Margaret Leighton, Michael Redgrave, Michael Gough, Edward Fox *cin* Gerry Fisher *m* Michel Legrand

In this Edwardian costume drama Losey uses a covert affair between the daughter of Norfolk gentry (Julie Christie) and a local farmer (Alan Bates) to tease forth the prejudices and moral hypocrisy of the British class system. This adaptation of L.P. Hartley's novel benefits from strong performances – not least from the young Dominic Guard through whose eyes the action is viewed – and an atmosphere of pregnant suggestion that is greatly assisted by Michel Legrand's distinctive score.

Monsieur Klein 1976, 123 min

cast Alain Delon, Jeanne Moreau, Suzanne Flon, Michel Lonsdale, Juliet Berto, Francine Bergé *cin* Gerry Fisher *m* Egisto Macchi, Pierre Porte

Set against the backdrop of the Vichy-French deportation of Jews in 1942, *Monsieur Klein* follows a successful art dealer as he finds himself haunted by his Jewish namesake who even occupies his apartment when he is not there. The art dealer is forced to defend himself against accusations that he is Jewish in a film that, like the best Losey, places the beleaguered individual on the very edge of society and psychology.

Lou Ye
China, 1965–

Unlike his contemporaries Zhang Yuan (*Beijing Bastards*, 1993) and Wang Xiaoshuai (*The Days*, 1993), whose work exhibits an urgent realism, Lou Ye's films exist in their own meta-universe, not so much China as *Chinatown*. One of the leading lights of the so-called "Sixth Generation" of Chinese film-makers, Lou makes movies that ooze with postmodern know-how, channelling Alfred Hitchcock, Wong Kar-Wai, *film noir* and the *nouvelle vague*.

Like other Sixth Generation filmmakers, Lou depicts the economic boom as experienced by China's city dwellers – frankly and unromantically. This candid examination has led to him – and many of his contemporaries – experiencing some local difficulties with the censors, who delayed the release of Lou's first film, *Weekend Lover* (1995). In 2000, he experimented with a subjective camera technique in *Suzhou River*, shooting much of the action from the perspective of an unseen narrator, a bold narrative gambit rarely deployed since Robert Montgomery's *Lady In The Lake* (1946). Also delayed by censors, this intricate arabesque remains the high point of the director's career so far. *Purple Butterfly* (2004), a magnificently moody chunk of Baroque set in 1930s Shanghai, focused on a switchboard operator who moonlights for a resistance group against the Japanese occupation. Complications ensue when a Japanese agent who enters the picture just happens to be her ex-lover.

Reality has often seemed to be an arbitrary construction in his films, but Lou finally faced facts with *Summer Palace* (2006). The first film from the mainland to depict the famous protests in Tiananmen Square in 1989, it was screened at Cannes without the permission of the Chinese Film Bureau. The government duly kicked up the inevitable fuss, but the film couldn't live up to the controversy, with some critics complaining that world events were merely a backdrop to a sprawling and saggy tale of star-crossed love. LH

Suzhou River (Suzhou he) 2000, 83 min

cast Xun Zhou, Hongshen Jia, Zongkai Hua, Anlian Yao, An Nai *cin* Yu Wang *m* Jörg Lemberg

Suzhou River is like Hitchcock's *Vertigo* (1958) filtered through Wong Kar-Wai's *Chungking Express* (1994). Lou deftly grafts together parallel love stories that are both hopelessly and enjoyably contrived. Two men fall for a flighty dancer who dresses as a mermaid. One is the unseen and unnamed narrator, the other a courier who loves her because she's the exact double of a woman he once loved. The stories-within-stories are presented in a giddy mixture of high style and hard cuts that make reality seem appropriately fluid, like a vivid and feverish dream.

Arthur Lubin
US, 1898–1995

Arthur Lubin's varied career embraces Abbott and Costello, *Phantom Of The Opera* and two garrulous equines. He became a director in 1934 after a decade of acting, and exhibited a breezy and efficient touch in his often escapist films. His finest directo-

rial effort, *Black Friday* (1940) was a weird mix of Frankenstein, Jekyll and Hyde and gangsters. He then took on Universal's new comedy team Abbott and Costello and dealt well with the undisciplined and hyperactive Costello in several films from 1941 and 1942. *Phantom Of The Opera* (1943) was his biggest critical success, while *New Orleans* (1947) somewhat whitened the history of jazz, casting Billie Holiday as a maid. *Francis* (1949), about a talking mule, spawned six sequels (1951–56), all but the last directed by Lubin. From the late 1950s he moved increasingly into television, with one popular project being *Mr Ed*, a series about a talking horse. JR

Black Friday 1940, 70 min, b/w

cast Boris Karloff, Bela Lugosi, Stanley Ridges, Anne Nagel, Anne Gwynne *cin* Elwood Bredell *m* Hans Salter

A fantastically baroque film but, though Boris Karloff and Bela Lugosi headline, the latter appears only intermittently and the film really belongs to Stanley Ridges as a genial professor whose life is saved by a brain transplant – but it's a gangster's brain! Does the professor remember where the gangster hid the loot? Ridges' transformation is completely convincing and the lurid atmosphere is helped by the expressive lighting and cinematography.

Ernst Lubitsch
Germany, 1892–1947

Revered in his lifetime as an artist on a par with Chaplin and René Clair, Ernst Lubitsch was successful from first to last, and probably had more influence over American movie comedy of the Hollywood Golden Age than anyone.

His career goes back to early-twentieth-century Berlin, where he studied under Max Reinhardt and became a movie comedy star himself as the character known as "Meyer". He started directing during World War I, and had a series of hits with the Polish-born actress Pola Negri in lavish historical pageants like *Madame Du Barry* (aka *Passion*, 1919), *Anna Boleyn* (1920) and *Das Weib des Pharao* (*Loves Of Pharoah*, 1920). At the same time he showed his versatility with light comedies that anticipated his Hollywood career, including *Die Austernprinzessin* (*The Oyster Princess*, 1919), a satire on American manners that was the first to exhibit the famed "Lubitsch Touch". Between 1915 and 1923 he made more than thirty films, and was considered to be among the most successful directors in the world.

Hollywood was alert to the quality and popularity of German films, and at the behest of the silent movie star Mary Pickford Lubitsch became one of the first European filmmakers lured West (spending much of his silent career at Warner Bros). In fact their collaboration was a failure, but his second film, *The Marriage Circle* (1923), was a sensation and set the tone for the quintessential "Jazz Age" comedies that followed. These Lubitsch silents may be rare treasures – reviewing *Heaven Can Wait* in 1943, James Agee lamented that it "is not up to his best, nothing has been for nearly twenty years". But based only on his sound films Lubitsch remains a master.

Switching to Paramount, he directed Maurice Chevalier and Jeanette MacDonald in a series of charming operettas, beginning with *The Love Parade* (1929), the first musical to integrate song and action. By the time of *Trouble In Paradise* (1932) and *Design For Living* (1933) the name Lubitsch was synonymous with urbane sophistication, and the "Lubitsch Touch" was already fabled.

In the broadest terms, the term denoted a well-groomed, "Continental" elegance. Almost all of Lubitsch's films were set in Europe, though this was a notional place where Gary Cooper and James Stewart felt right at home. "I prefer Paris, Paramount, to Paris, France", Lubitsch said. The protagonists' "class" is likewise a charade, a cover for drives that are invariably mercenary or sexual: in Lubitsch comedies, the plot motors are most often imposture, mistaken identity and/or infidelity. The pre-Production Code films assumed an adult interest in sex, but with an insouciant tone that translated well enough into the discrete insinuations of post-Code screwball comedy.

But the Touch is more than that: the films' tone and elegance derives just as much from the imaginative, askew point of view implicit in camera placement and cutting (Lubitsch pre-planned all his shots and acted out the parts for his performers). He worked on principles of misdirection and multiplication, pulling one joke out of another as if it were a magician's top hat.

A generation of filmmakers followed in Lubitsch's tracks – Billy Wilder (who scripted several Lubitsch films) being his most devoted disciple. Critics at the time felt that Lubitsch's 1940s films lacked the zest of what had come before, but the more gentle ironies and the delicate emotional modulations in *The Shop Around The Corner* (1940), *Heaven Can Wait* (1943) and *Cluny Brown* (1946) now look like something more than gay diversions. TC

Trouble In Paradise 1932, 83 min, b/w
cast Herbert Marshall, Miriam Hopkins, Kay Francis, Charles Ruggles, Edward Everett Horton *cin* Victor Milner *m* W. Franke Harling

While some of Lubitsch's early-1930s sex comedies now seem a little mannered in their urbanity, this sophisticated screwball wears its amorality with honour. Jewel thieves Marshall and Hopkins move in on the loaded Francis, but her charms threaten to break up a blissful partnership. Although the Marshall-Francis attraction isn't consummated, the film is steeped in sex and is decidedly pre-Production Code.

Ninotchka 1939, 110 min, b/w
cast Greta Garbo, Melvyn Douglas, Ina Claire, Bela Lugosi, Sig Ruman, Felix Bressart, Alexander Granach *cin* William H. Daniels *m* Werner R. Heymann

This is Lubitsch's best-known film, courtesy of the improbable tagline "Garbo Laughs!" And quite lustrous she is too, as the grave Communist apparatchik seduced by frivolous capitalist charmer Melvyn Douglas during a diplomatic mission in Paris. *Ninotchka* was written by Billy Wilder and Charles Brackett (with Walter Resich), and might easily be a Wilder movie. It's too schematic and not as funny as its reputation suggests, but only a curmudgeon could resist its worldly-wise insouciance.

The Shop Around The Corner 1940, 97 min, b/w
cast James Stewart, Margaret Sullavan, Frank Morgan, Joseph Schildkraut, Felix Bressart, Sara Haden *cin* William H. Daniels *m* Werner R. Heymann

A gem, and the romantic comedy against which all others should be judged, this sweet, sad valentine to love is set in Budapest. Here shop clerks Stewart and Sullavan bicker relentlessly, oblivious to the fact they're actually conducting a lonely hearts correspondence with each other. From such trifles Lubitsch concocts a charming, delicately observed picture that's close to Hollywood perfection.

To Be Or Not To Be 1942, 99 min, b/w
cast Carole Lombard, Jack Benny, Robert Stack, Felix Bressart, Lionel Atwill, Sig Ruman, Stanley Ridges *cin* Rudolph Maté *m* Werner R. Heymann

In Warsaw the Tura theatre troupe's latest play is abruptly cancelled when Germany storms Poland. Lubitsch was condemned at the time for having the bad taste to make light of Herr Hitler, but this audacious black comedy now looks like his bravest satire, as well as his funniest film. Carole Lombard and Jack Benny make one of the great screwball couples as a diva and a ham who conspire to foil the Führer.

George Lucas
US, 1944–

With his good friend Steven Spielberg, George Lucas can be considered the co-inventor of the movie blockbuster. His science-fiction epic *Star Wars* (1977) surpassed Spielberg's *Jaws* (1975) as the highest-grossing film of all time and became a cultural milestone for a generation. *Star Wars* is a Manichean moral tale that, despite taking place "a long time ago, in a galaxy far, far away", became as deeply ingrained in the popular psyche as any Greek myth or Bible parable, and far more easily translated into must-have merchandise.

The release of *Star Wars* also marked the start of a 22-year hiatus from directing for Lucas, whose previous two features were the kind of low-budget personal projects more readily identified with his fellow "movie brats" of the 1970s, such as Brian De Palma and Francis Ford Coppola. The latter's American Zoetrope studio produced Lucas's debut, *THX 1138* (1971), a movie Lucas shot when he was just 25. This austere, strongly atmospheric riff on George Orwell's *1984* conjured a uniformed, tyrannically regulated future, where the hero (Robert Duvall) falls afoul of the authorities after falling in love – an emotion that his society has tried to stifle with medication.

After the dystopic future shock of *THX 1138*, Lucas began to re-imagine the past. The poster tagline for his teen ensemble piece *American Graffiti* (1973) was "Where were you in '62?" – the year the 18-year-old Lucas barely survived a car accident that put an end to his racing ambitions. Using a palette that Lucas described as "juke-box-like – very garish, bright blue and yellow and red", the nocturnal movie catalogues bittersweet adolescent rites of passage while celebrating the aimless joys of "cruising". *Graffiti* proved to be a big hit despite Universal's initial judgement that the movie was "unreleasable". The studio then famously passed on Lucas's thirteen-page treatment for a little movie he was calling *Star Wars*, which later earned $323 million at the box office for Fox. Here the essential forces of good and evil were embodied by the woodenly virtuous Luke Skywalker (Mark Hamill) and the asthmatic man-in-black Darth Vader (voiced by James Earl Jones).

"I hate directing", Lucas confessed to *Rolling Stone* magazine in 1980. "It's like fighting a fifteen-round heavyweight bout with a new opponent every day." During his two decades out of the director's chair, Lucas produced scores of films (including the Indiana Jones series), built up his peerless digital-effects studio Industrial Light & Magic (which created the cyborg in *Terminator 2*, the dinosaurs in *Jurassic Park* and the digital waves in *The Perfect Storm*) and founded Skywalker Ranch, a complex of studios where directors can write, edit and mix their films and where Lucas's state-of-the-art THX sound reproduction system was developed.

Lucas's return to directing with *Star Wars: Episode I – The Phantom Menace* (1999) was at once dispiritingly inept and, of course, phenomenally successful. Mark Hamill once quipped, "I have a sneaking suspicion that if there were a way to make movies without actors, George would do it". The movie met Hamill's prediction halfway by inhabiting an almost entirely digitally created universe, a computer game crypt utterly devoid of human interest, warmth, passion or humour. Terrible reviews and disappointed audiences mattered little; licensing agreements alone ensured a monetary bonanza for *Phantom Menace* and its equally turgid successors, *Star Wars: Episode II – Attack Of The Clones* (2002) and *Star Wars: Episode III – Revenge Of The Sith* (2005). Ironically, in the rigid, hermetic totality of its morality and aesthetics, the second *Star Wars* trilogy imagined a distant past as suffocating as the future that Lucas imagined in *THX 1138*. jw

American Graffiti 1973, 110 min
cast Richard Dreyfuss, Candy Clark, Ron Howard, Paul LeMat, Cindy Williams, Charles Martin Smith, Harrison Ford *cin* Ron Eveslage

A highly eventful night in the life of a group of teenage friends in 1962, Lucas's ensemble hit created a lasting template for the period coming-of-age film with its wall-to-wall rock'n'roll soundtrack and young stars with bright futures (Richard Dreyfuss and Harrison Ford among them). Several of the characters seem wistfully reluctant to let go of the present moment – a hesitation the movie transforms into nostalgic regret, harkening back to a lost era of American innocence.

Star Wars 1977, 125 min
cast Mark Hamill, Harrison Ford, Carrie Fisher, Peter Cushing, Alex Guinness, Peter Mayhew, David Prowse *cin* Gilbert Taylor *m* John Williams

Despite the cardboard acting (with the exception of Harrison Ford as Han Solo, charismatic in his constant irritation), a pace that might be described as stately and a sci-fi aesthetic that was dated even in 1977, Lucas's epic fable struck a resounding chord with a generation of young fans via its primal theme of good battling evil, its stirring special effects and its arsenal of suspenseful action sequences.

Baz Luhrmann
Australia, 1962–

On the strength of three films, supplemented by some prominent stage, advertising and even recording work, Baz Luhrmann has secured an international reputation as one of the most flamboyant directing talents ever to emerge from the Antipodes. He is a stylistic magpie with a flair for camp, and his work reflects his love of musicals and melodrama.

Luhrmann trained as an actor at Sydney's National Institute of Dramatic Arts (NIDA), where he devised an early version of *Strictly Ballroom*, his affectionate homage to ballroom dancing. His play became a stage hit in Sydney and was reworked for the screen in 1992. A surprise smash at the Cannes Film Festival, Luhrmann's feelgood directorial debut became an international sleeper hit.

Throughout his career, Luhrmann has worked with two long-term collaborators: Catherine Martin, a costume and set designer whose visual flair is so instrumental to all his work; and scriptwriter/composer/lyricist Craig Pearce, who has co-written three of his movies. The trio have mounted several acclaimed opera productions, including a version of Benjamin Britten's *A Midsummer Night's Dream*, and it was that Shakespeare adaptation that prompted Luhrmann to make his rollicking, modern-day version of *Romeo And Juliet* in 1996. Officially titled *William Shakespeare's Romeo + Juliet*, the film's frenetic, MTV-style pacing and the casting of teen pin-up Leonardo DiCaprio ensured a remarkable degree of box-office success for a Shakespeare adaptation.

Emboldened by *Romeo + Juliet*'s success and backed by 20th Century Fox, Luhrmann embarked on his most ambitious but patchiest film, *Moulin Rouge!* (2001), a visually spectacular out-and-out musical starring Nicole Kidman and Ewan McGregor. The production was a troubled one: Luhrmann's father died on the first day of shooting, Kidman broke two ribs and smashed a knee, and the cost of re-shoots and the lavish production design are rumoured to have pushed it way over budget. Reviews were decidedly mixed, and the film was slow to take off in the US, but it went over spectacularly well in international territories such as India and Russia. It was to be the last of his "red curtain" films – a reference to the trilogy's use of theatrical artifice and quasi-Brechtian self-consciousness.

After *Moulin Rouge!*, Luhrmann mounted a production of *La Bohéme* in New York, shot a commercial for Chanel No. 5 with Kidman and began planning a biopic about Alexander the Great, rumoured to star DiCaprio. However, the project was shelved in the wake of Oliver Stone's poorly received film *Alexander* (2004). LH

Strictly Ballroom 1992, 94 min

cast Paul Mercurio, Tara Morice, Bill Hunter, Pat Thomson, Gia Carides, Peter Whitford *cin* Steve Mason *m* David Hirschfelder

A near-perfect slice of kitsch, this underdog tale stars Paul Mercurio as a wayward ballroom dancer who longs to dance his own outlawed steps, and chooses Tara Morice's wallflower as his unlikely partner to compete in the Pan-Pacific Grand Prix. A riot of spangles, glitter and spray-stiffened hair, the film minces on just the right side of irony while its abiding warmth and tight screenplay help it to hold up as surprisingly solid viewing years later.

William Shakespeare's Romeo + Juliet 1996, 120 min

cast Leonardo DiCaprio, Clare Danes, Harold Perrineau, Pete Postlethwaite, Miriam Margolyes, John Leguizamo *cin* Donald McAlpine *m* Nellee Hooper

Resetting Shakespeare's school syllabus favourite in the present day in a vaguely Californian-looking "Verona Beach", complete with Hawaiian shirts and shiny guns, was a stroke of genius on Luhrmann's part. Though hip and relentlessly inventive, *Romeo + Juliet* managed to remain faithful enough to please Bard buffs and features strong performances from stars Leonardo DiCaprio and Claire Danes, alongside scene-stealing turns by Harold Perrineau as Mercutio and John Leguizamo as Tybalt.

Moulin Rouge! 2001, 127 min

cast Nicole Kidman, Ewan McGregor, John Leguizamo, Jim Broadbent, Richard Roxburgh *cin* Donald M. McAlpine *m* Craig Armstrong

So lavish, hysterically edited and crammed with detail that it almost becomes annoying, Luhrmann's operatic confection casts Nicole Kidman as a consumptive *fin-de-siècle* showgirl who falls in love with Ewan McGregor's starry-eyed poet. The film's key conceit is to have the characters singing wilfully anachronistic pop and rock tunes, such as Nirvana's "Smells Like Teen Spirit", The Police's "Roxanne" and Elton John's "Your Song", which

sometimes works and sometimes just comes off as naff. Still, you've got to love a movie that has Jim Broadbent singing "Like A Virgin".

Sidney Lumet
US, 1924–

Trained in television, immersed in theatre and often inspired when working with leading acting talent, Sidney Lumet's filmography – a variable but impressive forty films – demonstrates the value of collaborative creativity and professional production. He deserves to be recognized as one of the greatest social chroniclers of his native New York.

The son of veteran Yiddish actor Baruch Lumet, he was educated at Columbia and the Actors Studio. After war service he ran an actors' group off-Broadway, directed summer-stock theatre and taught acting, joining CBS in 1950 and making a name with television dramas such as *You Are There*, *Best Of Broadway* and *The US Steel Hour*.

In 1956 producer Henry Fonda offered Lumet the opportunity to direct *12 Angry Men* (1957). After a succession of indifferent projects with theatrical themes, Lumet made *Long Day's Journey Into Night* (1962), which had a strong script and fine performances from Katharine Hepburn, Jason Robards and Ralph Richardson. Depicting a family riven by drug addiction, illness and alcoholism, all filmed in claustrophobic period drawing rooms, the Eugene O'Neill adaptation seemed to reiterate classical monochrome values in the age of Godard.

The 1960s and 70s were Lumet's heyday. Following the Cold War thriller *Fail-Safe* and the urban drama *The Pawnbroker* (both 1964), *The Hill* (1965), starring Sean Connery, was a sweaty contest of wills in a British internment camp in North Africa, photographed in penetrating detail by Oswald Morris. Connery showed Lumet his mettle again in *The Offence* (1973), another absorbing face-off in which a CID interrogator is haunted by the testimony of a suspected child molester, played by Ian Bannen. *Bye Bye Braverman* (1968) was an underrated vignette, in which a group of New York friends face up to middle age at a friend's funeral.

The gritty New Hollywood-style *Serpico* (1973) saw Lumet assume the role of chronicler of the New York justice system which he later embellished in *Dog Day Afternoon* (1975), *Prince Of The City* (1981), *The Verdict* (1982) and *Q&A* (1990). The latter delineated the New York status quo in all its expedients and allegiances with the mosaic diligence of Robert Altman or John Sayles. Like many of Lumet's later works, most notably the masterly *Network* (1976), regret permeates *Running On Empty* (1988), a rites-of-passage drama charting a young man's response to his parents' political activism. Since *Q&A*, the quality of the still-prolific Lumet's work has failed to match that of his glory days, but he remains an industry elder of compelling reputation. RA

12 Angry Men 1957, 120 min, b/w

cast Henry Fonda, Lee J. Cobb, Ed Begley, E.G. Marshall, Jack Klugman, Jack Warden, Martin Balsam, John Fielder, Joseph Sweeney *cin* Boris Kaufman *m* Kenyon Hopkins

From a nineteen-day shoot on a $343,000 budget, Lumet retrieved a crisp and focused record of a murder jury's deliberations that attempted to square a pre-war liberalism derived from the Dead End Kids with the complacency of the Affluent Society. An ensemble cast featured career-best turns from Lee J. Cobb and Joseph Sweeney, supported by the young Jack Warden and Martin Balsam and overseen by Fonda's liberal icon, all filmed in sweaty close-up by Boris Kaufman.

Fail-Safe 1964, 112 min, b/w

cast Henry Fonda, Dan O'Herlihy, Walter Matthau, Frank Overton, Edward Binns, Fritz Weaver, Larry Hagman *cin* Gerald Hirschfeld

Though overshadowed by its near contemporary, Stanley Kubrick's blackly comic *Dr Strangelove* (1963), *Fail-Safe* remains a tortured study of Cold War brinkmanship in the shadow of the Bomb. Henry Fonda's US president is burdened with a Pentagon gaffe of horrific proportions, and, while the humans sweat it out, the machines home in on Moscow. One of a TV-trained generation, Lumet understood cramped face-offs amid realistic compositions.

The Pawnbroker 1964, 115 min, b/w

cast Rod Steiger, Geraldine Fitzgerald, Jaime Sanchez, Brock Peters, Thelma Oliver, Baruch Lumet, Juano Hernandez *cin* Boris Kaufman *m* Quincy Jones

A daring pre-New Hollywood transplantation of *nouvelle vague* cutting and camerawork, *The Pawnbroker* found Rod Steiger's Holocaust survivor dealing with his demons in a Lower East Side prey to ethnic dislocation and gun crime. If the young killer in Lumet's first feature *12 Angry Men* is driven by desperation, here the whole city lives on the edge. Shot with *cinéma vérité* immediacy, the inner city becomes an archetype for hell in the twentieth century.

Dog Day Afternoon 1975, 130 min

cast Al Pacino, John Cazale, Sully Boyar, Penelope Allen, Beulah Garrick, Carol Kane, Charles Durning, James Broderick *cin* Victor J. Kemper

Based on a true story, *Dog Day Afternoon* sees bank robber Al Pacino besieged in a bank by the authorities after a bungled heist, the proceeds of which were intended to pay for a sex-change operation for his lover. Set in a fragmenting New York close to bankruptcy and in the shadow of the Attica prison riots, the film sees Pacino at the peak of his powers.

Network 1976, 121 min

cast Faye Dunaway, William Holden, Peter Finch, Robert Duvall, Wesley Addy, Ned Beatty, Arthur Burghardt *cin* Owen Roizman *m* Elliot Lawrence

Generated from Paddy Chayefsky's screenplay – and one of America's most eviscerating self-examinations – *Network* milked pure paranoia out of the sparks that fly when the nation's top anchorman loses it on air and

Henry Fonda faces down Lee J. Cobb in Sidney Lumet's ensemble classic *12 Angry Men*.

is subsequently exploited by the TV company for ratings. Acting as if her life depended on it, Faye Dunaway offers one of the most compelling performances in 1970s American cinema.

Ida Lupino
UK, 1918–95

Crowned "Queen of the Bs" by one feminist critic and "sexist" by another, Ida Lupino was one of the first female writer-directors in Hollywood and the first woman to direct herself. With her wide-eyed pixie looks, Lupino played ingénue roles throughout the 1930s, before moving on to play a series of hard-hitting, insolent dames in classics such as *They Drive By Night* (1940) and *High Sierra* (1941). Finally fed up with the roles she was getting, she displayed the reckless independence that came to characterize her career and formed her own production company, with the express intention of making socially conscious dramas.

When director Elmer Clifton suffered a mild heart attack three days into shooting *Not Wanted* (1949), which controversially charted the plight of a single mother, Lupino took up the reins (though she wasn't credited). Like her next three directorial projects, *Not Wanted* adopted a vigorous, quasi-documentary approach, radically shooting in urban backwaters and focusing on topically relevant issues. *Never Fear* (1949) concerned a dancer struck down by polio, *Outrage* (1950) was Hollywood's first serious study of a rape victim, and *Hard, Fast And Beautiful* (1951) was about a pushy mother and her tennis star daughter. Each film was about the place of women in society, but whether or not the director was reinforcing the patriarchal status quo is the subject of much heated debate because love and marriage are the solutions to the protagonist's problems in two of the films.

These social dramas were not popular with distributors, so Lupino reluctantly took the helm of the claustrophobic *noir The Hitch-Hiker* (1953), the least socially committed, yet most aesthetically pleasing, of her seven films. The critical and commercial failure of her next project, *The Bigamist* (1953), and her production company's financial difficulties then led Lupino to work as a television director. Her final film, the Catholic boarding-school comedy *The Trouble With Angels* (1966), had less of a feminist subtext than Dorothy Arzner's not dissimilar *The Wild Party* (1929), which was made decades earlier. Lupino's critical reputation and radical kudos suffered in comparison to her predecessor, and it was sadly only after her death that she was rediscovered and her work reclaimed. LH

The Hitch-Hiker 1953, 71 min, b/w
cast Edmond O'Brien, Frank Lovejoy, William Talman, José Torva, Sam Hayes, Jean Del Val *cin* Nick Musuraca *m* Leith Stevens

In this *noir* arabesque, two fishing buddies pick up a hitchhiker who turns out to be a cold-blooded psychopath. Lupino's claustrophobic hold tightens its grip as a tense battle of wits is played out as the trio drive down to Mexico. Rich in sinister dread and psychological detail, this is Lupino's finest hour.

David Lynch
US, 1946–

David Lynch is routinely described as the man who exposed suburbia's dark underbelly; he is the director who placed a severed ear amongst the manicured lawns, red roses and white picket fences of small-town America.

Growing up in those small towns, Lynch never did discover any severed ears in his garden and has always regarded his childhood as the happiest he's ever been. So, if you're looking for an autobiographical explanation for his obsession with graphic violence, it can perhaps be located on the run-down, crime-ridden streets of Philadelphia, where he attended art college (the usually saturnine Lynch becomes uncharacteristically animated when recalling his deep-seated fear and loathing of the city).

At college, he made the transition from painting to animation, creating the short film *The Grandmother* (1970) for the American Film Institute. He then started to write his first feature *Eraserhead* (1977). Filmed at weekends over five years, *Eraserhead* brought together the team he has worked with for most of his career – set designer Jack Fiske, cinematographer Frederick Elmes and sound designer Alan Splet (a low, unsettling drone is a key component of Lynch's aesthetic). A Kafkaesque fable about a man with vertical hair who has to take care of a small, needy monster, *Eraserhead* was the morbid expression of Lynch's unease about fatherhood.

A cult success, *Eraserhead* led directly to Mel Brooks employing Lynch to direct *The Elephant Man* (1980), a genuine tear-jerker thanks in part to John Hurt's performance and Freddie Francis's exquisite monochrome photography. However, the emotional impact is ultimately a result of the sparkling collision between opposing forces: Lynch's alienating avant-garde aesthetic and the story's inherent sentimentality. And then there was *Dune* (1984), an ambitious, flawed and undeniably camp adaptation of Frank Herbert's sci-fi epic. Despite the fact that producer Dino de Laurentis took that film out of the director's hands and re-cut it, the two worked together again on the film that's most associated with all things Lynchian – *Blue Velvet* (1986).

Blue Velvet spawned a sub-genre of films with dark suburban underbellies, resurrected the career of Dennis Hopper and sparked earnest public debate about the representation of male violence against women. However, it also led to a case of mistaken identity. Many saw Lynch as an ironic, anything-goes postmodernist, and when he declared he was a Reaganite, many assumed he was joking – he wasn't. The final scene in *Blue Velvet* comes closest to revealing the director's secret heart: a frankly sentimental, distinctly un-ironic reunion of mother and son shot in slow motion and soft focus. This is arguably the key to understanding David Lynch, the radical artist with conservative values.

Lynch himself became as much a cult hit as *Blue Velvet*, with his unique, almost extraterrestrial take on the English language, his Eagle Scout politeness, his magnificent quiff and his tie-free, fully buttoned shirts, he was much in demand on the talk-show circuit. The television series *Twin Peaks* (1990) continued his fascination with small-town America. The first series was a global hit and struck a surreal chord with the general public, but the second took off on a few too many loopy tangents for most people, losing millions of baffled viewers along the way. The film, *Twin Peaks: Fire Walk With Me* (1992), was made without co-creator Mark Frost, and the main character, played by Lynch's alter ego Kyle MacLachlan, was relegated to a cameo. Without his innocent investigator, the story lost both its quirky charm and its centrifugal force.

This was also true of the road movie *Wild At Heart* (1990), which had the same volatile mixture as *Blue Velvet*: straight-faced kitsch; a charged atmosphere thick with sinister dread; dialogue starched with aphorisms; lowlifes inhabiting a heightened reality; the fault lines of the rational world fissuring under the pressure of subconscious desires; the thin skin of civility pierced by nightmares; phantasmagorical imagery augmented by the haunting refrains of Angelo Badalamenti's ethereal score; fierce sex; and orgiastic violence. However, there was one key difference. In *Blue Velvet*, our tour guide through hell was the clean-cut Jeffrey who shared and reflected our shock and awe, our horrified fascination with the luridly compelling events that unfolded. In *Wild At Heart*, the first time we see Nicolas Cage's Sailor, he's excitedly bashing out the brains of a black gangster, thus disturbing the all-important balance between charming innocence and outré violence, and seriously bringing into question his credentials as our avatar.

After the critical failure of the *Twin Peaks* film, Lynch returned with his most inscrutable and oneiric work, *Lost Highway* (1997). An extraordinary realization of Lynch's obsession with doubles, the film was essentially a Möbius strip: a paranoid saxophonist (Bill Pullman) apparently kills his wife (Patricia Arquette) and is thrown in jail, where he morphs into a teenage boy who falls in love with Arquette's doppelgänger. An amiably eccentric diversion for the director, the appropriately named *The Straight Story* (1999) was the true tale of a man who drives hundreds of miles across America by lawn mower to be reunited with his estranged brother.

Then, with *Mulholland Drive* (2001) Lynch was definitely, and almost defiantly back on track. Lynch transformed the Hollywood satire into a murder mystery, with two aspiring actresses becoming modern-day Nancy Drews when they discover a dead body in a motel. As in many of his movies, the part of the amateur sleuth is also played by the viewer. And again, the mystery is never fully solved or properly explained. *Inland Empire* (2006) was less successful. Murky in its visuals, plotting and thinking, it was both self-indulgent and self-parodic. Embarrassingly, but understandably, no company wanted to distribute this three-hour epic of cinematic navel-gazing in the US, and the director had to release it himself. Clearly, the "machine" that Lynch has claimed gives him most of his ideas is in need of urgent repair. LH

Eraserhead 1977, 89 min, b/w

cast Jack Nance, Charlotte Stewart, Laurel Near, Allen Joseph, Jeanne Bates, Judith Anna Roberts *cin* Herbert Cardwell, Frederick Elmes *m* David Lynch

Excavated deep from the abyss of David Lynch's guilt-ridden, over-caffeinated id, *Eraserhead* is the authentically disturbing expression of a young father's horror of responsibility and domesticity. An everyday tale of a young man with vertical hair, his wife, their needy, monstrous child and the Lady In The Radiator is crammed with sick and incidental pleasures: the industrial symphony of clanging machine noises, the man-made chicken that alarmingly oozes dark, viscous goo and the baby itself, a sticky mutant cloned in hell: half animal embryo and half extraterrestrial.

Blue Velvet 1986, 120 min

cast Kyle MacLachlan, Isabella Rossellini, Dennis Hopper, Laura Dern, Hope Lange, Dean Stockwell *cin* Frederick Elmes *m* Angelo Badalamenti

Amateur detectives Jeffrey Beaumont (Kyle MacLachlan) and Sandy Williams (Laura Dern) try to trace the owner of a severed ear, which leads Jeffrey into the weird and frightening world of Dennis Hopper's monstrous Frank Booth. As unsettling and troubling as *Blue Velvet* genuinely is, this synthesis of Luis Buñuel, Edward Hopper and Sigmund Freud is constructed around a series of comforting old-fashioned opposites: day/night, surface/depth, blonde/brunette, innocence/corruption, good/evil, and Lynch only blurs these distinctions in order to ultimately restore them to their "proper" place.

Wild At Heart 1990, 124 min

cast Nicolas Cage, Laura Dern, Diane Ladd, Willem Dafoe, Isabella Rossellini, Harry Dean Stanton *cin* Frederick Elmes *m* Angelo Badalamenti

Elvis meets the Wicked Witch of the West, as an ex-con (Nicolas Cage) and his squeeze (Laura Dern) hit the road pursued by killers employed by her hellish mother. Driven by a hot eroticism, the pleasures of this film are mostly derived from its detours and cameos: Willem Dafoe as a psychopath toxically mixing oil and sleaze; Sherilyn Fenn as a dazed-and-confused car-crash victim dying from her injuries; and Crispin Glover as Cousin Dell, placing cockroaches down his underpants.

Mulholland Drive 2001, 147 min

cast Justin Theroux, Naomi Watts, Laura Elena Harring, Ann Miller, Dan Hedaya, Mark Pellegrino *cin* Peter Deming *m* Angelo Badalamenti

Spoiler alert: the first half of the film is Diane's dream. She has idealized herself as Betty, a strong-willed, talented actress who takes charge of her relationship with Rita/Camilla. Everything that occurs until they open the blue box is a dream – then the cowboy tells Diane to wake up. When she awakes, the truth is told in flashback: Camilla is the real star, Diane never made it as an actress, and she hired a hit man to kill Camilla when she left her for the film director. Or that's the theory.

Adrian Lyne

UK, 1941–

The 1980s crest of Adrian Lyne's career (which started in commercials) pinpoints the moment that the accelerated editing, gleaming surfaces and consumerist titillation of advertising began to penetrate the big-screen realm. In the case of *Flashdance* (1983), the movie was an advertisement – a feature-length promo for its wildly popular soundtrack. Lyne's most profitable films go down like a Big Mac and leave a styrofoam aftertaste, despite occasional pretensions to nouvelle cuisine.

Smoothing out the herky-jerky rhythms and wayward tone of his awkward girl-gang debut, *Foxes* (1980), Lyne enjoyed a big hit with *Flashdance*, which made an icon of Jennifer Beals in her off-the-shoulder top and leotard as the dancing welder with a dream. For a time, Lyne had the Reagan-era zeitgeist in his pocket. The similarly soundtrack-driven *9½ Weeks* (1985) paired off Mickey Rourke and Kim Basinger for compulsive steamy sex in richly appointed locations, and the infamous *Fatal Attraction* (1987) actually convinced a few members of the cognoscenti that it had something to say about modern marriage and desire. The hysterical cautionary tale against adultery was a touchstone for Lyne, who attempted variations on the theme with *Indecent Proposal* (1993) and *Unfaithful* (2002). In between, he tackled the ghosts of Vietnam in the exploitative post-traumatic thriller *Jacob's Ladder* (1990) and delivered a timid remake in *Lolita* (1997). JW

Fatal Attraction 1987, 120 min

cast Michael Douglas, Glenn Close, Anne Archer, Ellen Hamilton Latzen, Stuart Pankin, Ellen Foley *cin* Howard Atherton *m* Maurice Jarre

The scourge of adultery gets its own *Reefer Madness* (1936) in Lyne's lurid tale of a slick, married lawyer (Michael Douglas) who sleeps with a frizzy-haired (read: crazy) colleague (Glenn Close) and, when he ends the fling, opens a Pandora's box of woman-scorned clichés – and a few new variations, including bunny stew. The recipient of several Oscar nominations and the cover of *Time*, the movie is at least an invaluable time-capsule relic.

Kevin Macdonald

UK, 1967–

Kevin Macdonald has made documentaries that jangle more nerves and pump more adrenalin than any recent Hollywood blockbuster. Macdonald is the grandson of the legendary filmmaker Emeric Pressburger and the brother of Andrew Macdonald, who produced *Shallow Grave* (1994), a film that Kevin was originally slated to direct. When Danny Boyle got the job instead, Macdonald moved into documentaries, making a series of acclaimed TV films (mainly about directors), including a highly personal celebration of his grandfather's career, *The Making Of An Englishman* (1995).

He was then catapulted into the spotlight when his cinema debut, *One Day In September* (1999), unexpectedly snatched the Oscar for best documentary from the favourite, *The Buena Vista Social Club* (1999). *September* is the enthralling chronicle of the events surrounding the murder of eleven Israeli athletes at the 1972 Munich Olympics. Macdonald also pulled off the phenomenal coup of securing the only on-camera interview with the lone surviving terrorist. The director immediately earned a reputation for himself as a filmmaker who could make a documentary with the dynamic narrative strategies and edge-of-your-seat tension of the most riveting Hollywood thriller, a trend he happily continued with *Touching The Void* (2003).

Despite Macdonald's forays into fiction in his documentaries, he surprised critics with the assured maturity on display when he made his first feature film, *The Last King Of Scotland* (2006), a political thriller set in 1970s Uganda. He returned to documentaries in 2007 with *My Enemy's Enemy*, an investigation into the post-war activities of the infamous Gestapo commander Klaus Barbie. But with Hollywood calling – thanks to the awards and critical acclaim heaped upon *The Last King Of Scotland* – further fiction features are undoubtedly on the cards. LH

One Day In September **1999, 95 min**

with Michael Douglas, Ankie Spitzer, Jamal Al-Gashey, Gerald Seymour, Alex Springer *cin* Alwin Küchler, Neve Cunningham *m* Alex Heffes

In 1972, the Palestinian terrorist group Black September held eleven Israelis hostage in an apartment in the Olympic village under the gaze of the watching world. Macdonald adroitly charts the blunders that led to the athletes' deaths, revealing that the rescue operation was stymied by a lack of communication between police marksmen and, indeed, the lack of a plan. The film is, in turn, astonishing and disturbing, the only false note being Michael Douglas's overemphatic narration.

Touching The Void **2003, 106 min**

with Joe Simpson, Simon Yates, Richard Hawking *cast* Brendan Mackey, Nicholas Aaron, Ollie Ryall *cin* Mike Eley, Keith Partridge *m* Alex Heffes

In 1985 Simon Yates and Joe Simpson attempted to climb one of the Andes' most daunting mountains the old-fashioned way, by simply attaching themselves to a rope. But when Simpson fell down a cliff face, Yates had to make the decision to cut the rope and send his friend to almost certain death. Using reconstruction with actors and interviews with the protagonists, Macdonald ratchets up the tension to almost asphyxiating levels as Simpson tries to haul his broken body from its icy grave to the safety of base camp.

The Last King Of Scotland **2006, 121 min**

cast James McEvoy, Forest Whitaker, Kerry Washington, Gillian Anderson, Simon McBurney *cin* Anthony Dod Mantle *m* Alex Heffes

Forest Whitaker deservedly won an Oscar for his eye-opening performance as General Idi Amin, the Ugandan dictator and alleged cannibal. Capturing both his considerable charm and his terrifying egomania, Whitaker overshadows James McEvoy, who stars as a Scottish doctor and chancer who becomes one of the president's men in this taut adaptation of Giles Foden's novel. Macdonald's vibrant direction is note-perfect until the film's climax when giddy and gory melodrama start to get the better of him.

Alexander Mackendrick

US, 1912–93

The buoyantly cynical vision of Alexander Mackendrick brought a consistently subversive note to the often cosy world of Ealing Studios in the three brilliant comedies he made for the studio.

Born in the US but raised in Scotland, Mackendrick started off in advertising and, with his cousin Roger MacDougall, made short propaganda films during World War II. Joining Ealing Studios in 1946 as a scriptwriter, he made his directorial debut three years later with *Whisky Galore!* (1949), a deftly orchestrated battle of wits between a small band of Scottish islanders and an English Home Guard officer who comes between them and 50,000 cases of shipwrecked whisky. Like all Mackendrick's films, this spirited romp exhibited a gleeful, heartfelt cynicism and subtle moral complexity. The bad guys are pitiless and venal, but the innocents aren't entirely likeable either. Single-minded to the exclusion of everything else, his characters are often lost in a fog of self-indulgence, whether their narrow focus is on a cargo of whisky, a pet parrot or a miraculous invention (as in his 1951 masterpiece *The Man In The White Suit*). Mackendrick's only straight drama for Ealing, *Mandy* (1952), focused on a deaf girl whose parents fall out over the decision to send her to an institution. Here, the director's cynicism can be seen in the selfish lawyer who fabricates evidence about the mother having an affair.

The Maggie (1954) was another Scottish film about contested cargo. A game of cat-and-mouse is played out between the owners of a ramshackle old tug and their dissatisfied American client, and all the protagonists are breezily painted in different shades of deviousness. But they pale into insignificance besides the villains in *The Ladykillers* (1955), five of the most nonchalantly malevolent characters in Ealing history. Mackendrick cleverly veiled the script's breathtaking misanthropy in Ealing charm, but after he quit the studio to make the scabrous *Sweet Smell Of Success* (1957), he swiftly stripped away any last vestiges of whimsy.

Sadly, the corruscating *Sweet Smell Of Success* was a box-office failure, and Mackendrick's bad fortune continued. He was fired from both *The Devil's Disciple* (1959) and *The Guns Of Navarone* (1961) – from the latter for being too much of a perfectionist – and eventually returned to work for Michael Balcon on *Sammy Going South* (1963). However, according to his biographer Philip Kemp, there was a crucial difference of opinion between producer Balcon, who wanted a simple adventure, and the director who imagined the picture as "an inward odyssey of a deeply disturbed child". The resulting compromise met with indifferent reviews.

Ever since he had met writer Richard Hughes in the 1940s, Mackendrick wanted to film an adaptation of his novel *High Wind In Jamaica*. Its theme of a child's capacity to maintain innocence in the face of danger and indifference, could equally be applied to several of Mackendrick's more naïve characters. Unfortunately, 20th Century Fox had envisioned a cuter, more Disneyfied movie, and they cut almost a quarter of the 1965 film and reshuffled the rest. His final film *Don't Make Waves* (1967), a dippy comedy about Tony Curtis's lusty attempts to woo skydiver Sharon Tate, was a sad note on which to end his directorial career and Mackendrick later claimed he was tricked into making it.

When a final attempt to film his pet project about Mary, Queen of Scots collapsed, he quit filmmaking altogether, claiming he was spending 95 percent of his time getting films made and only 5 percent making them. Mackendrick spent the rest of his working life as the head of the film department at California Institute of the Arts. He proved to be an inspiring if demanding teacher, bringing the same dedicated craftsmanship and perfectionism to his teaching as he did to his best movies. LH

Whisky Galore! 1949, 82 min, b/w

cast Basil Radford, Joan Greenwood, Jean Cadell, Gordon Jackson, James Robertson Justice, Wylie Watson *cin* Gerald Gibbs *m* Ernest Irving

Wartime stringencies mean that the inhabitants of the Isle of Todday are suffering from a lack of whisky, when a ship carrying 50,000 cases of the stuff suddenly runs aground on their shores. Captain Waggett (Basil Radford) valiantly attempts to protect the contraband, but the best efforts of the Home Guard are no match for thirsty Scots. Hearty and gently subversive, this is the slightest of Mackendrick's three Ealing masterpieces.

The Man In The White Suit 1951, 85 min, b/w

cast Alec Guinness, Joan Greenwood, Cecil Parker, Michael Gough, Ernest Thesiger, Vida Hope *cin* Douglas Slocombe *m* Benjamin Frankel

When laboratory menial Sidney Stratton (Alec Guinness) invents a material that can never wear out or get dirty both the unions and management unite against him in a spirit of self-preservation. Dazzled by the brilliance of his great, white invention, the naïve stubbornness of Guinness's inventor becomes a threat to property and to life. Mackendrick brings his customary sharpness to this powerful satire on British industrial conservatism and moral cowardice.

The Ladykillers 1955, 97 min

cast Alec Guinness, Cecil Parker, Herbert Lom, Peter Sellers, Danny Green, Katie Johnson, Jack Warner, Frankie Howerd *cin* Otto Heller *m* Tristram Cary

Five thieves planning a train robbery in London's King's Cross (while masquerading as rehearsing musicians) decide they're going to have to kill their little old landlady before she tells the police their secret in this classic black comedy. Alec Guinness as creepy, toothy Professor Marcus leads the gang of sinister, but befuddled, crooks – oaf One Round, teddy boy Harry, old rogue The Major and spiv Louis – who prove no match for their intended victim, that politely interfering, parrot-obsessed representative of Edwardian England, Mrs Wilberforce (Katie Johnson).

Sweet Smell Of Success 1957, 96 min, b/w

cast Burt Lancaster, Tony Curtis, Susan Harrison, Martin Milner, Sam Levene, Barbara Nichols *cin* James Wong Howe *m* Elmer Bernstein

Burt Lancaster is spectacularly sinister as omnipotent gossip columnist J.J. Hunsecker, who employs oleaginous press agent Sidney Falco (a superbly two-faced Tony Curtis)

M

to break up his sister and her musician boyfriend by planting stories about him in the newspaper. Mackendrick's dark heart is finally revealed through the combination of James Wong Howe's stunning *noir* cinematography, Clifford Odets' gutter poetry and two of the most irredeemably venal characters ever committed to celluloid.

David Mackenzie

UK, 1966–

After making his first two feature films, David Mackenzie was momentarily seen by some as British cinema's great white hope – a reputation he largely stymied with his third effort *Asylum* (2005). Frustrated at the lack of opportunities for British filmmakers (after making three shorts), the director took the guerrilla option and shot his *petit guignol* thriller, *The Last Great Wilderness* (2002), on digital video with a tight budget. Although the film received mixed reviews, Mackenzie's vivid and assured direction proved to be an effective calling card. In 2002 he was handed a £4 million budget and a cast of British A-list talent to realize his dream of adapting *Young Adam*, an earthy novel by boho writer and fellow Scot Alexander Trocchi. This claustrophobic psychodrama benefited from a winning combination: it was both literary and sexy. His next movie was another adaptation of a novel set in the 1950s that once again throbbed with sexual infidelity. The resulting *Asylum* was an overheated slice of English gothic about a psychiatrist's wife falling for one of his patients, a worryingly old-fashioned treatment of mental illness that itself displayed alarming signs of hysteria. LH

Young Adam 2002, 98 min
cast Ewan McGregor, Tilda Swinton, Peter Mullan, Emily Mortimer, Jack McElhone, Therese Bradley *cin* Giles Nuttgens *m* David Byrne

In the claustrophobic confines of a coal barge, an incorrigible charmer (Ewan McGregor) seduces his best friend's wife, while flashbacks reveal his raunchy affair with another woman (Emily Mortimer). Although Mackenzie exhibits a maturity beyond his years, his over-reverential approach is, arguably, at odds with the explicit content. The director only really lets his hair down in the notorious scene where McGregor lustfully splashes custard and ketchup over Mortimer's naked body.

John Mackenzie

UK, 1932–

Although he's made films set in Dallas, South America, LA and the Mediterranean, Scottish director John Mackenzie remains best known for 1979's London gangster film *The Long Good Friday*. Starring Bob Hoskins as an East End gangster whose plans to attract American (Mafia) investment in the Docklands fall apart spectacularly over the course of an explosive Easter weekend, this is one of the definitive London films. It also marked a turning point in Mackenzie's career, propelling him to Hollywood after a decade directing dramas and plays for the BBC, mostly in the realist mode he learned from Ken Loach on *Cathy Come Home* (1966). These included several contributions to the drama series *Play For Today* and a powerful adaptation of Scottish hardman Jimmy Boyle's autobiography *A Sense Of Freedom* (1979). Predictably, perhaps, Mackenzie's subsequent international films lacked the grit and urgency of his 1970s work, and many went straight to video. *The Last Of The Finest* (aka *Blue Heat*, 1990) and *Ruby* (1992) were among his better efforts. TC

The Long Good Friday 1979, 114 min
cast Bob Hoskins, Dave King, Helen Mirren, Bryan Marshall, Derek Thompson, Eddie Constantine *cin* Phil Meheux *m* Francis Monkman

Bob Hoskins tears up the screen as the East End's answer to Little Caesar, Harold Shand. Harold has big plans: London will become Europe's capital, and the Docklands will host the 1988 Olympics. All he needs is a little foreign investment. But when Mafia boss Eddie Constantine arrives to give him the once-over Harold finds himself on the receiving end of a gang war he knows nothing about. It's a brutal film, with shocking explosions of violence, but it's also got a keen, implosive sense of the ridiculous ("Colin never hurt a fly. Only when it was necessary").

Gillies MacKinnon

UK, 1948–

Gillies MacKinnon combines Ken Loach's social conscience with Mike Leigh's feeling for character. He first attracted industry plaudits for *The Playboys* (1992), set in an Irish village where Robin Wright's unmarried mother must choose between love and conformity. Characteristically for MacKinnon, the protagonists are torn between liberating fantasies and the mire of reality. External stresses on relationships were prominent again in MacKinnon's Hollywood debut, *A Simple Twist Of Fate* (1994). Transposing George Eliot's novel *Silas Marner* to contemporary America, the film sees Steve Martin's reclusive cabinet-maker thrust into fatherhood when an orphan stumbles into his life.

Tough, gritty situations have dominated most of MacKinnon's more recent films. *Trojan Eddie* (1995) pits Stephen Rea's hard-nosed chancer against Richard Harris's underworld boss; *Small Faces* (1996), though obscured by *Trainspotting*, sets a richly observed rite of passage amid the rough estates and diminished prospects of 1960s Glasgow; *Regeneration* (1997) describes compromised life on the Western Front; and *Pure* (2002) is an unsentimental portrait of smack addiction seen through a child's eyes. One departure from this general theme

335

was *Hideous Kinky* (1998), in which Kate Winslet plays a hippy dragging her daughters through the souks and sands of Morocco. This change of tone didn't really work, however: the film seems as wayward and unfocused as its main protagonist. RA

Regeneration 1997, 114 min

cast Jonathan Pryce, James Wilby, Jonny Lee Miller, Stuart Bunce, Tanya Allen, David Hayman cin Glen MacPherson m Mychael Danna

Based on Pat Barker's World War I novel, *Regeneration* tells of a doctor working with shell-shocked soldiers in a Scottish asylum and his relationship with poet Siegfried Sassoon, who has been committed there for expressing anti-war views. Sensitively exploring the blinkered medical attitudes of the day and the horrors of war (the broken bodies and mud of Flanders are painted in sepia tones), this is powerful heritage cinema.

Alison Maclean

Canada, 1958–

Alison Maclean has dealt with disturbed souls in an impervious world. Moving to New Zealand at 14, she studied film and sculpture at Auckland University. Award-winning shorts led to the feature *Crush* (1992). Surviving a car accident, an assertive American (Marcia Gay Harden) assumes the identity of her injured friend and works her way into the lives of a writer and his daughter. After this success, Maclean moved to America, working on television series – including *Homicide: Life On The Street* and *Sex And The City* – and Natalie Imbruglia videos. Maclean returned to cinema with *Jesus' Son* (1999), a meditative piece based on a collection of short stories by Denis Johnson. Her output since has included *Persons Of Interest* (2004), a documentary dealing in sober detail with American Muslims in detention. Maclean is a technically imaginative and compassionate filmmaker. RA

Jesus' Son 1999, 107 min

cast Billy Crudup, Samantha Morton, Denis Leary, Holly Hunter, Dennis Hopper, Jack Black cin Adam Kimmel

Well-meaning FH (short for Fuckhead) survives a car crash and recalls episodes from his drugged-up, dropped-out life in 1970s America. Billy Crudup is superb in the lead role, and Samantha Morton is great as FH's lover. With an impressive supporting cast including Jack Black and Holly Hunter, this is a superb desultory poem of drifting, loss and redemption.

John Madden

UK, 1949–

John Madden, the director of the multiple-Oscar-winning *Shakespeare In Love* (1998), developed an interest in the Bard early in his career when he formed the Oxford and Cambridge Shakespeare Theatre Company after leaving university. In the mid-1980s, he established a name for himself by making quality television dramas, and later earned his reputation as a director of actors and a consummate craftsman with a self-effacing style. In other words, he is a very British director. Although he'd already made two films – the austere Edith Wharton adaptation *Ethan Frome* (1993) and the disastrous McCarthy-era *Golden Gate* (1994) – it was *Mrs Brown* (1997) that brought Madden to the attention of Hollywood. The Weinstein brothers bought the distribution rights to *Mrs Brown*, which tastefully dished the dirt on Queen Victoria's relationship with an irrepressible Scotsman, and then handed Madden the reins to *Shakespeare In Love*. After his giddy Oscar success, Madden came back down to earth with the critical and commercial flop *Captain Corelli's Mandolin* (2001). The director must shoulder much of the blame, as it was he who insisted on changing the ending of Louis de Bernières' novel. Returning to the theatre, Madden directed the London production of David Auburn's *Proof* and, in 2005, reunited with Gwyneth Paltrow to make the disappointing film version of the play. LH

Shakespeare In Love 1998, 123 min

cast Joseph Fiennes, Gwyneth Paltrow, Judi Dench, Ben Affleck, Colin Firth, Simon Callow, Geoffrey Rush cin Richard Greatrex m Stephen Warbeck

Scripted by Tom Stoppard, this ribald comedy about a young noblewoman who pretends to be a man in order to get a part in Shakespeare's latest production, *Romeo And Ethel*, is ripe with intellectual chutzpah and intertextual game-playing. Madden directs with aplomb, and Gwyneth Paltrow is a delight – and proves that her English locutions in *Emma* (1996) and *Sliding Doors* (1998) were no fluke.

Guy Maddin

Canada, 1956–

"The fluency with which Maddin speaks a dead movie-language suggests he suffers from a most plangent nostalgia, that he has spent most of his life looking backward through misty eyes": this is Guy Maddin, his own best critic, reviewing a retrospective of his films in *The Village Voice* in 2001. Teeming with fever dreams and mortified flesh, luxuriating in an oneiric confusion of amnesia, romantic regret and the ghosts of cinema past, Maddin's films are rapturous and possessed by the faraway spirits of silent and early sound cinema.

His first feature, *Tales From The Gimli Hospital* (1988), in which a smallpox-like epidemic ravages a Manitoba town, was a cult smash (it played for a year at a Greenwich Village cinema). *Archangel* (1990), which nestled beneath a snowy, forgetful World War I haze, and *Careful* (1992), "a pro-incest mountain *träumerei*" according to Maddin, were characterized by shimmering, often languid tableaux, glimpsed through a lens sometimes covered with gauze or Vaseline.

Since the failure of his first 35mm film, *Twilight Of The Ice Nymphs* (1997), the editing pace and sheer overload of images in his work have accelerated, and Maddin has been unstoppable. *Dracula: Pages From A Virgin's Diary* (2002) adapted a Royal Winnipeg Ballet production into a frenzied, (mostly) black-and-white silent melodrama. *Cowards Bend The Knee* (2002) locked *noir*, Eisenstein-style montage and confessional autobiography in a sordid back room for a thrashing *ménage à trois*. *The Saddest Music In The World* (2003) evoked Eisenstein trying his hand at screwball, with a little help from Busby Berkeley. And *Brand Upon The Brain!* (2006) – like *Cowards*, an autobiographical silent film – told the story of a young boy named Guy Maddin who lives in a lighthouse-cum-orphanage teeming with sinister plots and misfiring hormones. JW

Archangel 1990, 90 min
cast Kyle McCulloch, Kathy Marykuca, Sarah Neville, Ari Cohen, Michael Gottli, David Falkenberg *cin* Guy Maddin

Mourning his sweetheart and the loss of a leg after World War I, Canadian Lt John Boles (Kyle McCulloch, poignantly blank) arrives in a Russian Arctic outpost where a few faithful stragglers keep on fighting; befogged by mustard gas and amnesia, Boles mistakes his nurse for his late girlfriend – the first of many romantic mix-ups in what Maddin has named the favourite of his films. Hypnotic and hallucinatory, it includes a few priceless set pieces, including a strangulation-by-intestines and a rainstorm of bunny rabbits.

The Saddest Music In The World 2003, 99 min
cast Mark McKinney, Isabella Rossellini, Maria de Madeiros, David Fox, Ross McMillan, Louis Negin *cin* Luc Montpellier *m* Christopher Dedrick

In Maddin's most linear narrative to date, a down-on-his-luck Broadway producer (Mark McKinney) and his nymphomaniac, amnesiac girlfriend (Maria de Madeiros) descend on Depression-era Winnipeg to enter a contest to find the world's saddest music, cooked up by a double-amputee beer baroness (Isabella Rossellini) who is outfitted with glass legs bubbling with ale. "It's like I'm painting things just by looking at them", muses one character, and the same goes for Maddin whenever he peers through his camera.

Dušan Makavejev
Serbia (formerly Yugoslavia), 1932–

"I see the cinema as a guerrilla operation. Guerrilla against everything that is fixed, defined, established, dogmatic, eternal." So said Dušan Makavejev, the anarchist, collagist, essayist, controversialist, who is, arguably, the most important director to come out of the former Yugoslavia. His fame rests on five early films that went wildly off the beaten track of traditional storytelling, digressing into lectures and documentary and making use of found footage from old movies. These boisterous exercises manifested a Godardian cross-referencing glee, but were edited with the systematic astringency of Eisenstein. Makavejev dealt in contradictions rather than conclusions, apparently regarding meaning as another dusty monolith to be shelved alongside political doctrines and conventional narrative – a dangerous strategy even in the relatively "liberal" 1960s and 70s.

After several experimental short films and documentaries, Makavejev's debut feature, *Man Is Not A Bird* (1965), concerned the sexual odyssey of a Soviet engineer in Yugoslavia, with characteristic digressions on love and stage hypnotism. With *The Switchboard Operator* (1967) the director came into his exuberant, kaleidoscopic own, with a tragic tale of a cross-cultural love affair combined with lectures from sexologists and criminologists and asides on rat-catching and strudel-making. In *Innocence Unprotected* (1968) he took footage from the first Serbian talkie, which was filmed clandestinely in 1943 during the German occupation, and edited it together with reminiscences of its lead actor and director, Dragoljub Aleksić – a strongman who used to hang by his teeth from planes. He also added a third, contextualizing element of documentary footage made following the Nazi invasion of Serbia.

Makavejev's next film, *W.R.: Mysteries Of The Organism* (1971) brought him international attention but also state intervention. Fearing for his liberty, he left Yugoslavia the day after the film was banned, remaining in exile for seventeen years. The contention concerned a documentary portion of the film about the controversial psychoanalyst Wilhelm Reich, who argued that repressed sexuality was the root cause of political oppression. Makavejev's attitudes to sex and gender became an issue during the filming of *Sweet Movie* (1974), when lead actress Carol Laure walked off the set, complaining about the sex scenes she had been asked to take part in. The movie incorporated two stories, one involving a cult, the members of which like to defecate on dinner plates, and another about a communist pirate ship, captained by a character called Anna Planeta, who systematically seduces and kills young boys. It was the last of Makavejev's delirious, stuffed-to-the-brim collages. Since then, his narratives have become linear, his surrealism muted, and his energy diffused.

His most commercially successful film, *Montenegro* (1981), zeroed in on a bored American housewife in Sweden. *The Coca-Cola Kid* (1985) was a contemporary fable about a ruthless executive who finds a form of redemption in the Australian outback. Offering the promise of acerbic delights, its satire was rather dull and blunt. Makavejev returned from exile with *Manifesto* (1988) – based on the Emile Zola story "For A Night Of Love" – which was filmed in Belgrade. He once again addressed the subject of communism in *The Gorilla Bathes At Noon* (1993), about a Russian soldier lost in post-war Berlin. For some critics, the last two films represent a return to form; for many others, Makavejev is stuck in the past, an anarchist in need of a worthy adversary. LH

The Switchboard Operator (Ljubavni slucaj ili tragedija sluzbenice P.T.T.) 1967, 69 min, b/w
cast Eva Ras, Slobodan Aligrudić, Ruzica Sokić, Aleksander Kostić, Zivojin Aleksić *cin* Aleksandar Petković *m* Dušan Aleksić

Izabela, a young switchboard operator, sets up home with a rat-catcher called Ahmed. They live happily until a friend reads her fortune and predicts that she will have an affair. The film is more conventionally and emotionally involving than most early Makavejev movies, despite the presence of Brechtian alienation techniques – such as characters directly addressing the camera, and lectures on phallic adoration and mattress stuffing.

W.R.: Mysteries Of The Organism (W.R. – Misterije organizma) 1971, 86 min, b/w and col
with Wilhelm Reich *cast* Milena Dravić, Ivica Vidović, Tuli Kupferberg, Zoran Radmilović *cin* Aleksandar Petković, Pega Popović *m* Bojana Marijan

Opening as a documentary about Wilhelm Reich, the film switches to the story of a young Yugoslav devotee of the doctor's philosophy who liberates a politically indoctrinated and sexually repressed Soviet skater, with alarming results. What seemed radically dangerous then now seems charmingly quaint, particularly in its insistence that personal and political liberation can be achieved through bigger and better orgasms.

Montenegro 1981, 96 min
cast Susan Anspach, Erland Josephson, Bora Todorović, Per Oscarsson, John Zacharias, Svetozar Cvetković *cin* Tomislav Pinter *m* Kornell Kovach

Susan Anspach plays the desperate American housewife of a rich Swedish businessman who finds herself in the Zanzi Bar club, run by guest workers from Yugoslavia. Encountering a form of sexual liberation she cannot cope with, she turns to murder. Far gentler in its narrative gambits than his Yugoslav films, it's as if Makavejev only really blossoms in difficult conditions. As fellow East European director Jirí Menzel once said: "Communism is good for filmmaking."

Mohsen Makhmalbaf
Iran, 1957–

One of Iran's most acclaimed filmmakers of recent years, Mohsen Makhmalbaf was born in a poor district of Tehran and became politically active at an early age. At 15 he established an underground militia opposing the Shah's regime, and at 17 he was shot and arrested during a fight with a policeman. Makhmalbaf was sent to prison, where he spent more than four years – a period in which he read voraciously. Released following the Islamic Revolution of 1979, he wrote novels, stories and screenplays.

Early films – *Repentance* (1982), *Fleeing From Evil To God* (1984) – were politically didactic and cinematically crude. Generic, popular projects followed. *Boycott* (1985) was a thriller glorifying

Islamic values and drawing upon Makhmalbaf's experience of incarceration. *The Cyclist* (1987) was about a poor Afghan driven to take a job with a circus, riding a bicycle nonstop. *The Peddler* (1987) saw Makhmalbaf begin to question the hegemony of Iran's theocracy. *Marriage Of The Blessed* (1989) criticized the regime for its indifference towards veterans of the Iran-Iraq War. If *Once Upon A Time, Cinema* (1992) was content to celebrate the art of film, his subsequent work was marked by an increasingly sophisticated political awareness. *A Time Of Love* (1990) and *The Nights Of Zayandehroud* (1991) got Makhmalbaf into trouble for their depictions of sex and for challenging the Revolution.

The mid-1990s were a turning point. *Salaam Cinema* (1995), a *cinéma-vérité* account of auditions for a film, found Makhmalbaf pondering his role as an artist. *Gabbeh* and *A Moment Of Innocence* (both 1996) made him an international festival name and a Western arthouse draw. That year, Makhmalbaf also began teaching filmmakers from home, including daughter Samira, now a highly regarded director in her own right. The Makhmalbaf dynasty also includes another daughter, Hana (who directed *Joy Of Madness*, 2003), his wife Marzieh Meshkini (director of *The Day I Became A Woman*, 2000 and *Stray Dogs*, 2004) and his son Maysam who is an editor and cameraman.

Kandahar (2001), released the year of 9/11 and the US incursion into Afghanistan, was a powerful film that added further to Makhmalbaf's Western cachet. Shocked by conditions in Afghanistan, Makhmalbaf also made documentaries in the country, including *The Afghan Alphabet* (2002), charting children's lives in a border town. He has since returned his focus to Iran, resulting in films such as *Sex and Philosophy* (2005), an allegorical dance film about love and fidelity, with the choreography being used to explore the emotions of three women in love with the same man. This marks something of a change of direction, one that evinces an increasingly poetic take on Iranian experience. RA

Gabbeh 1996, 74 min
cast Shaghayeh Djodat, Hossein Moharami, Abbas Sayah, Rogheih Moharami *cin* Mahmoud Kalari *m* Hossein Alizadeh

A *gabbeh* is a style of thick, triple-knotted carpet from southern Iran, and this film begins as a documentary about the people who weave them. But the fabulous colours and textures of the *gabbeh* are really a starting point to reflect upon popular legends and desires. The result is a portrait of an Islamic culture far removed from chadors and the austerity of fundamentalism – a fantasia lushly evoking the spirits and forms of Sufi theology.

A Moment Of Innocence (Noon va Goldoon) 1996, 78 min
cast Mirhadi Tayebi, Ali Bakhsi, Ammar Tafti, Maryam Mohamadamini *cin* Mahmoud Kalari

When Mirhadi Tayebi turned up to audition for *Salaam Cinema*, Makhmalbaf recognized him as the policeman he

Set among the carpet-weaving tribes of southeastern Iran, *Gabbeh* has all the rich colours and directness of folk art.

had hospitalized two decades earlier. The result was this unusual film, which revisits the skirmish from the perspective of both protagonists. We learn that the policeman was in love with the woman used as a decoy during the attack, and that the young firebrand may have been too. A deftly made meditation on the nature of memory and coincidence and the tangled relations between politics, passion and art.

Kandahar (Safar e Ghandehar) 2001, 85 min

cast Nelofer Pazira, Hassan Tantaï, Sadou Teymouri, Hoyatala Hakimi *cin* Ebrahim Ghafori *m* Mohammad Reza Darvishi

Released soon after 9/11 and the US invasion of Afghanistan, *Kandahar* follows an Afghan expatriate as she searches for her sister in a country ravaged by Taliban extremists. The film contains many potent scenes, the most memorable of which sees landmine victims desperately scurrying across the desert to reach an airdrop of prosthetic limbs.

Samira Makhmalbaf

Iran, 1980–

Samira Makhmalbaf espouses using cameras to open up societies. The daughter of Iranian New Wave auteur Mohsen Makhmalbaf, she grew up in a unique atmosphere of cinematic and political ideas. As a child, she appeared in her father's *The Cyclist* (1987). Having little faith in her teachers or the curriculum, she left school at 14. Educated from home, she became part of the Makhmalbaf Film House, a film school and production facility that would nurture her and her stepmother, the director Marzieh Meshkini.

After making video shorts, Samira assisted on Makhmalbaf's *The Silence* (1998). That same year, her debut feature, *The Apple*, became an international festival and arthouse sensation. Lauded by the Western press as a precocious new talent, Samira was invited to sit on festival juries and fêted as the latest star in the Iranian efflorescence. Soon after, she picked up the directing prize at Cannes for *Blackboards* (2000), which explored the experience of teachers on the perilous Iran-Iraq border, using nonprofessionals and actual locations. If some have queried Samira's directing identity (Mohsen has co-written and edited her films), her emphasis on hidden lives is unique.

In 2002, Samira directed the Iranian segment of the French portmanteau commemoration *11'09"01*. Her 2003 feature *Five In The Afternoon* follows the fortunes of a young Afghan woman who defies tradition by professing a desire to become president. Behind the image of poster girl for arthouse realism, Samira Makhmalbaf is a democratic radical in a world of franchise cinema and fundamentalist intolerance. RA

The Apple (Sib) 1998, 85 min

cast Massoumeh Naderi, Zahra Naderi, Ghorban Ali Naderi, Azizeh Mohamadi *cin* Ebrahim Ghafori

Responding to a news item in which two girls were freed after twelve years incarceration by their father in a suburb of Tehran, the 17-year-old Makhmalbaf went there and shot this beautiful film using the actual protagonists. With a touch of her father's symbolism (a dangling apple, the fruit of temptation) Samira records the wide-eyed girls with sensitivity and intelligence.

Blackboards (Takhté siah) 2000, 85 min

cast Said Mohamadi, Bahman Ghobadi, Behnaz Jafari, Rafat Moradi *cin* Ebrahim Ghafori *m* Mohammad Reza Darvishi

Teachers wander the dangerous Iraqi border in Iranian Kurdistan in search of students, their blackboards strapped to their backs as cover against gunfire. As events unfold, it becomes clear that this is simultaneously a portrait of a bleak place caught up in an ongoing crisis and a persuasive take on the place of education in a hazardous world. Ambitious and highly impressive for a director still only 19.

Terrence Malick

US, 1943–

Almost as legendary for his silence as for his films, Terrence Malick has created a myth around himself worthy of Stanley Kubrick. He began his career as a philosophy teacher, studying the subject at Harvard and Oxford before going on to teach at the Massachusetts Institute of Technology. At the same time – the late 1960s – he worked as a journalist and was one of the first graduates of the recently founded American Film Institute.

His first film in the director's seat, *Badlands* (1973) was an esoteric and elegiac take on the lovers-on-the-run sub-genre. Hailed as one of the finest directorial debuts ever, *Badlands* drew up the Malick blueprint: an oddly serene collision of clinical violence and radiant beauty, in which nature bears mute witness to the casual brutality of human beings. The camera painted pictures of transfixing lyricism, while a dreamy voiceover is seemingly at odds with the images it accompanies.

Days Of Heaven (1978) reshaped a *noir* staple – lovers plotting the death of a rich husband – into a rapturous paean to nature as both provider and destroyer. Shot by Nestor Almendros and Haskell Wexler mostly in magic-hour light – the moments after sunset where the dying light confers a hazy languor and melancholic resonance on its subjects – it's considered one of the most sheerly beautiful of 1970s feature films. It took two years to edit, although for some critics the result was just too picture-perfect. The terse, slyly poetic voiceover by Linda Manz that holds the whole thing together was only added as an afterthought.

And then Malick disappeared from view. Refusing all requests for interviews, he became one of cinema's most enigmatic figures. It appears that during his twenty-year sabbatical he started work on a great folly, a quixotic attempt to document the creation of the universe, for which he reportedly filmed natural phenomena from all over the globe, paid for by Paramount and mysteriously abandoned in 1983. Rather less mystically, he wrote an early draft of the Jerry Lee Lewis biopic *Great Balls Of Fire!* (1989).

Malick was gently coaxed out of retirement in 1998 by producers Robert Geisler and John Robardeau. Offered a list of projects to chose from, he plumped for an adaptation of James Jones's World War II novel *The Thin Red Line*, which deals with the defeat of the Japanese at Guadalcanal. Assembling his own regiment of stars in the Australian outback, Malick abandoned the script, finding the essence of the film in multiple takes and, once again, in meticulous editing.

The New World (2005) damaged, possibly irrevocably, the myth of Malick. The contemplative, quasi-philosophical narration and familiar billowing blades of sun-dappled grass were all present and correct, but there was a difference: the rhapsodic shots of nature complement rather than counterbalance the loved-up narrative. Some critics believed that the director had finally succumbed to self-parody, painfully revealing his limited repertoire of tics and tropes; others were entranced. LH

Badlands 1973, 94 min

cast Martin Sheen, Sissy Spacek, Warren Oates, Ramon Bieri, Alan Vint, Gary Littlejohn *cin* Tak Fujimoto *m* Carl Orff, George Aliceson Tipton

Real-life killers Charles Starkweather and Caril Ann Fugate, who murdered eleven people in the mid-1950s, are here transformed into Martin Sheen's self-mythologizing Kit

Field of action: Sean Penn and Nick Nolte hold *The Thin Red Line*.

Carruthers and Sissy Spacek's frighteningly naïve Holly Sargis. When Holly's father objects to their love, Kit kills him in cold blood, and the two embark on a cross-country murder spree. Filtered through the prism of Holly's skewed personality, the whole film seems to exist in a cinematic hinterland that is neither naturalistic nor surreal, but a place that is uniquely Malick's own.

Days Of Heaven 1978, 94 min

cast Richard Gere, Brooke Adams, Sam Shepard, Linda Manz, Robert Wilke, Jackie Shultis, Stuart Margolin *cin* Nestor Almendros *m* Ennio Morricone

Two lovers (Richard Gere and Brooke Adams) work in the wheat fields of a dying farm owner (Sam Shepard). When the farmer falls for Adams, the lovers plot for her to marry him and take his money when he dies. However, the marriage gives him a new lease of life... Influenced by *Sunrise*, F.W. Murnau's classic story of a love triangle, and by Malick's own time as a farm worker, every frame of this bucolic, gothic tragedy shimmers with a mournful resonance, as if all the characters are unwittingly sowing the seeds of their own destruction.

The Thin Red Line 1998, 170 min

cast Sean Penn, Adrien Brody, James Caviezel, Ben Chaplin, John Cusack, Nick Nolte, Woody Harrelson, George Clooney *cin* John Toll *m* Hans Zimmer

Many viewers couldn't see beyond the narrative sprawl, philosophical monologues and stories of behind-the-scenes cuts and chaos of this unique war movie. Yet Malick's direction clearly packs the requisite genre punch, while the voiceovers act as an adroit counterpoint. The director insisted on filming only in natural light, so something as simple as sunlight proceeding slowly across a field inspires an unlikely transcendental awe. A masterpiece – there's nothing flawed about it.

Louis Malle

France, 1932–95

Although he was a contemporary of the *nouvelle vague* directors, Louis Malle's filmmaking was always more rooted in classical prototypes and he was never interested in innovation for innovation's sake.

Scion of a wealthy sugar dynasty, Malle received a Catholic education. He went on to read political science at the Sorbonne, an experience reflected in his films, which candidly anatomize the bourgeoisie. Upon graduating from IDHEC, the French national film school, Malle was picked by oceanographer Jacques Cousteau to co-direct, shoot and edit his documentary *Le monde du silence* (*The Silent World*, 1956). He also assisted on Robert Bresson's *A Man Escaped* (1956).

Malle's first solo directed feature was *Ascenseur pour l'échafaud* (*Lift To The Scaffold*, 1957), a thriller starring Jeanne Moreau as a tough modern woman bent on murder. It was distinguished by Henri Decäe's moody cinematography of a Paris free from tourist cliché and embellishment. Critic Georges Sadoul saw the film as the harbinger of a truly modern sensibility and identified Malle as the most promising director of the new generation.

Malle's next film, *Les amants* (*The Lovers*, 1958), treated middle-class female adultery in a uniquely nonjudgemental way, couching its tryst between Jeanne Moreau's bored socialite and Jean-Marc Bory's young man in classical tracking shots and acute observation.

Based on Raymond Queneau's verbally dexterous novel, *Zazie dans le métro* (1960) follows Catherine Demongeot's vivacious 12-year-old heroine across a madcap Paris alive with jump cuts and in-jokes. Starring Brigitte Bardot and focusing on a film star not unlike "BB", *Vie privée* (*A Very Private Affair*, 1962) denounced the alienating consequences of modern celebrity. The next year's *Le feu follet* (*The Fire Within*, 1963) was Malle's most mature statement on the times.

After *Viva Maria* (1965), which paired Moreau and Bardot in a rollicking confection of sex and Mexican politics, Malle took a long trip to India out of which came the celebrated documentary television series *Phantom India* (1968). Shown in cinemas abroad, this informative account of a complex nation was well received, although the Indian government objected to its uncompromising presentation of poverty. Also controversial was *Le souffle au coeur* (*Murmur Of The Heart*, 1971), in which a young man's sexual liberation follows an incestuous incident with his mother. Appearing in the wake of Marcel Ophüls' eviscerating documentary on wartime collaboration *The Sorrow And The Pity* (1969), *Lacombe, Lucien* (1973) was a difficult and insightful portrait of a teenage boy caught between an elitist Resistance and pragmatic collusion with Vichy.

Moving to America in the late 1970s, Malle caused a sensation with *Pretty Baby* (1978), set in a prewar New Orleans red-light district and detailing the sexual maturity of Brooke Shields' child prostitute. Starring Susan Sarandon – Shields' mother in *Pretty Baby* – *Atlantic City* (1980) was a character study in which Burt Lancaster's ageing hood fetches up in a resort which has known better days. *My Dinner With André* (1981) was a curio in which avant-garde theatre director André Gregory and actor Wallace Shawn played themselves talking over lunch.

The autobiographical *Au revoir les enfants* (1987) was Malle's last great film. In his final three films, he explored seminal themes of guilt, hypocrisy and modern alienation. Released amid celebrations of the bicentenary of the French Revolution, the Renoiresque *Milou en mai* (*Milou In May*, 1989) was a wistful romp in a Midi manor following an old matriarch's death, set as the country erupted with student revolution in May 1968. *Damage* (1992) featured a strong performance from Jeremy Irons as a weak-willed MP who falls for his son's French girlfriend, magnetically played by Juliette Binoche. Based on Josephine Hart's steamy bestseller, David Hare's script was nevertheless adept at the hesitancies of the British in the realm of sexual etiquette.

M

Jazz in the movies

With fairgrounds and variety shows as its early venues, cinema was commonly seen as a lowbrow art form, and it's unsurprising that it became associated with popular music – or, indeed, music "from the wrong side of the tracks". F.W. Murnau's *Sunrise* (1927), for instance, is a masterly romantic melodrama in which a simple farmer is lured to the (jazz-blaring) big city by a loose woman who urges him to kill his wife: Hugo Reisenfeld's appropriately decadent score provides a brassy contextualizing shorthand. In later movies, jazz would lend an apparent period authenticity, transporting us back in time as effectively as the costumes and sets. Witness the Scott Joplin rags popularized by *The Sting* (1973) – despite the fact that they were actually written decades before the era in which the film was set. This approach also suits biopics, such as *The Benny Goodman Story* (1955), Bertrand Tavernier's Dexter Gordon movie *'Round Midnight* (1986) and Clint Eastwood's 1988 Charlie Parker film *Bird*. Naturally there are also hundreds of notable documentaries and concert films such as *Jazz On A Summer's Day* (1960), *A Great Day In Harlem* (1994) and *Triumph Of The Underdog* (1998) about Charles Mingus.

The 1920s was the decade known as "the jazz age". Musicians played on-set music to get everyone in the right mood, and often appeared on screen (albeit silently) before *The Jazz Singer* (1927) – with its misnomer of a movie title – heralded the arrival of sound cinema. Famous performers began appearing in jazz interludes, and showbiz musicals such as the *Gold Diggers* series became popular, but jazz rarely drove the drama musically, and black performers were cut from prints distributed in the southern US. Following in the wake of the short programme-fillers that were set to classical music, producer Walter Lantz's 1940s *Swing Symphonies* were animations set to jazz hits, and Norman McLaren's pioneering animation *Begone Dull Care* (1949) featured the music of Oscar Peterson.

In the 1950s jazz reached its cinematic high point. Frank Sinatra portrayed a junkie drummer in Otto Preminger's *The Man With The Golden Arm* (1955), which featured a tough Elmer Bernstein soundtrack. Bernstein also wrote the score for *Sweet Smell Of Success* (1957), featuring (as themselves) The Chico Hamilton Quintet. Crime and jazz seemed to make great bedfellows: *noir* classic *The Big Combo* (1955) had a big-band score by David Raksin while Henry Mancini provided Latin jazz for Orson Welles's *Touch Of Evil* (1958). The *Pink Panther* man also gave the following year's *Peter Gunn* its drive, whilst *Anatomy Of A Murder* (1959) benefited from a masterpiece of a score by none other than Duke Ellington.

Meanwhile, in Europe John Barry moved from pop to jazz with *Beat Girl* (1958) and the following year Martial Solal scored Jean-Luc Godard's quintessence of cool, *A bout de souffle*. Jazz was often unrelated to the narrative but, after discussions with director Robert Wise, John Lewis wrote a truly integrated score for the interracial heist movie *Odds Against Tomorrow* (1959). On Louis Malle's *Ascenseur pour l'échafaud* (*Lift To The Scaffold*, 1957), Miles Davis's group improvised on previously written themes and Chico Hamilton provided some wonderfully edgy music for Roman Polanski's swinging London shocker *Repulsion* (1965). Malle's *Milou en mai* (1989) has a very different kind of jazz score – a far fluffier one – by Stéphane Grapelli. In the 1960s popular jazz merged with pop but Barry's understated music for *Petulia* (1968) still deserves a mention. The turn that mainstream jazz took in the 1970s – towards fusion and funk – was harder to place in cinema. Often it threatened to overwhelm the film. But in *The Taking of Pelham One Two Three* (1974) David Shire gave us an uncompromising big-band clash of atonality and funkiness.

Few jazz composers managed to develop regular film-scoring careers, but there are exceptions: Jim Jarmusch's regular collaborator John Lurie; the occasionally New Age-ish Mark Isham; and trumpeter-turned-director Mike Figgis, who often scores his own films. Despite jazz's American roots, European composers such as Krzysztof Komeda and Michel Legrand have also written splendid jazz scores – Komeda's highly groovy soundtrack for Polanski's *Cul-de-sac* (1966) being well worth a listen. As jazz entered the mainstream it was no longer seen as transgressive or cool, but the boundaries continued to be pushed – Howard Shore and Ornette Coleman's music for David Cronenberg's adaptation of William Burroughs' junkie nightmare *Naked Lunch* (1991) being an excellent case in point. But as jazz has lost popularity it has been less and less frequently used in films, except for special assignments: evoking the past in *LA Confidential* (1999) or in Francis Ford Coppola's overblown and underrated *The Cotton Club* (1989). One diehard is, of course, Woody Allen who compiles the soundtrack to many of his films from his own eclectic record collection. JR

Vanya On 42nd Street (1994) followed André Gregory's rehearsal of Chekhov's play in a decrepit Broadway theatre. With leads splendidly played by Julianne Moore and George Gaynes, the film recapitulated Chekhovian ennui and disappointment on the cusp of a new century. RA

Ascenseur pour l'eschafaud (Lift To The Scaffold) 1957, 89 min, b/w

cast Maurice Ronet, Jeanne Moreau, Georges Poujouly, Lino Ventura, Yori Bertin, Ivan Petrovich *cin* Henri Decaë *m* Miles Davis

Julien Tavernier (Maurice Ronet) murders his girlfriend's husband, but gets stuck in a lift as he's leaving the scene of the crime. At the exact same time, two teenagers steal his car and shoot a German tourist, while his girlfriend (Jeanne Moreau) wanders the streets wondering what has happened to him and thinking the worst. All three plot lines are juggled with amazing assurance and the whole film is bound together by a breathtaking Miles Davis score.

Les amants (The Lovers) 1958, 88 min, b/w

cast Jeanne Moreau, Alain Cuny, José Villalonga, Jean-Marc Bory, Judith Magre, Gaston Modot *cin* Henri Decaë *m* Johannes Brahms

Almost the epitome of French arthouse chic, this story of an affair between a bored middle-class wife and mother (Jeanne Moreau) and a bold young student (Jean-Marc Bory) suggests the passing of the mantle of French cinema to a new generation of filmmakers, while still tipping its hat to the *ancien régime*'s classical verities of handsome camerawork and literate acting.

Le feu follet (The Fire Within) 1963, 110 min, b/w

cast Maurice Ronet, Lena Skerla, Yvonne Clech, Hubert Deschamps, Jeanne Moreau, Alexandra Stewart *cin* Ghislain Cloquet *m* Erik Satie

Dissecting the feelings of a suicidal alcoholic as he drops in on Parisian friends for the last time, Malle puts the personal and public psychology of modern France under the microscope. Acted with subtle compassion by Maurice Ronet and crisply shot by Ghislain Cloquet, this is one of the very best films to emerge from France in this period.

Atlantic City 1980, 105 min

cast Burt Lancaster, Susan Sarandon, Kate Reid, Michel Piccoli, Hollis McLaren, Robert Joy *cin* Richard Ciupka *m* Michel Legrand

Nostalgia for the past suffuses this tale of Burt Lancaster's ageing mobster befriending young hippies in hock to the Mob. Set against the fading kitsch of an Atlantic City on the cusp of monetarism, this is perhaps the proper descendant of Lancaster's post-war films in which the old guard gave way to the ruthless sheen of corporate gangsterism.

Au revoir les enfants (Goodbye, Children) 1987, 104 min

cast Gaspard Manesse, Raphael Fejtö, Francine Racette, Stanislas Carré de Malberg, Philippe Morier-Genoud *cin* Renato Berta

This semi-autobiographical piece must be one of the most poignant statements on childhood ever made. Drawing upon Malle's time in a Carmelite school, it follows young Julien's realization that his little Jewish friend Jean will know death long before he does. Malle's feeling for the vicissitudes of the French status quo was never more acute, nor more sorrowful.

Milou en mai (Milou In May) 1989, 108 min

cast Michel Piccoli, Miou-Miou, Michel Duchaussoy, Dominique Blanc, Harriet Walter, Bruno Carette *cin* Renato Beta *m* Stéphane Grappelli

Belonging to the *cinéma de patrimoine* strand of 1980s heritage cinema that spawned *Jean de Florette* et al., this bucolic portrait of an aristocratic family gathering at a country estate following the death of the old matriarch perhaps lacks the insight of Jean Renoir's work, but it does have all of his faith in people, despite the revolution brewing outside.

David Mamet
US, 1947–

A latter-day master of the hard-boiled one-liner, David Mamet established himself as one of America's most profane and talented dramatists with *Glengarry Glen Ross*, *American Buffalo* and *Sexual Perversity In Chicago* (all of which have been filmed by other directors, with mixed results). Although he still writes plays, Mamet has been more prolific as a screenwriter and script doctor. His scripts include *The Postman Always Rings Twice* (1981), *The Verdict* (1982), *The Untouchables* (1987), *Wag The Dog* (1997), *The Edge* (1997), *Ronin* (1998, as Richard Weisz) and *Hannibal* (2001). Starting with *House Of Games* (1987), he has also written and directed films every couple of years.

Congenitally unsentimental, with a cynical suspicion of the world of appearances and a combative, frankly un-PC insistence on the war between the sexes, Mamet hammers out his highly charged dialogue on an old-fashioned typewriter, and has been known to rehearse his actors with a metronome to ensure they stick to his rhythm. As a director, he has favoured unemotional, clipped, tight-lipped actors like Joe Mantegna and William H. Macy, as well as his two wives, Lindsay Crouse and Rebecca Pidgeon.

Although his plays tend to be static affairs, in his original screenplays Mamet clings to the principle that action speaks louder than even his finely honed (and frequently unprintable) words. "Film, as opposed to theatre, is intrinsically a melodramatic medium", he has said, and there is an echo of Graham Greene's distinction between his serious novels and his "entertainments" in Mamet's slightly condescending approach to cinema. He has a propensity for clever, twisty thrillers like *Heist* (2001) and *The Spanish Prisoner* (1997), although it is worth noting that his plots repeatedly hinge on elaborate charades, stings designed to con the audience. It's a device that crops up in both these films, as well as in *House Of Games*, *State And Main* (2000) and *Spartan* (2004). In Mamet's universe, the viewer does well to remember the advice proffered in *House Of Games*: "What I'm talking about comes down to a more basic philosophical principle: Don't trust nobody." TC

House Of Games 1987, 102 min

cast Lindsay Crouse, Joe Mantegna, Mike Nussbaum, Lilia Skala, J.T. Walsh, Steve Goldstein *cin* Juan Ruiz Anchía *m* Alaric Jans

Psychiatrist Margaret Ford (Lindsay Crouse) has it out with the gambler who has driven one of her patients to despair. But on entering the House of Games Margaret is soon seduced by the apparently pragmatic Mike (Joe Mantegna) and finds herself sitting in on a card game looking for "tells". Mamet's first film as director is a little stiff and self-conscious, but it's put together with such fiendish cynicism that the detached, objective tone is certainly appropriate.

Spartan 2004, 107 min
cast Val Kilmer, Derek Luke, William H. Macy, Ed O'Neill, Tia Texada, Kristen Bell *cin* Juan Ruiz Anchía *m* Mark Isham

Although it scarcely got the release it deserved, this gripping political thriller shows just how far Mamet has developed as a director. *Spartan* is a dynamic and highly charged piece of storytelling that practically storms out of the gate. When the president's daughter is kidnapped, dedicated Special Ops agent Val Kilmer is put on the case, but the world of international politics proves every bit as duplicitous as Mamet's usual beat.

Rouben Mamoulian
Georgia (formerly Russian Empire), 1897–1987

Rouben Mamoulian was one of the most significant Hollywood directors of the 1930s and 40s, but his legacy has been hotly contested. There's no question that from his very first film, *Applause* (1929), he was fascinated by the technical possibilities of film and seized upon (and helped develop) several key innovations. But his sheer stylistic variety means that he does not slot easily into an auteurist framework and, as a result, some critics have claimed that he never quite lived up to his early potential. His cause has not been helped by a reputation for difficultness – he made only sixteen films and was fired from at least three more – and his tendency to blow his own trumpet just a little too loudly.

If he had never made a film, Mamoulian would be remembered as one of the great Broadway directors – of musicals in particular. Having studied with the legendary theatrical pedagogue Konstantin Stanislavsky in Moscow, Mamoulian arrived in the US (after a brief spell in London) in 1923. He directed the play *Porgy* in 1927 and its more famous operatic incarnation *Porgy And Bess* eight years later. He was also responsible for the premieres of two ground-breaking shows, *Oklahoma!* (1943) and *Carousel* (1945) (but did not direct the film versions of either). He hit Hollywood in 1929, at the invitation of Paramount boss Adolph Zukor, initially as a dialogue coach. *Applause* was an astonishingly confident and competent debut, with Mamoulian transcending the mawkish limitations of this back-stage musical with fluid camerawork and a rich soundtrack. The director went on to pioneer the use of aural flashbacks in his gangster movie *City Streets* (1931) and made the first Hollywood feature film in three-colour Technicolor, *Becky Sharp* (1935).

His three finest films of the 1930s, and arguably his whole career, covered three different genres and were made in consecutive years. *Dr Jekyll And Mr Hyde* (1931), is deliriously inventive in its use of wipes and point-of-view shots, while the transformation scenes of doctor to beast are a dizzying combination of sound and vision involving a revolving camera, double and triple exposures and an amplified heartbeat. *Love Me Tonight* (1932) is Mamoulian's masterpiece, a frothy musical fantasy set in France which was ground-breaking in the way it integrated all the varied elements – musical set pieces in particular – into a fluid and coherent whole. It was followed by the seventeenth-century costume drama *Queen Christina* (1933), in which Mamoulian cleverly exploited the offscreen mystique of his star, Greta Garbo, while celebrating her fragile, iconic beauty.

If these are Mamoulian's most celebrated films, then there are plenty more that are well worth watching. The 1930s saw two more excellent musicals in *The Gay Desperado* (1936) and *High, Wide And Handsome* (1937), the latter a highly original hybrid, an operetta-Western telling of the struggle between farmers and railroaders in the Pennsylvania oilfields of the 1850s. In 1940 came *The Mask Of Zorro*, a fine swashbuckler in which Tyrone Power's Zorro is pitted against the suave villainy and balletic swordplay of Basil Rathbone. It was followed the next year by another Power vehicle, *Blood And Sand*, a bullfighting saga remarkable for its lurid and painterly use of Technicolor. The failure of *Summer Holiday* (1948), a coming-of-age musical loosely based on Eugene O'Neill's play *Ah, Wilderness!*, did little for his reputation and he only directed one more film, *Silk Stockings* (1957), a musical adaptation of Lubitsch's *Ninotchka* (1939) starring Fred Astaire and Cyd Charisse. RB

Dr Jekyll And Mr Hyde 1931, 98 min, b/w
cast Frederic March, Miriam Hopkins, Rose Hobart, Holmes Hobart *cin* Karl Struss *m* Herman Hand

The finest of the many adaptations of Robert Louis Stevenson's novella. Frederic March is remarkable as the doctor whose scientific experiments into the good and evil sides of man's nature result in his transformation into a psychotic monster. It's a pre-Hays Code film, which means that the sexual desire of the feral Mr Hyde is made pretty explicit and there's one sustained shot of the dangled leg of prostitute Ivy (Miriam Hopkins) that's especially effective at conveying the disturbed state of his mind.

Love Me Tonight 1932, 104 min, b/w
cast Maurice Chevalier, Jeanette MacDonald, Charles Ruggles, Charles Butterworth, Myrna Loy *cin* Victor Milner *m* Richard Rogers

In a brilliant opening, Mamoulian orchestrates a "symphony of sounds" which vividly evokes the busy life of a Parisian street, before homing in on Maurice Chevalier (as the tailor Courtelin) singing "The Song Of Paree". It's typical of the director's imaginatively fluid approach to what is essentially an operetta, releasing it from stage-bound conventions via sweeping tracking shots. He's greatly aided by the onscreen chemistry of his stars, Chevalier and Jeanette MacDonald (as a lovesick princess) and one of Rodgers and Hart's most endearing scores.

Queen Christina 1933, 97 min, b/w

cast Greta Garbo, John Gilbert, Ian Keith, Lewis Stone, Elizabeth Young, C. Aubrey Smith *cin* William Daniels *m* Herbert Stothart

Garbo was reunited with her co-star and former lover John Gilbert in this highly fanciful account of Queen Christina's abdication from the throne of Sweden. Playing off the sexual ambiguity of her persona – she's dressed as a boy for much of the film – Garbo dominates the movie, with Mamoulian's camerawork gracefully allowing her to shine. There are two particularly outstanding moments – the scene in which Christina, after a tryst with her lover, wanders around the room "memorizing" it; and, most famously, the closing shot of her impassive, mask-like face as she sails away into exile.

Silk Stockings 1957, 117 min

cast Fred Astaire, Cyd Charisse, Janis Paige, Peter Lorre, Jules Munshin *cin* Robert Bronner *m* Cole Porter

There was a twenty-year difference between Cyd Charisse and Fred Astaire (he was 58) but the two still generate the requisite romantic sparks and illuminate the screen with their effortlessly graceful dancing. She plays Ninotchka, a humourless Russian on a mission to retrieve three commissars from the decadent West; he plays Steve Canfield, a movie producer determined to melt her frosty exterior. Director Mamoulian proves himself a master of Cinemascope, even managing to successfully parody it in the number "Stereophonic Sound".

James Mangold

US, 1963–

James Mangold has made a number of sincere and engaging small-scale dramas marked by an appealing old-fashioned sensibility. After graduating from CalArts, where he studied under Alexander Mackendrick, he won an internship at Disney but became disenchanted with the studio and quit after a year to further his studies at Columbia University. Milos Forman was one of his teachers and it was with him that he began developing his first two films *Heavy* (1995), which would go on to win the best director award at the Sundance Festival, and *Cop Land* (1997). The latter, his first major studio release, was a solid police drama led by Sylvester Stallone. *Girl, Interrupted* (1999) starred Angelina Jolie and Winona Ryder as inmates of a mental hospital for young women. Jolie won an Oscar for her performance, and indeed Mangold's ability to coax believable performances from his actors is one of his greatest strengths as a director. The time-travel romance *Kate And Leopold* (2001) and the generic thriller *Identity* (2003) were less successful. But he returned to form with *Walk The Line*, a brilliantly performed biopic of Johnny Cash starring Joaquin Phoenix and Reese Witherspoon. JC

Heavy 1995, 105 min

cast Pruitt Taylor Vince, Shelley Winters, Liv Tyler, Deborah Harry, Joe Grifasi, Evan Dando *cin* Michael Barrow *m* Thurston Moore

An overweight young man (Pruitt Taylor Vince), who lives with his mother (Shelley Winters) and works as a chef in her diner, falls in love with beautiful new waitress Callie (Liv Tyler). Gently paced and very well acted, *Heavy* is a charming, slightly quirky film that successfully captures the quiet desperation of lives on the edge.

Walk The Line 2005, 105 min

cast Joaquin Phoenix, Reese Witherspoon, Ginnifer Goodwin, Dallas Roberts *cin* Phedon Papamichael *m* T Bone Burnett

An authoritative account of country singer Johnny Cash's early years – his upbringing in Arkansas, his troubled relationship with his father, his fights with various addictions and his redemption at the hands of fellow singer (and eventual wife) June Carter. The biopic trajectory may be predictable but the performances of the two leads (Phoenix and Witherspoon) have the conviction to make the pair's struggle for success genuinely moving.

Joseph L. Mankiewicz

US, 1909–93

A young writer at Paramount and Metro, Joseph Leo Mankiewicz was promoted to producer at MGM in 1936. "I said I wanted to write and direct, but Louis B. Mayer said, 'No, you have to produce first. You have to crawl before you can walk.'"

Was Mayer capable of such wit? The remark sounds suspiciously like a line from a Mankiewicz movie, from *All About Eve* (1950) or perhaps *The Barefoot Contessa* (1954). Nevertheless, Mayer's decision may well have determined the kind of director Mankiewicz became; it's always apparent that he was a writer first, a producer second, and a director last. In a Mankiewicz picture the dialogue does all the talking. And rich, polysyllabic, epigrammatic talk it is too.

As a writer in the 1930s, Mankiewicz had turned his hand to everything from Jack Oakie comedies to the gangster movie *Manhattan Melodrama* (1934) and the farming tale *Our Daily Bread* (1934). As a producer, Fritz Lang's *Fury* (1936), George Cukor's *The Philadelphia Story* (1940) and several Frank Borzage romances vouch for his classy sensibility. Switching to 20th Century Fox he was finally allowed to direct; first up was the gothic melodrama *Dragonwyck* (1946), then three films written by Philip Dunne. The bittersweet supernatural love story *The Ghost And Mrs Muir* (1947) is the first to sustain the refined, elegant and ironic tone that became Mankiewicz's distinctive voice.

He really hit his stride with *A Letter To Three Wives* (1949), a shrewd marriage comedy in the Lubitsch manner (but with added acid) for which

Mankiewicz won both writing and directing Oscars. If *All About Eve* is his best – and best-known – film, it's because his witty, bitchy bons mots flow naturally from self-dramatizing theatre folk. But even second-tier Mankiewicz rates high on the scales: films such as *House Of Strangers* (1949), *People Will Talk* (1951), *5 Fingers* (1952), *Guys And Dolls* (1955), *There Was A Crooked Man* (1970) and *Sleuth* (1972). He didn't originate any of this material, but he was a careful and intelligent director who played to his own strengths.

Mankiewicz's literary qualities have led to his over- and underestimation as critical fashions have ebbed and flowed. His is a theatrical and artificial screen world, and in his films life often seems like a parlour game – or a debating club. But he knew how to stage a scene and he generally drew the best out of performers. Prolix and preachy on occasion, he was Darryl F. Zanuck's worst choice to try to salvage the Elizabeth Taylor spectacular *Cleopatra* (1963), presumably because he'd drawn such a fine performance from her in *Suddenly Last Summer* (1959). It's the one big blot on his copybook, and adjusting for inflation still the most expensive movie ever made. Mankiewicz wasn't known as an over-spending director (unlike Rouben Mamoulian who he replaced on the film) but in this particular case it could be said that the talk did not come cheap. TC

The Ghost And Mrs Muir 1947, 104 min, b/w

cast Rex Harrison, Gene Tierney, George Sanders, Edna Best *cin* Charles Lang Jr *m* Bernard Herrmann

A deftly directed rom-com which cleverly parodies several genres (notably the gothic *noir*) while managing to avoid too much whimsy. Gene Tierney plays the widow Mrs Muir who strikes up a relationship with the ghost of the previous owner, the grizzelled Captain Gregg (Rex Harrison), who gets her to write his story and saves her from the machinations of über-cad Miles Fairley (George Sanders). Bernard Herrmann's endearing score is the icing on the cake.

A Letter To Three Wives 1949, 103 min, b/w

cast Kirk Douglas, Linda Darnell, Ann Sothern, Paul Douglas, Jeanne Crain, Jeffrey Lynn, Thelma Ritter *cin* Arthur Miller *m* Alfred Newman

Three wives congregate for a children's picnic and receive a letter from a fourth (voiced by the unseen Celeste Holm), who maliciously informs them that she has run off with one of their husbands – but neglects to mention whose. Mankiewicz was fond of the flashback structure (his brother Herman co-wrote *Citizen Kane*), and also relished the catty complexity of "the women's picture". The first wife (Crain) is rather callow, but the film picks up in wit and tension as it goes on.

All About Eve 1950, 138 min, b/w

cast Bette Davis, Anne Baxter, George Sanders, Celeste Holm, Thelma Ritter, Marilyn Monroe *cin* Milton Krasner *m* Alfred Newman

Arguably the best backstage melodrama of them all, this story of a young actress on the make seems to have been dipped in acid before the cameras rolled. Bette Davis is the uncomfortably peaking diva Margo Channing, and it's probably her finest role: formidable and narcissistic, but

also vulnerable and all too aware that age is against her. Anne Baxter is the young ingénue who insinuates herself into Margo's circle – and George Sanders very nearly steals the show as sardonic critic Addison DeWitt.

Guys And Dolls 1955, 150 min

cast Marlon Brando, Frank Sinatra, Jean Simmons, Vivian Blaine, Stubby Kaye, Robert Keith *cin* Harry Stradling *m* Frank Loesser

Gambler Nathan Detroit (Marlon Brando) needs $1000 to secure a venue for this week's sporting fixture, "the oldest established permanent floating crap game in New York". Sky Masterson (Frank Sinatra) accepts a bet that Nathan can't persuade Sally Army missionary Sarah Brown (Jean Simmons) to go with him to Havana. Then there's Miss Adelaide (Vivian Blaine), Nathan's intended. Brando can't really sing and Mankiewicz allows it all to go on too long, but the choreography is dazzling and the cast truly stellar.

Anthony Mann
US, 1906–67

Along with the work of his close contemporaries Sam Fuller and Nicholas Ray, Anthony Mann's films best express the psychic turmoil engendered in a generation of American men who lived through two world wars and the Great Depression to arrive at the domestic affluence of the Eisenhower era. And it was in the 1950s that each reached a sustained creative pitch after an apprenticeship in the studio system and valuable exposure to *film noir* stylistics.

Mann came up from the New York theatre scene as an actor and director, worked as a talent scout for David O. Selznick, and was an assistant director at Paramount in the early 1940s. He went on to make (reputedly entertaining) B-pictures at Universal, RKO and Republic. Auteurist critics have excavated the cycle of *noir* movies he made from 1947 to 1950, including *Desperate*, *Railroaded!*, *T-Men* (all 1947), *Raw Deal* (1948) and *He Walked By Night* (1949, co-directed with Alfred Werker). Tight, economical suspense pictures with an angsty undertow, these are particularly of interest for Mann's collaboration with the expressionist cinematographer John Alton, whose taste for chiaroscuro and stark, dramatic compositions indelibly inflected Mann's *mise en scène*. Director and cinematographer applied the same *noir* filter to the French Revolution in the remarkable *Reign Of Terror* (aka *The Black Book*, 1949).

But for all the excellence of his thrillers, Mann's reputation rests on seven or eight Westerns which he made over the next decade, especially five with James Stewart: *Winchester '73* (1950), *Bend Of The River* (1952), *The Naked Spur* (1953), *The Far Country* (1954) and *The Man From Laramie* (1955). In these exemplary films, Stewart comprehensively broke from his pre-war nice-guy image to play driven, fiercely independent protagonists with a psychotic streak embedded in part-tragedy – *noir* antiheroes transplanted to the frontier and to some

M

extent redeemed (though often not quite rehabilitated) through cathartic violence directed at a more extreme sociopathic projection of themselves. These so-called "psychological Westerns" redefined the genre, and provide the bridge between Fordian foundation myth and Peckinpah's angry lamentations.

If the antagonists in the Westerns reflect the violent strain in Mann's B-thrillers, the world they inhabit is the antithesis of the claustrophobic urban nocturnes of *film noir*. More than any other Western director, including Ford, Mann roots character and action in the physical landscape of the American West, which he often photographed in Technicolor and CinemaScope. Asked about the genesis of *The Naked Spur* in 1967, Mann talked about the land: "We were in magnificent countryside – in Durango – and everything lent itself to improvisation … I wanted to show the mountains, the waterfalls, the forested areas, the snowy summits … the characters emerge more fully from such an environment." Crucially, this isn't empty pictorialism; in these films man and nature are congruent, each an extension of the other.

Despite that reference to improvisation, Mann's Westerns are classical in structure and consciously (sometimes self-consciously) evoke Greek tragedy – not for nothing is one of them called *The Furies* (1950). That may go some way to explain the director's subsequent elevation into the lofty realms of the big-budget 70mm historical epic with *El Cid* (1961) and *The Fall Of The Roman Empire* (1964). Both are superior examples of the type, but neither is immune to the elephantiasis endemic in this genre.

Even at the height of his powers Mann was perfectly capable of turning out banal and anodyne films – *The Glenn Miller Story* (1953), *Serenade* (1955). He was less reckless than Fuller, less passionate than Ray, yet in the framework of the Western he hit on an almost perfect form with more consistency than either of his peers – and fuelled it with pain. TC

Raw Deal 1948, 82 min, b/w

cast Dennis O'Keefe, Claire Trevor, Marsha Hunt, John Ireland, Raymond Burr *cin* John Alton *m* Paul Sawtell

It's easy to believe Dennis O'Keefe as a minor-league loser, set up to take the fall by a racketeer (Raymond Burr). He escapes prison with the help of his girl (Claire Trevor) and takes Marsha Hunt as hostage – thereby adding a romantic triangle to his other problems. Although all of Mann's collaborations with John Alton are worth seeing, this is the strongest story, developing in tension and character as it goes on. It's also the most undiluted and sadistic of the *noir* thrillers Mann made.

Reign Of Terror (aka The Black Book) 1949, 89 min, b/w

cast Robert Cummings, Richard Basehart, Richard Hart, Arlene Dahl, Norman Lloyd, Charles McGraw *cin* John Alton *m* Sol Kaplan

Probably Mann's oddest film, this is also one of his most enjoyable. Made at the same time as the *noir* thrillers that

were beginning to get him noticed, this historical B-movie applies a similar shadowy lighting style and curt, brutal tempo to the French Revolution. Robert Cummings is a double agent (another characteristic Mann trope) in the service of the Republic who infiltrates the inner circle of the tyrannical Robespierre (Richard Basehart).

Border Incident 1949, 96 min, b/w

cast Ricardo Montalban, George Murphy, Howard Da Silva, James Mitchell, Charles McGraw *cin* John Alton *m* André Previn

Although the script is fairly mundane, that only enhances the feeling that this semi-documentary-styled thriller remains pertinent some sixty years on. Two federal agents, one American and one Mexican, collaborate to thwart the smuggling of illegal Mexican workers into the US, where they are exploited and, in some cases, murdered. Most striking is the elemental violence Mann extracts from the countryside – a sign of things to come.

The Naked Spur 1953, 91 min

cast James Stewart, Janet Leigh, Robert Ryan, Ralph Meeker, Millard Mitchell *cin* William C. Mellor *m* Bronislau Kaper

The presence of Ryan and Meeker in this most intense and neurotic Mann Western signals its affinity with the *noir* cosmos. Stewart is a bounty hunter, Howard Kemp, spurred on by greed and hatred. Ryan represents a big payday, but he's clever – and genial – enough to play the dour Kemp's allies off against each other. Janet Leigh watches on, appalled. Filmed entirely in exteriors, it's a prime example of Mann's sensitivity to landscape as an expression of emotion.

The Far Country 1954, 97 min

cast James Stewart, Ruth Roman, Walter Brennan, John McIntire, Corinne Calvet, Jay C. Flippen *cin* William H. Daniels *m* Joseph Gershenson

Again Stewart represents naked self-interest as a single-minded prospector who refuses any social responsibility, even as the gold-rush town in which he finds himself is rife with murder and corruption. His heroism comes late in the day – too late to save his friend, old-timer Walter Brennan. Set in the Pacific Northwest in 1896, right at the tail end of the Western's time-period, *The Far Country* reads like a coded critique of ruthless capitalism, yet it unfolds with transparent lucidity.

Man Of The West 1958, 100 min

cast Gary Cooper, Lee J. Cobb, Julie London, Arthur O'Connell, Jack Lord, Royal Dano *cin* Ernest Haller *m* Leigh Harline

In Mann's penultimate and most punishing Western Cooper is, essentially, one of Stewart's tormented heroes a few years down the line, after they've exhausted their fury and returned to civilization. Then he meets a figure from his past, Doc Tobin (Cobb), a patently unreformed outlaw with whom he used to ride. Drawing on the contrasting acting styles of Cobb and Cooper, Mann fashions a powerful and fascinating drama probing the extent to which the man of the West can ever truly renounce his past.

Delbert Mann

US, 1920–

Delbert Mann contributed two landmark films to 1950s American cinema and then never quite hit a home run again.

In the early 1950s he made a name for himself as a director of live TV drama. Most notably, he directed two acclaimed Paddy Chayefsky teleplays, *Marty* (starring Rod Steiger) and *The Bachelor Party*, part of NBC's *Philco Television Playhouse* series. It was by adapting these two plays for the big screen that Mann made his move into feature-film directing. *Marty* (1955) was a smart movie that tapped into the zeitgeist, its intimacy and realism inspiring a run of similar films. It won the Palme d'Or, as well as four Oscars, including best director for Mann and best actor for Ernest Borgnine who played Marty. In the accomplished *The Bachelor Party* (1957), a group of friends on a stag night share their fears and aspirations.

Mann directed a number of feature films in the late 1950s and early 1960s, but none lived up to the promise of his first two films. It was in his direction of actors that Mann was at his best. His focus was on the realistic presentation of personal relationships, rather than anything approaching visual fireworks, and his films tended to lack energy and flair. Loneliness, loyalty and the passage of time were recurring themes. From the late 1960s onwards, Mann's work was mainly for the small screen. He directed countless TV movies, including versions of *Heidi* (1968), *David Copperfield* (1969) and *Jane Eyre* (1970). His version of *All Quiet On The Western Front* (1979) lacked the urgency and tragedy of the 1930 movie adaptation. JC

Marty 1955, 91 min, b/w

cast Ernest Borgnine, Betsy Blair, Esther Minciotti, Joe De Santis, Karen Steele, Jerry Paris *cin* Joseph La Shelle *m* Roy Webb

Marty (Ernest Borgnine) is on the verge of lonely middle age when he falls in love and everything changes. The film was a breath of fresh air at a time when Hollywood was producing epics to counter the growing impact of television. It was adapted by Paddy Chayefksy from his own teleplay.

Michael Mann
US, 1943–

To see a recent Michael Mann film is to witness big-time American cinema at its glossiest and most engrossing. While audiences flock to these starry movies, critics have praised them for their visual and narrative integrity.

Unusually for an American filmmaker, Mann trained at the London International Film School. In 1965 he began directing commercials and documentaries in Britain, including coverage of the May 1968 unrest in Paris which found its way onto US network news. Documentary aesthetics would later inform his feature films, many of which draw upon true stories. After winning the Cannes Jury Prize in 1970 with his experimental short *Jaunpuri*, Mann moved into television, writing episodes of *Starsky And Hutch*, *Crime Story* and *Vegas*. Building a dependable reputation, he directed his first telefeature in 1979. *The Jericho Mile* was the story of a penitentiary inmate who struggles against prejudice and the system to attain Olympic standard as an athlete. Its depiction of the vivid micro-culture of the prison would feed into his masterwork, *Heat* (1995).

Mann's first theatrical feature was *Thief* (1981), based on a police anecdote and featuring James Caan as a career criminal driven to sacrifice everything when a mobster cheats him. A detailed record of criminal procedure, it indulged Mann's career-long interest in the nature of professional dedication. It was followed by *The Keep* (1983), a stylized World War II horror film. Mann was executive producer on that essential 1980s crime series *Miami Vice*, whose rock-music-fuelled, pastel-hued, sun-soaked Miami ambience drew accusations of empty stylistics. His next feature, *Manhunter* (1986), similarly luxuriated in the alluring surfaces of the era, but beneath the sheen was an exploration of weightier ideas that won its director recognition as a serious filmmaker. As with many of his films, Mann wrote the screenplay himself.

The James Fenimore Cooper adaptation *The Last Of The Mohicans* (1992) put Daniel Day-Lewis's Hawkeye amid a densely realized colonial environment of forest canopy and sudden visceral death, providing further evidence of Mann's predilection for realistic but cinematic universes and fatal irrevocability. In 1989 Mann's television thriller *LA Takedown* depicted the rivalry between a cop and his career-thief opposite, a scenario explored with depth and gravitas in *Heat*, which confirmed Mann's A-list status. Pairing *Heat*'s Al Pacino with Russell Crowe, *The Insider* (1999) was based on the true story of a tobacco-company executive who brought his employers to book for perjuring themselves over the harmful effects of nicotine. Again, Mann generated an aestheticized reality of corporate lounges and incipient paranoia which recalled the 1970s political thrillers of Alan J. Pakula and Costa-Gavras.

Built around a layered performance from Will Smith, *Ali* (2001) evoked the period between 1964 and 1974 when Cassius Clay, later Muhammad Ali, became a world-champion boxer and a focus for African-American pride. It was followed by the Tom Cruise thriller *Collateral* (2004), which gained Mann his best opening weekend yet, but received a mixed response from critics. *Miami Vice* (2006) confidently updated the 1980s flash of his flagship TV show with post-Iraq surveillance technology and sheer firepower. Solid, dependable and exciting, Mann continues to define the modern thriller. RA

Manhunter 1986, 120 min

cast William Peterson, Kim Greist, Joan Allen, Brian Cox, Dennis Farina, Stephen Lang, Tom Noonan *cin* Dante Spinotti *m* Michael Rubini, Reds

The famous forerunner of *The Silence Of The Lambs* (1991), *Manhunter* is quintessential Mann. Focusing on the troubled sensibility of a forensics expert brought out of retirement to catch a malevolent serial killer, it is a gripping portrayal of the standoff between professional and private life, civilization and moral wilderness.

Heat 1995, 171 min

cast Robert De Niro, Al Pacino, Val Kilmer, Jon Voight, Amy Brenneman, Wes Studi, Dennis Haysbert *cin* Dante Spinotti *m* Elliot Goldenthal

Celebrated as the film which paired Pacino and De Niro on screen for the first time, *Heat* is a ferociously involving cat-and-mouse game between Pacino's grizzled career cop and De Niro's precision-driven corporate thief. Shot with architectural acuity against the azure towers of LA's financial centre, this is one of the greatest American films of the last 25 years.

The Insider 1999, 158 min

cast Russell Crowe, Al Pacino, Christopher Plummer, Diane Venora, Philip Baker Hall, Lindsay Crouse *cin* Dante Spinotti *m* Pieter Bourke, Lisa Gerrard

A gripping real-life account of the individual amid the vicissitudes of corporatism, *The Insider* stars Russell Crowe as rogue tobacco executive and whistleblower Jeffrey Wigand and Al Pacino as crusading journalist Lowell Bergman who battles CBS complicity in the cover-up. The leads simmer with righteous rage and the film takes on the distorted patina of a recurring nightmare. A modern masterpiece.

Ali 2001, 159 min

cast Will Smith, Jamie Foxx, Jon Voight, Mario Van Peebles, Ron Silver, Jeffrey Wright *cin* Emmanuel Lubezki *m* Lisa Gerrard, Pieter Bourke

Ali evokes *cinéma-vérité* aesthetics as it follows the boxer's fortunes from the civil rights struggle to the end of the Vietnam War. Masterfully photographed by Emmanuel Lubezki, its analysis of male confrontation reaches its apotheosis in the climactic fight with George Foreman in Zaire.

Collateral 2004, 120 min

cast Tom Cruise, Jamie Foxx, Jada Pinkett Smith, Mark Ruffalo, Peter Berg *cin* Dion Beebe, Paul Cameron *m* James Newton Howard

Shot on high-definition video, *Collateral* is steeped in the bluish Los Angeles light that has become synonymous with Mann. Jamie Foxx is a cab driver who picks up Tom Cruise's contract killer and is instructed to ferry him to each hit as he sabotages a federal prosecution. Tackling some of Mann's favourite themes, the film dramatizes the dispute between professional expertise and public obligation amid an impersonal urban architecture against which modern man must define his worth, remaining always an outsider.

Benoît Mariage

Belgium, 1961–

When *The Carriers Are Waiting* (1999) was released, critics made predictable noises about surrealism and René Magritte. After all, the bittersweet curio concerned a man who bullies his son into breaking the world door-opening record. But Benoît Mariage claimed that in the movie "we stick with the real; we stay right down to the earth!" And indeed, many of the oddball elements are drawn straight from the director's own life. Mariage was once a newspaper photographer who, to get the right picture, would follow freakish weather and photograph car crashes. His first forays into moving pictures had been as a documentary filmmaker, and after the global arthouse success of *The Carriers Are Waiting* Mariage returned to his roots with *Nemadis, The Years Without News* (2000), a film about the lives of Mauritanian nomads. His second flight into fiction, *L'autre* (*The Missing Half*, 2003), an unpredictable domestic drama about a woman who decides to abort one of her twins, was punishingly slow but strangely intriguing. LH

The Carriers Are Waiting (Les convoyeurs attendent) 1999, 94 min, b/w

cast Benoît Poelvoorde, Morgane Simon, Bouli Lanners, Dominique Baeyens *cin* Philippe Guilbert *m* Stéphane Huguenin, Yves Sanna

In order to win the family a car, a newspaper photographer (Poelvoorde) decides to enter his son into a competition to beat the world record for opening and closing a door, which stands at 40,000 times in 24 hours. Evocatively shot in lustrous monochrome, and inhabiting the same postindustrial blight as fellow-Belgian filmmakers the Dardennes brothers, Mariage's hyperreal comedy winningly exudes a melancholic charm, absurdist grace and gnarly poetry.

José Mojica Marins

Brazil, 1929–

Director, writer and producer José Mojica Marins – better known by his screen name Zé do Caixão (Coffin Joe) – is the face of Brazilian horror. His offbeat underground work, using sex and horror to explore personal and political issues, has been banned and vilified since his first shocker, *At Midnight I'll Take Your Soul* (1963). His most extreme nightmare is *Awakening Of The Beast* (1970). Tired of not being taken seriously, he later dedicated himself to videos, short stories, political candidacy, comic books, telenovela acting, TV terror shows and pornography. Critical perception changed following the award-winning documentary *Coffin Joe: The Strange World Of José Mojica Marins* (2001). After 29 variable features with no financial help from Brazil's subsidized film production sector, the Ministry of Culture co-funded *Devil's Reincarnation* (2007). AJ

At Midnight I'll Take Your Soul (A meia-noite levarei sua alma) 1963, 84 min

cast José Mojica Marins, Magda Mei, Valéria Vasquez, Nivaldo Lima, Ilídio Martins Simões *cin* Giorgio Attilli *m* Salatiel Coelho

In this experimental, sacrilegious and sensational film, grave-digger Coffin Joe (Marins) embarks on the first of his obsessive supernatural searches for the ideal woman to give birth to his perfect son. Marins took on the lead role after the original actor backed out.

M

Chris Marker

France, 1921–

Perhaps more than anyone in this book, Chris Marker is his own author, an autonomous auteur who makes films, he says, "in communion with himself". Shying away from interviews, and rarely photographed, he is an elusive and infinitely suggestive figure hovering just off camera, allowing us a glimpse here and there of what strikes him as pertinent.

He was born Christian François Bouche-Villeneuve. There is a suggestion that he served as a paratrooper during World War II. We know he was a professional photographer and writer in the 1950s, when he began to edge towards filmmaking in close collaboration with Alain Resnais. Along with Resnais and Agnès Varda he was one of the Rive Gauche (Left Bank) directors, who were initially considered more politically oriented than the *Cahiers* critics of the *nouvelle vague*. A communist in the 1960s, Marker has ruefully explored the fate of that ideology in *A Grin Without A Cat* (1977) and the melancholy *The Last Bolshevik* (1992).

His first films were very loosely ethnographic documentaries, but already in *Letter From Siberia* (1957) he had begun to shade his images with a subjective first-person commentary, sometimes wry, reflective and associative. In one sequence in that film an identical image is replayed three times with contradictory narrations, one upbeat, one critical, the third neutral. "What is truth?", the film asks. In another early *cinéma vérité* landmark, *Le joli mai* (*Pretty May*, 1963), Marker mingled vox-pop interviews with other "found" footage touching on political issues.

French critic André Bazin called *Letter From Siberia* "an essay documented by film", and five decades on Marker remains the foremost practitioner of the essay film. It is a paradox that this most intensely private and camera-shy personality should devote the best part of his life to first-person cinema. But Marker is present in these films as an absence: a disembodied voice, an eye without a face (the voice is not his voice, the "I" not necessarily his "I"). His major theme is memory – especially memory mediated in the age of photography. An anthropologist and traveller, he is intensely curious about the world. A philosopher, he draws connections between what he sees, what he remembers, and what he thinks. A poet, he reassembles observations, memories and thoughts to bring out their mystery as well as their meaning.

Like many of his generation, Marker is a devout cinephile. Hitchcock's *Vertigo* (1958) is one touchstone in his work. It crops up first in Marker's famous photo-montage *La jetée* (*The Pier*, 1962) and later in *Sans soleil* (*Sunless*, 1983) and his CD-ROM *Immemory* (1997). He has also made several portraits of filmmakers, including Akira Kurosawa (*A.K.*, 1985) and Andrei Tarkovsky (*A Day In The Life Of Andrei Arsenevich*, 2000).

If he's drawn to the manner in which these masters remake the world in their own image, commanding armies, orchestrating elaborate camera movements and destroying cities, Marker himself seems happiest at home doodling with a video camera, his computer and his beloved cat… (cats and owls are constant talismans in his work). Marker has always experimented with the methods and applications of cinema, creating interactive CD-ROMs, art installation pieces and animated computer graphics. In his eighties now, he deserves to be recognized as the first twenty-first-century filmmaker. TC

La jetée (The Pier) 1962, 28 min

cast James Kirk, Hélène Chatelain, Davos Hanich, Jacques Ledoux, William Klein *cin* Chris Marker, Jean Chiabaud *m* Trevor Duncan

Marker's best-known work is not an essay film at all, but a science-fiction story composed entirely (save for one flicker of movement) in still images captured on the director's Pentax. Set some time before and some time after World War III, it hinges on a brief encounter at Orly airport, a moment that passes in the blink of an eye. Terry Gilliam directed a lavish Hollywood adaptation, *Twelve Monkeys*, in 1995.

Sans soleil (Sunless) 1983, 100 min

with Alexandra Stewart *cin* Sana Na N'Hada, Danièle Tessier, Jean-Michel Humeau, Mario Marret *m* Michel Krasna, Mussorgsky, Sibelius

Marker's masterpiece, *Sans soleil* travels far and wide, ranging from ethnographic observations on tribal ceremonies in Africa and the incongruous shrines you still find in high-tech Tokyo to ruminations on the San Francisco locations of Hitchcock's *Vertigo* and notes for a speculative science-fiction film in Iceland. Evocative of W.G. Sebald's *Rings Of Saturn* and Bruce Chatwin's *The Songlines*, it's tied together by Marker's perennial obsession with time, memory and image culture.

Garry Marshall

US, 1934–

A classic entertainment industry all-rounder, Garry Marshall started off as a jazz drummer in his own band. He then started supplying gags for a host of comics, including Joey Bishop, going on to write for a series of highly successful TV comedy shows and sitcoms including *The Dick Van Dyke Show*, *The Lucy Show* and *I Spy* (all in the 1960s). In the next decade he was executive producer, writer and director on *The Odd Couple* (1970–75), had a similar role on *Happy Days* (1975–78) and created *Mork And Mindy* (1978–82), the series that made Robin Williams a star. Marshall has pursued a parallel career as a character actor, notably in the TV series *Murphy Brown* (1994–97) and recently as the voice of Buck Cluck in the animated feature *Chicken Little* (2005).

His first outing as a director was the manic hospital comedy *Young Doctors In Love* (1982). He scored something of a cult success with *The Flamingo Kid* (1984), a light coming-of-age comedy set in the 1960s and starring a young Matt Dillon. By the end of the decade Marshall had found his niche as an adroit purveyor of rom-coms that were a sly balance of comedy and sentimentality. *Overboard* (1987) was a screwball vehicle for Goldie Hawn and Kurt Russell, while *Beaches* (1988) paired up Bette Midler, as larger-than-life entertainer CC, with Barbara Hershey as an ambitious WASP lawyer. His big breakthrough, however, was *Pretty Woman* (1990), a tart-with-a-heart variation on the Cinderella theme which made Julia Roberts a superstar. Marshall was now hot property – the virtual king of chick flicks – but with his subsequent films, including the unconvincing *Frankie And Johnny* (1991), the predictable *The Runaway Bride* (1999) and the saccharine excess of the two *Princess Diaries* films (2001, 2004), he seemed to lose his winning touch. RB

Pretty Woman 1990, 119 min
cast Richard Gere, Julia Roberts, Ralph Bellamy, Jason Alexander, Hector Elizondo, Laura San Giacomo *cin* Charles Minsky *m* James Newton Howard

Vivian (Julia Roberts) is a streetwalker who plies her trade on Sunset Blvd. Asked for directions by Edward (Richard Gere), a workaholic millionaire, she finishes up at his hotel (though sex is not what he's after). Intrigued, he hires her to be his escort for business functions, and as she gets into the role her self-esteem grows and his hard surface starts to crack. This is a film about vulnerability, in which the two stars gel perfectly and Marshall maintains a delicate balance between fairy-tale romance and reality.

George Marshall
US, 1891–1975

A parodist of grace and humility, George Marshall awaits proper discovery. A Hollywood extra from 1912, he graduated via larger roles to writing stories and screenplays. By 1916 he was directing Harry Carey Westerns, and on his return from service in World War I he helmed a couple of Ruth Roland serials as well as features including the comedy *Why Trust Your Husband?* (1921) and the Western *Don Quickshot Of The Rio Grande* (1923). Specializing in comedy and action shorts, he was supervising director of shorts first at Fox and later at Pathé during the 1920s.

Throughout his career – in which he directed over 140 films – Marshall proved adept at the unobtrusive scene-setting and direction in which stars thrived. From the 1930s to the 1950s, he oversaw vehicles for Laurel and Hardy (*Towed In The Hole*, 1932), James Stewart and Marlene Dietrich (*Destry Rides Again*, 1939), W.C. Fields (*You Can't Cheat An Honest Man*, 1939), Alan Ladd and Veronica

Lake (*The Blue Dahlia*, 1946), Bob Hope (*Monsieur Beaucaire*, 1947), Jerry Lewis and Dean Martin (*My Friend Irma*, 1949) and Glenn Ford (*The Gazebo*, 1959). The crowd-pleasing junket *Star-Spangled Rhythm* (1942) showcased every Paramount contract player from Bing Crosby to Betty Hutton. Marshall was the obvious choice to direct *The Perils Of Pauline* (1948), Hutton's tribute to silent matinee daredevil Pearl White. His decline echoed that of the big Depression and wartime audiences. In *The Sheepman* (1959) Glenn Ford looked as incongruous as a sheep in cattle country, and by the 1960s Marshall seemed more at home on the TV treadmill than he did steering the weakest story in the portmanteau epic *How The West Was Won* (1962). RA

Destry Rides Again 1939, 94 min, b/w
cast James Stewart, Marlene Dietrich, Charles Winninger, Brian Donlevy, Una Merkel, Mischa Auer *cin* Hal Mohr *m* Frank Skinner

Released in 1939, the year of the Western (*Jesse James*, *Stagecoach*), this was an astute spoof oater. When James Stewart's wimpish marshal comes to the frontier town of Bottleneck, his quiet words and philosophy must do battle against Brian Donlevy's six-shooter. Marlene Dietrich reprises her *Blue Angel* temptress, and her catfight with Una Merkel remains a spectacle of rare delight. The film revived Dietrich's career and made Stewart an even bigger star.

The Blue Dahlia 1946, 98 min, b/w
cast Alan Ladd, Veronica Lake, William Bendix, Howard Da Silva, Hugh Beaumont, Doris Dowling *cin* Lionel Lindon *m* Victor Young

A rare *film noir* from George Marshall, this Raymond Chandler adaptation is as dark and deadly as any of the returning war vet movies made in the 1940s. Alan Ladd pursues the killer of his faithless wife through rainy LA streets, stumbling upon Veronica Lake and in the process consolidating their lucrative star pairing. Playing Ladd's buddy and psychotic alter ego, William Bendix is outstanding as one of the era's greatest casualties, a regular guy with a steel plate in his head and a furious temper.

Neil Marshall
UK, 1970–

With an unswerving eye for which horror clichés work and which are ripe for witty reinvention, Neil Marshall has carved out a niche as the premiere Brit Splat Packer. Inspired variously by *Raiders Of The Lost Ark* (1981), James Herbert novels, Sam Raimi and Peter Jackson, he shot his first productions on Super 8 film in his back garden. He went on to study animation and filmmaking at Newcastle Polytechnic. His graduation short, the zombie shocker *Brain Death* (1992), attracted the attention of producer/director Bahrat Nalluri, who asked Marshall to co-write his thriller *Killing Time* (1995). Marshall ended up working as editor on the film's chaotic shoot, an experience that convinced him he wanted to direct. He wrote and directed the short film *Combat* (1999), funding it by editing films such as *Ravine* and *Bully* (both 1999). His sensational feature debut was *Dog Soldiers* (2002), a black comedy werewolf shocker that he had begun writing in 1996. It was followed by the critically acclaimed *The Descent* (2005) and the futuristic action horror *Doomsday* (2007). AJ

Dog Soldiers 2002, 105 min
cast Sean Pertwee, Kevin McKidd, Liam Cunningham, Emma Cleasby, Thomas Lockyer, Darren Morfitt *cin* Sam McCurdy *m* Mark Thomas

A group of soldiers on weekend manoeuvres in Scotland stumble across a pack of werewolves and fend off their savage attacks until dawn. Scary, funny and exciting, this is *An American Werewolf In London* meets *Zulu*, with touches of John Ford.

The Descent 2005, 99 min
cast Shauna MacDonald, Natalie Mendoza, Alex Reid, Saskia Mulder, Nora Jane Noone, Myanna Buring *cin* Sam McCurdy *m* David Julyan

A six-woman caving expedition is pursued underground by a breed of bloodthirsty creatures. Through a series of high-impact shocks and intelligently constructed panic attacks Marshall expertly mines every fear and phobia. This dark, vicious and cruel masterpiece is a truly chilling experience.

Tonie Marshall
France, 1951–

Tonie Marshall shines an incisive light into the hidden lives of modern France. Critically identified with the French "New New Wave" of directors committed to documenting everyday society, she has produced a solid body of work, at the heart of which are a series of tough-minded female survivors.

The daughter of 1940s star Micheline Presle and American actor William Marshall, she started out as an actress. Her directing and writing debut came in 1989 with the police comedy *Pentimento*, starring Antoine de Caunes. *Pas très Catholique* (*Not Very Catholic*, 1994), which follows a woman detective as she stumbles on a son she hasn't seen for years, couched perennial "feminine" issues about ageing and committing in a comic format. Picking up on the family motif, *Enfants de salaud* (*Bastard Brood*, 1996) was a comedy starring Nathalie Baye, François Cluzet and a miraculous Molly Ringwald, in which half-siblings are brought together by their father's court appearance. Played out in the female preserve of a beauty salon, *Vénus beauté (institut)* (*Venus Beauty*, 1998) swept the 1999 César Awards. But neither *Au plus près du paradis* (*Nearest to Heaven*, 2002), in which Catherine Deneuve plays a woman reconciling with an old flame, nor the comedy *France boutique* (2003) have consolidated Marshall's international reputation. She remains one of the undiscovered treasures of French cinema. RA

Vénus beauté (institut) (Venus Beauty) 1998, 107 min
cast Nathalie Baye, Bulle Ogier, Samuel Le Bihan, Jacques Bonnaffé, Mathilde Seigner, Audrey Tautou *cin* Gérard de Battista *m* Khalil Chahine

The Venus beauty salon becomes a microcosm for the emotional psyche of France in this nicely observed portrait of the ups and downs of its staff, a "family" of the romantically injured, insulted yet hopeful. Nathalie Baye's Angèle is a touching portrait of what happens when you're in your forties but still feel like a 16 year old inside.

Andrew Marton
Hungary (formerly Austro-Hungarian Empire), 1904–92

Billy Wilder cracked, "Action scenes in my films are limited to a secretary being chased around the desk by her boss – and even then I call Andrew Marton." Born Endre Marton, in Budapest, Marton would become the most highly prized second-unit director in Hollywood, largely responsible for the Dunkirk sequence in *Mrs Miniver* (1942), the combat footage in *A Farewell To Arms* (1951) and *55 Days At Peking* (1963), and (with stuntman Yakima Canutt) the thrilling chariot races in William Wyler's *Ben-Hur* (1959) and Anthony Mann's *The Fall Of The Roman Empire* (1964). When Nicholas Ray was fired from the last of these, Marton took over and, according to Ray, "did heroic work". Marton developed his skills as an editor on Ernst Lubitsch's *The Student Prince* (1927) and *Eternal Love* (1929). He directed his first film that same year, and alternated those duties for a spell. Jewish, he fled Germany for Britain and then Hollywood. He went on to direct a dozen features solo – including the romantic adventure *Green Fire* (1954), starring Gene Kelly, and *The Thin Red Line* (1964) – but he is best remembered for his showpiece contributions to other filmmakers' work. TC

The Thin Red Line 1964, 99 min
cast Keir Dullea, Jack Warden, James Philbrook, Ray Daley, Robert Kanter *cin* Manuel Berenguer *m* Malcolm Arnold

The first adaptation of James Jones's Guadalcanal novel may have been eclipsed by the more poetic 1998 Terrence Malick version, but it offers an interesting point of comparison and in some scenes communicates a properly jaundiced vision of war. Dullea is Private Doll, whose anti-authoritarian instincts are dulled by exposure to the killing factory. Jack Warden is the hard-bitten Sergeant Welsh.

Rudolph Maté
Poland (formerly Austro-Hungarian Empire), 1898–1964

Rudolph Maté is best known for his cinematography, but as a director he excelled in many genres. He entered filmmaking in Hungary as assistant cameraman to director Alexander Korda in 1919. He was later apprenticed to cinematographer Karl Freund in Berlin, before moving to France as cameraman on Carl Dreyer's *Mikael* (1924), *La passion de Jeanne d'Arc* (1928) and *Vampyr* (1932). He also co-photographed Fritz Lang's "metaphysical" drama *Liliom* (1934). In Hollywood from 1935 as a lighting cameraman, Maté shot many classics including *Stella Dallas* (1937) and *Gilda* (1946). In 1947 he began directing. His moody look and feeling for action suited the emerging trend for punchy thrillers shot on location such as *The Dark Past* (1948), *D.O.A.* (1949) and *Union Station* (1950). *When Worlds Collide* (1951) was an effective science fiction in which humans face extinction as a dying star hurtles towards Earth. *The Violent Men* (1955) neatly balanced a range war shot in CinemaScope and Technicolor against Barbara Stanwyck's adulterous intrigues. RA

D.O.A. 1949, 83 min, b/w

cast Edmond O'Brien, Pamela Britton, Luther Adler, Beverly Campbell, Lynn Baggett, Willing Ching *cin* Ernest Laszlo *m* Dimitri Tiomkin

Upon discovering that he has ingested poison and has only hours to live, Edmond O'Brien's businessman hurtles through a living nightmare as he investigates his own death. Shot on LA and San Francisco locations and propelled by Dimitri Tiomkin's jazzy score, this remains a powerful minor moment in the history of *film noir*.

Elaine May
US, 1932–

Elaine May is one of a depressingly rare species in American cinema: an actress who is also a writer and director. Of the four films she's directed, two were forcibly wrested from her by the studio, and another was one of the most famous box-office bombs in cinema history.

May had one of the worst career experiences imaginable following the completion of her directorial debut. *A New Leaf* (1970), was taken from her and re-edited by the studio, Paramount. May was so unhappy with the result that she filed a lawsuit to have her name removed from the credits. Nevertheless, even shorn of its darker elements, this black comedy about a playboy (Walter Matthau) and his dastardly plot to marry and murder an heiress and botanist (May), still sparkles with the writer's pin-sharp, neurotic humour, while riffing on her favourite subject, that of betrayal.

Taken from a Neil Simon script, her next project, *The Heartbreak Kid* (1972), painfully and compellingly charted a newly married man's desperate pursuit of a comely coquette played by Cybill Shepherd. However, *Mikey And Nicky* (1976), was again re-edited by Paramount, being released in a form that the director considered unfinished.

A few years later, Columbia may well have wished they had done the same thing with *Ishtar* (1987). Receiving some of the worst reviews ever, this comedy behemoth only took a tiny percentage of its enormous budget. May has never again directed, sticking instead to scriptwriting. She was reunited with her former comedy partner Mike Nichols on *The Birdcage* (1996) and *Primary Colours* (1998) – she as scriptwriter, he as director-producer – but their old magic seemed to have vanished. LH

Mikey And Nicky 1976, 106 min

cast Peter Falk, John Cassavetes, Ned Beatty, Rose Arrick, Carol Grace, William Hickey, Sanford Meisner *cin* Victor J. Kemper *m* John Strauss

Mikey (Peter Falk) comes to the rescue of Nicky (John Cassavetes), who's in hiding from a gangster he's betrayed, but things aren't quite what they seem. Paramount wrested the film from the famously indecisive May in the editing-room; the director's cut was finally seen in 1980. It's the best John Cassavetes film that Cassavetes never made.

Ishtar 1987, 107 min

cast Warren Beatty, Dustin Hoffman, Isabelle Adjani, Charles Grodin, Jack Weston, Tess Harper, Carol Kane *cin* Vittorio Storaro *m* John Strauss

Ishtar went hugely over budget and months over schedule, reportedly because May was unhappy with the shape of the sand dunes and the size of the camels. Critics crowned it one of the worst films ever made. It's not. Early scenes are genuinely funny, and it's only when the action shifts to North Africa that it loses its way.

John Maybury
UK, 1958–

John Maybury can be bracketed among a small band of filmmakers which emerged in the late 1980s and 90s eschewing the naturalism of Ken Loach et al. in favour of the magical illusions of Powell and Pressburger, and the avant-garde aesthetic of Derek Jarman.

An art college student at the height of punk, Maybury decided to become a filmmaker after going to a Sex Pistols gig in London at which the experimental *Magick Lantern Cycle* films of Kenneth Anger were screened. The Anger touch was evident in his subsequent shorts *Pagan Idolatry* (1984) and *Tortures That Laugh* (1986), but so too was the painterly influence of Derek Jarman, who gave Maybury his first camera, a Super 8, and employed him as production designer on his punk odyssey *Jubilee* (1977).

His debut feature, *Love Is The Devil* (1998), told the love story of artist Francis Bacon and thief George Dwyer, and seemed to announce a major talent in British cinema. The Bacon estate refused to allow any of his paintings to be used in the film, but with characteristic chutzpah Maybury managed to allude to the Bacon aesthetic by shooting the faces of characters in the warped reflections of ashtrays or through cracked windows, capturing that "face-melt" effect. "A Powell and Pressburger Carry On" is how the director, with typical ebullience, summed up his own film.

Maybury didn't make another film for seven years. Fortunately, Steven Soderbergh rang. A fan of *Love Is The Devil*, the director of *sex, lies, and videotape* invited Maybury to direct *The Jacket* (2005) for his production company. This overloaded time-travel thriller was proficiently made but didn't bear any of the Maybury touches. There was, disappointingly, little to be seen of his mercurial talent. LH

Love Is The Devil 1998, 90 min

cast Derek Jacobi, Daniel Craig, Tilda Swinton, Anne Lambton, Annabel Brooks *cin* John Mathieson *m* Ryuichi Sakamoto

The story of an odd couple: Francis Bacon (Jacobi, in a role he was born to play) and the burglar George Dwyer (Craig) who broke into Bacon's studio one night and stayed for several years. It's a film of continual invention – the sound of a cigarette being exhaled morphs into the steam of a Turkish bath – without being coldly clever or overly pleased with itself. A real achievement.

Archie Mayo

US, 1891–1968

The former stage actor Archie Mayo was one of those directors that Anne Baxter – quoted in the magazine *Film Dope* – called a "canner": "Do the take, do the cover shot, reverse angle, close-up and get in the can. Like sardines." Of the 79 films Mayo made, a couple are notable for early appearances of a future big star in just the kind of role they would later be famous for: James Cagney first tried the gangster's uniform on for size in Mayo's *Doorway To Hell* (1930), as did neophyte mobster Humphrey Bogart in the film that launched his career, *The Petrified Forest* (1936). Mayo, however, had no say in the casting, and Bogie's big chance was entirely down to the stubborn perseverance of star Leslie Howard, who had played alongside him in the stage production. Both films are in fact somewhat workaday, their interest being chiefly historical. LH

The Petrified Forest 1936, 83 min, b/w

cast Leslie Howard, Bette Davis, Humphrey Bogart, Genevieve Tobin, Dick Foran, Charley Grapewin, Porter Hall *cin* Sol Polito *m* Bernard Kaun

Deadly armed robber Duke Mantee, broodingly played by Bogart, holds wandering writer Leslie Howard and waitress Bette Davis hostage in a gas-station restaurant in the middle of the desert. Signposting the new direction for the cinematic gangster as a man on the run, this slow melodrama is not really a gangster movie per se, but figuratively and literally about the death of the intellectual.

Paul Mazursky

US, 1930–

The *echt* 1960s swingers comedy *Bob & Carol & Ted & Alice* (1969) set the congenial tone for Paul Mazursky's polite satires, inflected by the nuances of European art cinema and the neuroses of American-Jewish humour. For much of his career, the writer-director has traced the fallout from the sexual revolution, from group encounters to single parenthood: the affable married lothario George Segal in *Blume In Love* (1973); the *ménage à trois* in *Willie And Phil* (1980); and John Cassavetes glumly retreating to an island with his daughter in *Tempest* (1982). Sophisticated, solipsistic and achingly poignant, Mazursky's satires often lack the spite and spike to stick to their targets. It seems that the director plays better in a minor key, as his delicate touch lightened the Stygian gloom of the post-Holocaust fable *Enemies: A Love Story* (1987) and the blue funk of *An Unmarried Woman* (1978). However, his collaboration with that other chronicler of Manhattan miseries Woody Allen, on *Scenes From A Mall* (1990), was a grave disappointment.

Mazursky's films often contain plenty of autobiographical detail. In the follow-up to *Bob & Carol & Ted & Alice*, *Alex In Wonderland* (1970), he operated in the grey area between autobiography and self-indulgence in his story of a novice director who's just had a big hit and doesn't know what to make for his second film. Having begun his career in films as an actor in Stanley Kubrick's debut *Fear And Desire* (1953), reaching a career high two years later in *Blackboard Jungle* (1955), he subsequently drew heavily on this period of his life in *Next Stop Greenwich Village* (1976), which follows a young actor's move to Manhattan's bohemian quarter.

Positioned between arthouse and mainstream, *Moscow On The Hudson* (1984) and the remake of Jean Renoir's *Boudu Saved From Drowning* (1932), *Down And Out In Beverly Hills* (1986), have been notable commercial successes for him. LH

Bob & Carol & Ted & Alice 1969, 105 min

cast Natalie Wood, Robert Culp, Elliott Gould, Dyan Cannon, Horst Ebersberg *cin* Charles E. Lang *m* Quincy Jones

Mazursky's directorial debut was both a phenomenal success and a cultural barometer. Swinger Robert Culp informs his wife Natalie Wood of his sexual indiscretions, an action that, oddly, liberates their marriage. They then try to open the eyes of their more conventional friends, Elliott Gould and Dyan Cannon, with alarming and fitfully funny results in this hit-and-miss affair.

An Unmarried Woman 1978, 124 min

cast Jill Clayburgh, Alan Bates, Michael Murphy, Cliff Gorman, Pat Quinn, Kelly Bishop, Lisa Lucas *cin* Arthur J. Ornitz *m* Bill Conti

Jill Clayburgh is left to look after her teenage daughter when her husband dumps her for a younger woman. After

3

a series of unsuitable suitors, she finds companionship with artist Alan Bates. However, the highlights are the scenes with Clayburgh's three thirtysomething girlfriends, whose chatty, catty, men-obsessed confabs may have given the makers of *Sex And The City* a few ideas.

Jim McBride
US, 1941–

Jim McBride's highly erratic but idiosyncratic career includes the seminal mock documentary *David Holzman's Diary* (1967), *Breathless* (1983) and the mainstream sleeper *The Big Easy* (1987), as well as several "lost" underground films, some under-the-radar TV and straight-to-video movies, and an early episode of the hit show *Six Feet Under* (2001).

McBride's first film, *David Holzman's Diary*, purports to be just that, a *vérité* self-portrait filmed by a young cinema nut obsessed with his friends Eclair and Nag(ra). A devotee of Godard, Holzman decides to film his daily reality in order to make sense of his life. Instead he only messes it up further.

Shot in five days on a budget of $2500, *David Holzman's Diary* is a playful, original, prescient take on the limits of *cinéma vérité*, with sharp insights into still-current debates about film, voyeurism and "reality". Save for brief runs in Paris and New York, this underground classic never had theatrical distribution, but as a film-school staple it has been highly influential. You could call it the first "mock doc", although the first postmodern *film vérité* may be closer to the mark.

McBride's follow-up, *My Girlfriend's Wedding* (1969), was a genuine documentary about his then girlfriend's green-card marriage of convenience. Next came a guerrilla-style post-apocalypse movie, *Glen And Randa* (1971), and the lowbrow sex comedy *Hot Times* (1974), into which he smuggled numerous references to the movies he had tried and failed to get produced in the interim. Sadly *Hot Times* didn't make it any easier to get backing for his most cherished project, an adaptation of Walker Percy's Louisiana novel *The Moviegoer*. During this period McBride was also developing his screenplay for a remake of Jean-Luc Godard's *A bout de souffle*, a project that finally came to fruition as *Breathless* in 1983.

A legit Hollywood director now, McBride signed up to direct *The Big Easy* (1987), a formula script by Daniel Petrie Jr starring Dennis Quaid. It was his first and only hit. A further collaboration with Quaid, the Jerry Lee Lewis biopic *Great Balls Of Fire!* (1989), was styled as an exuberant rock'n'roll musical, but this quirky experiment bombed (in part because the public balked at the non-judgemental approach to the Killer's 13-year-old bride) and McBride's feature-film career was stopped in its

tracks. His subsequent work has been relegated to low-budget films for TV, cable and video. TC

David Holzman's Diary 1967, 73 min, b/w
cast L.M. Kit Carson, Penny Wohl, Louise Levine, Fern McBride, Eileen Dietz, Mike Levine *cin* Michael Wadleigh

David wants truth 24 times a second. He films his neighbours, his friends, his girlfriend – until she walks out in disgust. Mostly he films himself. But his relationships with Eclair and Nag(ra) aren't as fulfilling as he hoped. McBride's underground classic is a playful riff on solipsistic cinephilia and voyeurism, anticipating the current craze for reality TV – save that Holzman is fictional.

Breathless 1983, 100 min
cast Richard Gere, Valerie Kaprisky, William Tepper, John P. Ryan, Art Metrano, Robert Dunn *cin* Richard H. Kline *m* Jack Nietzsche

Richard Gere and Valerie Kaprisky play the American–French lovers in McBride's much-maligned adaptation of Godard's seminal film. *Breathless* is best appreciated as a self-conscious Americanization, a flip Angelino mirror image of the French classic. This pop artefact centres on Gere's preening, narcissistic hustler. Like him, it's bursting with energy and ultimately about as substantial as a doughnut – which is partly the point.

The Big Easy 1987, 101 min
cast Dennis Quaid, Ellen Barkin, Ned Beatty, Ebbe Roe Smith, John Goodman, Lisa Jane Persky *cin* Affonso Beato *m* Brad Fiedel

The Big Easy marries a conventional internal affairs plot with a screwball romantic comedy dynamic: "serious", uptight DA Ellen Barkin tangles with frivolous, loose homicide dick Dennis Quaid. McBride switched the location from Chicago to New Orleans and encouraged his cast to have fun with the material, pulling off a genuinely fresh and lively mainstream movie in the process.

Leo McCarey
US, 1898–1969

Leo McCarey's supervision of 1930s and 40s Hollywood comedies is more akin to contract studio authorship than independent auteurism.

After holding various jobs in the film industry, McCarey began writing gags and directing Charlie Chase two-reelers at the Hal Roach studio in 1923. Three years later, he became Roach's vice president and supervisor of comedy production, a role in which he allegedly brought Laurel and Hardy together for *Wrong Again* (1929) and *Big Business* (1929). In 1929 McCarey graduated to features and hit his stride. With a winning combination of zany humour and popular sentiment, he directed some of the era's biggest star vehicles: *The Kid From Spain* (Eddie Cantor, 1932), *Duck Soup* (Marx Brothers, 1933), *Six Of A Kind* (W.C. Fields, 1934), *Belle Of The Nineties* (Mae West, 1934) and *The Milky Way* (Harold Lloyd, 1936).

McCarey knew an effective script when he read one. Directed by McCarey and co-written by Delmer

Daves and Donald Ogden Stewart, the Irene Dunne and Charles Boyer weepie *Love Affair* (1939) is one of few Hollywood releases to be remade without revision (it also helped that McCarey co-wrote the original story). But after the war the adroit lines and sentimental glow which had ensured McCarey's place as one of Hollywood's most successful directors no longer worked. While the Bing Crosby and Barry Fitzgerald feuding priest caper *Going My Way* (1944) won McCarey Oscars for writing and directing, it was mush. And the sequel – *The Bells Of St Mary's* (1945) – was not only pious but felt like an apologia for Catholic manipulation of the New York real estate market.

Yet, with Billy Wilder, McCarey remains one of only five directors to win the Hollywood hat-trick of best picture, best director and best screenplay Oscars. Jean Renoir perhaps best summed up McCarey's grasp of what the people thought they wanted: "Leo McCarey is one of the few directors in Hollywood who understands human beings." RA

Duck Soup 1933, 70 min, b/w
cast The Marx Brothers, Margaret Dumont, Louis Calhern *cin* Henry Sharp *m* Bert Kalmar, Harry Ruby

An utterly demented political satire about a bankrupt state, Freedonia, that is "saved" by wealthy Mrs Teasdale with the condition that her friend Rufus T. Firefly (Groucho Marx) is appointed dictator. As the master of the wise-cracking put-down, Groucho is blessed with his best-ever script, while Chico and the silent Harpo pursue their particular brand of physical humour with maniacal energy. The mirror sequence (in which Harpo tries to convince Groucho that he's his reflection) has to be seen to be believed.

Ruggles Of Red Gap 1935, 91 min, b/w
cast Charles Laughton, Mary Boland, Charlie Ruggles, ZaSu Pitts, Roland Young, Leila Hyams *cin* Arthur Hornblow Jr *m* Ralph Rainger

When Marmaduke Ruggles (Charles Laughton), a very English butler, is won in a poker game, he fetches up in Red Gap, an American western backwater where they have regular "beer busts" and just love his recitation of the Gettysburg Address. So full of character, and characters – Mary Boland, Charlie Ruggles, ZaSu Pitts (singing "By The Light Of The Silvery Moon") – that in our unsubtle times it feels like the hilarious missing link to another world.

The Awful Truth 1937, 91 min, b/w
cast Irene Dunne, Cary Grant, Ralph Bellamy, Alexander D'Arcy, Cecil Cunningham, Molly Lamont *cin* Joseph Walker *m* George Parrish

With undiminished vigour and a feeling for innuendo that Lubitsch must have envied, this is a key moment in the Hollywood remarriage genre. Less frenetic than Howard Hawks's *His Girl Friday* (1940), McCarey's screwball comedy of manners in which Cary Grant and Irene Dunne's sophisticated couple decide to divorce, then do all they can to sabotage the other's marriage plans, is a miracle of timing and repartee. The film won McCarey a directing Oscar.

McGehee & Siegel
Scott McGehee: US
David Siegel: US

Scott McGehee and David Siegel must rank as the oddest of contemporary cinema's odd couples. Unlike other notable two-headed directors they're not brothers and they don't even have any formal training in film, just a love of movies. McGehee has degrees in English literature and rhetoric; Siegel in architecture and fine art.

While working as waiters, in 1989 the pair had a reckless moment and made a short film, without having any idea how to use the equipment. After only one more trial run, they secured the finance, from tips and friends, to make their debut feature, the witty, intelligent *noir* thriller *Suture* (1993). Despite the film's critical success, however, their career appeared to stall.

After a number of failed projects, the duo finally completed *The Deep End* in 2001. More *film bleu* than *film noir*, the sumptuous camera shots of glittering water and glass adroitly reflect the filmmakers' postmodern interplay of brilliant surfaces within the story. The pair stepped out of the shadows of *noir* with *Bee Season* (2005), a disappointing curio about a young girl whose mystical powers come in useful in a national spelling competition. LH

Suture 1993, 96 min, b/w
cast Dennis Haysbert, Mel Harris, Sab Shimono, Dina Merrill, Michael Harris, David Graf, Fran Ryan *cin* Greg Gardiner *m* Cary Berger

After meeting for the first time at their father's funeral, Vince plots to kill his half-brother Clay and take his identity. He is confident his plan will work because they look so alike – the fact that Clay is black and Vince is white is something no one seems to notice. Clay survives a bomb but is burnt beyond recognition. Waking up with amnesia and a different identity, he has to come to terms with his new self. The directors deftly use race to explore consensual reality: what can you do if everyone else says that black is white?

The Deep End 2001, 100 min
cast Tilda Swinton, Goran Visnjić, Jonathan Tucker *cin* Giles Nuttgens *m* Peter Nashel

Believing that her young son has killed his homosexual lover, Tilda Swinton removes the body and the evidence. However, a dark stranger claims he has proof of murder, demands money and gets more than he bargained for. Awash with liquid imagery – Lake Tahoe, a dripping tap – the directors almost drown in their own cleverness, but are rescued by Swinton's superbly nuanced performance.

Norman Z. McLeod
US, 1898–1964

In the annals of American screen comedy, Norman Z. McLeod succeeded James W. Horne as a shepherd of comic talents. He entered Hollywood as an animator and gag writer on the Christie comedies, and rapidly found his niche. His experience as a fighter pilot in World War I then led to him assisting William A. Wellman on *Wings* (1927) and collaborating with Howard Hawks and Lewis Seiler on *The Air Circus* (1928). He began directing from 1928, and his name shows up on a string of very funny movies at all the major studios – MGM, Goldwyn, Hal Roach and Paramount – throughout the next two decades.

McLeod worked with the best of the era: the Marx Brothers (*Monkey Business*, 1931, and *Horse Feathers*, 1932), W.C. Fields (*It's A Gift*, 1934), Cary Grant (*Topper*, 1937), Constance Bennett (*Merrily We Live*, 1938), Eleanor Powell (*Lady Be Good*, 1941) and Ann Sothern (*Panama Hattie*, 1942). Towards the end of the 1940s, he nurtured new rising stars: Danny Kaye (*The Kid From Brooklyn*, 1946, and *The Secret Life Of Walter Mitty*, 1947) and Bob Hope (*The Paleface*, 1948, and *My Favorite Spy*, 1951), as well as directing one of the best Hope-Crosby "Road" movies, *Road To Rio* (1947). His career spanned the evolution of comedy from madcap to meet-cute to mutually assured destruction. McLeod's flexibility and lack of theme or style confirm his generic status as an all-round comedy director. RA

It's A Gift 1934, 73 min, b/w
cast W.C. Fields, Kathleen Howard, Jean Rouverol, Julian Madison, Baby LeRoy *cin* Henry Sharp *m* John Leipold

The great Fields is at his most curmudgeonly and misanthropic in this tale of Harold Bissonette, a dipsomaniac grocer hounded by his snobbish wife (Kathleen Howard) and generally done down by everybody that crosses his path. He dreams of escape to California, but when his dream comes true he still has his family in tow and (needless to say) there's plenty still to vex him. The brilliant set pieces include the disastrous visit of blind Mr Muckle (Charles Sellon) to the store and Harold's thwarted attempts to take a quiet nap on his porch.

The Secret Life Of Walter Mitty 1947, 110 min
cast Danny Kaye, Virginia Mayo, Boris Karloff, Fay Bainter, Ann Rutherford, Thurston Hall, Gordon Jones, Florence Bates *cin* Lee Garmes *m* David Raksin

After World War II, Hollywood's preoccupation with fraught masculinity fuelled *film noir* and Western alike, while nicely showcasing the obligatory lovelies. In Norman Z. McLeod's adaptation of James Thurber's short story, Danny Kaye stars as the pathologically shy publisher's assistant whose fantasy life takes on a sheen of tragicomedy when Virginia Mayo's distressed heiress enters his life, bringing real adventure. Along with Billy Wilder's *Seven Year Itch* (1955), this is the antidote to the post-war angst of the "little man".

John McNaughton
US, 1950–

Construction worker turned stills photographer John McNaughton raised $200,000 to make *Henry: Portrait Of A Serial Killer* (1986) and waited four years to get it released and critically acclaimed. None of his work since, as producer, writer or director, has matched its cool, raw power or high profile. Subsequent directing credits include the film of Eric Bogosian's one-man show *Sex, Drugs, Rock & Roll* (1991), the sci-fi shocker *The Borrower* (1991), the mob comedy *Mad Dog And Glory* (1993) and the twisted, torrid thriller *Wild Things* (1998), which caused something of a stir with its sex and violence. He has also directed the TV crime series *Without A Trace* and *Homicide: Life On The Streets*, and the "Haeckel's Tale" episode of the *Masters Of Horror* TV series. More recently the comedy *Speaking Of Sex* (2001), in which Bill Murray plays a sex counsellor, was one of several low-key excursions into other areas that also included the documentary *Condo Painting* (1998) and the mobster teleplay *Lansky* (1999), starring Richard Dreyfuss. AJ

Henry: Portrait Of A Serial Killer 1986, 83 min
cast Michael Rooker, Tom Towles, Tracy Arnold *cin* Charlie Lieberman *m* Ken Hale, Steven A. Jones, Robert McNaughton

Henry is loosely based on the real exploits of sociopath Henry Lee Lucas and Otis, his white trash partner in a series of brutal murder sprees. McNaughton follows in the footsteps of such first-time directors as *The Texas Chain Saw Massacre*'s Tobe Hooper, using disturbing visions of urban horror to repulse and shock viewers into dealing with their secret fears and unspoken anxieties.

John McTiernan
US, 1951–

A key player in the explosion of action cinema in the 1980s, John McTiernan directed a series of unfussy, no-nonsense spectaculars showcasing the likes of Arnold Schwarzenegger and Bruce Willis.

His first feature film, which he also wrote, was the fantasy horror *Nomads* (1986), starring Pierce Brosnan. It was a flop. He followed it up with the popular *Predator* (1987), a supercharged action horror starring Schwarzenegger as the head of a crack commando squad in the Central American jungle who find themselves hunted by an all-seeing primal beast. *Die Hard* (1988) defined an entire genre, with Bruce Willis smart-talking his way through a stand-off in an office block on Christmas Eve. *The Hunt For Red October* (1990) was another box-office hit.

Last Action Hero (1993) starred Schwarzenegger as a movie hero who breaks through into the real world. The derivative concept was clumsily handled.

His next, the sequel *Die Hard: With A Vengeance* (1995), was no match for the original. *The Thomas Crown Affair* (1999) was a fairly enjoyable remake of the 1968 film, but McTiernan's more recent films – a remake of the 1975 hit *Rollerball* (2002) and the army investigation thriller *Basic* (2003) – have been rather routine. JC

Die Hard 1988, 131 min

cast Bruce Willis, Alan Rickman, Bonnie Bedelia, Reginald Veljohnson, Alexander Godunov *cin* Jan DeBont *m* Michael Kamen

It is Christmas Eve in Los Angeles. In town for the holidays, tough New York cop John McClane (Bruce Willis) finds himself caught up in a hostage situation in an office block and is forced into a game of cat and mouse with a group of terrorists led by Hans Gruber (Alan Rickman). Tense, noisy and intelligent.

The Hunt For Red October 1990, 134 min

cast Sean Connery, Alec Baldwin, Sam Neill, Scott Glenn, James Earl Jones, Joss Ackland *cin* Jan DeBont *m* Basil Poledouris

The commander of the Russian navy's newest submarine (Sean Connery) engages in a claustrophobic battle of wills when he sets about defecting to the US. McTiernan handles the somewhat over-complicated plot with aplomb, producing a smart adaptation of Tom Clancy's novel.

Shane Meadows

UK, 1972–

Doing his own thing, Shane Meadows has steered clear of industry wisdom to write and direct his first five and a half features all in the vicinity of his home towns, Nottingham and Uttoxeter in Staffordshire (he ventured as far as Derbyshire for *Dead Man's Shoes*, 2004). Fresh, funny and true, these films represent some of the best cinema to come out of Britain in the last decade.

Meadows left school without any O-levels and later dropped out of art school (though this is where he met future leading man Paddy Considine). He found his vocation volunteering at Nottingham's Intermedia Film and Video production facilities, where he had access to camcorders and editing equipment. He taught himself how to make short films – usually Pythonesque comic vignettes which he churned out at the rate of one a month – and found backing to make the 60-minute featurette *Small Time* (1996). Developed through improvisatory methods similar to those of Ken Loach and Mike Leigh, *Small Time* is characterized by an authentic working-class naturalism, jocular, absurdist and irreverent, but with a residue of pent-up anger that occasionally breaks out in scenes of disturbing male violence.

All Meadows' feature films have stayed true to the ways and means of *Small Town*, save for the addition of a star (Bob Hoskins in the mono-

chrome *TwentyFourSeven*, 1997), or stars (Robert Carlyle, Ricky Tomlinson, Kathy Burke, Shirley Henderson and Rhys Ifans in the disappointingly campy *Once Upon A Time In The Midlands*, 2002). Strikingly, these mainstream interlopers have been Meadows' least convincing characters, whereas the likes of Thomas Turgoose, as 12-year-old Shaun in Meadows' acclaimed "comeback" film *This Is England* (2006) – another bruising look at troubled masculinity – have invariably impressed. TC

A Room For Romeo Brass 1999, 90 min

cast Andrew Shim, Ben Marshall, Paddy Considine, Frank Harper, Vicky McClure, Julia Ford, James Higgins *cin* Ashley Rowe *m* Nick Hemming

Coming-of-age movies come in all shapes and sizes, but this tale of two 12-year-old Midlands chums who fall under the influence of a dodgy older mentor is a real original. You can tell Meadows lived and breathed this story, as much for the joy it takes in childhood pranks as for the frightening psychosis exposed in Considine's shocking, intense performance.

Dead Man's Shoes 2004, 90 min

cast Paddy Considine, Gary Stretch, Toby Kebbell, Stuart Wolfenden, Andrew Shim, Neil Bell *cin* Danny Cohen *m* Aphex Twin

The failure of *Once Upon A Time In The Midlands* evidently didn't put Meadows off the idea of British Westerns – this is *High Plains Drifter* in Derbyshire. Considine (who wrote the script) is Richard, a squaddie who returns to the small town where he grew up to wreak revenge on the local thugs who abused his simpleton brother, Anthony (Toby Kebbell). A strain of black comedy makes us complicit in Richard's actions, but at the same time we wonder just how far he is going to go. This time, Meadows doesn't pull his punches.

This Is England 2006, 100 min

cast Thomas Turgoose, Stephen Graham, Jo Hartley, Andrew Shim, Vicky McClure, Joseph Gilgun *cin* Danny Cohen *m* Ludovico Einaudi

Another strong feature, this in effect tells the same old story of an impressionable young lad led astray by bad influences. In this case it's a lonely 10-year-old who falls in with a gang of skinheads after his dad has been killed in the Falklands. At first they seem a benign lot, but after a split the boy finds himself in the wrong crowd of BNP thugs. This is Meadows' most autobiographical film to date.

Julio Médem

Spain, 1958–

Julio Médem is a teller of fabulous tales of kismet and coincidence. His films' playful complexities are matched by their symbolism – which doesn't mean they are hard to watch: puzzling they may be, punishing they are not. Sensual, stimulating, often erotic, occasionally funny, Médem's films invite viewers to lie back, relax and allow sound and images to wash over them.

Médem fell in love with cinema when he saw *The Spirit Of The Beehive* (1973) by the great Basque director Victor Erice. Inspired, he experimented with his father's Super 8 camera, continuing to make short films after studying medicine and finally making his debut feature, *Vacas* (*Cows*), in 1992. Here Médem intricately and ambitiously stitches together four stories that span several generations and stretch the viewer's willingness to believe with a narrative chutzpah and thematic bravado. *Vacas* is possibly unique in cinema history for a series of shots that are seen from the point of view of a cow. Following this, *The Red Squirrel* (1993) – in which a failed rock star successfully persuades a beautiful amnesiac that she's his girlfriend until fragments from her old life frighteningly re-emerge – was in part filmed from the titular rodent's viewpoint.

Médem has said that ideas come to him as he's about to fall asleep, and of all his films, the quirky, metaphysical *Tierra* (*Earth*, 1995) seems most to occupy that nebulous space between concrete reality and the abstract fantasy of dreams. *Lovers Of The Arctic Circle* (1999) was a Byzantine, head-spinning mix of geography, geometries and symmetries, and the pinnacle of Médem's achievements to date. He continued to challenge the viewer in *Sex And Lucía* (2001) where the imagery and the narrative remain as elusive as ever, and the hazy intensity of the Mediterranean sun adds to the sensual overload. He then confounded expectations and courted national controversy when he made the documentary *Basque Ball, Skin Against Stone* (2003). Made up of interviews with victims, critics and supporters of the Basque separatist organization ETA, the film was angrily condemned as apparent pro-separatist propaganda. Asked why he made the film, Médem has said he needed to make a documentary about Basque politics in order to feel free to make fiction again. With *Caótica Ana* (2007) he returned to familiar and typically dizzy fictional territory. LH

Lovers Of The Arctic Circle (Los amantes del círcolo polar) 1999, 108 min
cast Najwa Nimri, Fele Martínez, Nancho Novo, Maru Valdivielso, Peru Médem, Sara Valiente *cin* Gonzalo F. Berridi *m* Alberto Iglesias

Ana and Otto live together as brother and sister, become lovers and split up. They go their separate ways until fate brings them together again in the Arctic. Médem maps out his plot with a series of dualities: the names of the protagonists are palindromes and the narration switches between Ana and Otto. The medley of synchronicity and absurdity and the incessant doubling would almost be too much if it wasn't orchestrated with such verve and aplomb.

Sex And Lucía (Lucía y el sexo) 2001, 128 min
cast Paz Vega, Tristán Ulloa, Najwa Nimri, Daniel Freire, Javier Cámara, Elena Anaya, Silvia Llanos *cin* Kiko de la Rica *m* Alberto Iglesias

This is another chaotic, possibly cosmic, story of two ill-starred lovers. But the confusion is magnified by Médem's fiendish narrative strategy: this is a tale twice told: once in a novel and again in fact, and the differences between the two versions are never really defined. This is Médem at his most wilfully capricious, doing a cinematic *pas de deux* that almost doubles as a parody of itself.

Deepa Mehta
India, 1950–

Deepa Mehta epitomizes the new generation of Indian directors making films for a global audience. Based in Toronto since 1973, she made her feature debut, *Sam And Me*, in 1991. It told the story of an Indian immigrant to Canada who forms an unlikely friendship with an elderly Jewish man, for whom he works as a carer. Though Mehta has made other well-received films since, such as the romance *The Republic Of Love* (2003), she is best known for her "elements" series. The first of these films was the lesbian-themed *Fire* (1996). *Earth* (1998) was an accomplished look at the India/Pakistan partition through a child's eyes. Filming of *Water* (2005), about the plight of widows in 1930s India, was forcibly interrupted when activists accused the film of being anti-Hindu. Undeterred, Mehta shot the film in Sri Lanka. It was nominated for best foreign-language film at the 2007 Oscars. NR

Fire 1996, 108 min
cast Nandita Das, Shabana Azmi, Kulbhushan Kharbanda, Javed Jaffrey, Ranjit Chowdhury *cin* Giles Nuttgens *m* A.R. Rahman

Sita marries video-store owner Jatin, who lives with his brother and sister-in-law Radha. The brothers have no time for their wives, and gradually Radha and Sita are drawn into a lesbian relationship. The film enraged Indian fundamentalists for its frank depiction of forbidden love and also for a scene in which a manservant masturbates in front of the brothers' paralysed mother while she watches religious TV programmes.

Earth 1998, 110 min
cast Maia Sethna, Nandita Das, Aamir Khan, Rahul Khanna, Kitu Gidwani, *cin* Giles Nuttgens *m* A.R. Rahman

Set in the simmering political cauldron of Lahore, 1947, just before the traumatic partition of India and Pakistan, *Earth* looks at the increasing divide between Hindus and Muslims as the reality of separation draws closer. Based on Bapsi Sidhwa's bestselling autobiographical novel, the story is seen through the eyes of a young girl from the neutral Parsee community.

Fernando Meirelles
Brazil, 1955–

Having worked steadily for decades in television and commercials, Fernando Meirelles made an incendiary breakthrough as a feature director with *City Of God* (2002). Co-directed with Kátia Lund, *City Of God* was a blood-drenched international hit that spanned three decades of vicious drug wars and offhand slaughter in a slum district of Rio. Meirelles had used a similar episodic structure and mosaic-style editing for his previous feature, *Domésticas*

Li'l Zé (Leandro Firmino da Hora) points the gun in Meirelles' hard-hitting *favela* drama *City Of God*.

(*Maids*, 2001), which he co-directed with Nando Olival. The film wove together the stories of five different maids in São Paulo – each woman being an interface between the city's privileged enclaves and its "invisible" underclass.

With the vast majority of its young performers drawn from the real-life Rio *favelas* (slums) that the film depicts (by all accounts, the actors could also be credited as "creative consultants"), *City Of God* has the raw immediacy of a war correspondent's footage, albeit filtered through a post-MTV sensibility. Undeniably propulsive, the film is long on style but, as some reviewers pointed out, short on characterization and larger social context. (Meirelles also directed four episodes of the spin-off TV series *City Of Men*.)

Meirelles may have taken this criticism to heart, because his first English-language film, an assured adaptation of John Le Carré's *The Constant Gardener* (2005) starring Ralph Fiennes and Rachel Weisz, exuded a controlled moral outrage at a pharmaceutical company's exploitation of a poor African country. Still, as in *City Of God*, the notion of using endemic poverty and violence as the material for slick entertainment remained a source of tension and ambivalence within the movie itself as well as in its critical reception. JW

City Of God (Cidade de deus) 2002, 130 min
cast Matheus Nachtergaele, Seu Jorge, Alexandre Rodrigues, Leandro Firmino da Hora *cin* César Charlone *m* Antônio Pinto, Ed Côrtes

The title of Meirelles' lurid, decade-hopping jigsaw of a movie comes from the ironic nickname of Rio's sprawling *favelas*; a dangerous gangland where drug abuse, rape and violent early death are everyday facts of life. Punctuated with body-slamming jump cuts and grisly use of the "bullet-time" photography popularized by *The Matrix* movies, this is visceral, sensational filmmaking.

The Constant Gardener 2005, 129 min
cast Ralph Fiennes, Rachel Weisz, Hubert Koundé, Danny Huston, Daniele Harford *cin* César Charlone *m* Alberto Iglesias

A mild-mannered British diplomat (Ralph Fiennes) unravels a vast conspiracy following the murder of his activist wife (Rachel Weisz), who had been poised to uncover a scheme to use Kenya's poor and sick as unwitting experimental subjects for a new drug. Meirelles cuts through the dense intrigue with a galloping momentum, concussive camerawork and a vivid colour-coded palette.

Georges Méliès
France, 1861–1938

Magician Georges Méliès tried to buy the Lumière brothers' *cinématographe* invention after he attended their first public screening on

December 28, 1895. When they refused, he built his own. He didn't stop with the camera either. Setting up his own company, he built a glass studio in the grounds of his home in Montreuil, and went on to write, direct, photograph and act in well over 500 films between 1896 and 1913. (Most were subsequently lost to posterity when he fell on hard times and sold the negatives.)

Méliès' illusionist tricks were wildly popular and influential – and often pirated. Many of them hinged on his reportedly accidental discovery of stop-motion and double exposure (running the film through the camera twice to overlay two images), by which means he was able to make people and objects disappear in the blink of an eye. He was also a talented artist and a vivid designer capable of devising spectacular fantasy tableaux. His range of subjects included melodrama, "reconstructed newsreels", literary adaptations, docudramas, horror and comedy, as well as the sci-fi fantasy of his most famous film, *A Trip To The Moon* (1902). Other notable films were *L'affaire Dreyfus* (*The Dreyfus Affair*, 1899), the comedy *L'homme à la tête en caoutchouc* (*The Man With The Rubber Head*, 1902) and the fantasy adventure *A la conquête du Pôle* (*The Conquest Of The Pole*, 1912).

Despite his innovations – which included such techniques as dissolves, fades and time-lapse photography – Méliès never fully realized the potential of montage to move beyond the staginess of theatre and immerse the audience in the action, and his films have a static, flat quality. Unable to keep pace with developments in film language, he fell into neglect and poverty before the surrealists rediscovered him in the early 1930s and honoured him as one of their own. TC

A Trip To The Moon (Le voyage dans la Lune)
1902, 14 min
cast Victor André, Bleuette Bernon, Brunnet, Jeanne d'Alcy, Henri Delannoy, Depierre *cin* Michaut, Lucien Tainguy

This is Méliès' most famous film, not least for the iconic image of a rocket ship protruding from the eye of the Man in the Moon. Inspired by Jules Verne, this 14-minute science fantasy combines live action, animated and optical special effects and hand-tinted colour frames. It is a witty spectacle, but hard to follow as a piece of storytelling (some versions include a narrator, which is probably how Méliès expected the film to be understood). *Impossible Voyage* (1903), about a trip to the sun, was cinema's first sequel.

Jean-Pierre Melville
France, 1917–73

On his seventh birthday, Jean-Pierre Melville's father gave him a 9.5mm movie camera, and making and watching movies soon became an all-consuming interest.

In 1937 Melville was drafted into the French army, remaining until France was invaded by Germany in 1940. During the Occupation he served in the Resistance and joined the Free French forces, taking part in the invasion of Italy in 1943 and in the liberation of Lyon, the location for his Resistance drama *Le silence de la mer* (*The Silence Of The Sea*, 1947). The shame of invasion and the twisted wartime allegiances of a France divided between Vichy compromise and clandestine resisters informed the taciturn melancholy of this first work.

Melville set up his own production facility in 1945, inaugurating a fiercely independent and iconoclastic career. Early works are marked by low budgets, skeleton crews, real locations and no stars. He doubled as director and cameraman, and wrote or co-wrote all but one of his films. With his debut, he emphasized subterranean dynamics using bottom-lit close-ups, initiating a characteristically unspoken impacted quality. Shot on actual locations and distributed beyond the usual channels, the film impressed the emerging generation – Robert Bresson, Alain Resnais and Eric Rohmer acknowledging its influence.

Based on Jean Cocteau's novel and co-written by Cocteau, *Les enfants terribles* (*The Strange Ones*, 1950) rehearsed the incestuous longing of a brother and sister mired in a Paris sick room. The film is fraught and highly strung, while the legacy of surrealism plays through Cocteau into cinematographer Henri Decaë's imagery. Part of the intellectual climate of 1940s Paris, surrealism and existentialism would resurface throughout Melville's career. *Les enfants terribles* led to more lucrative projects, such as *Bob le flambeur* (*Bob The Gambler*, 1956). The first truly Melvillian work, *Bob* was an almost documentary realist account of a Pigalle criminal planning a fateful casino heist. The *nouvelle vague* loved the film and Godard invited Melville to act in *A bout de souffle*.

There is a watchful, feline air about Melville's cat-and-mouse conflicts, and from *Le doulos* (*The Finger Man*, 1962), which finds Jean-Paul Belmondo's stool pigeon caught in the dirty light between police and thieves, Melville embarked on a string of classic works. Sixties Melville featured Lino Ventura, Serge Reggiani, Yves Montand and Alain Delon – the brightest actors of their generation to appear on French screens. Shot on location with a steely grace by Marcel Combes, *Le deuxième souffle* (*Second Breath*, 1966) follows Ventura's old hood as he looks to leave the country after one more job but finds himself too mired in underworld allegiances to escape. Ventura reappeared in *L'armée des ombres* (*Army In The Shadows*, 1969), but for future cinephiles, Delon would be the quintessential face of Melville's underworld. The dry trench-coated monosyllables and bleached-out look of *Le Samouraï* (1967), with Delon's impervious hit man

M

moving through the slick streets and bars of 1960s Paris, has come to epitomize French *film noir*. Lean and precise, it was Delon again in *Le cercle rouge* (*The Red Circle*, 1970) and *Un flic* (*Dirty Money*, 1972).

Critic Raymond Durgnat has said of Melvillian heroes that they are "cool cats that walk by themselves". Martin Scorsese, Quentin Tarantino and Michael Mann all acknowledge a debt to Melvillian codes and dynamics, and it is difficult to imagine revisionist *noir* without Melville. RA

Bob le flambeur (Bob The Gambler) 1956, 95 min, b/w

cast Roger Duchesne, Isabelle Corey, Daniel Cauchy, Guy Decomnle, André Garret, Claude Cerval *cin* Henri Decaë *m* Eddie Barclay, Jo Boyer

Treading a fine line between the cops and the crooks while maintaining a rigid personal code, Roger Duchesne's eponymous high roller plays out the compromises of the Occupation in a post-war world awaiting the definition that only action brings. *Bob* is an archetypal Melville film in its feeling for American idioms, the despair of the pulp novelette and the potency of cheap music.

Léon Morin, prêtre (Léon Morin, Priest) 1961, 128 min, b/w

cast Jean-Paul Belmondo, Emmanuelle Riva, Irène Tunc, Nicole Mirel, Gisèle Grimm, Marco Behar, Monique Bertho *cin* Henri Decaë *m* Martial Solal

In a small town under occupation an angry young woman goes to church and speaks profanities in the confessional. A priest tries to reach her with books and provocative remarks until one day, clearing out the attic, she has a vision… Built out of short crisp scenes and a performance in which Emmanuelle Riva positively aches, this portrait of the travails of perfection in an imperfect world is as measured as anything Melville accomplished.

Le Samouraï 1967, 95 min

cast Alain Delon, Nathalie Delon, François Périer, Cathy Rosier, Jacques Leroy *cin* Henri Decaë *m* François de Roubaix

An overt homage to *film noir* which self-consciously references the classic *This Gun For Hire* (1942) while exploring Melville's own obsessive themes of isolation and betrayal. Delon takes on the Alan Ladd role playing the ultimate hit man – ice cold, laconic and operating by his own codes of honour. His look is perfectly complemented by the muted colours of Henri Decaë's cinematography.

L'armée des ombres (Army In The Shadows) 1969, 143 min

cast Lino Ventura, Paul Meurisse, Jean-Pierre Cassel, Simone Signoret, Claude Mann *cin* Pierre Lhomme, Walter Wottitz *m* Éric Demarsan

Melville's tribute to the wartime "resistants" sees the codes of Maquis and gangster hopelessly enmeshed. Ventura and Simone Signoret gave career-best performances, Ventura as the Lyon Resistance leader determined to find out who betrayed him to the Gestapo, while Melville's account of lives underground tips over into nightmare. The film in which the French love of crime comes into most succinct contact with national myths.

Le cercle rouge (The Red Circle) 1970, 150 min

cast Alain Delon, Bourvil, Gian Maria Volontè, Yves Montaud, Paul Crauchet, Paul Amiot, Pierre Collet, Andrè Ekyan *cin* Henri Decaë *m* Eric Demarsan

On the day before his release, Alain Delon's career criminal is told of a jewel heist being set up on the outside. So begins an enterprise in which the codes and rituals of the underworld are corroded by greed and distrust. By this point in his career, Melville had reduced the drama to an almost geometrical pattern, its Place Vendôme climax the perfect nocturnal snatch.

Sam Mendes

UK, 1965–

Frequently lauded as a wunderkind, Cambridge-educated Sam Mendes first made his name as a theatre director. His enviable CV included directing Dame Judi Dench in *The Cherry Orchard*, Ralph Fiennes in the Royal Shakespeare Company's *Troilus And Cressida* and, as artistic director of the Donmar Warehouse, overseeing Nicole Kidman's sensation-stirring London stage debut – replete with nude scene – in David Hare's Arthur Schnitzler adaptation *The Blue Room*. All while still in his twenties.

Hollywood inevitably beckoned, and young master Mendes responded with *American Beauty* (1999), which made a near sweep of the top Academy Awards; the rumpled and modest best director dedicated his statuette to Billy Wilder, whose *Sunset Blvd* (1950) – like *American Beauty* – also used the device of a voiceover from its dead protagonist. Mendes finally stumbled somewhat with the glum gangster-vigilante saga *Road To Perdition* (2002), with Tom Hanks cast against type as a formidable hit man in Depression-era Chicago. But after marrying Kate Winslet in 2003 he returned to form with the unconventional war movie, *Jarhead* (2005), an adaptation of Anthony Swofford's memoir of the first Gulf War. JW

American Beauty 1999, 122 min

cast Kevin Spacey, Annette Bening, Thora Birch, Wes Bentley, Mena Suvari, Pete Gallagher, Allison Janneu *cin* Conrad L. Hall *m* Thomas Newman

Sad-sack clock-watcher Lester Burnham (Kevin Spacey) gives the finger to the banal materialism of aspirant suburbia and his emasculating, bitchy wife (Annette Bening): he smokes pot with a teenage neighbour, lusts after his daughter's minxy friend and takes a job in a burger bar. Mendes, helped by cinematographer Conrad Hall, used lush, oversaturated colours and tableau-like compositions to add an expressionist effulgence to Alan Ball's script, which keeps to the quippy rhythms of a self-consciously edgy sitcom.

Chris Menges
UK, 1940–

The distinguished British cinematographer Chris Menges graduated from ITV's current affairs programme *World In Action* (where he shot a number of documentaries about South Africa). He was cameraman on Ken Loach's *Poor Cow* (1967), then worked with the Czech cinematographer Miroslav Ondrícek on Lindsay Anderson's *If....* (1968).

Influenced by the Czech New Wave, he and Loach adopted a more lyrical, sympathetic style for *Kes* (1969), and would subsequently collaborate on half a dozen films. Menges was a key figure in the (briefly) resurgent British cinema of the early 1980s, shooting Alan Clarke's *Made In Britain* (1982), Neil Jordan's *Angel* (1982), Bill Forsyth's *Local Hero* (1983) and *Comfort And Joy* (1984), and Roland Joffe's *The Killing Fields* (1984) and *The Mission* (1986). He also had a stint as camera operator on *The Empire Strikes Back* (1980).

In 1988 he directed his first narrative feature, *A World Apart*, and was rewarded with the Grand Jury Prize at Cannes. Subsequent efforts have met with muted enthusiasm: the Key West-set drama *CrissCross* (1992), the sensitive adoption story *Second Best* (1994) and *The Lost Son* (1999), which starred Daniel Auteuil as a French private eye in London who stumbles across a child porn operation. Still in demand as a cinematographer, Menges is a sensitive filmmaker with more interest in people than stories. TC

A World Apart 1988, 113 min
cast Barbara Hershey, Jodhi May, Jeroen Krabbé, Linda Mvusi, Tim Roth *cin* Peter Biziou *m* Hans Zimmer

Jodhi May shines here as 13-year-old Molly, a South African white girl growing resentful that her mother (Barbara Hershey) spends more time at ANC meetings than with her. Shawn Slovo's autobiographical script finds a useful, oblique angle on apartheid, and Menges lets the issues filter through character without diluting their importance. Hershey is also impeccable as the tough, torn mother.

Jirí Menzel
Czech Republic (formerly Czechoslovakia), 1938–

Jirí Menzel's adventures in motion pictures have been as bittersweet as those of his film's melancholic protagonists. He'd made a classic of the Czech New Wave of the mid-1960s, *Closely Observed Trains* (1966), which took the Oscar for best foreign film in 1967. Then, after the Soviet tanks rolled into Prague in 1968, bringing a swift and brutal end to the limited freedoms that Czechs had begun to enjoy, Miloš Forman, Ivan Passer and other fellow-graduates of the Prague Film Academy went into exile, but Menzel defiantly stayed at home. For his troubles, his acerbic comedy *Larks On A String* (1969), set in a re-education camp for reactionaries, was banned from cinemas, while the director was prevented from working.

Menzel was only allowed behind a camera again after he recanted his earlier views and made a socialist realist film, *Who Looks For Gold* (1975). Following this, he made several movies, including two with the screenwriter of *Closely Observed Trains*, Bohumil Hrabal: *Cutting It Short* (1980) and *Snowdrop Festival* (1983). The best of his later films, *My Sweet Little Village* (1987), was a huge hit in his home country and garnered an Oscar nomination. Like most of his post-1968 movies, it was set in the countryside, and comically charts the attempts of a Communist apparatchik to take over the house of a village idiot and turn it into his summer residence. With the Velvet Revolution in 1989, the end of Communism meant the end of state subsidies, and Menzel found it increasingly difficult to find the funding for his idiosyncratic films, making only three features since. His most recent, *I Served The King Of England* (2006), was another wry adaptation of a Hrabal novel. LH

Closely Observed Trains (Ostre sledované vlaky) 1966, 92 min, b/w
cast Václav Neckár, Jitka Bendová, Vladimír Valenta, Josef Somr, Libuše Havelková, Alois Vachek *cin* Jaromir Sofr *m* Jirí Šust

These are the sexual misadventures of Miloš Hrma, a somewhat gormless apprentice train guard in Nazi-occupied Bohemia. Menzel peoples the screen with gentle eccentrics, observing them with a wry detachment and muted exuberance, while offsetting the whimsy with a lingering darkness: the Nazis promise to kill any station employee who neglects his duties. This minor masterpiece contains one of the most delightful moments of erotic chutzpah in the history of cinema, when a signalman merrily rubber-stamps the bare legs and bottom of his happy young lover.

William Cameron Menzies
US, 1896–1957

Though he is best known as a hugely influential Hollywood production designer, there's a persuasive case to be made for William Cameron Menzies to be recognized as the co-director of several classics credited solely to others, namely Victor Fleming's *Gone With The Wind* (1939) and Sam Wood's *Kings Row* (1942) and *For Whom The Bell Tolls* (1943). In Menzies' meticulous storyboards, not only the set design but also the camera angles and lenses, lighting schemes and editing sequences were all fastidiously specified – all determined long before the director called "Action!" As Thomas Schatz writes, Menzies "effectively defined the role and status of the art director (and later, the production designer) within the studio production system."

In the films for which Menzies combined the roles of designer and director, his actors often seemed somewhat adrift – as in *Things To Come* (1936) and *The Maze* (1953). *Things To Come* is a prophecy of war derived from H.G. Wells, in which the futurist Art Deco sets are the unbilled stars of the show, and *The Maze*, his final film as director, is a gothic 3-D mystery that was hobbled by a clunky denouement. One of Menzies' most engaging directorial projects is *Invaders From Mars* (1953), a beguiling child's-eye view of an alien invasion and a low-budget precursor to 1955's *Invasion Of The Body Snatchers*. JW

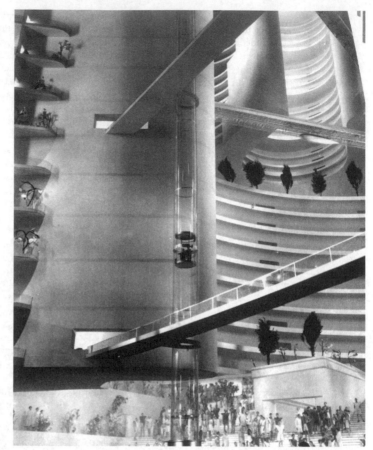

The stunning, futuristic sets are the most memorable aspect of *Things To Come*.

Things To Come 1936, 96 min, b/w

cast Raymond Massey, Ralph Richardson, Edward Chapman, Margaretta Scott, Cedric Hardwicke, Sophie Stewart *cin* Georges Périnal *m* Arthur Bliss

The producer Alexander Korda commissioned Menzies for this prestigious production of H.G. Wells's classic science-fiction meditation *The Shape Of Things To Come*. A prophetic vision of London, here renamed "Everytown", under the looming shadow of a devastating world war, the film lacks a certain human touch, but remains impressive for its grim prophetic overtones, adroitly executed set pieces and, of course, Menzies' vast, gleaming sets.

Márta Mészáros

Hungary, 1931–

Márta Mészáros made her mark with sensitive portrayals of women's lives behind the Iron Curtain. In 1936 her family moved to Stalinist Russia, with disastrous consequences: her mother died, and her father, an artist, was executed. After education at the VGIK film school in Moscow, Mészáros made newsreels, shorts and documentaries in Hungary and Romania, some of them with her first husband Laszlo Karda. She married the director Miklós Jancsó in 1960 (they divorced in 1973), and later joined Group 4, the feature arm of the state film studio Mafilm. Her debut feature, 1968's *The Girl*, was a *vérité* account of an orphan's search for selfhood, characterized by plain camerawork, rambling narration and spare dialogue. It signalled Mészáros's preoccupation with women's fortunes amid the oppressive environment of Cold War Hungary. *Adoption* (1975) details the relationship between a young woman and an older woman who seeks to adopt a child. It won the Golden Bear at the Berlin Film Festival. In *Nine Months* (1976) an unmarried woman leaves her lover to have a baby alone, and is remarkable for showing actress Lili Monori actually giving birth on camera.

In 1982 Mészáros began her "Diary" trilogy, explicitly addressing post-war Hungarian politics. The first was *Diary For My Children* (1984), an account of state brutality in the Stalinist era that won Mészáros the Special Jury Prize at Cannes. *Diary For My Loves*

(1987) recalled her experiences at film school during the repressive 1950s in Hungary. The autobiographical trilogy concluded in 1990 with *Diary For My Father And Mother*, which explored the events of the 1956 Hungarian uprising through a mix of newsreel, archive footage and fictional narrative. In 2000 Mészáros added a prequel to the story, *Little Vilna: The Last Diary*. Mészáros's preoccupation with women's lives continues to mark her work, finding echoes in the output of celebrated "feminist" filmmakers from Gillian Armstrong to Samira Makhmalbaf. In 2007, the Berlin Film Festival honoured Mészáros with a Berlinale Camera award. RA

Diary For My Loves (Napló szerelmeimnek)
1987, 130 min, b/w and col
cast Zsuzsa Czinkóczi, Agnes Csere, Anna Polony, Jan Nowicki, Irina Kouberskaya, Mari Szemes, Pál Zolnay *cin* Nyika Jancsó *m* Zsolt Döme

Márta Mészáros's grave realism has challenged Western critics, and her second autobiographical film diary follows her alter ego, an aspirant filmmaker resolutely played by Zsuzsa Czinkóczi. She loses her lover in the purges of the dark 1950s and faces 1956 with stoicism and a determination to put the realities of post-war Hungary on the screen, whatever Communist Party bosses think. The result is a bold melding of *vérité* newsreel, psychology and emotional truths.

Russ Meyer
US, 1922–2004

Dubbed "King Leer" by some, Russ Meyer may have been the director who popularized the skin flick but he was also one of the only true *auteurs* in America and his work has even been hailed by feminists for its portrayal of strong women characters. While some directors have a stylistic tic or set of thematic concerns that define their work, Meyer can be identified by one authorial obsession: big breasts.

Meyer honed his craft in the army as a combat cinematographer, and his wartime work is rated very highly indeed. In peacetime he became an industrial filmmaker, then went on to shoot centrefolds for *Playboy*. Gaining a reputation as the best flesh photographer in the business, he was invited to make moving pictures. Meyer effectively invented the skin flick as a box-office phenomenon with *The Immoral Mr Teas* (1959), a film about a man blessed with X-ray vision who uses his superhuman powers to look through women's clothing. The director continued in the same lecherous vein with *Eve And The Handyman* (1961), which he wrote, directed, produced and edited.

In the mid-1960s, Meyer took a quantum leap with a quartet of Southern-gothic tales populated by the rawest of rednecks, which peerlessly experimented with proper dialogue and real acting (of sorts): *Lorna* (1964), *Mudhoney* (1965), *Motor Psycho* (1965) and *Faster, Pussycat! Kill! Kill!* (1965). The latter is a masterpiece of camp excess. Its subversive combo of libidinous, feral and powerful young women and incompetent, impotent young men led the feminist critic B. Ruby Rich to laud it as "an unexpected celebration of bad-girl empowerment", and a print was bought by the Museum of Modern Art in New York for its permanent collection.

The financial success of *Vixen* (1968) piqued the interest of 20th Century Fox who, surprisingly, put the drive-in king under contract. Meyer responded to his new-found respectability by making one of the most joyfully perverse – and, indeed, perverted – films the studio has ever released, *Beyond The Valley Of The Dolls* (1970). Disappointingly, he then followed it up with *The Seven Minutes* (1971), a serious attempt at a courtroom drama. Meyer even apologized for the film's artistic pretensions later, explaining: "I made the mistake of reading my reviews."

Stung by the commercial failure of *The Seven Minutes*, he reverted to his winning formula of pneumatic chests, cheesy puns, knockabout slapstick, sermonizing voiceovers and appearances by "Martin Bormann". But what joins all these films together in unholy union is a magnificent, casually and truly cinematic eye; Meyer was an artist almost despite himself. His work became coarser and grubbier in the late 1970s, but he never resorted to hard-core pornography. "I don't find what goes on below the waist to be that visual", he once told his friend, the critic Roger Ebert. *Beyond The Valley Of The Ultravixens* (1979) turned out to be Meyer's last feature. He never completed his magnum opus, *The Breast Of Russ Meyer*, but instead put his life in print with his self-published three-volume autobiography, *A Clean Breast*. LH

Faster, Pussycat! Kill! Kill! 1965, 83 min, b/w
cast Tura Satana, Haji, Lori Williams, Susan Bernard, Stuart Lancaster, Paul Trinka *cin* Walter Schenk *m* Paul Sawtell, Bert Shefter

Three strippers, driving hard and fast across the desert, happen upon a heterosexual couple. Varla, the leader, kills the young man with her bare hands, takes the girl hostage and inveigles her in a plot to steal the fortune of The Dirty Old Man and his half-witted muscle-bound son Vegetable. Directed with pop-art zeal and exuberant gusto, Meyer here reveals himself to be one of the great landscape artists of late-twentieth-century cinema.

Beyond The Valley Of The Dolls 1970, 109 min
cast Dolly Read, Cynthia Myers, Marcia McBroom, John La Zar, Michael Blodgett, Pam Grier *cin* Fred J. Koenekamp *m* Stu Phillips

One of the most ridiculously sublime movies ever made about a rock band, the plot, about the misadventures of girl group The Carrie Nations, soon becomes a delirious medley of orgies, transvestism and decapitation. Scripted by critic Roger Ebert, it's replete with such gems as "you will drink the black sperm of my vengeance". The nihilistic kitsch of Meyer's major-studio debut represents the pinnacle of the camp *Guignol* that infected American cinema in the early 1970s.

Nancy Meyers
US, 1946–

A story editor for producer Ray Stark when she met TV writer Charles Shyer, Nancy Meyers suggested they collaborate on the script for a Goldie Hawn vehicle. *Private Benjamin* (1980) was a box-office hit, and the screenplay (also written by Harvey Miller) was even nominated for an Oscar.

The "Shmeyers" became a team, and were married in 1980. Together they penned a series of mildly amusing, sentimental family comedies in the tradition of Garson Kanin and Ruth Gordon, among them *Irreconcilable Differences* (1984), *Baby Boom* (1987), *Father Of The Bride* (1991) and the woeful *I Love Trouble* (1994).

Shyer took a director credit on most of these, but Meyers took over on the remake *The Parent Trap* (1998) – the same year the couple separated. Mel Gibson engaged her to helm *What Women Want* (2000), but the solo outing *Something's Gotta Give* (2003), which she also wrote, was a smarter answer to that question. Both films were financially successful, leaving Meyers enviably well placed as she enters her sixties. TC

Something's Gotta Give 2003, 128 min
cast Diane Keaton, Jack Nicholson, Keanu Reeves, Frances McDormand, Amanda Peet *cin* Michael Ballhaus *m* Hans Zimmer

Diane Keaton was Oscar-nominated for her engaging turn as a divorced playwright of a certain age, whose man troubles take a dramatic turn when her daughter's septuagenarian boyfriend has a heart attack in her home – and is ordered to recuperate in situ. It's light entertainment pure and simple, but unusual for its focus on a mature couple, and for its female perspective. The stars are good value too.

Oscar Micheaux
US, 1884–1951

One of eleven children born to former slaves in Illinois, Oscar Micheaux proved to be a multiple trailblazer, forging westward to set up a homestead in South Dakota before becoming the first African-American to make a feature-length film – in both the silent and talkie formats. He made more than forty films in just thirty years, often raising funds door-to-door showing his stills or scripts (just as he had once sold his novels to his neighbours in South Dakota) and carrying his film cans from theatre to theatre. As Richard Corliss wrote, "In the 30-plus years of race cinema, there was only one black man with the drive and doggedness to write, produce, direct, finance and distribute his own films ... In some many ways, Micheaux was the D.W. Griffith of race cinema. And also its Edward D. Wood Jr."

Micheaux's films are invaluable historical artefacts – the melodrama *Within Our Gates* (1919), the earliest surviving film by a black American, is a powerful riposte to D.W. Griffith's racist *Birth Of A Nation*. They are a tribute to an artist's perseverance against all odds. But they're also Bad Movie benchmarks, due to a combination of meagre resources, lack of technical know-how and Micheaux's decided indifference to the niceties of film grammar and realistic performance style. A chronic shortage of film stock meant that too many first takes had to be considered, in Ed Wood's own words, "Perfect!" The wear and tear of time and the scissorings of film censors and exhibitors have also battered the films, sometimes beyond narrative coherence (if they possessed it in the first place).

The typical Micheaux film is a roughshod melodrama with Chinese boxfuls of sub-plots. A characteristic entry is *The Girl From Chicago* (1932), a stilted, convoluted, gaffe-stacked, yet undeniably intriguing remake of his own silent film *Spider's Web* (1926). Micheaux regular Carl Mahon stars as Alonso White, a secret service agent assigned to investigate a crime boss in Mississippi who sweeps a schoolteacher off her feet and carries her away to good-time Harlem. The teacher's landlady follows, plays the numbers, wins big, but gets framed for a murder actually committed by the crime boss's girlfriend, who also happens to be in town...

Micheaux did not aim to set himself apart from Hollywood's sensationalism, but instead emulated its heated melodrama, musical routines and eroticism, while managing to avoid the studio stereotyping of African-Americans. There was an element of bourgeois moralizing in his films, but they nonetheless tackled such difficult themes as interracial romance, gambling, prostitution, rape and lynching.

Micheaux never had much success attracting top-flight black talent to his no-budget productions, but the silent 1925 picture *Body And Soul* features the film debut of the magnificent Paul Robeson, in dual roles as a womanizing preacher and his saintly brother. Robeson's huge charisma raises *Body And Soul* above much of Micheaux's other work, as does the sheer socio-emotional sweep of *God's Step Children* (1938), a melodrama of passing that, despite its blunders and convolutions, achieves a cumulative poignancy. JW

God's Step Children 1938, 69 min
cast Jacqueline Lewis, Ethel Moses, Alice B. Russell, Charles Thompson, Carman Newsome, Gloria Press, Laura Bowman *cin* Lester Lang

Lifting much from Fannie Hurst's novel *Imitation Of Life* and its 1934 screen version, this is the life story of light-skinned Naomi, who pines for the son of the woman who raised her and longs to "pass" in the white world that rejects her. The film takes a complex stance towards Naomi's anguish; beyond the ropey staging and technical difficulties, one can glimpse a rich, strange, sad achievement.

Roger Michell

South Africa, 1956–

Roger Michell is an enigma wrapped inside a mystery wrapped inside a film director. How else can we explain a man who has made films as diverse as the Hollywood action thriller *Changing Lanes* (2002), the heart-warming rom-com *Notting Hill* (1999) and the taboo-breaking tale of inter-generational desire that was *The Mother* (2003)? His early BBC television work was similarly eclectic, including *The Buddha Of Suburbia* (1993) and *Persuasion* (1995). Like that other craftsman of British cinema, Stephen Frears, Michell cuts his directorial cloth according to the script: all nervy hypertension in *Changing Lanes* and calm restraint in *The Mother*.

Whether it's a potent political drama, as in *Titanic Town* (1998) or an uneven literary adaptation such as *Enduring Love* (2004), each of his films is imbued with thought, craft and little imposition of the man behind the camera. Even if the director himself is hard to fathom, we know what we will get from a Roger Michell film: it will be intelligent, well acted and very middlebrow. *Venus* (2006) is exactly that: the story of an ageing thespian's infatuation with a teenager which secured Michell some kudos and its lead, Peter O'Toole, an Oscar nomination. LH

Titanic Town 1998, 100 min

cast Julie Walters, Ciaran Hinds, Ciaran McMenamin, Nuala O'Neil, Jaz Pollock, James Loughran, Barry Loughran *cin* John Daly *m* Trevor Jones

A middle-aged Belfast mother, splendidly played by Julie Walters, single-handedly tries to bring peace to her neighbourhood in the early 1970s only to incur the violent wrath of IRA-supporting locals. Michell's feature debut is a subtle, nuanced evocation of the Northern Irish Troubles and the impact they had on a daily and domestic level. The result is politically balanced, if tonally uneven.

Notting Hill 1999, 124 min

cast Julia Roberts, Hugh Grant, Hugh Bonneville, Emma Chambers, James Dreyfuss, Rhys Ifans, Tim McInnerny *cin* Michael Coulter *m* Trevor Jones

Michell and writer Richard Curtis have been heavily criticized for creating a Notting Hill that was almost exclusively white, and presenting a Britain that was easy on the American eye. Despite the whitewash, this boy-meets-megastar fantasy is a guilty pleasure, and Hugh Grant displays a comic timing that is worthy of his near namesake, Cary.

Takashi Miike

Japan, 1960–

Confrontation is Takashi Miike's default mode. Slick with all manner of bodily secretions, his films share a *raison d'être* in the remotest extremes of physical dismemberment, sadomasochism, volcanic psychopathology and the dark art of the sick joke. Even his warp-speed work ethic is in your face – the grind-house savant averages four to seven celluloid disturbances per year. The high-demand Japanese home entertainment market has encouraged the voluminous output of Miike and other proponents of the straight-to-video "V-cinema". In Miike's case, the abbreviation brings plenty of other words to mind: violent, viral, venereal. Or even vomit – when *Ichi The Killer* (2001) screened at the Toronto International Film Festival, the movie's reps handed out promotional sick-bags, perhaps chiefly concerned with potential audience reactions to the scene in which a man is hung from hooks and then doused with boiling oil.

After an apprenticeship that included two stints as Shohei Imamura's assistant director, Miike carved out his niche specializing in ultraviolent yakuza (Japanese Mafia) plots featuring cartoonish performances delivered at coke-binge tempos; he has compared his editing style to that of a DJ scratching and mixing records. His first theatrical release, *Shinjuku Triad Society* (1995), dealt in cops-versus-criminals mayhem but was set within the shadowy, bloody underworld of the human organ trade. Thereafter, Miike just kept on outdoing himself in the disgustingness stakes. *Dead Or Alive* (1999) included such delightful scenes as an exploding stomach and a woman drowning in her own faeces in a toddler's plastic pool. *Audition* (1999) showcased amputation, puncture of the eyes and a man eating puke. The wicked reality-TV parody *Visitor Q* (2001) depicted incest, necrophilia, anal rape (by microphone) and projectile lactation.

In recent years Miike has been able to startle audiences simply by reining in his now-familiar assault tactics, and has proven himself remarkably versatile over a range of genres, including the musical (*The Happiness Of The Katakuris*, 2001) and the Ealing-style comedy (2002's *Shangri-La*, which commented on the Japanese financial crisis). *The Bird People In China* (1998), shot in the mountains of China's Yunnan province, is Miike's most beautiful film. The oddly touching *Gozu* (2003), though featuring a typical cavalcade of eccentrics and mutants, had none of the director's usual accompanying gore. The aggressively experimental *Big Bang Love* (2006) presented the violence and homoeroticism within a gothic prison complex as a metaphor for contemporary Japanese society. Even stripped of shock value, Miike's work rarely lacks surprises. JW

Dead Or Alive (Hanzaisha) 1999, 105 min

cast Riki Takeuchi, Sho Aikawa, Renji Ishibashi, Hitoshi Ozawa, Susumu Terajima, Ren Osugi *cin* Hideo Yamamoto *m* Koji Endo

A Tokyo police detective gets caught between yakuza and Triad gangsters in this pile-up of hyper-speed ultra-violence, which is book-ended by flabbergasting scenes of sex and death (often combined) and cut with startling measures of sentimentality (the cop needs money for his

367

daughter's operation). Bound to twinge even the steeliest viewer's gag reflex, the movie begat two equally frenzied sequels.

Audition (Ôdishon) 1999, 115 min

cast Ryo Ishibasahi, Eihi Shiina, Miyuki Matsuda, Renji Ishibashi, Tetsu Kuremura, Jun Kunimura *cin* Hideo Yamamoto *m* Koi Endo

In search of a new wife, a Japanese widower stages a bogus acting audition and eventually discovers a gorgeous former ballerina who seems like the perfect mate … until the mask falls away, revealing a sadistic empress of the torture room. Miike's atypically calm, sombre pace gives precious little indication of the infernal spectacle – or one-sided battle of the sexes – to come. There are torments here that even Dutch painter Hieronymus Bosch might have deemed excessive.

The Happiness Of The Katakuris (Katakuri-ke no kofuku) 2001, 113 min

cast Kenji Sawada, Keiko Matsuzaka, Shinji Takeda, Naomi Nishida, Tetsuro Tamba, Naoto Takenaka *cin* Hideo Yamamoto *m* Koji Makaino

A skewed tribute to both the resilience of blood ties and *The Sound Of Music*, Miike's warped musical unfolds at a family-run countryside inn where the oddly high mortality rate (and even odder causes of death – suicide by room key, a sex-induced heart attack et al.) leaves the proprietors with numerous bodies to dispose of. Featuring claymation and a chorus line of corpses, the film strikes a positive, can-do attitude – there's no apparent irony in that title.

Ichi The Killer (Koroshiya Ichi) 2001, 129 min

cast Tadanobu Asano, Nao Omori, Shinya Tsukamoto, Sabu, Alien Sun, Susumu Terjima *cin* Hideo Yamamoto *m* Karera Musication

Young yakuza henchman Kakihari (ubiquitous Japanese heart-throb Tadanobu Asano), a bleach-blonde sadomasochist, is looking for his mentor's killer: the notorious Ichi, a lachrymose slice'n'dice machine of a gangster who has lethal blades attached to his shoes. Based on Hideo Yamamoto's manga, this is perhaps Miike's most comprehensive and inventive catalogue of fleshly indignities. Given the director's penchant for atrocity, that's saying quite a lot.

Nikita Mikhalkov

Russia (formerly Soviet Union), 1945–

Nikita Mikhalkov has had a hugely successful directorial career, becoming the best-known filmmaker in Russia. He made his directorial debut, *At Home Among Strangers* (1974), after learning his craft on student shorts. Of the numerous films he's made since, several have attained the status of minor classics. Often sourced from literary masterpieces they are rooted in Chekhovian complexities and last-act ironies. *A Slave Of Love* (1976) won him international kudos. The remarkable *An Unfinished Piece For Mechanical Piano* (1976), based on Chekhov's first play *Platonov*, told the poignant tale of a school-teacher who visits friends at a country house (a familiar Mikhalkov location) only to discover that his old sweetheart has been invited, bring-

ing an unwelcome and unsettling reminder of his early promise. *Oblomov* (1979), an ambitious adaptation of Ivan Goncharov's four-part novel which was previously deemed unfilmable, meditatively and unhurriedly focused on a wealthy landowner who refuses to get out of bed. *Dark Eyes* (1987), a bittersweet, beautifully modulated adaptation of several of Chekhov's short stories, starred Marcello Mastroianni as a former idealist seriously compromised by wealth and comfort who rashly embarks on a short, idyllic affair with a young woman, which may or may not change his whole life.

Just when critics had got Mikhalkov pegged as a maker of subtle fables of bourgeois decadence, he made *Urga* (1990), which was part character study, part melodrama and part landscape art. With *Burnt By The Sun* (1994) the director returned to familiar territory: the country house and the summer setting. His acknowledged masterpiece, it deservedly won the Oscar for best foreign film. One year on, Mikhalkov won a seat in the Russian parliament, as a member of the Our Home Is Russia party, and four years later he was hotly tipped to succeed the ailing President Yeltsin. Backed by rich and powerful supporters, Mikhalkov claimed he would run for president if the people so wished. This coincided with the release of the sumptuous epic *The Barber Of Siberia* (1998), in which he cast himself as Tsar Alexander III, pictured riding into the Kremlin on a white steed in one scene. If it was intended as propaganda for its director, it didn't succeed, nor did critics favour the film. Putin became president, and Mikhalkov didn't make another film for at least another eight years. LH

A Slave Of Love (Raba lyubvi) 1976, 94 min

cast Elena Solovei, Rodion Nakhapetov, Alexander Kalyagin, Oleg Basilashvili *cin* Pavel Lebeshev *m* Eduard Artemiev

In 1917, a film crew are shooting a silent movie in the Crimea, at the time of the Bolshevik seizure of Moscow. A spoiled actress undergoes a political re-education by her lover, a Bolshevik cameraman, who's been filming atrocities by the White Guard. When he's executed, she must decide whether or not to continue his dangerous work. While the plot rings a propagandist note, Mikhalkov proves himself to be the master of capturing a hazy, languorous summer's day.

Burnt By The Sun (Utomlyonnye solntsem) 1994, 134 min

cast Nikita Mikhalkov, Ingeborga Dapkounaite, Nadia Mikhalkov, Oleg Menchikov, Andre Oumansky *cin* Vilen Kaliuta *m* Edouard Artemiese

Mikhalkov stars as Sergei Kotov (with his own daughter Nadia playing his child), a hero of the Bolshevik revolution living an idyllic life of privilege and quiet authority in his country house, cocooned from the terror of Stalin's bloodiest purges. The domestic, bucolic existence is disturbed by the appearance of his young wife's former lover, Dmitri, a member of Stalin's secret police. The real reasons for his visit soon become horribly apparent in this complex, melancholic drama, which is hypnotically dotted by staggering imagery, such as the large portrait of Stalin which hangs surreally from a hot air balloon.

M

Lewis Milestone
Moldova (formerly Russian Empire), 1895–1980

Lewis Milestone is one of few Hollywood directors to have worked from the silents to the 1960s. Though he claimed few plaudits for his originality, he was hardly ever out of work and rarely disappointed either his studio masters or audiences.

Educated in Germany, Milestone emigrated to America in 1913 before serving in the US army where he picked up his photographic skills. After screenwriting and editing work in Hollywood he took the reins of his first film, *Seven Sinners* (1925), before landing *Two Arabian Nights* (1927), which earned the only Academy Award for comedy direction ever to be dished out.

Swiftly adapting to sound, he hit his stride with the first and most openly political of his numerous war films, *All Quiet On The Western Front* (1930) – an inventive adaptation of Erich Maria Remarque's novel. His next film, *The Front Page* (1931), has since been overshadowed by Howard Hawks' version of the Ben Hecht newsroom stage play (*His Girl Friday*, 1939), but Milestone really shone with his measured adaptation of John Steinbeck's classic *Of Mice And Men* (1939).

The 1940s saw Milestone bogged down in combat movies set in Norway (*Edge Of Darkness*, 1943), the Ukraine (*The North Star*, 1943) and Japan (*The Purple Heart*, 1944), though the best (*A Walk In The Sun*, 1945) was set in Italy. With the war over, Milestone moved with the times once again, helming *The Strange Love Of Martha Ivers* (1946), a smouldering *noir* that starred Barbara Stanwyck and Kirk Douglas. Having returned, with disappointing results, to the works of Remarque (*Arch Of Triumph*, 1948) and Steinbeck (*The Red Pony*, 1949), Milestone followed through with more war films, an Australian adventure, *Kangaroo*, and a passable stab at a lavish *Les Misérables* (both 1952).

After a fallow period during the late 1950s, the Rat-Pack heist movie *Ocean's 11* (1960) once again propelled him to the front ranks of Hollywood directors. However, he might have preferred to remain in the background. Brought onto the troubled set of *Mutiny On The Bounty* (1962) after Carol Reed departed, he had to contend with Marlon Brando staging his own mutiny. This rambling, largely unsuccessful three-hour version of the story was to be his last feature. RC

All Quiet On The Western Front 1930, 138 min, b/w
cast Lew Ayeres, Louis Wolheim, John Wray, Slim Summerville, Russell Gleason *cin* Arthur Edeson

Milestone used the studio's budget and more to pay for a Universal Studios World War I battleground, which on screen looked and felt confusing, dangerous and muddy. A veteran of the US Army Signal Corps, he used his experience to good effect, taking his cue from the antiwar message of Remarque's novel and not letting up. For many critics it is the first great war film.

Of Mice And Men 1939, 106 min, b/w
cast Lon Chaney Jr, Burgess Meredith, Bob Steele, Charles Bickford *cin* Norbert Brodine *m* Aaron Copland

Far closer to the Depression-era spirit of the novel than the 1992 remake, Milestone's version was released roughly two years after the book's original publication. If the narrative moves a little ponderously for today's tastes, the acting, particularly from Lon Chaney Jr as simple gentle giant Lenny, still packs a punch.

John Milius
US, 1944–

John Milius is a member of an endangered species in modern Hollywood: right-wing, liberal-baiting, gun-toting and once described by critic Andrew Sarris as a "gifted barbarian". One of his professed great regrets was not being able to fight in the Vietnam War (although he did it vicariously by co-writing 1979's *Apocalypse Now*). His films are unashamedly mythic, proudly exhibiting an old-fashioned grandeur and ambition despite his being a USC graduate and thus part of the "movie brat" coterie.

For some critics, he has never bettered his debut, *Dillinger* (1973), while in *The Wind And The Lion* (1975) Milius found an epic setting and genre to match his sweeping, grandiose themes. *Big Wednesday* (1978) was a sprawling tale of the lives of three surfers, as women and the Vietnam War come between them and the waves. *Conan The Barbarian* (1982) was a unique mix of Arnold Schwarzenegger's musculature, pseudo-Nietzschean philosophy and sword-and-sorcery camp. Proving to be Milius's biggest hit, he'd finally discovered his supersized niche in the comic-book form. Critics dubbed the director a fascist – he prefers "Zen fascist" or "anarchist" – when they saw *Red Dawn* (1984), his Reaganite paranoid conspiracy thriller in which the Soviet Union invades a small town in Colorado. *Farewell To The King* (1989) was Milius's own version of *Apocalypse Now* (1979), as Nick Nolte played a Colonel Kurtz figure, an army deserter who is reluctantly but stoically drawn into the war against the Japanese during World War II. Milius was nominated for an Oscar for his contribution to the screenplay.

It seemed inevitable that Milius would eventually direct his own Vietnam pic. *Flight Of The Intruder* (1991) zeroed in on two navy pilots who make the "moral decision" of defiantly bombing Hanoi against military orders and are court-martialled for their troubles. Bombast once again got the better of Milius and he hasn't directed a feature film since, working instead on TV, writing and producing the typically overwrought *Rome*. Milius says he's been blacklisted by liberal Hollywood, but the simple fact is his films don't make money any more. And that's just the law of the jungle. LH

Dillinger 1973, 107 min
cast Warren Oates, Ben Johnson, Michelle Phillips, Cloris Leachman, Harry Dean Stanton, Richard Dreyfuss *cin* Jules Brenner *m* Barry DeVorson

Warren Oates evinces his usual gruff charm as Dillinger, the swarthy antihero who became a redneck Robin Hood when he robbed banks in the Great Depression and dramatically escaped prison. Riffing on Milius's favourite theme – self-mythology – the drama's abrasive energy and low-budget grit are an appropriately seedy counterpoint to the jaunty rhythms of *Bonnie And Clyde* (1967).

The Wind And The Lion 1975, 119 min
cast Sean Connery, Candice Bergen, Brian Keith, John Huston, Geoffrey Lewis, Steve Kanaly, Roy Jenson *cin* Billy Williams *m* Jerry Goldsmith

Candice Bergen and her two sons are kidnapped in Morocco by Arab bandit Sean Connery. It soon becomes an international incident and President Teddy Roosevelt personally intervenes. The director was brought up hearing stories from his dad about the gung-ho heroics of Roosevelt; this is a handsomely mounted fictional epic in the mould of Joseph Conrad and an unabashed hymn to imperialism.

Claude Miller
France, 1942–

Jean-Luc Godard's former tea boy, Claude Miller is one of the *nouvelle vague*'s finest alumni, and he forged an intimate bond with François Truffaut, working as production manager on four of his films. With thrillers such as the Ruth Rendell adaptation *Betty Fisher And Other Stories* (2001), Miller expertly applied that French polish of sophisticated *cinéma vérité* to the stark mechanics of pulp fiction. *Garde à vue* (*Under Suspicion*, 1981), an asphyxiatingly tense refit of John Wainwright's novel about the interrogation of a man accused of two child sex murders, scored him a resounding critical and commercial hit. Patricia Highsmith was the source for *Dites-lui que je l'aime* (*This Sweet Sickness*, 1977), an intriguing tale of warped, self-destructive love.

Miller often populates his screen with bent-out-of-shape characters, such as the lovesick detective on the lonesome trail of a pathological beauty in *Mortelle randonnée* (*Deadly Run*, 1983), who can't batten down the hatches on their torrid emotions. This is even the case in non-thriller material like *The Accompanist* (1992), an atmospheric and complex psychodrama about a young pianist who desperately tries to keep the lid on her explosive envy

for the singer she accompanies.

There is another Miller trope: the upheavals of adolescence, as depicted in *The School Trip* (1998), *An Impudent Girl* (1985), *La petite Lili* (2003) and his acclaimed debut *The Best Way To Walk* (1975), a potent evocation of the power play between two young counsellors in a summer camp. It's depicted most famously, perhaps, in *La petite voleuse* (*The Little Thief*, 1988), which brought Miller's connection with Truffaut satisfyingly full circle, being the completion of a project that the great director started just before he died. LH

La petite voleuse (The Little Thief) 1988, 109 min
cast Charlotte Gainsbourg, Didier Bezace, Simon de la Brosse, Raoul Billerey, Chantal Banlier *cin* Dominique Chapuis *m* Alain Jomy

Miller inherited this project from François Truffaut and wrote a script from his mentor's thirty-page synopsis, adding elements that reflected Truffaut's troubled early life. The result, which charts a young thief's salvation through photography, is a fitting, sensitive and poignant tribute to one of cinema's bona fide talents.

Betty Fisher And Other Stories (Betty Fisher et autres histoires) 2001, 103 min
cast Sandrine Kiberlain, Nicole Garcia, Mathilde Seigner, Luck Mervil, Edouard Baer *cin* Christophe Pollock *m* François Dompierre

Nicole Garcia is coolly magnificent as the monstrously selfish and clinically insane mother who visits her daughter, Sandrine Kiberlain, on the day that her grandchild dies. Miller tightens his grip without recourse to kneejerk thriller gimmicks, but with an adroit economy of narrative that renders his casual mode of address intensely compelling.

George Miller
Australia, 1945–

In his first feature film and its two sequels (the 1979 original *Mad Max*, 1981's *Mad Max 2: The Road Warrior* and 1985's *Mad Max Beyond Thunderdome*), George Miller created an endlessly adaptable icon: the leather-clad desert combatant roaring through a post-apocalyptic landscape. As Australian critic Adrian Martin wrote, "No other Australian films have influenced world cinema and popular culture as widely and lastingly as George Miller's *Mad Max* movies". According to Martin, *Mad Max*'s blood flows through the veins of filmmakers as diverse as the Coen brothers, Tsui Hark, Luc Besson and Guillermo Del Toro. For his part, Miller has cited Akira Kurosawa's samurai films, Joseph Campbell's mythological archetypes and Buster Keaton's *The General* (1927) as the inspirations behind his dystopian adventures in the near future.

Miller began making short films while still working as a doctor, and edited the original *Mad Max* film at home. Made for less than $400,000,

M

the movie held the record for the highest profit-to-cost ratio for some twenty years. It introduced audiences to Mel Gibson as the titular cop who earns the "Mad" in his moniker after the murder of his wife and child turns him from reluctant highway badass to full-tilt avenging angel. The well-received sequel, *The Road Warrior*, saw Max become the reluctant saviour of an isolated oil-refining community, but the third and, for the time being, final entry in the series, *Beyond Thunderdome* (co-directed with George Ogilvie), disappointed diehard fans by toning down the violence, introducing cute kids and including Tina Turner songs on the soundtrack.

In Hollywood, Miller also directed "Nightmare at 20,000 Feet", the standout segment of the omnibus *Twilight Zone: The Movie* (1983); *The Witches Of Eastwick* (1987), a fun, trashy all-star adaptation of the John Updike bestseller; and *Lorenzo's Oil* (1992), a harrowing family medical drama. *Babe: Pig In The City* (1998) failed commercially but eventually won a significant critical following, while *Happy Feet* (2006) was a hit at the box office and was Oscar nominated too. JW

Mad Max 1979, 93 min
cast Mel Gibson, Joanne Samuel, Hugh Keays-Byrne, Steve Bisley, Tim Burns, Roger Ward, Vince Gill *cin* David Eggby *m* Brian May

Hot, dust-blown and perfumed with petroleum, Miller's speed-demon debut (victim of some atrocious dubbing for its American release) envisions an almost-lawless future where the separation between cops and criminals is as easily blurred as a line in the dirt. The nominal lead driver of this demolition derby is the vengeful highway patrolman Max Rockatansky (Mel Gibson), but the main characters are really the souped-up vehicles themselves, roaring through one chase scene after another.

Mad Max 2: The Road Warrior 1981, 94 min
cast Mel Gibson, Bruce Spence, Vernon Wells, Emil Minty, Mike Preston, Kjell Nilsson, Virginia Hey, Syd Heylen *cin* Dean Semler *m* Brian May

This sequel arguably improves on the original film, taking shape as a siege drama: desolate "road warrior" Max happens upon a desert outpost with coveted gas reserves that's under constant assault from a nasty gang of thugs clad in leather and chainware. Like the laconic but stout-hearted gunslingers of yesteryear's Westerns, Max decides to stay and help, setting the stage for yet more sensational chase sequences.

Babe: Pig In The City 1998, 96 min
cast Magda Szubanski, James Cromwell, Mickey Rooney *(voices)* E.G. Daily, Steven Wright *cin* Andrew Lesnie *m* Nigel Westlake

An urban sequel that proved to be far darker than the beloved pastoral original, *Babe: Pig In The City* (1998) was a dismal failure at the box office, but won a significant critical following, thereby reinforcing Miller's auteurist standing. Michael Sragow named it the best film of the year in *SF Weekly* and David Edelstein was particularly effusive in *Slate*: "This is my candidate for the most overlooked big-budget film of the decade, maybe of the century. Pearls before swine, indeed."

Anthony Minghella
UK, 1954–

"A writer who directs", in his own estimation, Anthony Minghella has, at various stages of his career, evoked both Noel Coward and David Lean: Coward's blithe spirit and classy romantic eloquence; Lean's petit-bourgeois fascination with how the other half lives, his love of scale and grandeur.

Brought up on the Isle of Wight, the son of a family of Italian immigrants, Minghella studied literature at the University of Hull and went on to teach drama there in the 1970s. His first play, *Mobius The Stripper*, was staged at Hull in 1975. His West End debut, *Made In Bangkok*, came eleven years later, by which time he had started to write for radio and TV, finding success with episodes of the acclaimed *Inspector Morse* series (1987–90) and Jim Henson's *The Storyteller* (1988).

His first feature, *Truly Madly Deeply* (1991), was a low-budget BBC TV film, a British answer to Jerry Zucker's *Ghost* (1990). Juliet Stevenson's authentic portrait of bereavement was balanced with a typically sardonic turn from Alan Rickman as her late lamented, who shows up at her ratty flat with his dead mates to watch videos. Sweet in both senses, according to taste, *Truly Madly Deeply* went on to have theatrical exposure in Britain and the US, and Minghella was wooed to direct the modest romantic comedy *Mr Wonderful* (1993) in Hollywood – to date the only film which he did not also write, and on which he did not have final cut.

Then he teamed up with producer Saul Zaentz to take on Michael Ondaatje's dense, difficult World War II novel *The English Patient* (1996). With its complex patterning of flashbacks and relationships, this represented a considerable leap in scale and ambition, but Minghella handled it with great composure. The film went on to win nine Oscars, including best picture and best director.

Since then he has carved out a niche for himself at the literary end of middlebrow with *The Talented Mr Ripley* (1999), an overly decorous adaptation of Patricia Highsmith's novel with Matt Damon, Gwyneth Paltrow, Cate Blanchett and Jude Law, and an equally handsome but top-heavy return to war-torn romance, *Cold Mountain* (2003), with Law again, Nicole Kidman and Renée Zellweger. Beautifully crafted (Minghella has built up a fine team of collaborators including cinematographer John Seale, editor Walter Murch and costume designer Ann Roth), all three movies earned Oscar attention, and were strongly supported by the Miramax company. More recently, Minghella has opted to shift gears again with *Breaking And Entering* (2006), an original screenplay and his first contemporary film in thirteen years. TC

The English Patient 1996, 160 min
cast Ralph Fiennes, Kristin Scott Thomas, Juliette Binoche, Willem Dafoe, Naveen Andrews, Colin Firth *cin* John Seale *m* Gabriel Yared

During World War II, a Canadian nurse (Binoche) decides to stay in an abandoned, bombed-out monastery to care for a dying, terribly burned patient (Fiennes). At first he remembers little of what brought him there, but as time passes he is swept up in painful memories of a pre-war love affair in Egypt. Minghella's free adaptation of Michael Ondaatje's poetic novel is a moving, evocative love story played out in tiny fragments against an epic backdrop of war and history.

The Talented Mr Ripley 1999 139 min
cast Matt Damon, Jude Law, Gywneth Paltrow, Cate Blanchett, Philip Seymour Hoffman, Jack Davenport *cin* John Seale *m* Gabriel Yared

Anthony Minghella adapted Patricia Highsmith's first Tom Ripley novel to show the sociopathic fraud at his insidious best. Although born on the wrong side of the tracks, Ripley (Matt Damon) is mistaken for an Ivy Leaguer and seizes on an invitation to go to Europe to bring home an old Princeton buddy (Jude Law) that he's never met. Trouble is Dickie's playboy lifestyle turns out to be just to Ripley's taste. The film is well cast, beautifully appointed, intelligent and suspenseful but, allowed to sprawl, it loses its edge.

Vincente Minnelli
US, 1903–86

Vincente Minnelli has influenced directors from Pedro Almodóvar to Martin Scorsese. Above all, he was a stylist. From his debut – the musical *Cabin In The Sky* (1943) – onwards, the consummate craftsman effortlessly flitted from genre to genre as a contract director. He proved equally adept at biting Hollywood satires, such as *The Bad And The Beautiful* (1952) and *Two Weeks In Another Town* (1962), charming domestic comedies like *Father Of The Bride* (1950) and *Designing Women* (1957), intense psychological dramas such as *The Cobweb* (1955) and even biopics (*Lust For Life*, 1956). He is, however, best known for two things: his tempestuous marriage to Judy Garland and his musicals.

In 1940 Minnelli was invited to MGM by the great lyricist and producer Arthur Freed. Freed became Minnelli's mentor, and with his support Minnelli directed some of the greatest musicals in Hollywood history: *Meet Me In St Louis* (1944), *The Band Wagon* (1953) and the best picture Oscar-winners *An American In Paris* (1951) and *Gigi* (1958). Characterized by their colour-saturated elegance and the sophisticated choreography of Minnelli's mobile camera, even his lesser musicals – *Ziegfield Follies* (1946), *The Pirate* (1948), *Brigadoon* (1954) – and the monochrome *Madame Bovary* (1949) had their eye-popping moments, such as Jennifer Jones waltzing in near-madness in the lusty Flaubert adaptation.

The main unifying element of his 37 films is an elaborate design aesthetic. The director's impressive knowledge of art history is evident in his films' fantastic sets and fabulous costumes and in the recreated scenes from Van Gogh paintings in *Lust For Life*. But it's also there in his mix-and-match palette. With their lavish colours, heightened senses and fluid camera, Minnelli's films were like diurnal reveries, often using dream sequences, as with Fred Astaire's ornate nightmare in *Yolanda And The Thief* (1945) and the seventeen-minute dream ballet that was the audacious climax of *An American In Paris*. Never bashful about their artifice or lack of authenticity, they often took place in a past or in a country that could never exist in such picture-perfect form, like his rose-tinted simulacra of boho Paris in *An American In Paris* or the dream of American wholesomeness in *Meet Me In St Louis*. Minnelli's talent for design probably owes something to his days spent as a window-dresser, as a costume designer for cine-variety shows, and as art director at Radio City Music Hall.

Minnelli's career continued into the 1960s and 70s, when it was well past its sell-by date. His later films include such tosh as the Elizabeth Taylor/Richard Burton melodrama *The Sandpiper* (1965), his final musical, the Barbra Streisand vehicle *On A Clear Day You Can See Forever* (1970), and *A Matter Of Time* (1976), which starred his daughter Liza Minnelli. LH

Meet Me In St Louis 1944, 113 min
cast Judy Garland, Margaret O'Brien, Leon Ames, Mary Astor, Tom Drake, Lucille Bremer *cin* George Folsey *m* Ralph Blane, Hugh Martin and others

A family in St Louis at the turn of the twentieth century have to decide whether to move to New York when dad gets a promotion. Judy Garland sparkles as daughter Esther, while Tom Drake is in fine form as the beau next door. Made to warm the cockles of American hearts in the midst of war, the sunniest of Minnelli's musicals has its subversive element, provided by troubled daughter Tootie (Margaret O'Brien), cruelly killing off her dolls and demolishing her snowmen.

An American In Paris 1951, 114 min
cast Gene Kelly, Leslie Caron, Oscar Levant, Nina Foch, Georges Guetary *cin* Alfred Gilks, John Alton *m* George Gershwin

Struggling artist Gene Kelly tries to prise himself from the grip of wealthy gadfly Nina Foch and get his mitts on ingénue Leslie Caron. This bohemian satire is deliciously laced with a breathtaking cynicism: Foch, for instance, buys Kelly's affections for the price of an exhibition. There are exuberant song-and-dance numbers aplenty, such as "I Got Rhythm", and a climactic daydream ballet that takes a jubilant, nonstop tour of French art history.

The Bad And The Beautiful 1952, 116 min, b/w
cast Kirk Douglas, Lana Turner, Barry Sullivan, Dick Powell, Gloria Grahame, Walter Pidgeon, Gilbert Roland *cin* Robert Surtees *m* David Raksin

This is the other side of the musical coin: the monochrome nightmare to the Technicolor dream. It's a deliciously mordant *film à clef*, based on the juiciest of Hollywood gossip. Minnelli's melodrama can switch in the blink of an eye from

The Hollywood musical

From the first major talkie, *The Jazz Singer* (1927), the birth of the musical was, unsurprisingly, synchronous with the invention of sound, with technology and content dancing cheek to cheek; though it was unclear at first who was taking the lead.

With a whole new genre on its hands and no one to put on the show, Hollywood wisely pursued a vigorous recruitment policy of importing much of its talent from Broadway, whether it was songwriters such as Richard Rodgers and Lorenz Hart or, later, stars such as Gene Kelly and choreographers like Bob Fosse and Stanley Donen. Indeed, the fledgling form was swiftly reinvigorated by one early stage émigré: Busby Berkeley. With a mobile camera that moved as elegantly as his dancers, Berkeley's spectacular extravaganzas crackled with a heady mix of choreography, geometry and cheap titillation. From his birds-eye-view camera, nestled in the studio roof, his hoofers were miraculously transformed into abstract patterns and suggestive shapes. He ingeniously misapplied his army drill training to dance numbers, and rushed his lens through chorus girls' splayed legs, persuading them to suggestively manipulate huge bananas and wear nothing but large coins.

In the early to mid-1930s, Berkeley's lavish, lewd musicals were fantastically popular entertainment, an escapist and exotic diversion from the Great Depression, though the numerous backstagers made it clear that the show people were struggling too. In the late 1930s, a more chastened Berkeley moved to MGM, helping Judy Garland and Mickey Rooney to put on the show in *Babes In Arms* (1939) and three other cheesily innocuous outings. Meanwhile, Fred Astaire and Ginger Rogers donned tuxedos and evening dresses, danced cheek to cheek with sinuous grace, and took the musical into the rarefied atmosphere of high society in *Top Hat* (1935) and beyond.

The next golden age dawned after the war (heralded by *Meet Me In St Louis*, 1944), when MGM reinvented itself as the home of the musical. The company's *éminence grise* was producer Arthur Freed. Never once venturing behind the camera himself, he arguably stamped his imprimatur on every film produced by his legendary unit, after joining Louis B. Mayer's company as an associate producer on *The Wizard Of Oz* (1939). The hallmarks of a Freed Unit musical were exuberant screwball wit (especially in scripts penned by Adolph Green and Betty Comden), stunning innovations in the movement of dancers and cameras, and experimental production numbers that went way beyond the dictates of narrative or logic. In lively fare such as *The Harvey Girls* (1946), *Easter Parade* (1948) and *Annie Get Your Gun* (1950), many critics have argued that Freed was as much the director as the filmmakers he hired.

Arguably only a handful of directors managed to impose their personal preferences on the MGM musical. Vincente Minnelli's output was sophisticated, oneiric and self-aware, disguising a sly cynicism beneath the dazzling surface of art-historical references in *Meet Me In St Louis*, *The Band Wagon* (1953) and the Oscar-winners *An American In Paris* (1951) and *Gigi* (1958). Stanley Donen and Gene Kelly, meanwhile, brought a breath of fresh air to the musical. The decision to film some of *On The Town* (1949) actually on the town and not in a studio mock-up of New York was genuinely revolutionary, perfectly suiting star and co-director Gene Kelly's radical dance style – athletic, earthy and brimming with blue-collar vitality, eschewing top hat and tails for T-shirts, khakis and uniforms. However, the film studios were both the location and the subject for Donen, Kelly and Freed's finest hour, *Singin' In The Rain* (1952), which was arguably the greatest musical of all time. The 1950s had other highlights – such as the Rodgers and Hammerstein adaptations *Carousel* (1951) and *The King And I* (1956) – but the emergence of Frank Sinatra and Elvis Presley added few innovations to the genre and failed to produce any major classics.

The 1960s started well with *West Side Story* (1961) and *The Sound Of Music* (1965), but by the end of the decade big-budget belly flops like *Dr Dolittle* (1967), *Star!* (1968) and *Paint Your Wagon* (1969) weren't in sync with a counterculture that was listening to rock'n'roll. Nor was Francis Ford Coppola's *Finian's Rainbow* (1968), which featured a 69-year-old Fred Astaire in the lead. In the Vietnam era, musicals could no longer offer a glossy escape from uncomfortable realities, and the old studio system, which had once relied upon musicals as much-needed money-spinners, finally lost faith in them. Since then, Hollywood has had a musical hit every few years on average, including Bob Fosse's *Cabaret* (1972) and Randal Kleiser's *Grease* (1978). However, even when *Chicago* (2002) won an unexpected Oscar for best film, fellow Broadway hits *The Producers* and *Rent* (both 2005) couldn't emulate its sparkling achievements, or even the box-office figures of their stage productions. So, recent break-out hits such as *Moulin Rouge!* (2001) and *Dreamgirls* (2006) would seem to represent a sustained curtain call and farewell bow, rather than an encore. LH heightened reality to hysteria, not least in the scene where Lana Turner's car drives madly out of control.

Lust For Life 1956, 122 min
cast Kirk Douglas, Anthony Quinn, James Donald, Pamela Brown, Everett Sloane, Niall MacGinnis, Jill Bennett cin Freddie Young m Miklós Rózsa

Kirk Douglas chews up the pastoral scenery as Vincent Van Gogh, going into angsty overdrive as the tormented genius. This, however, is as much a work of painterly abstraction as it is overripe melodrama, a tale told in colours as much as dialogue. By the end, Douglas seems to inhabit a virtual reality of inky black crows and intense yellow wheat fields, as if he has miraculously stepped into a Van Gogh canvas.

Minnelli at Maxim's: a silver-haired Maurice Chevalier lays on the charm in *Gigi*, Lerner and Loewe's homage to *fin-de-siècle* Paris.

Gigi 1958, 116 min
cast Leslie Caron, Maurice Chevalier, Louis Jourdan, Hermione Gingold, Jacques Bergerac cin Joseph Ruttenberg m Alan Jay Lerner, Frederick Loewe

Minnelli starts as he means to go on with a nod and a wink, as Maurice Chevalier stops the action, addresses the audience directly and breaks into "Thank Heaven For Little Girls". This sets the audacious tone for a musical ripe with sparkling cynicism, vibrant peacock colours, chintzy furniture and Cecil Beaton costumes. The director proves himself to be one of cinema's great window-dressers, eschewing close-ups for mid-shots that luxuriate in the splendour of the opulent decor.

Some Came Running 1958, 136 min
cast Frank Sinatra, Dean Martin, Shirley MacLaine, Martha Hyer, Arthur Kennedy, Nancy Gates, Leora Dana cin William H. Daniels m Elmer Bernstein

Frank Sinatra and Dean Martin are a long way from their Rat Pack here: Ol' Blue Eyes is a pugnacious writer returning from war and acclimatizing to changes in a small town, where he has some unfinished business with his older

brother. Before he knows it, he's part of a love triangle with Shirley MacLaine and schoolteacher Martha Hyer. If this sounds all very *noir*, Minnelli, typically, glosses the picture in a carnival of blues, oranges and silvers.

Hayao Miyazaki
Japan, 1941–

Hayao Miyazaki is a filmmaker whose appeal goes way beyond fans of anime – that all too often impenetrable Japanese genre. His work includes some of the most charming kids' movies you could hope to see: animated films which make Disney seem simple-minded. And over the past decade, he has notched up two superb fantasy films – *Princess Mononoke* (1997) and *Spirited Away* (2001)– that leave other sci-fi-oriented anime trailing in their wake. He is a huge figure in Japan, where *Spirited Away* is the highest grossing film of all time.

Two things distinguish Miyazaki's films: their look, which sets the goggle-eyed characters of anime within astonishing painterly backdrops; and the ambiguity of plot and characterization, which propels even the simplest tales beyond a 2-D moral compass. There is an innocence and ecological awareness in the work, too, that is engaging and moving, however absurd or mystifying the narrative context. And for confirmed Miyazaki fans – who will happily watch the more obscure films in Japanese versions – there is a joy in recognizing the director's familiar motifs: the movement of the wind across grass or forests, the delight in flight and flying machines of all kinds (Miyazaki's father was an aviation engineer), and strong, wilful female characters – often young girls or grannies. In more recent movies, there have been ever more elaborate fantasy characters, creating a kind of alternative Japanese eco-mythology, conjuring up spirits of nature such as river or forest gods.

Born in a Tokyo commuter town, Miyazaki got his first job as an artist at Toei Animation, where he

M

met Isao Takahata, with whom he has collaborated throughout his career. The duo moved to studio A Pro in 1971, where they produced TV episodes of the Japanese pulp crime series, *Lupin III*. This led to Miyazaki's film debut, a Lupin spin-off feature, *The Castle Of Cagliostro* (1979), which set out his store with its creative animation, fantastical staging and humour. It was followed by the sci-fi adventure, *Nausicaä Of The Valley Of The Wind* (1984), based on Miyazaki's own manga comic. This introduced a more serious, indeed doom-laden, plotline of nature corrupted by humans and warfare.

On the strength of *Nausicaä*, Miyazaki was able to set up his own animation company, Studio Ghibli, which has produced all his subsequent films, as well as work by Takahata and others. His own first film for Ghibli was *Laputa: Castle In The Sky* (1986), a lyrical fantasy of two children seeking a magical floating island. But it was *My Neighbour Totoro* (1988) that was the breakthrough success for Ghibli and Miyazaki. For all the cuteness, it is

hard to conceive of Disney ever producing a tale quite like this: a story of two young sisters, whose mother is in hospital, and who explore a world that hovers between excitement and terror.

Miyazaki kept the magic intact with his next kids' outing, the delightful *Kiki's Delivery Service* (1989), about a trainee witch and her cat. This gave full rein to his love of flight sequences, as did *Porco Rosso* (1992), an odd movie, even within the Miyazaki canon, about an anti-fascist aviator who has the head of a pig. Little of this prepared audiences for Miyazaki's masterpiece, *Princess Mononoke*, a distinctly grown-up and at times violent anime which is set in medieval Japan. At its heart, as in *Nausicaä*, is an ecologically troubled world, where nature and its animal spirits are at war with human incursions. The largely hand-drawn animation is stunning, whether evoking the forests and settlements, the battles (which recall Akira Kurosawa's *Kagemusha*, 1980), or the panoply of odd characters. Morally, too, everything is

Contemporary animation

Over the past fifteen years, computer animation has powerfully asserted itself, reaching an undeniable critical mass as a cultural force. Yet still we are romanced by the old-world charms of cel animation. One of the major players in cel animation is currently the Japanese production outfit Studio Ghibli, and its most celebrated director is without a doubt Hayao Miyazaki. A left-leaning, socially orientated filmmaker heavily influenced by Western children's literature, Miyazaki has the stature of Walt Disney in his own country and, whilst he claims he has no real interest in the reach of his films beyond Japan, over the last five years his work has secured a growing interest in Europe and North America. His films *Princess Mononoke* (1997), *My Neighbour Totoro* (1988) and *Spirited Away* (2001) are lavishly designed, dreamy movies that place the fantastic in our contemporary lives. There is a richness to the background visuals that entrances and transports – in the Japanese anime tradition the visual backgrounds are as meaningful as the actions of a film's characters.

In the UK, animation remains an important part of the film industry. The Aardman Studios, creators of the Wallace and Gromit characters and *Chicken Run* (2000) are well known, but British animation has a long and distinguished history. The studio of John Halas and Joy Batchelor is still justly celebrated for its pioneering adaptation of George Orwell's novel *Animal Farm* in 1954. More recently, the animator Suzie Templeton produced a stunning stop-motion version of Prokofiev's *Peter And The Wolf* for Channel 4 Films.

A sharp contrast to the work of Ghibli and Aardman is the sparkling, computer-generated aesthetic of the California-based Pixar Animation Studio. Pixar started life as part of George Lucas's filmmaking operation in the early 1980s. It has a distinct visual and narrative style, and directors John Lasseter and Brad Bird have proved their status as animation visionaries, wrapping new technology around traditional narratives. Whereas the *Toy Story* films (1995 and 1999) were situated literally in the childhood world of imagination and play, *The Incredibles* (2004) celebrated the uniqueness of one's individuality. *Finding Nemo* (2003) and *Monsters Inc* (2001) were both far larger-than-life stories that had potent themes about the bonds of family, whether natural or surrogate. Amidst the visual fireworks that are the hallmark of all good animation, these films also have heart and soul.

Indeed, the great strength of animation is not its ability to mimic reality but instead to transform what we see around us: in doing so it gets to the essence of things, and what it is to be alive. This is applicable as much to the joyous, jazz-influenced abstractions of Norman McLaren as it is to the existentialist grotesqueries of Jan Svankmajer, or indeed to the work of Ladislaw Starewicz and Caroline Leaf. The French filmmaker Michel Ocelot is a name that also deserves more recognition. His work overtly roots itself in animation's tradition – most notably in the work of Lotte Reiniger (who rendered silhouettes magically articulate in the fantastical 1928 animation *The Adventures Of Prince Achmed*). Ocelot's most recent film, *Azur et Asmar* (2006), is a visually stunning and politically savvy adventure about race and understanding. JC

ambivalent and complex: the villains are all too full of redeeming qualities.

Miyazaki announced his retirement after *Mononoke*, but while on vacation, so he says, he found the inspiration for *Spirited Away*. This was the first of his films to be released to international acclaim – oddly perhaps, for it is an intensely Japanese movie. After its hugely successful release, Miyazaki retired again, but re-emerged to complete *Howl's Moving Castle* (2004), based on Diana Wynne Jones' fantasy novel, after its original director at Ghibli left the project. It is arguably his least satisfying film, and it came as no surprise when Studio Ghibli announced that he would be working on a final project, *Ponyo On A Cliff*. Slated to appear in Japan in summer 2008, it seems to be a return to children's filmmaking, with a story about a young boy and a princess goldfish, set largely at sea. ME

The Castle Of Cagliostro (Rupan sansei: Kariosutoro no shiro) 1979, 100 min

cast (English voices) David Hayter, John Snyder, Richard Epcar, Dorothy Elias-Fahn, Dougary Grant *cin* Hirokata Takahashi *m* Yuji Ono

This is a fun movie: an animated James Bond/Tintin-style adventure featuring the master thief Lupin III and his sidekicks, who must rescue the beautiful Princess Clarisse from the impregnable castle of the evil Count Cagliostro. The detailing is wonderfully drawn and authentic throughout. Steven Spielberg, no less, is said to have described its opening scene as the best car chase in movie history.

My Neighbour Totoro (Tonari no Totoro) 1988, 86 min

cast (English voices) Dakota Fanning, Elle Fanning, Timothy Daly, Pat Carroll, Lea Salonga, Frank Welker *cin* Hisao Shirai *m* Joe Hisaishi

The hand-crafted animation of this life-enhancing children's movie is simply astonishing. Benevolent, mute, slightly fierce-looking forest sprites called "Totoros", which can be seen only by children, act as guardians for two sisters while they wait for their mother to come home from hospital. The film has many beauties, not least the touching relationship between the girls and their dad, who seems entirely open to the possibility that Totoros exist. A Disney movie would feel obliged to resolve all the issues, but Miyazaki's film, like life itself, is deliberately inconclusive.

Princess Mononoke (Mononoke him) 1997, 134 min

cast (English voices) Billy Crudup, Claire Danes, Gillian Anderson, Minnie Driver, Billy Bob Thornton, John DiMaggio *cin* Atsushi Okui *m* Joe Hisaishi

Mononoke was a quantum leap for Miyazaki, as he turned for the first time to a film for an adult audience. Set in fourteenth-century Japan, it features astonishing battle scenes as the animal gods of the forest, led by a girl warrior (Mononoke), confront iron miners who are polluting and destroying their universe. Perhaps its most impressive quality is that, for all the ecological messages, you are never quite sure who is good or evil. To their credit, Dreamworks released the English-language version uncut, with a star voice cast for the dub.

Spirited Away (Sen to chihiro no kami-kakushi) 2001, 125 min

cast (English voices) Daveigh Chase, Jason Marsden, David Ogden Stiers, Susan Egan, Bob Bergen, Tara Strong *cin* Toshio Suzuki *m* Joe Hisaishi

Although *Spirited Away* features many of his regular themes and motifs, its bizarre creations are not the most obvious introduction to Miyazaki's work. It is a strange tale of a sulky girl who finds herself lost in a world populated by Japanese spirits, gods and witches, and, like Dorothy in Oz or Lewis Carroll's Alice, has to find a way back to reality. Her adventures are fantastic and, at times, very alien to a Western viewer. But the girl's journey, and her personal growth, are ultimately moving, even if you can't quite figure out what has been going on.

Kenji Mizoguchi
Japan, 1898–1956

Jean-Luc Godard anointed him "the greatest of Japanese filmmakers"; one critic has dubbed him the Shakespeare of cinema. Kenji Mizoguchi made so many films that even he lost count: he once estimated that he'd made 75 movies, while others claim it was 86. The reason for this apparent discrepancy is that many pre-war films have been lost or destroyed. Those that survive are all worth tracking down: Mizoguchi is one of cinema's finest aesthetes, poets and pessimists.

Mizoguchi's favourite subject is undoubtedly women: wives locked in loveless marriages (1951's *The Lady From Musashino*), daughters falling from grace (1952's *The Life Of Oharu*), self-sacrificing lovers (1939's *The Story Of The Late Chrysanthemums*) and above all, abused geishas (too many to list). Regarded by some as a proto-male-feminist, Mizoguchi gave a more prosaic reason for his ongoing fascination with downtrodden females: "While I was working with Nikkatsu, the company already had Murata Minoru making films which featured a hero, so, for balance, they made me make films featuring a heroine." (He did try to make movies about samurai, like *The 47 Ronin*, 1941, but with limited success.) Other critics claim that Mizoguchi is more sadist than feminist, that his films are little more than a series of endurance tests for his permanently stoic heroines (and that arguably only Lars von Trier's female characters have suffered more for his art). These critics draw on Mizoguchi's personal life as evidence of his misogyny: a serial frequenter of geisha houses, Mizoguchi would habitually bully his actresses, and desperately tried to prevent his lover and muse Kinuyo Tanaka from becoming a director. But the films also present us with contradictory evidence. Here is a director who possessed a searing empathy with his lonely outcasts (significantly, his older sister was sold to a geisha house, and it was her job that initially funded his studies in art). In masterpieces such as *The Life Of Oharu*, and near-masterpieces such as *Osaka Elegy* (1936), *Sisters Of The Gion* (1936), *Gion Festival Music* (1953) and *Street Of Shame* (1956) all Mizoguchi's beleaguered heroines emerge from their long ordeal with their dignity and moral superiority (if nothing else) intact.

Mizoguchi is undeniably the master of the sequence shot. Like Miklós Jancsó and Bela Tarr after him, he is one of cinema's finest choreographers of camera. The director often limited himself to one shot per scene: an elegant, hypnotic glide on a track or crane, while maintaining a tactful distance from the overheated melodrama, like a Japanese scroll painting. A classic Mizoguchi shot starts on high above a roof or wall and moves earthwards, where it meets the protagonists and tracks them at ground level with graceful and deceptive ease. Its precision adds to the creeping sense of predestination, that characters' movements are already mapped out and governed by an invisible and greater force. Conversely, the director seemed almost allergic to close-ups, making easy identification with the suffering protagonist difficult, if not impossible. Added to that, he possessed the eye of a trained painter, creating a tension between the finely wrought elegance of his camerawork and the unrelenting squalor of his subject matter. The result was an eerie confluence between formalism and fatalism, best seen in films like *Sansho The Bailiff* (1954) and above all his greatest film, *Ugetsu* (1953). Its strange, ethereal beauty moved critic David Thomson to claim it could even rival *Citizen Kane* as the greatest film ever made. LH

The Story Of The Late Chrysanthemums (Zangiku monogatari) 1939, 142 min, b/w
cast Shotaro Hanayagi, Kokichi Takada, Gonjuro Kawarazaki, Kakuko Mori *cin* Yozo Fuji, Shigeto Miki *m* Shiro Fukai, Senji Ito

The director's greatest pre-war movie puts the spotlight on a mediocre actor, Kikunosuke, living in the dark shadow of his adopted father, Kikugoro V, a stage legend. When he falls in love with a nurse, the unfortunate thesp becomes the black sheep of the family. Down-and-out in Tokyo and the provinces, a struggling actor in a rep company of no repute, Kikunosuke's pain is as exquisite as Mizoguchi's camerawork, which is never less than sublime.

The Life Of Oharu (Saikaku ichidai onna) 1952, 148 min, b/w
cast Kinuyo Tanaka, Toshirô Mifune, Tsukie Matsuura *cin* Yoshimi Hirano, Yoshimi Kono *m* Inchiro Saito

Oharu, a courtesan, and Katsunosuke, a commoner, are in love. But feudal Japan is a place with a minute social snobbery matched only by its cruelty. The local warlord is displeased. Katsunosuke pays for his impudence with his head, Oharu with her happiness. When she and her family are exiled, it sets off a train of humiliations and bereavements that leave poor Oharu literally staggering under the weight of her grief. This is *Breaking The Waves* set in seventeenth-century Japan: unrelenting, grim and bewitching.

Ugetsu (Ugetsu monogatari) 1953, 94 min, b/w
cast Kinuyo Tanaka, Masayuki Mori, Machiko Kyo *cin* Kazuo Miyagawa *m* Inchiro Saito, Fumio Hayasaka, Tamekichi Mochizuki

There's blood on the streets, but Genjuro and his daft friend Tobei couldn't be happier that war is on its way. They ditch their stoical wives to seek their fortunes without so much as a backward glance. Cringing Tobei becomes a samurai general. Vain Genjuro's skills as a potter, meanwhile, win him the love of the mysterious Lady Wasaka. She's as beguiling as the pale moon of the title, and as unattainable. Daylight reveals the extent of Genjuro and Tobei's delusions in Mizoguchi's seminal and enchanting fable.

Sansho The Bailiff (Sanshô dayû) 1954, 120 min, b/w
cast Kinuyo Tanaka, Yoshiaki Hanayagi, Kyoko Kagawa, Eitaro Shindo *cin* Kazuo Miyagawa *m* Fumio Hayasaka, Tamekichi Mochizuki

According to Mizoguchi expert Mark Le Fanu, *Sansho* completes the great triptych that includes *Oharu* and *Ugetsu*. Although the eponymous character is little more than a bit part, he still manages to play a significant role in the lives of the protagonist: a tax collector who enslaves the children of an exiled governor. All the characters, however, are figures in an unforgiving landscape, painted by one of cinema's most uncompromising artists.

Jacinto Molina
Spain, 1934–

Writer, producer, director and actor (under the more famous name Paul Naschy), Jacinto Molina remains the best-known face of Spanish horror. The stocky ex-weightlifter was cast as an extra in various sword-and-sandals epics and B-movies before becoming the key actor in Iberian horror. He played a host of classic horror characters, including Dracula, the Phantom of the Opera, Jack the Ripper, the Devil, Frankenstein's monster, Dr Moreau and Mr Hyde. But his signature role is Count Waldemar Daninsky, a Polish werewolf he portrayed in eleven gothic adventures from *Hell's Creatures* (1968) to *Tomb Of The Werewolf* (2004). His sporadic directorial career (often under the name Jacinto Molina Alvarez) began with *Inquisition* (1976). His Hammer-influenced aesthetic is pretty conventional, although *Latidos de pánico* (*Panic Beats*, 1983) and *El aullido del diablo* (*Howl Of The Devil*, 1987) are strange cult items. AJ

Inquisition (Inquisición) 1976, 94 min
cast Paul Naschy, Daniela Giordano, Mónica Randall, Ricardo Merino, Tony Isbert, Julia Saly *cin* Miguel Fernández Mila *m* Máximo Barratas

This is *Witchfinder General* Spanish-style, with judge Naschy brutalizing and torturing his way through the French region of Carcassone as his perversions become his undoing. Naschy doubles as the Devil in the fire-and-brimstone sequences, which are loaded with sadistic sex and nasty nipple-severing violence.

Latidos de pánico (Panic Beats) 1983, 94 min
cast Paul Naschy, Julia Saly, Lola Gaos, Silvia Miró, Paquita Ondiviela, Manuel Zarzo *cin* Julio Burgos *m* Moncho Alpuente, Servando Carballar

An ancestral spirit, a sixteenth-century, devil-worshipping, blood-drinking knight, returns to wreak murderous havoc on the household of Alaric de Marnac. Both Alaric and his ancestor are played by Naschy in this odd confection of gothic horror, gratuitous nudity and shocking gore.

Dominik Moll
Germany, 1962–

Having directed only a few films at somewhat lengthy intervals Dominik Moll has shown a knack for depicting awkward social encounters that slowly build in menace and insinuation into an explosion of emotional and physical violence. After *Intimité* (*Intimacy*, 1994), based upon a story by Jean-Paul Sartre, Moll helmed the well-received *Harry, He's Here To Help* (2000), a claustrophobic psychological thriller that showed the filmmaker to be an attentive student of Hitchcock and Chabrol. He followed up with another fractious and tense exercise in controlled paranoia in the shape of *Lemming* (2005), a disturbing four-hander reminiscent of Roman Polanski, with a terrifying performance from Charlotte Rampling as the plot's nightmare catalyst. JW

Harry, He's Here To Help (Harry, un ami qui vous veut du bien) 2000, 117 min
cast Sergi Lopez, Laurent Lucas, Mathilde Seigner, Sophie Guillermin, Liliane Rovère, Michel Fau *cin* Matthieu Poirot-Delpech *m* David Sinclair Whitaker

On holiday with his wife and bratty kids, stressed-out Michel (Laurent Lucas) runs into wealthy Harry (Sergi López), apparently an old school friend whom Michel can't quite remember. Harry buys his pal a new car and encourages him to rediscover his teenage writing ambitions, but his deep interest in Michel's wellbeing soon starts to take on a frightening intensity in Moll's darkly funny thriller.

Lukas Moodysson
Sweden, 1969–

The maker of one of the most popular films in recent Scandinavian history, Lukas Moodysson was once dubbed "the most hated man in Sweden". His debut *Show Me Love* (1998) was far more tender than its original Swedish title, *Fucking Åmål*, would suggest, being a finely calibrated study of the burgeoning relationship of two 16-year-old schoolgirls amidst the boredom and bigotry of a small Swedish town. A phenomenal success in its home country, where it rang as many cash tills as *Titanic*, it was declared by Ingmar Bergman to be "a young master's first masterpiece". Moodysson didn't return the compliment, however, claiming that lipsticked

miserablists The Cure were more of an influence on him than any filmmaker – although, in unguarded moments, he does begrudgingly admit to admiring Ken Loach. *Show Me Love* was festooned with awards. At one ceremony, the director lambasted the Swedish film industry for its elitism, complaining particularly about the choice of an opera house as the venue for the shindig. When the tuxedoed audience began to boo, Lukas stormed off stage, raising his middle finger as a parting gesture.

A sort of rapprochement began with the release of *Together* (2000). Its comedic confluence of 1970s politics, fashions, facial hair and Abba instilled a warm glow of nostalgia in audiences around the Western world. It may well have given people the wrong idea of Moodysson as a purveyor of feelgood irony. He soon put them straight with *Lilya 4 Ever* (2002), which plunged the audience remorselessly into misery. The director continued where he left off with *A Hole In My Heart* (2004), set once again in a squalid flat, and taking as its subject another offshoot of the sex industry. Detailing the production of an amateur porn movie, Moodysson acknowledged its voyeurism, opting for a militantly up-close-and-personal approach that was almost suffocating in its intensity and nihilism. The director entered experimental territory – and some would argue an artistic cul-de-sac – with the little-seen *Container* (2006), in which sound and image were divorced and meaning obfuscated. LH

Show Me Love (Fucking Åmål) 1998, 89 min
cast Alexandra Dahlstrom, Rebecka Liljeberg, Erica Carlson, Matthias Rust *cin* Ulf Brantås

A Swedish movie about teenage lesbians, Moodysson's debut may well disappoint viewers with certain expectations. This is an innocent, life-enhancing movie about small-town claustrophobia and adolescent torpor. Alexandra Dahlberg and Rebecka Liljeberg are particularly affecting as the bored beauty and the shy outsider whose lives are turned around when one kisses the other to win a bet.

Together (Tillsammans) 2000, 106 min
cast Lisa Lindgren, Gustav Hammarsten, Mikael Nyqvist, Jessica Liedberg, Ola Norell, Shanti Roney, Emil Moodysson, Cecilia Frode *cin* Ulf Brantås

A mother takes her two children from their alcoholic father and joins a commune where washing up is considered by some to be a bourgeois act. Lampooning the loony excesses of the 1970s Left, this warm comedy was a big hit amongst ex-radicals. Despite its inherent conservatism, the humour is sweet and gentle while its tonal shifts are poignantly modulated.

Lilya 4 Ever 2002, 109 min
cast Oksana Akinshina, Artiom Bogucharskij, Ljubov Agapova, Lilia Sinkarjova, Elina Benenson *cin* Ulf Brantås *m* Nathan Larson

Somewhere in the former USSR, young Lilya has been abandoned by her mother, who has vamoosed to the US, and begins to turn tricks for a living. A white knight appears in the form of Alexei, who sweeps her off to Sweden. There she realizes that she has been conned yet again, as she's locked up in a squalid flat, repeatedly raped and forced into prostitution. Moodysson stringently removes the gloss from the image of Sweden as a haven of sexual liberation.

Michael Moore
US, 1954–

The polemical satirist and *agent provocateur* Michael Moore is perhaps the most contentious filmmaker in the United States. An old-school socialist who endorsed Ralph Nader in the 2000 presidential race (but turned to John Kerry in 2004), Moore is also an inveterate self-publicist who puts himself front and centre in his films. With his trademark baseball cap, stubble and baggy blue jeans, he is an instantly recognizable figure – a leftist icon with a popular touch.

Moore has tried his hand at narrative fiction filmmaking – the poorly received *Canadian Bacon* (1995) riffed on a US attack on its neighbour to the north. But it is his documentary features, books and TV shows that have made him famous, especially his first film *Roger & Me* (1989), about the impact of General Motors factory closures on his home town Flint, *Bowling For Columbine* (2002) and the Cannes Palme d'Or winner *Fahrenheit 9/11* (2004), the first documentary to make more than $100 million at the US box office.

Infuriated right-wingers complain that Moore's satiric and political purposes distort journalistic principles. Supporters counter that Moore is a necessary corrective to the conservative institutional bias in traditional media outlets. To the extent that his nonfiction films play fast and loose with the facts, there are grounds for caution; Moore often gets carried away by his own slick rhetoric. But he makes no bones about his agenda, and he has a knack for bringing the bigger picture into dramatic focus. His movies impress with their keen sense of the absurd, their adroit construction and their direct engagement with the issues of our time, whether that be corporate capitalism run amok (*Roger & Me*; his TV series *TV Nation* and *The Awful Truth*), gun culture (*Bowling For Columbine*), George W. Bush's war on terror (*Fahrenheit 9/11*) or health care (*Sicko*, 2007). TC

Bowling For Columbine 2002, 120 min
with Michael Moore, Charlton Heston, Marilyn Manson, Matt Stone, James Nichols, Barry Glassner *cin* Brian Danitz, Michael McDonough *m* Jeff Gibbs

What begins as a response to the shootings at Columbine High School widens out into an essay on American gun lore, the culture of fear, and the widening social gap between rich and poor. Moore himself has a tendency to shoot from the hip – and isn't above taking pot shots at easy targets either – but at least he also asks questions later.

Fahrenheit 9/11 2004, 110 min
with Michael Moore, George W. Bush, Jim McDermott, Porter Goss, John Conyers, Tammy Baldwin *cin* Mike Desjarlais *m* Jeff Gibbs

Moore's blockbuster documentary was a polemical sledge-hammer aimed at scuppering George W. Bush's re-election campaign in 2004. Despite breaking records at the box office, *Fahrenheit 9/11* fell short of its aim. Moore failed to find the smoking gun that would incriminate the president, and had to make do with innuendo about his dealings with the Saudis instead. The movie is on much firmer ground when it explores how the administration fostered paranoia and curtailed civil liberties after September 11, and makes an emotional case against the war in Iraq.

Nanni Moretti
Italy, 1953–

Nanni Moretti, Robert Benigni and Maurizio Nichetti are the trinity of Italian actors/writers/directors who are routinely compared to Buster Keaton and Woody Allen. But Moretti, significantly, has spiced his drollery with ideology, accompanying his pratfalls with politics.

After a series of short films made on Super 8 in the early 1970s, Moretti made a name for himself by developing an alter ego called Michele Apicella, a tactless former political activist brimming with opinions and self-importance. He introduced himself in *I Am An Autocrat* (1976), a low-budget behind-the-scenes peak at an experimental theatre troupe. Here, and in *Ecce bombo* (1978), Moretti hit the bull's-eye among post-1968 radicals who saw themselves in the painfully earnest intellectuals talking themselves into a political cul-de-sac. Michele's role in subsequent movies transformed from film to film. He was a Felliniesque director making a biopic of Freud's mother in *Sweet Dreams* (1981), a teacher interfering in the lives of his colleagues in *Bianca* (1983) and in *Red Lob* (1989) he was a water-polo player and communist activist who suffers from amnesia. Its game of water polo nimbly doubled as an allegory for the demise of the political party.

International success only arrived when Moretti dropped Apicella to play himself. The autobiographical *Dear Diary* (1994) won him the best director award at Cannes and he continued in essay form for the quirky and culturally astute *Aprile* (1998), which juxtaposed the left-wing victory in the Italian election and the birth of his child. Book-ended with the director's attempts to make a musical about a communist pastry chef, *Aprile* didn't have the Jennifer Beals moment that made its predecessor such a capricious delight. *The Son's Room* (2001) eschewed self-reflexivity for a straight narrative and won the Palme d'Or. However, in 2006 Moretti suffered the fate of the satirist who likes to operate on the cutting edge when *Il caimano* (*The Caiman*) became a victim of changing circumstances. The subject of

M

his intended satire, Italian Prime Minister Silvio Berlusconi, had left office by the time the film was released internationally, so what was meant to be edgy and contemporary suddenly became a timepiece – and a flawed one at that. LH

Dear Diary (Caro diario)1994, 100 min

cast Nanni Moretti, Renato Carpentieri, Antonio Neiwiller, Jennifer Beals, Alexandre Rockwell, Carol Mazzacurati *cin* Giuseppe Lanci *m* Nicola Piovani

Moretti's ecstatic blurring of reportage and fiction is divided into three sections, beginning with Moretti scooting around Rome on his Vespa, bumping into Jennifer Beals and informing her that *Flashdance* saved his life. In part two, he searches in vain for tranquillity on the Lipari Islands; while in part three the tone shifts dramatically as Moretti documents his year-long battle with an apparent cancer.

The Son's Room (La stanza del figlio) 2001, 100 min

cast Nanni Moretti, Laura Morante, Jasmine Trinca, Giuseppe Sanfelice, Silvio Orlando, Claudia Della Seta *cin* Giuseppe Lanci *m* Nicola Piovani

Moretti plays it straight as a well-heeled psychoanalyst whose comfortable existence falls apart when his son dies in a diving accident. As director, Moretti catches the quotidian rhythms and details of domestic life before the accident, and continues in the same mode in the horrified aftermath, documenting the fitting of the coffin, for instance, with a stark dispassion. It's this ordinariness that resonates so painfully, the film placing its visual metaphors lightly. Genuinely stunning.

Errol Morris

US, 1948–

One might say that Errol Morris's filmmaking career was secured on a dare. When Morris told his friend Werner Herzog about the difficulties he had finding financing for his projects, Herzog replied that Morris should simply forge ahead, "and the day I see the finished work" the German director added, "I am going to eat my shoe". The finished work turned out to be *Gates Of Heaven* (1980), a droll and richly detailed portrait of the proprietors and clients of two pet cemeteries. Herzog also held up his end of the bargain, immortalized in Les Blank's 1980 short *Werner Herzog Eats His Shoe*.

Morris brought strains of ironic comedy to the documentary format, an innovation that would inform the work of nonfiction filmmakers such as Michael Moore and Chris Smith. Even in a film as unsettling as *Mr Death: The Rise And Fall Of Fred A. Leuchter* (1999), about the eponymous capital-punishment technologist and Holocaust denier, Morris manages to incorporate touches of gallows humour – the opening credits sequence, lit by lightning, casts Leuchter as a mad scientist straight out of a 1950s B-movie. But Morris's deadpan comic sensibilities never cheapen his material. *Gates Of Heaven* is at once amused and impressed by its subjects' some-times overwrought dedication to their deceased cats and dogs, and his second film, *Vernon, Florida* (1981), is a tapestry of the eccentric inhabitants of the titular backwater that never descends into snide grotesquerie.

Appropriately for a former philosophy student who once paid the rent as a private investigator, Morris has consistently produced work that poses questions about the very limits of knowledge and self-knowledge. *A Brief History Of Time* (1991), a delightful elucidation of Stephen Hawking's cosmic bestseller, and *Fast, Cheap & Out Of Control* (1997), a brilliant four-hander on a disparate group of specialists (a topiary artist, a mole-rat expert, a robot scientist and a lion tamer), melds scientific and philosophical inquiry to reach cockeyed epiphanies. Meticulous and quietly shocking, *The Thin Blue Line* (1988) virtually solved a murder and helped set free Randall Adams, a Texas man serving a life sentence for a crime he didn't commit.

Winner of an overdue documentary Oscar for Morris, *The Fog Of War* (2003) incorporated many of his instantly recognizable motifs: no narration, an agitated Philip Glass score (Morris favours the composer for his gift of evoking "existential dread"), a revelatory treasure trove of archival footage and its use of the "Interrotron". This is Morris's name for a camera setup that enables the subject – in this case, former US Secretary of Defense Robert S. McNamara – to speak directly into the camera. Depending on the context, the much-vilified McNamara comes across as both mediator and warmonger; with characteristic reticence, Morris allows the viewer to deliver the final judgement. JW

The Thin Blue Line 1988, 101 min

with Randall Adams, David Harris, Edith James, Dennis White, Don Metcalfe *cin* Stefan Czapsky *m* Philip Glass

In the wrong place at the wrong time, Randall Adams landed on Death Row for a murder he didn't commit: the 1976 shooting of a Dallas cop. Former detective Morris takes up the case, and pieces it together with forensic precision and the aid of stunningly incisive interviews with law-enforcement officials, Adams himself and chief witness David Harris. Harris's tape-recorded near-confession to the crime at the film's end stands as one of the most chilling moments in documentary history.

The Fog Of War 2003, 106 min

with Robert S. McNamara, Errol Morris *cin* Peter Donahue, Robert Chappell *m* Philip Glass

These "eleven lessons from the life of Robert S. McNamara" are culled from some 23 hours of interviews with the former US Secretary of Defense, now elderly and looking to account for his role in the American war in Vietnam. In its studied even-handedness, its intelligent ambivalence, the film offers not answers but evidence, and was especially timely for having been released not long after the launch of the precedent-setting "pre-emptive war" in Iraq.

Paul Morrissey
US, 1938–

Paul Morrissey is not just the director of a handful of movies attributed to Andy Warhol. The Fordham University graduate had already made a number of short films about the New York underground (including 1963's *Taylor Mead Dances*) before he met Warhol at a screening in the mid-1960s. The two were briefly co-managers of rock band the Velvet Underground, and collaborated on numerous anti-aesthetic, anti-narrative slices of low life, including the celebrated film marathon *Chelsea Girls* (1966), which came in at a total of 210 formless minutes. Morrissey's solo feature debut, *Flesh* (1968), was the first of a trilogy of zero-budget, zeitgeist experiments which were roughly cut and badly acted by junkies, hustlers and transvestites. *Flesh*, *Trash* (1970) and *Heat* (1971), were erotic hymns to the enigmatic, narcissistic and charismatic Joe Dallesandro and his sculpted body, turning the male form into an object of affection to such an unparalleled degree that they soon became transgressive landmarks in gay cinema. Morrissey often wielded the camera himself in these and many of his other films.

While the Warhol-Morrissey collaboration *Women In Revolt* (1971) charted the travails of three transvestites, *Heat* nodded in the general direction that the director's career would follow in the 1970s, being a more polished narrative and an overwrought parody of *Sunset Blvd* (1950). *Flesh For Frankenstein* (1973) and *Blood For Dracula* (1974) were camp *Guignol* carnivals – delirious, kitsch spectaculars laden with gore. *The Hound Of The Baskervilles* (1978) was the first of Morrissey's films not to carry the "Andy Warhol Presents" brand. This Sherlock Holmes spoof, with Peter Cook and Dudley Moore, was sadly elementary in its clumsy script and clunky direction. Hustlers continued to be Morrissey's cinematic currency in *Madame Wang's* (1981), *Forty Deuce* (1982), and gangland cult item *Mixed Blood* (aka *Cocaine*, 1985). Morrissey has since extended his range to the Mafia (1988's *Spike Of Bensonhurst*) and to an eighteenth-century composer (1985's *Beethoven's Nephew*). Many of his latter-day films, however, belong to a very different underground than those of four decades ago: the straight-to-video ghetto. LH

Flesh 1968, 105 min
cast Joe Dallesandro, Geraldine Smith, Maurice Bradell, Louis Waldon, Geri Miller, Candy Darling, Jackie Curtis, Patti Darbanville *cin* Paul Morrissey

In which Joe Dallesandro turns tricks to pay for an abortion for the girlfriend of his lesbian wife. Morrissey's camera dwells lovingly on Dallesandro's buff, naked body while quietly and hypocritically tut-tutting the commodification of Dallesandro's studly flesh by the other characters.

Tender, shocking and melancholic, *Flesh* tests the boundaries of cinema, though it might just test the patience of a contemporary audience.

Trash 1970, 103 min
cast Joe Dallesandro, Holly Woodlawn, Jane Forth, Michael Sklar, Geri Miller, Andrea Feldman *cin* Paul Morrissey

With her stratospherically over-the-top performance, transvestite Holly Woodlawn easily steals the film from the nearly narcoleptic Dallesandro. An outrageous confluence of *cinéma vérité*, camp humour, shock tactics and conservative politics, it was also a clear influence on early John Waters.

Peter Mullan
UK, 1959–

As an actor, Peter Mullan has worked with such great British filmmakers as Ken Loach, Danny Boyle, Michael Winterbottom, John Boorman and Mike Figgis. As the director of two remarkable feature films, he has proved himself their peer.

A working-class Scottish lad, he was turned down by the National Film School, and instead studied social economics and drama at university. It wasn't until his mid-thirties that film work started to come in. His resolute, dogged, emotional performance in Loach's *My Name Is Joe* (1998) brought him international attention (and a best actor award at Cannes).

By then he had already directed three grim, intense short films – the best of which was *Fridge* (1995) – and his first feature, *Orphans* (1997). If the shorts are clearly indebted to Loach's social realism, *Orphans* takes its story of four siblings burying their mum somewhere else entirely, veering from melodrama to black comedy, from absurdism to out-and-out surrealism like a drunk's dark night of the soul.

Searing, original and out of control, *Orphans* was a bold debut; it may have helped Mullan purge his wilder instincts. At any rate, his systematic condemnation of Catholic repression in *The Magdalene Sisters* (2002) was all the more powerful for the focus and discipline with which it was filmed. TC

The Magdalene Sisters 2002, 119 min
cast Geraldine McEwan, Eileen Walsh, Anne-Marie Duff, Nora Jane Noone, Dorothy Duffy, Britta Smith *cin* Nigel Willoughby *m* Craig Armstrong

Set in Ireland in the early 1960s, this follows the experience of three teenage girls who make the mistake of being raped, or impregnated outside marriage, or simply too pretty, and are consequently packed off to a Magdalene laundry by their families for open-ended "purification". This is a prison movie, in effect, with the Roman Catholic Church holding the keys. It won the Golden Lion at the Venice Film Festival.

M

Robert Mulligan
US, 1925–

Overlooked by critics for decades, Robert Mulligan is finally being seen as a distinctive voice in post-war American cinema.

After war service as a radio officer, Mulligan studied radio communication while holding down a job as a copyboy at *The New York Times*. He then joined CBS as a messenger, working his way up to become a star director of television drama. Mulligan's first feature was *Fear Strikes Out* (1956), an intimate account of a baseball player's nervous breakdown. Steeped in Freudian symbolism and the father-son confrontation that characterizes 1950s Hollywood melodrama, *Fear Strikes Out* saw Anthony Perkins reaching for the quiet mania that would define his 1960s persona.

Though lacking the political commitment of post-war liberals like Stanley Kramer and Martin Ritt, Mulligan's sensitivity with personal dynamics and feeling for the past are clearly evident. *Love With The Proper Stranger* (1963) and *Baby, The Rain Must Fall* (1964) find melodrama reaching beyond the histrionic and visual excess of 1950s Sirk and Minnelli, generating what increasingly seems a "cooler", searching look. Starring Steve McQueen and, respectively, Natalie Wood and Lee Remick – all actors capable of quiet grace – and taking the jazz and rockabilly life as their backdrop, these works benefit from nuanced monochrome cinematography of their Italian-American and Texan small-town milieux.

The attention to historical detail and the American vernacular scene marks *To Kill A Mockingbird* (1962), producer Alan J. Pakula and Mulligan's most famous collaboration. *Inside Daisy Clover* (1965) saw Natalie Wood essaying the rise and decline of a 1930s musical star with subtle understatement. And *Up The Down Staircase* (1967) pivots around Sandy Dennis's strong turn as an idealistic teacher negotiating the tribulations of a public school in a New York slum neighbourhood.

In a New Hollywood of jazzier aesthetics and political commitment, *The Pursuit Of Happiness* (1970) follows Michael Sarrazin's odyssey from college boy to convict. If the result was too meditative for some, *Summer of '42* (1971) offered a nostalgic exploration of a teenager's rite of passage with a war widow, and became one of Mulligan's biggest hits. *The Other* (1972) tempered its pastoral 1930s settling with an eerie mood of disquiet as a young boy learns to empathize with the violent world around him. *Same Time, Next Year* (1978) charted a 25-year tryst between Ellen Burstyn and Alan Alda's adulterers with the literacy associated with 1930s romantic comedy. Mulligan's last film, *The Man In The Moon* (1991), was both Reese Witherspoon's debut and a return to a humanistic treatment of young love. RA

To Kill A Mockingbird 1962, 129 min, b/w
cast Gregory Peck, John Megna, Frank Overton, Rosemary Murphy, Ruth White, Mary Badham *cin* Russell Harlan *m* Elmer Bernstein

Adapting Harper Lee's novel of racial prejudice in Depression-era Mississippi, Mulligan, screenwriter Horton Foote and cinematographer Russell Harlan create a world inhabited by all the fears, desires and trinkets of childhood, as seen through the subjective eye of Mary Badham's child observer, Scout. Its bite-sized incidents recalling the action of memory and the television aesthetics of Mulligan's early career, few films make a more searching plea for childlike innocence in the modern world.

F.W. Murnau
Germany, 1888–1931

Friedrich Wilhelm Murnau is not just a poet of motion, but "the greatest film director the Germans have ever known" in the words of legendary critic Lotte Eisner. For some, modern cinema begins with Murnau.

After World War I, he formed a production company with actor Conrad Veidt and made his directorial debut, *Der Knabe in Blau* (*The Boy In Blue*, 1919). Of his twenty subsequent films, nine are lost, and four are masterpieces. *Nosferatu* (1922), a classic of German expressionism, put Murnau in the same premier league as Fritz Lang and G.W. Pabst. Heavy with shadows and fraught with dread, every frame is insinuated with that somnambulistic sense of being suspended between reverie and reality, an intoxicating sensation that would permeate much of Murnau's work. That impression of an alternative universe was evoked partly by the director's peerless use of real locations (rather than studio sets), resulting in a film that was neither wholly fantastic nor entirely naturalistic, but an alchemical fusion of artifice and verisimilitude. Magic, in other words. Murnau also made use of negative footage to uncanny effect.

With *The Last Laugh* (1924) Murnau made another giant step in the progress of cinema. He "unchained" the camera, allowing it to mimic the movements of a character with its own subjective point of view. He abandoned intertitles in favour of telling the story solely through images, and used miniatures, superimpositions and false perspective in scenes of everyday life to heighten reality to oneiric effect: a twilight zone dictated by dream logic. With its use of long takes, depth of field and fluent camerawork, *The Last Laugh* quickly became a must-see movie for awed cinematographers and directors. It brought Murnau to the attention of studio boss William Fox, who immediately offered him a contract. Murnau made two more films in

Germany, an adaptation of Molière's *Tartuffe* (1926) and *Faust* (1926), a near-masterpiece with a plethora of dazzling special effects which hit their spectacular heights with Faust and Mephistopheles' breathtaking flight over town and country.

In America, Murnau was granted artistic licence by Fox to make *Sunrise* (1927) and he created what is, according to *Cahiers du cinéma*, "the single greatest masterwork in the history of cinema". It was, however, a commercial disaster, and Murnau's creative freedom proved to be a chimera. A new ending was imposed upon *Four Devils* (1928), while *City Girl* (aka *Our Daily Bread*, 1930), was finished by another director. Murnau broke his contract with Fox and ultimately dipped into his own pocket to fund *Tabu* (1931). Initially directed with Robert Flaherty, who eventually left the project, it was another song of two lovers – a Polynesian Romeo and Juliet who escape from their elders when they decree that the girl must remain a virgin for the gods. Murnau's ballad of idyll and doom was his fourth and final masterpiece. He was killed in a car crash a week before the premiere. It was, in some ways, appropriate that the director died with silent cinema, as the clumsy technology of early sound films, which returned the medium to its static, theatrical roots may well have killed off the powers of a director who once declared that he wanted to rid cinema of the stage and the word. LH

Nosferatu (Nosferatu: eine Symphonie des Grauens) 1922, 88 min, b/w

cast Max Schreck, Alexander Granach, Gustav von Wangenheim, Greta Schröder *cin* Fritz Arno Wagner *m* James Bernard

With his cadaverous skull and hollowed-out eyes, Max Schreck is so convincing as the Dracula-like character Count Orlok that the movie *Shadow Of The Vampire* (2000) speculated, strangely plausibly, that the enigmatic actor really was a vampire. According to critic Lotte Eisner, the themes of repression and sexuality that flow throughout this definitive vampire movie reverberated in very personal ways for Murnau, whose homosexuality had to remain a dark secret due to Germany's punitive, homophobic laws.

Destroyed by the sun: the final death throes of the cadaverous Count Orlock (Max Schreck) in Murnau's *Nosferatu*.

The Last Laugh (Der letze Mann) 1924,
90 min, b/w

cast Emil Jannings, Maly Delschaft, Max Hiller, Emilie Kurz, Hans
Unterkircher, Olaf Storm *cin* Karl Freund *m* Guiseppe Becce

This masterpiece of flowing lyricism and heady invention
tells the tale of a broken man, a demoted hotel porter
(Jannings). The very first shot has the camera whizzing
down in a lift and darting across the lobby and through
the doors of the hotel in which the film is set, a shot
apparently accomplished with the use of a bicycle. In a
later scene, Murnau audaciously attached the camera to
Freund's body, to ingeniously convey Jannings's drunken,
woozy stupor.

Sunrise: A Story Of Two Humans 1927,
95 min, b/w

cast George O'Brien, Janet Gaynor, Margaret Livingstone, Bodil Rosing,
J. Farrell MacDonald *cin* Charles Rosher, Karl Struss *m* Hugo Riesenfeld

A village man is convinced by a city temptress to drown
his wife. He then has second thoughts. Murnau constructed his impressive sets, of the village and the city,
on twenty acres of the Fox studio backlot, and joined the
two locations with a rail track a mile long. This facilitated
one of the most celebrated single shots in cinema history
as a tram trundles from the country, past a lake, straight
into the bustling heart of the city. *Sunrise* hums with
similarly dazzling innovations, but it's much more than
the sum of its technical parts. This is a film that can make
a modern audience swoon in admiration.

Myrick & Sánchez
Daniel Myrick: US, 1964–
Eduardo Sánchez: Cuba, 1968–

Myrick and Sánchez made the most notorious,
and successful, low-budget feature ever. Both
filmmakers from a young age, they met while studying film at the University of Central Florida. Myrick
cut his teeth with cinematography and editing on
the fringes of the industry, while Sánchez directed
unreleased student films. *The Blair Witch Project*
(1999) began as a website telling the "true" story
of a series of murders attributed to an eighteenth-
century witch ostracized by a Maryland community. Convincing in its historical and documentary
veracity, the website rapidly generated a cult following. By the time the film appeared, there was
worldwide interest and it made a fortune for Myrick
and Sánchez (its estimated $60,000 budget gener-
ated worldwide revenue of close to $250 million).
Few contemporary filmmakers have toyed with cinema's contract between artifice and experience with
such shrewdness and such eerie precision. Despite
rumours of a *Blair Witch* sequel or prequel, subsequent work from the duo has been slow to appear,
although Sánchez directed solo in 2006 on the sci-fi
monster movie *Altered*. RA

The Blair Witch Project 1999, 81 min

cast Heather Donahue, Joshua Leonard, Michael C. Williams *cin* Neal
Fredericks *m* Tony Cora

Taking its premise from an urban legend and following a
group of filmmakers intrigued, then traumatized, by what
they find in the woods, this ragged, light-blasted conundrum of tape and Super 8 returned horror cinema to its
psychological premises. Tapping into millennial anxiety,
Myrick and Sánchez reiterated the role of the woman as
the traditional vessel of American horror. The result chilled
a generation to the core.

Mira Nair

India, 1957–

Mira Nair was originally a documentarian, and the documentary maker's commitment to making sense of life as it is lived powerfully underpins her vivid, often beautiful films. Influenced by the Italian neo-realist filmmakers, Nair's films dramatize and document cultures, their frequent clashes, misunderstandings and connections. Another preoccupation is the tensions between the traditional and the modern.

Nair studied at Delhi University and then at Harvard, where her thesis project was a documentary short, *Jama Masjid Street Journal* (1979), about a traditional Muslim community in Old Delhi. Other early documentaries include *India Cabaret* (1985), about two striptease dancers, and *Children Of A Desired Sex* (1987), about the abortion of female foetuses. Nair's international breakthrough was the drama *Salaam Bombay!* (1988), an outstanding debut film which won the Camera d'Or at Cannes for best first feature. Her next film, *Mississippi Masala* (1991), was about an Indian family forced to leave Uganda during the rule of Idi Amin who settle in the American South. She also directed a short film inspired by the death of the South African Communist leader Chris Hani, *The Day The Mercedes Became A Hat* (1993).

The Perez Family (1995) was a Hollywood studio melodrama about Cuban families coming to Miami. *My Own Country* (1998) was another story of immigrants in contemporary America. Nair returned to her documentary roots with *The Laughing Club Of India* (1999), which explored the phenomenon of clubs where people meet for organized therapeutic laughter. Nair then experienced her biggest success with the lavish *Monsoon Wedding* (2001), a teeming family-gathering movie in which all the disparate strands were beautifully integrated. In 2002, Nair contributed a piece to *11'09"01*, in which eleven directors looked at the effects of 9/11 on people around the world. The lively *Vanity Fair* (2004), an adaptation of a classic nineteenth-century novel, was a change of direction. Starring Reese Witherspoon as plucky social climber Becky Sharp, it looked stunning but lacked Nair's usual incision. *The Namesake* (2006) was a return to form and to Nair's perennial theme of the challenges facing Indian immigrants abroad – in this case New York. JC

Salaam Bombay! 1988, 113 min
cast Safiq Syed, Sarfuddin Qurassi,Raju Barnad, Raghubir Yadav, Aneeta Kanwar *cin* Sandi Sissel *m* L. Subramaniam

A classic slice-of-life realist drama about a child's journey from innocence to experience, *Salaam Bombay!* follows the life of a street kid called Krishna who is abandoned by his family and ends up in the Bombay slums. Through a panoply of characters, city life is revealed in all its energy and desperation. The film was shot in Bombay using child actors recruited from the streets.

Monsoon Wedding 2001, 113 min
cast Naseeruddin Shah, Lillete Dubey, Shefali Shetty, Vijay Raaz, Tilotama Shome, Vasundhara Das *cin* Declan Quinn *m* Mychael Danna

A number of stories intertwine as an upper-class family in Delhi prepare for an extravagant wedding. The film explores familiar Nair territory: culture clash and the relationship between tradition and modernity. Luxuriating in wedding paraphernalia – from flower petals to henna tattoos – the film nevertheless has a rough home-movie quality imparted by the loose hand-held camerawork.

Hideo Nakata

Japan, 1961–

Largely devoid of new ideas, Hollywood studios have never hesitated in simply reheating and re-serving the proven hits of other countries, and in Hideo Nakata they've found a gold mine. Never exactly simpatico with subtitles, American audiences didn't get the chance to see Nakata's original version of *Ring* (1998) – a tale of a viral videotape and the highest-grossing Japanese horror film of all time – or his equally unnerving *Dark Water* (2002) in cinemas, and instead had to settle for the big-budget remakes, which couldn't match the originals for slow-burn intensity or subcutaneous dread.

Although he's best-known as a leading light of J-horror (his 1996 debut, *Ghost Actress*, prowled a haunted movie set), Nakata has in fact ranged across many genres and tones, directing *Sleeping Bride* (2000), a sweet-souled teenage fairy tale, *Sadistic And Masochistic* (2000), a documentary on the porn director Masaru Konuma, and *Chaos* (1999), a Tokyo *noir* which spun a convoluted netting of double- and triple-crosses.

Both based on novels by Kôji Suzuki, *Ring* and *Dark Water* also share a similar emotional core – a fragile single mother's guilt-ridden relationship with her only child – and divine fear from the mythic and monstrous properties of water (tracing their respective mysteries back to a disused well and a water tower). Nakata himself helmed the Dreamworks sequel-to-the-remake *The Ring Two* (2005), in which a high point of sorts is reached when the heroine and her son are besieged in their car by a crazed herd of computer-generated deer. Perhaps permanently lured by the siren call of Hollywood, Nakata has several English-language films in the works; thankfully, only one is a remake. JW

Ring (Ringu) 1998, 95 min

cast Nanako Matsushima, Miki Nakatani, Hiroyuki Sanada, Yuko Takeuchi, Hitomi Sato *cin* Ichiro Hayashi *m* Kenji Kawai

A grainy avant-garde video is killing its viewers, who are later found with their faces contorted into Munch-like masks of fear. News reporter Asakawa (Nanako Matsushima) begins to investigate the curse, endangering her gruff ex-husband and their young son. Nakata's instant horror classic works by gradually increasing the levels of expertly calibrated dread and withholding visual information, and has a fiendish climax that matches David Cronenberg's *Videodrome* (1983) in its uncanny televisual terror.

Dark Water (Honogurai mizu no soko kara) 2002, 101 min

cast Hitomi Kuroki, Rio Kanno, Mirei Oguchi, Asami Mizukawa, Fumiyo Kohinata *cin* Junichiro Hayashi *m* Kenji Kawai

Mired in a child-custody battle, Yoshimi (Hitomi Kuroki) moves with her daughter to a dank, underlit apartment complex where the spectacular plumbing problems may, in fact, be the effluvia of an angry ghost. A bracing study of Yoshimi's isolation and paranoia, the movie implicitly sifts the guilty, sorrowful fallout of a broken home; its jolts are all the more forceful for being delivered from a recognizable emotional source.

Mikio Naruse

Japan, 1905–69

Despite being little-known in the West, Tokyo-born Mikio Naruse was one of the most prolific and accomplished Japanese directors of the twentieth century, chalking up nearly ninety films in four decades.

Although his earlier, pre-war movies, such as

Wife, Be Like A Rose (1935), are undoubtedly more experimental and visually dynamic, Naruse's most interesting films were produced during the 1950s, Japanese cinema's golden era. Many can be described as *shomin-geki* – tragic working-class dramas – which often focus on a female protagonist in an unfolding family saga. This is one of several factors that have led commentators to compare his output to that of Yasujiro Ozu. And though there are undoubtedly narrative parallels between Ozu's *Tokyo Story* (1953) and Naruse's heartbreaking *Sound Of The Mountain* (1954), it is perhaps more telling that both Ozu and Naruse, as well as many of their contemporaries, were working within a nation in flux.

In post-war Japan, tradition and modernity were battling for supremacy, and this was a tension played out each day, in every city and town, behind the closed shoji screens of the family unit. Both Naruse and Ozu rendered this cultural transition in a rich palette of visual metaphors, wherein traditional and modern costume, as well as scene settings, could be used to reflect the conflicts of values between younger and older generations and between husbands and wives. In Naruse's films the results are often bleak and depressing, perhaps echoing the hardships of his own working-class background. Yet they remain a compelling and powerful body of work. PB

Repast (Meshi) 1951, 97 min, b/w

cast Setsuko Hara, Ken Uehara, Yukiko Shimazaki, Yôko Sugi, Akiko Kazami *cin* Masao Tamai *m* Fumio Hayasaka

When a thoroughly modern niece (Shimazaki) comes to stay, the gulf between Michiyo (Hara) and her drippy husband (Uehara) becomes all too apparent. Hara's performance is breathtaking and culminates in an edge-of-the-seat "should-I-stay-or-should-I-go?" scene, made all the more dramatic by the accompanying thud of a ceremonial drum. The real star of the show, however, is the family's little manx cat.

Sound Of The Mountain (Yama no oto) 1954, 96 min, b/w

cast Setsuko Hara, Sô Yamamura, Ken Uehara, Yôko Sugi, Teruko Nagaoka *cin* Masao Tamai *m* Ichirô Saitô

Based on the novel by Nobel-winning author Yasunari Kawabata, this film makes no attempt to offer hope to a family as it is gradually split apart. The lead female "desperate housewife" role is again taken by the wonderful Setsuko Hara, though the tale is equally about her ageing father-in-law (Yamamura) and the solace the pair find in each other's friendship. A beautifully played, beautifully shot classic.

Gregory Nava

US, 1949–

Born in San Diego, on the Mexican–US border, and of Mexican–Basque heritage, Gregory Nava was a prize-winning UCLA film student and became one of the first Latin American directors in Hollywood, winning plaudits (and an Academy Award nomination) for his second feature, *El norte* (*The North*, 1983). Not all Nava's work has been overtly political – his debut feature, the micro-budgeted *The Confessions Of Amans* (1977), was a medieval fable, and his third feature, the torrid *A Time Of Destiny* (1988), was out and out melodrama. Indeed, he is actually a stylized, visually adventurous filmmaker. But inevitably the ambitious generational saga *My Family* (1995), the biopic *Selena* (1997) and the TV series *American Family* (2002) have assumed more cultural importance as a barometer of Latin American integration than for their artistic merits. *Selena*, about the murdered Tejano singer Selena Quintanilla-Pérez, was a breakthrough role for Jennifer Lopez in America. Nava also has a co-writing credit on Salma Hayek's Kahlo biopic, *Frida* (2002). TC

El norte (The North) 1983, 139 min

cast Zaide Silvia Gutierrez, David Villalpando, Ernesto Gomez Cruz, Lupe Ontiveros *cin* James Glennon *m* The Folkloristas, Malecio Martinez

Written with Nava's long-term partner Anna Thomas, this is the moving story of two Guatemalan teenagers, a brother and sister who make the perilous journey through Mexico and over the border to start a new life in the US – the north of the title. A ground-breaking film for its downbeat reverse angle on American life, *El norte* is surprisingly lyrical in its approach, with an epic poetic style reminiscent of John Ford.

Ronald Neame
UK, 1911–

The history of British cinema could be told through the prism of Ronald Neame's sixty-year career. Born into the business – his mother was a silent film star and his father a director – Neame got his first job in film in his teens working on Alfred Hitchcock's *Blackmail* (1929) when the silent film became a talkie midway through the shoot. He rapidly established a reputation as a cinematographer on dozens of films – including the George Bernard Shaw adaptations *Pygmalion* (1938) and *Major Barbara* (1941). David Lean edited the latter and the two men worked together on Lean's directorial debut (with Noel Coward), *In Which We Serve* (1942), before forming a company, Cineguild, with producer Anthony Havelock-Allan. Neame photographed three films for Lean, was the co-screenwriter on *Brief Encounter* (1945) and produced the Dickens adaptations *Great Expectations* (1946) and *Oliver* (1948).

When the two fell out, Neame turned to direction, making a confident debut with the atmospheric thriller *Take My Life* (1947). Neame was always an unflashy director, allowing his actors the scope to give strong performances. His best films were made in the 1950s. *The Card* (1952) is a skilful adaptation of Arnold Bennett's rags-to-riches saga starring Alec

Guinness (a Neame regular), while *The Man Who Never Was* (1957) tells the real-life wartime saga of how a British naval intelligence plot succeeded in duping the Nazis. Best of all was *The Horse's Mouth* (1958) an adaptation of Joyce Carey's rumbustious novel in which Alec Guinness was at his best as the curmudgeonly boho painter Gulley Jimson. Guinness gave a less effective character turn as the irascible Scottish officer in *Tunes Of Glory* (1960), handing command of his regiment over to John Mills.

The 1960s was Neame's leanest decade but among several duds *The Chalk Garden* (1964) and *The Prime Of Miss Jean Brodie* (1969) both stand out as solidly professional and raised above the ordinary by strong performances. Neame had had mixed fortunes in Hollywood but with *The Poseidon Adventure* (1972) he hit the jackpot. This nail-biting action saga in which an ocean-going liner is hit by a freak wave and ten trapped passengers manage to survive launched a flotilla of disaster movies and gave Shelley Winters fans a shot in the arm. The film's success led to further Hollywood outings of which the best are *The Odessa File* (1974), a thriller about a protected Nazi assimilated within post-war German industry, and *Hopscotch* (1980), a lame comedy with Walter Matthau as an embittered CIA operative. LH

The Horse's Mouth 1958, 95 min

cast Alec Guinness, Kay Walsh, Renee Houston, Mike Morgan, Robert Coote, Ernest Thesiger *cin* Arthur Ibbetson *m* Kenneth V. Jones

Not as gutsy as the original novel, this is, nonetheless, a lively exploration of the painterly psyche – up there with Vincente Minnelli's *Lust For Life* (1956) and Robert Day's *The Rebel* (1961). Guinness, who also scripted the movie, gives his all as the obsessive and decidedly un-PC Gulley Jimson, maintained in his pursuit of art by a stalwart band of British character actors. The London locations are a delight and John Bratby's paintings provide the final touch of authenticity.

The Poseidon Adventure 1972, 117 min

cast Gene Hackman, Ernest Borgnine, Red Buttons, Shelley Winters, Carol Lynley, Roddy McDowell *cin* Harold E. Stine *m* John Williams

The Poseidon Adventure is arguably the greatest disaster movie of the 1970s. Neame was clearly the right man to steer this behemoth through the choppy waters of a big-budget production. In both the small scenes of domestic tension and the mighty set pieces, as Reverend Scott (Gene Hackman) tries to lead survivors through the hull of an upturned cruise ship to light and safety, the director maintains a sure touch.

Jean Negulesco
Romania, 1900–93

Dubbed "The Prince of Melodrama" at a 1984 retrospective, Jean Negulesco excelled at the torrid emotionalism of 1940s star vehicles. In the 1920s he was painting in Paris, reputedly at Modigliani's studio. In 1927 he went to America to exhibit, drifting to Hollywood in the early 1930s where he did second-unit work on *A Farewell To Arms* (1932). After some screenwriting work, he was chosen by Warner Bros to direct *The Maltese Falcon* (1941), but was fired in favour of John Huston.

Singapore Woman (1941) was his first directing credit. If this was a piece of tawdry exotica, *The Mask Of Dimitrios* (1944) began a string of mature, sophisticated melodramas featuring world-weary Continentals amid a textured and smoke-filled *mise en scène*. Negulesco was good at steering studio divas through ersatz dream worlds. Resurrecting the shadowy half-life of Warner Bros' *Casablanca*, *The Conspirators* (1944) saw Paul Henreid's Resistance hero fetch up in Lisbon to have a fling with Hedy Lamarr. In *Humoresque* (1946) Joan Crawford plays the jaded arts patron to John Garfield's surly violin-playing genius. *Three Strangers* (1947) was an allegory revolving around a sweepstake ticket. The Oscar-winning *Johnny Belinda* (1948), starring Jane Wyman as a deaf-mute, seems shrill compared with these subtle gems.

Moving to 20th Century Fox in 1948, Negulesco had brief epiphanies with *Road House* (1948), starring Ida Lupino, the dank *Britannia Mews* (1949), featuring Maureen O'Hara, and *Three Came Home* (1950), in which Claudette Colbert suffered nobly in a Japanese internment camp. But the CinemaScope 1950s were not Negulesco's era and despite hits like Marilyn Monroe's *How To Marry A Millionaire* (1953) and the Dorothy Maguire weepie *Three Coins In The Fountain* (1954), the old magic was no longer there. RA

The Mask Of Dimitrios 1944, 95 min, b/w

cast Zachary Scott, Peter Lorre, Sydney Greenstreet, Faye Emerson, George Tobias *cin* Arthur Edeson *m* Adolph Deutsch

Shot like *Casablanca* by Warner Bros cinematographer Arthur Edeson and pairing *The Maltese Falcon's* Peter Lorre and Sydney Greenstreet, this moody Eric Ambler adaptation unfolds in flashback as mystery writer Lorre pieces together the murder of Zachary Scott's seedy criminal mastermind amid chiaroscuro sets and fatalistic dialogue.

Roy William Neill
US, 1887–1946

Born at sea off the coast of Ireland (his father was the ship's captain), Roland de Gostrie adopted his anglicized stage name as a child performer. He became an assistant to movie pioneer Thomas Ince in 1915, and directed his first film, *A Corner In Colleens*, a year later. Neill made 150 features, forty of them silent, and all of them B-movies. He worked at MGM, Columbia and Universal, and for five years in Britain, for Gainsborough and Warner Bros-First

National (coming within a hair's breadth of directing a Launder-Gilliat script which Alfred Hitchcock would turn into *The Lady Vanishes*). Returning to Hollywood when war broke out, Neill worked at Universal on several horror movies – most notably *Frankenstein Meets The Wolf Man* (1943) – and was assigned by the studio to take over its Sherlock Holmes series, starring Basil Rathbone and Nigel Bruce. He distinguished himself as both director and producer, crafting eleven of these crisp, atmospheric updates on Conan Doyle. Neill died in 1946, shortly after completing *Black Angel*, an effective *film noir* starring Dan Duryea and Peter Lorre. TC

The Scarlet Claw 1944, 74 min, b/w

cast Basil Rathbone, Nigel Bruce, Gerald Hamer, Paul Cavanagh, Arthur Hohl, Miles Mander *cin* George Robinson *m* Paul Sawtell

Although Neill toned down the World War II propaganda aspects of the Holmes series, he infused these contemporary films with the Victorian atmospherics of the original stories, so that even this Canadian-set yarn (which Neill co-wrote) has the authentic snap and crackle. Purists may balk at Nigel Bruce's buffoonish take on Dr Watson, but the contrast with the lean, cerebral, curt (but still affectionate) Rathbone plays very well. Stylish and inventive, this is arguably the best of a dependably entertaining series.

Mike Newell
UK, 1942–

Mike Newell has made a speciality of depicting men and women trying to liberate themselves from the strictures of their worlds. A stage and television director, Newell trained at Granada Television from 1964. Along with the likes of Ken Loach and Mike Leigh, he was one of a generation of filmmakers that cut its teeth on soaps such as *Coronation Street* and plays by John Osborne, Jack Rosenthal and David Hare.

After the success of the made-for-TV adaptation *The Man In The Iron Mask* (1977), Newell directed *The Awakening* (1980), a derivative genre horror film pairing Susannah York with Charlton Heston and revolving around the excavation of an Egyptian mummy's tomb. Tracing the notorious case of a New Zealand farmer who shot several people dead and went on the run in the 1940s, *Bad Blood* (1981) was more effective. In the Ruth Ellis biopic *Dance With A Stranger* (1984) Newell turned to the exploration of British manners and mores that would distinguish his biggest hit, the comedy phenomenon *Four Weddings And A Funeral* (1994).

The Good Father (1986) starred Anthony Hopkins as a disgruntled father who embarks on a legal battle to even the odds with his ex-wife and to see his son. If it eventually cops out on the negative implications of its war of the sexes, it nevertheless left its post-feminist audience feeling uncomfortable. Based on the Timothy Mo novel, 1988's *Soursweet* essayed the tensions of being Chinese in modern Britain and added to a strand of British output that valiantly challenged Thatcherism's monocultural assumptions. Then came *Enchanted April* (1991), a flawed indulgence in which Joan Plowright, Miranda Richardson, Polly Walker and Josie Lawrence were 1920s Brits ensconced in an Italian villa.

With *Four Weddings* and *An Awfully Big Adventure* (1995) – a black comedy (also starring Hugh Grant) about backstage love triangles in post-war Liverpool – Newell won over both audiences and critics. Moving to Hollywood, the director was entrusted with big-budget, starry vehicles, beginning with the intelligent Mafia exposé *Donnie Brasco* (1997). But 1999's *Pushing Tin* was an uncertain hybrid of macho posturing in which John Cusack's strutting air-traffic controller clashes with Billy Bob Thornton's backwoods Iron John figure. Giving Thornton his head, it was a mishmash of actors in search of a theme.

Mona Lisa Smile (2003) found Julia Roberts coaching the girls at a repressive 1950s American college in how to achieve self-determination. In 2005, Newell became the first British director to helm an entry in the Harry Potter franchise with *Harry Potter And The Goblet Of Fire*. As a director, Newell has shown himself especially adept at emotional drama, humorous satire and the serendipities of life and performance. RA

Dance With A Stranger 1984, 102 min

cast Miranda Richardson, Rupert Everett, Ian Holm, Matthew Carroll, Tom Chadbon *cin* Peter Hannan *m* Richard Hartley

Essaying the 1955 case of Ruth Ellis, the last woman to be hanged in Britain, this dingy, claustrophobic film catches the patina of British life as post-war austerity was turning to post-Suez modernity. But Miranda Richardson's nervy performance also asks whether things have really changed for women forced to choose between patriarchy and the options promised in 1980s Britain.

Four Weddings And A Funeral 1994, 117 min

cast Hugh Grant, James Fleet, Simon Callow, John Hannah, Kristin Scott Thomas, David Bower *cin* Michael Coulter *m* Richard Rodney Bennett

Finding bemused bachelor Hugh Grant mired in the social norms of green-belt Britain, this hugely successful, extremely funny film adeptly pricked the bubble of Little England. However, it was never less than an affectionate mirror of 1990s Britain as it courted a prevailing fondness for a panoply of eccentrics, National Trust properties and romantic love.

Donnie Brasco 1997, 126 min

cast Al Pacino, Johnny Depp, Michael Madsen, Bruno Kirby, James Russo, Anne Heche, Zeljko Ivanek, Gerry Becker *cin* Peter Sova *m* Patrick Doyle

Steeped in the streetwise hieroglyphics of Paul Attanasio's script and the washed-out colours of cinematographer Peter Sova's Brooklyn, this is Mike Newell's best film, a compelling character study in which Johnny Depp's undercover cop is taken under ageing Mafioso Al Pacino's wing

and is ethically compromised by the experience. For its strength and assurance, it recalls the New York thrillers of Sidney Lumet.

Fred Niblo
US, 1874–1948

Although he only came to direction in his midforties, Fred Niblo was responsible for a handful of distinguished silent films, most famously the spectacular epic *Ben-Hur: A Tale Of The Christ* (1925), but he failed to survive the transition into the sound era. His career began in vaudeville, working for the legendary "father" of American musical comedy George M. Cohan, whose sister he married. He moved into the movies in 1917, joining the company of producer Thomas Ince, for whom his second wife Enid Bennett worked as an actress. Niblo continued to act in both his own films and in two opposite his wife, directed by Victor Schertzinger. A couple of films for Douglas Fairbanks, *The Mark Of Zorro* (1920) and *The Three Musketeers* (1921), stand out as among the best of the great swashbuckler's career. He provided similarly intelligent support for Rudolph Valentino in the bullfighting romance *Blood And Sand* (1922) and for Ramon Novarro in *Thy Name Is Woman* (1924) and *The Red Lily* (1924), the latter a classic tearjerker about separated young lovers in which Enid Bennett gives one of her strongest performances.

Ben-Hur, starring Novarro, was Niblo's finest hour. Based on Lew Wallace's bestselling 1880 novel, it tells of the friendship and then bloody rivalry between Jewish prince Judah Ben-Hur and the Roman Messala against the backdrop of Rome and Palestine at the time of Jesus. Shot in Italy and California for the newly formed MGM, *Ben-Hur* took two years to complete and was the most expensive silent film ever made. More than one second-unit director was involved but Niblo should be credited for turning a potential disaster into a major success. Subsequent films included the Greta Garbo vehicle *The Temptress* (1926), *Camille* (1926), starring Norma Talmadge in the title role, and *The Enemy* (1927) with Lillian Gish. But Niblo's career as a director gradually ground to a halt and in his final years he returned to acting. RB

Ben-Hur: A Tale Of The Christ 1925, 143 min, b/w and col

cast Ramon Novarro, May McAvoy, Francis X. Bushman, Betty Bronson, Claire McDowell *cin* Clyde De Vinna

A spectacular combination of action and piety that more than holds its own against William Wyler's 1959 remake. Novarro's sultry athleticism is countered by Francis X. Bushman's tough-guy Messala, but it's the action set pieces that really stick in the memory – the battle at sea and above all the famous and incredibly thrilling chariot race.

Andrew Niccol

New Zealand, 1964–

Screenwriter of *The Truman Show*, about a man whose entire life is a made-for-television construct, Andrew Niccol is clearly fascinated by the appearance or simulation of perfection; in his still-young career, he has sought to create pristine surfaces in order to break them. *Gattaca* (1997) imagines a future apartheid between test-tube babies with perfect DNA and naturally conceived imperfects (with Uma Thurman as the exemplar of genetic supremacy). In *S1m0ne* (2002), Niccol concocts a flat-footed media satire, full of in-jokes, about a past-it director (Al Pacino) who creates a computer-simulated superstar actress. ("I am the death of the real", she declares, appropriating Baudrillard.) With the confused, distended *Lord Of War* (2005), Niccol changed gears somewhat, making a quasi-sympathetic protagonist out of an amoral international arms dealer (Nicolas Cage). Once again, the writer-director showed that he's unafraid to lunge for the "big subjects", but the jury is out as to whether or not he can handle them once they're in his grasp. JW

Gattaca 1997, 101 min

cast Ethan Hawke, Uma Thurman, Alan Arkin, Jude Law, Loren Dean, Gore Vidal, Ernest Borgnine *cin* Slawomir Idziak *m* Michael Nyman

In a not-so-distant totalitarian future where genetically perfect "Valids" lord over flawed "In-valids", myopic would-be astronaut Jerome (Ethan Hawke) swaps identities with a paralysed "Valid" (Jude Law). Niccol's debut as a writer-director pleases with its neo-retro production design and makes surprisingly few concessions to generic action thrills, but it's short on ideas and coherence and gets side-tracked by a lame murder-mystery plot.

Maurizio Nichetti

Italy, 1948–

One of Italy's favourite comedy performers and directors, Maurizio Nichetti deftly elides silent slapstick buffoonery with elaborate plot constructions. His directorial debut, *Ratataplan* (1979), which silently charted the comic misadventures of a waiter, was a hilarious marriage of Jacques Tati and Buster Keaton. In the grotesque media satire *Ho fatto splash* (1980), Nichetti's was the only character who didn't speak, while in *Tomorrow We Dance* (1983) he finally got to utter in one of his own movies. With *The Icicle Thief* (1989) and *Volere volare* (*To Want To Fly*, 1991) the director finally translated his phenomenal domestic popularity into international success. It was, however, short-lived. Comedies such as *Stefano Quantestori* (1993) and *Luna e l'altra* (*Luna And The Others*, 1996) graced cinemas in his homeland, but in the rest of the world, Maurizio Nichetti is conspicuous by his absence. LH

The Icicle Thief (Ladri di saponette) 1989, 98 min

cast Maurizio Nichetti, Caterina Sylos Labini, Heidi Komarek, Frederico Rizzo, Renato Scarpa *cin* Maria Battistoni *m* Manuel De Sica, Franco Godi

A director called Maurizio Nichetti is interviewed on Italian television to discuss his neo-realist homage, *The Icicle Thief*, which is being shown on TV for the first time. After a power outage, the worlds of crass commercials and austere art film merge, as a blonde model from a car advert wanders into the black-and-white movie, with her colour intact. The resulting chaos is a riot of technical and narrative innovation, stuffed with cheap gags, expensive effects and priceless satire.

Volere volare (To Want To Fly) 1991, 96 min

cast Angela Finocchiaro, Maurizio Nichetti, Mariella Valentini, Patrizio Roversi, Remo Remotti *cin* Roberto Brega

Maurizio (Nichetti), a shy sound engineer, meets a hooker called Martina who has cornered the market in kinky requests. On their first date, our hero's hands morph into two cartoon characters with lives of their own and the rest of his body soon follows. Frisky and charming, the film's dazzling technical innovations don't quite find their analogue in a script which soon exhausts its supplies of narrative twists.

Mike Nichols

Germany, 1931–

While still a student at the University of Chicago, Mike Nichols got involved with the Compass Players, a highly influential theatre group that focused on improvisational comedy. Fellow student Elaine May was also a member and the two went on to form a ground-breaking comedy duo which culminated in their 1960 stage show *An Evening With Mike Nichols And Elaine May*, which ran for eight months on Broadway. The couple ended their performing partnership shortly after, with Nichols gravitating towards theatre direction. Responsible for several Broadway hits throughout the 1960s, he formed a particularly successful relationship with comedy playwright Neil Simon.

Perhaps unsurprisingly, his work in the cinema has focused on fast-talking comedies with a satiric edge that allow plenty of room for acting pyrotechnics. *Who's Afraid Of Virginia Woolf?* (1966) and *The Graduate* (1967) opened his movie career with a pair of cinematic aces that few directors have ever matched. The director crashed spectacularly down to earth with the unfairly vilified *Catch-22* (1970). This ambitious anti-war satire, based on Joseph Heller's bestselling novel, had some extremely funny performances within its labyrinthine narrative structure. Nichols plugged back into the cultural mainframe and critical favour with an astute look

Z

at contemporary sexual mores in *Carnal Knowledge* (1971). But his success was short-lived. The sub-aquatic curio *The Day Of The Dolphin* (1973) and the frantic Warren Beatty/Jack Nicholson farce *The Fortune* (1975) were judged unloved duds. Nichols didn't even complete his next movie, abruptly abandoning the Neil Simon-scripted *Bogart Slept Here* two weeks into the project. He didn't make another fictional feature film for eight years, returning instead to the theatre and television.

The director regained his mojo with *Silkwood* (1983). But this was a different Mike Nichols, his camera muted and unobtrusive. This well-mannered, self-effacing style worked to subtle effect in the Meryl Streep melodrama about a whistle-blowing nuclear-facility worker, but it has often resulted in bland mediocrity. *Biloxi Blues* (1988), *Working Girl* (1988), *Postcards From The Edge* (1990) and *The Birdcage* (1996) all had their hard edges softened out resulting in mainstream anonymity. The latter was Nichols' official reunion with Elaine May as scriptwriter, though she had been his uncredited script doctor since the disappointing *Heartburn* (1986). The critical verdict on their Bill Clinton satire *Primary Colors* (1998) was "close, but no cigar", while *Wolf* (1994) exploited Jack Nicholson's lupine qualities to very little effect. And Nichols has produced a couple of authentic turkeys: the senti-mental *Regarding Henry* (1991), about a brain-damaged lawyer, and *What Planet Are You From?* (2000), a lame sci-fi comedy. The TV drama *Wit* (2001), about a terminally ill academic (subtly played by Emma Thompson), was a sensitive return to form. Nichols has also continued to thrive on Broadway, winning more Tonys than any other director, though his pedestrian adaptation of Patrick Marber's stage play *Closer* (2004) – a cynical foray into the battle of the sexes – was not the *Carnal Knowledge* for the twenty-first century that it could have been. LH

Who's Afraid Of Virginia Woolf? 1966, 132 min
cast Elizabeth Taylor, Richard Burton, George Segal, Sandy Dennis *cin* Haskell Wexler *m* Alex North

Nichols was chosen by Elizabeth Taylor to direct her as the bitter wife of Richard Burton's dipso history professor. The couple then drunkenly eviscerate each other in front of guests George Segal and Sandy Dennis. Haskell Wexler's Oscar-winning monochrome photography lacquers another layer of intensity to Edward Albee's corruscating text, while the fact that the whole shouting match is acted out by a tempestuous real-life couple adds a frisson of voyeuristic pleasure.

The Graduate 1967, 108 min
cast Anne Bancroft, Dustin Hoffman, Katharine Ross, William Daniels, Murray Hamilton *cin* Robert Surtees *m* Paul Simon, David Grusin

In its withering attack on the materialist values of middle-class Americans and its courting of a youth audience

Who's afraid? Richard Burton gets Elizabeth Taylor and George Segal in his sights in *Who's Afraid Of Virginia Woolf?*

through its Simon and Garfunkel soundtrack, this is one of the defining Hollywood films of the 1960s. It also launched the career of Dustin Hoffmann as the freaked-out, shambling graduate of the title who is torn between predatory suburban housewife Mrs Robinson (Anne Bancroft) and her good-as-gold daughter (Katharine Ross).

Carnal Knowledge 1971, 97 min

cast Jack Nicholson, Candice Bergen, Art Garfunkel, Ann-Margret, Rita Moreno, Cynthia O'Neal, Carol Kane *cin* Giuseppe Rotunno

Jules Feiffer's caustic script charts the bitter disintegration of relationships over the years between boorish college friends – cocksure sexist Jack Nicholson and insecure sexist Art Garfunkel – and their conquests, Candice Bergen and Ann-Margret. One of the first films to recognize that counterculture ideals had tragically curdled, Nichol's scabrous comedy is a surprisingly adult critique of chauvinistic male assumptions about women.

Gaspar Noé
Argentina, 1963–

The latest bad boy of French cinema was actually born in Buenos Aires to an artist father and bourgeois family, and he arrived in Paris via New York. Gaspar Noé attended film school, briefly studied philosophy and formed his own cottage film industry, wherein he writes, directs, edits and operates the camera. The forty intense minutes of his short film *Carné* (1991) zeroed in on a butcher who looks after his mentally handicapped daughter. He fatally misinterprets the blood on her skirt caused by menstruation, immediately comes to the conclusion that she's been raped and kills an innocent passer-by. The winner of the Cannes short film prize, he substantially reworked it into *Seul contre tous* (*I Stand Alone*, 1998). Filmed over three years and shot whenever the director could scrape together enough money to buy film stock, Noé's feature debut was a *succès de scandale* on its release. He relentlessly pounded the reeling audience with salvo after salvo of ferociously sick imagery. After making a hardcore short to promote safe sex, *Sodomites* (1998), Noé managed to top his outrageous debut in 2002. "*Irreversible* might be the most homophobic movie ever made" and "one of the nastiest films ever released" were two typical reactions. The bone of critical contention was a nine-minute rape scene, shot in one unflinching take.

Critics put him in the same brat pack as nihilistic novelist Michel Houellebecq, and the same question has been asked of both – are they more than the sum of their shock tactics? Noé seems to fancy himself as a bit of a philosopher: a quote from Friedrich Nietzsche appears on one of *Seul contre tous*'s intertitles. And there may be a connection, as all of Noé's male protagonists are reduced to their animal form; they each suffer from the psychological state that Nietzsche classified as "ressentiment", a skewed view

of the world engendered by the desire for revenge. Unfortunately, the sullen director doesn't help himself – or any critics who'd like to take him seriously – when he makes such adolescent statements as "all history is written in sperm and blood". LH

Seul contre tous (I Stand Alone) 1998, 92 min

cast Philippe Nahon, Blandine Lenoir, Frankye Pain, Martine Audrain, Zaven, Jean-François Rauger, Guillaume Nicloux *cin* Dominique Colin

After leaving his pregnant mistress in a bloody heap, a racist, homophobic butcher hotfoots it to Paris. The film was praised by some critics, who detected shades of *Taxi Driver*; and others who regarded it as a political allegory – actor Philippe Nahon does indeed resemble Jean-Marie Le Pen, leader of the right-wing National Front – or as a critical dissection of masculinity.

Irreversible 2002, 97 min

cast Monica Belluci, Vincent Cassel, Albert Dupontel, Jo Prestia, Philippe Nahon, Stéphane Drouot, Jean-Louis Costes, Gaspar Noé *cin* Benoît Debie

A young man (Cassel) and his friend seek revenge on the gay pimp who raped his girlfriend (Bellucci). A simple enough story, but Noé's narrative gambit (or gimmick) is that his tale is told backwards, à la *Memento*, in twelve single, semi-improvised takes. The rape scene is, at least, shot at a distance and at an uncomfortable angle, and the actress was reportedly in charge of its violent choreography. Far less defensible is the climactic, visceral moment, in which the director doesn't flinch or cut away (an illusion created by digital effects).

Christopher Nolan
UK, 1970–

Christopher Nolan has swiftly established himself as one of the brightest hopes for Hollywood storytelling as the movies enter their second century. His first feature, *Following* (1998), was a shoestring independent production; the fourth, *Batman Begins* (2005), was a mega-budget blockbuster.

Nolan grew up on both sides of the Atlantic, the son of an American mother and a British father, and was making short Super 8 films from the age of 7. Shortly after graduating from university in London he made *Following*, set in the capital's Soho district. Shot on 16mm, in black and white, it tells the story of a blocked writer's encounter with a burglar who insists on showing off his expertise at "reading" people through their possessions. Presented in flashbacks and flashforwards, it is a clever thriller tailored to the strictures of zero-budget filmmaking. It was enough to secure a move to Hollywood and a reasonable budget for *Memento* (2000). Nolan's brother Jonathan had written a short story about a man with short-term memory loss. From this kernel Christopher crafted a fiendish puzzle picture with brief scenes shown in reverse chronological order alternating with flashbacks steadily moving forward in time. In

Shocksploitation in contemporary French cinema

Around the turn of the new millennium, a certain corner of French cinema took a perverse pleasure in breaking taboos, merrily transgressing societal norms with a series of shock tactics that delighted in saying the unsayable and showing the unshowable. "You have thirty seconds to leave the cinema" announced a title card before the climax of Gaspar Noé's *Seul contre tous* (*I Stand Alone*,1998). By this point of the film, the audience would have already been deluged by a flood of racist and homophobic invective and would have witnessed the movie's misanthropic protagonist repeatedly beating his lover's pregnant belly until she miscarried on the floor of their apartment. They would be wondering how it could possibly get any worse. It does, of course. But Noé managed to outdo himself with his next film. The grim centrepiece of *Irreversible* (2002) was a rape scene that lasted nine gruelling minutes, shot in one long, unblinking take. It also featured a revoltingly violent scene in which a man's face falls apart, caved in by several ferocious blows with a fire extinguisher.

The class of 2000 broke the final screen taboo, and made censorship history, by finally showing the male member in a state of arousal, a part of life that had previously only been the preserve of hard-core pornography. Catherine Breillat utilized real sex and quasi-philosophizing in *Romance* (1999). Concerning a schoolteacher's sexual and sadomasochistic journey of self-discovery, it starred the porn legend Rocco Siffredi. He cropped up again in *Anatomie de l'enfer* (*Anatomy Of Hell*, 2004), in which he received an eye-opening biology lesson in the secrets of the female body from his inamorata/employer. In the film's undisputed highlight, she dunks a used tampon in a glass of water and invites him to drink a cordial of her menstrual blood. Which he does. Patrice Chéreau introduced French frankness to British cinema with the graphic oral sex of *Intimité* (*Intimacy*, 2001), while the male member was paraded in all its tumescent glory in Leos Carax's *Pola X* (1999) and Bertrand Bonello's *Le pornographe* (*The Pornographer*, 2001), whose eleven-second "cum shot" was controversially cut by the British Board of Film Classification.

Despite the new candour (or because of it), sex never appeared as an erotic act, but as functional and desperate at best. Sex was explicitly equated with revulsion in Cédric Kahn's *L'ennui* (1998), which posited the sexual act as a joyless exercise in neurosis, self-destruction and power play. The logical and predictable conclusion of this new cinema of disgust was to twin sex with violence. In the visceral, unflinching and ground-breaking *Baise-moi* (2000), co-directed by porn industry veteran Coralie Trinh Thi and author Virginie Despentes, a hooker and porn star hit the road on a sex and killing spree. The allegedly unsimulated sex was as sadistically brutal as the eye-watering violence. Bruno Dumont's *Twentynine Palms* (2003), a Californian road trip with lots of breaks for restless rutting, climaxed in a grisly crescendo of male rape and horror-movie gross-out. Sex and death were again controversially allied in Claire Denis's *Trouble Every Day* (2001), in which a serum extracted from the human libido transformed sexual desire into cannibalistic and vampiric urges. Marina De Van wrote and directed the asphyxiatingly intense *Dans ma peau* (*In My Skin*, 2002), in which she starred as a self-harmer who snacked on her own flesh (and thus carved out an unintentionally apt metaphor for a national, narcissistic cinema that was eating itself).

Perhaps directors like De Van belong to a long, venerable tradition of artists hoping to *épater le bourgeoisie*: France is of course the country that gave us the Marquis de Sade and Michel Houellebecq. But does the work of this new school add up to more than just shock tactics and braying? For some critics, it represented a hysterical overreaction to the corseted gentility of French heritage cinema that had reigned in the 1990s. For Noé and his peers, the real target was an American cinema that was becoming less and less provocative. For other critics, this new extreme cinema was a passive-aggressive manifestation of decadence, the piercing death rattle of white, bourgeois culture, stripped of the liberal values that both informed and inspired middle-class directors. In the words of writer James Quandt, this last gasp of sensationalism was "a narcissistic response to the collapse of ideology in a society traditionally defined by political polarity and theoretical certitude". In other words, little more than a gross-out national product of some rude boys and bad girls. LH

part a dazzling formal exercise in storytelling, the film riffs on questions of truth, memory and the construction of identity that crop up in all Nolan's work to date.

Insomnia (2002), with Al Pacino and Robin Williams, was a more modest success, a capable but relatively straightforward remake of Norwegian filmmaker Erik Skjoldbjaerg's 1997 midnight-sun noir. (This is the only one of his films to date that Nolan has not written himself.) Entrusted with reinvigorating the moribund Batman franchise, Nolan exceeded all expectations with *Batman Begins*, an intelligent, resonant take on modern mythology and the power of nightmares. *The Prestige* (2006) lived up to its title. A classy, unpredictable item about feuding Edwardian magicians, it was another tricksy piece of sleight of hand, brimming with savoir-faire and smartly disavowing its own showmanship.

A mainstream filmmaker with a left-field sensibility and a fascination with narrative, Nolan looks ideally placed to emulate the success of someone like Steven Soderbergh. He may go farther still. TC

Memento 2000, 113 min

cast Guy Pearce, Carrie Anne Moss, Joe Pantoliano, Mark Boon Jr, Stephen Tobolowsky *cin* Wally Pfister *m* David Julyan

Leonard Shelby (Guy Pearce) tries to piece together clues to identify his wife's murderer. He is hampered in this project by short-term memory loss, which means he can't remember anything beyond a fifteen-minute span. Structured along two alternating timelines running in opposite directions, and with the hero in effect beginning again from scratch in every scene, *Memento* is a virtuoso piece of story scrambling. Critics loved it, and this low-budget indie flick became a cult sleeper.

Batman Begins 2005, 141 min

cast Christian Bale, Liam Neeson, Gary Oldman, Cillian Murphy, Michael Caine *cin* Wally Pfister *m* James Newton Howard, Hans Zimmer

Eschewing Tim Burton's fairy-tale vision and avoiding Joel Schumacher's terminal camp, Nolan elects to take Batman seriously. That is, he explores the making of a living legend, through tragedy, training and moral conviction. It's a film about terrorism too: how fear preys on society, and the fine distinction between justice and revenge. This is absorbing, confident filmmaking on a blockbuster scale.

The Prestige 2006, 130 min

cast Christian Bale, Hugh Jackman, Michael Caine, Scarlett Johannson, Piper Perabo, David Bowie, Andy Serkis *cin* Wally Pfister *m* David Julyan

Nolan is up to his old tricks again in this teasingly clever and original suspense movie about obsession and identity. Edwardian-era magicians Borden and Angier are friends and collaborators, until an escapology trick goes wrong and Angier's wife is drowned on stage. From then on their rivalry knows no bounds. *The Prestige* is constructed as a postmodern puzzle, framing stories within stories and flashbacks within flashbacks, and presenting us with at least two unreliable narrators – one of whom is the victim in the murder trial that opens the film.

Chris Noonan
Australia, 1952–

By 1995, Chris Noonan had some twenty years of intermittent television work under his belt, including the 1987 mini-series *Vietnam* (featuring a teenaged Nicole Kidman) and the award-winning *Stepping Out*, an hour-long document of mentally challenged performers taking the stage at the Sydney Opera House. Nothing in his résumé would have marked him out as the go-to man for a heartwarming charmer about a talking pig who wins a sheepherding contest, and no plot outline of *Babe* (1995) would have distinguished it as an intergenerational box-office hit and best picture Oscar nominee. *Babe* looked set to become a one-off hit for Noonan, as it took him a decade to return to the director's chair for the disappointing *Miss Potter* (2006), starring

Renée Zellweger as beloved British author and illustrator Beatrix Potter. JW

Babe 1995, 89 min

cast James Cromwell, Magda Szubanski *(voices)* Christine Cavanaugh, Miriam Margoyles, Danny Mann *cin* Andrew Lesnie *m* Nigel Westlake

Saved by chance from the abattoir by Farmer Hoggett (James Cromwell), a baby pig (plaintively voiced by Christine Cavanaugh) is quasi-adopted by a sheepdog, who teaches him the trade, and wins the trust of the sheep community with his bravery and good manners. Adapted from Dick King-Smith's novel *The Sheep-Pig*, this comic adventure builds a surprising degree of breath-holding suspense during the climactic sheep-herding contest.

Khyentse Norbu
Bhutan, 1961–

Khyentse Norbu is unique in the history of cinema, being the only Buddhist lama to make movies. The director discovered at the age of 7 that he was the reincarnation of a nineteenth-century saint, and since then his full title has been His Eminence Dzsongsar Jamyang Khyentse Rinpoche. Or Rinpoche – Precious One – for short. Educated at a monastery, Norbu saw his first film at the age of 19 and discovered a love of film when studying in London. There he met producer Jeremy Thomas, who employed him as a consultant on Bernardo Bertolucci's *Little Buddha* (1994). It was Thomas who bankrolled Norbu's debut, *The Cup* (1999). With only a four-week course in filmmaking to fall back on, Norbu had to call on a higher power to make key decisions: divination. His next film, *Travellers And Magicians* (2003) was an enchanting road movie set in Bhutan, and although it was similarly lauded by critics, Norbu has no plans to give up the day job. LH

The Cup (Phörpa) 1999, 94 min

cast Kunsang Nyima, Pema Tshundup, Jamyang Lodro, Neten Chokling, Orgyen Tobgyal, Lama Chonjor *cin* Paul Warren *m* Douglas Mills

In a monastery in the foothills of the Himalayas, a football-mad monk does everything in his earthly powers to watch the World Cup on television. *The Cup* was written in English and translated into Tibetan. Norbu employed the monks to play variations on themselves, and they all proved to be natural actors. The first film ever from Bhutan, a country with only three cinemas, is an enchanting, captivating hymn to film's ability to act as a window to another world.

Phillip Noyce
Australia, 1950–

One of a number of Australian directors who successfully made the transition to Hollywood in the 1980s, Phillip Noyce is at his best when fusing the personal and the social.

Noyce established himself on home turf with two key films in the Australian film revival of the 1970s: the racism drama *Backroads* (1977) and *Newsfront* (1978), which explored social history through the lens of newsreel cameras. The aesthetically ambitious *Heatwave* (1982), which pitted activists against developers in a sizzling Sydney, demonstrated an interest in social causes evident throughout Noyce's career. *Shadows Of The Peacock* (1987) charted a woman's journey of self-discovery after she finds out her husband has been unfaithful. At the end of the 1980s Noyce broke into the American film industry with two movies: the excellent thriller *Dead Calm* (1988), starring Sam Neill and Nicole Kidman, and the action movie *Blind Fury* (1989), starring Rutger Hauer as a blind swordsman inspired by Japan's Zatoichi character. He hit the big time with *Patriot Games* (1992), starring Harrison Ford as American intelligence agent Jack Ryan. His emphasis on big-budget action and thriller material continued with the Tom Clancy adaptation *Clear And Present Danger* (1994), *The Saint* (1997), in which the 1960s TV character was revived, and the routine serial killer movie *The Bone Collector* (1999). After a disappointing run of films in the second half of the 1990s he seems to have renewed his creativity with *Rabbit-Proof Fence* (2002). Based on the true story of three aboriginal girls, it fused the personal and the political with great force. In the same year, he directed the Graham Greene adaptation *The Quiet American*, which won Michael Caine an Oscar nomination for best actor. *Catch A Fire* (2006) was a taut drama set in apartheid-era South Africa. JC

Newsfront 1978, 110 min

cast Bill Hunter, Chris Haywood, John Dease, Gerard Kennedy, Wendy Hughes, John Ewart *cin* Vincent Monton *m* William Motzing

A highly effective and inspiring period piece, *Newsfront* follows the careers of two Australian newsreel cameramen, Len and Frank Maguire, between 1948 and 1956. Integrating actual newsreel footage with new material, the film succeeds in being both dramatic and acutely aware of social and political history.

Rabbit-Proof Fence 2002, 93 min

cast Everlyn Sampi, Tianna Sansbury, Ningali Lawford, Laura Monaghan, Myarn Lawford, Kenneth Branagh *cin* Christopher Doyle *m* Peter Gabriel

With echoes of Noyce's early outback film *Backroads*, *Rabbit-Proof Fence* delighted many Australian critics – some of whom were never sold on his Hollywood fare – with its sympathetic story of three aboriginal girls of the so-called "stolen generation" separated from their families by Christian zealot authorities. The girls endeavour to walk the 1200 miles back home guided only by the fence of the title. Gabriel's subtle music and Doyle's camera add clout and class to an enterprise which demonstrates conviction and accomplishment in equal measure.

Pat O'Connor
Republic of Ireland, 1944–

Since his TV drama *A Ballroom Of Romance* (1982) won a BAFTA, Irish director Pat O'Connor has divided his time between Hollywood and his homeland. The streets of Belfast provided the backdrop for the explosive *Cal* (1984), which crossed sectarian lines and announced O'Connor's talent for handling character actors. He further demonstrated this knack in *A Month In The Country* (1987) – a beautifully paced take on J.R. Carr's novel which co-starred Kenneth Branagh and Colin Firth as two traumatized World War I veterans working in the grounds of an English country church – and the Irish Civil War saga *Fools Of Fortune* (1990). A string of misfiring Stateside comedies followed, including *Stars And Bars* (1988), *The January Man* (1989) and *Sweet November* (2001), which starred a miscast Keanu Reeves. However, O'Connor returned to safer ground with *Circle Of Friends* (1995), an adaptation of Maeve Binchy's Catholic-inflected rite of passage novel, and *Dancing At Lunghansa* (1998), which featured Meryl Streep. But while these films contained characteristic moments of intensity, their pastoralism was frowned upon by those critics keen for O'Connor to return to the mean streets of Ulster. RC

Cal 1984, 81 min
cast Helen Mirren, John Lynch, Donal McCann, John Kavanagh, Ray McAnally *cin* Jerzy Zielinski *m* Mark Knopfler

Northern Ireland's politics don't loom too large in a film that on release felt like a breath of fresh air in a largely stagnant period for UK and Irish cinema. Cal (a Catholic) falls passionately for Marcella, a Catholic librarian whose protestant husband was recently killed by an IRA gunman. It was Cal who drove the killer's car. Helen Mirren won best actress at Cannes but it's John Lynch's guilty haunted face and Bernard MacLaverty's screenplay that stand out most in O'Connor's most dynamic and engaging feature.

Damien O'Donnell
Republic of Ireland, 1967–

It may seem surprising that a Dublin-born director had his breakthrough hit with a film about a mixed-race Pakistani family living in Salford in the north of England in the 1970s. However, this unusual cultural mix proved to be inspired and Damien O'Donnell's feature debut, *East Is East* (1999), became an award-winning hit. His first short film, *35 Aside* (1995), about a young boy who doesn't like football, had given an early glimpse of O'Donnell's ability to champion the outsider, and similar themes pervaded *East Is East*. Since then he has continued in the same comedy-drama vein with the low-budget road movie *Heartlands* (2002) and the bittersweet *Inside I'm Dancing* (2004), about two young disabled men struggling for independence. ED

East Is East 1999, 96 min
cast Om Puri, Linda Bassett, Jordan Routledge, Archie Panjabi, Emil Marwan, Chris Bisson, Jimi Mistry *cin* Brian Tunfao *m* Deborah Mollison

George Khan (Om Puri), a Pakistani chip-shop owner living in Salford in 1971, seems to be happily married to his white English wife (Linda Bassett). However, his struggles to raise his six sons and one daughter as good Muslims are exacerbated by their varied desires to integrate into British society. O'Donnell achieves a fine balance between humour and drama by empathizing with his characters, and creates a touching portrait of a family learning to deal with their multiculturalism.

Damien Odoul
France, 1968–

A published poet who reportedly had no formal training in cinema, Damien Odoul made his first short at the age of 19. Then, after constructing such poetic and experimental arabesques as *La Douce* (1988) and *Elegeia: Chant de deuil* (*Elegy: Song Of Mourning*, 1995), the director unexpectedly quit filmmaking. Six years later, he released *Le souffle* (*Deep Breath*, 2001). Like François Truffaut's debut

Les quatre cent coups (*The 400 Blows*, 1959), it drew heavily on the director's own troubled youth – Odoul had also been expelled from various schools as a young tearaway. The newcomer's synthesis of mucky realism and magical transcendence enchanted many critics who detected, with a certain wistful nostalgia, the poetic intensity and uncommercial purity of Robert Bresson. The majority of reviewers, however, have been underwhelmed by Odoul's subsequent work. *Errance* (2003) sprawled elliptically and often obtusely as the director followed the decline of a womanizing, alcoholic Algerian war veteran. *En attendant le deluge* (*After We're Gone*, 2004), in which a dying man commissions a private performance of his favourite play in his old chateau, left many critics baffled, bothered and a bit bored. LH

Le souffle (Deep Breath) 2001, 77 min
cast Pierre-Louis Bonnetblanc, Dominique Chevallier, Maxime Dalbrut, Jean-Claude Lecante, Jean Milord, Stéphane Terpereau *cin* Pascale Granel

David, a snotty delinquent from the city, spends a summer on his uncle's farm. Opening with shots of the rolling French countryside in bucolic monochrome, the sense of dreamy pastoral is disrupted somewhat abruptly by the close-up of a live sheep having its throat cut, setting the disturbing tone for a film that bubbles toxically with cruelty and resentment just beneath its immaculate surface.

Kihachi Okamoto
Japan, 1923–2005

Though a little-known figure outside of Japan, Kihachi Okamoto was an adept and versatile director of films across a range of genres, usually of the action variety. These include fast-paced crime thrillers such as *Procurer Of Hell* (1961), samurai warrior films like *Samurai Assassin* (1965) and World War II action films such as *Fort Graveyard* (1965). He was also capable of producing satirical material, as in *The Elegant Life Of Mr Everyman* (1963) and – in particular – *Human Bullet* (1968), an incisive attack on the military focusing on a Japanese soldier selected for a kamikaze mission.

As for many of his generation, World War II made an indelible mark on him. Called up from university in 1943, he was thrust into action when the Pacific war was at its bloodiest and only just survived a US air attack. In 1947 he joined the Toho Studios where he worked as an assistant director for, among others, Mikio Naruse and Ishiro Honda. The melodrama *All About Marriage* (1958) was his debut movie but he made a greater impact the following year with *Desperado Outpost* (1959), a war film about disgruntled soldiers, and the hard-hitting yakuza film *Boss Of The Underworld* (1959). Of his many chanbara (sword fight) films, *Sword Of Doom* (1966) is regarded as his masterpiece and one of the most significant contributions to the samurai genre. NN

Sword Of Doom (Dai-bosatsu tôge) 1966, 119 min, b/w
cast Tatsuya Nakadai, Yuzo Kayama, Michiyo Aratama, Toshirô Mifune, Yôko Naito *cin* Hiroshi Murai *m* Masaru Satô

A brooding samurai classic rich in atmosphere and tension, *Sword Of Doom* is a showcase for Okamoto's considerable skills as a director. It is full of memorable set pieces, including the blistering depiction of an ambush on a woodland path lined with swordsmen. The lead actor Tatsuya Nakadai carries genuine menace as a samurai endowed with prodigious swordsmanship, but a cold, cold heart.

Annette K. Olesen
Denmark, 1965–

Annette Olesen has the honour of being probably the last director to make a film according to the ten rules of filmic purity (the Vows of Chastity) as outlined by Lars von Trier and Dogme 95. The Danish National Film School graduate learned her trade making adverts, shorts and documentaries, first earning her spurs on the award-winning, Mike Leigh-inspired *Minor Mishaps* (2002). The script was hewn from months of rehearsal and improvisation and was shot on digital film, with hand-held cameras. It had the abrasively quirky feel of a Dogme film, so it was perhaps unsurprising that Olesen then joined the brotherhood which had sworn abstinence from artificial lighting and superficial action, and vowed to obey Lars von Trier's restrictive rules. *In Your Hands* (2004) was the most austere of the 34 films that had received the official Dogme certificate. Punishing and emotionally scarring, it centred on two women – one a prisoner, the other the chaplain – in a women's prison. An essay on faith and the possibility of miracles in the modern age, it painfully recalled the religious agonies and ecstasies of Denmark's greatest and most austere filmmaker, Carl Theodor Dreyer. Her next film, *1:1* (2005), addressed the tensions between locals and Islamic immigrants in Copenhagen. In a moment of cultural synchronicity, it was released internationally just as demonstrations spread around the world in violent reaction to the publication in a Danish newspaper of sacrilegious cartoons featuring the Prophet Muhammad. LH

Minor Mishaps (Små ulykker) 2002, 109 min
cast Jørgen Kill, Maria Würgler Rich, Henrik Prip, Jesper Christensen, Jannie Faurschou, Vigga Bro, Karen-Lise Mynster *cin* Morten Søborg *m* Jeppe Kaas

Olesen's muted, amiable melodrama was the result of months of improvisation with only the vaguest notion – that the finished product should be about a sense of loss. From eighty hours of video, scriptwriter Kim Fupz Aakeson fashioned a two-hour screenplay about the emotional aftermath of bereavement. An ageing male nurse loses his wife of 46 years; Olesen charts the effect it has on him and his dysfunctional family with an astringent eye and unusual wit.

Manoel de Oliveira
Portugal, 1908–

Manoel de Oliveira, one of the most original and profound artists working in cinema, was never more prolific than after turning 80, thereafter writing and directing one film a year into his late nineties. He was making up for lost time. During the years of António Salazar's dictatorship (1932–68), Oliveira was condemned to long periods of silence and inactivity. It was only in 1972, four years after Salazar's death, that he was able to fully explore his principal themes of desire, fear, guilt and perdition, underscored by the very Portuguese sentiment of the "consolation of melancholy".

Oliveira was born in Oporto, a coastal city which inspired a number of his films. His first feature, *Aniki-Bobo* (1942), followed the adventures of street urchins growing up in the slums of Oporto and on the banks of the River Duoro. Made in the year that the term "neo-realism" was coined in Italy, it contains many characteristics of that movement, with much location shooting and unaffectedly natural performances from local children. In his documentary *Oporto Of My Childhood* (2001), Oliveira revisited the city, filming it as though it didn't exist any more except through the eyes of memory.

Many of his films are adaptations of literary works which – while maintaining the nature of the original text – destroy conventional narrative with long takes and fixed shots of beautifully composed images. In *The Letter* (1999), an updating of the seventeenth-century French novel *La Princesse de Clèves*, the lingering shots allow the viewer time to observe the conflict between love and honour, carnality and spirituality. *Francisca* (1981), based on a romantic novel about a triangular relationship, also fulfils Oliveira's aim to create a synthesis of literary, musical and pictorial elements.

Despite his late renaissance as a filmmaker, Oliveira now enjoys a worldwide reputation and he has garnered a plethora of awards, including the Venice Film Festival's Golden Lion "for his whole works" in 1985. Among his later films are *A Talking Picture* (2003), which has an international cast on a cruise ship speaking five languages, and *Belle toujours* (2006), a delightful and belated sequel to Luis Buñuel's *Belle de jour* (1967). RBe

Abraham Valley (Vale Abraão) 1993, 187 min
cast Leonor Silveira, Cécile Sanz de Alba, Luís Miguel Cintra, Ruy de Carvalho, Luís Lima Barreto *cin* Mário Barroso *m* Richard Strauss

The film, a stylized reworking of Flaubert's *Madame Bovary*, set in the wine-growing region of modern-day Portugal, continued Oliveira's exploration of doomed love, one of his favourite themes. Ema (Leonor Silvera), an attractive but innocent girl, marries a doctor whom she does not love. Bored and lonely, she takes a lover. Poetic and haunting,

with an extraordinary use of landscape, this is, despite its length, one of Oliveira's most successful films.

I'm Going Home (Je rentre à la maison) 2001, 90 min
cast Michel Piccoli, Catherine Deneuve, John Malkovich, Antoine Chappey, Leonor Baldaque *cin* Sabine Lancelin

Made in French, this is one of Oliveira's most approachable, poignant and personal works – a meditation on ageing and the theatre, personified by Michel Piccoli, as a septuagenarian actor trying to deal with old age, and refusing to compromise his principles. This involves his rejecting a lucrative role in a vulgar TV mini-series and accepting instead to play Buck Mulligan in a film of James Joyce's *Ulysses*, to which he is tragicomically unsuited.

Laurence Olivier
UK, 1907–89

While the screen performances of England's most renowned modern stage actor were often more than a little hammy, as a director he made two films that should alone place him in the pantheon of great British filmmakers. Laurence Olivier's life-long love of Shakespeare, and eagerness to do something useful for the war effort, led to his *Henry V* (1944). Henry's rousing "once more unto the breach" battle cry did indeed act as a rallying call to a nation that had been brutally pummelled by the Blitz. *Henry V* reflected, and stiffened, the stoic values of a country at war. His introspective *Hamlet* (1948), on the other hand, mirrored post-war disillusionment just as effectively as the *films noirs* of the period, while also memorably adopting their deep-focus monochrome intensity. *Richard III* (1955) was the least cinematic and most disappointing of his Shakespearean adaptations, his camera doing little more than letting four knighted thespians do their thing. His next film, *The Prince And The Showgirl* (1957), was a stiff curio. The plot about the collision of two different worlds – royalty and showbiz – unhappily reflected the mismatched acting styles of its leads: Marilyn Monroe, an alumna of the Actors Studio, and Olivier, who only saw madness in the Method. *Three Sisters* (1970) was little more than a record of a National Theatre production of Chekhov's play. It was a disappointment from a director whose debut had unexpectedly embraced the expressive possibilities of cinema rather than simply using it as a tool to record his own theatrical genius. LH

Henry V 1944, 137 min
cast Laurence Olivier, Renée Asherson, Robert Newton, Leslie Banks, George Robey, Esmond Knight *cin* Robert Krasker *m* William Walton

In a great *coup de cinéma* the film begins with a stage production at the Globe. Olivier then audaciously opens the action out into the bloody, physical reality of battle at Agincourt, with hundreds of extras bringing the play to vibrant life. Prime Minister Winston Churchill wanted any lines that were critical of the English leader to be removed, but even if Olivier's Henry does suffer from one-dimensionality, it's more than compensated for by his sheer chutzpah and filmic invention (with occasional nods to Eisenstein in the battle scenes).

Hamlet 1948, 155 min
cast Laurence Olivier, Eileen Herlie, Basil Sydney, Jean Simmons, Felix Aylmer, Stanley Holloway *cin* Desmond Dickinson *m* William Walton

There are Freudian overtones here in the erotic frisson between Olivier and his screen mother, played by Eileen Herlie (who was almost thirteen years his junior). This is a lean, nimble version, with a constantly prowling camera that emphasizes the psychological at the expense of the political: the behind-the-scenes power games have been boldly excised, as have the characters Rosencrantz and Guildenstern, resulting in an exuberantly claustrophobic experience.

Ermanno Olmi
Italy, 1931–

The son of peasants, Ermanno Olmi worked as a clerk in the Edison-Volta electrical plant, and later began to make documentaries for the firm. His last film for the company was also his first feature; *Il tempo si è fermato* (*Time Stood Still*, 1959), in which an older and a younger man bond while working as watchmen overseeing a hydroelectric dam project. *Il posto* (*The Job*, 1961) drew upon Olmi's own experience, with the young protagonist negotiating the grind of a bureaucratic workplace.

The director's characteristic sensitivity is evident in 1963's *I fidanzati* (*The Engagement*), an account of a young couple who are engaged to be married but are driven apart by the need to seek work in another town. Observing its protagonists with a patient regard for little triumphs and failures, the film recalled the simple camerawork and non-professional actors of the neo-realist Vittorio De Sica. Yet Olmi's preoccupation with peasant dignity generates a mystical quality, and his warm though spare compositions are a pious reply to the fashionable ambivalence of his contemporary, Michelangelo Antonioni. Olmi's critique of the industrial environment suggests not the blank despair of Antonioni's *The Red Desert* (1964) but rather the bemusement of humanity before the blight of Italy's post-war boom.

While an obvious statement of faith like Rod Steiger's portrayal of Pope John XXIII in *A Man Named John* (1965) seemed overly reverent, when Olmi returned to the tribulations of the soil – *The Tree Of Wooden Clogs* (1978) – he tapped into more characteristic roots. The film was a return to cinema after ten years languishing in the relative obscurity of Italian TV. *The Legend Of The Holy Drinker* (1988) was driven by a strong performance from Rutger Hauer as a tramp given money by a kindly stranger, but diverted by worldly things from repaying the debt. As a parable against materialism, it seemed timely, winning the Venice Golden Lion. RA

Il posto (The Job) 1961, 99 min, b/w
cast Sandro Panzeri, Loredana Detto, Tullio Kezich *cin* Lamberto Caimi *m* Pier Emilio Bassi

A year after Billy Wilder's *The Apartment* interrogated the moral logics of the corporate era, Ermanno Olmi's young protagonist seemed like a modern-day Buster Keaton, quietly registering the alienation around him. Finding moments of tender humour – especially in his relationship with colleague Loredana Detto – Olmi generated a tapestry of human sensibility amid the fury of the modern world. It made an international impact.

The Tree Of Wooden Clogs (L'albero degli zoccoli) 1978, 186 mins
cast Luigi Ornaghi, Francesca Moriggi, Omar Brignoli, Antonio Ferrari, Teresa Brescianini, Giuseppe Brignoli, Carlo Rota *cin* Ermanno Olmi

Regarded at the time as a conservative riposte to Bernardo Bertolucci's *1900*, this fresco of peasant life admits neither flashy performance nor set-piece spectacle as it patiently records the weave of man and the seasons with all the grace and innocence of a child's prayer. The result – a sober and majestic tribute to a lost world – returned Italian cinema to its neo-realist roots and won the Palme d'Or at Cannes.

Marcel Ophuls
Germany, 1927–

In his masterwork *The Sorrow And The Pity* (1969), Marcel Ophuls laid bare the conscience of post-war France. The film's success helped shape both the modern investigative documentary and contemporary French films on World War II – not least Louis Malle's powerful fiction film *Lacombe, Lucien* (1974).

The son of director Max Ophuls, Marcel had a peripatetic childhood, which commentators have suggested facilitated his objective documentary accounts of the French national psyche. After education at Hollywood High while his father worked for the studios during the 1940s, Marcel served with the US occupying forces in Japan. When the family returned to Paris in 1950 Marcel became an assistant to Julien Duvivier and Anatole Litvak, and worked on John Huston's *Moulin Rouge* (1952) and his father's *Lola Montès* (1955). Through François Truffaut, Ophuls got to direct an episode of the portmanteau film *Love At Twenty* (1962). There followed the commercial hit *Banana Peel* (1964), a detective film starring Jeanne Moreau and Jean-Paul Belmondo. With a slump in box-office fortunes, Ophuls turned to television news reporting and a documentary on the Munich crisis of 1938: *Munich* (1967). He then embarked on his examination of France under Nazi occupation, *The Sorrow And The Pity*. Although he enjoyed making entertainments, Ophuls became identified as a documentarian, using a characteristically sober interview style to resolve disparate experiences into a persuasive argument. *A Sense Of Loss* (1972) looked at Northern Ireland, while *The Memory Of Justice* (1973) was an ambitious comparison of US policy in Vietnam and the atrocities of the Nazis. Disagreements with his French backers over interpretation led Ophuls to smuggle a print to New York where it was shown privately. Legal wrangles left him disappointed and financially broke and Ophuls turned to university lecturing. In the mid-1970s he began producing documentaries for CBS and ABC. His feature documentary *Hotel Terminus: The Life And Times Of Klaus Barbie* (1988) won an Oscar, since when he has made a damning interview film with two senior East German Communists, *November Days* (1981) and a ruminative look at how journalists cover war, *The Trouble We've Seen* (1994). RA

The Sorrow And The Pity (Le chagrin et la pitié) 1969, 262 min, b/w
cin André Gazut, Jürgen Thieme

Banned from French television for decades, Marcel Ophuls' account of the Nazi occupation revealed a wartime France in which people collaborated to get by. Combining German newsreel footage and interviews with witnesses, ranging from a Wehrmacht captain to bystanders on the street, it remains a textured and compassionate revision of wartime heroics that would influence everything from the acclaimed British television series *The World At War* to Jacques Audiard's *Un héros très discret* (*A Self-Made Hero*, 1996).

Max Ophuls
Germany, 1902–57

Max Ophuls had a romantic sensibility that is among the most astute in all cinema, while his flowing, generous camera style reinforces the poetic intensity of his films. Regularly dismissed as a mere stylist, his reputation has soared over the last 25 years and he is now regarded as a master of the doomed love story, able, like Douglas Sirk, to transcend the limitations of the stereotypic "women's film".

Ophuls started off as an actor but from 1924 turned to stage direction working in both Germany and Austria. By 1929 he was working at Berlin's UFA studios initially as Anatole Litvak's dialogue director. He made half a dozen films in Germany, including *Dann schon lieber Lebertran* (1931) scripted by Emeric Pressburger, the best of which was the commercially successful melodrama *Liebelei* (1932), which is tinged with a forlorn mood unique to the director. With the Nazis coming to power in 1933, the Jewish Ophuls (whose real name was Oppenheimer) left Germany for France and embarked on a peripatetic career, the fruit of which – *La signora di tutti* (*Everybody's Woman*, 1934), *La tendre ennemie* (*The Tender Enemy*, 1936), *Werther* (1938) – is marked by nostalgia for a vanishing sensibility and distinguished by sinuous camera movement.

Following the fall of France in 1940, Ophuls left for Hollywood where his talents were largely unappreciated. After an abortive experience with Howard Hughes (he was fired from *Vendetta* after a few days), the director made the swashbuckler *The Exile* (1947) starring Douglas Fairbanks Jr. There followed three of the most pleasing American films of the post-war years. Although it is derived from the conventions and clichés of the studio genre picture, the bittersweet melodrama *Letter From An Unknown Woman* (1948) has entered the canon, making Ophuls' name synonymous with the possibility of personal expression in Hollywood. Ophuls suffused the dark dramas *Caught* and *The Reckless Moment* (both 1949) with the fragility of romantic illusion played out in a complex web of camera moves and surface detail. In the former, Barbara Bel Geddes plays an impressionable model who marries a vicious entrepreneur played by Robert Ryan, while in the latter Joan Bennett's middle-class housewife becomes involved with James Mason's shady blackmailer. Both films stealthily contrast workaday post-war America with the hidden yearnings of women's souls.

Ophuls returned to France in 1950 and here his distinctive preoccupations and style blossomed, beginning with *La ronde* (1950), an international success despite running into censorship problems. Three Guy de Maupassant stories inspired 1951's *Le plaisir*, its portmanteau form enabling Ophuls to indulge his feeling for a lost *fin-de-siècle* world. In one an old man relives romantic reverie in a dance hall. In another the women of a brothel spend a blissful day in the Normandy countryside. In the third a model commits suicide for the love of an artist. Arguably, for his control of narrative space and for their affecting orchestration of romantic regret, Ophuls' 1950s films were his most consummate. *Madame de...* (1953) returned to the Second Empire Paris of dashing officers and ornate ritual, amid which Danielle Darrieux's earrings become a roving metaphor for the mechanisms of fate. *Lola Montès* (1955) traced the discrepancy between the graceful recollections of its nineteenth-century adventuress and her tawdry fate as the spectacle in a circus. Ophuls makes the camera seem to paint narrative as the fluid disposition of space, extravagantly laced with decor and sentiment.

While preparing *Montparnasse 19* (1958), Ophuls died of a rheumatic heart disorder. Director Jacques Becker took over the project and dedicated the film to his illustrious predecessor. If Ernst Lubitsch, Erich von Stroheim and to a lesser extent Billy Wilder evoked a courtly Old Europe that died as the cinema was being born, none felt the demise of such grace and gentility as acutely as Ophuls. RA

Liebelei 1932, 87 min, b/w

cast Wolfgang Liebenener, Magda Schneider, Luise Ullrich, Olga Tschechowa, Gustaf Gründgens *cin* Franz Planer *m* Theo Mackeben

A young impressionable girl falls deeply in love with a dashing young lieutenant and it drives them both to the summit of happiness and the depths of despair. Almost an essay on the fragility of human satisfaction, this polished romance established patterns of longing and loss that would become Ophuls' trademarks.

Letter From An Unknown Woman 1948, 87 min, b/w

cast Joan Fontaine, Louis Jourdan, Mady Christians, Marcel Journet, Art Smith, Carol York, Howard Freeman *cin* Franz Planer *m* Daniele Amfitheatrof

Out of the dime-store melodramatics of Joan Fontaine's hidden yearning for Louis Jourdan's errant concert pianist, Ophuls weaves a powerful reflection on the nature and transience of human love. Filming amid the tenements and parks of Hapsburg Vienna, cinematographer Franz Planer's mobile camera interacts with Alexander Golitzen's art direction to bring the city to glorious life, while Ophuls reveals a world torn between brute reality and the poetry of tender subjectivity.

The Reckless Moment 1949, 114 min, b/w

cast Joan Bennett, James Mason, Geraldine Brooks, Henry O'Neill, Shepperd Strudwick *cin* Burnett Guffey *m* Hans J. Salter

A restrained domestic melodrama focusing on Lucia Harper (Joan Bennett), a well-meaning but controlling housewife who tries to cover up her daughter's accidental killing of an unsuitable lover. James Mason plays petty criminal Martin Donnelly sent to blackmail the family but instead falling for Lucia. The lightest of *films noirs* but with a strong script that delivers a consistent darkness and Ophuls' direction adding a layer of hypnotic and lyrical beauty.

La ronde 1950, 92 min, b/w

cast Anton Walbrook, Simone Signoret, Serge Reggiani, Simone Simon, Daniel Gélin, Danielle Darrieux *cin* Christian Matras *m* Oscar Straus

A celebration of the circle in both structure and content, this chain of passion and seduction swirls through nineteenth-century Vienna enlivening Arthur Schnitzler's metaphorical play of love and desire. Ophuls' iconography of carousels and waltzes is held together by master of ceremonies Anton Walbrook's all-knowing narration, resulting in the auteur's quintessential work.

Lola Montès 1955, 140 min

cast Martine Carol, Peter Ustinov, Anton Walbrook, Ivan Desny, Will Quadflieg *cin* Christian Matras *m* Georges Auric

This is seminal Ophuls; a spectacular piece of artifice that turns the biopic on its head as the story of Lola – courtesan, dancer and legendary *femme fatale* – unfolds from the confines of a circus act. By living in the interstice between her romantic memories and her present degradation, the film dwells with unmatched cinematic flair in the unhappy place where hope and despair meet, where love encounters its own end.

Mamoru Oshii
Japan, 1951–

Among the most influential directors of anime in recent times, Mamoru Oshii has achieved recognition well beyond the animation niche, and that's not just because he also has some acclaimed live-action features under his belt. It is perhaps not too farfetched to suggest that his *noir*-ish sci-fi anime *Ghost In The Shell* (1995) might be the missing link between *Blade Runner* (1982) and *The Matrix* (1999).

Criticized by some for his heavy philosophizing, Oshii is nonetheless a true sci-fi auteur, and takes the themes with which he grapples – principally the interface between humans and technology – very seriously. That said, although his anime films largely jettison the comic elements of the original mangas, Oshii is not entirely immune to humour, allowing his pet bassett hound prominent roles in some of his films, albeit in animated form.

Early directing credits included the TV series *Urusei yatsura* (*Those Obnoxious Aliens*) and two feature spin-offs in 1983 and 1984. Oshii's dark futuristic vision was expressed to the full in the robot-themed *Patlabor I* and *II* (1989 and 1993), direct precursors to *Ghost In The Shell*. Interspersed with these anime projects were a few live-action movies. The fourth of these, *Avalon* (2001), about an addictive and potentially lethal futuristic computer game, was selected to appear at Cannes. *Ghost In The Shell 2: Innocence* (2004) went one better, gaining the rare distinction for an animated feature of competing for the Palme d'Or. Oshii's next movie indicated an unexpected change of tack: the oddball anime *Amazing Lives Of The Fast Food Grifters* (2006) depicts a succession of freeloaders scamming a noodle stall owner. NN

Ghost In The Shell (Kôkaku kidôtai) 1995, 82 min

cast (English voices) Atsuko Tanaka, Akio Ôtsuka, Tamio Ôki, Iemasa Kayumi, Kôichi Yamadera, Tesshô Genda *cin* Hisao Shirai *m* Kenji Kawai

One of the most influential anime movies ever made, *Ghost In The Shell* crystallizes all the attributes – and some would argue pretensions – of Mamoru Oshii. Arresting animation and an assured control of pace and atmosphere create a memorable futuristic world of cops, cyborgs and hackers, but in his journeys into philosophical territory Oshii is striving for something much deeper.

Nagisa Oshima
Japan, 1932–

Nagisa Oshima, scion of an educated middle-class family, was drawn into radical politics while at university, where he studied political science and law. In 1954, he joined the Shochiku film company as an assistant director. It was a time when Japan was torn between its indigenous codes and traditions, and the manners and mores of the West, following the departure of the American occupying forces in 1952. Post-war Japanese cinema, then experiencing a boom, reflected this tension.

Oshima's first feature, 1959's *A Town Of Love And Hope*, was a lean, angry critique of class oppression centring on a young boy forced to sell pigeons to survive. An iconoclast from the start, Oshima had a political sophistication that exceeded that of the internationally fêted *nouvelle vague* filmmakers, of whom he was a contemporary. The director, in his 25 films over the next decade, criticized the staid Japan of tradition, the Japan of Akira Kurosawa and of Yasujiro Ozu, with its weight of ethical and aesthetic courtesies. He soon became a spokesman for the *nuberu bagu*, or Japanese New Wave, and edited a magazine criticizing industry attitudes and practices. Preoccupied with the problems of youth and its disillusionment with older values, Oshima's work during this period took its cue from real experience, teetering between realism and fantasy and emphasizing violence and sex. Deliberately evoking Alain Resnais, *Night And Fog In Japan* (1960) criticized the the US-Japanese military alliance. When the film failed at the box office, Oshima became increasingly regretful over the Left's impact on the young, leaving

Shochiku to freelance and experiment widely. He then formed his own company, Sozosha, in partnership with his wife, the actress Akiko Koyama, a key figure in his evolving repertory company.

Oshima's international reputation dates from 1968 when the angry and explicit *Death By Hanging* was shown out of competition at Cannes. Putting a modern image of the Japanese urban experience before a foreign audience, *Diary Of A Shinjuku Thief* (1969) followed the exploits of a young man who steals for sexual satisfaction, becoming involved with a girl who is complicit in his erotic fantasy. Godardian in its collage effect, it was influenced by the events of May 1968 in Paris, and by Western youth culture generally. In 1969 *Boy* explored the feelings of a child corrupted by his itinerant criminal family, blaming the problems of a wayward generation on the material consequences of the post-war settlement. *Ceremony* (1972) examined in allegorical style the post-war fortunes of a family in which characters represent competing political perspectives, while weddings and funerals become the focus for singularly Japanese rites and responses.

With the dissolution of Sozosha in 1973 and the establishment in 1975 of Oshima Productions, the director began to get involved in international co-productions. This move, however, detracted from the sensitivity to indigenous experiences found in his ear-

Pushing the boundaries: Tatsuya Fuji and Eiko Matsuda in the unrestrained *Ai no corrida*.

lier work. For some critics, even Oshima's erotic masterpiece *Ai no corrida* (*In The Realm Of The Senses*, 1976) seemed to play gratuitously to the Western arthouse crowd. *Empire Of Passion* (1978) seemed a peculiarly personal response to his prosecution following the Japanese release of his previous film, detailing the fate of an adulterous couple who commit murder and are plagued by the authorities and the old husband's ghost. Less sure of itself, *Merry Christmas Mr Lawrence* (1982) tapped into the contemporary Western Orientalist fad typified by Ruichi Sakamoto's growing résumé, including the score for this dissection of wartime dynamics in a Japanese POW camp. Arguably, David Bowie's "stranger in a strange land" also played into Oshima's preoccupation with children out of their depth. In 1986 Oshima managed to raise some controversy again with the uneasy comedy *Max, mon amour* (1986), which caused its share of outrage by depicting Charlotte Rampling romancing an ape.

By now the president of the Japanese directors' guild and a respected film theorist and critic, Oshima had become an established figure in the industry. After a break from feature filmmaking of fourteen years, *Gohatto* (*Taboo*, 1999) again centred on a beautiful child, this time a young soldier whose beauty causes havoc among his comrades. No other Japanese director has charted the moral and psychological consequences of post-war Japanese history with such passion and insight. RA

Death By Hanging (Koshikei) 1968, 117 min, b/w

cast Yun Yun-Do, Kei Sato, Fumio Watanabe, Toshiro Ishido, Masao Adachi, Mutsuhiro Toura, Hosei Komatsu *cin* Yashuhiro Yoshioka *m* Hikaru Hayashi

Employing Brechtian devices to create distance from his distressing material, Nagisa Oshima details the execution of a Korean immigrant sentenced to death for the rape and murder of two Japanese girls. When the hanging goes wrong, the situation's absurd implications are reminiscent of the surreal Western comedies of the period, while the power of the film's condemnation of Japanese racism remains undiminished.

Ai no corrida (In The Realm Of The Senses) 1976, 108 min

cast Tatsuya Fuji, Eiko Matsuda, Aoi Nakajima, Meika Seri, Taiji Tonoyama, Hiroko Fuji, Naomi Shiraishi, Kyoko Okada *cin* Hideo Ito *m* Minoru Miki

Oshima shocked censors and audiences with this tale of the unrestrained sexual passion of a couple exploring the boundaries of physical desire. An analogy for the virile culture of pre-war Japanese militarism, it was banned by US Customs on the eve of the New York Film Festival and was the subject of a long-running censorship tussle in Britain. Today, the film stands as one of the most unabashed treatments of taboo in film history.

Gohatto (Taboo) 1999, 101 min

cast Takeshi Kitano, Ryuhei Matsuda, Shinji Takeda, Tadanobu Asano *cin* Toyomichi Kurita *m* Ryuichi Sakamoto

Ryuhei Matsuda plays Kano, a young man inducted into the Shogunate militia in the 1860s whose loveliness causes

sexual anarchy to break out among his colleagues. Witty and precocious, the film brought an unflinching eye to bear on the possibilities of gender and role play.

Katsuhiro Ôtomo
Japan, 1954–

If there is one Japanese anime above all others responsible for finally breaking the form in the West, it has to be Katsuhiro Ôtomo's *Akira* (1988). A watershed work in so many ways, it has also proved something of a millstone for its creator, who has struggled to match its success in the two decades since. Fear of unfavourable comparison was perhaps the reason why he chose to follow it up with a live-action feature, the entertaining horror-comedy *World Apartment Horror* (1991), which followed a lowly yakuza's attempts to forcefully evict the residents of a tower block, some of whom appear to be supernatural.

Ôtomo returned to anime in 1995, contributing a segment to the acclaimed portmanteau *Memories*, which was based on his manga. Expectations were sky-high for *Steamboy* (2004), his first anime feature since *Akira*, but its retro-futurist Victorian London setting couldn't satisfy the sci-fi fans, and the plot was too dense to appeal to a younger audience. Nonetheless, the film had moments of bravura artistry and breathless excitement. The live-action fantasy *Bugmaster* (2006) followed a travelling healer who rids people of plague-carrying bugs. Fans may crave a true sequel to *Akira*, but Ôtomo remains a ground-breaking artist who remembers the value of drama and entertainment while exploring the themes that fascinate him. NN

Akira 1988, 124 min

cast (voices) Mitsuo Iwata, Nozomu Sasaki, Mami Koyama, Tesshô Genda, Hiroshi Ôtake, Kôichi Kitamura *cin* Katsuji Misawa *m* Shoji Yamashiro

In a futuristic Tokyo a biker gang find themselves involved in a top-secret government project named "Akira", which leads to one of their members becoming endowed with psychic powers. It is up to the bikers' leader, Kaneda, to rescue his friend. Ôtomo's first major work catapulted him to international renown, and in the West at least remains arguably the most famous anime film to date.

Idrissa Ouédraogo
Burkina Faso (formerly Upper Volta), 1954–

Hailing from the African cinematic hotbed of Burkino Faso – which for some 38 years has hosted Africa's premier film festival in Ouagadougou – Idrissa Ouédraogo hit the festival big time with his third feature, *Tilaï* (1990). Winner of the Cannes Special Jury Prize, its stark village scenario strongly identified the director with the sub-genre of African village films. *Yaaba* (1989) was a film cut from similar cloth, this time focusing on old women ostracized by a prejudiced village community. European critical interest, however, led to concerns that the still camera focus and beautifully filmed landscapes reflected only the picturesque view of Africa. Unfair though this was, Ouédraogo has subsequently utilized a more mobile camera and the lower profile of later work with overseas viewers suggests that if any fault exists it lies not with the filmmaker. He has in any case responded more to the concerns of African audiences who he declared didn't want to see more "poetic and contemplative films". The somewhat brisker *Le cri du coeur* (*The Heart's Cry*, 1994), set in France and Mali, dramatized the disaporic tensions in many Africans' lives, whereas *Samba Traoré* (1992), with its criminal protagonist on the make, and *Kini And Adams* (1997), a grim English-language tale of two friends caught in a rural-versus-urban tug-of-war, also reflect this change of tack towards the modern. But they retain the director's customary deft handling of a mixed ensemble of professional actors and first-timers, particularly children. Ouédraogo is a key figurehead of African cinema and he remains productive, as evidenced by his invited contributions to prestige portmanteau films – most recently *11'09"01* (2002), about reactions to the September 11 terrorist attacks. RC

Tilaï (The Law) 1990, 81 min

cast Rasmane Ouédraogo, Ina Cissé, Roukietou Barry, Assane Ouédraogo *cin* Jean Monsigny, Pierre Laurent Chenieux *m* Abdullah Ibrahim

After a spell away from his village, Saga (Rasmane Ouedraogo) returns to find his intended wife Nogma (Ina Cissé), married to his father. The two young lovers secretly reunite, setting in chain a tragic set of events riven with conflicting loyalties and moral dilemmas. Memorable imagery, a sparse, evocative score and Ouédraogo's unsentimental handling combine to great effect.

François Ozon
France, 1967–

Frequently and inaccurately described as yet another bad boy of French cinema, François Ozon is really its cheeky imp, sporting both the appearance and the directorial presence of a naughty pixie. He used to make movies, on his father's Super 8 camera, in which most of his family would take acting parts and often wind up dead. A number of critics have seized upon these films as early signifiers of a familiar trope of Ozon's – the lingering death of the nuclear unit.

After attending the FEMIS film school, the director made a number of celebrated shorts, among them the 42-minute *See The Sea* (1997) which quietly hummed with sinister intentions and muted passions. His feature debut, *Sitcom* (1998), was in effect Pasolini's *Theorem* reimagined with a large white rat taking Terence Stamp's role: a bourgeois family were transformed almost instantly by contact with the rodent. Ozon was quickly wrangled by critics into the school of late-1990s neophytes who were trying their damnedest to *épater le bourgeoisie*. *Criminal Lovers* (1999) featured bondage, rape and cannibalism in a truly grim fairy tale, in which *Natural Born Killers* (1994) suddenly morphed into "Hansel And Gretel". *Water Drops On Burning Rocks* (2000) exuded a new sense of maturity, successfully retooling an unproduced play by Rainer Werner Fassbinder, that austerely mimicked his one-set staginess and unapologetic theatricality.

Ozon finally discovered his own voice in *Under The Sand* (2000) which placed Charlotte Rampling at the centre of a mystery, carefully orchestrated to tease and beguile with the merest hints of psychological motivation and narrative exposition. The director returned to base camp with the entertaining kitsch overload of *8 Women* (2002). By contrast, the hazily erotic *Swimming Pool* (2003) seemed like an extension of *Under The Sand*. The director worked closely with Charlotte Rampling again: she played a fusty crime writer whose creative sojourn in Provence is disturbed by a dreamy young girl whose untrammelled sexuality both irritates and intrigues the spinster. Ozon distilled his elliptical and psychological games-playing to its purest essence in *5 x 2* (2004), literally leaving blanks for the audience to fill in, while *Time To Leave* (2005) defied Ozon-watchers by being a conventional and disappointing tale of a gay photographer who's been diagnosed with terminal cancer. LH

Under The Sand (Sous le sable) 2000, 95 min

cast Charlotte Rampling, Bruno Cremer, Jacques Nolot, Alexandra Stewart *cin* (Winter) Jeanne Lapoirie, (Summer) Antoine Héberlé *m* Philippe Rombi

Rampling is glacially magnificent as Marie, a middle-aged woman whose husband mysteriously disappears one day on the beach when she is taking a nap. Marie doesn't seem to care whether he committed suicide or ran away – she continues her life as if he were alive, or at least a constant presence. Long stretches of daily life are conducted without words, and seemingly without significance, but are yet freighted with a haunting poignancy.

8 Women 2001, 111 min

cast Catherine Deneuve, Isabelle Huppert, Emmanuelle Béart, Fanny Ardant, Virginie Ledoyen, Danielle Darrieux *cin* Jeanne Lapoirie *m* Krishna Levy

Ozon is at his most impish in this kitsch, colour-saturated, Agatha Christie-style mystery set to music. A middle-aged man is discovered with a knife in his back and eight immaculately groomed *femmes fatales* are the unusually glamorous suspects. While most of the eight – many of France's topmost leading ladies – play variations on their screen personas only Huppert transcends herself as the pinched, bitter spinster who spits out her sniffy cynicism like machine-gun fire.

5 x 2 2004, 90 min
cast Valéria Bruni-Tedeschi, Stéphane Freiss, Françoise Fabian, Michael Lonsdale, Géraldine Pailhas *cin* Yorick Le Saux *m* Philippe Rombi

Here are five scenes from a marriage, from the couple's first meeting to a bitter, post-divorce encounter. There is nothing in between each episode – no exposition and no explanation – and the audience is left to its own devices to solve the mystery of the painful dissolution of an idyllic love affair. To add to the enigma, Ozon's tale is told backwards in the mode of Christopher Nolan's *Memento* (2000) and Gaspar Noé's *Irreversible* (2002) – although Harold Pinter's play *Betrayal* provided the director's starting point.

Yasujiro Ozu

Japan, 1903–63

According to Wim Wenders, Yasujiro Ozu is "cinema's sacred treasure". He's similarly revered by Jim Jarmusch and Hou Hsiao-Hsien. His masterpiece, *Tokyo Story* (1953), is regularly voted as one of the greatest films of all time in the UK's *Sight & Sound* magazine poll, held once a decade. And yet, for many film-goers, Ozu's work is as daunting as Sunday night homework.

The reason for this is that Ozu's films largely defy the description "movie". Very little moves in them, especially the camera. Both banal and ceremonial, they revel in domestic detail and mundane rituals, particularly the drinking of tea or sake. Oddly elliptical, they often miss out important chunks of narrative, like Noriko's climactic wedding in *Late Spring* (1949). And watching a few Ozu films back-to-back can feel like watching the same movie over and over again, like a film buff's *Groundhog Day* – with the same stock company (especially actress Setsuko Hara, a beacon of dough-faced innocence and virtuous tradition), the same themes, the same situations and often the same character names (Noriko being particularly popular).

Ozu used to compare himself to a chef who makes nothing but tofu, and he wasn't exaggerating. All his late films contain exactly the same ingredients: shots of trains, empty streets, telegraph wires and washing hanging on a line. Famously, he placed the camera a few inches from the ground, as if the viewer were sitting on a traditional tatami mat. His compositions are rigorously spare and often defiantly symmetrical, usually filmed in long, continuous takes. Co-written with Kôgo Noda, his stories almost exclusively centre on the breakdown of the Japanese family, often as a result of modernization and urbanization. Children leave the nest to form new families (often at their father's request), children disappoint their parents, parents burden their children, parents die, and the cycle of life goes unerringly on. Variations on these familial themes appear in *Late Spring*, *Early Summer* (1951), *Tokyo Story*, *Equinox Flower* (1958), *Good Morning* (1959), *Late Autumn* (1960) and his final film *An Autumn Afternoon* (1962). These subject-motifs and their treatment have been linked by some critics to Zen Buddhism. Whatever the truth of this, they certainly invite – even compel – contemplation from the viewer.

But it wasn't always this way. Before the war, Ozu had gained a reputation as a maker of comedies, the Japanese equivalent of his hero Ernst Lubitsch. The satire *I Was Born, But…* (1932), about two young boys' loss of respect for their father, is often considered his first masterpiece. Other comic films include the broad, slapstick college farce *I Flunked, But…* (1930) and *What Did The Lady Forget?* (1937), about a "modern" young woman who comes to stay with her aunt and uncle. He also turned his hand to crime movies (*Walk Cheerfully*, 1930, *Dragnet Girl*, 1933), thrillers (*That Night's Wife*, 1930) and melodramas (*Woman Of Tokyo*, 1933, *A Passing Fancy*, 1933). These genre works are usually forgotten when critics discuss Ozu the transcendental artist and stringent minimalist.

Ozu's output was curtailed by military service during World War II and he was to emerge by the end of the decade as a filmmaker with a simpler and purer technique. His work is ultimately that of a serious director, who achieves his effects through the steady accumulation of fine details. And what seems like repetition is in fact refinement, an artist rigorously perfecting his craft. Methodical, patient and wearing, Ozu hits us with a sucker punch when we least expect it. Masterpieces like *Tokyo Story* and *Late Spring* build slowly and deceptively towards emotional devastation that will have any sentient being reeling in their seat. Even if you don't believe, as Paul Schrader argues in his book *Transcendental Style In Cinema*, that watching an Ozu film is a religious experience, it certainly is an experience – demanding, mesmerizing and rewarding – that is matchless in the history of cinema. LH

Late Spring (Banshun) 1949, 108 min, b/w
cast Setsuko Hara, Chishu Ryu, Yumeji Tsukioka, Haruko Sugimura, Hohi Aoki, Jun Usami *cin* Yuharu Atsuta *m* Senji Ito

Everyone agrees that Noriko's devotion to her father is admirable – but it's time she married. We wait for a love story to arrive amongst the quiet preparations for dinner, the patching of trousers and catching of trains. But it never comes – because it's already under our noses. Wily Ozu's greatest love story is a hymn to filial love. Outwardly as innocent as Noriko's white socks, it delivers a devastating emotional punch.

Early Summer (Bakushû) 1951, 135 min, b/w
cast Setsuko Hara, Chishu Ryu, Chikage Awajima, Kuniko Miyake, Ichiro Sugai, Chieko Higashiyama *cin* Yuharu Atsuta *m* Senji Ito

Spring turns to summer, and somewhere out in the Ozu universe, another Noriko (always the same, always different) reaches marriageable age. But this is a bolder Noriko, wittily chatting back to Aya, her sharp best friend. Summer seems a bolder season altogether: "Idiot!" Noriko's nephews

From the ground up: a typical low-angle shot in a restrained moment from Ozu's poignant *Tokyo Story*.

shout at their uncle, delighted by the old boy's apparent deafness. The family are scarred by war, but (unusually for Ozu) they're prepared to embrace rather than just endure change. The eternal Noriko shows them how.

Tokyo Story (Tôkyô monogatari) 1953, 136 min, b/w

cast Setsuko Hara, Chishu Ryu, Chieko Higashiyama, So Yamamura, Kyoko Kagawa *cin* Yuharu Atsuta *m* Kojun Saito

An elderly couple travel to Tokyo to visit their grown-up children. But the siblings – from hard-faced salon owner Shige to self-important doctor Koichi – have no time for their parents. The visit is a polite disaster. Only saintly Noriko, their widowed daughter-in-law, welcomes them, but even her kindliness cannot insulate them from the cold truth: they are not wanted, and the selfish younger generation are a profound disappointment. A poignant classic.

Equinox Flower (Higanbana) 1958, 118 min

cast Shin Saburi, Kinuyo Tanaka, Ineko Arima, Yoshiko Kuga, Kaiji Sada, Chieko Naniwa *cin* Yuharu Atsuta *m* Kojun Saito

Ozu's first colour movie is a shock to the system. The aggressive vibrancy of his film stock robs his pictures of their previous minimalist intensity, and there's another surprise too. This potent drama centres on a father who *doesn't* want his daughter to get hitched and does everything in his power to prevent the marriage. One thing remains the same, though: the emotional sucker punch that Ozu packs in the final frames.

Good Morning (Ohayô) 1959, 94 min

cast Keiji Sada, Yoshiko Kuga, Chishu Ryu, Kuniko Miyake, Koji Shidara, Masahiko Shimazu *cin* Yuharu Atsuta *m* Toshiro Mayuzumi

One of the most charming, eccentric and fleet-footed of all Ozu's works, this gentle comedy unfolds in a series of delightful vignettes and pen portraits. At its centre are two schoolboys who fart at will and stage a silent protest when their father doesn't buy them a television set. Nearby is a poisonous busybody who mounts a campaign against a neighbour she suspects of stealing funds from the local club. A droll and singular vision of Japanese suburbia.

G.W. Pabst

Czech Republic (formerly Austro-Hungarian Empire), 1885–1967

Georg Wilhelm Pabst was once as highly regarded as his contemporaries F.W. Murnau and Fritz Lang, but his reputation has not weathered nearly as well. Today he is mainly celebrated for *Pandora's Box* (1928), a lurid tale of sexual beguilement and self-destruction in which the incandescent performance of Louise Brooks proved Pabst's undoubted abilities as a director of women.

Pabst came to film direction at the age of 38, after a successful career as an actor and theatre director – including a stint in New York directing German-language plays. His films of the interwar years are sometimes described as realist, but their *mise en scène* is often claustrophobic and oppressive and his viewpoint essentially pessimistic. *Joyless Street* (1925), in which Greta Garbo plays a young middle-class woman who contemplates prostitution to save her family from destitution, explored the desperation caused by post-war inflation. *Geheimnisse einer Seele* (*Secrets Of A Soul*, 1926), an early application of Freudian ideas in film, examined a man's morbid obsession with murdering his wife and contained some startlingly effective dream imagery. Pabst's own preoccupation with the psychosexual found its most complete expression in *Pandora's Box*, an adaptation of Frank Wedekind's controversial play of 1904. Having chosen American actress Brooks for *Pandora's Box* by virtue of her frank and natural sexuality and her distinctly modern beauty, Pabst employed her again for *Diary Of A Lost Girl* (1929), a melodramatic tale of corrupted innocence that attacked bourgeois sexual hypocrisy.

With the arrival of sound, Pabst's films became even more overtly message-based. *Westfront 1918* (1930) was a powerful attack on the inhumanity of war that was even more hard-hitting than Lewis Milestone's *All Quiet On The Western Front* (1930). Pabst's venture into musical territory with a version of Brecht and Weill's anticapitalist satire,

The Threepenny Opera (1931), was rather heavy-handed, but the same year saw the release of his last great cinematic achievement *Kameradschaft* (*Comradeship*). Returning to the theme of pacifism, the film tells the story of how a group of German miners on the Franco-German border came to the rescue of their French counterparts following a disaster. Although often criticized as a simplistic celebration of worker solidarity, it was a remarkably atmospheric and detailed look at the grimness of mining which, in its use of both professional and nonprofessional actors, anticipated Italian neo-realism.

Needless to say the sentiments of both *Westfront 1918* and *Kameradschaft* did not tally with the views of National Socialism, so when the Nazis came to power Pabst headed for France, where he made two films, before moving to the US. Unlike several of his Austro-German colleagues, he found little success in Hollywood, making just one film, *A Modern Hero* (1934), for Warner Bros. Three more films in France preceded his contentious return to Austria, where he shot *Komödianten* (1941) and *Paracelsus* (1943) within the confines of Nazi control. In the post-war period Pabst went some way to redeem his standing with *Der Prozess* (*The Trial*, 1948), which attacked anti-Semitism, and *Der letzte Akt* (*The Last Ten Days*, 1955) about Hitler's final days in power. RB

Pandora's Box (Die Büsche der Pandora)
1928, 100 min, b/w
cast Louise Brooks, Fritz Kortner, Franz Lederer, Carl Goetz, Krafft Raschig, Alice Roberts *cin* Günther Krampf

As the seductive gamine Lulu – a showgirl who is both amoral yet a kind of innocent – American starlet Louise Brooks created one of the most enduring and archetypal of screen figures. The embodiment of pure sexuality, Lulu cuts a swathe through a series of weak-willed and emasculated men. A claustrophobic Berlin (where she works as a burlesque performer) and the fog-filled streets of London (where she meets her end at the hands of Jack the Ripper) provide a suitably oppressive backdrop.

Al Pacino

US, 1940–

It's not all that surprising that the three films Al Pacino has directed have been stage adaptations. Theatre is his first love. Even at the start of his film superstardom in the 1970s he would bounce between cinema and theatre. In 1985, following the devastating failure of Hugh Hudson's historical blockbuster *Revolution*, Pacino returned to the theatre, and put a lot of his own money into the film adaptation of Heathcote Williams's play *The Local Stigmatic* (1990), which he co-directed with David Wheeler. The movie was never intended for general release and, although the Museum of Modern Art has a copy, it reportedly can only screen it with Pacino's consent. At least another of his labours of love, *Looking For Richard* (1996), was indeed intended for public consumption. *Chinese Coffee* (2000), on the other hand, was an adaptation of an Ira Lewis play that has rarely been screened – whether this is by design or default it is hard to say. LH

Looking For Richard 1996, 112 min

with Al Pacino, Kevin Spacey, Winona Rider, Alec Baldwin, Harris Yulin, Aidan Quinn, John Gielgud, Kevin Kline *cin* Robert Leacock *m* Howard Shore

Pacino makes ebullient and engaging company as we join him in his search for the truth about the character of Richard III, one of Shakespeare's most complex villains. He interviews people on the street, as well as Oxford dons and John Gielgud. He visits Stratford and discusses how to play a scene with Kevin Spacey, before finally acting the role alongside Alec Baldwin and Winona Ryder. Pacino's quixotic spirit, fierce intelligence and infectious enthusiasm make this much more than just a Hollywood legend's vanity project.

Marcel Pagnol

France, 1895–1974

A native of Provence – whose culture he did much to promote through his plays, films and novels – Marcel Pagnol was a filmmaker who believed in the supremacy of the word, seeing the arrival of sound as a means of extending the playwright's art. This unashamed literary bias has led to him being dismissed by certain cineastes (in particular the tyros of the *nouvelle vague*), but he is responsible for two great classics of French cinema, *César* (1936) and *The Baker's Wife* (1938), and was the first filmmaker to be elected to the Académie Française.

Pagnol wrote his first play at the age of 15 before taking up his father's career as a teacher. Appointed to a school in Paris in 1922, he was able to give up teaching a few years later following the success of his plays *Marius* and *Topaze* in 1929. *Marius* was the first in a trilogy of plays set against the docks of Marseille; it was followed by *Fanny* (1931) and *César* (1936). Together they followed the lives of fishmonger Fanny, her seafaring boyfriend Marius, her older admirer Panisse and Marius's father César. The trilogy's acute and often comic observations of provincial, working-class life (with authentic language to match) plus its larger-than-life performances proved a winning combination and the film rights were soon snapped up. *Marius* was filmed by Alexander Korda in 1931, but when Pagnol was excluded from involvement in *Topaze* (1933), he formed his own company and hired Marc Allégret to direct *Fanny* in 1932. Pagnol himself helmed *César*, the most serious, but also the most moving, of the three.

As well as filming his own work, Pagnol adapted four stories by fellow Provençal writer Jean Giono beginning with *Joifroi* in 1933. Their most famous collaboration was the sublime *The Baker's Wife*, a bittersweet comedy about a baker who stops working when his much younger wife leaves him for a shepherd. The film is a virtual summary of the director's virtues as a filmmaker: a simple story, lively dialogue and, above all, strong well-rounded characters – fleshed out by a group of regular performers, many with their roots in music hall. Pagnol's films may be technically unadventurous but that is more than compensated for by their affectionate comedy and underlying humanity. RB

César 1936, 121 min, b/w

cast Raimu, Pierre Fresnay, Orane Demazis, André Fouché, Fernand Charpin, Edouard Delmont *cin* Willy *m* Vincent Scotto

The third film of Pagnol's Marseille series sees the arrival of a new character, Césariot (André Fouché), a young man seeking the identity of his real father. Finely balanced on the edge of melodrama and sentimentality, the film hinges on the attempts by café owner César (Raimu) to reconcile father, mother and son – not least because he is the boy's grandfather. A poignant tale of shame, regret and misunderstanding that is raised to the highest level by the fine ensemble acting.

The Baker's Wife (La femme du boulanger) 1938, 116 min, b/w

cast Raimu, Ginette Leclerc, Charles Moulin, Fernand Charpin, Robert Vattier, Robert Bassac, Charles Blavette *cin* Georges Benoit *m* Vincent Scotto

Another scrutiny of human foibles and weaknesses, but this time observing the community living in a Provençal village rather than Marseille. The star, once again, is Raimu – this time as a cuckolded baker who decides to stop working – and if anything his performance is even more astounding than in *César*. As the disgruntled villagers do their best to get him to resume bread-making, Raimu uses his clown's body and expressive face to register his pain in a way that wrings every meaning out of the term tragi-comic.

P

Alan J. Pakula
US, 1928–98

Sometimes it feels like a filmmaker must be hard-wired into the zeitgeist. In a five-year spell in the 1970s, Alan J. Pakula directed three popular thrillers that didn't just reflect political tensions, they anticipated and amplified the fear and disillusionment of the times. These films are commonly known as "paranoia thrillers", although there was nothing delusional about the last of them. *All The President's Men* (1976) documented the *Washington Post*'s investigation into the Watergate break-in, a true story that paralleled the contemporaneous fictional crimes and cover-ups in *Klute* (1971) and *The Parallax View* (1974).

If Pakula had a knack for telling conspiracy stories – and his collaboration with cinematographer Gordon Willis was surely the key to it – he was evidently an intelligent, cultured individual who tried to explore other facets of life in his work, though not always with the same success. He started out as an animator before moving into production, notably for director Robert Mulligan. *To Kill A Mockingbird* (1962) was nominated for the Oscar for best picture, and set the hallmark for a series of adult dramas with pedigree writers like Horton Foote and Gavin Lambert. Pakula turned director in 1969 with an adaptation of John Nichols' novel *The Sterile Cuckoo*. He later earned an Oscar nomination for best screenplay with his meticulous, tasteful but deeply problematic adaptation of William Styron's Holocaust novel, *Sophie's Choice* (1982).

With the industry losing interest in dramas – and adults – in the 1980s Pakula seemed out of touch, and fell back on the kind of potboiler thrillers he could direct in his sleep: he brought craftsmanship but little conviction to *Presumed Innocent* (1990), *Consenting Adults* (1992), *The Pelican Brief* (1993) and *The Devil's Own* (1997). If there is buried treasure in his career, the undiscovered gems are the three pictures he made after *All The President's Men*: the romantic comedy *Starting Over* (1979) and two further collaborations with *Klute* Oscar-winner Jane Fonda, a subtle, realistic Western, *Comes A Horseman* (1978), and one more conspiracy thriller, the flawed but fascinating *Rollover* (1981).

Pakula died in a freak auto accident at the age of 70 – the kind of death that would have set alarm bells ringing in his films. TC

Klute 1971, 114 min
cast Jane Fonda, Donald Sutherland, Roy Scheider, Charles Cioffi, Shirley Stoler, Vivian Nathan *cin* Gordon Willis *m* Michael Small

More than just a spine-tingling exercise in urban paranoia (though it is that too), Pakula's film thrives on a different kind of tension: the tension between the demands of a woman-in-peril scenario, and Jane Fonda's authoritative portrayal of actress/call girl Bree Daniels as an emancipated woman. It's clear that in some ways Bree herself is the real threat. Fonda won the Oscar for the part, probably the most important in her career.

The Parallax View 1974, 102 min
cast Warren Beatty, Paula Prentiss, Hume Cronyn, William Daniels, Kenneth Mars *cin* Gordon Willis *m* Michael Small

The most lucid and ingenious, the most deeply, creepily satisfying of paranoia thrillers, *The Parallax View* posits an assassination corporation behind (one presumes) the murders of John and Robert Kennedy and Martin Luther King. Reporter Joe Frady (Warren Beatty) is on to Them, or so he believes… Pakula and cinematographer Gordon Willis elaborate an oblique but unmistakeable unease with each and every frame.

All The President's Men 1976, 138 min
cast Dustin Hoffman, Robert Redford, Jack Warden, Martin Balsam, Hal Holbrook, Jason Robards, Jane Alexander *cin* Gordon Willis *m* David Shire

Critic David Thomson is surely right when he complains that America would have been better served with a Watergate movie that focused on politics, not heroic reporters. Nevertheless, on its own terms this ominous, compelling film of Bob Woodward and Carl Bernstein's book remains a useful record of chicanery and attempted cover-up, and the dedication and integrity of the journalists who broke the story.

Euzhan Palcy
Martinique, 1958–

With *A Dry White Season* (1989), Euzhan Palcy became the first black woman to make a Hollywood studio feature film. Born in Martinique, she worked there as a TV writer and director before studying at the Sorbonne in Paris, where she met François Truffaut. He advised her in the production of her feature debut *Rue cases nègres* (*Sugar Cane Alley*, 1983). The film's enthusiastic reception – including a César award for best first film – took her straight to America. Set in apartheid South Africa, *A Dry White Season* starred Marlon Brando and Donald Sutherland; Brando elected to work for free. More recent works include *Siméon* (1992) and *Aimé Césaire: A Voice For History* (1994), a documentary about the Martinican writer and politician. Palcy continues to direct – mainly for TV – and has the notable distinction of having a cinema in Paris named after her. JC

Rue cases nègres (Sugar Cane Alley) 1983, 103 min
cast Garry Cadenat, Darling Legitimus, Douta Seck, Joby Bernabé, Francisco Charles *cin* Dominique Chapuis *m* Groupe Malavoi

A vibrant and affecting adaptation of the novel by Joseph Zobel. The film focuses on a young boy, Jose, who works the sugar cane plantations of Martinique with his grandmother in the 1930s. Jose is determined to escape this way of life and so dedicates his life to study. A charming dramatization of a little-documented world, the film eschews sentimentality in favour of a sensitive social realism.

Jafar Panahi
Iran, 1960–

After serving as Abbas Kiarostami's assistant director on *Through The Olive Trees* (1994), Jafar Panahi made two features of his own that further developed the narrative perfected in Kiarostami's *Where Is My Friend's House?* (1987), in which a child embarks on an obstacle-laden quest. Both *The White Balloon* (1995) and *The Mirror* (1997) concerned the trials and tribulations of little girls in crowded Tehran streets (respectively, one on a mission to buy a goldfish and one trying to find her way home after school); their stressful journeys, shot in "real time", are thrillers that double as microcosmic portraits of the city.

The Circle (2000) showed what might happen to these vulnerable but formidably strong-willed girls once they grew up. An inflammatory indictment of women's repression under the theocratic Iranian regime, it won plaudits abroad but was banned at home. The mordant, perfectly calibrated *Crimson Gold* (2003) – as with *The White Balloon*, the screenplay was by Abbas Kiarostami – also took a circular shape, beginning with the suicide of a mentally unbalanced pizza-delivery man during a botched robbery and then backtracking to account for his terrible end. Like *The Circle*, *Offside* (2006) addressed women's exclusion from society in Iran, but this time Panahi added comic and optimistic overtones to the action. JW

The Circle (Dayereh) 2000, 90 min
cast Maryiam Oarvin Almain, Nargess Mamizadeh, Fereshteh Sadr Orafai, Monir Arab, Elham Saboktakin *cin* Bahram Badakhshani

Panahi's spin on *La ronde* constructs an existential Alcatraz, depicting the daily lives of women in Iran as a journey through a labyrinthine prison. Despite the schematic framework, the film is a piece of bracing, heightened social realism; though propelled by fatalist dread, it's also a raw cry of defiance, and a fine introduction to Panahi's uniformly excellent body of work.

Offside 2006, 93 min
cast Sima Mobarakshai, Safar Samandar, Shayesteh Irani *cin* Rami Agami, Mahmoud Kalari *m* Yuval Barazani, Korosh Bozorgpour

Iranian women are banned from attending soccer games in Iran, so perhaps it's fitting that Panahi's spirited movie was banned from Iranian cinemas. In this rowdy day-in-the-life, various women disguised as men try to gain admission to a World Cup qualifier – and they mostly fail, though the movie's visual gags and wry banter make it clear that they're hardly defeated in being caught out. The women here are appealing and complicated, asserting their rights – and their love of sport – through wily subterfuge.

Danny & Oxide Pang
Hong Kong, 1965–

The phenomenon of pan-Asian fusion is not limited to restaurants. Arguably, the Pang brothers typify this noodle bar approach more than any other directors, liberally seasoning their work with stylistic tics and tropes from Hong Kong, Japan and Thailand. Indeed, Danny works in Hong Kong, and Oxide in Thailand.

Both twins worked in advertising – Danny as an editor and Oxide as a colourist and director. The latter's career move to Thailand eventually resulted in an opportunity to write and direct his debut feature, *Who Is Running?* (1997), a karmic genre movie in which the hero is informed by a Buddhist monk that he can only change his bad luck by saving the lives of five people. The critical and commercial success led to the brothers' most renowned work as co-directors. *Bangkok Dangerous* (1999) and *The Eye* (2002) displayed their chameleon-like qualities; the gangster movie owed a neon-hued debt to Wong Kar-Wai, while the supernatural chiller took its eerie cue from Japanese horror movies like Hideo Nakata's *Ring* (1998). Often the problem with any sort of fusion, whether in cinema or cookery, is that the result can be a blandly indistinct stew of influences, disappointingly free of national or individual characteristics. And this is certainly the case with much of the Pang brothers' formulaic output. Only Oxide's *Abnormal Beauty* (2004) has punched above its generic weight. This *Crash*/*Silence Of The Lambs* hybrid about a woman who takes illicit photos of car crash victims and comes to the attentions of a serial killer at least did something innovative with a familiar recipe. LH

Bangkok: Dangerous 1999, 108 min
cast Pawalit Mongkolpisit, Premsinee Ratanasopha, Patharawarin Timkul, Pisek Intrakanchit *cin* Decha Srimantra *m* Orange Music

A deaf-mute variation on the familiar theme of the loneliness of the contract killer, a story at least as old (in Western cinema) as *This Gun For Hire* (1942). While technically impressive – the dialogue adds up to less than twenty minutes and the set pieces display a certain brio and bravado – there is something contemptuously familiar about the posturing hit men, neon aesthetic and steely cityscape. The blur of action is cut so hard and so fast that it ends up like a cheap fairground ride in the Wong Kar-Wai theme park. But it's thrilling nonetheless.

The Eye (Gia gwai) 2002, 99 min
cast Lee Sinje, Lawrence Chou, Chutcha Rujinanon, Candy Lo, Pierre Png, Edmund Chen, So Yut-Lai, Ko Yin-Ping *cin* Decha Srimanta *m* Orange Music

The brothers Pang have transplanted another generic trope – when body parts go bad – and grafted on a patina of weird Japanese elegance. A blind violinist has a cornea transplant and begins to see dead people being carted off by the Grim Reaper. The atmosphere is suitably eerie and the shock effects provide enough bangs for our bucks. And even if they are slavishly copying other directors' styles, at least here the Pangs prove themselves to be master forgers.

P

Sergei Parajanov
Georgia (formerly Soviet Union), 1924–90

Sergei Parajanov is a visionary heir to Alexander Dovzhenko and a reminder that the persecution of film directors in the Soviet Union didn't end with the death of Stalin.

Born to an Armenian family, Parajanov studied film at the State Institute of Cinematography under Lev Kuleshov. His first four feature films all complied with the official doctrines of socialist realism: *Andriesh* (1955), *The First Lad* (1959), *Ukrainian Rhapsody* (1961) and *Flower In The Stone* (1963). And then came *Shadows Of Our Forgotten Ancestors* (1964), a lyrical invocation of the spirit of Dovzhenko, whose film *Earth* (1930) was sensually evoked in Parajanov's bucolic, folkloric and delirious love song to the Ukrainian landscape. With its rejection of traditional narrative and symbolic use of camera movement, *Shadows* was a film of startling originality. Winning several awards, Parajanov quickly became a local celebrity, a human rights activist and a problem to the authorities, not least when he refused to dub his film into the Russian language.

Several projects were rejected by Soviet apparatchiks and the director was, in effect, exiled to Armenia. There he made his most defiantly anti-realistic, idiosyncratic and formalist picture, *The Colour Of Pomegranates* (1969), a sublimely hypnotic and exquisitely opaque masterpiece. The film was taken from him by the authorities and given to another director to re-edit and make fit for public consumption. An export ban was imposed upon the offending work, and that was just the start of Parajanov's troubles.

In 1974, he was arrested on several charges including "trafficking in art objects" and homosexuality, though the director always maintained that his real crime was surrealism. Condemned to hard labour for five years, the director served all but one, and was freed after an international campaign. (Parajanov's prison stories later became a screenplay for Yuri Ilyenko's film *Swan Lake: The Zone*, 1990.) Banned from filmmaking, Parajanov was rearrested in 1982 and again only allowed his liberty after foreign intervention. Permitted to work in Georgia, he applied the *Pomegranates* template to *The Legend Of The Suram Fortress* (1984), an intoxicating blend of ecstatic imagery and narrative opacity based on a medieval Georgian legend. Parajanov continued in the same hyperreal vein with his short *Arabesques On The Pirsomani Themes* (1986) and *Ashik Kerib* (*Kerib The Minstrel*, 1988), the gnomic tale of a wandering minstrel which showcased Parajanov's innovative use of dance and ritual. *Kerib* was the distillation, if not quite the perfection, of the film-maker's artistic idiosyncrasies. As with the works of his hero Pasolini, watching the film is like seeing the world through a different lens. LH

Shadows Of Our Forgotten Ancestors (Teni zabytykh predkov) 1964, 95 min
cast Ivan Nikolaichuk, Larissa Kadochnikova, Tatiana Bestaeva, Spartak Bagashvili *cin* Viktor Ilienko *m* Y. Shorik

It's less self-consciously painterly than *Pomegranates* – Parajanov's effervescent camera can hardly stay still – while the plot, a Carpathian Romeo and Juliet, is even approachable to Western audiences. What the two films share is the director's yen for super-saturated colours, mystical symbols, and religious rituals and his uncanny ability to evoke the hallucinatory qualities of a fever dream.

The Colour Of Pomegranates (Tsvet granata, aka Sayat Nova) 1969, 73 min
cast Sofico Chiaureli, Melkon Aleksanian, Vilen Galstian, Giorgi Gegechkori *cin* Suren Shakhbazian *m* Tigran Mansurian

There's a linear narrative about the life of the eighteenth-century Armenian poet Sayat Nova buried in this extraordinary film's symbolic textures, which are defiantly rooted in Armenian culture and folklore. The fact that the story is fiendishly difficult to decipher never becomes a problem, as this is a film to bask or bathe in. Parajanov's lyrical imagery – pages of books flapping on the roof of an old house like birds readying for flight, the blood-red juice of pomegranates slowly saturating the fabric of a pure white tablecloth – have all the intensity, ebullience and logic of a lucid and delirious dream.

Chan-Wook Park
South Korea, 1963–

Also known as Park Chan-Wook, this South Korean director has rapidly become the figurehead for a new wave of sophisticated ultra-violent films from East Asia.

Originally a film critic, Park shot to fame in his homeland with *Joint Security Area* (aka *JSA*, 2000), which was both a murder mystery (of sixteen North Korean guards) and a subtle plea for harmonious relations between the two Koreas. It was a polished film graced with characteristic touches of cinematic flair: unusual camera angles, a man freezing in mid-air, a grisly scene in a morgue. The massive success of the film, which dealt with a subject that was taboo in South Korea, set Park on the road to making his "Vengeance" trilogy: *Sympathy For Mr Vengeance* (2002), *Oldboy* (2003) and *Lady Vengeance* (2005). Though it is reductive to make the case that there is a template for Park's vengeance films, it is true to say that they all contain shocking violence, nausea-inducing physicality – the eating of a live squid in *Oldboy* being a signature example – and punishing levels of physical and psychological cruelty.

Predictably, Quentin Tarantino became an immediate Park fan, and unsuccessfully attempted to steer the Cannes jury towards awarding *Oldboy* the Palme

P

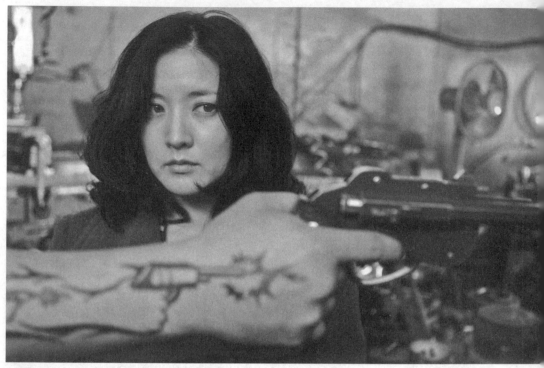

Lady Vengeance: the culmination of Chan-Wook Park's "Vengeance" trilogy was a typical melée of complex plotting and extreme violence.

d'Or in 2004. Just as predictably, fingers were pointed at the film following the Virginia Tech massacre and the release of pictures of the perpetrator, disturbed South Korean student Seung-Hui Cho, that were similar to images from the film.

Western focus on the "Vengeance" trilogy has, however, blinded viewers to Park's wider oeuvre, which has touched on horror, science fiction, historical drama and fantasy, with the afterlife being a favourite theme. In 2006, *I'm A Cyborg But That's OK* even ventured into the reaches of romantic comedy, although the feel-good factor was corrupted by the fact that Park's characters live in a mental institution. South Korea's finest remains a director to watch out for. RC

Oldboy 2003, 120 min
cast Choi Min-Sik, Ji-Tae Yu, Ji Dae-Han, Oh Dal-Su, Kang Hye-Jeong *cin* Jeong Jeong-Hun *m* Jo Yeong-Wook

Not really the sicko outrage of media legend, *Oldboy* is still a very queasy, yet thrilling, ride. Oh Desai (Choi Min-Sik) has been incarcerated in a single room for fifteen years, apparently the leading suspect in his wife's murder. When he is suddenly released, he goes on the rampage, intoxicated with hatred for his unknown jailor and a desire for revenge. The plausible denouement (or at least what stands for one in the world of exotic horror), the career-defining turn from the ravaged-looking Choi and the consistently stunning imagery ensure that the film's cult status feels well earned.

Nick Park
UK, 1958–

In over twenty years with Aardman Animations, Nick Park has become the star creator of the Bristol-based studio's lovingly detailed claymation adventures. His films crackle with droll wit, slapstick action, endearing anthropomorphism and a certain lightly worn nostalgia for the commercial artefacts and interior design of post-war England.

Park's films are also literally inventive, wheezing and creaking with delightfully complex, ad hoc contraptions, like Techno Trousers (in *The Wrong Trousers*, 1993) and the Knit-o-Matic (in *A Close Shave*, 1995). These two gadgets come courtesy of Wallace, the cheese-loving amateur inventor (voiced by Peter Sallis) who, together with his mute, long-suffering dog Gromit, is the star of Park's Oscar-winning shorts. In the first Wallace & Gromit animation, *A Grand Day Out* (1989), Wallace builds a spaceship in his basement to take them on a trip to the moon, which holds a special attraction for him because, after all, it's made of cheese. In another early triumph, Park won his first Oscar for the claymation short *Creature Comforts* (1990), which depicted life at the zoo using unscripted interviews with human members of the "great British public".

Five years in the making, Aardman's first feature film, *Chicken Run* (2000), includes a daring escape sequence that Park and co-director Peter Lord designed as a homage to *Raiders Of The Lost Ark* (1981). Indeed, Park's films brim with cinematic references. The shadowy, rain-drenched *The Wrong Trousers*, arguably the best of the short Wallace & Gromit films, borrows from classic *noir* and Hitchcock in its tale of a villainous penguin who embroils Wallace in a diamond heist, while *Chicken Run* recasts stop-motion poultry in clever reworkings of scenes from *Stalag 17* (1953) and *The Great Escape* (1963). Wallace and Gromit also remain productive and on top form; in 2005, they starred in their first feature-length film, the splendid *Wallace & Gromit In The Curse Of The Were-Rabbit*. JW

Chicken Run 2000, 84 min

cast (voices) Mel Gibson, Julia Sawalha, Jane Horrocks, Miranda Richardson, Phil Daniels *cin* Dave Alex Riddett *m* John Powell, Henry Gregson-Williams

Enlisting the aid of on-the-lam American rooster Rocky (voiced by Mel Gibson), Ginger the chicken (Julia Sawalha) and her friends hatch a plan to escape from the grim prison camp known as Tweedy's Farm. Despite a few broad concessions to the American market, Aardman's first feature-length film preserves all the charm and quirk of the studio's shorts, and revels in both its suspenseful action sequences and a joyous swing-dance set piece.

Wallace & Gromit In The Curse Of The Were-Rabbit 2005, 85 min

cast (voices) Peter Sallis, Helena Bonham Carter, Ralph Fiennes, Peter Kay, Nicholas Smith *cin* Tristan Oliver, Dave Alex Riddett *m* Julian Nott

The scatty inventor and his mute, sensible best friend finally get the feature-length treatment. (Park co-directs with Steve Box.) As co-proprietors of a humane pest-control service, Wallace and Gromit are busy enough keeping their town's prizewinning vegetable patches safe from munching rabbits, but then a mysterious, ravenous beast starts wreaking havoc on the local gardens. This is a joyous, exquisite movie, and so crammed with delightful detail that it rewards multiple viewings.

Alan Parker

UK, 1944–

The work of Alan Parker has invited critical epithets from gut-wrenching and heart-warming to toe-tapping. This is a man who has made a whole movie about bowel movements. Parker is an enemy of pretension, a campaigner against the cerebral tendency of British cinema, mockingly referring to avant-garde films as "instant narcolepsy".

A working-class boy who worked his way up the advertising industry, making hundreds of commercials along the way, Parker was running his own production company by the time he was 26. In 1973, he funded his own short film, *No Hard Feelings*, and

in 1976 he made his feature debut, *Bugsy Malone*. A truly idiosyncratic gangster comedy with a cast of kids and a roster of songs, it established a musical theme that would run through much of Parker's subsequent career. With *Fame* (1980), *Pink Floyd – The Wall* (1982), *The Commitments* (1991) and *Evita* (1996), it seems that the erstwhile adman has found his métier in the musical. However, Parker can also craft a story, being both a screenwriter and a published novelist. Critics, though, have spotted an unfortunate yen for cinematic hyperbole in his non-musicals. Certainly, *Midnight Express* (1978) was oversized and overwrought, harrowing as it was.

The big message movie seems to be a happy medium for Parker, as he proved in the powerful Civil Rights film *Mississippi Burning* (1988). At times, as with *Birdy* (1984), it feels as if Parker has plugged directly into the central nervous system of his audience. And there does seem to be a contract with the viewer not unlike that between an advertiser and a consumer. Even though it knows it's being emotionally manipulated, the audience goes along with Parker for the ride. He pulled the strings so masterfully in *Angel Heart* (1987) that most people couldn't see the twist coming. Yet he was unable to pull off the same trick with *The Life Of David Gale* (2003). The Kevin Spacey death-row drama was one of the director's relatively few commercial disappointments, along with the bowel-obsessed *The Road To Wellville* (1994), while *Shoot The Moon* (1981), *Come See The Paradise* (1990) and *Angela's Ashes* (1999) showed that the audience doesn't really tune in when Parker is playing in minor key. LH

Midnight Express 1978, 121 min

cast Brad Davis, Randy Quaid, John Hurt, Irene Miracle, Bo Hopkins, Paolo Bonacelli, Paul Smith *cin* Michael Seresin *m* Giorgio Moroder

A testimony to Parker's inimitable powers as a wrangler of the audience's emotions is that he makes us feel sorry for an American drugs tourist. *Midnight Express* is based loosely on the true story of Billy Hayes, played with intense vulnerability by Brad Davis, who's caught trying to smuggle drugs out of Turkey. He experiences every circle of hell in a barbaric jail, where he befriends an eccentric inmate (John Hurt) who tells him about the "midnight express".

Mississippi Burning 1988, 127 min

cast Gene Hackman, Willem Dafoe, Frances McDormand, Brad Dourif, R. Lee Ermey, Gaillard Sartain, Stephen Tobolowsky *cin* Peter Biziou *m* Trevor Jones

Gene Hackman and Willem Dafoe are both magnificent as sparring partners in the FBI who investigate the disappearance of three Civil Rights workers in Mississippi in 1964. This no-frills feature was based on a true story and Parker was in campaigning mode. There is something dubious about a do-good movie in which white cops come to the rescue of poor, almost mute blacks who can't help themselves. Others may take a more pragmatic view, that this is a rare Hollywood film that deals with one of the most shameful episodes of recent American history.

413

The Commitments 1991, 118 min
cast Robert Arkins, Michael Aherne, Angeline Ball, Maria Doyle, Dave Finnegan, Bronagh Gallagher, Andrew Strong *cin* Gale Tattersall

Parker shows that he can do gritty realism like the best of British, applying his showman's sensibility to Roddy Doyle's small-scale novel of a young soul band trying to make the big time in Dublin. Sixty-four bands were auditioned, as well as 1500 young musicians: the nonprofessional actors, especially lead singer Andrew Strong, exhibit an ebullient, energetic charm.

Trey Parker
US, 1969–

When Trey Parker and buddy Matt Stone write juvenile, scatological jokes for actors, it's just not funny. Yet put that same gross-out humour in the mouths of cartoon children, and it's not only funny, but authentically transgressive and taboo-breaking. The former film student at the University of Colorado is unlikely to be remembered for *Cannibal – The Musical* (1993), a toe-tapping celebration of a nineteenth-century prospector who was the only American to be convicted of cannibalism. Nor indeed, for *Orgazmo* (1997) about a Mormon porn star. Both films would have been consigned to the overflowing trash can of Hollywood history if it hadn't been for a cartoon short called *The Spirit Of Christmas* (1995). A video greetings card commissioned by a TV executive, in which a cartoon Jesus and Santa slug it out over the meaning of the holiday, it became a cult must-have item amongst Hollywood cognoscenti. It begat the TV series *South Park* which in turn begat the feature film *South Park: Bigger, Longer And Uncut* (1999).

After their own dismal attempt at film stardom in *BASEketball* (1998), Parker and Stone wisely stuck with animation. Their puppet-animated response to Bush's war on terror took no prisoners. *Team America: World Police* (2004) began with a storming Jerry Bruckheimer parody and speculated with puerile tongue in cheek that liberal actors Sean Penn, Tim Robbins and Susan Sarandon have been brainwashed by North Korea's leader Kim Jong Il. Concluding with belligerent jingoism, it is best enjoyed as part homage, part parody of Gerry Anderson's Thunderbirds Superdynamation style, which it superficially so resembles. LH

South Park: Bigger, Longer And Uncut 1999, 81 min
cast (voices) Trey Parker, Matt Stone, George Clooney, Mary K. Bergman, Isaac Hayes, Minnie Driver, Eric Idle *m* Trey Parker

It's a minor, profane miracle that this film succeeds at all and it does so by ratcheting up the TV series' bad taste and invention, while hitting its satiric targets with an assured maturity. Just when you think the depths have been finally reached, new levels of bad taste are somehow plumbed: Winona Ryder's novelty act with ping-pong balls,

for instance, and the gay relationship beween Saddam Hussein and Satan.

Gordon Parks
US, 1912–2006

Gordon Parks has the distinction of being the first African-American to direct a major box-office hit. A photojournalist with *Life* magazine from 1948 to 1968, Parks directed his first film, *The Learning Tree*, in 1969. Based on his own memoir of growing up black in Kansas, it was deemed "culturally significant" by the US Library of Congress in 1989. His great commercial success, *Shaft* (1971), naturally spawned a sequel – *Shaft's Big Score!* (1972) – which was a tepid attempt to cash in on Richard Roundtree's black private-eye cool. (Roundtree's third outing in the role, 1973's *Shaft In Africa*, was directed by John Guillermin.) Both films, however, announced the emergence of a new African-American screen persona. *Leadbelly* (1976) was an emasculated portrait of the American blues folk singer Huddie Ledbetter, from a director whose penchant for storytelling seldom found adequate screen vehicles. His son was Gordon Parks Jr, the director of that other African-American box-office success, *Superfly* (1972). RA

Shaft 1971, 100 min
cast Richard Roundtree, Moses Gunn, Charles Cioffi, Christopher St John, Gwenn Mitchell, Lawrence Pressman *cin* Urs Furrer *m* Isaac Hayes

Ultra-cool private detective Richard Roundtree's investigation of a gangland kidnapping amid the Bronx turf wars never lets up, powered along by a slick Isaac Hayes score. The film takes its realist cues from the new maverick Hollywood thrillers of the era, and has come to epitomize "blaxploitation". But for Gordon Parks, it was "just a Saturday night fun picture which people go to see because they want to see the black guy winning." Exhausting its box-office allure, the franchise fetched up on primetime television and was remade by John Singleton in 2000.

Pier Paolo Pasolini
Italy, 1922–75

Pier Paolo Pasolini is a great filmmaker, one of cinema's true artists, and yet he has arguably made only one really great film. There's a very good reason for this apparent paradox. What Pasolini was attempting, as a novelist, poet and director, was so insanely ambitious and experimental that it veered into the quixotic. He was trying to rewrite the language of film and construct his own cinema of poetry. This was not to be a lyricism stuffed with chocolate-box beauty, but a difficult, gnarly poetry that wasn't easy to consume. And like all true experiments, it didn't always work.

A gay, Marxist atheist, Pasolini was the son of an army officer and a schoolteacher, a profession he himself took up until he was expelled for allegedly having sexual relations with some of his pupils. He moved to Rome in the early 1950s, where he delighted and scandalized the country with his explicit and iconoclastic novels and poetry. His novels celebrated the lowlife *ragazzi* – pimps, hustlers, thieves – to whom the middle-class intellectual Pasolini swore sexual and artistic allegiance. This criminal milieu was the subject of his first two films, *Accattone* (1961) and *Mamma Roma* (1962), incandescent and evocative studies of a thief and a prostitute respectively. Both represented a decisive move away from the neo-realism of Vittorio De Sica and Roberto Rossellini to a more mythic realism. Amid the dank squalor of Pasolini's unflinching naturalism, his protagonists were occasionally and incongruously posed like divine subjects in religious iconography, as in the famous "La ricotta" episode in Pasolini's contribution to the portmanteau film *RoGoPaG* (1962). He took this potent aggregation of religion and neo-realism to its logical conclusion with *The Gospel According To St Matthew* (1964), easily the finest screen representation of the life of Christ and the director's masterpiece.

Revealing a cinematic dexterity that hasn't always been recognized, he elegantly adopted a different mode of address with *Hawks And Sparrows* (1965), a charming, allegorical picaresque featuring the subversive presence of elderly clown Totò and Pasolini's lover, Ninetto Davoli, whose goofy exuberance would be a near-constant feature of the director's subsequent movies.

Oedipus Rex (1967) represented the other half of the mythic realism equation, taking Sophocles' tragedy and inflecting it with a neo-realist grit, with Franco Citti as the king, bristling with the same coarse vitality and luminous anger that he displayed in *Accattone*. Pasolini book-ended the tragedy with scenes from the twentieth century, not for a one-size-fits-all universalism, but for a specific contemporary resonance, echoing a theme that would resonate throughout his work, the tragedy of the individual in an alienating, industrial society.

Theorem (1968) and *Pigsty* (1969) were myths of Pasolini's own making, while *Medea* (1970) continued to mine the psychoanalytical and ideological seams of Greek tragedy. Then, Pasolini really surprised everyone, by entering the mainstream. The "Trilogy Of Life" was for him a zesty celebration of sex and youth before industrial capitalism had transformed the human body into a saleable commodity. *The Decameron* (1971) was a phenomenal hit in both arthouses and grind houses as well as local fleapits, and unexpectedly spawned many cheap porno imitations, ie saleable commodities. Pasolini applied the same gleefully bawdy and intellectually rigorous template to *The Canterbury Tales* (1972), which concluded with a scene surely unmatched in any national cinema, of the Devil's giant bottom farting out the damned. (Pasolini was to stand trial on charges of obscenity on account of the film.) *Arabian Nights* (1974), however, was the delirious apotheosis of the trilogy. With its Chinese box structure of interweaving stories, it was a heady brew of joyous copulations, aching melancholy and fantastic invention. It proved to be the end of both the trilogy and a particular ideology for the director. In his *mea culpa* essay "Disavowal Of The Trilogy Of Life", Pasolini irascibly declared that the sexual liberation he had previously celebrated was a twentieth-century chimera, another product of capitalist consumerism.

Pasolini continued this iridescent anger – with both himself and a generation who had allowed themselves to become little more than consumers – in *Salò, Or The 120 Days Of Sodom* (1975), a despairing howl of nihilism whose unrelenting onslaught of torture, barbarity and sadism made it one of the most controversial works ever made. It was banned in many countries, including Britain, where a highly censored version could be seen only in film clubs with a prologue pedantically explaining the historical background and informing the audience that it was full of symbols they wouldn't understand. It was released in Italy, but by then its creator was already dead, apparently murdered by one of his beloved *ragazzi*, Pino Pelosi. For some, however, the startling inconsistencies in Pelosi's confession pointed to political assassination. Pasolini was a popular, outspoken newspaper columnist and had recently called for the prosecution of government leaders. In 2005, Pelosi claimed in a television interview that he was merely a bystander to the murder carried out by others who accused the director of being a "dirty communist" while they callously beat him to death. The case of Pasolini's murder was subsequently reopened.

In his theories of film, Pasolini argued that the conventions of classical Hollywood cinema had become so entrenched that they seemed to be not just the preferred but the *natural* way to construct a narrative, shoot a scene or edit a sequence. In this conventional cinema – what he dubbed the cinema of prose – the goal was naturalism and the form was invisible. In his Marxist cinema of poetry, by contrast, Pasolini brought the viewer's attention to the means of filmic production and more importantly tried to construct a way of seeing that couldn't be immediately codified or commodified. As Bernardo Bertolucci, an assistant on *Accattone*, said, working with Pasolini was like watching cinema being invented on set. This meant putting cameras in the "wrong" place, encouraging a degree of amateurism, and making mistakes in the editing so there was a pronounced lack of continuity or fluidity.

Pasolini contaminated, disrupted and corrupted the unified narrative, prioritizing irrationality and dream logic over psychological cohesion, like the good Freudian he always was. If *The Gospel According To St Matthew* is Pasolini's only perfectly unified movie, there are moments, transcendent epiphanies, in all his films where the audience sees the world startlingly anew, and that, surely, is a defining characteristic of art. LH

The Gospel According To St Matthew (Il vangelo secondo Matteo) 1964, 142 min, b/w
cast Enrique Irazoqui, Margherita Caruso, Susanna Pasolini, Marcello Morante, Mario Socrate *cin* Tonino Delli Colli *m* J.S. Bach, Mozart, Prokofiev

Pasolini presents Jesus as an angry young man, a messiah for the countercultural times. The film brims with Marxist poetry and immediacy, not just in Enrique Irazoqui's blistering performance as Jesus, but in the harsh realism of the crucifixion sequence, as Pasolini relentlessly evokes the real pain of nails being hammered into flesh.

Theorem (Teorema) 1968, 98 min
cast Terence Stamp, Silvana Mangano, Massimo Girotti, Anne Wiazemsky, Laura Betti, Andrés José Cruz *cin* Giuseppe Ruzzolini *m* Ennio Morricone

Pasolini's potent Marxist fable about the paralysing effect of beauty on capitalist society is probably more relevant than ever in this celebrity-obsessed, nip-tuck age. Terence Stamp is at his most criminally handsome and Zen-like as the Christ/Devil figure who enters a bourgeois house and seduces the members of the household one by one. When he mysteriously leaves, the family unit spectacularly implodes, while the maid (played by Pasolini favourite Laura Betti) starts to levitate above the house.

Pigsty (Porcile) 1969, 100 min
cast Pierre Clémenti, Jean-Pierre Léaud, Alberto Lionello, Ugo Tognazzi, Anne Wiazemsky *cin* Tonino Delli Colli *m* Benedetto Ghiglia

A mordant, transgressive and pessimistic satire on two very different consumer societies: the first on the slopes of Mount Etna in the fifteenth century, where cannibal Pierre Clémenti throws the heads of his victims into the volcano and soon attracts a following who ritually repeat his actions, until the Church intervenes, and he is himself eaten by dogs. In the second – even more controversial – episode, Jean-Pierre Léaud plays the son of a West German industrialist who can only be sexually aroused by pigs until they eventually devour him. It would be difficult to miss the metaphor.

Medea 1970, 118 min
cast Maria Callas, Giuseppe Gentile, Laurent Terzieff, Massimo Girotti, Margareth Clementi, Anna Maria Chio, Luigi Barbini *cin* Ennio Guarnieri

Along with *Oedipus Rex* this surely must rank as one of the most idiosyncratic versions of a Greek myth, not just for Pasolini's Freudian and Marxist take, but for its confluence of theatrical minimalism and bizarre costume design. Euripides' tragedy is presented as a clash of ideologies between Medea (a tempestuous Maria Callas), representing magic and myth, and the rational and civil Jason. Pasolini stretches out the silences, allowing the camera to linger on his hallucinatory version of a mythic landscape.

The Decameron (Il decamerone) 1971, 111 min
cast Franco Citti, Ninetto Davoli, Angela Luce, Patrizia Capparelli, Pier Paolo Pasolini *cin* Tonino Delli Colli *m* Pier Paolo Pasolini, Ennio Morricone

Taking a selection of tales from Boccaccio's original text, Pasolini wove them into a complex, ribald and euphoric celebration of storytelling, self-reflexivity and sex. If ever one film was meant for two distinct audiences, it's this. Amid all the bountiful nudity and firm, tender flesh, there is a feast for the mind too in Pasolini's earthy metaphors and his scabrous baiting of the Church and bourgeoisie.

Salò, Or The 120 Days Of Sodom (Salò, o le centoventi giornate di Sodoma) 1975, 117 min
cast Paolo Bonicelli, Giorgio Cataldi, Umberto P. Quintavalle *cin* Tonino Delli Colli *m* Ennio Morricone

Pasolini's adaptation of the Marquis De Sade's novel transposes the story to Fascist Italy. The plot is frighteningly simple: Fascists ritually and sexually humiliate naked teenagers. The children are stripped, immersed in barrels of shit and put on leashes and all fours like dogs. *Salò* begs the question: in what way were Pasolini and his film crew different from the Fascist tormentors they were depicting?

Ivan Passer
Czech Republic (formerly Czechoslovakia), 1933–

To see *Intimate Lighting* (1965) or *Cutter's Way* (1981) is to open a window onto the work of a great undiscovered director, a master of mood and nuance, very subtle, funny and poignant. Yet Ivan Passer has been toiling in the Hollywood trenches for more than three decades, with just a dozen mostly negligible (and some very bad) movies to show for it.

Passer was a shining light of the Czech New Wave, writing the screenplays for Milos Forman's acclaimed *A Blonde In Love* (1965) and *The Fireman's Ball* (1967), and directing his own screenplay for *Intimate Lighting*, about a musician returning to his home town with his betrothed. All three films are naturalistic comedies balancing satire and affection, and evidence that Passer was at least Forman's equal. After 1968 he made his way to the US with the aid of producer Carlo Ponti. His first Hollywood film, *Born To Win* (1971), is a drug movie with slapstick sequences, starring George Segal, Paula Prentiss and a young Robert De Niro – worth a look. Police movie *Law And Disorder* (1974) also has its followers. But subsequent efforts trace a sinking talent. Passer stopped writing and seems to have settled for mediocrity, save for the rare occasions when the material rekindles his enthusiasm: *Cutter's Way*, most notably, and the Emmy-winning TV movie *Stalin* (1992) are the standouts. TC

Cutter's Way 1981, 109 min
cast Jeff Bridges, John Heard, Lisa Eichhorn, Ann Dusenberry, Stephen Elliott, Nina Van Pallandt *cin* Jordan Cronenweth *m* Jack Nitzsche

Steeped in post-Vietnam malaise, this haunting neo-*noir* murder mystery makes evocative use of Santa Barbara locations and has three indelible characters in the bronzed, indecisive Bone (Bridges), the jaded Mo (Eichhorn) and John Heard's volatile, alienated Viet vet Cutter. Bone thinks he saw rich industrialist J.J. Cord murder a girl, and Cutter insists that he do something about it. It's a conspiracy movie in the 1970s paranoia mode, but with a radical thrust that digs in deep.

Pawel Pawlikowski

Poland, 1957–

Pawel Pawlikowski is a celebrated British director and the victim of a case of mistaken identity. When critics saw *Last Resort* (2000) they anointed him the rightful heir to Ken Loach and Mike Leigh. In fact, Pawlikowski is an outspoken critic of social realism, declaring instead that his films "aspire to the condition of a dream". An austere asylum-seeker drama, *Last Resort* was rooted in autobiography – Pawlikowski and his mother had moved from Poland to Britain when he was 15. In the early 1990s he made a series of award-winning documentaries for the BBC, including *Moscow Pietushki* (1990), *Dostoevsky's Travels* (1991) and *Serbian Epics* (1992), which have become festival favourites. Later in the decade he made his feature debut with the little-seen love story *The Stringer* (1998). Lauded as a major British talent after the release of *Last Resort*, he was hired to direct the Plath biopic *Sylvia*, but abandoned ship soon after Gwyneth Paltrow came on board. The critical success of his next film, *My Summer Of Love* (2004), and the critical drubbing of the Plath hagiography confirmed that Pawlikowski possesses an astute understanding of cinema. LH

My Summer Of Love 2004, 86 min
cast Natalie Press, Emily Blunt, Paddy Considine, Dean Andrews, Michelle Byrne, Paul Antony-Barber, Lynette Edwards *cin* Ryszard Lenczewski

A poignant character study of two girls from either side of the class divide – posh, pretentious and charismatic Tamsin (Emily Blunt) and impetuous urchin Mona (Natalie Press). Loosely based on a Helen Cross novel, the film was mainly improvised on set. Reality is given the quality of fable just as in Milos Forman's *Loves Of A Blonde* (1965), a defining film for Pawlikowski, who possesses the same gift for small details and piquant observations as his mentor.

Alexander Payne

US, 1961–

A leading light in the "new New American cinema" which also includes Steven Soderbergh, David O. Russell and Paul Thomas Anderson, Alexander Payne has refrained from parading technique or his own importance; his films are modestly mounted but deceptively penetrating satires on Middle-American mores.

Born and raised in Omaha, Nebraska, Payne set each of his first three films in his home state. In the case of *Election* (1999) and *About Schmidt* (2002) that involved wholesale changes to source novels set in New Jersey and New York respectively. "I read a book and throw it away", he has said. "I then create my own version of the book."

Despite this apparent loyalty to his roots, Payne seems significantly alienated from both the vacuity of the area's consumer culture and the flat, barren landscape that surrounds it. The local population don't come off any better. His first film, *Citizen Ruth* (1996), was a scathing satire on the self-serving hypocrites on both sides of the abortion debate, one of the bravest and least sentimental American movies of the 1990s.

Election (1999) is an acerbic comedy about political chicanery in a high-school presidential contest. It's a particularly resonant Clinton-era artefact, shot through with a sour, ironic take on sexual desire that is another Payne trait. Sold as a teen comedy, *Election* was, like *Citizen Ruth*, a box-office non-event. According to Sharon Waxman's book *Rebels On The Backlot*, Paramount head of production John Goldwyn confessed that "*Election* is the best movie we've made in the past ten years, and it's a movie we have no interest in repeating".

Despite this, Payne has successfully insisted on final cut, and continues to get his films made his way. Casting Jack Nicholson in *About Schmidt* won him a larger audience, and the popular *Sideways* (2004) garnered rave reviews. *Sideways* also brought Payne his first Oscar nominations, for best director and (with regular writing partner Jim Taylor) for best adapted screenplay. TC

About Schmidt 2002, 125 min
cast Jack Nicholson, Kathy Bates, Hope Davis, Dermot Mulroney, Howard Hesseman, June Squibb *cin* James Glennon *m* Rolfe Kent

Jack Nicholson is Schmidt, an embittered, widowed pensioner with a dim estimation of the human race in general and his prospective son-in-law in particular. Renting a Winnebago, he drives from Omaha to Denver for the wedding, still hoping he can make his daughter see sense. A fascinating adaptation of Louis Begley's much more upscale novel, this comedy gradually reveals itself as a tragedy of American isolation.

Sideways 2004, 127 min
cast Paul Giamatti, Thomas Haden Church, Virginia Madsen, Sandra Oh, Marylouise Burke, Jessica Hecht *cin* Phedon Papamichael *m* Rolfe Kent

Again, a comedy about a disaffected male, caught up in his own neuroses and disdainful of the superficial culture around him. Miles (Giamatti) is a middle-aged wine snob, divorced, and potentially alcoholic. That his best friend Jack (Haden Church) is as shallow as a Petri dish sums up his plight. A week of wine and golf in Napa prior to Jack's wedding affords Miles a chance to reconnect with the opposite sex. Although it's as cynical about men as Payne's other films, *Sideways* is warmer and more optimistic, its moments of low farce balanced with subtle emotional epiphanies.

417

Sam Peckinpah

US, 1925–84

He was the West's great elegist, a poet who became notorious for violence. The poetry and the violence were not quite inextricable, but closely intertwined, and Sam Peckinpah's biographers have found their roots buried in his childhood on a ranch in Fresno, California. There, Peckinpah learned to ride and hunt with the men in his family. His grandparents on both sides had been pioneers in their youth, though his father was a lawyer and his maternal grandfather became a congressman.

If Peckinpah imbibed the romance of the West early, he also learned how brutal the company of men can be, and how repressive were the strictures of that old-time religion his mother liked to preach. These themes come up in his work time and again. For all that he was a genre specialist, Peckinpah considered himself at war with the studios – against the odds, he made some of the most personal films that ever escaped from Hollywood. Honest too: somewhere in the mix of Cable Hogue (Jason Robards), Benny (Warren Oates in *Bring Me The Head Of Alfredo Garcia*), David Sumner (Dustin Hoffman in *Straw Dogs*) and Pat Garrett (James Coburn) a self-portrait emerges, tormented, angry, noble and inadequate. "Bloody Sam", they called him, and his work was an open wound.

Judging by his heroes, and his blatant distaste for the modern world, Peckinpah may have felt he lived out of his time, but TV in the 1950s presented the perfect epoch for a young writer to earn his spurs churning out scripts for *Gunsmoke, Have Gun Will Travel, Broken Arrow, The Rifleman* and *The Westerner* (the series he created in 1960).

Peckinpah's first five features were Westerns, and watching the sixth, *Straw Dogs* (1971), it's obvious how deeply the genre was ingrained in his *mise en scène*, for all that this controversial revenge thriller is ostensibly set in 1970s Cornwall. Self-consciously, and with all due ceremony, he buried the genre that he loved – he took a small role as an undertaker in *Pat Garrett And Billy The Kid* (1973) who announces his intention to "leave the territory" – but couldn't resist digging up the corpse in his very next picture, the gothic Mexican nightmare *Bring Me The Head Of Alfredo Garcia* (1974).

Even in his first films, *The Deadly Companions* (1961) and *Ride The High Country* (1962) Peckinpah's West is on borrowed time. It's autumn and the sun is always setting. Like John Ford, Peckinpah cherishes the memory, the mirage of the frontier (a utopia enshrining male camaraderie, wine, women and song which he invariably posits south of the border, in Mexico), but unlike Ford he can't turn his head from the mercenary betrayal of that dream, as cattle barons, Puritans and horseless carriages annex this wilderness.

In the conflict between the town people and the outlaws, Peckinpah identified exclusively with the outlaws, the mavericks like Billy the Kid, the Wild Bunch and rodeo rider Junior Bonner who placed freedom over all else. (Needless to say, all of them were men.) But he was smart enough to know there was as much Pat Garrett in him as the Kid: when Garrett shoots his old friend and comrade, he shoots himself in the mirror too, a self-loathing gesture James Coburn took directly from Peckinpah's own behaviour.

The violence in Peckinpah flows naturally out of this tension between the free and the repressed, the savage and the civilized. In his use of multi-camera set-ups, slow motion, and a radically multi-perspectival, cubist montage he forged an entirely new idiom for its depiction on screen: shocking, hyperbolic and cathartic. Not five years before *The Wild Bunch* (1969), Hollywood still had qualms about showing blood. Pointing to the TV news images from Vietnam and the assassination of the Kennedys, Peckinpah claimed the artist's responsibility to mirror society. The shock waves from his cinematic fusillade may have died down but its influence remains prevalent, and there's no question it cemented Peckinpah's persona in the popular imagination.

The Ballad Of Cable Hogue (1970) and *Junior Bonner* (1972) reveal the other side of the filmmaker – rueful, funny, even tender – but audiences preferred the mayhem of *Straw Dogs* and *The Getaway* (1972), and in truth Peckinpah himself was riven with demons. An alcoholic, he was intensely paranoid and undoubtedly his own worst enemy. By the mid-1970s he was addicted to cocaine, and his last films – with the partial exception of *Cross Of Iron* (1977) – are empty and shambolic.

An uncompromising artist, Peckinpah attempted to ride roughshod over the studios and they retaliated in kind. *Major Dundee* (1964) and *Pat Garrett And Billy The Kid* were substantially recut in their original theatrical versions, and even *The Wild Bunch* was not immune from rough treatment. Two decades after his death, his reputation is higher than ever, and most of his films are now available in handsome DVD editions, painstakingly restored to better reflect his original intentions, with admiring documentaries and scholarly commentaries from his legion of biographers. Had he enjoyed the luxury of hearing his own eulogy, like Cable Hogue, it's unlikely he'd have done anything differently. TC

Ride The High Country 1962, 93 min

cast Randolph Scott, Joel McCrea, Ronald Starr, Mariette Hartley, R.G. Armstrong, Edgar Buchanan *cin* Lucien Ballard *m* George Bassman

Peckinpah's second feature is already a mature, accomplished, autumnal work, rehearsing many of what would become his staple themes, albeit on a more intimate scale. The bonds of male friendship are tested as civilization encroaches on the West. "All I want is to enter my house justified", Steve Judd (McCrea) tells his old friend Gil Westrum (Scott), perhaps the most profound moral sentiment in any Peckinpah film. The character is based on the director's father, who died shortly before filming.

The Wild Bunch 1969, 145 min
cast William Holden, Ernest Borgnine, Robert Ryan, Edmond O'Brien, Warren Oates, Jaime Sanchez *cin* Lucien Ballard *m* Jerry Fielding

Vietnam brought carnage to the television evening news. Peckinpah put it on the big screen, in multiple angles, agonizing slow motion, and stinging vehemence. In the process, he revolutionized movie violence. Yet for all its martial horrors, the film exerts a rueful, tender melancholy as the old West passes into history and, in their death throes, the old timers finally acknowledge their collusion in its demise.

The Ballad Of Cable Hogue 1970, 121 min
cast Jason Robards, Stella Stevens, David Warner, Strother Martin, Slim Pickens, L.Q. Jones, R.G. Armstrong *cin* Lucien Ballard *m* Jerry Goldsmith

Peckinpah's own favourite film, this is another allegorical Western, but in a completely different register. It's a comedy and a love story, the slow-motion violence replaced with sequences sped up for farcical effect. Left to die in the desert, Hogue finds water where there isn't any, and sets up shop selling it to the passing stagecoach. Having fallen in love with local prostitute Hildy (Stevens), his ballad of choice is a schmaltzy love song, "Butterfly Mornings".

Junior Bonner 1972, 103 min
cast Steve McQueen, Robert Preston, Ida Lupino, Joe Don Baker, Barbara Leigh, Ben Johnson *cin* Lucien Ballard *m* Jerry Fielding

Probably Peckinpah's most underrated film, and, save for a barroom brawl, his least violent. It's a modern-day Western with McQueen in the title role as a cowboy on the rodeo circuit returning to his home town in Texas to find his old man (Preston) turfed out of the house, and his brother (Baker) getting rich off real estate. "I'm working on my first million and you're still working on eight seconds", Curly tells him.

Pat Garrett And Billy The Kid 1973, 121 min
cast James Coburn, Kris Kristofferson, Bob Dylan, Slim Pickens, Katy Jurado, Richard Jaeckel *cin* John Coquillon *m* Bob Dylan

Peckinpah knew the West was spent. But no one, not even John Ford in *The Man Who Shot Liberty Valance* (1962), composed such a beautiful, aching, anguished lament as this. Kris Kristofferson and James Coburn administer the funeral rites, but gauge the mood from the New Mexico sunsets, Bob Dylan's haunting dirges and Slim Pickens expiring in the arms of Katy Jurado.

Bring Me The Head Of Alfredo Garcia 1974, 112 min
cast Warren Oates, Isela Vega, Gig Young, Robert Webber, Helmut Dantine, Emilio Fernandez *cin* Alex Phillips *m* Jerry Fielding

Critically reviled in the US, banned in Germany, Argentina and Sweden, and a *cause célèbre* for certain cultists, Peckinpah's most extreme, nightmarish and candid film is even now too raw and ragged to rest quietly in whatever plot we've set aside for this *bête noir* director. Warren Oates got the role of his life (playing Peckinpah, essentially) as Benny, a cuckolded piano player who decapitates the corpse of his lover's ex in return for a million dollars and finds something like dignity in seeing the job through.

Pat Garrett (James Coburn) administering the last rites to Billy the Kid (Kris Kristofferson) – and the Western – in *Pat Garrett And Billy The Kid*.

Arthur Penn
US, 1922–

In 1967 Arthur Penn changed the face of popular American cinema. Keen on theatre from high school, Penn formed a drama group in the army during World War II. At Black Mountain College he was exposed to radical currents that would shape his subsequent work. Tuition at the Actors Studio laid the groundwork for the psychologically motivated "interior" performances of his best films, introducing him to actors such as Gene Hackman who would figure in the New Hollywood

renaissance to come. From 1951 Penn was a floor manager in television before building a reputation for drama.

His feature debut was *The Left Handed Gun* (1958), a Billy the Kid story originally written as a television play by Gore Vidal. Rereading the legendary outlaw as a mixed-up juvenile turning to crime, Penn cast Method-trained actor Paul Newman as Billy. The result was a fraught, visceral treatment of a character desperate to live up to his public image. Using the device of Hurd Hatfield's "yellow journalist" as the story's chronicler, Penn brought to the foreground the brutal history of the mythological American past, a theme that would

Arthur Penn and the rise of New Hollywood

Arthur Penn's *Bonnie And Clyde* (1967) is widely regarded as the harbinger of what became known as New Hollywood. It had a rollicking, youthful sensibility and a self-conscious nostalgia for classical Hollywood, tempered by some of the cool ennui of European arthouse. *Bonnie And Clyde* defined the New Hollywood cinephile temperament, while its disaffection, beauty and savagery spoke directly to a generation of its particular discontents. Subsequent New Hollywood films – Dennis Hopper's *Easy Rider*, George Roy Hill's *Butch Cassidy And The Sundance Kid*, John Schlesinger's *Midnight Cowboy*, Sam Peckinpah's *The Wild Bunch* (all 1969) – all revolved around anti-heroes at odds with the times. The lacerating gunfire of Penn's movie would echo throughout New Hollywood Westerns, from the genre revisionism of Philip Kaufman's *The Great Northfield Minnesota Raid* (1971) to Penn's later *The Missouri Breaks* (1976).

Penn was a filmmaker who bridged the years between the industry-raised picture-makers of golden era Hollywood and the educated media-savvy auteurs of the late-1960s. Radicalized in his youth, he learned from making live television how to apply modern ideas about society and psychology to timeworn genres. His movies were attuned to the sensibilities of the culture at large: *The Left Handed Gun* (1958), *The Miracle Worker* (1962), *Mickey One* (1965) and *The Chase* (1966) combined intensely felt performances with powerful accounts of disaffection and loneliness. Quite apart from its stunning acting, *The Miracle Worker* told a story of carefully understated and realistic human development; it anticipated the rawness of New Hollywood actors such as Sissy Spacek, Jack Nicholson and Harvey Keitel. The murky *Mickey One* featured Warren Beatty as a paranoid nightclub comedian; it predicted the 1970s conspiracy thrillers that now seem like New Hollywood's political legacy. *The Chase* also rehearsed a perennial New Hollywood dilemma; the fate of the ethical individual mired in a world resolutely hostile to individual self-expression. Such a dilemma would be felt in Hal Ashby's explorations of outsiderdom *Harold And Maude* (1971) and *Being There* (1979), in Martin Scorsese's *Mean Streets* (1973), and in Brian De Palma's *Carrie* (1976).

In Penn's *The Left Handed Gun*, Paul Newman's troubled outlaw is approached by a popular historian keen to turn this life into dime-store legend. This historicization of the American past is developed in *Bonnie And Clyde's* incessant family snapshots and Bonnie's "poetic" missives to the press. Penn's *Little Big Man* (1970) took historical revisionism to epic proportions. The rewriting of the past would be a key feature of New Hollywood filmmaking: from the Youngers having their photographs taken before clanking traction engines in *The Great Northfield Minnesota Raid*, to the historian scribe of Robert Benton's Civil War movie *Bad Company* (1972). But film history, too, was an active preoccupation of New Hollywood films. *Bonnie and Clyde* bedecked Faye Dunaway and Warren Beatty in the contents of classic Hollywood's dressing-up box, seated them in gleaming old roadsters and even used back projection for the car windows. In Peter Bogdanovich's *The Last Picture Show* (1971) and *Paper Moon* (1973), New Hollywood revelled in the sepia past.

Another change that New Hollywood rang was its celebration of minor characters. *Bonnie And Clyde* featured a roster of young actors whose distinctive faces and quirky mannerisms saw a new generation departing from the polished demeanours and diction of classical casting. Whilst Dunaway became a face of mainstream fashion in the United Artists-distributed *The Thomas Crown Affair* (1968), and Beatty became a top-league Hollywood leading man, it was the likes of Michael J. Pollard, Gene Hackman and Estelle Parsons who wrote the "jus' folks" hymn sheet from which the new sensibility sang. That Penn's currency did not last beyond the 1970s suggests that, as a movement, New Hollywood drew its lifeblood from these actors, and the directors who knew them best. RA

characterize New Hollywood films from Penn's own *Bonnie And Clyde* (1967) onwards.

The Left Handed Gun was badly reviewed, and Penn returned to TV and theatre work. Four years later he triumphantly returned to the big screen with 1962's *The Miracle Worker* (1962), based on the Broadway hit that explored the difficult relationship between the deaf and blind Helen Keller and her teacher Annie Sullivan. Their unsentimental and raw spontaneity earned both Anne Bancroft and Patty Duke Academy Awards. Influenced by the *nouvelle vague*, but presaging the 1970s conspiracy thriller, *Mickey One* (1965) found Warren Beatty playing a nightclub comedian with a persecution complex. Its allegorical quality looked forward to *The Chase* (1966), a Western that was one of the most prescient American films of the 1960s. However, it was Penn's 1930s-set Texan crime drama *Bonnie And Clyde* that rewrote history in a devastatingly topical way.

In 1969, *Alice's Restaurant* was one of the era's most underrated films, as it linked 1960s counterculture with the radicalism of Penn's youth. *Little Big Man* (1970) chronicled the fortunes of a 121-year-old survivor of the Battle of Little Big Horn. Dustin Hoffman gave an extraordinary performance in the title role of this revisionist Western that, like Penn's best work, emptied American history of decades of establishment mythology. Few thrillers have seemed at once so desultory and so powerful as 1975's *Night Moves*, which gained its potency from detective Gene Hackman's growing realization that the restoration of law and order is too meagre in a post-Watergate world of wholesale corruption.

Bringing screen icons Marlon Brando and Jack Nicholson together, Penn's last Western, *The Missouri Breaks* (1976), was also his last great film. *Four Friends* (1981) was a nuanced portrait of life in the early 1960s that confronted the contradictions of post-war America. It is a measure of Penn the auteur's decline that it bears the most emphatic stamp of screenwriter Steve Tesich's recollections. *Target* (1985) starred Hackman as a beleaguered husband searching for his missing wife in a shadowy, dangerous Paris, while *Dead Of Winter* (1987) was a disappointing genre thriller with none of the historical purchase or feeling for the audience that made Penn such a great communicator. RA

The Chase 1966, 133 min
cast Marlon Brando, Robert Redford, Jane Fonda, E.G. Marshall, Angie Dickinson, Janice Rule *cin* Joseph La Shelle *m* John Barry

In a Texan town divided by bigotry and myopia, Marlon Brando's sheriff protects escaped convict Robert Redford amid a maelstrom of historical tensions and allegiances, topically reflecting the height of the Civil Rights struggle, the escalating war in Vietnam and the mid-1960s rebellion of American youth.

Bonnie And Clyde 1967, 111 min
cast Warren Beatty, Faye Dunaway, Michael J. Pollard, Gene Hackman, Estelle Parsons *cin* Burnett Guffey *m* Charles Strouse

Shot on Texan locations and alternating between rollicking humour and savage violence, this crime drama defined a generation and depicts the outlaw pair as a couple of crazy kids out for kicks. The film perplexed studio executives by heralding the youth-oriented, low-budget auteur movies that would change the industry, though intriguingly it was offered to Jean-Luc Godard and François Truffaut before Penn took it on. Steeped in a vernacular nervous energy that seems thoroughly native, it is a landmark in modern American cinema.

Alice's Restaurant 1969, 111 min
cast Arlo Guthrie, Pat Quinn, James Broderick, Michael McClanathan, Geoff Outlaw, William Obanhein *cin* Michael Nebbia *m* Arlo Guthrie

One of the three films for which Penn was nominated for a best director Oscar, *Alice's Restaurant* is an ode to 1960s counterculture. Expanding folk singer Arlo Guthrie's anti-Vietnam paean of the same name into a picaresque tale of adventures on America's back roads, this meandering movie echoes his father Woody Guthrie's wanderings during the Depression, which were filmed by Hal Ashby in *Bound For Glory* (1976).

Night Moves 1975, 99 min
cast Gene Hackman, Jennifer Warren, Susan Clark, Edward Binns, Harris Yulin, Melanie Griffith, James Woods *cin* Bruce Surtees *m* Michael Small

One of the most melancholy films of the post-Watergate era, *Night Moves* pushed the already dark mythology of *film noir* into even murkier extremes. Harry Mosby (Gene Hackman) is hired to find an errant teenager, but when he finally tracks down the testy Lolita (Melanie Griffith), she mocks apple-pie Hollywood innocence and drives the already ambivalent private detective into an unfathomable moral labyrinth.

The Missouri Breaks 1976, 125 min
cast Marlon Brando, Jack Nicholson, Randy Quaid, Kathleen Lloyd, Frederic Forrest, Harry Dean Stanton *cin* Michael Butler *m* John Williams

Thomas McGuane's quirky script and Marlon Brando's eccentric and psychotic hired gunman add up to a demystification of outlawry that remains key to the New Hollywood output. Bloody violence and genuine horror complete the demythologizing of the history of the American West, and this is one of the last great Westerns.

Sean Penn
US, 1960–

Easily one of his generation's finest performers, Sean Penn has also proved himself a skilled director of actors in wintry, despairing films full of high-intensity roles, such as his debut, *The Indian Runner* (1991), a good brother/bad brother tragedy inspired by the ominous Bruce Springsteen song "Highway Patrolman". His gift for soulful characterization is often let down by sluggish pacing, overwrought scripting and staging, and a faintly morbid attraction to lurid, loaded material; *The*

Crossing Guard (1995) and *The Pledge* (2001) both focused on the violent death of a child and the cravings for vengeance that follow in its wake, and his contribution to the omnibus *11'09"01* (2002) was grievously misconceived. Penn remains a promising director, however, and can be credited with guiding Jack Nicholson to two of his best latter-day performances (in *The Crossing Guard* and *The Pledge*). *Into The Wild* (2007) was Penn's adaptation of Jon Krakauer's bestseller about a man's tragic journey into the Alaskan wilderness. JW

The Pledge 2001, 124 min

cast Jack Nicholson, Benicio Del Toro, Patricia Clarkson, Robin Wright Penn, Helen Mirren, Aaron Eckhart *cin* Chris Menges *m* Hans Zimmer

Utterly unmoored by the appalling murder of a little girl, veteran cop Jack Nicholson swears to the child's mother (Patricia Clarkson) that he will find the killer. Penn's adaptation of Friedrich Dürrenmatt's novella is cluttered and often hackneyed, but it's anchored magnificently by Nicholson, who sets aside his usual muggy shtick in favour of a brilliant slow-burn interpretation of a man whose psyche begins to unravel as his desire for revenge hardens.

D.A. Pennebaker
US, 1925–

Donald Alan Pennebaker is one of the pioneers of Direct Cinema, the fly-on-the-wall style of documentary filmmaking that emerged in the late 1950s. With Albert Maysles he invented a lightweight camera that facilitated his style of documentary-making: hand-held, observational and intimate. Shorn of both a narrator and an interviewer, his stories seem to tell themselves in a series of unguarded moments, as if the finished product was the result of some form of filmic serendipity. This is, of course, a carefully crafted illusion – Pennebaker is an arch and subtle manipulator, possessed of an enviable ability to sift through hours of material to divine the right narrative and turn the spotlight on just the right characters.

Pennebaker's early work included a spell at Drew Associates, where he worked on the JFK vs Hubert Humphrey election film *Primary* (1960). Thereafter, he has made a speciality out of music documentaries, including concert films for David Bowie and Depeche Mode. *Don't Look Back* (1967), about Bob Dylan, is undoubtedly the standout movie. He cemented his reputation with the first feature-length account of a rock festival, *Monterey Pop* (1969). *Energy War* (1977), about President Carter's fuel policy, lasted a full five hours. The fact that Pennebaker could parlay hours of official yakking and government strategy into a genuinely gripping 300 minutes is testimony to his unique and quiet genius. *Town Bloody Hall* (1979) was the record of a riveting debate between Norman Mailer and a panel

of feminists. *The War Room* (1993) made a celebrity of Clinton's presidential campaign strategist James Carville. TV work and a couple more music features followed: *Down From The Mountain* (2000), focusing on bluegrass performers, and *Only The Strong Survive* (2002), with various Stax soul legends. Since 1979, his films have been co-directed by his wife Chris Hegedus. LH

Don't Look Back 1967, 96 min, b/w

with Bob Dylan, Joan Baez, Donovan, Albert Grossman, Alan Price, Allen Ginsberg *cin* Howard Alk, Jones Alk, D.A. Pennebaker

Pennebaker goes along for the ride as His Bobness tours England in 1965. We see Dylan on-stage and back-stage, jamming, rehearsing and taking the mick out of folk singer Donovan, who's a running joke throughout the doc. The undeniable highlights, though, involve the star's testy relationship with the British press, who act as if an alien has just landed in Blighty, and Dylan's iconic cue-card rendition of "Subterranean Homesick Blues".

Town Bloody Hall 1979, 85 min

with Norman Mailer, Germaine Greer, Jill Johnston, Diana Trilling, Jacqueline Ceballos *cin* Jim Desmond, D.A. Pennebaker, Mark Woodcock

Filmed in 1971, but deemed unusable until Chris Hegedus went to work on it in the editing suite, this gripping documentary chronicles the electrifying encounter between self-confessed male chauvinist pig Norman Mailer and three renowned feminists, plus a town hall full of liberal sympathizers scenting blood. Billed as a knockout match between pitbull Norman and the equally pugnacious Germaine Greer, the show is stolen by Jill Johnston who puts on a bravura display of lesbian affection that seems to (temporarily) silence the seen-it-all Mailer.

The War Room 1993, 96 min

with James Carville, George Stephanopoulos, Mary Matalin, Bill Clinton *cin* Nick Doob, D.A. Pennebaker, Kevin Rafferty

Pennebaker and Hegedus initially wanted to make a film about presidential candidate Bill Clinton, but were denied access and told they could film his staff instead. They had the good fortune to encounter chief strategist and belligerent lizard James Carville, the self-styled Ragin' Cajun, who became the hectoring, motor-mouthed star of their show. But there's a twist worthy of Ernst Lubitsch, as Carville's fiancée Mary Matalin is his opposite number in the Republican camp, and their across-the-barricades love affair provides the movie with its unlikely heart.

Nelson Pereira dos Santos
Brazil, 1928–

The most prominent director of Brazil's Cinema Novo movement of the 1960s and 70s, Nelson Pereira dos Santos is an elder statesman of Brazilian cinema.

After studying at the Paris film school, Pereira dos Santos relocated to Rio de Janeiro and joined the efforts to create a distinctive, popular national cinema. A documentary emphasis marked his first feature, *Rio 40 graus* (*Rio, 40 Degrees*, 1955), and his follow-up, *Rio sona norte* (*Rio North Zone*, 1957), told a deliberately gritty, but rather more emotive, story about a samba composer struggling with the poverty of favela life and looking for his big break. Similarly, *Vidas secas* (*Barren Lives*, 1963), the director's most celebrated film, took its cue from Italian neo-realism with its tale of impoverished rural life.

All of Pereira dos Santos's films demonstrate his declared ambition to participate in national life through "culture and politics". He was credited with being the "heart" and "conscience" of the new cinema movement that burgeoned around him, although it was his fellow countryman Glauber Rocha who proved to be its premier theorist.

With the exception of the *noir* film *Boca de ouro* (*Gold Mouth*, 1963), Pereira dos Santos focused on comedy and drama throughout the 1960s, before raising his international profile with *How Tasty Was My Little Frenchman* (1971), a black comedy spiced with cannibalistic and colonial contexts that looked back at the Brazilian past. Thereafter, he worked in a variety of genres, with a penchant for biopics on Brazilian cultural figures. Although Pereira dos Santos remains one of South America's most influential directors, the recent conspiracy thriller *Brasília 18%* (2006) failed to reverse a declining international interest in his later works. RC

Vidas secas (Barren Lives) 1963, 103 min
cast Atila Iório, Maria Ribeiro, Orlando Macedo, Jofre Soares, Gilvan Lima *cin* Luiz Carlos Barreto, José Rosa *m* Leonardo Alencar

In the dusty and barren landscape of northeastern Brazil, a family and their memorable dog wander in search of sustenance and dignity in this adaptation of a novel by Graciliano Ramos. The high-contrast cinematography, which emphasizes the bleak but brightly lit environment, underlines the oppression created by the landowners, police and clergy. The solution to these ills – land reform – is largely unmentioned, with the silences and the searing images left to speak for themselves.

Frank Perry
US, 1930–95

In the 1960s Frank Perry epitomized the possibility of personal integrity and genuine autonomy in American filmmaking. Apprenticed as a stage manager and producer, Perry entered filmmaking as a production assistant, then co-producing the television documentary series *Playwright At Work*. Emerging from theatre and often adapting books, Perry's features tend to the literary. *David And Lisa* (1962) generated plaudits and an Oscar nomination for best director for its sensitive, ultimately Freudian examination of the love between two disturbed adolescents. The allegorical *The Swimmer* (1968), starring Burt Lancaster, was followed by the suburban satire *Diary Of A Mad Housewife* (1970) and *Doc* (1971), a New Hollywood spin on the Wyatt Earp-Doc Holliday story. With these three films Perry hit on the era's predilection for low-budget sincerity. He was part of the New York school of directors, with an East Coast sensibility that has its roots in post-war precursors to *cinéma vérité*. Perry largely lost his way in the 1970s, excepting in part *Rancho Deluxe* (1974), in which Jeff Bridges features as one of two cattle-rustling rebels. The scathing biopic *Mommie Dearest* (1981) – starring Faye Dunaway as Joan Crawford – divided audiences and critics. Among his later films, the Susan Sarandon satirical whodunnit *Compromising Positions* (1985) explored Reagan-era suburban sexual mores. After having been diagnosed with cancer, Perry ended his career with a documentary on his battle with the illness, 1992's *On The Bridge*, which recalls his freshest, most affecting work. RA

The Swimmer 1968, 95 min
cast Burt Lancaster, Janet Landgard, Janice Rule, Tony Bickley, Marge Champion, Nancy Cushman *cin* David Quaid *m* Marvin Hamlisch

Based on a short story by John Cheever, this allegorical, absorbing curio follows Burt Lancaster's eccentric odyssey across the swimming pools of suburban Connecticut. The regretful melancholy of a generation suffuses the vividly evoked green-belt idyll to reflect on the dreams and disappointments of the era.

Wolfgang Petersen
Germany, 1941–

Not many cut-down TV series are now regarded as movie classics, but *Das Boot* (1981) is one of them. Written and directed by Wolfgang Petersen, *Das Boot* was a gripping, authentic portrait of life on board a U-boat during World War II. Originally five hours in length (six fifty-minute episodes), *Das Boot* was re-edited into a 149-minute movie version that proved surprisingly popular in the US and Britain. Petersen was nominated for two Oscars, and the film for four more.

Das Boot was the culmination of a decade spent in German TV at a time when Fassbinder, Herzog, Kluge and Schlöndorff were resurrecting German cinema (most often with TV funding). Despite Petersen's success, few of his early works have been seen outside German-speaking countries.

Based on Michael Ende's children's book, *The NeverEnding Story* (1984) was aimed at international audiences, and found them. But Petersen's first official Hollywood production, the sci-fi race allegory *Enemy Mine* (1985) proved a disappointment, and the amnesia mystery thriller *Shattered* (1991), which he also wrote, was simply preposterous. He hasn't been tempted to take a screenplay credit since.

In The Line Of Fire (1993) put this faltering career back on track. A slick vehicle for Clint Eastwood, it consolidated his reputation as a suspense director, and he's traded on it ever since. Petersen's movies may reveal a tin ear for dialogue, but the actors in his movies always have more pressing concerns to worry about: a deadly virus (*Outbreak*, 1995), an attempt on the president's life (*Air Force One*, 1997), or fifty-foot waves (*The Perfect Storm*, 2000). In 2004 he signed Brad Pitt and Eric Bana for the muscular historical epic *Troy*. Expensive and glossy, the film turned out to be little more than workmanlike; a CGI epic that failed to generate excitement or find contemporary resonance. In 2006 he returned to the waves for *Poseidon*. TC

Das Boot (The Boat) 1981, 209 min

cast Jürgen Prochnow, Herbert Grönemeyer, Klaus Wennemann, Hubertus Bengsch, Martin Semmelrogge *cin* Jost Vacano *m* Klaus Doldinger

Undoubtedly Petersen's major achievement, this is probably the best submarine movie of them all. Adept use of the Steadicam complements the intense, dripping claustrophobia of the location. Petersen's own screenplay pleads understanding for captain and crew (no Nazis here), but the characterization is solid, and the tension builds palpably over the lengthy running time. Twenty-five years after its release, *Das Boot* is just outside the Top 50 in the Internet Movie Database's rankings for the best films ever made.

In The Line Of Fire 1993, 129 min

cast Clint Eastwood, John Malkovich, Rene Russo, Dylan McDermott, Fred Dalton Thompson, John Mahoney *cin* John Bailey *m* Ennio Morricone

Veteran secret service agent Clint Eastwood was there when John F. Kennedy was shot, and he's not about to let assassin John Malkovich make him relive the nightmare. Petersen handles this absorbing cat-and-mouse game with complete assurance, drawing out parallels between the (rather verbose) killer and the bodyguard, and capitalizing on his star's age and experience. It's a precise, shrewdly realized piece of work, based on the best script to come Petersen's way (by Jeff Maguire).

Maurice Pialat

France, 1925–2003

Hardly the most celebrated of the French filmmakers to emerge in the 1960s, the difficult, volatile, uncompromising Maurice Pialat has cast a long shadow. Comparisons with John Cassavetes are appropriate. Pialat's crucial influence on post-*nouvelle vague* French cinema – on Cyril Collard, Catherine Breillat, Xavier Beauvois, Erik Zonca, Laurent Cantet and a whole slew of actors from Gérard Depardieu on down – has not been properly understood.

A painter before he was a filmmaker – though he was scarcely a pictorialist – Pialat was 43 before he made his first feature, *L'enfance nue* (*Naked Childhood*, aka *Me*, 1968). (However, his 1960 documentary short *L'amour existe* (*Love Exists*), with its pessimistic portrait of tower blocks and of the rich and poor, had won a prize at the Venice Film Festival.) *L'enfance nue*, a portrait of a foster child sliding into delinquency, was followed by the six-hour TV serial *La maison des bois* (*The House In The Woods*, 1970–71), a landmark for those that have seen it. Pialat then made the searing semi-autobiographical *Nous ne vieillirons pas ensemble* (*We Won't Grow Old Together*, 1972) and *La gueule ouverte* (*The Mouth Agape*, 1974), the latter a staggeringly unfiltered response to his mother's terminal illness.

In these films Pialat achieved a propulsive, convulsive naturalism, his acute social observation trumped with an intense, pitiless honesty. Even his admirers admit auteur Pialat, who wrote and often acted in his own films, wasn't a conventional storyteller. His tumultuous, raw, ragged dramas were all about capturing – or rather, unleashing – hard emotional truths. One common strategy was to shoot in long, nearly unendurable takes. He also had a penchant for disorienting elliptical transitions, often highlighting the perverse, contradictory aspects of human behaviour. Mixing professional and amateur actors, Pialat not only encouraged improvisation and the rawness of his actors, he also engineered startling eruptions of anger and violence on camera, often directed at himself – Sophie Marceau, who starred in *Police* (1985), famously complained her director was "a sadomasochistic pervert".

Pialat regular Depardieu also starred in *Police*, which found disturbing similarities between his Paris cop and the underworld, and in *Loulou* (1980), which revisited the unhappiness of modern love. In *Sous le soleil de Satan* (*Under Satan's Sun*, 1987), Depardieu effectively essayed the turmoil of a priest trying to redeem Sandrine Bonnaire's young murderess, and the film won the Palme d'Or at Cannes. Jacques Dutronc's artist in *Van Gogh* (1991) portrayed brilliantly the "difficult" creator, while its riverside scenes were an obvious tribute to the Renoirs, *père et fils*.

The relationships in Pialat's features are almost always abrasive, erratic and traumatic, fuelled by burning resentment and the impulse towards self-destruction. "Love does not exist", Pialat's nameless father tells his onscreen daughter (Bonnaire) at the end of *To Our Loves* (1983), although the film has already amply demonstrated all the pain and confusion that trails in its wake (and let's not forget the name of Pialat's first documentary – *Love Exists*). "He is the only filmmaker who tells the truth about love", claimed Depardieu. RA & TC

Nous ne vieillirons pas ensemble (We Won't Grow Old Together) 1972, 110 min

cast Marlène Jobert, Jean Yanne, Christine Fabréga, Patricia Perangeli, Jacques Galland *cin* Luciano Tovoli *m* Joseph Haydn

Jean (Yanne) is a filmmaker, married, but in a long-term relationship with Catherine (Jobert), a younger woman

P

whom he routinely bullies and undermines. They break up – and then he realizes he wants her back. Reconciliation is succeeded by recrimination in a cycle of anguished intimacy that draws in Catherine's parents and Jean's estranged wife. It's a probing, painfully honest film about a man's compulsion to destroy his love.

Loulou 1980, 105 min
cast Isabelle Huppert, Gérard Depardieu, Guy Marchand, Humbert Balsan, Bernard Tronczyk *cin* Pierre William Glenn, Jacques Loiseleux

In this riposte to the idealism of 1968 and the upheavals of the Giscard d'Estaing years, a bourgeois woman takes up with a boorish drifter for sex, booze and kicks. Pairing Gérard Depardieu with Isabelle Huppert and leavening his story with social observation, Pialat produced a finely honed commentary for the times in which his drunken protagonists lurch into the dark suburbs and French cinema hastens toward a *fracture sociale*.

To Our Loves (A nos amours) 1983, 95 min
cast Sandrine Bonnaire, Evelyne Ker, Maurice Pialat, Dominique Besnehard, Anne-Sophie Maillé, Cyril Collard *cin* Jacques Loiseleux *m* Henry Purcell

You don't so much watch this study of that which we like to call "love" as experience it. Intellectually dispassionate, it's an emotional hurricane, with a revelatory performance from the 17-year-old Sandrine Bonnaire at its core. The product of a broken home (her father – Pialat – is an emotional wrecking ball), Suzanne careers from one boyfriend to another, her promiscuity outraging her mother and her brother. The climactic family get-together is unforgettable.

Police 1985, 113 min
cast Gérard Depardieu, Sophie Marceau, Richard Anconina, Pascale Rocard, Sandrine Bonnaire, Franck Karoui *cin* Luciano Tovoli *m* Henryk Gorecki

Depardieu is a Paris cop who beats up Tunisian drug dealers and does deals with their lawyers. But when he falls for Sophie Marceau's venal drug courier, Pialat characteristically homes in on the play of the social and the sexual. Catherine Breillat wrote this complex and layered *policier* and it is not difficult to see that the legacy of social rage and behavioural detail has passed down to the next generation.

Sous le soleil de Satan (Under Satan's Sun) 1987, 93 min
cast Gérard Depardieu, Sandrine Bonnaire, Maurice Pialat, Alain Artur *cin* Willy Kurant *m* Henri Dutilleux

Pialat's Palme d'Or winner is based on a novel by Georges Bernanos, whose work inspired Robert Bresson's *Diary Of A Country Priest* (1950) and *Mouchette* (1966). In his fourth film for Pialat, Depardieu is Father Donissan, a nineteenth-century priest whose devotion could be either madness or saintliness. It's an Old Testament religion Pialat presents here – the Devil himself whispers in Donissan's ear one night – but fraught with the terror of doubt, the impotence of mankind.

Jean-Marie Poiré
France, 1945–

In 1993 Jean-Marie Poiré trounced *Jurassic Park* at the French box office with his bawdy time-travelling comedy, *Les visiteurs*. The son of film producer Alain Poiré, Jean-Marie began his career as a scriptwriter. Contributing screenplays for a distinguished roster of French directors, including Edouard Molinaro, Michel Audiard and Gérard Oury, led to his feature debut, *Les petits câlins* (*The Little Wheedlers*, 1978). Josiane Balasko, who worked with him on this production, introduced the director to the *café-théâtre* troupe "Le Splendid", which numbered among its members future collaborator Christian Clavier.

Poiré's comedies are characterized by irreverent wordplay and social ridicule. Early national successes were *Les hommes préfèrent les grosses* (*Men Prefer Fat Girls*, 1981), which he co-wrote with Balasko, and *Père Noël est une ordure* (*Santa Claus Is A Louse*, 1982), based on an ensemble piece created by Le Splendid. This cult success was remade as *Mixed Nuts* (1994) in Hollywood by Nora Ephron with Steve Martin, although further attempts to popularize Poiré in America have failed. In 2001, Poiré himself directed *Just Visiting*, an English-language remake of his 1993 hit, again starring Jean Reno and Christian Clavier, but it was not a success. RA

Les visiteurs (The Visitors) 1993, 107 min
cast Christian Clavier, Jean Reno, Valérie Lemercier, Marie-Anne Chazel, Christian Bujeau, Isabelle Nanty *cin* Jean-Yves Le Mener *m* Eric Levi

When sorcery finds a twelfth-century knight (Jean Reno) and his grubby squire (Christian Clavier) fetching up in modern-day France, the scene is set for wholesale slapstick and wicked social satire. Clavier also essays his prissy twentieth-century descendant, while Valérie Lemercier is both the girl Reno loved and lost and a bourgeois modern wife. The most successful French film in almost half a century, it spoke to a country sure of its cultural bearings.

Roman Polanski
France, 1933–

The quintessential Roman Polanski film is a penned-in chamber drama where the air is thick with foreboding, sexual pathology and senseless violence. Within Polanski's shock corridors, the strong prey upon the weak (with an evil glee that borders on the grimly comic in the 2005 Dickens adaptation *Oliver Twist*) or, less often, the weak perceive a threat that exists only in the passageways of a disordered mind. His interest in pagan ritual and occult superstition adds yet more dark intrigue to a critical mass of suspicion, displacement, mental illness and everyday human cruelty, though Polanski's pitch-black sense of humour usually lurks in the shadows.

Polanski often employs very few major characters in a discrete or isolated setting: two men and a woman on a boat in his debut feature, *Knife In The Water* (1962); dissimilar couples facing off on an island in *Cul-de-Sac* (1966) and on an ocean liner in *Bitter Moon* (1992); solitary rent-payers terrorized by their habitat – or so it seems – in *Repulsion* (1965) and *The Tenant* (1976). His *Knife In The Water* co-screenwriter, Jerzy Skolimowski, reinforced this strict containment of space, time and dramatis personae, though it's also a trend evident in Polanski's early shorts, including *Two Men And A Wardrobe* (1958), collected on Criterion's two-disc edition of *Knife In The Water*.

The director's life has accumulated such a litany of tragedy and scandal that his personal travails have often threatened to overshadow his work, and have no doubt informed it. When he was 8, his mother threw him from a train bound for Auschwitz, where she later died (his father survived); the boy thereafter lived by his wits in the ghetto and then in the Polish countryside, hidden by various families. (An alternative account has Polanski being pushed through a barbed-wire fence by his father.) His blood-soaked adaptation of *Macbeth* (1971) is widely interpreted as a cathartic echo of the horrendous murder of his pregnant wife, Sharon Tate, at the hands of the Manson family in 1969.

Less than a decade later, Polanski fled the US to avoid statutory rape charges involving a 13-year-old girl (he took up permanent residence in France to avoid extradition), a disgrace that adds a rumbling subtext to a filmography that teems with corrupted sexuality. In *Chinatown* (1974), the nominal *femme fatale* bears her father's child; in *Repulsion*, a lone woman's sexual anxiety takes on nightmare proportions; in *Rosemary's Baby* (1968), Mia Farrow's character is sedated and then apparently raped by her own husband ("It was kinda fun in a necrophile sort of way", he quips, accounting for the scratches on her body). In *Repulsion*, Catherine Deneuve inhabits a psychically charged apartment similar to Farrow's in *Rosemary's Baby*, with the same incessant ticking clock, piano scales forever playing in the distance and nightmare assaults.

Polanski's latter-day career has not generated the same returns as his heyday: *Tess* (1979) was a deeply felt if overlong adaptation of the Thomas Hardy tragedy; *Frantic* (1988) an artful exercise in Hitchcockian paranoia; *The Ninth Gate* (1999) a pulpy amusement starring Johnny Depp as a rare-book dealer trying to track down surviving copies of a satanic text. Forty years after the release of his first feature, Polanski depicted the Nazi-era Warsaw of his childhood in *The Pianist* (2002), the best of his recent films. (He had previously declined an invitation to direct *Schindler's List*, 1993.) He won the directing Oscar for this confrontation with the indelible traumas of his early life, but of course, another ghost from the past prevented him from picking up the award in person. JW

Knife In The Water (Noz w wodzie) 1962, 94 min, b/w

cast Jolanta Umecka, Leon Niemczyk, Zygmunt Malanowicz *cin* Jerzy Lipman *m* Krzysztof T. Komeda

A bored middle-aged couple invite an insolent young hitchhiker aboard their boat, and the stage is set for a litany of mind games, power trips and ugly displays of passive-aggression. Polanski's foreboding, tightly wound debut established the tone for his entire career. It also made the cover of *Time* magazine, which says as much about the position that international auteurist cinema occupied in 1960s mainstream culture as it does about the film's individual impact.

Repulsion 1965, 104 min, b/w

cast Catherine Deneuve, Yvonne Furneaux, John Fraser, Ian Hendry, Patrick Wymark *cin* Gilbert Taylor *m* Chico Hamilton

Filmed in London's fashionable South Kensington, *Repulsion* is a kind of counter-image to the idea of swinging London. Catherine Deneuve plays Carol, a manicurist who shares a flat with her older, sexually active sister. Increasingly repulsed by any form of physical contact, she retreats into isolation and paranoiac delusions. In a *tour de force* of wide-angled close-ups and obtrusive sounds, Polanski forces us to share Carol's disturbed and disturbing viewpoint.

Rosemary's Baby 1968, 137 min

cast Mia Farrow, John Cassavetes, Ruth Gordon, Sidney Blackmer, Maurice Evans, Ralph Bellamy *cin* William A. Fraker *m* Krzysztof Komeda

Faithfully adapting Ira Levin's bestseller, Polanski's first major Hollywood-backed feature is a slow-burn of psychological menace, imagining the birth of Satan as a plot engineered by an innocent woman's nosy neighbours and her reptilian husband (John Cassavetes). Once the seed is planted, Rosemary (Mia Farrow), with her Falconetti-style crop and chalky pallor, is posed as a phantom in wait, her pregnancy a sexually transmitted disease that will breed a plague.

Chinatown 1974, 131 min

cast Jack Nicholson, Faye Dunaway, John Huston, Perry Lopez, John Hillerman, Darrell Zwerling *cin* John A. Alonzo *m* Jerry Goldsmith

Regarded as both the first neo-*noir* and the last "studio picture", this masterful revision of the 1940s hard-boilers looks on as depravity incarnate Noah Cross (John Huston) takes control of Los Angeles' water supply and causes a severe drought, and macho private eye Jake Gittes (Jack Nicholson) gets everything tragically wrong. Polanski and screenwriter Robert Towne beat their chosen genre senseless and dump it in the wilds of Greek tragedy, though Towne objected to the unforgettable, nearly nihilist finale.

The Pianist 2002, 149 min

cast Adrien Brody, Thomas Kretschmann, Emilia Fox, Michal Zebrowski, Ed Stoppard, Maureen Lipman *cin* Pawel Edelman *m* Wojciech Kilar

Based on the memoirs of Wladyslaw Szpilman, Polanski's spellbinding revisitation of the Nazi-occupied Poland of his childhood splits roughly in half: one part a foredoomed depiction of Szpilman family life in Warsaw as the vice of fascist oppression tightens, the other a cogent study of terrified isolation as Szpilman (Adrien Brody), starved and incrementally dehumanized, hides out in the abandoned apartments of the ravaged city.

Sydney Pollack

US, 1934–

Sydney Pollack can be relied upon to elicit star turns, Oscars, box-office dollars and, occasionally, zeitgeist-defining films. He studied at the Neighborhood Playhouse School of the Theatre under Sanford Meisner, later teaching there. In the late 1950s he was acting in television, but a small role in *War Hunt* (1962) brought Pollack into contact with Robert Redford, with whom he would work extensively. Working as the dialogue coach on John Frankenheimer's *The Young Savages* (1961) fostered his interest in directing, but Pollack marked time directing episodes of a variety of popular television series before his 1965 feature debut, *The Slender Thread*.

The Tennessee Williams adaptation *This Property Is Condemned* (1966) teamed director Pollack with star Redford, launching a partnership that lasted into the 1990s. Pollack emerged as a Hollywood player with his 1969 Depression-era allegory *They Shoot Horses, Don't They?* (starring Jane Fonda and Michael Sarrazin), a commentary on contemporary America. In *Jeremiah Johnson* (1972) Redford played a tenderfoot trying to survive in the Utah Rockies in the 1850s. The film had a documentary feel for nature which recalled Robert Flaherty and presaged Redford's own environmental concerns. A key release of its day, *The Way We Were* (1973) was a love story in which Barbra Streisand's 1930s Jewish radical and Redford's liberal WASP writer weather the crises of fascism and McCarthyism dressed up in period costumes and overlaid with Streisand's hit single. With hindsight, few appeals to the counterculture seemed more condescending than this lucrative soap.

The Yakuza (1974) – a Japanese-American gangster fusion – showed Pollack's mettle as a genre filmmaker of grace and polish, and paired Japanese crime movie star Ken Takakura with Robert Mitchum. This was followed by *Three Days Of The Condor* (1975), which remains one of the most compelling of the 1970s conspiracy thrillers. *The Electric Horseman* (1979) found Jane Fonda's reporter following Redford's disillusioned rodeo star into the wilderness in a project that degenerated into mush after a promising start. Dustin Hoffman's crossdressing antics in comedy mega-hit *Tootsie* (1982) felt like a fantasy plea, as more and more American women negotiated the gender wars. Showered with awards, including the best director Oscar for Pollack, the Redford-Meryl Streep vehicle *Out Of Africa* (1985) was worthy but dull.

The 1990s saw Pollack executive-producing solid projects: *The Fabulous Baker Boys* (1989), *Sense And Sensibility* (1995), *The Talented Mr Ripley* (1999).

Meanwhile, as an actor, Pollack gave effective turns for Woody Allen (*Husbands And Wives*, 1992), Robert Altman (*The Player*, 1992) and Stanley Kubrick (*Eyes Wide Shut*, 1999). But his later directorial projects seemed self-important – *The Firm* (1993) – or redundant – *Sabrina* (1995), *Random Hearts* (1999). Only 2005's *The Interpreter* evoked the old narrative and thespian panache and spoke to the times. RA

Three Days Of The Condor 1975, 117 min
cast Robert Redford, Faye Dunaway, Cliff Robertson, Max von Sydow, John Houseman, Addison Powell *cin* Owen Roizman *m* Dave Grusin

Released in the wake of Watergate, this exercise in paranoia portrayed the consequences of trusting no one. Robert Redford is a researcher translating for the CIA. When he leaves for lunch one day, he returns to discover that all his colleagues have been gunned down. On the run in a wintry New York, he kidnaps the trusting Faye Dunaway and tries to piece together the puzzle. Crisply shot on location, this taut exercise fused Hitchcockian suspense with a very contemporary disquiet.

Tootsie 1982, 116 min
cast Dustin Hoffman, Jessica Lange, Teri Garr, Dabney Coleman, Charles Durning, Bill Murray, Sydney Pollack *cin* Owen Roizman *m* David Grusin

An out-of-work actor (Dustin Hoffman) masquerades as a woman to get a part on a top TV show, but as the soap opera's ratings go through the roof, his private life goes into meltdown – particularly when he starts to fall for his female co-star (Jessica Lange). Ignore the film's simplistic implications and you're left with a feel-good distraction for the *Kramer vs Kramer* era which just aches to do the right thing.

The Interpreter 2005, 128 min
cast Nicole Kidman, Sean Penn, Catherine Keener, Jesper Christensen, Yvan Attal, Earl Cameron *cin* Darius Khondji *m* James Newton Howard

Nicole Kidman interprets for the UN, specializing in obscure African dialects. One evening, she overhears whispers of a plot to assassinate an African head of state during a conference. While its brinkmanship evokes Hitchcock, the world of Pollack's film is definitely very contemporary, as dictators murder innocents in dusty townships. Few films catch the rage and sorrow of the post-9/11 status quo like Pollack's.

Abraham Polonsky

US, 1910–99

Abraham Polonsky is one of the most spectacular victims of the anti-Communist witch-hunts that swept Hollywood shortly after World War II. He was blacklisted three years after he made his first film, *Force Of Evil* in 1948, and did not direct another film until *Tell Them Willie Boy Is Here* in 1969. Polonsky never denied that he was a Communist, and in his key works – both as scriptwriter and director – he explored the ways in which rapacious capitalism derails the American Dream and destroys people's lives.

Having worked in radio as a scriptwriter, Polonsky got a job at Paramount on the strength of his anti-Nazi novel *The Enemy Sea* (1943). After working on a feeble Marlene Dietrich vehicle, *Golden Earrings* (1947), he was teamed up with director Robert Rossen and actor John Garfield for *Body And Soul* (1947), a powerful – if stagey – boxing movie in which the protagonist fights his way out of poverty only to fall foul of the Mob. The film was made for Garfield's own independent production company and led to Polonsky getting the nod for its next project, *Force Of Evil*, which he both scripted and directed. Garfield played a swanky lawyer who rises from his New York slum background, but is seduced by the lure of riches from a mobster client.

Subpoenaed to appear before the House Un-American Activities Committee (HUAC) in 1951, Polonsky refused to name fellow Communists (indeed, his Marxist beliefs never deserted him), and his inevitable blacklisting followed. He survived the next couple of decades by writing scripts for both TV and film under a pseudonym, most notably writing *Odds Against Tomorrow* (1959), Robert Wise's fine *film noir*. Polonsky's name returned to the credits for the first time on Don Siegel's cop movie *Madigan* (1968) and, the following year, he returned to the director's chair for *Willie Boy*, a Western with a strong social conscience. It was hailed (by most) as a remarkable comeback and was followed by his last film, *Romance Of A HorseThief* (1971), about a pair of early twentieth-century Polish-Jewish horse thieves and their attempts to get the better of some Russian cavalry officers. RB

Force Of Evil 1948, 78 min, b/w

cast John Garfield, Thomas Gomez, Beatrice Pearson, Marie Windsor, Roy Roberts *cin* George Barnes *m* David Raksin

One of the great *films noirs*, *Force Of Evil* is a powerful Cain and Abel story in which Thomas Gomez plays the big brother, Leo Morse, who has sacrificed his own happiness to help his lawyer brother, Joe (John Garfield), succeed. Both men operate on the wrong side of the law, but Leo is full of guilt while Joe revels in it – that is until Leo's life is threatened by the Mob. An intense study of duplicity and corruption, the film is raised to the level of tragedy by its cool look (inspired by Edward Hopper) and its oddly poetic voiceover.

Tell Them Willie Boy Is Here 1969, 98 min

cast Robert Redford, Katharine Ross, Robert Blake, Susan Clark, Barry Sullivan, Charles McGraw *cin* Conrad Hall *m* Dave Grusin

As President Taft visits California, a young Paiute Indian (Robert Blake) kills a man in self-defence and runs off with his daughter. Whipped up by the press, a full-scale manhunt ensues led by the reluctant Sheriff Cooper (Robert Redford) who attempts to maintain his distance from the gung-ho antics of the posse. Beautifully filmed by Conrad Hall, much of it in the desert, this is a film that sides with the outsider and questions the supposedly improving effects of civilization.

Gillo Pontecorvo
Italy, 1919–2006

With its consummate melding of suspense and documentary techniques, and its insights into the struggle between colonial martial law and the resistance, *The Battle Of Algiers* (1965) is Gillo Pontecorvo's masterpiece. This classic of political cinema still retains so much currency that it was screened to military strategists in the Pentagon four decades after it was made. Sadly, Pontecorvo produced nothing to equal it in a career that was neither prolific nor consistent.

Pontecorvo was born in Pisa, the son of a wealthy Jewish businessman. With Italy turning fascist he fled to Paris, where he worked as a journalist and as an assistant to the Dutch documentarist Joris Ivens and the French thriller director Yves Allégret. He joined the Communist Party in 1941 and returned to Italy to become a leader of the Partisans in Milan. After the war, Roberto Rossellini's *Paisà* (1946) inspired him to buy a 16mm camera and he began making documentaries in 1953.

In 1957 he made his first narrative feature, *The Wide Blue Road*, a fishing melodrama starring Yves Montand. *Kapo* (1959) was an attempt at a realistic Holocaust drama, in which the young Susan Strasberg (Broadway's first Anne Frank) becomes a "Kapo" – a prisoner charged with keeping her fellow inmates in line. Powerful in its depiction of the camps, the film was marred by a conventional romance in its second half.

No such diversions throw *The Battle Of Algiers* off course. Working without stars (only Jean Martin, the French colonel, had acted professionally before) and on the very streets where the events depicted had taken place a few years earlier, Pontecorvo conveyed the deadly cat-and-mouse game between occupier and "terrorist" in stark dramatic strokes. And although he didn't make any bones about where his sympathies lay, the film is scrupulously fair. Banned in France for many years, and censored in both Britain and the US, *The Battle Of Algiers* was celebrated by international left-wing movements throughout the late 1960s and beyond.

Four years later, *Queimada!* (*Burn!*, 1969) again explored colonialism and resistance, this time in the eighteenth-century Antilles. It was re-edited by the studio, United Artists, and barely released. Ten years later, Pontecorvo's final film, the Basque thriller *Ogro* (1979), received scant attention outside the Mediterranean. TC

The Battle Of Algiers (La battaglia di Algeri)
1965, 117 min, b/w

cast Brahim Haggiag, Jean Martin, Yacef Saadi, Samia Kerbash, Ugo Paletti *cin* Marcello Gatti *m* Ennio Morricone, Gillo Pontecorvo

Pontecorvo's use of real locations, nonprofessional actors and hand-held camera gives this drama the immediacy

P

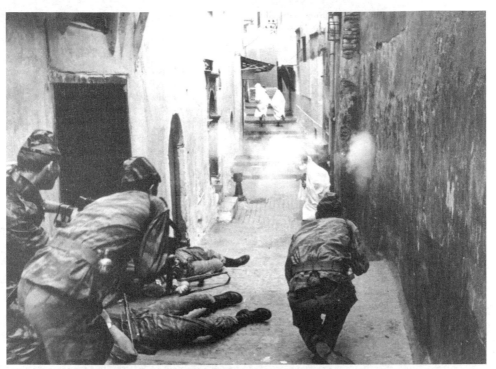

With its documentary-style visuals, including filming on the city streets where the real events took place, *The Battle Of Algiers* is startling in its directness.

of breaking news. It is just as current today, with its hard, level-headed examination of the clandestine war between Arab "terrorist" resistance fighters and a Western occupying force. The film earned Pontecorvo an Oscar nomination and more or less invented the "political thriller" sub-genre, influencing Steven Spielberg's *Schindler's List*.

Queimada! (Burn!) 1969 132 min
cast Marlon Brando, Evaristo Marquez, Norman Hill, Renato Salvatori, Dana Ghia *cin* Marcello Gatti, Giuseppe Bruzzolini *m* Ennio Morricone

Marlon Brando's Englishman William Walker ferments revolution in the Portuguese Antilles, but then returns ten years later to repress the rebel leader he himself created. The film's production was fraught with difficulties. United Artists wanted to cast Sidney Poitier, but Pontecorvo insisted on a native peasant, Marquez, who struggled to deliver a performance. The 132-minute Italian-language print has recently been restored, although you lose some of Brando's adventurous performance in the dubbing.

Edwin S. Porter
US, 1870–1941

The story of Edwin Porter, one of cinema's pioneers, itself plays out like a silent film in which the hero comes to the aid of a damsel in distress – the distressed maiden, in this case, being cinema itself. Before Porter's *The Great Train Robbery* in 1903, the majority of silent shorts were comedy routines, showcases for special effects, or excerpts from stage plays. The novelty was beginning to wear off, and the nascent film business was already starting to slump. Porter saved the industry by his innovative use of cross-cutting between parallel scenes to give a story impetus and suspense. The result was not only the first Western movie but also possibly the most popular film in box-office history until *The Birth Of A Nation* in 1915.

Porter had started out as a projectionist. When a fire destroyed his projector and thus his travelling show in 1900, he joined the Edison Manufacturing Company. Originally hired as a technician, he was soon promoted to director and producer. His *The Life Of An American Fireman* (1903) used both fiction and footage of a real blaze, while *The Dream Of A Rarebit Fiend* (1906) was influenced by the surrealism of French director Georges Méliès. As the film industry developed, Porter's artistic limitations as a director began to surface and the rise of the studios dealt the death blow to his career. In 1915, he left filmmaking to return to his first love, projectors. The stock market crash of 1929 decimated his manufacturing business, and Porter died in obscurity two decades later. LH

The Great Train Robbery 1903, 12 min, b/w
cast John Manus Dougherty Sr, A.C. Abadie, Gilbert M. Anderson, Justus D. Barnes *cin* Edwin S. Porter, Blair Smith

The film is based on a real train robbery by Butch Cassidy and the Wild Bunch in 1900, which netted them $5000. In Porter's movie, a group of cowboys hijack a train, blow up its safe, take the valuables and shoot the driver. Help is summoned, and the bandits are tracked down and killed. In the final shot Justus D. Barnes points a gun directly at the camera and starts to shoot. This early *coup de cinéma* allegedly prompted much ducking and fainting in the aisles. In the fast-paced action and climactic chase sequence can be seen the seeds of the Hollywood action movie.

Sally Potter
UK, 1949–

Experimental, intellectual, formally challenging and politically correct, Sally Potter's films are an antidote to what she calls the "crawling realism" of British cinema. Leaving school at 16 to make films, Potter, ever the polymath, went on to become a dancer, performance artist and composer before returning to cinema at the end of the 1970s. Her breakthrough, *Orlando* (1992), took seven years from script to screen, receiving spiritual guidance and moral support from her heroes Michael Powell and Emeric Pressburger in the drawn-out process. Their very un-British love of illusion and distaste for naturalism is a clear influence on Potter's sensual and self-conscious fable of a nobleman who lives for 400 years, first as a man and then as a woman.

Potter's musical training came in handy five years later on her next film, *The Tango Lesson*, for which she composed the music. She also took the starring role as a director called Sally who falls in love with a dancer while making a film about tango. And yes, Potter did indeed fall in love with her instructor while making a film about tango. Boldly self-reflexive or maddeningly self-indulgent depending on your pretension threshold, *The Tango Lesson* is certainly unique in British cinema. In contrast, *The Man Who Cried* (2001) had few friends. A $15 million film with an international cast including Johnny Depp and Christina Ricci, this terribly arch eve-of-war melodrama has since been criticized by its own director, who felt that she lost artistic control in return for a larger budget.

On 12 September 2001, Potter started writing her personal response to the events of the previous day. The result was *Yes* (2004), about a passionate affair between an American woman and a Middle-Eastern man. The film boasts a militantly capricious and typically Potteresque innovation: all the characters speak in iambic pentameter. But, as is the case with so much of Potter's work, most critics admired the intellectual and cinematic ambitions even if they couldn't bring themselves to fully love the film. LH

Orlando 1992, 93 min
cast Tilda Swinton, Billy Zane, John Wood, Lothaire Bluteau, Charlotte Valandrey *cin* Alexei Rodionov *m* David Motion, Sally Potter

Based on Virginia Woolf's fable and alleged billet-doux to the androgynous writer Vita Sackville-West, Potter's sweeping drama stars Tilda Swinton in a career-defining performance as the Elizabethan nobleman who cannot wither or grow old. But he can, apparently, change sex. Knowing, opulent, intellectually ambitious and emotionally charged, *Orlando* succeeds in being both transparently theatrical and boldly cinematic.

Yes 2004, 100 min
cast Joan Allen, Simon Abkarian, Sam Neill, Shirley Henderson, Sheila Hancock, Samantha Bond *cin* Alexei Rodionov *m* Philip Glass, Sally Potter

The story of an illicit tryst between a white, middle-class woman and a Lebanese surgeon who, despite his qualifications, can only find work as a chef in London. This tender, erotic melodrama embraces the very "now" themes of terrorism, racism, immigration, tolerance and capitalism, and captured the hearts and minds of many critics unaccustomed to using both at the same time. Others, however, carped that the story was so gossamer-thin that it couldn't carry the philosophical weight of these heavy-duty topics.

Dick Powell
US, 1904–63

In the course of just twenty years Dick Powell went from Busby Berkeley musical star to *film noir* tough guy to action director. The former band vocalist and musician made his film debut in 1932, becoming a staple of the Warner Bros backstage musical. Freed from that treadmill, Powell sought straight roles, and excelled as Philip Marlowe in Edward Dmytryk's *Murder, My Sweet* (aka *Farewell My Lovely*, 1944). He made his directorial debut with *Split Second* (1953), which credibly blended the thriller and science-fiction B-movie. After *You Can't Run Away From It* – a tame 1956 remake of *It Happened One Night* – and the 1957 submarine classic *The Enemy Below* came *The Hunters* (1958), a Korean War drama distinguished by Robert Mitchum's laconic presence. Like Ida Lupino, Powell's facility with punchy stories suited television well. He also directed *The Conqueror* (1956), which starred John Wayne as Genghis Khan. This adventure was filmed near an atomic test site in Utah, and later Powell, along with a number of others involved in the shoot, developed cancer. RA

The Enemy Below 1957, 97 min
cast Robert Mitchum, Curt Jurgens, Al Hedison, Theodore Bikel, Russell Collins, Kurt Kreuger, Frank Albertson *cin* Harold Rosson *m* Leigh Harline

Robert Mitchum's weary destroyer captain doggedly pursues a German U-boat under the command of Curt Jurgens. Shot in CinemaScope and suffused with tension, complex allegiances and rivalries, this remains one of the most riveting, suspenseful examples of that often overlooked genre, the submarine movie. It is also Dick Powell's finest achievement as a director.

Powell & Pressburger

Michael Powell: UK, 1905–90
Emeric Pressburger: Hungary (formerly Austro-Hungarian Empire), 1902–88

"I am not a film director with a personal style, *I am the cinema*", Michael Powell famously declared. With equal parts hubris and humility, Powell proposed himself as the conductive vessel for occult currents of sight and sound. He became Britain's greatest cinema visionary, the bulk of his finest output a collaboration with the Hungarian émigré Emeric Pressburger. They teamed up as independent producers, calling themselves The Archers, with Pressburger taking on most of the scripting while Powell handled directorial duties.

Like most visionaries, Powell was regarded with varying degrees of scorn and suspicion during many of his productive years. It took an appreciative group of cinephile Americans to invite a reassessment, which flowered with the 1979 restoration of Powell's virtual career-ender *Peeping Tom* (1960) – a project partly financed by the director's biggest champion, Martin Scorsese, whose longtime editor Thelma Schoonmaker married Powell in 1984.

"They are, for the most part, fairy tales", Powell once said of his films. Certainly during the mid-to-late-1940s high tide of their collaboration, many of Powell and Pressburger's movies took the form of fables, tracking wide-eyed wanderers through strange and bewitching forests: gold-digging city gal Wendy Hiller marooned in the superstitious Scottish Western Isles in *I Know Where I'm Going!* (1945); airman David Niven on the stairway to the monochrome hereafter in *A Matter Of Life And Death* (1946); the band of nuns bewildered and aroused in the Himalayan mountains in *Black Narcissus* (1947). Fittingly, it was a Hans Christian Andersen tale ripe with luxuriant tragedy, *The Red Shoes* (1948), that allowed the Englishman to perfect his brand of ecstatic formalism.

After early encounters with Rex Ingram and Alfred Hitchcock (Powell had a screenwriting hand in the latter's *Blackmail*, 1929), Powell began his directing career in the 1930s with "quota quickies", so named because they were made and screened by parliamentary decree as a safe haven for home-made British filmmaking against the advance of the post-sound Hollywood juggernaut. Powell signalled his graduation from the B-movie workshop with *The Edge Of The World* (1937). Shooting the film in Scotland's Shetland Islands under punishing conditions, Powell animated his stunning location footage with double exposures, time-lapse flourishes and ghosts, and hinted at the gothic inflections

that would add frisson to much of his later work. The film caught the eye of Alexander Korda, who played matchmaker between his fellow Hungarian Pressburger and Powell. The duo's first film together, *The Spy In Black* (1939), appeared the week that World War II broke out.

Powell and Pressburger's wartime films – made under the aegis of the Ministry of Information – were never mere patriotic tracts. *Contraband* (1940) conjured a roaming underground party atmosphere in blackout London; the highly eccentric *A Canterbury Tale* (1944) is set in rural Kent and throws together three new arrivals – a "Land Girl", an American GI, and a British soldier – united in their efforts to identify the mysterious figure who pours glue on the hair of any girl out after dark. *The Life And Death Of Colonel Blimp* (1943) angered Winston Churchill with its gentle mocking of a fuddy-duddy career soldier. Startlingly, several of these films featured sympathetic, rounded German characters, as well as a stylistic embrace of German expressionism. In *The Spy In Black*, the audience is nudged to identify with Conrad Veidt's World War I spy, while in *49th Parallel* (1941) a community of émigré Germans in Canada resists the attempts of a fanatical German U-boat captain to persuade them of the virtues of Nazism. And it's a German (Anton Walbrook) who (in *Colonel Blimp*) delivers both the hushed paean to England and the exhortation to victory against the Nazis by any means necessary.

Powell's ideal, he said, was the "composed film", a symphonic current of sound and image, sought most overtly in *The Red Shoes* and his equally extravagant account of Offenbach's opera *The Tales Of Hoffmann* (1951). A revisitation of their oeuvre reveals many motifs and refrains, as one would find in a symphony. Foremost of these is a gothic gift for rendering the familiar strange, but there is also an uncanny attunement to the animal world, from the startling image of a falcon disembowelling a rabbit in *I Know Where I'm Going!* to the fox hunt that sets the tone of feverish flight and pursuit in *Gone To Earth* (1950).

Remarkably for a team so often concerned with the masculine toils of war, Powell and Pressburger also achieved strong and sensitive female characterizations. The quintessential P&P woman in a nutshell: serious, loyal, fiercely focused, a little out of breath. Kim Hunter beatifies her in *A Matter Of Life And Death*; Deborah Kerr embodies her in triplicate in *Colonel Blimp*, and in fifty years ages not a day; Kathleen Byron, so terrifyingly hysterical as Kerr's nemesis in *Black Narcissus*, plays her in *The Small Back Room* (1949), a spare, acerbic study of an alcoholic, self-loathing bomb-disposal expert. A black-and-white breather after the carnival of *The Red Shoes*, *The Small Back Room* captures both a damaged individual psyche and a troubled national mood. It's an often overlooked

P

431

The delirious Himalayan vision of *Black Narcissus* was created entirely at Pinewood Studios.

gem amid Powell's bigger and brighter sparklers, and named by the director himself as one of his favourites. JW

The Life And Death Of Colonel Blimp 1943, 157 min

cast Roger Livesey, Anton Walbrook, Deborah Kerr, John Laurie, Roland Culver, James McKechnie, Ursula Jeans *cin* Georges Périnal *m* Allan Gray

Inspired by a newspaper cartoon character, Powell and Pressburger's first Technicolor production follows career soldier Clive Candy (Roger Livesey) from the Boer conflict through two world wars, as he maintains a tender friendship with a former German soldier (Anton Walbrook) and hangs on for dear life and dignity to perilously outdated notions of soldiering and conflict. The film is cleverly framed by a Home Guard war exercise that Candy is nominally running from his club.

A Matter Of Life And Death (aka Stairway To Heaven) 1946, 100 min

cast David Niven, Kim Hunter, Roger Livesey, Raymond Massey, Marius Goring, Robert Coote, Abraham Sofaer *cin* Jack Cardiff *m* Allan Gray

A celestial accounting error allows doomed RAF pilot David Niven to miraculously escape from a plane crash. By the time the upstairs office figures out the mistake, the young man has fallen for American radio operator Kim Hunter in this playful heaven-and-earth love story, commissioned by the War Office to bolster Anglo-American relations. The film is hindered only by Raymond Massey's blustering as legal counsel for the afterlife.

Black Narcissus 1947, 100 min

cast Deborah Kerr, Flora Robson, Jean Simmons, Sabu, David Farrar, Jenny Laird, Esmond Knight, Kathleen Byron *cin* Jack Cardiff *m* Brian Easdale

Powell and Pressburger's prowess as masters of illusion reached a peak here, as they used painted backdrops to transform Pinewood Studio's sets into a Himalayan palace convent still thick with the phantom fumes of its past life as a bordello. Led by Deborah Kerr, a beleaguered order of nuns begins to unravel as they are dizzied by the heat, wind and high altitude of their new home and seduced by their own memories and latent desires.

The Red Shoes 1948, 133 min

cast Anton Walbrook, Moira Shearer, Marius Goring, Leonid Massine, Albert Basserman, Robert Helpmann *cin* Hein Heckroth *m* Brian Easdale

Flame-haired ballerina Moira Shearer falls under the obsessive spell of Svengali-like ballet impresario Anton Walbrook in this astounding rendition of a Hans Christian Andersen tale. *The Red Shoes* achieves an orgiastic fusion of folklore, music, dance, design, costumery, painting and photography, a Total Art of cinema pirouetting brazenly through the cooling wreckage of Total War. Perhaps predictably, producer J. Arthur Rank thought the film a disaster, and granted it neither a premiere nor an official poster.

Peeping Tom 1960, 109 min

cast Karl Böhm, Anna Massey, Maxine Audley, Moira Shearer, Esmond Knight, Michael Goodliffe, Brenda Bruce *cin* Otto Heller *m* Brian Easdale

Powell worked without Pressburger for his most notorious film, which was scripted by World War II codebreaker Leo Marks and essentially ended the director's career in

Britain. A young amateur filmmaker slaughters a series of women using a blade attached to his tripod – a murder technique that forces the victim to watch her own death. It's a gruesome thesis on voyeurism as the look that kills, and it's hauntingly self-reflexive: Powell's original title was *The Filmmaker*.

Udayan Prasad
India, 1953–

Few British directors have figured the compromises of multiculturalism in difficult times as surely as Udayan Prasad. Born in India, Prasad moved to the UK as a young child. He graduated from the National Film and Television School, and began his career directing television documentaries, followed by dramas, notably for BBC's *Screen Two* series. Prasad's feature debut – *Brothers In Trouble* (1995) – was set among Pakistani and Bengali immigrants in the early 1960s, and traced the fortunes of "illegals" negotiating life in a Midlands town. The film's progression from squat half-life to the bright sunshine of an apparently pleasant land is carefully charted. Prasad followed this with the popular *My Son The Fanatic* (1997), based on a Hanif Kureishi story and one of the most underrated features in a year touted for its "Britflick" renaissance. His 2001 film, *Gabriel And Me*, was a less than successful adaptation of Lee Hall's acclaimed BBC radio play, *I Luv You Jimmy Spud*, about a young boy who aspires to become a guardian angel. RA

My Son The Fanatic 1997, 86 min
cast Om Puri, Rachel Griffiths, Akbar Kurtha, Stellan Skarsgård, Harish Patel, Bhasker Patel, Sarah Jane Potts *cin* Alan Almond *m* Stephen Warbeck

His son is turning to fundamentalism for answers, his wife is preparing to return to India and he is playing errand boy to a gangster. Then cabbie Om Puri finds himself falling in love with a regular customer, a prostitute played by Rachel Griffiths. This daring film faced up to the realities of a status quo being fragmented by the strains of cultural grievance and generational dispute. It was an image of an increasingly obvious trend in contemporary, multicultural Britain.

Otto Preminger
Austria (formerly Austro-Hungarian Empire), 1906–86

Otto Preminger played a concentration camp commander in his friend Billy Wilder's *Stalag 17* (1953), and reputedly played a similar role on his own sets, where he was feared by actors and technicians alike. Yet if he was tyrannical behind the scenes, Preminger's films are notably cool, objective, and open to interpretation. Even in his suspense pictures, he shies away from manipulation, preferring to tease out ironies and ambiguities. The son

of a successful prosecutor, he lays out the case and allows the audience to judge for themselves.

Like Ernst Lubitsch, Preminger was a Viennese Jew and a graduate of Max Reinhardt's company (when Reinhardt left Vienna for Hollywood, Preminger succeeded him). He directed one film in Austria, *Die grosse Liebe* (*The Great Love*, 1931), but moved to the US in 1935, initially to Broadway, and then to 20th Century Fox, where he became a recalcitrant protégé of Darryl F. Zanuck.

His first B-movies are by and large forgotten, and a falling out with Zanuck took him back to theatre, but in 1944 he was allowed to replace Rouben Mamoulian as director on *Laura*, a major picture he was producing for Fox. The film was a hit (and is now regarded as a classic) and Preminger went on to direct a series of highly regarded crime thrillers and melodramas at the studio.

Although this was at the height of the *film noir* period, Preminger's approach to staple *noir* elements like obsession and neuroses is altogether more detached than the norm. *Fallen Angel* (1945), *Whirlpool* (1950) and *Angel Face* (1952) are crisp, classy productions, probing rather pat psychological scenarios for every ounce of complexity. With his penchant for long takes and smooth, level tracking movements, Preminger remains above the expressionist *noir* fever dream as practised by Robert Siodmak or Joseph H. Lewis. His preference for casting Dana Andrews (five times) and Gene Tierney (three times) in these films is instructive: they share an opacity that can be stolid and suggestive, perverse and imperturbable.

When Preminger struck out on his own as one of the first and foremost independent producer-directors he became famous for transgressive subject matter. Whether out of commercial instinct or social conscience, Preminger gave the League of Decency and the Production Code more headaches than any other filmmaker of the 1950s. Nevertheless, his movies' sensationalist aspects are redeemed by the integrity of the performances and a serious, mature interest in breaking down social taboos.

The Moon Is Blue (1953) was a slight, even trivial comedy, but its frank discussion of the heroine's virginity put it beyond the pale for the censors. Preminger fought them and won. *Carmen Jones* (1954) and *Porgy And Bess* (1959) were all-black musicals. *The Man With The Golden Arm* (1955) was the first honest depiction of drug addiction. *Bonjour Tristesse* (1958) implies incestuous desire. *Anatomy Of A Murder* (1959) is a courtroom drama hinging on rape and sexual promiscuity. And for *Exodus* (1960), an epic about the founding of Israel, Preminger broke the blacklist to hire screenwriter Dalton Trumbo.

Going into the 1960s, Preminger gravitated towards an epic canvas, with big, ensemble casts, long running times and broadsheet subjects: senate confirmation hearings and homosexuality in *Advise And Consent* (1962); the Catholic Church in *The Cardinal* (1963). These later films are distinguished by his command of CinemaScope composition and strong casting, even if they fall squarely in the tradition of middlebrow "prestige" pictures. Preminger made another half a dozen films between 1967 and 1979, about which the least said the better. It had been an important career, as influential as any in terms of dragging Hollywood out of its ivory tower to confront the social realities of the day. TC

Laura 1944, 88 min, b/w
cast Dana Andrews, Gene Tierney, Clifton Webb, Judith Anderson, Vincent Price, Dorothy Adams *cin* Joseph La Shelle *m* David Raksin

After a couple of false starts, this was where everything came together for Preminger. A murder mystery in which the cop falls in love with the corpse and his number-one suspect, it's a delectably perverse item, absurd and artificial yet somehow quintessentially metropolitan, presided over with snobby condescension by Clifton Webb's Waldo Lydecker. David Raksin's haunting melody takes it to another, quite unexpected, level.

Angel Face 1952, 91 min, b/w
cast Robert Mitchum, Jean Simmons, Mona Freeman, Herbert Marshall, Leon Ames, Barbara O'Neil *cin* Harry Stradling *m* Dimitri Tiomkin

Although Preminger couldn't wait to break out of the studio system, the half a dozen suspense movies he made under it represent his most consistently accomplished work. *Angel Face* is the best of them, a Freudian thriller about an ambulance driver – Mitchum – sucked in by angelic heiress Jean Simmons. Cast definitively against type, she turns in the performance of her career. And the ending is a stunner.

Bonjour Tristesse 1958, 94 min
cast Deborah Kerr, David Niven, Jean Seberg, Mylène Demongeot, Juliette Greco, Geoffrey Horne *cin* Georges Périnal *m* Georges Auric

Never widely acclaimed in the US, Preminger's film of the teenage Françoise Sagan novel was adored by the French auteurists – which is why Preminger's protégée, Jean Seberg, wound up peddling the *Herald Tribune* on the Champs-Elysées in Godard's *A bout de souffle* (1959). Here she's 17-year-old Cécile, plotting to keep her playboy father to herself. Preminger shoots the present in black and white and the flashback in Technicolor, and makes startlingly adept use of the CinemaScope format.

Anatomy Of A Murder 1959, 160 min, b/w
cast James Stewart, Lee Remick, Ben Gazzara, Arthur O'Connell, Eve Arden, George C. Scott, Kathryn Grant *cin* Sam Leavitt *m* Duke Ellington

The first of Preminger's epics, and arguably his masterpiece. A courtroom drama, it pits traditional Hollywood star James Stewart as the defence attorney against Methodical up-and-comers George C. Scott (prosecuting) and Ben Gazzara (defendant). There's little doubt army sergeant Mannion killed the man who, he says, raped his wife (Lee Remick), but the law may find room for leniency in this case. The acting exchanges are riveting but so is Preminger's clinical, lucid account of the process of the trial.

Alex Proyas
Egypt, 1963–

Marrying cutting-edge technical resources to a pulpy-baroque sensibility, Alex Proyas often allows style to dictate substance; his films, as is the case with many a former music-video director, are often the sum of their flash and flair. He's most at home in the speculative environs of the near future, as in *Spirits Of The Air, Gremlins Of The Clouds* (1989), an ambient remix of *Mad Max* (1979) in which a small group of lost souls wanders the post-apocalyptic outback (Proyas was raised in Australia from the age of 3). His next feature, *The Crow* (1994), gave every 1990s Goth teen a new favourite movie with its story of a murdered rock star seeking vengeance from beyond the grave. The film sadly gained another dimension of spooky pathos – and perhaps an added kick at the box office – following the death of 28-year-old star Brandon Lee in a freak on-set accident.

Proyas favours expressionist production design, skewed angles and jagged shadows and silhouettes, adding more jitters via lightning-quick cutting, as in the gothic *noir* film *Dark City* (1998). The film was inspired by Proyas's recurrent childhood nightmare in which "alien puppetmasters" called the Strangers would invade his bedroom, move the furniture around and possibly rearrange the contents of his mind or personality too. In *Dark City*, this bad dream is the reality for an entire unwitting metropolis. Proyas changed pace with *Garage Days* (2002), a bouncy, hyperspeed adventure about an Aussie band angling for their big break, but returned to cold, gleaming sci-fi surfaces for the Isaac Asimov update *I, Robot* (2004), a Will Smith vehicle stalled by glaring product placement, clunky exposition and CGI with a lot of its seams showing. JW

Dark City 1998, 100 min
cast Rufus Sewell, Kiefer Sutherland, Jennifer Connelly, Richard O'Brien, Ian Richardson, Colin Friels, William Hurt *cin* Dariusz Wolski *m* Trevor Jones

Amnesiac John Murdoch (Rufus Sewell) wakes up next to a total stranger who also happens to be a mutilated corpse. With the police in pursuit, he begins his own investigation into the murder, having no idea who committed the crime or whether the people around him actually are who they claim to be. This is Proyas's elaborate tribute to Fritz Lang and *Metropolis* (1927), a derivative but splendidly paranoid city symphony.

Vsevolod Pudovkin
Russia, 1893–1953

Vsevolod Pudovkin divides critics. For some he is a visual poet second only to Alexander Dovshenko in the pantheon of early Soviet cinema. For others, his theories are far more interesting than his films.

After working with Russian film pioneer Vladimir Gardin, Pudovkin joined Lev Kuleshov's legendary film workshop at the State Film School in 1922. He wrote and acted in his mentor's *Mr West In The Land Of The Bolsheviks* (1924) and *The Death Ray* (1925), before making his directorial debut with the innovative and ebullient comedy short *Chess Fever* (1925). Pudovkin's reputation as a director rests on three films: *Mother* (1926), *The End Of St Petersburg* (1927) and *Storm Over Asia* (1928), which all chart the political awakening of a naïve individual. In *Mother*, set in 1905, a woman comes to see the ideological error of her ways and heroically joins the struggle after informing on her son to the police.

In his films and theoretical writing, Pudovkin finessed Kuleshov's theory of montage, ie that the meaning of a shot is constructed by its context: place a shot of an actor next to one of a bowl of steaming soup and he will seem hungry. Pudovkin put this hypothesis into glorious practice in the police search in *Mother*, cutting tensely between the protagonist's worried face and her son's secret stash of weapons. These ideas were in diametric opposition to Eisenstein's concept of montage. Whereas Eisenstein's theories celebrated dissonance and conflict, Pudovkin emphasized harmony, using montage to create narrative and psychological cohesion. Intended for propaganda purposes (to raise the awareness of the mainly illiterate masses), his parallel editing now seems crude and obvious: venal, overfed bosses juxtaposed with the starving nobility of the workers. But his splicing techniques really paid dividends in the impressive battle scenes in *The End Of St Petersburg* and *Storm Over Asia*, which possessed a dynamic energy and visceral charge. The key difference between him and Eisenstein, however, was that Pudovkin zeroed in on the individual, making vivid use of the close-up and contextualizing shots to reveal psychological nuances.

Neither sound nor Stalin were kind to Pudovkin: his experiment with the new technology, *Deserter* (1933), was condemned for its formalism, while more objective critics agreed that the director was primarily a visualist adrift in the new technology. The following year the director was injured in a car accident in which his regular scriptwriter Nathan Zarkhi was killed. Thereafter Pudovkin never fully regained his touch and spent the rest of his career churning out films on the propaganda production line. LH

Mother (Mat) 1926, 90 min, b/w
cast Vera Baranovskaya, Alexander Chistyakov, Ivan Koval-Sambrsky, V. Chuvelyov, Anna Zemtzova, Nikolai Batalov, *cin* Anatoli Golovnya

Loosely based on a Maxim Gorky novel, this tells the story of a downtrodden working woman's politicization. When her actions lead to the arrest of her revolutionary son (Nikolai Batalov), the Mother (Vera Baranovskaya) decides to assist his escape. Pudovkin's political vision locates individual effort and sacrifice in the heart of the revolutionary cause. Dramatically edited, the final sequence sees the Mother take up the flag from a fallen worker and stand defiantly resisting the Tsarist troops.

The End Of St Petersburg (Konyets Sankt-Peterburga) 1927, 80 min, b/w
cast A.P. Chistyakov, Vera Baranovskaya, Ivan Chuvelyov, V. Chuvelyov, V. Obolensky *cin* Anatoli Golovnya, K. Vents

Both Eisenstein and Pudovkin were commissioned to celebrate the tenth anniversary of the revolution, and the differences between this and *October* are telling. Whereas in Eisenstein's film the masses were the protagonist and the only recognizable individual was Lenin, Pudovkin tells the story of the revolution through the trajectory of an individual farm lad, as his political consciousness is miraculously raised.

Storm Over Asia (Potomok Chingis-Khan) 1928, 102 min, b/w
cast Valeri Inkishinov, I. Inkishinov, A. Chistyakov, A. Dedintsev, Anna Sudakevich, K. Gurnyak, Boris Barnet, V. Tzoppi, V. Ivanov *cin* A.N. Golovnya

This story of a Mongolian revolt against the British Empire is by far the most conventionally gripping of Pudovkin's films. Even his heavy-handed political juxtapositions have their desired effect, cutting knowingly between the religious rituals of a monk putting on his costume for a Buddhist ceremony and the wife of a bloated British army chief donning her perfumed finery.

The Brothers Quay

Timothy Quay: US, 1947–
Stephen Quay: US, 1947–

Responsible for some of the most memorable animated films ever made, identical twins Stephen and Timothy Quay specialize in surreal, challenging visions. Born in Philadelphia in 1947, they attended the Royal College of Art in London in the 1960s. There they met Keith Griffiths, who has produced much of their work since their debut, *Nocturna Artificialia* (1979).

Strongly influenced by animators such as Walerian Borowczyk and Ladislaw Starewicz, the Quays delight in the medium's ability to explore the unconscious. Uninterested in linear narrative, they are inspired more by music and dance than literary texts, though they have adapted Franz Kafka, Bruno Schulz and Robert Walser.

Most of the Quays' films are animated shorts, such as *The Cabinet Of Jan Svankmajer* (1984), which explores the great Czech animator's aesthetic philosophies via a series of stylized vignettes. Other examples, such as *Rehearsals For Extinct Anatomies* (1987), *The Comb* (1990) and *In Absentia* (2000), are impossible to summarize and hard to forget. These are playfully sinister films with seemingly crucial action happening slightly offscreen, or outside the camera's typically narrow depth of focus.

The brothers' live-action features are just as original, tantalizing and visually startling. The first, *Institute Benjamenta* (1995), shot in silvery, luminescent black and white, adapts Robert Walser's novel *Jakob Von Gunten* into a tale of a would-be servant enrolling at a crumbling boarding school run by a pair of siblings with a fetishistic interest in deer. MB

The Street Of Crocodiles 1986, 21 min
cast (voice) Feliks Stawinski *cin* Quay Brothers, Jonathan Collinson *m* Leszek Jankowski

Widely regarded as the Quays' masterpiece, this adaptation of Bruno Schulz's story shows a hesitant traveller exploring a shadowy but strangely alluring town, where reality slips and slides and nothing, not even the screws holding everything together, behaves as expected.

The Piano Tuner Of Earthquakes 2005, 98 min
cast (voices) Amira Casar, Gottfried John, Assumpta Serna *cin* Nic Knowland *m* Trevor Duncan, Christopher Slaski

The Quays' second feature begins with the kidnapping of an opera singer before repairing to an isolated villa full of bizarre automatons. Piano tuner Felisberto is hired to repair them, but he discovers that there's more to them, the villa and its mysterious owner Dr Emmanuel Droz than meets the eye.

Michael Radford

India, 1946–

The story of Michael Radford is not so much one of rise and fall, as one of rise and fall, and rise and fall, and partial rise again. Born in India to an army family, Radford was brought up in the Middle East and Scotland. After studying at the newly established National Film School, he spent a number of years as a documentary maker, before his first fictional feature, *Another Time, Another Place* (1983), announced him as a burgeoning new British talent. With the following year's *noir*-tinged *Nineteen Eighty-Four*, an impressively designed and modulated adaptation of George Orwell's dystopian novel, the writer-director fulfilled that promise.

However, Radford's next film, *White Mischief* (1987), represented a spectacular fall from critical grace. A languorous, stilted evocation of colonial decadence in wartime Kenya, it died a commercial death and Radford didn't make another film for seven years. Unable to find work in Britain, he eventually resurfaced in Italy, where he engineered one of the great comebacks in recent cinema history. *Il postino* (*The Postman*, 1994) became the highest grossing non-English-language film in the world, and one of only a handful of foreign-language movies to receive an Oscar nomination for best film.

Hollywood immediately opened its wallet to Radford – but in choosing to direct *B. Monkey* (1996), he made an unlucky decision. The project already had a whiff of *film maudit* about it, as the original director had walked, and Radford soon discovered why Harvey Weinstein earned the soubriquet "Harvey Scissorhands" when the Miramax boss re-edited the tale of obsessive love and shelved it for three years. During that time, Radford once again found himself back at square one. In 2000, he made *Dancing At The Blue Iguana*, a low-budget, semi-improvised drama about strippers, which sparkled with a zesty spirit, but ultimately seemed more rewarding for the actors than the audience. Radford's reputation received a boost with his assured and handsomely mounted production of *The Merchant Of Venice* (2004), which was blessed with a barnstorming performance from Al Pacino as Shylock. LH

Another Time, Another Place 1983, 102 min

cast Phyllis Logan, Giovanni Mauriello, Denise Coffey, Tom Watson, Gianluca Favilla, Gregor Fisher *cin* Roger Deakins *m* John McLeod

In an isolated area of Scotland, the arrival of three Italian prisoners of war represents an exotic, magical escape to a cloistered farmer's wife, luminously played by Phyllis Logan. As she hesitatingly embarks on a passionate affair with one of them, it stirs up feelings of guilt and liberation. Radford effortlessly evokes the stifling atmosphere and striking landscape with a deliberate, contemplative pace and a series of immaculately framed compositions.

Il postino (The Postman) 1994, 108 min

cast Massimo Troisi, Philippe Noiret, Linda Moretti, Maria Grazia Cucinotta, Renato Scarpa, Ana Bonaiuto *cin* Franco di Giacomo *m* Luis Enrique Bacalov

Radford charts the relationship between exiled Chilean poet Pablo Neruda and a simple Italian postman, whom he verses in literary metaphors and the art of seduction. It's impossible to separate this charming, bucolic film from the fate of actor and co-writer Massimo Troisi, who refused a heart transplant in order to finish the movie, but died just after filming was complete. There's a low-key, mournful resonance to his performance as the postman, which is echoed poignantly in Radford's meditative directorial approach.

Bob Rafelson

US, 1933–

Bob Rafelson directed, and enabled, some of the richest American cinema of the post-studio era. Born into a New York Jewish family and the nephew of Ernst Lubitsch's frequent screenwriter Samson Raphaelson, Rafelson attended Dartmouth College before breaking into television. Although Rafelson wrote additional dialogue for Shakespeare and Ibsen adaptations, it was the wacky hit TV series *The Monkees* (1966–68) that made his name. The Beatles-derived pop group – conceived and groomed especially for the show – starred in Rafelson's first feature, *Head* (1968). The film was an exercise in

Outsider Jack Nicholson plays Chopin on the road to somewhere else in *Five Easy Pieces*.

fashionable psychedelia leavened with the sardonic attitude of co-writer Jack Nicholson, with whom Rafelson would make his best films.

Five Easy Pieces (1970) was one of the finest works of its day and won the New York Film Critics best director prize. It was produced by BBS, an independent company formed by Rafelson, Bert Schneider and Steve Blauner dedicated to promoting American directors' cinema. The history of BBS epitomizes both what was best about New Hollywood and what became of the American art cinema that it spawned. The company produced Nicholson's *Drive, He Said* (1970), Peter Bogdanovich's *The Last Picture Show* (1971) and Rafelson's *The King Of Marvin Gardens* (1972), which typified the observant regional realism that BBS briefly stood for.

The director's subsequent work has been patchy. Bearing something of the loose observational tenor of his earlier work, *Stay Hungry* (1976) found Jeff Bridges' property speculator investing in a gym and its muscle men, led by Arnold Schwarzenegger. Rafelson's remake of *The Postman Always Rings Twice* (1981) has been unfairly neglected, while 1981's *Black Widow* – despite its formulaic competition between Theresa Russell's *femme fatale* and Debra Winger's FBI agent – remains effective neo-*noir*. *No Good Deed* (2002) was a disappointing thriller starring Samuel L. Jackson, but Rafelson's name is still synonymous with the New Hollywood of the 1970s. RA

Five Easy Pieces 1970, 98 min

cast Jack Nicholson, Karen Black, Billy "Green" Bush, Fannie Flagg, Sally Ann Struthers, Marlena MacGuire, Richard Stahl, Lois Smith *cin* Laszlo Kovacs

Driven by Jack Nicholson's studied portrayal of an intelligent man stranded between the desolate pleasures of blue-collar America and the rarefied air of his elitist family, this was one of the most poignant examinations of the American legacy to come out of New Hollywood. Rebellion has never seemed so contingent, futile and misunderstood.

The King Of Marvin Gardens 1972, 104 min

cast Jack Nicholson, Bruce Dern, Ellen Burstyn, Julia Anne Robinson, Scatman Crothers *cin* Laszlo Kovacs

Two brothers, one a small-time chancer (Bruce Dern), the other a reflective late-night radio presenter (Jack Nicholson), compare notes against the backdrop of an Atlantic City in kitschy decay. Like the best of New Hollywood, the film is imbued with the desultory air afflicting America in the midst of Vietnam and on the eve of Watergate. Crucially, it is also a metaphor for the perennial tug of commerce and art in American cinema.

The Postman Always Rings Twice 1981, 121 min

cast Jack Nicholson, Jessica Lange, John Colicos, Michael Lerner, John P. Ryan, Anjelica Huston, William Traylor *cin* Sven Nykvist *m* Michael Small

Simmering with the sexuality that liberated American cinema during the 1970s, this remake of the Lana Turner-John Garfield *film noir* is both more *noir* and nearer to the sensuality of James M. Cain's source novel. Fuelled by the chemistry and presence of Jack Nicholson and Jessica

R

Lange, and refined by the dusty Depression images of Ingmar Bergman's regular cinematographer Sven Nykvist, this is an underrated highlight of Rafelson's career.

Kevin Rafferty
US, 1948–

Documentary filmmaker Kevin Rafferty has specialized in producing investigative documentaries about American lifestyle and values. He made his name with the compilation documentary *The Atomic Café* (1982), which he co-directed with Jayne Loader and his brother Pierce Rafferty. He provided budding filmmaker Michael Moore with advice and camerawork on his breakthrough documentary feature *Roger & Me* (1989). *Blood In The Face* (with Anne Bohlen and James Ridgeway, 1991) was an exposé of white supremacists in America. It was followed by *Feed* (1992), a fly-on-the-wall look at the New Hampshire presidential primary elections, and *The Last Cigarette* (1999), an entertaining look at the tobacco industry in America. ED

The Atomic Café 1982, 80 min
with Dwight D. Eisenhower, Lyndon Johnson, Nikita Khrushchev, Richard Nixon, Ronald Reagan

Co-directed with Jayne Loader and Pierce Rafferty, *The Atomic Café* tells the fascinating story of the US government's attempts to get the public to embrace the nuclear bomb as part of their lives. A compilation of footage from government and military films of the 1940s and 50s, alongside excerpts from television and radio shows, the film is an amusing, sometimes jaw-dropping, if not chilling, document of paranoid propaganda.

Sam Raimi
US, 1959–

Long before Wes Craven mixed the slasher flick with deconstructive comedy in the *Scream* franchise, Sam Raimi was both practising and parodying horror-film conventions with his *Evil Dead* movies. Everything kicks off in *The Evil Dead* (1981) when a group of college-age friends inadvertently summon demonic wood spirits that possess and derange them, one by one. Raimi's low-budget feature debut drew a gory, frightening caricature of the imagery and human behaviour native to the horror genre, while inventing a novel strain of plant pathology – one poor girl is raped by a tree. The first sequel, *Evil Dead II: Dead By Dawn* (1987), is essentially a rousing slapstick remake of the original film, with highlights including an eyeball popping out of a zombie's mouth and landing in a screaming woman's mouth, and hero-by-default Ash (Bruce Campbell) chopping off his own possessed hand, which then chases him and tries to stab him.

The director made one more *Evil Dead* film, *Army Of Darkness* (1993), a decade after the original. This third instalment is an action comedy in which Ash – now equipped with a chainsaw for a hand – time-travels back to England in the Middle Ages. Raimi's first major-studio picture, *Darkman* (1990), is similarly heavy on kinetic action sequences in its tale of a disfigured scientist seeking revenge on those responsible for his mutilation. After the zippy Western pastiche *The Quick And The Dead* (1995), Raimi made an artistic breakthrough with the wintry neo-*noir A Simple Plan* (1998), about small-town friends who find $4 million in the wreckage of a crashed plane – a discovery that proves to be a Pandora's box of moral rot and terrible violence. Raimi began another franchise – this time on a mega-budget scale – when he landed the director's chair for *Spider-Man* (2002). His fun, proficient adaptation of the Marvel superhero comic book became the big summer blockbuster of 2002, and Raimi was quickly signed up for the sequels, which appeared in 2004 and 2007. JW

The Evil Dead 1981, 86 min
cast Bruce Campbell, Ellen Sandweiss, Betsy Baker, Richard DeManincor, Theresa Tilly *cin* Tim Philo *m* Joseph LoDuca

Ensconced in a remote cabin in the woods, a group of friends discover the "Book of the Dead" and accidentally unleash the local fiendish spirits, resulting in demonic possession – which, it seems, is best cured with a few swift blows from a dull axe. Positively swimming in blood, the movie surpasses its low production values and meagre budget with resourceful, nimble camera placement and movement – especially whenever the film takes the demons' point of view.

Spider-Man 2002, 121 min
cast Tobey Maguire, Willem Dafoe, Kirsten Dunst, James Franco, Rosemary Harris, Cliff Robertson, J.K. Simmons *cin* Don Burgess *m* Danny Elfman

After a fateful spider bite turns him into an arachnid superhero, high school student Peter Parker (Tobey Maguire) battles the shape-shifting Green Goblin (Willem Dafoe) while nursing his crush on gorgeous girl-next-door Mary Jane Watson (Kirsten Dunst). The speedy, serviceable action scenes pit an air-surfing Green Goblin against the web-spinning Spidey, but like most high-end Hollywood action productions, the film relies too heavily on CGI, resulting in a certain anonymity.

Harold Ramis
US, 1944–

What can we make of the director of both *Groundhog Day* (1993) and *Bedazzled* (2000)? While the former was the sparkling antithesis of the Hollywood production-line mentality, the latter reeked of stale formulae and focus-group mediocrity.

Harold Ramis started promisingly in the late 1960s with the Second City comedy troupe and went on to script the National Lampoon radio show and the movie *National Lampoon's Animal House* (1978). His writing career reached its glorious zenith with the deliriously inventive *Ghostbusters* (1984) which he co-wrote with Dan Aykroyd. Sadly, his workaday directorial style hasn't shown the same innovation, and his movies – which stand or fall according to the quality of the writing – have been depressingly hit and miss. *National Lampoon's Vacation* (1983) and *Club Paradise* (1986) could have been contenders, while clone comedy *Multiplicity* (1996) was a decent premise in search of a plot. And Ramis didn't possess the necessary chutzpah to make a decent job of *The Ice Harvest* (2005).

His early work – such as the cult golfing comedy *Caddyshack* (1980) – was characterized by gently anarchic and politely bawdy comedies that pivoted around an anti-authoritarian figure (usually Bill Murray, who brings out the best in Ramis). But in the 1990s and 2000s, the director spoke in interviews of wanting to make films with meaning. His later projects have certainly articulated a crisis in masculinity: witness Robert De Niro's mob boss consulting shrink Billy Crystal in *Analyze This* (1999) and *Analyze That* (2002). LH

Groundhog Day 1993, 101 min

cast Bill Murray, Andie MacDowell, Chris Elliott, Stephen Tobolowsky, Brian Doyle-Murray, Marita Geraghty *cin* John Bailey *m* George Fenton

Jaded weatherman Bill Murray is trapped in space and time, endlessly waking up each morning on the same day in the same small town. He soon learns to use this eternal cycle to get to know everything about the object of his dubious affection, Andie MacDowell. This is a film brimming with minor miracles – the level of mad, cerebral invention actually increases the longer it goes on, so that it's both funny and clever, and authentically philosophical. And it rewards repeat viewing.

Lynne Ramsay
UK, 1969–

Even in her National Film and Television School graduation short, *Small Deaths* (1996), Lynne Ramsay's acutely original eye for the telling moment is immediately apparent. Ramsay's work bears some of the hallmarks of the social realist school of British naturalism – her two features and three shorts all share her own working-class Scottish background – but she is a more sensual, liberated filmmaker than Mike Leigh or Ken Loach; her camera is more agile, her cutting more flexible, her imagination more poetic.

A photographer by training, Ramsay opted for the cinematographer course at NFTS, but quickly realized she had made a mistake and persuaded her tutors to allow her to make her own film. *Small Deaths* went on to win a prize for best short at

Cannes, and her two follow-ups (*Kill The Day*, 1996, and *Gasman*, 1997) were also highly acclaimed. The shorts' elliptical narratives and oblique perspectives on the emotional epiphanies of childhood led naturally into her first feature, *Ratcatcher* (1999). Set in Glasgow in 1973 during a dustmen's strike, the film presents us with an inarticulate young urchin from a deprived background who carries his own burden of guilt after a childish game has fatal consequences.

Morvern Callar (2002) allowed her to stretch, although this adaptation of Alan Warner's novel about a supermarket girl who cuts up her dead lover's body and takes off on a voyage of self-discovery revealed some uncertainty in its handling of narrative, and was generally less warmly received. Despite this, and a prolonged silence during which Ramsay flirted with an adaptation of Alice Sebold's novel *The Lovely Bones* (ultimately passing), she remains one of the most inspiring prospects of her generation. TC

Ratcatcher 1999, 94 min

cast William Eadie, Tommy Flanagan, Mandy Matthews, Leanne Mullen, John Miller *cin* Alwin Kuchler *m* Rachel Portman, Carl Orff

Ramsay's acclaimed first feature is a distinctive contribution to the cinema of childhood. The social squalor of the setting is not allowed to drown out moments of reverie and flashes of surrealism. Mixing professional and non-professional actors, and working with her regular collaborators cinematographer Alwin Kuchler and editor Lucia Zucchetti, Ramsay catches at something both mundane and allusive.

Jean-Paul Rappeneau
France, 1932–

Jean-Paul Rappeneau's cinema is a rogues' gallery of belligerent, charming, vulnerable and chivalrous men, boisterously epitomized by the antihero of his most celebrated film, *Cyrano De Bergerac* (1990). It was Gérard Depardieu's hell-raising take on the eponymous beaky wordsmith that brought Rappeneau to the rapt attention of the outside world. However, the director had been making award-winning, money-spinning comedies in France for over two decades.

After working as an assistant for a movie producer, Rappeneau made numerous industrial films and one short, *Chronique provinciale* (1958), but he eventually came to prominence as Louis Malle's scriptwriter on *Zazie dans le métro* (1960). His directorial debut, *A Matter Of Resistance* (1966), was a saucy war comedy in which bored housewife Catherine Deneuve gamely wards off advances from both a Nazi commandant and a Resistance leader. The French Revolution romp *The Scoundrel* (1971) was a sign of swashbuckling things to come, while the amiable screwball farce *Call Me Savage* (1975) starred Yves Montand as a typical Rappeneau hero – a gruff, bellicose, but ultimately decent, sociopath whose island retreat is invaded by vivacious runaway Deneuve.

Eight years after *All Fired Up* (1982), which also starred Montand, Rappeneau made *Cyrano De Bergerac*, one of France's most expensive productions and biggest hits. Working on a larger canvas, Rappeneau had finally come of age, and getting the blockbuster bit between his teeth, he successfully imbued *The Horseman On The Roof* (1995) with the same broad sweep and big-budget élan. In 2003, he returned to the war comedy with *Bon Voyage*, a curiously disappointing farce set in a Bordeaux hotel where the great and the not so good of Paris find temporary refuge after the Nazi invasion. LH

Cyrano De Bergerac 1990, 138 min

cast Gérard Depardieu, Jacques Weber, Anne Brochet, Vincent Perez, Roland Bertin, Philippe Morier-Genoud *cin* Pierre Lhomme *m* Jean-Claude Petit

Gérard Depardieu's rabble-rousing portrayal of a warrior poet with a prominent proboscis is considered by many to be the definitive Cyrano. While his ebullient grandstanding overshadows co-stars Anne Brochet and Vincent Perez, he's matched for outrageous panache and sheer verve by Rappaneau's swirling and sinuous camerawork, which comes into its own in the nimbly choreographed fight sequences. The director skilfully abbreviates Edmond Rostand's lengthy play without losing its exquisite poetry.

The Horseman On The Roof (Le hussard sur le toit) 1995, 136 min

cast Olivier Martinez, Juliette Binoche, Claudio Amendola, Pierre Arditi, Isabelle Carré, François Cluzet *cin* Thierry Arbogast *m* Jean-Claude Petit

Upon its release, this rousing tale of love in the time of cholera was the most expensive French film ever made. Olivier Martinez is suitably dashing as an Italian officer who comes to the rescue of a luminous, married countess (Juliette Binoche). As they gallop across the South of France in search of her husband, a will they/won't they scenario plays out in an overture of intimate exchanges and stolen glances. *The Horseman* is opulent and extravagant, but also suitably grisly in its unflinching depiction of the devastating effects of cholera.

Irving Rapper
UK, 1898–1999

Some directors are less well known than their films. British-born Irving Rapper is one such man, best known for his romantic melodramas in the tradition of Frank Borzage, George Cukor and Michael Curtiz. Rapper began his career as an actor and director on Broadway, but moved to Hollywood in the 1930s. Joining Warner Bros as a dialogue coach, he soon became an assistant director and worked with Michael Curtiz, whom he acknowledged as mentor. His first two films as director were modest, *Shining Victory* and *One*

Foot In Heaven (both 1941). But he is now known mainly for his films with Bette Davis, including *Now, Voyager* (1942), *The Corn Is Green* (1945), in which she played a Welsh schoolteacher, and the concert hall melodrama *Deception* (1946). The highlight of his work in the following decade was 1958's *Marjorie Morningstar*, featuring the luminescent Natalie Wood. His long career lasted into the 1970s. Despite sometime theatricality, Rapper's work had all the narrative flow, rich acting and crisp monochrome cinematography of Warner Bros at its zenith. RA

Now, Voyager 1942, 117 min, b/w

cast Bette Davis, Paul Henreid, Claude Rains, Gladys Cooper, Bonita Granville, John Loder, Ilka Chase, Patrick Lee *cin* Sol Polito *m* Max Steiner

Played out against the backdrop of a richly evoked Boston high society, this archetypal women's picture sees Bette Davis transformed from mother-dominated plain Jane to sexy socialite in the flick of a cigarette. As the woman who finds love, only to sacrifice it, the star was never better. She's ably supported by Claude Rains as the sympathetic psychiatrist who helps her break out of her shell, while Paul Henreid is the object of her devotion.

Mani Ratnam
India, 1956–

Unlike the garish excesses of most South Indian cinema, Mani Ratnam's films – most of which are in the Tamil language – are models of subtlety. After a quiet debut, Ratnam broke through with *Mouna ragam* (*A Silent Symphony*, 1986), a sensitive study of the break-up and subsequent reaffirmation of a marriage. His next two films – the *Godfather*-esque *Nayakan* (*Hero*, 1987) and the sibling rivalry tale *Agni nakshatram* (1988) – became huge critical and commercial successes and firmly established him as a bankable filmmaker with arthouse sensibilities. He followed them with *Gitanjali* (1989), a tender love story between two people who don't have long to live, and *Anjali* (1990), which saw him working with a large cast of children for the first time.

Roja (1992), a sensitive look at the Kashmir issue, was Ratnam's all-India breakthrough film. His best-known film, *Bombay* (1995), came next. The politically themed *Iruvar* (*The Duo*, 1997) and *Dil se* (*From The Heart*, 1998, his first Hindi film) did not achieve anything near the ecstatic response accorded to *Bombay*. *Alai payuthey* (*Waves*, 2000) saw Ratnam tackling the issue of marriage again, while *Kannathil muthamittal* (*A Peck On The Cheek*, 2002) returned to political themes with its story of a child's search for her mother set against the backdrop of ethnic strife in Sri Lanka. A quasi-biopic of a controversial businessman, *Guru* (2007) was Ratnam's first Hindi-language film to be a major success. Whatever the themes of his films, Ratnam is at his best when exploring the nuances of human relationships. NR

Bombay 1995, 141 min

cast Arvind Swamy, Manisha Koirala, Nasser, Kitty, Tinnu Anand, Akash Khurana *cin* Rajiv Menon *m* A.R. Rahman

A love story between a Hindu man and a Muslim woman set against the backdrop of the 1993 sectarian violence in Bombay, this film caused controversy with its thinly veiled portrayals of fundamentalist leaders and its realistic depictions of interreligious riots. The couple's twin sons, who are brought up to respect both religions, bring their warring Hindu and Muslim grandfathers together, and the film's message of tolerance – combined with A.R. Rahman's chart-busting songs – led to considerable box-office success.

Brett Ratner
US, 1969–

Brett Ratner's relatively small but hugely popular body of work is characterized by fast-paced, wilfully populist pieces with a streetwise sensibility.

Following a distinguished career as a director of music videos, Ratner made his debut feature, *Money Talks*, in 1997. A comedy about a hapless con man who is accused of having organized a prison break, it was the first of several collaborations with Chris Tucker. *Rush Hour* (1998) teamed Tucker with Jackie Chan in a buddy cop movie packed with smart-ass banter and Chan's legendary stunt work. Ratner directed the two inevitable sequels in 2001 and 2007. *The Family Man* (2000) was an unusual project for Ratner – a sentimental drama starring Nicolas Cage. The Hannibal Lecter horror *Red Dragon* (2002) was followed by *After The Sunset* (2004), a diamond heist thriller starring Pierce Brosnan and Salma Hayek. Next, Ratner took the reins on the special effects extravaganza *X Men 3: The Last Stand* (2006). JC

Red Dragon 2002, 124 min

cast Edward Norton, Ralph Fiennes, Anthony Hopkins, Emily Watson *cin* Dante Spinotti *m* Danny Elfman

In this atmospheric, well-judged prequel to *The Silence Of The Lambs* (1991) Hannibal Lecter (Anthony Hopkins) teams up with a retired FBI agent (Edward Norton) to track down a serial killer named The Tooth Fairy (Ralph Fiennes). Ratner's film captures the sense of impending doom and also elicits some strong performances.

Nicholas Ray
US 1911–79

A man aflame runs direct to camera. A girl of 16, stripped to the waist, is whipped by three teenagers. Two cars packed with kids race towards each other in a dark tunnel, skidding into a head-on crash. None of these opening sketches from Nicholas Ray's original story outline made it into *Rebel Without A Cause* (1955), save for the heavily modified "chicky race", but you get a sense of what he was after: chaos, danger and transgression. The French title for the film was *La fureur de vivre* – the rage to live – and though Eric Rohmer complained about the change in the pages of *Cahiers du cinéma*, Ray was nothing if not fervent.

Two years before, also in *Cahiers*, Jacques Rivette had noted Ray's "taste for paroxysm, which imparts something of the feverish and impermanent to the most tranquil of moments". This strain of existential agitation captured the imagination of the young *Cahiers* auteurists, for whom Ray became an object of veneration. "The cinema is Nicholas Ray", declared Jean-Luc Godard, and François Truffaut, Rohmer and Rivette all concurred: here was a bona fide post-war outsider poet, violent and solitary, infusing all manner of stories – Westerns, *noir* thrillers, melodramas, war movies – with his own indelible stamp. To wit: psychological complexity, visual intelligence, and a romantic-fatalist, mythopoetic sensibility carried to extravagant dramatic flourishes. Ray could take a low-budget Republic Western like *Johnny Guitar* (1954), shoot it full of Freud, Greek tragedy and Joe McCarthy, and end up with a camp baroque classic unlike anything else in the genre.

They Live By Night (1948), *Born To Be Bad* (1950), *On Dangerous Ground* (1951), *Rebel Without A Cause, Hot Blood* (1956), *Bigger Than Life* (1956), *Bitter Victory* (1957), *Wind Across The Everglades* (1958), *The Savage Innocents* (1960). You don't need to see these films (in one or two isolated cases it may be better that you don't) to appreciate the poetry in Ray's filmography. Like the doomed but intense romances that permeate the movies, his career was short but passionate: twenty movies in fifteen years, half a dozen of them either great or very close to it. By 1963 he was through in Hollywood, and practically spent as a creative force, though he continued to teach and write, and collaborated with his students to make *We Can't Go Home Again* (another poetic and self-mythologizing name) in 1974.

Born Raymond Nicholas Kienzle, Ray studied for a few months with the architect Frank Lloyd Wright (when pressed, he suggested his facility for CinemaScope might be attributed to Wright's influence). He worked in radio, researched American folk music, did some left-wing theatre in New York, and was shown the way around a movie set by Elia Kazan who let him observe the filming of *A Tree Grows In Brooklyn* (1945). He served in the Office of War Information under John Houseman, and it was Houseman who gave him his break on *They Live By Night*, a potent *noir* about a young couple on the margins of society. It remains one of the great first films.

Film noir: from out of the shadows

When World War II ended and American films reappeared in Europe, certain French writers identified a marked darkening of tone and style in Hollywood crime pictures. The critic Nino Frank, writing in August 1946, dubbed these films *film noir*, noting a new psychological complexity and moral ambiguity in such films as *The Maltese Falcon* (1941), *Murder My Sweet* (1944), *Double Indemnity* (1944) and *Laura* (1944).

Needless to say, Hollywood directors didn't set out to make *films noirs* – what they were making were thrillers, mysteries and romantic melodramas. But if you compare the crime films of the 1930s with those of the 1940s and 50s (the so-called classic era of *film noir*), the differences are as marked as the similarities. While the earlier films often portrayed criminals as troubled, complex characters, their emphasis was largely on the action and the moral conclusion was always pretty clear: crime did not pay. However, later crime films – although subject to the same restrictions – were more morally blurry, with their protagonists struggling much more existentially with issues of anxiety, guilt and betrayal.

There was also a noticeable difference in the visual qualities of the new crime films, particularly in the way they were lit. In a typical *film noir*, high-contrast lighting was often used to create deep enveloping shadows, while at the same time oddly angled shots could suggest a sense of strangeness or subjectivity. The city at night was the archetypal *noir* location; the dark, rain-soaked streets reflecting the harsh glare of neon. Within this claustrophobic, threatening atmosphere, *noir*'s characters fought for survival. Scenarios often centred around a doomed relationship, in which a weak-willed man – a petty crook, a private eye, a returning war veteran – is ensnared by a *femme fatale*, irresistible but dangerous, who lures him into a scheme that invariably spirals out of control.

The cynicism that pervades much of *noir* was largely derived from one of its main sources – the hard-boiled crime fiction of the 1930s, with its greater realism, terse language and dubious heroes. Dashiel Hammett, Raymond Chandler and James M. Cain exemplified this school of writing, and many of their works were adapted for the screen. Another major determinant of the *noir* style was the wave of Austro-German directors that arrived in Hollywood to escape Nazism. Figures like Fritz Lang, Robert Siodmak, Otto Preminger and Billy Wilder brought both an outsider's perspective to American life and, arguably, a more experimental style, which had its roots in the distortions and extreme subjectivity of expressionism.

Home-grown directors were no less important in the creation of *film noir*, but it is significant that the first acknowledged *noir* masterpiece – John Huston's version of Hammett's novel *The Maltese Falcon* – employed a range of camera "tricks" that revealed an awareness of both German expressionism and Sergei Eisenstein. The same is even truer of Orson Welles's *Citizen Kane* (1941), a film that exerted a powerful influence on *noir*, not least in its use of elaborate tracking shots, long takes, complex design and flashback narration.

But it would be wrong to reduce *noir* to a formulaic juggling of its various components. The very best *noirs* employed some or all of these elements to powerful and disturbing effect, and by frequently focusing on individuals living on the margins, they were able to give a voice to some of the fears and anxieties bubbling beneath the surface of society. Many of those involved in the making of what are now thought of as *films noirs* were on the left (sometimes the far left) of the American political spectrum. Directors like Abraham Polonsky, Jules Dassin, Edward Dmytryk and Nicholas Ray all made films that raised important social issues (such as racial intolerance) and provided an often critical perspective on traditional American values – from capitalism to the nuclear family. Such films acted as an antidote to the complacent optimism of the early 1950s, but many of those who made them fell foul of the wave of anti-communism that swept the country in the post-war period.

Film noir is thought to have "ended" with Orson Welles's *Touch Of Evil* in 1958. Thereafter, a few films were made that fit fairly neatly into the *noir* rubric, but by the 1960s this had become a trickle. The emergence of a more permissive society, a greater emphasis on youth culture and Hollywood's preoccupation with Technicolor spectacle all contributed to making *noir* seem anachronistic. It would take another decade before a generation of self-consciously cine-literate directors would fully embrace its revival in the form of neo-*noir*. RB

Ray's politics should have got him into trouble during the blacklist, but the patronage of RKO boss Howard Hughes was his protection. Instead, his own self-destructive urges got the better of him. A charismatic and promiscuous bisexual, Ray lived it like he told it: on dangerous ground. He even had an affair with Edie Wasserman, the wife of agent and studio executive Lew Wasserman, said to be the most powerful man in Hollywood.

Godard said that, alone among directors, if cinema hadn't existed, Ray would have invented it. Yet Ray's great work was all made within the studio system, putting an expressionist skew on the highly codified lexicon of American genre moviemaking. Towards the end of the 1950s Ray appeared to be

Adolescent confusion: a troubled James Dean finds solace with Natalie Wood in *Rebel Without A Cause*.

pushing for something else – you can see him edging to break new thematic and formal ground in the eco-parable *Wind Across The Everglades* and the ethnographic *The Savage Innocents* – but unlike his close contemporary Orson Welles, he failed to make that reinvention Godard believed him to be capable of.

Moving to Europe, he made two so-so epics for Samuel Bronston, *King Of Kings* (1961) and *55 Days At Peking* (1963), but collapsed on the set of the latter. He would live for another two decades, an artist in premature retirement. An alcoholic and a drug addict, he played up to his legendary status as a maverick and an outsider, but outsiders can't make movies without help, and Ray seemed unwilling or unable to find any. TC

They Live By Night 1948, 95 min, b/w

cast Cathy O'Donnell, Farley Granger, Howard da Silva, Jay C. Flippen *cin* George E. Diskant *m* Leigh Harline

This lyrical, romantic *film noir*, based on Edward Anderson's Depression-era novel, set the template for the "couple on the run" sub-genre. Ray stresses the innocence and fallibility of his young lovers Bowie and Keechie (Granger and O'Donnell): they're locked in a passionate embrace in the film's very first shot, before an ominous voiceover shatters the mood: "This boy and this girl were never properly introduced to the world we live in."

In A Lonely Place 1950, 93 min, b/w

cast Humphrey Bogart, Gloria Grahame, Frank Lovejoy, Jeff Donnell, Carl Benton Reid *cin* Burnett Guffey *m* George Antheil

Bogart stars as Hollywood screenwriter Dixon Steele, who finds himself a suspect when a hat-check girl he had picked up is found murdered. Although a *noir* atmosphere permeates the movie, Ray and screenwriter Andrew Solt keep the murder investigation in the background, focusing instead on the relationship between Dix and Laurel (Grahame), a girl across the way who falls in love with him, even if she can't entirely trust him. This love story feels remarkably modern: Dix and Laurel are passionate and tender one minute, violent and fearful the next.

On Dangerous Ground 1951, 82 min, b/w

cast Ida Lupino, Robert Ryan, Ward Bond, Charles Kemper, Ed Begley *cin* George Diskant *m* Bernard Herrmann

The title refers to mental as well as environmental terrain in this flawed but vital thriller. Ryan gives a blistering performance as the city cop on the verge of a crackup who finds a bruised sort of redemption on a case in upstate New York involving Lupino's blind woman and her retarded brother. For once, Ray's forthright romanticism teeters into sentimentality, but the point is hard-won, almost cathartic in its intensity. Bernard Herrmann's score was said to be the composer's favourite work.

The Lusty Men 1952, 113 min, b/w

cast Robert Mitchum, Susan Hayward, Arthur Kennedy, Arthur Hunnicutt, Frank Faylen *cin* Lee Garmes *m* Roy Webb

Along with Sam Peckinpah's *Junior Bonner* (1972), this is Hollywood's only honest rodeo picture, stressing the hardship and danger of life on the circuit. In one of his finest roles, Robert Mitchum is the ex-rodeo champ who pulls his broken bones back to his home in Texas, where he falls in with an enthusiastic cowhand (Kennedy) and teaches him the ropes, to the displeasure of the cowboy's wife (Hayward). Beautiful black-and-white photography by Lee Garmes.

Rebel Without A Cause 1955, 111 min

cast James Dean, Natalie Wood, Sal Mineo, Jim Backus, Ann Doran, Corey Allen, Dennis Hopper *cin* Ernest Haller *m* Leonard Rosenman

"You're tearing me apart" rails Jim Stark (Dean) at his middle-class parents. "If he had the guts to knock Mom cold once, then maybe she'd be happy and stop picking on him", he mumbles. Yet Dean himself represents a softer, more sensitive masculinity than his macho peers. The film's psychodynamics can feel coercive, but in grasping for tragedy it does tap an intense adolescent poetry of sexual confusion and frustration. Dean is extraordinary, iconic – and was dead before the movie even opened.

Bigger Than Life 1956, 95 min

cast James Mason, Barbara Rush, Walter Matthau, Robert F. Simon, Christopher Olsen *cin* Joseph MacDonald *m* David Raksin

Patriarchal society gets a thorough working over in Ray's typically bold domestic melodrama. James Mason is a respected small-town schoolteacher whose repressed frustration and megalomania are magnified tenfold under the influence of the "wonder drug", cortisone. More than just an "issue" movie, the film lifts the lid on middle-class complacency and debilitating conformity, even as it warns of the fascistic impulses that might fester underneath such suppression ("God was wrong", rails Mason).

Satyajit Ray
India, 1921–92

Satyajit Ray is India's most renowned director. His films represent the serious arthouse strand in Indian cinema, in contrast to the *masala* mainstream of Bollywood.

Ray was still working as an illustrator and copywriter for an advertising firm when he made his debut, *Pather panchali* (1955). Funded in part by the sale of his wife's jewellery, and made at weekends over the course of three years, the production would have probably carried on in the same piecemeal fashion if it hadn't been for John Huston. On a visit to India, the director of *The African Queen* saw rough cut footage and his enthusiastic support for the work-in-progress caused an unlikely chain reaction that resulted in the West Bengal government funding the rest of the film. It was a sensation on release, both at home and abroad, meaning Ray was finally able to quit his day job.

Ray was never popular throughout India – the commercial success of his pictures was restricted by his use of the Bengali language, as opposed to the more widely spoken Hindi. But even though the language was specific to his region, Ray's films spoke clearly to discriminating Western cinema-goers (the director once admitted that his international audience helped him survive as a filmmaker). This is not really surprising, as Ray learned his craft by not only studying Vittorio De Sica's *Bicycle Thieves* (1948) but also lapping up American movies, especially those of John Ford and Frank Capra. And although there is little of Hollywood's influence to be seen in the leisurely pace and the local subject matter, it's very much evident in the melodramatic impulses and deft ability to quietly craft a narrative. There is a French connection too, in the humanist lens of his mentor Jean Renoir, whom Ray had assisted on *The River* (1951).

In all, Ray made over thirty films, writing, directing and editing them, designing the sets and eventually composing his own scores. The Apu trilogy films – *Pather panchali*, *Aparajito* (*The Unvanquished*, 1956) and *The World Of Apu* (1959) – are the best known. But Ray's oeuvre includes a number of other standout films. In *The Music Room* (1958) a lonely widowed landlord puts on lavish concerts in his crumbling mansion. *Devi* (1960) was a disturbing fable of devotion and deification. *Charulata* (*The Lonely Wife*, 1964) returned to the theme of loneliness, this time in the figure of a neglected wife. The magisterial *Days And Nights In The Forest* (1970) told the story of four young men from the city whose lives are quietly but fundamentally transformed when they holiday in the country. *Distant Thunder* (1973) was a captivating, curiously uplifting domestic drama set against the Bengal famine of 1943. Another historical film, *The Chess Players* (1977) was the cheerfully eccentric tale of two Indian noblemen complacent in the face of British designs on their territory. *The Home And The World* (1984) was a compelling, slow-burning chamber piece about the Indian practice of purdah. His later career was marked by severe illness. A loose adaptation of Henrik Ibsen's *An Enemy Of The People* in 1989 represented a brave comeback, and *The Stranger* (1992) was a graceful final feature.

Above all, Ray revealed himself to be a director of moments. At their best, his films burned with a sensuous, incandescent quality, mastering one of cinema's most uncanny magic tricks, the illusion that the camera is somehow able to capture the light from inside a human being. If he wasn't nicknamed "Ray of Light", then he should have been. He has been classified as a neo-realist but, in truth, Ray belongs to an older tradition of fatalistic pantheism, displaying an appreciation of nature and misery reminiscent of the novels of Thomas Hardy. Despite its sour tragedies and unrelenting poverty, Ray's universe is a world of wonder. So it's not surprising to discover that he was also a children's illustrator, or that this middle-class director was accused of an immoral alchemy, of turning poverty into beauty. The distinct lack of an overt political agenda also aggravated some left-wing critics. Instead, Ray evinced a warm humanism often transmitted through a deceptively simple yet profoundly resonant close-up of the human face: cinema's *lingua franca*. LH

Pather panchali 1955, 115 min, b/w
cast Subir Bannerjee, Kanu Bannerjee, Karuna Bannerjee, Uma Das Gupta, Chunibala Devi *cin* Subrata Mitra *m* Ravi Shankar

An impoverished writer has to leave his wife to look for work in the big city, leaving his children (Apu and his fruit-stealing sister) to their own devices, with tragic consequences. The tracks of Vittorio De Sica's *Bicycle Thieves* are evident throughout this spare, episodic classic, which at times segues effortlessly from neo-realism to expressionism, evoking the magic of a child's world with the same eerie enchantment as another masterpiece from 1955, Charles Laughton's *Night Of The Hunter*.

Aparajito (The Unvanquished) 1956, 110 min, b/w
cast Pinaki Sengupta, Smaran Ghosal, Kanu Bannerjee, Karuna Bannerjee, Santi Gupta, Ramani Sengupta *cin* Subrata Mitra *m* Ravi Shankar

In what initially feels like a documentary on city life in the subcontinent, Apu takes on the role of wide-eyed ethnographer, spying on his neighbours and observing obscure rituals. When his father dies, he returns reluctantly to village life, but eventually vacillates between town and country, much to the chagrin of his lonely mother. It's in the city that the movie really comes to sweaty life, with Ray revealing an eye for squalid yet remarkable detail, his deep-focus photography immersing the viewer head-first in the hubbub of urban India.

The World Of Apu (Apur sansar) 1959, 117 min, b/w
cast Soumitra Chatterjee, Sharmila Tagore, Alok Chakravarty, Swapan Mukherjee, Dhiresh Majumdar *cin* Subrata Mitra *m* Ravi Shankar

The third part of the Apu trilogy possesses less of the universal resonance that Ray had previously mined so successfully, but remains a remarkable and lyrical achievement nonetheless. Now a young man, Apu is struggling to pay the rent working as a writer. When he attends a wedding at which the groom goes mad, Apu is drafted in as a substitute husband. His new wife doesn't take to his down-at-heel lifestyle at first, but soon their domestic difficulties turn into something else: bona fide tragedy.

The Music Room (Jalsaghar) 1958, 100 min, b/w
cast Chabi Biswas, Padma Devi, Pinaki Sengupta, Tulsi Lahari *cin* Subrata Mitra *m* Ustad Vilayat Khan, Asis Kumar, Robin Majumder, Dakhin Mohan Takhur

Making a perfect double bill of yearning with *Charulata*, *The Music Room* zeroes in on a lonely widower named Biswambhar Roy, the last of the landlord class. His only real companions are his memories and the guests who attend the lavish concerts that he regularly holds in the fading glory of his music room. The rest of the time Biswambhar rattles around his ramshackle mansion like an Indian Charles Foster Kane. Spare, evocative and exquisitely plangent.

Charulata (The Lonely Wife) 1964, 117 min, b/w
cast Soumitra Chatterjee, Madhabi Mukherjee, Shailen Mukherjee, Shyamal Ghoshal, Gitali Roy *cin* Subrata Mitra *m* Satyajit Ray

Ray's diary of a lonely housewife springs a couple of surprises: the song halfway through the movie that seems to be either a nod to or a parody of Bollywood conventions, and Ray's free-form style, which gives the film a *nouvelle vague* quality, as it gently oscillates between edgy, lyrical and impressionistic moods. The overwhelming sense of yearning, however, is almost too much to bear.

Robert Redford
US, 1936–

The golden boy of 1970s cinema, the *éminence grise* of American indies, Robert Redford made a typically laconic start to his filmmaking career, dropping out of college and only drifting into acting after living in Europe for a year as a struggling artist. He learned his trade in TV and on stage, upgrading to leading actor on film in the mid-1960s, but once *Butch Cassidy And The Sundance Kid* (1969) had conferred superstar status upon him, Redford was not slow in taking control.

After problems with the studio on *Tell Them Willie Boy Is Here* (1969), Redford formed his own production company, Wildwood. The flaxen-haired film idol has continued to maintain his distance from Hollywood by setting up the Sundance Institute and Festival, which has nurtured and promoted a whole generation of independent filmmakers. Quentin Tarantino and Steven Soderbergh are the most famous alumni of Sundance, though it has to be said that the festival winners are usually of the worthy but dull variety. It's an earnestness which is sadly in evidence in Redford's own directorial efforts. This propensity for solemnity, however, didn't stop *Ordinary People* (1980) from unexpectedly snatching the best director Oscar from under the noses of both Martin Scorsese and David Lynch.

Redford's directorial style often mirrors his screen presence: distant, good-looking and laid-back. Too often, however, laid-back turns to lax, especially when the script itself is rambling, as with the tedious *The Milagro Beanfield War* (1988). Sometimes the films, possibly like Redford himself, can be too handsome for their own good. While the unexpectedly enchanting hymn to fly-fishing *A River Runs Through It* (1992) boasted imagery that was genuinely Edenic, the same Montana landscape was the object of soft-focus platitudes in the interminable *The Horse Whisperer* (1998). Both were suffused with a New Age spiritualism which found its full, cringing expression in *The Legend Of Bagger Vance* (2000) in which Will Smith was wincingly miscast as a caddy with mystical powers. It's in *Quiz Show* (1994) that Redford's laconic directing style has

R

really paid dividends, which suggests perhaps that he should ditch the pastoral and mystical, and concentrate on the coruscating and satirical. LH

Ordinary People 1980, 124 min

cast Donald Sutherland, Mary Tyler Moore, Judd Hirsch, Timothy Hutton, M. Emmet Walsh, Elizabeth McGovern, Dinah Manoff *cin* John Bailey

The relationship between husband and wife Donald Sutherland and Mary Tyler Moore slowly corrodes after the death of their teenage son; worst affected, though, is their younger son, Timothy Hutton, who suffered a psychological meltdown after the boating accident. Although it's finely calibrated, impeccably sensitive and immaculately acted, this film is best remembered for beating Martin Scorsese's *Raging Bull* to the best picture Oscar in 1980.

Quiz Show 1994, 132 min

cast John Turturro, Rob Morrow, Ralph Fiennes, Paul Scofield, Elizabeth Wilson, Mira Sorvino, Martin Scorsese *cin* Michael Ballhaus *m* Mark Isham

Based on a true scandal in which the producers of the 1950s TV quiz show *Twenty-One* regularly and blithely rigged the outcome to get ratings. Lecturer Charles Van Doren (Ralph Fiennes) is the latest unbeaten champion to benefit from the scam. When he becomes an audience favourite and poster boy for intellectualism, he incurs the jealous wrath of previous champ Herbie Stempel, who blows the whistle on the whole corrupt enterprise. Magnetic and adroit, the tight script benefits from the director's measured, forensic approach.

Carol Reed

UK, 1906–76

Peter Bogdanovich once described *The Third Man* (1949) as "the greatest non-auteur film ever made", thereby implying that Carol Reed was more technician than artist. The reasons for such a dismissal derive from the significant cultural prejudices embedded in auteurism, including the antipathy of *Cahiers du cinéma* critics towards British cinema, the reluctance of the British film establishment to embrace auteur theory and the distracting presence in *The Third Man* of the archetypal auteur, Orson Welles, as Harry Lime.

However, if we look at Reed's career as a whole, we may also conclude that he was deprived of the basic continuities that allowed Hollywood directors of his generation to flourish within the studio system. Reed made three masterpieces in three years (1947–49), but rather lost his way in the 1950s, partly due to the demands of Hollywood backers and calls to make films with greater international appeal. At any rate, as the first film director to be knighted, Reed had no need to press his artistic credentials, even if his critical reputation seesawed.

The illegitimate son of leading actor Herbert Beerbohm Tree and his mistress May Pinney, Reed made his stage debut at age 17. Three years later he joined writer Edgar Wallace's theatre company,

working as a stage manager and script adaptor, as well as an actor. In the early 1930s, he joined Associated British Talking Pictures at Ealing Studios, and he began directing "quota quickies" in 1935. Reed invested these low-budget production-line pictures with enough style to earn some recognition, and by the release of his sixth feature, *Bank Holiday* (1938) – a cheeky British variation on MGM's all-star ensemble piece *Grand Hotel* (1932) – he was already showing real creative command.

Working with more ambitious material for *The Stars Look Down* (1939), an independently financed adaptation of A.J. Cronin's novel, Reed mixed uneven romantic melodrama with a surprisingly authentic portrait of a coal-mining community and a call for nationalization to "purge the old greeds". This foray into social realism was soon discarded for the Hitchcockian espionage thriller *Night Train To Munich* (1940), written by the team behind *The Lady Vanishes* (1938), Frank Launder and Sidney Gilliat. With the outbreak of World War II, Reed devoted himself primarily to propaganda and training films, but also made the popular David Niven war movie *The Way Ahead* (1944).

Going into the war as one of British cinema's most promising talents, Reed emerged as a mature and masterly filmmaker – and as an artist. However much his consecutive master works – *Odd Man Out* (1947), *The Fallen Idol* (1948) and *The Third Man* (1949) – owe to their talented screenwriters, it is clear that these pictures are Reed's vision fully realized on screen. Furthermore, they share a view of the world that is informed by war and death: a world in which friendships and love affairs only beget anguished betrayals and cruel disillusionment. The expressionist camera angles and chiaroscuro effects that Reed and his cinematographers Robert Krasker and Georges Périnal favoured in these films mirrored the *noirs* being made in America in the same period. However, his location shooting also firmly rooted these suspense thrillers in post-war Europe – indelibly so in the Vienna of *The Third Man*. All three films also exude a thoroughly British appreciation for eccentric character parts; among his other virtues, Reed was a fine director of actors.

The Fallen Idol and *The Third Man* were both made in collaboration with the writer Graham Greene, who proved to be one of Reed's most auspicious partners. Co-produced by Alexander Korda and David O. Selznick, *The Third Man* marked a high point not only in Reed's career, but also in the history of British cinema. Indeed, a 1999 British Film Institute poll of writers, academics and experts voted it the best British film ever made.

Post-*Third Man*, Reed's career went into a long, slow decline, with each subsequent film marking a gradual fall from grace, from the interesting, flawed Joseph Conrad adaptation *Outcast Of The Islands* (1952) and the *Third Man*-esque *The Man Between*

R

(1953) to the whimsical poetic realist fable *A Kid And Two Farthings* (1955) and the disappointing Hollywood outing *Trapeze* (1956).

A modest reunion with Greene for *Our Man In Havana* in 1959 arrested this decline, perhaps suggesting that Reed's other 1950s projects had suffered because of the quality of their writing. However, this brief return to form was halted three years later when Reed came off worst in a battle of wills with Marlon Brando on the set of *Mutiny On The Bounty* (1962). *The Agony And The Ecstasy* (1965), starring Charlton Heston as Michelangelo, was judged to be altogether too much agony, and not enough ecstasy. The old-fashioned but popular musical *Oliver!* (1968) played to Reed's strengths for Dickensian eccentricity and atmosphere, won

the Oscar for best picture over Stanley Kubrick's *2001: A Space Odyssey* and John Cassavetes's *Faces* and finally gifted Reed, at the end of his career, with his first – and only – best director Oscar. TC

Odd Man Out 1947, 116 min, b/w

cast James Mason, Robert Newton, Cyril Cusack, Kathleen Ryan, F.J. McCormick *cin* Robert Krasker *m* William Alwyn

IRA man Johnny McQueen (James Mason) is wounded in a botched robbery. Hunted down through the streets, he is given shelter by some, shown the door by others – but who can he trust? The first of Reed's vertiginous, expressionist suspense pictures, *Odd Man Out* is a baroque, nightmarish allegory. In the end, what makes Johnny the odd man out is that he's dying; the bars and back rooms of Belfast become some kind of purgatory.

The Fallen Idol 1948, 92 min, b/w

cast Bobby Henrey, Ralph Richardson, Michèle Morgan, Jack Hawkins *cin* Georges Périnal *m* William Alwyn

Although it's less well known than *The Third Man*, this may be Reed's most controlled and moving film. Bobby Henrey plays the lonely son of an ambassador whose affection for the friendly butler Baines (Ralph Richardson) brings ruination when he suspects his friend of murdering his wife. The film explores ambivalent relationships across class, cultural and generational divides through the eyes of an innocent – but far from unsullied – child.

The Third Man 1949, 104 min, b/w

cast Joseph Cotton, Alida Valli, Orson Welles, Trevor Howard, Bernard Lee *cin* Robert Krasker *m* Anton Karras

Legend has it that, after seeing Reed's dazzling post-war thriller, the director William Wyler sent his colleague a spirit level… all those crazy, lopsided camera angles, as if the world was out of kilter. Perhaps it was. This is such a seductive classic, so stylish and urbane, that it's easy to overlook the ugly bare bones of a story that begins and ends with a funeral in the ruins of Old Europe, the sense of fetid corruption underlying it all, and the sorry victims of Harry Lime's penicillin racket. But then that's exactly what the film is about: the charming face of evil, the smile that conceals a switchblade.

The lower depths: the net closes in on racketeer Harry Lime (Orson Welles) in the final moments of *The Third Man*.

R

Oliver! 1968, 146 min
cast Mark Lester, Ron Moody, Oliver Reed, Jack Wild, Shani Wallis, Harry Secombe, Hugh Griffith *cin* Oswald Morris *m* Lionel Bart

This popular musical take on Dickens' *Oliver Twist* is just good enough to make you wish Reed had been allowed to do the book instead. Lionel Bart's songs are catchy (including "Consider Yourself" and "As Long As He Needs Me"), but Panavision and Technicolor showstoppers tend to work against Dickens' bleak picture of Victorian poverty and exploitation. There's strong character work though, and production designer John Box excelled himself. The film won five Oscars, including best picture and best director.

Michael Reeves

UK, 1943–69

Michael Reeves was one of the great missed opportunities of British cinema. Entering films in various roles, he worked in Europe and England, but his break came in Italy, when he co-wrote and was second assistant director on *Crypt Of Horror* (1964), starring Christopher Lee and Donald Sutherland. He was only 20 when he co-wrote and directed his first feature, 1965's *The She-Beast*, which starred the "Queen of Scream", Barbara Steele. *The Sorcerers* (1967), which Reeves also co-wrote, followed. In this horror with a sci-fi twist, Boris Karloff and Catherine Lacey played a diabolical couple conducting an experiment who use perverse forms of mind control on Ian Ogilvy. Trading in the vicious and the vicarious, this dizzying meditation on cinema looked forward to Kathryn Bigelow's 1995 epic *Strange Days*. Reeves's masterpiece, *Witchfinder General* (1968), helped redefine the horror genre. While preparing his next film, *The Oblong Box* (subsequently taken over by Gordon Hessler and released in 1969), Reeves died of a drug overdose. He was only 24. RA

Witchfinder General 1968, 88 min
cast Vincent Price, Ian Ogilvy, Rupert Davies, Hilary Dwyer, Robert Russell, Nicky Henson *cin* John Coquillon *m* Paul Ferris

Resonant with the dour skies and vast horizons of its East Anglian setting, this was an evocation of religious and sexual repression during the English Civil War. Reeves conjures a fecund poetry out of the collision of prejudice and fear as Vincent Price's vengeful witch-hunter scours the land for marks of the witch. It remains one of the richest British horror movies.

Carl Reiner

US, 1922–

As a gag writer, Carl Reiner is a showbiz legend, on a comedy par with his contemporary and erstwhile colleague Mel Brooks. As a film director, he's been eclipsed by his son, Rob Reiner.

The former Broadway actor joined Sid Caesar's *Your Show Of Shows* as a scribe alongside Woody Allen and Brooks, with whom he devised the cult sketch series *The 2000 Year Old Man*. After creating the popular sitcom *The Dick Van Dyke Show*, Reiner turned his comedic, quietly surreal talents to cinema, making his directorial bow with *Enter Laughing* (1967) adapted from his own autobiographical novel of the same name. As a filmmaker, Reiner's golden age was in the late 1970s and early 1980s when he collaborated with Steve Martin on four classics of unabashed stupidity and sly philosophy: *The Jerk* (1979), *Dead Men Don't Wear Plaid* (1982), *The Man With Two Brains* (1983) and *All Of Me* (1984). He also co-wrote the middle two of these.

Either side of this fecund period, Reiner made films that swung from the good (*Oh God!*, 1977 and *Where's Poppa*, 1970) to the godawful (*Bert Rigby, You're A Fool*, 1989, and *Fatal Instinct*, 1993). However, most of his movies occupy the middle ground of genial mediocrity: *The One And Only* (1978), *Summer Rental* (1985), *Summer School* (1987), *Sibling Rivalry* (1990) and *That Old Feeling* (1997). He has also continued to act, appearing in such films as Woody Allen's *Bullets Over Broadway* (1994) and Steven Soderbergh's *Ocean's Thirteen* (2007). LH

Dead Men Don't Wear Plaid 1982, 89 min
cast Steve Martin, Rachel Wood, Alan Ladd, Carl Reiner, Barbara Stanwyck, Ray Milland, Ava Gardner *cin* Michael Chapman *m* Miklós Rózsa

Not the funniest of his collaborations with Steve Martin, this is nonetheless fiendishly clever and genuinely ground-breaking, constructed like a crazed jigsaw of clips from old *films noirs*. Martin plays a private eye investigating the bizarre disappearance of a mad scientist and cheese-maker. Along the way, he enlists the help of Humphrey Bogart (culled ingeniously from *In A Lonely Place*, *Dark Passage* and *The Big Sleep*), comes face to face with James Cagney (from *White Heat*), Alan Ladd (*This Gun For Hire*) and Burt Lancaster (*The Killers*) and effortlessly charms Lana Turner (*Johnny Eager*), Bette Davis (*Deception*) and Barbara Stanwyck (*Sorry, Wrong Number*).

Rob Reiner

US, 1947–

Rob Reiner is American comedy's arch humanist. The son of actor-director Carl Reiner and raised in show business, he began his career in regional theatre and minor comedy roles on television. His movie acting debut was in his father's 1967 comedy, *Enter Laughing*. But his breakthrough came in 1971, playing the vexed liberal son-in-law to conservative hard-hat Archie Bunker in the long-running television series *All In The Family*. As an actor, Reiner tended to appear in warm-hearted fare with a Jewish sense of irony, and this tone would also generally mark his directed work.

Reiner's 1983 debut was the seminal *This Is Spinal Tap*, which astutely spoofed the rock documentary and became a midnight classic. The road movie *The Sure Thing* (1985) updated Frank Capra's *It Happened One Night* (1934), with John Cusack and Daphne Zuniga playing students hitching across America and falling in love to the strains of Tin Pan Alley tunes. The film's sparky dialogue rivalled that of Reiner's hit romantic comedy *When Harry Met Sally...* (1989). The rite-of-passage movie *Stand By Me* (1986) was a paean to youth based on a Stephen King short story. Featuring River Phoenix and Kiefer Sutherland, it marked Reiner's big commercial breakthrough. Although 1987's *The Princess Bride* was ostensibly a children's fantasy, it contained enough spoofery to be recognizably Reiner.

The 1990s saw Reiner's industry clout grow, but releases such as the Tom Cruise courtroom drama *A Few Good Men* (1992) and the Civil Rights apologia *Ghosts Of Mississippi* (1996) now seem bland. Conversely, the James Caan-Kathy Bates two-hander *Misery* (1990) – based on another Stephen King tale – milked chilling suspense from a writer's incarceration by an obsessed fan. *The American President* (1995) played like contemporary Capra, and was a lesson in liberal populism, as Michael Douglas's president fell for Annette Bening's political lobbyist. Again invoking memories of movies past, *Rumour Has It...* (2005) found Jennifer Aniston's heroine wondering whether *The Graduate* (1967) was based on her parents' relationship. The best of Reiner's films make audiences feel special, step on nobody's toes and are advertisements for the milk of human kindness. RA

This Is Spinal Tap 1983, 82 min

cast Christopher Guest, Michael McKean, Harry Shearer, Rob Reiner *cin* Peter Smokler *m* Christopher Guest, Michael McKean, Harry Shearer, Rob Reiner

Stunning in its parody of the jumped-up egos and pumped-up noise of heavy metal bands, this "rockumentary" charts in *cinéma vérité* fashion the decline of an English rock band beset by endemic rivalries and aesthetic misjudgements. Director, star and co-writer Rob Reiner's hilarious sense of the absurd tempers this cult classic.

When Harry Met Sally... 1989, 95 min

cast Billy Crystal, Meg Ryan, Carrie Fisher, Bruno Kirby, Steven Ford, Lisa Jane Persky, Michelle Nicastro *cin* Barry Sonnenfeld *m* Marc Shaiman

When Harry (Billy Crystal) met Sally (Meg Ryan), it was the start of a ten-year "courtship", hindered by his romantic reluctance and her finicky romanticism. Richard Rodgers and Lorenz Hart show tunes provided the background as the pair pondered whether men and women can ever be friends without sex getting in the way. The film grossed more than $100 million and made big stars of the two leads.

Karel Reisz
Czech Republic (formerly Czechoslovakia), 1926–2002

One of the founders of the Free Cinema documentary movement, Karel Reisz later dismissed it as "a PR exercise that touched a nerve". And yet, like Tony Richardson, he ended up being defined by the movement as much as he defined it.

Spirited out of Czechoslovakia just before the Nazi invasion, Reisz came to Britain at the age of 12, leaving behind his parents, who would both die in a concentration camp. He claimed that it was his experience as a teacher that made him realize that British movies of the 1950s were not reflecting the lives of the people he taught. With Richardson, Lorenza Mazzetti and Lindsay Anderson, he formed the Free Cinema group, whose manifesto declared their intention to make films that were both for and about a working class that had been largely neglected by its national cinema. Reisz and his colleagues were also active film critics, with Reisz writing for *Sight & Sound* and completing a landmark volume, *The Technique Of Film Editing*, in 1953. Reisz contributed the documentary short *Momma Don't Allow* (1955) (co-directed with Richardson) to Free Cinema's inaugural and iconoclastic event at the National Film Theatre in 1956. Two years later, the acclaimed *We Are The Lambeth Boys* (1958) documented the activities of a Lambeth youth club.

It was with his first fiction feature, *Saturday Night And Sunday Morning* (1960), that Reisz really stamped his mark on British cinema. The definitive film of new realism, it was to be the director's only visit to the kitchen sink. Forming a production company with the film's star Albert Finney, he took the unwise decision of remaking Emlyn Williams's psycho-drama *Night Must Fall* (1964), and immediately lost all the impetus gained from their first collaboration. The director subsequently caught a serious dose of modishness with the time-capsule curio *Morgan: A Suitable Case For Treatment* (1966), a wacky confluence of madness, gorillas and Marx. But worse was to follow: his biopic of Isadora Duncan, *Isadora* (1968), was cut so savagely by the studios that Reisz was put off making films for several years.

Against all the odds, his career was reborn in the US with two minor-key classics: *The Gambler* (1974), a bruising tale of Dostoevsky-inspired self-destruction, and *Who'll Stop The Rain?* (1978), a thriller full of sour beauty about two desperate Vietnam vets and an ill-fated heroin deal. Reisz completed his comeback with the magnificent *The French Lieutenant's Woman* (1981). But once again he signally failed to capitalize on the success, following it up with two bizarre choices: the Patsy Cline

R

British social realism: keeping it real

Critics have often bemoaned the dominance of social realism in the British national cinema; not enough Michael Powell and Emeric Pressburger-style fantasy, too many gritty realist dramas. However, as with most sweeping generalizations, there is more than a grain of truth amid this critique of British filmmaking.

Karel Reisz was one of a number of directors involved in the Free Cinema movement of the 1950s, which was launched in 1956 by Reisz, Lindsay Anderson, Tony Richardson and Lorenza Mazzetti. These key directors, and their associates, produced imaginative, short documentary films, shot in a grainy *cinéma vérité* style with inexpensive 16mm technology, which typically featured working-class people at work and play. They looked back to the strong wartime documentary tradition epitomized by Humphrey Jennings, who had built on the foundations laid by the great John Grierson who established Britain as a centre of excellence for documentary-making in the 1930s. Reisz moved from documentaries to fiction features in 1960, with *Saturday Night And Sunday Morning*, as part of a burgeoning New Wave of British filmmaking, one of several such movements worldwide. The British New Wave lacked the intellectual ambition and free editing style of the *nouvelle vague* and the pathos of Italian neo-realism, but it shared with both a move towards greater location shooting and a suspicion of gloss and artifice. It also had a distinctly British focus on the lower end of the traditional English class system.

Other significant early films of this social realist movement were Richardson's *A Taste Of Honey* (1961) and *The Loneliness Of The Long Distance Runner* (1962), John Schlesinger's *A Kind Of Loving* (1962) and Anderson's *This Sporting Life* (1963). All but *A Taste Of Honey* (from a play by Shelagh Delaney) were based on novels, but the most important literary adaptation of the British New Wave was Richardson's 1959 film of John Osborne's landmark play *Look Back In Anger*. Staged at the Royal Court in 1956, it set the tone for films reflecting the "Angry Young Men" vogue of the period, which was evidenced in the New Wave's emphasis on the lives and frustrations of northern working-class men, and its often less-than-sympathetic handling of female characters.

The radical political mood of the moment was felt across all areas of the media. British television, with its public service obligations, played a key role in the cultural movements of the period, providing employment for a new generation of directors and opportunities for developing alternative models of low-key realism. Ken Loach, a torchbearer for realistic and social-cause filmmaking, was one of several directors to benefit from working for the BBC, finding himself in the national spotlight after making the ground-breaking TV drama *Cathy Come Home* (1966). By the end of the 1960s, films like Loach's *Kes* (1969) vied for attention with those of the extravagant "romantic" director Ken Russell, while Reisz and Richardson were moving towards literary adaptations and lighter fare. And although Anderson's *If....* (1968) retained the political anger of the early 1960s, its hypothetical public school revolution moved well away from social realism's tales of ordinary people living ordinary lives.

The 1970s were not significant years for realism in British cinema, with the impetus shifting to television, but in the 1980s Loach was joined by Mike Leigh, who hit his stride in 1988 with *High Hopes*. Leigh remains an important force in British social realism to the present day, making down-to-earth films from 1995's *Secrets And Lies* to 2002's *All Or Nothing*. Filmmakers of the 1980s and early 90s were inspired by the social concerns raised by the politics of Margaret Thatcher's Conservative regime, and were aided by an injection of cash into the industry courtesy of the newly created Channel 4, with its edict to provide distinct, provocative and socially diverse programming. The undoubted *chef d'oeuvre* of this financing was Stephen Frears's *My Beautiful Laundrette* (1985).

As British film production rose in the 1990s, Loach returned to prominence with a series of films about the struggles of those at the wrong end of the social ladder: *Riff-Raff* (1990), *Raining Stones* (1993) and, best of all, *My Name Is Joe* (1998). Gary Oldman's fierce *Nil By Mouth* (1997) and Lynne Ramsay's more lyrical *Ratcatcher* (1999) were bleak, but brilliant, highlights of the decade. At the other end of the spectrum, Mark Herman's *Brassed Off* (1996) and Peter Cattaneo's *The Full Monty* (1997) mixed comedy with themes of working-class conflict, unemployment and alienation, and Damien O'Donnell's *East Is East* (1999) added multicultural clashes to the mix. Of the new generation of realists, the most convincing is the streetwise Shane Meadows, whose DIY aesthetic has made use of the economies of digital video. *A Room For Romeo Brass* (1999) was one of several films to announce his talents, and his mature, semi-autobiographical *This Is England* (2007) has kept Britain's tradition of social realism fresh and pertinent. ED & RC

biopic *Sweet Dreams* (1985), and an Arthur Miller-scripted dud, the inappropriately titled *Everybody Wins* (1990). After that film's box-office and critical failure, Reisz wisely decided to concentrate on theatre for the rest of his life. LH

Saturday Night And Sunday Morning 1960, 89 min, b/w

cast Albert Finney, Shirley Anne Field, Rachel Roberts, Hylda Baker, Bryan Pringle, Norman Rossington *cin* Freddie Francis *m* John Dankworth

Albert Finney burns up the screen as the fighting-fit, cocksure and belligerent young toolmaker Arthur Seaton (motto: "Don't let the bastards grind you down"; personal philosophy: "What I'm out for is a good time. All the rest is propaganda"). Specializing in shagging and small-scale, pyrrhic victories, he knows he will eventually be ground down by the society he so boisterously rails against. What plot there is sees Seaton flip-flopping between married woman Rachel Roberts and perky ingénue Shirley Anne Field.

The French Lieutenant's Woman 1981, 127 min

cast Jeremy Irons, Meryl Streep, Leo McKern, Penelope Wilton, Hilton McRae, Emily Morgan, Charlotte Mitchell *cin* Freddie Francis *m* Carl Davis

Other directors had puzzled over ways to adapt John Fowles' meta-fiction, with its pick'n'mix endings, but without success. It was Reisz's brainwave (surprisingly not screenwriter Harold Pinter's) to make a film within a film. Irons and Streep play two actors starring in an adaptation of Fowles' novel whose love scenes continue after the cameras have stopped rolling, as life begins to mirror art.

Ivan Reitman
Slovakia (formerly Czechoslovakia), 1946–

Canadian-raised Ivan Reitman is a reliable manufacturer of slick, high-concept comedies that usually offer undemanding enjoyment but sometimes descend into cynicism, mawkishness, or both. Reitman began in the B-movie sector in Canada – he produced David Cronenberg's first two films and helmed the self-explanatory *Cannibal Girls* (1973). He then directed Bill Murray in a number of comedies: as the wacky counsellor in the mushy summer-camp farce *Meatballs* (1979), the slacker boot-camper in *Stripes* (1981) and an eccentric scientist-turned-ghost exterminator in *Ghostbusters* (1984), a supremely confident horror-comedy with cutting-edge special effects.

Thereafter, Reitman took on many projects that relied heavily on cutesy, underdeveloped gimmicks (and helmed *Ghostbusters*' fat and lazy sequel in 1989). In *Twins* (1988), virtuous, beefy Arnold Schwarzenegger and oily lil' Danny DeVito are… twins! In *Kindergarten Cop* (1990), macho policeman Arnie goes undercover… at a kindergarten! In *Junior* (1994), Arnie gets pregnant… except he's a man! Reitman's better films have tended to leave Schwarzenegger out of the equation: *Dave* (1993) handed Kevin Kline a plum dual role as both the sleazy US president and the ordinary schmo who's enlisted to impersonate him, while the desert-island thriller *Six Days Seven Nights* (1998) halfway overcame its ludicrous contrivances via the sparky screwball chemistry between stars Harrison Ford and Anne Heche. Subsequent films including the superhero comedy *My Super Ex-Girlfriend* (2006) have mined the same comic vein. JW

Ghostbusters 1984, 105 min

cast Bill Murray, Dan Aykroyd, Sigourney Weaver, Harold Ramis, Rick Moranis, William Atherton *cin* Laszlo Kovacs *m* Elmer Bernstein

A trio of paranormal researchers set up shop as exorcists ridding their seedy, beloved New York of assorted spirits, ghouls and demons. The spectral effects still hold up and Bill Murray ad-libs merrily as the dissolute and rather nasty Dr Venkman. Though you have to wonder about the political acumen of a major motion picture that makes a villain out of the Environmental Protection Agency.

Edgar Reitz
Germany, 1932–

A key figure in New German Cinema, Edgar Reitz grew up in the provincial Hunsrück area of West Germany before studying in Munich. Despite his involvement with the radical Oberhausen Manifesto that called for a new form of cinema, Reitz's work remained largely unnoticed outside of Germany for many years, with neither his experimental filmmaking, his documentaries nor his historically inclined features making much of a mark in the 1960s.

His filmmaking pace quickened in the 1970s, and his work also began to earn more attention. His 1977 film *Zero Hour* explored the plight of post-war villagers in eastern Germany who were mistreated by both Russian and American allies. *Germany In Autumn*, (1978) a collaborative state-of-the-nation film set against the backdrop of the Baader-Meinhof terrorist activities was co-directed with Rainer Werner Fassbinder, Volker Schlöndorff, Alexander Kluge and several others. It served as a useful reminder of Reitz's political interests. However, towering over these – and all of his other works – was Reitz's epic historical *Heimat* (*Homeland*, 1984) series.

Filmed on 35mm stock, *Heimat* was screened as a two-part film at European film festivals and in several major German cities in 1984, before appearing as an eleven-part series on German television to huge audiences and widespread acclaim. Reitz's choice of title was significant, as it was a reference to the rural, nostalgic *Heimatfilme* genre of the 1950s. Part critique of the *Heimatfilme*, part critique of the genre's critics, the film sought to reclaim a sense of modern German history and a German identity not solely consisting of guilty silence. An even more ambitious sequel, *The Second Heimat: A New Generation*, followed in 1992. German reunification provided a central theme of *Heimat 3: A Chronicle Of Endings And Beginnings* (2004), though *Heimat Fragments: The Women* (2006) has passed largely unnoticed outside Germany. Never really designed for big box-office success, Reitz's work has, nevertheless, proved influential and has set a very high benchmark for sustained historical drama. RC

Heimat (Homeland) 1984, 924 min, b/w and col

cast Marita Breuer, Dieter Schaad, Michael Lesch, Eva Maria Bayerswaltes, Rüdgiger Weigang *cin* Gernot Roll *m* Nikos Mamangakis

Reitz's history from the margins – concerning the fictional village of Schabbach in the Hunsrück region – is tremendously cinematic. Crisp monochrome and colour photography and subtle, incisive editing brings the lives of the Simon family into sharp focus with much convincing period detail. Using an episodic structure, Reitz drew extensively on his own family's collective history and used local amateurs with the right faces and accents alongside name actors. *Heimat* is richly deserving of all the plaudits it received.

The Second Heimat: A New Generation (Die zweite Heimat: Chronik einer Jugend) 1992, 1509 min

cast Henry Arnold, Salome Kammer, Noemi Steuer, Franziska Traub *cin* Christian Reitz, Gernot Roll, Gérard Vandenberg *m* Nikos Mamangakis

Reitz and co-director Robert Busch move the action from the village of Schabbach to the artistic student community of Munich in the 1960s and early 70s. The story follows Hermann Simon's career as a conductor/composer and his various friendships and relationships, most notably with elusive cellist Clarissa Lichtblau. Its hard to convey the Proustian richness of this mammoth series which combines the appeal of the ongoing investment in characters afforded by a soap opera with the wide canvas of a screen epic. It is claimed as the longest complete film ever to be shown commercially.

Jean Renoir

France, 1894–1979

Son of the impressionist painter Pierre-Auguste, Jean Renoir was born with the advent of cinema itself. He went on to make more than forty films, stretching from the silent era to 1970. During his creative peak in the 1930s his abundant virtues were often overlooked, but Orson Welles, Charlie Chaplin and François Truffaut would all name him the greatest of filmmakers and he was probably the single most influential model for the *nouvelle vague*.

He was a self-effacing, unpretentious popular artist who worked across every genre, distinguishing each with his profoundly sympathetic yet often pessimistic humanism. "Everyone has their reasons", the avuncular Octave (played by Renoir himself) famously remarks in *La règle du jeu* (*The Rules Of The Game*, 1939), though the rider is often forgotten: "That is the terrible thing in this world."

Renoir sometimes claimed he came to make films in order to immortalize his first wife, Catherine Hessling, who had been his father's last model. In *La fille de l'eau* (*Whirlpool Of Fate*, 1925) and *Nana* (1926) he did just that – but he also fell in love with the cinema, a relationship that far outlasted his marriage.

Cinema was a fashionable pursuit among the children of the French intelligentsia at the time. Jean's brother Pierre was an actor in films and theatre, his other brother Claude became a film producer, and Pierre's son Claude would photograph many of Jean's most beautiful films. Many – even most – of Renoir's closest collaborators were also old friends, including his assistant director Jacques Becker, the composer Joseph Kosma and editor Marguerite Houllé. In these circles, filmmaking may have been more of a vocation than a job, and though he modestly drew a distinction between his father's artistry and his own, Renoir maintained some distance from the constraints of the industry. His private collection of his father's paintings was gradually depleted as he scrambled to finish his films his way.

Renoir's silent pictures ran the gamut from social realism to fantasy, but he came into his own in the 1930s with the arrival of synchronous sound recording. Reflecting on the dozen movies Renoir made between 1931 and the outbreak of World War II, the critic Gilbert Adair commented: "There is no other instance in the history of the cinema of a filmmaker who, for so long, could do no wrong. It seemed, for the Renoir of the interwar years, that the masterpiece was simply his speciality."

In terms of genre, politics and themes, these films roam far and wide, from the outrageous farce *Boudu Saved From Drowning* (1932) to the lyrical, impressionistic *Partie de campagne* (*A Day In The Country*, 1936). But even as early as *La chienne* (*The Bitch*) in 1931 we find Renoir seeking to transcend the artificial divisions between comedy and tragedy in a vividly detailed, spontaneous-seeming rendering of the ongoing chaos and confusion of everyday life. For all that the bourgeoisie attempt to assert some sort of order over their affairs, anarchic emotions and desires make a mockery of such affectations – and meanwhile glaring inequities go unaddressed. His lovers and charlatans alike carry on obliviously, "dancing on the precipice of a volcano", as Renoir described the characters in *La règle du jeu*.

The grandson of a tailor, Renoir had no class snobbery, and his films reveal his fondness towards all social strata, though perhaps he preferred the bonhomie and *joie de vivre* of the servants' quarters. As the political climate polarized during the 1930s he endorsed the Popular Front in spirited celebrations of working-class solidarity such as *The Crime Of Monsieur Lange* (1936) and *La vie est à nous* (*The People Of France*, 1936).

However, if there is an overarching agenda across Renoir's films of the 1930s it is first and foremost aesthetic rather than political: even from the beginning he was drawn to shooting on actual locations, experimenting with the long take, deep-focus compositions and the travelling shot. While not unique to Renoir, these techniques did run counter to the much faster editing style in Hollywood at the time, and research shows his cutting rate is also markedly slower than that of his colleagues in France.

R

André Bazin, his most influential champion, observed that "Renoir found a way to reveal the hidden meaning of people and things without destroying the unity that is natural to them." By pushing people together in the frame, placing them in their own environment, and within a single flowing take, Renoir discreetly composed his own open, inclusive, egalitarian analysis of social structures. This strategy was perfectly realized in his two most famous films, the humanist masterpiece *La grande illusion* (1937) and the satiric country house comedy *La règle du jeu*. Both evince a depth and subtlety of feeling that transcends their relatively conventional scenarios. The former was declared "cinematographic enemy no.1" by Nazi propaganda minister Josef Goebbels, who objected to its depiction of German officers and ordered that the original negative be seized. The latter scandalized the audience at its premiere (according to Renoir someone tried to burn down the cinema in protest) and was cut by thirteen minutes at the behest of the distributor. Later it was banned in France for being too demoralizing. It only resurfaced in its restored form in the late 1950s, at which time it was recognized as one of the greatest films ever made.

Fortunately, Renoir's experience and his gift for self-renewal allowed him to overcome such vicissitudes. He left Paris the day the Germans entered the city, and after a period in Lisbon he arrived in the US in 1941. If his Hollywood movies feel somewhat marooned, exiled from the sociopolitical discourse which had inspired his films in France, nevertheless *The Southerner* (1945), *The Diary Of A Chambermaid* (1946) and *The Woman On The Beach* (1947) are all at least interesting negotiations with his new studio-mediated reality.

Renoir's reputation in his home country had declined in this period, partly because of his self-imposed exile. Nearly 60, he returned to France by way of India, where he made *The River* (1951), his first colour film. Although critics have stressed his influence on neo-realism, his later films revel in artifice and spectacle. This is especially true of his trilogy of films about the theatre – *The Golden Coach* (1953), *French Cancan* (1955) and *Eléna et les hommes* (*Paris Does Strange Things*, 1956). Perhaps the key to Renoir's "realism" was always to be found in his love of actors, and it was in theatrical performance that he found a modernist metaphor for the way behaviour is shaped and channelled by society, the ephemeral flux of emotions and the elusive, endlessly challenging art of living.

Renoir directed for another fourteen years, and although this period does not contain his best work, he continued to develop his style; *Le déjeuner sur l'herbe* (1959) was notable for its use of pastel colours, while the same year's *Le testament du Dr Cordelier* saw Renoir modernizing by using multiple cameras for the first time. TC

La chienne (The Bitch) 1931, 91 min, b/w

cast Michel Simon, Janie Marèse, Georges Flamant, Roger Gaillard, Magdeleine Bérubet *cin* Theodor Sparkuhl

A henpecked office clerk and Sunday painter, Legrand (Simon) is seduced by Lulu (Marèse) at the behest of her pimp. He sets her up in a studio-apartment and worries about how to extricate himself from his wife while Lulu sets about cashing in on his paintings… Is it a tragedy or a comedy? Two puppets in the film's prologue fail to agree – and in fact Renoir's supremely diffident film is both. Fritz Lang remade the story as *Scarlet Street* (1945).

Boudu Saved From Drowning (Boudu sauvé des eaux) 1932, 81 min, b/w

cast Michel Simon, Marcelle Hainia, Séverine Lerczinska, Jean Gehret, Max Dalban, Jean Dasté *cin* Marcel Lucien *m* Raphael

An affable middle-class bookseller saves a tramp (Simon) from drowning in the Seine and invites him into his home. Once ensconced, the incorrigible Boudu plays havoc with the household, seducing his benefactor's wife and maid, and turning all good intentions on their head. A genuinely anarchic farce with a larger-than-life performance from Simon at its centre, this has been called Renoir's most Buñuelian film. It was remade by Paul Mazursky as *Down And Out In Beverly Hills* (1988).

Partie de campagne (A Day In The Country) 1936, 40 min, b/w

cast Sylvia Bataille, Georges D'Arnoux, Jane Marken, André Gabriello, Jacques Brunius, Jean Renoir *cin* Claude Renoir *m* Joseph Kosma

Ostensibly unfinished, Renoir's lyrical forty-minute take on a Maupassant short story is a perfect movie as it stands. During a picnic by the river, a young Parisian leaves her family and fiancé for a brief, sensuous dalliance with another man. This is Renoir's most lovely "impressionist" picture – in the words of François Truffaut, "a film of pure sensation; each blade of grass tickles our face".

The Crime Of Monsieur Lange (Le crime de Monsieur Lange) 1936, 80 min, b/w

cast René Lefèvre, Florelle, Jules Berry, Marcel Levesque, Odette Talazac, Henri Guisol *cin* Jean Bachelet *m* Joseph Kosma

Amédée Lange (René Lefèvre) writes a comic strip – *Arizona Jim* – for a small printing press run by the venal and corrupt Batala (Jules Berry). In trouble with his creditors, Batala does a runner, and the workers take over the press to run it as a collective. They are so successful that Batala returns to claim the profits… Written by Jacques Prévert, this may not have the subtleties of later Renoir, but its breathless all-for-one approach is impossible to resist.

La grande illusion (Grand Illusion) 1937, 114 min, b/w

cast Jean Gabin, Dita Parlo, Pierre Fresnay, Erich von Stroheim, Jean Dasté, Marcel Dalio *cin* Christian Matras *m* Joseph Kosma

Based on the stories of one of Renoir's old war comrades, this World War I prison drama was long hailed as one of the greatest films ever made. With working-class hero Jean Gabin sharing a cell with middle-class Jew Marcel Dalio and the aristocratic Pierre Fresnay, under the beady monocle of Commandant Erich von Stroheim, it is as much about class as it is about escape, while the war itself is implied rather than shown. The beautiful, moving last act follows Gabin and Dalio trekking across the Alps towards freedom.

R

La bête humaine (The Human Beast) 1938, 100 min, b/w

cast Jean Gabin, Simone Simon, Fernand Ledoux, Blanchette Brunoy, Julien Carette, Jean Renoir *cin* Curt Courant *m* Joseph Kosma

A picture that was influential on American *film noir*, this updates Emile Zola's novel from the 1890s to the 1930s. A story about a crime of passion involving railway engineer Jacques Lanthier (Gabin) and his lover Séverine (Simon), it fitted into the pessimistic cycle of poetic realism popularized by Marcel Carné and Julien Duvivier. Atmospheric, hard-edged, yet tender, it presents another side of Renoir. It was remade by Fritz Lang as *Human Desire* in 1954.

La règle du jeu (The Rules Of The Game) 1939, 110 min, b/w

cast Marcel Dalio, Nora Gregor, Jean Renoir, Roland Toutain, Paulette Dubost *cin* Jean Bachelet *m* Mozart, Saint-Saëns, Johann Strauss

François Truffaut called this "the credo of film lovers, the film of films, the most despised on its release and the most valued afterward". The film unfolds as a light country house farce, but it's a farce with teeth, ripping into the antiquated old-world class system, the mores and manners which keep people in their place. Not that Renoir judges: the tone is reminiscent of the mixture of "irony and tenderness, humour and sensuality" that Jean observed in his father's paintings. On the eve of World War II, the human comedy is played out here in all its complex cross-purposes.

The River 1951, 99 min

cast Nora Swinburne, Esmond Knight, Arthur Shields, Suprova Mukerjee, Thomas E. Breen, Patricia Walters *cin* Claude Renoir *m* M.A. Partha Sarathy

A US/Indian co-production about an English colonial family living on the banks of the Ganges in the 1920s. "I wanted to be a witness to a civilization that wasn't based on profit", Renoir said. Here he reflects on that subtle passage from childhood, when "time slipped away unnoticed", to maturity, when past and future put the present in its place. In its emphasis on the daily rhythms of life and the passing of the seasons, this is Renoir's most timeless film. It is also his most painterly. Shot in Technicolor by his nephew, Claude Renoir, it is often exquisitely beautiful.

The Golden Coach (Le carosse d'or) 1953, 103 min

cast Anna Magnani, Odoardo Spadaro, Nada Fiorelli, Dante, Duncan Lamont, George Higgins *cin* Claude Renoir *m* Vivaldi

Anna Magnani is Camilla, an actress in a commedia dell'arte troupe that washes up in eighteenth-century Peru. The New World is not all they had been led to expect – they even have to build their own theatre. Again, a surface frivolity choreographed to the music of Vivaldi covers a melancholy meditation on love, art and life.

Le déjeuner sur l'herbe 1959, 91 min

cast Paul Meurisse, Regine Blaess, Helene Duc, Charles Blavette *cin* Georges Leclerc *m* Joseph Kosma

The title invites us to think of impressionism, and this lyrical, bucolic film – shot in colour, in and around Renoir's childhood estate – evokes a sublime, earthy pantheism. But *Déjeuner* is also a strikingly modern comedy pitting sensuality against scientific rationalism. Meurisse plays an esteemed scientist, touted as the next president of Europe, who advocates the eugenics of artificial insemination for future generations, until he falls under the spell of a chambermaid.

Alain Resnais
France, 1922–

The words that are often employed to describe Alain Resnais' films – cryptic, difficult, labyrinthine – would have once sold a movie to an audience. Now, nothing is more likely to instil dread into the hearts of film-goers and make them head straight for the multiplex. And there you might find Resnais himself, because ever since he was a small boy, the archetypal arthouse director has loved popular cinema and trash culture.

Brought up on a strange brew of musicals, comic books and Proust, the son of a chemist entered France's first film school, IDHEC, where he studied editing, though he has since claimed that everything he knows about splicing techniques he learned from graphic novels. After leaving college, he directed a series of documentaries that culminated in the masterpiece *Night And Fog* (1955), one of the most haunting evocations of the horrors of Auschwitz. Juxtaposing contemporary, wistful shots of the abandoned camp with raw archival footage, and the painful recollections of a concentration camp survivor, it secured Resnais' reputation as cinema's time and memory man.

Proustian themes return eternally throughout his fictional work, and in *Hiroshima mon amour* (1959) Resnais' sinuous and sensual tracking shots find their narrative analogue in the fluid synthesis of memories and the here and now. While the plot of *Hiroshima* was ultimately and disappointingly conventional, *L'année dernière à Marienbad* (*Last Year In Marienbad*, 1961) took abstraction to new byzantine levels. A puzzle that can never be solved, *Marienbad* elaborately blurs not just the past and present but the syntactical differences in the traditional cinematic lexicon between subjective and objective points of view – in other words, seeing is not believing, or possibly, only seeing is believing. Resnais' work – which is perhaps also in debt to the ideas of philosopher Henri Bergson and screenwriter Marguerite Duras – invites such cerebral knot-twisting. His Left Bank political interests, modernist outlook and interest in serious literature (reflected in his use of *nouveau roman* novelist Alain Robbe-Grillet to script *Marienbad*) also marked Resnais out from the other *nouvelle vague* directors with which he was bracketed.

The past weighs like a nightmare on the brains of most of Resnais' haunted characters. In the convoluted, fragmented and naturalistic *Muriel* (1963), Hélène invites an old lover back to her house and discovers that he's not quite the man she remembered. In the sensual and semi-accessible *La guerre est finie* (*The War Is Over*, 1966) ageing anti-Franco activist Yves Montand is trapped in political limbo, seeing

The Holocaust on film

Whether as subject matter or influence, actual footage or dramatized fiction, the Nazis' horrific programme for the extermination of European Jewry has shaped a wide range of films. Its first acknowledgement on screen was probably "Concentration Camp" Erhardt, the ominous Nazi buffoon in Ernst Lubitsch's *To Be Or Not To Be* in 1942, three years before the concentration camps were liberated. They were finally unequivocally revealed to the world via the monochrome footage of skeletal survivors and piles of corpses in the US government propaganda film *Nazi Concentration Camps* (1945), directed by George Stevens. From the footage of the 1940s up to *Schindler's List* (1993), the contents of archives established a perception of the Final Solution as being an almost unwatchable spectacle of human degradation and misery. Alain Resnais' *Night And Fog* (1955) contrasted a muted Eastman-color present with grainy images of yesterday, while the commentary struggled to articulate such unspeak-able events. At only 32 minutes, Resnais' film became a touchstone for television documentaries such as 1974's *The World At War*, counselling wariness in the treatment of this difficult history. In Stanley Kramer's *Judgement At Nuremberg* (1961), Hollywood turned history into a lesson in liberal sentiments, featuring as it did prestige histrionics from Marlene Dietrich, Montgomery Clift and Spencer Tracy.

Relaxation of censorship in the 1960s and 70s provoked unflinching treatments of this terrible history. Sidney Lumet's *The Pawnbroker* (1964) tried to meld the gritty horrors of Resnais with the cool new world of 1960s *cinéma vérité* as Rod Steiger's embittered camp survivor struggled with his demons. As the search for war criminals made headlines, releases such as Ronald Neame's *The Odessa File* (1974), John Schlesinger's *Marathon Man* (1976) and Franklin J. Schaffner's *The Boys From Brazil* (1978) turned the horrors of Nazism into the stuff of fashionable conspiracy theory thrillers, featuring more histrionic turns from the likes of Laurence Olivier, Maximilian Schell and Gregory Peck. Liliana Cavani's *The Night Porter* (1973) saw the Holocaust rehearsed as an S&M relationship between Charlotte Rampling's former child camp victim and Dirk Bogarde's former SS officer. By the 1980s, enough time had passed for the Final Solution to be the background of primetime television in *Holocaust* (1978), or turned into the stuff of women's picture romance in *Sophie's Choice* (1982) – notwithstanding that film's har-rowing central scene.

Infinitely more haunting were the to-camera testimonies of camp survivors and bystanders in Claude Lanzmann's documentary *Shoah* (1985). Breaking with the tradition of using archive footage and eventually distancing himself from Resnais' example, Lanzmann's film derives its power from the accumulation of verbal detail. Living in the poignant interstices between anguished recollection and slow tracks over innocent-seeming meadows, Lanzmann's was a sobering response to post-Resnais tabloid horrors. Another documentary confront-ing the limits of responsibility and the ambivalence of modern evil was Marcel Ophuls' *Hotel Terminus: The Life And Times Of Klaus Barbie* (1987). Rigorous and detailed in its account of the war criminal returned to face trial in France, it was another sobering episode in the quest for a responsible Holocaust cinema. Inevitably, Steven Spielberg's *Schindler's List* begged the question of whether commercial aesthetics were adequate to the horrors of history. But Liam Neeson's complex performance as the war profiteer who recognized the wisdom of saving Jews to work for him never goes for easy answers, while Janusz Kaminski's monochrome suffering is in its way as evocative as *Shoah*'s talking heads. The documentary *Into The Arms Of Strangers* (Mark Jonathan Harris, 2000) combined the contemporary testimonies of children rescued from Nazi Europe with rare newsreel of them coping with life in Britain and their feelings of guilt, relief and loss.

Subsequent Holocaust films have negotiated *Schindler*'s influence with varying success. Francesco Rosi's *The Truce* (1996), in its awe-stricken fashion, evoked liberal post-war responses, with John Turturro's careworn per-formance as Primo Levi seeming too limp to be a credible protagonist. *Life Is Beautiful* (Roberto Benigni, 1997) was a comic fantasy trading on Benigni's ingenuous innocence. *Apt Pupil* (Bryan Singer, 1997) asked difficult questions of history as a young man smitten with Nazism tracks down a war criminal to his suburban neighbour-hood, while Holocaust survivor Roman Polanski's traditional narrative approach in *The Pianist* (2002) won him the best director Oscar. RA

no future in the nostalgic past, or hope in the nihil-istic present. *Je t'aime, je t'aime* (1968) was the literal articulation and exploration of Resnais' themes of time travel, and the closest he has come to producing a work from the sci-fi genre that has surely been an influence on his thematic obsessions. A man takes part in a Wellsian experiment with a time machine only to be lost in an alternative universe of his own fragmented memories. There were more experiments in *Mon oncle d'Amérique* (*My American Uncle*, 1980) as a behavioural psychologist attempts to prove that "the living being is a memory which acts".

In *Providence* (1977), Resnais' first film in English, fact and mischievous fiction coalesce in the mind of a dying novelist. The script was by David Mercer, signalling a move towards using playwrights rather than novelists as collaborators, leading to a more theatrical and conventional mode of address. *Smoking/No Smoking* (1993) was an ambitious adaptation of Alan Aykbourn's intricate examination of choice and consequence, *Intimate Exchanges*. Resnais teamed up with Aykbourn again on the hectic comedy of manners *Coeurs* (*Private Fears In Public Places*, 2006). *On connaît la chanson* (*Same Old Song*, 1997) was written by the husband-and-wife playwriting team of Agnès Jaoui and Jean-Pierre Bacri; while *Mélo* (1986) took as its source a play from 1929 and is one of the many minor works on Resnais' CV, along with *Life Is A Bed Of Roses* (1983), *Love Unto Death* (1984) and *Pas sur la bouche* (*Not On The Lips*, 2003). At least with *I Want To Go Home* (1989) Resnais finally addressed his long favourite interest when he trained his lens on an American cartoonist in Paris. LH

Hiroshima mon amour 1959, 90 min, b/w

cast Emmanuelle Riva, Eiji Okada, Stella Dassas, Pierre Barbaud, Bernard Fresson *cin* Michio Takahashi, Sacha Vierny *m* Georges Delerue, Giovanni Fusco

In the stunning opening, the scene of two lovers entwined is discordantly juxtaposed with documentary footage of the scorched victims of the atomic bomb, while the hypnotic tracking shots and Sacha Vierny's angular monochrome compositions evoke an unlikely and vibrant sensuality. After the long, bravura opening Marguerite Duras' script quickly turns to melodrama, ponderously documenting the love affair between a French actress and Japanese architect both scarred by the war.

L'année dernière à Marienbad (Last Year In Marienbad) 1961, 94 min, b/w

cast Delphine Seyrig, Giorgio Albertazzi, Sacha Pitoëff, Françoise Spira, Karin Toche-Mittler, Pierre Barbaud *cin* Sacha Vierny *m* Francis Seyrig

As static, inky and elemental as a cartoon strip, for some this gnomic puzzle about two people, X and A, who may or may not have been lovers the previous year is the high watermark of modernist filmmaking. For others it's the very definition of cinema as fashion shoot, as elegantly empty as the ornate corridors that the camera obsessively dollies down. It's much more rewarding, or at least pleasurable, to regard the whole loopy narrative as a sci-fi film, in which X has unknowingly entered a parallel universe where the trees and statues cast no shadows and relations between time and space have irrevocably broken down.

La guerre est finie (The War Is Over) 1966, 121 min, b/w and col

cast Yves Montand, Ingrid Thulin, Geneviève Bujold, Jean Dasté, Dominique Rozan, Jean-François Rémi *cin* Sacha Vierny *m* Giovanni Fusco

Like many of Resnais' characters, Montand's Diego is "groping around in the fog", utterly lost in a miasma of unreliable memories and unavoidable commitments. Unlike his comrades, he wants to escape the past. "Spain isn't the dream of 1936, it's the sad truth of 1965" he irascibly declares in one of the film's more telling lines. Disillusioned and isolated, he seeks the security of sex with both his wife and free radical Geneviève Bujold.

Providence 1977, 110 min

cast Dirk Bogarde, Ellen Burstyn, John Gielgud, David Warner, Elaine Stritch, Cyril Luckham *cin* Ricardo Aronovich *m* Miklós Rózsa

A dying novelist takes revenge on his family by dreaming up surreal, spiteful narratives involving his two sons, his daughter-in-law and a werewolf. Self-pitying and brimming with suppositories, his imagination runs away with itself and his grip on his own characters steadily loosens. Malevolent, self-loathing and winningly charismatic, John Gielgud ismagisterial as the film's centrifugal force. And as with *Arthur* (1981), *Providence* shows that no one uttered a profanity quite like Gielgud.

On connaît la chanson (Same Old Song) 1997, 120 min

cast Pierre Arditi, Sabine Azéma, Jean-Pierre Bacri, André Dussollier, Agnès Jaoui, Lambert Wilson, Jane Birkin *cin* Renato Berta *m* Bruno Fontaine

Bouncing between the innovative and conventional, eight self-deluding members of the *petit bourgeoisie* suddenly burst into popular songs in this spirited homage to Dennis Potter's *The Singing Detective*. This is Resnais' most commercially successful film and a key component of the second part of his career in which he eschewed glacial modernism for charming and convivial froth.

Carlos Reygadas
Mexico, 1971–

When *Battle In Heaven* (2005) was shown at Cannes, its opening scene shocked many critics. In uncomfortable close-up, the camera pans down the corpulent body of an old man until it alights on his erect penis, which is being energetically sucked by an alluring nymphet with a tear in her eye. It wasn't just the explicitness of the sex, or the gaping difference in age, beauty and body size that offended many, but the fact that this odd couple were played by nonprofessional actors.

The film's director was Carlos Reygadas. For some critics, he is the Mexican Robert Bresson, making films that are stark, spiritual and often incandescent. For others, his movies are exploitative, turgid and self-regarding. A product of Mexico's upper class and a former member of the national rugby team, Reygadas trained as lawyer, and worked in the foreign service in Brussels before leaving to become a filmmaker. His first film, *Japón* (2002), provided a taste of things to come. Like *Battle*, it made use of real sex and non-actors. But both the unsimulated copulation and the use of debutants were very important for the young director, being employed in the service of an unflinching commitment to reality. The neophyte thespians have no screen persona to hide behind, and Reygadas doesn't even furnish them with a script beforehand, so their performances are constantly and brutally raw. The director also strips away every vestige of fiction, including, to a large extent, plot, which he regards as a marketing device, to reveal another layer, possibly spiritual or metaphysical – at least, that's what his defenders will tell you. LH

Japón 2002, 133 min

cast Alejandro Ferretis, Magdalena Flores, Yolanda Villa, Martin Serrano, Rolando Hernández *cin* Diego Martínez Vignatti, Thierry Tronchet

A middle-aged man travels to a Mexican village to commit suicide. He lodges with an elderly lady at the top of a hill, masturbates, exchanges pleasantries with the locals, has sex with the elderly lady and then kills himself. The bleached-out visuals and mellifluous tracking shots exert a hallucinatory grip and the meditative pace and religious aspirations could conceivably classify this film as an example of Bressonian transcendentalism. But its unflinching depiction of slaughtered animals and sex acts also place it firmly in the exploitation sub-genre that has seeped into arthouse cinema in the last decade.

Dick Richards

US 1936–

The word "promising" can be a curse to any creative artist, often sounding the death knell for their talent and/or career. Take "promising film director" Dick Richards. By 1975, he'd already notched up two cult hits and a commercial smash with his first three films. Twelve years later, his career had faltered so badly that it came to a sad full stop.

An army photographer in Korea, Richards was already an acclaimed fashion snapper and adverts director when he made his debut, *The Culpepper Cattle Company* (1972). A fine example of the downbeat anti-Western that was in countercultural vogue in the disillusioned Vietnam War era, it was followed by *Rafferty And The Gold Dust Twins* (1973). A quirky, endearing road movie in which an ex-marine is kidnapped by two women, *Rafferty* secured, like its predecessor, both a cult audience and the epithet that no newcomer wants to hear. Scaling the box-office heights with *Farewell, My Lovely* (1975), Richards proceeded to execute a belly flop with *March Or Die* (1977), a foreign legion flick which suffered from a terminal case of the clichés. The slasher thriller *Death Valley* (1982) was the very definition of mediocrity, while the family drama *Man, Woman And Child* (1983) failed to excite. *Heat* (1986) was to be his final film. LH

Farewell, My Lovely 1975, 95 min

cast Robert Mitchum, Charlotte Rampling, John Ireland, Sylvia Miles, Anthony Zerbe, Harry Dean Stanton *cin* John A. Alonzo *m* David Shire

Reverential to the point of pastiche, this hat-doffing tribute to the hard-boiled genre features a remarkable alignment of stars, both behind and in front of the camera. Robert Mitchum is suitably iconic and bullishly laconic as

Phillip Marlowe, playing on his past record as a *noir* hero. Production designer Dean Tavoularis, whose fastidious eye for fine period detail gave *The Godfather* that meticulous sense of place is at his most vibrantly evocative here, while *Chinatown*'s cinematographer John A. Alonzo once again conjures up a magical *noir* universe of louche, doomed romanticism.

Tony Richardson

UK, 1928–91

There are some directors who are so umbilically linked to a cinematic movement or historical moment that when that time has passed, they seem to be brutally cut adrift. The theatrical and filmic work of Tony Richardson defined the new wave of British grainy realism, but he dramatically lost his way when he left the kitchen sink.

Richardson's *annus mirabilis* came in 1956, when he turned out a couple of works that defined a generation, kick-started two movements and gave bullish expression to the thwarted intellectual and physical energies pulsating through austere, postwar Britain. First, his ground-breaking documentary *Momma Don't Allow* (1955), co-directed with Karel Reisz, was shown as part of the revolutionary Free Cinema programme at the National Film Theatre to awed acclaim, and secondly his iconoclastic Royal Court production of John Osborne's equally radical play *Look Back In Anger* was experienced as a time bomb in the lap of the theatrical establishment. The film rights inevitably became much sought-after property, and rather than sell to the American studios, Osborne and Richardson set up Woodfall Films to make their own adaptation. The result was a faithful record of a blistering performance by Richard Burton in 1958. The same was true of their next collaboration, *The Entertainer* (1960), with Laurence Olivier burning up the screen as a dead-end vaudevillian.

As a director, Richardson made significant contributions to the kitchen sink genre with his poignant, minor-key adaptation of Shelagh Delaney's slice of provincial poetry *A Taste Of Honey* (1961) and Alan Sillitoe's *The Loneliness Of The Long Distance Runner* (1962). For many, though, Richardson's masterpiece is *Tom Jones* (1963). The film signalled a break from rainy northern realism and the beginning of the tricksy modishness that, together with the influence of the *nouvelle vague*, would set the template for British cinema for the duration of the decade. It won Oscars for best film, director and script. But while his next film, the Evelyn Waugh adaptation *The Loved One* (1965), possessed a quirky, acerbic charm, it was a box-office disaster.

Without a realist footing or social purpose, his subsequent films of that decade often exhibited a directorial uncertainty, nervously hiding behind the smoke and mirrors of stylistic flamboyance. Difficult works were adapted into ambitious failures: Jean Genet's *Mademoiselle* (1965), Marguerite Duras' *The Sailor From Gibraltar* (1967) and Vladimir Nabokov's *Laughter In The Dark* (1969). While *Hamlet* (1969) was modest but stagy, *Ned Kelly* (1970), starring Mick Jagger, was another misfire. *The Charge Of The Light Brigade* (1968) recalled past promise, while *Joseph Andrews* (1977) represented a desperate return to *Tom Jones* author Henry Fielding and former glories. Crude, lumpen and embarrassing, it reflected how far both Richardson and British cinema had fallen in just over a decade. American films like *The Border* (1982), *The Hotel New Hampshire* (1982) and the posthumously released *Blue Sky* (1994) were unrecognizable as works from the director of *A Taste Of Honey*. LH

The Loneliness Of The Long Distance Runner
1962, 104 min, b/w
cast Michael Redgrave, Tom Courtenay, Avis Bunnage, Alec McCowen, James Bolam, Joe Robinson, Dervis Ward *cin* Walter Lassally *m* John Addison

Tom Courtenay is suitably spiky as one of the bolshie males that British social realism seemed to specialize in, this time in the form of a borstal boy who discovers a sense of liberation in cross-country running. Entered into a race by the governor, he ultimately commits an act of symbolic, potent and pointless defiance. This wintry melodrama contains many of the classic kitchen sink/angry young man components: surly interior monologues, urban blight, and characters permanently trapped in domestic hell.

Tom Jones 1963, 97 min
cast Albert Finney, Susannah York, Hugh Griffith, Edith Evans, Joan Greenwood, Diane Cilento *cin* Walter Lassally *m* John Addison

Albert Finney is aptly boisterous as the hero of Henry Fielding's eighteenth-century satire, especially in the fabled food and foreplay scene where he and Joyce Redman whet their carnal appetites with some unrefined table manners. While the realism of the Free Cinema movement is evident in the mud-splattered evocation of rural life, the freeze frames, speeded-up moments and direct addresses to camera not only ushered in a new, zesty style of British cinema but heralded a hedonistic release from the post-war pressure cooker that had put a lid on the sexual and intellectual ambitions of angry young men.

The Charge Of The Light Brigade 1968, 141 min
cast Trevor Howard, Vanessa Redgrave, John Gielgud, Harry Andrews, Jill Bennett, David Hominess, Ben Aris *cin* David Watkin *m* John Addison

A sweeping, uneven panorama of the lives, events, mistakes and political machinations that contributed to one of Britain's greatest heroic failures. Class conflict, rough justice and illicit love all spice the brew, while Richardson finds visual metonyms for the hierarchical social structure throughout, epitomized by the climactic battle when Lord Raglan and his retinue picnic on a hill above a valley of death, observing the slaughter below like a morbid equestrian event. In slavish adherence to 1960s modishness, the action is bizarrely punctuated by cartoons which act as a form of surreal exposition.

Leni Riefenstahl
Germany, 1902–2003

Arguably the most controversial filmmaker of the twentieth century, Leni Riefenstahl may not have been Hitler's lover but she certainly wrote him a love letter in the form of a breathless, craven documentary, *Triumph Of The Will* (1935). She is more than a filmmaker, she's a litmus test – the contested ground between those who believe you can separate aesthetics from ideology and those who argue that propaganda, especially Nazi propaganda, should never be considered art.

A dancer for legendary impresario Max Reinhardt, Riefenstahl was recovering from an injury when she saw one of Arnold Fanck's *Bergfilms* (mountain movies), *Der Berg des Schicksals* (*Peaks Of Destiny*, 1924). With characteristic ambition and an opportunist's chutzpah, Riefenstahl tracked down Fanck and persuaded him to cast her in his next movie, *The Holy Mountain* (1926), where she performed her own stunts, learned how to climb mountains and film scenes. She continued to act until her directorial debut, *The Blue Light* (1932), in which she starred as a social outcast who holds the secret to a mysterious blue light emanating hypnotically from a mountain range in the Italian Dolomites.

In the same year she attended a rally addressed by Adolf Hitler that resulted in an epiphany of seemingly orgasmic proportions, which she would later detail in her autobiography: "It seemed as if the earth's surface were spreading out in front of me, like a hemisphere that suddenly splits apart in the middle, spewing out an enormous jet of water, so powerful that it touched the sky and shook the earth. I felt quite paralysed." Displaying her instinctive will to succeed, Riefenstahl wrote Hitler a fan letter. In their subsequent meeting, he told her that she should make films for him when he came to power. And when he did become chancellor, Riefenstahl exploited the new opportunities in the film industry that the Jewish exodus had afforded. And then her ambition became truly Faustian.

Her first production for the Nazis, *Victory Of Faith* (1933), documented a party rally and was essentially a sketchbook for *Triumph Of The Will*, a misty-eyed record of the 1934 Nuremberg rally which has been hailed as the greatest propaganda film ever made. If we can judge Riefenstahl's Nazi-era work in purely aesthetic terms, then *Triumph Of The Will* is overshadowed by her next documentary *Olympia* (1938), a record of the 1936 games in Berlin. The initial reaction was awed and rapturous, and the film won the best picture award at the Venice Film Festival. However, its release in the US coincided with the events of Kristallnacht in which German Jews were systematically attacked

459

and murdered. In the first taste of the controversy she would experience for the rest of her long life, Riefenstahl was publicly shunned outside Germany and *Olympia* quietly ignored.

Her conduct during the war itself is the subject of some speculation. At the beginning, she accompanied German troops into Poland with a film crew, but somewhat incongruously spent the rest of the war making an opera called *Tiefland*, in which she cast herself as a gypsy girl seduced by a venal landowner. Riefenstahl always denied knowledge of Nazi atrocities, even when it was later revealed that the gypsies she'd employed as extras had been incarcerated in a concentration camp and were not long afterwards despatched to their deaths in Auschwitz. However, recent research suggests that she cannot have been ignorant of their fate. After the war, she was held under house arrest for several years. *Tiefland* was finally released in 1954. It was the last proper film she'd ever make. Numerous projects folded due to lack of financial support, and she spent much of her time in Africa working on photographic books about the Nuba. A pariah in the German film business, she was, in her mind, a convenient, high-profile scapegoat, as she protested in Ray Müller's documentary *The Wonderful, Horrible Life Of Leni Riefenstahl* (1993).

Riefenstahl successfully reinvented herself as a still photographer, spending the rest of her life scuba diving and refusing to apologize for her past. She made a home movie of her subaquatic adventures, *Underwater Impressions* (2002), at the age of 98. LH

Triumph Of The Will (Triumph des Willens)
1935, 114 min, b/w

with Adolf Hitler, Otto Dietrich, Josef Goebbels, Hermann Göring, Rudolf Hess, Heinrich Himmler, Viktor Lutze *m* Herbert Windt

Horribly hyped as a work of art, and invaluable as a document of mass hysteria and hypnosis, it's difficult to gauge who the creator of *Triumph Of The Will* really is – Riefenstahl or Hitler. After all, the Nazis supplied the iconography, the designer costumes, the leads, the extras and even the aesthetics, creating a Busby Berkeley-like mix of symmetry and choreography. Riefenstahl's unique contribution seems to be a few sinuous tracking shots and soft-focus homoeroticism. It is, also, one of the greatest horror movies ever made.

Olympia **1938, 201 min, b/w**
with Jack Beresford, Velma Dunn, Ernest Harper, Adolf Hitler, Käthe Köhler, John Lovelock, Jesse Owens, Matthias Volz *m* Herbert Windt

Split over two parts, "Festival Of Nations" and "Festival Of Beauty", and taking almost two years to edit the 250 miles of footage, this ground-breaking documentary is a catalogue of startling innovations as Riefenstahl placed some of her thirty cameramen in ditches, on rollerskates, atop flagpoles and under water, while mounting a camera on a miniature hot-air balloon to capture some much-vaunted aerial shots.

Wolf Rilla
Germany, 1920–2005

Wolf Rilla directed one of the best horror movies made in Britain. The son of actor Walter Rilla, who brought his family to Britain in 1934, Wolf was educated at Cambridge and joined the BBC in the early 1950s. After his feature debut, the Dennis Price crime drama *Noose For A Lady* (1952), Rilla made thrillers, social problem pictures and comedies, displaying an eye for composition and narrative space, as well as an ability to handle actors.

The Raymond Huntley comedy vehicle *Glad Tidings* and the thriller *Marilyn* both followed in quick succession in 1953. George Sanders starred in the latter *film noir* as a man betrayed by his adulterous wife. *Marilyn* evoked Tay Garnett's *The Postman Always Rings Twice* (1946), and made clever use of chiaroscuro lighting. Rilla's 1955 movie, *The Blue Peter*, proposed Outward Bound training for juvenile delinquents. The director recalled his own experience as a Cambridge student in 1958's *Bachelor Of Hearts*, in which Hardy Kruger loses himself in a fling with Sylvia Syms. *Piccadilly Third Stop* (1960) detailed a heist with thrilling sequences on the London Underground, but it is *Village Of The Damned* (also 1960) that ensured Rilla's place in British cinematic history. Post-1960, Rilla's output was unremarkable. Only in *Cairo* (1963), in which George Sanders attempts to rob Tutankhamun's tomb, was there any inspiration. RA

Village Of The Damned **1960, 77 min, b/w**
cast George Sanders, Barbara Shelley, Martin Stephens, Michael Gwynn, Laurence Naismith, Richard Warner *cin* Geoffrey Faithfull *m* Ron Goodwin

A quiet English village undergoes a mysterious day-long trance, followed by the unexpected birth of twelve very unusual children. Eerily similar in appearance, the new arrivals also share telepathic and kinetic powers. Wolf Rilla's chiller – based on John Wyndham's novel *The Midwich Cuckoos* – is atmospheric and quietly powerful. Offering no explanation or reflection, it could be read as a cautionary tale for a British film industry forced to address the teenage audience.

Arturo Ripstein
Mexico, 1943–

Before the country's cinematic revolution at the beginning of the twenty-first century, there was a 1960s wave of Mexican cinema led by Arturo Ripstein. The son of a film producer, the young Arturo's life was transformed when his father introduced him to Luis Buñuel. An assistant on *The Exterminating Angel* (1962) when he was just 18, Ripstein received a more formal education in filmmaking at Mexico City's university, UNAM. A director with impeccable connections, his debut was co-written by Gabriel García Márquez and Carlos Fuentes, while Buñuel acted as "godfather". The story of an ex-prisoner who wants to go straight but first has to face the aggrieved father of the man he killed, *A Time To Die* (1965) has been dubbed by one critic as "the most precocious debut of the Mexican cinema".

Ripstein's films are populated by a marginal constituency of grotesques, drag queens, homosexuals, loners and losers who often self-destruct at the push of a button. His universe is claustrophobic and cluttered. He regularly attacks two of Mexico's most revered institutions: the family and the soap opera. For his sins, he is berated or ignored by a public reared on Hollywood soft-corn.

Since his debut, Ripstein has made over forty features and numerous documentaries. Highlights include *The Castle Of Purity* (1973), about a father who imprisons his family from the outside world for their own good; the gay cult item *The Place Without Limits* (1978), scripted by novelist Manuel Puig; *Life Imprisonment* (1979), a blistering *film noir* about police corruption which is for many Ripstein's masterpiece; *Realm Of Fortune* (1986), his first collaboration with regular scribe and wife Paz Alicia Garciadiego; and his breakout hit, *Deep Crimson* (1996). LH

Deep Crimson (Profundo carmesí) 1996, 109 min
cast Daniel Giménez Cacho, Regina Orozco, Marisa Paredes, Giovanni Florido, Verónica Merchant *cin* Guillermo Granillo *m* David Mansfield

Based on the true story of the "Lonely Hearts Killers" who preyed on lonely widows. Regina Orozco and Daniel Giménez Cacho play two of the most unappealing leads in recent cinema history: he's bald, she's obese and they're even uglier on the inside. But it's not just the protagonists or the subject matter that make this unsettling viewing. The photography lies somewhere between sepia and sordid, the dominant colour is the muted yellow of old, neglected newspapers, the light is too harsh in some places and too dim and sickly in others, while the long takes and fluid camera make for a genuinely queasy experience.

Guy Ritchie
UK, 1968–

Guy Ritchie left school at 15 with a GCSE in film – his only qualification – and entered the industry as a runner. He made several commercials and music videos, then a short film, *The Hard Case* (1995). It was sufficiently vigorous to persuade Trudie Styler to invest in his feature debut, *Lock, Stock And Two Smoking Barrels* (1998). Rejected by British distributors, the flash, brash crime-world comedy *Lock, Stock* was saved by Tom Cruise, whose endorsement ("This movie rocks!") encouraged Columbia to pick up the film for North America.

In the UK, Polygram saw the light and found they had a smash hit on their hands (over £11 million on first release).

Ritchie reprised the formula in *Snatch* (2000): larger-than-life characters up to no good; multiple plot lines colliding; big, "Look, Ma!" camera moves; lots of laddish laughs… and Brad Pitt as an unintelligible Irishman. More polished than his debut, *Snatch* was another big hit. But *Swept Away* (2002), a remake of Lina Wertmüller's 1975 desert island sex comedy starring Ritchie's new wife, Madonna, proved a critical and commercial disaster, and the long-gestating *Revolver* (2005) was another misfire, a return to British gangsterland, but with incoherent philosophical pretensions. TC

Lock, Stock And Two Smoking Barrels 1998, 105 min
cast Jason Flemyng, Dexter Fletcher, Nick Moran, Jason Statham, Steven Mackintosh *cin* Tim Maurice-Jones *m* John A. Hughes, John Murphy

A wide-boy caper comedy about four working-class lads in hock to a gangster for half a million pounds, *Lock, Stock* is rough around the edges and rough in the centre too. But it delivers colourful characters (Hatchet Harry, Barry the Baptist, Dog, Plank) in an ingenious crisscross plot full of splashy moves and lots of laughs, and it doesn't dawdle either.

Martin Ritt
US, 1914–90

Martin Ritt epitomized the Depression-bred liberalism that moulded post-war Hollywood. While a student, he befriended Elia Kazan, joining his Group Theater as an actor. Following war service, Ritt made his Broadway directing debut in 1946, and directed a number of stage and television dramas until 1951, when he was blacklisted for communist affiliations. He then taught for a number of years at the Actors Studio, working with students who included Joanne Woodward, Lee Remick, Rod Steiger and future regular collaborator Paul Newman. In 1957, he was permitted to return to the industry, and made his film directing debut with *Edge Of The City*, a convincing waterfront drama starring Sidney Poitier and John Cassavetes that simmered with contemporary racial tensions.

Ritt's reputation rests on a series of literate studies of social issues, including *The Long Hot Summer* (1958). This William Faulkner adaptation starred Paul Newman, and marked the beginning of a series of films the two made together. In 1961 Newman essayed the jazz life in *Paris Blues* (1961), followed by the classic *Hud* (1962) and 1966's *Hombre*, an intelligent plea for racial harmony between whites and Indians spectacularly shot by James Wong Howe in Death Valley. Ritt's continuing versatility was showcased in the decent John le Carré adaptation *The Spy Who Came In From The Cold* (1965) and the Mafia-themed *The Brotherhood* (1968), starring Kirk Douglas.

The period drama *The Molly Maguires* (1970) was followed by further films about socially conscious characters: James Earl Jones as the legendary boxer Jack Johnson in *The Great White Hope* (1970); Jon Voight's teacher in a Carolina backwater in *Conrack* (1974); Woody Allen's nebbish torn over the contradictions of the McCarthy era in *The Front* (1976). The Oscar-winner of the decade, however, was Sally Field's union organizer in *Norma Rae*. Released in 1979 as Reagan's New Right was rising to prominence, it seemed a forlorn reminder of past struggles. None of his later films, from *Back Roads* (1981) to *Stanley & Iris* (1990), were able to match it. Ritt's compassionate observation of backwoods American lives has left a legacy that can be seen in independent films from Billy Bob Thornton's *Sling Blade* to the work of John Sayles. RA

Hud 1962, 111 min, b/w
cast Paul Newman, Melvyn Douglas, Patricia Neal, Brandon de Wilde, Whit Bissell, John Ashley *cin* James Wong Howe *m* Elmer Bernstein

Handsomely shot on Texan locations by James Wong Howe and acted with grounded conviction by Paul Newman and Melvyn Douglas, this is the story of a rancher's dispute with his hard-drinking errant son. As a study of the passing of a heritage, it ranks with John Huston's *The Misfits* of the preceding year.

The Molly Maguires 1970, 124 min
cast Richard Harris, Sean Connery, Samantha Eggar, Frank Finlay, Anthony Zerbe, Bethel Leslie, Art Lund *cin* James Wong Howe *m* Henry Mancini

Set in Pennsylvania mining country in 1876, this account of the rivalry between a company informer and a saboteur, robustly played by Richard Harris and Sean Connery, catches the ambivalence in the play of conscience and corruption that so often sullies political causes. Again, Howe's cinematography and Ritt's direction recall the gritty realism of Warner Bros in its heyday.

Norma Rae 1979, 114 min
cast Sally Field, Beau Bridges, Ron Leibman, Pat Hingle, Barbara Baxley, Gail Strickland, Morgan Paull *cin* John A. Alonzo *m* David Shire

Although less successful in its evocation of political activism than *The Molly Maguires*, Sally Field's portrayal of a real-life Dixie mill worker was an Oscar-winning triumph. She brings nuance and conviction to her depiction of an uneducated working woman's emerging feminism and empowerment, and is ably supported by Ron Leibman as a New York-based Jewish union organizer.

Jacques Rivette
France, 1928–

Of all the *Cahiers du cinéma* writers who became filmmakers in the 1950s, Jacques Rivette has been the most consistently uncompromising. The length of his films militated against their widespread distribution and has ensured that they remain appreciated by a small though fanatical coterie. Rivette has been cited by no less than François Truffaut as being the spark that ignited the *nouvelle vague*; he was the first *Cahiers* critic to make a short (*Aux quatre coins*, 1949), and the director of what his contemporaries considered the archetypal *nouvelle vague* feature, *Paris nous appartient* (*Paris Belongs To Us*, 1960), which was started before both *Les 400 coups* (1960) and *A bout de souffle* (1959).

While working as a critic, Rivette served a short-film apprenticeship and assisted Jean Renoir on *French Cancan* (1955) before making his feature debut with *Paris nous appartient*, which was shot guerrilla-style over two years. He was editor-in-chief of *Cahiers* between 1963 and 1965. Once controversial for its perceived anti-Catholic bias, *La religieuse* (*The Nun*, 1965) now appears his most conventional film. Rivette's mature style was established by the 252-minute *L'amour fou* (1968), a pivotal work in his oeuvre that revolves around rehearsals for a stage production, in turn observed by television cameras making a documentary.

Rivette's key works are dauntingly long and bewilderingly complex in their structure and philosophical concerns. The unreleased *Out 1: Noli me tangere* (1971), for example, ran to thirteen hours, and the "short version" – *Out 1: Spectre* (1972) – came in at over four. *Celine And Julie Go Boating* (1974) seems modest at just over three hours. Together they add up to one of cinema's most sustained enquiries into the nature and possibilities of film form, which would influence the likes of directors Jean-Marie Straub and Chantal Akerman.

His output over the next two decades was less ambitious, if more audience-friendly: the quixotic quasi-thriller *Le pont du nord* (1981) and a return to the theatre in *L'amour par terre* (*Love On The Ground*, 1984). The oblique fantasies of the *Duelle/Noroît* diptych (1976) were a partial exception to this trend, while *The Gang Of Four* (1988) marked a return to form. The unexpected international hit *La belle noiseuse* (*The Beautiful Troublemaker*, 1991) was followed by the two-part, six-hour *Jeanne la pucelle* (1994), which proffered a revisionist take on the Joan of Arc legend that omitted coverage of the usually pivotal trial. The part-musical *Haut bas fragile* (1995) and *Secret défense* (1997), an update of the Greek Elektra myth, led to the late masterpiece *Va savoir* (*Who Knows?*, 2001), a suitably Pirandellian take on a Pirandello play in which six characters fall in love in a series of interlocking triangular relationships. MB

Paris nous appartient (Paris Belongs To Us) 1960, 140 min, b/w
cast Betty Schneider, Gianni Esposito, Françoise Prévost, Daniel Crohem, François Maistre *cin* Charles L. Bitsch *m* Philippe Arthuys

Rivette's debut feature started as he meant to go on. Based around a theatrical troupe rehearsing Shakespeare's

Pericles at its centre, the film spins a web of intrigue and paranoia involving a mysterious apparent suicide, a death foretold and a political conspiracy that may only exist in overly impressionable minds, but that nonetheless casts a long shadow over the proceedings. Although later Rivettes may be more assured, the Cold War elements of this film make it an enthralling time capsule.

Celine And Julie Go Boating (Céline et Julie vont en bateau) 1974, 194 min

cast Juliet Berto, Dominique Labourier, Bulle Ogier, Marie-France Pisier, Barbet Schroeder *cin* Jacques Renard *m* Jean-Marie Sénia

The ideal starting point for Jacques Rivette newcomers, this sees librarian Dominique Labourier teaming up with magician Juliet Berto to investigate both a mysterious house and the significance of the domestic melodrama that is playing out there in a seemingly endless loop. Whole PhD theses could be written about Rivette's self-reflexive analysis of cinematic narrative, but they'd probably miss the film's effervescent *joie de vivre*: few heavyweight art movies are this much fun.

La belle noiseuse (The Beautiful Troublemaker) 1991, 238 min

cast Michel Piccoli, Jane Birkin, Emmanuelle Béart, Marianne Denicourt, Marie Belluc, David Bursztein *cin* William Lubtchansky

Temperamental artist Michel Piccoli is persuaded to come out of retirement after meeting Emmanuelle Béart, who inspires him to complete a long-abandoned painting after she sheds her clothes in his studio. The running time is amply justified by Rivette's unprecedentedly detailed scrutiny of the entire artistic process, complete with false starts and conceptual rethinks. The faint-hearted may prefer the two-hour *Divertimento*, assembled from alternative takes.

Va savoir (Who Knows?) 2001, 154 min

cast Jeanne Balibar, Marianne Basler, Hélène de Fougerolles, Catherine Rouvel, Jacques Bonnaffé, Sergio Castellitto *cin* William Lubtchansky

A near-perfect late masterwork, *Va savoir* revisits familiar Rivette themes but presents them with such quicksilver deftness that they seem entirely fresh. Once again, a theatrical rehearsal is the backdrop for Rivette's tale, this time of six characters and their interlocking philosophical and amorous entanglements, plus a jewel-theft sub-plot that is ultimately resolved via a memorable vodka-fuelled "duel". This is probably the closest Rivette will ever come to a slapstick farce.

Jay Roach
US, 1957–

Though he disowned what was to be his first feature, *Zoo Radio* (1990), after undue meddling from the film's writer-producer, the ever-capable Jay Roach bounced back quite profitably with two highly successful comedy franchises: *Meet The Parents* (2000) (with its 2004 sequel, *Meet The Fockers*) and the Bond-spoofing *Austin Powers* trilogy (1997–2002). As demonstrated by the clumsily shot hockey scenes in the David-versus-Goliath sports drama *Mystery, Alaska* (1999), Roach hasn't got a keen eye for action sequences, and his suc-

cessful comedies are largely driven by their scripts and their stars. JW

Austin Powers: International Man Of Mystery 1997, 95 min

cast Mike Myers, Elizabeth Hurley, Robert Wagner, Michael York, Mimi Rogers, Seth Green *cin* Peter Deming *m* George S. Clinton

British secret agent Austin Powers (Mike Myers) and his nemesis, Dr Evil (also played by Myers), were cryogenically frozen in the 1960s and awake in the resolutely unswinging 1990s in this agreeable farce. There are several splendid set pieces – the psychedelic/*Hard Day's Night*-style opening is a hoot, and Dr Evil makes some rather astounding confessions at group therapy – but the toilet humour rapidly wears thin.

Meet The Parents 2000, 108 min

cast Robert De Niro, Ben Stiller, Blythe Danner, Teri Polo, James Rebhorn, Jon Abrahams, Owen Wilson *cin* George Folsey *m* Randy Newman

Roach's comedy capitalizes on Ben Stiller's unfailingly inventive, and often quite touching talents as an all-occasion punching bag. Here martyrdom ensues by way of a painfully awkward stay with his girlfriend's parents (Robert De Niro and Blythe Danner). Roach often sabotages good punch lines with setups that honk like oncoming trucks, and the film's intermittent nastiness back-pedals into a sentimental resolution, but watching Stiller get the girl – or being seriously injured trying – always has its pleasures.

Tim Robbins
US, 1958–

The son of a folk singer, Tim Robbins studied theatre at UCLA and co-founded stage troupe The Actors Gang not long after graduation. Since his film debut, *No Small Affair* (1984) the lanky actor has lent his boyish looks and occasionally menacing air to such films as *Jacob's Ladder* (1990), *The Player* (1992), and *The Shawshank Redemption* (1994). With his partner Susan Sarandon, he has been caricatured as Hollywood's archetypal bleeding-heart liberal, most savagely and iconoclastically in Trey Parker and Matt Stone's *Team America: World Police* (2004). In 1993, the couple were temporarily banned from the Oscars after they used the awards as a platform to speak out on behalf of Haitian HIV sufferers who were incarcerated in Guantanamo Bay.

To judge by appearances, it would seem that Robbins' movies are an extension of his political programme. But the director would passionately disagree. For him, a "political film" is one-sided and polemical, whereas he definitely regards his movies as non-partisan and even-handed. There was some evidence of this ideological balancing act in his directorial debut *Bob Roberts* (1992), in which Robbins was charismatic and outwardly insouciant as a right-wing country-and-western singer who styles himself as the anti-Bob Dylan. Wry, spiky songs like "The Times Are Changing… Back" echoed the

On death row: a murderer (Sean Penn) opens his heart to Sister Helen Prejean (Susan Sarandon) in *Dead Man Walking*.

witty, reactionary ditties of the conservative country star played by Henry Gibson in Robert Altman's *Nashville* (1975), and it's no surprise to learn that watching Altman's rangy, sprawling satire was an epochal moment in Robbins' life. The impeccable sense of fair play was most in evidence in the death penalty drama *Dead Man Walking* (1995), in which Robbins skilfully avoided the traps of tub-thumping pieties, while the influence of Altman was most apparent in *Cradle Will Rock* (1999), an ensemble piece that nimbly cut between multiple story strands and characters of various political hues. LH

Dead Man Walking 1995, 122 min

cast Susan Sarandon, Sean Penn, Robert Prosky, Raymond J. Barry, R. Lee Ermey, Celia Weston, Lois Smith *cin* Roger Deakins *m* David Robbins

Susan Sarandon won an Oscar for her astringently raw performance as Sister Helen Prejean, the nun campaigning for a stay of execution for noxious, racist killer Matthew Poncelet (Sean Penn). Based on a true story, this is by no means the bleeding-heart opus one might have feared. Penn is truly repellent and the opinions of the victims' vengeful families are treated with genuine respect. The issues are afforded their true complexity, and even though Robbins' conclusions are not surprising, he offers no easy, pious solutions.

Cradle Will Rock 1999, 133 min

cast Hank Azaria, Rubén Blades, Joan Cusack, John Cusack, Cary Elwes, Philip Baker Hall, Cherry Jones *cin* Jean-Yves Escoffier *m* David Robbins

The true story of John Houseman and Orson Welles's failed attempt to stage the left-wing musical *The Cradle Will Rock* with money from the Federal Theater Project is only one thread in a hugely impressive tapestry that details the thorny relationship between art and politics. In another strand, millionaire Nelson Rockefeller naïvely commissions

Marxist Diego Rivera to paint a mural in his corporate headquarters, only for the Mexican painter to cheekily bite the capitalist hand that feeds him.

Bruce Robinson
UK, 1945–

Anyone familiar with *Withnail & I* (1986) will know all about Bruce Robinson's early career as a penniless, bibulous and malnourished actor. The perennial student favourite was based on his own squalid experiences living in a half-derelict flat with a fellow thesp who was versed in the classics and pickled in alcohol. Like "I", Robinson was by far the more successful of the two actors, enjoying roles in Franco Zeffirelli's *Romeo And Juliet* (1968) and François Truffaut's *The Story Of Adèle H* (1975). Truffaut's film heralded the end of Robinson's acting career as he decided to concentrate on his writing. Ten years later, one of his screenplays finally made it onto a projector. The phenomenal, award-strewn triumph of Roland Joffé's Cambodian War film *The Killing Fields* (1984) paved the way for his autobiographical opus, *Withnail*.

His sudden success, however, had a sad analogue in a swift decline. *How To Get Ahead In Advertising* (1988), about an ad exec who alarmingly grows a talking boil on his neck, was a film of two very different halves, one a surreal, pin-sharp satire and the other a limp polemic. Critics and audiences were bemused. Legend has it that the plot of his next movie, *Jennifer 8* (1992), was hastily finalized on the way to a pitch meeting with Hollywood studio bosses. The anonymous thriller was sufficiently disappointing not to get a theatrical release in the UK, and was the last film he directed. Concentrating instead on his writing, Robinson has reportedly penned numerous screenplays, although only a few, like *In Dreams* (1998), have been produced. None, though, are ever likely to be quoted verbatim and ad nauseam in Britain's student unions. LH

Withnail & I 1986, 107 min
cast Richard E. Grant, Paul McGann, Richard Griffiths, Ralph Brown, Michael Elphick, Daragh O'Malley *cin* Peter Hannan *m* David Dundas, Rick Wentworth

Robinson was still living in the decadent squalor that his cult classic mordantly evokes when he wrote the first draft of *Withnail* as a novel about two out-of-work thespians who go on holiday by mistake. Behind all the boisterous mayhem, rampant homophobia and memorable, oft-quoted dialogue ("As a youth, I used to weep in butchers' shops.") lies a systematic, quiet symbolism, for instance, only one light on the odd couple's battered car is working, and it's certainly not the one on Withnail's side.

Phil Alden Robinson
US, 1950–

From air force to high flier, Phil Alden Robinson's route to Hollywood has certainly been circuitous. The maker of *Field Of Dreams* (1989) cut his directorial teeth in the US Air Force, where he wrote and produced training films. Back among civilians, he worked as a TV news anchorman and made commercials and industrial films. His first screenplay, *All Of Me* (1984) was written for Steve Martin and directed by Carl Reiner, while his second was for Bob Clark's *Rhinestone* (1984), which teamed odd couple Dolly Parton and Sylvester Stallone.

He made his directorial debut with *The Woo-Woo Kid* (1987), an amiable comedy based on the true story of a 14-year-old bigamist who became a tabloid sensation during World War II. *Field Of Dreams* slowly evolved into heart-warming cult classic, and after completing *Sneakers* (1992), a spirited, old-fashioned caper movie, Robinson didn't make another film for ten years. Instead he turned his attentions to the Balkan conflict for a TV documentary and developed numerous projects for television. His return to the big screen was typically unpredictable, when he extended Tom Clancy's Jack Ryan franchise with *The Sum Of All Fears* (2002), adding little to the series. LH

Field Of Dreams 1989, 106 min
cast Kevin Costner, Amy Madigan, Gaby Hoffman, Ray Liotta, Timothy Busfield, James Earl Jones, Burt Lancaster *cin* John Lindley *m* James Horner

Kevin Costner is in his Gary Cooper Everyman mode as the Iowa farmer who builds a baseball pitch in the middle of a corn field in tribute to his dead dad, a former player. The film's most memorable line, "if you build it, he will come",

turns out to have eerie consequences when ghosts from the Chicago White Sox team who famously threw the 1919 World Series make an unscheduled appearance. Rich in sentiment, metaphors, and opportunities for tears, Alden's humour thankfully diverts the melodrama away from the group hug of a movie that it so easily could have become.

Glauber Rocha
Brazil, 1938–81

Theorist, idealist, visionary and cinematic provocateur Glauber Rocha was a quintessentially 1960s figure. Fired up by anti-colonial sentiment and the avant-garde innovations of the *nouvelle vague*, Rocha became the young firebrand of Brazilian Cinema Novo. As was the custom of the times, he wrote a passionate manifesto in 1965 called "The Aesthetics Of Hunger", arguing against the imperialist values inherent in cinema, and he set about the task of creating a new kind of cinema with "an idea in the head and a camera in the hand".

Unlike many political filmmakers, Rocha's methods were extravagant, including heavy-handed allegory, severe and speedy montage, and incendiary theatrics. His films also reflected an interest in Afro-Brazilian religion and ritual. After his 1962 feature debut *Barravento* (*The Turning Wind*), which put him at the centre of a cinematic revival, he upped the stakes with *Black God, White Devil* (1964), a loose story about people caught between a "devil" and a "god" in the dry wilderness of northeastern Brazil in the 1940s. The film has since topped a magazine poll for the best Brazilian film ever made.

Rocha's third feature, *Land In Anguish* (1967), was a political allegory set in a city in a fictitious Latin American country which targeted corrupt political leaders. His next film, the visionary *Antonio das Mortes* (1969), returned to rural northeastern Brazil and celebrated a bandit, or "warrior saint", fighting against his military employers as an ideal of revolutionary resistance. Rocha left his home country in 1971, following a significant increase in repression and tighter censorship by the military government in 1968, however he had already travelled extensively (making the fiercely anti-colonialist *The Lion Has Several Heads* in Congo-Brazaville in 1970). After returning to Brazil in 1975, Rocha made his last film, *The Age Of The Earth* (1980), which was yet another intense and symbolic assault on the senses. RC

Antonio Das Mortes (O Dragão da Maldade Contra o Santo Guerreiro) 1969, 95 min
cast Maurício do Valle, Odete Lara, Othon Bastos, Hugo Carvana, Jofre Soares, Lorival Paris *cin* Affonso Beato *m* Marlos Nobre

Like a fevered messianic cross between the works of Alejandro Jodorowsky and Sergio Leone, this is, in many ways, a sequel to *Black God, White Devil*. In other ways, it is not: gone are the stark black-and-white photography and muted realism of its predecessor (which many critics rate above *Antonio*). However, the compensations are substantial, with more frenetic Catholicism, folklore, politics, dance and music being spiced up together to create a distinctly Brazilian brew. About as left field as you can get.

Alexandre Rockwell

US, 1957–

Alexandre Rockwell is one of several Sundance Festival darlings from the early 1990s who never seemed able to capitalize on their early success. His *In The Soup* won the festival's Grand Jury Prize in 1992. A rough-hewn black-and-white comedy, its theme was one close to many of his fellow filmmakers' hearts – the trials and tribulations of getting a movie off the ground. Rockwell's subject moved from a struggling director to struggling actors in *Somebody To Love* (1994), and he contributed one segment of the ill-fated portmanteau *Four Rooms* (1994). His improvisatory approach earned diminishing returns, however, and his next feature, *Louis And Frank* (1998), went virtually straight to video. *In The Soup* star Steve Buscemi remained loyal to the director, however, popping up in *Somebody To Love* as a drag queen and in *13 Moons* (2002) as Bananas the clown. JW

In The Soup 1992, 96 min, b/w
cast Seymour Cassel, Steve Buscemi, Jennifer Beals, Will Patton, Stanley Tucci, Jim Jarmusch, Carol Keane, Elizabeth Bracco *cin* Phil Parmet *m* Mader

Behind on the rent for his rat-hole apartment, aspiring director Aldolfo Rollo (Steve Buscemi) puts his 500-page script *Unconditional Surrender* up for sale, attracting the attentions of would-be producer Joe (Seymour Cassel), a tactile, Mob-connected con man whose enthusiasms for making and spending money keep pushing Aldolfo's ambitions to the sidelines. Rockwell's comedy of errors is charming and loose-limbed, and he fosters a brilliant rapport between Buscemi's put-upon straight man and Cassel's charming, fleet-footed swindler.

Franc Roddam

UK, 1946–

Best known as the director of *Quadrophenia* (1979), Franc Roddam could be considered one of the people responsible for inventing reality TV, being among the directors of Britain's first real-life soap, *The Family*. After leaving the BBC, the erstwhile copywriter and graduate of the London Film School immediately hit cinematic pay dirt with his feature debut. Based loosely on The Who's concept album, *Quadrophenia* succinctly articulated the theme that would mark out Roddam's career: the frayed ties of male bonding.

With his cult success, Roddam was inundated with offers, and after wading through three hundred scripts, he opted for *The Lords Of Discipline* (1983). Set in an American military school in the early 1960s, it explored institutionalized racism to harrowing effect. After receiving another critical thumbs up, the director went seriously off piste with *The Bride* (1985), a risible feminist revision of James Whale's *Bride Of Frankenstein* (1935). The director returned to more familiar territory with *War Party* (1988), an adroit contemporary retooling of the Western in which modern-day Native Americans are hunted down by the law after a re-enactment goes horribly wrong. Then in 1992 he took Patrick Meyer's play about mountaineering, *K2*, and filmed it on the world's most treacherous mountain. The action adventure took a tumble at the box office, and Roddam returned to television on both sides of the Atlantic. LH

Quadrophenia 1979, 120 min
cast Phil Daniels, Leslie Ash, Philip Davis, Mark Wingett, Sting, Ray Winstone, Garry Cooper, Gary Shail, Toyah Willcox *cin* Brian Tufano

Phil Daniels instantly acquired iconic status as Jimmy, the workaday Mod who prepares for the annual Bank Holiday Battle of Brighton by engaging in his own war of attrition with sullen girlfriend Leslie Ash. Roddam's documentary training reveals itself in the improvised dialogue, while Sting is unusually convincing as Ace, the Modfather. Aside from the performances and the carefully orchestrated fight sequences, the real pleasure is in the details: the scooters, the suits, the pills, the discs and the rituals. The film's release serendipitously coincided with a Mod revival in Britain.

Robert Rodriguez

US, 1968–

A leading proponent of DIY cinema, and since 2001 a passionate advocate for digital filmmaking, Robert Rodriguez is redefining what it means to be a filmmaker. At the same time, for all his talent and energy, his output is scattershot and often disappointing.

The third child in a family of ten, Rodriguez showed an early talent for drawing, and for many years wrote a comic strip inspired by his siblings, *Los hooligans*. His first feature, *El Mariachi* (1992), became an indie legend when it was picked up by Columbia for distribution. A Tex-Mex shoot-em-up in a tongue-in-cheek Sergio Leone style, it was made on a budget of just $7000, which Rodriguez raised by participating in clinical drug trials.

If this headline-grabbing figure fails to include the costs of postproduction, it still gives a fair indication of Rodriguez's home-movie-style enterprise. A studio remake/sequel, *Desperado* (1995), came in at $7 million. Shortly afterwards Rodriguez was offered the reins on the $40 million swashbuckler *The Mask Of Zorro*, which he rejected when the studio refused to let him make the film more cheaply.

R

Frequently running foul of the unions, Rodriguez routinely writes, directs, edits, scores, records, shoots, designs and produces his movies himself – all from his home base, Troublemaker Studios. He even wrote a book on the making of *El Mariachi*, the aptly titled *Rebel Without A Crew*. His taste is for pulp: spaghetti Westerns, horror movies, comic books and sci-fi (see his 1998 film *The Faculty*). His style is a camped-up version of Leone's baroque compositions, with ostentatious camera moves out of Orson Welles, Sam Fuller and the Coen brothers, and rapid MTV-style montage – it's not so much postmodern as pop-modernist. His own *Ten Minute Film School* series (2004) reveals that props, costumes, sets and special effects – almost all the traditional elements of *mise en scène* – are digitally painted in during postproduction. He's still a cartoonist at heart, which is why his juvenile *Spy Kids* films (2001–2003) represent his most accomplished work.

Befriended by Quentin Tarantino when *El Mariachi* and *Reservoir Dogs* both played at Sundance, Rodriguez shared the bill with him on the portmanteau film *Four Rooms* (1995), directed Tarantino's vampire script *From Dusk Till Dawn* (1996) and composed the score for *Kill Bill: Vol 2* (2004). Tarantino directed a single scene in Rodriguez's innovative comic-styled *Sin City* (2005) – not coincidentally, it was the most human scene in the picture. They teamed up again for the lurid double feature *Grindhouse* (2007). Again, the contrasts were marked. In his segment, *Planet Terror* – a tribute to Z-grade zombie schlock – Rodriguez used digital effects to reproduce scratched and battered second-run celluloid and jammed the movie with so much lurid mayhem that audiences didn't know where to look. But while Rodriguez amps everything up, Tarantino tamps it down so that we care about his characters. It's the difference between empty pastiche and what we might call, for old time's sake, "a real movie". TC

El Mariachi 1992, 81 min

cast Carlos Gallardo, Consuelo Gomez, Jaime de Hoyas, Peter Marquardt *cin* Robert Rodriguez *m* Robert Rodriguez

A travelling mariachi guitar player is mistaken for a violent gunman, with fatal results. Although it's difficult to separate the film from its legendary (and somewhat mythical) low-budget origins, this tongue-in-cheek, hard-boiled spaghetti shoot-em-up is exhilaratingly styled. Rodriguez is energized by technical challenges, and his facility made this one of the great calling-card movies.

Sin City 2005, 124 min

cast Mickey Rourke, Bruce Willis, Clive Owen, Jessica Alba, Benicio del Toro *cin* Robert Rodriguez *m* John Debney, Graeme Revell, Robert Rodriguez

Co-directed with the legendary comic-book author Frank Miller (Rodriguez was expelled from the Directors Guild after insisting on this), *Sin City* hides its big-name cast under synthetic make-up and uses digital technology to replicate the inky black-and-white graphics of the original. Upping the ante on the corruption and sleaze endemic in *film noir*, this is ironic, hyperbolic, charbroiled retro-reactionary pulp fiction.

Nicolas Roeg
UK, 1928–

Nicolas Roeg is one of the romantics of modern cinema. His early career was a veritable pilgrim's progress through the industry. After projectionist duties in the army, he joined a minor studio as an office boy and apprentice editor. He then went to MGM's UK branch and, by 1959, had gone from clapper boy to cinematographer. During the 1960s, Roeg worked on a range of films, including David Lean's *Lawrence Of Arabia* (1962), Roger Corman's *The Masque Of The Red Death* (1964), François Truffaut's *Fahrenheit 451* (1966), John Schlesinger's *Far From The Madding Crowd* (1967) and Richard Lester's *Petulia* (1968). While the atmospheric desert milieu of *Lawrence* was later echoed in the Australian outback of Roeg's *Walkabout* (1970), his first film as director was *Performance* (also 1970), a paean to 1960s psychedelia co-directed with Donald Cammell.

Roeg once described cinema as a "time machine" and his reputation is founded on an adventurous play with temporality and desire, a phantasmagoria of choppy time frames and unanchored visions. The results have varied from visionary to self-indulgent. Beginning with a father driving his children into the desert for a picnic, and then trying to kill them, *Walkabout* does not explain human motivation any more than it explains who is witnessing its bizarre imagery. Following the children as they negotiate the wilderness and encounter its Aboriginal inhabitants, Roeg's cinematography and Antony Gibb's editing play out the consequences of time and thought as a jumble of primeval associations.

In 1973's *Don't Look Now*, Roeg's interrogation of traditional surfaces seemed even bolder. The prospect of subjectivity adrift in a defamiliarized world marked *The Man Who Fell To Earth* (1976), in which a strikingly androgynous David Bowie starred as an alien negotiating an America of cheap motels, billboards and rampant venality. Continuing Roeg's project of revising narrative, *Bad Timing* (1980) was a murder investigation in which Art Garfunkel's obsessive relationship with Theresa Russell is pored over by Harvey Keitel's detective voyeur. Roeg's distinctive vision is little compensation for the film's misogyny.

Russell married Roeg in 1982, and became his star and muse in much of his subsequent work. Doubts about the artistic efficacy of the director-muse arrangement seem exemplified by their

R

relationship. *Eureka* (1982) was a messy, obscure reflection on wealth and meaning. *Insignificance* (1985) put Albert Einstein, Marilyn Monroe, Joe DiMaggio and Senator Joseph McCarthy in a 1954 hotel room for some sexual and political intrigue leavened with weighty observations on time and the cosmos. The result was intermittently interesting. *Castaway* (1986) dispensed with the director's usual pyrotechnics to explore the consequences when Oliver Reed's desert-island misogynist is landed with Amanda Donohue as his Woman Friday, and remains one of Roeg's most watchable films.

In 1988's *Track 29*, Russell starred as a childless wife disturbed when Gary Oldman, who might be her illegitimate son, turns up on her doorstep. As with many of Roeg's films, *Track 29* was intriguing because one is unsure of the objective provenance of its events, but ultimately it could not overcome the criticism of pandering to Russell. More successful was *The Witches* (1989), a witty Roald Dahl adaptation in which a boy and his grandmother share a hotel with Anjelica Huston and her coven, who are plotting to turn England's children into mice. Russell starred more successfully in 1992's *Cold Heaven*, a promising thriller of marital infidelity and metaphysical tangle that revealed the director's unexpected facility with genre. There has been little

cheer for Roeg aficionados since, with neither the lifeless Romania-set drama *Two Deaths* (1995) or the Fay Weldon adaptation *Puffball* (2007) measuring up to earlier glories.

Roeg remains one of the last links that modern British cinema retains with the experimentalism of 1960s European cinema. RA

Performance 1970, 105 min
cast James Fox, Mick Jagger, Anita Pallenberg, Michele Breton, Ann Sidney, John Bindon, Stanley Meadows *cin* Nicolas Roeg *m* Jack Nitzsche

Shelved by Warner Bros for two years, this was meant to be an amalgam of two proven film formulae, the gangster flick and the "Swinging London" movie. What was delivered was a work of visionary excess, with James Fox's vicious hit man fetching up in the Chelsea basement of Mick Jagger's rock star. Overlaid with a sexual and narcotic haze, the result is a power play of terrible and unforgettable consequence.

Walkabout 1970, 123 min
cast Jenny Agutter, Lucien John, David Gulpilil, John Meillon *cin* Nicolas Roeg *m* John Barry

A teenage girl (Jenny Agutter) and her younger brother (Lucien John) are inexplicably abandoned in the Australian outback by their father who torches his car and kills himself. Their ensuing struggle for survival is aided by an Aboriginal boy (David Gulpilil) undergoing "walkabout". Beautifully filmed by Roeg in a dreamily elliptical fashion, the film sensitively explores ideas of lost innocence and the irreconcilable gap between nature and civilization.

Three's company: Mick Jagger enjoys a bohemian bath night with Anita Pallenberg and Michele Breton in *Performance*.

Don't Look Now 1973, 110 min

cast Julie Christie, Donald Sutherland, Hilary Mason, Massimo Serato, Clelia Matania, Renato Scarpa *cin* Anthony Richmond *m* Pino Donaggio

If that title seems too knowing, Roeg's intention here is to reveal the metaphysical substance of innocent events as an architect (Donald Sutherland) and his wife (Julie Christie) flee England after the accidental death of their little girl. They arrive in a wintry Venice that is caught in a web of unearthly resonance. Few horror films have explored the hurt at the heart of the uncanny with such a sense of sorrow.

The Man Who Fell To Earth 1976, 138 min

cast David Bowie, Rip Torn, Candy Clark, Buck Henry, Bernie Casey, Jackson D. Kane *cin* Anthony B. Richmond

A visually impressive essay on the potential of modernist cinema, Roeg's story of an alien (David Bowie) falling from grace in a fallen world remains the most compelling portrait by a foreign director of a simulated and displaced America.

Eric Rohmer

France, 1920–

The perception that French cinema consists largely of earnest polo-necked students discussing philosophy via well-crafted epigrams owes much to the films of Eric Rohmer. But such stereotyping oversimplifies a surprisingly varied body of work. Although best known for the cycles *Moral Tales* (six films, 1962–72), *Comedies And Proverbs* (six films, 1980–86) and *Tales Of The Four Seasons* (four films, 1989–98), he has also dabbled in political satire (*The Tree, The Mayor And The Mediatheque*, 1993), German-language costume drama (*The Marquise of O*, 1976), French Revolutionary intrigue (*The Lady And The Duke*, 2001) and World War II espionage (*Triple Agent*, 2003). The hyperstylized medieval fable *Perceval* (1978) was another anomaly in his work. Told in verse and song, it follows the fortunes of a young Welshman from ingenuous youth to Arthurian knight, his naïvety echoed by a spartan visual treatment that consciously recalls medieval tapestries. In a career in which the quality of films has remained consistently high, *Love In The Afternoon* (1972), *A Summer's Tale* (1996) and *The Green Ray* (1986) vie with numerous other titles from *Claire's Knee* (1970) to *A Winter's Tale* (1992) for recognition as the best of many understated masterpieces.

Born Jean-Marie Maurice Scherer (his pseudonym fused Erich von Stroheim with pulp novelist Sax Rohmer), he began as a teacher, journalist and critic, editing *Cahiers du cinéma* from 1957 to 1963. Rohmer was in at the beginning of *nouvelle vague* developments with his short *Présentation, ou Charlotte et son steak* (1951), which starred a young Jean-Luc Godard. Older than his *nouvelle vague* colleagues, he took longer to break into feature films; his first attempt at a feature, *Les petites filles modèles*,

was abandoned in 1952, and he finally made his debut with *The Sign Of Leo* in 1959. It was another decade before he gained widespread renown. This came partway through the *Moral Tales*, when *My Night With Maud* (1969) achieved international recognition and an Oscar nomination.

Rohmer has remained remarkably consistent ever since. As his films have become sparer and simpler (often shot in 16mm with a tiny budget and crew), his themes and characters have grown more nuanced. Working largely independently and with great economy of style, he has repeatedly created complex and subtle parts for actresses, to the extent that he has been seen as an auteur with a uniquely feminine touch. His uncannily empathetic understanding of young people's preoccupations gives no hint of his own advancing age (he was 60 when he began his second cycle, nearly 80 when he finished the third), aside from the moral, philosophical and spiritual richness of the films they inhabit.

Rohmer's awareness of human relationships is matchless, especially the intricate verbal games people play when trying to justify their desires. For his characters, the mind too often tries to trump the heart, and therein lies both their appeal and their tragedy. Rohmer's reputation has fluctuated without ever reaching great heights or depths, his output being in general less overtly flashy and provocative than that of his great French peers Truffaut, Godard and Resnais. For some, he is a quiet conservative in a radical throng. Now approaching his nineties, he shows little sign of declining in productivity, though with his great cycles behind him the emphasis appears to be more on historical drama – as in *Les amours d'Astrée et de Céladon* (2007) – than on contemporary mores. MB

My Night With Maud (Ma nuit chez Maud)
1969, 110 min, b/w

cast Jean-Louis Trintignant, Françoise Fabian, Marie-Christine Barrault, Antoine Vitez, Léonide Kogan, Guy Léger *cin* Nestor Almendros

After becoming fascinated by a blonde woman whom he sees in church, devout Catholic Jean-Louis Trintignant becomes immune to the considerable physical and intellectual charms of Françoise Fabian, despite the fact that she is clearly a perfect match for him. This is the wittiest and most formally elegant of Rohmer's *Moral Tales*, with Nestor Almendros's black-and-white photography as crisp as the snow that settles on wintry Clermont-Ferrand.

Claire's Knee (Le genou de Claire) 1970, 105 min

cast Jean-Claude Brialy, Aurora Cornu, Béatrice Romand, Laurence de Monaghan, Michèle Montel, Gérard Falconetti *cin* Nestor Almendros

How does a diplomat get to perform a distinctly undiplomatic act? That's the dilemma facing thirtysomething Jean-Claude Brialy as he becomes obsessed with the idea of caressing the knee of the teenage Laurence de Monaghan (first encountered at eye level as she climbs a ladder), but in strictly chaste circumstances. He's no Humbert Humbert, but a typical Rohmer male, focusing on a single act as a surrogate for a whole lexicon of unspoken desires.

A Full Moon In Paris (Les nuits de la pleine lune) 1984, 101 min

cast Pascal Ogier, Tchéky Karyo, Fabrice Luchini, Virginie Thévenet, Christian Vadim *cin* Renato Berta *m* Elli, Jacno

Another classic exploration of the way relationships malfunction, *A Full Moon In Paris* stands halfway between the simple structures of the earlier *Moral Tales* and the looser more improvised quality of Rohmer's later films. Louise (Pascale Ogier) claims to love her laconic, stay-at-home boyfriend but wants to have more fun. She rents a Paris apartment to allow herself more freedom but, inevitably, things go wrong. The performances are as nuanced as ever but there's an extra degree of humour, especially in the scenes involving Ogier and her self-absorbed, intellectual friend Octave (Fabrice Luchini).

An Autumn Tale (Conte d'automne) 1998, 112 min

cast Marie Rivière, Béatrice Romand, Didier Sandre, Alain Libolt, Alexia Portal *cin* Diane Baratier *m* Claude Marti, Gérard Pansanel

Not unlike Yasujiro Ozu's last films (especially *Late Autumn*, 1960), the final entry in Rohmer's *Tales Of The Four Seasons* cycle is about middle-aged friends Marie Rivière and Béatrice Romand and how their concern for their own and their offspring's future happiness leads to an ill-advised matchmaking scheme and multiple misunderstandings. The wedding party climax is a masterpiece of visual and emotional choreography, seemingly tying up loose ends while leaving things tantalizingly open.

Jean Rollin

France, 1938–

Born into a family of actors and artists, Jean Rollin's early encounters with books, paintings and cinema inspired him with a love of the "fantastique" (a French genre combining fantasy and horror elements). *Le viol du vampire* (*Queen Of The Vampires*, 1967) marked his feature debut. A collage of sublime surrealism, horrific stagy set pieces, lesbian nudity, ridiculous monotone dialogue and arty pretension, it became a *succès de scandale* and initiated a Rollin formula: subsequent titles included *La vampire nue* (*The Nude Vampire*, 1970), *Vierges et vampires* (*Requiem For A Vampire*, 1971) and *Le frisson des vampires* (*Sex And The Vampire*, 1971). His films and others' imitations of them even came to be known as "Rollinades" in the press. Much of Rollin's output in the 1970s was hard-core porn, released under the pseudonym Michel Gentil (his full name is Jean Michel Rollin le Gentil). *Fascination* (1979), *Le lac des morts vivants* (*Zombie Lake*, 1981) and *La morte vivante* (*The Living Dead Girl*, 1982) were gory attempts to reclaim his tarnished reputation. After a fallow period exacerbated by health problems, *La fiancée de Dracula* (*Fiancée Of Dracula*, 2002) proved nothing had changed. AJ

Lèvres de sang (Lips Of Blood) 1975, 88 min

cast Jean-Loup Philippe, Annie Briand, Nathalie Perrey, Martine Grimaud *cin* Jean-François Robin *m* Didier William Lepauw

Quintessential Rollin. A young man (Jean-Loup Philippe) is haunted by dreams of his vampire sister and embarks on a quest to find her. This ode to macabre eroticism is laced with ethereal gothic romance and surreal Oedipal nightmares.

Mark Romanek

US, 1959–

Highly respected for his pop videos (for Madonna, REM and Johnny Cash, among others), Mark Romanek has yet to achieve the same success in movies. After working as an assistant on Brian De Palma's *The Fury* (1978) and *Home Movies* (1980), Romanek directed his feature debut, the odd cult movie *Static*, in 1985. Co-written with *Home Movies* star Keith Gordon, it was about a man who claims to pick up TV signals from God. Romanek didn't direct another feature film until 2002, when he made the intriguing *One Hour Photo*, starring Robin Williams. TC

One Hour Photo 2002, 96 min

cast Robin Williams, Connie Nielsen, Michael Vartan, Dylan Smith *cin* Jeff Cronenweth *m* Reinhold Heil, Johnny Klimek

Stanley Kubrick's influence is evident in this austere, strange, chilly film about a photo counter employee, Sy (Williams), who becomes obsessed with what seems to be the perfect suburban family, the Yorkins, who are regular customers. Befriending their young son Jake (Dylan Smith), Sy discovers that the family is not everything he had assumed – so he sets about putting matters to right. The conception is intriguing, but as it pitches into thriller territory the film loses its credibility.

Eddie Romero

Philippines, 1924–

Impressed by Eddie Romero's stories for the Philippines Free Press, legendary director Gerardo de Leon talked him into writing a screenplay. The resulting film, *Ang maestra* (*The Teacher*, 1941), was a hit, and marked the start of a successful partnership that would last decades. Romero's solo directing debut was *Ang kamay ng diyos* (*The Hand Of God*, 1947). When the Philippine film industry collapsed in the 1950s, Romero and de Leon moved to Hollywood, where they produced, wrote, directed and distributed a variety of Philippine-shot exploitation movies including *Brides Of Blood* (1968), *The Big Doll House* (1971), *Black Mama, White Mama* (1972), *The Twilight People* (1973) and *Beyond Atlantis* (1973). Returning to the Philippines, Romero directed his historical masterpiece *Ganito kami noon, paano kayo ngayon?* (*This Is The Way We Live*, 1976). He also associate-produced *Apocalypse Now* (1979). AJ

Beast Of Blood 1971, 90 min

cast John Ashley, Celeste Yarnall, Eddie Garcia, Liza Belmonte, Alfonso Carvajal, Bruno Punzalan *cin* Justo Paulino *m* Tito Arevalo

The last of the insane "Blood Island" trilogy, *Beast Of Blood* features a mad doctor (Eddie Garcia) who grafts a new head onto a chlorophyll-blooded monster. The hero (played by John Ashley) must journey to the heart of the island to track down the source of the mayhem. Hilarious trash, the film was promoted with sick bags.

George A. Romero

US, 1940–

George Romero is the director who, in the words of Stephen King, took horror "out of Transylvania". Before Romero's *Night Of The Living Dead* (1968), the genre was stuck in a world of old counts, fake bats and creaking doors. Romero's monsters were not mutants from outer space or ancient bloodthirsty aristocrats, but average Joes, "the neighbours who were unlucky" in the words of the director. His toxic combination of gory effects, documentary techniques and zeitgeist subtexts took the horror movie to new extremes of realism and contemporary relevance.

Made in 1968, the year of Black Power and student protests, *Night Of The Living Dead* was "the most literal possible image of America devouring itself" according to a contemporary review. "Snapshots of the time" is how Romero likes to describe his subsequent series of political and cerebral splatter movies. *Dawn Of The Living Dead* (1978) was a lacerating satire on consumerism and arguably the high point of the series. *Day Of The Dead* (1985) took Reaganite obsessions with science and the military and twisted them into a claustrophobic story involving mad scientists and sadistic experiments. George W. Bush's "War on Terror" was the satirical focus of *Land Of The Dead* (2005). Written before the events of September 11, 2001, new lines were added ("we don't negotiate with terrorists") to freight it with topical significance. With its unsubtle and muddled metaphors, it showed why subtexts and allegories should always be buried deep beneath the surface.

The leader of the zombie pack had been making films since the age of 14, when his 8mm debut, *The Man From The Meteor* got Romero into trouble with the local police after he set fire to a dummy and dropped it from the roof of his parents' apartment block. In the early 1960s, Romero set up his own production company in Pittsburgh, making commercials and industrial films, which became his training ground.

Away from the flesh-eaters, Romero's work is a mixed bag of misfires and minor masterpieces. The follow-up to *Night Of The Living Dead*, *There's Always Vanilla* (1971), was an ill-advised foray into

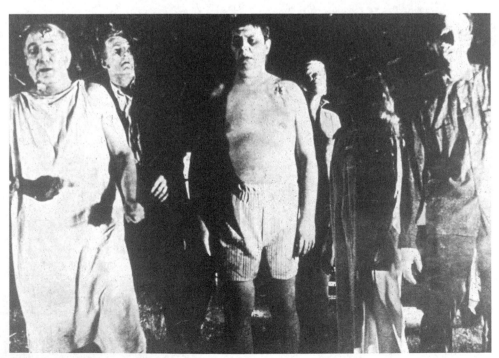

Neighbours from hell: Romero's zombies take to the streets in *Night Of The Living Dead*.

romantic comedy territory. *Jack's Wife* (1972) was the diary of a mad housewife with witchcraft spicing an uneven brew. With *The Crazies* (1973) Romero was back on firmer ground, with a virus spreading disease and social unrest across America. *Martin* (1977), the best of his non-zombie fare, was a queasy tale of a young man who has convinced himself that he's a twentieth-century vampire. *Knight Riders* (1981) was a truly unusual and not entirely successful synthesis of modern-day bikers and Arthurian mythology. The uneven *Creepshow* (1982) showed why portmanteau movies are hard to get right. In *Monkey Shines* (1988), which remains the best of late Romero, a simian takes grisly revenge on behalf of his paraplegic owner. *The Dark Half* (1992) was a superior Stephen King adaptation. Romero has found it difficult to secure funding for his movies which haven't starred the living dead, but the little seen, poorly reviewed horror movie *Bruiser* (2000) has possibly shown why. LH

Night Of The Living Dead 1968, 96 min, b/w
cast Duane Jones, Judith O'Dea, Karl Hardman, Marilyn Eastman, Keith Wayne, Judith Ridley *cin* George A. Romero *m* Scott Vladimir Licina

Attacked by a zombie in a graveyard, Barbara is rescued by a truck driver, and the duo board themselves up in what appears to be a deserted house, only to discover the presence of other survivalists. Soon the threat is from inside as well as out, as the humans prove to be their own worst enemies. The tragically ironic and despondent ending is another reason why Romero's first film was a bloody revolution in American cinema.

Dawn Of The Dead 1978, 126 min
cast David Emge, Ken Foree, Scott H. Reiniger, Gaylen Ross, David Crawford, David Early, Richard France, Howard Smith *cin* Michael Gornick *m* Goblin

Four survivors from *Night Of The Living Dead*'s plague of flesh-eating zombies take refuge in a shopping mall which soon becomes their Alamo. They have to defend it not just from the undead, but also from a post-apocalyptic gang of leather-clad bikers. In the mall, zombies still continue to shop as if nothing has changed in their lives. Romero admits his satire on consumerism is "so unsubtle it's like a pie in the face", nevertheless it's immensely enjoyable on both an allegorical and visceral level.

Bernard Rose
UK, 1960–

British filmmaker Bernard Rose's work is thoughtful, inventive and engaging, with a real affinity for mood. His first two films, the thrillers *Body Contact* (1987) and *Paperhouse* (1988), were moody and memorable. He broke through to bigger leagues with *Chicago Joe And The Showgirl* (1990), in which a young American soldier and a London hooker team up for a crime and murder spree. *Candyman* (1992) was a very effective and intense horror film based on a short story by Clive Barker.

Rose has also directed a well-received Beethoven biopic – *Immortal Beloved* (1994), starring Gary Oldman – and a classically styled but disappointing adaptation of *Anna Karenina* (1997). *Ivansxtc* (2000) was shot on digital video, of which Rose is an enthusiastic exponent. He followed it with the disappointing film-within-a-film horror *Snuff-Movie* (2005). JC

Candyman 1992, 98 min
cast Virginia Madsen, Tony Todd, Xander Berkeley, Kasi Lemmons, DeJuan Guy, Vanessa Williams *cin* Anthony B. Richmond *m* Philip Glass

Relocating Clive Barker's short story "The Forbidden" to Chicago, Rose received plaudits for this taut horror in which researcher Helen Lyle (Virginia Madsen) investigates the urban legend (or is it?) of a killer called the Candyman. Tense and multilayered, *Candyman* boasts a score from renowned composer Philip Glass, which adds some additional auditory class to proceedings.

Ivansxtc 2000, 93 min
cast Danny Huston, Peter Weller, Lisa Enos, Joanne Duckmann, Angela Featherstone *cin* Ron Forsythe, Bernard Rose *m* Matt Schultz, Elmo Webber

A loose adaptation of Leo Tolstoy's novella *The Death Of Ivan Ilyich*, this powerful character piece charts the disintegration of Hollywood agent Ivan Beckman (Danny Huston), whose hedonistic, frenzied life goes into freefall when he is diagnosed with cancer. Real Hollywood agents were said to be dismayed by the harsh light in which their profession was cast – as well as by the low budget that, if replicated across the industry, would reduce their incomes.

Stuart Rosenberg
US, 1927–

Stuart Rosenberg is little more than a proficient craftsman who has enjoyed a respectable career. He worked in the booming TV drama field in the late 1950s and early 60s, directing episodes of *Alfred Hitchcock Presents…*, *The Twilight Zone* and *The Naked City*. A strike halted production on his first feature, *Murder, Inc* (1960), which was finished by his producer Burt Balaban. *Cool Hand Luke* (1967) is a modern classic, and the movie for which he will be remembered. Paul Newman (who played Luke) respected him enough to collaborate on a series of interesting projects, though none of them really clicked: the political satire *WUSA* (1970), the comedy Western *Pocket Money* (1972) and the thriller *The Drowning Pool* (1975). Rosenberg scored a box-office hit with *The Amityville Horror* (1976), and made a couple more watchable films – the prison drama *Brubaker* (1979) and the crime romp *The Pope Of Greenwich Village* (1984) – before retirement. TC

Cool Hand Luke 1967, 126 min
cast Paul Newman, George Kennedy, J.D. Cannon, Lou Antonio, Strother Martin, Jo Van Fleet, Clifton James *cin* Conrad Hall *m* Lalo Schiffrin

This is an iconic role for Paul Newman: a cocky rebel on a chain gang in the Deep South. Luke doesn't just refuse to buckle under, he does so with a smug grin which invites punishment and admiration (he's a brother in arms to Jack Nicholson's Randle McMurphy in *One Flew Over The Cuckoo's Nest*, 1975). If Rosenberg's fondness for zooms now looks dated, numerous memorable sequences and rich supporting characters cement the film's enduring status.

Francesco Rosi
Italy, 1922–

No other director has negotiated Italian politics with the insight of Francesco Rosi. Working his way up through the industry, he assisted on Luchino Visconti's neo-realist classic *La terra trema* (*The Earth Trembles*, 1948), which later influenced his investigations of the "Southern Question", and also worked for Michelangelo Antonioni and Mario Monicelli. Rosi's 1958 directorial debut *La sfida* (*The Challenge*) was a realist fiction exploring the manipulation of the fruit and vegetable market in Naples by the Camorra, or Neapolitan Mafia. It won the Special Jury Prize at Venice. His follow-up, *I magliari* (*The Weavers*, 1959), focused on Italian immigrants scraping a living in post-war Germany.

However, the director's breakthrough didn't come until 1961, with *Salvatore Giuliano*, in which he returned to the fraught issue of Sicilian and southern

Italian economic backwardness during the post-war boom. Here Rosi also began to develop *cine-inchiesta*, an investigative technique in which questions, doubts and ambiguities are raised about Italian political and criminal allegiances. Using actual witnesses and non-linear associational narratives, Rosi proposed "a second phase of neo-realism", a critical attitude interrogating national realities rather than merely revealing them. *Hands Over The City* (1963) was a compelling account of municipal corruption in which Rod Steiger's financier works a construction industry scandal to his advantage.

If Rosi has not always been comfortable with literary adaptations – *More Than A Miracle* (1967), *Carmen* (1984), *The Truce* (1996) – he responded to Italy's industrial strife and political violence in the 1970s with further investigations of the status quo. In *Uomini contro* (*Men Against*, 1970), Rosi used a story of officer-soldier conflict during World War I as an indictment of the class structure. *The Mattei Affair* (1972) was remarkably prescient, and shared the Palme d'Or at Cannes. *Lucky Luciano* (1973) characteristically saw its nominal figure as a vessel in which all the symptoms of the Italian and American political agendas coalesced.

Illustrious Corpses (1976) followed the serial murder of judges in politically sensitive Sicilian Mafia trials. *Christ Stopped At Eboli* (1979) tried,

Sicilian landscape: through an oblique exploration of a notorious bandit's death, *Salvatore Giuliano* raised questions about poverty, crime and politics in southern Italy.

like Ermanno Olmi's *The Tree Of Wooden Clogs* the same year, for a politically inflected rural fantasia on southern Italy. The ponderous *Three Brothers* (1980) and the disastrous Gabriel García Márquez adaptation *Chronicle Of A Death Foretold* (1987) were thin variations on the fractured perspectives of history explored in Rosi's earlier work. Rosi's political agenda and its influence can be observed in the work of directors ranging from Costa-Gavras to Sidney Lumet, while his incendiary portraits of Sicily reverberate in Francis Ford Coppola's *The Godfather* trilogy. RA

Salvatore Giuliano 1961, 125 min, b/w
cast Frank Wolff, Salvo Randone, Federico Zardi, Pietro Cammarata, Fernando Cicero, Sennuccio Benelli *cin* Gianni Di Venanzo *m* Piero Piccioni

The story of the Sicilian bandit gunned down in 1950 and the subsequent political strife between conflicting factions and interests. The film begins with the aftermath of Giuliano's death and the preparation of his corpse and follows through to the trial of his cronies. The gangster's short trajectory from brigand to popular hero to right-wing terrorist allows Rosi to anatomize the forces that continued to rend Italian public life.

The Mattei Affair (Il caso Mattei) 1972, 115 min
cast Gian Maria Volonté, Luigi Squarzina, Peter Baldwin, Franco Graziosi, Gianfranco Ombuen, Elio Jotta *cin* Pasqualino De Santis *m* Piero Piccioni

Enrico Mattei was an entrepreneur whose premature death in a 1962 air crash was widely regarded as the action of foreign oil companies unhappy with Mattei's championing of Italian interests over international cartels. While giving a superb performance, regular collaborator Gian Maria Volonté never detracts from Rosi's rigorous inquest.

Herbert Ross
US, 1927–2001

Herbert Ross has been compared with Hollywood craftsmen Michael Curtiz and George Cukor and he had a notable facility with the genres that we associate with the old studios. However, his work tapped into specifically modern sensibilities.

A former actor and dancer, Ross choreographed Broadway and Hollywood musicals including *Carmen Jones*, *Funny Girl* and *Inside Daisy Clover*. His first directed film was 1969's *Goodbye, Mr Chips*, a glutinous remake of the Sam Wood-Robert Donat vehicle that was as dated as the pairing of Peter O'Toole and Petula Clark was desperate. Other projects that drew on Ross's musical training were either underwhelming (*The Turning Point*, 1977), bloated (*Pennies From Heaven*, 1981) or ill-judged (*Footloose*, 1984).

Ross was far more comfortable in his pairings with writer Neil Simon, which included the "odd couple" movie *The Sunshine Boys* (1975), and two movies exploring the sexual dynamics of post-feminism – the Richard Dreyfuss-Marsha Mason comedy *The Goodbye Girl* (1977) and the portmanteau *California Suite* (1978). When working without Simon, Ross demonstrated that he was sympathetic to the woes of modern romance in the Barbra Streisand-George Segal screwball *The Owl And The Pussycat* (1970) and the Woody Allen-scripted *Play It Again, Sam* (1972). He ventured into other territory too: *The Last Of Sheila* (1973) was a cunning thriller, and his Sherlock Holmes picture *The Seven Percent Solution* (1976) has been seen as camp, interestingly revisionist, or both. Following in the tradition of the great "women's pictures", both *Steel Magnolias* (1989) and *Boys On The Side* (1995) also displayed their director's sensitivity to the experiences of American women negotiating the options bequeathed by the 1970s. RA

Play It Again, Sam 1972, 86 min
cast Woody Allen, Diane Keaton, Tony Roberts, Jerry Lacy, Susan Anspach, Jennifer Salt, Joy Bang *cin* Owen Roizman *m* Billy Goldenberg

Based on Woody Allen's play and steeped in the nostalgia then sweeping American popular culture at large, the account of the nebbish pilgrim's progress through the sexual jungle in Humphrey Bogart's shadow marked a retreat from the New Hollywood antics of early Allen. Herbert Ross directed with restraint and empathy for the gender wars that Allen would shortly make his own.

The Goodbye Girl 1977, 110 min
cast Richard Dreyfuss, Marsha Mason, Quinn Cummings, Paul Benedict, Barbara Rhoades, Theresa Merritt *cin* David M. Walsh *m* David Grusin

When Richard Dreyfuss's struggling actor and Marsha Mason's jilted dancer are thrown together in a New York apartment, the romantic chemistry and laughs bounce off the walls, wryly observed by Mason's endearing daughter Quinn Cummings. Dreyfuss's performance – including his hilarious portrayal of a gay, lisping Richard III – earned him the best actor Oscar.

Roberto Rossellini
Italy, 1906–77

Roberto Rossellini was christened "the father of modern film" by *Cahiers du cinéma*. Along with Jean Renoir, he was the most important influence on the *nouvelle vague* directors – and beyond them, on Michelangelo Antonioni and anyone who thinks seriously about realism and humanism in cinema, from the Dardenne brothers to Lars von Trier and the other members of the Dogme collective. Yet Rossellini is probably better known today as the father of Isabella, and for his marriage to Ingrid Bergman.

The popular notion that *Rome, Open City* (1945) represents the first salvo in the revolutionary Italian neo-realist movement is too simplistic: the elements of the style were already largely in place by the time of Luchino Visconti's *Ossessione* (1942).

Indeed history has tended to gloss over the three features Rossellini had previously made under the auspices of Mussolini's Fascist regime – *The White Ship* (1941), *A Pilot Returns* (1942) and *The Man With The Cross* (1943).

Nevertheless, *Rome, Open City* represents a landmark in neo-realism. The strictures of filming under the dying days of the German occupation largely dictated the style of Rossellini's film: its low-grade, grainy texture (he bought whatever stock he could find from photographic shops), the "on the streets" locations (the Germans had set up barracks in Rome's studios), and its hand-held camera style. However, none of this detracts from the courage, power and conviction of this remarkable film, which is both a searing political melodrama and an authentic record of a particular time and place.

Rossellini's next film, *Paisà* (1946), still contains trace elements of melodrama, but this tapestry of six vignettes from the liberation of Italy is markedly devoid of propaganda: using nonprofessional actors and developing his scenarios across the length of the country, Rossellini fashioned a vivid picture of devastation and survival. Applying similar methods to post-war Germany, he produced an even more desolate, nihilistic chronicle of the times in *Germany, Year Zero* (1947). Together, this trilogy of films stand as one of the great achievements of the Italian neo-realist movement for their direct engagement with contemporary social issues at a time of global upheaval.

Ingrid Bergman – at the time, perhaps the most famous actress in the world – was so moved by *Paisà* that she wrote to Rossellini and offered her services, even though her Italian, she said, was limited to "Ti amo". Rossellini accepted the invitation, and they embarked on *Stromboli* (1950), in which Bergman played a Lithuanian refugee who marries a poor Italian fisherman but bridles at the austere conditions on the volcanic island which is his home. Although both were already married, Rossellini and Bergman fell in love and she became pregnant with his child. The world was scandalized and denunciations flew thick and fast. Despite – or because of – the publicity, the public rejected *Stromboli*.

By now Rossellini had broken from the neo-realists. Rejecting their prescriptive doctrines, he moved away from overtly reformist political cinema in favour of psychological realism – a transition for which many critics were unprepared, demanding as it did a more active, engaged form of viewing. Stripping away the props of artifice, plot and screenplay, Rossellini brought a more concerted focus to bear on the individual in his or her world. Meaning became a function of camera placement and movement, the observation of the character in his or her environment.

Bergman starred in five more Rossellini films before their own marriage foundered. Each in its own way was built on the director's relationship with the actress and the themes of marriage, identity, communication and isolation. The best of them is *Voyage To Italy* (1954), in which an English couple (Bergman and George Sanders) with an ailing marriage briefly reconcile while touring southern Italy. Rossellini ignited further scandal through his affair with and subsequent marriage to screenwriter Somali Das Gupta, during the making of his documentary *India* (1958).

With only a couple of exceptions, Rossellini devoted the last twenty years of his life to historical reconstructions and documentaries, many of them made for television. In these later films, Rossellini applied the techniques of neo-realism and psychological realism to illuminate the lives of great men in history. He also worked with zoom lens techniques to give the past an intimacy that complemented the intellectual heft of his screenplays. Among the best of these projects were *The Rise To Power Of Louis XIV* (1966), *Socrates* (1970), *Blaise Pascal* (1971), *Cartesio* (*Descartes*, 1974) and *The Messiah* (1975). Although they have been highly praised and had some limited cinematic release, sadly these films are hard to see today. *Italy: Year One* (1974) was a final return to the big screen, tracing the career of the country's first post-war prime minister, Alcide De Gasperi. TC

Rome, Open City (Roma, città aperta) 1945, 100 min, b/w

cast Anna Magnani, Francesco Grandjacquet, Marcello Pagliero, Aldo Fabrizi, Maria Michi *cin* Ubaldo Arata *m* Renzo Rossellini

Rossellini initially set out to make a documentary about a priest in the Resistance. But the project evolved into a drama as the underground war raged on. A Communist leader hides out from the Nazis with the support of a group including a lithographer, Francesco (Grandjacquet), his wife Pina (Magnani) and a priest, Don Pietro (Fabrizi), but death follows on his heels.

Germany, Year Zero (Germania anno zero) 1947, 78 min, b/w

cast Edmund Moeschka, Franz Krüger, Barbara Hintz, Werner Pittschau, Erich Gühne *cin* Robert Julliard *m* Renzo Rossellini

Rossellini's final "war" film was shot in the rubble of Berlin. A 12-year-old boy (Edmund Moeschka) struggles to care for his family under impossible circumstances, eventually turning to patricide and suicide. Devastating images of defeat, solitude and abandonment cast a long shadow over this child's fate. In one scene a recording of a Hitler speech echoes over the apocalyptic landscape.

Francis God's Jester (Francesco guillare di Dio) 1950, 83 min, b/w

cast Aldo Fabrizi, Arabella Lemaitre, Nazario Geraldi, Roberto Sorrentino *cin* Otello Martelli *m* Renzo Rossellini

Also known as *The Flowers Of Saint Francis*, this delightful, frequently comical portrait of St Francis of Assisi strips away the reverend solemnity associated with biblical films to express what Rossellini called "the playfulness … the liberation the spirit finds in poverty, in the absolute separation from human things". Simple but profound, the film features many Franciscan monks in the cast. It was Rossellini's own favourite, and has been highly praised by Martin Scorsese and Pier Paolo Pasolini (it was surely an influence on their religious films).

Stromboli 1950, 107 min, b/w

cast Ingrid Bergman, Mario Vitale, Renzo Cesana, Mario Sponza *cin* Otello Martelli *m* Renzo Rossellini

Ingrid Bergman plays a young Lithuanian woman who marries an Italian fisherman (Mario Vitale) as her quickest way out of a refugee camp. But she finds it difficult to adjust to the hard life under the volcano on the island of Stromboli. For his first film with Bergman, Rossellini put her in much the same situation as her character: she was deprived of all the luxuries to which a Hollywood star would be accustomed, and thrown in without a script.

Voyage To Italy (Viaggio in Italia) 1954, 100 min, b/w

cast Ingrid Bergman, George Sanders, Maria Mauban, Paul Muller, Leslie Daniels, Natalia Ray *cin* Enzo Serafin *m* Renzo Rossellini

An affluent middle-aged British couple tour southern Italy while a family inheritance is sold – but the solitude of the trip exposes the fault lines in their marriage. Among the ancient Roman sites, the wife (Bergman) comes to her own emotional epiphany. Practically plot-less, *Voyage To Italy* cuts deeper than any melodrama. Critic Laura Mulvey has called it "the first modern film".

Robert Rossen
US, 1908–66

Robert Rossen's post-war thrillers shepherded Warner Bros social realism into the modern era of corporate crime. Born to Russian-Jewish parents on New York's Lower East Side, Rossen was briefly a boxer before becoming a playwright and then a screenwriter. His feeling for the nexus of milieu and character tinges almost all of his screenplays, including *Marked Woman* (Lloyd Bacon, 1937), *They Won't Forget* (Mervyn LeRoy, 1938), *The Roaring Twenties* (Raoul Walsh, 1939) and *A Walk In The Sun* (Lewis Milestone, 1946).

During the 1930s, Rossen was associated with the Communist Party, but severed his affiliation in 1945. Nevertheless, he was forced to testify to the House Un-American Activities Committee (HUAC) two years later. Under the shadow of a subpoena, he drew on his past for his hard-hitting directorial debut *Johnny O'Clock* (1947) and the same year's *Body And Soul*, which was scripted by Abraham Polonsky. His subsequent project, *All The King's Men* (1949), evoked the career of 1930s Louisiana governor Huey Long, charting the rise and fall of the Southern demagogue, and won the best picture Oscar.

Blacklisted in 1951, Rossen named names two years later – an act he deeply regretted – and sustained himself by working in foreign locations for *Mambo* (1954) and *Alexander The Great* (1956), until he regained his critical stock and industry cachet with *The Hustler* (1961). The poolroom drama hinged on Paul Newman's fine performance and, in turn, made the actor a 1960s icon. Allegedly a troubled man by then, Rossen died without knowing that his final film *Lilith* (1964) – in which Warren Beatty's therapist is drawn to Jean Seberg's enchanting patient – had appeared in a *Cahiers du cinéma* Top 10 list. RA

Body And Soul 1947, 105 min, b/w

cast John Garfield, Lilli Palmer, Anne Revere, Hazel Brooks, William Conrad, Joseph Pevney *cin* James Wong Howe *m* Hugo Friedhofer

John Garfield's boxer, fighting his way up from a Brooklyn candy store, realizes that the world is not enough. Boxing was Hollywood's stock metaphor for proletarian struggle, and this Manichean tale of post-war transcendence crisply reflects the dilemma of the contract director with something to prove working in a studio system sold on the quick fix.

The Hustler 1961, 135 min, b/w

cast Paul Newman, George C. Scott, Jackie Gleason, Piper Laurie *cin* Gene Shufton *m* Kenyon Hopkins

"Fast" Eddie Felson (Paul Newman) lives on his wits as a small-time poolroom hustler, that is until ruthless promoter Bert Gordon (George C. Scott) gets hold of him and matches him against the legendary Minnesota Fats (Jackie Gleason). Will Eddie succeed or will his self-destructive impulses get the better of him? Rossen skilfully conjures up both the addictive lure and the sleaze of smoke-filled pool halls, where competition becomes a metaphor for the way men prey upon each other.

Lilith 1964, 114 min, b/w

cast Warren Beatty, Jean Seberg, Peter Fonda, Kim Hunter, Anne Meacham, James Patterson, Jessica Walter *cin* Eugen Schüfftan *m* Kenyon Hopkins

This reworking of the legend of the manipulating woman plays out in an asylum, where Jean Seberg twists therapist Warren Beatty around her little finger. Playing evocatively with distinctions between sanity and madness, this departure for Rossen is perhaps the director's tribute to the beleaguered soul in a corrupted garden. An enduring curio, it was Seberg's favourite of all her work.

Eli Roth
US, 1972–

Brought up on 1970s schlock, Eli Roth shot his first video horror, *Splatter On The Linoleum*, at age 11. After graduating from NYU film school, he worked in film production, learning his craft on movies such as Robert Redford's *Quiz Show* (1994), Betty Thomas's *Private Parts* (1997) and Martin Brest's *Meet Joe Black* (1998). In Los Angeles he managed to scrape together funding for the TV animation series *Chowdaheads* (1999) and *The Rotten Fruit* (2003). During this period he also worked as

The Splat Pack

When the small independent Lionsgate Films released Eli Roth's *Cabin Fever* in 2003, it become a major distributor overnight. But *Cabin Fever* was just one of the many surprise hits for which the "Splat Pack" have been responsible. Adapted from the description of Herschell Gordon Lewis and George A. Romero's pioneering early work as "Splatter Films", the Splat Pack was an expression coined by the horror-film critic Alan Jones in *Total Film* magazine to describe the new wave of low-budget horror filmmakers that appeared to be on a mission to bring back hard-core violence in the face of the watered-down, sound-designed shockers that ruled the multiplexes. The key directors in this group are Roth, Neil Marshall (*The Descent*, 2005), Alexandre Aja (*Switchblade Romance*, 2003, *The Hills Have Eyes*, 2006), Rob Zombie (*House Of 1000 Corpses*, 2003, *The Devil's Rejects*, 2005), Greg McLean (*Wolf Creek*, 2005) and James Wan, Leigh Whannell and Darren Lynn Bousman (the *Saw* series, 2004–06). They repeatedly clashed with ratings boards, especially America's notorious MPAA, whose controversial decisions on the portrayal of sex were exposed in *This Film Is Not Yet Rated* (2006). Their films continued to find substantial box-office success, however, and provided maximum returns on budgets that were loose change by Hollywood standards, working in a genre long considered the bastard stepchild of the movie business.

They were a young, well-educated and close-knit community, and had all grown up on a diet of extreme exploitation horror, containing epic levels of torture, terror and depravity. Looking to make the cheapest movie they could upon graduating, James Wan and Leigh Whannell came up with the minimal plot device of placing two strangers in a dirty bathroom with a chainsaw, and *Saw* (2004) was born. Darren Bousman was a frustrated writer toiling in the lowliest behind-the-camera posts, who scripted the most deliberately offensive, violent screenplay because he had nothing to lose. It ended up being rewritten as *Saw II* (2005). It's evidence of what every true Splat Packer knows: if their horror movie is to go the distance, most film-goers must recommend that others *not* go see it.

Old-school genre directors such as John Carpenter, Brian De Palma and Wes Craven owed their inspiration to the more refined work of Alfred Hitchcock, producer Val Lewton and the Hammer House of Horror. But in their formative cine-literate years the Splat Pack had been watching movies such as Abel Ferrara's *The Driller Killer* (1979), Italian cannibal shockers and video nasties. They had seen their guru/mentor Quentin Tarantino emulate their schlock idols and determined to go down the same grind-house route. It is no surprise that *Cabin Fever* captured the attention of Tarantino, who befriended Roth, offered advice and ended up as the executive producer for his *Hostel* films.

Man's inhumanity to man is the common theme of the Splat Pack's raw and brutal horrors. There's nothing supernatural or sci-fi about them: they derive from people doing unspeakable things to themselves and others. However, that's not to say that neo-horror is crudely made vile trash for geeks only. Ever since its 1950s heyday, the horror genre has acted as a sneaky conduit for subversive ideas, a vital component of their shock value. *Hostel* (2005) is a case in point: it has been seen by some critics as a metaphor for the Iraq War and the anti-American attitudes it has fostered. AJ

---

an assistant to director David Lynch. It was through his association with Lynch that he raised $1.5 million to make his feature debut, *Cabin Fever*, the most profitable horror film of 2003. With *Hostel* (2005), he moved into horror-porn (or "gorno") in a story of some backpackers in Slovakia who find themselves on the receiving end of some hard-core torture. Highly successful, it spawned a sequel, *Hostel Part 2*, in 2007. Roth has gained a prominent advocate in the form of Quentin Tarantino, who dubbed him the "future of horror". In 2007 Roth directed a fake trailer segment for Tarantino and Robert Rodriguez's *Grindhouse* project. AJ

Cabin Fever 2003, 93 min

cast Rider Strong, Jordan Ladd, Cerina Vincent, Joey Kern, James DeBello, Arle Verveen *cin* Scott Kevan *m* Angelo Badalamenti, Nathan Barr

Five students party at an isolated forest cabin and get systematically struck down by a deadly flesh-eating virus.

From its *Evil Dead* location and *Night Of The Living Dead* narrative tricks to its *Deliverance* atmosphere and use of songs from *The Last House On The Left*, Roth's fever dream is a blood-soaked blast.

Bimal Roy
Bangladesh (formerly India), 1909–66

The Vittoria De Sica of Hindi cinema, Bimal Roy masterfully orchestrated poignant and lyrical hymns of Indian neo-realism. Even though his subjects were marginal and occasionally criminal, he filtered the miserable travails of these victims of the caste system through a poetic, almost romantic sensibility. Born to moneyed landowners in Bengal, Roy had to up sticks and find work in Calcutta when his family were cheated out of their wealth. Finding employment at the New Theatres Studio, Roy quickly established himself as a talented photographer of still and moving pictures, forming a formidable partnership with director P.C. Barua, notably on *Devdas* (1936).

In 1943 Roy made *Bengal Famine*, a powerful documentary about the famine that had devastated the region, displaying a social commitment that would become the hallmark of his subsequent work. Class conflict was a running battle in Roy's movies: his heroes would often find themselves locked in an internecine struggle with a boss or landowner. In *Udayer pathey* (*The New Dawn*, 1944) the sister of a rich industrialist defies her family by falling in love with a radical novelist. Strident and unflinching in its naturalism, it was a commercial success and a milestone in Indian cinema. Roy made a few more movies in Calcutta until the city's film industry dwindled, and moved to Bombay in 1951. It was about this time that he saw De Sica's *Bicycle Thieves*, a film that had a profound and lasting effect on Roy. The Italian director's neo-realist influence was most evident in *Do bigha zamin* (*Two Acres Of Land*, 1953), Roy's undisputed masterpiece.

In 1955, Roy unexpectedly returned to a film he had photographed for Barua twenty years earlier, *Devdas*. Even though it is the one film of Roy's that has crossed national borders, it wasn't his most commercially successful work. That honour goes to *Madhumati* (1958) an evocative and atmospheric ghost story about a man who is haunted by the death of his lover. Criticized for the marked absence of Roy's usual social critique, the story revolves around a villainous, venal boss, in this case the owner of a timber estate played by Bollywood's legendary film villain, Pran. In Roy's last feature film, the excellent *Bandini* (1963) a prison doctor falls for one of the inmates, the Bollywood star Nutan, and discovers the tragic reasons that led her to kill in cold blood. LH

Do bigha zamin 1953, 142 min, b/w

cast Balraj Sahni, Nirupa Roy, Ratan Kumar, Murad *cin* Kamal Bose *m* Salil Choudhury

Described as one of the founding films of Hindi cinema, this is the powerful tale of a father who has to move to Calcutta to repay a loan. He lives in abject poverty as a rickshaw driver while his son becomes a shoeshine boy. Bristling with a sense of social justice, Roy's masterpiece is all the more poignant for its autobiographical inflections.

Devdas 1955, 159 min, b/w

cast Dilip Kumar, Vyjayanthimala, Motilal, Suchitra Sen, Nasir Hussain, Murad, Kanhaiyalal, Moni Chatterjee *cin* Kamal Bose *m* Sachin Dev Burman

In one of the ten versions of Sarat Chandra Chatterjee's classic novel, *Devdas*, an impish boy spends an idyllic childhood with his neighbour Paro. When his antics become too much for his family he's sent away. Returning as a man, Devdas and Paro instantly fall in love but are prevented from marrying because of the caste system's social regulations. With a muted grandeur, Roy's mellifluous black-and-white photography is achingly lyrical and beautifully modulated.

Bandini 1963, 157 min, b/w

cast Nutan Behi, Ashok Kumar, Dharmendra, Raja Paranjpe *cin* Kamal Bose *m* S.D. Burman

A prison doctor falls in a love with a beautiful prisoner (luminous screen legend Nutan Behi) and gradually discovers why this apparent innocent is doing time for murder. The tale is told in flashback, Roy's dexterous ability with narrative matched only by his expressionistic use of sound and vision, which seems to get inside the head of its tormented female protagonist during the celebrated murder sequence.

Patricia Rozema
Canada, 1958–

The product of a Dutch Calvinist upbringing, Patricia Rozema poignantly explores the interface between idolatry and cinema in her films. A former journalist, she has scripted all her features to date. Her first film, the short *Passion* (1985), established Rozema's preoccupation with hidden love. After various industry assignments – including a stint as David Cronenberg's assistant director on *The Fly* (1986) – she received funding for her auspicious feature debut, *I've Heard The Mermaids Singing* (1987), for which she won the Prix de la Jeunesse at Cannes.

Rozema's less certain *White Room* (1990), was an arty exercise in which a male voyeur attempted to understand a woman's reclusive silence, while *When Night Is Falling* (1995) crystallized her interest in stylistic finesse. The director's contribution to the 1990s Jane Austen revival was *Mansfield Park* (1999), for which she drew upon Austen's own commentaries. It featured Frances O'Connor's thoroughly modern portrayal of an outsider amid a society of sham sophistication, and like Rozema's best work it showed a graceful regard for the vicissitudes of human communication. RA

I've Heard The Mermaids Singing 1987, 83 min, b/w and col

cast Sheila McCarthy, Paule Baillargeon, Ann-Marie MacDonald, John Evans, Brenda Kamino, Richard Monette *cin* Douglas Koch *m* Mark Korven

Sheila McCarthy is fetching as the gauche temporary secretary and would-be photographer who falls for gallery manager Paule Baillargeon. With her vivid fantasy life, dreams and obsession with her new boss, outsider McCarthy embodies Patricia Rozema's themes of confession and adoration. The result is a mesmerizing, subtle film with keenly observed relationships.

When Night Is Falling 1995, 94 min

cast Pascale Bussières, Rachael Crawford, Henry Czerny, David Rox, Don McKellar, Tracy Wright, Clare Coulter *cin* Douglas Koch *m* Lesley Barber

When repressed academic Pascale Bussières meets Rachael Crawford's delicious carnival performer, the spin on the marital and sexual status quo is wrought with visual tropes of warm and delightful calibre. This tale of lesbian self-realization is magical, intoxicating and romantic.

John Ruane
Australia, 1952–

After graduating from film school, John Ruane spent ten years trying to realize his film projects, finally acquiring enough funding to make *Feathers* (1987), a fifty-minute adaptation of a Raymond Carver story. But the international success of his debut *Death In Brunswick* (1991) sits in sharp contrast to the fate of his next release, *That Eye, That Sky* (1994), a mystical outback oddity that stubbornly remained a local film for local people. *Dead Letter Office* (1998) at least made it to the shelves of video shops around the globe. It is set in a shady, neglected nook of the Australian Post Office where all the undelivered mail ends up, a place that the new recruit (Miranda Otto) knows all too well, as it was the final destination of her childhood letters to her absent father. Languorous and sweetly surreal, the film never quite delivered on its intriguing promise, which may also be true of Ruane himself. LH

Death In Brunswick 1991, 109 min
cast Zoe Carides, Sam Neill, John Clarke, Yvonne Lawley, Nico Lathouris, Nicholas Papademitriou *cin* Ellery Ryan

The most successful of Ruane's explorations of marginalia, with characters who inhabit an emotional (and occasionally literal) hinterland. Sam Neill exudes a shabby charisma as the slovenly Carl Fitzgerald, a constant disappointment to his mother who finally gets a job as a cook in a club – where he's attacked by the bouncer, falls for the boss's wife and accidentally kills the kitchen assistant. Off-centre, uneven and unnerving, the narrative of this black comedy shuffles awkwardly and endearingly along, not unlike its unkempt protagonist.

Alan Rudolph
US, 1943–

Alan Rudolph has directed a string of beguiling, idiosyncratic movies – including the multilayered thriller fantasy *Trouble In Mind* (1987), *The Moderns* (1991), set in the art world of 1920s Paris, and the complex character study *Mrs Parker And The Vicious Circle* (1994) – but he has had only one certifiable hit, the sexy, soulful *Choose Me* in 1984. Even arthouse cognoscenti either love him or loathe him – or both; no two film buffs seem to agree whether *Afterglow* (1997) is sublime or just silly, and that goes double for *Equinox* (1992).

A child of the system (his father, Oscar, was a TV director), Rudolph worked his way up through the ranks, making a couple of cheapo horror flicks in the early 1970s. He might have been just another studio hack but for Robert Altman, who took him on as an assistant director for *The Long Goodbye* (1973), *California Split* (1974) and *Nashville* (1975).

When Rudolph went back to directing (with Altman his frequent producer), he realized he had unlearned the Hollywood way.

As writer and director, Rudolph creates a distinctive comic universe that is nearly as populous but more romantic and artificial than Altman's; his playful, poetic scripts glisten with puns, surreal non sequiturs and arch literary conceits. Borrowing ingredients from farce – amorous doublings, mistaken identities and coincidences – Rudolph nevertheless steers his films towards melancholy and regret. He makes movies about real emotions but insists on the artifice surrounding them. They are self-conscious fairy tales for grown-ups, illusions for the disillusioned. In a word (and both connotations may apply): precious. TC

Choose Me 1984, 114 min
cast Genevieve Bujold, Keith Carradine, Lesley Ann Warren, Patrick Bauchau, Rae Dawn Chong *cin* Jan Kiesser *m* Luther Vandross

Romantic complications among the LA demimonde: Eve runs a bar and rents out a room to incognito radio therapist Dr Nancy Love. Both women are much taken with the genuinely strange stranger Mickey, who may or may not be a compulsive liar. The film was made in under a month for just $750,000. With its jazzy nocturnal mood and sexy soul score from Luther Vandross, this is the Rudolph movie that almost everyone gets, and a good starting point for further forays into his work.

Raúl Ruiz
Chile, 1941–

Raúl Ruiz is nothing if not prolific. Between the ages of 17 and 20, he wrote one hundred plays, on a bet. Later in his life he decided to make one hundred films by the time he was 50, and when he achieved that feat, to make more films than all the other Chilean directors combined.

Ruiz started in avant-garde theatre in Chile, worked in Chilean and Mexican television, made a couple of short films, then directed his feature debut. *Tres tristes tigres* (*Three Sad Tigers*, 1968) is an atypically realistic film for a director now known for his strident assaults on all things conventional. A Marxist and confidant of President Allende, Ruiz fled the country after General Pinochet's brutal coup. In France, he made numerous films for television, as well as taking commissions from various festivals, finding work wherever he could get it.

With so many projects comes an inevitable lack of quality control. Ruiz expert Jonathan Rosenbaum admits that the director "doesn't even seem to care whether what he's doing is good or not". And there have been some eye-watering disasters, like his American erotic thriller *Shattered Image* (1998). Even fans admit that most of his pictures are blueprints rather than fully developed films, preferring, like critic Jonathan Romney, to regard his oeuvre as a "permanent work in progress", a jumbled assemblage of recurring themes, images and narrative gambits. Ruiz does everything in his power to rob the cinematic apparatus of its realistic components, employing unreliable narrators, unusual camera filters and cheap special effects, channelling the work of Orson Welles, Luis Buñuel and author Jorge Luis Borges to help him in his anarchic quest.

The sad irony is that even though Ruiz has made so many films, only a very few are available for home entertainment. The best of these are *Genealogies Of A Crime* (1997), *Time Regained* (1999) and *Comedy Of Innocence* (2000), but his earlier work includes some gems too. *The Hypothesis Of The Stolen Painting* (1978) was originally commissioned as a documentary on novelist and philosopher Pierre Klossowski, but when the subject went on holiday, Ruiz reportedly improvised this gnomic drama in which six paintings are reproduced as *tableaux vivants* and an unseen narrator meticulously deciphers their secret codes. Stories are transformed into a labyrinth of digressions in the narratively opaque and visually stunning *Three Crowns Of The Sailor* (1983). And there were more tall tales in *Three Lives And Only One Death* (1996) starring Marcello Mastroianni, times four: in one life he's a professor who leads a double life as a beggar; in another he's a husband held against his will for twenty years by the fairies living in a nearby apartment. Welcome to the world of Raúl Ruiz. LH

Genealogies Of A Crime (Généalogies d'un crime) 1997, 114 min

cast Catherine Deneuve, Michel Piccoli, Melvil Poupaud, Andrzej Seweryn, Bernadette Lafont, Monique Mélinand *cin* Stefan Ivanov *m* Jorge Arriagada

Catherine Deneuve is suitably enigmatic as a lawyer who likes to take on hopeless causes, but has never won a case. In this instance, her project is a young man who allegedly killed his mother. The dead woman was an analyst and would fastidiously record her son's movements when he was a child, concluding when he was only 5 years old that he would grow up to be a killer. In an instance of Ruiz's obsession with mirror images and identity exchanges, Deneuve plays the dead woman in flashback.

Time Regained (Le temps retrouvé) 1999, 162 min

cast Catherine Deneuve, Emmanuelle Béart, Vincent Perez, John Malkovich, Pascal Greggory, Marcello Mazzarella *cin* Ricardo Aronovich *m* Jorge Arriagada

This sensual, dreamy, spellbinding cinematic approximation of the last volume of Marcel Proust's *A la recherche du temps perdu* finds the author lost in recollections of his love for Gilberte, and his encounters with her regal, sexy mother Odette and the decadent sadist Baron De Charlus. To emphasize the fluidity of time and the fallibility of memory, Ruiz moves the furniture woozily around Proust as he lies on his death bed and the narrative darts around with the haphazard logic of memory.

Comedy Of Innocence (Comédie de l'innocence) 2000, 103 min

cast Isabelle Huppert, Jeanne Balibar, Charles Berling, Edith Scob, Nils Hugon, Laure de Clermont-Tonnerre *cin* Jacques Bouquin *m* Jorge Arriagada

The 9-year-old child of a petit-bourgeoisie couple suddenly announces that he's not their son and demands to be taken to his real mother. When his two mothers meet, his "new" mum reveals that he is the reincarnation of her child who drowned two years earlier. Ruiz takes a slight story and masterfully suffuses it with an eerie sense of hypnotic reverie, partly through the use of his trademark tracking shots. This is one of Ruiz's most conventional and linear offerings, but this surprising discipline makes the experience no less unsettling.

Richard Rush
US, 1930–

A maverick talent, Richard Rush was nominated for the best director Oscar for *The Stunt Man* (1980), but was derided for his next – and last – film, the clunky erotic thriller *Color Of Night* (1994). A directors' director, he has attracted the admiration of an unlikely collection of big names: Ingmar Bergman called the campus comedy *Getting Straight* (1970) "the best American film of the decade", Stanley Kubrick raved about the influential, splenetic buddy cop movie *Freebie And The Bean* (1974), and François Truffaut loved *The Stunt Man*. Nevertheless, despite his obvious aspiration to entertain, Rush's mainstream career has stuttered along haphazardly. He made six films in 24 months in 1967–68, including *Hell's Angels On Wheels*, with Jack Nicholson, and *The Fickle Finger Of Fate*, with Tab Hunter, but then just four more features over the next three decades. He left the 1990 Mel Gibson production *Air America* (which he wrote).

One of the first graduates from UCLA's film programme, Rush founded a company making advertisements and industrial films, then sold up to write and direct *Too Soon To Love* (1960), which he managed to sell to UIP, and which featured Jack Nicholson's second screen performance. Riding the drive-in boom, Rush made half a dozen "youth pictures" in the 1960s. His own perspective on the hippie movement may be garnered from *Getting Straight*, in which Elliott Gould plays a graduate student caught up in the maelstrom and madness of the times. Rush claims, with cinematographer Laszlo Kovacs, to have invented "rack focus" in this period (pulling focus from foreground to background without changing the frame). But although there are inspired touches in many of his films, only *The Stunt Man* sustains the invention and intelligence of which Rush was capable. TC

The Stunt Man 1980, 131 min

cast Peter O'Toole, Steve Railsback, Barbara Hershey, Allen Garfield, Alex Rocco, Sharon Farrell, Adam Roarke *cin* Mario Tosi *m* Dominic Frontière

One of the most exhilarating and audacious movie-movies, *The Stunt Man* was a long-cherished project based on a novel by Paul Brodeur. It's the story of a Vietnam deserter who escapes arrest and falls in with a film crew. Director Eli Cross (Peter O'Toole) knows a pawn when he sees one and gives him a job as a stunt man. In true dream-factory fashion he ends up in bed with the leading lady (Hershey). A whirligig, carnivalesque comedy, *The Stunt Man* slips in serious reflections on manipulation and artifice amid a plethora of brilliantly choreographed action sequences.

David O. Russell
US, 1958–

The inhabitants of David O. Russell's excitable comedies plunge into bewildering swamps of addled moral confusion, and must talk or fight their way out. Like his contemporaries Spike Jonze and Charlie Kaufman, Russell wagers that the most refined medium for picking apart the big quandaries – the fiction of the self, the definition of necessity and the possibility of leading a meaningful life – is the wacky comedy, and he has thus far located ample humour in such unlikely material as incest, war and existential dread.

Russell spent his twenties as a labour and literacy activist in Nicaragua and the American northeast. His first film, *Boston To Panama* (1985), was a short video documentary about Central American immigrants in Boston, where he taught English as a second language. His debut feature, *Spanking The Monkey* (1994), concerned the increasingly fraught and sordid relationship between a college student and his injured mother. Shot for an initial cost of about $80,000, this black-comic film remains one of the unlikeliest winners of the Audience Award in Sundance history. Fractious family dynamics also powered the delightfully unhinged *Flirting With Disaster* (1996), in which adoptee and new father Ben Stiller crisscrosses the US in search of his birth parents.

Russell's next two films not only harnessed the slapstick, absurdist energies of *Flirting With Disaster*, but also revealed Russell's political acumen. In *Three Kings* (1999), a cynical heist plot engineered by a crew of American soldiers in the first Gulf War becomes a humanitarian rescue mission. And the unclassifiable *I Heart Huckabees* (2004) – centred on an earnest environmental activist whom Russell based on his younger self – sweats bullets of big ideas and big emotions, pepped up by existential anxiety, Zen dilemmas and George W. Bush-era liberal despondency. JW

Spanking The Monkey 1994, 100 min

cast Jeremy Davies, Alberta Watson, Carla Gallo, Benjamin Hendrickson *cin* Michael Mayers *m* David Carbonara

Bullied by his sleazy dad and stupid friends, a frustrated pre-med student (Jeremy Davies) gets stuck at home for the summer playing nursemaid to his sullen yet sultry mum (Alberta Watson), who has a broken foot and her own smothered ambitions to stew over. Mother and son share a seething, claustrophobic frustration that boils over into proscribed lust and morning-after revulsion in Russell's audacious debut, still his darkest and most studiously misanthropic film to date.

Flirting With Disaster 1996, 92 min

cast Ben Stiller, Patricia Arquette, Téa Leoni, Mary Tyler Moore, George Segal, Alan Alda, Lily Tomlin *cin* Eric A. Edwards *m* Stephen Endelman

"The mystery of your unknown self is about to unfold": so adoption adviser Tina (Téa Leoni) promises adoptee and new father Mel (Ben Stiller) at the start of Russell's splendid screwball comedy, which ensures that Mel's cross-country identity investigation is thwarted at every possible turn. Disaster spills over with hilarious talk and outlandish incident, reaching its delirious climax with an LSD-spiked frenzy of dinner-table catastrophe and much switching of spouses and cars.

Three Kings 1999, 115 min

cast George Clooney, Mark Wahlberg, Ice Cube, Nora Dunn, Jamie Kennedy, Mykelti Williamson *cin* Newton Thomas Siegel *m* Carter Burwell

After they find a treasure map protruding from an Iraqi captive's ass, Desert Storm soldiers George Clooney, Mark Wahlberg and Ice Cube go in search of the loot and stumble through the ugly aftermath of the war they've ostensibly finished fighting. This dark, morally inquisitive comedy was the first major American studio release to question seriously the motivations behind the first American invasion of Iraq and the deadly chaos left in victory's wake.

Ken Russell
UK, 1927–

Ken Russell's contribution to British cinema is both unique and delirious. The controversial showman yoked the power of classical music to baroque, sensational images in ways that would suggest he has some form of cinematic synaesthesia. It's as if Russell has no conscious filter, no internal mechanism for knowing which associations work and which don't – for instance, realizing that having Roger Daltrey ride the back of a twelve-foot phallus in *Lisztomania* (1976) is not a good idea.

Russell heard his first piece of classical music on the radio while recovering from a nervous breakdown in his early twenties. "With music came pictures, dream images when I closed my eyes", the director has revealed. Duly inspired and fully recovered, he studied ballet, became a still photographer, and made a couple of short films – *Peepshow* (1956) and *Amelia And The Angel* (1957) – which earned him a place as a director on the BBC's legendary arts programme, *Monitor*. Here he made numerous films on

R

a variety of subjects, in particular uniting music and imagery in a series of iconoclastic documentaries on Elgar, Debussy, Bartok, Isadora Duncan and Richard Strauss. His first three features, *French Dressing* (1964), *Billion Dollar Brain* (1967) and *Women In Love* (1969) were partly means to an end: to produce a biopic of Tchaikovsky. He eventually got to make *The Music Lovers* (1971) when he pitched the film to an American studio as "the story of a homosexual who falls in love with a nymphomaniac". *Mahler* (1974) and *Lisztomania* continued in the same vein, translating the lives of composers into outré tableaux peopled by nuns, Nazis, Jesus Christ and Charlie Chaplin. He maintained his assault on the musical genre with the unexpectedly charming Busby Berkeley homage, *The Boyfriend* (1971) and audacious, taste-free rock opera *Tommy* (1975).

Easily Britain's most infamous director, Russell's reputation as an "appalling talent" was sustained by his contentious masterpiece *The Devils* (1971) and his sanguine biopic of sculptor Henri Gaudier-Brzeska, *Savage Messiah* (1972). After the clattering disappointment of *Valentino* (1977), the 1980s were not kind to Russell. *Altered States* (1980), starring William Hurt as a hallucinating scientist, was followed by the sex satire *Crimes Of Passion* (1984), the English romantics romp *Gothic* (1986), the horror *Lair Of The White Worm* (1988) and the D.H. Lawrence adaptation *The Rainbow* (1989). All these films had their ecstatic moments, but were defeated by the industry's new puritanical insistence on linear narrative and realistic characters, neither of which were Russell's strong points. *Whore* (1991) was his last film to get a real cinematic release, and latterly he's been making films on a camcorder with dolls, toys and friends in his New Forest studio, which also doubles as his conservatory. LH

Women In Love 1969, 130 min
cast Alan Bates, Oliver Reed, Glenda Jackson, Jennie Linden, Eleanor Bron, Alan Webb, Vladek Sheybal *cin* Billy Williams *m* Georges Delerue

Russell claimed never to have heard of D.H. Lawrence when he was asked by United Artists to direct this adaptation, but he displays a clear kinship with the author in his devotion to earthy lusts and English landscapes. Atavistic and lyrical, the rest of the film has been overshadowed by Oliver Reed and Alan Bates' famous naked wrestling bout in the warm glow of an open fire.

The Music Lovers 1971, 123 min
cast Richard Chamberlain, Glenda Jackson, Christopher Gable, Max Adrian, Izabella Telezynska *cin* Douglas Slocombe *m* Tchaikovsky

Russell's Tchaikovsky biopic focuses on the dysfunctional relationship between the troubled homosexual composer (Richard Chamberlain) and his starstruck, highly sexed wife (Glenda Jackson). The director more than matches Tchaikovsky's heart-on-sleeve music with some wonderfully over-the-top set pieces, including the moment when the pianist Rubinstein (Max Adrian) trashes the piano concerto that Tchaikovsky has just performed, as the composer's patroness (Izabella Telezynska) gazes impassively from the hall balcony.

The Devils 1971, 111 min
cast Vanessa Redgrave, Oliver Reed, Dudley Sutton, Max Adrian, Gemma Jones, Murray Melvin *cin* David Watkin *m* Peter Maxwell Davies

In set designer Derek Jarman's clinical vision of the convent of Loudon, reforming priest Oliver Reed is put on trial and tortured on the rack by Christopher Logue's Cardinal Richelieu against a backdrop of demented, masturbating nuns whose hysteria is matched only by Russell's febrile imagination. A four-minute sequence where naked, hysterical nuns rape a statue of Christ was banned by British censors, but even the sanitized version was condemned by critic Alexander Walker as "monstrously indecent" and when the two met on a television debate, Russell famously attacked Walker with a rolled-up newspaper.

Mahler 1974, 115 min
cast Robert Powell, Georgina Hale, Lee Montague, Miriam Karlin, Rosalie Crutchley, Gary Rich *cin* Dick Bush

It was Ken Russell's great misfortune to be born in Britain. If he had been born anywhere else in Europe, he probably would have been heralded as the rightful heir to Fellini, or at least as a cult auteur whose faults would have been forgiven for his idiosyncratic and unique contribution to the evolution of cinema. *Mahler* is a classic example with its Nazi nuns, sacrilegious crucifixion scene and actress Georgina Hale emerging fully formed from a cocoon. Even if it doesn't all quite work, it's at least a welcome tonic to the dyspeptic realism of traditional British cinema.

The priest Mignon (Murray Melvin) keeps a watchful eye on the neurotic nuns – one of the more restrained moments from *The Devils*.

Gene Saks
US, 1921–

A former actor who still occasionally appears in films – he can be spotted in Woody Allen's *Deconstructing Harry* (1997) – Gene Saks began directing on Broadway in 1963, and his films are mostly stage adaptations. His film debut, *Barefoot In The Park* (1967), was based on a Neil Simon comedy, and initiated a long partnership with the playwright. Putting earnest young Robert Redford in a New York apartment with nubile Jane Fonda toyed with the possibilities of the sexual revolution, but the film settled instead for comfy marital habit. However, the same year's hugely successful Jack Lemmon-Walter Matthau comedy, *The Odd Couple*, was a joyously philosophical riposte to the generation gap.

Matthau also starred in *Cactus Flower* (1969), seeming to be perplexed by modern sexual mores as he tried to seduce kooky, Oscar-winning Goldie Hawn. *Last Of The Red Hot Lovers* (1972) showcased fine performances from Alan Arkin (as a fortysomething restaurateur wanting a fling) and Sally Kellerman, but moved along as predictably as a primetime television show. *Brighton Beach Memoirs* (1986), inspired by Simon's Brooklyn childhood, had its decent moments, but wasn't as touching as it ought to have been, and neither was *A Fine Romance* (aka *Tchin Tchin* or *A Touch Of Adultery*, 1991), which unusually teamed Julie Andrews and Marcello Mastroianni. A middle-class Jewish sensibility pervades Saks's oeuvre, which at its best is a showpiece for comic actors. RA

The Odd Couple 1967, 105 min
cast Jack Lemmon, Walter Matthau, John Fiedler, Herbert Edelman, David Sheiner, Larry Haines *cin* Robert B. Hauser *m* Neal Hefti

The rapport between fastidious Jack Lemmon and slob Walter Matthau is at the heart of this comedy. The pair play out the bachelor dream of all-night poker, while battling like your favourite aunt and uncle over beer on the rug. It occasionally feels like the pilot to the long-running TV series that followed, but Lemmon and Matthau still shine as one of the great double acts of American comedy.

Walter Salles
Brazil, 1956–

One of the impressive generation of Latin-American directors who began to win an international reputation in the late 1990s (others include Fernando Meirelles, Alejandro Gonzáles Iñárritu and Alfonso Cuarón), Walter Salles is a shrewd, talented, highly articulate filmmaker. His best work to date has grown out of a desire to explore and understand Brazilian society and national identity. The son of a diplomat, Salles spent many formative years outside Brazil, and it will be interesting to see if he can make "international" films without sacrificing his edge.

Salles began in the documentary field, spending ten years making films for Brazilian and European television. He made an inauspicious fiction debut with the thriller *Exposure* (1991). Teaming with writer-director Daniela Thomas, he found his feet with two hybrid thrillers, *A Foreign Land* (1996) and *Midnight* (1998). Both mixed genre stylization with social realism, reflecting the gaping disparities across Brazilian society through parallel stories of men and women. For some these represent Salles's best work.

Central Station (1998), a solo effort, made Salles's name on the festival and arthouse circuits. It focused on the relationship between Dora, a retired schoolteacher, and Josué, a 9-year-old boy who needs her help to find his father in the Brazilian interior. The scenario is reminiscent of Italian neo-realism, and Salles allowed enough time during shooting to "discover" the film as they went along. A similar strategy produced the strongest material in his handsome Che Guevara biopic *The Motorcycle Diaries* (2004). In between, he directed the visually stunning, self-consciously mythic vendetta piece *Behind The Sun* (2001). *Dark Water* (2005) was a strange choice for his first English-language Hollywood film, a muted, thoughtful remake of Hideo Nakata's clammy shocker that disappointed horror fans. TC

Central Station (Central do Brasil) 1998, 113 min
cast Fernanda Montenegro, Vinícius de Oliveira, Marilia Pêra, Soia Lira, Othon Bastos *cin* Walter Carvalho *m* Jacques Morelenbaum, Antônio Pinto

A miraculously unsentimental movie about a young boy who turns to the only person he knows in Rio after his (illiterate) mother is killed in an accident: the woman who wrote a letter to his father on her behalf. Dora (Montenegro) wants none of him – she never even posts the letters she writes for the peasants – but is ultimately guilt-tripped into a road journey across the country. Along the way, she becomes almost human again.

The Motorcycle Diaries (Diarios de motocicleta) 2004, 126 min
cast Gael García Bernal, Rodrigo de la Serna, Mía Maestro, Mercedes Morán, Lucas Oro, Jean-Pierre Noher *cin* Eric Gautier *m* Gustavo Santaolalla

Based on the memoirs of Ernesto "Che" Guevara and Alberto Granada, who as young men in 1952 set out from Buenos Aires to travel the length of South America – more than 8000km – on a 1939 Norton 500 motorcycle. Improvised on the road, *The Motorcycle Diaries* is a spirited journey which treats the revolutionary icon as an idealistic, romantic young medical student, an easy rider politicized by what he sees en route. It's clearly a prestige film made for mass consumption, but honourably so.

Gabriele Salvatores
Italy, 1950–

After decades of the highest achievement, Italian cinema slumped into mediocrity in the 1980s and 90s. Gabriele Salvatores is one of the better local filmmakers of this era, his predilection for middlebrow literary adaptations somewhat offset by adventurous aesthetic choices. Salvatores came to prominence as a theatre director at the Teatro dell'Elfo in Milan, only making a definitive break for the cinema in 1989, with *Marrakech Express*. *Mediterraneo* (1991) won the Oscar for best foreign film for its schmaltzy account of eight bumbling Italian soldiers washed up on a Greek island during World War II. *Puerto escondido* (1992) was a Mexican crime drama, and had a bit more edge. *Teeth* (2000) was a luridly styled comic nightmare about a middle-aged man with huge teeth (Salvatores dreamed this one up himself). *I'm Not Scared* (2003) was a more audience-friendly proposition, and his first film in a decade to earn distribution in the US. In *Quo Vadis, Baby?* (2005) Salvatores stepped into *film noir* territory, with a tale of a hard-drinking fortysomething female private detective investigating her sister's suicide. TC

I'm Not Scared (Io non ho paura) 2003, 108 min
cast Giuseppe Cristiano, Mattia Di Pierro, Adriano Conserva, Fabio Tetta, Giulia Matturo *cin* Italo Petriccione *m* Ezio Bosso

Southern Italy, summer. A boy happens across another child, the hostage in a kidnapping, who is chained up in a cave on an old, disused farm. They strike up a friendship, but Michele is not sure how best to help or who can be trusted. With its bold primary colours and gothic atmospherics, this adaptation of Niccolò Ammaniti's best-selling novel is clearly influenced by child's-eye reveries *The Night Of The Hunter* (1955) and *To Kill A Mockingbird* (1962).

Mark Sandrich
US, 1900–45

Mark Sandrich was adept at keeping the banter sharp, no matter how unlikely his Hollywood musical comedies got. From 1927 he made countless comedy shorts, including such Lupino Lane two-reelers as *Monty Of The Mounted* (1927) and *Hello Sailor* (1927), before making his feature debut with *Runaway Girls* (1928). After the arrival of sound interrupted his career, Sandrich returned to shorts. *So This Is Harris!* (1932), which he co-wrote as well as directed, chronicled a risqué golf course rivalry that presaged the japery of Fred Astaire and Edward Everett Horton, and won an Academy Award for best comedy short.

Talking his way back into features, the director was soon doing well with the Fred Astaire-Ginger Rogers RKO musical cycle. Played out against Van Nest Polglase's Art Deco-inspired sets and timed to Astaire and Hermes Pan's deft dance routines, these comedies of mistaken identity and romantic by-play were propelled by the charm of their two stars and the lyricism of Irving Berlin, George Gershwin and Jerome Kern's songbooks. *The Gay Divorcee* (1934), *Top Hat* (1935), *Follow The Fleet* (1936), *Shall We Dance* (1937) and *Carefree* (1938) were all scintillating episodes in a legendary screen partnership. In *Holiday Inn* (1942), Sandrich teamed Astaire and Bing Crosby for the first time and introduced Berlin's popular, Oscar-winning hit "White Christmas", by which time the director was also serving as his own producer.

The romantic flag-waver *So Proudly We Hail* (1943) starred Claudette Colbert, Paulette Goddard and Veronica Lake as noble nurses, and in the follow-up, *I Love A Soldier* (1944), Goddard alternated between welding and suffering. Sandrich had just started work on the musical *Blue Skies* (1946) when he died of a heart attack, but Stuart Heisler took over the production, which saw Astaire and Crosby vying for Joan Caulfield to some great Berlin tunes. RA

Top Hat 1935, 100 min, b/w
cast Fred Astaire, Ginger Rogers, Edward Everett Horton, Erik Rhodes, Eric Blore, Helen Broderick, Thomas Ricketts *cin* David Abel *m* Irving Berlin

Propelled by the absurd prospect of Fred Astaire's musical showman chasing Ginger Rogers' fashion model across Europe in order to persuade her that he is not married,

The charming onscreen magic of Ginger Rogers and Fred Astaire in *Top Hat*.

festival. Sasanatieng continued in kitsch mode with the disappointing *Citizen Dog* (2005), a hyper-realistic delirium of colours, musical numbers and digital effects which tried to do for Bangkok what Jean-Pierre Jeunet's *Amélie* (2001) did for Paris. The aptly titled *The Unseeable* (2006) has yet to receive significant exposure outside Thailand. LH

Tears Of The Black Tiger
2000, 101 min

cast Chartchai Ngamsan, Stella Malucchi, Supakorn Kitsuwon, Arawat Ruangvuth *cin* Nattawut Kittikhun *m* Amornbhong Methakunavudh

The opening shot of the heroine's supersaturated pink dress in a world starved of colour sets the postmodern, flamboyant tone for this tale of Black Tiger, a sensitive gunslinger destined never to find happiness with his childhood love. The candy-coloured kitsch and ironic nods to classic Thai Westerns are regularly and incongruously punctuated by scenes of slow-motion carnage set against Dalí-esque backdrops that may well have given Douglas Sirk pause.

this is as deft and classy as the song-and-dance series gets. Edward Everett Horton, Erik Rhodes and the wonderful Eric Blore provide able support as equally absurd stooges. Blessed with unforgettable Irving Berlin tunes – "Cheek To Cheek", "Isn't This A Lovely Day?" – *Top Hat* smashed all box-office records and was pure screen magic.

Wisit Sasanatieng
Thailand, 1964–

Wisit Sasanatieng is the leading light of New Thai Cinema. Dormant since the 1980s, the local film industry was reinvigorated when he wrote the 1950s crime drama *Dang Bireley And The Young Gangsters* (1997). Directed by old college friend Nonzee Nimibutr, it exceeded all previous domestic box-office tallies. The duo then proceeded to surpass their own record with their next collaboration, *Nang Nak* (1999), a ghost story about a soldier who returns from service to live with his dead wife. The newly energized industry made its mark on international cinema with films by the Oxide brothers and Pen-ek Ratanaruang, and while Sasanatieng's own directorial debut, *Tears Of The Black Tiger* (2000), fared badly in the domestic market, it travelled well. A cult hit at Cannes, it was the first Thai film ever to be shown at the

Peter Sasdy
Hungary, 1935–

Peter Sasdy came to prominence with his BBC adaptation of Isaac Asimov's *The Caves Of Steel* (1964). Its cinematic flair brought him to the attention of Hammer Films, who recruited him to direct *Taste The Blood Of Dracula* (1970), *Countess Dracula* (1971), starring an on-form Ingrid Pitt, and *Hands Of The Ripper* (1971). A perfectionist who had a hard time within the Hammer organization, he directed the only movie to be made under the banner of Christopher Lee's Charlemagne Productions, *Nothing But The Night* (1972). *Doomwatch* (1972), which was adapted from a BBC series, *I Don't Want To Be Born* (aka *The Devil Within Her*, 1975), in which Joan Collins gave birth to a demonic baby, and *Welcome To Blood City* (1977) paled in comparison to Sasdy's small-screen adaptation of Nigel Kneale's *The Stone Tape* (1972), which is considered one of the scariest TV programmes ever made. Similarly, his late film projects, such as the Harold Robbins adaptation *The Lonely Lady* (1982), compared poorly with his extensive and varied television work. AJ

S

Taste The Blood Of Dracula 1970, 95 min

cast Christopher Lee, Ralph Bates, Linda Hayden, Geoffrey Keen, Gwen Watford, Peter Sallis *cin* Arthur Grant *m* James Bernard

Three elderly satanists bring Dracula back to life and soon come to regret having done so. This Prince of Darkness tale is well above average, skilfully unravelling Victorian society to expose the hypocrisy within. As always, Christopher Lee plays the bloodthirsty count.

Hands Of The Ripper 1971, 85 min

cast Eric Porter, Angharad Rees, Jane Merrow, Keith Bell, Derek Godfrey, Dora Bryan, Marjorie Rhodes *cin* Kenneth Talbot *m* Christopher Gunning

A psychiatrist (Eric Porter) takes an interest in the case of Jack the Ripper's daughter (Angharad Rees), a disturbed young woman who appears to be following in her father's murderous footsteps. *Hands Of The Ripper* is classic 1970s Hammer horror – graphic and truly scary.

Carlos Saura

Spain, 1932–

Carlos Saura is the grand old man of Spanish cinema and a prime example of how severe restrictions can bring out the art and cunning in a film director, or as Czech director Jirí Menzel puts it, "oppression stimulates". Saura's films were often packed with metaphors and a magic realist blur of truth and fantasy. A left-wing filmmaker working under the Franco regime, the ex-still photographer defied the fascist dictator's apparatchiks through a combination of guile and symbolism, writing one script for the state censors and one for the actors. It was a lesson he learned early; his provocative neo-realist-influenced study of delinquency, *Los golfos* (*The Hooligans*, 1959), received excited interest at Cannes in 1960, prompting the Francoists to withhold the film for two years.

The stunning apotheosis of this devious methodology was *The Hunt* (1966) in which three Francoists embark on a rabbit hunt on the old killing fields of the Civil War, and are gradually overwhelmed by a sense of guilt and impending bloodshed. And when his *The Garden Of Delights* (1970) was banned domestically, Saura sneaked a print out of the country and showed it at the New York Film Festival, where it attracted so much critical attention that the Spanish authorities were embarrassed into releasing it at home. A corrosive satire about a businessman who's forgotten the number to his Swiss bank account, it starred his then-wife and muse, Geraldine Chaplin. Together they made nine films, including the award-winning *Peppermint frappé* (1967) and *Cousin Angelica* (1974). The collaboration reached its zenith with *Cría cuervos* (*Raise Ravens*, 1976), which was released a year after the death of Franco. That momentous event was partly responsible for a sea change in Saura's style: it saw an end to his ingenu-

ous allegory and political commitment and, for some critics, to his extraordinary talent.

Of all his post-Franco films, only *¡Ay, Carmela!* (1990) touched upon the history of the Spanish Civil War, while his most famous works have been the trilogy of hermetically sealed musicals starring dancer and choreographer Antonio Gades: *Blood Wedding* (1981), *Carmen* (1983) and *El amor brujo* (*Love, The Magician*, 1986). Saura says he makes musicals because the genre encourages experiment and artifice, and he's also made several lesser examples of the form, including *Sevillanas* (1992), *Flamenco* (1995) and *Tango* (1998). He has, though, experimented with other forms, flirting with comedy in *Mama Turns 100* (1979), neo-realism in *Deprisa, deprisa* (1980), Freudian drama in *Sweet Hours* (1982), historical epic in *El Dorado* (1990) and biopic in *Goya In Bordeaux* (1999). LH

Cría cuervos (Raise Ravens) 1976, 110 min

cast Geraldine Chaplin, Ana Torrent, Conchi Perez, Maite Sanchez, Héctor Alterio, Germán Cobos *cin* Teo Escamilla *m* Federico Mompoll

The past and present slowly merge in this hypnotic, atmospheric and allegorical portrait of stolen innocence. In a typical Saura blur, Geraldine Chaplin plays both the ghost of her mother and her own adult daughter – her Ana is haunted by childhood memories of a distant father she came to loathe, and the summer she spent with her sisters in the care of an aunt after his heart attack.

Carmen 1983, 101 min

cast Antonio Gades, Laura del Sol, Paco de Lucía, Cristina Hoyos, Juan Antonio Jimenez *cin* Teodoro Escamilla *m* Paco de Lucía

This art/life amalgam starts out as a documentary on the rehearsals for a flamenco version of *Carmen*. However, Saura's mode of address subtly alters as the production's director, played by Antonio Gades, falls for the leading dancer, also called Carmen, and events on and off stage begin their own intimate dance, mirroring each other's movements until real life becomes as melodramatic as Bizet's fabled opera.

¡Ay, Carmela! 1990, 103 min

cast Carmen Maura, Andres Pajares, Gabino Diego, Maurizio De Razza, Miguel A. Rellan, Edward Zentara *cin* José Luis Alacane *m* Alejandro Massó

Almodóvar's muse Carmen Maura is in fine fettle as the feisty, blousy Carmela, who forms a vaudevillian act with her husband and travels the country during the Civil War, entertaining Republican soldiers. When they are caught by nationalist troops, they have to swear allegiance to Franco and entertain the opposition to escape punishment.

Claude Sautet

France, 1924–2000

Claude Sautet is modern cinema's greatest miniaturist. A former social worker and sometime music critic, he attended the French film school IDHEC in the late 1940s. After producing and writing for television, he directed an experimental short before

S

making his name as a screenwriter and script doctor, collaborating on such films as Georges Franju's *Eyes Without A Face* (1960) and Jacques Deray's gangster classic *Borsalino* (1970). Sautet's early works as a director tended towards genre exercises – *The Big Risk* (1960), *Guns For The Dictator* (1965) – while a feeling for genre persists across his oeuvre.

Always a script collaborator as well as a director, Sautet began a series of astutely observed character studies in the early 1970s that recalled in their tact and classical *mise en scène* a latter-day Jacques Becker. *Les choses de la vie (The Things Of Life*, 1969) revolved around Michel Piccoli's portrait of midlife banality, with Sautet advancing this story of bourgeois adultery through a measured observation of psychology and environment. *César et Rosalie* (1972) threatened to become swamped in glossy Claude Lelouch aesthetics, filtering the pain and regret of an eternal triangle through Yves Montand and Romy Schneider's sensitive performances. *Mado* (1976) focused on the tense, shifting dynamics between a prostitute and her businessman client against the backdrop of financial intrigue.

The father and son drama, *Un mauvais fils (A Bad Son*, 1980), recalled the underworld milieu of early Sautet fims, while its accumulation of detail now seems typical of the director's later work. Awash with the modulations of a Ravel trio, *Un coeur en hiver (A Heart In Winter*, 1992) was a patient examination of relationships that paid off in international arthouse cachet. *Nelly et Monsieur Arnaud* (1995) paired Michel Serrault and Emmanuelle Béart as an elderly writer and his typist, carefully charting the evolving rapport to its bitter outcome. Sautet's work kept alive the grace and humility of the French *cinéma d'intime*. RA

Un coeur en hiver (A Heart In Winter) 1992, 104 min

cast Daniel Auteuil, Emmanuelle Béart, André Dussollier, Elisabeth Bourgine, Brigitte Catillon, Myriam Boyer *cin* Yves Angelo *m* Philippe Sarde

A romantic triangle in all but name, this polished account of a couple teetering on the brink of love pits the opacity of Daniel Auteuil's reclusive violin restorer against the impulsiveness of Emmanuelle Béart's brilliant young soloist. The result is an absorbing analysis of missed opportunities and lives passing by.

Victor Saville
UK, 1897–1979

An important producer and writer, Victor Saville also had a directing career that peaked with a set of classic British 1930s entertainments. Displaying a particularly deft hand with his female stars – ranging from Jessie Matthews via Madeleine Carroll to Rita Hayworth – he also showed a propensity for making socially aware films often based on popular novels.

His first major directing credit was for the silent comedy *The Arcadians* (1927) before he moved into sound with the hugely successful British spy thriller *The W Plan* (1930). In the early 1930s, Saville made films for the Gaumont-British studios, headed by his old colleague Michael Balcon. Though 1933's *I Was A Spy* didn't achieve the accolades of *The W Plan*, the director showed his versatility with the feisty feminist tale of a Lancashire mill town *Hindle Wakes* (1931); J.B. Priestley's theatrical drama *The Good Companions* (1933); and the musicals *Evergreen* (1933) and *First A Girl* (1935), starring Jessie Matthews. After co-directing the prestige costume drama *The Dictator* (1935) for independent producer Ludovico Toeplitz, he set up his own company, making films for Alexander Korda to distribute. He went on to direct a handful of movies, including the spy drama *Dark Journey* (1937) and Winifred Holtby's *South Riding* (1938), a scathing and passionate critique of social conditions in Britain, before giving up the director's chair in the late 1930s in favour of producing.

With *The Citadel* (1938), based on a novel by A.J. Cronin, and *Goodbye, Mr Chips* (1939), based on a novel by James Hilton, under his producer's belt, Saville, who was now based in the US, returned to directing. Highlights of his later directorial career include the musical *Tonight And Every Night* (1945) with Rita Hayworth, and big-budget literary adaptations such as A.J. Cronin's sentimental *The Green Years* (1946) and Rudyard Kipling's *Kim* (1950). His directorial career ended with the limp amnesiac drama *The Long Wait* (1954) and the equally poor biblical epic *The Silver Chalice* (1955).

Respected for his professionalism, versatility and his deft ability to weave social issues into polished entertainments, Saville had the distinction of being one of a select handful of British director-producers to make it within the studio system. JR

The Good Companions 1933, 113 min, b/w

cast Jessie Matthews, Edmund Gwenn, Mary Glynne, John Gielgud, Percy Parsons *cin* Bernard Knowles *m* George Posford, Douglas Furber

Having met inadvertently, an unlikely trio comprising a sacked millworker (Edmund Gwenn), young schoolteacher (John Gielgud) and shy spinster (Mary Glynn) decide to throw in their lot with a band of down-at-heel travelling entertainers, called The Dinky-Doos. Changing their name to "The Good Companions", the group go from strength to strength thanks to the effervescent talents of the delightful Susie Dean (Jessie Matthews). A classic backstage musical, memorable – among much else – for the sound of Gielgud's clipped tones asking, "What's a Dinky-Doo?"

First A Girl 1935, 80 min, b/w

cast Jessie Matthews, Sonny Hale, Anna Lee, Griffith Jones, Alfred Drayton, Constance Godridge *cin* Glen MacWilliams *m* Louis Levy

A stage-struck woman becomes a female impersonator (Jessie Matthews cross-dressing as a man who is cross-dressing as a woman!), but romantic complications follow. The risqué sexual ambiguity, infectious song-and-dance

S

routines and hilariously catastrophic stage-show finale make it unmissable. A chic remake of Reinhold Schünzel's *Victor und Victoria* (1933), which Blake Edwards bawdily remade as *Victor/Victoria* starring Julie Andrews in 1982.

John Sayles
US, 1950–

John Sayles reveals America in all its social and cultural variety. And while it is simplistic to call his work educational, the veracity and seriousness of his films encourage a more comprehensive outlook in the spectator. Before moving into filmmaking, Sayles held a number of jobs and gained a working knowledge of real people, bringing a rare behavioural density to his films. His role as a screenwriter-for-hire on a variety of generic offerings – Roger Corman's *Battle Beyond The Stars* (1980), Joe Dante's *The Howling* (1981), Bill Forsyth's *Breaking In* (1989) and as script doctor on *Apollo 13* (1995) and *The Mummy* (1999) – has helped fund his independent directorial projects. Aside from writing, directing and editing, he has also taken minor roles in his own films and those of his contemporaries Spike Lee and Jonathan Demme. Sayles's writing experience – his novel *Union Dues* (1977) received a National Book Award nomination – also introduced a literary quality to his work, fleshing out his regional portraits, if occasionally leaving potential characters dormant.

Sayles began working in genre movies, writing scripts for Roger Corman from 1977, which enabled him to make his directorial debut, *The Return Of The Secaucus Seven*, in 1979. Focusing on a group of 1960s radicals coming of age as the New Right ascended, *Secaucus Seven* became a festival hit, and could be seen as the model for Lawrence Kasdan's *The Big Chill* (1983). Self-discovery was also the theme of *Lianna* (1983), which examined, with pain and humour, a married woman's realization that she loves another woman.

Appearing as the "Brat Pack'" cycle brought fresh impetus to the teen movie, *Baby It's You* (1983) explored issues of cultural assimilation through an affair between a Jewish student (Rosanna Arquette) and a dapper Italian-American (Vincent Spano). Shot in dirty light by Sayles's regular cinematographer Haskell Wexler, *Matewan* (1987) charted in bloody detail a 1920s West Virginia labour dispute. Again, Sayles focused on the multicultural implications, rather than the class war, as migrant workers fought for equal rights.

The Chicago White Sox throwing the 1919 baseball World Series at the behest of big business and the Mob was the event that marked the end of American innocence in Sayles's eyes, and he dramatized this fall from grace in 1988's *Eight Men Out*. Three years later, *City Of Hope* dissected the sociopolitical implications behind a New Jersey city facing redevelopment, and the following year, Sayles broadened his fan base with *Passion Fish* (1992), which related in tragicomic detail a New York soap star's paraplegia following an accident.

With the Irish fairy tale *The Secret Of Roan Inish* (1993), the director became heir to the Robert Flaherty school of poetic documentary. Two years later, *Lone Star* presented a rich portrait of Texan border politics. The investigative *Men With Guns* (1997) went south of the border, opting for Spanish and Mayan dialogue. Starting out in familiar territory as a small-scale drama set in an Alaskan town, *Limbo* (1999) unexpectedly transforms into a thriller played out against the stark backdrop of a remote inlet; it was one of Sayles's less successful films. *Sunshine State* (2002) presented the arrival of developers at a Florida resort as a force of nature in a rapacious world. Based on his own short story, *Casa de los babys* (2003) featured Sayles's typically intelligent female roles, as three women venture to South America in search of babies to adopt. The portrayal of political intrigue at a Colorado gubernatorial campaign in 2004's *Silver City* struck a nerve during the bitter presidential contest that same year.

For an American cinematic tradition besotted with mavericks but constrained by corporations, Sayles's oeuvre sets an example of genuine independence. RA

City Of Hope 1991, 130 min
cast Vincent Spano, Joe Morton, Tony Lo Bianco, Barbara Williams, Stephen Mendillo, Chris Cooper *cin* Robert Richardson *m* Mason Daring

John Sayles's modern American epic dexterously orchestrates multiple story strands and draws compelling performances from his strong, unstarry ensemble cast. Taking the political and personal temperature of a fictitious New Jersey community on the edge of municipal disintegration, Sayles still succeeds in highlighting the individual.

Lone Star 1995, 135 min
cast Chris Cooper, Elizabeth Peña, Joe Morton, Matthew McConaughey, Kris Kristofferson, Stephen Mendillo *cin* Stuart Dryburgh *m* Mason Daring

After a skeleton is dug up on the edge of town, sheriff Chris Cooper is forced to reassess the events that led to the killing, uncovering resentments that fracture his Texan town racially and politically. Written with vernacular verve and shot with a fine sense of widescreen space by cinematographer Stuart Dryburgh, Sayles's screenplay received an Oscar nomination.

Sunshine State 2002, 141 min
cast Edie Falco, Jane Alexander, Ralph Waite, Angela Bassett, James McDaniel, Mary Alice *cin* Patrick Cady *m* Mason Daring

Whilst evoking Altman's multi-handed multi-stranded worlds, Sayles manages to sidestep any actorly showmanship to locate his actors firmly in the reality of a Florida beach resort torn between a complex past and a future in hock to the property developers. Absorbing and poignant.

S

Franklin J. Schaffner
Japan, 1920–89

Franklin J. Schaffner worked in a wide variety of genres, from domestic dramas to adventure epics. His ability to combine the personal and the visually expansive has drawn comparisons with David Lean.

An acclaimed director of American TV drama in the 1950s, Schaffner began directing feature films in the early 1960s. He hit his stride in 1964 with *The Best Man*, which was adapted from a stage play by Gore Vidal. An energetic, engrossing and surprisingly visually engaging movie, *The Best Man* explored life on the campaign trail as two candidates (Henry Fonda and Cliff Robertson) battle it out for presidential nomination. In contrast to this small-scale drama, Schaffner's next movie, *The War Lord* (1965), was an epic, medieval drama starring Charlton Heston as the eleventh-century Norman lord of the title. The director also turned his hand to the traditional biopic and the literary adaptation, filming *Nicholas And Alexandra* about the last tsar of Russia in 1971 and the quiet, family drama *Islands In The Stream*, based on an Ernest Hemingway novel in 1977.

Schaffner's most famous films, however, are *Planet Of The Apes* (1968), *Patton* (1969) and *Papillon* (1973) – three classics of American cinema. Combining visual imagination with satirical bite, *Planet Of The Apes* starred Charlton Heston as an astronaut who awakes on a planet governed by an ape culture with a strong military inclination, while *Patton* was a character study of the eponymous World War II commander starring an Oscar-winning George C. Scott. *Papillon*, about life in a French penal colony, featured standout performances from Dustin Hoffman and Steve McQueen. It was, however, the last highlight of Schaffner's career, which declined steadily over the following two decades with such misfires as *The Boys From Brazil* (1978) and *Sphinx* (1981). JC

Planet Of The Apes 1968, 112 min
cast Charlton Heston, Roddy McDowall, Kim Hunter, Maurice Evans, James Whitmore, James Daly, Linda Harrison *cin* Leon Shamroy *m* Jerry Goldsmith

Astronaut Charlton Heston finds himself marooned, Gulliver-style, on a planet where talking apes lord it over subjugated, and entirely mute, humans. This classic dystopian tale, which brutally turns evolutionary theory on its head, climaxes with one of the most visually arresting twists in cinematic history. Far superior to its many sequels and Tim Burton's 2001 hi-tech remake.

Patton 1969, 170 min
cast George C. Scott, Karl Malden, Stephen Young, Michael Bates, Michael Strong, James Edwards *cin* Fred Koenekamp *m* Jerry Goldsmith

With an Oscar-winning screenplay by Francis Ford Coppola and Edmund H. North, this is an epic film examining the forces that drove General George S. Patton (George C. Scott) during his legendary military campaigns in World War II. Schaffner (who also won an Oscar, for best director) served under Patton's command in Sicily, which may partially account for the film's authenticity.

Fred Schepisi
Australia, 1939–

Fred Schepisi's life story is the archetypal tale of a director who had a couple of successes in his home country, then went to Hollywood where his promise never fully materialized. Educated in a seminary, Schepisi dropped his monastic ambitions for the world of advertising, where he worked his way up from copywriter to managing director of his own agency. He returned to his religious roots with his first two cinematic outings, "The Priest", an award-winning episode of the portmanteau movie *Libido* (1973), and *The Devil's Playground* (1976) in which he drew from the well of his own youthful experiences in the monastery.

The lyrical and brutal *The Chant Of Jimmie Blacksmith* (1978) attracted international attention. Schepisi predictably moved to Hollywood, where he ended up making a Willie Nelson Western, *Barabarosa* (1982), and the equally incongruous *Iceman* (1984), a sensitive drama about a thawed-out Neanderthal. Next came *Plenty* (1985), a critically acclaimed version of a David Hare play in which an ex-Resistance member (Meryl Streep) struggles to adapt to post-war life. Schepisi's subsequent career has been a mixture of the good, the bad and the indifferent. On the credit account: the Steve Martin comedy *Roxanne* (1987), the Australian-set *A Cry In The Dark* (1988), spy thriller *The Russia House* (1990), Manhattan society satire *Six Degrees Of Separation* (1993) and the Michael Caine-Bob Hoskins drama *Last Orders* (2001). On the debit side: *IQ* (1994), *Fierce Creatures* (1997) and *It's All In The Family* (2003). Schepisi clearly doesn't repeat himself when it comes to subject matter, or style, preferring to adapt his visual idioms to the demands of the story. If there are defining characteristics in his eclectic career, they would be solid craftsmanship, immaculate performances and a talent that hasn't yet fully developed. LH

The Chant Of Jimmie Blacksmith 1978, 122 min
cast Tommy Lewis, Freddy Reynolds, Ray Barrett, Jack Thompson, Angela Punch, Steve Dodds *cin* Ian Baker *m* Bruce Smeaton, Peter Caroll

Half Aborigine, half white, Jimmie is systematically abused by every white Australian he comes across, including the pregnant woman who cons him into marriage. Unable to take it any more, he seeks revenge on white people, regardless of age, gender or innocence. Almost incongruously beautiful and thematically complex, Schepisi's drama makes uncomfortable viewing, not just because of its startling violence, but because it leaves our liberal sympathies in a state of bewildered flux.

S

The Russia House 1990, 122 min

cast Sean Connery, Michelle Pfeiffer, Roy Scheider, James Fox, John Mahoney, Michael Kitchen, J.T. Walsh *cin* Ian Baker *m* Jerry Goldsmith

Playwright Tom Stoppard luxuriates in the labyrinthine complexities of John le Carré's spy novel, while Sean Connery essays a classic le Carré character: drunk, out of his depth and aiming for salvation. He's a dipsomaniac British book publisher sent notebooks by a Soviet editor, Michelle Pfeiffer, in the hope that he will help her friend, a renegade Russian scientist, by publishing the military secrets contained therein. His knightly ambitions go quickly awry as he becomes a pawn in a fiendishly complex game played out between American and Russian intelligence.

Last Orders 2001, 109 min

cast Michael Caine, Tom Courtenay, David Hemmings, Bob Hoskins, Helen Mirren, Ray Winstone, JJ Feild *cin* Brian Tufano *m* Paul Grabowsky

Schepisi rounded up the cream of British acting talent to flesh out his poignant adaptation of Graham Swift's Booker Prize-winning novel about four regulars at a local pub. When one of them (Caine) dies, the others make a slow pilgrimage to Margate to scatter his ashes, and along the way memories flash back to the war and secrets are painfully revealed. It is one of the few screenplays Schepisi has written.

Lone Scherfig

Denmark, 1959–

After Lone Scherfig's first two features, *Kajs fødselsdag* (*The Birthday Trip*, 1990) and *Når mor kommer hjem* (*On Our Own*, 1998), garnered some festival success, she was approached by the guardians of the "Vow of Chastity" manifesto to make a film under the Dogme 95 banner. With the award-winning *Italian For Beginners* (2001), Scherfig not only intruded on the male domination of Dogme, but also took the movement into new territory, producing a light, romantic comedy to counter Dogme's otherwise earnest canon. (Annette Olesen and Susanne Bier have since followed in her footsteps and joined Dogme's female contingent.) Her first English-language feature, *Wilbur Wants To Kill Himself* (2002) was filmed in Scotland, and was a black comedy about a man looking after his suicidal brother and their dilapidated bookshop. However, she reverted to her native Danish to make her next film, *Hjemve* (*Just Like Home*) in 2007. ED

Italian For Beginners (Italiensk for begyndere) 2000, 112 min

cast Anders W. Berthelsen, Anette Støvelbaek, Ann Eleonora Jørgensen, Peter Gantzler *cin* Jørgen Johansson

An eclectic group of lonely hearts take Italian classes in Copenhagen, partly as a pretext for finding love and happiness. But first they must experience death, loss and reconciliation. Scherfig adheres to Dogme rules by using local settings, natural light and a hand-held camera. But unlike some of her Dogme colleagues she doesn't allow the burdens of her characters to overwhelm the audience, and finds just the right lightness of touch to produce a feel-good film.

John Schlesinger

UK, 1926–2003

Discussing the unifying themes of his eclectic career, John Schlesinger once declared he was interested in characters who make "a kind of compromise, making the best of a situation while retaining the safety valve of fantasy". It's a description that could equally apply to a director whose career was marked by iconoclastic movies, minor-key masterpieces, and the artisan's need to work constantly, even if it meant compromise and making the best of a bad script.

An amateur magician and filmmaker, Schlesinger left Oxford University to tread the boards in Britain, Australia and New Zealand, notching up a few film appearances along the way. After a successful stint as a director for the legendary BBC arts programme *Monitor*, he won the Golden Lion at the Venice Film Festival for his documentary about a day in the life of Waterloo train station, *Terminus* (1961). Its unexpected success brought him to the attention of producer Joseph Janni, who employed Schlesinger to helm two significant additions to the kitchen sink genre, *A Kind Of Loving* (1962) and *Billy Liar* (1963).

There was always something of the outsider and arriviste in Schlesinger, a fact he would frequently note himself. That craftsman's cool versatility, though, would serve him well in a quartet of films that would carve his name in the cinematic pantheon: *Darling* (1965), the splendidly scenic Thomas Hardy adaptation *Far From The Madding Crowd* (1967), *Midnight Cowboy* (1969) and *Sunday, Bloody Sunday* (1971). He overreached with the tinseltown tale of ambition *The Day Of The Locust* (1975), whose failure was assuaged by the box-office takings for the generic thriller *Marathon Man* (1976). After the measured success of *Yanks* (1979), a drama about GIs in Britain, Schlesinger proceeded to make one of Hollywood's most fabled disasters, *Honky Tonk Freeway* (1981), whose phenomenal failure cruelly exposed the director's Achilles heel – a lack of personal style or overarching vision. Possessing a gentle knack with actors, he was often only as good as his script, unable to do more than polish the surface if the raw material was weak. This flaw was brought into sharp focus with the poor quality of subsequent Hollywood projects, *The Falcon And The Snowman* (1985), *The Believers* (1987), the saving grace *Madame Sousatzka* (1988), *Pacific Heights* (1990) and *An Eye For An Eye* (1996). His British literary-based television work of the same period has aged rather better – including an adaptation of Stella Gibbons's *Cold Comfort Farm* in 1995. Schlesinger's film career reached its nadir with his final movie, the Madonna vehicle *The Next Best Thing* (2000),

S

which was an intensely stressful experience for the 74-year-old director, who was already frail. Not long after, Schlesinger suffered a debilitating stroke and died three years later. LH

Darling 1965, 127 min

cast Dirk Bogarde, Laurence Harvey, Julie Christie, Roland Curram, Alex Scott, Basil Henson, Helen Lindsey *cin* Kenneth Higgins *m* John Dankworth

There are films of their time and films about their time. Schlesinger's chilly dissection of Swinging London unfortunately inhabits the former camp. The years have not been kind to *Darling*, while Michelangelo Antonioni's forensic analysis of the same milieu, *Blow-Up* (1966), only improves with age. The gulf in class exposes the difference between artist and artisan, with Schlesinger in hock to the film fashions of the period, instantly labelling his material with a sell-by date. That said, in its day this was considered to be a bona fide masterpiece and Julie Christie won an Oscar as the vacuous model who sleeps her way to success.

Midnight Cowboy 1969, 113 min

cast Jon Voight, Dustin Hoffman, Sylvia Miles, Brenda Vaccaro, John McGiver, Barnard Hughes, Ruth White *cin* Adam Holender *m* John Barry

In the best possible sense, Schlesinger was the directorial equivalent of a sponge, here soaking up the abrasive edge and heroin chic of Paul Morrissey's films, which he reproduced with a Hollywood veneer and sound professionalism. The first X-rated movie to win the best film Oscar, it details with aching poignancy the brittle dreams of naïve stud Jon Voight and squalid opportunist Dustin Hoffman, whose damaged lives amongst the beautiful people reveal the cold, clammy side of the counterculture coin.

Sunday, Bloody Sunday 1971, 110 min

cast Glenda Jackson, Peter Finch, Murray Head, Peggy Ashcroft, Maurice Denham, Vivian Pickles, Frank Windsor *cin* Billy Williams *m* Ron Geesin

Schlesinger's most personal film, wherein Peter Finch plays a gay, Jewish doctor who falls for the same man as divorcee Glenda Jackson. Unfortunately, the contested object of desire is the inert Murray Head, who sorely lacks that confluence of mystery and handsome vacuity that Terence Stamp brought to Pier Paolo Pasolini's *Theorem* (1968). It was, though, ground-breaking in its depiction of a homosexual man as complicated and normal rather than melodramatic and doomed, and was reportedly responsible for many young men having the courage to come out.

Marathon Man 1976, 126 min

cast Dustin Hoffman, Laurence Olivier, Roy Scheider, William Devane, Marthe Keller, Fritz Weaver, Richard Bright *cin* Conrad Hall *m* Michael Small

The credit for the success of this paranoid conspiracy thriller is due in no small part to scriptwriter William Goldman, not to mention Schlesinger's uncanny ability to work with the best writers the industry had to offer. Graduate student Dustin Hoffman finds himself in trouble as he enters his late brother's shadowy world of intrigue, and falls into the dentist's chair of ex-Nazi Laurence Olivier. Gripping and appropriately glossy, it's above all a testament to the chameleon qualities of its unlikely director.

The cold side of the countercultural coin: Dustin Hoffman and John Voight in *Midnight Cowboy*.

S

Volker Schlöndorff
Germany, 1939–

Volker Schlöndorff is not afraid to tackle the literary behemoth. Where other directors have feared to tread, he has grappled manfully with Marcel Proust, Günter Grass and Margaret Atwood.

There is something sympathetic, almost altruistic, in the way Schlöndorff sacrifices the notion of personal style to cut his cinematic cloth according to the work he's adapting. In that way he's very different from his New German Cinema contemporaries – Rainer Werner Fassbinder, Werner Herzog, Wim Wenders – whose work can often be identified from a few shots and whose cinematic personality is infused in every frame. While Schlöndorff's self-effacement is admirable, it's also deeply problematic, because ultimately his films live or die on the strength of their scripts. There are no auteur flourishes to savour, or even cling to.

A former director of television news reports, Schlöndorff built up his film experience as an assistant to Louis Malle, Alain Resnais and Jean-Pierre Melville. His feature debut was *Young Törless* (1966), an adaptation of Robert Musil's novel about sadistic bullying at a boys' boarding school which won the International Critics Prize at Cannes. Schlöndorff raised his international profile again with *The Lost Honour Of Katharina Blum* (1975), his adaptation of Heinrich Böll's novel about tabloid sensationalism and the climate of paranoia in 1970s Germany. He co-directed *Katharina Blum* with his wife Margarethe von Trotta, who injected an additional political edge into his work. This was the first of Schlöndorff's three great films, the other two being *The Tin Drum* (1979) and *Swann In Love* (1984).

The success of *Tin Drum* triggered Schlöndorff's relocation to the US, with its bigger budgets, but he returned to Germany in 1992 to manage the Neubabelsberg Studios after divorcing von Trotta. However, since making *Swann In Love* in the mid-1980s, only *Voyager* (1991), his well-polished version of Max Frisch's novel of regret and incest, *Homo Faber*, has piqued the interest of critics and audiences. Other projects, such as *A Handmaid's Tale* (1990), trail the faint whiff of compromised failure; and some, like *Legend Of Rita* (2000), have barely interested international distributors. LH

The Lost Honour Of Katharina Blum (Die verlorene Ehre der Katharina Blum) 1975, 106 min
cast Angela Winkler, Mario Adorf, Jürgen Prochnow, Dieter Laser, Heinz Bennent, Hannelore Hoger *cin* Jost Vacano *m* Hans Werner Henze

Schlöndorff and co-director (and spouse) Margarethe von Trotta adopt the *cinéma vérité* mode of dirty realism to fashion this abrasive, urgent report on the manufacture of paranoia in 1970s Germany. After a one-night stand with a terror suspect, a young woman is accused of harbouring anarchist groups by both the police and a tabloid newspaper, who make up quotes, disturb her dying mother in hospital and prompt a vicious local hate campaign against her.

The Tin Drum (Die Blechtrommel) 1979, 142 min
cast David Bennent, Mario Adorf, Angela Winkler, Daniel Olbrychski, Charles Aznavour, Heinz Bennent *cin* Igor Luther *m* Maurice Jarre

Schlöndorff's masterstroke was to cast a young boy as the child who never grows up, rather than a dwarf, as prospective directors had suggested. Looking like he's wandered off the set of *Village Of The Damned*, David Bennent is properly demonic as the man-child who witnesses the capitulation of his Polish city to the Nazis. What's striking about this solid adaptation of Günter Grass's epic novel is not the shocking nature of its controversial scenes of underage sexuality, but their unlikely and impeccable good taste.

Swann In Love (Un amour de Swann) 1984, 110 min
cast Jeremy Irons, Ornella Muti, Alain Delon, Fanny Ardant, Marie-Christine Barrault, Anne Bennent *cin* Sven Nykvist *m* Hans Werner Henze

Schlöndorff certainly has guts, attempting a segment of one of the most hallowed texts of modern literature – Proust's *A la recherche du temps perdu*. Unlike Raúl Ruiz's woozily impressionistic *Time Regained* (1999), Schlöndorff plays his Proust straight, aiming squarely for emotional candour, and often succeeding. Jeremy Irons stars as the eponymous dandy who scandalizes society by falling in love with a comely prostitute.

Julian Schnabel
US, 1951–

A controversial neo-expressionist painter and sculptor who came to fame as a member of the 1980s New York art scene, Julian Schnabel turned to filmmaking with *Basquiat* (1996), a biopic about his friend and rival Jean-Michel Basquiat, who died from drugs at 28. His second film, *Before Night Falls* (2000), was also a portrait of a tortured artist, in this case the gay Cuban writer Reinaldo Arenas. Both are as confidently composed as you would expect, conventional in structure, centred on sympathetic lead performances (by Jeffrey Wright and Javier Bardem respectively), and overladen with starry supporting casts. In 2007 Schnabel came away from the Cannes Film Festival with the best director prize for his French made *Le scaphandre et le papillon* (*The Diving Bell And The Butterfly*), based on the memoir by *Elle* magazine editor Jean-Dominique Bauby, who woke up from an accident to find himself completely paralysed save for one eye. TC

Before Night Falls 2000, 133 min
cast Javier Bardem, Johnny Depp, Sean Penn, John Ortiz, Michael Wincott, Najwa Nimri *cin* Javier Pérez Grobet, Guillermo Rosas *m* Carter Burwell

Schnabel was in the unusual position of being able to entirely fund his second film himself. Like his first, *Before Night Falls* is an unapologetically empathic, romantic and

S

opaque biopic. Reinaldo Arenas was a committed revolutionary whose talent and sexual proclivities upset the Castro regime. The film's buoyant, enraptured visual sensibility is more assured than the kitschy symbolism in *Basquiat*, and this is clearly a labour of love. Bardem brings Arenas's sensuality and intellectual curiosity to vivid life.

Victor Schonfeld
US

B rought up in a middle-class Jewish New York family, Victor Schonfeld's documentaries caused bitter controversy wherever they were shown. After working on an Israeli kibbutz as a teenager, he moved to London where he became a filmmaker and met future wife and co-producer Jennifer Millstone. Schonfeld's first brush with controversy was prompted by the release of *The Animals Film* (1981), an unflinching and forensic examination of the treatment of animals in farms, laboratories and factories, the production of veal and the use of monkeys in scientific experiments. Controversially giving voice to the Animal Liberation Front, it raised consciousness and hackles in equal measure when shown on British television. Schonfeld risked even greater controversy with his next project when he returned to Israel and spent three years making *Shattered Dreams: Picking Up The Pieces* (1988). Examining the explosive issues surrounding the Palestinian crisis, the film made clear Schonfeld's support for a two-nation solution, and he was duly attacked by conservative Jewish groups. LH

Shattered Dreams: Picking Up The Pieces
1988, 173 min
with Jack Class *cin* Peter Greenhalgh, Amnon Salomon, Dani Schneur *m* Shalom Hanouch

Over the course of almost three hours, Schonfeld interviews Palestinians and Israelis of all political hues. He talks to right-wing rabbi Meir Kahane (who advocates the expulsion of all Arabs), and to peace activists and the families of dead soldiers. All this is juxtaposed with sepia archive footage of original Zionist settlers tilling the land and building a Utopia that was lost in the subsequent bloodshed. What exactly happened to that dream is the subject of this vivid, poignant and over-long analysis.

Paul Schrader
US, 1946–

R aised under the austere teachings of Calvinism, Paul Schrader didn't see a film until he was 18 – though he certainly made up for lost time, gorging on cinema and other earthly pleasures as one of the "movie brats" of the decadent 1970s. Once he started making his own films, his religious upbringing left a persistent watermark: his sober, cerebral movies typically concentrate on people in

desperate straits, the possibility of their redemption and the forms their deliverance or damnation may take. Unsurprisingly, Schrader is a devotee of Robert Bresson: *American Gigolo* (1980) and *Light Sleeper* (1992) both refer to the French master's *Pickpocket* (1959), and Schrader's influential 1972 book *Transcendental Style In Film* treated Bresson alongside Yasujiro Ozu and Carl Theodor Dreyer.

A Schrader archetype is the solitary wanderer in a foreign, threatening (under)world. In *Hardcore* (*The Hardcore Life*, 1979), a religiously devout businessman descends into the porn and sex-trade underground to find his daughter; in *American Gigolo*, Richard Gere takes a similar tour to uncover the person who's framing him for murder; in *Cat People* (1982), Nastassja Kinski tracks down her estranged brother in a sleazy, voodoo-suffused corner of New Orleans. In the fascinating but underseen *Mishima: A Life In Four Chapters* (1985), Schrader discovered in the extreme-right-wing Japanese patriot, novelist and *seppuku* artist Yukio Mishima a trajectory of physical and spiritual transfiguration to rival his scripts for Martin Scorsese (*Taxi Driver*, 1976, *Raging Bull*, 1980, and *The Last Temptation Of Christ*, 1988). Schrader has also proved himself an unsentimental chronicler of working-class life in films as disparate as *Blue Collar* (1978), *Light Of Day* (1987) and *Affliction* (1997), the latter a bleak, beautifully performed adaptation of a Russell Banks novel.

Schrader has kept busy as a director in recent years. *Auto Focus* (2002) was a peek beneath the Hollywood underbelly, where *Hogan's Heroes* TV star Bob Crane (played by Greg Kinnear) fell prey to sex addiction and a sordid death. *Dominion: Prequel To The Exorcist* (2005) bombed on release but earned a cult following, while *The Walker* (2007) starred Woody Harrelson as a male escort who becomes embroiled in a murder investigation. JW

Hardcore (aka The Hardcore Life) 1979,
108 min
cast George C. Scott, Peter Boyle, Season Hubley, Dick Sargent, Leonard Gaines, David Nichols *cin* Michael Chapman *m* Jack Nitzsche

After his daughter disappears on a church-sponsored trip, Calvinist businessman George C. Scott hires a private investigator (Peter Boyle) and discovers, to his profound horror, that she played a starring role in a porno film. Scott then undertakes a desperate journey through the LA underbelly in search of his child in Schrader's redemptive parable, which shares subtle affinities with his script for Scorsese's *Taxi Driver*.

Affliction 1997, 108 min
cast Nick Nolte, James Coburn, Sissy Spacek, Willem Dafoe, Mary Beth Hurt, Jim True, Marian Seldes *cin* Paul Sarossy *m* Michael Brook

Small-town policeman Wade (a terrific Nick Nolte) is a failed husband and father, an impotent cop and a child of violence, still lumbering under the long shadow of his abusive-drunk father (James Coburn). Convinced that an apparently accidental hunting death is actually the tip of a murderous local real-estate conspiracy, Wade feeds an obsession that he imagines will right his standing but that, ultimately, only hastens his doom in Schrader's bold, grim and painful study.

Barbet Schroeder

Iran, 1941–

Barbet Schroeder – who has a small role as a car salesman in Jean-Luc Godard's *Les carabiniers* (1963) – began his film production company, Les Films du Losange, the same year at the age of 23. Born to Swiss-German parents in Iran, and educated at the Sorbonne, Schroeder had been published in *Cahiers du cinéma* and knew many of the figures in the *nouvelle vague*. As a producer, he is responsible for some of the best work by Eric Rohmer, including *My Night With Maud* (1969) and Jacques Rivette (*Céline And Julie Go Boating*, 1974) as well as Rainer Werner Fassbinder's *Chinese Roulette* (1976).

His work as a director, though eclectic and ambitious, has generally been less accomplished. He himself prefers the word "adventurer" to auteur. Made in Germany, *More* (1969) is the story of a heroin addict. *La vallée* (1972), with music by Pink Floyd, sent a group of hippies down to New Guinea. *Maîtresse* (1976) candidly explored ideas about control and love in the context of the S&M subculture, mixing genuine doms and submissives with actors Bulle Ogier and Gérard Depardieu. These early features were interspersed with a handful of equally interesting documentaries, including *Idi Amin Dada* (1974) and *Koko, A Talking Gorilla* (1978).

Having moved to the US, Schroeder cast Mickey Rourke as Charles Bukowski in the authentically scummy *Barfly* (1987), then enjoyed his biggest success with *Reversal Of Fortune* (1990), a judiciously non-judgemental account of the Claus von Bulow trial. The director carved out a niche for himself as a purveyor of serious crime drama, but the virtues in films like *Single White Female* (1992), *Kiss Of Death* (1995) and *Murder By Numbers* (2002) are all premeditated: in the (variable) scripts and the casting, not in what the French call the "realization". He is still primarily a producer rather than a director. The limitations of this period, however, are thrown into relief by *Our Lady Of The Assassins* (2000), a courageous, outrageous film Schroeder shot on high-definition video on location in Colombia, based on the novel by Fernando Vallejo. TC

Reversal Of Fortune 1990, 111 min
cast Jeremy Irons, Glenn Close, Ron Silver, Annabella Sciorra, Uta Hagen, Fisher Stevens, Jack Gilpin *cin* Luciano Tovoli *m* Mark Isham

In 1979 the wealthy American socialite Sunny von Bulow fell into a coma from which she would never awake. Her husband Claus (Jeremy Irons) was tried and convicted of attempted murder, then won an appeal with the help of star lawyer Alan Dershowitz (Ron Silver). Brilliantly scripted by Nicholas Kazan (son of director Elia Kazan), *Reversal Of Fortune* is a teasing, tantalizing comedy of manners narrated by Sunny (Glenn Close). It doesn't tell us anything particularly new about the case, but engages instead with its insights into high society and the legal process. Irons won the best actor Oscar for his performance.

Joel Schumacher

US, 1939–

Joel Schumacher's life is the classic rags to riches story of the American dream. Born into poverty in a tough district of New York, Schumacher's father died when he was only 4, leaving his mother to work almost nonstop to support herself and her only child. Joel paid his own way through art college and landed a job as window-dresser in one of Manhattan's swankier department stores. Leading a lifestyle of drugs and alcohol in the late-1960s, the party animal lived the high life with Andy Warhol and had several near-death experiences.

One day in the early 1970s, as Joel likes to tell it, he decided to become a film director, quit the world of window display and packed his bags for Hollywood. There he started as a costume designer, notably on Woody Allen's *Sleeper* (1973), and graduated to screenwriter. His feature screenwriting debut was the musical *Sparkle* (1976). By the time it was released, he'd already written and directed a biopic of Bugsy Siegel's moll, *The Virginia Hill Story* (1974), for television, though it would be another seven years before he was hired to helm a feature film, *The Incredible Shrinking Woman* (1981). A decade later he was reportedly the most commercially successful director in Hollywood, with a slew of blockbusters to his name.

There is a "let's do the show right here" bravado to his résumé; Schumacher has fearlessly tackled a range of films with brio, panache and the visual chops of a window designer. He's made the taut John Grisham adaptations *The Client* (1994) and *A Time To Kill* (1996), the mediocre romantic comedy *Cousins* (1989), the remarkable howl of urban angst *Falling Down* (1993), the deathly romance *Dying Young* (1991) and the kitsch comic-book spectacular *Batman Forever* (1995). There are some discernible characteristics aside from journeyman versatility: Schumacher has an eye for young talent, making three definitive Brat Pack movies, *St Elmo's Fire* (1985), *The Lost Boys* (1987) and *Flatliners* (1990). And after the fiasco of *Batman & Robin* (1997), in which the director was unmasked as the Caped Crusader's worst enemy, Schumacher performed both a *mea culpa* and *volte face*.

Subsequent projects were low-key, dissonant and largely free of flash: the queasy snuff movie thriller *8MM* (1999), the transvestite chamber piece *Flawless*

S

(1999), the gritty Vietnam pic *Tigerland* (2000), the ingeniously conceived thriller *Phone Booth* (2002), the worthy true crime story about the murder of an Irish journalist, *Veronica Guerin* (2003) and the spooky paranoia thriller *The Number 23* (2006). However, *The Phantom Of The Opera* (2004) received a critical drubbing by some. LH

St Elmo's Fire 1985, 108 min

cast Emilio Estevez, Rob Lowe, Andrew McCarthy, Demi Moore, Judd Nelson, Ally Sheedy *cin* Stephen H. Burum *m* David Foster

Together with John Hughes's *The Breakfast Club* (1984), this film is the quintessential product of the 1980s Brat Pack, the gang of young actors that included Emilio Estevez, Rob Lowe and Ally Sheedy amongst its superbly coiffed members. Here the gang play college graduates who have to deal with the harsh realities of adult life against a backdrop of neon lighting and adult orientated rock. Unabashedly stylish and painfully 1980s.

Falling Down 1993, 115 min

cast Michael Douglas, Robert Duvall, Barbara Hershey, Frederic Forrest, Tuesday Weld, Lois Smith *cin* Andrzej Bartkowiak *m* James Newton Howard

Sticking out like a sore thumb in Schumacher's filmography, this is undoubtedly his masterpiece. This is *Taxi Driver* for the multiplex, articulating the anger of the silent majority about traffic gridlock and breakfasts at burger bars becoming unavailable on the stroke of 11.30am. Even if it ultimately cops out with psychological explanations for its protagonist's psychotic reactions, *Falling Down* is not the first Hollywood film to lose its nerve, and we're more than compensated by the film's numerous anarchic pleasures.

Batman Forever 1995, 121 min

cast Val Kilmer, Jim Carrey, Tommy Lee Jones, Nicole Kidman, Chris O'Donnell, Michael Gough *cin* Barbara Ling *m* Elliot Goldenthal

When studio execs decided that Tim Burton's introspective visions were turning punters off the *Batman* franchise, they called on Schumacher to amp up the pizzazz. And the first thing the ex-costume designer did was to sex up the Caped Crusader's rubber suit with the addition of nipples and a codpiece. The unsightly bulges, however, were overshadowed by Jim Carrey's outrageous turn as The Riddler, proving once again that the comic-book universe is the best place for the comedian's oversized antics. Schumacher kept a rein on his kitsch instincts – something he spectacularly failed to do in the follow-up.

Ettore Scola

Italy, 1931–

A member of the Italian Communist Party who began his career writing for humorous magazines, Ettore Scola has created a richly varied body of work that shows a consistent interest in the impact of historical events on individual lives. His early comedies proved that he could be a perceptive observer of social and sexual absurdities, but his more recent films have sometimes been suffocated by blandly tasteful production values and a lack of narrative pace.

Scola started in film as a writer, providing largely comic material for directors such as Dino Risi and Antonio Pietrangeli. His first film as a director was *Se permetete parliamo di donne* (*Let's Talk About Women*, 1964), a bittersweet comedy in which Vittorio Gassman played nine different roles. In the 1970s, Scola became increasingly adept at directing comedies of manners with a satirical edge, such as *Dramma della gelosia* (*The Pizza Triangle*, 1970), in which Monica Vitti is lusted after by both Marcello Mastroianni and Giancarlo Giannini, and *La più bella serata della mia vita* (*The Most Wonderful Evening Of My Life*, 1972) about three magistrates who decide to sharpen their skills even though they are now retired. *C'eravamo tanto amati* (*We All Loved Each Other So Much*, 1974) was an affectionate homage to post-war Italian cinema seen through the eyes of three friends, while the prizewinning *Brutti, sporchi e cattivi* (*Down And Dirty*, 1976) was the blackest of comedies about the brutish lives of an impoverished family on the outskirts of Rome.

As his international reputation grew, Scola's films became more ambitious – and arguably more pretentious. *Una giornata particolare* (*A Special Day*, 1977), in which Sophia Loren played a careworn housewife who befriends a homosexual radio journalist (Mastroianni) on the day of Hitler's visit to Mussolini in 1939, divided critics, with some regarding it as the director's masterpiece, others as a particularly clodhopping allegory. *Le bal* (1982), an attempt to conjure vignettes of France's twentieth-century history through the prism of a Parisian ballroom was even more freighted with symbolism – even though not a word is spoken. *La nuit de Varennes* (*That Night In Varennes*, 1982) was a more conventional look at a slice of French history, focusing on Louis XVI and Marie Antoinette's attempt to escape from Paris following the French Revolution.

Although Scola has remained an active filmmaker into the twenty-first century, since *La nuit de Varennes* only the autobiographical *La famiglia* (1987), a slow-moving look at one middle-class Italian family through three generations, has made any impact outside of his home country. RB

Dramma della gelosia (The Pizza Triangle) 1970, 107 min

cast Marcello Mastroianni, Monica Vitti, Giancarlo Giannini, Manuel Zarzo, Merisa Merlini *cin* Carlo Di Palma *m* Armando Trovajoli

This film is both an homage to, and a satire on, the typical *commedia all'italiana*, with emotions and performances writ large and histrionic. A triangular relationship, involving a communist bricklayer (Marcello Mastroianni), a flower seller (Monica Vitti) and a pizza chef (Giancarlo Giannini), is told in flashback by the three protagonists. As in many of Scola's comedies, the story veers alarmingly between the hilarious and the tragic.

S

La nuit de Varennes (That Night In Varennes)
1982, 150 min
cast Marcello Mastroianni, Jean-Louis Barrault, Hanna Schygulla, Harvey Keitel, Jean-Claude Brialy *cin* Armando Nannuzzi *m* Armando Trovajoli

A star-studded costume picture that is both visually dazzling and intellectually stimulating. In 1791, two coaches trundle along the road from Paris to Verdun, one carrying the escaping king and queen of France, the other an assorted group of celebrities, including the ageing Casanova, the radical Thomas Paine, the writer Restif de la Bretonne and an Austrian countess. Their conversations range from the revolution to their personal hopes and fears, and the effect is like eavesdropping on a great historical moment.

Martin Scorsese

US, 1942–

For three decades Martin Scorsese has been at the forefront of American cinema, its most avid champion and respected standard-bearer, and often its most electrifying practitioner.

For all his oft-expressed love for the Golden Age of Hollywood, Scorsese has been influenced just as greatly by outsiders such as Orson Welles and John Cassavetes, and foreigners such as Michael Powell and Roberto Rossellini. (He has paid tribute to American and Italian cinema in two long, authoritative documentary films – *A Personal Journey With Martin Scorsese Through American Movies*, 1995, and *My Voyage To Italy*, 1999 – and has plans to devote a third to British cinema.) The most cine-literate of directors, he has also been among the most formally restless and exploratory, evolving an obsessive-compulsive *mise en scène* based on dynamic, agile camerawork and radical, staccato editing rhythms attuned to his innovative, informed and highly influential use of rock, pop and classical music.

Few studio filmmakers have pushed the expressive range of celluloid to such limits – and outside the studios no one enjoys access to such an exciting aesthetic arsenal. His virtuosity is clear, and represents a thrilling synthesis of the cinematic effects he has absorbed since childhood. Nevertheless, the question mark that looms over Scorsese's career is an old one: to what extent is the artist compromised by the business? Has Hollywood empowered Scorsese's art, or co-opted the promise of a putative American New Wave?

To his credit, Scorsese has never stopped asking himself these questions. Inevitably there have been highs and lows in his long, relatively prolific but only intermittently successful career (it comprises more than twenty narrative features and half a dozen major documentary projects). If he hasn't had the kind of commercial success enjoyed by his movie-brat peers Francis Ford Coppola, George Lucas and Steven Spielberg, he hasn't pandered to the audience either.

Famously, he almost joined the priesthood as a young man. Instead, he decided his true calling was the cinema, although religious symbolism and the search for spiritual redemption permeate his films. "You don't make up for your sins in church, you do it in the streets, you do it at home. The rest is bullshit and you know it", declared his alter ego, Charlie Cappa (Harvey Keitel) in *Mean Streets* (1973) – which is, along with his feature debut *Who's That Knocking At My Door* (1967), the most autobiographical film in the Scorsese canon.

Mean Streets is the first of Scorsese's "godless men" gangster triptych, completed by *GoodFellas* (1990) and *Casino* (1995). Charlie is diligently making his way in the Mob, looking out for his screw-up cousin Johnny Boy (Robert De Niro), and secretly carrying on with Johnny's epileptic sister, Teresa (Amy Robinson). At the same time, he's telling it like it is to the Lord: "It's all bullshit apart from the pain…" How deeply did Scorsese identify with Charlie? In his prayers, the actor's voice is mixed in with the director's to the point where they become one. But don't overlook the film's exuberance, the propulsive, inventive camerawork (including the most euphoric drunk scene ever shot), the declamatory use of rock music, and the comic shtick between Keitel and a firecracker De Niro. Scorsese can't help rhapsodizing over a pool-hall squabble that degenerates into violence. However reasonable Charlie may be, we're drawn to the quixotic, infuriatingly irresponsible Johnny Boy.

In the push and pull between these two characters we find the first embodiment of the dynamic which agitates so much of Scorsese's work – between the intellectual and the animalistic, the repressed and the anarchic, the sacred and the profane. This duality explains the ambivalence in Scorsese's vision, which is torn between respect for classical Hollywood tradition and reflecting modern, countercultural experience (see, for example, 1977's revisionist musical *New York, New York*).

This tension is worked through most compellingly in the rebarbative relationships between Robert De Niro and Joe Pesci in *Raging Bull* (1980), *GoodFellas* and *Casino*, not coincidentally the definitive Scorsese films in the public imagination. In these films Scorsese both identifies with and distances himself from his transgressors to forge a sensational, subjective cinema that simultaneously repels and attracts.

Raging Bull is the ultimate "Method" movie in ways that go well beyond performance. "I was bleeding internally all over and I didn't know it. My eyes were bleeding, my hands, everything except my brain and my liver … then I realized I was La Motta, I'd make the movie about me", Scorsese said, referring to his drug problems in the late 1970s. The film is a portrait of the brute male animal, inarticulate, phobic, battering his head against the walls. But

S

Martin Scorsese and Robert De Niro

Martin Scorsese and Robert De Niro are the most famous of all modern actor/director partnerships. Together they were responsible for *Mean Streets* (1973), *Taxi Driver* (1976), *Raging Bull* (1980) and *GoodFellas* (1990) – and that's only half the pair's joint tally. Their best work is an electrifying symbiosis of Method acting and directorial verve, producing a dynamism of intense ferocity.

The pair grew up just a few streets apart in New York's Little Italy, but they only met years later when Scorsese was introduced to De Niro by Brian De Palma, who had already made three films with the actor. And yet *Mean Streets* seems like a debut, for both star and director. The electricity that De Niro generated as Johnny Boy – totally wired and frighteningly unpredictable – was matched in its intensity by the kinetic energy of the director's virtuoso camerawork and editing. Then, beginning with *Taxi Driver*, De Niro was Scorsese's main man for four consecutive features. In *Taxi Driver*, they created their most famous and oft-quoted antihero, the slowly simmering cabbie Travis Bickle. *New York, New York* (1977) was a departure for both, being Scorsese's only musical. De Niro played an old-fashioned leading man, all good looks and charm, with only a hint of edge. It was a classic Method performance: De Niro learnt to play the saxophone and even started gigging incognito. But the critics were unmoved, leaving Scorsese in a depression that would eventually land him in hospital. At his nadir, he decided that *Raging Bull* would be his last feature, a valediction to an abortive career. What it turned out to be was Scorsese's redemption, both personal and professional. He has since credited the film with saving his life. This is thanks in no small part to the performance of De Niro, for whom the La Motta biopic was a personal project. Committed as ever to the Method, De Niro trained as a boxer for a year, entering three fights and winning two. He famously put on 55 pounds to play the pugilist in later life by eating his way around France and Northern Italy, and even helped the director to rewrite Paul Schrader's script.

Since the 1990s De Niro has showed increasing signs of mellowing. In *GoodFellas* (1990), he left it to Joe Pesci to be the film's source of unnervingly psychotic energy. He persuaded Scorsese to direct *Cape Fear* (1991), but this was no *Raging Bull*. *Casino* (1995) had the epic scope, and was in some ways convincing, yet at the same time seemed like a tired reprise of *GoodFellas* for both actor and director. The Method has become too obvious in the actor; no De Niro performance goes without the actor shrugging his shoulders, and as one critic put it, screwing up his face as if his nostrils have been assaulted by a terrible smell.

Perhaps it is *Raging Bull*'s successor – the vastly underrated *The King Of Comedy* (1983) – that boasts De Niro's greatest turn. Scorsese has made the point himself, anointing De Niro's portrayal of Rupert Pupkin his "best performance ever". Pupkin, a comedian with alarming delusions of grandeur, is corny, oily and chilling.

De Niro and Scorsese haven't worked together since 1995 (unless you count their vocal double act in the 2004 children's animation *Shark Tale*). De Niro was too old to play the part originally intended for him in 2002's *Gangs Of New York*, as the project was at least twenty years in gestation, and Scorsese seems to have found his new alter ego in the unlikely shape of Leonardo DiCaprio (who starred in *The Aviator*, 2004, and *The Departed*, 2006, as well as *Gangs*). Meanwhile, De Niro has moved into light comedy – often with stunning effect (as in Jay Roach's *Meet The Parents*, 2000). He's even ventured behind the camera himself, with *A Bronx Tale* (1993) and *The Good Shepherd* (2006), but although De Niro's directorial efforts have been impressive, Scorsese is unlikely to have any sleepless nights worrying about being eclipsed by his former star. LH

at least it allows for a shot at redemption – "I was blind and now I see" – a possibility which has all but evaporated in the moral desert of *Casino*, with its nihilistic matrix of greed and self-delusion.

Brilliant but ungiving, *Casino* looks like a self-rebuke, a violent recoil from the exhilarating amoral rush of Scorsese's most popular film, *GoodFellas*, whose opening voiceover declares: "As far back as I can remember I always wanted to be a gangster." *Casino* is altogether more objective – the first hour delineates the organization of crime with an almost documentary rigour – and altogether less enamoured of its self-destructive wise guys. At the time Scorsese was widely perceived to be treading water, but looked at alongside *GoodFellas*, *Casino* seems

the fuller and more mature work, the American epic he knew he had inside him.

Beyond these modern classics, Scorsese has applied himself to a wide range of subjects with varying degrees of success – though he's never as comfortable as when he's making films about the Italian-American community he knows so intimately. The intense creative high of the 1970s – which also included the "women's picture" *Alice Doesn't Live Here Anymore* (1974) and the neo-*noir* vigilante fantasy *Taxi Driver* (1976) – was succeeded by a relatively fallow period in the 1980s, when his prospects were jeopardized by the poor returns on both *Raging Bull* and *The King Of Comedy* (1983). In 1983 *The Last Temptation Of Christ* was cancelled just days

The finest of collaborations: Martin Scorsese and Robert De Niro at work on the set of *Taxi Driver*.

S

before shooting was due to commence (five years later, Scorsese was able to resurrect the project).

The comedy thriller *After Hours* (1985) was followed by *The Color Of Money* (1986), a flashy but superficial sequel to *The Hustler* (1961) with Paul Newman mentoring Tom Cruise. Neither film was commensurate with Scorsese's reputation. When he finally got *The Last Temptation Of Christ* made in 1988 the merits of the film were overshadowed by the controversy of its depiction of a human Jesus struggling to accept his divinity. Nevertheless, the film seemed to recharge Scorsese. His 44-minute short *Life Lessons* in the portmanteau film *New York Stories* (1989) was a hyperactive portrait of an ageing established artist and his relationship with a much younger woman.

Scorsese's remake, *Cape Fear* (1991), in which a psychopathic Robert De Niro terrorizes lawyer Nick Nolte, seemed intended to capitalize on the momentum from *GoodFellas*; it was the director's most cynical, ugly film, and his most financially successful. If the Edith Wharton costume drama *The Age Of Innocence* (1993) reclaimed his artistic credibility, *Kundun* (1997) proved too exotic for most audiences. In contrast, *Bringing Out The Dead* (1999) almost felt like self-parody.

Scorsese began the twenty-first century with two expensive period epics, both produced by Harvey Weinstein and starring Leonardo DiCaprio: *Gangs Of New York* (2002) and *The Aviator* (2004). Both are audacious and extravagant entertainments, but they shy away from the darker, more disturbing elements buried in their hearts. Uneven and dissatisfying, Scorsese's recent films don't measure up to his best work. In fact he's made richer, more satisfying and more personal films in the documentary field, most notably his fascinating, empathetic but appalled portrait of the young Bob Dylan transcending his roots, *No Direction Home* (2005). If Scorsese seemed to have lost his way, *The Departed* marked a return to familiar terrain – the gangster milieu – and in more ways than one, a return to form. It was enough, at any rate, to scoop the Academy Award for best director that had eluded him so many times before. Regardless of the merits of the film, few would maintain it was any more than his due. TC

Mean Streets 1973, 110 min

cast Harvey Keitel, Robert De Niro, Amy Robinson, Richard Romanus, David Proval *cin* Kent Wakeford *m* Eric Clapton, Rolling Stones

This is where Martin Scorsese hit his stride. After a decade on the brink, he made his breakthrough by bringing it all back home: Little Italy, 1973. An urgent, edgy look at the lower echelons of the Mob, it was the director's first, unforgettable collaboration with Robert De Niro. The actor's brash Johnny

Boy is an anarchic loudmouthed hustler: shooting at the lights of the Empire State Building, boogieing in the street, he's intensely alive yet implacably bent on self-destruction.

Taxi Driver 1976, 112 min
cast Robert De Niro, Cybill Shepherd, Harvey Keitel, Albert Brooks, Martin Scorsese *cin* Michael Chapman *m* Bernard Herrmann

Scorsese's expressionist, hallucinatory rendition of an infernal New York puts us in the head of Travis Bickle (Robert De Niro), one of the iconic characters of the 1970s, an empty existential cipher loosely based on failed assassin Arthur Bremer. The vision is worthy of Baudelaire: putrid, corrupt, but also irresistible. The city is a cesspool, the taxi cab a coffin.

New York, New York 1977, 153 min
cast Liza Minnelli, Robert De Niro, Lionel Stander, Barry Primus, Mary Kay Place *cin* Laszlo Kovacs *m* John Kander, Fred Ebb

De Niro is sax-man Jimmy Doyle in Scorsese's unexpected, underrated musical – a tribute to 1940s razzamatazz directed in the raw, tumultuous style of John Cassavetes. Doyle is an irresistible egoist who woos and wows Liza Minnelli's singer Francine Evans. Funny and furious by turns, De Niro revels in the opportunity to exhibit his range and humour without sacrificing his emotional authenticity; the breakdown of the relationship takes the genre into new ground.

Raging Bull 1980, 129 min, b/w and col
cast Robert De Niro, Joe Pesci, Cathy Moriarty, Frank Vincent, Nicholas Colasanto, Theresa Saldana *cin* Michael Chapman

Six years and six films after *Mean Streets* propelled him into the maelstrom of Hollywood success – and emerging from his own near-fatal drug problem – Martin Scorsese made what he believed could be his last movie. Its subject is Jake La Motta, the Bronx Bull, a graceless but indomitable boxer who never quit beating himself up. Punishing, painful and pitiless, with the ultimate Method performance from De Niro at its core, *Raging Bull* is in many ways the culmination of the American psycho-realist tradition – but it's realism pushing through towards spiritual transcendence.

The King Of Comedy 1983, 109 min
cast Robert De Niro, Jerry Lewis, Sandra Bernhard, Diahnne Abbott, Shelly Hack, Ed Herlihy *cin* Fred Schuler *m* Robbie Robertson

An austere anti-comedy about a manic would-be TV personality, Rupert Pupkin (De Niro), who kidnaps his idol Jerry Lewis (playing a fictional version of himself) at gunpoint then delivers his shtick to a captive audience. Clamping down his usually hyperactive camera, Scorsese creates an uncomfortable, claustrophobic satire on fame and celebrity culture that also reflects obliquely on John Hinkley's obsession with Jodie Foster. Way ahead of its time, *The King Of Comedy* was dubbed "flop of the year" by *Entertainment Tonight*.

GoodFellas 1990, 145 min
cast Robert De Niro, Ray Liotta, Joe Pesci, Lorraine Bracco, Paul Sorvino, Frank Sivero, Gina Mastrogiacomo *cin* Michael Ballhaus

Firing on all cylinders, Scorsese taps the exhilaration and exhaustion of the 1980s in this brazen, euphoric gangster movie – a biopic inspired by writer Nicholas Pileggi's interviews with low-level Mafioso Henry Hill. On a technical level the structure, the amoral voiceover and the breathtakingly bold editing strategies come together spectacularly, and Joe Pesci's portrait of a psychopath is absolutely unforgettable. For a younger generation of fans,

this is Scorsese's most gratifying film – older viewers may bemoan the lack of depth.

The Age Of Innocence 1993, 138 min
cast Daniel Day-Lewis, Michelle Pfeiffer, Winona Ryder, Richard E. Grant, Joanne Woodward (narrator) *cin* Michael Ballhaus *m* Elmer Bernstein

Although some felt this Edith Wharton adaptation was an anomaly, Scorsese investigates the manners and mores of nineteenth-century New York society with the same rapt attention he brings to lowlife mobsters. A tragic story about a gentleman (Day-Lewis) who allows the love of his life to slip away under the influence of social conventions, this is arguably Scorsese's most beautiful and moving work.

Casino 1995, 178 min
cast Robert De Niro, Joe Pesci, Sharon Stone, James Woods, Don Rickles, Alan King, Kevin Pollak *cin* Robert Richardson

If *Mean Streets* seemed like a riposte to the grandiosity of *The Godfather* (1972), *Casino* attempts to emulate Francis Ford Coppola's epic scale and ambition. Revisiting the wise-guy milieu for the third time, Scorsese tells the story of Ace Rothstein and Nicky Santoro (De Niro and Pesci), two New York hoodlums who become major players in the history of Las Vegas. Here the sociological detail is married to a more coherent moral vision of tragic hubris and iniquity.

Kundun 1997, 134 min
cast Tenzin Thuthob Tsarong, Gyurme Tethong, Tulku Jamyang Kunga Tenzin, Tencho Gyalpo *cin* Roger Deakins *m* Philip Glass

The odd one out in the Scorsese canon, *Kundun* tells the story of the Dalai Lama's life, from his birth into a poor farming family in the Amdo province of Tibet in 1935 and his recognition as the reincarnation of the thirteenth Dalai Lama two years later, through the Chinese Communist invasion of Tibet in 1950, to his exile to Dharamsala in northern India in 1959. It's a simple story. Yet it's an exotic, strange picture, a film of dreams, portents and visions, a trance-movie in search of transcendence.

Gangs Of New York 2002, 168 min
cast Leonardo DiCaprio, Daniel Day-Lewis, Cameron Diaz, Jim Broadbent, John C. Reilly, Henry Thomas *cin* Michael Ballhaus *m* Howard Shore

Two decades after he first talked about bringing Herbert Asbury's history of criminal mid-nineteenth-century New York to the screen, Scorsese found the backer he needed in Harvey Weinstein's Miramax. His most expensive film has an epic scale but is compromised by conventional blockbuster elements, a weak romantic sub-plot, and a running time that feels rushed even at 168 minutes. Nevertheless, it's a compelling effort, half frontier Western, half gangster movie, with a momentous portrait of villainy from Day-Lewis.

The Departed 2006, 151 min
cast Leonardo DiCaprio, Matt Damon, Jack Nicholson, Mark Wahlberg, Martin Sheen, Vera Farmiga *cin* Michael Ballhaus *m* Howard Shore

The title is a raffish Bostonian synonym for "the deceased". But it equally describes the movie's troubled double agents – mirror images of each other played by Leonardo DiCaprio and Matt Damon – who have put family and home behind them. They are driven, self-made men who nevertheless can't escape their roots. This remake of the fiendishly contrived Hong Kong thriller *Infernal Affairs* (2002) is arguably a knock-off of a knock-off, but it's a thoroughly compelling piece of storytelling, a prestige B-movie elevating chicanery to absurd heights.

S

Ridley Scott
UK, 1937–

Ridley Scott is one of the most successful British directors working in Hollywood today. Part of that British "invasion" of the early 1980s that included Alan Parker and Adrian Lyne, Scott is one of a generation of directors who graduated from television commercials to participate in the high-concept American cinema of the multiplex era.

He was educated at West Hartlepool College of Art and London's Royal College of Art where he studied film. Scott's very first film was a British Film Institute short called *A Boy And A Bicycle* (1966), an exercise for camera and voiceover that seemed functional rather than indicative of any unique take on human experience. In the mid-1960s Scott joined the BBC as an art director, graduating to director on a number of popular TV series, including *Z Cars* and *The Informer*. He then established Ridley Scott Associates, a production facility for creating commercials with which he began to make a name. Noted for their visual panache and smart conceits, Scott's British commercials, notably the award-winning Hovis bread ads with Depression back-to-backs to the strains of Dvořák, played to a cine-literate audience with an intelligent but easily digestible message. In 1984 Scott's Apple Mac ad, with its Orwellian "Big Brother" theme, would make broadcasting history when it aired on American TV during Super Bowl night.

Scott broke into features in 1977 with *The Duellists*, a Joseph Conrad adaptation in which two Napoleonic officers, played by Harvey Keitel and Keith Carradine, embark on a series of duels on the battlefields of Europe. Although the director seemed less interested in narrative and characterization than in his visuals, Scott's debut still won best first film at Cannes that year. The elaboration of style and surface continued in Scott's first two Hollywood projects, arguably his best films, *Alien* (1979) and *Blade Runner* (1982). Boldly designed and visually slick, they generated models of the future that continue to pervade the culture.

Like the best Hollywood product, Scott's work caught something of the zeitgeist. If the Tom Cruise fairy tale *Legend* (1985) was misjudged, *Someone To Watch Over Me* (1987) was a gripping thriller. Infused with 1980s Hollywood morality, it contrasted a lowly New York cop (Tom Berenger) with a fabulously rich Manhattan socialite (Mimi Rogers) to entertaining if unconvincing effect. *Black Rain* (1989) was an exciting yakuza thriller starring Michael Douglas as an American cop chasing his prey across a futuristic Osaka. The characteristic, glistening postmodern imagery confirmed Scott as one of the most influential chroniclers of all that is corrupt, yet the film's racial politics leave much to be desired.

Thelma And Louise (1991) was a rollicking story in which second-wave feminism at last found a seat at the multiplex. The sluggish and politically debatable *1492: Conquest Of Paradise* (1992) commemorated Columbus's voyage to the Americas and starred Gérard Depardieu and Sigourney Weaver. In 1996's effective rite-of-passage picture *White Squall*, Jeff Bridges coaches a bunch of young sailors through their paces and a spectacular storm at sea. Then came *GI Jane* (1997), an over-hyped comic strip in which Demi Moore sets out to prove her mettle by surviving Marine Corps basic training to become one of the guys.

More nuanced and benefiting from state-of-the-art CGI, *Gladiator* (2000) rejuvenated the sword-and-sandals genre with all the feeling for narrative space of a David Lean epic. It remains a key film for its meld of brutal action and meditative calm in Russell Crowe's star persona. *Hannibal* (2001) was a lumbering sequel to Jonathan Demme's *The Silence Of The Lambs* (1990), but found room for satire in the attempt to place Anthony Hopkins's ascetic Lecter within the conventions of a post-*Se7en* Hollywood thriller. If Scott has had difficulty reconciling seductive surfaces with complex narratives, he has always known how to play the Hollywood game of attending to visual pleasure while catering to the popular intellect.

Returning to the digestible narratives of prime-time news, *Black Hawk Down* (2001) reread the bungled 1993 US military raid on Mogadishu as a video game proclaiming American superiority in a year of bitter recriminations. The Nicolas Cage con-man comedy *Matchstick Men* (2003) seemed cute by comparison. Returning to the historical ground of *1492* and *Gladiator*, *Kingdom Of Heaven* (2005) was an ambitious but dull coming-of-age drama set during the Crusades. For a director whose work has so often provided Western parlour homilies prettified with striking visuals, this one crudely played to an America bent on its post-9/11 world-historical mission. It was in striking contrast to the following year's cosy adaptation of Peter Mayle's Provençal jaunt, *A Good Year* (2006), starring Russell Crowe. Crowe also starred, with Denzel Washington, in *American Gangster* (2007), a 1970s-set drug-running thriller. RA

Alien 1979, 117 min
cast Tom Skerritt, Sigourney Weaver, Veronica Cartwright, Harry Dean Stanton, John Hurt, Yaphet Kotto *cin* Derek Vanlint *m* Jerry Goldsmith

Benefiting from H.R. Giger's astonishing creature and a claustrophobic setting, this unbearably tense face-off between the tired crew of an intergalactic mineral freighter and a voracious alien life form reread B-science fiction as an old dark house horror movie set in space. Feisty Sigourney Weaver has been standing up to our worst demons ever since.

S

Close encounters of the sci-fi kind

Ridley Scott's *Alien* (1979) and *Blade Runner* (1982) are widely regarded as being among the finest science-fiction movies ever made. Yet, in many respects, they seem to strive not to be sci-fi at all. *Alien*, though ostensibly a high-calibre sci-fi tale, is in reality an almost perfectly choreographed horror movie: replace its repulsively corporeal monster with a homicidal maniac and the space station with an isolated haunted house and the sci-fi veneer drops away. Similarly, *Blade Runner* is the key film in what has been dubbed the "tech" *noir* sub-genre, its sci-fi plot overlain with lavish neo-*noir* trimmings – rain, shadows and classic plot hooks such as double identities and treachery – and the sense of estrangement which haunted sci-fi movies made during the Cold War replaced by *noir*-ish pessimism about global capitalism.

Sci-fi has always found space for alien monsters, robots and futuristic societies. But whereas many earlier sci-fi films, such as Jack Arnold's *It Came From Outer Space* (1953), were largely dependent upon the wow factor of their intergalactic locations, future Earth scenarios or man-meets-alien plots, in later years sci-fi elements have increasingly been used as pegs upon which any story – from horror to comedy – can be hung.

George Lucas's *Star Wars* (1977) marked the beginning of this trend towards cross-genre fertilization, propelling sci-fi at light speed towards fantasy and especially action. Critics even detected in the franchise the frontier spirit of the Western (and its close cousin the samurai film), with its emphasis on duty, honour and comradeship. Roland Emmerich's *Independence Day* (1996) took things further, using a battery of CGI effects (though not better scripting) to update the fighter pilot films of World War II in an out-and-out patriotic war movie: Washington versus the aliens. This emphasis on special effects can also be seen in films such as Michael Bay's *Armageddon* (1998) which unite sci-fi with the action movie; in James Cameron's *Terminator* films (1984, 1991) much of the excitement focuses on traditional action-movie set pieces such as one-on-one combat and great escapes. The most successful original sci-fi film of recent times, the Wachowski brothers' *The Matrix* (1999), is undeniably a science-fiction movie in terms of its futuristic gloss and man-versus-machine mythology, but it is at the same time a powerful conspiracy-theory thriller. Steven Spielberg's *Minority Report* (2002) and Alex Proyas's *I, Robot* (2004) are essentially fast-paced thrillers in which the science fiction elements motivate the not hugely convincing plots. *Minority Report* also emulates *Blade Runner*'s use of *noir*-ish high-contrast light and shadows, as does Proyas's trenchcoat-draped *Dark City* (1998). Michael Winterbottom's *Code 46* (2003) is set in a classic *noir* location (Shanghai) and centres on a doomed and rather *noir*-ish love affair.

Steven Spielberg has been responsible for another key trend in the multiplex transformation of sci-fi, his *Close Encounters Of The Third Kind* (1977) and *E.T. The Extra-Terrestrial* (1982) foregrounding child protagonists, thus pushing the genre towards the wholesome family entertainment category. Whereas the former was in many respects an inspired and belated piece of homespun Americana preaching a message of tolerance, the latter had elements of a clever *Lassie* remake, with its coming-of-age theme and entertaining story of kids fooling adults who just don't understand. A close neighbour to the kids' movie is the sci-fi comedy strand which includes Barry Sonnenfeld's *Men In Black* (1997) and Joe Dante's *Explorers* (1985). Another recent trend has been the proliferation of comic-book movies: Bryan Singer's *X-Men* (2000), Sam Raimi's *Spider-Man* (2002) and Stephen Norrington's *The League Of Extraordinary Gentlemen* (2003), as well as films featuring older favourites such as Batman and Superman, have blended sci-fi with action, fantasy and knowing humour.

Spielberg's *War Of The Worlds* (2005) was an unusual return to "classic" sci-fi, with its updating of H.G. Wells's story of alien attack. But although the film made decent use of tried-and-tested material, it could be argued that such an approach marks something of a dead end for a genre whose essence lies in novelty and the future. PB

Blade Runner 1982, 117 min

cast Harrison Ford, Rutger Hauer, Sean Young, Edward James Olmos, M. Emmet Walsh, Daryl Hannah *cin* Jordan Cronenweth *m* Vangelis

A visionary crime picture set on the slick, rainy streets of Los Angeles in 2019, this adaptation of Philip K. Dick's novel *Do Androids Dream Of Electric Sheep?* saw Harrison Ford's crumpled "blade runner" charged with the job of tracking and destroying four replicant menials, escaped from an off-world colony. A 1992 director's cut sharpened the film's *noir*-ish feel for the poetry of love and death, removing the voiceover narration and reinforcing this dark fable's reputation as a modern classic.

Thelma And Louise 1991, 129 min

cast Susan Sarandon, Geena Davis, Harvey Keitel, Michael Madsen, Christopher McDonald *cin* Adrean Biddle *m* Hans Zimmer

Geena Davis and Susan Sarandon are a housewife and a waitress fleeing domestic commitments, whose carefree weekend road trip takes a violent turn and becomes an on-the-run road-movie adventure. Although an entertaining and original spin on "women's pictures", this popular 1990s chick flick ultimately didn't rock the patriarchal boat too much, but did capture the spirit of the decade.

S

Gladiator 2000, 155 min

cast Russell Crowe, Joaquin Phoenix, Connie Nielsen, Oliver Reed, Richard Harris *cin* John Mathieson *m* Hans Zimmer

A peplum epic for our times, this multi-Oscar-winning face-off between Russell Crowe's honourable Roman general and a weak, power-hungry imperial usurper (Joaquin Phoenix) rereads ancient history and the epic gladiator battles of Rome's Colosseum as a corporate *mano-a-mano* wrangle, pressing all the right PC buttons but never losing sight of the body count.

Tony Scott
UK, 1944–

Tony is both Ridley Scott's younger brother and an ersatz version of the *Alien* director. His films are more crass, brazen and thrilling, with an insistent focus on steely surfaces, shiny objects and military hardware. An art college and film school graduate, he learned his craft making commercials for his sibling's advertising company, and the influence shows. His debut, *The Hunger* (1983), was a sapphic vampire movie shot like a perfume commercial, complete with billowing curtains and inexplicable doves. Dying an inelegant death at the box office, Scott's career was rescued by auteur producers Don Simpson and Jerry Bruckheimer, who secured his services for *Top Gun* (1986). A phenomenal, epochal hit, it provided the blueprint for Scott's Boy's Own aesthetic, a maximum power cinema fuelled by insane amounts of adrenaline and testosterone.

At his best, Scott hard-wires his movies straight into the central nervous system, as he did with the terrific paranoid conspiracy thriller *Enemy Of The State* (1998), *Crimson Tide* (1995) and the CIA action drama *Spy Game* (2001). It's all the more surprising when this fail-safe formula fails, as it did in *Beverly Hills Cop 2* (1987), *Days Of Thunder* (1990), *The Last Boy Scout* (1991), *The Fan* (1996), *Revenge* (1996), *Man On Fire* (2004), *Domino* (2005) and *Déjà Vu* (2006). Arguably, Scott's great contribution to cinema was to spot the talent in Quentin Tarantino, buying the screenplay for *True Romance*, which gave the boy wonder the financial means to go to work on *Reservoir Dogs*. However, when Scott made *True Romance* years later, in 1993, he didn't adapt his hyperactive style to the deliberate rhythms of Tarantino's script and managed to lose the sparkling dialogue in a miasma of smoke, neon sheen and rapid editing. LH

Top Gun 1986, 110 min

cast Tom Cruise, Kelly McGillis, Val Kilmer, Anthony Edwards, Tom Skerritt, Michael Ironside, Rick Rossovich *cin* Jeffrey Kimball *m* Harold Faltermeyer

A fevered hybrid of Reaganite ideology and hardware porn, *Top Gun* is a bravura tale in which flying instructor Kelly McGillis falls in glossy love with maverick pilot and top-gun wannabe Tom Cruise, aka "Maverick". But as Quentin Tarantino famously pointed out in the indie comedy *Sleep With Me* (1994), the real love in this movie is the one that dare not speak its name – that of Maverick and his ice-cool pilot adversary Val Kilmer, aka "Ice". All surface sheen and pumped action, this is the quintessential 1980s action movie.

Crimson Tide 1995, 115 min

cast Denzel Washington, Gene Hackman, Matt Craven, George Dzundza, Viggo Mortensen, James Gandolfini *cin* Dariusz Wolski *m* Hans Zimmer

More military chest-beating from Scott, Simpson and Bruckheimer. Russian rebels threaten the US, and a nuclear sub is sent out to deliver a pre-emptive strike. The radio goes on the blink leaving the crew to decide the future of the planet. A gung-ho sea dog (Hackman) and his more considered second-in-command (Washington) engage in cod-Socratic dialogue and the movie turns into an ethics lesson interrupted by some steroidal action.

George Seaton
US, 1911–79

Initially an actor, George Seaton encouraged some strong performances in a range of films. Following a radio stint in 1933 – under his birth-name, George Stenius – as the voice of the Lone Ranger, he moved to New York to write. Employed as a contract writer by MGM, he contributed, uncredited, to the script of the Marx Brothers' *A Night At The Opera* (1935), and, credited, to *A Day At The Races* (1937). After a stint at Columbia in the early 1940s, he settled at 20th Century Fox in 1943, where he received an Oscar nomination for screenwriting *The Song Of Bernadette* (1943).

It was 1945 before he got his directing break with the Betty Grable musical *Diamond Horseshoe*; two years later he wrote and directed the classic Christmas tear-jerker *Miracle On 34th Street*. *For Heaven's Sake* (1950) was a light comedy about angelic intervention in a troublesome birth, while *The Country Girl* (1954), which stripped some of the glamour from show business, won Oscars for Grace Kelly's acting and Seaton's screenplay. In the 1960s, as well as a couple of tolerable entertainments, Seaton made the World War II espionage drama *The Counterfeit Traitor* (1962) and the happy virus comedy *What's So Bad About Feeling Good?* (1968). In 1970, *Airport*, with its all-star cast, improbable scenarios and hammy clichés, set the model for the blockbuster disaster movies to come, and three years later, the Western *Showdown* was his final film. JR

Miracle On 34th Street 1947, 96 min, b/w

cast Maureen O'Hara, John Payne, Edmund Gwenn, Gene Lockhart, Natalie Wood, Porter Hall *cin* Lloyd Ahern, Charles Clarke *m* Cyril Mockridge

Though it missed out on best picture, *Miracle* picked up Oscars for original story, screenplay and supporting actor (odd, as he plays Santa Claus) Edmund Gwenn. The setup – Macy's Santa claims to be the real thing, and has to defend himself against charges of insanity – is corny, and we all know how it will end, but this matters little in a work of such homespun charm.

S

Susan Seidelman

US, 1952–

Susan Seidelman remains a poignant symbol of the possibilities of independent filmmaking in America. After majoring in fashion design at Drexel Institute of Technology, she worked for a Philadelphia television station before studying film at New York University. An award-winning short, *And You Act Like One Too* (1976), announced her interest in women's lives and voices. Beginning with a $10,000 inheritance, Seidelman made her first feature – *Smithereens* – on 16mm for $80,000 in 1982. Producing, co-writing, directing and editing, she drew on her own experience of New York's Lower East Side for this story of a young woman determined to break into the music scene. Shot on the streets and subways and driven by its frisky editing and soundtrack by The Feelies, it was an energetic poem to late 1970s SoHo and became a surprise hit at Cannes.

Then came the punk comedy *Desperately Seeking Susan* (1985). It was a 1980s phenomenon that was made for $5 million and raked in $30 million. It propelled Seidelman into the big time, but her subsequent studio films represent in some way a betrayal of her gifts. *Making Mr Right* (1987) is intermittently interesting, with its absurd scenario about a PR executive falling for an android, and does shed some light on the heterosexual dynamic. But nothing can be said for the disastrous *She-Devil* (1989), a completely misguided Hollywood adaptation of Fay Weldon's *The Life And Loves Of A She-Devil*.

Alongside increasing television work came projects such as the 1993 short *The Dutch Master*, starring a disillusioned Mira Sorvino who becomes intrigued by a young man in a Dutch painting. It received an Academy Award nomination for best live-action short and was subsequently re-released in the 1994 portmanteau feature *Erotic Tales*. In *Gaudi Afternoon* (2001), Judy Davis plays an American translator in Barcelona who sets out on the trail of a missing husband. Davis's journey of self-discovery seemed to crystallize what Seidelman's films have meant to her audience. RA

Desperately Seeking Susan 1985, 103 min
cast Rosanna Arquette, Madonna, Aidan Quinn, Mark Blum, Robert Joy, Laurie Metcalf, Anna Levine *cin* Ed Lachman *m* Thomas Newman

Challenging suburban conformity with the same acuity Steven Soderbergh would bring to *sex, lies and videotape* (1989), this early salvo in the US indie revolution was a "Girl's Own" story of wit and verve. Pairing Rosanna Arquette as the suburban housewife looking for something different with Madonna as a ragtag street angel, and mixing it up in a mistaken identity conceit, Seidelman brought screwball comedy bang up to date.

Ousmane Sembène

Senegal, 1923–2007

Ousmane Sembène was the father of modern African cinema, a novelist, a documentarian, a director, and above all a teacher. The self-educated son of a fisherman, he fought in World War II, then worked in the docks of Marseille, which provided both a political education and the subject for his first novel, *The Black Docker* (1956). He wrote nine other novels, including the classic *God's Bits Of Wood* (1960). Despite their popularity, Sembène decided that if he was going to reach his mostly illiterate West African audience he needed to make movies. So, at the age of 40, he joined the VGIK film school in Moscow. Colonialism, patriarchy and government corruption were subsequently the targets of his satirical, Marxist lens.

Sembène never took the easy option, preferring thorny complexity to Manichean rigidity, offering possible solutions rather than comforting conclusions for a continent trapped between the stifling traditions of the past and the corrupt bureaucracies of the present. As he said himself, cinema is a "mirror, so my people can take responsibility and solve their own problems". Unsurprisingly, movies like *Xala* (1974) have often been censored or banned in his home country, Senegal.

After making three short films, Sembène made his feature debut, the *vérité*-style *Black Girl* (1965). It told the despairing story of a Senegalese woman working as a maid for a Riviera couple who discovers that colonialism is alive and well among the French bourgeoisie. *Mandabi* (*The Money Order*, 1968), the first feature film in an African language, was based on his own novel about a man trapped in Dakar who's prevented from cashing a money order by the frustrating machinations of corrupt government mandarins. The same moneyed class was mercilessly parodied in *Xala*, in which an African businessman has his car washed and radiator filled with Evian, while adjoining streets are teeming with beggars. Sembène was bold enough to hold up a satirical mirror to religion, or at least to the people who use the Muslim faith for their own selfish ends.

In his *chef-d'oeuvre*, *Ceddo* (1977), Senegalese villagers stoically try to resist conversion to Islam, while his last film, *Mooladé* (2004), revealed the medieval barbarity behind the "Islamic" practice of female circumcision. This award-winning masterpiece was the second part of his (now unfinished) "Heroism Of Daily Life" trilogy, which began with *Faat Kiné* (2000), another feminist fable about the stigma of being a single mother in African society. The director's wrath, however, was not just reserved for Africans. Sembène returned to the subject of World War II, both to attack the colonial power and to excavate a forgotten piece of history in two films of exquisite power: an African village's doomed rebellion against conscription to the French army in *Emitai* (1971) and a French massacre of African war heroes in *Camp de Thiaroyé* (1988). LH

Xala 1974, 123 min

cast Thierno Leye, Seune Samb, Miriam Niang *cin* Georges Caristan, Orlando R. López, Seydina D. Saye, Farba Seck *m* Samba Diabara Samb

There's something distinctly Buñuelian about the opening of this scathing, nonchalant satire, in which a group of African businessmen in newly independent Senegal take over the previously French-run chamber of commerce in the name of socialism and are instantly corrupted by suitcases brimming with cash handed to them by their former colonial oppressors. One of the businessmen, the laconically corrupt El Hadji, then suffers from impotence on the night of his wedding to his third wife. Believing he is the victim of a curse, he seeks the help of local healers.

Moolaadé 2004, 124 min

cast Fatoumata Coulibaly, Maïmouna Hélène Diarra, Salimata Traoré, Dominique Zeïda, Mah Compaoré *cin* Dominique Gentil *m* Boncana Maïga

Against a bustling cacophony of goats, chickens and drums, and etched in sunny colours, Sembène's final film effortlessly evokes the hubbub of village life in West Africa. Four young girls seek sanctuary from "purification" – circumcision – with a woman who refused to have her own daughter mutilated. Invoking the spell of protection, she places herself in conflict with her peers who try to find ways to destroy her powers. Sembène's mature, complex analysis of medieval practices versus Western freedoms unfolds with a fable-like simplicity and clarity.

Mrinal Sen
Bangladesh (formerly India), 1923–

One of the great triumvirate of Bengali filmmakers (along with Satyajit Ray and Ritwik Ghatak), Mrinal Sen is easily the most political of the three. After dabbling in journalism, Sen joined the Marxist-leaning Indian People's Theatre Association, which took agitprop plays to isolated rural areas, and became a member of the Communist Party. After making several openly Marxist-themed Bengali films, Sen burst upon the Indian national consciousness with the Hindi-language *Bhuvan Shome* (1969), a spare film in which an uptight urban widower finds emotional salvation amongst simple village folk when he goes on a rural hunting expedition. Around this time, Sen and several of his contemporaries attempted to develop a socially engaged "Parallel Cinema" to compete with mainstream Bollywood.

The 1970s and 80s were Sen's most fertile phase; he placed Bengali middle-class concerns against the larger backdrop of urban political unrest in such films as *Calcutta 71* (1971), *Ek din pratidin* (And

Quiet Rolls The Dawn, 1979), *Akaler sandhane* (*In Search Of Famine*, 1980) and *Kharij* (*The Case Is Closed*, 1982). The influence of directors François Truffaut, Glauber Rocha, Fernando Solanas and Robert Bresson is also evident in many of the films from this period. Sen's commitment to political issues in his work meant that he had an intellectually fractious relationship with Ray, who was avowedly apolitical in his filmmaking. NR

Akaler sandhane (In Search Of Famine) 1980, 115 min

cast Smita Patil, Sreela Majumdar, Dhritiman Chatterjee, Satya Banerjee *cin* K.K. Mahajan *m* Salil Choudhury

A film crew goes to a small village in Bengal to shoot a recreation of the 1943 famine (man-made by the British as food was diverted for World War II troops). The reality the crew encounter is shockingly far removed from their urban Calcutta lives. The masterful film-within-a-film structure enables a critique of the way in which the story of the famine has been retold – both in other films such as Satyajit Ray's *Ashani sanket* (*Distant Thunder*, 1973) and in this film itself.

Mack Sennett
Canada, 1880–1960

Nicknamed the "King of Comedy", Mack Sennett created the template for Hollywood comedy in the early years of the movies. Largely improvised and with the loosest of structures, Sennett's films were fast and furious, always involved slapstick and usually culminated in a riotous chase sequence. He was also a great discoverer of talent and launched the film careers of – among others – Harry Langdon, Roscoe "Fatty" Arbuckle, Ben Turpin, and Charlie Chaplin.

After a brief career as a vaudeville actor in New York, Sennett joined Biograph Studios in 1908 where he worked for D.W. Griffith, initially as a performer, and later as a writer and director of comedy films. Four years later, he left to form his own company, Keystone, taking with him a number of Biograph actors, including the versatile comedienne Mabel Normand (his lover at the time). Between 1912 and 1935, Sennett produced, directed, wrote and performed in hundreds of films, many of them shorts, and was responsible for the first ever full-length comedy film, *Tillie's Punctured Romance* (1914), which starred Normand, Chaplin and Marie Dressler.

Producing mainly short films, Keystone was highly prolific – once a comic formula had been established it would be repeated in every conceivable permutation. Characters were the broadest of stereotypes and included the wide-eyed Normand in domestic situations opposite either Chaplin or Arbuckle, the cross-eyed Ben Turpin whose roles burlesqued other movie stars, and, most famously, the anarchic band of incompetent policemen known as the Keystone Kops. Sennett was also aware of the drawing power of sex, and pretty young women – the Mack Sennett Bathing Beauties – would frequently appear en masse for the flimsiest of reasons and in the flimsiest of costumes.

In 1915 Keystone became a part of Triangle (a company formed by Sennett, Griffith and Thomas Ince). Sennett left just two years later but continued to produce large numbers of comedy films as an independent. Perhaps unsurprisingly, given the physical nature of his comedy, Sennett's career declined spectacularly in the 1930s following the arrival of sound. RB

Tillie's Punctured Romance 1914, 73 min, b/w

cast Charlie Chaplin, Mabel Normand, Marie Dressler, Mack Swain, Charles Bennett, Chester Conklin *cin* Hans F. Koenekamp, Frank D. Williams

The first ever comedy feature film accurately shows Sennett's strengths and weaknesses. It stars Marie Dressler as a naïve country girl, Tillie, who is fleeced by city slicker Chaplin with the help of his girlfriend Mabel (Mabel Normand). The humour is predictably broad, much of it derived from the fact that Dressler was a rather solid 45-year-old, but there are some good set pieces, including Tillie getting tipsy, Chaplin attacking a tiger-skin rug and the inevitable appearance of the Keystone Kops.

Coline Serreau

France, 1947–

Coline Serreau has directed some of the most provocative and exportable films in modern French cinema. The daughter of theatre people, she divided her studies between academic pursuits – literature, music – and the performing arts – dance and trapeze. After acting in the 1970s, her first directed feature was *Mais qu'est-ce qu'elles veulent?* (*But What Do They Want?* 1977), a documentary in which women talk about their lives and aspirations.

A product of the post-1968 *café-théâtre* performance tradition, Serreau's satirical panache would combine with an astute political sense to interrogate patriarchal values. *Pourquoi pas!* (*Why Not!* 1977) focused on a *ménage à trois*, showing something of Serreau's utopian idealism. In 1985, *Trois hommes et un couffin* (*3 Men And A Cradle*) out-grossed *Rambo* in France, and earned Serreau her first César. It was a huge hit when successfully remade in Hollywood as *Three Men And A Baby* by Leonard Nimoy in 1987. *Romuald et Juliette* (1989) took issue with cut-throat corporate politics as Daniel Auteuil's white executive forms a strategic, then romantic, partnership with his black cleaning woman.

In 1992's *La crise*, Vincent Lindon starred as a yuppie husband who loses his job and his wife on the same day, but finds regenerative friendship with a down-and-out young man. Lindon also took the lead in Serreau's 1996 sci-fi comedy, *La belle verte* (*The Good Green World*, 1996). The director herself also appears, playing an alien who comes to Earth to bring a utopian message about how the planet could be. Lindon, an actor adept at portraying middle-class male vulnerability, starred in 2001's *Chaos*, in which a bourgeois couple witness an Algerian prostitute being beaten in the street. In 2003, the belated sequel to *3 Men, 18 ans après* (*18 Years Later*), did not repeat the original's box-office success.

Serreau's accessible comedies put women's perspectives on masculine manners before a mainstream audience. In 2004, she was made a chevalier in the *Légion d'honneur*. RA

3 Men And A Cradle (3 hommes et un couffin) 1985, 106 min

cast Roland Giraud, Michel Boujenah, André Dussollier, Philippine Leroy-Beaulieu *cin* Jean-Yves Escoffier, Jean-Jacques Bouhon

Three swinging bachelors suddenly and unexpectedly find themselves with a baby to care for and, to complicate matters, gangsters and the cops are also interested in the infant's cradle. Serreau's riotous caper pressed all the right buttons, while hilariously skewering the "New Man" of the 1980s.

Romuald et Juliette 1989, 112 min

cast Daniel Auteuil, Firmine Richard, Pierre Vernier, Maxime Leroux, Gilles Privat *cin* Jean-Noël Ferragut

In this tale of an ousted executive (Auteuil) and his affair with his office cleaner (Richard) Serreau once again took the moral temperature of her times: it's both a warm, surprisingly astute romantic comedy and also a pointed critique of yuppie brinkmanship.

Steven Shainberg

US

With its dazzling combination of risqué subject matter and self-conscious verve, Steven Shainberg's S&M oddity *Secretary* (2002) contained all the attention-seeking chutzpah of a debut that doubles as a calling card to major Hollywood studios. And for all the attention his real debut received six years earlier it may as well have been the director's first film, because up until the eye-catching moment when Maggie Gyllenhaal bends over an office desk to be severely reprimanded for her typing errors, the director's career had been largely unremarkable.

After graduating from Yale with a degree in East Asian studies, Shainberg took the now traditional route to Hollywood: film school, MTV, adverts and shorts. Shainberg had the prescience, however, to acquire the rights to three Jim Thompson novels just before they became much sought-after property in the mid-1990s. *Hit Me* (1996), his adaptation of the crime writer's opus *A Swell-Looking Babe*,

S

about a bellhop caught up in a heist, was dismissed as yet another failed attempt to pilfer from Quentin Tarantino. Once his first film had been quietly forgotten, Shainberg made his second debut with *Secretary* – this time with the desired effect, successfully grabbing the attention of the industry, the critics and the public alike. His success also enabled him to corral a bona fide Hollywood star – Nicole Kidman – for his next project, *Fur* (2006), a fantasy inspired by the life of photographer Diane Arbus. However, the film was a dud, crammed with moments of stale surrealism. LH

Secretary 2002, 104 min
cast James Spader, Maggie Gyllenhaal, Jeremy Davies, Patrick Bauchau, Stephen McHattie, Oz Perkins *cin* Steven Fierberg *m* Angelo Badalamenti

A self-harming ingénue, Maggie Gyllenhaal, is hired as a secretary by James Spader, discovers there's more to the job than typing and filing and soon adds S&M to her CV. However, the relationship between boss and underling subtly alters over time, making it difficult to detect who exactly is the S and who is the M. The grand master of sexual dysfunction and erotic displacement, Luis Buñuel, knew that the kinky should always come out of the ordinary; unfortunately Shainberg overeggs the surrealistic effects with a second-hand dreamscape. Startling and refreshing, nonetheless.

Jim Sharman
Australia, 1945–

Jim Sharman left the circus, where his father had his own travelling sideshow, to join the theatre. A graduate of the National Institute of Dramatic Arts in Sydney, he quickly established himself as an acclaimed director of avant-garde theatre and continued in experimental mode with the kooky sci-fi musical film *Shirley Thompson Versus The Aliens* (1972). Moving to England to direct a stage version of *Jesus Christ Superstar*, he met actor Richard O'Brien, who approached him with a musical he'd been working on. *The Rocky Horror Show* was meant to run for a limited period as a workshop performance in the tiny Royal Court Upstairs, but transferred first to a large London venue and then to the US. The 1975 film version gradually built up a devoted following, but its phenomenal cult success has placed Sharman's subsequent film career firmly in the shade.

After helming two gothic dramas, *Summer Of Secrets* (1976) and *The Night, The Prowler* (1978) in Australia, Sharman reunited with O'Brien in an attempt to recapture *Rocky Horror*'s anarchic spirit and box-office takings. *Shock Treatment* (1981) didn't live up to either the transgressive promise of its title or its predecessor's achievements, and Sharman returned to Australia and to the theatre. LH

The Rocky Horror Picture Show 1975, 100 min
cast Tim Curry, Susan Sarandon, Barry Bostwick, Richard O'Brien, Jonathan Adams, Nell Campbell *cin* Peter Suschitzky *m* Richard O'Brien

A young couple, Brad and Janet, enter the alternative universe of Dr Frank'N'Furter, a transvestite from the planet of Transexual in the galaxy of Transylvania, who has created the perfect man, Rocky Horror, with the help of his twisted assistants. This is definitely not a movie to watch home alone, simply because without a crowd clad in stockings and suspenders rabidly quoting the lines, boisterously joining in the songs, firing off water pistols and throwing rice at the appropriate moments, it just isn't the same delirious experience.

Don Sharp
Australia, 1922–

An eclectic and unassuming craftsman, Don Sharp would seem to be the dictionary definition of the journeyman director. But this is selling him short: his films are, for the most part, directed with brio and muscular authority, and have attracted particular admiration from British critic and screenwriter David Pirie. After acting in Australia, Sharp moved to Britain, and found his directorial home at Hammer Studios, which welcomed dependable artisans who could work with low budgets, tight schedules and occasionally inebriated actors. *The Kiss Of The Vampire* (1963), *The Devil-Ship Pirates* (1964) and *Rasputin: The Mad Monk* (1966) all bore the mark of an indomitable professional, as did non-Hammer fare such as *Witchcraft* (1964), which featured Lon Chaney Jr, and *The Face Of Fu Manchu* (1965). In the 1970s, Sharp made the cult Hell's Angels horror film *Psychomania* (aka *The Deathwheelers*, 1971), before establishing himself as a reliable director of enjoyably efficient thrillers such as *Callan* (1974), *Hennessy* (1975) and *The Thirty-Nine Steps* (1978). Sharp continued his career into the 1980s, working in television in Hollywood. LH

The Face Of Fu Manchu 1965, 89 min
cast Christopher Lee, Nigel Green, Joachim Fuchsberger, Karin Dor, Tsai Chin, Howard Marion Crawford *cin* Ernest Steward *m* Christopher Whelan

After witnessing the execution of his deadly nemesis Fu Manchu (Christopher Lee), Sir Nayland Smith (Nigel Green) returns to London, only to get an eerie sense of déjà vu, as a string of familiar crimes are committed. Improbably exciting and politically incorrect, this is Sharp's best film.

The Thirty-Nine Steps 1978, 102 min
cast Robert Powell, David Warner, Eric Porter, Karen Dotrice, John Mills, George Baker, Ronald Pickup, Timothy West *cin* Harry Pottle *m* Ed Welch

Drawing upon his pulling power as television's Jesus Christ (*Jesus Of Nazareth*, 1978), Robert Powell plays the third filmic incarnation of John Buchan's luckless hero Richard Hannay, the archetypal innocent caught in a web of international intrigue. While Sharp's version is a pale shadow of Hitchcock's *noir*-ish 1935 original, he clearly

S

learnt from the mistakes of Ralph Thomas's pedestrian 1959 remake, firmly keeping the pedal to the metal all the way through to the outlandish climactic set piece on the clock face of Big Ben.

Jim Sheridan
Republic of Ireland, 1949–

A prolific playwright and theatre director, and co-founder of Dublin's Project Arts Centre, Jim Sheridan moved to New York in 1982, an experience that provided the inspiration for the loosely autobiographical *In America* (2004), and the name of his production company, Hell's Kitchen.

Sheridan's lead in *In America* is played by Paddy Considine – he is a passionate, driven, impetuous, loving, funny and deeply wounded individual. Similar working-class heroes crop up in all Sheridan's films: the afflicted artist Christy Brown (Daniel Day-Lewis) in his acclaimed debut, *My Left Foot* (1989); the wrongly convicted Republican Gerry Conlon (Day-Lewis again) in *In The Name Of The Father* (1993), and the Lear-ish Bull McCabe (Richard Harris) in *The Field* (1990).

Whatever their faults (and Sheridan often strains for effect), you can feel the full force of his personality in these films, and they established Sheridan as a bona fide actors' director. Politically, he has tackled the Troubles with consistent conviction and integrity. While *In The Name Of The Father* used some dubious dramatic shorthand, it's substantially more honest than the case that put Conlon in jail for fifteen years. *The Boxer* (1997) was a worthy, if somewhat laborious attempt to disavow sectarian violence. Sheridan also wrote Mike Newell's *Into The West* (1992), wrote and produced Terry George's *Some Mother's Son* (1996), and was an executive producer on Paul Greengrass's *Bloody Sunday* (2002).

After all this, Sheridan inexplicably agreed to direct the gangsta rapper 50 Cent in the pseudo-biopic *Get Rich Or Die Tryin'* (2005), a colossal error in judgement and a lousy movie. TC

My Left Foot 1989, 103 min
cast Daniel Day-Lewis, Brenda Fricker, Ray McAnally, Ruth McCabe, Fiona Shaw, Eanna MacLiam, Alison Whelan *cin* Jack Conroy *m* Elmer Bernstein

Born paralysed with cerebral palsy, Christy Brown is encouraged to learn to express himself through the use of his functional left foot by his indomitable mam. He grows up to become a published writer and a painter, and falls in love with his nurse. Sheridan (who also co-wrote the screenplay with Shane Connaughton) avoids most of the pitfalls associated with these triumph of the underdog scenarios: the triumphs here are few and hard-won, and the underdog is arrogant, prickly and an alcoholic. The film dares to be funny as well as painful.

Kaneto Shindo
Japan, 1912–

The reputation of the underappreciated Kaneto Shindo can only grow as the rediscovery of his films continues apace. He has directed over forty movies and written two hundred scripts in a career spanning over half a century, but his most fruitful period was also Japan's – the 1960s. Landmark works such as *Naked Island* (1960), *Onibaba* (1964) and *Kuroneko* (1967) deserve to be considered among the finest Japanese films of the era, and mark out Shindo as a director of rare ability.

Before becoming a director, Shindo worked with Kenji Mizoguchi as a screenwriter and assistant director, and even completed a documentary on the filmmaker in 1975. His mentor's influence is reflected in the numerous strong women characters in his own films (many played by his wife, Nobuko Otowa). Shindo's earlier works, including his autobiographical debut, *The Story Of My Loving Wife* (1951), dwelt on the impact of the atom bomb on Hiroshima, whereas several of his films from the 1970s concerned the role of sex in society. All of his acknowledged classics from the 1960s demonstrate his mastery of *mise en scène*, light, pacing, and especially sound. *Naked Island*'s sparse use of dialogue adds to its power; *Onibaba*'s percussion-led soundtrack amplifies its disturbingly unconventional horrors. Both *Onibaba* and *Kuroneko* also highlight Shindo's weirdly offbeat sensibility, and his magnificent sense of the eerie. NN

Naked Island (Hadaka no shima) 1960, 94 min, b/w
cast Nobuko Otowa, Taiji Tonoyama, Shinji Tanaka, Masanori Horimoto *cin* Kiyomi Kuroda *m* Hikaru Hayashi

Shindo's stark depiction of a peasant family's existence on a barren waterless coastal island is both an exposé of the poverty of the times, and a perfect marriage of style and content. Containing almost no dialogue, the film relies on the power of Shindo's images, such as the pseudo-documentary sequence depicting the endless transportation of fresh water to the parched soil of the island, and an assured pace that effectively conveys the rhythms of the protagonists' lives.

Onibaba 1964, 103 min, b/w
cast Nobuko Otowa, Jitsuko Yoshimura, Kei Sato, Jukichi Uno, Taiji Tonoyama *cin* Kiyomi Kuroda *m* Hikaru Hayashi

This bizarre, arresting movie packs an unsettling punch. Set in an undefined wartime past, a mother and daughter-in-law survive by selling the weapons and armour of soldiers they murder by luring them into a deep hole in the ground, concealed by the seven-foot-tall grass around their home. When a neighbour returns from the war with the news that the son (and husband) of the family has died, a dark sexually charged emotional triangle is established. The film is rich in eerie atmosphere, the sinister long grass rustling ominously throughout, its menace such that it feels as if it is almost alive.

Esfir Shub
Russia, 1894–1959

Esfir Shub is the mother of the modern compilation documentary. She entered the Soviet film industry in 1922 as an editor, adjusting American imports to make them "appropriate" for Soviet audiences. Sergei Eisenstein and Dziga Vertov's ideas on montage would be highly influential. Commissioned to work on newsreel and documentary footage of the pre-Soviet period for the tenth anniversary of the Revolution, she made *The Fall Of The Romanov Dynasty* (1927) and *Lev Tolstoy And The Russia Of Nicholas II* (1928). Shub's achievement was to generate a sense of ironic detachment through pointed juxtapositions of shots assisted by the narration, often written by her.

The official insistence on dry socialist realism meant Shub was criticized for "formalism", and for a time she was dismissed as merely an editor, thus denying her a due authorial credit for her work. However, in 1935 she was officially recognized for her contribution to Soviet film art. Her compilations marked the progress of the Revolution – *The Great Way* (1927), *Today* (1930), *Komsomol – Patron Of Electrification* (1932). In *Spain* (1939) she compiled footage from Soviet cameramen covering the Spanish Civil War. *Twenty Years Of Soviet Cinema* (1940), a collaboration with Vsevelod Pudovkin, reviewed the achievements of her generation.

Although not a major innovator, Shub's work reached big audiences, and her legacy can be felt in the editorializing zeal of such contemporary documentary filmmakers as Michael Moore. RA

The Fall Of The Romanov Dynasty (Padenie dinastii Romanovykh) 1927, 65 min, b/w
with Emperor Franz Josef, Kaiser Wilhelm II, V.I. Lenin, Tsar Nicholas II

Part of Esfir Shub's legacy was to preserve footage that otherwise would have been destroyed or lost. This "montage of film document", the result of tireless months of trawling

A close-up of Jitsuko Yoshimura captures the eerie menace of Shindo's *Onibaba*.

through the archives, charted the period from 1913 to 1917 during which Tsar Nicholas II lost his grip on the state and the aristocracy lost power. With often humorous and piquant associations and resonances, Shub highlighted the pathos of this time while investing Russia's progress towards Bolshevism with genuine emotional intensity.

M. Night Shyamalan
India, 1970–

In the CGI era, few directors suggest the possibility of the metaphysical so convincingly and with such compassion as M. Night Shyamalan. He was given a Super 8 camera as a child, and had made 45 films by the age of 17, vowing to become the next Spielberg. After studying film at New York University, Shyamalan made his first feature with the backing of his wealthy parents. *Praying With Anger* (1992)

S

was written and directed by Shyamalan, who also starred as a young Indian-American who returns to the old country to visit his ancestral home. It evinced a developed grasp of *mise en scène*, a magic-realist visual sensibility and a preoccupation with the metaphysical that would become characteristic of the Shyamalan style.

Less artistically successful, and fraught with studio politics at Miramax, *Wide Awake* (1998) portrayed the spiritual dimension of a young boy dealing with the death of his beloved grandfather. Shyamalan's sensitivity towards his child protagonists, most notably in *The Sixth Sense* (1999), and his ability to combine weighty themes with accessible emotions are reminiscent of his hero Spielberg. It is a formula that has made him one of Hollywood's most successful creators.

After his visionary blockbuster, Shyamalan again collaborated with Bruce Willis for 2000's *Unbreakable*. Willis's train crash survivor becomes the unwitting fixation of Samuel L. Jackson's comic-book obsessive in what was an ambitious experiment in audience manipulation. The protagonist and the audience are left to ponder the emotional and psychological consequences for the unusually gifted hero. *Signs* (2002) found another uncertain hero, this time Mel Gibson, playing a minister who has lost his faith and is flummoxed by the crop circles that mysteriously form on his land. This aroused our curiosity but was eventually an empty ploy.

Adept at generating strangeness in the modern world, Shyamalan can, at his most metaphysical, leave us wanting more in the way of underpinning credibility. *The Village* (2004) focuses on a small Pennsylvania backwoods community in which a truce between the villagers and the creatures that inhabit the woods begins to unravel after a violent act. In 2006's *Lady In The Water*, a sea nymph fetches up in an apartment building's swimming pool. Shyamalan is the most high profile proponent of the imaginative turn Hollywood horror cinema has taken in the wake of *The Blair Witch Project* (1999). RA

The Sixth Sense 1999, 107 min
cast Bruce Willis, Haley Joel Osment, Toni Collette, Olivia Williams, Donnie Wahlberg, Glenn Fitzgerald *cin* Tak Fujimoto *m* James Newton Howard

This sombre tale of a boy coming to terms with the fact that he sees the dead forges a touching rapport between young Haley Joel Osment and Bruce Willis, playing the psychologist to whom he turns. Shot in Shyamalan's adopted home town of Philadelphia, the film is imbued with a stealthy unease and a mounting premonition of sadness, making it one of the most striking mainstream horror movies in years.

The Village 2004, 108 min
cast Joaquin Phoenix, Bryce Dallas Howard, Adrien Brody, Sigourney Weaver, William Hurt *cin* Roger Deakins *m* James Newton Howard

This account of a village terrorized by "those we don't speak of" – destructive entities that live in the adjoining woods – takes its cue from *The Blair Witch Project* (1999) and its politics from the post-9/11 ethos of Homeland Security. The result is chilling and odd.

George Sidney
US, 1916–2002

"Sidney has ruined more good musicals with more gusto than any director in history", according to critic Andrew Sarris. While other musical directors, such as Vincente Minnelli and Busby Berkeley, have been honoured with auteur status, George Sidney has never been regarded with much acclaim.

The "anonymous and inveterate iconoclast", as *Film Comment* has dubbed him, worked his way up from MGM messenger boy to director in the 1930s. After his best-forgotten feature debut *Free And Easy* (1941), Sidney established himself as an inventive director of MGM musicals with the Gene Kelly vehicles *Thousands Cheer* (1943) and *Anchors Aweigh* (1945) and the Esther Williams "waterworks" of *Bathing Beauty* (1944). Under the aegis of producer and genius Arthur Freed and others, the director churned out a slew of musical classics – *The Harvey Girls* (1946), *Annie Get Your Gun* (1950), *Show Boat* (1951) and *Kiss Me Kate* (1953) – occasionally drawing breath to make non-musicals such as *The Three Musketeers* (1948) and *Scaramouche* (1952).

When Sidney left MGM for Columbia, the quality of his films dropped, with *Pal Joey* (1957) being the only high point in a muddle of mediocrity. He bounced back briefly when he returned to MGM for the Elvis Presley extravaganza *Viva Las Vegas* (1964). His supporters argue that almost every Sidney movie boasts a moment of anarchic, self-referential glee that's genuinely worthy of Jean-Luc Godard, whether it's Gene Kelly dancing with Jerry Mouse in *Anchors Aweigh*, or the final reel of *The Swinger* (1966) suddenly rewinding and miraculously saving its two leads from a fatal car crash. Appropriately, Sidney quit filmmaking in 1968 (making his final film, the Tommy Steele vehicle *Half A Sixpence*, the previous year), just when the death knell was sounding for the classic big-budget film musical. LH

Anchors Aweigh 1945, 143 min
cast Gene Kelly, Frank Sinatra, Kathryn Grayson, José Iturbi, Leon Ames, Henry Armetta *cin* Robert Planck, Charles Boyle *m* Georgie Stoll

A cameo by one of MGM's stars, Jerry of *Tom And Jerry* fame, impishly steals this film from under the noses of Frank Sinatra and Gene Kelly, who play two sailors on shore leave who find love in Hollywood. Jerry's big moment arrives in a delirious fantasy sequence in which Gene and Jerry miraculously dance side by side. It's one of the most genuinely ecstatic and ground-breaking moments in American cinema history.

S

Scaramouche 1952, 115 min

cast Stewart Granger, Eleanor Parker, Janet Leigh, Mel Ferrer, Henry Wilcoxon, Lewis Stone, Nina Foch *cin* Charles Rosher *m* Victor Young

During the period of the French Revolution, Stuart Granger seeks revenge on the Marquis who killed his best friend while hiding out with a troupe of actors. At its giddy best, this is essentially a musical without a song, like the famous climactic sword fight that clocks in at a stupendous six minutes and fifteen seconds, and is almost as exquisitely choreographed and as exuberantly inventive as anything you'll find in an Arthur Freed production.

Pal Joey 1957, 111 min

cast Frank Sinatra, Kim Novak, Rita Hayworth, Barbara Nichols, Elizabeth Patterson *cin* Harold Lipstein *m* Richard Rogers, Lorenz Hart

From the very first scene, in which Frank Sinatra is thrown out of town for propositioning a minor, Sidney's vulgarity runs throughout this lurid film version of Rodgers and Hart's 1940 Broadway musical. Sinatra is a penniless singer and rake who plays doubles with both icy, nubile dancer Kim Novak and wealthy widow Rita Hayworth.

Don Siegel
US, 1912–91

One of an unofficial school of tough, terse genre marksmen (he was born the same year as fellow B-movie heavies Samuel Fuller and André de Toth), Don Siegel cranked out 35-plus features in as many years, usually as a director for hire and often on quick, low-budget shoots. His various studio contracts often left him little in the way of project selection or control over their final outcome. Siegel was forced to add reassuring book ends to his chilling McCarthy allegory *Invasion Of The Body Snatchers* (1955), and he was the first person to use the Directors Guild of America's credit pseudonym "Allen Smithee", for *Death Of A Gunfighter* (1969), after Siegel argued that star Richard Widmark had assumed creative authority over the film.

Yet even under confining circumstances, Siegel was able to carve out an auteurist niche for himself, with his gift for lean and lissome montage (he had previously worked as a film editor), his startlingly matter-of-fact approach to onscreen violence and his knack for icy atmospherics (best showcased in *Body Snatchers*). A late developer – notwithstanding his solid feature debut, *The Verdict* (1946), starring Peter Lorre and Sidney Greenstreet – Siegel worked best with male actors like the ageing John Wayne in *The Shootist* (1976), and he had difficulty creating memorable women's roles.

The commercially successful run of five films he made with his protégé and friend Clint Eastwood raised Siegel's standing and increased his creative capital in Hollywood. (Siegel played a small role as a bartender in Eastwood's 1971 directorial debut, *Play Misty For Me*, and Eastwood dedicated 1992's *Unforgiven* to Siegel's memory.) Siegel later made a conscious effort to claim authorship for his work by using the opening title "A Siegel Film", which also became the title of his posthumously published autobiography.

Remarkably for a career largely beholden to contract assignments, Siegel's oeuvre does repeatedly return to familiar themes. These include the perils and hypocrisies of macho entitlement (examined with particularly dark enchantment in *The Beguiled*, 1971, which starred Eastwood as a Union soldier in the Civil War-era American South) and the legal and moral compromises often struck by those entrusted to enforce the law and uphold social mores (especially in the informal police trilogy *Madigan*, 1968, *Coogan's Bluff*, 1968, and *Dirty Harry*, 1971). In Siegel's world, combatants on opposing sides of the law can bear an unsettling resemblance to one another, be they prison authorities and rebel prisoners in *Riot In Cell Block 11* (1954) and *Escape From Alcatraz* (1979) or the ruthless cop and his lowlife targets in *Dirty Harry*. The latter created an authoritarian icon during one of the most tumultuous eras in America's history, and remains Siegel's most famous – and famously quotable – film. JW

The Big Steal 1949, 71 min, b/w

cast Robert Mitchum, Jane Greer, William Bendix, Ramon Novarro, Patric Knowles, John Qualen *cin* Harry J. Wild *m* Leigh Harline

This fizzy chase caper can be thought of as a comic spin on Jacques Tourneur's despondent *noir Out Of The Past* (1947), revisiting one of its settings (Mexico) and recruiting several of its personnel (Robert Mitchum, Jane Greer and screenwriter Daniel Mainwaring). Mitchum is the wiseacre framed for theft and Greer the dame who accompanies him across Mexico, as he pursues the real culprit but is hunted in turn by a world-weary lawman.

Invasion Of The Body Snatchers 1955, 80 min, b/w

cast Kevin McCarthy, Dana Wynter, Larry Gates, Carolyn Jones, King Donovan, Virginia Christine *cin* Ellsworth J. Fredricks *m* Carmen Dragon

A doctor (Kevin McCarthy) discovers that locals who lately "don't seem themselves" have in fact been replaced by invading aliens in this unnerving sci-fi benchmark, taken from a Daniel Mainwaring script and shot in just nineteen days for a mere $300,000. Released in the thick of the Cold War, the movie's allegory is intriguingly ambiguous – the pod people could be interpreted either as Communists or red-baiting reactionaries.

Dirty Harry 1971, 101 min

cast Clint Eastwood, Harry Guardino, Reni Santoni, John Vernon, Andy Robinson, John Larch, John Mitchum *cin* Bruce Surtees *m* Lalo Schifrin

Laconic and scowling, Clint Eastwood is Harry Callahan, the maverick cop packing a .44 Magnum who dispenses rough justice to the hippie detritus of San Francisco with little patience for constitutional protections and other such liberal niceties. Not quite "fascist", as per its reputation, the film is nevertheless ambivalent at best towards its reactionary antihero and remains troubling for its essential endorsement of vigilantism.

S

Brad Silberling

US, 1963–

After working on TV series including *NYPD Blue*, Brad Silberling got his feature filmmaking break when his work attracted the attention of Steven Spielberg, who hired him to direct *Casper* (1995). Silberling has made just a handful of films to date, but all are marked by a stylish visual sense and an engaging warmth. Even *Casper*, so steeped in fantasy, keeps a hold on the human core of the story. His politely received second feature *City Of Angels* (1997) was an interesting adaptation of Wim Wenders' *Wings Of Desire* (1987). Silberling has also directed *Moonlight Mile* (2002), a family drama starring Jake Gyllenhaal, Susan Sarandon and Dustin Hoffman. He returned to fantasy with *Lemony Snicket's A Series Of Unfortunate Events* (2004) starring Jim Carrey, and more recently has directed the intriguing *10 Items Or Less* (2006), about an actor (Morgan Freeman) researching a role as a supermarket employee who becomes captivated by one of the checkout girls. JC

Casper 1995, 100 min

cast Christina Ricci, Bill Pullman, Eric Idle, Cathy Moriarty, Chauncey Leopardi, Amy Brenneman *cin* Dean Cundey *m* James Horner

Silberling brings the comic-book character Casper the Friendly Ghost to the big screen with humour and sentiment. Deploying high-end computer animation to render the spectral characters, the film found opportunities to suggest something more melancholy beneath its slapstick energy.

Bryan Singer

US, 1965–

The startling transformation of Bryan Singer from arthouse auteur to major Hollywood player is not unlike that of Clark Kent removing his nerdy glasses and suddenly turning into the Man of Steel with unbelievable powers. Singer started making 8mm films in his teens and studied at both the School of Visual Arts in Manhattan and the University of Southern California. There, he made a short with old pal Ethan Hawke, *Lion's Den* (1988), a calling card to the industry that led directly to Singer securing the funds for his debut, *Public Access* (1992). A subtle, unsettling tale of a mysterious stranger who uses a local cable TV show to expose a small town's dirty secrets, it shared the Grand Jury Prize at the Sundance Film Festival. It was written by school friend and former detective Christopher McQuarrie, and the duo teamed up again to commercial success and cult adulation with *The Usual Suspects* (1995).

After his damp squib adaptation of a Stephen King novella, *Apt Pupil* (1998), Singer made an unexpected and confusing career move, taking charge of the special-effects behemoth *X-Men* (2000). The result was a treacly morass of exposition, a franchise being prepared for liftoff. At least the sequel *X2* (2003) delivered more bangs for its fans' bucks. Like his hero Steven Spielberg, the director seems to have acquired a taste for blockbusters, with the popcorn-spilling thrills of *Superman Returns* (2006) completing his unlikely transformation into a Hollywood power-player. LH

The Usual Suspects 1995, 106 min

cast Gabriel Byrne, Kevin Spacey, Stephen Baldwin, Chazz Palminteri, Pete Postlethwaite, Giancarlo Esposito *cin* Tom Sigel *m* John Ottman

Five heist veterans, brought together for a police line-up, are commissioned to steal $91 million dollars of drug money by the enigmatic and possibly satanic crime lord Keyser Söze. Their story is told in flashback, narrated by Verbal Kint (Spacey), a small-time con man under police interrogation. But as the labyrinthine plot unfolds it becomes clear that nothing is as it seems…

John Singleton

US, 1968–

Was it beginner's luck? At the age of 24, John Singleton became the youngest person ever to be nominated for the best director Oscar for *Boyz N The Hood* (1991), a semi-autobiographical tale of growing up in crime-ridden South Central Los Angeles. But he has yet to make a film to match this promising debut.

Singleton's weakness for sentimentality, the easy assignment of blame and last-reel tragedy – only hinted at in *Boyz* – was laid bare in the facile romance-cum-road movie *Poetic Justice* (1993), starring Janet Jackson as a bereaved young poet, and in *Higher Learning* (1995), a bluntly schematic portrait of a college campus as a volatile microcosm of society. Presented as a companion piece to *Boyz*, the muddled but interesting *Baby Boy* (2001) clumsily delved into the issue of socially enforced infantilism among young black men. However, Singleton has otherwise become an action-pulp journeyman: *Shaft* (2000) turned the suave PI of yore into a vigilante detective with busy fists; *2 Fast 2 Furious* (2003) was a mind-numbing derby sequel; and the family revenge drama *Four Brothers* (2005), much like the *Shaft* remake, took a discomfiting pleasure in indiscriminate vigilantism. JW

Boyz N The Hood 1991, 107 min

cast Laurence Fishburne, Cuba Gooding Jr, Ice Cube, Morris Chestnut, Nia Long, Tyra Ferrell, Angela Bassett *cin* Chuck Mills *m* Stanley Clarke

Growing up under the eye of his strict father (Laurence Fishburne) in rough-and-tumble South Central LA, Tre (Cuba Gooding Jr) tries to keep on the straight and narrow, despite the example set by his hard-drinking, gun-toting, trash-talking pals like Doughboy (Ice Cube). The movie

S

instantly established Singleton as wunderkind of the moment. It's well-acted and heartfelt, even if the atmosphere contains some whiffs of misogyny and the recirculated air of the after-school special.

Robert Siodmak
Germany, 1900–73

A chronicler of dangerous gentility and grimy urban streets, Robert Siodmak thrived on the serendipities of control and experiment that were characteristic of the Hollywood studio system. After acting in the theatre, he entered the German film industry in 1925 as a title writer for Hollywood imports. The next year he graduated to editor, then co-directed (with Edgar G. Ulmer) *Menschen am Sonntag* (*People On Sunday*, 1929), a naturalistic account of Berliners at play, scripted by his brother Curt and Billy Wilder. *Abschied* (*Farewell*, 1930) was set in a Berlin boarding house and similarly overlain with a realist patina. It foresaw the eerie *petit bourgeois* interiors of later Siodmak films, but 1931's *Stürme der Leidenschaft* (*Storms Of Passion*) indicated the psychological focus of the director's American work.

Siodmak left for Paris shortly after the Nazis came to power, and of all the Middle-European émigrés, he had the most productive time in the French capital. Highlights included the Danielle Darrieux musical *La crise est finie* (*The Slump Is Over*, 1934) and *Pièges* (*Snares*, 1939), a detective mystery – with musical interludes – featuring Maurice Chevalier. Stylistically, *Pièges* anticipated the long takes and classical *mise en scène* in Siodmak's remarkable run of Hollywood thrillers.

Fleeing to Hollywood in 1939, Siodmak marked time in Paramount B-pictures before moving to Universal where *Son Of Dracula* (1943) and the camp *Cobra Woman* (1944) hint at the dual personalities and compromised light of his later films. *Phantom Lady* (1944), *The Suspect* (1944) and *The Spiral Staircase* (1945) explore buried passions in dark milieux. Each has a feeling for character and personal doom redolent of Jacques Tourneur rather than the literal violence and cynicism of Alfred Hitchcock and Fritz Lang. Deanna Durbin's favourite film was 1944's *Christmas Holiday*, in which her picket-fence teen image was startlingly subverted in a steamy New Orleans setting. In *The Dark Mirror* (1946) Olivia de Havilland played twin sisters, one malevolent, one good. The prowling camera in the opening scene

Burt Lancaster: power and vulnerability

Burt Lancaster's outstanding athletic prowess won him a scholarship to New York University, but he was a performer at heart, and he soon gave up his place in order to form an acrobatic act with his childhood friend Nick Cravat. By the time he made his film debut in *The Killers* (1946) – following war service and a brief stint on Broadway – Lancaster was in his early thirties, still in his physical prime, but without the callowness of youth. It was this combination of power and the vulnerability of a man who has lived and suffered that director Robert Siodmak latched onto in *The Killers* and in their second film together, *Criss Cross* (1949). In both of these *films noirs*, Lancaster plays an essentially good man who is lured off the rails by the love of a bad woman, and in each performance he managed to suggest a degree of inner turmoil that gave the films an added tragic dimension. Lancaster's last outing for Siodmak was the ebullient swashbuckler *The Crimson Pirate* (1952), which exploited his graceful athleticism to the full, opposite his old acrobatic partner Nick Cravat.

The 1950s was Lancaster's greatest decade, during which he not only formed his own production company (he was one of the first post-war stars to do so), but also received the kind of meaty roles that allowed him to show his full range as an actor. *From Here To Eternity* (1953) may be famous for his clinch in the foam with Deborah Kerr, but the sensitivity of his performance as the nice-guy Sergeant Warden won him a deserved Oscar nomination. A couple of darkly cynical Westerns for Robert Aldrich, *Apache* (1954) and *Vera Cruz* (1954), prompted Lancaster to have a shot at directing. The result, *The Kentuckian* (1955), about a frontiersman who heads off to Texas with his son was worthy rather than exciting, and – other than the unremarkable murder mystery *The Midnight Man* (1974) which he co-directed with Roland Kibbee – it was his only directorial credit. Three years later came *Sweet Smell Of Success* (1957), in which Lancaster gave, what is for many, his greatest performance, as the ruthless and amoral J.J. Hunsecker, a society columnist who coolly wrecks the lives of those around him.

By all accounts, Lancaster could be extremely prickly and difficult to work with, but he was able to synthesize this aspect of his personality with the charismatic good looks and muscular physique that had been his calling cards. As his looks faded in middle age, he seemed even more distinguished an actor, exuding gravitas and authority, notably as a nineteenth-century Sicilian aristocrat in Luchino Visconti's *The Leopard* (1963). There were several duds in his later years, but his beautifully observed performance as an elderly self-deluding crook in Louis Malle's *Atlantic City* (1980) was one of several distinguished codas to a remarkable career. RB

discovers a corpse in a darkened room, typifying Siodmak's penchant for ominous clutter.

Ella Raines, Charles Laughton and George Sanders did some of their best work for Siodmak. Set in Edwardian London, *The Suspect* sees Laughton's decent husband driven to murder his shrewish wife amid the prim setting of imperial drawing rooms and terraces. In *The Strange Affair Of Uncle Harry* (1945), Sanders plays the weak brother of a possessive hypochondriac who falls for Ella Raines's city sophisticate. The possibility of horror lingers beneath the labyrinthine surfaces of Siodmak's detailed rooms and conflicted figures. For the pure dread of its opening sequence in which Burt Lancaster awaits his own execution, *The Killers* (1946) looks forward to the brutal crimes and crisp locations of post-war films by Jules Dassin and Samuel Fuller.

While *Criss Cross* (1949) is arguably Siodmak's masterpiece, *The File On Thelma Jordon* (1949) is a plodding melodrama redeemed by Barbara Stanwyck at her most duplicitous. Though disillusioned with the age of CinemaScope, Siodmak's final English-language film was a gloriously light-hearted Technicolor swashbuckler, *The Crimson Pirate* (1952), which reunited him with Burt Lancaster. He returned to Germany two years later where, despite the frissons of the mass murderer drama *The Devil Strikes At Night* (1957), his work never achieved the same spellbinding quality. Expressed through the velvet blacks and greys of Woody Bredell and Nicholas Musuraca's cinematography, Siodmak's cinema of suggestion forms the link between 1930s Universal horrors and the Cold War *film noir* of the 1950s. RA

Phantom Lady 1944, 87 min, b/w

cast Franchot Tone, Ella Raines, Alan Curtis, Thomas Gomez, Fay Helm, Aurora, Andrew Tombes, Elisha Cook Jr *cin* Woody Bredell *m* Hans J. Salter

Ella Raines memorably plays a devoted secretary seeking to find the mysterious woman of the title, who can clear her boss of murder. In her first starring role, the seductive Raines descends into an underworld steeped in shadow and desire, assisted in her quest by Franchot Tone.

The Spiral Staircase 1945, 83 min, b/w

cast Dorothy McGuire, George Brent, Ethel Barrymore, Kent Smith, Rhonda Fleming, Gordon Oliver, Elsa Lanchester *cin* Nicholas Musuraca *m* Roy Webb

This chiller set in a New England mansion finds Dorothy Maguire's mute heroine pursued through grand rooms and gloomy passages by a maniac intent upon eradicating imperfection. If it all looks back to Universal's *The Old Dark House*, George Brent's professor reminds us of more modern horrors.

The Killers 1946, 105 min, b/w

cast Edmond O'Brien, Ava Gardner, Burt Lancaster, Albert Dekker, Sam Levene, Vince Barnett *cin* Woody Bredell *m* Miklós Rózsa

One of the darkest, most fatalistic films of its era, you watch *The Killers* less for its hackneyed narrative than for its extraordinary mood of pessimism and dark despair.

The opening sequence – the killing of ex-boxer "the Swede" (Burt Lancaster) – contains the kernel of the Hemingway short story, and remains a textbook *film noir* moment.

Criss Cross 1949, 98 min, b/w

cast Burt Lancaster, Yvonne de Carlo, Dan Duryea, Stephen McNally *cin* Frantz Planer *m* Miklós Rózsa

Burt Lancaster is Steve Thompson, an easy-going guy unable to get over his ex-wife Anna (Yvonne de Carlo), even though she has hooked up with reptilian hoodlum Slim Dundee. Steve dreams up the plans for a payroll heist as an excuse when Slim catches him with Anna – and from that moment on he is sucked into a vortex of crime, jealousy and deceit. On one level an archetypal *noir*, this film is unusual for the way its protagonists teeter on the brink of a normal life, before succumbing to the destructive lure of criminality.

Ramesh Sippy
India, 1947–

Though he has made several accomplished films in his long career, Ramesh Sippy will forever be known as the director of *Sholay* (1975). The greatest hit ever in the history of Indian cinema, it was, until recently overtaken by Aditya Chopra's *Dilwale dulhania le jayenge* (*The Big Hearted Will Win The Bride*, 1995), the longest-running Indian film ever, showing for 286 consecutive weeks in one Mumbai cinema. Son of the veteran producer G.P. Sippy, he began his career with the mature romance *Andaz* (*The Gesture*, 1971). The rollicking comedy *Seeta aur Geeta* (1972) followed. Then came *Sholay*, which marked the start of his association with the legendary Amitabh Bachchan. A nonentity when the film began shooting, Bachchan was a superstar by the time it was released.

Sadly, Sippy was never able to replicate the film's success. The big-budget, James Bond-like *Shaan* (1980), though very competent, was not a patch on its predecessor, nor was the brooding *Shakti* (1982) or the love-triangle-themed *Saagar* (1985). Not to be deterred, Sippy turned to television and made the monumental family saga *Buniyaad* (1987). After returning to the big screen for a string of forgettable films, he turned producer. NR

Sholay 1975, 204 min

cast Sanjeev Kumar, Dharmendra, Hema Malini, Jaya Bhaduri, Amitabh Bachchan, Amjad Khan *cin* Dwarka Divecha *m* R.D. Burman

Often dubbed a "curry Western", *Sholay* is essentially a revenge drama in which a former police officer hires two small-time crooks to capture the dreaded bandit Gabbar Singh who had decimated his family. Blending elements of Akira Kurosawa's *Seven Samurai* (1954), John Ford and Sergio Leone with uniquely Indian humour, music and emotion, Sippy pulled off that rare feat – a film that almost every Indian knows scene by scene, line by line.

Sholay's star: Amitabh Bachchan

It's only appropriate that Ramesh Sippy's *Sholay* (1975), the greatest hit in the history of Hindi cinema, in terms of both box-office returns and cultural impact, stars the greatest movie actor that Hindi cinema has ever known. Son of the renowned poet Harivansh Rai Bachchan, Amitabh started his adult life quietly enough, working in the shipping industry in Calcutta. A burning desire to become a star brought him to Bombay (now Mumbai). After debuting as one of the seven leads in K.A. Abbas's war-themed *Saat Hindustani* (1969), Bachchan made an impact in a supporting role in Hrishikesh Mukherjee's *Anand* (1970) starring the then superstar Rajesh Khanna. A string of box-office failures followed. Then star screenwriting duo Salim Khan and Javed Akhtar noticed him in a fight sequence in the comedy *Bombay To Goa* (1972) and recommended him to director Prakash Mehra. Though he was the third or fourth choice for the role, Mehra cast Bachchan in *Zanjeer* (1973), in which he played an intense, terse cop who battles corruption by day and his childhood demons by night. The role firmly cast Bachchan in the mould of the "angry young man" who takes on the system, and he was praised by the masses and intelligentsia alike. Hit upon hit followed, not in the least, of course, being *Sholay*, in which he played a laconic small-time crook with a ready supply of sardonic one-liners.

By the late 1970s, Bachchan had evolved into an all-singing, all-dancing, wisecracking, showboating, heart-string-tugging entertainer, a process that began with Manmohan Desai's *Amar Akbar Anthony* (1977). After he suffered a near-death experience on the set of Desai's *Coolie* (1983) all of India prayed for him and heaved a sigh of relief when he recovered. Around the same time, his childhood friend Rajiv Gandhi became prime minister of India and persuaded Bachchan to enter politics. The experience was a disaster and also coincided with ill-health and a waning film career, with disappointing movies from former stalwarts such as Desai's *Gangaa Jamunaa Saraswathi* (1988), Mehra's *Jaadugar* (1989) and Sippy's *Akayla* (1991). After a slump through most of the 1990s, Bachchan reinvented himself again in 2001 as the host of *Kaun banega karodpati*, the Indian version of *Who Wants To Be A Millionaire*. He became a national favourite again and roles commensurate with his age were specially written for him. Always a consummate actor, he won acclaim for his roles in films such as Karan Johar's *Kabhi khushi kabhie gham* (2001), Ravi Chopra's *Baghban* (2003), Sanjay Leela Bhansali's *Black*, Ram Gopal Varma's *Sarkar* (both 2005), and Johar's *Kabhi alvida naa kehna* (2006). Today Bachchan is revered as the elder statesman of Hindi cinema and has been heaped with encomiums as varied as doctorates, the Légion d'honneur and a wax likeness in Madame Tussaud's amongst others. His son Abhishek Bachchan and daughter-in-law, former Miss World Aishwarya Rai, are also big Bollywood stars in their own right. In 1999 a BBC Online poll saw Bachchan being voted as Star of the Millennium, beating off challenges from contenders such as Laurence Olivier, Marlon Brando, Marilyn Monroe and Charlie Chaplin by a large margin. At 65, he continues to be busier than his younger Bollywood contemporaries and is an ever-present face in India, staring down from countless billboards and television commercials. NR

Douglas Sirk
Germany, 1897–1987

In the 1950s, Douglas Sirk was regarded as little more than a mass producer of three-hankie weepies that were devoured by the public and derided by critics. In the 1970s, by which time auteur theory allowed critics to take their guilty pleasures seriously, Sirk was born again, reassessed as an artist, proto-feminist and sly social commentator. He became one of the most influential directors of that period, and arguably every decade since, numbering Rainer Werner Fassbinder, John Waters, Pedro Almodóvar, Todd Haynes and François Ozon amongst his acolytes. Unlike with some other directors, fans didn't have to read against the grain or stretch credibility to detect signs of intelligent life; the cerebral and subversive elements were like depth charges, carefully and consciously planted by Sirk, a European intellectual and contemporary of Brecht.

Born in Hamburg to Danish parents, Claus Detlef Sierck quickly established himself as one of Germany's most renowned stage directors of the 1920s and 30s, translating Shakespeare and staging Shaw, Pirandello and his colleague Bertolt Brecht. A left-wing intellectual with a Jewish wife, it would have been logical and reasonable for him to lead the creative exodus from Hitler's Germany. Instead, he stayed on for several years and worked under the Nazis, becoming a successful and sought-after movie director and making several films for the Neubablesberg Studios. His masterpiece from that period, *Zu neuen Ufern* (*To New Shores*, 1937), starring Zarah Leander as a singer punished for the sins of her lover, proved to be his last German film.

He fled to Holland in 1937, under the pretext of scouting for locations, and made one movie, *Boefje* (1939). When the advance of the Wehrmacht made it impossible for him to stay, he left on the last boat to America. Sirk initially moved to Hollywood to remake one of his German films, and when the

S

deal collapsed he fell into the unlikely profession of alfalfa farmer, which he would later describe as being one of the happiest periods of his life. Sirk was finally employed by Hollywood to direct *Hitler's Madman* (1943) and to pen scripts for Columbia. His stock in the industry began to rise with a trilogy of films he helmed starring George Sanders: *Summer Storm* (1944), *Scandal In Paris* (1946) and *Lured* (1947). As good as those films were, it was in his work with Universal Studios that signs of "Sirkness" began to emerge.

Initially hired as a comedy director, his critical reputation ultimately rests on four melodramas – *Magnificent Obsession* (1954), *All That Heaven Allows* (1955), *Written On The Wind* (1956) and *Imitation Of Life* (1959) – in which characters lead lives of quiet desperation and stifled passions behind an opulent social veneer. Even though these tear-jerkers were ripe, often overripe, with knowing dialogue, expressionist photography, sumptuous set-dressing, and ludicrous plot twists, the point of Sirk's directorial self-awareness wasn't, as is often the case with his acolytes, ironic gamesmanship or camp braggadocio. So, even in a plot as self-evidently berserk as *Magnificent Obsession*, the director could detect and convey intimations of Greek tragedy. The purpose of his violently saturated colours and ridiculously lavish decor wasn't just to underscore the emotional intensity of a scene, but also to serve as a constant, Brechtian reminder of the story's artifice.

Even though his "women's pictures" were major money-spinners, Universal still employed Sirk to dabble in other genres: the 3-D Western *Taza, Son Of Cochise*, the Attila the Hun biopic *Son Of The Pagan* (both 1954), the comedy adventure *Captain Lightfoot* (1955), the war film *A Time To Love And A Time To Die* (1957), and *The Tarnished Angels* (1958), a potent adaptation of William Faulkner's novel, *Pylon*. Many critics share Sirk's opinion that the latter was his greatest triumph. A bleak, despairing essay on failure and betrayal, *The Tarnished Angels* saw Rock Hudson (a frequent Sirk lead) cast against type as a tawdry reporter in 1930s New Orleans who is intoxicated by the hedonistic lifestyle of a team of stunt-flyers.

Even though *Imitation Of Life* was a huge commercial success, Sirk unexpectedly moved to Switzerland, partly for reasons of health. There, he returned to the theatre and taught at the Munich Film School, living long enough to see that his efforts had not been wasted, as critics finally looked beneath the surface sheen and soap operatics and realized that the heightened style, mythic dimensions, intricate symbolism, zeitgeist allegories and social satire were not just happy accidents. LH

All I Desire 1953, 79 min

cast Barbara Stanwyck, Richard Carlson, Lyle Bettger, Maureen O'Sullivan, Lori Nelson, Marcia Henderson *cin* Carl Guthrie *m* Joseph Gershenson

Barbara Stanwyck is typically majestic as a blousy, vulnerable burlesque dancer who left her husband and kids to pursue an acting career, but returns to the family fold with "bruises on her illusions". Meaty one-liners like "they're not going to bury me in this provincial burgh!" prove that even a minor Sirk melodrama is crammed full of his subversive trademarks.

Magnificent Obsession 1954, 108 min

cast Jane Wyman, Rock Hudson, Barbara Rush, Otto Kruger, Agnes Moorhead, Paul Cavanagh *cin* Russell Metty *m* Frank Skinner

In this typical Sirkian combination of genuine sincerity and honest subversion, playboy painter Rock Hudson falls for the blind Jane Wyman after being indirectly responsible for her husband's death. He later renounces his hedonistic ways and returns to his vocation as a brain

Pillow talk: Rock Hudson and Lauren Bacall embrace in Sirk's emotionally overwrought melodrama *Written On The Wind*.

Melodrama: appealing to the emotions

These days, the term "melodramatic" is used mostly to dismiss a film as improbable, excessive or worthless. This belies the fact that melodrama as a film genre is as worthy as any other, and as an aesthetic it infuses countless movies, from Westerns through epics to comedy. Drawing on influences as wide ranging as Greek tragedy and sentimental Victorian novels, melodrama was a hugely popular theatrical form in the late nineteenth century. Like slapstick comedy, which had its roots in vaudeville, it adapted easily to the silent movies. Placing a heavier emphasis on expressive gestures and visual iconography than on dialogue and naturalism, early movie melodramas such as those by D.W. Griffith involved overwrought situations and often tragic outcomes. Stories of good versus evil were told using familiar motifs and archetypes and exaggerated, stylized performances. The aim of melodrama was never realism but rather to create intense emotional impact. It had a huge influence on the women's movies, family dramas and chick flicks that followed.

Filmmakers like D.W. Griffith, F.W. Murnau and Frank Borzage developed the form, their innovations in editing and cross-cutting taking melodrama away from the realm of theatre and towards a more cinematic language. In *Way Down East* (1920), Griffith used the close-up to achieve emotional effect for the first time, zooming in on Lillian Gish's anguished face. Other key silent melodramas included *A Fool There Was* (1915), featuring a young Theda Bara, the first and quintessential vamp; Griffith's *Hearts Of The World* (1918), *True Heart Susie* (1919), *Broken Blossoms* (1919) and *Orphans Of The Storm* (1922) – all of which starred the delicately expressive Lillian Gish; Frank Lloyd's *Madame X* (1920), a classic tale of fallen virtue; Erich von Stroheim's *Greed* (1924); King Vidor's war movie *The Big Parade* (1925); and F. W. Murnau's exquisite *Sunrise* (1927).

During the 1930s, with many films being based on popular women's novels, the point of view of the female protagonist was increasingly foregrounded, and by the end of the decade the "women's movie" was a cinematic force to be reckoned with. Stars such as Barbara Stanwyck, Bette Davis, Joan Crawford, Greer Garson and even the exotic Greta Garbo provided strong points of identification for female audiences. Popular themes included wronged women who sought revenge, or fallen women who sought redemption. Doomed romances and fatal diseases abounded – George Cukor's *Camille* (1936), for example, gave Garbo her finest role as the tragic courtesan, while Edmund Goulding's *Dark Victory* (1939) saw Bette Davis suffering in typically fine form. In maternal melodramas like King Vidor's *Stella Dallas* (1937), with Barbara Stanwyck, and numerous Bette Davis movies, including Edmund Goulding's *The Old Maid* (1939) and *The Great Lie* (1941), the key love relationship was between mothers and – usually – daughters.

After World War II, melodrama and *film noir* became familiar bedfellows. After her stunning turn in Michael Curtiz's *Mildred Pierce* (1945), playing the mother who is all but destroyed by her fierce love for her daughter, Joan Crawford starred in the increasingly shadowy melodramas *Humoresque* (Jean Negulesco, 1946), *Possessed* (Curtis Bernhardt, 1947) and *Sudden Fear* (David Miller, 1952). No less dark, David Lean's melancholy study of repression and loss, *Brief Encounter* (1945), provided a particularly British take on melodrama. The genre's hallmarks of barely contained hysteria, tragic suffering and stylized visual aesthetics found another flowering in consumerist post-war America. In Hollywood, the form ripened to bursting point, with Douglas Sirk providing the richest crop. Vincente Minnelli, best known for his gaudy MGM musicals, also ripped open the American Dream with studies of hopeless desperation: frustrated women obsessing about home furnishings in *The Cobweb* (1955); desperate men in crisis in *The Bad And The Beautiful* (1952) and *Some Came Running* (1958).

While modern audiences might reject the overwrought stylings of those earlier films, the popular appeal of the so-called "women's movies" – or chick flicks, as they are now known – remains undiminished. From Herbert Ross's *The Turning Point* (1977) through James L. Brooks' *Terms Of Endearment* (1983) to James Cameron's *Titanic* (1997), there has always been big money to be made from a skilful, and shameless, appeal to the emotions. In Europe, directors like Rainer Werner Fassbinder and Pedro Almodóvar have paid immaculate tribute to Douglas Sirk, as has US indie director Todd Haynes, whose ravishing *Far From Heaven* (2002) evoked 1950s melodrama without resorting to pastiche. Aspects of melodrama are everywhere, from Ang Lee's *Brokeback Mountain* (2005), which boldly wrung a three-hankie weepie out of the love between two cowboys, to the showstopping musical numbers and ordinary-girls-done-good heroics of Bill Condon's *Dreamgirls* (2006) and the emotionally devastating Sirkian theatrics of Zhang Yimou's *Curse Of The Golden Flower* (2006). sc

surgeon, which comes in handy in the unbelievable denouement. Even Sirk said this remake of John Stahl's 1935 original was "a damned crazy story if there ever was one".

All That Heaven Allows 1955, 89 min
cast Jane Wyman, Rock Hudson, Agnes Moorhead, Conrad Nagel, Virginia Grey, Charles Drake, Gloria Talbott *cin* Russell Metty *m* Frank Skinner

Frustrated widow Jane Wyman falls for her youthful Thoreau-esque gardener Rock Hudson. After a prelapsarian idyll with him in the country, she returns to her small town to face the tutting disapproval of her children and friends. The whole delirious enterprise hums with the sort of piquant subtlety that was sadly lost on contemporary critics: Sirk conveys Wyman's domestic entrapment by framing her against windows and doors, and most famously and gloriously by capturing her reflection in that most potent symbol of suburban entropy, the television set.

Written On The Wind 1956, 99 min
cast Lauren Bacall, Robert Stack, Dorothy Malone, Rock Hudson, Robert Keith, Grant Williams *cin* Russell Metty *m* Frank Skinner

Robert Stack plays a playboy and constant disappointment to his oil-baron father, who has all but adopted Rock Hudson as the son he always wanted. Stack, however, has the one thing Hudson wants in the world, Lauren Bacall; while Stack's alcoholic sister, Dorothy Malone, will do anything to get her hooks into Rock. The elegantly demented result is a swirling miasma of mirror images, thwarted passions, castrating father figures and symbols of phallic potency.

Imitation Of Life 1959, 125 min
cast Lana Turner, John Gavin, Sandra Dee, Juanita Moore, Susan Kohner, Daniel O'Herlihy, Troy Donahue *cin* Russell Metty *m* Frank Skinner

Steely greys dominate the palette, exaggerating the discontented cynicism that seeps through almost every frame of this bittersweet tale of two single mothers – a white woman and her black maid – who live together in a crummy flat. With his deployment of such obvious racial stereotypes, it's hard to gauge whether Sirk was intending to be sincere or satirical in rendering Moore's character as a model of subservient perfection.

Abderrahmane Sissako
Mauritania, 1961–

Abderrahmane Sissako is one of the brightest talents to emerge in African cinema in over a decade. After studying film in Moscow and making the graduation short, *Le jeu* (*The Game*, 1990), he began his directorial career proper with the feature *October* (1993) and the documentary *Rostov-Luanda* (1998), which follows the director in search of a long-lost friend in Angola.

After relocating to France, Sissako directed *La vie sur terre* (*Life On Earth*, 1998), a short observational docudrama that runs the gamut from a Paris shopping mall to a Malian village. Further indirect commentary on African–European relations followed in the slow, but wry, *Waiting For Happiness* (2002), which won the international critics' Un Certain Regard prize at the Cannes Film Festival. It was a superbly shot, low-key drama set in Mauritania, and its understated charm and reflections on exile quickly brought the director to prominence.

Sissako's subtle and largely implicit criticism of the developed world took a much more direct form in 2006 in the charismatic and daring *Bamako*. Audaciously putting the World Bank, the International Monetary Fund and other Western institutions on trial in the courtyard of a mud-walled house in Mali's capital, the film counterpoints the daily struggles of a young Malian couple with the proceedings of the wig-clad court debating the impact of debt repayments on the continent. Sissako has also produced two films, *Abouna* (*Our Father*, 2002) and *Daratt* (*Dry Season*, 2006), for Chadian director Mahamat-Saleh Haroun. RC

Waiting For Happiness (Heremakono) 2002, 96 min
cast Khatra Ould Abdel Kader, Maata Ould Mohamed Abeid, Mohamed Mahmoud Ould Mohamed *cin* Jacques Besse *m* Oumou Sangare

Young Abdallah is passing time in a Mauritanian village by the sea, with which he is unfamiliar, before emigrating to Europe. Sissako's camera seeks out the various locals and drifters who cross his path, including a Chinese man with a penchant for singing karaoke. Not unlike Mahamat-Saleh Haroun's *Abouna*, the film's imagery is placed centre stage, and there is considerable beauty – although next to no narrative – for those with the patience to keep watching. A portrait of life, and nothing but.

Alf Sjöberg
Sweden, 1903–80

Once Sweden's most significant active filmmaker, Alf Sjöberg is nowadays best known for his contribution to Ingmar Bergman's career – he directed Bergman's first script – than for his own. Part of the reason that Sjöberg has become little more than a footnote in Bergman Studies is the marked lack of consistency in style, theme and quality, especially in the latter half of a career that spanned forty years and eighteen films.

His directorial debut, *The Strongest* (1929), was a tale of seal hunters that deftly welded documentary and fiction in the grand manner of Robert Flaherty, but there are four films in particular that are striking testaments to his neglected talent. *The Road To Heaven* (1942) an energetic fantasy about an innocent tempted by the Devil on the titular road, left an impression on the young Bergman, who two years later scripted *Torment* (aka *Frenzy*, 1944) for his mentor. In this stark allegory about fascism, that looks as if it has been mediated through the angular, fevered chiaroscuro of German expressionism, a student and his prostitute girlfriend are tormented by a sadistic teacher. Imbued with gritty lyricism, *Only A Mother* (1949) charted the spiralling descent of a sturdy peasant woman, while *Miss Julie* (1951) is for many the pinnacle of Sjöberg's career. All of these films were part of the period from 1944 to 1956, before he was eclipsed by his acolyte. And although *The Judge* (1960) was respectfully received, Sjöberg's final film, *The Father* (1969), was panned by critics. LH

Miss Julie (Fröken Julie) 1951, 90 min
cast Anita Björk, Ulf Palme, Märta Dorff, Lissi Alandh, Anders Henrikson, Inga Gill, Åke Fridell *cin* Göran Strindberg *m* Dag Wirén

On midsummer's eve in a Swedish manor house, a count's daughter, Julie, seduces a servant, Jean, and plans to run away with him. In the morning light, she comes to realize that their social and emotional differences are intractable, and cuts her throat. To August Strindberg's austere, gloomy play Sjöberg adds both a pulse and a back story that illustrates Julie's unhappy childhood. These scenes are unquestionably the director's greatest triumph, eliding past and present – often in the same shot – with a dreamy, Wellesian fluency.

Vilgot Sjöman
Sweden, 1924–2006

Vilgot Sjöman's ground-breaking movie *I Am Curious – Yellow* (1967) was a key film in the sexual revolution in cinema. The subject of a famous trial after US Customs seized prints, its subsequent landmark victory set a legal precedent that allowed Hollywood to make X-rated studio pictures.

A former clerk and prison orderly, Sjöman was a novelist and screenwriter who won a film scholarship to UCLA in 1956. In the US, he also served an apprenticeship on George Seaton's *The Proud And The Profane* (1956). Upon his return, Sjöman worked as Ingmar Bergman's assistant on *Winter Light* (1962), and made his debut with *The Mistress* (1962). Controversy followed the release of the sexually explicit *491* (1964), which was banned in Sweden for its frank content, and the incest saga *My Sister, My Love* (1966). Since the iconoclastic *I Am Curious – Yellow* and the following year's *I Am Curious – Blue* (yellow and blue being the colours of the Swedish flag), a number of Sjöman's films took full advantage of the newly relaxed censorship laws. *Till Sex Do Us Part* (1972) peaked with a wild orgy involving the Royal Swedish Opera Company performing *Rigoletto*. Following in the same vein as *Till Sex Do Us Part*, titles such as *A Handful Of Love* (1974) and *Taboo* (1977) give some indication of the direction that Sjöman's career took in subsequent years. LH

I Am Curious – Yellow (Jag är nyfiken) 1967, 121 min, b/w
cast Lena Nyman, Börje Ahlstedt, Peter Lindgren, Vilgot Sjöman, Holger Löwenadler *cin* Peter Wester *m* Bengt Ernryd

A sociologist, Lena, questions members of the public about the Swedish class structure, in between engaging in bountiful sex with her boyfriend in various locations (in a pond, up a tree) in this film-within-a-film that's fuelled by a Godardian anarchic energy. Even though the once outré scenes now possess the same dusty appeal as quaint Victorian erotica, director Mike Figgis, who was "completely and utterly blown away" by the film, has nominated Sjöman's ode to sexual and political liberation as one of three movies that every budding filmmaker should see.

Victor Sjöström
Sweden, 1879–1960

When Ingmar Bergman cast Victor Sjöström as the elderly professor in *Wild Strawberries* (1957), he forged a link between two great eras of Swedish cinema. Initially a stage actor and director, Sjöström signed a contract with the production company Svenska Bio in 1912. In three years he made 31 films, of which just three survive, including the ground-breaking *Ingeborg Holm* (1913), whose vivid depiction of a woman's descent into insanity following the legally sanctioned seizure of her children led to a change in the law. Sjöström made (and usually acted in) a further ten Swedish films, including the hugely successful *The Sons Of Ingmar* (1919) and the masterly *The Phantom Carriage* (1921), before moving to Hollywood in 1923. With fellow Swede Mauritz Stiller, he had raised the profile of his country's cinema to a rare high, and had become internationally renowned for imagery that was both realistic and expressionistic.

Anglicizing his name to Victor Seastrom, he continued to make psychologically acute literary adaptations, such as the Lon Chaney vehicle *He Who Gets Slapped* (1924) and the elemental *The Wind* (1928). Other notable Hollywood films included *The Scarlet Letter* (1926), with Lillian Gish, *The Divine Woman* (1927), with Greta Garbo, and his sole talkie *A Lady To Love* (1930), with Edward G. Robinson. Unhappy with the visual restrictions imposed by the coming of sound, Sjöström returned to Sweden in 1930 and wound down his directing career. In his final decades he took up acting again, also becoming the artistic director of Svensk Filmindustri from 1943 to 1949. *Wild Strawberries* was his final credit, and a perfect epitaph. MB

The Phantom Carriage (Körkarlen) 1921, 92 min, b/w
cast Victor Sjöström, Hilda Borgström, Tore Svennberg, Astrid Holm, Lisa Lundholm, Tor Weijden *cin* J. Julius

The best known of Victor Sjöström's silent Swedish melodramas, this turned Nobel laureate Selma Lagerlöf's novel into an expressionist nightmare whose double-exposed special effects were a technical marvel at the time. Sjöström himself plays the Scrooge-like central character, condemned to drive the title vehicle as it gathers up the souls of the recently departed. It was reputedly Ingmar Bergman's favourite film, and he borrowed both Sjöström and its flashback structure for his own masterpiece *Wild Strawberries* (1957).

He Who Gets Slapped 1924, 78 min, b/w
cast Lon Chaney, Norma Shearer, John Gilbert, Tully Marshall, Ruth King, Marc McDermott, Ford Sterling *cin* Milton Moore

Sjöström's second Hollywood film stars Lon Chaney as a scientist whose life is destroyed by his wife's affair with his sponsor. Humiliated, he becomes a circus clown and gets slapped for real, before he falls in love with a fellow

S

performer (Norma Shearer). As a historical footnote, this was the first film produced by the Metro-Goldwyn-Mayer studio, and the first to sport its famous lion, Leo.

The Wind 1928, 85 min, b/w

cast Lillian Gish, Lars Hanson, Montagu Love, Dorothy Cumming, William Orlamond, Edward Earle *cin* John Arnold

Sjöström's most famous American film is aptly titled, as the wind is in many ways the central character, howling around and through the sand-strewn desert shack in which Virginian Lillian Gish ends up. Her involvement with a handsome stranger leads to rape, manslaughter and some of Sjöström's most memorable set pieces, especially the frantic sandstorm burial. Sadly, MGM vetoed the original ending in favour of an unconvincing happy one, but it's a minor blemish.

Erik Skjoldbjaerg

Norway, 1964–

Born in Tromsø in Norway, Erik Skjoldbjaerg studied at the National Film and Television School in the UK. His debut feature, *Insomnia* (1997), proved one of the most well-received genre films to come out of Europe in the past decade. The film's success took Skjoldbjaerg to the US, where he made *Prozac Nation* (2001), an adaptation of Elizabeth Wurtzel's memoir about her clinical depression. Pulled from theatrical distribution by Miramax, it has met with a lukewarm reception on DVD. He was invited to direct the 2002 American studio remake of *Insomnia*, but declined, and the job went to Christopher Nolan. Skjoldbjaerg returned to Norway for *En folkefiende* (*Enemy Of The People*, 2005), which inventively updated Ibsen's 1882 play with its story of a TV celebrity who moves back to his home town to set up a water bottling business but finds his integrity tested by a conflict of interests. JC

Insomnia 1997, 97 min

cast Stellan Skarsgård, Sverre Anker Ousdal, Gisken Armand, Bjørn Floberg *cin* Erling Thurmann-Andersen *m* Geir Jensen

Skjoldbjaerg's smart approach to *Insomnia* was to make what he called "a reverse *film noir*". Daylight not darkness is the harbinger of duplicity as a cop investigating a murder case in northern Norway struggles with sleep deprivation on account of the ever-present daylight. The film is visually stark and downbeat, and rather than emphasize the wide sweep of the Norwegian landscape Skjoldbjaerg instead opts for a stifling claustrophobia – to great effect.

Jerzy Skolimowski

Poland, 1938–

There is a short, piquant scene in *Deep End* (1970) which distils the very essence of Jerzy Skolimowski. The film's young protagonist throws a cutout of a topless woman into a swimming pool, and as soon as he jumps on top of it, the cardboard magically transforms into acquiescent, desirable flesh. And a movie which had been all semi-improvised naturalism makes a similar metamorphosis into slow motion and dream sequence. That sparkling collision of realism and surreal fantasy permeates the director's best work.

Skolimowski basically stumbled into filmmaking after a fortuitous meeting with Andrzej Wajda. After co-writing and acting in the director's *The Innocent Sorcerors* (1960), Skolimowski was persuaded to attend the Łódź Film School, where he met Roman Polanksi, and shared writing duties on *Knife In The Water* (1962). Skolimowski's first two films were intensely personal affairs, with the director effectively playing a version of himself called Andrzej Leszezyc, preparing for the army in *Rysopsis* (aka *Identification Marks: None*, 1964) and preparing for a boxing match in *Walkover* (1965). For some critics, his masterpiece from this early period is *Barrier* (1966), an impressionistic and nightmarish vision of Warsaw filtered through the alienated perspective of a lonely medical student.

After the Belgium-made modish curio *Le départ* (1967), which won a Golden Bear at the Berlin Film Festival, Skolimowski made the important allegorical chamber piece *Hands Up!* (1967). It was banned by the Polish government, a decision that prompted the director to leave the country. Since then, his career has divided into compromised international co-productions – *The Adventures Of Gerard* (1970), *King, Queen, Knave* (1972), *Torrents Of Spring* (1989) and *Ferdydurke* (1991) – and films set in Britain. *Deep End*, *The Shout* (1978), *Moonlighting* (1982) and *Success Is The Best Revenge* (1984) are the best of Skolimowski's later work, while the award-winning *The Lightship* (1985) encapsulated one of the director's recurring themes, centring on a power struggle in a hermetic world. LH

Deep End 1970, 88 min

cast Jane Asher, John Moulder-Brown, Diana Dors, Karl Michael Vogler, Christopher Sandford *cin* Charly Steinberger *m* Cat Stevens

A shabby municipal baths in London provides Skolimowski with the perfect metaphors of surface and depth to expose the sexual fever that lies beneath the façade of British suburban life. A 15-year-old school leaver working at the baths discovers that part of his job is to service middle-aged ladies (such as Diana Dors). It's all too much for him, and he starts to stalk his surly, coquettish colleague, causing trouble for both her fiancé and her married lover.

The Shout 1978, 86 min

cast Alan Bates, Susannah York, John Hurt, Robert Stephens, Tim Curry *cin* Mike Molloy *m* Rupert Hine, Anthony Banks, Mike Rutherford

British social realism is the last place you'd expect to find magic. But Skolimowski adopts the hand-held, observational approach of the kitchen-sink genre to recount the story of a dark stranger (Bates), who enters the lives of

S

sound artist (Hurt) and his wife (York). A power struggle plays out between the two men in a chamber piece with all the essential Skolimowski ingredients: dissonance, claustrophobia and an unsettling, charged atmosphere.

Moonlighting 1982, 97 min

cast Jeremy Irons, Eugene Lipinski, Jiri Stanislav, Eugeniusz Haczkiewicz, Denis Holmes, Jenny Seagrove cin Tony Pierce-Roberts m Stanley Myers

With an uncertain accent that flip-flops between posh and Polish, Jeremy Irons plays the leader of a team of immigrant workers who have come to Britain illegally to renovate their boss's London home, just before martial law is declared in their home country. Appearances can be deceptive with Skolimowski and what appears to be naïve realism conceals an intricate colour coding: in his muted, restrained palette, the only truly vibrant colour is the bright red of Solidarity, the Polish union.

Pål Sletaune

Norway, 1960–

Within a fine tradition of Nordic miserabilism, Pål Sletaune is at the Aki Kaurismäki end of the gloomy spectrum. Evincing the same grimly ironic, blue-collar squalor of the Finn's minor-key universe, Sletaune peoples his films with the saddest procession of losers, nerds and misfits to have graced the cinema for many a year, most of them even lacking the one shred of stoic dignity that Kaurismäki's laconic heroes cling to. After the acclaimed short *Eating Out* (1993), his debut, *Junk Mail* (1997), set the trend and the high watermark for his lugubrious style. Postmen rarely come off well in films and TV, but *Junk Mail* boasted one of the slackest, most misanthropic protagonists ever to carry a mailbag, and became an international success. His subsequent films, however, haven't travelled as well, even though they're crammed with similarly dark material. In *You Really Got Me* (2001), a loser whose girlfriend has just left him unwisely gets mixed up in a plot to kidnap a rock star. In *Next Door* (2005), another recently dumped loser is seduced by his two lusty female neighbours, and events soon take a sharp turn for the spooky and sadomasochistic. LH

Junk Mail (Budbringeren) 1997, 83 min

cast Robert Skjærstad, Andrine Sæther, Per Egil Aske, Eli Anne Linnestad, Trond Høvik, Henriette Steenstrup cin Kjell Vassdal m Joachim Holbelk

Postman Roy is a magnificent comic creation. Lazy, slovenly and smelly, he eats food straight out of tins, and spends his spare time reading other people's mail and stalking a deaf woman named Line. When he finds the keys to her apartment and lets himself in, he sets off a chain of events that quickly becomes a bleak and convoluted comedy of errors, as Line turns out not to be the naïve ingénue he had taken her for.

Kevin Smith

US, 1970–

Even Kevin Smith admits he's not much of a director. His visuals are functional at best. His staging and cutting are flat and clunky. Performances are often amateurish (Smith – whose Silent Bob alter ego has appeared in most of his films – is something of a professional amateur himself). Yet he immediately established himself as a touchstone filmmaker for Generation X with his debut, *Clerks* (1994), a zero-budget black-and-white comedy about bored youths working in a convenience store, chewing the fat about sex, comic books, porno, *Star Wars* and ice hockey.

Smith's obscene, scatological humour – he doesn't self-censor – struck a chord and helped define a new era in American comedy. Unlike the Farrelly brothers, whose equally puerile *Dumb & Dumber* was released the same year, Smith wrote credible characters instantly recognizable to the young suburbanites who make up his core audience.

Clerks was a Sundance pick-up for Miramax and became a cult hit. The director's follow-up, *Mallrats* (1995), which transfers the slacker action to a shopping mall, was savaged by the critics but became a hit on video. He salvaged his reputation with the more mature romantic comedy *Chasing Amy* (1997), starring Jason Lee and Ben Affleck, and explored his own unconventional brand of Catholicism in *Dogma* (1999), with Alanis Morissette as God.

Smith has continued to oscillate between broad stoner comedy – *Jay And Silent Bob Strike Back* (2001), the disappointing *Clerks II* (2006) – and stabs at more nuanced romantic comedy – *Jersey Girl* (2004) – with mixed results. Meanwhile, he continues to actively cultivate his fan base through his popular website – www.viewaskew.com – his graphic novels, his podcasts and his essay writing. TC

Clerks 1994, 92 min, b/w

cast Brian O'Halloran, Jeff Anderson, Marilyn Ghigliotti, Lisa Spoonauer, Jason Mewes, Kevin Smith cin David Klein m Scott Angley

A day in the life of Dante and Randal, two New Jersey dropouts holding down dead-end jobs in a Quick-Stop convenience store and the neighbouring RST Video, obsessing on the finer points of pornography and the Force (*Star Wars*). Looking every bit as cheap as the $28,000 it cost to make, buoyed up with spectacularly vulgar humour, it is perfectly of a piece with the lives of the characters it portrays.

Alan Smithee

US, 1967–

Alan (or Allen) Smithee was a pseudonym authorized by the Directors Guild of America (DGA) to be used when a Hollywood director wanted to

S

remove his or her name from a film. The cause of such situations has usually been producer interference, as was the case when Robert Totten was replaced by Don Siegel on the set of *Death Of A Gunfighter* (1969). Neither director wished to be associated with the resultant film and the name Allen Smithee was born as a way of resolving the matter.

Before allowing the Smithee name to be used, the DGA would assess whether the film has been removed from the control of the director, to ensure that the pseudonym was not being used simply to conceal directorial failures. The director also had to agree not to go public on the reasons for the disassociation. Use of the Smithee name accelerated in the 1980s and 90s and was also used widely in television.

In 1997 *An Alan Smithee Film: Burn Hollywood Burn* was released. In this satire on Hollywood, a director called Alan Smithee attempts to disown a film but is told he must use the pseudonym Alan Smithee. Amusing premise apart, the film was true to the Smithee tradition and turned out to be a complete turkey. Its director Arthur Hiller then capped it all by asking for (and being granted) a Smithee for the way the film had been edited. In response to the publicity the Smithee name received as a result of the film the DGA subsequently replaced it with a variety of pseudonyms, the first of which was Thomas Lee for the film *Supernova* (1999), directed in fact by Walter Hill. However, the Smithee name is still used from time to time. Debate persists over Smithee's origins. Some claim the name is an anagram of "The Alias Men", while others assert that it was a variation on the name originally suggested in relation to *Death Of A Gunfighter*, Al Smith, with the extra letters being added to ensure a real director would never emerge with the name. RC

Death Of A Gunfighter 1969, 100 min
cast Richard Widmark, Lena Horne, John Saxon, Michael McGreevey, Darkeen Carr *cin* Richard E. Lyons *m* Oliver Nelson

One of the many ironies of Smithee's career is that his first film may actually be his best. An old-school lawman working in a town bent on its own civilizing mission has to fight his corner after he kills a drunk in self-defence. *The New York Times* famously hailed the film's sharp direction. It is no masterpiece but Richard Widmark shines as Marshal Frank Patch in an intriguing film that reflects on the decline of the old West.

Michele Soavi
Italy, 1957–

A member of the wealthy Olivetti family, Michele Soavi began his film career as an actor in Italian exploitation fare such as Lucio Fulci's *Paura nella città dei morti viventi* (*City Of The Living Dead*, 1980). After a minor part in cult director/producer Joe D'Amato's *Rosso sangue* (*Absurd*, 1981), he was hired to write *Ator l'invincible* (*Ator The Fighting Eagle*, 1982) for him. It was D'Amato who produced Soavi's feature debut, *Deliria* (*Stagefright*, 1987), a deliberate ode to the films of Dario Argento. A lifetime fan of Argento's work, Soavi became his second assistant director on *Tenebrae* (1982) and first assistant on *Phenomena* (1985). He also directed the documentary *Dario Argento's World Of Horror* (1985) and acted in *Phenomena* and *Opera* (1987). Argento produced *The Church* (1989) and *The Sect* (1991) for Soavi, but these films were both unlike anything in the Argento canon. They led to what is perhaps his greatest work, *Dellamorte dellamore* (*Cemetery Man*, 1994). The illness of his son forced Soavi to retire from the industry for five years. He made his return via well-received TV movies and the feature *Arrivederci amore, ciao* (*The Goodbye Kiss*, 2006). AJ

The Sect (La setta) 1991, 115 min
cast Herbert Lom, Kelly Curtis, Mariangela Giordano, Michel Adatte, Carla Cassola *cin* Raffaele Mertes *m* Pino Donaggio

A young schoolteacher (Kelly Curtis) becomes the instrument of a sinister cult, led by Moebius Kelly (Herbert Lom), who are seeking the birth of the Antichrist. High on surreal originality and suspense, *The Sect* is sensational, cerebral and unusually affecting.

Dellamorte dellamore (Cemetery Man) 1994, 105 min
cast Rupert Everett, Anna Falchi, François Hadji-Lazaro, Mickey Knox, Fabiana Formica *cin* Mauro Marchetti *m* Manuel De Sica

Cemetery caretaker Rupert Everett kills his perfect woman and is cursed to see her face wherever he goes. This grotesque comedy mixes gross-out zombie gore with the quixotic irreverence of Jeunet and Caro's *Delicatessen* (1991). It is weird, wild and wonderful stuff.

Steven Soderbergh
US, 1963–

More than any other single film, *sex, lies, and videotape* (1989) crystallizes the American independent renaissance of the late 1980s and early 1990s. Shot in Baton Rouge, Louisiana, for a little over $1 million by first-timer Steven Soderbergh, this relatively low-budget "regional" film was cerebral, dense with talk and utterly devoid of cheap thrills (notwithstanding the title and Miramax's racy promotional campaign). Yet it created a sensation at the Sundance Film Festival in 1989 and won the Palme d'Or for its stunned 26-year-old director. "I guess it's all downhill from here", Soderbergh famously quipped in his Cannes acceptance speech.

For the better part of a decade, his self-deprecating line appeared to be somewhat accurate: in commercial terms, at least, Soderbergh entered a decade-

S

long slump after the box-office success of *sex, lies*. His adventurous career has come to represent all the triumphs and perils of auteurist filmmaking in America. As he climbed his way back to the top directorial ranks with the Oscar-winning one-two punch of *Erin Brockovich* and *Traffic* in 2000, Soderbergh brought an idiosyncratic touch to familiar genre material, striking an implicit détente between the arthouse and the mainstream, whereby aesthetic integrity and bottom-line exigencies meet halfway.

Soderbergh followed *sex, lies* with *Kafka* (1991), a nightmarish yet playful thriller that mixed biop-

The rise of the independents

At the end of the 1980s, Hollywood was caught up in buddy movies, sci-fi blockbusters and family fare. Untried directors with artistic whims, conversation-heavy scripts and compromised heroes were not at the top of producers' shopping lists. Some wonderful and successful American independent movies were made during the decade – the Coen brothers' *Blood Simple* (1984), for instance, or Jim Jarmusch's *Stranger Than Paradise* (1984) – but relatively few broke into suburban cinemas, or out of the specialist press.

Arguably, the film that changed all that was Steven Soderbergh's *sex, lies, and videotape* (1989), a clever domestic drama featuring more navel-gazing and less nudity than its title would suggest. It won the Palme d'Or at Cannes, jury president Wim Wenders commenting that the movie gave him "confidence in cinema". Soderbergh left the gong under his chair, but, bullishly marketed by producers Miramax, *sex, lies, and videotape* broke out of the arthouse ghetto and went on to make $50 million worldwide.

It was precisely this collision of mainstream and alternative, and the idea that moves made outside of the Hollywood system could attract big audiences, that made the independent cinema of the 1990s so intoxicating and successful. In 1991, Sundance's increasingly influential Grand Jury Prize went to Todd Haynes's kaleidoscopic *Poison*, whose story lines conflated sex and violence, angering the political Right and helping inaugurate the New Queer Cinema. Elsewhere, filmmakers who were prepared to take a chance found themselves blinking in the glare of success. Robert Rodriguez sold *El Mariachi* (1992), whose quick cuts, simple sets and amateur cast were dictated by a budget of just $7000, to Columbia and benefited from their vast promotional and distribution resources. Richard Linklater's largely plotless *Slacker* (1991) caught the Generation X zeitgeist and found its twentysomething existentialists held up as symbols of the age. Other filmmakers took advantage, including Hal Hartley, Gregg Araki, Susan Seidelman and Jon Jost.

If Sundance was vital to filmmakers, allowing them to attract distribution deals, marketing budgets and press attention, a number of independent producers were vital in getting films onto the street. Christine Vachon, a fiercely driven New Yorker, produced *Poison*, Larry Clark's messy, nihilistic *Kids* (1995), Todd Solondz's *Happiness* (1998), which tackled the tricky issue of paedophilia, and Kimberley Peirce's *Boys Don't Cry* (1999), personally indemnifying the Toronto Film Festival when it was threatened by lawsuits for screening the film.

If one company dominated the era, it was Miramax. Founders Bob and Harvey Weinstein picked up an astonishing number of brilliant – and highly successful – films in the 1990s, including Quentin Tarantino's *Reservoir Dogs* (1992), Kevin Smith's Sundance-winning *Clerks* (1994) and Gus Van Sant's *Good Will Hunting* (1997). Yet for all their energy, marketing genius and knack for spotting movies that could sweep their way to centre stage, the Weinsteins were not universally popular. Harvey's brutal cuts earned him the nickname "Scissorhands": Tarantino struggled to get *Reservoir Dogs*' ear-carving torture scene past him, while David O. Russell – whose brilliantly uncomfortable *Spanking The Monkey* (1994) was produced by Fine Line after Miramax turned it down – complained that "they treat you like used Kleenex".

However, the Weinsteins' editorial approach was nothing compared to what was to come. Once it became clear there was money to be made, the established studios moved in. In 1993 – shortly before *Pulp Fiction* (1994) made Quentin Tarantino a major Hollywood player – Disney bought Miramax. Within a few years, most of the big studios had an "independent" wing (for example Fox Searchlight), squeezing the genuine independents and heaping pressure on filmmakers to create movies to their – and the Oscars' – requirements. Sundance, now swollen into a vast jamboree, handed out badges reminding forgetful attendees to "Focus on Film" in 2007.

Yet, while the climate changed, the influence of the first wave – and its reminder that intelligent, offbeat films could still get an audience – was profound. The success of *Being John Malkovich* (1999), *Donnie Darko* (2001), *Secretary* (2002), *Little Miss Sunshine* (2006) and a hundred other gems strung between the mainstream and the left field is hugely heartening. Hits like *The Blair Witch Project* (1999) and *Fahrenheit 9/11* (2004, dropped by the Disney-run Miramax and picked up by indie giant Lionsgate) proved that independent producers can smash box-office records. As long as there is a mainstream, there will always be an underground. Where it rises next is anyone's guess. JS

ic and adaptation, and *King Of The Hill* (1993), a poignant Depression-era story of a boy coping without his parents in a fleabag hotel. Both films flopped (*Kafka* especially suffered a critical drubbing), hampered by unreasonable expectations and uncommercial subject matter. Even Soderbergh himself disliked *The Underneath* (1995), a chilly remake of Robert Siodmak's *Criss Cross* (1949). The director had reached an impasse, and what followed was a painful self-administered shot of adrenaline called *Schizopolis* (1996), in which writer-director-star Soderbergh dismantled narrative, identity, language and his own dead marriage.

After *Schizopolis* and a collaboration with Spalding Gray on *Gray's Anatomy* (1996), the revitalized Soderbergh delivered a pair of sinuous, witty thrillers: the sexy-cool *Out Of Sight* (1998), with Jennifer Lopez and George Clooney as a federal agent and her bank-robbing quarry, and *The Limey* (1999), with Terence Stamp as a Cockney avenging angel seeking the truth behind his daughter's mysterious death. Both lost money for their distributors, but were widely considered terrific films that simply hadn't found their audience – not a problem for the $100-million-plus grossers *Erin Brockovich* and *Traffic*. *Brockovich* won Julia Roberts the best actress Oscar for her brassy turn as a crusading legal secretary, while *Traffic*, which weaves three colour-coded storylines from various battlefields in the American drug war, won Soderbergh the best director Oscar.

After *Traffic*, Soderbergh could write his own ticket. He has since used his clout to finance other independent-minded filmmakers through Section Eight, the production company he set up with his frequent star Clooney (backing Gary Ross's *Pleasantville*, 1998, and Todd Haynes's *Far From Heaven*, 2002, among many others). Since 2000, Soderbergh has continued to draw on his informal ensemble company (including Clooney, Roberts, Don Cheadle and Luis Guzmán) and alternated between crowd-pleasing cash cows and more idiosyncratic endeavours: from the jaunty all-star pageantry of *Ocean's Eleven* (2001) and its self-reflexive sequels (2004, 2007) to the avant-garde misfire *Full Frontal* (2002), the lovely Andrei Tarkovsky remake *Solaris* (2003) and *The Good German* (2006), a monchrome homage to 1940s studio classics set in post-war Berlin. Soderbergh's non-franchise activities continue to prove that he hasn't yet sacrificed art for industry. JW

sex, lies, and videotape 1989, 96 min

cast James Spader, Andie MacDowell, Peter Gallagher, Laura San Giacomo, Ron Vawter, Steven Brill *cin* Walt Lloyd *m* Cliff Martinez

Ann (MacDowell) is a sexually repressed housewife whose slick yuppie husband, John (Gallagher), is having an affair with her free-spirited sister, Cynthia (San Giacomo). When John's enigmatic high-school friend Graham (Spader) arrives in town, Ann's outwardly perfect life and marriage begin to unravel – all the more when she discovers Graham's hobby of videotaping women discussing their sexual histories.

Schizopolis 1996, 96 min

cast Steven Soderbergh, Betsey Brantley, David Jensen, Mike Malone *cin* Steven Soderbergh *m* Cliff Martinez, Jeff Rona, Steven Soderbergh

Unclassifiable, synopsis-proof and shot on a shoestring budget, this shape-shifting experiment in narrative fragmentation finds Soderbergh himself playing both an office drone working for a Scientology-like corporation and a dentist who's having an affair with the drone's wife (played by Soderbergh's real-life ex Betsy Brantley). Adultery, identity slippage and corporate hegemony all cast long shadows over the verdant lawns of suburbia in Soderbergh's deadpan, fascinating and stunningly dense whatchamacallit.

Out Of Sight 1998, 118 min

cast George Clooney, Jennifer Lopez, Ving Rhames, Don Cheadle, Dennis Farina, Albert Brooks, Steve Zahn *cin* Elliot Davis *m* David Holmes

Comely federal marshal Jennifer Lopez and bank robber George Clooney fall for each other in this droll Elmore Leonard adaptation. The two stars have a potent chemistry – established during their first "date" in the boot of a car – and the film is given an oneiric quality by Soderbergh's use of tinted stock and filters, fragmentary editing and frequent discontinuity between sound and image, which was also used to hypnotic effect in the following year's *The Limey*.

Erin Brockovich 2000, 130 min

cast Julia Roberts, Albert Finney, Aaron Eckhart, Marg Helgenberger, Cherry Jones, Veanne Cox *cin* Edward Lachman *m* Thomas Newman

Especially for its first hour or so, this rabble-rousing biopic gives star vehicles a good name – it's a smooth, quietly angry thriller about corporate malfeasance with a sly script and nimble hand-held photography by Ed Lachman. But the movie contrives far too many "you-go-girl" speeches for the scantily clad Julia Roberts; over and over again, she gets on her high horse and cusses up a storm 'til they give her the bleepin' Oscar already.

Traffic 2000, 147 min

cast Michael Douglas, Don Cheadle, Benicio Del Toro, Luis Guzmàn, Dennis Quaid, Catherine Zeta-Jones *cin* Steven Soderbergh *m* Cliff Martinez

This ambitious, vérité-style reworking of a Channel 4 miniseries braids three tales from different sides of the Central American drug trade: Michael Douglas is the new drug tsar whose daughter's escalating habit is his dirty little secret; Catherine Zeta-Jones is a pregnant Californian wife who discovers her husband's a coke lord; and Benicio Del Toro is a supremely capable Mexican cop. With a different colour stock for each strand, *Traffic* can be schematic, but it's also lush with deftly staged incident and telling detail.

Solaris 2003, 99 min

cast George Clooney, Natascha McElhone, Jeremy Davies, Viola Davis, Ulrich Tukur *m* Steven Soderbergh *m* Cliff Martinez

Something terrible has befallen the crew of a space station, and when George Clooney's bereaved psychologist goes to investigate, he discovers the ghost or reincarnation of his dead wife (Natasha McElhone). This plangent retelling of Stanislaw Lem's sci-fi spin on the Orpheus myth arguably improves on Andrei Tarkovsky's 1972 film version – it's pensive, elegant and enormously moving, which are not normally qualities one would expect from a film co-produced by James Cameron.

S

Iain Softley

UK, 1958–

Is it too preposterous to advance the theory that there are two Iain Softleys? The director who gave us the acclaimed British costume drama *The Wings Of The Dove* (1997) and the one who turned out the by-the-numbers Hollywood thriller *The Skeleton Key* (2005).

Softley's British debut *Backbeat* (1994) hummed with youthful vibrancy and potential, but his American introduction, the unremarkable cyberthriller *Hackers* (1995), was instantly forgettable. Yet Softley's third film, the Henry James adaptation *The Wings Of The Dove*, was hailed by some as a modern classic.

His two most recent American movies repeated this puzzling pattern. *K-Pax* (2001) began with a tantalizing premise – mental patient Kevin Spacey may or may not be a visitor from another planet – but dissipated its intrigue in a feel-good blend of group hugs, New Age platitudes and mad-but-happy clichés. Four years later, *The Skeleton Key* was a routine, mediocre chiller written by Ehren Krueger. You can't help but wonder why Softley hasn't written any screenplays since his impressive debut, *Backbeat*.

If there is a unifying element to Softley's variable output, it is the design concept of his films – the impressively holistic approach to theme, decor and lighting. Seeing this, it's not surprising to learn that he was a painter in his teens and a set designer for amateur dramatic productions while studying English at Cambridge University.

Perhaps the differences between the British Softley and the Hollywood version have little to do with the director himself and more to do with the demands and modus operandi of the two different film industries. LH

Backbeat 1994, 100 min

cast Sheryl Lee, Stephen Dorff, Ian Hart, Gary Bakewell, Chris O'Neill, Scott Williams *cin* Ian Wilson *m* Don Was

This is a Beatles biopic with a difference. Softley focuses on the band's salad days in Hamburg, when the fifth Beatle, Stuart Sutcliffe, met art student Astrid Kirchherr. Their relationship gave birth to the mop-top haircut and turned them into the Fab Four, Sutcliffe opting for painting over music. Softley sketches in the characters of McCartney, Harrison and Pete Best with a sharp economy of detail, training his lens, instead, on the doomed lovers and the scabrous, jealous Lennon.

The Wings Of The Dove 1997, 102 min

cast Helena Bonham Carter, Linus Roache, Alison Elliott, Elizabeth McGovern, Michael Gambon *cin* Eduardo Serra *m* Edward Shearmur

This lean adaptation of Henry James's novel sees a scheming couple (Bonham Carter and Roache) plot to inherit the wealth of a dying American heiress. Softley updates the book by eight years to 1910, bringing in a modern world of cars, wristwatches and a more open acknowledgement of sex. With its compromised motivations of lovers locked in a toxic embrace, the plot resembles James M. Cain at his misanthropic best, a cue Softley exploits by filtering the narrative through a fevered *film noir* prism.

Alexander Sokurov

Russia (formerly Soviet Union), 1951–

Alexander Sokurov is "one of the saviours of the serious cinema" according to writer Susan Sontag. And he certainly takes himself seriously, even if critics sometimes don't. Up until 1987 and the liberating effects of *glasnost*, all his films received chilly official treatment (his 1978 diploma piece, *The Lonely Voice Of A Man*, for example, was banned by Soviet authorities for being formalist). It wasn't until the release of *Mother And Son* in 1997 that Sokurov entered wider Western consciousness. By then he'd already amassed an impressive body of work, including numerous documentaries and features such as *Days Of The Eclipse* (1988). Since 1997, his films have both intoxicated and infuriated critics with their opaque narratives, spiritual tropes and formal compositions: filming behind panes of painted glass in *Mother And Son*, the one-take wonder in *Russian Ark* (2002) and the sepia-tinged, dream-like tonality of *Father And Son* (2003).

His preference for long takes and a mobile camera are redolent of his late friend Andrei Tarkovsky, the subject of his documentary *Moscow Elegy* (1987). The legendary director, though, is a rare cinematic influence. Sokurov prefers to mine inspiration from classical music, painting and literature, citing Dostoevsky, Chekhov, Tolstoy and Rembrandt as his peers. The director seems to think of himself as a questing genius in the Romantic tradition, and the influence of painter Caspar David Friedrich was certainly evident in the haunting *Moloch* (1999), which tried to make common sense of the lives of Eva Braun and Adolf Hitler as they weekend with Himmler and Goebbels at Berchtesgaden (at one point Hitler declares "we will beat death", thus enunciating one of Sokurov's recurring themes).

Part of a proposed historical tetralogy, *Moloch* was followed by *Taurus* (2001), a solemn essay on power, corruption and the last days of Lenin, limned in sickly pea greens. Sokurov selects colours and hues to complement his themes, which sometimes means that form and content are equally murky. *The Sun* (2005), for instance, was shot almost exclusively in evening light to gloomily evoke the end of an era as Emperor Hirohito, in the aftermath of Hiroshima and Nagasaki, makes his previously unthinkable decision to admit defeat and renounce his divinity. *Aleksandra* (2007), a Chechnya-set war film without a war, echoed aspects of the hypnotic 328-minute marathon *Spiritual Voices* (1995), which touched on the reality of being a soldier.

S

Spiritualist genius or over-solemn cineaste, Sokurov is unique in contemporary cinema, a genuine throwback to a more challenging and auterist era of filmmaking. LH

Mother And Son (Mat i syn) 1997, 73 min

cast Aleksei Ananishov, Gudrun Geyer *cin* Aleksei Fedorov *m* Glinka, Otmar Nussio, Giuseppe Verdi

Sokurov casts a mesmerizing spell with this simple tale of a loving son who carries his dying mother in his arms from their cabin to a nearby wood, where they reminisce. As well as with meditative takes, the director practises his transcendentalism through typical Sokurovian means: distorting and softening his image with the help of painted glass and an anamorphic lens, and elevating background noise to the level of sonic poetry. Sublime.

Russian Ark (Russkiy kovcheg) 2002, 88 min

cast Sergey Dreiden, Maria Kuznetsova, Leonid Mozgovoy *cin* Tilman Büttner *m* Mikhail Glinka, Peter Tchaikovsky, G. Persella, Georg Philipp Telemann

An unseen narrator (Sokurov) and a French diplomat meander through the ornate majesty of the Hermitage museum in St Petersburg. As they do, history springs miraculously to life, with the help of 2000 actors. The time-shifting journey through Russian culture was all shot in a single, unbroken, mellifluous take. What we see is the fourth attempt, and given the fact that Sokurov and crew only had two days in the Hermitage to set up and shoot, it is an immense achievement.

Father And Son (Otets i syn) 2003, 83 min

cast Andrey Shchetinin, Alexei Nejmyshev, Alexander Rasbash *cin* Alexander Burov *m* Andrei Sigle

In a rooftop apartment, the relationship between an army veteran father and soldier son plays out in a series of mysterious glances and physical exercises, as if the two exist in a hermetically sealed universe that is entirely of their own making. This carefully modulated chamber piece is militantly impressionistic, genuinely unique and undeniably homoerotic, no matter what the director says about critics reading a homosexual subtext where none was intended.

Fernando E. Solanas

Argentina, 1936–

For over four decades the filmmaking of Fernando E. Solanas has pursued a radical left-wing agenda. In collaboration with the Cine Liberación collective, Solanas and co-director Octavio Getino made the acclaimed epic documentary *La hora de los hornos* (*The Hour Of The Furnaces*, 1968), which exposed violence and corruption in Argentina. The two men then wrote the manifesto "Towards A Third Cinema", rejecting the values of both Hollywood and European auteur films in favour of a more revolutionary style. They continued to make films in the service of the revolutionary cause until Juan Perón's return to power in 1973, after which Solanas transferred his immense energies to fictional films. His active support of Perón forced him into exile in Paris in 1976, an experience which inspired *Tangos,*

The Exile Of Gardel (1985). In 1988 he won the best director prize at Cannes for *Sur* (*The South*). Despite taking political office following an assassination attempt in 1991, Solanas continued to direct. His thoughtful Latin American road movie *The Voyage* (1992) was nominated for the Palme d'Or, while his more recent work has comprised documentaries focusing on Argentinian history and the social realities of life in South America. ED

Sur (The South) 1988, 127 min

cast Miguel Angel Sola, Susu Pecoraro, Phillippe Léotard, Lito Cruz, Ulises Dumont *cin* Félix Monti *m* Astor Piazzolla, Fernando Solanas

A political activist is released after five years in jail. Before his painful reunion with his wife he spends a night of reflection wandering the streets of a city during which people from his past appear to him in flashback. Solanas beautifully weaves an episodic, dream-like meditation on melancholy, loss and love.

Todd Solondz

US, 1959–

Everybody's either a bully or a weakling, and the weaklings will gladly become bullies if given half the chance: such is the human strain as seen through the microscope of Todd Solondz, cinema's bard of the New Jersey suburbs. The geek's revenge passion play *Welcome To The Dollhouse* (1996) bravely made its dorky whipping post Dawn Weiner just as capable of cruelty as her tormenters. In the even chillier climes of *Happiness* (1998), Solondz stage-managed a deadpan freak show in which the most sympathetic character just happened to be a child molester.

Before he'd turned 30, Solondz – who once considered becoming a rabbi and later taught English to Russian immigrants – wrote, directed and starred in his first feature, *Fear, Anxiety & Depression* (1989). His debut was the derivative product of a Woody Allen acolyte, though its title neatly encapsulated the dominant moods of the more successful Solondz works to come: *Dollhouse* won the Grand Jury Prize at Sundance and *Happiness* earned an unexpected PR boost when its nervous original distributor dumped it.

After *Happiness*, Solondz had to strain ever harder to shock. In the schematic, self-reflexive *Storytelling* (2001), a black teacher and his white creative-writing student engage in rough, indeterminately consensual sex while he orders her to scream "Nigger fuck me hard!" In *Palindromes* (2004), young Aviva – played by eight different actors – has an abortion under parental pressure and then escapes to an orphanage-cum-Bible camp for disabled kids. The rotating cast conceit ensures that Aviva is little more than a wheedling cipher, the hollow centre of a self-satisfied cacophony of sentimentality and snide contempt. JW

S

Welcome To The Dollhouse 1996, 88 min

cast Heather Matarazzo, Victoria Davis, Christina Brucato, Christina Vidal, Siri Howard, Brendan Sexton Jr *cin* Randy Drummond *m* Jill Wisoff

Persecuted by classmates and teachers, overlooked by her parents and hopelessly in love with an older hunk, Dawn "Weiner Dog" Weiner is the movie's bespectacled face of pubescent forbearance and pain (and perhaps her writer-director's alter ego). *Dollhouse* is a uniquely subjective experience: depending on their memories of early adolescence, viewers may interpret it as an expressionist horror film, a painfully realist rendering of the social acid bath that is junior high school, or both.

Happiness 1998, 139 min

cast Jane Adams, Dylan Baker, Lynn Flynn, Philip Seymour Hoffman, Ben Gazzara, Louise Lasser, Jared Harris *cin* Maryse Alberti *m* Robbie Kondor

Though it hinges on three sisters (and their dysfunctional extended network of family, friends and neighbours), Solondz's cavalcade of pathology is less Chekhovian than Buñuelian in its matter-of-fact misanthropy. Packing in rape, murder, suicide and child abuse, *Happiness* actively provokes outrage in its portrayal of a paedophile (Dylan Baker) as a sympathetic suburban dad doing his best. A brattish stunt on Solondz's part, perhaps, but it's also darkly comic proof that even monsters have souls.

Barry Sonnenfeld
US, 1953–

Barry Sonnenfeld is a mainstream comedy director whose career oscillates between deft, hip hits like *Get Shorty* (1995) and *Men In Black* (1997) and bland misfires like *Wild Wild West* (1997) and *Big Trouble* (2002).

A graduate of the New York University film school, Sonnenfeld made industrial films and pornos (he claims to have directed nine porn films in nine days) before photographing the Coen brothers' first three features – *Blood Simple* (1984), *Raising Arizona* (1987) and *Miller's Crossing* (1990) – which were each acclaimed for their visual ingenuity and cinematic style. He was also the cinematographer on Rob Reiner's *When Harry Met Sally...* (1989) and *Misery* (1990), among several others.

In 1991, Sonnenfeld turned to directing with *The Addams Family*, an episodic black comedy based on the ghoulish *New Yorker* comic strip. A sequel, *Addams Family Values*, followed two years later. However, it wasn't until he made the Elmore Leonard Hollywood thriller *Get Shorty* in 1995 that Sonnenfeld proved he could pull all the elements together. At his best, Sonnenfeld is an insouciant filmmaker whose sly sense of humour redeems inherently superficial material; but he can also push too far into caricature and slapstick silliness – and his recent Robin Williams comedy vehicle *RV* (2006) certainly falls into the latter camp. TC

Get Shorty 1995, 105 min

cast John Travolta, Gene Hackman, Rene Russo, Danny DeVito, Dennis Farina, Delroy Lindo, James Gandolfini *cin* Peter Larkin *m* John Lurie

One of the more successful adaptations of crime novelist Elmore Leonard, this has John Travolta as Miami loan shark Chili Palmer pitching true-crime stories to schlock Hollywood producer Harry Zimm (Gene Hackman). Sonnenfeld sets a light, breezy tempo and evidently appreciates Leonard's knowing, satiric take on Tinseltown, preserving the author's beloved backchat without letting the movie get too talky or self-conscious.

Men In Black 1997, 98 min

cast Will Smith, Tommy Lee Jones, Linda Fiorentino, Vincent D'Onofrio, Rip Torn *cin* Don Peterman *m* Danny Elfman

A big hit that wittily keyed into America's obsession with alien lifeforms and New York's obsession with itself. Will Smith is a cop initiated into the secrets of the universe by his new partner, Agent K (Tommy Lee Jones). This odd-couple partnership supplies regular laughs, while Sonnenfeld has a lot of fun with eye-popping special effects. The 2002 sequel, *Men In Black II*, which saw Jones leave the Men in Black and become a postman, was funny, but forgettable.

Carlos Sorin
Argentina, 1944–

Carlos Sorin has made Patagonia his own personal cinematic territory. Ever since his debut, *A King And His Movie* (1986), the ad-maker and TV director has staked his claim, setting his films in the empty plains, huge skies and surreal desolation of southern Argentina. Given the fact that vast tracts of flat, featureless land dominate the region, it's not surprising that three of those films have been road movies.

In the eccentric picaresque *Eversmile New Jersey* (1989), Daniel Day-Lewis played an Irish dentist from New Jersey who travels across the alien landscape by motorbike (his sidecar doubles as a dentist's chair) to inform the locals about the benefits of oral hygiene. *Historias minimas* (2002) told the charming and rambling tale of three people making a 200-mile pilgrimage to San Julián. In *Bombón el perro* (2004), meanwhile, a laconic unemployed mechanic finds a new lease of life when he's given a huge white mastiff and starts to compete in dog shows. Things go awry when the mutt, who has no problem with deportment and walkies, needs a leg up in the stud department. Sorin returned to road movies in 2006, with the offbeat *El camino de San Diego* (*The Road To San Diego*), in which the main character, Tati, sets off in search of soccer legend Diego Maradona. LH

Historias minimas 2002, 91 min

cast Javier Lombardo, Antonio Benedicti, Javiera Bravo, Julia Solomonoff *cin* Hugo Colace *m* Nicolás Sorin

Three disparate characters – a single mum on her way to a game show, an old man looking for his long-lost dog and

S

an opportunistic salesman – make the long journey to the city of San Julián. Sorin employs nonprofessional actors, framing the small details of his characters' domestic lives by the dwarfing immensity of the landscape. The result is deeply humanistic and subtly critical of a country where everyone has their price.

Penelope Spheeris
US, 1945–

Though her career traces its own precipitous decline into a bottomless pit of lamebrain comedy, Penelope Spheeris can take credit for three singularly bleak, angry films that came out of her interest in the American punk music scene in the late 1970s/early 1980s: the felicitously named documentary *The Decline Of Western Civilization* (1980); the Roger Corman-produced punk drama *Suburbia* (1984); and the killing spree exploitation flick *The Boys Next Door* (1985). Not coincidentally, these were her first three films.

Greek-American by birth (director Costa-Gavras is a cousin), Spheeris grew up travelling with her father's carnival, the Magic Empire. After studying film at UCLA, she produced skits for Albert Brooks on the first season of the long-running comedy TV show *Saturday Night Live* in 1975.

Intrigued by LA's punk rock scene, Spheeris went on to write, direct and edit *The Decline Of Western Civilization*, a valuable record of bands like The Circle Jerks, The Germs, Fear and Phranc. The first of two follow-ups, *The Metal Years* (1988) was strictly generic, but *Part III* (1998) gave us a harrowing update on the plight of ordinary punk fans nearly twenty years on. Both *Suburbia* and *The Boys Next Door* (featuring a young Charlie Sheen) stayed true to a nihilistic punk ethos, mixing acidic social commentary with exploitation film elements. Although these early features are heavy-handed, they are reminders of a vital, provocative sub-Hollywood cinema that existed even into Reagan's second term.

With the demise of that exploitation arena, Spheeris gravitated back towards comedy, contributing to scripts for the blue-collar sitcom *Roseanne* (1990) and, on the big screen, hitting the jackpot with *SNL* spin-off *Wayne's World* (1992). Subsequent efforts – populist comedies like *Black Sheep* (1996), with Chris Farley, and *The Kid & I* (2005), a vehicle for Tom Arnold – tend to underline Spheeris's own comment on the commentary track of the *Suburbia* DVD: "I was a good director, until I sold out." Meanwhile, she also continues to make rock documentaries – *We Sold Our Souls For Rock 'n' Roll* (2001) lays bare the major rock festival Ozzfest – as well as regularly working in TV. TC

Suburbia 1984, 94 min
cast Chris Pedersen, Bill Coyne, Jennifer Clay, Timothy O'Brien, Wade Walston, Flea, Christina Beck *cin* Tim Suhrstedt *m* Alex Gibson

Spheeris made the transition to narrative features with this Roger Corman-produced portrait of a gang of punks who call themselves T.R. – The Rejected. Living in an abandoned suburban development alongside a metaphorical pack of wild dogs, The Rejected carry the scars of abuse, intolerance and violence, and there's no question that the writer-director is on their side of the tracks. Look out for Flea, from the Red Hot Chili Peppers, in a supporting role. With music from The Vandals.

Steven Spielberg
US, 1946–

Steven Spielberg was always a filmmaker. He made his first short at age 10, screened one of his early 8mm efforts for his wildly enthusiastic Boy Scout troop at age 12 and had completed a 140-minute feature called *Firelight* by age 15 (or 17 by other accounts). Spielberg began his professional career in television in the late 1960s, and made the short *Amblin* in 1968, which won an award at the Venice Film Festival, led to a seven-year deal with Universal and gave him the name for the production company he co-founded in 1984. In 1971, he directed the feature-length *Duel* for the small screen. The coolly effective suspense tale of a crazed truck was well-received and eventually won a theatrical release, having been expanded with four addditional scenes. His proper debut feature, *The Sugarland Express* (1974), wherein a kidnapping sparks a media circus, faltered at the box office, but just a year later he returned with *Jaws* (1975). The rest is history.

In addition to co-founding a major studio (DreamWorks SKG) and producing scores of films for other directors, Spielberg is responsible for several of the top-grossing movies of all time. Many movies of his staggeringly profitable career have not merely been popular flicks but, in fact, compulsory-attendance cultural events – from the box-office behemoths *Jaws*, *Close Encounters Of The Third Kind* (1977), *Raiders Of The Lost Ark* (1981), *E.T. The Extra-Terrestrial* (1982) and *Jurassic Park* (1993) to the sober, worthy period pieces *Schindler's List* (1993), *Amistad* (1997) and *Saving Private Ryan* (1998). Together with George Lucas's *Star Wars* (1977), Spielberg's movies have been credited with changing the direction of the entire American film industry, juvenilizing the mainstream and setting it on a course of summer blockbusters, spin-off merchandising and big-splash opening weekends.

Even when depicting the Holocaust, slavery in America or the infernal battlefields of World War II in his serious, honourable period projects, Spielberg cannot resist sweetening his bitter his-

S

John Williams and Steven Spielberg

With dozens of awards, including five Oscars, to his name, John Williams has composed many of the most iconic film scores in cinema's history. Williams began his musical career working as a film soundtrack pianist, which led to film orchestration and then to television composition. His first Oscar came in 1972 for his adaptation of *Fiddler On The Roof*. The 1970s brought disaster movies like *The Poseidon Adventure* (1972) and 1974's *Earthquake* and *The Towering Inferno*: though the genre is now widely derided, the films were often extremely popular and Williams's music fitted perfectly. Yet at the same time Williams was also creating more intimate and experimental music for films such as Robert Altman's psychodrama *Images* (1972).

Williams has scored all but two of Steven Spielberg's films, beginning with his first feature, *Sugarland Express* (1974). For *Jaws* (1975) the soundtrack's obsessively accelerating two-note motif generated real fear and garnered Williams another Oscar, but his music for Hitchcock's last film, *Family Plot* (1976), was less successful. George Lucas's *Star Wars* (1977) was, despite its futuristic setting, very much based on 1930s adventure serials (with a debt to Akira Kurosawa's *The Hidden Fortress*, 1958, as well) so Williams's orchestral score fittingly uses leitmotifs from the tradition of Golden Age composers such as Erich Korngold and, by influence, Richard Wagner. It became the best-selling orchestral soundtrack album ever and Williams returned for the rest of the cycle. The three *Indiana Jones* films (1981, 1984 and 1989) are in the same swashbuckling mould. Even when he scored only part of a series – *Superman* (1978), for instance, and the first three *Harry Potter* films (2001, 2002 and 2004) – his themes continue to feature in subsequent instalments. While scores like the Oscar-winning *E.T. The Extra-Terrestrial* (1982) are traditional, he is not afraid to experiment – even in populist films such as *Close Encounters Of The Third Kind* (1977), which the composer has said is one of his favourites. Its famous five-note motif is a mainstay of spoofs and there is a rumour that NASA regularly beams it into space, hoping for a return intergalactic communication. But there is a lot more to the score, including sections of dissonant noise and echoes of the ethereal György Ligeti pieces used in Stanley Kubrick's *2001: A Space Odyssey* (1968). In 1993 Williams showed his versatility again, working on two dizzyingly different Spielberg projects: *Jurassic Park* and *Schindler's List*. The latter, with its Jewish-tinged violin concertino, won Williams another Oscar, as did *Saving Private Ryan* (1998), another score for Spielberg. JR

tory lessons with mawkishness and ameliorating sentiment. He is a director of action-adventure nonpareil, but can never fully adapt his boyish temperament to weightier material. No matter his setting or subject, we're always in Spielbergland, a world of magical make-believe where Tom Hanks can face down a German tank with a single pistol and where the "showers" at Auschwitz are really showers after all.

Promisingly, his recent work has ranked among his most interesting. *A.I. Artificial Intelligence* (2001) was a fascinating blend of mother-child pathology and discordant sensibilities, *Minority Report* (2002) had a delicious nasty streak and *Catch Me If You Can* (2002) whipped up a mischievous, delightful froth. *War Of The Worlds* (2005) re-established the director as the reigning architect of disaster, and *Munich* (2005) was an anguished look back at the terrorist attack on the 1972 Munich Olympics that posed difficult questions about the nature of vengeance. JW

Jaws 1975, 124 min

cast Roy Scheider, Robert Shaw, Richard Dreyfuss, Lorraine Gary, Murray Hamilton, Carl Gottlieb, Jeffrey Kramer *cin* Bill Butler *m* John Williams

Still Spielberg's most exhilarating film, the first summer blockbuster is a well-oiled, perfectly calibrated monster-movie machine, building terror by concealment (nearly an hour passes before we get a full look at the shark) and adding blackly comic textures (often in the person of sat-

urnine seaman Robert Shaw). Spielberg toys with viewer complicity too – he delights in his shark's-eye camera and the opening kill carries a sexual undertow that's rare in this remarkably chaste director's oeuvre.

Raiders Of The Lost Ark 1981, 115 min

cast Harrison Ford, Karen Allen, Wolf Kahler, Paul Freeman, Ronald Lacey, John Rhys-Davies, Denholm Elliott *cin* Douglas Slocombe *m* John Williams

Spielberg's rollicking escapade has as much whizz-bang excitement in a single set piece as an entire summer's worth of bloated blockbusters. Roving archaeologist Indiana Jones (Harrison Ford) races to reach the Lost Ark of the Covenant and its magical powers before the Nazis can get their hands on it, which launches a timeless action adventure combining lost-civilization intrigue, concussive action, sight gags, special effects, inebriated romance and that big boulder.

E.T. The Extra-Terrestrial 1982, 115 min

cast Henry Thomas, Dee Wallace, Robert MacNaughton, Peter Coyote, Drew Barrymore *cin* Allen Daviau *m* John Williams

Returning to the paranormally inflected American suburbia of *Close Encounters*, Spielberg's record-breaker is a boy-meets-alien love story that established the director's recurrent fixation with the child in search of respite from cosmic loneliness. Despite a few jarring low-comedy interludes (not to mention the regrettable CGI effects tacked onto the 2002 re-release), *E.T.* earns its emotional dividends, not least because Spielberg coaxes charmingly unaffected performances from his young actors, especially Henry Thomas as Elliot.

S

Schindler's List 1993, 195 min, b/w

cast Liam Neeson, Ben Kingsley, Ralph Fiennes, Caroline Goodall, Jonathan Sagalle, Embeth Davidtz *cin* Janusz Kaminski *m* John Williams

Spielberg finally won a directing Oscar for his epic about industrialist Oskar Schindler (Liam Neeson), who saved more than a thousand Jews from the death camps during World War II. Especially during the first hour, Spielberg brings a measure of cold *vérité* immediacy and dry, savage wit to the material, but his maudlin tendencies eventually win out, and it's puzzling why a would-be definitive work on the Holocaust only casts Jews as, at best, flatly drawn supporting players.

Saving Private Ryan 1998, 170 min

cast Tom Hanks, Tom Sizemore, Matt Damon, Edward Burns, Barry Pepper, Adam Goldberg, Ted Danson *cin* Janusz Kaminski *m* John Williams

The best and worst of Spielberg: the justly celebrated D-Day overture is one of the most stunning battlefield immersions ever committed to celluloid, but the rest of Spielberg's undoubtedly heartfelt testament to Allied fortitude is a hackneyed patchwork of war-movie clichés, anchored by Tom Hanks's saintly Everyman. The film never seriously questions the morality of sacrificing half a dozen men to save one, while its present-day book ends reach a punishing level of bathos.

A.I. Artificial Intelligence 2001, 146 min

cast Haley Joel Osment, Frances O'Connor, Jude Law, William Hurt, Sam Robards *cin* Janusz Kaminski *m* John Williams

Spielberg inherited this science-fiction fable (based on a Brian Aldiss story) from Stanley Kubrick, and the result is a strange and affecting meld of two diametrically opposed filmmaking styles. As the robot-boy David, the preternatural Haley Joel Osment carries this tragic tale of an abandoned child and his desperate attempts to make-believe his way to perfect family happiness. (The last half-hour or so is completely unnecessary – for the better, more Kubrick-like ending, switch the DVD player off when little David dives into the sea.)

Minority Report 2002, 145 min

cast Tom Cruise, Max von Sydow, Steve Harris, Neal McDonough, Colin Farrell, Samantha Morton *cin* Janusz Kaminski *m* John Williams

An eye-popping futurama spilling over with visual invention, left-field wit and scuzzy bits of business (not to mention a few plot gaps in the space-time continuum), this is Spielberg's most enjoyable film since *Raiders Of The Lost Ark*. It adapts Philip K. Dick's tale of a "Pre-Crime" unit headed up by John Anderton (Tom Cruise), who makes arrests before crimes happen – until one of his in-house psychics predicts Anderton's part in an imminent murder.

John M. Stahl
US, 1886–1950

John Stahl stands in the shadows of Douglas Sirk, who haunts the official history of celluloid melodrama. While some critics argue that he deserves better, cynics have suggested that the title of Stahl's 1934 film *Imitation Of Life* perfectly sums up his bloodless *mise en scène*.

A director from 1914, his filmography divides almost perfectly between silent and sound films, with 23 made before pictures began to talk, and 22 made after. However, it's for the latter half that he is best known, particularly for his string of sentimental dramas from the 1930s that helped to define the weepie. His best films had at their hearts women

Steven Spielberg directing Tom Cruise and Samantha Morton in the visually inventive sci-fi film *Minority Report*.

who could survive anything that melodrama threw at them, whether it was single mums Margaret Sullavan and Claudette Colbert in *Only Yesterday* (1933) and *Imitation Of Life*, or Irene Dunne stoically waiting for her man in *Back Street* (1932). Three of Stahl's films were later remade by Sirk – *Imitation Of Life*, *Magnificent Obsession* (1935) and *When Tomorrow Comes* (1939). Comparisons are, of course, inevitable, and this is where Stahl loses out, his direction having remained resolutely average.

Most of his soaps were models of restraint, with the camera observing the action from an elegant distance. In tandem with a stately pace, Stahl's austere approach has prompted comparisons with Carl Theodor Dreyer, Yasujiro Ozu and Robert Bresson – but only by a handful of critics. The Christian missionary drama *The Keys Of The Kingdom* (1944) and the musical *Oh, You Beautiful Doll* (1949) demonstrated Stahl's range outside of weepies, but the variable quality of his 1940s output hasn't helped his neglected reputation, with *Leave Her To Heaven* (1945) being one of the few recommended films of his later years. LH

Back Street 1932, 92 min, b/w

cast Irene Dunne, John Boles, June Clyde, George Meeker *cin* Karl Freund *m* David Broekman, James Dietrich

In this finely calibrated adaptation of Fannie Hurst's novel, Irene Dunne waits patiently for her wealthy lover, played by Stahl regular John Boles. But he shows no signs that he will ever leave his wife – or that he has feelings for anyone but himself – and she wastes away her life in quiet martyrdom.

Only Yesterday 1933, 106 min, b/w

cast Margaret Sullavan, John Boles, Edna May Oliver, Billie Burke *cin* Merritt B. Gerstad *m* C. Bakaleinikoff

Contemplating suicide after losing everything in the Wall Street Crash, John Boles discovers a letter on his desk from former lover Margaret Sullavan, who, as we discover in flashback, Boles had failed to recognize after returning from World War I. A series of coincidences and plot twists drive the narrative to its climactic sucker punch.

Leave Her To Heaven 1945, 110 min

cast Gene Tierney, Cornel Wilde, Jeanne Crain, Vincent Price *cin* Leon Shamroy *m* Alfred Newman

Displaying one of the most violent examples of the Electra complex in the history of melodrama, Gene Tierney marries Cornel Wilde simply because he looks like her dead dad. She soon turns into a jealous and possessive Janus, who won't let anyone come between her and her father figure. Agilely directed and limned in a hyper-real palette, the result is a slick piece of solemn kitsch.

Richard Stanley

South Africa, 1966–

Richard Stanley is arguably better known for the *Sturm und Drang* surrounding his movies than he is for the films themselves. And yet it all started

so well. An acclaimed director of music videos, his low-budget debut, *Hardware* (1990), rapidly became a cult hit. Things started to go wrong after his next picture, *Dust Devil* (1992), had wrapped. A gory and visionary fable about a mystical serial killer in the Namibian desert, it was stuck in post-production limbo after Palace Pictures suddenly went bust. An American print finally surfaced in a version that seriously displeased its maker, and Stanley eventually dipped into his own pockets to release a director's cut.

But that was nothing compared to the difficulties he encountered on his next project. What happened during the making of his H.G. Wells adaptation, *The Island Of Dr Moreau* (1996), has since passed into movie folklore. After widely reported problems with the star Val Kilmer, Stanley was sacked from the project after only four days of shooting and replaced by the veteran John Frankenheimer. Undeterred, Stanley infiltrated the set dressed in a monster costume and stayed in character for the whole shoot, right under the noses of unsuspecting producers. And that's how he ended up as an extra on a movie that he was slated to write and direct. After this bruising experience, Stanley concentrated on documentaries. LH

Hardware 1990, 93 min

cast Dylan McDermott, Stacey Travis, John Lynch, William Hootkins, Iggy Pop *cin* Steven Chivers *m* Simon Boswell

In a riot-torn, dystopian future, a scavenger buys his artist girlfriend the head of an android for one of her sculptures, without realizing that it's been programmed to kill. The piece of military hardware hastily assembles itself a new body and turns her apartment into a bloodbath. An inimitable and delirious synthesis of MTV, Tarkovsky and *The Terminator* (1984), Stanley expertly glosses over the lack of budget and story with a pulsating narrative drive that consists of hard cuts and extreme violence.

Ladislaw Starewicz

Lithuania (formerly Russian Empire), 1882–1965

Ladislaw Starewicz had a charming – if disconcerting – boyhood fascination with magic lanterns and insects. As he grew up, this obsession became the starting point for an extraordinary career in the cinema. In 1910, he attempted to film a stag beetle fight. When one of the beetles died during production, he revived the corpse through stop-motion animation. Starewicz became an animation innovator, his feature breakthrough *The Tale Of The Fox* (1930) predating Disney's *Snow White And The Seven Dwarfs* by seven years. His output was prodigious and his intricately designed films all come wrapped in a beguiling, eerie spirit.

Born in Vilnius in Poland, Starewicz later moved to Moscow, where he made films including *The Beautiful*

Leukanida (1912) and *The Dragonfly And The Ant* (1913). After the Russian Revolution, he emigrated to France, settling in Fontenay-sous-Bois. There, he wrote his screenplays, designed and built puppets and sets, and animated his models. He generally worked single-handed, though his daughter Irène eventually collaborated with him. He worked typically in the short film format and most of his works were made for children. His French films include *Frogland* (1923), *Nose To The Wind* (1956) and *Winter Carousel* (1958). One of his best-known creations is *The Mascot* (1934), which had some success in America. But when courted by animation studios there, the quirky visionary declined in favour of maintaining total artistic control. He has influenced Henry Selick, the Brothers Quay and Jan Svankmajer. JC

The Tale Of The Fox (Le roman de Renard)
1930, 65 min, b/w
cast (voices) Claude Dauphin, Romain Bouquet, Sylvain Itkine *cin* Ladislaw Starewicz *m* Vincent Scotto

A stunningly detailed version of the folk tale in which the titular fox runs rings round the king, who wants him imprisoned for his cunning ways. It spent ten years in pre-production and took eighteen months to shoot, and the animation is remarkable even by today's CGI-assisted standards.

Michael Steinberg
US, 1959–

In his best work Michael Steinberg reproduces something of the sexual mania and psychological acuity of Woody Allen and Hal Ashby. The child of movie aficionados, he was raised on 1960s and 70s American cinema. While working his way through college playing poker, he attended a film class, was impressed by F.W. Murnau and Erich von Stroheim screenings and began dabbling in Super 8 filmmaking. His studio passport was *Nightwatch*, shot on 16mm at the UCLA Film School, the alma mater of his hero Francis Ford Coppola.

Steinberg's feature debut was *The Waterdance* (1991), which he co-directed with Neal Jimenez. Based on Jimenez's experience as a paraplegic, this telling, if sentimental, piece explored the issue of disability with sensitivity and insight, won the audience award at the Sundance Film Festival and found its way into the *New York Times* Top 1000 US films list. Also well regarded was Steinberg's study of listless modern youth, 1993's *Bodies, Rest & Motion*. A sensational conceit, *Wicked* (1998) starred Julia Stiles as a teenager who takes her dead mother's place and seduces her father. Steinberg also produced Rory Kelly's ensemble comedy *Sleep With Me* (1994) and co-produced *There's Something About Mary* (1998) for the Farrelly brothers. His feeling for the moods of the intelligent young awaits the right vehicle. RA

Bodies, Rest & Motion 1993, 94 min
cast Bridget Fonda, Eric Stoltz, Tim Roth, Phoebe Cates, Alicia Witt, Scott Johnson *cin* Bernd Heinl *m* Michael Convertino

Perhaps a metaphor for actors on the way up, this portrait of people living on the social outskirts of an Arizona town featured telling turns from its cast of indie hopefuls. Steinberg invests the energy of his film with a coolly observed slacker dynamic.

Josef von Sternberg
Austria (formerly Austro-Hungarian Empire), 1894–1969

No one in this history of cinema has been photographed with such passionate intensity as Marlene Dietrich was by Josef von Sternberg. She was more than an inamorata, she was his creation. "I am Marlene", he once famously declared. He then spent the rest of his career trying to prove that he was his own man.

Moving from Vienna to the US as a child, von Sternberg worked in the New York film industry as an editor, then made training films for the army during World War I. He gravitated to Hollywood afterwards, and his first film was the grim social document *The Salvation Hunters* (1925). It came to the attention of Charlie Chaplin who released it through United Artists. In a series of movies – the best examples of which are *The Last Command* (1928), *The Docks Of New York* (1928) and *Thunderbolt* (1929) – he then showcased his opulent brand of cinema: women with ice in their veins, bizarre love triangles, striking compositions sublimely achieved through a deft play of light and shadow, and a vivid sense of place constructed with a fastidious eye for detail and clutter. His masterpiece of the silent period, *Underworld* (1927), is for many historians a cinematic landmark: the first modern gangster film.

In 1929, von Sternberg travelled to Germany to make a film at the request of actor Emil Jannings. At a theatre production, he was intoxicated by the lead actress, Marlene Dietrich, and cast her in the film. And although he would later claim that she was a complete unknown when he discovered her, in truth she had already appeared in a number of silents. *The Blue Angel* (1930) was a phenomenal hit in Germany and a moderate success in its English-language version.

Once in America, nothing in the von Sternberg frame was as luminous as Dietrich's immaculately arranged visage; the light seemed to come from within her. She remained a fantasy figure throughout their seven-film collaboration and Dietrich perfectly embodied Sternberg's love of paradox. She could be both mannish and all woman; she was infinitely superior to the men around her, whether

S

it was in *Morocco* (1930) as a curiously androgynous cabaret singer, or in *Dishonoured* (1931) as the glamorous Mata Hari-like spy who coolly adjusts her make-up in front of the firing squad. In *Shanghai Express* (1932), their most commercially successful pairing, Dietrich sacrificed her dignity on the altar of masochistic desire; she played the martyr again in *Blonde Venus* (1932), the weakest of their collaborations, as a devoted mother who only consorts with Cary Grant to pay for her sick husband's medical expenses.

The Scarlet Empress (1934), a baroque, visually opulent tale of Catherine the Great, remains the masterpiece of their partnership. However, it is 1935's *The Devil Is A Woman* – centred on a middle-aged army captain (who possesses an uncanny resemblance to von Sternberg) and his masochistic obsession with Dietrich's Spanish coquette – that is now held up as a mirror for the director and star's torrid, doomed relationship. This and the short *The Fashion Side Of Hollywood* (1935) were disappointments, and Dietrich was labelled box-office poison.

After the end of their partnership, von Sternbeg toiled with a flawed but fascinating adaptation of *Crime And Punishment* (1935) and the tepid comedy *The King Steps Out* (1936), finally coming a cropper on *I, Claudius* (1937), a fabled fragment in cinema history with Charles Laughton all set to give the performance of his career until the project folded after star Merle Oberon was involved in an automobile accident. With *The Shanghai Gesture* (1941), von Sternberg tried too hard to make a masterpiece that would prove he was more than the man who "discovered" Dietrich. The director wound up making two mediocre films for Howard Hughes, *Macao* (1952) and *Jet Pilot* (1957), both of which were humiliatingly re-edited. Von Sternberg had to plough his own money into *The Saga Of Anathan* (1953) about a group of Japanese survivors marooned on an island, refusing to believe that World War II is over. While it will never eclipse the seven films he made with Dietrich, this deeply carnal and deliriously abstract melodrama brought critical acclaim near the end of his career. LH

Underworld 1927, 80 min, b/w

cast George Bancroft, Evelyn brent, Clive Brook, Larry Semon, Fred Kohler Helen Lynch *cin* Bert Glennon

Bank robber Bull Weed (George Bancroft) aids a down-and-out lawyer (Clive Brook), who in return becomes his right-hand man but then falls for his boss's girlfriend Feathers (Evelyn Brent). A violent showdown occurs when the volatile gangster discovers the truth. Scripted by ex-crime reporter Ben Hecht, this is an influential milestone in the gangster genre, generating great mileage out of what would become perennial themes of *film noir*: conflicts of love and loyalty.

The Blue Angel (Der blaue Engel) 1930, 106 min, b/w

cast Emil Jannings, Marlene Dietrich, Kurt Gerron, Rosa Valetti, Hans Albers *cin* Günther Rittau, Hans Schneeberger *m* Friedrich Hollaender

Dietrich's role in this masterpiece is so archetypal – stockings, suspenders, top hat and decadent sexuality – that it's a shock to see the film and not the legend. The star is podgy and is rarely afforded a close-up, but she has rather eclipsed the film itself, which is a shame, as this is really Emil Jannings' movie. As the pompous and lonely college professor who gives up his day job to be Dietrich's clown, a support act in her life and her work, his performance aches with poignancy.

The Scarlet Empress 1934, 104 min, b/w

cast Marlene Dietrich, John Lodge, Sam Jaffe, Louise Dresser, C. Aubrey Smith, Gavin Gordon, Olive Tell, Ruthelma Stevens *cin* Bert Glennon

Based on Catherine the Great's diaries and with inter-titles giving the impression of historical authenticity, this regal drama actually takes place in a fairy-tale world, complete with gargoyles for furniture. Hans Dreier's sets are glorious. Close-ups of Marlene Dietrich's face radiating beneath a veil are genuinely breathtaking in their rapturous intensity, though she has little to do as the German girl called up by the empress of Russia to marry her peculiar son and produce an heir. The sketchy narrative skirts gracefully around the edges of kitsch in a heightened state of near delirium that now seems decades ahead of its time.

George Stevens
US, 1904–75

Best known as a "prestige" filmmaker from Hollywood's post-war period, George Stevens had already made his mark as one of the top screwball directors of the 1930s. However, his experiences documenting the war in Europe – his 16mm colour footage of the liberation of the Dachau concentration camp was presented as evidence at the Nuremberg war trials – marked something of a shift in his career.

Born into an acting family, Stevens became a cameraman at the age of 17, and was soon shooting Laurel and Hardy shorts (and contributing gags) at the Hal Roach Studios. Having moved to RKO in the early 1930s, Stevens was hand-picked by one of the studio's biggest stars, Katharine Hepburn, to direct her as Booth Tarkington's eponymous social climber in *Alice Adams* (1935). The following year, he was entrusted with Fred Astaire and Ginger Rogers' *Swing Time*, their fifth – and arguably their best – film together. *Vivacious Lady* (1938), *Woman Of The Year* (1942), *The Talk Of The Town* (1942) and *The More The Merrier* (1943) consolidated his reputation as an adept comedy craftsman. He even got away with the vastly over-budget adventure yarn *Gunga Din* (1939), though the years have not been kind to its colonialist politics.

After the war, Stevens formed Liberty Films with fellow directors Frank Capra and William Wyler. Although the company soon foundered, it signalled

S

his desire for greater autonomy. He largely realized that ambition, becoming one of the most proactive presidents of the Directors Guild of America on questions of artistic rights – for example, in 1965 he waged a million-dollar lawsuit against America's leading television networks for the manner in which they broadcast films.

Never very prolific, Stevens made only eight features between 1945 and his death in 1975, half of these in the first ten-year span. His process was slow and methodical, involving himself in every aspect of preproduction, then shooting each scene from dozens of different setups, "finding" the film in the editing. (He took a year to edit his 1953 Western, *Shane*.) If this was labour-intensive, Stevens' productions boasted a technical sophistication that was ahead of their time. The use of layered sound effects in *Shane*, the close-ups and lap dissolves in *A Place In The Sun* (1951), and the epic framing of *Giant* (1956) all testify to his consummate technique. The stars' performances in *A Place In The Sun* and *Giant* (which both earned Stevens best director Oscars) also demonstrated the director's willingness to fold Method acting into the mainstream.

Stevens' classical humanism – exemplified by *The Diary Of Anne Frank* (1959) – and his mainstream success did not commend him among auteurists, although a recurring preoccupation with the outsider has been discerned in *Alice Adams*, *Shane*, *A Place In The Sun* (Montgomery Clift as George Eastman) and *Giant* (James Dean as Jett Rink). It is true, however, that Stevens' later work was often lugubrious and heavy-handed, its sobriety not really matched by insight or revelation. His elephantine 225-minute, all-star biblical movie *The Greatest Story Ever Told* (1965), about the life of Jesus Christ, was a miscalculation of epic proportions that he spent five years making and another five years recovering from. TC

Swing Time 1936, 103 min, b/w
cast Fred Astaire, Ginger Rogers, Victor Moore, Helen Broderick, Eric Blore, Betty Furness, George Metaxa *cin* David Ames *m* Jerome Kern

A quintessential Fred Astaire and Ginger Rogers musical. It takes a while to find its feet, but once Jerome Kern and Dorothy Fields' songs kick in there's no looking back. Highlights include "Pick Yourself Up", "The Way You Look Tonight", "A Fine Romance", the blackface "Bojangles In Harlem" number (with four Freds), and the climactic "Never Gonna Dance". The plot… is immaterial.

The More The Merrier 1943, 104 min, b/w
cast Jean Arthur, Joel McCrea, Charles Coburn, Richard Gaines, Bruce Bennett, Frank Sully, Clyde Fillmore *cin* Ted Tetzlaff *m* Leigh Harline

Stevens' screwball comedies didn't have the satiric edge of the very best of them, but he was a shrewd visual storyteller, and invested this romantic comedy with a palpable sweetness. Inspired by wartime accommodation shortages in Washington DC, the movie finds Jean Arthur sharing an apartment with both Joel McCrea and Charles Coburn, with the older Coburn playing the role of mischievous matchmaker. All three performances are cherishable.

A Place In The Sun 1951, 122 min, b/w
cast Montgomery Clift, Elizabeth Taylor, Shelley Winters, Anne Revere, Raymond Burr, Herbert Hayes *cin* William Mellor *m* Franz Waxman

Determined to make something of himself, George (Clift) takes a job in his uncle's firm. But before he can break into the family's charmed inner circle and fall in love with socialite Angela (Taylor) he becomes embroiled with a factory girl (Winters). Pregnant, she threatens to ruin everything… The film wallows rather in its romantic despair (courtesy of Theodore Dreiser's source novel, *An American Tragedy*), but its architecture is impressive: subtle sound design; overlapping dissolves to juxtapose different class strata; rhapsodic close-ups of a 17-year-old Taylor.

Shane 1953, 118 min
cast Alan Ladd, Van Heflin, Jean Arthur, Brandon de Wilde, Jack Palance, Elisha Cook Jr, Ben Johnson *cin* Loyal Griggs *m* Victor Young

One of the most famous and iconic Westerns, *Shane* takes staple genre elements like gun lore and the conflict between small farmers and cattle barons, and treats them with some seriousness. Stevens found an affecting viewpoint for the story in the eyes of young Brandon de Wilde, the boy who idolizes righteous gunslinger Shane (Alan Ladd) without fully comprehending the impact this handsome stranger has on his mother and father (Arthur and Heflin). It's a self-conscious classic, but still resonates with all the hope and yearning of that unforgettable ending.

Robert Stevenson
UK, 1905–86

Having started his long filmmaking career in the silent era, Robert Stevenson became one of the last in-house studio directors with his long tenure at the Walt Disney Studios from 1957 until 1976.

A science student at Cambridge, Stevenson became fascinated by movies when researching audience psychology for his graduate thesis. He began writing screenplays, and turned director in 1934. *King Solomon's Mines* (1937) put him on Hollywood's radar, and he moved there permanently two years later, directing *Tom Brown's School Days* (1940) and the melodrama *Back Street* (1941) with Charles Boyer and Margaret Sullavan. In the 1940s, he embarked on more adult fare, and had the honour of directing Orson Welles as a creditable Mr Rochester in *Jane Eyre* (1944). There were continuing hints of darkness in the *noir*-ish *Walk Softly, Stranger* (1950) and the notorious red-scare melodrama *I Married A Communist* (1949), which boasted fine cinematography courtesy of Nicholas Musuraca.

In the 1950s, Stevenson directed up to a hundred TV episodes of such shows as *Gunsmoke*, *Alfred Hitchcock Presents* and *General Electric Theatre*. He was a modest, self-effacing director, a safe pair of hands who put the audience first and who became very proficient at hybrid productions incorporating live-action and animated effects. (Stanley Kubrick is said to have studied *Mary Poppins*, 1964, while preparing *2001: A Space Odyssey* in 1968.) In 1957,

S

Disney brought Stevenson in to direct the live-action family adventure *Johnny Tremain*. He went on to helm almost all of the studio's live-action, family-friendly hits over the next two decades, including *Old Yeller* (1957), *The Absent-Minded Professor* (1961), the Oscar-nominated *Mary Poppins*, *That Darn Cat* (1965), *The Love Bug* (1968), *Bedknobs And Broomsticks* (1971), *One Of Our Dinosaurs Is Missing* (1976) and his last feature, *The Shaggy DA* (1976). In 1977, *Variety* declared Stevenson "the most commercially successful director in the history of movies", but by that time his brand of decorous, anodyne slapstick was already past its heyday. TC

Mary Poppins 1964, 139 min

cast Julie Andrews, Dick Van Dyke, David Tomlinson, Glynis Johns, Hermione Baddeley *cin* Edward Colman *m* Richard M. Sherman, Robert B. Sherman

A dark story of a dysfunctional family, its lovable, lonely moppets neglected by their preoccupied father and suffragette mother, *Mary Poppins* is nowhere near as sugary as its detractors claim. This particular dream world – where chalk pavement pictures come to life, carousel horses run free and anarchic chimney sweeps rampage through the parlour – is a place where the shadowy side of childhood is laid bare rather than denied. The movie's sheer barnstorming energy secured it thirteen Oscar nominations and five wins, including best actress for lead Julie Andrews.

Ben Stiller

US, 1965–

The son of comedy double act Jerry Stiller and Anne Meara, Ben Stiller made his film acting debut in Steven Spielberg's *Empire Of The Sun* (1987). As an actor, he has carved a niche for himself as a comedy neurotic, peddling a nervy brand of hapless angst. His filmmaking career began in the 1990s with serious intentions, but Stiller has recently bowed to the inevitable and bridged the gap between his comic and directorial personas. For his directorial debut, 1994's *Reality Bites* (in which he also co-starred), Stiller added Hollywood gloss to the kind of slacker talking picture pioneered by Richard Linklater. The dark comedy *The Cable Guy* (1996) made headlines when star Jim Carrey's $20 million fee became public knowledge. Notably lacking in levity, easy laughs and obvious box-office appeal, it was a huge flop and an industry embarrassment. Stiller evidently learnt his lesson, and fully embraced his inner idiot in his third directorial effort, *Zoolander* (2001). LH

Zoolander 2001, 90 min

cast Ben Stiller, Owen Wilson, Christine Taylor, Will Ferrell, Milla Jovovich *cin* Barry Peterson *m* David Arnold

Stiller and frequent collaborator Owen Wilson star as rival male models, New Age Hansel and has-been Derek Zoolander. The latter is brainwashed into killing the prime minister of Malaysia who objects to the clothes industry's use of sweatshops and child labour.

Whit Stillman

US, 1952–

With just three films to his credit in sixteen years – the most recent one in 1998 – John Whitney Stillman seems likely to remain a fringe figure, though his admirers would probably define themselves as a clique, not a cult.

To date, all of his films have been urbane and sophisticated ensemble comedies set amid the privileged preppie class to which he belongs: the son of a debutante and a Democrat politician, Stillman is a Harvard graduate (school of '73).

In his first film, *Metropolitan* (1990), Stillman memorably describes this class as the doomed "upper *haute bourgeoisie* – or UHB". Although the portrait involves self-mockery, it's not so much satire as comedy of manners; in the tradition of his literary heroes, Jane Austen and Samuel Johnson, Stillman is a conservative at heart, proposing old-fashioned chivalry, friendship and good conversation as the true attributes of a civilized society.

Although it was independently financed on a meagre budget, *Metropolitan* has more in common with the elegant drawing-room comedies of the 1930s than the other credit-card movies being made in the late 1980s. The difference wasn't just Stillman's patrician upbringing, but also his age: he was in his late thirties at the time, looking back on the deb party scene he had tasted nearly two decades before.

Barcelona (1994), another "end of an era" movie, this time set during the dying days of the Cold War, drew on his experiences as an American in Spain when he worked as a sales agent for artists and filmmakers. *The Last Days Of Disco* (1998) returned to New York and functioned as an informal follow-up to *Metropolitan*, this time focusing on Chloë Sevigny and Kate Beckinsale as two disaffected rich girls contemplating their navels in 1980s Manhattan. TC

Metropolitan US, 1990, 98 min

cast Edward Clements, Carolyn Farina, Chris Eigeman, Taylor Nichols, Allison Parisi, Dylan Hundley *cin* John Thomas *m* Tom Judson and Mark Suozzo

Stillman's first film is still his most satisfying. Tom (Clements) is an impoverished socialist with an Ivy League education. Against his principles, he finds himself at a debutante ball, and is befriended by a group of attractive, witty preppies who insist he join them for more of the same. Although some of the performances feel green (and Stillman's arch, erudite dialogue can be unforgiving), the nuanced, charming *Metropolitan* conjures a distinct social set and allows us to see beyond its callow surface.

S

Oliver Stone
US, 1946–

Oliver Stone's flashy epics of American affairs have generated controversy across the media. Stone developed a taste for history early in life and in 1965 dropped out of Yale to enlist for the Vietnam War. That year "in country" (1967–68) determined his outlook and his often bitter reflections on the United States. While studying film at New York University (where Martin Scorsese was a teacher), Stone made the short *Last Year In Vietnam* (1971). Grind-house exploitation fare followed – *Seizure* (1974) and *The Hand* (1981).

By the mid 1980s, Stone's screenplays – *Midnight Express* (1978), *Scarface* (1983), *Year Of The Dragon* (1985) – were exploring genre violence and masculine conflict, establishing Stone as a Hollywood player in the process. *Platoon* (1986) reaped commercial success and the best director Oscar for its down-and-dirty account of a grunt's Vietnam tour. Stone continued to examine unresolved national traumas in 1986's *Salvador*, an excoriating indictment of the Reagan administration's role in El Salvador.

Wall Street (1987) consolidated the director's position as a media commentator on the national temper; with Gordon Gecko's mantras "Lunch is for wimps" and "Greed is good" becoming the shorthand of a decade. After these high-profile spectacles, *Talk Radio* (1988) was a modest attempt to study the conflicting voices of the airwaves. Eric Bogosian's provocative radio host reconciled perennial Stone concerns with a discourse on the status quo. It proved a welcome antidote to the previous year's wacky and saccharine *Good Morning, Vietnam*. *Born On The Fourth Of July* (1989) viewed Vietnam through the perspective of an embittered paraplegic veteran. It provided Tom Cruise with an Oscar-nominated role and won Stone another best director Academy Award.

Although critically drubbed, *The Doors* (1991) was powered by a searching performance by Val Kilmer as 1960s icon Jim Morrison. Stone, however, has rarely afforded interesting roles for women, and here Meg Ryan looked singularly out of place playing Pamela Courson. With its conspiracy theory mindset, *JFK* (1991) raised a storm among critics and historians. It was an absorbing potpourri of documentary footage and Hollywood reconstruction, centred on Kevin Costner's earnest portrayal of New Orleans DA Jim Garrison's attempt to revise the Warren Commission's findings following the 1963 Kennedy assassination. As with *Nixon* in 1995, this tautly cut and dazzlingly postmodern history lesson seemed to many observers to be inaccurate, self-indulgent and paranoid. But as Stone himself observed, his epic takes are no more engineered than the interpretations proffered by historians themselves.

Following his ponderous attempt to see the Vietnam War through Vietnamese eyes in *Heaven And Earth* (1993), *Natural Born Killers* (1994) found Stone revelling in the seductions of post-MTV image manipulation and a swamp of ethical relativity. Quentin Tarantino disowned his screenplay, and the film came across as the nth degree of 1990s "New Violence". With Woody Harrelson and Juliette Lewis starring as a modern-day Bonnie and Clyde, it was difficult to discern where the exploitation ended and the critique began. Decline followed. Starring Sean Penn, the revisionist *film noir U Turn* (1997) was a disappointment. The Al Pacino-Cameron Diaz vehicle *Any Given Sunday* (1999) had more visual rhetoric than its commonplace tale of American football ethics could justify. However, *Comandante* (2003) was an interesting, characteristically visual documentary about Fidel Castro.

The sword-and-sandal epic *Alexander* (2004) begged questions about Stone's repeated criticisms of nationalism in an era of American adventures in the Middle East. *World Trade Center* (2006) contained little examination of the tensions that contributed to 9/11. Instead, we got a tense, sweaty Nicolas Cage flick about the last two survivors dug out from Ground Zero, prompting the unusual spectacle of right-wing commentators actually praising the liberal iconoclast. RA

Salvador 1985, 122 min
cast James Woods, James Belushi, Michael Murphy, John Savage, Elphidia Carrillo *cin* Robert Richardson *m* Georges Delevue

When Richard Boyle (James Woods), an American journalist in search of kicks, drives with a buddy south of the border to El Salvador, he is unprepared for the horror that awaits him. A powerful indictment of US policy in Latin America and a searching, sensitively acted portrait of a man rediscovering responsibility.

Platoon 1986, 120 min
cast Tom Berenger, Willem Dafoe, Charlie Sheen, Forest Whitaker, Francesco Quinn, John C. McGinley *cin* Robert Richardson *m* Georges Delerue

Oliver Stone's bitterly relentless depiction of a new recruit's experiences on the pitiless battlefields of Vietnam was a critical and commercial hit. Stone's personal experiences and insights coloured his movie and its "war is hell" ethos contributed to a wave of Hollywood heart-searching over America's Southeast Asian experience.

Wall Street 1987, 126 min
cast Michael Douglas, Charlie Sheen, Daryl Hannah, Martin Sheen, Terence Stamp, Hal Holbrook *cin* Robert Richardson *m* Stewart Copeland

Oliver Stone puts a novel spin on the cliché of the boy spoilt by money in this story of callow bond trader Bud Fox (Charlie Sheen) seduced by Michael Douglas's corporate shark. There is a piquancy to the casting of Martin Sheen as Bud's union rep father. Stone fills the film's swirling spaces with all the tackiness and gloss of a generation with too much money and too little taste. The result is one of the key films of the era.

S

Nixon 1995, 192 min

cast Anthony Hopkins, Joan Allen, Powers Boothe, Ed Harris, Bob Hoskins, E.G. Marshall, David Paymer *cin* Robert Richardson *m* John Williams

Revolving around Anthony Hopkins's towering performance as President Richard M. Nixon, this is a modern epic that ranks alongside *The Godfather* (1972). A fluent collage of *vérité* and reconstruction dramatizes the political and psychological tensions that wrought the politician. From his booze and aspirin refuge as the Watergate scandal looms, Nixon reflects on his career, while Joan Allen gives director Oliver Stone his most well-rounded female character, playing the long-suffering Pat Nixon.

Straub & Huillet

Jean-Marie Straub: France, 1933–
Danièle Huillet: France, 1936–2006

The collaborative team of Jean-Marie Straub and Danièle Huillet (they married in 1959) made films that are among the most austere and politically radical in the history of cinema. This means that their work is virtually unknown outside the festival circuit, the one exception being *The Chronicle Of Anna Magdalena Bach* (1968) an account of the last thirty or so years of the working life of great German composer J.S. Bach. The film makes no attempt to dramatize, and presents Bach's music within its original performance context.

Straub and Huillet first met at the Lycée Voltaire in Paris in 1954. By the 1960s, the pair were living in Germany so that Straub could avoid national service in France. Their first two films, the short *Machorka-Muff* (1963) and the full-length *Nicht versöhnt oder Es hilft nur Gewalt wo Gewalt herrscht* (*Not Reconciled*, 1965), were attacks on Germany's militarism and its inability to confront its Nazi past, both derived from texts by Heinrich Böll. The minimal anti-style immediately apparent in these two films – the flatly delivered performances, restrained camerawork and unpredictable edits – would remain consistent throughout their joint career.

Straub and Huillet's uncompromising approach was conceived in opposition to conventional filmmaking. Traditional forms of cinematic expression were seen by them – as by Jean-Luc Godard post-1968 – as serving the dominant ideology. The idea of manipulating the viewer into some form of emotional identification with the subject was an anathema. Instead, they offered a more Brechtian, alienating style which demanded that viewers engage with what was seen to create their own meaning. The couple's aim was to make their audience think rather than emote.

In their occasional films based on classic texts, such as Corneille's play *Othon* (1970), what is heard and what is seen often have only a tangential relationship to each other. This refusal to pander to the "needs" of the viewer means that on the rare occasions that their films are screened they are frequently met with incomprehension and sometimes hostility. Their aim, to arrive at some kind of documentary truth, had a purity and an integrity of purpose, but more often than not left audiences befuddled and confused. RB

The Chronicle Of Anna Magdalena Bach
1968, 93 min, b/w

cast Gustav Leonhardt, Christiane Lang, Paolo Carlini, Ernst Castelli *cin* Ugo Piccone, Saverio Daimanti, Giovanni Canfarelli *m* J.S. Bach

On the one hand a celebration of Bach's music and on the other a meditation on the impossibility of "recreating" history, *Chronicle* stands at the opposite end of the spectrum from such composer biopics as Milos Forman's *Amadeus* (1984). Despite the attempts at authenticity in both costumes and musical performance, the artifice of filmmaking is always made apparent – from the uninflected voice-over of Anna Magdalena (Bach's wife) to the use of back-projection. The result, starkly simple and lacking any narrative thread, is both insightful and surprisingly moving.

Erich von Stroheim

Austria (formerly Austro-Hungarian Empire), 1885–1957

It's an appropriate irony that Erich von Stroheim is best known in the public imagination for his role as Gloria Swanson's faithful, slightly sinister Teutonic butler in *Sunset Blvd* (1950). Appropriate because the director was acting all of his adult life, both on and off screen, until the two became a delirious blur. As many historians have noted, the director's greatest work of fiction was the character of Erich von Stroheim.

Born simply Erich Stroheim, he inserted the "von" when he landed in America in the late 1900s to suggest an aristocratic background. Rather than being the son of an Austrian officer, as he claimed, he was actually the son of an Austrian milliner who specialized in straw hats. That fantasy continued in front of the camera, where he played a series of dastardly noblemen, notably for D.W. Griffith. Von Stroheim's forte was the horrible Hun with a monocle, a scar and a bad attitude. A seducer of women and destroyer of reputations, his arrogance was deeply etched into his "aristocratic" countenance, fashioning himself as "the man you love to hate". Appropriately, he played an Austrian civil guardsman in own directorial debut *Blind Husbands* (1919), seducing the wife of a rich American. The complete auteur, von Stroheim wrote, acted, directed and designed the costumes and the sets in many of his subsequent movies. Each, with the notable exception of *Greed* (1924), possessed an inimitable confluence of opulence, cynicism, squalor, aristocracy, and sexual fetishism in a Ruritanian country. But above all, they demonstrated an unblinking commitment to realism.

S

Von Stroheim's dedication to verisimilitude resulted in a suffocating welter of period detail and a radical naturalism, the consequences of which were expense and length, both of which got him into trouble with studios. Of his subsequent movies, only one was released in the form that von Stroheim had originally conceived. *Foolish Wives* (1922), in which the director practically rebuilt Monte Carlo on the backlot, was cut by Universal by a third. He was fired by Universal's boy wonder producer Irving G. Thalberg from *Merry-Go-Round* (1923) and decamped to the Goldwyn Company to make *Greed*, only for his nemesis to follow him to the newly minted Metro-Goldwyn-Mayer. Estimates for the initial version ran between seven to ten hours, and when Thalberg asked for a trim, von Stroheim brought it in at a mere four hours. Unimpressed, Thalberg took the film from the director and ensured it was edited down to a manageable 140 minutes. *The Merry Widow* (1925) was the only von Stroheim work since his debut to be brought in on schedule and budget. *The Wedding March* (1928) was another opulent prince-and-pauper romance that was heavily slashed.

Joseph Kennedy (father of the future president John F. Kennedy) bankrolled *Queen Kelly* (1931) for his lover Gloria Swanson, and the production went spectacularly over the agreed financial and time limits. Von Stroheim was fired by Swanson and the film wasn't fully completed at that time, although extracts found their way into *Sunset Blvd* (1950) and a reconstructed version was finally released in 1985. The director completed only one more film, *Walking Down Broadway*, which was his only talkie, but he was given his cards from that, too. It was released as *Hello Sister* (1933) a year later. LH

Greed 1924, 140 min, b/w
cast ZaSu Pitts, Jean Hersholt, Gibson Gowland, Dale Fuller, Tempe Pigott, Silvia Ashton, Chester Conklin *cin* Ben Reynolds, William H. Daniels

Based on Frank Norris's novel *McTeague*, the relationship between three friends dramatically fissures when one of them wins the lottery, which leads to an astonishingly realized and supremely ironic climax in Death Valley. The delicious irony of Erich von Stroheim's pedantic obsession with radical verisimilitude is that the events actually appear to take place inside the febrile imagination of a controlling intelligence. Universally acclaimed as a masterpiece now, it was at the time derided as the "filthiest, vilest, most putrid picture in the history of the motion picture business".

The Merry Widow 1925, 113 min, b/w
cast Mae Murray, John Gilbert, Roy D'Arcy, Josephine Crowell, George Fawcett *cin* Oliver Marsh, William H. Daniels, Ben Reynolds, Ray Rennahan

In von Stroheim's most commercially successful film, the director was consistently unfaithful to Franz Léhar's operetta, emphasizing his own obsessions with sexual dysfunction, sadism and naturalism. In a typical von Stroheim fantasy land called Monteblanco, two princes vie for the affections of a showgirl. She becomes the merry widow of the title after a licentious baron (and foot fetishist) keels over on their wedding night. This is a baroque, uneven and bawdy romp.

Queen Kelly 1931, 101 min, b/w
cast Gloria Swanson, Walter Byron, Seena Owen, William von Brincken, Madge Hunt *cin* Gordon Pollock, Paul Ivano, Ben Reynolds, Gregg Toland

Prince Walter Byron falls in love with sweet convent girl Gloria Swanson, but is betrothed to be married to mad queen Seena Owen. Byzantine action ensues, and the film originally ended with an attempted suicide. This epic of fairy tale and fetishism was only shown in Europe at the time; its first showing in America was after the release of *Sunset Blvd*, which featured some footage from this film.

John Sturges
US, 1910–92

"I've been lucky", John Sturges once remarked about his public perception, "they always remember the good ones and forget the bad ones." This is certainly true of a director whose name will forever be associated with action movies of the highest stripe, including *Bad Day At Black Rock* (1955), *Gunfight At The OK Corral* (1957), *The Magnificent Seven* (1960) and *The Great Escape* (1963). And yet these are only four movies from a CV that includes another forty.

Starting out in RKO's blueprint and editing department, Sturges made numerous documentaries during the war and returned to Hollywood as a director on crime thriller *The Man Who Dared* (1946). In a career that spanned three decades, he worked in a number of genres, even turning his attention to romantic drama (*By Love Possessed*, 1961), heavyweight literary adaptations (*The Old Man And The Sea*, 1958) and a superior chunk of sci-fi (*Marooned*, 1969). Most are best forgotten, and thankfully have been. But it is the action movies that exude a memorable deft efficiency, notably *Never So Few* (1959), *Joe Kidd* (1972) and *The Eagle Has Landed* (1976).

At his best, he orchestrated his gung-ho action movies like delicate symphonies, expertly counterpointing loud bangs with quiet anticipation, set pieces with slow burn. There was an eloquent simplicity to his narrative thrust, which usually centred on a moral code of man's-gotta-do chivalry, where the reluctantly righteous often dispensed a brand of gruff justice. With CinemaScope, Sturges was a master of his domain, demonstrating a rugged compositional elegance and an unerring ability to frame his brawny, stoic characters in a finely calibrated choreography of macho assertion. LH

S

Bad Day At Black Rock 1955, 81 min

cast Spencer Tracy, Robert Ryan, Anne Francis, Dean Jagger, Lee Marvin, Ernest Borgnine *cin* William C. Mellor *m* André Previn

In the first American film to deal with the controversial subject of the mistreatment of Japanese-Americans during World War II, one-armed veteran Spencer Tracy arrives at an isolated community to give a Japanese-American farmer the medal of honour that his late son won in the conflict, only to discover he's disappeared in mysterious circumstances.

The Magnificent Seven 1960, 138 min

cast Yul Brynner, Eli Wallach, Steve McQueen, Charles Bronson, Robert Vaughn, Brad Dexter, James Coburn *cin* Charles Lang *m* Elmer Bernstein

Mexican farmers hire a team of gunslingers to protect them from slimy Eli Wallach and his desperadoes. In this remake of Akira Kurosawa's *Seven Samurai* (1954), Sturges masterfully builds the tension through the steady accumulation of significant details and character traits, and engineers the sort of long fuse action movie that simply doesn't exist any more. The climactic shoot-out is impossibly poignant.

The Great Escape 1963, 173 min

cast Steve McQueen, James Garner, Richard Attenborough, James Donald, Charles Bronson, James Coburn *cin* Daniel L. Fapp *m* Elmer Bernstein

This had been a pet project of the director since the publication in 1950 of Paul Brickhill's nonfiction book that detailed the outlandish escape of 76 prisoners of war from Stalag Luft Nord. It is testament to Sturges's immaculate craftsmanship that this near-three-hour film still ratchets up the tension no matter how many times it is seen, leaving the audience to hope against hope that Steve McQueen's motorbike will miraculously make it over the barbed wire.

Preston Sturges
US, 1898–1959

Though he wasn't the first writer who moved, within the confines of the studio system, into directing, Preston Sturges was certainly one of the most successful. Starting in 1940, he made seven smash hits in four years, inspired screwball comedies which rank among the funniest films ever made. Then he switched studios, lost his touch and ran out of luck. Sturges was a child of the studio system, but in treating it as his playground he invited his own expulsion; the system couldn't countenance such a prodigious upstart for long. By 1950 his Hollywood career was over. He died nine years later at the age of 60.

Perhaps because his own life had a screwball kilter, swinging between great affluence and failure, Preston Sturges had a knack for undercutting sentimental Hollywood cliché with astute irony and social satire. No one had a keener sense of the absurd. His had been an unusual childhood, in some ways similar to the upbringing of another great talent who enjoyed carte blanche in Hollywood for a short spell at much the same time: Orson Welles. Both were the children of independent, "artis-

tic" women who instilled in them a love of high culture from an early age. In Sturges's case, Mary Desti was a great friend of Isadora Duncan and Aleister Crowley, and young Preston spent much of his childhood among the bohemian Riviera set and at boarding schools for American expatriates in Europe. (He himself avowedly preferred the company of his stockbroker stepfather.)

By his own admission a gadfly in his youth, Sturges created a kiss-proof lipstick while working for his mother's cosmetics company, the first in a wide range of commercially unviable inventions. He sold some songs, and then, recovering from appendicitis at the age of 30, decided to become a playwright. He had a Broadway hit with *Strictly Dishonorable* (1929). He made headlines shortly afterwards when he eloped with heiress Eleanor Hutton, but this, the second of four marriages, quickly foundered.

Sturges's writing career seemed to going the same way when he wrote a spec script inspired by his ex-wife's grandfather, the cereal tycoon C.W. Post. *The Power And The Glory* (directed by William K. Howard, 1933) uses an innovative non-chronological flashback structure that influenced Welles's approach to *Citizen Kane* eight years later.

Among the dozen scripts credited to Sturges in the 1930s, *The Good Fairy* (1935), *Diamond Jim* (1935), *Easy Living* (1937) and *Remember The Night* (1940) are notable, though Sturges himself was unhappy with the results. By now firmly established as one of the most gifted writers in Hollywood, he sold his screenplay *The Great McGinty* (1940) for $1 on condition that he also direct it – beating Billy Wilder and John Huston to the punch by a year. A satire on political corruption, the movie was a popular and critical smash, and Sturges was on his way – he wrote and directed three films within a year, all hits, as well as opening his own luxury Hollywood restaurant, The Players.

Sturges specialized in anarchic comedies mixing sophisticated banter with lowbrow slapstick. He excelled at the former, and distributed his wisecracks generously: bit players like William Demarest, Eric Blore, Jimmy Conlin and Franklin Pangborn were as much a part of the Sturges universe as any movie star. Everybody gets their word in. Like his peers, Ernst Lubitsch and René Clair, but more audacious and empowered by his success, he also took great delight in subverting the prohibitions of the Production Code. The critic James Agee noted that with 1944's *The Miracle Of Morgan's Creek* – a farce about the predicament of a small-town girl who, after drinking too much "lemonade", is impregnated with sextuplets by an unknown soldier – Sturges had "raped the Hays Office in its sleep". But Sturges didn't just poke fun at prudery: his films are best appreciated as a satiric riposte to the sanctimony of American wartime propaganda. In both *Morgan's*

Creek and its companion piece *Hail The Conquering Hero* (1944), quintessential nebbish Eddie Bracken emerges as an endearing but hapless home-front hero, a dim, redoubtable loser, and a refreshing antidote to the vaunted John Wayne warrior.

For half a decade Sturges could do no wrong, and Paramount made him one of the highest-paid men in America. But he balked when they tried to impose financial and artistic restraints, and the relationship deteriorated further when they shelved his downbeat biopic of the anaesthetics pioneer William Morton, *The Great Moment* (1944), for two years. A partnership with Howard Hughes produced only one film, *The Sin Of Harold Dibblebock* (1947). Starring Harold Lloyd, it was well reviewed but withdrawn and recut by Hughes (who released it five years later as *Mad Wednesday*). Sturges wrote (uncredited) *Vendetta* (1950) for Max Ophuls, took over the direction at Hughes's insistence, and was promptly fired after the two men fell out over money.

Moving to Fox, deprived of the stable of Paramount contract players who were such an integral part of his movies, Sturges made *Unfaithfully Yours* (1948), a black comedy about a jealous conductor (Rex Harrison) fantasizing about murdering his wife (Linda Darnell). It was as perfectly executed a piece of filmmaking as anything he had done, but was too cruel for its time and rejected by the audience. A Betty Grable comedy Western, *The Beautiful Blonde From Bashful Bend* (1949) was Sturges's only film in colour, and an unhappy experience. Another flop, it marked the end of his Hollywood career, and he retired to Paris to lick his wounds. His last picture, *Les carnets du Major Thompson* (1955) is reputedly very poor, and, perhaps mercifully, virtually impossible to see.

Although Sturges's most highly regarded film today is probably *Sullivan's Travels* (1941), a characteristic, and very funny, put-down of self-importance and commercial self-interest, the film is marred by atypical and rather glib moralizing. In fact *The Lady Eve* (1941) and *The Palm Beach Story* (1942) are his most perfect creations, brilliantly ironic and amoral sex comedies about impoverished inventors, daffy millionaires and priceless dress sense. In Sturges's films, clothes may not make the man (though time after time his heroes put on uniforms that don't quite fit) but they can be the making of a beautiful woman: with nothing but their wits and their wardrobes, Barbara Stanwyck and Claudette Colbert secure a first-class berth for life. Sturges would be the last person to begrudge them their good fortune. Despite everything, the happy ending was one convention to which he preferred to stay true. TC

Joel McCrea and Veronica Lake get a dose of reality in *Sullivan's Travels*.

The Great McGinty 1940,
82 min, b/w

cast Brian Donlevy, Muriel Angelus, Akim Tamiroff, Allyn Joslyn, William Demarest *cin* William Mellor *m* Frederick Hollander

Brian Donlevy plays hobo Dan McGinty, whose record-breaking efforts at repeat voting commend him to Akim Tamiroff's Mob boss. Eventually installed as state governor, complete with a pre-selected bride, McGinty makes the mistake of falling in love with his honest wife. Her virtue will be his ruination. Related in flashback, Sturges's first film as writer-director is an omnivorous satire on corruption and marked his intentions to bring dramatic realism into American comedy. Sturges won an Oscar for the screenplay.

The Lady Eve 1941, 97 min, b/w

cast Barbara Stanwyck, Henry Fonda, Charles Coburn, Eugene Pallette, William Demarest, Eric Blore *cin* Victor Milner

Henry Fonda's millionaire ophiologist returns from pursuing reptiles up the Amazon and falls for Barbara Stanwyck's 24-carat gold-digger (literally: she trips him up). Apprised of her conniving ways, he dumps her, only to take the fall a second time when she exacts revenge masquerading as the British aristocrat Lady Eve Sidwich. Prime Sturges, this semi-affectionate mockery of class pretension marked the full flowering of his splendidly egalitarian "stock company" of players.

Sullivan's Travels 1941, 90 min, b/w

cast Joel McCrea, Veronica Lake, Robert Warwick, William Demarest, Franklin Pangborn *cin* John Seitz *m* Charles Bradshaw, Leo Shuken

Unhappy with churning out hits like *Ants In Your Plants Of 1939*, Hollywood director John L. Sullivan (McCrea) announces that his next picture – *O Brother, Where Art Thou?* – will celebrate the Common Man. He raids the wardrobe department to camouflage himself as a hobo and sets out on the road, studio entourage in his wake, meeting a down-on-her-luck Veronica Lake en route. Having escaped his studio minders, Sullivan gets a more severe dose of reality than he banked on. Although the film strays into the didactic "message movie" territory it is supposed to be satirizing, the dialogue is tart and sharp, with some uproarious scenes of slapstick.

The Palm Beach Story 1942, 88 min, b/w

cast Claudette Colbert, Joel McCrea, Mary Astor, Rudy Vallee, Sig Arno, Robert Warwick, Jimmy Conlin *cin* Victor Milner *m* Victor Young

Sex and money drive this sublimely silly apotheosis of screwball comedy in which worldly-wise Claudette Colbert transfers her attentions (if not her affections) from her talented but penniless husband Joel McCrea to billionaire Rudy Vallee. The delightfully eccentric ensemble includes Vic Potel's "Wienie King", Mary Astor as the man-eating Princess Centimillia, Sig Arno's European gigolo Toto, and the anarchic "Ale & Quail Club". A clear influence on Billy Wilder's *Some Like It Hot* (1959).

The Miracle Of Morgan's Creek 1944, 99 min, b/w

cast Eddie Bracken, Betty Hutton, Diana Lynn, William Demarest, Porter Hall *cin* John Seitz *m* Charles Bradshaw, Leo Shuken

Trudy Kockenlocker (Hutton) does her bit for the boys going off to war and then some – she wakes up married to someone she doesn't remember (but may be called Ratziwatski) and definitively pregnant. At least her previously shunned admirer Norval (Bracken) will do everything in his limited power to help. By sticking to the letter of the Production Code Sturges somehow got away with this most outrageous travesty of small-town morality.

Hail The Conquering Hero 1944, 101 min, b/w

cast Eddie Bracken, William Demarest, Ella Raines, Raymond Walburn, Franklin Pangborn, Georgia Caine *cin* John Seitz *m* Werner Heymann

Woodrow Lafayette Pershing Truesmith (Bracken) is mortified to fail to live up to his father Hinky Dink Truesmith's military exploits in the Great War. Invalided out of the service by hay fever, Woodrow hasn't the heart to tell his mother the truth and can't see his way home, until six marines take pity on him and propose an elaborate but surely harmless charade. Sturges's satire on politics and the cult of personality is one of his finest achievements, all the more remarkable for its conspicuously ironic stance on wartime heroics.

Unfaithfully Yours 1948, 105 min, b/w

cast Rex Harrison, Linda Darnell, Kurt Kreuger, Barbara Lawrence, Rudy Vallee, Lionel Stander *cin* Victor Milner *m* Alfred Newman

Renowned conductor Sir Alfred de Carter (Harrison) contemplates merciless revenge on his beloved wife Daphne (Darnell) three times over the course of a concert: once to Rossini, once to Wagner, and once to Tchaikovsky. He tries to put these dark fantasies into action, resulting in a highbrow farce that is one for the connoisseurs. The protagonist was inspired by Sir Thomas Beecham, but he is not a million miles away from Sturges himself.

Elia Suleiman
Israel, 1960–

Brought up in Nazareth, Elia Suleiman moved to New York where he taught himself the history of cinema, majoring in Robert Bresson, Yasujiro Ozu and Michelangelo Antonioni. A maker of intimate documentaries and fiction, the inspiration for his work is provided by ideas, impressions and thoughts jotted down in a notebook. But whereas most other directors might use them to compose a fully formed, unified work, Suleiman replicates his notes on screen, adopting a scattershot, abstract and sketchy approach. *Chronicle Of A Disappearance* (1996) capriciously welded fact to fiction as it poignantly charted the director's return to Nazareth from America, and won the prize for best debut at the Venice Film Festival. But it was *Divine Intervention* (2002) that, on two separate occasions, thrust the director unwillingly into the headlines. First for a scene in which Suleiman's girlfriend magically and controversially turns into a ninja and vanquishes a platoon of Israeli soldiers. And secondly, when the Academy announced that it would be ineligible for nomination for the best foreign-language film Oscar, as it didn't consider Palestine to be a country. This might give the impression that Suleiman's work is forensic and polemical, whereas it is actually absurd, personal and allegorical. LH

Divine Intervention 2002, 92 min

cast Elia Suleiman, Manal Khader, George Ibrahim, Amer Daher, Jamel Daher *cin* Marc-André Batigne

Beginning with a disarming scene in which Santa Claus is stabbed to death on a Palestinian wasteland, Suleiman's abstruse narrative unfolds in a series of comically unsettling vignettes. "E.S.", as the director likes to fashion himself, spits out a peach pip which causes a tank to blow up and sends a balloon with Palestinian leader Yasser Arafat's face over a military checkpoint.

Seijun Suzuki

Japan, 1923–

A brilliant nonconformist, Seijun Suzuki was a B-movie director at the Nikkatsu Studio in the late 1950s and 60s whose work became increasingly abstract. Assigned lurid pulp melodramas and yakuza thrillers, Suzuki mixed up deliriously tacky rhapsodies of colour, design and sound with absurdist gags and choreographed action scenes, then scrambled this highly artificial *mise en scène* through surreal editing patterns. In 1967 he was fired by Nikkatsu for his "incomprehensible" work, and didn't make another feature for ten years.

The director's decadent style has been compared to pop art and to contemporaneous films made by Jean-Luc Godard. He has also been influenced by the traditional Japanese performing arts kabuki and Noh. Earlier Suzuki (he sometimes made four films a year) invest more in conventional theme and story, albeit with a modern, antimilitarist sympathy for the underdog, and still with a strong subversive lilt and outré colour and design. He hit his creative peak in the last four years at Nikkatsu. From *Youth Of The Beast* (1963) and the *Flesh* trilogy (1964–66) to his best-known films, *Tokyo Drifter* (1966) and *Branded To Kill* (1966), he gravitated towards postmodern pastiche, parody and camp. His 1980 film *Tsigoineruwaizen* (aka *Zigeunerweisen*) is deemed a masterpiece in Japan, but has gone virtually unseen in the West, while more recent pictures like *Pistol Opera* (2001) and *Princess Raccoon* (2005) trade on past glories.

Suzuki remains one of cinema's most cherished anomalies, an experimentalist and subversive who worked on the film factory production line. On a formal level, his delirious expressionist style, dazzling widescreen compositions and conceptual daring remain an energizing source for directors as different as Kitano Takeshi, Jim Jarmusch, Wong Kar-Wai and John Woo. TC

Tokyo Drifter (Tokyo nagaemono) 1966, 83 min

cast Tetsuya Watari, Chieko Matsubara, Hideaki Nitani, Ryuji Kita *cin* Shigeyoshi Mine *m* So Kaburagi

If you see only one Suzuki movie, this should be it – a whacked-out yakuza thriller about a reformed assassin, "Phoenix" Tetsu (Tetsuya Watari), who is pulled back into the game to save his old boss. The stunning art direction, endlessly replayed theme song and bold colour palette suggest a musical more than a thriller. Suzuki's refusal to play the material straight prompted the studio to dispense with his services a year later.

Branded To Kill (Koroshi no rakuin) 1966, 91 min, b/w

cast Jo Shishido, Nanbara Koji, Ogawa Mariko, Annu Mari, Isao Tamagawa *cin* Kague Nagatsuka *m* Naozumi Yamamoto

A mournful gangster thriller mutates into something else entirely as "Number Three Killer" (Jo Shishido) becomes obsessed with a *femme fatale* and squares up for a showdown with "Number One". This was the final nail in the coffin for Nikkatsu: Suzuki abandons any pretence at shooting the hackneyed script and just lets his imagination run riot.

Jan Svankmajer

Czech Republic (formerly Czechoslovakia), 1934–

Exploring dream logic through an arresting, unsettling fusion of animation, puppetry and live action, Jan Svankmajer's films possess a visceral intensity and humour, occupying a realm where horror and fantasy meet. Inspired by Federico Fellini, Georges Méliès and Eastern European traditions of puppetry, Svankmajer formally and thematically subverts expectations about animation and, like Walt Disney, is fascinated by the fairy-tale form. He is also strongly influenced by surrealists such as Luis Buñuel.

Svankmajer began by working in theatre and was powerfully inspired by the Czech Surrealist Group. In the early 1960s he shifted into filmmaking with the short film *The Last Trick* (1964). Many other films followed, including the short *The Flat* (1969), in which a man is caught in a room with an antagonistic chair and a bowl of soup, and the puppet-based *Don Juan* (1970). Between 1973 and 1980 the Communists deemed his work subversive and he produced no films, but in 1983 his fortunes revived when his *Dimensions Of Dialogue* won the Grand Prize at France's prestigious Annecy Animation Festival for its claymation pyrotechnics and audacious treatment of ordinary objects coming to life. Since then Svankmajer's reputation has grown, though his work continues to find only a limited audience through arthouse screenings and DVD.

Svankmajer's key film remains *Alice* (1988), a sinister spin on Lewis Carroll's novel. For the director, Carroll's childish scenarios proved compelling. Since that film's breakthrough success, Svankmajer has made the feature-length pieces *Faust* (1994), *Conspirators Of Pleasure* (1996), *Little Otik* (2001) and *Lunacy* (2005), the last a subversive De Sadean exploration of societal norms set in an insane asylum. His work has inspired filmmakers as diverse as Terry Gilliam, the Brothers Quay and Tim Burton. JC

Alice (Neco z Alenky) 1988, 86 min

cast Kristyna Kohoutova *cin* Svatopluk Maly

This intense adaptation of *Alice In Wonderland* uses predominantly found objects as "puppets". Socks, skulls and a stuffed rabbit all parade mesmerizingly through a fetid, bleak fantasy world. Call it whimsical body horror. The film now stands as a masterpiece of animation.

Little Otik (Otesánek) 2001, 132 min

cast Veronika Zilková, Jan Hartl, Kristina Adamcová, Jaroslava Kretschmerová *cin* Juri Galvanek *m* Carl Maria von Weber

Based on a Czech fairy tale, *Little Otik* trades on horror conventions to explore what happens when a childless couple "adopt" a log that looks like a baby. Parental anxieties are gleefully, almost cruelly, explored, as is our compelling urge to procreate.

Jan Sverák

Czech Republic (formerly Czechoslovakia), 1965–

The son of actor-writer Zdenek Sverák, Jan Sverák studied documentary filmmaking at the Prague film school FAMU before concentrating on documentary-tinged fiction. He made several well-regarded films including the touching *Obecná skola* (*Elementary School*, 1991) – loosely based on his father's childhood in post-World War II Czechoslovakia – which was nominated for the Oscar for best foreign-language film. The surreal *Akumulátor 1* (1994), a sci-fi satire on the power of television, was popular in his home country, but his success was largely local until the charming *Kolya* (1996) won him an Oscar. After some acting work, Sverák directed *Dark Blue World* (2001), about two Czech pilots fighting in the Battle of Britain. Well received by those who saw it, it nonetheless failed to live up to the standard set by *Kolya*. JR

Kolya (Kolja) 1996, 105 min

cast Zdenek Sverák, Andrei Chalimon, Libuse Safránková, Ondrej Vetchý, Stella Zázvorková *cin* Vladimir Smutný *m* Ondrej Soukup

The touching, if unadventurous, story of a grumpy old man (played by the director's father, who also wrote the script) and a charming moppet for whom he is suddenly made unwillingly responsible. Needless to say, the old musician's cynical heart is softened by the lad's innocence in the face of the Soviet occupation of Prague, but the performances avoid the sentimentality that could so easily have scuppered the picture.

István Szabó

Hungary, 1938–

Of all the great post-war Hungarian directors, István Szabó is the best-known to Western audiences. In the early 1960s, Szabó began working at the Béla Balázs Studio (named after the eminent film theorist), which was designed to promote new Hungarian directors. Szabó's short films garnered accolades on the festival circuit, and his first feature, *The Age Of Daydreaming* (1964), showed the influence of François Truffaut. In *Father* (1966) Szabó began to address the generational history that has been his keynote. A young man's memories of his wartime Resistance hero father are refined as he learns to become his own man. If his 1970s work, such as *Love Film* (1970) and *Budapest Tales* (1977), seemed more overtly lyrical and symbolist, films such as *Confidence* (1979) combine a feeling for intimate dynamics – the tentative relationship between a Resistance fugitive and a refugee – with urgent thriller tropes.

Szabó's exploration of personal identity fed into the three works (all starring Klaus Maria Brandauer) that form the director's renowned "Central European trilogy": *Mephisto* (1981), *Colonel Redl* (1984) and *Hanussen* (1988). Together they provide a snapshot history of the region from the end of the Austro-Hungarian Empire to the eve of World War II. Self-betrayal proves the undoing of both Redl and the clairvoyant Hanussen. Redl forsakes his lowborn identity to advance through the Hapsburg officer class, eventually succumbing to the deceit. Crisply shot by Szabó's regular cinematographer Lajos Koltai and consummately acted by Brandauer, *Hanussen* follows a wounded ex-soldier whose gift gains him admission to the drawing rooms of Weimar Germany, yet he brings strife as he predicts the rise of Nazism.

Directing English-language international co-productions in the 1990s – *Meeting Venus* (1991), *Sunshine* (1999) – has diminished the power of an oeuvre that derived its original urgency from the convolutions of indigenous European events. Only *Sweet Emma, Dear Böbe* (1992) reclaimed the intimacy of the past as it explored the fortunes of two Hungarian women teachers in the post-Communist transition who are forced to drop Russian from the curriculum and learn English. Its portrait of a society exchanging grey conformity for rampant exploitation reveals Szabó's ambivalence towards the new Europe. *Taking Sides* (2001) starred Harvey Keitel and was a return to *Mephisto* territory. In 2004 Szabó offered another fine role for an actress in *Being Julia*, for which Annette Bening received an Oscar nomination and won a Golden Globe. Few directors have addressed the realities of twentieth-century European history with such sensitivity and grace. Szabó continued his exploration of the Hungarian status quo in *Rokonok* (2006), in which a government functionary suddenly finds an unbidden gang of relatives on his doorstep, all hoping for favours. RA

Mephisto 1981, 144 min

cast Klaus Maria Brandauer, Ildikó Bánsági, Krystyna Janda, Rolf Hoppe, György Cserhalmi, Péter Andorai *cin* Lajos Koltai *m* Zdenkó Tamássy

An actor associates himself with the Nazi regime for the sake of his career and is forced to compromise his art and his friends. Klaus Maria Brandauer gives an increasingly constrained performance, portraying a sensitivity to the dynamics of the master–slave relationship required by fascism. The film is based on Karl Mann's novel about German screen actor Gustaf Gründgens.

S

Isao Takahata

Japan, 1935–

Isao Takahata is the co-founder of Studio Ghibli, Japan's most commercially – and many would say artistically – successful anime house. He established the studio in 1985 with Hayao Miyazaki, with whom he had been working in film and TV since the 1960s. Most of the duo's earlier work focused on children's stories, which included a hugely popular animated series called *Panda! Go Panda!* (1972), inspired by Pippi Longstocking, and an anime version of *Heidi* (1974). However, at Ghibli, Takahata forged a different path, creating films for a largely adult market, with realism often coming to the fore.

His debut for Ghibli was *Grave Of The Fireflies* (1988), based on a semi-autobiographical novel by Akiyuki Nosaka. It was originally released as a double bill with Miyazaki's gorgeously cute *My Neighbour Totoro*: it was a bizarre pairing, for Takahata's bleak wartime tale is hardly a children's film. *Fireflies* does, however, share *Totoro*'s painterly style and its evocative detailing of everyday life and objects. Since their release, both films have come to be considered among the greatest anime. *Fireflies* has been interpreted in various ways – as an allegory of Japan's madness during the war or as an apology for its involvement – but it is clearly about the horrors of war and its personal tragedies.

Takahata's follow-up, *Only Yesterday* (1991), is reminiscent of Haruki Murakami's novels, with its story of a Tokyo office worker taking a holiday on a farm and reflecting on her childhood in the countryside. It was acclaimed for the way in which it intercut realist narrative with expressionist sequences, evoking the character's imagination. *Pom Poko* (1994), however, returned to the world of fantasy. An eco-fable in which a magic band of raccoons try to disrupt property developers taking over their hillsides, it has some wonderful tableaux and a fair amount of humour, but it never quite approaches the Miyazaki league. In 1999, Takahata directed *My Neighbors The Yamadas*, a lightweight family comedy created in comic strip-style animation. He has also produced many Ghibli films, including Goro Miyazaki's *Tales From Earthsea* (2007). ME

Grave Of The Fireflies (Hotaru no haka) 1988, 88 min
cast (English voices) Rhoda Chrosite, Amy Jones, J. Robert Spencer, Veronica Taylor *cin* Nobuo Koyama *m* Yoshiro Mamiya

Fireflies tells the story of two orphans struggling to survive in the last months of World War II. The fireflies of the title provide comfort for the children (who live in a cave-shelter), and mirror the bombs that rained down upon their home at the opening of the film. But that is as far as the whimsy goes: this is an almost brutally poignant film about children growing up out of their depth, and about the folly of pride taking precedence over reason. It is also Takahata's masterpiece.

Lee Tamahori

New Zealand, 1950–

Lee Tamahori is a New Zealand filmmaker who won international plaudits for his early work – such as his first feature, *Once Were Warriors* (1994) – and went on to build a Hollywood career. Like compatriot Roger Donaldson, Tamahori works confidently in genre forms, notably thrillers. His Hollywood debut was *Mulholland Falls* (1996), a crime flick set in the 1940s, and subsequent titles have included kidnapping drama *Along Came A Spider* (2001), action movie *XXX: State Of The Union* (2005) and *Next* (2007), a foray into sci-fi. Alongside *Once Were Warriors*, Tamahori's best efforts have included the James Bond film *Die Another Day* (2002) and *The Edge* (1997), written by David Mamet, in which two men struggle to survive in the American wilderness. More recently, he made the science-fiction thriller, *Next* (2007), starring Nicolas Cage and Julianne Moore. JC

Once Were Warriors 1994, 99 min
cast Rena Owen, Temuera Morrison, Mamengaroa Kerr-Bell, Julian Arahanga *cin* Stuart Dryburgh *m* Murray Grindlay, Murray McNab

Once Were Warriors explores contemporary Maori culture and the marginalization New Zealand's Maori people often suffer from. Based on a novel by Alan Duff, and received with enthusiasm on its release, this is intense realist cinema that manages to represent the edgy allure of a specific milieu, while also perceptively chronicling its downsides. Leads Temuera Morrison and Rena Owen are outstanding.

Alain Tanner
Switzerland, 1929–

Although his career has taken him to Britain, Spain, France and Portugal, Alain Tanner is one of the most engaged and committed Swiss filmmakers.

The son of an actress and a painter, Tanner studied socioeconomics prior to a three-year spell in London where he worked for the British Film Institute and became friendly with the leading lights in the Free Cinema movement. He and his compatriot Claude Goretta even co-directed an impressionistic documentary portrait of London in the Free Cinema style, *Nice Time* (1957), about Piccadilly Circus at night. Tanner returned to Switzerland by way of France, which was then in the throes of the *nouvelle vague*. Back home, he directed more than forty television *vérité* documentaries on a wide variety of subjects. In 1968, he quit broadcasting and set up as an independent director, founding Groupe 5 with four other Swiss filmmakers, including his friend Goretta.

Tanner's first feature film was *Charles Dead Or Alive* (1969), about a middle-aged industrialist who drops out of society in self-disgust. Both *The Salamander* (1971) and *Jonas qui aura 25 ans en l'an 2000* (*Jonah Who Will Be 25 In The Year 2000*, 1976) were co-written with British art theorist John Berger. Like his other films from this militant period they are marked with Brechtian, socialist ideas and the formal influence of the great modernist directors Robert Bresson and Roberto Rossellini. They are also much preoccupied with the place of Switzerland as a neutral zone at the heart of western Europe, although paradoxically this often shows itself in the congenital rootlessness of Tanner's wandering protagonists. In *Messidor* (1978), for example, two young female hitchhikers meet and resolve to see how long they can survive without money – an experiment that is soon corrupted by exploitation and violence.

In the 1980s, Tanner's cinema demonstrated a shift from politics to the personal, especially in a series of very explicit films exploring sexuality co-written with actress Myriam Mézières. Frank and "poetic", *A Flame In My Heart* (1987) and *The Diary Of Lady M* (1992) are risqué, and borderline risible, hard-core art films. *Light Years Away* (1981), a *Jonas* follow-up set in the year 2000, won the Special Jury Prize at Cannes. Tanner's collaborations with writer Bernard Comment – *Fourbi* (1996), *Requiem* (1998), *Jonas et Lila, à demain* (1999), a homage to his 1976 movie, and *Paul s'en va* (2004), in which the spirit of a missing semiology lecturer speaks through his students – recall his earlier work. These, along with another

erotic film with Mézières, *Fleurs de sang* (*Flowers Of Blood*, 2002) have not been widely distributed. TC

Jonas qui aura 25 ans en l'an 2000 (Jonah Who Will Be 25 In The Year 2000) 1976, 115 min
cast Jean-Luc Bideau, Rufus, Miou-Miou, Jacques Denis, Myriam Mézieres *cin* Renato Berta *m* Jean-Marie Sénia.

Tanner's most popular film ruminates on the lost dreams of May 1968. A group of radicals from that era get together and reflect on the roads they have travelled; the small ways in which they are struggling to make a difference. Wry, funny and sad, it's one of the best movies to come out of that time.

Quentin Tarantino
US, 1963–

Few modern directors have created such a furore with so few films. After moving to California as a child, Quentin Tarantino dropped out of high school and got a job in a video store. There he developed an extensive knowledge of movies and cultivated relationships with patrons from the film industry. The short *My Best Friend's Birthday* (1987) launched Tarantino into filmmaking.

His feature debut came with the heist thriller *Reservoir Dogs* (1991) which he wrote, directed and acted in. A hit at Sundance, the film established Tarantino as a media sensation, a sharp-witted, precocious auteur plying audience and interviewer with the gems and anecdotes of a childhood spent watching B-movies and bad television. The film's protracted and splenetic face-offs and flip attitude to violence gave rise to a widespread media debate about the "Tarantino Effect", which his screenplay for Tony Scott's *True Romance* (1993) and the bitterly contested script for Oliver Stone's *Natural Born Killers* (1994) only fuelled.

The world awaited Tarantino's second feature. When *Pulp Fiction* arrived in 1994, it made a fortune and received the Palme d'Or at Cannes, a best director Academy Award nomination, and the best original screenplay Oscar for Tarantino and co-writer Roger Avary. Branded the legatee of Martin Scorsese's pop-cultural allusiveness, Tarantino conferred mainstream respectability on the obsessive referencing of the moving image. His industry chutzpah and unabashed junk fetish would be felt in US indies from Kevin Smith to Nicole Holofcener. Becoming a studio insider through his association with arch indie facilitator Miramax, Tarantino also had a regular presence as an actor in such films as Robert Rodriguez's *Desperado* (1995) and *From Dusk Till Dawn* (1996), the latter of which he also scripted and executive produced.

Following the muddled plot lines and dismal showing of 1995's portmanteau film *Four Rooms*, for which he shared directing credits with Rodriguez, Allison Anders and Alexandre Rockwell, Tarantino seemed to evolve with *Jackie Brown* (1997), a paean to 1970s blaxploitation icon Pam Grier. Starring Grier as a money-smuggling flight attendant who finds an ally in Robert Forster's burnt-out bail bondsman, *Jackie Brown* belied the cruel and superficial flash of Tarantino's earlier work. It instead focused on the poignant prospect of middle-aged people making a last bid for control of their lives.

With their chapter format, *Kill Bill Vol 1* (2003) and *Kill Bill Vol 2* (2004) evoked the narrative skill of a director who once aspired to write novels. Uma Thurman's crack assassin vows to kill those who shot her, her fiancé, her unborn child and the whole congregation at her wedding, with the violent, highly stylized action inspired by Tarantino's beloved Hong Kong martial arts cinema. Demonstrating a consummate handling of story and editing, the *Kill Bill* films' narrative bravura and visceral pleasures left their indelible mark on the American multiplex.

In 2005 Tarantino guest-directed for Rodriguez on *Sin City*, adapted from the Frank Miller graphic novels set in a modern municipal hell. Collaborating again in 2007, Rodriguez and Tarantino released *Grindhouse* in the US, a double-feature tribute to the slasher-horror exploitation films of their youth. However, *Death Proof*, Tarantino's segment of the film, was shown separately at the Cannes Film Festival and released as a stand-alone feature in the UK and much of the rest of the world.

The most notorious of the US indies, Tarantino has mixed wit, violence and cinephilia into an incendiary cocktail that rewrote the multiplex mantra of the post-*Jaws* era. RA

Reservoir Dogs 1991, 99 min
cast Harvey Keitel, Tim Roth, Michael Madsen, Chris Penn, Steve Buscemi, Lawrence Tierney, Randy Brooks, Kirk Baltz *cin* Andrzej Sekula

Inspired by Stanley Kubrick's 1956 thriller *The Killing* and influenced by Ringo Lam's *City On Fire* (1989), Quentin Tarantino boldly elided the actual hold-up to concentrate on the build-up and the bloody aftermath. Featuring an eclectic line-up of modern villains, *Reservoir Dogs* is fuelled by demotic dialogue, trash pop and nearly unbearable blood-letting.

Pulp Fiction 1994, 154 min
cast John Travolta, Samuel L. Jackson, Uma Thurman, Harvey Keitel, Tim Roth, Amanda Plummer, Maria de Medeiros *cin* Andrzej Sekula

Tarantino's signature work is a potpourri of trash novelettes, set to the strains of cheap but potent pop. The director skilfully orchestrated three interlinked stories in which underdogs put one over on underworld villains, while the ensemble cast give some of the most memorable performances of their generation. The standout, however, is John Travolta, making a triumphant comeback in partnership with Samuel L. Jackson.

Jackie Brown 1997, 154 min
cast Pam Grier, Samuel L. Jackson, Robert Forster, Bridget Fonda, Michael Keaton, Robert De Niro, Michael Bowen *cin* Guillermo Navarro

Tarantino's best film is a well-wrought thriller that also manages to be a poem to middle-aged disappointment. An adaptation of an Elmore Leonard novel, *Jackie Brown* forgoes Tarantino's typical stylized violence to concentrate on the characters. Pam Grier was never better than as the eponymous ageing flight attendant who finds herself caught between the cops and the Mob and – yearning for a new life and a big cash payout – decides to pit one against the other.

Kill Bill Vol 1 2003, 111 min
cast Uma Thurman, Lucy Liu, Vivica A. Fox, Daryl Hannah, David Carradine, Michael Madsen, Julie Dreyfus *cin* Robert Richardson *m* RZA

Returning with a vengeance to the blood-letting and fanboy cinephilia of his early work, Tarantino riffs on action movie aesthetics in both his *Kill Bill* films. He places Uma Thurman's vengeful, yellow-tracksuit-clad assassin – who was gunned down on her wedding day by the (primarily female) killers of the Deadly Viper Squad – at the centre of a melange of B-movie tropes, anime sequences, martial arts stunt moves and violent, blood-splattered balletic mayhem. Superficial but dazzling.

Andrei Tarkovsky
Russia (formerly Soviet Union), 1932–86

The son of a poet, Andrei Tarkovsky himself would often wax metaphysical about the poetry of cinema, citing Robert Bresson, Aleksander Dovzhenko, Kenji Mizoguchi, Luis Buñuel and Akira Kurosawa as supreme practitioners of the art. Most critics would add Tarkovsky's own name to that prestigious list. For even though his narratives were often wilfully opaque, his imagery was sublime and genuinely visionary.

Andrei Tarkovsky studied under Mikhail Romm at VGIK, the Soviet state film school in Moscow, and his diploma film, *The Steamroller And The Violin* (1961), won a prize at the New York Film Festival. When his first feature film, *Ivan's Childhood* (1962) shared the Golden Lion at the Venice Film Festival, the director's future seemed assured. Yet he only made six more features in the next 24 years, and the fate of his next film was all too typical of a career defined by frustration. *Andrei Rublev* (1966) was shelved for several years by Soviet authorities, who viewed it as a potent allegory of the artist's plight under the Communist regime.

Although he managed to exploit the demise of socialist realism that gradually followed Stalin's death in 1953, Tarkovsky's films were too formalist and individual for totalitarian tastes. Decades later, *Solaris* (1972), *Mirror* (1974) and *Stalker* (1979) still suffered from the same chilly official indifference. The director's patience with government control finally snapped when he was making *Nostalgia*

(1983) in Italy and demanded more time in the country. When the request was refused, he defected to the West – but the Soviets got their revenge by having Sergei Bondarchuk ensure that *Nostalgia* missed out on the Palme d'Or at Cannes (it won the less prestigious Special Jury Prize instead). Whether Tarkovsky really would have had more joy in the profit-oriented, bottom-line cinema of the free market, we'll never know. He was already dying of lung cancer in 1986 when he made *The Sacrifice* in Sweden, and was too ill to receive the Grand Jury Prize at Cannes.

There is no doubt that when watching a Tarkovksy film, you are in the presence of a visionary (and according to some observers, the self-aggrandizing director knew it all too well himself). This vision was expressed in key elements which were often repeated from film to film in a highly personal symbolism: fire, water, wind, mirrors, dream sequences, spilt milk, levitation, foliage moving under water, references to old paintings and the flow of black and white to colour. Despite their recurrence, these sublime images exert a hypnotic hold, tightening their hallucinatory grip as events steadily unfold. This is partly due to the luxurious length of the takes (up to ten minutes in *The Sacrifice*). For Tarkovsky, cinema "was the only art that operates with the concept of time".

This physical and empirical sense of time passing imbued scenes with an in-built evanescence, an instant, aching nostalgia for a moment whose end we've just witnessed. At their mesmerizing best, these meandering shots invoke in an audience a sort of cinematic and spiritual transcendence. And this, no doubt, was Tarkovsky's aim, as he believed that "the purpose of art is to improve a man spiritually". It's a religious epiphany he was also intending for his characters, because even though many of his films are about outward journeys (*Andrei Rublev*, *Solaris* and *Stalker*, for instance) they act as a mirror for the journey within. In the intensely personal *Mirror*, the director deftly employs all the tricks of the illusionist's trade to evoke the scattershot nature of memory: slow motion, surreal imagery, scenes shot in diffused wintry light or in the hazy languor of the magic hour and, above all, through a series of startling metamorphoses. While the dialogue in *Nostalgia* was portentously trite, Tarkovsky's themes of memory, longing and identity are perfectly articulated through his awe-inspiring and spellbinding frescoes.

Unfortunately, Tarkovsky's spirituality was often expressed in dialogue that was as leaden and prosaic as his images were supple and allusive, displaying an alarming weakness for thematic exposition, grandiose statements and generalizations. Occasionally the big psychological truths Tarkovsky was aiming for could be easily reduced to simple truisms. Despite his creating a stunning and credible alternate universe in *Stalker*, the film's moral can be expressed as "be careful what you wish for". Given this unfortunate literalism, it's much more truthful and useful to think of Tarkovsky as less of a poet and more of a composer, whose work can be absorbed bodily and emotionally. For all their cerebral musings and metaphysical *pensées*, Tarkovsky's works bypass the head and travel straight to the heart, transporting us to new levels and states in exactly the same quasi-mystical way that a symphony can magically, inexplicably, induce an out-of-body experience. LH

Ivan's Childhood (Ivanovo detstvo) 1962, 95 min, b/w

cast Kolya Burlyaev, Irma Rausch, Valentin Zubkov, Yevgeny Zharikov, Valentina Malyavina *cin* Vadim Iusov *m* Vyacheslav Ovchinnikov

In this, the most naturalistic of all Tarkovsky's works, a young orphan working as a spy for the Russians on the German front is adopted by a group of officers who try to send him away from the danger zone. The director's idea of socialist realism is to shoot everything with an angular, up-tight chiaroscuro look, which he peppers with a few

Ivan's Childhood is suffused with Tarkovsky's poetic vision of landscape.

delirious dream sequences with near mystical results. The vibrancy and fluency of the camerawork, however, stands in contrast to the stiffness and formality of Tarkovsky's later years.

Andrei Rublev 1966, 182 min, b/w and col
cast Anatoli Solonitsyn, Ivan Lapikov, Nikolai Grinko, Nikolai Sergeyev, Irma Rausch, Kolya Burlyaev *cin* Vadim Iusov *m* Vyacheslav Ovchinnikov

Itinerant fifteenth-century painter Andrei Rublev travels across a turbulent and violent landscape to finally arrive at a spiritual and creative transcendence. Tarkovsky's lustrous, deep-focus frames are filled with less ponderousness than his later films, while his mobile camera is more at ease with itself. His imagery exerts a mesmerizing grip in a series of stunning set pieces, from the opening wonder of a balloon flight, through the violence of the Tatar attack on Vladimir Cathedral to the culminating casting of the great bell.

Solaris 1972, 166 min
cast Natalya Bondarchuk, Donatas Banionis, Jüri Järvet, Anatoli Solonitsyn, Vladislav Dvorjetski, Nikolai Grinko *cin* Vadim Iusov *m* Eduard Artemiev

A scientist travels to the planet Solaris, which seems to give life to the contents of his unconscious mind. When his dead wife makes an unscheduled appearance, he blasts her off into space. But when she returns a second time, his resistance is lowered and he commences a love affair with a woman he knows is make-believe. It was left to Steven Soderbergh in his underrated 2002 remake to mine the devastating emotional resonances of this intriguing scenario; Tarkovsky instead goes for the big philosophical themes.

Mirror (Zerkalo) 1974, 106 min
cast Margarita Terekhova, Philip Yankovsky, Oleg Yankovsky, Ignat Daniltsev, Nikolai Grinko, Larisa Tarkovskaya *cin* Georgi Rerberg *m* Eduard Artemiev

A dying man sets a bird free, a gust of wind flattens a field of corn, a woman washes her hair. *Mirror* is the most personal and poetic of all Tarkovsky's films, a meditation on Russian history and his own life – in particular his relationship with his father, Arseny, whose poems form a counterpoint to the film's startling images. Intercutting archive and new material, and mixing colour with black and white, the film is fragmentary and imagistic in a way that suggests the pure subjectivity of dreams and reflection.

Stalker 1979, 163 min, b/w and col
cast Aleksandr Kajdanovsky, Anatoli Solonitsyn, Nikolai Grinko, Alisa Frejndlikh *cin* Aleksandr Knyazhinsky *m* Eduard Artemiev

The Stalker takes the Writer and the Scientist through the Zone to the Room, where all their dreams will apparently come true. Although this is the most hackneyed of Tarkovsky's sci-fi variations, the trio's perilous journey – bizzarely guided by a metal nut attached to a bandage – soon takes on levels of Beckettian absurdity. Tarkovsky's Zone is an extraordinary yet believable world, while the "real world", meticulously etched in high-contrast monochrome, resembles a hand-crafted lithograph to such an astonishing degree that it's a shock when something stirs in its perfectly realized frames.

The Sacrifice (Offret) 1986, 149 min
cast Erland Josephson, Susan Fleetwood, Tommy Kjellqvist, Allan Edwall, Valérie Mairesse, Gudrún Gísladóttir *cin* Sven Nykvist *m* J.S. Bach

Faced with the apocalypse, a journalist prays to God to spare humanity and offers to kill his young son in return. When the disaster is averted, he has to decide whether to keep to his end of the bargain. Shot on the island of Faro by Ingmar Bergman's favourite cinematographer, the film tries to channel the Swedish grandmaster, but Tarkovsky loses his own voice in the process. Without his trademark expressionist imagery, he cannot retain his vice-like grip on our senses and we're left with dialogue that strives for Chekhovian significance with predictably insipid results.

Béla Tarr
Hungary, 1955–

Glacial, existential and sombre, Béla Tarr's work has drawn comparisons with other masters of the still life: Andrei Tarkovsky, Jim Jarmusch and Aki Kaurismäki. This former student of the Hungarian Academy of Theatre and Film started out in social-realist mode, and his films – inert and punishingly slow – have only recently gained a reputation for stark abstraction. Tarr's feature debut *Family Nest* (1979), *The Outsider* (1981) and *The Prefab People* (1982) all focused on some form of domestic meltdown; the latter, which documents the painful break-up of a factory worker's marriage, is generally regarded as the high point of Tarr's claustrophobic and naturalistic early works.

Damnation (1988) heralded a new painterly style for Tarr, ripe with formal eloquence and metaphor. His panoramic long takes are hypnotically redolent of the exquisitely choreographed shots of fellow Hungarian director Miklós Jancsó. His palette is inky, the pace funereal and the characters a product of their bleak environment. When they do speak, their utterances are mostly gnomic and occasionally telling. A line from *Damnation*, "Stories are all stories of disintegration" handily sums up the sense of decay that languorously permeates that picture and subsequent works.

This slow-motion approach found its fullest expression in the 430-minute *Sátántangó* (1994), an intense, nightmarish masterwork about a disintegrating rural community that falls under the spell of a messianic huckster. *Werckmeister Harmonies* (2000), clocking in at a mere two and a half hours, remains the accessible face of Béla Tarr. Not far behind is *The Man From London* (2007), Tarr's noirish and idiosyncratic take on Georges Simenon's novel about a witness to a murder who takes home a bag of cash and soon wishes he hadn't.

The tableaux approach and mesmerizing effects of the Hungarian director's *mise en scène* have prompted comparisons with Tarkovsky, which Tarr promptly dismissed on the very reasonable grounds that he doesn't share the Russian master's spiritual leanings. Indeed, Tarr is reluctant to freight his films with any sort of meaning or significance, even though critics have spied allegories about the collapse of Communism in his latest pictures. There really doesn't seem to be any good reason, however, not

547

to take Tarr at his word, and regard his recent works as belonging to the same surreal, apolitical and hermetically sealed universe as David Lynch's *Eraserhead* (1976). And they're none the worse for that. LH

Damnation (Kárhozat) 1988, 120 min, b/w

cast Miklós B. Székely, Vali Kerekes, Hédi Temessy, Gyula Pauer, György Cserhalmi *cin* Gábor Medvigy *m* Mihály Víg

Like Jim Jarmusch on tranquillizers, Béla Tarr's mobile camera tracks the desperate lives of a barfly and the singer at his local watering hole (the aptly named Titanik) who embark on, or rather sink into, a torpid, treacherous affair. Their self-loathing and blue-collar misery will be familiar to anyone who's seen a few films by Aki Kaurismäki, except Tarr makes the gloomy Finn seem like a lightweight when it comes to cinematic inertia and human entropy. Tarr's glare is steely, hypnotic and proves, without doubt, that he is the master of the art of monotony.

Werckmeister Harmonies (Werckmeister harmóniák) 2000, 145 min, b/w

cast Lars Rudolph, Peter Fitz, Hanna Schygulla, János Derzsi, Djoko Rossich, *cin* Gábor Medvigy, Jörg Widmer, Patrick de Ranter *m* Mihály Víg

Tarr's fable unravels in a series of deep-focus monochrome tableaux, as the appearance of a stuffed whale and his owner, an enigmatic messiah figure called the Prince, has a devastating, apocalyptic effect on the inhabitants of a small, dreary Hungarian town. The title refers to the composer Andreas Werckmeister whose theories about tonality formed the basis of Western music, and the attempts by one of the town's inhabitants to recreate the sound of music before Werckmeister. This is one of the many eccentricities in a film that in turn seduces and unsettles, lulling susceptible viewers into a deep and satisfying trance.

Frank Tashlin

US, 1913–72

"**H**enceforth, when you talk about a comedy, don't say 'It's Chaplinesque'; say loud and clear, 'It's Tashlinesque.'" So said Jean-Luc Godard in a review of *Hollywood Or Bust* (1956).

A hero of the *nouvelle vague*, Frank Tashlin was one of the first animation directors to make the transition to live action successfully. As many critics have pointed out, there's little difference between the two forms in the Tashlin canon: whether his movies are populated by humans or cartoons, they all exist in a parallel universe with its own unique laws of physics, where gravity is defied, logic is reversed and slapstick is king. He worked his way up from errand boy to animator at Fleischer Studios, but left his mark at Warner Bros, where he forged his own signature style. After a brief stint as a gag man for Hal Roach's studio, Tashlin oversaw the development of Porky the Pig at Warner Bros. In addition, he scripted Mickey Mouse's first feature, *Mickey And The Beanstalk* (1940) and made the last monochrome Looney Tune, *Puss N' Booty* (1943).

After World War II, Tashlin returned to live action as a writer for the Marx Brothers, among others, and even found the time to pen a few children's books. His big directorial break came when Bob Hope asked him to re-shoot much of *The Lemon Drop Kid* (1951) after Sidney Lanfield had made a hopeless hash of the screenplay, which Tashlin co-wrote. His first credit as a live-action director appears on *The First Time* (1952), but he really discovered his métier working with Jerry Lewis. Hired to direct two of the best of Lewis's comedies with Dean Martin – *Artists And Models* (1955) and *Hollywood Or Bust* – he discovered in the hyperactive comedian the sort of oversized exuberance and supple elasticity previously only found in cartoon characters.

Tashlin made six more films with Lewis alone: *Rock-A-Bye Baby* (1958), *The Geisha Boy* (1958), *Cinderfella* (1960), *It'$ Only Money* (1962), *Who's Minding The Store?* (1963) and *The Disorderly Orderly* (1964). All are models of delirious anarchy and mawkish sentiment (with the latter increasing as the years rolled by). At the same time, Tashlin found another cartoon in human form, the impossibly pneumatic Jayne Mansfield, whose breasts became the subject of much snickering innuendo in *The Girl Can't Help It* (1956) and *Will Success Spoil Rock Hunter?* (1957). The 1960s were largely years of decline, during which he made a couple of Doris Day films and the seafaring comedy *The Private Army Of Sergeant O'Farrell* (1968) with Bob Hope.

Tashlin once defended his juvenile humour on the grounds of social satire, but this didn't convince every critic. He is often dismissed as a vulgarian who executed a hypocritical double back-flip by simultaneously pandering to the lowbrow tastes he was lampooning. Certainly his satire was never subtle. Consumerism, television and what the director described as "the nonsense of what we *call* civilization" were all attacked with the lightness of touch of a cartoon sledgehammer. Recently Tashlin's critical stock has fallen. Somewhat unjustly, because as gross-out humour still rings the cash-tills of multiplexes and Hollywood seems hellbent on turning all its blockbusters into live-action cartoons, the work of Frank Tashlin has never seemed more relevant or apposite. LH

Son Of Paleface 1952, 95 min

cast Bob Hope, Jane Russell, Roy Rogers, Trigger, Douglas Dumbrille, Bill Williams, Lloyd Corrigan *cin* Harry J. Wild *m* Lyn Murray

This sequel to the 1948 spoof Western *The Paleface* (which Tashlin co-wrote) is one of Bob Hope's funniest films. As Junior Potter, the usual cowardly blunderer he'd perfected over the years, Hope is patronized and outsmarted by the curvaceous Jane Russell – a saloon gal and gang leader – as well as the warbling Roy Rogers and his legendary horse, Trigger. Tashlin injects his customary flair, which mocks every Western convention with increasingly surreal inventiveness.

Will Success Spoil Rock Hunter? 1957, 94 min

cast Tony Randall, Jayne Mansfield, Betsy Drake, Joan Blondell, John Williams, Henry Jones *cin* Joe MacDonald *m* Cyril J. Mockridge

Beginning with Tony Randall playing all the instruments on the 20th Century Fox fanfare, this frenetic farce continues in playful postmodern vein when he later reduces the CinemaScope format to a TV-size pin hole as part of a lecture addressed directly to the audience. Television is one of the many targets in this broad satire on celebrity, advertising and a culture driven mad by sex, as Randall plays a desperate adman who's willing to do anything to get movie star Jayne Mansfield to endorse a new beauty product.

Cinderfella 1960, 90 min

cast Jerry Lewis, Ed Wynn, Judith Anderson, Anna Maria Alberghetti, Henry Silva, Robert Hutton, Count Basie *cin* Haskell Boggs *m* Walter Scharf

One of the most enduringly popular of Jerry Lewis's collaborations with director Frank Tashlin, this farcical take on the Cinderella story is enhanced by the presence of jazzman Count Basie and Ed Wynn as the "fairy godfather". The film rejoices in some classic Lewis moments (the staircase descent, for example), but the comedian's appeal remains a specialized taste.

Jacques Tati

France, 1907–82

An unlikely amalgam of Buster Keaton and Jean-Paul Sartre, Jacques Tati almost single-handedly kept the clowning tradition of silent cinema alive in the age of sound, while inventing an unlikely existential hero, Monsieur Hulot.

Tati started out as a mime in music hall. After a series of shorts, he made his feature debut with *Jour de fête* (1949). This whimsical farce starred the director as a hapless postman who attempts to introduce modern methods of efficiency to a militantly old-fashioned French village. By no means a classic, it serves as a taster for the Tati universe. Driven by its own quantum physics whereby every action has a chain reaction, the story is a variation on the director's favourite theme, the clash between sleepy tradition and flinty modernity.

Tati's first masterpiece, *Monsieur Hulot's Holiday* (1953), introduced the world to Hulot, a human cartoon cloaked in the uniform of the absent-minded: whatever-the-weather raincoat, pipe dangling at a forgetful angle and trousers haphazardly flapping at half-mast. Hulot is permanently at odds with the modern, mechanized world, and yet he himself could be an automaton run on clockwork, with his impossibly jaunty stride, his wind-up tennis serve and his mechanical method of doffing his hat to every woman he meets. Hulot appeared in nearly all Tati's subsequent films. In *Mon oncle* (*My Uncle*, 1958), however, he is just one of several central figures, with his relative's modernist house and its fiendishly inventive gadgets taking the starring role.

From this moment onwards, Tati's gags had the tendency to be as cold and clinical as the culture he was satirizing. His continuing obsession with modernity would be the end of him. To make *Playtime*

At odds with the world: Jacques Tati (right) is the human cartoon in *Monsieur Hulot's Holiday*.

(1967), he built his own miniature city, a glass and steel metropolis on the outskirts of Paris. Tati hoped that this vast set would become a film studio after the picture wrapped. Instead, the French government knocked it down to build a road. Unfortunately, the clown had put his own money into the project, signing over his entire back catalogue to a bank in return for a sizeable loan. When *Playtime* didn't return a profit, the films were sequestered and Tati declared himself bankrupt. Somehow, he found the finance to make *Traffic* (1971), a hit-and-miss road movie in which Hulot drives a gizmo-laden camper van from Paris to an automobile show in Amsterdam. It was to be his last significant feature film, but there was a happy ending (of sorts) for Tati: he lived long enough to see his back catalogue bought from the bank by a movie company and re-released to rapturous and rightful acclaim. LH

Monsieur Hulot's Holiday (Les vacances de Monsieur Hulot) 1953, 114 min, b/w
cast Jacques Tati, Nathalie Pascaud, Michèle Rolla, Louis Perrault, André Dubois *cin* Jacques Mercanton, Jean Mousselle *m* Alain Romans

Hulot is the eye of a comedy hurricane in a French seaside resort, resulting in a series of immaculately timed sight gags, running jokes and social observations. Ever a perfectionist, Tati carried on tinkering with this comedy years after it was releaded, even inserting a clever pastiche of *Jaws* in 1978.

Mon oncle (My Uncle) 1958, 110 min
cast Jacques Tati, Jean-Pierre Zola, Adrienne Servantie, Alain Bécourt, Lucien Fregis *cin* Jean Bourgoin *m* Alain Romans, Franck Barcellini

Mon oncle consists of a series of sketches connected only by Hulot's (occasionally peripheral) presence and loosely sutured to the theme of sterile modernity versus untamed nature. The star attraction is the minimalist home with its suburban pretensions and labour-saving devices, the product of Tati's talent for delirious invention. The result is ingenious, if not hilarious; which is not to say that the film is not the work of a visionary, questing genius. Just a genius it's hard to warm to.

Playtime 1967, 126 min
cast Jacques Tati, Barbara Dennek, Rita Maiden, Jacqueline Lecomte, Valérie Camille *cin* Jean Badal, Andréas Winding *m* Francis Lemarque

Steely grey modernism is, once again, the target of Tati's piquant satire: the 1960s desire to pen everybody in the same minimalist box, be it in an airport, hotel, restaurant or home. The observations about call-centre architecture are depressingly more relevant than ever. And the ingenious soundtrack is classic Tati, a silly symphony of amplified effects and muffled dialogue.

Bertrand Tavernier
France, 1941–

A critic and press agent before he became a filmmaker (he worked for producer Georges de Beauregard before going freelance), Bertrand Tavernier enjoyed a front-row seat during the height of the *nouvelle vague*, and rubbed shoulders with such giants as Howard Hawks, John Ford and Michael Powell on their French press tours. He is one of the most active advocates for cine-literacy in France, and is the co-author of the classic text *50 ans de cinéma américain*.

Despite his background, as a filmmaker Tavernier found that he inclined to the older school of classical French cinema – exemplified by his early collaboration with screenwriters Pierre Bost and Jean Aurenche (who had been disparaged by François Truffaut as examplars of the despised "cinéma du papa"), an association which continued long after both men died. (Tavernier filmed Bost's novel *A Sunday In The Country* in 1984, and Aurenche is a significant character in 2002's *Laissez-passer*.)

Although he directed a couple of shorts as contributions to portmanteau features as early as 1964, it wasn't until ten years later that he made his feature debut, *The Watchmaker Of St Paul*, a smart, well-crafted Simenon adaptation starring Philippe Noiret and set in Tavernier's native Lyon. He's made very nearly a film a year ever since, refuting categorization by hopping from realist contemporary dramas to nostalgic period pieces, a cop thriller, a swashbuckler, a couple of war films, documentaries on subjects ranging from Parisian housing projects, Mississippi culture, and the Algerian War, and even a prescient slice of science fantasy, *Deathwatch* (1980).

If this eclecticism signals some restlessness, Tavernier brings to almost everything intellectual curiosity, passionate conviction, and authorial restraint. He very rarely shows his hand with the camera, yet his subtle widescreen compositions eloquently position his protagonists in a wider social and historical context. His essential humanism did not preclude plunging into the dark misanthropic universe of *noir* novelist Jim Thompson for the disturbingly funny *Clean Slate* (1981).

If quality French drama is itself a known brand on the international arthouse circuit, a genus in which *A Sunday In The Country*, *Round Midnight* (1986) and *These Foolish Things* (1990) all fit quite happily, Tavernier began to kick against that with 1992's police procedural *L.627*, a project inspired by his own son Nils' drug problems, and shot in the breathless hand-held documentary style that would soon become fashionable again. *The Bait* (1995), which won the Golden Bear at the Berlin Film Festival, and *It All Starts Today* (1999) were further attempts to refocus urgent attention on pressing social issues. It might be noted in passing that Tavernier's efforts to stay *au courant* do not immunize him from charges of sexism (although it is also true he has collaborated regularly with his ex-wife, the screenwriter Colo Tavernier). TC

Clean Slate (Coup de torchon) 1981, 128 min

cast Philippe Noiret, Isabelle Huppert, Jean-Pierre Marielle, Stéphane Audran, Eddy Mitchell *cin* Pierre William Glenn *m* Philippe Sarde

Cinema's boldest, and best, adaptation from the hard-boiled pulp fiction of Jim Thompson. Tavernier transplanted *Pop.1280* from the American West to French colonial Senegal in 1938. Noiret (in one of six films he made with the director) is a slobbish sheriff, a local joke and cuckold whose apparent impotence puts him above (or below) suspicion when he embarks on a disturbingly calm killing spree – wiping the slate clean, as he sees it. Scripted by Jean Aurenche.

A Sunday In The Country (Un dimanche à la campagne) 1984, 90 min

cast Sabine Azéma, Louis Ducreux, Michel Aumont, Genevieve Mnich, Monique Chaumette, Thomas Duval *cin* Bruno de Keyser *m* Gabriel Fauré

Based on Jean Bost's novel, *A Sunday In The Country* is a lovely, graceful mood piece about an elderly, faintly dissatisfied painter (Ducreux) welcoming his children and grandchildren home a few years before World War I. You can draw parallels between Bost (and even the director) and the artist – a classicist who faintly regrets having failed to join the avant-garde – though there aren't many roads Tavernier has not explored in his long and varied career.

Round Midnight (Autour de minuit) 1986, 133 min

cast Dexter Gordon, Francois Cluzet, Gabrielle Haker, Sandra Reeves Phillips, Lonette McKee, Herbie Hancock *cin* Bruno de Keyser *m* Herbie Hancock

Set in 1959 and loosely based on the relationship between Parisian jazz fan Francis Paudras and Bud Powell, this is one of the best films about jazz, and one of Tavernier's most popular works. Real-life saxophone legend Dexter Gordon is an extraordinary presence as the alcoholic bebop great, a towering, teetering bear-like figure who speaks in his slow, unpredictable rhythm but often with great charm and warmth. He cleans up for a while under his acolyte's devoted friendship, but for how long?

The Taviani Brothers

Vittorio Taviani: Italy, 1929–
Paolo Taviani: Italy, 1931–

Sons of a Tuscan lawyer who was persecuted by the Fascists, the Taviani brothers studied liberal arts at the University of Pisa and became interested in cinema after seeing Roberto Rossellini's neo-realist classic *Paisà* (1946). Although they began collaborating on documentaries in the 1950s and made a number of acclaimed features in the 1960s and early 70s – including *Under The Sign Of Scorpio* (1969), *St Michael Had A Rooster* (1972) and *Allonsanfan* (1974) – their international breakthrough came with the Palme d'Or winner *Padre Padrone* in 1977, a film emblematic of their utopian belief in change.

If their work has become less political over time, the Tavianis' methods and sensibilities have remained consistent over four decades. They alternate directing duties on a scene-by-scene basis. Their films are rooted in neo-realism and a peculiar Italian regionalism, but they are also fused with idiosyncratic experimental and fabulist elements, a Brechtian theatricality as close to Fellini as to Rossellini. Indeed, they are drawn to melancholy period pieces adapted from Tolstoy, Pirandello and Goethe. Key recurring themes in the Tavianis' work include tradition, patriarchy, the dignity of labour and the importance of memory and imagination.

Their most popular films include *The Night Of San Lorenzo* (1982), a magical bedtime story; the exquisite *Kaos* (1984), based on stories by Pirandello; *Good Morning, Babylon* (1987), their first English-language movie and a love song to silent cinema; *Night Sun* (1990), a tale of spiritual grappling adapted from Tolstoy, and *Fiorile* (1993), a sumptuous family saga set in Tuscany. In 2007, they released *La masseria delle allodole* (*The Lark Farm*), a family drama set during the Armenian genocide of 1915. TC

Padre Padrone 1977, 113 min

cast Fabrizio Forte, Omero Antonutti, Saverio Marconi, Marcella Michelangeli, Gavino Ledda *cin* Mario Masini *m* Egisto Macchi

The true story of Gavino Ledda, an illiterate Sardinian shepherd who grew up to become a professor of linguistics by way of military service. This Cannes prizewinner casts an unsentimental eye over the ignorance and poverty of rural life, exemplified by the hero's own autocratic father (the title translates as "Father Master"). Although the emotive soundtrack is sometimes clumsy, the Tavianis' primitivism is a conscious strategy that ultimately bears results.

Good Morning Babylon (Good morning Babilonia) 1987, 113 min

cast Vincent Spano, Joaquim De Almeida, Greta Scacchi, Desiree Becker, Charles Dance *cin* Giuseppe Lanci *m* Nicola Pionvani

This tale of two inseparable brothers is evidently one of the Tavianis' most personal films. Nicola (Vincent Spano) and Andrea (Joaquim De Almeida) are Tuscan stonemasons who come to America in search of work and wind up in Hollywood, creating the sets for D.W. Griffith's *Intolerance* (1916). This nostalgic fable turns sour before the end, but its rhapsodic vision of the early days of moviemaking is worth savouring.

André Téchiné

France, 1943–

André Téchiné is a widely respected French art-house director. A former critic with *Cahiers du cinéma* and a professor at the national film school IDHEC, Téchiné made his first feature *Paulina s'en va* (*Paulina Is Going*) in 1969. After working in television and theatre, Téchiné established a key theme with his 1975 film *Souvenirs d'en France* (*French Provincial*). Focusing on a family from the 1930s to the 1970s,

Téchiné explored the relationship between wider and personal histories. The film starred Jeanne Moreau, and the director's work has since been distinguished by affording fine actresses key roles.

In 1977, *Barocco* elicited critical plaudits for its elegant look, but Téchiné has often been criticized for his cold *mise en scène*, particularly in *The Brontë Sisters* (1979). By now a key director of the post-*nouvelle vague* generation, Téchiné won the best director prize at Cannes and the César for *Rendez-vous* (1985), a sexy *noir* melodrama replete with the seductive surfaces of the era. *The Scene Of The Crime* (1986), starring Catherine Deneuve, revolved around a young boy who encounters two escaped convicts. Deneuve also appeared in *Ma saison préférée* (My Favourite Season, 1993), which explored tensions between estrangement and natural affection as a family await the death of their elderly mother. In *Les voleurs* (Thieves, 1996), amid Téchiné's reconstruction of traditional thriller conventions, Deneuve played a philosophy professor who becomes sexually involved with a young working-class woman.

J'embrasse pas (I Don't Kiss, 1991) and the rite of passage drama *Wild Reeds* (1994) brought a sober eye to representations of homosexuality, the former being a not entirely successful tale of a young man's moral downfall as a rent boy in Paris. *Alice et Martin* (1998) depicted a powerful romance between two damaged people, and is one of Juliette Binoche's finest moments. *Strayed* (2001), which chronicled the fortunes of a family living in a deserted chateau after the fall of France in World War II, saw Téchiné teasing out the social and psychological consequences and coaching a superb performance from Emmanuelle Béart. Gérard Depardieu starred as an old flame who tracks Deneuve to an evocative Tangiers in *Changing Times* (2004), while Béart returned for *Les témoins* (The Witnesses, 2007), an AIDS drama set in 1980s Paris.

Few modern French directors balance individual feelings with the wider social picture with such emotional finesse and visual intelligence. RA

Wild Reeds (Les roseaux sauvages) 1994, 114 min

cast Frédéric Gorny, Gaël Morel, Elodie Bouchez, Stéphane Rideau, Michèle Moretti, Jacques Nolot *cin* Jeanne Lapoirie

Set in André Téchiné's native southwest during the closing events of the Algerian War in 1962, the film charts the shifting allegiances and passions of a class of students about to graduate. Featuring natural performances from Elodie Bouchez, Gaël Morel and Stéphane Rideau, and imbued with a Renoiresque feeling for the fleeting moment, this is one of the best French films about being young in an unhappy world.

Julien Temple
UK, 1953–

There haven't been many British directors who have taken such a sudden fall from critical grace as Julien Temple. The leap from *The Great Rock'n'Roll Swindle* (1979) to *Absolute Beginners* (1986) turned into one of the most spectacular belly flops in British film history. While the former was a vibrant and cocksure debut, the latter has come to symbolize everything that was hollow about 1980s excess and directorial hyperbole. The critical reception of the two set the pattern for the rest of Temple's career.

A graduate of Cambridge University and the National Film School who started out making pop videos, Temple found his niche with widely applauded documentaries, while his forays into fiction failed to register a positive blip on the critical radar. His second Sex Pistols documentary, *The Filth And Fury* (2000) acted as a corrective to *Swindle*, allowing John Lydon in particular to set the record straight. *Glastonbury* (2006) was a colossal and impressive enterprise, sculpting a documentary from thousands of hours of amateur, archive and professional footage from three decades of the music festival. Temple also co-directed the Amnesty International comedy and music compilation, *The Secret Policeman's Other Ball* (1982).

On the fiction side, Temple specializes in energetic, callow movies such as *Earth Girls Are Easy* (1988), a sci-fi musical comedy that screamed out to be a cult hit. But no one was listening. *Bullet* (1995) went straight to video. By making a biopic about director Jean Vigo (*Vigo: A Passion For Life*, 1997), music video director Temple was always going to suffer in comparison to his iconoclastic hero. Bristling with Temple's characteristic gusto, *Pandaemonium* (2000) reduced poets Coleridge and Wordsworth to artistic clichés in ill-fitting wigs, and *Joe Strummer: The Future Is Unwritten* (2007), about the lead singer of punk band The Clash, was a welcome return to home turf. LH

The Great Rock'n'Roll Swindle 1979, 104 min

with Malcolm McLaren, Sid Vicious, John Lydon, Steve Jones, Paul Cook, Ronald Biggs, Jess Conrad *cin* Adam Barker-Mill

Crowned by *Variety* as the *Citizen Kane* of rock'n'roll movies, this boisterous romp through the brief history of the Sex Pistols is suitably anarchic in form and exhausting in its insistent energy. Shot during the band's last year and compiled after their demise, it combines archive footage – their potty-mouthed, career-making appearance on Reg Grundy's TV show – with Sid Vicious's electrifying version of "My Way", Steve Jones palling up with Ronnie Biggs in Brazil and spoof ads for Sex Pistols products.

Hiroshi Teshigahara

Japan, 1927–2001

Unlike many of his contemporaries, Hiroshi Teshigara was anything but prolific – in a lengthy career he made fewer than ten features. However, his best work still resonates with unnerving power and dazzling invention. His early feature *Pitfall* (1962) was a satirical piece about an eerie town whose inhabitants are tainted by corruption, for which he devised a style he called "documentary fantasy" to capture the experimental existentialism of the screenplay. *Pitfall* paved the way for Teshigara's best-known film – the incomparable *Woman Of The Dunes* (1964) – which was awarded the Special Jury Prize at Cannes and received two Oscar nominations, including best director.

Teshigara continued with *The Face Of Another* (1966), an unsettling exploration of identity about a man who has a new, completely different face constructed for him after being burned in a laboratory fire. His altered behaviour – not always for the better – indicates his new appearance may be altering his personality. This was followed in 1968 by *The Ruined Map* which was filmed in colour and CinemaScope and was distinguished by the clever conceit of a private eye whose life starts to resemble that of the man he is hired to track down. Teshigara had a quiet 1970s, before returning with a documentary on the Spanish artist Antonio Gaudí in 1984. He then made two admired historical features: *Rikyu* (1989), about a sixteenth-century Buddhist tea master's calming influence on a firebrand warlord, and its sequel *Basarah – Princess Goh* (1992). NN

Woman Of The Dunes (Suna no onna) 1964, 123 min, b/w

cast Eiji Okada, Kyôko Kishida, Hiroko Ito, Koji Mitsui, Sen Yano, Kinzo Sekiguchi *cin* Hiroshi Segawa *m* Tôru Takemitsu

An unforgettable cinematic experience, *Woman Of The Dunes* is an ambiguous work, open to a myriad of interpretations. The film is one of unearthly power, telling the story of an entomologist trapped by villagers and forced to live with a woman in a house hemmed in by sand dunes unforgettably captured by Hiroshi Segawa's lens. It comes across like a bizarre nightmare, as the man tries to escape his strange prison while beginning a sexual relationship with the woman who is his captor, with the house, all the while, threatened by the daily advances of the sand.

Gerald Thomas

UK, 1920–93

Gerald Thomas's directorial career is dominated by the thirty phenomenally successful *Carry On* films. Although he directed several decent B-movies, including *Time Lock* (1957) with a young Sean Connery, it's for his comedy films that he is best remembered.

The *Carry On* series defined a particular brand of vulgar British comedy and created a troupe of fine character actors, among them Sid James, Barbara Windsor, Kenneth Williams, Charles Hawtrey, Hattie Jacques, Kenneth Connor and Joan Sims. Behind the scenes, the franchise boasted producer Peter Rogers, composer Eric Rogers and screenwriters Norman Hudis and Talbot Rothwell, who all contributed to the films' success.

After World War II, Thomas became an editor, before directing the children's film *Circus Friends* (1956). Two years later, *Carry On Sergeant*, about a squad of bumbling National Servicemen, became an unexpected success, despite the critics' sniffy response to its seaside postcard humour. *Carry On Nurse* (1959) was its quickly planned sequel, and soon the franchise was rivalled in popularity only by the Bond films. With more than a whiff of music hall about them, the *Carry On* films gleefully lampooned movie genres and British institutions, most enjoyably in *Cleo* (1964), *Screaming, Cowboy* (both 1966), *Up The Khyber* (1968) and *Matron* (1972). *Carry On At Your Convenience* (1971) hit one false note with its easy swipes at trade unions.

The gradual redundancy of sly innuendo in an increasingly permissive society made *Carry On Emmannuelle* (1977) a sad final gasp for the series, and Thomas began compiling clips for TV "specials". *The Second Victory* (1986) was a rare serious film, before an ill-conceived attempt to revive the *Carry On* corpse in the 1990s with *Columbus* (1992). With most of the iconic stars dead, *Columbus* used newer alternative comedians – including the master of modern innuendo, Julian Clary – but to no great effect. JR

Carry On Cleo 1964, 92 min

cast Sid James, Amanda Barrie, Kenneth Williams, Kenneth Connor, Joan Sims, Charles Hawtrey *cin* Alan Hume *m* Eric Rogers

The protracted saga of the Burton-Taylor epic *Cleopatra* (1963) was ripe for *Carry On* treatment, and the spoof has an unusually lavish look since Thomas was able to use sets from the original movie. The series regulars throw themselves wholeheartedly into the predictable melange of innuendo, lavatorial humour and squirm-inducing puns. The highest of the highlights is Kenneth Williams's rendition of Caesar's cry: "Infamy, infamy – they've all got it in for me!"

Ralph Thomas

UK, 1915–2001

The brother of *Carry On* director Gerald, the prolific Ralph Thomas covered a wider range of styles with varying success. After a variety of jobs in the industry, Thomas turned to directing with three so-so comedies at Gainsborough Studios, where he formed a lasting working relationship with Rank producer Betty E. Box. He upped his game in 1950 with the strange pursuit thriller *The Clouded Yellow*. Highlights of his mixed output include the first of six medical comedies, *Doctor In The House* (1954), and the solidly Dickensian *A Tale Of Two Cities* (1958). Dirk Bogarde starred in *Two Cities*, the first few *Doctor* comedies, and several of Thomas's other films, including the spy spoof *Hot Enough For June* (1963). The slightly saccharine *Conspiracy Of Hearts* (1960), in which a group of nuns save Jewish children from the Holocaust, contrasts with *No Love For Johnnie* (1961), a dark story of a cynical politician. It was Thomas's last good film, though none scraped the barrel quite as noisily as the execrable penis-transplant story *Percy* (1971) which, incredibly, sprouted a sequel. JR

The Clouded Yellow 1950, 95 min, b/w

cast Trevor Howard, Jean Simmons, Kenneth More, Barry Jones, Sonia Dresdel, André Morell *cin* Geoffrey Unsworth *m* Benjamin Frankel

Post-war British films often had a dark undertow, and this story of a spy who becomes a butterfly cataloguer after the war spirals into strange territory when he becomes mixed up in a murder. Trevor Howard is excellent in one of his characteristic troubled-man performances, while Jean Simmons' fragile heroine is the equal of her outing as Ophelia in Olivier's *Hamlet* (1948).

Richard Thorpe
US, 1896–1991

The work of the immensely prolific and famously efficient Richard Thorpe is almost devoid of personality. His technique was simply to shoot until something went wrong and then pick up with increasingly closer shots until everything was done.

In 1923, Thorpe started writing and directing, making dozens of low-budget Westerns, comedies and crime dramas, sometimes under the pseudonym Frank L. Inghram. His MGM films, if no more inspired, were more impressively staged; the incoherence of *Tarzan Escapes* (1936) is due to reshoots after preview audiences were revolted by the violence. In addition to his four Tarzan films, Thorpe directed four Esther Williams musicals, Elvis Presley's *Fun In Acapulco* (1963) and Hedy Lamarr's *White Cargo* (1942). A capable director of swashbucklers, he also filmed Robert Taylor, who was once a major MGM star, in *Ivanhoe* (1952) and *Quentin Durward* (1955), and completed a remake of the Ruritanian romance *The Prisoner Of Zenda* (1952) amongst his 128 features and six serials.

Thorpe's best work includes *The Thin Man Goes Home* (1944), the most comedic of the *Thin Man* series, and two Mario Lanza films: *The Great*

Caruso (1951) and *The Student Prince* (1954). The swashbuckling *Knights Of The Round Table* (1953) was MGM's first widescreen film, while 1957 saw him direct two contrasting musicals: *Ten Thousand Bedrooms*, which threatened to destroy Dean Martin's career, and *Jailhouse Rock*, a triumph for the young Elvis. Thorpe retired ten years later. JR

Jailhouse Rock 96 min, 1957, b/w

cast Elvis Presley, Judy Tyler, Vaughn Taylor, Dean Jones, Jennifer Holden, Mickey Shaughnessy *cin* Robert Bronner *m* Jeff Alexander, Lieber and Stoller

With a full hand of knockout songs, this is by far the best of Elvis's films. The sheer magnetic gusto of his hip-swivelling, nostril-flaring, thigh-trembling, sneering performance overcomes the ridiculousness of the story – after being imprisoned for murder, Elvis finds a guitar and rock stardom. Presley himself choreographed the iconic title song.

Tian Zhuangzhuang
China, 1952–

One of the leaders of the so-called Fifth Generation of Chinese filmmakers, Tian Zhuangzhuang nonetheless hasn't lit up world cinema as spectacularly as his contemporaries Zhang Yimou or Chen Kaige. But that's possibly due to a shortage of output, which wasn't entirely Tian's decision. While Zhang and Chen suffered from sporadic state interventions in their careers, they were at least allowed to make films. Tian was, in effect, banned for almost ten years after *The Blue Kite* (1992) became a global success. Tian was the son of two famous actors (his father was also chief of the Beijing Film Studios), yet his parents' prominent position didn't prevent him from being sent to the country for re-education during the cultural revolution.

Along with Zhang and Chen, Tian was one of the first students of the Beijing Film Academy when it opened for the first time in twelve years in 1978. And although they're lumped together under a generational banner, there are important stylistic differences between them. While his contemporaries demonstrated a dazzling eye for opulence and artifice, Tian quietly emphasized naturalism and ethnography with his semi-documentary reports on distant tribes: Inner Mongolia in *On Hunting Ground* (1984) and Tibet in the stunning *The Horse Thief* (1986). The latter, which mesmerized Western audiences, employed nonprofessional actors, and controversially depicted Buddhist practices outlawed by the authorities. It's been suggested that the director made his next four films as a penance to the state, and Tian has admitted in an interview that he made *Travelling Players* (1987), *Rock Kids* (1988), *Illegal Lives* (1990) and *The Last Eunuch* (1991) as a hired hand.

His next film, the extraordinary *The Blue Kite*, was a distinctly personal affair, and landed him in big trouble with the authorities. Detailing the disastrous effects of Mao's Great Leap Forward on a librarian's family from the perspective of their young son, the political and domestic panorama was banned. A rough cut was reportedly smuggled to a Dutch film company who put the final touches to the picture with the help of the director's notes. Then, as the film was being released around the world, Tian was himself blacklisted. As a result of the film's international success and a letter that Tian had signed calling for the release of political prisoners, he was banned from making films for a year, while laboratories and studios were officially barred from contact with the director. For the other nine of his missing years, he produced and mentored a new generation of filmmakers, and made a triumphant return with the asphyxiatingly intense and notably apolitical re-make of Fei Mu's 1948 classic, *Springtime In A Small Town* (2002). In 2004, he returned to the documentary form with a poignant survey of the isolated and endangered way of life on the Tibetan border in *Tea-Horse Road Series: Delamu* (2004). LH

Springtime In A Small Town (Xiao cheng zhi chun) 2002, 116 min

cast Jingfan Hu, Jun Wu, Bai Qing Xin, Xiao Keng Ye, Si Si Lu *cin* Pin Bing Lee *m* Li Zhao

A seriously ill man lives with his distant wife in a house whose crumbling façade is matched for decrepitude only by the state of their marriage; a cuckoo enters the threadbare nest in the form of his old friend, who also happens to be her ex-lover. The constantly moving camera is an adroit counterpoint to their still lives. Eschewing anything approaching a close-up, Tian keeps the audience at a literal distance from the characters in this small but perfectly formed chamber piece of silent yearning, stifled passions and aching regret.

Moufida Tlatli

Tunisia, 1947–

Search through the credits of some of the most important Arab films of the 1980s and 90s and chances are you'll find Moufida Tlatli's name featured prominently as editor. Tlatli spent the first two decades of her career cutting celluloid for the likes of Michel Khleifi, Férid Boughedir, Merzak Allouche and Abdellatif Ben Ammar. She transcended all of them, however, with her own rich and textured directorial debut, *The Silences Of The Palace* (1994). With its depiction of a beautiful servant girl growing up in the prince's palace towards the end of French colonial rule in Tunisia, the film established Tlatli as one of the Arab world's leading female filmmakers. Her second directorial effort, *The Season Of Men* (2000), was another masterful account of Arab women cossetted by living in a patriarchal society. AJa

The Silences Of The Palace (Samt el qusur) 1994, 128 min

cast Hend Sabri, Amel Hedhili, Najia Ouerghi, Ghalia Lacroix, Sami Bouajila, Kamel Fazaa *cin* Youssef Ben Youssef *m* Anouar Brahem

Tlatli's account of women living in a 1950s palace, where they are expected to clean, cook and indulge the sexual needs of its male inhabitants, is a vivid, impassioned look at the injustices meted out to Arab women. Moving from the present day to the last years of French colonialism in Tunisia via a series of flashbacks, *The Silences Of The Palace* justifiably brought Tlatli to international prominence and launched the career of the then 14-year-old Hend Sabri, who plays the young servant girl through whose eyes we witness court life.

Johnnie To

Hong Kong, 1955–

Johnnie To is the tortoise to John Woo's hare. While Woo brought a new wave of Hong Kong cinema to the eyes of the outside world and blazed brilliantly in Hollywood, his contemporary To remained loyal to the local film industry, and is only now getting recognition in the West. Part of the reason is that while Woo has mostly stuck to his guns with action movies and "heroic bloodshed", To has mixed and matched his genres throughout his career. Ever since his stuttering debut, the martial arts adventure *The Enigmatic Case* (1980), the director has dabbled in romances like *Love On A Diet* (2001), straight comedies such as *Eighth Happiness* (1988) and comedy horror stories like *My Left Eye Sees Ghosts* (2002). *Heroic Trio* (1993) was a delirious comic-book adventure starring three of Hong Kong's leading ladies: Michelle Yeoh, Maggie Cheung and Anita Mui. It brought him briefly to the attention of the West and in particular to director Oliver Assayas (who paid homage to To in 1996's *Irma Vep*).

However, it was only after he formed the Milkyway Image production company in 1996 that To was able to make personal projects, such as the series of films that reclaimed the "heroic bloodshed" territory originally staked out by Woo. In *Running Out Of Time* (1999) and *Fulltime Killer* (2001), To took a fistful of Triad clichés and successfully gave them a cynical, postmodern overhaul. And he's performed the same service on a series of action movies: *A Hero Never Dies* (1998) – a baroque, brutal, and convoluted tale of betrayal, sacrifice and amputation – and *The Mission* (1999), in which five bodyguards of a Triad leader bond in their quiet periods, only to discover that one of them is having dangerous liaisons with the boss's wife. The unusually realistic Triad movie *Election* (2005) cemented To's international reputation and led the prolific director straight to *Election 2* (2006). LH

Fulltime Killer (Chuen jik sat sau) 2001, 100 min

cast Andy Lau, Takashi Sorimachi, Simon Yam, Kelly Lin, Cherrie Ying, Lam Suet, Teddy Lin *cin* Cheng Siu-keung *m* Alex Khaskin, Guy Zerafa

Co-directed with regular scribe Wai Ka-fai, this is the Johnnie To model to a tee – part innovation, part derivation. Takashi Sorimachi is a haunted, alienated hit man who desperately regrets the lack of human warmth that his lonely profession necessitates. Andy Lau, a flash, leather-clad upstart killer, loves one thing more than the movies, and that's his job. A violent game of cat and mouse is played out on the streets of Hong Kong as Lau tries to oust Sorimachi from his position as Asia's number one assassin.

Election (Hak se wui) 2005, 100 min

cast Tony Leung Ka Fai, Simon Yam, Louis Koo, Nick Cheung, Lam Ka Tung, Cheung Siu Fai, Lam Suet *cin* Cheng Siu-keung *m* Lo Tayu

The election for the new chairman of the Wo Shing Triad turns into a bloody, internecine struggle for power between the two main candidates, Tony Leung Ka Fai's Big D and Simon Yam's Lok. Navigating a series of twists and turns, the narrative gradually reveals its gangster heroes – the so-called men of honour – to be little more than overgrown kids dealing in drugs, prostitution and industrial quantities of hypocrisy. A potent mixture of action and ethics.

James Toback

US, 1944–

"**M**ost movies", director, screenwriter and author James Toback has claimed, "are in the territory of evasion rather than expression." By contrast, this notorious gambler, ladies' man and sports fan's uneven but engaging films take his obsessions to full stretch. Toback's networking skills have stood him in good stead throughout: sent to interview American footballer and actor Jim Brown, he ended up living with the star and writing his biography. He wrote the script for *The Gambler* (1974), which starred James Caan, but it was not until his directorial debut, *Fingers* (1978), that Toback really made his name.

Fingers' meandering style – the movie is essentially a few days in the life of a pianist-cum-loan shark – is echoed in much of his later work. Yet although the amiably duff rom-com *The Pick-up Artist* (1987) enjoyed some box-office success, Toback produced little of note in the 1980s. The 1990s were more productive: after picking up an Oscar nomination for his script for Warren Beatty's *Bugsy* (1991), he directed the improvisational love-triangle drama *Two Girls And A Guy* (1997) and *Black And White* (1999). Featuring a sprawling cast including Elijah Wood, Mike Tyson, Claudia Schiffer, Brook Shields, Method Man and Toback regular Robert Downey Jr, *Black And White* explored issues of race and identity. Since then Toback has tackled fixed basketball games in *Harvard Man* (2001) and sexuality in *When Will I Be Loved* (2004). JS

Fingers 1978, 90 min

cast Harvey Keitel, Jim Brown, Tisa Farrow, Michael V. Gazzo, Tanya Roberts, Georgette Muir *cin* Michael Chapman

Torn between his desire to be a concert pianist and his father's Mob connections, Jimmy Angelilli (Harvey Keitel) prepares for an audition, has girl trouble and does his best to collect debts in an intense character study that has become a cult classic.

Ricky Tognazzi

Italy, 1955–

Declaring that "cinema should intervene in reality", Ricky Tognazzi is rightly celebrated for two films that brought to light the ugly sides of Italian society: football hooliganism and the Mafia. The son of Ugo Tognazzi (star of Edouard Molinaro's *La cage aux folles*, 1978), Ricky started his film career as an actor himself, making his screen debut at the age of 8 in the portmanteau *RoGoPaG* (1963). He acted alongside his father in Bernardo Bertolucci's *Tragedy Of A Ridiculous Man* (1981) and continues to appear in film and television productions.

Tognazzi made his directorial debut in 1989 with *Piccoli equivoci* (*Little Misunderstandings*). His next film, *Ultrà* (*Hooligans*, 1991), empathetically and controversially probed the mind-set of football hooligans. It shared the best director award at the Berlin Film Festival with Jonathan Demme's *The Silence Of The Lambs*. Alighting on an even more contentious issue, *La scorta* (*The Escort*, 1994) was one of three films released in just twelve months that tackled the issue of judges who risked their lives to bring the Mafia to justice (Margarethe von Trotta's *The Long Silence* and Alessandro Di Robilant's *Law Of Courage* being the other two).

In both these films, Tognazzi set up generic conventions only to upset them. As he explained in an interview: "We have to get away from the banal and offer people something real." The stark reality for Tognazzi is that these are his only feature films to have made much of a mark internationally. Outside Italy, little has been seen of *Vite strozzate* (*Strangled Lives*, 1996), *Canone inverso* (*Making Love*, 2000) and *Io no* (2003). Tognazzi returned to the subject of the Cosa Nostra and to the figure who inspired *La scorta*, the assassinated judge Giovanni Falcone, in a co-production with the American television company HBO called *Excellent Cadavers* (1999). Although a solid effort, it was not the return to form his fans had been hoping for. LH

Ultrà (Hooligans) 1991, 100 min

cast Claudio Amendola, Ricky Memphis, Gianmarco Tognazzi, Giupi Izzo, Alessandro Tiberi, Fabrizio Vidale *cin* Alessio Gelsini *m* Antonello Venditti

In an admirable commitment to realism, Ricky Tognazzi auditioned hundreds of real-life football hooligans and shot scenes during the 1990 World Cup in Italy to lend authentic-

T

ity to this supercharged tale of group dynamics amid Roma fans as they prepare for battle with the "ultras" of Juventus. Although the film is studded with predictably violent set pieces, Tognazzi's focus rests on the relationship between Claudio Amendola, the head of the hooligans, and his best friend Ricky Memphis, who appears to have robbed him of both his leadership and his girlfriend while he was in prison.

La scorta (The Escort) 1994, 96 min

cast Enrico Lo Verso, Claudio Amendola, Ricky Memphis, Carlo Cecchi, Leo Gullotta, Tony Serandeo *cin* Alessio Gelsini *m* Ennio Morricone

After his predecessor has been murdered, judge Carlo Cecchi arrives in Sicily and is at first wary of employing bodyguards. However, they soon form an unofficial team of investigators, and things start to go seriously awry when they discover corruption and Mafia collusion in their own justice department. Tognazzi masterfully racks up the tension with the simple yet effective ploy of keeping the Cosa Nostra off screen, as a constant unsettling presence, who only make themselves known, as they do in real life, through assassinations and car bombs.

Giuseppe Tornatore

Italy, 1956–

Often set on his native Sicily, Giuseppe Tornatore's films – which he often also scripts – are concerned with men finding their place in the world and are, depending on your outlook, either sentimental or gently nostalgic.

After some acting work in his teenage years, Tornatore became a photographer, then a television director before his first feature, the gangster thriller *Il camorrista* (*The Professor*, 1985). The semi-autobiographical hymn to movies *Cinema Paradiso* (1988) brought him international success. In the next year's *Everybody's Fine* a Sicilian pensioner (Marcello Mastroianni) travels around Italy visiting his children before returning home to report laconically that "Everybody's fine". The overworked thriller about amnesia *A Pure Formality* (1994) is mainly notable for performances by Gérard Depardieu and Roman Polanski. *The Legend Of 1900* (1998), a fantasy about a ship-bound jazz pianist, was an attempt on the international market but despite outstanding design and photography, Tim Roth's strong central performance and Ennio Morricone's beautiful score, it was a little too self-indulgently whimsical for many, and audiences preferred the smaller scale, gently erotic coming-of-age drama *Malèna* (2000). After a lull, Tornatore made *La sconosciuto* (*The Unknown Woman*, 2006), a critically acclaimed thriller about a Ukrainian immigrant nurse. JR

Cinema Paradiso (Nuova Cinema Paradiso) 1988, 124 min

cast Philippe Noiret, Salvatore Cascio, Jacques Perrin, Marco Leonardi, Agnese Nano, Leopoldo Trieste *cin* Blasco Giorato *m* Ennio Morricone

A famous film director returns to his Sicilian birthplace for the funeral of the local cinema projectionist and reminisces about his childhood friendship with the dead man. Balancing ambition with restraint, the film benefits from Morricone's lovely main theme, which has become a classic. The original 155-minute Italian release was a flop, but the shorter international version deservedly won the Oscar for best foreign-language film. The 1991 director's cut (175 minutes) fills out some plot lines but also adds padding.

Roberta Torre

Italy, 1962–

Comparatively few Italian directors have risked life and limb to tackle the subject of the Mafia. Only one, Roberta Torre, has made a musical about

The magic of the movies: Salvatore Cascio helps out projectionist Philippe Noiret in *Cinema Paradiso*.

them. A graduate of the Milan Film School, the director settled in Palermo, the capital of Sicily and the power base of the Cosa Nostra, in 1991 and has made films about the city ever since.

After completing a few documentaries, Torre based her first feature, *To Die For Tano* (1997) on the true story of gangster Tano Guarrasi. Despite the presence of nonprofessional actors, including a few mobsters, the result was about as far from the sober observations of neo-realism as it's possible to get. A high-kitsch musical, it garnered three awards at the Venice Film Festival. Torre continued in the same vein with *South Side Story* (2000), which relocated *Romeo And Juliet* from Verona to Palermo with a culture-clash musical about a Nigerian prostitute and a street singer. The director returned to the subject of organized crime with *Angela* (2001). LH

Angela 2001, 91min
cast Donatella Finocchiaro, Andrea Di Stefano, Mario Puella, Toni Gambino, Erasmo Lobello, Matteo Gulino *cin* Daniele Cipri *m* Andrea Guerra

Based on a true story from the 1980s, Roberta Torre zeroes in on a trophy wife who's little more than a drugs mule for her Mafiosi husband, who's running his narcotics operation from the family shoe shop. Donatella Finocchiaro courts serious danger when she embarks on a passionate affair with one of his foot soldiers, unaware that their trysts are the subject of police surveillance. With the exception of some surreal, studio-based driving sequences, Torre forsakes her usual self-conscious exuberance for an urgent, hand-held realism that also packs a powerful genre punch.

Jacques Tourneur
France, 1905–77

Son of film director Maurice Tourneur, Jacques Tourneur became the most illustrious graduate of Val Lewton's unit at RKO, where the producer and his team developed a new sub-genre of psychological horror film in the 1940s. A fragrant fog of implacable menace gathers in Tourneur's Lewton-era trilogy: *Cat People* (1942), *I Walked With A Zombie* (1942) and *The Leopard Man* (1943). The viewer is left free to conclude that these films' sinister events are products of either supernatural influences or overactive imaginations steeped in folklore and myth – or some self-fulfilling combination of the two.

The director seemed to be fascinated by strangers in strange lands, fugitives and newcomers adapting – often messily – to unfamiliar environments. Creating shadowy milieux partly to veil low-budget sets, Tourneur and cinematographer Nicholas Musuraca located their films' sense of foreboding in pure light and darkness. This was most memorable in *Cat People*'s scary swimming-pool scene: the water's reflections undulate on the surrounding walls while the room's amniotic echoes mingle and

blur with the slow growl of an unseen beast.

Tourneur and Musuraca teamed up again – this time without Lewton – for *Out Of The Past* (1947), starring Robert Mitchum as the fatalist narrator. A quintessential *noir*, the film is an intricate pile-up of connivance and betrayal, in which, as in Tourneur's horror films, the characters are haunted by ghosts of their own conception. Flashback-driven and choked with smoke ("Cigarette?" Kirk Douglas asks Mitchum; "Smoking", Mitchum replies, holding up his cig), *Out Of The Past* is endlessly fascinating in its convolutions and in the bizarre psychology of Mitchum's antihero. He seems to will his own destruction; you can hear it in his bedroom voice when Jane Greer asks if he believes her lies: "Baby, I don't care."

Tourneur worked across several genres during the 1940s and 50s, his credits including the Technicolor Western *Canyon Passage* (1946) and the post-war thriller *Berlin Express* (1948), which featured startling footage of the rubble-strewn German metropolis. *Nightfall* (1956) fruitfully revisited *Out Of The Past*'s flashback structure and hounded antihero, and *Night Of The Demon* (1957), like Tourneur's RKO horror films, pits reason against superstition, with Dana Andrews as a skeptical psychologist delving into a satanic cult. *Night Of The Demon* continued Tourneur's onscreen interest in occult ritual (best captured in the voodoo intrigues of *I Walked With A Zombie*) and plumbed the distinction that *Cat People*'s doomed Irena makes between "the mind and the soul". Unfortunately, the American producer (who retitled the film *Curse Of The Demon*) tacked on anticlimactic glimpses of the monster, though Tourneur's fans would have better appreciated the director's sense of nocturnal ambiguity. JW

Cat People 1942, 73 min, b/w
cast Simone Simon, Kent Smith, Tom Conway, Jane Randolph, Elizabeth Russell, Hack Holt, Alan Napier *cin* Nicholas Musuraca *m* Roy Webb

Irena (the perfectly feline Simone Simon) marries nice guy Oliver (Kent Smith) but refuses to consummate the union, believing herself to be the descendant of a Serbian race of "cat people". Sinuous and splendidly underlit, the first of producer Val Lewton's horror films is a mesmerizing Freudian psychodrama in which the return of the repressed is comprised of erotic desire, sexual jealousy and historical atrocity.

I Walked With A Zombie 1943, 68 min, b/w
cast Frances Dee, James Ellison, Tom Conway, Edith Barrett, Christine Gordon, Theresa Harris, Darby Jones *cin* J. Roy Hunt *m* Roy Webb

In Lewton and Tourneur's spin on *Jane Eyre*, sweet-souled nurse Betsy (Frances Dee) takes a job in the West Indies, where the indigenous voodoo-practising locals – and evidently a few of the Anglo transplants – believe that Betsy's semi-comatose charge, Jessica (Christine Gordon), is the walking dead. With its ghostly cinematography and hypnotic drumbeats forever in the distance, the movie blurs superstition and reality, faith and truth.

Out Of The Past (aka Build My Gallows High)
1947, 97 min, b/w

cast Robert Mitchum, Jane Greer, Kirk Douglas, Rhonda Fleming, Richard Webb, Steve Brodie, Virginia Huston *cin* Nicholas Musuraca *m* Roy Webb

After *femme fatale* Jane Greer shoots him and absconds with $40,000 of his money, suave gang boss Kirk Douglas hires near-somnambulant private eye Robert Mitchum to track her down in Acapulco – but Mitchum falls for her himself. Built upon Daniel Mainwaring's novel and sharp script (and further polished by hard-boiled maestro James M. Cain), this benchmark *noir* glints with diamond-hard dialogue, deadpan wit and existential mystery.

Robert Towne

US, 1934–

Robert Towne is one of Hollywood's most renowned screenwriters and script doctors, performing emergency surgery on dozens of movies, most famously Arthur Penn's *Bonnie And Clyde* (1967) and Francis Ford Coppola's *The Godfather* (1972). Starting as a writer for Roger Corman, he used television series such as *The Man From U.N.C.L.E.* as a training ground in the 1960s, and produced a stunning trio of film scripts in the mid-1970s: *The Last Detail* (1973), *Chinatown* (1974) and *Shampoo* (1975).

His films as a writer-director, however, simply cannot compete with his achievements as a scribe. Even though they all display Towne's rare ability to render three-dimensional characters, movies such as *Personal Best* (1982) – a faintly lewd tale of two young lesbian athletes – and *Tequila Sunrise* (1988) have met with mixed reviews.

Without Limits (1998) was widely trumpeted as a rare film about sporting failure (being a biopic of maverick runner Steve Prefontaine), but disappointingly the result was another American success story and an advert for Nike (Prefontaine's coach founded the sportswear company). Towne was replaced as the director of the *Chinatown* sequel *The Two Jakes* (1990) by Jack Nicholson, but recently returned to the milieu of 1930s California with *Ask The Dust* (2006). An adaptation of John Fante's cult novel and a personal project he'd been planning for over thirty years, the uneven results unfortunately didn't improve Towne's poor track record with critics. LH

Tequila Sunrise 1988, 115 min

cast Mel Gibson, Michelle Pfeiffer, Kurt Russell, Raul Julia, J.T. Walsh, Arliss Howard, Arye Gross, Gabriel Damon *cin* Conrad Hall *m* David Grusin

Robert Towne develops the triangular relationship between charismatic drug dealer Mel Gibson, persistent cop and old school friend Kurt Russell and ice queen Michelle Pfeiffer with rare precision. The nuances of character and themes of friendship and treachery are sketched in with the skill and attention to detail that have become Towne's trademarks.

Tran Anh Hung

Vietnam, 1962–

Three features in twelve years – including the Venice Golden Lion winner *Cyclo* (1995) – have made Tran Ang Hung Vietnam's most prominent filmmaker. He was born in Da Nang, but moved with his family to France at the age of 12, where he continues to live and work. Nevertheless, all three of his French-backed films have been set in his native land and in his native tongue.

The first of these, *The Scent Of Green Papaya* (1993) evocatively recreated a 1950s Saigon household in a Paris studio. His third feature, *At The Height Of Summer* (aka *The Vertical Ray Of The Sun*, 2000), evokes a similar sensuous, reflective mood for all that it charts the amorous misadventures of three sisters and their partners over a month. Languorous and painterly (ravishingly shot by Mark Ping-Bin Lee), the film finds harmony prevailing over discord.

Cyclo is the odd one out, a very violent, graphic immersion in the urban squalor of contemporary Ho Chi Minh City, although even here Tran's poetic transcendentalist eye ensures a very different kind of gangster movie, a fluid nightmare that has aptly been described as a Vietnamese *Taxi Driver*. TC

The Scent Of Green Papaya (L'odeur de la papaye verte) 1993, 104 min

cast Tran Nu Yên-Khê, Man San Lu, Thi Loc Truong, Anh Hoa Nguyen, Hoa Hoi Vuong *cin* Benoît Delhomme *m* Tôn Thât Tiêt

Mui (played as an adult by Tran's muse and wife, Tran Nu Yên-Khê) is inducted into domestic service for a bourgeois family as a 10-year-old peasant girl. Over the years, her chores (especially cooking rice and papaya for the family) become more than servitude; they assume a spiritual dimension. That Tran allows us to intuit this through simple observation and sensual, evocative camerawork (including gliding travelling shots and delicate macro close-ups) is indicative of his subtle, refined aesthetic.

Cyclo (Xich lo) 1995, 129 min

cast Le Van Loc, Tran Nu Yên-Khê, Tony Leung, Nguyen Nhu Quynh *cin* Benoît Delhomme *m* Tôn Thât Tiêt

Starting with a premise indebted to Vittorio De Sica's *Bicycle Thieves* (1948), this sensational anti-thriller immerses us in the urban squalor of Ho Chi Minh City. Tony Leung's gangster Poet is the pivotal figure who draws both a dispossessed pedicab driver and his sister down into a fetid, feverish underworld. More overtly than Tran's other films, this is a political as well as existential vision, a fluid, violent nightmare about poverty and neglect.

At The Height Of Summer (A la verticale de l'été) 2000, 112 min

cast Tran Nu Yên-Khê, Nhu Quynh Nguyen, Le Khanh, Quang Hai Ngo, Chu Hung, Manh Cuoung Tran *cin* Mark Ping-Bin Lee *m* Tôn Thât Tiêt

Lou Reed's "Pale Blue Eyes" ushers in this beautiful, humid, decidedly tranquil film about three Vietnamese sisters and their relationships. Set over a thirty-day period between anniversaries honouring their mother and their father, the

559

drama touches on adulteries, pregnancy, and even a hint of incestuous desire. Yet Tran defuses these melodramatic elements to focus on a more subtle intimacy: "I wanted my film to feel like a caress", he said. "It had to have a gentle smile floating through it."

Lars von Trier

Denmark, 1956–

A natural provocateur, Lars Trier added the "von" to his name at the age of 20, less as a homage to Stroheim or Sternberg than as an act of effrontery and mischief; this reportedly deeply neurotic, phobic individual is also a daring exhibitionist. This propensity for pushing his ego to the fore has made von Trier a controversial figure, but also, with Pedro Almodóvar and Emir Kusturica, one of the three most acclaimed European filmmakers of his generation. He is certainly the most famous Danish director since Carl Theodor Dreyer. Though their sensibilities are very different, Dreyer's influence has been important – indeed, in 1988 von Trier filmed Dreyer's adaptation of *Medea* for television.

That the young von Trier was raised by his communist mother to make decisions for himself may go some way to explain his fondness for setting himself artistic parameters. These are by no means limited to the "Vows of Chastity" he developed with Thomas Vinterberg to form the basis of the Dogme 95 Manifesto. In his so-called "America Trilogy", which to date only consists of *Dogville* (2003) and *Manderlay* (2005), von Trier dispensed with all but the most rudimentary *mise en scène*, filming his actors on a sparsely decorated soundstage. Kick-starting the 2003 essay film *The Five Obstructions*, he challenged his old film school lecturer, director Jørgen Leth, to remake a short subject in five specific idioms. And in *The Boss Of It All* (2006) he invented something he called "Automavision": a camera that randomly selects its own frame from eight pre-programmed variants.

All this is a far cry from von Trier's earlier work. *The Element Of Crime* (1984) was a baroque artifice, a labyrinthine neo-*noir* with Wellesian camera angles, long, flowing takes and a hypnotic voiceover. Similarly, *Europa* (1991; known as *Zentropa* in the US) used a barrage of expressionist optical effects – back projection, colour and monochrome within the same frame – to create a weird, claustrophobic nightmare vision of Germany in the aftermath of World War II. Both films won technical awards at the Cannes Film Festival, and von Trier was also named best director for the latter. Zentropa, the name of the German railway company in *Europa*, became the name of the production company he formed with Peter Aalbaek Jensen.

The most dramatic shift came through the brilliant TV series *The Kingdom* (1994), a hospital soap opera with a surreal Lynchian twist. Abandoning the meticulously planned visual frames of his first features, *The Kingdom* embraced a hand-held camera and jump cuts to create a *vérité* feel. (It was influenced, von Trier said, by the first season of the ground-breaking Barry Levinson TV cop show *Homicide*.)

This aesthetic volte-face was formalized by the Dogme Manifesto in 1995, which espoused a puritanical back-to-basics ethos that, among other strictures, banned genre filmmaking and post-production artifice. The next feature, *Breaking The Waves* (1996), wasn't strictly a Dogme project, but in many ways it anticipated the naturalistic look and melodramatic flavour of future Dogme productions, albeit on a grander scale. For the first time in von Trier's cinema characters and emotions seemed as important as style and technique.

The powerful story of an innocent bride brought up in a strict religious community on the Isle of Skye, it was also the first of von Trier's controversial "Golden Heart" films, in which a purely good heroine is subjected to the vicissitudes of a cruel fate. This schema (which also applies to 1998's *The Idiots*, 2000's *Dancer In The Dark* and to some extent also to *Dogville* and *Manderlay*) has attracted predictable criticism on the grounds of misogyny, though it can also be read as the reverse: von Trier's female identification figure is in open revolt against a repressive patriarchal regime.

The international success of *Breaking The Waves* included an Oscar nomination for actress Emily Watson and the Grand Jury Prize at Cannes. The

Nicole Kidman faces up to a cruel fate in von Trier's sparse *Dogville*.

The Dogme connection

Lars von Trier concocted the idea of Dogme with his younger colleague Thomas Vinterberg in March 1995. It turned out to be hugely influential and surprisingly far-reaching, catching the imagination of young filmmakers all over the world. Both as a brand and as an artistic ethos, Dogme 95 became the cornerstone for the success of von Trier's company Zentropa and helped launch several Danish filmmakers on the international stage, including Vinterberg himself, Susanne Bier, Søren Kragh-Jacobsen and Kristian Levring.

The Dogme Manifesto started a little misleadingly, with a denunciation of auteurism and a call for collectivism. It was von Trier's intention to get a new New Wave rolling, so the movement had to be bigger than any individual, and von Trier was at the time by far the best-known Danish filmmaker. Then the manifesto really got down to brass tacks: "Today a technological storm is raging, the result of which will be the ultimate democratization of cinema." This was a reference to the impact of digital video, which was just beginning to make itself felt. Framed against the centenary of cinema, Dogme was a pre-emptive strike claiming the potential of that technological revolution to revitalize cinema. The problem, according to the Dogme brethren, was that the medium had become inherently decadent: "The movie has been cosmeticized to death ... the 'supreme' task of the decadent filmmakers is to fool the audience." What the Dogme Manifesto proposed was a back-to-basics corrective, by denying filmmakers the technological tricks and dramaturgical crutches which had put a wall between mainstream cinema and the real world. The means to this end was a "Vow of Chastity" in the form of ten rules:

1. Shooting must be done on location. Props and sets must not be brought in.
2. The sound must never be produced apart from the images, or vice versa.
3. The camera must be hand-held.
4. The film must be in colour. Special lighting is not acceptable.
5. Optical work and filters are forbidden.
6. The film must not contain superficial action. (Murders, weapons, etc must not occur.)
7. Temporal and geographical alienation are forbidden. (That is to say that the film takes place in the here and now.)
8. Genre movies are not acceptable.
9. The film format must be Academy 35mm.
10. The director must not be credited.

Most if not all of the Dogme-certified films broke at least one or two of these rules – the last one more than any. But the general thrust was clear, and indeed common to many oppositional movements in the history of cinema: neo-realism, Free Cinema, *cinéma vérité* and the *nouvelle vague* all emphasized, to varying degrees and extents, that to retain its validity cinema must return to the real.

The first two Dogme films, Vinterberg's *Festen* (*The Celebration*) and von Trier's *The Idiots*, both premiered in the main competition at Cannes in May 1998. They provoked considerable debate and Vinterberg's film won the Jury Prize. Kragh-Jacobsen's *Mifune* (1999) and Levring's *The King Is Alive* (2000) followed shortly afterwards, and soon there were films being made under the Dogme banner in South Korea, Argentina, France, Spain and the US. There have now been more than two hundred.

Yet none have matched the impact of the first dozen Dogme films, and none of the founding Dogme brethren have made more than one film in that idiom. Vinterberg's next was *It's All About Love* (2003), which might have been conceived as Dogme's polar opposite. But the point had been made. Dogme put Danish cinema back on the map, but more importantly, it paved the way for the widespread acceptance of the low-budget, hand-held aesthetic that digital video made available to all. TC

subsequent Palme d'Or for the experimental musical *Dancer In The Dark* and the astonishing success of the Dogme brand propelled von Trier to the forefront of European cinema, though he remains a *bête noir* for many Anglo-American critics.

Is he an arch manipulator and a charlatan? Von Trier has certainly been guilty of the first charge, but his probing, deterministic view of man's inhumanity to man has an appropriate moral severity,

and his bold, experimental aesthetic impulses are undoubtedly a shot in the arm for the European art film tradition. TC

Breaking The Waves 1996, 159 min

cast Emily Watson, Stellan Skarsgård, Katrin Cartlidge, Jean-Marc Barr, Adrian Rawlins *cin* Robby Müller *m* Joachim Holbek, David Bowie (songs)

Set in a remote Calvinist community in northwest Scotland in the 1970s, this intense love story is like a sexually explicit Carl

Dreyer film: innocent Bess (Watson, extraordinary) marries oil rigger Jan (Skarsgård). When he is paralysed in an accident he begs Bess to find sexual satisfaction elsewhere, and she does so, believing it to be God's will. Shot in CinemaScope but with a constantly moving hand-held camera and disorienting jump cuts, *Breaking The Waves* offers a strange but potent mixture of naturalism, melodrama and metaphysics.

The Idiots 1998, 117 min

cast Bodil Jørgensen, Jens Albinus, Anne Louise Hassing, Troels Lyby, Nikolaj Lie Kaas *cin* Casper Holm, Jesper Jargil, Kristoffer Nyholm, Lars von Trier

Von Trier's only official Dogme film is a disturbing story about a group of middle-class dropouts "spassing out" – that is, acting as if they are mentally retarded. This tasteless extended prank functions as some form of regression therapy and provocative performance art. It's bitingly funny in places, irritatingly juvenile in others – part of the film's interest lies in figuring out those lines to your own satisfaction. It's also a raw metaphor for the madness of moviemaking, with Albinus as the group's dislikeable leader an obvious analogue for the director.

Dogville 2003, 178 min

cast Nicole Kidman, Paul Bettany, James Caan, Patricia Clarkson, Ben Gazzara, Chloë Sevigny *cin* Anthony Dod Mantle *m* Antonio Vivaldi

A Brechtian morality tale about a gangster's daughter, Grace (Kidman), who seeks refuge in the tiny eponymous backwoods community. Shielded by Tom (Bettany), an earnest aspiring writer, she wins the support of the townspeople by pitching in with the chores, but this apparent Eden shows a different face when the going gets tough, and the locals exact an ever-higher price for their hospitality. Filmed on a large, empty soundstage and narrated with jovial irony by John Hurt, this is adventurous, innovative filmmaking, a devastating, determinist fable about sin, transgression and punishment.

Rose Troche
US, 1964–

In the mid-1990s *Go Fish* looked as though it would kick-start a lesbian feature cinema. After studying film, photography and industrial design at the University of Illinois, Rose Troche co-wrote this lesbian lifestyle comedy with Guinevere Turner, who also starred. In 1994 it made history by becoming the first film to be signed for distribution during the Sundance Film Festival, initiating the frenetic deal-making that would characterize the US indie scene for the rest of the decade. Becoming a hit with lesbian and straight arthouse audiences, it led to *Bedrooms And Hallways* (1998), a sexual roundelay set in London's bedsit-land and starring Jennifer Ehle. Less conspicuously than in Troche's 1994 film, *Bedrooms And Hallways* set out to revise mainstream presumptions and prejudices about sex and gender.

But after all the talk of Troche and Turner kindling a new women's cinema, Troche's subsequent work, including *The Safety Of Objects* (2001) – a bland relationship drama starring Glenn Close and Dermot Mulroney – has found limited distribution. Paying

her way with television – *The L Word*, *Six Feet Under* – Troche remains another of those US indie directors who is seldom seen but never forgotten. RA

Go Fish 1994, 83 min, b/w

cast V.S. Brodie, Guinevere Turner, T. Wendy McMillan, Migdalia Melendez, *cin* Ann T. Rossetti *m* Brendan Dolan, Jennifer Sharp, Scott Aldrich

This grainy-toned film emerged out of the lesbian video avant-garde, and is one of the most refreshing and vital debuts of the 1990s. Upbeat, sexy and romantic, it begins where coming-out dramas have traditionally ended, following the fortunes of Guinevere Turner, a feisty *femme fatale* and aspirant writer, as she searches for love.

Fernando Trueba
Spain, 1955–

Accepting the Oscar for best foreign-language film for *Belle époque* in 1992, dedicated film buff Fernando Trueba said: "I would like to believe in God in order to thank him. But I only believe in Billy Wilder, so… thank you Mr Wilder." A former film critic for *El país*, Trueba made his first feature film at the age of 24. *Opera prima* (*First Work*, 1980) was a sexy youth comedy that, along with the films of Fernando Colomo, helped launch the *comedia madrileña* style. Such films were both contemporary and irreverent, and marked a complete break from the Franco era.

Much more conventional than his contemporary Pedro Almodóvar, Trueba's work is nonetheless similarly obsessed with sex, albeit from a more patriarchal vantage point, as he demonstrated in the popular hit, *Sé infiel y no mires con qiuén* (*Be Wanton and Tread No Shame*, 1986). He was also keen to diversify and tried his hand at a dark psychological thriller with *The Mad Monkey* (1990), his first English-language film. The results were decidedly mixed and he returned to sex comedies, hitting the sweet spot with his next picture, *Belle époque*.

Hollywood beckoned, by way of Antonio Banderas and Donald Westlake's screwball comedy *Two Much* (1995) – a misfire that sent Trueba straight back to Spain, where he remains a powerful industry figure. In recent years he has dedicated himself to a series of music documentaries exploring Latin jazz, flamenco and Brazilian pop. TC

Belle époque 1992, 109 min

cast Jorge Sanz, Fernando Fernán Gómez, Maribel Verdú, Ariadna Gil, Penélope Cruz *cin* Joe Luis Alcaine *m* Antoine Duhamel

In 1931, an ageing artist, Manolo (Gómez), shelters a young deserter from the royalist army (Sanz) – a handsome lad who is welcomed with open arms by each of the old man's four daughters. Despite the conventional farce structure, this romantic, wistful comedy does tweak assumptions just enough to amuse, even if the character of Manolo as a complacent anarchist with nothing much to rebel against does seem a little unconvincing.

François Truffaut

France, 1932–84

The result of an unwanted pregnancy, François Truffaut's early life of delinquency and criminality would be faithfully and vividly charted in his feature debut *The 400 Blows* (1959). He never knew his real father and was virtually adopted by the pioneering writer on film André Bazin, who transformed the film-loving truant into a notoriously acerbic critic for *Cahiers du cinéma*. It was in that journal that he attacked the overly literal and literate "tradition of quality" that had stagnated the post-war French film industry and outlined "la politique des auteurs" (or auteur theory) which controversially asserted that directors were the authors of their own work, even artists formerly regarded as B-movie hacks. Many of Truffaut's reviews for *Cahiers* established a new pantheon of auteur-directors in which Jean Vigo, Jean Renoir, Alfred Hitchcock, Howard Hawks and Nicholas Ray loomed large.

In addition to putting his ideas into practice in *The 400 Blows*, Truffaut also became the driving force behind the emerging *nouvelle vague*, writing the story for Jean-Luc Godard's *A bout de souffle* (1959) and producing Jacques Rivette's *Paris nous appartient* (*Paris Is Ours*, 1960). The success of *The 400 Blows* (for which he won the best director prize at Cannes) led to international recognition and to one of the most unusual director-actor relationships in the history of cinema. Truffaut became a mentor to the film's young star in exactly the same way that Bazin had been *his* surrogate father. Jean-Pierre Léaud would dress in Truffaut's old clothes and star in many of his movies, most significantly reprising the character of Antoine Doinel (the protagonist of *The 400 Blows*). Following the "Antoine and Colette" episode in the portmanteau picture *Love At Twenty* (1962), Antoine was revisited in *Stolen Kisses* (1968), *Bed And Board* (1970) and *Love On The Run* (1979). Indeed, this unique bond between director and alter ego was so strong that Léaud reportedly suffered a breakdown within days of Truffaut's death in 1984.

As a director, Truffaut was highly influenced by both Jean Renoir and Alfred Hitchcock. The impact of the latter was most obvious in pulpy, idiosyncratic neo-*noirs* such as *Shoot The Pianist* (1960), *The Bride Wore Black* (1967) and *Confidentially Yours* (1983). Renoir's open-hearted, fair-minded humanism, on the other hand, left its mark on *Jules et Jim* (1962), *The Wild Child* (1970) and *The Last Metro* (1980). The divisions are not schematic, however, *La peau douce* (*The Soft Skin*, 1964), for instance, is cut, framed and scored like Hitchcock, but is full of the humanistic foibles of Renoir.

While Truffaut's entire oeuvre is a mix and match of generic conventions and naturalistic observations, a common bond unites a collection that ranges eclectically from sci-fi (*Fahrenheit 451*, 1966) to costume melodramas (*The Story Of Adéle H*, 1975). Even though *The 400 Blows*, *The Wild Child* and *Small Change* (1976) are his only films about children, most of Truffaut's male characters have never left tumescent adolescence, diverting their youthful energies and naïve single-mindedness into an obsessive, one-eyed pursuit of sex. The title of Truffaut's 1977 comedy *The Man Who Loved Women* applied not only to the over-sexed director himself but to almost all his hapless avatars. For example, in a forlorn bid to woo the unresponsive object of his affection, Jean-Pierre Léaud moves into a hotel across from her apartment in "Antoine et Colette", while in *Mississippi Mermaid* (1969), Jean-Paul Belmondo falls hopelessly in love with Catherine Deneuve, the con artist who stole his money and attempted to poison him. Truffaut's women are strong-willed, placed on a pedestal and have a catalytic, often cataclysmic, effect on their male counterparts. The result is that *l'amour* is never less than *fou*. Whether it is Doinel's troubled love life, the unhappy threesomes in *Jules et Jim* and *Anne And Muriel* (1971), or Gérard Depardieu's self-destructive adultery in *The Woman Next Door* (1981), a Truffaut film rarely ends happily.

As he showed in *Day For Night* (1973), the Oscar-winning paean to the joys and frustrations of filmmaking, Truffaut never lost his love of cinema. However, as his career progressed – and he took acting roles in such Hollywood blockbusters as Spielberg's *Close Encounters Of The Third Kind* (1977) – he was accused by some (notably Jean-Luc Godard) of lapsing into the kind of script-led, polished commercialism that he had once lambasted. Yet Truffaut was always a committed cineaste, who remained, up to his death from a brain tumour at just 52, totally at ease with the revolutionary filmic language he had helped create. His critical reputation may have slipped slightly in some quarters, but the magnitude of his achievements as both theorist and auteur should not be underestimated. LH

The 400 Blows (Les quatre cents coups) 1959, 100 min, b/w

cast Jean-Pierre Léaud, Claire Maurier, Albert Rémy, Guy Decomble, Patrick Auffay, Georges Flamant *cin* Henri Dacaë *m* Jean Constantin

The 400 Blows bristles with spontaneity and *nouvelle vague* energy. The autobiographical resonances are easy to spot in the story of 13-year-old Antoine Doinel. Faced with a distracted mother and hostile teachers, he finds sanctuary in the cinema and the novels of Balzac. Drifting into truancy and petty theft, he's placed in a home for juvenile delinquents, and it's from here that he runs away, along the beach and into film history. The poignant freeze-frame

Cahiers du cinéma and the nouvelle vague

The term *nouvelle vague* (or New Wave) was coined by French journalists to describe a disparate group of young filmmakers who, in the mid- to late-1950s, seemed intent on overturning the conventions of French cinema and replacing it with a freer, more radical approach. The key figures were identified as François Truffaut, Jean-Luc Godard, Jacques Rivette, Eric Rohmer and Claude Chabrol, all of whom began as critics for the film magazine *Cahiers du cinéma* under the fatherly eye of theorist André Bazin. It was in the pages of *Cahiers* that Truffaut's influential essay, "A Certain Tendency Of French Cinema", first appeared in January 1954. It ridiculed the "tradition of quality", evident in films by the likes of Claude Autant-Lara and Jean Dellanoy, in which the script was paramount and the emphasis was on psychological realism and tasteful, artistic production values. Truffaut also invoked Alexandre Astruc's 1948 article, "Le camera stylo", which had encouraged filmmakers to use the camera as an author would use a pen to impart a personal signature upon their work. The so-called *politique des auteurs* became a central concept of the *Cahiers* critics and, in turn, of the *nouvelle vague*, and led them to create their own – hotly disputed – pantheon of significant auteur-directors. This included respected figures, such as Jean Renoir and Alfred Hitchcock, as well as directors widely seen as journeymen or hacks in the US, such as Samuel Fuller, Edgar G. Ulmer and Frank Tashlin.

The first of the *Cahiers* critics to complete a feature film was Chabrol with *Le beau Serge* (1958), followed the next year by Truffaut and his autobiographical *The 400 Blows* (*Les quatre cent coups*). Both films focused on the trials and tribulations of youth, were largely filmed on location, and had a rough-hewn freshness that was in part due to the cinematography of Henri Decaë who, along with Raoul Coutard, was the cameraman of choice for several *nouvelle vague* classics. Rohmer's downbeat account of an American in Paris, *Le signe du lion* (1959), came next, followed by Rivette's *Paris nous appartient* (1960). But the film that, for many, most completely epitomizes the *nouvelle vague* style is Godard's *A bout de souffle* (*Breathless*, 1959), which was based on a story by Truffaut. The film's most startling feature was the jump cut, whereby part of a scene was cut from the middle of a take, so that the action on screen suddenly jumped forward, or a shot would abruptly cut to a close-up. The result was a restless, nervous energy that added a spontaneous, improvised quality to the narrative. *A bout de souffle* is also deliberately conscious of American culture – popular and otherwise. The antihero is an existential hoodlum who reads William Faulkner and is obsessed with the screen style of Humphrey Bogart.

While the *nouvelle vague* filmmakers were certainly radical in terms of stylistic innovation, their films lacked much of a political dimension, preferring instead to pay tribute to the conventions of Hollywood B-movies – as in *Shoot The Pianist* (1960), Truffaut's melancholy *film noir*. An increasingly political edge did emerge in Godard's work in the mid-1960s, by which time most of his fellow *nouvelle vague* auteurs were beginning to be subsumed into the cinematic mainstream. Chabrol continued fashioning ever more sophisticated variations on Hitchcockian themes, Rohmer refined his tales of intellectual and sexual misunderstandings and Truffaut continued to pore over the longings and inadequacies of the troubled male psyche. Only Rivette and Godard have maintained any real commitment to experimentation and the reinvention of cinematic language. RB

as he looks directly and uncertainly into the camera is one of the most celebrated parting shots in the cinematic canon.

Shoot The Pianist (Tirez sur le pianiste) 1960, 81 min, b/w

cast Charles Aznavour, Marie Dubois, Nicole Berger, Michèle Mercier, Albert Rémy, Claude Mansard *cin* Raoul Coutard *m* Georges Delerue

In typical *nouvelle vague* fashion, this is more of a playful, urgent essay on (rather than faithful adaptation of) David Goodis's pulp novel *Down There*. However, it is by some degrees less self-conscious and iconoclastic than Jean-Luc Godard's wholesale deconstruction of the gangster genre in *A bout de souffle*. Truffaut's film is more conventional, enjoyable and respectful in its devotion to American cinema than the work of his Marxist colleague. That said, zesty invention, jump cuts and in-jokes cram this *noir*-ish tale of a pianist (Charles Aznavour) who gets caught up in the underworld thanks to his lowlife brother.

Jules et Jim 1961, 106 min, b/w

cast Jeanne Moreau, Oskar Werner, Henri Serre, Marie Dubois, Vanna Urbino, Sabine Haudepin *cin* Raoul Coutard *m* Georges Delerue

Of all Truffaut's films about mad love, this is the most emotionally irresistible. In the intoxicating form of the impetuous free spirit played by the magnificent Jeanne Moreau, it rejoices in one of the most capricious and vivid of all the headstrong women who have populated the director's oeuvre. Oskar Werner and Henri Serre both fall for her freewheeling but elusive charms. Only Werner gets to marry her, but when this inevitably goes wrong, they invite Serre to join them in one of the most celebrated *ménages à trois* in cinema history.

Anne And Muriel (Deux anglaises et le continent) 1971, 132 min

cast Jean-Pierre Léaud, Kika Markham, Stacey Tendeter, Sylvia Marriott, Marie Mansart, Philippe Léotard *cin* Néstor Almendros *m* Georges Delerue

This gentle period piece bridges the gap between Truffaut's wild youth and stolid maturity. It's based on a novel about a troubled threesome by author Henri-Pierre Roché (who also wrote *Jules et Jim*). While the narrator is a typical Truffaut character – clipped, dispassionate, omniscient – the level of mad invention is reduced to a few trademark iris shots, where the screen is reduced to the size of a pin-hole. That said, there are familiar pleasures in the jerky, puppet-like charms of Jean-Pierre Léaud, who becomes the object of stifled affection for the two sisters of the title.

Day For Night (La nuit américaine) 1973, 116 min

cast Jacqueline Bisset, Valentina Cortese, Dani, Alexandra Stewart, Jean-Pierre Aumont, Jean Champion *cin* Pierre-William Glenn *m* Georges Delerue

All of the director's films were, in some way, about the processes of cinema, but surprisingly this is the only Truffaut film to be explicitly about the production of a movie. Among the rich tapestry of characters, themes and sub-plots, Truffaut himself plays the director, while Jean-Pierre Léaud is reassuringly lovelorn as the star infatuated by leading lady Jacqueline Bisset. The winner of the Academy Award for best foreign film, the finely calibrated light comedy leads to inevitable tragedy.

The Last Metro (Le dernier métro) 1980, 131 min

cast Catherine Deneuve, Gérard Depardieu, Jean Poiret, Heinz Bennent, Andréa Ferréol *cin* Néstor Almendros *m* Georges Delerue

This was a personal project for Truffaut, in which he recreated the Paris he knew under the Nazi Occupation. Catherine Deneuve has to run her Jewish husband's theatre while he is hiding in the cellar. The arrival of charismatic, womanizing actor Gérard Depardieu represents a different kind of threat altogether. Although immaculately filmed and researched, it's hard not to agree with critics who said that at the end of his life Truffaut was making exactly the same kind of "quality" movies that he railed against three decades earlier.

Douglas Trumbull

US, 1942–

A visionary scientist and an unlucky filmmaker, Douglas Trumbull was brought from animating science films for NASA to supervise visual effects on Stanley Kubrick's *2001: A Space Odyssey* (1968). One of the core team of four special effects supervisors, Trumbull oversaw the climactic stargate sequence, and shortly afterwards was installed as director in his own right on *Silent Running* (1971). The film was a box-office flop, and though he turned down the opportunity to contribute to *Star Wars* (1977) he returned to special effects work on *Close Encounters Of The Third Kind* (1977), *Star Trek: The Motion Picture* (1979) and *Blade Runner* (1982).

Trumbull's only other feature, *Brainstorm* (1983) was marred by the accidental death of Natalie Wood during the shoot, and was only completed after the insurers backed the filmmaker against his own studio. The movie's intriguing premise posited a machine capable of recording and playing back emotional stimulation – an idea which resurfaced thirteen years later in Kathryn Bigelow's *Strange Days*. It is a theme that Trumbull continues to work through in his career outside feature films, as he explores the potential of immersive media in theme park virtual-reality rides and his patented large-format, sixty frames-per-second Showscan process. TC

Silent Running 1971, 89 min

cast Bruce Dern, Cliff Potts, Ron Rifkin, Jesse Vint *cin* Charles F. Wheeler *m* Peter Schickele

This memorable, atypical sci-fi film features Bruce Dern as a constant gardener, lovingly tending his greenhouses in space, all that remains of the earth's ecology. Three drones, Huey, Louie and Dewey, are his only companions. Though there is little dialogue, the script boasts three notable credits: Michael Cimino and Deric Washburn (*The Deer Hunter*) and Steven Bochco (TV's *Hill Street Blues*). Pointedly set in 2001, it's a gentle, affecting piece of work.

Tsai Ming-Liang

Malaysia, 1957–

Alongside Edward Yang and Hou Hsiao-Hsien, Tsai Ming-Liang has propelled Taiwanese film to the front ranks of arthouse cinema with his self-contained plot-averse brand of auteurist filmmaking. All of his films inhabit a world of contemporary urban angst and disconnection. They are not easy on the viewer – but they are not meant to be – and their moods can be hard to pin down. And although renowned for their difficult and sometimes harrowing subjects and slow fly-on-the wall pacing (often unpunctuated by dialogue), some of Tsai's films have included musical numbers and been characterized as "sweet", rather than miserablist.

Growing up in the small Malaysian town of Kuching, Tsai became familiar with East Asian and Hollywood films before moving to Taipei to study film and drama. Among the directors he encountered there were Robert Bresson, Michelangelo Antonioni and François Truffaut, and he has been compared to them all. Tsai's first feature, *Rebels Of The Neon God* (1993), introduced the main elements of his universe: ubiquitous water, cramped decaying apartments, thwarted or nonexistent communication and Taiwanese youth drifting along on a tide of unsatisfying hedonism. Water, in particular, is a key trope, indicating both an absence of companionship and a psychologically toxic environment. In *Vive l'amour* (1994), the director eavesdropped on three lonely singles; in his best, but grimmest, film, *The River* (1997), a nuclear family slowly disintegrates; and in *The Hole* (1998), strangers struggle to connect. Sexually uncertain but curious, Tsai's characters often reflect the homosexual themes that took a more direct form in his television documentary on AIDS, *My New Friends* (1995).

By the turn of the century, Tsai had accumulated an international following, as well as a core of regular actors that included Lee Kang-Sheng and Yang Kuei-Mei. *What Time Is It There?* (2001), a muted fable on grief, included a homage to Truffaut, with scenes set in Paris and a wordless cameo from Jean-Pierre Léaud. Despite demonstrating a lighter touch, Tsai's films were now also showing signs of diminishing artistic returns, as evident in *Goodbye Dragon Inn* (2003) and the watermelon-strewn *The Wayward Cloud* (2005). The latter also surprised some reviewers with its decidedly unerotic, but full-on, porn industry scenes. *I Don't Want To Sleep Alone* (2006) – which could stand as a general motif for Tsai's world of unrequited lovers – took his mix of urban ennui to Kuala Lumpur (and upset the Malaysian government which threatened to ban it). Tsai's work manages to elicit wildly contrasting responses, from utterly disengaged to ecstatic. RC

The River (Heliu) 1997, 124 min
cast Lee Kang-Sheng, Miao Tien, Lu Hsaio-Ling, Chen Chaorong, Chen Siang-Chyi *cin* Liao Peng-Jung

A father, mother and son who can't relate to each other have to deal with the son's mysterious neck pain (brought on by the waters of the polluted Tanshui river) and a leaking ceiling that won't abate in what is perhaps Tsai's finest film. Although absorbing, *The River* is the director's bleakest Taipei tale, but also the most attentive to plot – and it includes a remarkable denouement. It won the Special Jury Prize at the Berlin Film Festival.

The Hole (Dong) 1998, 95 min
cast Yang Kuei-Mei, Lee Kang-Sheng, Miao Tien, Tong Hsiang-Chu *cin* Liao Peng-Jung

After a mass exodus from Taipei, a man and a woman living separately in a crumbling apartment block decide to remain, and are forced to acknowledge each other's presence through a hole left in the floor by a plumber, while it, of course, rains constantly. Fantasy song-and-dance sequences liven up this lonely dystopian scenario and help to create a mordantly witty allegory that even offers some hope amid Tsai's customary drenchings.

Tsui Hark
Vietnam, 1950–

A pivotal figure on the Hong Kong movie scene since the early 1980s, Tsui (pronounced "Choy") Hark is the most suc-

cessful of the region's New Wave filmmakers, a prolific director and producer with more than fifty credits to his name. An inventive recycler with a flair for colourful spectacle, Tsui has re-energized traditional Chinese popular forms, and produced blockbuster hits in almost every local genre.

Born in Vietnam, Tsui lived in Hong Kong for three years from the age of 14, then studied filmmaking in Austin, Texas. Returning to Hong Kong, he became a director at the influential TV station TVB alongside future New Wave figures like Ann Hui, Ringo Lam, Patrick Tam and Yim Ho.

Beginning with *The Butterfly Murders* in 1979, Tsui's first three features were political allegories dressed up with dazzling imagery and pulpy scenarios. Critics were impressed, but each movie flopped. In 1983, *Zu: Warriors From The Magic Mountain* was another commercial failure, but in tricking out traditional Chinese myth with comically extravagant, eye-popping special effects, the film more or less invented what would become a staple Hong Kong genre. That genre's biggest hit, Tony Ching's *A Chinese Ghost Story* (1987) was a Tsui production. So was John Woo's equally influential gangster drama *A Better Tomorrow* (1986), which spawned two sequels and myriad imitators in what fans dubbed the "heroic bloodshed" film.

Former martial arts champion Jet Li as hero Wong Fei Hung displays his extraordinary athleticism in *Once Upon A Time In China*.

Famously hands-on as a producer at his Film Workshop company, to the point of alienating director John Woo on *A Better Tomorrow* and replacing the esteemed King Hu on *Swordsman* (1990), Tsui can claim solo credit for the hit Cantonese musical comedies *Shanghai Blues* (1984) and *Peking Opera Blues* (1986), as well as the martial arts epic *Once Upon A Time In China* (1991), which made Jet Li a star.

Tsui wasn't immune to the problems of the Hong Kong film industry in the early 1990s, and like John Woo he tried his hand in Hollywood with the assistance of action star Jean-Claude Van Damme, but neither *Double Team* (1997) nor *Knock Off* (1998) mustered a script worthy of his imagination. Tsui's recent work is consistent with the early films' interest in traditional Chinese mythology, identities in flux, and pure visual storytelling, but there is also a suspicion that he has been profligate with his talent: his films are routinely scrappy and chaotic, rushing in several directions at once. TC

Once Upon A Time In China (Wong Fei Hung) 1991, 134 min

cast Jet Li, Biao Yuen, Rosamund Kwan, Jacky Cheung, Steve Tartalia *cin* Tung-Chuen Chan, Wilson Chan, David Chung *m* Romeo Diaz, James Wong

Resurrecting one of the most popular Chinese heroes, doctor/martial artist Wong Fei Hung, Tsui places him in Hong Kong in 1875, and pits him against pirates working with Western colonials (the British and the Americans are the bad guys here). For all its ambitious scope and acute sense of history, the movie is choppy and uneven, but the action sequences are extraordinary, in particular a fight scene in a warehouse full of ladders.

Shinya Tsukamoto
Japan, 1960–

Cult director Shinya Tsukamoto is the ultimate auteur: he writes, directs, designs, photographs, edits and most often stars in nightmare movies that stream like a series of convulsive psychotic episodes.

For Tsukamoto, alienation is above all visceral. His art is intense, aggressive, and gut-felt. Like novelist J.G. Ballard and the early films of David Cronenberg, his work is consumed with the collision between technology and the flesh. His breakthrough movie was the surreal 16mm underground classic *Tetsuo: The Iron Man* (1988), a key text for students of "body horror". *Tetsuo II: Body Hammer* (1992) was a bigger-budget, colour sequel/remake, though still in the shock-cut, dynamic fast-forward aesthetic that is his signature style.

In *Tokyo Fist* (1995) Shinya and his brother Koji hammered each other in what is probably cinema's most single-minded fight scene, and in *Bullet Ballet* (1998) a middle-class worm turns into a gun-fixated

revenge junkie after his girlfriend shoots herself and he's mugged by a gang of street punks.

The period thriller *Gemini* (1999) marked a change of pace, and a more developed narrative than usual, but with *A Snake Of June* (2002) Tsukamoto was back on his obsessive-compulsive beat, this time delving into the erotics of voyeurism and masturbation. TC

Tetsuo: The Iron Man 1988, 67 min, b/w

cast Tomoroh Taguchi, Kei Fujiwara, Nobu Kanaoku, Shinya Tsukamoto *cin* Shinya Tsukamoto, Kei Fujiwara *m* Chu Ishikawa

Although this 16mm monochrome underground film is not the most accessible Tsukamoto movie (*Tetsuo II: Body Hammer* is in some ways a better point of entry), it is an extraordinary debut and a clear statement of intent. A nightmarish fantasy about man fusing with machine, it runs out of narrative gas about halfway through, but there's no stopping the flow of disturbing and bizarre imagery that pours out of Tsukamoto's head. The obvious comparison is with David Lynch's *Eraserhead* (1976) – though Lynch didn't ram a thick metal bolt into his own thigh on camera.

Stanley Tucci
US, 1960–

If as an actor Stanley Tucci continues to intrigue, as a director he is in danger of becoming a one-hit wonder. His acting career goes back to *Prizzi's Honor* (1985) and includes memorable turns in films ranging from *The Pelican Brief* (1993) to *The Devil Wears Prada* (2006). In 1995 he impressed critics as the co-director (with Campbell Scott) of *Big Night*, a film with thespian delights as enticing as the aromas of Italian cuisine. Disappointingly, Tucci has not delivered since. *The Imposters* (1998), co-starring Oliver Platt and Tucci, contained entertaining moments involving the likes of Steve Buscemi and Lili Taylor, but its period screwball ocean-liner conceit sank. *Joe Gould's Secret* (2000) presented an intermittently keen portrait of a writer's life, along with a line-up that included Ian Holm, Patricia Clarkson and Steve Martin. RA

Big Night 1995, 109 min

cast Stanley Tucci, Tony Shalhoub, Minnie Driver, Ian Holm, Isabella Rossellini, Caroline Aaron, Marc Anthony *cin* Ken Kelsch *m* Gary DeMichele

Brothers Stanley Tucci and Tony Shalhoub are restaurateurs on the skids in 1950s New Jersey. While one sees the culinary art as a spiritual quest, the other wants material wealth. The big night in question revolves around the visit of a celebrity, whose patronage might save their establishment. With its long-take preparations and soft-focus theatricality, few food movies generate such a metaphysical flavour. This poem to gastronomy finds the supporting cast in top form.

T

567

Frank Tuttle
US, 1892–1963

Frank Tuttle is a classic example of a good jobbing Hollywood director, who could be relied upon to make films on time, within budget and to a consistently high standard. He was employed by Paramount for over twenty years and made over seventy films, but today is almost solely remembered for the film that launched the Alan Ladd–Veronica Lake partnership, *This Gun For Hire* (1942).

Involved in acting and directing while a student at Yale, Tuttle started out as a screenwriter at Jesse L. Lasky Productions (later Paramount) in 1921, moving on to direction the following year with *The Cradle Buster*, which he also wrote. He soon established a reputation for producing strong and lively material for Paramount's female stars, most notably Clara Bow, Bebe Daniels, Gloria Swanson and Louise Brooks. But he was extremely versatile, and he made the transition to sound with ease; *The Green Murder Case* (1929), for instance, was one of the best thrillers of the early talkie period. After making the successful comedy-musical *Roman Scandals* for Goldwyn in 1933, Tuttle resumed a partnership with Bing Crosby, directing him in five musicals, including one of his best, *Here Is My Heart* (1934). Other highlights of the period included a well-paced and stylish adaptation of Dashiel Hammett's *The Glass Key* (1935).

Summoned to appear before the House Un-American Activities Committee (HUAC) in 1947, Tuttle admitted to being a member of the Communist Party and his career hit the rocks. A brief sojourn in Europe resulted in an American-French co-production, *Gunman In The Streets* (1950), and in 1951 he was called to testify in front of HUAC again. Despite the fact that he named several fellow travellers, Tuttle's film career did not resume until the mid-1950s, when he made a handful of movies for Warner Bros, the best being the *noir* police procedural *A Cry In The Night*, starring Raymond Burr and Edmond O'Brien. RB

This Gun For Hire 1942, 80 min, b/w
cast Alan Ladd, Veronica Lake, Robert Preston, Laird Cregar, Tully Marshall *cin* John F. Seitz *m* David Buttolph

An unsmiling Alan Ladd is Phillip Raven, a near-psychotic hit man who loves only his cat. Double-crossed by the man who hired him, he falls in with singer Ellen Graham (Veronica Lake), who helps him evade the police, but is actually working undercover as a federal agent. While the film never quite lives up to its electrifying opening, Ladd's "angel of death" was the prototype for a number of cool assassins, culminating in Jean-Pierre Melville's open homage in *Le samouraï* (1967).

Tom Tykwer
Germany, 1965–

When *Run Lola Run* (1998) achieved critical and commercial success, it seemed like a shot of adrenaline for world cinema, a film that took on new forms and big themes.

Tom Tykwer had been honing his skills since the age of 11, when he started to experiment with his family's Super 8 camera. After his feature debut, the intense and award-winning psychodrama *Deadly Maria* (1993), the ex-cinema programmer produced a quartet of films that explored the same themes at varying speeds, at different lengths and with mixed results. *Wintersleepers* (1997) introduced audiences to his motifs: coincidence, blind chance and enduring love. In a brooding essay on identity, memory and the impact of choice, Tykwer traced the cause and unexpected effects that a car crash has on the lives of six people.

Run Lola Run parlayed those themes into a higher concept and a phenomenal global hit, the most commercially successful film in Germany since Wolfgang Petersen's *Das Boot* (1981). But *The Princess And The Warrior* (2000) seemed like a marathon to Lola's sprint, with the director putting his would-be lovers through a long and protracted series of contrivances and near-death experiences.

His next project was *Heaven* (2002), the first part of a trilogy which the Polish director Krzysztof Kieślowski was developing with Krzysztof Piesiewicz at the time of his death. It was another tale of lovers conjoined by outrageous fortune: a woman who tried to kill the drug dealer responsible for her husband's death and the sympathetic policeman who helps her escape from custody. Although the two directors share an interest in coincidence, Tykwer lacks Kieślowski's subtle approach to metaphor and the end result was uneven. Undeterred by the mixed reviews and public indifference, Tykwer embarked upon his second English-language feature. But *Perfume*, his 2006 adaptation of Patrick Süskind's novel, similarly divided critics and audiences. LH

Run Lola Run (Lola rennt) 1998, 80 min
cast Franka Potente, Moritz Bleibtreu, Herbert Knaup, Nina Petri, Armin Rohde *cin* Frank Griebe *m* Tom Tykwer, Johnny Klimek, Reinhold Heil

Franka Potente has only twenty minutes to get 100,000 Deutschmarks to a local gangster or her drug-dealing boyfriend will probably be killed. Video-game logic drives Tom Tykwer's breakneck narrative, so when the story ends, the scenario starts all over again. Potente becomes an arthouse Lara Croft, desperately charging through an urban obstacle course to complete her mission. Suffused with a kinetic energy, small changes and seemingly insignificant choices create a massive ripple effect in the three different versions of the same setup.

Liv Ullmann

Japan, 1938–

The Norwegian actress/writer/director Liv Ullmann is best known for starring in the films of Ingmar Bergman (with whom she has a daughter). The few films she has directed are firmly in the tradition of the European arthouse, grappling with morality in meditative, painterly and sensitively acted films reminiscent of Bergman and Carl Theodor Dreyer. Having directed the "Parting" episode in *Love* (1982), a portmanteau picture directed by six women, Ullmann made her feature debut in 1992 with the period drama *Sofie*, about a young woman's struggle for autonomy in nineteenth-century Denmark. In 1995 she followed the epic romance *Kristin Lavransdatter*, set in medieval Norway, with a one-minute contribution to *Lumière And Company*, a celebration of the centenary of cinema made by forty directors. Her next two films were both scripted by Bergman: *Private Confessions* (1996) centred on his parents' fractious marriage, while *Faithless* (2000) – her biggest success to date – was a melancholy study of divorce. JR

Faithless (Trolösa) 2000, 154 min
cast Lena Endre, Erland Josephson, Krister Hendriksson, Thomas Hanzon, Michelle Gylemo, Juni Dahr *cin* Jörgen Persson

A typically Bergmanesque story, combining autobiography with fiction, *Faithless* tells of a writer, called Bergman, who becomes engrossed in his own story about a woman's painful infidelity and custody battle. Long-time collaborators Josephson and Ullmann bring an appropriate intensity and poeticism to the morally complex tale.

Edgar G. Ulmer

Czech Republic (formerly Austro-Hungarian Empire), 1904–72

Some directors work on a shoestring; the prodigiously talented and resourceful Edgar G. Ulmer often had to settle for the lint from the laces. Some of Ulmer's films were shot in less than a week for next to nothing (it took four days and $8,000 to produce 1939's *Moon Over Harlem*). Yet, rather miraculously, he usually succeeded in putting a personal signature on movies made under extremely cramped conditions, in a wide variety of languages (Ukrainian, Yiddish, Spanish, Italian) and genres (science fiction, melodrama, crime, comedy, horror, musicals, historical epic).

A Jew raised in Vienna and educated by Jesuits, Ulmer studied both architecture and philosophy while working as an actor and set designer, which included a spell in the company of the great theatrical producer Max Reinhardt. He was a key player in interwar German cinema, serving as production designer on F.W. Murnau's *The Last Laugh* (1924) and as a set designer on Murnau's *Sunrise* (1927) and Fritz Lang's *Metropolis* (1927) and *M* (1931). He also joined forces with Robert Siodmak to co-direct *Menschen am Sonntag* (*People On Sunday*, 1929), a day-in-the-life portrait of Berlin that boasted a screenplay by Billy Wilder and Curt Siodmak.

In America, Ulmer directed arguably the best of Universal's 1930s horror films, *The Black Cat* (1934), a gothic frightener pairing Bela Lugosi and Boris Karloff. Shortly thereafter, he was blackballed after his affair with (and subsequent marriage to) Shirley Kassler, who was then wed to the nephew of Universal boss Carl Laemmle. However, Ulmer never stopped working. After moving to New York, he directed a timeless suite of Yiddish films, including the sublime Lithuanian pastoral *Green Fields* (1937) and the bittersweet, incandescent *The Light Ahead* (1939), about a star-crossed young shtetl couple.

Back on the fringes of Hollywood, Ulmer made in excess of one hundred low-budget films earning himself the title "King of Poverty Row". These ranged from *Bluebeard* (1944), with John Carradine as a nineteenth-century Parisian painter who kills his models, the *noir*-ish melodrama *The Strange Woman* (1946), with Hedy Lamarr as an unusually complicated and sympathetic *femme fatale* in 1820s Maine, to the bizarrely fog-bound sci-fi *The Man From Planet X* (1951). Ulmer's most revered work remains the benchmark *noir* film *Detour* (1945), a

Hollywood expressionism: a startled Dr Werdegast (Bela Lugosi) confronts his fears in *The Black Cat*.

no-budget, no-exit four-hander with a world-class case of the cold sweats. "Money – you know what that is, it's the stuff you never have enough of", laments the antihero in the hard-boiled voiceover, as if commenting on the film's financial outlay; but like so much of Ulmer's work, *Detour* makes a virtue of necessity. JW

The Black Cat (aka The House Of Doom)
1934, 66 min, b/w

cast Boris Karloff, Bela Lugosi, David Manners, Lucille Lund, Julie Bishop, Egon Brecher *cin* John J. Mescall *m* Heinz Roemheld

In this pre-eminent 1930s Universal horror film, recently released prisoner of war Bela Lugosi and a pair of American honeymooners brave the death-haunted environs of Boris Karloff's Hungarian fortress-cum-mansion, constructed on a bloody World War I battlefield. Startlingly dark and graphic for its time, Ulmer's sinuous filmic face-off brings the jagged angles, ghostly shadows and post-war nightmares of German expressionist cinema to Hollywood.

Detour 1945, 68 min, b/w

cast Tom Neal, Ann Savage, Claudia Drake, Edmund MacDonald, Tim Ryan, Esther Howard, Pat Gleason *cin* Benjamin Kline *m* Leo Erdody

All that hapless nightclub pianist Al (Tom Neal) wants is to get across America to his sweetheart in Hollywood. But after he accidentally causes a man's death, he gets entangled with witchy Vera (the fearsome, flinty-voiced Ann Savage), who knows his secret and uses it to blackmail him. Grimy and concise, and shot in six days under circumstances as threadbare as those of its hard-bitten characters, this cornerstone of American *noir* is as existentially bleak as Albert Camus' *The Stranger*.

Roger Vadim

France, 1928–2000

After the publication of his autobiography, *Bardot, Deneuve And Fonda: My Life With Three Of The Most Beautiful Women In The World*, Roger Vadim had the gall to complain that his work had been overshadowed by his lovers, and that people had forgotten what a good director he was.

Previously a stage actor, Vadim was working as an assistant for director Marc Allégret when he spotted the beautiful ingénue Brigitte Bardot. Married not long afterwards, he succeeded where other directors had failed and made his wife a global brand with *...And God Created Woman* (1956). By the time "Bardolatry" was an international epidemic in 1957, the pair were already divorced. Their professional partnership, however, lasted longer than their marriage: *The Night Heaven Fell* (1958), *Please, Not Now!* (1961) and *Warrior's Rest* (1962) all adhered to the same formula of tease and tedium.

From 1957 onwards, Vadim dedicated his time, in the words of Pauline Kael, to "turning each wife into a facsimile of the first". He showcased the talents of his lesser-known spouse, Annette Stroyberg, in a so-so modern update of *Dangerous Liaisons* (1959) and paraded Catherine Deneuve's unique combination of fire and ice in *Vice And Virtue* (1963). Jane Fonda's all-American coquettishness was on display in an anaemic version of *La ronde* (1964), *The Game Is Over* (1966) and *Barbarella* (1968), which represented the perky, high-kitsch zenith of their unlikely unison.

In 1971, Vadim made *Pretty Maids All In A Row*, a black comedy starring Rock Hudson as a football coach and part-time serial killer, which is for some critics the director's best film. After a disastrous attempt to revive the Bardot brand in *Don Juan 73* (1973), Vadim lost his powers both as a film and star maker. The old Svengali suffered an embarrassing failure trying to launch Cindy Pickett with 1980's *Night Game*. His working life came to an end with displeasing symmetry, with his final film being the in-name-only remake, *And God Created Woman* (1988), starring Rebecca De Mornay. LH

...And God Created Woman (Et Dieu... créa la femme) 1956, 95 min

cast Brigitte Bardot, Curt Jurgens, Jean-Louis Trintignant, Christian Marquand, Georges Poujouly *cin* Armand Thirard *m* Paul Misraki

Brigitte Bardot drives a small town mad with her coquettish ways and nude sunbathing, raising temperatures and flitting from one brother to another. Even though "BB" applies her trademark tinderbox mix of dangerous innocence and willing spectacle, Roger Vadim gives us surprisingly few close-ups, orchestrating most of the film in medium shots.

Barbarella 1968, 98 min

cast Jane Fonda, John Phillip Law, Anita Pallenberg, Milo O'Shea, Marcel Marceau, Claude Dauphin *cin* Claude Renoir *m* Bob Crewe, Charles Fox

Forty-first-century astronaut Jane Fonda is sent by the president of the Earth to track down Milo O'Shea who wants to destroy the world with his secret weapon. Although the plot in this set-bound, high-camp odyssey is merely a set of delirious contrivances to rob Fonda of her clothes, some grace notes are supplied by co-writer Terry Southern's mordant satire and winking dialogue.

Luis Valdez

US, 1940–

The pioneering playwright/filmmaker Luis Valdez, responsible for establishing "Chicano theatre", is most widely known for the musical biopic *La Bamba* – which, ironically, some have seen as Hollywoodizing the culture.

One of ten children born to migrant farm workers, Valdez became involved in agitational theatre in the 1960s. In addition to playwriting, he directed *Zoot Suit* (1981), based on his successful theatrical production about a miscarriage of justice in the 1940s. He transferred his play about Mexican history to the screen with *Corridos! Tales Of Passion And Revolution* (1987), and in 1991 modernized the nativity story for TV with *La Pastorela: The Shepherd's Play*. His 1994 movie version of the 1950s TV series *The Cisco Kid* made the lead (Jimmy

Smits) more respectable and less stereotyped than the original. JR

La Bamba 1987, 108 min
cast Lou Diamond Phillips, Esai Morales, Rosana de Soto, Elizabeth Peña, cin Adam Greenberg m Los Lobos, Carlos Santana, Miles Goodman

The story of the teenage Mexican-American rock'n'roll star Richie Valens, who was killed in the same plane crash as Buddy Holly, takes its title from one of his hits. It's a solid, enjoyable biopic, with a charismatic central performance from the young Lou Diamond Phillips and strong support from Esai Morales as his troubled brother. And the music is superb.

Jaco Van Dormael
Belgium, 1957–

A former clown, the talented Belgian filmmaker Jaco Van Dormael showed great promise with his first feature film, the acclaimed *Toto The Hero* (1991), a César and Caméra d'Or winner that he both wrote and directed. However, he garnered a more mixed reception five years later when he released *The Eighth Day* (1996), a European variation on Barry Levinson's *Rain Man* (1988), about the relationship between a stressed yuppie (Daniel Auteuil) and a man with Down's Syndrome (Pasquel Duquenne). One of the better films featuring a character with a disability, *The Eighth Day* begins rather like a Francis Veber comedy, before moving into melodrama territory. It was another decade before Van Dormael was able to announce that he would be making an ambitious and expensive English-language sci-fi picture. TC

Toto The Hero (Toto le héros) 1991, 91 min
cast Michel Bouquet, Jo De Backer, Thomas Godet, Mireille Perrier cin Walther van den Ende m Pierre Van Dormael

This dazzlingly inventive and intricate debut is the story of Thomas, an old man consumed by the notion that he was robbed of his birthright when nurses mixed him and another newborn up in a hospital emergency. Thomas grew up poor and unhappy, while his neighbour Alfred enjoyed a rich and happy life. Now nearing the end of the road, Thomas is set on murdering his usurper. Despite Thomas's bitterness, the movie is full of joyful, poetic and absurdist touches.

Melvin Van Peebles
US, 1932–

A prolific creative force, Melvin Van Peebles is a playwright, novelist, composer, actor and filmmaker. He is also a potent figure in the history of black American film.

He took "Van" into his name when he enrolled at the University of Amsterdam to study astronomy courtesy of the GI Bill (he already had a BA in English literature prior to his service in the US Air Force). In the 1950s he made several short films that came to the attention of Henri Langlois of the Cinémathèque Française. Langlois invited him to Paris, where he wrote three novels and made his first feature, *The Story Of A Three Day Pass* (1967), which centred on a black soldier's romance with a white French girl.

Van Peebles parlayed this into a contract with Columbia, who gave him a farce about a bigoted white businessman who wakes up one morning to find he's turned black. Shot in 22 days, *Watermelon Man* (1970) is an outrageous consciousness-raising comedy with some modish gimmicks. Van Peebles also contributed an exuberant score, nixed the studio ending ("it was all a bad dream!") and, crucially, realized the story's radical potential by persuading the studio to cast African-American comic Godfrey Cambridge, rather than Alan Arkin, in the lead.

The studio was sufficiently perturbed to cancel the director's three-picture deal. Undeterred, Van Peebles took his fee and invested it in the independent *Sweet Sweetback's Baadasssss Song* (1971), an underground film that became a box-office phenomenon – knocking Arthur Hiller's *Love Story* (1970) off the top of the chart, and, along with Gordon Park's *Shaft* (1971), starting the blaxploitation movie trend.

However, he couldn't repeat the trick. Writing and directing two Broadway musicals in two years, *Ain't Supposed To Die A Natural Death* (1971) and *Don't Play Us Cheap* (1973), Van Peebles found himself with consecutive Tony nominations for best musical book, and two commercial flops. He filmed the latter in 1973, but it received the most limited of releases (a Region 1 DVD snuck out in 2002 and has been well reviewed by the few who saw it).

Sadly Van Peebles wouldn't direct another film until the misbegotten *Identity Crisis* in 1989. It was written by his actor/director son, Mario, who also did much to rekindle interest in his father with *Baadasssss!* (2003), which dramatized the making of *Sweet Sweetback*. Father and son directed and acted in a film together, *Gang In Blue* (1996), about racism in the police force, but this was little seen. TC

Sweet Sweetback's Baadasssss Song 1971, 97 min
cast Melvin Van Peebles, Rhetta Hughes, John Amos, Simon Chuckster cin Robert Maxwell, Jose Garcia m Melvin Van Peebles

The most important independent feature film to emerge from the black consciousness ferment of the late 1960s and early 70s, *Sweet Sweetback* hits a radical groove and runs it down for nearly the film's entire 97 minutes. Long scenes of Sweetback (Van Peebles) running are mixed with bouts of explicit sex and clashes with the police. Psychedelic effects, split screens and an original Van Peebles score recorded by Earth, Wind and Fire add to the bitches' brew.

Gus Van Sant
US, 1952–

Directors often flip-flop between the demands of art and commerce, alternating personal projects with those that pay the bills. However, few of them have produced movies as violently and puzzlingly different as Gus Van Sant, prompting wry speculation in the press that there could, in fact, be two Gus Van Sants.

Van Sant's cinema is populated by hustlers, outsiders and beautiful, elegantly wasted losers. With an eye for male pulchritude, especially of the young, chiselled and dissolute variety, his movies are handsome paeans to lost boys. In the festival-winner *Mala Noche* (1985), made for just $25,000 dollars, Van Sant trained his lens on a store clerk who falls for a Mexican. He continued to make high art out of low life in *Drugstore Cowboy* (1989), which starred Matt Dillon as the leader of a group of junkies who rob pharmacies to feed their habits in the 1970s, and which brought Van Sant to mainstream attention.

He capitalized on that success with a more ambitious, left-field take on the same demimonde in *My Own Private Idaho* (1991). Van Sant followed this with the sort of ingratiatingly quirky, self-satisfied folly that filmmakers often concoct when success has gone to their head. His adaptation of Tom Robbins's cult novel *Even Cowgirls Get The Blues* (1993) got a big thumbs down from critics and audiences. The director's response was to make his first major studio project. *To Die For* (1995) poked cultivated, mordant fun at the culture of instant celebrity, as murderously ambitious weather girl Nicole Kidman corrals her teenage lover, Joaquin Phoenix, into killing her career-threatening husband.

In 1997, *Good Will Hunting* met with Oscar success and accusations of a mainstream sell-out. Heralded as a shot-by-shot simulacrum of Alfred Hitchcock's masterpiece, *Psycho* (1998) was only a ninety percent colour rendering of the original; its compromise left it somewhere between art installation and pointless Hollywood remake. Then, once again, Van Sant followed a critical and commercial disappointment by accepting the studio's shilling and directing *Finding Forrester* (2000). It proved to be the most cynical and glossy of all his commercial enterprises, a brazen attempt to repeat the *Good Will Hunting* formula with all the cloying elements of the original.

The director then produced three of his most experimental and defiantly uncommercial projects. Beginning with *Gerry* (2001), which tracked the movements of two friends lost in a desert, the director appropriated the languorously hypnotic real-time sequence shots of Béla Tarr. And like the Hungarian, he has allied these lazily hypnotic scenes with an apocalyptic prescience. This fluid mixture of anomie and mobility worked most successfully in *Elephant* (2003), in which the narrative tensions inherent in a prelude to a mass murder deftly supplied the necessary heft to balance the camera's inconsequential meanderings. Unfortunately, *Last Days* (2004), a languid survey of the final week of a rock star who bears an uncanny resemblance to Kurt Cobain, exhibited no such friction between form and content. Van Sant got the balance right with his next slow-motion picture, *Paranoid Park* (2007). Returning to *Elephant*'s milieu of disconnected youth, the director focused on an enigmatic skateboarder implicated in the death of a security guard.

If there is one thing that unites the two Van Sants, it is the pervasive sense of melancholic transience that is eloquently expressed in his trademark shots of clouds (in the perpetual motion of time-lapse photography), going nowhere fast. LH

My Own Private Idaho 1991, 104 min
cast River Phoenix, Keanu Reeves, James Russo, William Richert, Rodney Harvey, Chiara Caselli *cin* John Campbell, Eric Edwards *m* Bill Stafford

This near-masterpiece of impressionism has almost been overshadowed by the death of its star River Phoenix who overdosed a few years after its release. Phoenix immersed himself in the role of a white trash, narcoleptic hustler who buddies up with another rent boy (Keanu Reeves). While surreal intrusions stud the film, adeptly conveying the dazed subjectivity of its spaced-out protagonist, Van Sant is guilty of some overambition, and this almost groans under the weight of its own brilliance.

Good Will Hunting 1997, 126 min
cast Robin Williams, Matt Damon, Ben Affleck, Stellan Skarsgård, Minnie Driver, Casey Affleck, Cole Hauser *cin* Jean Yves Escoffier *m* Danny Elfman

Van Sant balances the demands of commercial and independent cinema with enviable dexterity in this Oscar-winning film. Matt Damon plays the janitor and reluctant mathematical genius, while Robin Williams is the psychologist who tries to get him in touch with his inner boffin. Their scenes together become a bit self-help and New Age, and they're the weakest part of a film that's much happier to hang out with the kids.

Elephant 2003, 81 min
cast Alex Frost, Eric Deulen, John Robinson, Elias McConnell, Jordan Taylor, Carrie Finklea, Nicole George *cin* Harris Savides

As we glide along with the artists, malcontents and bulimics on a typical school day, there's nothing to suggest that this is a prelude to a mass murder. Van Sant's roaming, non-judgemental camera doesn't even change its register when the killing starts. Many critics claimed that this Palme d'Or winner, inspired by the Columbine incident, offered no solutions or reasons for the massacre. In fact, Van Sant seems to point the finger at the usual suspects, with video games and the Internet playing a significant part in the killers' skewed view of the world. It's undoubtedly brilliant, but not quite as radical as it appears.

Agnès Varda
Belgium, 1928–

Agnès Varda has been dubbed the grandmother of the *nouvelle vague*. Her 1954 debut, *La pointe courte*, was an iconoclastic synthesis of ragged documentary and Bergmanesque fiction that ran counter to the French tradition of quality cinema, controversially using nonprofessional actors and real locations (as opposed to studio sets). But Varda had two strikes against her gaining full membership to the boys' club of the New Wave: her gender, and the fact that she was not a cinephile – she claimed to have only seen 20 to 25 films before she made her debut. Unlike Jean-Luc Godard and François Truffaut, she was more interested in life than movies.

She essayed a series of documentaries before her next feature, *Cleo From 5 to 7* (1961). Along with *Le bonheur* (*Happiness*, 1965), a visually sensuous exploration of a love triangle, it cemented Varda's reputation as one of the most important women directors in the history of cinema. Critic Amy Taubin, however, claims that "no one could ever make a case for Varda's consistency", pointing the finger at 1960s soufflés *Les créatures* (1966) and *Lions Love* (1969), and the feminist musical *One Sings, The Other Doesn't* (1977). Varda finally received universal acclaim with her masterpiece, *Vagabond* (1985), and with *Kung-Fu Master* (1987), a taboo-breaking study of a forty-something divorcee's affair with a 14-year-old boy, played by Varda's son Mathieu Demy. Her terminally ill husband, director Jacques Demy, was the subject of a poignant and ingenious 1991 tribute, *Jacquot de Nantes*, which was a fond collage of his life and movies.

The Gleaners And I (2000) was another documentary, a meditative, engrossing and meandering piece on the tradition of scavenging in France. Its subjects range from the nineteenth-century gleaners who picked up grain that had not been harvested, to a Michelin-starred chef who forages for fruit and herbs, and to the scavengers of Paris who rifle through the city's trash. Such was her attachment to these characters that Varda revisited them in 2002 for *The Gleaners And I: Two Years Later*. It's clear from the titles of these two documentaries that the director regards these treasure-hunters as her spiritual forebears. And her appropriation of form and content from essays, documentaries, paintings, life and occasionally movies to create her thought-provoking films does indeed make her one of cinema's great gleaners. LH

Cleo From 5 To 7 (Cléo de 5 à 7) 1961, 93 min, b/w and col
cast Corinne Marchand, Antoine Bourseiller, Dorothée Blanck, Dominique Davray, Michel Legrand *cin* Jean Rabier *m* Michel Legrand

Agnès Varda's hypnotic valentine to Paris is a rapturous, luminously photographed panorama of two hours in the life of a pampered young singer who wanders the streets as she waits for the results of a test for cancer. As Corinne Marchand meanders through the parks, cafés and shops, Varda demonstrates an exquisite photographer's eye for faces, buildings and the bustle of the city.

Vagabond (Sans toit ni loi) 1985, 106 min
cast Sandrine Bonnaire, Macha Méril, Yolande Moreau, Stéphane Freiss, Marthe Jarnais, Joël Fosse *cin* Patric Blossier *m* Joanna Bruzdowicz

Sandrine Bonnaire deservedly won a César for her role as a bloody-minded down-and-out woman found dead in a ditch one cold winter's morning. Her final days are reconstructed from the memories of the people who briefly encountered her. She is different things to different people, but above all she is a litmus test for their selfishness, an index of altruism. Featuring mostly nonprofessional actors, this film represents the epitome of Varda's deft ability to fuse naturalism with a photographer's eye for framing and colour.

Jacquot de Nantes 1991, 118 min, b/w and col
cast Philippe Maron, Edouard Joubeaud, Laurent Monnier, Brigitte de Villepoix *cin* Patrick Blossier, Agnès Godard *m* Joanna Bruzdowicz

Varda asked her husband Jacques Demy to write down his earliest memories when he was suffering from a terminal illness, and then transformed his recollections into a fine screenplay. The result is a perfect example of Varda's approach to cinema, as she deftly juxtaposes luminous reconstructions of Demy's childhood as a young cinephile in pre-war Nantes with scenes from his most famous films, including *The Umbrellas Of Cherbourg* (1964).

Ram Gopal Varma
India, 1962–

In a career spanning just 18 years the prolific Ram Gopal Varma has already chalked up 27 films as director and 42 as producer. The resulting output ranges from the dire to the brilliant. Much like Quentin Tarantino, Varma followed a stint working in a video store with a debut film that really made the industry sit up and take notice: *Shiva* (1989) was a violent, Telugu-language, campus-set Mafia tale. Crime is his forte, and he made several films in the genre before entering the world of Hindi films full time. Known for his off-kilter camera angles, under-lit spaces and maverick sensibilities, Varma never really joined the Bollywood mainstream, though he's worked with some of its top talent. He is best known for his Mumbai gangland epics *Satya* (1998), *Company* (2002) and *Sarkar* (2005). He has tried his hand at comedy with one notable success – *Rangeela* (1995) – and several times at horror, again with one success – *Bhoot* (2003). His production house, popularly known as the Factory, churns out films in Varma's favourite genres with new directors fashioned after his image. NR

Satya 1998, 170 min
cast J.D. Chakravarthi, Manoj Bajpai, Urmila Matondkar, Paresh Rawal *cin* Garard Hooper, Mazhar Kamran *m* Vishal Bharadwaj, Sandeep Chowta

Satya is an Everyman who arrives in the big bad city of Mumbai and falls in with the wrong crowd, ultimately landing up in jail. There, a gang boss takes a shine to him and, back outside, Satya becomes the city's premier fixer and hit man. His burgeoning love for the beautiful Vidya (Matondkar) must take a back seat. The film was a raw yet glamorized window into the Mumbai underworld and spawned many imitations – plenty of them from Varma's own production house.

Marcel Varnel
France, 1894–1947

French stage actor and director Marcel Varnel had a brief and unremarkable career in 1920s and early 1930s Hollywood. But, after moving to England, he carved a niche directing the most popular comic actors of the day: eight films with Will Hay; four with the Crazy Gang; three with Arthur Askey; and nine with George Formby. Among his best were Hay's *Oh, Mr Porter!* (1937) and Askey's *Band Waggon* (1940), but all these film were rumbustious affairs, often based on stage routines, and filled with a subversive mix of farcical chaos and verbal puns. Relying both on improvisation and sharp scripts, Varnel was able to keep the immediate energy of live comedy while showing an uncanny understanding of English humour. After World War II, his George Formby vehicles began to appear tired, and he returned to theatre directing before his untimely death in a motoring accident. Despite his immense success in Britain, he is almost completely unknown elsewhere. JR

Oh, Mr Porter! 1937, 85 min, b/w
cast Will Hay, Moore Marriott, Graham Moffatt, Sebastian Smith, Agnes Lauchlan *cin* Arthur Crabtree *m* Charles Williams

In Will Hay's best film a bumbling wheel-tapper is promoted beyond his ability to become stationmaster at a remote Irish halt. A set of improbable adventures with his incompetent stooges leads to them losing a train and encountering a band of IRA gunrunners. The delightful comedy and sly social and political commentary make this simultaneously a timeless pleasure and an insight into times past.

Francis Veber
France, 1937–

So many French films have been remade in America that several academic books have been dedicated to the subject. Francis Veber has the honour of having more films retooled by Hollywood than any other living French writer and director. Early in his directorial career, French critics compared him to Frank Capra, and he has continued to write most of his own screenplays. Six of his original scripts have been turned into uninspiring facsimiles, not including Billy Wilder's sad swansong *Buddy Buddy* (1981), which was based on Veber's stage play *Le contrat*. Something was definitely lost in translation when his debut, *Le jouet* (1976), was transformed into the shameful Richard Pryor vehicle *The Toy* (1982). Equally unfortunate was the Robin Williams-Billy Crystal film *Father's Day* (1997), a remake of Veber's 1983 film *Les compères*.

After directing four movies in France, Veber moved to America, believing that if Hollywood was going to remake his films, he should be the one to do it. He turned his 1986 film *Les fugitifs* into *Three Fugitives* (1989), but it met with little commercial success, as did *Out On A Limb* (1992), the first film for which he didn't write his own screenplay. Ironically, it was while he was living in America that Veber wrote his greatest French directorial success *Le dîner de cons* (1998). As both a play and a film, it brought him international attention. He followed it up with the equally scabrous, equally farcical, but not quite so successful *The Closet* (2001), in which executive Daniel Auteuil plays gay to avoid the sack. The irony is that neither of these films has been remade by Hollywood. Yet.

The odd couple crime caper *Tais-toi!* (*Shut Up!*, 2003), starring Gérard Depardieu and Jean Reno, and *La doublure* (*The Valet*, 2006), which fell back on Veber's stock comedy catalyst from *Le dîner de cons*, the character of François Pignon, look equally unlikely to be remade in the US, as they were both only partially successful. LH

Le dîner de cons (The Dinner Game) 1998, 80 min
cast Jacques Villeret, Thierry Lhermitte, Francis Huster, Alexandra Vandernoot, Daniel Prévost *cin* Luciano Tovoli *m* Vladimir Cosma

Each week Thierry Lhermitte and his smarmy friends organize a dinner, to which they invite unsuspecting dullards and let them expound on their boring obsessions. He brings accountant Jacques Villeret – who builds national monuments out of matchsticks – to the ritual humiliation, but his own world falls apart when his wife abruptly leaves him. Francis Veber conducts a masterclass in the art of farce, swiftly piling contrivance upon contrivance, until events spiral wildly and capriciously out of control.

Gore Verbinski
US, 1965–

An award-winning advertising director known best for the once-ubiquitous "Budweiser frogs", Gore Verbinski parlayed his success into a job at the DreamWorks studio. There he helmed palatable commercial fare such as the sweet if strenuous children's farce *Mouse Hunt* (1997) and the violent screwball comedy *The Mexican* (2001), which circumvented the lack of chemistry between stars Julia Roberts and Brad Pitt by conspiring to keep them apart as much as possible.

He next directed Naomi Watts in *The Ring* (2002), a remake of Hideo Nakata's 1998 horror phenomenon *Ringu*. The rehash preserved the central conceit – a mysterious video makes the rounds, causing its viewers to die seven days after watching it – but slicked up the dark, bleary original into a semi-linear MTV clip. A Disney World theme-park ride provided the source for Verbinski's biggest hit, *Pirates Of The Caribbean: The Curse Of The Black Pearl* (2003), which traded heavily on lead buccaneer Johnny Depp's voluptuous wit and spry spontaneity. In addition to helming two hugely successful *Pirates* sequels – *Dead Man's Chest* (2006) and *At World's End* (2007) – Verbinski also shot *The Weather Man* (2005), with Nicolas Cage as the titular meteorologist. JW

Pirates Of The Caribbean: The Curse Of The Black Pearl 2003, 143 min

cast Johnny Depp, Geoffrey Rush, Orlando Bloom, Keira Knightley, Jack Davenport, Kevin R. McNally *cin* Dariusz Wolski *m* Klaus Badelt

Resplendent in beaded dreadlocks and kohl, the indispensable Johnny Depp plays dastardly charmer Captain Jack Sparrow as a purring East End dandy in this otherwise overfed, action-tractioned swashbuckler. The basic plot sees Captain Jack forge an uneasy alliance with an earnest blacksmith (Orlando Bloom) to thwart a gang of hexed pirates led by the nefarious Barbossa (Geoffrey Rush), who've kidnapped a fair maiden (Keira Knightley) in an attempt to lift an Aztec curse.

Paul Verhoeven
Netherlands, 1938–

An extreme and controversial filmmaker, Paul Verhoeven made a name for himself in a country without a great filmmaking tradition, and in the 1980s and 90s became one of the most successful European moviemakers in Hollywood. At the same time, he has often been criticized for the graphic violence and sexual candour in his work, and remains notorious for the widely panned *Showgirls* (1995).

Growing up in the Netherlands during World War II, Verhoeven was on the sharp end of bombing raids from both German and Allied forces, and even underwent a mock execution by a German soldier. The son of a headmaster, he got a doctorate in maths and physics, but immediately dedicated himself to making films (during two years' military service he directed a twenty-minute enlistment film for the Dutch marine corps).

A devout cineaste, Verhoeven rejected the intellectual art cinema pioneered by the *nouvelle vague* while embracing the social liberalism that took hold in 1960s Amsterdam. His first feature, *Business Is Business* (1971), a larky comedy about prostitution, was hugely popular in the Netherlands, as was *Turkish Delight* (1973), a passionate, tragic love story adapted from the novel by Jan Wolkers, a Dutch Bukowski figure. With Rutger Hauer as a sculptor all but consumed with desire for his ex-girlfriend, the movie was as sexually frank as *Last Tango In Paris* (1972). One in three people over the age of 14 in the country saw the film – it remains the most popular Dutch movie ever made.

Collaborating with screenwriter Gerard Soeteman (who has written all Verhoeven's Dutch films) the director went on to make the realist historical piece *Katie Tippel* (1975) – one of a number of films he has made about women surviving destitution – the widely admired World War II drama *Soldier Of Orange* (1977), and the unapologetically trashy biker movie *Spetters* (1980). The most intriguing of his Dutch films is *The Fourth Man* (1983), a deliriously torrid and surreal melodrama about a homosexual Catholic novelist falling under the spell of black widow Christine – a prototype for Catherine Trammell in *Basic Instinct* (1992).

Verhoeven's local success and growing international reputation brought him to Hollywood. Wisely shying away from contemporary drama, he had a considerable hit with his second American movie, *Robocop* (1987). Ostensibly a sci-fi thriller, but also a political satire on the smiling face of Reaganomics, *Robocop* is as subversive as the very best graphic novels. The film spawned two inferior sequels, but Verhoeven had already moved on. *Total Recall* (1990) was another big-budget sci-fi extravaganza, this time starring Arnold Schwarzenegger. Based on a short story by Philip K. Dick, it mixed mainstream action spectacle with radical ideas about mind control and postmodern self-referentiality. It consolidated Verhoeven's growing reputation as one of the key players of the era.

Basic Instinct (1992), another hit, made Sharon Stone a star – though this time many reviewers were leery of the salacious content and controversies about the movie's politically incorrect portrait of a bisexual psychopath (complaints that inspired an apology from the film's screenwriter, Joe Eszterhas). Nevertheless, the film has some persuasive champions, including academic Camille Paglia, who celebrated it as a transgressive feminist text.

If the Dutchman enjoyed making mischief in puritanical America, he overplayed his hand in his next outing with Eszterhas, *Showgirls*. Too candid for the mainstream and too trashy for the critics, this was probably the most derided studio movie of the 1990s. Verhoeven would pull off one more genuinely subversive film in Hollywood – the sci-fi war movie *Starship Troopers* (1997) – but he was no longer seen as a safe pair of hands, and balked against the restraints imposed on *Hollow Man* (2000). Plans to make historical epics about the Crusades and the life of Christ came to nothing.

He returned to the Netherlands, where after a six-year gap he came back with the hugely successful *Black Book* (2006), a glossy World War II Resistance melodrama with a spunky Jewish heroine and enough cynicism to offend all vested interests. Prime Verhoeven. TC

Soldier Of Orange (Soldaat van Oranje) 1977, 149 min

cast Rutger Hauer, Jeroen Krabbé, Derek de Lint, Susan Penhaligon, Edward Fox *cin* Jost Vacano *m* Roger van Otterloo

Verhoeven's highly acclaimed epic about the reaction of various Dutch college friends to the unexpected German invasion. Some join the Resistance, one signs up for the SS, others don't survive. Eric (Hauer) escapes to London and returns as a spy in the service of his eccentric queen. Purportedly based on a true story, this is compelling stuff, but Verhoeven adroitly balances adventure elements with credible character nuances to fashion an engrossing dramatic account of a fraught period – to which he would return nearly thirty years later in the even more assured *Black Book*.

Robocop 1987, 102 min

cast Peter Weller, Nancy Allen, Daniel O'Herlihy, Ronny Cox, Kurtwood Smith, Miguel Ferrer *cin* Jost Vacano *m* Basil Poledouris

Detroit, sometime soon. Amid mounting violent crime, the Omni corporation has been entrusted with the police force, and quickly introduces its secret weapon: Robocop.

Part man, part machine, Robocop is an invulnerable and deadly crime-fighting tool imprinted with three foolproof directives: to uphold the law, serve the public trust, and protect the innocent. What could go wrong? Gory, fast-paced, and very funny, *Robocop* is also a fine piece of classical storytelling.

Total Recall 1990, 113 min

cast Arnold Schwarzenegger, Sharon Stone, Rachel Ticotin, Ronny Cox, Michael Ironside *cin* Jost Vacano *m* Jerry Goldsmith

Doug Quaid (Schwarzenegger) keeps dreaming about Mars – perhaps if he went there, he could sleep easy? It's just about affordable, with the purchase of memory implants – and Quaid can choose a custom-made ego trip to go with it. Based on Philip K. Dick's short story "We Can Remember It For You Wholesale" this mashes philosophy and violence with almost as much ingenuity as *Robocop*.

Starship Troopers 1997, 129 min

cast Casper Van Dien, Dina Meyer, Denise Richards, Jake Busey, Clancy Brown, Michael Ironside *cin* Jost Vacano *m* Basil Poledouris

This time Verhoeven transplants World War II to a sci-fi setting: strutting Aryan teen troopers take on giant bugs. And here's the kicker – it's our earthling heroes that turn out to be the fascists. Mixing satire, black comedy and gore, this offers an alternate angle on the nostalgia for the "Greatest Generation" as epitomized by movies like Steven Spielberg's *Saving Private Ryan* (1998). Written by Ed Neumeier of *Robocop* fame.

Black Book (Zwartboek) 2006, 145 min

cast Carice van Houten, Sebastian Koch, Thom Hoffman, Halina Reijn, Derek de Lint *cin* Karl Walter Lindenlaub *m* Anne Dudley

Verhoeven's first Dutch movie since he moved to Hollywood more than twenty years earlier. It's a World War II thriller

World War II in space: action and black comedy in Verhoeven's *Starship Troopers*.

about a beautiful Jew acting as an undercover agent (literally: she beds a sympathetic Nazi officer) for the Resistance. The film is a triumph, a tremendous piece of storytelling that's both old-fashioned and audacious. Life is a perpetual battle, it suggests, and mercenary self-interest is all you can really trust.

Marion Vernoux
France, 1966–

Marion Vernoux's work is sensitive to the economic vicissitudes of modern love. Born into a theatrical family, she broke into cinema as a production assistant and then a scriptwriter. The fate of men and women longing for connection, yet impeded by circumstance, recurs throughout her oeuvre. Her first feature was *Personne ne m'aime* (*Nobody Loves Me*, 1994), a feminist road movie about two sisters who lack emotional fulfilment and take to the road. Vernoux's first British hit was the Julian Barnes-inspired emotional triangle *Love, Etc* (1996). But its attempt to view modern relationships through a 1960s lens made for some obvious modernist posturing when compared to her best work. After scripting *Venus Beauty* (1998), Tonie Marshall's portrait of emotional ennui in a beauty parlour, Vernoux directed the touching *Rien à faire* (*Empty Days*, 1999). Karin Viard, Hélène Fillières and Sergi López starred in *Reines d'un jour* (*A Hell Of A Day*, 2001), a zany comedy of romantic manners. The Emmanuelle Béart comedy *A boire* (2003) suggested an ambition torn between box-office necessity and more challenging commitments. RA

Rien à faire (Empty Days) 1999, 103 min
cast Valeria Bruni Tedeschi, Patrick Dell'Isola, Sergi López, Florence Thomassin, Kelly Nornoy *cin* Dominique Colin *m* Alexandre Desplat

Unemployed factory worker Valeria Bruni Tedeschi and between-jobs executive Patrick Dell'Isola clandestinely meet in the local supermarket. Homing in on the passion and feints of their affair, Vernoux, assisted by Dominique Colin's bravura close-ups, offers a refreshing antidote to Parisian export confections. Emotionally honest and hard-headed about the realities of love in the "downsizing" 1990s, this offbeat film offers genuine surprises.

Dziga Vertov
Poland (formerly Russian Empire), 1896–1954

"I am eye. I am a mechanical eye." Dziga Vertov – the grandfather of *cinéma vérité* – was never short of an attention-grabbing line. A musician and a graduate in neurology, Vertov held the dialectic of artist and scientist in dynamic tension throughout his career, from his earliest sound experiments in 1916 in his "Laboratory of Hearing" at the Petrograd Psychoneurological Institute.

His first job in the film industry was to compile and edit the weekly newsreel series *Kinonedelya*, and it was at this time that he entered the orbit of Lev Kuleshov, just as he was working on his famous montage experiments. It wasn't long before Vertov formulated his own theories called Kino-Eye, and formed his own group to put his ideas into practice. Vertov synthesized Kuleshov's revolutionary ideas on montage with the symbolic abstractions of constructivism and the poetic influence of Vladimir Mayakovsky.

He asserted that fictional movies were fatal and as contagious as leprosy. The camera, he claimed, couldn't lie and was a mass producer of truth, infinitely superior to the flawed iris of human perception and that editing machines expressed another, deeper form of truth, by organizing and shaping the chaos of the universe. He and his brother Mikhail Kaufman travelled the Soviet Union, filming hundreds of hours of footage, catching life unawares. With his wife Elisaveta Svilova, he edited the images into constructivist canvases of symmetrical patterns, clean lines and messy reality, using slow motion, fast motion, animation, split screens, superimposition, rapid montage and every tool in the illusionist's trade in the service of reality. The result was a series of matchless newsreels under the umbrella Kino-Pravda, and the documentary films *Kino-Eye* (1924), *Stride, Soviet!* (1926), *A Sixth Of The World* (1926) and *The Eleventh Year* (1928).

But technical brilliance gave way to art, and Vertov began to refer to his films as cine-poems and cine-symphonies. This new emphasis on personal artistry over mass observation reached its startling apotheosis with *The Man With A Movie Camera* (1929). Unfortunately, his artistic crusade wasn't successful, as audiences weren't generally cine-literate enough to appreciate his Marxist message. Sound enabled him to return to his experiments in hearing with *Enthusiasm* (1931), which influenced Charlie Chaplin's *Modern Times* (1936), and *Three Songs Of Lenin* (1934), which sutured vox pops, newsreel and Ukrainian song to construct a hymn to the revolutionary leader on the tenth anniversary of his death. However, his later work couldn't match the success of his earlier films and was cold-shouldered by Stalin's regime under the new doctrine of socialist realism. Condemned for being too formalist, Vertov was forced back to square one, becoming an editor of prosaic newsreels. With most of his work unseeable, *The Man With A Movie Camera* is his principal legacy, but what a legacy it is. LH

Montage

A vivid and giddy celebration of both the modern city and state socialism, full of superimpositions and special effects, Dziga Vertov's *The Man With A Movie Camera* (1929) is arguably the most spellbinding use of montage in Soviet film history. Derived from the French word "monter" (to assemble), the concept appropriately incorporated at least two competing theories – those of Lev Kuleshov and Sergei Eisenstein. Although the former wasn't the first filmmaker to adopt montage techniques (that is usually credited to D.W. Griffith), he was the first to theorize them. During his workshop sessions at the state film school, VGIK, Kuleshov and his students would systematically dissect D.W. Griffith's *Intolerance* (1916), viewing it repeatedly, cutting it up and reassembling it. Satisfied that he'd discovered the inner workings of film narrative, Kuleshov devised an experiment to demonstrate the "Kuleshov Effect". With the assistance of future director Vsevolod Pudovkin, he took footage of the expressionless face of actor Ivan Mozhukin and spliced in shots of a woman lying in a coffin, a little girl playing with a teddy bear and a bowl of hot soup. When he showed the footage to an audience, they were all touched by Mozhukin's versatile acting, believing that he seemed grief-stricken, happy and hungry respectively. Of course, the actor's face never actually changed in any of the shots; all of his delicate emotions had been projected onto him by the audience. Thus, Kuleshov concluded, context was as crucial as content to the meaning of a film sequence, and the viewer had a key role to play in understanding the juxtaposition of the images.

A number of renowned filmmakers attended Kuleshov's workshops. One of them, Sergei Eisenstein, would devise his own theories of montage, which refined Kuleshov's establishing principles. Where Kuleshov emphasized harmony and unity, Eisenstein preferred dynamism and collision. For him, film was not constructed out of a series of building blocks but by a series of shocks or explosions in the engine of the narrative. Eisenstein conceived five types of montage, each with differing functions and effects: metric, rhythmic, tonal, overtonal and intellectual. The last – essentially a combination of shots that form an abstract concept in the mind of the viewer – was the most important. The style was best exhibited in *October* (1927), Eisenstein's celebration of the Russian Revolution. In the most famous example, close-ups of Alexander Kerensky, the head of the provisional government, are juxtaposed with footage of a mechanical peacock in order to suggest the man's preening vanity and self-deluding pride. However, the finest exponent of associational montage was Alexander Dovzhenko who, in *Arsenal* (1929) and *Earth* (1930), eschewed the cold ferocity and mechanical dialecticism with which Eisenstein imbued *Strike* (1924), *Battleship Potemkin* (1925) and *October*, to construct a cinema that was pantheistic, baroque and genuinely personal.

In the West, D.W. Griffith's approach to montage – as a way to propel the narrative forward – marched onwards. In the 1930s and 40s it almost became *de rigueur* to denote the passage of time with a shot of the leaves of a calendar falling away (or memorably being shot off by a machine gun in Howard Hawks's *Scarface*). Warner Bros even had its own Montage Department in the 1930s, which was headed by Don Siegel. Montage sequences have since become the laziest tool of easy shorthand for indolent directors. Perhaps the most overused trope of the romantic comedy is the "getting to know all about you" montage. This old chestnut typically incorporates shots of a loved-up stroll on a wave-tossed beach, and is unerringly accompanied by a song that is both soppy and expository (the words "falling" and "love" usually feature heavily), which screenwriters clearly hope will do their hard work for them. LH

The Man With A Movie Camera (Chelovek s kinoapparatom) 1929, 90 min, b/w

cin Mikhail Kaufman

From the very first shot of a photographer and his apparatus superimposed above a towering movie camera, it's clear that this isn't going to be a slice of life caught unawares. Vertov attempts to construct "a truly international absolute language based on its total separation from the language of theatre and literature", and in his mission to create pure cinema, he makes the viewer aware of the artificiality of the documentary approach. Above all, however, this is a hymn to city life and urgent modernity that's often dizzying in its choice of vertiginous angles and spellbinding in its use of kaleidoscopic superimpositions and startling juxtapositions.

Sandrine Veysset

France, 1967–

If Claire Denis has been dubbed the poetess of French women directors, Sandrine Veysset is the realist of the sisterhood. After studying literature and visual arts at the University of Montpellier and playing in a punk band in the 1980s, Veysset was befriended by Léos Carax, for whom she chauffeured and worked as an art director. In the early 1990s she designed sets for Carax's *Les amants du Pont-Neuf* (1991) and stage sets for Karim Dridi's portrait of immigrant life, *Bye-Bye* (1995). In 1992 she cast the children for Diane Kurys's *Après l'amour*, and sympathy for children and the disadvantaged characterizes Veysset's oeuvre. *Will It Snow For Christmas?* (1996) made a strong impression in transatlantic arthouses. In *Victor… pendant qu'il est trop tard* (*Victor… While It's Too Late*, 1998), a little boy flees abusive parents and finds refuge in the reluctant care of a prostitute.

Building on a reputation for nonjudgemental performances, and Hélène Louvart's *vérité* cinematography, *Martha… Martha* (2001) charts the painful consequences as a mother compulsively abandons her devoted husband and daughter. *Il sera une fois* (*Once Upon A Tomorrow*, 2005) featured Lucie Régnier, who also appeared in *Martha… Martha*, in a strongly scripted variation on a vision that combines the matter-of-fact with the transcendental. In her work, Veysset continues to be preoccupied with the social and familial consequences of globalization. RA

Will It Snow For Christmas? (Y aura-t-il de la neige à Noël?) 1996, 91 min
cast Dominique Reymond, Daniel Duval, Jessica Martinez, Alexandre Roger, Xavier Colonna, Fanny Rochetin *cin* Hélène Louvart *m* Henri Ancillotti

Following Claude Berri and Yves Robert's romanticized visions of Marcel Pagnol's Provence, this portrait of life on a southern farm is back-breaking and tragic. Scripted by Sandrine Veysset from her own experience, it quietly observes family life and work rituals as a woman tries to raise seven children, while their tyrannical father lives with another family in the next village. As the mother, Dominique Reymond works miracles in this moving and powerful film.

Charles Vidor
Hungary (formerly Austro-Hungarian Empire), 1900–59

Charles Vidor oversaw Rita Hayworth's finest screen moments. After serving his apprenticeship at UFA in Berlin, Vidor went to Hollywood in 1924, working his way up the studio ladder. Although uncredited, Vidor co-directed *The Mask Of Fu Manchu* (1932) with Charles Babin, and also directed the flawed, but intriguing, psychoanalysis movie *Blind Alley* (1939), though he was essentially marking time through the 1930s. However, over the next decade, he distinguished himself with the Ida Lupino murder mystery *Ladies In Retirement* (1941), and the Hayworth vehicles *Cover Girl* (1944) and *Gilda* (1946). Despite misfires such as the 1945 Chopin biopic *A Song To Remember* starring Cornel Wilde, as well as messy litigation with Columbia chief Harry Cohn, Vidor had a flair for stars and meshing musical numbers with drama. This talent is evidenced in the 1955 Ruth Etting biopic *Love Me Or Leave Me*, in which Doris Day fought off James Cagney's hoodlum manager. Ironically, Vidor died while on a project called *Song Without End* (1960), completed by the uncredited George Cukor. RA

Cover Girl 1944, 107 min, b/w
cast Rita Hayworth, Gene Kelly, Lee Bowman, Phil Silvers, Jinx Falkenburg, Leslie Brooks *cin* Rudolph Maté, Allan Davey *m* Jerome Kern, Ira Gershwin

A delightful mix of songs, laughs and rich Technicolor, this trifle traces chorus girl and model Rita Hayworth's rise to front-page fame. Hoofer Gene Kelly limbers up for the Arthur Freed-Stanley Donen opuses to come, while rehearsing all the brasher clichés of wartime entertainment.

Gilda 1946, 109 min, b/w
cast Rita Hayworth, Glenn Ford, George Macready, Joseph Calleia, Steven Geray, Joe Sawyer *cin* Rudolph Maté *m* Marlin Skiles, Edwin Wetzel

Glenn Ford's drifter fetches up in steamy Buenos Aires and finds himself in a *ménage à trois* with Rita Hayworth and her husband George Macready. The sexual suggestion was never more exotic, and Hayworth never more in thrall to her sensual persona, than in this key entry in Hollywood's *film noir* canon.

King Vidor
US, 1894–1982

King Vidor presents a problem for those critics who like to herd directors into the convenient pens that auteur theory has so solidly erected. Unusually eclectic, he flitted from the sober realism of *Street Scene* (1931) to the lurid melodramatics of *Duel In The Sun* (1946) via the women's picture *Stella Dallas* (1937). A yawning ideological gap also existed among his films, and David Thomson isn't the only critic to spot the ease with which Vidor could move from the neo-socialism of *Our Daily Bread* (1934) to the crypto-fascism of *The Fountainhead* (1949). It's quite typical of Vidor that the former, about the bitter travails of a farm commune, was condemned for being both left and right wing.

Vidor had various jobs in Hollywood – clerk, extra and gag writer – until he drummed up the finances for his debut, *The Turn In The Road* (1919). The director continued this spirit of independence when he set up his own mini-studio, the short-lived Vidor Village, and a decade later paid for the first all-black musical, *Hallelujah* (1929), out of his own pocket. But it was for a studio, MGM, that he produced his first film of note, *The Big Parade* (1925). One of the first American films to visit the trenches of World War I from an anti-war stance, this powerful silent's phenomenal success gave Vidor the clout to engineer his most ambitious and arguably greatest cinematic achievement, *The Crowd* (1928).

Vidor paid the mortgage by making three star vehicles for William Randolph Hearst's mistress, Marion Davies, as well as turning out the cloyingly sentimental box-office success *The Champ* (1931). He ended the decade by contributing the sepia

The symmetrical hell of office work traps protagonist James Murray in King Vidor's *The Crowd*.

"Over The Rainbow" sequence to *The Wizard Of Oz* (1939), and by filming a solid adaptation of A.J. Cronin's socially realistic novel, *The Citadel* (1938), which cemented his reputation as a committed consciousness-raiser. In contrast were the questionable heroics of his 1940 hymn to square-jawed bravado and blatant colonialism, *Northwest Passage* (one of the first films to use Technicolor on location). After the war he directed a series of movies that started at a delirious fever pitch and never let up, including the bizarre love-triangle melodrama *Beyond The Forest* (1949) starring Bette Davis, and the Jennifer Jones soap *Ruby Gentry* (1952), which was an attempt to return to the lurid glories of *Duel In The Sun*.

Given the impressive fact that he made more than fifty films in forty years, it's not surprising that defining qualities are hard to come by, but there are crumbs for auteurists. Apart from his striking visual sense, Vidor's films were often populated by individuals locked in a lifelong struggle. His career ended on a low note with a couple of epics, the heroic failure *War And Peace* (1956) and the arthritic *Solomon And Sheba* (1959). Although Vidor lived for another 23 years, he never completed another feature. LH

The Big Parade 1925, 141 min, b/w

cast John Gilbert, René Adorée, Hobart Bosworth, Claire Adams, Robert Ober, Claire McDowell, Tom O'Brien *cin* John Arnold, Hendrik Sartov

This masterpiece of the silent era traces the adventures of rich man's son John Gilbert, who joins the army. His initial experiences at the French front during World War I are unexpectedly bucolic, as he falls in love with a girl (René Adorée). King Vidor deftly emphasized the fairy-tale nature of their romance with shimmering depth-of-field photography, while the battle sequences are visually staggering.

The Crowd 1928, 104 min, b/w

cast Eleanor Boardman, James Murray, Bert Roach, Estelle Clark, Daniel G. Tomlinson, Dell Henderson, Lucy Beaumont *cin* Henry Sharpe

Everyman James Murray has big plans when he moves to the city, but is soon locked into a joyless marriage. When his daughter dies, he loses both his job and self-esteem. Vidor's formidable essay on the dehumanizing effects of modernity and the self-deception of an American dreamer is punctuated by some of his most striking imagery. One of the most famous shots in silent film has the camera entering an antiseptic office full of working stiffs clinically arranged in identical rows and zooms in on our hapless protagonist, forlornly trapped in a symmetrical hell.

Stella Dallas 1937, 106 min, b/w

cast Barbara Stanwyck, John Boles, Anne Shirley, Barbara O'Neil, Alan Hale, Marjorie Main, George Walcott *cin* Rudolph Maté *m* Alfred Newman

Social climber Barbara Stanwyck snares wealthy bore John Boles, but after a quick marriage she discovers that her lack of class denies her the entrée into high society that she'd always craved. Vidor's camera is curiously static, as if he doesn't want to detract from the plot's many intricacies or Stanwyck's nuanced and beautifully modulated performance in this emotionally devastating collision of social aspirations and cold reality.

Duel In The Sun 1946, 138 min

cast Jennifer Jones, Gregory Peck, Joseph Cotten, Lionel Barrymore, Lillian Gish *cin* Lee Garmes, Harold Rosson, Ray Rennahan *m* Dimitri Tiomkin

This lurid horse opera, nicknamed "Lust In The Dust", is dangerously overheated – but in a good way. Based on a novel by Niven Busch, who helped put the cowboy on the analyst's couch, *Duel In The Sun* sees beautiful half-breed Jennifer Jones torn between two brothers: Joseph Cotten, who represents domesticity and decency, and Gregory Peck, who is primal, dangerous and every shade of wrong. Limned in hues of violent red, from the scorched earth and fiery women to the hellfire sermonizing and blazing sunsets, this is wonderfully demented stuff.

The Fountainhead 1949, 114 min, b/w

cast Gary Cooper, Patricia Neal, Raymond Massey, Kent Smith, Robert Douglas, Henry Hull, Ray Collins *cin* Robert Burks *m* Max Steiner

Ayn Rand's adaptation of her own bestselling novel boasts one of the more bizarre love triangles in Hollywood history: that between visionary architect and impertinent egotist Howard Roark, media mogul Gail Wynand who believes in giving the public what they want, and his wife, an ice maiden who only married Wynand when her masochistic desires for Roark began to overwhelm her. As fantastically demented as *Duel In The Sun*, this is a heady brew of half-baked philosophy, right-wing polemics and superb design. Unmissable.

Jean Vigo
France, 1905–34

Jean Vigo is cinema's eternal auteur-poet. He was born the son of a celebrated anarchist and pacifist whose views led to his death in a prison cell in 1917. In frail health, Vigo moved to Nice for the air and warmer climate. There, he made *A propos de Nice* (1930) with his father-in-law's financial help. Influenced by Dziga Vertov's witty and lyrical interpretation of reality – Vertov's brother Boris Kaufman shot all of Vigo's films – the director's satire attacked the manners and mores of the bourgeoisie basking idly by the Mediterranean while the poor propped up the social edifice. Anticipating 1960s *cinéma vérité*, Kaufman used a concealed camera to catch candid images, while dissolves strip a woman bare to expose the ostentations of the rich. *Taris* (1931), Vigo's visual essay about Olympic swimmer Jean Taris, employed superimposition, dissolves and variable motion,

signalling a debt to the contemporary avant-garde, particularly the surrealists.

Financed by the Comte de Noailles, the features *Zéro de conduite* (*Nil For Conduct*, 1933) and *L'Atalante* (1934) fulfilled Vigo's father's legacy of social indignation, remaining singular classics of revolt. The director's last, troubled production led to his death, and Vigo never saw his work enjoy the subsequent adulation of cinephiles. His influence is evident among filmmakers ranging from Lindsay Anderson to Léos Carax. In France, the Prix Jean Vigo has been awarded each year since 1951 to encourage young and innovative filmmakers, in recognition of their independence of spirit and style. RA

Zéro de conduite (Nil For Conduct) 1933, 41 min, b/w

cast Jean Dasté, Robert Le Flon, Delphin, Du Verron, Blanchar, Léon Larive, Madame Emile, Michelle Fagard *cin* Boris Kaufman *m* Maurice Jaubert

Drawing on his own unhappy school days, Jean Vigo presents children who are witty, imaginative and anarchic, while their teachers are dwarfs, recidivists and grotesque dummies. This parable of freedom versus authority launched a scurrilous attack on the French status quo, and the film was banned, dubbed "anti-French" and not exhibited until 1945. It remains cinema's master narrative of adolescent rebellion.

L'Atalante 1934, 89 min, b/w

cast Michel Simon, Dita Parlo, Jean Dasté, Gilles Margaritis, Louis Lefèbvre *cin* Boris Kaufman, Louis Berger, Jean-Paul Alphen *m* Maurice Jaubert

Vigo took a genre love story of a couple setting up married life on a barge and turned it into a masterpiece of romantic longing. Pitched between the realism of the canals and drab suburbs of inter-war Paris and its protagonists' interior lives, this is illuminated by the sensitive performances. It took years for the film to appear in its intended form, but the result is like water in sunlight.

Christian Vincent
France, 1955–

Christian Vincent's best work combines psychological acuity with sociological commitment. Influenced by the militant politics of the 1970s, Vincent's life was changed by a screening of Jean Renoir's *La règle du jeu* (1939). After studying the sociology of film at the University of Paris, he attended the national film school IDHEC. Vincent then made shorts with Fabrice Luchini, Tonie Marshall and a young Julie Delpy, and also worked in regional television news. His first feature – *La discrète* (*The Discreet*, 1990) – won three Césars and was a box-office success. In it Luchini's bored author seduces a woman so as to have something to write about, but then falls in love.

Deriving its mood from the sexual politics of Choderlos de Laclos, *La discrète* displayed a sensitivity to gender interaction that would inform the director's 1992 film *Beau fixe* (*Set Fare*), in which four Parisiennes decamp to a country *manoir* to revise for their exams, and the Isabelle Huppert-Daniel Auteuil marital drama *La séparation* (1994). The latter also featured the up-and-coming Karin Viard, with whom Vincent made the highly enjoyable *Les enfants* (*The Children*) in 2005. Gérard Lanvin portrays a middle-aged teacher who meets Viard's estate agent for an affair played out in the empty rooms of un-let apartments. Vincent's blend of sex and society awaits proper recognition. RA

La séparation 1994, 88 min

cast Isabelle Huppert, Daniel Auteuil, Jérôme Deschamps, Karin Viard, Laurence Lerel, Louis Vincent, Nina Morato *cin* Denis Lenoir

Isabelle Huppert and Daniel Auteuil are a pair of *soixante-huitards* living in bourgeois comfort when cracks appear in their relationship. When she declares that she is having an affair, he thinks he can handle it. But gradually his cool unravels… Aloof and observational in its approach, this modern drama of the decline of ideals benefits from Huppert's trademark stillness and a performance of seething sadness from Auteuil.

Thomas Vinterberg
Denmark, 1969–

In 1995 Lars von Trier and Thomas Vinterberg made film history with the notorious Dogme 95 Manifesto. Vinterberg studied at the National Film School of Denmark, and his graduation short – *Sidste omgang* (*Last Round*, 1993) – won the jury award at the Munich International Festival of Film Schools. Announcing a preoccupation with families that would mark his best work, *The Boy Who Walked Backwards* (1994) found its protagonist, bereaved by his brother's death, realizing he can turn back time by walking backwards. The melding of melodrama and metaphysics comes to seem distinctively Vinterbergian. *The Greatest Heroes* (1996) was a patchy comedy thriller following a pair of bank robbers across Sweden with a long-lost daughter in tow. It starred Thomas Bo Larsen and Ulrich Thomsen, the brothers in Vinterberg's 1998 arthouse breakthrough *Festen* (*The Celebration*).

The Dogme "Vow of Chastity" challenged the illusionism and artifice of mainstream film aesthetics with a "back to basics" strategy of shooting authentic stories on location using available light and without directorial signature. While generating publicity for a new Danish cinema, the Dogme project came to seem symptomatic of a wider shift in 1990s cinema, that bore the influence of reality TV, the films of Harmony Korine and such sleeper hits as *The Blair Witch Project* (1999). Yet for Vinterberg, the Dogme rules did not set the tone for his subsequent oeuvre. *It's All About Love* (2002), co-written by *Festen* collaborator Mogens Rukov and

starring Joaquin Phoenix and Claire Danes, was a science fiction fantasy set in a chaotic future. As the couple's marriage flounders, a Lynchian dislocation sets in around them. Greeted by puzzled reviews, it was followed by the decidedly misjudged *Dear Wendy* (2004) starring Jamie Bell and Bill Pullman, in which a young pacifist is drawn to an abandoned handgun. The innocent abroad in a fallen world has become a recurrent theme in Vinterberg's bold and promising cinema. RA

Festen (The Celebration) 1998, 105 min

cast Ulrich Thomsen, Henning Moritzen, Thomas Bo Larsen, Paprika Steen, Birthe Neumann, Trine Dyrholm *cin* Anthony Dod Mantle *m* Lars Bo Jensen

When Ulrich Thomsen stands up at his father's sixtieth birthday party to pay tribute to the old man, everyone can imagine what's coming… But Thomsen tells a different story: one involving alienation, sibling mistrust and a father abusing a now dead sister. Monitoring the shock waves with a jerky, muddy image shot on Hi8 video and blown up to 35mm, Vinterberg presents a familiar tale of bourgeois breakdown. But he tempers it with just a hint of the ghostly as the sister "returns" in the night, suggesting that the right aesthetics can reveal the truth.

Luchino Visconti
Italy, 1906–76

Les parents terribles; *Tobacco Road*; *Figaro*; *Crime And Punishment*; *The Glass Menagerie*; *A Streetcar Named Desire*; *Rosalinda*; *Death Of A Salesman*; *Three Sisters*. These are just some of the stage productions Luchino Visconti directed between 1945 and 1954 – a range of work too rich and radical for any national cinema, but suggestive of this director's extraordinary reach.

Count Don Luchino Visconti di Modrone was born into one of the oldest families in Italy. His family crest – a serpent devouring a baby – adorned the very pillars of Milanese society; even the cathedral was founded by a Visconti. He grew up in a castle surrounded by a medieval village, the feudal idyll restored by his father, who had rescued the family's fortunes by marrying a rich industrialist's daughter. His older brother was an officer in Mussolini's armed forces. Luchino himself served briefly in the cavalry, then put together one of the best stables in horse racing.

Always interested in theatre and the arts, Visconti went to Paris in the late 1930s. Here he befriended Coco Chanel, met the film director Jean Renoir – who hired him as an assistant on his *Partie de campagne* (*A Day In The Country*, 1936) – transformed his politics (he became a Marxist), and revealed his true vocation. When he returned to Italy, Visconti immediately set about making his own films. First, an uncredited but authentically sleazy adaptation of James M. Cain's *The Postman Always Rings Twice*, which he called *Ossessione* (1942). Then, after the war, *La terra trema* (1948), a largely improvised drama funded by the Communist Party, and filmed with and among Sicilian fishermen. An overwhelmingly stark chronicle of a family that tries and fails to break out of the poverty trap, *La terra trema* is a masterpiece of neo-realism.

While he made two more films, *Bellissima* (1951) and *Rocco And His Brothers* (1960), that follow the lives of working-class characters, they were separated by the very different *Senso* (*The Wanton Countess*, 1954) – a tragic romance set in 1866 during the Austrian occupation of Venice. *Senso* was the first of Visconti's historical melodramas, films notable for the rich opulence of their *mise en scène* and the director's almost fetishistic attention to period detail. If this seems like a paradox, it should be remembered that although Visconti remained a committed communist throughout his life, he was always attended by five or six personal servants and never abandoned his love of beautiful objects. Farley Granger has reported that for months during the making of *Senso* the director had an entire villa in Vicenza furnished in the right style, with fresh flowers in every room every day. Claudia Cardinale has told how in *The Leopard* (1963), his attention to detail extended to the embroidered silk handkerchief tucked out of sight within her purse.

In truth, Visconti's taste for the heightened emotions of melodrama is no less pronounced in his earlier films. He was a great lover and director of opera, and his films are highly operatic in the intensity of feeling on display – often against the background of great historical events. It's an oeuvre that owes as much to Freud as it does to Marx. Visconti's homosexuality is also a key aspect of his vision. There's an uninhibited sensuousness about the way the camera dwells on beautiful young men in *La terra trema*, *Rocco And His Brothers* and, most obviously, in *Death In Venice* (1971), while *Senso* is almost entirely seen from the viewpoint of the lovelorn countess who is obsessed with Farley Granger's narcissistic pretty boy. Visconti was also profoundly marked by the irrevocable and bitter dissolution of his parents' marriage when he was a boy of 11 (unlike his siblings, Luchino took his mother's side), and almost all his films relate to the breakdown of family bonds and the (self-) destructive properties of love, pride and sex. These subjects are an almost abstract expression in his very last film *L'innocente* (1976).

Visconti's much more variable later films have been called "decadent", but decadence is their subject as well as their style: the rotting corruption of fascism in *The Damned* (1969), von Aschenbach's fatalistic dalliance in the cholera-ridden city in

The past meets the future: Sicilian aristocrat Prince Salina (Burt Lancaster) takes to the dance floor with the mayor's daughter Angelica (Claudia Cardinale) in Viscont's lavish costume drama *The Leopard*.

Death In Venice, King Ludwig of Bavaria's mad fantasies made real in *Ludwig* (1972). Best of all these late films is *Conversation Piece* (1974), in which a retired American professor (Burt Lancaster) has his solitary life interrupted by a bevy of *Dolce vita* types, led by an Italian marchesa, and is forced to question his whole system of values and beliefs. TC

Ossessione 1942, 140 min, b/w

cast Clara Calamai, Massimo Girotti, Juan de Landa, Dhia Cristiani *cin* Aldo Tonti, Domenico Scala *m* Giuseppe Rosati

Visconti's unofficial transposition of James M. Cain's *The Postman Always Rings Twice* to the Po Delta is strikingly naturalistic, earthy and carnal. Massimo Girotti as the drifter and Clara Calamai as his lover generate a tangible onscreen heat, but Visconti extends a degree of humanity to her overweight, restaurant-owning husband via an engaging scene in which he performs in a singing competition. Co-screenwriter Giuseppe de Santis evocatively described the film as steeped "in the air of death and sperm", and, predictably enough, it was banned by the Fascist authorities.

Bellissima 1951, 108 min, b/w

cast Anna Magnani, Walter Chiaria, Tina Apicella, Gastone Renzelli, Alessandro Blasetti *cin* Piero Portalupi *m* Franco Mannino

Anna Magnani is in superbly histrionic form as desperate mum Maddelena, determined to escape poverty and her abusive husband by getting her young daughter Maria (the diminutive Tina Apicella) into the movies. Answering an audition at the Cinecittà Studios in Rome, the two confront hundreds of other mothers and daughters with similar ambitions. Part sentimental women's picture, part satirical look at the hard-nosed reality of show business, the film is made memorable by the convincing intensity of the central mother-daughter relationship.

Senso (The Wanton Countess) 1954, 117 min

cast Alida Valli, Farley Granger, Heinz Moog, Rina Morelli, Christian Marquand *cin* Aldo Graziati, Robert Krasker *m* Anton Bruckner

Set in Venice and Verona on the eve of Garibaldi's expulsion of the Austrians, this sees Alida Valli's countess being seduced by a feckless young Austrian officer (Farley Granger) into betraying everything she believes in. This classy, operatic melodrama enacts a ferociously unstable, masochistic relationship, a recurring pattern in Visconti's work. Tennessee Williams and Paul Bowles are among six credited screenwriters, while extracts from Bruckner's *Seventh Symphony* provide the febrile accompaniment.

Rocco And His Brothers (Rocco e i suoi fratelli) 1960, 180 min, b/w

cast Alain Delon, Renato Salvatori, Annie Girardot, Katina Paxinou, Alessandra Panaro *cin* Giuseppe Rotunno *m* Nino Rota

Powerful social cinema, midway between Visconti's early neo-realist films and his taste for overtly operatic emotional melodrama. All but destitute, a southern family moves into shared lodgings in industrialized Milan, but blood ties will be ripped apart in this new environment. Even the saintly Rocco (Alain Delon) will be tainted by malign fate. Annie Girardot puts in a remarkable performance.

The Leopard (Il gattopardo) 1963, 177 min

cast Burt Lancaster, Claudia Cardinale, Alain Delon, Paolo Stoppa, Rina Morelli, Romolo Valli, Terence Hill *cin* Giuseppe Rotunno *m* Nino Rota

Visconti was ideally suited to film di Lampedusa's elegiac account of a nineteenth-century Sicilian aristocrat, Prince Salina (Burt Lancaster), and his struggles with historical change. The first half of this stately three-hour film shows us social upheaval through sweeping martial conflict, while the second takes place at the prince's summer retreat, and principally concerns marital arrangements for his nephew Tancredi (Alain Delon) to Angelica (Claudia Cardinale), the *nouveau riche* daughter of the mayor – ultimately a more radical change. One of the most beautiful and profoundly resonant films ever made.

Death In Venice (Morte a Venezia) 1971, 128 min

cast Dirk Bogarde, Björn Andresen, Silvana Magnano, Mark Burns, Marisa Berenson, Romolo Valli *cin* Pasqualino di Santis *m* Gustav Mahler

In Visconti's adaptation of Thomas Mann's novella, the central character is now a composer experiencing a creative and spiritual crisis, rather than a writer. Holidaying alone in Venice, Aschenbach (a twitchily neurotic Dirk Bogarde) struggles with his feelings for a beautiful young Polish boy (Björn Andresen). Does he represent an ideal of perfection or are the composer's feelings simply carnal? The film's emphasis on opulence, courtesy of superb art direction and Mahler's poignant music, effectively highlights Aschenbach's isolation, but dilutes the ambiguity and complexity of the original story.

Wachowski Brothers

Larry Wachowski: US, 1965–
Andy Wachowski: US, 1967–

Their sole previous directing credit was the laddish, calculating thriller *Bound* (1996), starring the very game duo of Jennifer Tilly and Gina Gershon as lipstick lesbians on the make. Yet in 1999, the no-profile Wachowski brothers unleashed the cult-spawning phenomenon *The Matrix*, a surprise smash hit driven by an irresistible premise: life as we know it is mere machine-generated illusion. The sleek gadgetry and state-of-the-art special effects provided part of the draw, of course: the film pioneered, in Hollywood at least, "bullet-time" photography, the instantly famous (and endlessly parodied) visual effect whereby Matrix inhabitants can dodge bullets in slo-mo or freeze in mid-leap. But *The Matrix* script also offered food for the mind – this was surely the first Joel Silver production to ponder evolutionary psychology, Descartes' brain-in-a-vat scenario, Plato's allegory of the cave and Baudrillard's "desert of the real", all the while positing Keanu Reeves as the saviour of the human race.

The press-shy Wachowskis claim they'd always planned the Matrix story as a trilogy, but *The Matrix Reloaded* (2003) and *The Matrix Revolutions* (2003), shot back-to-back, reeked of desperate bloat. They increasingly sacrificed momentum and coherence for pseudo-Zen pontification – the latter courtesy of Laurence Fishburne's blowhard elder Morpheus – and numbing action-sequence onslaughts. The Wachowskis also wrote the prolix screenplay for *V For Vendetta* (2006), a big-screen adaptation of the graphic novel by Alan Moore, who was sufficiently displeased with the final result that he had his name removed from the credits. JW

The Matrix 1999, 136 min
cast Keanu Reeves, Laurence Fishburne, Carrie-Ann Moss, Hugo Weaving, Gloria Foster, Joe Pantoliano, Marcus Chong *cin* Bill Pope *m* Don Davis

Machines are harvesting humans as energy sources, keeping them unawares by pumping a "computer-generated dream world" directly into their brains. A small band of resistance fighters tag computer hacker Neo (Keanu Reeves) as mankind's saviour from the evil mechanoids. Fuelled by the amphetamine rush of future shock and gravity-defying martial arts, *The Matrix* bests most mainstream action sagas.

George Waggner
US, 1894–1984

After cranking out a batch of mostly forgotten Westerns and frontier yarns, predominantly for Universal, George Waggner directed a pair of horror films starring Lon Chaney Jr in 1941: *Man-Made Monster*, in which Chaney played an electrically controlled robot-beast, and *The Wolf Man*, which cemented the actor's fame and was the last in Universal's foundational quartet of horror films (alongside *Dracula*, *Frankenstein* and *The Mummy*). After these career standouts, Waggner's later credits included the middling but fun Western *The Fighting Kentuckian* (1949) – which assembled an unlikely cast of John Wayne, Oliver Hardy and Vera Ralston – and the Department of Defense propaganda artefact *Red Nightmare* (1962). Waggner worked chiefly in television from the mid-1950s onwards. JW

The Wolf Man 1941, 70 min, b/w
cast Lon Chaney Jr, Evelyn Ankers, Claude Raines, Patric Knowles, Bela Lugosi, Fay Helm *cin* Joseph Valentine *m* Hans Salter, Frank Skinner

Returning to his family's ancestral home in Wales, Larry Talbot (Lon Chaney Jr) is bitten by a gypsy/dog (played by Bela Lugosi). Once Larry begins to transform into the eponymous hairy hybrid, his struggle to contain his warring selves provides the film with an endlessly renewable allegory. The fog-choked film is suffused with a sadness and rich subtext that almost match that of James Whale's *Frankenstein* (1931).

Andrzej Wajda
Poland, 1926–

Arguably Poland's finest director, Andrzej Wajda has crafted films that crackled with historical significance and zeitgeist urgency, and he's often seemed as much a war reporter, social commentator or sly satirist as a maker of fictions.

Wajda was a Resistance fighter during World War II, and this experience lent his subsequent war films an edge of visceral authenticity and poignant intensity. After the conflict, he studied painting at the Fine Arts Academy in Krakow and transferred to the film school in Łódź, where he honed his talents on shorts. The first of his great war trilogy, *A Generation* (1955), gave a role to Roman Polanski, who has since said of the film, "Polish cinema began with it." Naturalistic, painterly and violent, it focused on the formation of a political consciousness and a youth Resistance group in Poland in 1942. The uncompromisingly bleak *Kanal* (1957) followed the Polish partisans into the sewers, while the highly stylized and heavily symbolic *Ashes And Diamonds* (1958) completed the sequence. This astonishing trio remains the aesthetic high point of the director's career, painting war as shambolic and random.

With an enviable dexterity, the director has worked in different genres throughout his long and controversial career. Each diverse work bears the Wajda imprimatur of a trained artist's visual eloquence: the psychological youth drama *Innocent Sorcerers* (1960); *Siberian Lady Macbeth* (1961) in which a peasant takes a lover and kills her father-in-law and husband; and *Everything For Sale* (1969) a self-reflexive movie about a filmmaker called Andrzej. However, Wajda's most celebrated later films grapple with Polish history (*Landscape After Battle*, 1970, and *Man Of Marble*, 1977), mythology (*The Wedding*, 1972) or contemporary crises (*Rough Treatment*, 1978). The most famous of these – and the film with which he is most frequently associated – is 1981's *Man Of Iron*. Less a movie than an urgent, courageous and corrosive report on the political crisis in Poland, it won the Palme d'Or just before martial law was declared.

In the politically unstable period that followed, Wajda worked abroad in both film and theatre. His most famous work in quasi-exile was the Franco-Polish co-production *Danton* (1982). This potent and engrossing historical drama about the struggle for control of the French Revolution had obvious parallels with contemporary events in Poland, when the trade union movement Solidarity provided a powerful oppositional voice to the Communist government.

The end of Communism was a mixed blessing for Wajda. He won a seat in the senate for the Solidarity party, but his films drew in far fewer punters now they had to compete with American imports in the newly opened free market. Films such as the Holocaust drama *Korczak* (1990) piqued little public interest. Then in 1999 he made an unexpected and triumphant return to domestic box-office glory with the record-breaking *Pan Tadeusz* (based on the narrative

poem by Polish national poet Adam Mickiewicz), which was seen by six million Poles on its cinematic release alone. In 2002, he employed Roman Polanski once again as an actor in the farce *Revenge*, bringing both mercurial careers full circle. LH

Ashes And Diamonds (Popiol i diament)
1958, 109 min, b/w
cast Zbigniew Cybulski, Ewa Krzyzewska, Adam Pawlikowski, Bogumil Kobiela, Waclaw Zastrzezynski *cin* Jerzy Wójcik *m* Filip Nowak, Jan Krenz

At the end of World War II, a Resistance group has a final assignment: to assassinate a Communist Party leader who is considered too close to Moscow. In a hotel to carry out the hit, Zbigniew Cybulski enters into a relationship with the comely barmaid that may have serious consequences for his mission. Etched in high-contrast monochrome, Andrzej Wajda sutures *film noir* chiaroscuro onto a war movie, sensually overloading it with startling images that teeter on the baroque.

Landscape After Battle (Krajobraz po bitwie)
1970, 111 min
cast Daniel Olbrychski, Stanislawa Celinska, Aleksander Bardini, Zygmunt Malanowicz, Tadeusz Janczar *cin* Zygmunt Samosiuk *m* Zygmunt Konieczny

Survivors from a World War II concentration camp are interned by the Americans, who are afraid they may misuse their freedom and seek retribution on their old captors. Soon the only difference between their new and old jailors is the difference in uniform. Wajda zeroes in on a bloody-minded and psychologically disturbed poet who falls in love with one of the new female internees. From the extraordinary dialogue-free opening – when the prisoners celebrate their liberation to the strains of Vivaldi – the sense of the absurd permeates every frame of this extraordinary film.

Man Of Iron (Czlowiek z zelaza) 1981, 152 min
cast Jerzy Radziwilowicz, Krystyna Janda, Marian Opania, Irena Byrska, Wieslawa Kosmalska *cin* Edward Klosinski *m* Andrzej Korzynski

A loose sequel to 1977's *Man Of Marble* adopts the same narrative framework of a reporter's investigation, but rather than searching for the truth, the journalist constructs lies and conducts a smear campaign against Poland's burgeoning unions. With a memorable cameo by Lech Walesa, this is as much a historical document and a force for good as it is a movie. But while it succeeds as the former, it disappoints as the latter, as if buckling under the enormous weight of its political responsibilities. However, it both raised Western consciousness about Solidarity and acted as a political rallying call in its home country.

Danton 1982, 136 min
cast Gérard Depardieu, Wojciech Pszoniak, Anne Alvaro, Patrice Chéreau, Roger Planchon , Alain Mace *cin* Igor Luther *m* Jean Prodomidesi

Screenwriter Jean-Claude Carrière insisted that Wajda should not overemphasize the parallels between the French Revolution and the power struggles in contemporary Poland, but for those around in the 1980s it is hard not to see Danton as a Lech Walesa figure and Robespierre as General Jaruzelski. The focus is very much on the relationship between these contrasted figures, with Gérard Depardieu bringing a fleshy immediacy to the title role, while Wojciech Pszoniak as Robespierre is steely control personified. Despite its length and over-wordy script, this is one of the finest films about the French Revolution.

W

Raoul Walsh
US, 1887–1980

When the critics from *Cahiers du cinéma* were conferring auteur status upon erstwhile Hollywood hacks, they tended to favour the sort of macho directors whose lives were as rugged and red-blooded as the films they made. Raoul Walsh was the epitome of the brawny, no-nonsense maverick who demonstrated a vigorous sense of adventure both on and off screen. As a teenager, he interrupted his studies to travel on his uncle's schooner, and hopped off the boat to become a cowboy in Mexico and a wrangler for a trail herd that wound its way to Texas. Here, he entered show business with a travelling stage company and finally drifted into Hollywood as a cowboy actor, working for D.W. Griffith both behind and in front of the camera, notably as John Wilkes Booth in *The Birth Of A Nation* (1915).

As a director, Walsh was a pioneer. He helped to formulate the prototype of the gangster movie with *Regeneration* (1915) and helmed other notable silent films including *The Thief Of Bagdad* (1924), *What Price Glory* (1926) and *Sadie Thompson* (1928). He also gave John Wayne his first big break, in *The Big Trail* (1930). But the 1930s weren't kind to Walsh, and it was only when he moved to Warner Bros at the end of the decade that signs of a personal style within an anonymous studio product began to surface.

His forte was the action picture, fuelled by an abrasive energy and gruff decency, in which two-fisted heroes defined their own moral code in an indifferent universe. With a trio of gangster movies, he took the genre to new heights: *The Roaring Twenties* (1939), *High Sierra* (1941) and *White Heat* (1949). Walsh displayed a natural affinity with tough-guy actors, bonding with alpha males James Cagney (*Manpower,* 1941), Humphrey Bogart (*They Drive By Night,* 1940) and especially Errol Flynn – *They Died With Their Boots On* (1941), *Gentleman Jim* (1941) and *Objective Burma!* (1945). Walsh's personal experiences instilled authenticity in Westerns such as *Pursued* (1947) and *Colorado Territory* (1949). Although he remained an active director into the early 1960s, his career tailed off after he left Warner Bros in the mid-1950s and he made few films of note.

Walsh lost his right eye in 1929 (the result of a collision between his car and a jack rabbit), and his signature eye-patch enhanced his reputation as a macho filmmaker whose life was as hard and as fast as the films he directed. The director – who made more than one hundred movies in a career that spanned 52 years – was forced to retire in 1964 when he lost the sight in his remaining eye. LH

Ida Lupino and a world-weary Humphrey Bogart plan their getaway in Walsh's groundbreaking *noir*, *High Sierra*.

The Thief Of Bagdad 1924, 155 min, b/w

cast Douglas Fairbanks, Julianne Johnston, Anna May Wong, Snitz Edwards, Charles Belcher *cin* Arthur Edeson *m* Lee Erwin

Arguably this is a Walsh film in name only, since it was made for Douglas Fairbanks's own company and is completely geared to his then-enormous appeal as the most balletic of swashbucklers. It is also a mesmerizing example of imaginative design from William Cameron Menzies, who combines a wealth of influences – from Russian ballet orientalism to Art Deco – to create a truly magical world as the backdrop for the extraordinary adventures of Fairbanks's thief and his attempts to win the hand of the Caliph's daughter (Julianne Johnston).

High Sierra 1941, 100 min, b/w

cast Ida Lupino, Humphrey Bogart, Alan Curtis, Arthur Kennedy, Joan Leslie, Henry Hull, Henry Travers *cin* Tony Gaudio *m* Adolph Deutsch

A landmark in the history of crime movies and in Humphrey Bogart's career, *High Sierra* marked the end of the gangster's era as king of the Hollywood backlot. It ushered in the age of the *film noir* antihero – on the run and out of luck. For the first time, Bogart lost his sneering malevolence and acquired the jaded decency that became his stoic trademark. A former public enemy number one, Bogart flees with Ida Lupino after an armed robbery goes wrong. Writers W.R. Burnett and John Huston suffused the film with world-weary cynicism, and Walsh injected it with pace.

They Died With Their Boots On 1941, 142 min, b/w

cast Errol Flynn, Olivia de Havilland, Arthur Kennedy, Charles Grapewin, Gene Lockhart, Anthony Quinn *cin* Bert Glennon *m* Max Steiner

General George Armstrong Custer could have been created as an archetypal Walsh hero, especially as dashingly portrayed by Errol Flynn. Historical accuracy wasn't the point, and Walsh directs with a strong sense of the sweeping drama of the Old West, taking full advantage of his cast of hundreds and outdoor locations. There's also a sentimental poignancy to the scenes Flynn shares with his co-star Olivia de Havilland, playing Custer's devoted wife.

White Heat 1949, 111 min, b/w

cast James Cagney, Virginia Mayo, Edmond O'Brien, Margaret Wycherly, Steve Cochran, John Archer, Wally Cassell *cin* Sidney Hickox *m* Max Steiner

When James Cagney made a reluctant return to the gangster genre after ten years, he insisted that Walsh be the director and that his character have some form of psychosis. So the writers gave him a king-size Oedipus complex, and his beloved mother is one of his gang of armed robbers. It all ends in the greatest climax in gangster film history, with Cagney atop a gleaming gas tank, taunting the police, crackling with coiled energy and shouting the immortal line, "Made it, Ma! Top of the world!"

Charles Walters

US, 1911–82

Charles Walters is a conundrum. The director of two classic musicals – *Easter Parade* (1948) and *High Society* (1956) – he is rarely referred to as a great director, and is certainly not in the class of Vincente Minnelli. The explanation, perhaps, lies in the fact that these enduringly popular films were made under the aegis of producer Arthur Freed.

Walters took the logical journey to becoming a director of musicals. He started out as a dancer and choreographer on Broadway and made his Hollywood debut as a hoofer and dance director on *Seven Days' Leave* (1942). Walters perfected his craft as the dance director on Minnelli's *Meet Me In St Louis* (1944) and staged "On The Atchison, Topeka And The Santa Fe" in George Sidney's *The Harvey Girls* (1946), the number that critic Pauline Kael once crowned, "one of the most triumphant sequences in screen-musical history". Walters' sensitivity to performance also endeared him to MGM's biggest stars, and he crafted his routines with intuitive rhythm, spirit and style.

Walters graduated to director on 1947's *Good News*, an average campus musical comedy, before reuniting Fred Astaire and Ginger Rogers for the disappointing *The Barkleys Of Broadway* (1949). He also enjoyed a close relationship with Judy Garland on the sets of both *Easter Parade* and *Summer Stock* (1950), the latter an ebullient fantasy about a farm girl treading the boards and finding fame. Walters was nominated for a best director Oscar for the Leslie Caron carnival musical romance, *Lili* (1952), and he both directed and danced with Joan Crawford in *Torch Song* (1953). When the popularity of musicals began to wane, he moved to light, pacy comedies, including the Doris Day vehicle, *Don't Eat The Daisies* (1960) and Cary Grant's last film, *Walk Don't Run* (1966).

Most of Walters' films pass a Sunday afternoon amiably enough, but every underdog has its champion. The director has been canonized by critic Douglas McVay, who praises his sinuous verve and invention in musical numbers and claims that *High Society*, *Summer Stock*, *Good News* and *The Belle Of New York* (1952) "arguably entitle Charles Walters to a position alongside Minnelli and Donen." Few would agree. LH

Easter Parade 1948, 103 min

cast Judy Garland, Fred Astaire, Peter Lawford, Ann Miller, Jules Munshin, Clinton Sundberg, Richard Beavers *cin* Harry Stradling *m* Irving Berlin

Fred Astaire plays a dancer who trains Judy Garland to be his next protégée, just to spite his former partner Ann Miller. While the age difference – 23 years – is mildly alarming (Gene Kelly was due to star), this remains a perennially popular musical. Walters' champion Douglas McVay admits that this Irving Berlin musical "tends to lack real visual style, and to be somewhat uninventive in the treatment of many of its routines". Audiences, however, loved and love it.

Lili 1952, 81 min

cast Leslie Caron, Mel Ferrer, Jean-Pierre Aumont, Kurt Kasznar, Zsa Zsa Gabor, Amanda Blake, Alex Gerry *cin* Robert Planck *m* Bronislau Kaper

Teenage orphan Leslie Caron joins a carnival troupe and falls in love with the puppets, but sadly not the puppetmaster who yearns silently for her. Instead she is attracted to the magician with a tangled love life. This elegant slice of whimsy has considerable charm, though Walters had to persuade Dore Schary, head of production at MGM, to make it. It was the director's favourite of all his films.

High Society 1956, 107 min
cast Bing Crosby, Grace Kelly, Frank Sinatra, Celeste Holm, John Lund, Louis Calhern, Sidney Blackmer *cin* Paul C. Vogel *m* Cole Porter

James Stewart, Cary Grant and Katharine Hepburn, stars of 1940's *The Philadelphia Story*, on which this Cole Porter musical is based, are the very definition of a tough act to follow. However, Frank Sinatra, Bing Crosby and Grace Kelly (in her last film role) give this joyous musical an enduring appeal. Walters' moment of inspiration was to import "Well Did You Evah?" from the 1939 stage show *DuBarry Was A Lady*, which vies with "Who Wants To Be A Millionaire?" as this musical's high point.

Wayne Wang
Hong Kong, 1949–

Wayne Wang has always alternated between the mainstream and the personal in a manner that commentators never tire of referring to as his "Yin and Yang" approach. Critics watching the wheels grind on the machine-tooled Jennifer Lopez vehicle *Maid In Manhattan* (2002) could scarcely believe they were watching a film by the director of the subtle evocation of Chinese-American life, *Dim Sum* (1985) or the cheerfully improvised and warmly experimental *Blue In The Face* (1995).

Named after John Wayne by his film-obsessed father, Wang left Hong Kong to study art and film in California but returned to his homeland to direct TV series. Back in America, Wang made a name for himself as an astute surveyor of Chinese-American life. Off the cuff and exuding an effervescent charm, the micro-budgeted comedy thriller *Chan Is Missing* (1982) told the whimsical story of two cabbies desperately searching for a friend who has run off with their money, while *Dim Sum* was a restrained, intimate portrait of an elderly first-generation Chinese immigrant to San Francisco facing his mortality. It was followed by the first of Wang's startling juxtapositions, the all style/no substance thriller *Slam Dance* (1987). He returned to terra firma with *Eat A Bowl Of Tea* (1989), a so-so survey of post-war immigration, but then made the militantly uncommercial and surprisingly violent Hong Kong gangster satire *Life Is Cheap… But Toilet Paper Is Expensive* (1989). His next film was another radical change of direction – a Disney film, *The Joy Luck Club* (1993).

This, in turn, was followed by his most perfectly realized work, *Smoke* (1995). Later that year, *Blue In The Face* brought back most of the film's characters and seasoned the brew with cameos from Madonna, Jim Jarmusch and Lou Reed. Since then, and with the exception of *Chinese Box* (1997) and *The Centre Of The World* (2001), Wang has specialized in women's movies: *Anywhere But Here* (1999), *Maid In Manhattan* and *Last Holiday* (2006). Although the intentions have been honourable, the result has been bland factory fodder. Wang's stated reason for his eclectic method is that he doesn't like being labelled. But a few more films like these, along with the one-girl-and-her-dog movie *Because Of Winn-Dixie* (2005), and he could get stuck with the label no director wants: Hollywood hack. LH

The Joy Luck Club 1993, 139 min
cast Rosalind Chao, Chin Tsai, Kieu Chinh, Lisa Lu, France Nuyen, Lauren Tom, Tamlyn Tomita, Ming-Na Wen *cin* Amir Mokri *m* Rachel Portman

An intricate lattice of flashbacks illustrates the memories of three wealthy Chinese women (members of the titular mah jong club) and their American daughters, all of whom have suffered at the hands of violent, unfaithful or indifferent husbands. The production values are high, the cinematography is immaculate and the music tasteful – Wang's time-shifting drama has "quality" written through it – but it seems a little too calculating in its bid for critical praise and classic status.

Smoke 1995, 112 min
cast Giancarlo Esposito, José Zúñiga, Stephen Gevedon, Harvey Keitel, Jared Harris, William Hurt, Daniel Auster *cin* Adam Holender *m* Rachel Portman

Even though it's the least autobiographical, *this* is somehow the most resonant of all of Wang's "neighbourhood" pictures. The film began life when the director fell in love with a Paul Auster short story about a writer who's a regular at a Brooklyn tobacconist, which acts as a drop-in centre for locals to smoke stogies and tell their stories. Both Auster and Wang are credited as co-directors, and the evident pleasure that the cast and crew took in the filming translates to the screen.

Vincent Ward
New Zealand, 1956–

Visionary, quixotic and romantic, Vincent Ward likes to take things to extremes – geographically, narratively and visually. Trained as a painter, his films unite Andrei Tarkovsky's jaw-dropping imagery with Werner Herzog's wanderlust to spectacular effect. But there's a downside: Ward often sacrifices narrative cohesion to visual splendour.

After majoring in film at art school and making the short feature *A State Of Siege* (1978), Ward displayed his Herzogian credentials by spending two years as the only white man in a remote tribe of Maoris for the documentary, *In Spring One Plants Alone* (1979). With *Vigil* (1984), a disturbingly raw and plaintive coming-of-age story set on a Kiwi sheep farm, he became the first New Zealand director to have his work accepted for competition at Cannes.

Then he really started to get ambitious. *The Navigator* (1988) took four years to complete, while *Map Of The Human Heart* (1993) globe-

W

trotted thousands of miles from the Albert Hall to the Arctic Circle via Dresden. Ward returned to his painterly roots with the mawkish, pseudo-philosophical and genuinely extraordinary *What Dreams May Come* (1998), in which Robin Williams travelled through a Heaven and Hell re-imagined as *tableaux vivants* by Caspar David Friedrich, Dalí and Bosch.

Ward's idiosyncratic modus operandi can get him into trouble, however. He was sacked from *Alien³* (being replaced by David Fincher) after baffled producers couldn't understand why the action took place on a wooden planet. His troubled personal project, the New Zealand colonial period drama *River Queen* (2005), proved unsatisfactory for both the director and critics, and raised serious doubts about whether there's any easy place in the modern industry for a filmmaker with such an expansive and, indeed, expensive vision. LH

The Navigator 1988, 91 min, b/w and col
cast Bruce Lyons, Chris Haywood, Hamish McFarlane, Marshall Napier, Noel Appleby, Paul Livingston *cin* Geoffrey Simpson *m* Davood A. Tabrizi

Driven by a religious vision, fourteenth-century miners in Cumbria dig a tunnel to escape the imminent arrival of the Black Death and find themselves in twentieth-century New Zealand. Unfolding with a fable-like simplicity, the time-travel narrative is more or less a peg on which to hang some of director Vincent Ward's most sumptuous, magical and disturbing images.

Map Of The Human Heart 1993, 109 min
cast Jason Scott Lee, Robert Joamie, Anne Parillaud, Annie Galipeau, Patrick Bergin, Clotilde Courau, John Cusack *cin* Eduardo Serra *m* Gabriel Yared

Ward's soaring magnum opus tracks star-crossed lovers halfway across the world as a young Inuit falls in love with a half-Indian girl in a hospital in Montreal in the 1930s. They are parted, but ten years later he joins the Royal Air Force and they reunite in London. There are some awe-inspiring scenes – notably the bravura shot of the couple making love on top of a hot air balloon – and even the bombing of Dresden set piece bristles with a terrible beauty.

Régis Wargnier
France, 1948–

The French director is best known for a series of films that explore the yawning gap between cultures, filtered through the prism of lush, melodramatic excess that wins awards but clog the arteries of cynical film reviewers.

Régis Wargnier studied classics at the University of Nanterre and entered the film industry as an assistant to Claude Chabrol. His directorial debut, *La femme de ma vie* (*Women Of My Life*, 1986), was a lyrical essay on the devastating effects of alcohol on a marriage that won the César for best first work. After *Je suis le seigneur du château* (*I'm The King Of The Castle*, 1989), in which two boys battle over

bragging rights to a large mansion, Wargnier discovered his soap operatic métier with the Oscar-winning *Indochine* (1992). Made at a time when French cinema seemed to be particularly prone to donning costumes and exhuming the past, it represented the high point of a particular strain of heritage cinema that, like Jean-Jacques Annaud's *The Lover* (1992), filmed the sun setting on the French empire with a barely concealed nostalgia.

In *Une femme française* (1995) Emmanuelle Béart embarks on a series of affairs while her husband is fighting in World War II, and continues to be unfaithful after the conflict. This domestic drama crystallized the strengths and weaknesses of Wargnier's opulent brand of middlebrow cinema, with the director once again demonstrating a keen eye for scenery, but no feeling for character.

Wargnier returned to his keynote, culture-clash theme with *East-West* (1999), which unearthed a little-known and shameful moment in Soviet–French relations. More familiar failings were exposed in *Man To Man* (2005), which charted the fate of African pygmies shipped to Britain and treated as freak show specimens. Once again, Wargnier took a fascinating scenario and coated it so thickly with pseudo-painterly flourishes that most of the historical interest had all but vanished beneath several layers of melodramatic gloss. The contemporary Parisian plague thriller, *Pars vite en reviens tard* (*Seeds Of Death*, 2007), suggested a fresh direction, but still disappointed. LH

Indochine 1992, 154 min
cast Catherine Deneuve, Vincent Perez, Linh Dan Pham, Jean Yanne, Dominique Blanc, Henri Marteau *cin* François Catonné *m* Patrick Doyle

Plantation owner and graceful matriarch Catherine Deneuve is crushed when naval officer Vincent Perez chooses her adopted Indochinese daughter over her. When she conspires to have him packed off to a remote island, the daughter follows and has her political consciousness raised along the way. Many critics objected to the story's colonialist perspective, and the overbearing sense that the real tragedy was the end of empire. Despite its dubious ideological undercurrents, the surface does shimmer with a languorous beauty, and it was rewarded with the Academy Award for best foreign film.

East-West (Est-ouest) 1999, 125 min
cast Sandrine Bonnaire, Oleg Menshikov, Sergei Bodrov Jr, Catherine Deneuve, Tatiana Doguileva *cin* Laurent Dailland *m* Patrick Doyle

Wargnier's fictionalization of a little-known slice of post-war history is both poignant and resonant. A doctor (Oleg Menshikov), his wife (Sandrine Bonnaire) and their child are among the thousands of Russian émigrés in France who take up Stalin's offer of amnesty after World War II and return to the Soviet Union. As the family suffer the lingering death of life in a squalid room in Kiev, Bonnaire resolves to leave her adopted country and embarks on an affair with a young swimmer who plots to escape to the West.

Andy Warhol

US, 1928–87

Andy Warhol invented reality television. This may not be entirely true, but it's the sort of self-aggrandizing statement of which the artist would surely have approved. While the influence – if not the monetary value – of his art arguably may have waned, his avant-garde movies now seem more bizarrely pertinent and influential than ever. Much of cinema is about voyeurism, and Warhol made this more blatant, wielding his 16mm camera like a prurient Big Brother (both of the Orwellian and reality show kind) or a particularly cruel form of CCTV that doubled as an X-ray into the troubled souls of the junkies, transvestites and narcissists who peopled his screen. His oft misquoted prediction that in the future everyone will be famous for fifteen minutes now rings true, with most contestants having a shelf life of a month before their magazine fame is pulped and recycled for a new bunch of exhibitionists.

In the early 1960s, when the US avant-garde was exploring ideas of randomness and repetition, Warhol bought his first camera and simply trained it on his so-called superstars and let it run, reportedly walking away and returning when the reel of film had run out. Some films, like *My Hustler* (1965), *Vinyl* (1965) – an idiosyncratic adaptation of *A Clockwork Orange* – and *Lonesome Cowboys* (1968), nominally had plots. Others didn't bother with the pretence. Warhol zoomed in on conversations or naked bodies, or both, gleefully exploiting the combination that has made reality television such a winning formula – eavesdropping and nudity. The naked male customers of the aptly titled *Nude Restaurant* (1967) and 1969's *Blue Movie*, in which Viva and Louis Waldron have sex, merrily broke taboos. The magnum opus of this unblinking strain of underground cinema, *The Chelsea Girls* (1966), acts as a critical litmus test: it's either tediously self-indulgent or a bravura return to primitive cinema, depending on your tolerance for DIY aesthetics and druggy attention-seekers.

More likely to be screened in art galleries than in cinemas, Warhol's early work is typified by a series of real-time experiments that focused on a single subject, with a self-explanatory title: *Sleep* (1963) – six hours of poet John Giorno snoozing; *Eat* (1963) – painter Robert Indiana chewing a mushroom for 45 minutes; *Blow Job* (1963) – a man's face as he receives oral pleasure; and the towering zenith of one-shot cinema, *Empire* (1964) – eight hours of the Empire State Building shot from the forty-first floor of the skyscraper opposite. With their punishing length and determined emphasis on repetition, disengagement and amateurism, these home movies are clearly the grainy prototypes of the numerous video installations that have become a permanent fixture in galleries around the globe.

After making sixty films in the mid-1960s, Andy Warhol more or less retired from cinema after he was shot by Valerie Solanas in 1968. His main contribution after *Lonesome Cowboys* (1968) was to add his imprimatur to the narratively conventional movies of Paul Morrissey. LH

My Hustler 1965, 70 min, b/w

cast Paul America, Ed Hood, Joseph Campbell, John MacDermott, Ed Weiner, Geneviève Charbon, Dorothy Dean *cin* Andy Warhol

A middle-aged homosexual takes a blonde hustler to Fire Island with intent to seduce. His female neighbour and another stud take bets on who will be the first to have the strapping young man. In the second half, the two hustlers wash, shave, shower and ride the wave of homoerotic attraction that threatens to engulf the pair of them. This classic example showcases Warhol's unique instruction to actors: keep acting until the reel ends. The filmmaker reasoned that after a while they would stop pretending and gradually reveal their true selves.

The Chelsea Girls 1966, 210 min, b/w and col

cast Ondine, Angelina "Pepper" Davis, Ingrid Superstar, Albert René Ricard, Mary Woronov, International Velvet *cin* Andy Warhol *m* Velvet Underground

Each superstar (the name given to a young stray who drifted into the orbit of Warhol's studio, the Factory) is given twenty to thirty minutes to do their thing, which often means flaunt their stuff, take their clothes off or ramble inconclusively. The subjects are often as unfocused as the camera itself, which zooms in and out often for no discernible reason. Co-directed with Paul Morrissey.

Lonesome Cowboys 1968, 109 min

cast Viva, Taylor Mead, Tom Hompertz, Louis Waldon, Joe Dallesandro, Eric Emerson, Julian Burroughs, Francis Francine *cin* Paul Morrissey

For all the media hoopla about the gay cowboys of Ang Lee's *Brokeback Mountain* (2005), Warhol and Paul Morrissey did it 36 years earlier, mining the homosexual subtext that's an integral, unspoken part of the man's-gotta-do-what-a-man's-gotta-do genre. Joe Dallesandro and his gang come to town, rape Viva and hang out in this sloppy, improvised and ground-breaking spoof that bears some of the hallmarks of Morrissey's later burlesques such as *Flesh For Frankenstein* (1973).

John Waters

US, 1946–

Long before David Lynch and Todd Solondz exposed the livid underbelly of American suburbia, Baltimore-based cinema laureate John Waters giddily celebrated the violence, perversity and poor hygiene to be found just beyond the white picket fence. Any film from his 1970s run of underground provocations will serve up some permutation of cannibalism, incest, intravenous drug use, death by electric chair, religious blasphemy and sex with chickens. In *Multiple Maniacs* (1970), leading lady Divine (né Harris Glen Milstead) snarfs down human organs and is raped by a lobster; in the midnight-circuit blockbuster *Pink Flamingos* (1972), she eats a poodle dropping, then grins for the camera. "If someone vomits watching one of my films", Waters once wrote, "it's like getting a standing ovation."

The fearless Divine was the unrivalled star of stars in the informal repertory company of Waters' underground years. This included Mink Stole, Mary Vivian Pearce, David Lochary and the ample and elderly Edith Massey, resplendent in a revealing dominatrix ensemble in the surprisingly coherent *Female Trouble* (1974), which sends schoolgirl Divine on a rampage after she's denied a pair of cha-cha heels for Christmas. *Polyester* (1981) provided Waters' first piece of star casting – 1950s teen idol Tab Hunter as Divine's unreliable love interest – and a somewhat resistible gimmick: the film was presented in "Odorama", with scratch-and-sniff cards to be inhaled by audience members at designated moments.

Waters moved into the more respectable mainstream with *Hairspray* (1988), a Day-Glo slice of irreverent nostalgia and his last film with Divine (who died just a few weeks after the film's Baltimore premiere). The director soldiered on with *Cry-Baby* (1990), a spoof on *Grease* with Johnny Depp sending up his teen pin-up image, and *Serial Mom* (1994), with Kathleen Turner as a model housewife driven to murder by bad manners and faux pas. After earning mixed reviews for *Pecker* (1998) and *Cecil B. DeMented* (2000), Waters made something of a return to his outlaw roots in 2004 with the aptly titled *A Dirty Shame*, featuring Tracey Ullman as a concussed nymphomaniac and Selma Blair sporting Russ Meyer-worthy breasts. This gleefully outrageous film continued a theme in Waters' work that stretches back to *Pink Flamingos*: in the face-off between trash culture and the "straight" world, the ostensibly upstanding citizens are truly the most depraved. JW

Pink Flamingos 1972, 108 min

cast Divine, David Lochary, Mary Vivian Pearce, Mink Stole, Danny Mills, Edith Maney, Channing Wilroy, Cookie Mueller *cin* John Waters

In Waters' grotesque underground hit, made for a relatively lavish $100,000, two families compete for the coveted title of the "Filthiest People Alive": it's Divine's trailer-trash clan versus the Marbles, who run a baby-production factory in their basement. The movie leaves no doubt about where its sympathies lie in this particular contest, and crowns Divine's triumph in the notorious coda wherein she eats dog shit.

Hairspray 1988, 92 min

cast Divine, Debbie Harry, Sonny Bono, Ricki Lake, Colleen Fitzpatrick, Ruth Brown, Pia Zadora, Ric Ocasek, Mink Stole *cin* David Insley *m* Kenny Vance

Tracy Turnblad (Ricki Lake) is a "pleasantly plump" teen in early-1960s Baltimore who aches to strut her stuff on *The Corny Collins Show*; her bid to join the dance programme's

slender, lily-white ranks soon becomes fused with an integration campaign. Sweet-souled and rated PG, Waters' mainstream breakthrough tones down the spectacular bad taste of his earlier output – with the exception of the impeccably gaudy set design and costumes – and is the swan song of the irreplaceable Divine.

Peter Watkins
UK, 1935–

Will the critics of the future look back and wonder how it was that Peter Watkins laboured neglected, outside the system, for more than four decades?

A law unto himself, Watkins employs artistic strategems that are unique but remarkably consistent. From *Culloden* (1964) to *The Commune* (1999) he has created vivid, multifaceted, intellectually adventurous work by mixing dramatic and documentary techniques, presenting history as actuality drama with "real people" in place of actors, and adopting an interrogative (but subjective) voiceover commentary. He is still best known for his chilling BBC film about the potential effects of a nuclear attack on Britain, *The War Game* (1965), which won an Oscar for best documentary. Although it was withheld by the BBC for many years, the film was widely distributed and influential in the CND movement.

A radical political thinker who brooks no compromise, Watkins quit the BBC and went on to make provocative films in Sweden, Denmark, France and Canada, the best known of which is probably the war sports dystopia *Gladiators* (1969). *Privilege* (1967) and *Punishment Park* (1971), his only American film, are fascinating, prescient but somewhat clumsy narrative fictions about pop culture and authoritarianism respectively. Both films were rejected by contemporary audiences and barely distributed, sending Watkins back to nonfiction filmmaking, and polemically anti-commercial forms: *The Journey* (1987), for example, a fourteen-hour anti-nuclear project. Equally ambitious was his 2000 epic study of the Parisian anarchist government, *La commune (Paris, 1871)*. His masterpiece, however, remains *Edvard Munch* (1974) – and it's not a great leap to imagine that Watkins identified completely with this tortured and repudiated artist. As the director's work becomes more widely available on DVD, interest is increasing in this congenital refusenik. TC

Edvard Munch 1974, 210 min

cast Geir Westby, Gro Fraas, Erik Allum, Amund Berge, Kjersti Allum, Camilla Falk *cin* Odd-Geir Saether

To tell the story of the Norwegian painter Edvard Munch, Watkins employed a large cast of nonprofessional actors, some of whom share their own thoughts on the artist in direct-to-camera interviews. He imparts historical context in a dry BBC-style voiceover, and uses flashbacks to dramatize the formative traumas of Munch's life – the early

W

deaths of his mother and sister, his own near-death experience and a wretched love affair with a married woman. It is riveting, shot through with fascinating insights. Munch emerges not only as a brilliant artist but also as a prototypical tormented modern sceptic, scouring away at the surface of things to find some essential truth.

Apichatpong Weerasethakul

Thailand, 1970–

Unique, experimental, allusive and elusive, Apichatpong Weerasethakul's transcendental meditations blur boundaries and alter reality, using nonprofessional actors and long takes that stretch both time and audience patience. A star of the Thai New Wave, Weerasethakul studied architecture and designed dream houses, before studying art and film at the Chicago Art Institute, where he produced a series of avant-garde shorts.

His feature debut, the engrossing and increasingly eccentric documentary-drama *Mysterious Object At Noon* (2000), played a film version of the surrealists' game "exquisite corpse", as the director travelled through Thailand asking people to construct the next part of a bizarre fictional story. *The Adventures Of Iron Pussy* (2003) is the least typical of the director's output, being a camp, pastiche musical about the adventures of a drag queen and an action hero.

Weerasethakul's reputation rests on two films that are welded to a two-act structure that divides upon entrance to an enchanted forest. In *Blissfully Yours* (2002), which won the Un Certain Regard prize at Cannes, the opening credit sequence begins halfway through the movie, which changes narrative tack as the film's central couple enters a jungle near the border with Burma. The long-take naturalism is then spiked by bouts of intense lyricism, hard-core sex and superimpositions.

In 2004, *Tropical Malady* simply stunned critics, even those who had been hardened by the experience of watching *Blissfully Yours*. The first Thai film to be shown in competition at Cannes, *Tropical Malady* won the Special Jury Prize. By turns naturalistic and gnomic, tedious and magical, artless and pretentious, the film – like the director himself – divided opinions: is Weerasethakul a genius, a coquette or a trickster? The director continued to eschew narrative in favour of impressionism in 2006 with the autobiographical *Syndromes And A Century*, which was commissioned as part of the New Crowned Hope's project to mark the 250th anniversary of Mozart's birth. The film's long, hypnotic shots left some critics awestruck, yet finally convinced of Weerasethakul's talents. LH

Tropical Malady (Sud pralad) 2004, 119 min
cast Banlop Lomnoi, Sakda Kaewbuadee, Sirivech Jareonchon, Udom Promma *cin* Vichit Tanapanitch, Jarin Pengpanitch, Jean-Louis Vialard

Weerasethakul affects a grainy, faux naïvety as he charts the quotidian existence of a Thai soldier and his beau in the big city. Halfway through their love story, the celluloid seems to melt down, the screen goes black and realism gives way to magic and allegory. In an enchanted forest, the soldier tracks down a shamanistic spirit that takes on the form of both a glowing tiger and his naked lover. If there is a link between the two halves – and not all critics agree there is – it might be the predatory nature of desire.

Paul Wegener

Germany, 1874–1948

A profound influence on the 1930s horror movies put out by Universal Studios, stage actor Paul Wegener's dream-like films used sophisticated trick photography and often starred himself. He is best remembered nowadays for his third retelling of the Golem story. After making the Faustian *The Student Of Prague* (1913) with Stellan Rye, Wegener co-directed two Frankensteinian films, *Der Golem* (1915) and *Der Golem und die Tänzerin* (*The Golem And The Dancing Girl*, 1917). More myths followed: *Rübezahls Hochzeit* (*Rubezahl's Wedding*, 1916) and *Der Rattenfänger von Hameln* (*The Pied Piper Of Hamelin*, 1918), before his masterpiece, *Der Golem, wie er in die Welt kam* (*The Golem: How He Came Into The World*, 1920). Upon its release in the US in 1923, the film ran in New York for nearly a year. Wegener then turned to acting full-time before directing a few films in the late 1930s, including the biopic *King August The Strong* (1936). He later appeared in several propaganda films during the Nazi era, and was named an Actor of the Stage. JR

Der Golem: wie er in die Welt kam (The Golem: How He Came Into The World) 1920, 85 min, b/w
cast Paul Wegener, Albert Steinrück, Lyda Salmanova, Ernst Deutsch, Hans Stürm, Max Kronert *cin* Robert Babeerske *m* Hans Landsberger

This version of the Jewish folk tale about a sixteenth-century rabbi who makes a clay man to protect Prague's persecuted Jewish community is a clear precursor of the Frankenstein story, and this expressionist classic (co-directed with Carl Boese) was a model for James Whale's 1931 *Frankenstein*. In the title role the actor-director invests the clay man – here translated into an ungainly hulk with an unflattering haircut – with real pathos, while the subtle special effects leave the film hovering gently between realism and fantasy.

Peter Weir

Australia, 1944–

The 1970s was a fecund decade for Australian cinema, with the emergence of directors like

W

Phillip Noyce, Gillian Armstrong, Fred Schepisi, Bruce Beresford and George Miller. An industry that had been practically nonexistent started consistently producing twenty films a year. The most commercially successful and widely respected of the directors to emerge from this New Wave, Peter Weir is distinctive in finding dramatic situations that resonate with deeper philosophical, spiritual and environmental concerns.

Although it wasn't his first film (that was the previous year's black comic fantasy, *The Cars That Ate Paris*), *Picnic At Hanging Rock* (1975) introduced Weir to critics and filmgoers around the world: a spellbindingly atmospheric, enigmatic story about the disappearance of three girls and a teacher from a school trip in 1900. The movie's mystical sense of time and place notwithstanding, many viewers were convinced it was based on a true story (it wasn't). *The Last Wave* (1977) offered another warning about the precarious imbalance between modernity and the natural world, a theme that recurs in various guises throughout his career. It was the moving but relatively conventional war film *Gallipoli* (1981) that sealed his reputation at home as a kind of national totem. Ironically it would be his last Australian picture.

Weir's Hollywood output has been varied, if largely successful – *Dead Poets Society* (1989) and *Green Card* (1990), in particular, were box-office smashes – but at their best his films maintain a melancholy sense of the strange. *The Year Of Living Dangerously* (1982) sees foreign correspondent Mel Gibson in over his head in Indonesia. In the hugely popular *Witness* (1985) Philadelphia cop Harrison Ford goes undercover in an Amish community. In *The Mosquito Coast* (1986) a self-styled inventor (Ford again) takes his family into the jungle to get back to nature – with disastrous results. Jeff Bridges survives a plane crash and tries to rediscover the taste of strawberries in the haunting *Fearless* (1993), while in *The Truman Show* (1998) Jim Carrey discovers his whole life is a prefabricated sham. *The Truman Show* is one of Weir's many American films to deal with a man coping in an alien environment.

Weir has been nominated for five Academy Awards (four times as best director), most recently for *Master And Commander: The Far Side Of The World* (2003). TC

The Cars That Ate Paris 1974, 91 min

cast Terry Camilleri, John Meillon, Melissa Jaffa, Kevin Miles, Max Gillies *cin* John McLean *m* Bruce Smeaton

The film that practically kick-started the Australian New Wave, Weir's low-budget debut is an arty, offbeat horror-cum-Western B-movie – just one influence on George Miller's Mad Max movies – about a small town that survives, in various ways, off the proceeds of the many suspicious car accidents that occur there. Deliciously dark fun, revealing the skewed vision that runs through all the director's best work.

Picnic At Hanging Rock 1975, 115 min

cast Rachel Roberts, Vivean Gray, Helen Morse, Kirsty Child, Anthony Llewellyn-Jones *cin* Russell Boyd *m* Mozart, Beethoven

Valentine's Day, 1900: bedecked in white lace dresses and gloves, the young ladies of Appleyard College set out for a picnic at Hanging Rock, an Aboriginal holy place. Three girls and a teacher stroll off to explore the lower slopes; then there is a scream. A week later one ashen-faced girl is found, but she remembers nothing of what has happened. A hypnotic, tantalizingly mysterious film… all the more so since Weir went back and cut a further seven minutes out for his 1998 director's cut.

Witness 1985, 112 min

cast Harrison Ford, Kelly McGillis, Josef Sommer, Lukas Haas, Jan Rubes, Alexander Godunov, Danny Glover *cin* John Seale *m* Maurice Jarre

When an Amish child witnesses a murder, big-city police detective Harrison Ford has to go undercover in the community to ensure the boy's protection. Although the script could easily have furnished a generic fish-out-of-water cop thriller, Weir responds with such fascination to the Amish society that the film becomes something more captivating and mysterious. A wordless sequence in which the community comes together to build a wooden barn lingers long in the memory.

The Truman Show 1998, 103 min

cast Jim Carrey, Laura Linney, Ed Harris, Noah Emmerich, Natasha McElhone, Peter Krause *cin* Peter Biziou *m* Burkhard Dallwitz, Philip Glass

Jim Carrey is Truman Burbank, who from birth is the unwitting star of TV's most brazen reality show. Everyone around him is an actor, but Truman only has the vaguest sense that something is amiss. Screenwriter Andrew Niccol's sci-fi conceit satirized – and anticipated – the most extreme versions of reality TV, but Weir imbued it with a cosmic existential wistfulness.

Master And Commander: The Far Side Of The World 2003, 138 min

cast Russell Crowe, Paul Bettany, James D'Arcy, Edward Woodall, Chris Larkin *cin* Russell Boyd *m* Iva Davies, Christopher Gordon, Richard Tognetti

Although it's hardly Weir's most personal work, this scrupulously crafted adaptation of Patrick O'Brien's much-loved seafaring novels is an intelligent Boy's Own adventure for grown-ups. Set during the Napoleonic era, this is a fine vehicle for Russell Crowe and Paul Bettany in contrasting roles, the former as the judicious man of action, Captain Jack Aubrey, and the latter as the scientist, ship's surgeon Stephen Maturin. Nominated for ten Oscars, the film only came away with wins for cinematography and sound editing.

Orson Welles
US, 1915–85

No filmmaker has been more revered than Orson Welles – or more abused. For most of the twentieth century he was celebrated in the West as the man who directed "the greatest film ever made", *Citizen Kane* (1941). But that honour came at a price: *Kane* was his first film, and US critics, especially, chastised him for never matching it. Some even questioned whether it was genuinely his accomplishment in the first place.

Welles was a child prodigy (a cartoonist, poet and actor by the age of 10, according to a local newspaper) who became America's Boy Wonder… He was also a mythomaniac, a highly unreliable narrator of his own life. Almost all his films are about himself, and *The Magnificent Ambersons* (1942) is the only film he directed in which he doesn't appear. He most often cast himself as a monster, subtly insinuating a sympathy for the demagogue that his scenarios (and his offscreen politics) would seem to disavow. "We are made of opposites", Welles said. "We live between two poles. There is a philistine and an aesthete in all of us, and a murderer and a saint. You don't reconcile the poles, you just recognize them."

A professional actor from the age of 16, the young Welles created a sensation in the New York theatre with his audacious voodoo *Macbeth* production in Harlem in 1936. *Doctor Faustus* followed, and another triumph, *The Cradle Will Rock* (1937). With producer John Houseman he founded the Mercury Theatre, starting with an acclaimed antifascist production of *Julius Caesar* in November 1937. The Mercury Theatre on the Air also produced weekly radio plays, including the notorious Halloween adaptation of *War Of The Worlds*, which turned H.G. Wells's novel into a live news broadcast and panicked the entire nation in 1938. In addition, Welles found fame as the voice of radio sleuth The Shadow.

His fame did not go unnoticed in Hollywood, and in 1939 the 23-year-old was offered an unprecedented contract by RKO, granted artistic carte blanche to write, produce and direct; final cut guaranteed. A good many of his subsequent troubles may have been exacerbated by the jealousy, resentment and alarm this contract excited in the industry. In the event, Welles would only be allowed to sign off on one film under these terms – *Citizen Kane*.

The precise sphere and extent of *Kane*'s influence continues to be debated, but there is no question that this was the most sophisticated film to come out of the Hollywood studio system, both in conception and in execution. The use of deep focus was particularly striking (and might be attributed to cinematographer Gregg Toland who had previously used the technique on John Ford's *The Long Voyage Home*, 1940), but there are also many remarkable transitions and montage sequences. Coming from the radical theatre, Welles was well versed in expressionist lighting effects. His penchant for low camera angles perhaps unconsciously reproduced the view from the stalls. His radio experience had attuned him to acoustics in a way that was completely alien to Hollywood veterans. Crucially, as an outsider, and with no one standing over his shoulder, Welles

Dramatic deep focus photography in *The Magnificent Ambersons* courtesy of Welles and cinematographer Gregg Toland, with the spoiled George (Tim Holt) in the foreground watched by his mother (Dolores Costello).

had no inhibitions about what could and couldn't be achieved and how to go about it. He brought in his colleagues from the Mercury Theatre to cast the picture, all of them unknown to movie-goers. In that sense, this stunningly assured debut was an unrepeatable experiment.

The film is not just an aesthetic *tour de force*. Thematically, it's just as complex and mature. It's a film about Charles Foster Kane, or William Randolph Hearst, or George Orson Welles, but someone else is always telling it, and then someone else is retelling it from a different perspective: the lawyer, the friend, the ex-wife. "Rosebud", Kane's enigmatic last word, remains a potent symbol because the different meanings ascribed to it are none of them wrong: it's a snow globe; or a pretty girl imprinted on the memory; a nickname Hearst applied to his mistress, Marion Davies; and the lost piece of a vast jigsaw puzzle that may or may not explain anything.

The impossibility of accounting for someone's life may be the key Wellesian theme, along with the impossibility of measuring up to your own aspirations. Welles's dynamic, baroque style can be interpreted as a rush to deny or stave off a dark sense of nihilism, just as Kane himself fills up warehouses with *objets d'art*. "I began at the top and have been working my way down ever since", the director remarked with tongue-in-cheek self-effacement in *F For Fake* (1974). It's true he would never again enjoy the resources bestowed on him by RKO at the height of the factory system.

There is ample evidence in the ruins of *The Magnificent Ambersons* that this film could have raised the bar still higher. For two thirds of its running time this melancholy period piece is uncommonly droll and gracious. But Welles left the editing unfinished at the behest of Nelson Rockefeller to make *It's All True* in Brazil, an unfinished movie celebrating pan-American solidarity on the eve of World War II. A disastrous preview screening and an even more disastrous change in studio control sealed *Ambersons'* fate, and this dark, tragic story was cut by nearly an hour and given a new, happy ending – apparently all the original footage was destroyed.

Welles's tenure at RKO was over, and Hollywood made sure he never had final cut in America again. Even though they were made relatively cheaply, *The Stranger* (1946) and *The Lady From Shanghai* (1948) were both significantly altered in postproduction, as was Universal's *Touch Of Evil* in 1958. The evidence suggests that these changes invariably diluted the conviction of the films in question. Nor were many of these the films he would have chosen to make in the first place: given his head, Welles turned to literature, and Shakespeare above all, not paperback thrillers.

Dismayed by the wounds exacted on his work, and potentially in jeopardy from the McCarthy blacklist, Welles went into voluntary exile in Europe, and became, in effect, an independent filmmaker. He paid for *Othello* (1952) himself, by acting in other people's films – a strategy that forced him to drag the company all over Europe with him as they shot the picture piecemeal over a three-year period.

These strictures forced a change in style. *The Magnificent Ambersons* and even 1948's *Macbeth* (shot in 21 days at Republic) are distinguished by long, ornate travelling shots. With *Othello*, Welles was forced to sacrifice the organic unities of the sequence shot for an altogether more abbreviated, fragmentary editing dialectic based on sleight of hand, speed and distraction. He taught himself how to edit, and discovered magic in the Moviola. ("There's rhythmic structure, there's counterpoint, harmony and dissonance [to] a film", Welles enthused. "The Moviola is a musical instrument.")

Even in Europe, he lost control of *Confidential Report* (aka *Mr Arkadin*, 1955), arguably his most disappointing exercise, rerunning *Kane* as a flamboyant B-movie potboiler. The twisted *noir Touch Of Evil* was a reminder of what he could accomplish with a studio behind him, but inexplicably, the studio preferred to remind Welles what damage they could wreak.

In 1962, producers Alexander and Ilya Salkind gave him free rein to make Franz Kafka's *The Trial*, and he took the opportunity to vent his feelings of persecution and paranoia, even as he insisted that Josef K (a marvellously nervy Anthony Perkins) was guilty as sin. It's a curious, difficult, but mordantly funny film (you could make the case that all Welles's movies are comedies at heart).

Around this time Welles largely abandoned institutional filmmaking to shoot his own projects as he chose, with a bare-bones cast and crew, no shooting script, and no production deadline. The most famous title in this line was his *Don Quixote* project, but there were dozens more, including adaptations of *The Merchant Of Venice* and Karen Blixen's *The Dreamers*, comic sketches, magic routines, readings and fragments. Friends and enemies have speculated he developed completion anxiety, sabotaging himself before anyone else got the chance. In the case of the unseen thriller, *The Deep* (1970), there may be some truth in it. The prodigious and allegedly profligate Mr Welles always seemed a little in love with failure.

But *Chimes At Midnight* (1965) and *The Immortal Story* (made for French TV in 1968) prove that he was still capable of exquisite artistry, given support. And *F For Fake* is a ground-breaking, superbly pragmatic and dexterous comedy about art and truth largely derived from second-hand footage. There is real hope that another independent film, the autobiographical *The Other Side Of The Wind* (1972) will soon see the light of day.

Welles was a political figure all of his life, and numerous biographers are still fighting over which is the more appropriate myth: the self-destructive showboat who refused to buckle down or the mis-understood maverick too pure for the system. Both are probably true, but these legends tend to under-rate just how much Welles accomplished in a dozen astonishing films, even if he always left us hungry for more. TC

Citizen Kane 1941, 119 min, b/w

cast Orson Welles, Joseph Cotten, Agnes Moorehead, Everett Sloane, Ruth Warrick, Ray Collins *cin* Gregg Toland *m* Bernard Herrmann

Citizen Kane is different films to different people. Technically and aesthetically, the thrill of unbounded creativity is everywhere apparent. It is alive with promise and possibility, provocative, stimulating and open. Like those infinite mirror shots Welles is so fond of, *Kane* is all surface and infinite depth; irreducible. It's an epic tale, the story of a man's life, yet the narrative is easily told in a brief newsreel. It's a detective story, but we are the detective. To Jorge Luis Borges, *Kane* is "a labyrinth without a centre"; to Martin Scorsese and many, many others, an inspiration; to Pauline Kael, it "may be more fun than any other great movie" (though she famously gave the credit to Herman J. Mankiewicz, who co-wrote the script).

The Magnificent Ambersons 1942, 88 min, b/w

cast Tim Holt, Joseph Cotten, Agnes Moorehead, Dolores Costello, Anne Baxter, Orson Welles (voice) *cin* Stanley Cortez *m* Bernard Herrmann

RKO's desecration of Welles's second film may be the worst act of studio vandalism in Hollywood history. But even in this debased form, *Ambersons* is a wonderful film, a deeply moving adaptation of Booth Tarkington's novel charting the demise of a wealthy American family and the come-uppance of spoiled young George (Tim Holt), who has wrecked his mother's chance of happiness.

The Lady From Shanghai 1948, 87 min, b/w

cast Rita Hayworth, Orson Welles, Everett Sloane, Glenn Anders, Ted de Corsia *cin* Charles Lawton *m* Heinz Roemheld

"You need more than luck in Shanghai", muses Rita Hayworth, whose experiences in the city hover murkily in the background of her performance. The script is liberally sprinkled with such hard-boiled epigrams, while there's a wry detachment in the movie's pace and extravagant design. It was made virtually off-the-cuff, a crazy *film noir* to pay a debt to Columbia and, perhaps, to patch up his marriage to Hayworth: the picture is a love-hate letter to the iconic star. Michael O'Hara is as colourless a role as Welles ever gave himself, counterpointed by Everett Sloane's bitter, brilliant lawyer. Fractured as it is, this cine-matic hall of mirrors is endlessly diverting; Welles's camera is the ultimate scene-stealer.

Macbeth 1948, 103 min, b/w

cast Orson Welles, Jeannette Nolan, Dan O'Herlihy, Roddy McDowall, Edgar Barrier *cin* John L. Russell *m* Jacques Ibert

This is Welles's most underrated film, largely because he had the audacity to play fast and loose with the original, adding a character (Alan Napier as a Holy Father) and slash-ing back the text (though not as dramatically as the 89-minute version the studio put out). It is raw, fervid, pagan

and bold – some tracking shots are as inspired as anything he ever did. The erratic performances are the major flaw.

Othello 1952, 90 min, b/w

cast Orson Welles, Micheál MacLiammóir, Robert Coote *cin* Anchisi Brizzi, G.R. Aldo, George Fanto *m* Francesco Lavagnino, Alberto Barberis

Filmed over a three-year period in locations across Europe and Morocco while Welles stitched together the financing, *Othello* is a remarkably coherent and atmospheric movie, and it won the Palme d'Or at Cannes. With stunning pro-duction design by the great Alexandre Trauner, and a sin-gular baroque style that Welles imposed on the play, it also features an outstanding performance from MacLiammóir as the insidious Iago. Welles ruminated on the production in his (rare) documentary *Filming Othello* in 1978.

Touch Of Evil 1958, 112 min, b/w

cast Charlton Heston, Janet Leigh, Orson Welles, Joseph Calleia, Marlene Dietrich, Akim Tamiroff, Zsa Zsa Gabor *cin* Russell Metty *m* Henry Mancini

Welles returned to Hollywood for what turned out to be his final film within the studio system, a spectacu-larly seedy *noir* set on the US-Mexican border. It's a mystery thriller probing the ethics of putting justice ahead of the law, dominated by Welles's performance as the corrupt police detective Hank Quinlan. Famous for its opening five-minute tracking shot, the film is a triumph of atmosphere, graced with nuanced performances and a compelling narrative. Recut by Universal in postproduction, and mys-teriously dumped, the film was re-edited in 1998 in accord-ance with a 58-page memo Welles dictated at the time.

Chimes At Midnight 1965, 105 min, b/w

cast Orson Welles, Keith Baxter, Jeanne Moreau, John Gielgud, Margaret Rutherford *cin* Edmond Richard *m* Angelo Francesco Lavagnino

This autumnal masterpiece draws on the five Shakespeare plays in which Falstaff appears: *Richard II*; *Henry IV* parts one and two; *Henry V*, and *The Merry Wives Of Windsor*. Welles suggested he was "perhaps the only purely good character Shakespeare ever wrote", an interesting descrip-tion of a cowardly rogue and inveterate carouser. Of all the director's Shakespeare adaptations, this is certainly the richest, with sterling performances from an excellent inter-national cast (marred somewhat by problematic dubbing).

F For Fake (Vérités et mensonges) 1974, 85 min

cast Orson Welles, Oja Kodar, Elmyr de Hory, Clifford Irving *cin* François Reichenbach, Gary Graver *m* Michel Legrand

Welles's last great film, a witty essay about art, authentic-ity, truth, lies, hoaxes and forgeries, was ahead of its time. Welles had been invited to narrate a documentary by François Reichenbach about the art forger Elmyr de Hory, whose Picassos allegedly adorn the galleries of Europe and North America. Welles took over the film to reflect the revelation that de Hory's biographer, Clifford Irving, had been exposed as the hoaxer behind the recently published Howard Hughes autobiography.

William A. Wellman
US, 1896–1975

The poor man's Howard Hawks, "Wild Bill" Wellman excelled in hard-hitting, tough-talking action movies. A boisterous youth, he dropped out of high school to break into professional ice hockey. During World War I, Wellman drove an ambulance in the French Foreign Legion before becoming a pilot in the Lafayette Flying Corps, an adjunct of the Lafayette Escadrille, which was a famed haven for young Americans eager for combat prior to US involvement in the hostilities. Wellman broke his back when he was shot down and received the Croix de Guerre.

His Hollywood career was inspired by this heroic past. In the 1920s he was a wing walker with a flying circus and, according to an inaccurate but telling legend, he got his first role in a movie (1919's *The Knickerbocker Buckaroo*) after making a forced landing on Douglas Fairbanks's polo grounds. Tall, lean and weather-beaten, Wellman decided he didn't enjoy acting and persuaded Fairbanks to get him a job with the crew. Graduating from prop boy to assistant director, Wellman directed his first movie – *The Man Who Won* – in 1923.

Owing to the vicissitudes of film preservation, most of Wellman's silent films have been lost, but *Wings* (1927), which made his name as a director, has survived. This aerial warfare epic established one major type of Hollywood action movie: mind-blowing thrills, thin characterization and no place for women. Although flapper star Clara Bow featured on the ground, it was in the aerial sequences – shot over reproduction wartime trenches on Texan flats – that Wellman's heroic, daring world came vividly to life. It won Hollywood's first Academy Award for best picture.

Wellman quickly developed a reputation for his efficient handling of action and landscapes. A confrontational persona, he clashed with executives and took no nonsense from actors, once getting into a fist fight with Spencer Tracy. Like Hawks, he worked in many genres. In 1928 Wellman made *Beggars Of Life*, a story set on the road in which *Wings* star Richard Arlen tagged along with a murderer played by Louise Brooks, disguised as a man. The James Cagney vehicle *The Public Enemy* (1931), which was made for Warner Bros, helped establish the Depression-era gangster cycle. *Night Nurse* (1931) was a tense melodrama that saw Barbara Stanwyck driven to defend her infant charges against a vicious plot to kill them. Featuring a documentary naturalism, *Wild Boys Of The Road* (1933) was a sympathetic story of hobo life that signalled the awakening of Hollywood's social conscience.

In 1937 Wellman made the first version of *A Star Is Born*, and the Ben Hecht newspaper comedy *Nothing Sacred* for David O. Selznick, perhaps the only producer Wellman trusted. *Beau Geste* (1939) found Gary Cooper evoking Wellman's Foreign Legion experience in an exciting, nicely shot adventure yarn. Ginger Rogers' unscrupulous murder suspect gulls everyone in a rollicking tale of Chicago

ethics in 1942's subversive *Roxie Hart* (the source for the musical *Chicago*). However, the anti-lynch law argument *The Ox-Bow Incident* (1943) now seems didactic.

Based on war correspondent Ernie Pyle's memoirs, *The Story Of GI Joe* (1945) vividly evoked the mud and blood of modern warfare, featured a fine cameo by Robert Mitchum and influenced Samuel Fuller. The even more Fulleresque *Battleground* followed in 1949. The tense *Yellow Sky* (1948) saw bank robbers confronting an old prospector and his tomboyish daughter. Shot by Joseph MacDonald on blasted salt flats, it featured rich performances from Gregory Peck, Richard Widmark and Anne Baxter. The 1950s saw Wellman assigned increasingly mediocre Westerns – *Across The Wide Missouri* (1951) – and aviation pictures – *Island In The Sky* (1953), *The High And The Mighty* (1954). He was a daredevil in death as in life, and when he died his ashes were scattered from a plane. RA

The Public Enemy 1931, 84 min, b/w
cast James Cagney, Jean Harlow, Edward Woods, Donald Cook, Joan Blondell, Donald Cook *cin* Dev Jennings *m* David Mendoza

This was one of the films that forged the violent, dynamic model for a series of Warner Bros gangster programmers in the 1930s. Rocketing James Cagney to stardom as the archetypal tough guy Tom Powers and drawing on the ongoing history of Prohibition gangsterism, Wellman's seminal opus responsibly acknowledged the role of poor social conditions and historical misfortune in its portrait of an inner-city boy gone bad.

Nothing Sacred 1937, 75 min
cast Carole Lombard, Fredric March, Charles Winninger, Walter Connolly, Sig Rumann, Frank Fay, Troy Brown *cin* W. Howard Greene *m* Oscar Levant

When small-town girl Carole Lombard discovers she has radium poisoning she intends to spend the rest of her days living it up in New York. Instantly on her case is a reporter (incisively played by Fredric March) who knows how to milk the story for all it's worth. Writer Ben Hecht's acid reply to the Capra school of homespun heroism and cornball folksiness – one of the most cynical of 1930s newspaper comedies – benefits from a terrific turn from Lombard, plus a gallery of rustics with fewer scruples than a bootlegger.

Beau Geste 1939, 120 min, b/w
cast Gary Cooper, Ray Milland, Robert Preston, Brian Donlevy, Susan Hayward *cin* Theodor Sparkuhl, Archie Stout *m* Alfred Newman

Memorably opening with a shot of a desert fort eerily draped in corpses, Wellman's rousing, Foreign Legion adventure is a terrific showcase for star Gary Cooper's quiet integrity and taciturnity. Although *Beau Geste*'s heroics may seem oddly innocent to today's audiences, this recruiting poster of a film seems increasingly poignant in the light of the World War – and the war movies – that were to come.

Battleground 1949, 118 min, b/w
cast Van Johnson, John Hodiak, Ricardo Montalban, George Murphy, Marshall Thompson, Jerome Courtland *cin* Paul C. Vogel *m* Lennie Hayton

Steeped in the rawness of what seems like neo-realism and featuring genuine combat footage, this account of GIs

W

trapped in the wintry Ardennes by Hitler's final offensive is dirty and gruelling. A cast of post-war stalwarts give great performances, and it seems remarkable now that this was shot on the MGM backlot.

Wim Wenders

Germany, 1945–

Wim Wenders always seems to be on the move. In the course of his career he has made films in Japan, Portugal, Cuba, Italy, Russia, Australia, his native Germany, and the US. Not surprisingly, he called his film company "Road Movies".

Born just months after the end of World War II, Wenders became an art student, film critic and then a leading figure in the German New Wave of the 1970s. He left Germany at the end of that decade, just as the movement began to run out of steam. Less political than some of his colleagues, and an ardent cinephile with a love of John Ford, Nick Ray and rock'n'roll (in 1970 his first feature, *Summer In The City*, was dedicated to The Kinks), Wenders was already halfway to Hollywood before Francis Ford Coppola offered him a berth at his Zoetrope studio.

"The Yanks have colonized our subconsciousness", one of the characters remarks in his seminal *Kings Of The Road* (1976), an observation midway between critique and confession. That ambivalence was key to the listless disaffection pervasive in those early, aimless journey films: *The Goalkeeper's Fear Of The Penalty Kick* (1971), *Alice In The Cities* (1974), *Wrong Movement* (1975). Although less well-known than his international efforts, these are some of Wenders' most accomplished and rewarding pictures.

Collaborating from the very first with novelist Peter Handke and cinematographer Robby Müller, Wenders favoured long takes, taciturn, alienated protagonists and open-ended narratives. This was a deeply mittel-European sensibility. Yet increasingly he was drawn towards the dynamics of American genre filmmaking. That tension produced an imaginative Patricia Highsmith adaptation, *The American Friend* (1977), starring Dennis Hopper as the movies' least likely Tom Ripley, and featuring cameos by directors Nick Ray and Sam Fuller.

It was probably this film that prompted Coppola to assign Wenders to *Hammett* (1982), but the two men fell out, and Coppola re-shot much of it to his own liking. In a career limbo as the *Hammett* saga dragged on, Wenders made *The State Of Things* (1982) on the run. A film about a stalled film, it is one of his most underrated and most personal efforts. Produced in America with European financing, *Paris, Texas* (1984) crystallized the director's love affair with the wide-open spaces that inspire his deepest reveries. It won the Palme d'Or and was an arthouse hit across Europe. In the US, predictably, the response was less enthusiastic.

Returning to Berlin, Wenders hit on the idea of angels eavesdropping on the thoughts and prayers of this still-divided city's inhabitants. *Wings Of Desire* (1987) may be his most satisfying film because it brings his congenital rootlessness back home. It proved to be his biggest hit, and he won his second major prize in succession at Cannes (for best director). For many critics this would prove his peak. (His sequel *Faraway, So Close!*, 1993, did not come close.) His success made Wenders a fashionable commodity – he was now hanging out with the rock stars he used to listen to – and from here on his attempts to address sophisticated ideas about art, globalization, violence and communication mostly fail to flesh out their intellectual pretensions: *Until The End Of The World* (1991) was a massive philosophical sci-fi film shot across four continents. It was released in a theatrical 158-minute cut, though a (possibly more coherent?) 280-minute version has surfaced on DVD in Germany.

The End Of Violence (1997) was an illustrated thesis of a movie – but not a particularly convincing one. *The Million Dollar Hotel* (2000), based on an idea by U2's Bono, was a bizarre whodunnit set in a flophouse. *Land Of Plenty* (2004) laboured under the duress of its working title, *Angst And Alienation In America*. *Don't Come Knocking* (2005), starring Sam Shepard, proved to be a partial return to form, though it could also be seen as retreading past glories. Handsomely photographed and loaded with stars, these Beverly Hills art movies suggest that the perennial wanderer is going round and round in ever diminishing circles.

Wenders has also made numerous nonfiction films, often as side-projects, including *Lightning Over Water* (1980), about Nick Ray's slow death, *Tokyo-Ga* (1985) and *Notebook On Cities And Clothes* (1989). One of these nonfiction films, the music documentary *Buena Vista Social Club* (1999), has proved to be the director's only popular success since the 1980s. TC

Kings Of The Road (Im Lauf der Zeit) 1976, 175 min, b/w

cast Rüdiger Vogler, Hanns Zischler, Lisa Kreuzer, Rudolf Schündler *cin* Robby Müller, Martin Schafer *m* Axel Linstädt

Ennui is etched into the very landscape of the monochrome German hinterlands in this epic road movie, one of the touchstone European films of the 1970s. Vogler is Bruno, an electrician kept busy fixing broken cinema equipment in border-town theatres. He gives a lift to Robert (Zischler), depressed and aimless after the break-up of his marriage. They don't talk much and accomplish next to nothing together, but a bond is forged.

W

Harry Dean Stanton strides along the track with only the landscape for company in *Paris, Texas*.

The American Friend (Der Amerikanische Freund) 1977, 127 min

cast Dennis Hopper, Bruno Ganz, Lisa Kreuzer, Gérard Blain, Nicholas Ray, Samuel Fuller, Jean Eustache *cin* Robby Müller *m* Jürgen Knieper

Based on Patricia Highsmith's novel *Ripley's Game* (she was no fan, apparently), Wenders' most *noir*-ish movie features Dennis Hopper as an uncharacteristically dissolute Tom Ripley, art dealing and wheeling the vulnerably ill Ganz into a murder plot. Another Hopper, Edward, casts a shadow over Robby Müller's moody camerawork, while a couple of set pieces have a Hitchcockian bravado.

Paris, Texas 1984, 147 min

cast Harry Dean Stanton, Dean Stockwell, Hunter Carson, Nastassja Kinski, Aurore Clément *cin* Robby Müller *m* Ry Cooder

A lonely man strides through the Southwestern desert, in self-imposed exile for sins he can no longer recall. Nursed back to health by his brother, Travis attempts to heal the broken lives he has on his conscience. Think about the story too closely and the threads start to unravel, yet the film's patient attention to behaviour combined with Müller's enraptured response to the American landscape makes for a deeply felt authenticity. Cult supporting player Harry Dean Stanton is unforgettable in his only lead role. From a script by Sam Shepard, with a Ry Cooder score.

Wings Of Desire (Der Himmel über Berlin) 1987, 127 min, b/w and col

cast Bruno Ganz, Solveig Dommartin, Otto Sander, Curt Bois, Peter Falk *cin* Henri Alekan *m* Jürgen Knieper

There are angels over the streets of Berlin. One of them, Damiel (Bruno Ganz) is inspired to renounce his wings for the simple mortal pleasures of touch, and taste, and love. The idea is borderline cute, but the execution is sublime, from the layered, poetic-impressionistic soundtrack to the breathtaking black-and-white and colour cinematog-

raphy by the great Henri Alekan. Wenders' most popular film is also his best.

Lina Wertmüller
Italy, 1928–

In the 1970s Lina Wertmüller expressed all the drama of sex and politics in post-1968 Europe. The rebellious scion of an aristocratic Swiss family, Wertmüller was influenced by a school friend – who later married Marcello Mastroianni – to enrol at Rome's Theatre Academy. After she graduated in 1957, she toured Europe as a puppeteer and worked as an actress, director and playwright. During this time she first met actor Giancarlo Giannini, who would become key to her unique blend of comedy, operatic emotionalism and astute political commentary.

In 1962 Mastroianni persuaded Federico Fellini to hire Wertmüller as a production assistant on *8½*. Wooing the crew to Sicily, she shot her first film, *The Lizards* (1963), a tale of provincial lethargy owing something to Fellini's *I vitelloni*. Commercial assignments were followed by *The Seduction Of Mimi* (1972), in which Giannini's labourer gets involved with the Mob and communists to satirical effect. Wertmüller was rewarded with the best director prize at Cannes. *Love And Anarchy* (1973) found Giannini's male chauvinist in thrall to Mariangela Melato's siren.

Wertmüller's American success gathered momentum with *Swept Away... By An Unusual Destiny In The Blue Sea Of August* (1974), which detailed the

W

passionate face-off between a socialite and a communist marooned on a desert island. With *Seven Beauties* (1975), Giannini became a bigger international star and Wertmüller the first woman director to be nominated for an Academy Award. She became a cult figure, although not without feminist charges of political crudity. She had a talent to provoke, which helped raise her profile and ensured that she appealed to – and appalled – both left and right-wingers in Europe and America. *Blood Feud* (1978) continued her political account of Italian life, this time set against the backdrop of the beautiful Sicilian coast. While *Camorra: A Story Of Streets, Women And Crime* (1986) was a promising thriller marred by poor plotting, but distinguished by strong performances from Angela Molina and Harvey Keitel. Other recent projects – from 1989's *Crystal Or Cinders, Fire Or Wind, As Long As It's Love* to 2004's *Too Much Romance… It's Time For Stuffed Peppers* – have been more generic, showing little of the social and political acuity that has characterized the director's best work. However, Wertmüller, who writes all her own scripts, remains one of cinema's true independents. RA

Seven Beauties (Pasqualino settebelleze)
1975, 115 min

cast Giancarlo Giannini, Fernando Rey, Shirley Stoler, Elena Fiore, Piero Di Iorio, Enzo Vitale, Ermelinda De Felice *cin* Tonino Delli Colli *m* Enzo Jannacci

A riotous catalogue of masculine excesses, this was Giancarlo Giannini's greatest moment, a picaresque journey from social pariah to concentration camp inmate. Wertmüller's Oscar-nominated comedy is as carnivalesque and contentious as the director ever got.

James Whale
UK, 1889–1957

In *Bride Of Frankenstein* (1935), the sinister Dr Pretorius drinks "to a new world of gods and monsters". With those words he could also be toasting the cinema of James Whale, whose films often considered men suffering from a God complex and showed a fascination with physical infirmity and deformity. Whale was also one of the chief architects of the new world that was the horror talkie: his *Frankenstein* and Tod Browning's *Dracula* both appeared in 1931 and established Universal's 1930s monopoly on the genre. Current horror archetypes of the haunted house, the mad scientist and the lightning-lit laboratory all share a direct bloodline with imagery from Whale's movies (which, in turn, bore the deep influence of German expressionist decor and lighting schemes).

Surprisingly, Whale's films also glint with screwball wit, even at their spookiest. *The Old Dark House* (1932) strands a group of travellers in a gothic pile populated by a lunatic family, including the great Ernest Thesiger, who mines comedy gold from the unlikely line "Have a potato". While Whale's adaptation of H.G. Wells's *The Invisible Man* (1933) makes hilarious hay out of blundering cops, Claude Rains' thunderous voice and John P. Fulton's effects are truly the film's stars.

Whale's first theatrical experience was as a POW in a German prison camp during World War I; his feature debut was, unsurprisingly, an anti-war film, *Journey's End* (1930), adapted from the R.C. Sheriff play he had directed on the London stage. After the romantic tear-jerker *Waterloo Bridge* (1931), Whale enjoyed the splendid run of horror films that he is most famous for: *Frankenstein, The Old Dark House, The Invisible Man, Bride Of Frankenstein*. He also helmed *Remember Last Night?* (1935), a delicious black-comic mystery in which a man is found dead after a party so intoxicating that none of his fellow revellers remember it, and *Show Boat* (1936), a handsome version of the Jerome Kern-Oscar Hammerstein musical. He retired after the World War II drama *They Dare Not Love* (1941) and, except for a couple of brief returns to directing, concentrated on painting. In 1998 Ian McKellen gave a magnificent performance as Whale in Bill Condon's biopic *Gods And Monsters*, which poignantly imagined Whale's later years and introduced contemporary audiences to his work. JW

Frankenstein 1931, 71 min, b/w

cast Boris Karloff, Colin Clive, Mae Clarke, John Boles, Edward Van Sloan, Frederick Kerr *cin* Arthur Edeson *m* David Broekman, Bernhard Kaun

It will take many more years and many more parodies to dilute the uncanny effects of the first sound version of Mary Shelley's gothic novel. Boris Karloff's towering performance as the Monster is a Möbius strip of childlike vulnerability and inchoate rage, but the unwitting villain is, of course, Dr Frankenstein himself (Colin Clive), whose furtive grave-robbing and famous frenzied shrieks of "It's alive!" obliterate the line between man and monster.

Bride Of Frankenstein 1935, 75 min, b/w

cast Boris Karloff, Colin Clive, Valerie Hobson, Ernest Thesiger, Elsa Lanchester, Dwight Frye, Una O'Connor *cin* John Mescall *m* Franz Waxman

"It speaks!" Boris Karloff's creature wanders the countryside with an angry mob in pursuit and even makes a friend, while Dr Frankenstein and his new collaborator, Dr Pretorius (Ernest Thesiger), toil to produce a female mate for the Monster. The Bride's birth makes for a *tour de force* set piece, and Elsa Lanchester, crowned with electroshock hair and hissing like an angry swan, creates an icon out of mere minutes of screen time.

Robert Wiene
Germany, 1873–1938

Celebrated for one of the defining films of German expressionism, *The Cabinet Of Dr Caligari* (1919), Robert Wiene was also one of the

W

first in a long and perplexing line of directors who make one masterpiece, but never repeat that sparkling achievement. Critic Lotte Eisner, the champion of expressionism, decreed that Wiene was one of those second-rate directors whose first film "misled people into thinking them remarkably gifted".

Most horror aficionados since have shared her harsh opinion. Even his contribution to *Caligari* has been questioned: Fritz Lang, who was due to direct the movie, concocted the film's famous twist, while the picture's other coup, the celebrated angular canvas and board sets, were devised by a trio of designers

German expressionism

Watching *The Cabinet Of Dr Caligari* (1919) is to witness the crystallization of a potent visual vocabulary. All the key tropes of German expressionism are present and correct: macabre imagery hewn from nightmares, the sinister ubiquity of opaque shadows (actually painted onto the sets), and a twilight zone dominated by oblique angles and spatial distortions, consciously designed to disorient and intoxicate. These fantastic elements can be seen in numerous classics, such as Paul Wegener's *Der Golem* (1920), Fritz Lang's *Dr Mabuse, The Gambler* (1922), Paul Leni's *Waxworks* (1924), Henrik Galeen's *The Student Of Prague* (1926) and F.W. Murnau's *Faust* (1926). Expressionism had been the dominant form in most other German arts since 1910, most notably in the theatre of Max Reinhardt. But after Germany's defeat in World War I, the artistic form acquired a resonance with the whole zeitgeist, unexpectedly acting as a mirror for a country that had lost land, money and pride in the Versailles Treaty. This body blow to national confidence resulted in a morbid introspection and a renewed interest in mysticism.

Caligari was released in the year after the war ended. And Wiene's film was so strongly associated with expressionism that the style was alternately known as Caligarism. But *Caligari* was more than a design classic: the movie's philosophical undertow – its concerns with the individual's relationship with empirical reality – was disturbing and influential. The whole movie's action could simply have been located in the mind of its deluded protagonist. And this, for some critics, is the crux of expressionism: the subjective expression of an inner world, the fractured realities of the damaged. *Waxworks*, the masterpiece by painter and film director Paul Leni, was a portmanteau movie about three different historical figures, all filtered through a writer's febrile imagination. The stars of the show are undoubtedly the phantasmagorical sets but, according to the director, they weren't constructed exclusively for aesthetic reasons, but to render an internal landscape and events that cannot be seen "through everyday eyes". For others, expressionism is all about the startling chiaroscuro: the bold application of one strong key light amidst stygian gloom. *Nosferatu* (1922), directed by Murnau, took expressionism out of the studios and into the open air, while somehow retaining the intense poeticism and pervasive sense of diurnal nightmare, achieving a gothic alchemy by transforming the natural into the supernatural. And it gave the horror movie an instant icon in Count Orlok (played by Max Schreck) – a spectral, skeletal and curiously erotic presence with bat ears, rat teeth and scissor fingers. Indeed, expressionism specialized in creatures of the night, as found in *Der Golem*. But expressionism also influenced science fiction. Lang's *Metropolis* (1927), with its modernist and majestic vision of the city of the future (constructed from steel, concrete, glass and light) became one of the major building blocks of sci-fi.

Expressionism came to an end in the late 1920s following a shift in German cinema pioneered by F.W. Murnau and G.W. Pabst towards a new realism or objectivity ("Neue Sachlichkeit"). The demise of silent movies also played a part in expressionism's decline, as the invention of sound ushered in a more naturalistic and prosaic cinema. Then the Nazi party's ascension to power in 1933 had repercussions for both the German and American film industries, with the exodus of talent from one country to the other. Fritz Lang, Karl Freund, Billy Wilder and Robert Siodmak brought expressionism with them as they fled to Hollywood. The result was a hybrid of American pulp, wartime disillusion, French poetic realism and German *Sturm und Drang*: film noir. Early shadings of it can be detected in Lang's 1930s output, including *Fury* (1936) and *You Only Live Once* (1937), but expressionism really flourished again immediately after the war, once more holding up a mirror to national insecurities and psychic wounds. *Noir's* tales of betrayal, disillusionment and fevered desire adopted expressionism's destabilizing effects to reflect the frazzled identities and neurotic perspectives of its disturbed protagonists, particularly in such flashback classics as Siodmak's *Criss Cross* (1949) and Rudolph Maté's *D.O.A.* (1950).

Although its last gleamings can be detected in neo-*noirs* such as Ridley Scott's *Blade Runner* (1982), the natural heir to expressionism – and Murnau in particular – is arguably Werner Herzog. This legendary eccentric walked all the way from Munich to Paris to pay tribute to Lotte Eisner, the fabled critic and champion of expressionism, when she was seriously ill, and he even remade Murnau's *Nosferatu* in 1979 to make explicit the connection between New German Cinema and its dimly remembered predecessors. LH

W

and came about as the result of a decision by Erich Pommer necessitated by the frequent power cuts of the time.

Wiene studied law and became a theatre manager before joining the film industry as scriptwriter and director. *Caligari* was an instant classic, and Wiene profited by association. The film became notorious too. In his seminal book *From Caligari To Hitler*, critic Siegfried Kracauer blamed it for preconditioning the German psyche for the rise of Nazism – even though the film was banned under the Reich as "degenerate art". Wiene utilized the same angular set design in *Genuine* (1920) and helmed *Raskolnikov* (1923), a prestige adaptation of *Crime And Punishment*. The other movie for which Wiene is best known is *The Hands Of Orlac* (1926), in which Conrad Veidt plays a pianist who has a hand transplant, with murderous consequences.

In the late 1920s and early 1930s, Wiene specialized in light Lubitsch-like comedies. Fleeing the Nazis, he arrived in Britain where he planned a sequel to his greatest work, but he died in Paris not long afterwards, neither being able to remake *Caligari* or overcome it. At the time of his death he was working on *Ultimatum* (1938) with Erich von Stroheim; the film was completed by Robert Siodmak. LH

The Cabinet Of Dr Caligari (Das Cabinet des Dr Caligari) 1919, 58 min, b/w

cast Werner Krauss, Conrad Veidt, Lil Dagover, Friedrich Feher, Hans Heinz von Twardowski, Rudolf Lettinger *cin* Willy Hameister

The narrative – about a mad doctor who uses a fairground somnambulist to commit crimes for him – lacks the fluency and poetry of Fritz Lang and F.W. Murnau, and the direction is undeniably stagey. The angular set designs and the painted shadows add to the theatricality, but also represent a bold move away from naturalism and realism. It's the ending that's probably the most truly influential aspect of this classic horror film.

Billy Wilder

Poland (formerly Austro-Hungarian Empire), 1906–2002

Graduating from screenwriter to director and later producing his own work, Billy Wilder was a key Hollywood auteur and an astute commentator on America's manners and mores. Growing up in inter-war Vienna and exposed to American largesse and its burgeoning cultural influence, Wilder became infatuated with American music and movies. His expertise got him into journalism and in 1926 he accompanied band leader Paul Whiteman on the Berlin leg of a European tour.

Keeping his finger on the popular pulse, Wilder became a Berliner in taste and temperament, developing an attitude of worldly cynicism that would characterize his films. He broke into screenwriting with *People On Sunday* (1929), a vibrant account of young Berliners on their day off. Co-directed by Robert Siodmak and Edgar G. Ulmer, it remains a vital documentary-like slice of Weimar life and announced the emergence of a new filmmaking generation. In 1933 Wilder fled Nazi Germany and got the chance to direct in Paris. *Mauvaise graine* (*Bad Seed*, 1933) was a harbinger of films to come, with its frenetic tale of moral degradation anticipating both future compromised Wilder heroes and the freshness of the *nouvelle vague*.

Wilder arrived in Hollywood in 1934 and his screenwriting collaborations with Charles Brackett set sophisticated standards for the examination of sexual politics and human weakness in American comedy. *Midnight* (Mitchell Leisen, 1939), *Ninotchka* (Ernst Lubitsch, 1939), *Ball Of Fire* (Howard Hawks, 1941): Brackett and Wilder rapidly made a name for intelligent and commercial showcases for the likes of Gary Cooper, Greta Garbo and Barbara Stanwyck. As a director, Wilder combined the deft touch and knowing wit of Ernst Lubitsch (whom he acknowledged as an influence) with the pragmatic flow of classical Hollywood narrative in a resonant interrogation of American society.

Falling out with director Mitchell Leisen over Leisen's cavalier way with a script, Wilder goaded Paramount into giving him a directing assignment. *The Major And The Minor* (1942) was a slightly subversive tale in which Ray Milland's naïve army major falls for Ginger Rogers, who is improbably masquerading as a child. Wilder returned to the army with *Stalag 17* (1953), a comedy drama set in a POW camp, with director Otto Preminger heading up the German contingent. Disguise and deception would become key Wilder themes from the Audrey Hepburn confection *Sabrina* (1954) to the Agatha Christie courtroom drama *Witness For The Prosecution* (1957) and that raucous tribute to the Roaring Twenties, *Some Like It Hot* (1959). However, for some this cross-dressing classic signalled the coarsening of Wilder's output.

The writer-director's chronicle of post-war America was at its best when underpinning a portrait of American disappointment with a realism worthy of Erich von Stroheim. *Double Indemnity* powerfully set the trend in 1944. Despite gratuitous Oscar-seeking, *The Lost Weekend* (1945) derives its power from an alcoholic's sojourn among the apartments and storefronts of its Manhattan locations. *Sunset Blvd* (1950) is unremitting in its revelation of the rotten lives beneath the glitz of Hollywood, while *Ace In The Hole* (1951) is a corruscating indictment of "yellow" journalism.

Wilder formed a screenwriting partnership with I.A.L. Diamond that began with the Lubitschian boudoir confection *Love In The Afternoon* (1957)

Billy Wilder and Jack Lemmon

Billy Wilder once said that "Happiness is working with Jack Lemmon." No other director has made more of Lemmon's distressed urban schlemiel than Wilder. Born in 1925, Lemmon became the fresh-faced foil in Judy Holliday vehicles at Columbia during the 1950s before winning the best supporting actor Oscar for *Mister Roberts* in 1955. In Wilder's *Some Like it Hot* (1959), Lemmon fetched up on a Florida-bound express fleeing Chicago gangsters and competing with the devil-may-care Tony Curtis for the affections of Marilyn Monroe. Clad in a frumpy frock to foil the Mob while warding off the cockeyed advances of Joe E. Brown's besotted millionaire, Lemmon demonstrated a likeable wackiness that he was to finesse in his 1960 performance as C.C. "Bud" Baxter in Wilder's *The Apartment*. This portrayal of a corporate Everyman was to follow Lemmon for the rest of his career. The insurance clerk on the way up that he played summed up for the Kennedy era the urban *mensch* perplexed by the sexual minefields and fiscal imperatives of the affluent society.

Jack Lemmon's 1960s roles seemed to take their lead from Wilder, with whom he worked on the Parisian comedy *Irma La Douce* (1963). But while David Swift's romantic comedies *Under the Yum-Yum Tree* (1964) and *Good Neighbor Sam* (1964) gamely ventured beyond the coy rom-com template (as defined by Doris Day and Rock Hudson), Lemmon's other work progressed towards increasingly pathetic portraits of executive angst. In Blake Edwards' *Days Of Wine And Roses* (1963), he played a PR man whose drinking destroys his marriage. Richard Quine's *How To Murder Your Wife* (1965) took the aspirant playboy from *The Apartment* and turned him into that arch 1960s animal – the artist lothario. It remains one of the era's most pointed conjunctions of "mod" and misogyny. Wilder's *The Fortune Cookie* (1966) was a dark allegory of modern middle-class avarice, and established a screen partnership torn between Lemmon's inveterate anxiety and Walter Matthau's lugubrious moral brinkmanship. It was a relationship refined in *The Front Page* (1974), in which Matthau and Lemmon reprised the feints and thrusts of newspaper editor Walter Burns and star reporter Hildy Johnson from Lewis Milestone's 1931 original and Howard Hawks's 1940 adaptation *His Girl Friday*. The parallels between Matthau and Lemmon's urbane chicanery and the unfolding Watergate affair were clear to those who wished to see them.

A very enjoyable Neil Simon two-hander, Gene Saks's *The Odd Couple* (1968) placed the by-now familiar Lemmon-Matthau double act against the backdrop of the sexual revolution. Stuart Rosenberg's *The April Fools* (1969) let Lemmon's disillusioned Wall Street broker have his way with Catherine Deneuve. But what was cute in *The Odd Couple* now seemed desperate. Middle-class striving became middle-aged angst in Arthur Hiller's *The Out-Of-Towners* (1970), a modern horror story in which an Ohio executive is laid low by the exasperations of the city. *Avanti* (1972), again with Wilder, was a lighter take on midlife middle-class mores, but there was an Oscar for a dramatic role as a frustrated salaryman in John Avildsen's *Save The Tiger* (1973). In the 1970s, Lemmon generally measured the dismay of a post-war generation caught unawares by American decline, feminism and the ageing process. Costa-Gavras's *Missing* (1982) blew the lid on suburban complacency as a picket-fence patriot discovers what happened to his son during the US-sponsored Chilean junta. Lemmon's performances in Oliver Stone's *JFK* (1991) and Robert Altman's *Short Cuts* (1993) were serviceable, but he seemed increasingly temperamental, and Howard Deutch's *The Odd Couple II* (1998) was a lame attempt to resurrect a formula that could only work in the 1960s when the sexual revolution was still sexy. There were so-so reunions with Matthau in Donald Petrie's *Grumpy Old Men* (1993) and Howard Deutch's *Grumpier Old Men* (1995). Only in James Foley's *Glengarry Glen Ross* (1992) did Lemmon truly convince, his performance seeming like a plausible response to the downsizing savagery of today. RA

W

and reached its pinnacle with that fairy tale of modern mendacity, *The Apartment* (1960). Star Jack Lemmon would become Wilder's ideal model for the essentially decent American male compromised by the buying and selling of souls. *The Front Page* (1974) – a remake of Lewis Milestone's 1931 film, previously adapted by Howard Hawks as *His Girl Friday* (1940) – was a tribute to the grubby press offices of the director's youth, while the dynamic between Lemmon and Walter Matthau encapsulated the moral and sexual ambivalences of being a *mensch* in a sick world. Matthau's performance as the crooked lawyer in *The Fortune Cookie*

(1966) reminded more than one American critic of Richard Nixon.

In the 1970s, Wilder increasingly struggled to inhabit the times. *Fedora* (1978) was the Hollywood player's attempt to reprise the success of *Sunset Blvd* and his final film, *Buddy Buddy* (1981), was an intermittently funny stab at recreating the Lemmon-Matthau-Wilder magic. With his moral realism and feeling for the audience, Wilder taught American cinema to grow up, bridging the transition from the studio era to the corporatism of modern Hollywood. RA

America's dream girl: Tom Ewell struggles to cope with the proximity of Marilyn Monroe in *The Seven Year Itch*.

Double Indemnity 1944, 107 min, b/w

cast Fred MacMurray, Barbara Stanwyck, Edward G. Robinson, Porter Hall, Jean Heather, Tom Powers, Byron Barr *cin* John F. Seitz *m* Miklos Rozsa

This is a gripping *film noir* in which Fred MacMurray's insurance salesman relates how he murdered a client for money and for a woman. A prototype of the genre, it provides the link between the dank passions of 1930s French crime thrillers and the barren moral universe of post-war Los Angeles. Unusually shot in the city's suburban malls and marshalling yards, this is suffused with the dread of Barbara Stanwyck's peroxide *femme fatale* and endures as one of Hollywood's bitterest films.

Sunset Blvd 1950, 111 min, b/w

cast William Holden, Gloria Swanson, Erich von Stroheim, Nancy Olson, Fred Clark, Lloyd Gough, Jack Webb *cin* John F. Seitz *m* Franz Waxman

Wilder's poison-pen letter to Hollywood in decline was written from bitter experience and shot on Los Angeles days so bright they cruelly reveal the wrinkles in screen star Norma Desmond's face. But behind the tabloid story of William Holden's struggling screenwriter found face down in the diva's swimming pool there is another tale, that of the idealistic story editor Holden loved. Here, the innocent fatuities of the industry town confront the disappointments of savage experience.

Ace In The Hole 1951, 111 min, b/w

cast Kirk Douglas, Jan Sterling, Robert Arthur, Porter Hall, Frank Cady *cin* Charles Lang Jr *m* Hugo Friedhofer

No one gets out of this film with any dignity, least of all the ruthless journalist Charles Tatum (a brilliantly manic Kirk Douglas) who manipulates the attempted rescue of a man trapped undergound to further his flagging career. His venality is matched by the victim's insensitive wife (Jan Sterling) and a sheriff seeking to get himself re-elected. Largely filmed in the New Mexico desert, this remains one of the most cynical visions of human greed on film.

The Seven Year Itch 1955, 105 min

cast Marilyn Monroe, Tom Ewell, Evelyn Keys, Sonny Tufts, Robert Strauss, Oskar Homolka, Marguerite Chapman *cin* Milton Krasner *m* Alfred Newman

When executive Tom Ewell's wife and son go away for the summer, he swelters in Manhattan and Marilyn Monroe drops in for cocktails. Playing to America's male-menopausal dream and pushing at Production Code mores already in decline, Wilder's adaptation of George Axelrod's Broadway success cuts through the innuendo to find an oddly touching tale of male insufficiency.

Some Like It Hot 1959, 121 min, b/w

cast Jack Lemmon, Tony Curtis, Marilyn Monroe, Joe E. Brown, George Raft *cin* Charles Lang Jr *m* Adolph Deutsch

The most popular of all classic screen comedies, and arguably the greatest, has Jack Lemmon and Tony Curtis playing a couple of musicians who witness a gangland massacre and, in order to escape the Mob, disguise themselves as women and join an all-girl orchestra. A reason for sticking around appears in the voluptuous form of Marilyn Monroe as ukulele-playing Sugar Kane. Curtis's attempts to win her and Lemmon's attempts to lose the attentions of an elderly millionaire create some hilariously awkward situations which Wilder controls with the deftest of touches.

The Apartment 1960, 125 min, b/w

cast Jack Lemmon, Shirley MacLaine, Fred MacMurray, Ray Walston, Jack Kruschen, David Lewis *cin* Joseph LaShelle *m* Adolph Deutsch

Jack Lemmon is a dutiful insurance clerk in a generic Manhattan corporation. He is a young man on the way up – hard-working, resourceful, bright – who lends his apartment key to his superiors in exchange for possible promotion. But when he finds that Shirley MacLaine, the elevator girl he fancies, is having an affair with his boss, he becomes a *mensch* again. Crisply shot by Joseph LaShelle and played with humour and pathos by Lemmon and MacLaine, Wilder's film anatomized the manners and mores of the Space Age.

Bretaigne Windust
France, 1906–60

The role of Bretaigne Windust in Bette Davis's acting career has often been unfairly overlooked. Hailing from patrician roots and educated at Princeton, he co-founded the University Players in Massachusetts, whose number included Joshua Logan, Henry Fonda, Margaret Sullavan and James Stewart.

After acting and directing on Broadway, Windust went to Hollywood in the late 1940s to direct a string of likeable star vehicles. Davis essayed another of her languishing cultural types in Windust's debut, *Winter Meeting* (1948), in which she played a lovelorn New England poetess. That same year, she starred in his second film, the jaunty screwball comedy *June Bride*, alongside Robert Montgomery. In 1950, the director made two brisk comedies, *Perfect Strangers* with Ginger Rogers and *Pretty Baby* with Betsy Drake, which were set in the modern milieux of a jury room and an advertising agency, respectively.

With an uncredited Raoul Walsh, Windust co-directed 1951's powerful Humphrey Bogart vehicle *The Enforcer* (aka *Murder, Inc*). This *film noir* was inspired by contemporary revelations about the Mob, and introduced the argot of the "Syndicate" and a tenor of social decline reminiscent of post-war Fritz Lang. Windust gravitated to television work in the 1950s, where his rapport with actors saw him flourish. RA

June Bride 1948, 97 min, b/w

cast Bette Davis, Robert Montgomery, Betty Lynn, Jerome Cowan, Barbara Bates, Tom Tully, Fay Bainter *cin* Ted McCord *m* David Buttolph

When bickering ex-lovers Bette Davis and Robert Montgomery go to Indiana to cover a typical "hoosier" wedding for their magazine, the smarty-pants New Yorkers learn a thing or two about following their instincts… Fast, witty and right on the money, this film is a worthy echo of the pre-war remarriage strand of romantic comedy.

Michael Winner

UK, 1935–

Michael Winner is better known in Britain for his controversial politics and television appearances than for his films. Beginning as a film critic and entertainment columnist, Winner joined the BBC before breaking into the film industry making "nudies" and second features. Early work included *Play It Cool* (1962), a vehicle for Elvis clone Billy Fury, and *The Jokers* (1966), a screwball thriller in which Winner regular Oliver Reed and Michael Crawford plan to steal the crown jewels. It was scripted by the acclaimed British television writers Dick Clement and Ian Le Frenais, who also wrote Winner's 1968 war spoof *Hannibal Brooks*.

Winner's pacy, gimmicky style and his way with genre led him to Hollywood. *Lawman* (1971) was a gory, post-Peckinpah revenge Western starring Burt Lancaster. It anticipated *Death Wish* (1974), in which another Winner regular Charles Bronson plays a liberal man brutalized by the murder of his wife and daughter and intent on revenge. Square-jawed and laconic, Bronson, like Reed, was an ideal Winner protagonist, the decent man driven

to violence by circumstance and frustration. In *The Mechanic* (1972), he played an assassin who makes kills look like accidents, and in *The Stone Killer* (1973) he was a cop pitted against the Mob. Subsequently there have been *Death Wish* sequels (1981, 1985), glossy remakes and adaptations (*The Big Sleep*, 1978, *Appointment With Death*, 1988) and the feminist-baiting rape-revenge movie *Dirty Weekend* (1993).

While Winner exploited liberalizing 1970s attitudes towards sex and violence, his rampantly conservative solutions to modern malaise, lack of visual nuance and cynical number crunching have not encouraged critical plaudits. His oeuvre is a model of transient entertainment cinema. RA

Hannibal Brooks 1968, 102 min

cast Oliver Reed, Michael J. Pollard, Wolfgang Preiss, John Alderton, Helmut Lohner, Peter Carsten, Karin Baal *cin* Robert Paynter *m* Francis Lai

This saga, in which Oliver Reed's POW tries to escape to Switzerland with an elephant called Lucy, is the kind of wacky genre twist typical of 1960s cinema. The location photography in the Alps is attractive, Reed makes the most of his screen presence and the result is an engaging time-waster.

Michael Winterbottom

UK, 1961–

Michael Winterbottom's work has been both prolific and eclectic. Including television movies, he has made fourteen films in eleven years, thus emulating the fast-track approach of the *nouvelle vague* and his hero Rainer Werner Fassbinder.

After studying English at Oxford, he trained in film at Bristol and became an assistant to director Lindsay Anderson. Winterbottom then met producer Andrew Eaton, with whom he would later form Revolution Pictures. After both working in television, they made their first film together, *Butterfly Kiss* (1995). An early clue to Winterbottom's eclecticism lay in its genre: the lesbian serial killer British road movie. Overwrought in every department, the same fault lines were visible in another psychodrama, *I Want You* (1998), a sketchy yet unsubtle tale of *amour fou* in Margate. Of his intimate, contemporary melodramas, only the morose and nuanced *Wonderland* (1999) could be classified as a success, but it still lacks universal resonance.

Winterbottom's oeuvre doesn't defy classification completely, however. He has adapted Thomas Hardy twice, for instance: the emotionally raw and majestically photographed *Jude* (1996) and *The Claim* (2000), which boldly transposed *The Mayor Of Casterbridge* to the snowy desolation of the Sierra Nevada. These handsomely mounted and impressively choreographed period pieces are exceptions in Winterbottom's output. His increasing dependence upon low budgets and digital technology has determined his aesthetic, a sort of grainy informalism that allows him to respond to world events with an enviable speed.

The emotionally bruising and award-winning *In This World* (2002) dispensed with a script and employed two nonprofessional actors to chart the course of two Afghan illegal immigrants on their perilous 4000-mile journey to Britain. The powerful docudrama *The Road To Guantanamo* (2006) continued the tradition that Winterbottom started with *Welcome To Sarajevo* (1997), a deeply resonant and urgent report from the Bosnian conflict. In 2007, he made a splash at Cannes with *A Mighty Heart*, an electrifying drama about the last days of Daniel Pearl, an American journalist who was kidnapped and beheaded in Pakistan.

Digital cameras and low budgets have allowed Winterbottom to experiment with more formally innovative work, such as *24 Hour Party People* (2002) and *A Cock And Bull Story* (2005), a self-reflexive essay on the process of making a film of Laurence Sterne's *Tristram Shandy*. Given the speed with which Winterbottom turns out films, duds are an inevitability, such as *Code 46* (2003), a dystopian tale of genetic experiments without an original piece of cinematic DNA in its body; and the sexually explicit *9 Songs* (2004).

Quibbles aside, Britain is certainly lucky to have a director like Winterbottom, a genuine independent who works with autonomy, speed and at the edge of technology, politics and taste. Yet there isn't one of his films that wouldn't have benefited from more attention. It's tantalizing to think what he'd be capable of if he learned the art of patience. LH

Welcome To Sarajevo 1997, 102 min
cast Stephen Dillane, Woody Harrelson, Marisa Tomei, Emira Nusevic, Kerry Fox, Goran Visnjic, James Nesbitt *cin* Daf Hobson *m* Adrian Johnston

Based on the true story of ITN reporter Michael Nicholson who couldn't maintain the distance of his colleagues during the Bosnian conflict and eventually took an orphan home to London. Michael Winterbottom's fusion of real and reconstructed television footage packs the narrative with an urgent, emotional punch, but its early promise dissipates when the film leaves the war zone. The director, however, eschews cheap emotions and obvious dramatics in this staggering and moving work.

Wonderland 1999, 109 min
cast Shirley Henderson, Gina McKee, Molly Parker, Jan Hart, John Simm, Stuart Townsend *cin* Sean Bobbitt *m* Michael Nyman

Like Ingmar Bergman on a council estate, Winterbottom explores the lives of three South London sisters: a waitress (Gina McKee), a hairdresser (Shirley Henderson) and a housewife (Molly Parker), all locked into patterns of loneliness and entropy. Although the throb, gristle and energy of the city is perfectly captured in the grainy texture of the film, what's missing is the Swedish master's sense of poetry

and lingering depth. And while it's morose and nuanced, this misery fest doesn't quite possess the plangent ache of a great film about human folly and dysfunction.

The Claim 2000, 121 min
cast Wes Bentley, Milla Jovovich, Nastassja Kinski, Peter Mullan, Sarah Poley, Ron Anderson, Marty Antonini *cin* Alwin Küchler *m* Michael Nyman

Unofficial mayor and sheriff, Peter Mullan runs the nineteenth-century gold-rush town Kingdom Come in the Sierra Nevada mountains. His past comes back to haunt him in the shape of mother and daughter Nastassja Kinski and Sarah Polley. This elegaic drama reveals Winterbottom as a determined cinematic magpie, with nods to *Fitzcarraldo* and *McCabe And Mrs Miller*. Brimming with atypical flourishes of grandeur, *The Claim* comes within touching distance of greatness.

24 Hour Party People 2002, 117 min
cast Steve Coogan, Keith Allen, Rob Brydon, Enzo Cilenti, Ron Cook, Chris Coghill, Paddy Considine, Danny Cunningham *cin* Robby Müller

In this demented elegy to the legendary Manchester music label, Factory Records, there's no sense that the rise and fall of a band whose lead singer committed suicide is inherently more dramatic than the rise and fall of a band whose lead singer took an industrial quantity of drugs. Winterbottom and regular scribe Frank Cottrell Boyce chart the history of Joy Division and The Happy Mondays. Edgy, experimental and self-reflexive though it is, it's also self-satisfied and the mutual back-slapping provides the film's rhythm section.

Robert Wise
US, 1914–2005

His flexibility sometimes running to anonymity, Robert Wise was an agile jack of all trades who helmed many an award-winning smash hit. His auspicious beginnings included a stint as Orson Welles's editor on *Citizen Kane* (1941) and *The Magnificent Ambersons* (1942). Wise also played an important role within Val Lewton's horror unit at RKO, directing, among others, *The Curse Of The Cat People* (1944), a haunting child's-eye sequel to Lewton and Jacques Tourneur's *Cat People* (1942), and an adaptation of Robert Louis Stevenson's *The Body Snatcher* (1945), which teamed horror greats Boris Karloff and Bela Lugosi. His critical breakthrough came with the boxing movie *The Set-Up* (1949), which won the international critics and cinematography prizes at Cannes.

One of Wise's biggest early successes, the science-fiction classic *The Day The Earth Stood Still* (1951), sounded an early warning against nuclear proliferation, aided by a spooky Bernard Herrmann score. Wise returned to science-fiction sources often during his career, directing *The Andromeda Strain* (1971), adapted from Michael Crichton's novel about a deadly alien virus, and the serviceable television spin-off *Star Trek: The Motion Picture* (1979). Wise's redemptive boxing tale *Somebody Up There Likes Me* (1956) gave the dynamic Paul Newman his second film role (he took over after the original lead, James Dean, died in a car crash in 1955), and Susan Hayward won an Oscar for her sky-high performance in the death-row melodrama *I Want to Live!* (1958). However, when Wise returned to horror with *The Haunting* (1963), the most convincing character was the spooky Hill House itself, bumping and pulsating with paranormal activity.

Today, Wise's lavish musicals are his most widely seen and appreciated films, though the angular grace and jittery operatics of the multiple-Oscar-winning *West Side Story* (1961) can mostly be attributed to his co-director Jerome Robbins (who was fired midway through production). The saccharine, yet joyous Christmas perennial *The Sound Of Music* (1965) has proved itself to carry lasting appeal for both family audiences and camp-loving nostalgics. JW

The Curse Of The Cat People 1944, 70 min, b/w
cast Simone Simon, Ann Carter, Kent Smith, Elizabeth Russell, Julia Dean, Jane Randolph, Eve March, Sir Lancelot *cin* Nick Musuraca *m* Roy Webb

In this worthy sequel to 1942's *Cat People*, a lonely little girl, Amy (Ann Carter), finds a sympathetic imaginary friend in the ghostly form of her father's dead wife, Irena (Simone Simon), who believed herself to be the descendant of a Serbian feline race. Amy's parents start to believe she is falling victim to the same curse – real or imagined – that led to Irena's tragic demise. A quintessential Val Lewton frightener.

West Side Story 1961, 152 min
cast Natalie Wood, Richard Beymer, Russ Tamblyn, Rita Moreno, George Chakiris, Tony Mordente *cin* Daniel L. Fapp *m* Leonard Bernstein

Co-directed by choreographer Jerome Robbins, this beloved musical re-imagines William Shakespeare's *Romeo And Juliet* as a turf war between rival New York gangs, with lovers Natalie Wood and Richard Beymer caught on opposite sides of the fray. Leonard Bernstein's justly famed music builds up a sultry, sensational tension; Stephen Sondheim's lyrics and the supporting players are irresistible, and the dancing and acrobatics exhilarating.

The Haunting 1963, 152 min
cast Julie Harris, Claire Bloom, Richard Johnson, Russ Tamblyn, Fay Compton, Rosalie Crutchley *cin* Davis Boulton *m* Humphrey Searle

The Haunting is rated as one of the most frightening films ever made, with director Wise managing to squeeze every extra ounce out of that old staple the haunted house movie. An unlikely team of investigators occupies this one, led by Dr Markway (who trusts in science) but also including the repressed Eleanor – played by Julie Harris with an intensity that is frightening in itself. Gradually the house starts to make its presence felt, and the tension is ratcheted up to almost unbearable levels.

The Sound Of Music 1965, 174 min
cast Julie Andrews, Christopher Plummer, Richard Haydn, Eleanor Parker, Peggy Wood *cin* Ted McCord *m* Richard Rogers, Oscar Hammerstein

Feisty novice nun Maria (Julie Andrews) becomes governess to the seven children of rigid widowed Baron Von Trapp (Christopher Plummer) in this ever-popular Rodgers and Hammerstein musical, which manages to turn the fascist menace into a toothy kitsch-fest. Maria shows the kids a gentler touch, and soon has them harmonizing prettily, sporting matching outfits sewn from curtains and escaping the Nazis. The tunes are catchy, though.

Frederick Wiseman
US, 1930–

Arguably the greatest documentary maker in America, Frederick Wiseman's work comes with no added ingredients. No narration, no music, no inter-titles, no obvious narrative devices. With his unflinching eye and hand-held camera, the director seems to present us with raw, unmediated and bruising reality in the tradition of Direct Cinema. But this is only an appearance. As Wiseman is the first to point out, there's little *vérité* in his cinema, which is both highly selected and subjective.

Given the philosophical and physical impossibility of complete objectivity, some critics have wondered why his films aren't more partisan or prescriptive. For Wiseman, this is missing the point. He aims to reflect the shaded complexities of stark reality, offering viewers an immersive experience, allowing them to visit places they would never normally go and arrive at their own conclusions. He's made location reports from department stores, fashion houses and meat-processing plants in more than thirty films. But Wiseman is most successful when training his lens on bureaucracies and dwelling on the relationship between the individual and the state, including those people caught in a web of dehumanizing procedures, Kafkaesque systems and disabling hierarchies.

A graduate of Yale Law School, Wiseman gave up a career teaching law to make a self-financed documentary about the state prison for the criminally insane at Bridgewater, Massachusetts. *Titicut Follies* (1967), which became infamous when it was banned by the state judiciary, established his modus operandi: detached, observational and austere. It's a formula that served him well in *High School* (1968), *Law And Order* (1969), *Hospital* (1970) and the bleak army documentary *Basic Training* (1971).

The first of Wiseman's films to go past the ninety-minute mark, *Juvenile Court* (1973) challenged preconceptions in a way that is now one of the defining qualities of the director's work. *Welfare* (1975) clocked in at almost three hours, while *Near Death* (1989) – two minutes shy of six hours –was a compelling and gruelling account of the lives of four terminally ill patients and their doctors.

This contemplative, rambling approach works less well when the audience is invited to spend more than two hours in the company of fashion clotheshorses in *Model* (1980), but exerts a tight, emotional grip when a subject comes ready-made with inherent conflicts, social resonance and natural drama such as in *Public Housing* (1997) or *Domestic Violence* (2001). LH

Titicut Follies 1967, 85 min
cin John Marshall

Hugely controversial, this blisteringly raw, iconoclastic documentary revealed barbaric mistreatment of the mentally ill, who were regularly bullied and forced to wander around naked. In its most infamous and unforgettable scene, a Hungarian doctor force-feeds a patient by inserting a tube through his nose, while nonchalantly puffing away at a cigarette as the ash nearly falls into the tube itself. The reaction of the Massachusetts state officials once they saw the film was to ban it, on the grounds that inmates had not given consent. The ban ran until 1992 after a legal challenge.

Welfare 1975, 167 min
cin William Brayne

Frederick Wiseman has said that his films are about the theatricality of everyday experience and ordinary lives. Unsurprisingly, his films are crammed with dramatic monologues. His masterpiece culminates in a famous speech delivered by an ex-state employee who has waited 124 days for a welfare cheque after coming out of a mental institution, declaring that it's like waiting for Godot. This reference to Beckett crystallizes the sense of the impotent rage of individuals, whether social workers or their destitute clients, who are helpless and powerless in the face of an indifferent bureaucracy.

Wong Kar-Wai
China, 1958–

One of the most influential directors of the last few decades, Wong Kar-Wai has a signature style, a bristling neon aesthetic, that can be seen in films, adverts and music videos across the globe.

His debut, *As Tears Go By* (1989), was an adequate Hong Kong thriller, a visually unremarkable homage to Martin Scorsese's *Mean Streets* (1973) on which future action director Andrew Lau was cinematographer. It was Wong's second film, *Days Of Being Wild* (1991), that is, according to critic J. Hoberman, "the movie with which Wong Kar-Wai became Wong Kar-Wai". It's surely no coincidence that it was photographed by the highly individual Christopher Doyle, and includes the touches that have come to define Wong's oeuvre: an evanescent beauty rendered in smudges of blurry neon, a corrosive energy that almost blisters the celluloid, a wide-angle universe that seems to have been filtered through a fevered dream, and what Hoberman describes as "an underwater atmosphere".

Days also featured the stock company that would crop up in much of Wong's subsequent work: Leslie Cheung, Maggie Cheung and Tony Leung. It's Leung in particular who has become the face of Wong Kar-Wai, playing a string of handsome, lovelorn, doe-eyed losers in six of his films. Wong has been described as the "poet of time" and *Days Of Being Wild* is his first attempt to convey the transitory nature of human experience. Significantly, the melodrama is set in the early 1960s, which is sensually evoked by a warm nostalgia that runs oddly counter to Wong's own experiences. In 1963, the 5-year-old Wong moved to Hong Kong from Shanghai with his family, but his Mandarin-speaking parents were made to feel like outsiders in the Cantonese-dominated colony, and would spend much of their time in the local cinemas. It's been suggested that Wong's body of work represents an extraordinary act of wish fulfilment – that the director has created an alternative 1960s in his movies.

Chungking Express (1994) gave Wong Kar-Wai's trademark directorial style an international profile. The film was shot quickly during a two-month delay in the postproduction of his martial arts epic *Ashes Of Time* (1994). And the energy seems to have transferred itself to the film, as critics compared its quickfire *joie de vivre* to the cerebral, gleeful anarchy of early Jean-Luc Godard. The film's free-form nature was also due to the lack of a finished script; it's an on-the-hoof quality that has since become a characteristic of the director. *Chungking Express* and its unofficial sequel *Fallen Angels* (1995) have fractured narratives, variations on the theme of chaste love and permanent longing. They are both movies that invite contemplation; Wong Kar-Wai's films are frequently about individuals who have little to do but think – "beautiful losers" to borrow Leonard Cohen's phrase. It's a term that could apply to the gay lovers in the ironically titled *Happy Together* (1997), who constantly bicker in a Buenos Aires transformed into a pixelated, colour-saturated, down-at-heel Wong/Doyle universe.

In The Mood For Love (2000) was the maturation of the Wong/Doyle partnership. Wong's themes were summed up and given a melancholy burden of bittersweet nostalgia, and the film was blessed with fine acting from Tony Leung and a gracefully statuesque Maggie Cheung. It has a sense of maturity that's greatly aided by Doyle's deep-focus photography, which eschews the surface sheen that had, through cheap imitation, become a Hong Kong cliché. Its "sequel" *2046* (2004) took over five years to make, and was beset by problems – not all of them of the director's making. Even after showing it at Cannes, Wong went back and re-cut the film. During its long evolution, the sci-fi movie had morphed into a thriller about a Thai hit man, and finally into a more familiar tale about the impossibility of love for Tony Leung's character from *In The Mood For Love*.

Significantly Christopher Doyle wasn't the only cinematographer working on *In The Mood For Love* or *2046*, although it's hard to tell. So Doyle-like is the photography it's as if the director had bodily absorbed the Australian cinematographer. As if to prove the point, Wong's first movie without Doyle for two decades, *My Blueberry Nights* (2007), was poorly received by critics at Cannes. Reviewers found many things to criticize about the quirky American road movie, not least the unusual casting of singer Norah Jones in the lead, but also the absence of Doyle's signature style. LH

Into the limelight: cinematographers get their due

Given that film is primarily a visual medium, shouldn't directors share some of their credit with their cinematographers? Take the case of Wong Kar-Wai, for instance. Wong's debut, *As Tears Go By* (1989) was shot by future director Andrew Lau, but was visually unremarkable – another Triad movie from the Hong Kong production line. Wong Kar-Wai only became the director we all recognize in his second film, *Days Of Being Wild* (1991), an intoxicating confluence of lollipop colours and hyperreal reveries. It's certainly not coincidental that the film's director of photography was Christopher Doyle, as that same densely textured style – impressionistic, sensuous and shimmering – can be observed in many of the films he's worked on, from Chen Kaige's *Temptress Moon* (1996) to Phillip Noyce's *The Quiet American* (2002).

Citizen Kane (1941), the movie that regularly tops the critics' polls, was subtitled by its director as "A film by Orson Welles". Years later, critic Pauline Kael famously argued that writer Herman J. Mankiewicz deserved many of the plaudits for the film's success, and a persuasive argument can be made too for cinematographer Gregg Toland. The film's deep-focus photography, which miraculously keeps figures in both the foreground and background in pin-sharp focus, can be seen in the cinematographer's other movies, such as John Ford's *The Long Voyage Home* and *The Grapes Of Wrath* (both 1940). Toland's ground-breaking cinematography is an integral part of *Kane*'s classic status, and even Welles's biographer David Thomson admits that "it is clear that *Citizen Kane* could not have had its look or its élan without him". But Toland is just one of a number of cinematographers who have written their signature onto moving pictures – or who are forever associated with a certain innovation. Jack Cardiff virtually made Technicolor his own with a visually strident and intensely expressionistic palette, notably the blazing reds that throbbed with desire and portent in *Black Narcissus* (1947) and *The Red Shoes* (1948). John Alton mastered the art of darkness and defined the look of *film noir* with a Manichean chiaroscuro that had no place for shades of grey. Throughout Anthony Mann's *T-Men* (1947), *Raw Deal* (1948), *Reign Of Terror* (1949) and *Border Incident* (1949) and Joseph H. Lewis's *The Big Combo* (1955), faces were veiled and bisected by pitch-black shadows, while the Stygian gloom that monopolized Alton's frame allowed figures to emerge gradually if at all; often they remain enigmatic silhouettes, as if they weren't human but merely inky outlines sketched in a faded graphic novel.

Some directors have had a regular working relationship with the same cinematographer over several years. Ever since *Barton Fink* in 1991, the Coen brothers, for instance, have made good use of Roger Deakins. With one exception, Bernardo Bertolucci called upon the genius of Vittorio Storraro for his films from *The Spider's Stratagem* (1970) to *Little Buddha* (1993). In the 1970s, both Eric Rohmer and François Truffaut regularly relied upon the services of the legendary Néstor Almendros. However, it's a measure of how a film is a lot more than the sum of its visual tropes that there is little to link the flat naturalism of Truffaut's *Love On The Run* (1979) to the golden, evanescent beauty of Terrence Malick's *Days Of Heaven* (1978) – both photographed by Almendros – whereas both films are identifiably the work of their respective directors, consistent with their abiding themes and interests.

Furthermore, the history of cinema has not generally been kind to the work of cinematographers turned directors. With the exception of Nicolas Roeg, the results have not been heartening. Spielberg's regular cinematographer Janusz Kaminski may have helped construct one of the greatest battle scenes of cinema history in *Saving Private Ryan* (1998), but he came unstuck with his diabolical horror movie *Lost Souls* (2000). And even though Jack Cardiff won numerous awards for *Sons And Lovers* (1960), the rest of his directorial career veered from the workaday (*The Liquidator*, 1965) to the woeful (*Girl On A Motorcycle*, 1968). *Away With Words*, the 1999 movie directed by Christopher Doyle, was never properly released in cinemas and had only limited DVD distribution. It is considered something of a curate's egg, with hypnotic imagery but a shambolic narrative. Whatever its merits, its near total obscurity – combined with the fact that Doyle has never sat in the director's chair of a feature film since – reveals that this cinematographer, for one, needs directors such as Wong Kar-Wai as much as they need him. LH

W

Wong Kar-Wai's world of beautiful urban losers: Faye Wang reflected in *Chungking Express*.

Chungking Express (Chongqing senlin) 1994, 97 min

cast Brigitte Lin, Tony Leung, Faye Wang, Takeshi Kaneshiro, Valerie Chow *cin* Christopher Doyle *m* Frankie Chan, Roel A. Garcia

Brigitte Lin, iconic in dark glasses and blonde wig, looks for the courier who stole her cash and stash and bumps into "Cop 233" who's just self-consciously decided to fall for the next woman he meets. Dazzling in its cool exuberance and colour-saturated gloss, this neon paean to lost love is Wong's most exquisitely hypnotic work to date.

Fallen Angels (Duoluo tianshi) 1995, 96 min

cast Leon Lai, Michele Reis, Takeshi Kaneshiro, Karen Mong, Charlie Young, Chan Fai-Hung *cin* Christopher Doyle *m* Frankie Chan, Roel A. Garcia

This companion piece to *Chungking Express* has two more fragmentary narratives that occasionally intertwine. There's a bizarre love triangle between a dapper hit man, his infatuated agent and a punk called Baby; and the story of an ex-convict who reopens shops at night and a waif called Charlie. A visionary and virtuoso meditation on time, longing and loneliness, *Fallen Angels* is, depending on your point of view, either the stunning epitome or an excessive pastiche of the Wong Kar-Wai style.

In The Mood For Love (Huayang nianhua) 2000, 97 min

cast Maggie Cheung, Tony Leung, Rebecca Pan, Lai Chin, Siu Ping-Lam, Chin Tsi Ang *cin* Christopher Doyle, Lee Ping-Bin *m* Michael Galasso

There's a fleshy vibrancy to Doyle's photography that evokes a sense of the early 1960s as much as the hairdos and interior decor. Deep-focus photography brings out the hustle and bustle of city life. It's a truly sensual film, with sporadic moments of slow motion that heighten the narrative's hallucinatory quality. Tony Leung and Maggie Cheung conduct the most painfully chaste of affairs; it unfolds like a dream.

John Woo
China, 1946–

Quentin Tarantino once said that John Woo could direct action like Michelangelo could paint a ceiling. In *A Better Tomorrow* (1986) he put two guns in Chow Yun-Fat's hands and more or less invented what would become the "heroic blood-shed" sub-genre of Hong Kong thrillers, a type that reached its pinnacle in his hyperbolic *The Killer* (1989) and *Hard-Boiled* (1992).

Hollywood was impressed, and Woo was promptly imported to re-energize the local shoot-em-up. The director wears his influences on his sleeve: he fuses the stoic gangsters of Jean-Pierre Melville with the cathartic carnage of Sam Peckinpah and the flamboyant choreography in the films of Vincente Minnelli. US audiences were initially bemused, however, by expressionist rhetorical flourishes (swooping crane shots, zooms, freeze frames, multi-camera coverage and slow-motion replays) not commonly associated with Jean-Claude Van Damme flicks. *Hard Target* (1992) was at best a limited success (it's a Hong Kong movie in English, some complained), yet it is a measure of Woo's influence that much of his cinematic style has been reintegrated into the mainstream. *Broken Arrow* (1993) proved a major hit, and Woo won over the critics with *Face/Off* (1997), a playful, larger-than-life thriller with John Travolta and Nicolas Cage impersonating each other after mutual face transplants. But success comes with a price. *Mission: Impossible II* (2000) was little more than very expensive hack work, while the ambitious $120 million World War II drama *Windtalkers* (2002) was a massive flop. Woo's next – lacklustre – effort had the piquant title *Paycheck* (2003).

Is there more to John Woo than florid shoot-outs and corny sentiments? Some critics have suggested he's essentially a trumped-up second unit director. It took him a long time (nearly twenty years) to define himself in the Hong Kong industry, where he initially toiled on formulaic martial arts quickies and lowbrow comedies. However, a protégé of martial arts specialist Chang Cheh, he learned to choreograph action at the master's feet. And from *A Better Tomorrow* on, Woo (who is a devout Christian) also imparts great feeling to his Hong Kong movies: traditional Chinese values of honour, loyalty and respect are of paramount importance. Nor is he oblivious to the way in which these ideals are considered anachronistic in a modern capitalist society… despite body counts in the hundreds, Woo's films are deeply romantic, though that romance is usually homosocial, males bonding over a shared chivalric code. This moral subtext finds its most dramatic expression in the face-off (two characters holding guns to each other's head) that is Woo's signature scene. TC

A Better Tomorrow (Yingxiong bense) 1986, 95 min

cast Chow Yun-Fat, Leslie Cheung, Lung Ti, Emily Chu, Waise Lee, Fui-On Shing, Kenneth Tsang, Tsui Hark *cin* Wong Wing Hang *m* Joseph Koo

In outline a cops-and-robbers thriller harking back to the classical Hollywood gangster movie, *A Better Tomorrow* melded exaggerated violence with a floridly romantic – practically chivalric – take on male friendship and honour. Christened "heroic bloodshed" by fans, the sub-genre would become a staple of Hong Kong cinema in the next decade. The movie also made Woo's favourite actor Chow Yun-Fat a superstar: Alain Delon with a gun in each hand.

The Killer (Diexue shuang xiong) 1989, 111 min

cast Chow Yun-Fat, Danny Lee, Sally Yeh, Chu Kong, Paul Chu, Kenneth Tsang *cin* Wong Wing-Hang, Peter Pau *m* Lowell Lo

A hired assassin (Chow) accidentally blinds a nightclub singer, and moves to make reparation – though the cop on the case (Lee) is also hovering around the girl. The improbable mix of munitions and mutual sympathy, black comedy and heartfelt sincerity is very Woo, and somehow ennobles the outrageously pulpy material. It's another fine showcase for Chow Yun-Fat.

Bullet In The Head (Diexue jietou) 1990, 136 min

cast Tony Leung, Jacky Cheung, Waise Lee, Simon Yam, Fennie Yeun, Yolinda Yan *cin* Ardy Lam, Wilson Chan *m* James Wong, Romeo Diaz

Avowedly Woo's most personal film ("Tony Leung's character Ben is me"), this is the story of three friends who come of age in the gang-ridden Hong Kong of the late 1960s, fall foul of the law and end up smuggling drugs through Vietnam. The governing metaphor is spelt out in the title: Woo recreates the famous news photo of a Vietnamese man executed with a gun to his head, and ups the ante on the Russian roulette scene from Michael Cimino's *The Deer Hunter* (1978). Although sometimes incoherent and over-pitched, this is an intense and substantial movie, clearly intended to comment on Tiananmen Square and the imminent handover of Hong Kong to the mainland in 1997.

Face/Off 1997, 138 min

cast John Travolta, Nicolas Cage, Joan Allen, Alessandro Nivola, Gina Gershon, Dominique Swain, Nick Cassavetes *cin* Oliver Wood *m* John Powell

Woo's best American film is a delirious doppelgänger double-take, with cop Nicolas Cage and criminal John Travolta trading places (or is it the other way round?). The stars' larger-than-life role-playing is a lot of fun, but this tongue-in-cheek quality doesn't preclude philosophical seriousness – nor a little subversion as Travolta (playing Cage playing him) makes himself comfortable with the other man's wife and daughter.

Edward D. Wood Jr
US, 1924–78

The subject of Tim Burton's poignant 1994 hymn to defiant and flamboyant failure, Ed Wood has the dubious distinction of having made the worst film in the history of cinema, *Plan 9 From Outer Space* (1959). Like most of his movies, it drew on his personal stock company, a retinue of has-beens and lonely dreamers, led by the morphine-addled Bela Lugosi, unreliable psychic the Great Criswell, wrestler Tor Johnson and professional goth Vampira. This band of outsiders was responsible for such notorious disasters as *Bride Of The Monster* (1954) and *Night Of The Ghouls* (1959). All adhered to the same success-proof formula, being quickly and cheaply shot with cardboard sets, wretched acting and lamentable dialogue.

As well as *Plan 9*, *Glen Or Glenda* (1953) is Wood's other masterpiece of accidental surrealism. Beginning with Bela Lugosi intoning heavily about both the human condition and a big green dragon, it finally segued into a story of a misunderstood transvestite, played in full drag by Wood himself. (Cross-dressing was a subject close to the director's angora-clad heart, as Wood fought in World War II wearing a red bra and panties underneath his uniform, and liked to direct in a blonde wig.) To the film's poignant *crie de coeur* for social tolerance for transvestites, Wood added, in a signature flourish, shots of stampeding buffalo.

When his dreams of social acceptance as a director were finally thwarted, Wood penned sleazy pulp novels such as *Raped In The Grass* and helmed skin flicks such as *Necromania* (1971). A chronic alcoholic, he died of a heart attack two years before he was named the world's worst director and *Plan 9* the world's worst film in Harry and Michael Medved's iconoclastic book *The Golden Turkey Awards*. LH

W

Plan 9 From Outer Space 1959, 79 min, b/w

cast Gregory Walcott, Mona McKinnon, Duke Moore, Tom Keene, Carl Anthony, Paul Marco, Tor Johnson, Vampira *cin* William C. Thompson

Bela Lugosi died a few days into shooting this cinematic travesty about aliens resurrecting the dead. Undeterred, Wood endlessly repeated what footage he'd got, or else replaced him with a double: his wife's much taller chiropractor holding a cape over his face. The flying saucers are hubcaps, the gravestones are made of cardboard and the interior decor of the spaceship is a shower curtain. This is a film without a redeeming quality, except for the victory of sheer will over artistic talent, which in itself represents some kind of genius for self-delusion.

Sam Wood
US, 1883–1949

A major figure in his day, Sam Wood now tends to be damned with faint praise as a solid if unspectacular director, with a lot of good films to his name but no unqualified masterpieces. His cause has not been helped by the fact that he was one of Hollywood's most rabid anti-communists, blithely naming names to the House Un-American Activities Committee (HUAC) in 1947. Ironically, his most well-known films are his two Marx Brothers comedies, *A Night At The Opera* (1935) and *A Day At The Races* (1937), which would almost certainly have been funny whoever directed them.

After a brief acting career, Wood learnt his craft as an assistant to Cecil B. DeMille, getting his first shot at solo direction for Jesse L. Lasky Productions (later Paramount) on a series of vehicles for matinee idol Wallace Reid. He developed a reputation as a good director of women, and made nine films with Gloria Swanson, including *Beyond The Rocks* (1922), which paired her with Rudolph Valentino. With the advent of sound, Wood moved to MGM and scored a notable success with the sentimental tale of a dedicated schoolteacher, *Goodbye, Mr Chips* (1939). He was also entrusted with wrapping up *Gone With The Wind* (1939) when Victor Fleming got sick. It was on that film that he met legendary production designer William Cameron Menzies, who ensured the classy look of most of Wood's best films.

The early 1940s saw Wood handling more prestigious projects, and some of his finest films date from this period. *Kitty Foyle* (1940) won Ginger Rogers an Oscar for her dramatic role as a Philadelphia secretary who marries her rich socialite boss. That same year, Wood made *Our Town*, a respectable version of Thornton Wilder's play about life in an ordinary New Hampshire town. Small-town life was treated rather more darkly in *Kings Row* (1942), while *The Devil And Miss Jones* (1941) was another tale of class conflict, but this time a comedy starring a delightful Jean Arthur as a department store employee and Charles Coburn as

the store's owner working undercover as a salesman to investigate union activity.

Thereafter, Wood's work – while always solid – was fairly run-of-the-mill. *For Whom The Bell Tolls* (1943) was a slow-moving and uninspired version of Ernest Hemingway's Spanish Civil War tale – curious material for Wood since his own politics would have pitted him against the film's Republican hero (Gary Cooper). *The Pride Of The Yankees* (1942) and *The Stratton Story* (1949) were biopics of star baseball players, celebrating resolution in the face of adversity, and only the Victorian melodrama *Ivy* (1947), with Joan Fontaine playing against her usual victim type, rose above the ordinary. RB

A Night At The Opera 1935, 94 min, b/w

cast Marx Brothers, Kitty Carlisle, Allan Jones, Margaret Dumont, Walter Woolf King, Sig Ruman *cin* Merritt B. Gerstad *m* Herbert Stothart

It's questionable whether MGM really understood the Marx Brothers; did the production values need to be so lavish and were the romantic duo strictly necessary? Even so, this is one of their best films, with Groucho in sublime form as Otis B. Driftwood, an unscrupulous agent trying to sign Chico's rising young tenor, while also promising to get Margaret Dumont into society. Much madness ensues, from the contract dispute – with its "sanity clause" gag – to the final accident-filled performance of *Il trovatore*.

Goodbye, Mr Chips 1939, 113 min, b/w

cast Robert Donat, Greer Garson, Terry Kilburn, John Mills, Paul Henreid, Judith Furse *cin* Freddie Young *m* Richard Addinsell

A superb performance from 34-year-old Robert Donat (who has to age by more than sixty years over the course of the film) saves this story of Mr Chippings, an English prep school teacher and later headmaster, from descending too far into the mawkish. Greer Garson plays the love interest who makes the shy and retiring teacher emerge from his shell and eventually blossom. An unashamed celebration of teaching as a vocation, the film also tells of the emotional development of one man and those within his care.

Kings Row 1942, 127 min, b/w

cast Ann Sheridan, Robert Cummings, Ronald Reagan, Betty Field, Claude Rains, Charles Coburn *cin* James Wong Howe *m* Eric Korngold

The nearest that Wood came to greatness was this engrossing chronicle of the lives of five kids growing up in an American provincial town, whose hopes and ambitions become blighted in adult life by the jealousies and angst gnawing away beneath the surface. Ronald Reagan plays the overconfident Drake and Robert Cummings the earnest best friend who is called on to redeem his friends' broken lives at the end. One of Eric Korngold's finest and most moving scores provides the icing on the cake.

Geoffrey Wright
Australia, 1959–

Geoffrey Wright started out as a film critic before making his writer-director debut with the crude one-hour 16mm drama *Lover Boy* (1989). His first full-length feature, *Romper Stomper* (1992), explored Melbourne's neo-Nazi subculture. Starring future Hollywood giant Russell Crowe, it won a number of cult awards in Australia. *Metal Skin* (1994) dealt with illegal drag racing amongst social misfits in Altona, Victoria. Fired from directing the sci-fi blockbuster *Supernova* (2000), Wright made his Hollywood debut with *Cherry Falls* (2000). He returned to Australia for *Macbeth* (2006), a contemporary adaptation of Shakespeare's play set against the violent backdrop of Melbourne's criminal underworld. AJ

Romper Stomper 1992, 91 min

cast Russell Crowe, Daniel Pollock, Jacqueline McKenzie, Alex Scott, Leigh Russell *cin* Ron Hagen *m* John Clifford White

A group of racist skinheads led by the scarily charismatic Hando (Crowe) react badly to the rise of immigrant communities in Melbourne and go on the rampage. But their Vietnamese victims hit back, while a love triangle develops between Gabo (McKenzie), Davey (Pollock) and Hando. Subcultural and multicultural subtleties take a back seat in this violent, adrenaline-charged drama, which is staged with efficient but often soulless bravado.

Cherry Falls 2000, 93 min

cast Brittany Murphy, Jay Mohr, Michael Biehn, Gabriel Mann, Jesse Bradford, Douglas Spain *cin* Anthony B. Richmond *m* Walter Werzowa

When a dark secret is dredged up, murder and mayhem break out in the small town of Cherry Falls, and the sheriff's daughter, Jody Marken (Brittany Murphy), decides to investigate. Wright's bright and breezy direction adds an energetic, hip undertow to this sprightly teen shocker, smartly subverting its genre components with allegorical black humour and sly blood-letting.

William Wyler

Germany, 1902–81

William Wyler directed some of the most respected, and respectable, Hollywood films of the classical decades. Meeting Carl Laemmle, the head of Universal, while studying at the National Conservatoire of Music in Paris in 1920, Wyler was offered a New York publicity job. Moving to Hollywood, he climbed the industry ladder rung by rung, rising from prop man, grip, script clerk, cutter and casting director to assistant director on the Lon Chaney version of *The Hunchback Of Notre Dame* (1923). Wyler was also a production assistant on Fred Niblo's 1925 adaptation of *Ben-Hur*, which he would remake as the Charlton Heston sword-and-sandal epic in 1959.

While grinding out Western two-reelers, Wyler's reputation for "class" and the ability to elicit strong performances grew with his 1930 Western *Hell's Heroes* and the John Barrymore melodrama *Counsellor at Law* (1933). In 1934 Wyler married actress Margaret Sullavan, who starred in the light comedy *The Good Fairy* (1935), which might

count *Amélie* (2001) among its descendants. They divorced in 1936 and he would later marry actress Margaret Tallichet.

In 1936 he began a long association with producer Samuel Goldwyn that generated some of the most fêted Hollywood films of the 1940s. His first assignment was an adaptation of Lillian Hellman's play *The Children's Hour*. *These Three* (1936) starred Merle Oberon and Miriam Hopkins in roles Audrey Hepburn and Shirley MacLaine would reprise in Wyler's lesser 1961 remake. The director then began a historic collaboration with cinematographer Gregg Toland, on films such as *Dead End* (1937) and *Wuthering Heights* (1939), evolving the deep focus shooting technique. This facilitated a progression from the discrete shooting protocols and choppy editing of pre-war Hollywood to the naturalistic spatial and temporal continuity that would mark realist post-war cinema from Elia Kazan to Otto Preminger.

Unused to this method, actors fretted, earning Wyler the nickname "ninety-take Wyler". Notoriously falling out with Bette Davis, Wyler nevertheless made some of his best films with her. The antebellum drama *Jezebel* (1938) marks the bridge between feisty Depression Davis and the *grande dame* of wartime melodrama. The star gave a cunning turn in *The Letter* (1940), a plantation potboiler sultrily shot by Tony Gaudio that revolves around a woman who murders her lover. Wyler's consummate meld of emotion and narrative space also marks *The Little Foxes* (1941), and the director links the pre-war sentimentality of Frank Borzage and John M. Stahl with the expressionist canvases of Nicholas Ray and Vincente Minnelli.

Arguably, Wyler was at his best when the release was not freighted with industry cachet, allowing the simple generic pleasures to be enhanced by sheer craftsmanship. That poster tribute to plucky wartime Britain – *Mrs Miniver* (1942) – has not worn well, but the formulaic Gary Cooper vehicle *The Westerner* (1940) still entertains. *Detective Story* (1951) set pugnacious Kirk Douglas down for 24 cathartic hours in a sweaty box of a post-war police station, reprising the Warner Bros inner city Wyler essayed in Humphrey Bogart's Depression vehicle, *Dead End* (1937).

Before becoming a screen icon, Audrey Hepburn shone in the naturalistic fairy tale *Roman Holiday* (1953). After returning from war service, during which he made the celebrated air force documentary *The Memphis Belle* (1944), Wyler paid tribute to the war generation in *The Best Years Of Our Lives* (1946). Post-war literary adaptations were sometimes respectful but dull (*Ben-Hur*), but other effective examples were moulded out of compelling performances: *The Heiress* (1949) and *Carrie* (1952), adapted from Henry James and Theodore Dreiser respectively.

W

Gregory Peck and Audrey Hepburn negotiate love and the Spanish Steps in *Roman Holiday*.

Like many Hollywood directors, Wyler took advantage of the times. When gritty procedurals were all the rage, he replied with *Detective Story*. When widescreen Westerns were in demand, he made *The Big Country* (1958). When they relaxed the Production Code, he revised the lesbianism in *The Children's Hour* for a 1961 film adaptation. When they wanted a heist caper, he gave them Audrey Hepburn in *How To Steal A Million* (1966). But the results reaped generous recognition at the box office and the Oscar ceremonies. Nominated twelve times, Wyler won the best director prize on three occasions, for *Mrs Miniver*, *The Best Years Of Our Lives* and *Ben-Hur*. *Ben-Hur* in fact won eleven Oscars from twelve nominations.

For a director accused by critics of lacking a personal ideology, it seems ironic that Wyler's last good film was the Fanny Brice biopic *Funny Girl* (1968), in which Barbra Streisand plays the star who gains celebrity at the cost of self-knowledge. RA

Jezebel 1938, 105 min, b/w

cast Bette Davis, Henry Fonda, George Brent, Margaret Lindsay, Donald Crisp, Fay Bainter, Richard Cromwell *cin* Ernest Haller *m* Max Steiner

Bette Davis gives her all as the woman determined to get her man in what was an attempt to steal some of the thunder of *Gone With The Wind* (1939). It worked, and Davis claimed a best actress Oscar. Her relentless Southern belle is well supported by Henry Fonda and George Brent as the men she manipulates. The ballroom climax remains a key Davis moment as she outrages propriety in a flaming red (actually bronze) dress in the monochrome film.

Little Foxes 1941, 116 min, b/w

cast Bette Davis, Herbert Marshall, Teresa Wright, Patricia Collinge, Dan Duryea, Charles Dingle *cin* Gregg Toland *m* Meredith Willson

Wyler's adaptation of Lillian Hellman's Broadway hit is a layered and powerful dissection of familial decline in the deep South in the early years of the twentieth century. The moneyed Hubbards are a pretty nasty bunch, but Regina (Bette Davis) is the most ruthless and self-seeking of the lot. Although separated from her sick husband, Horace Giddens (Herbert Marshall), she needs his help to complete a suspect business deal and will stop at nothing to secure it. The sometimes stagey machinations are stealthily anatomized by Toland's textbook deep-focus photography, and Davis has never been better.

The Best Years Of Our Lives 1946, 171 min, b/w

cast Myrna Loy, Fredric March, Dana Andrews, Teresa Wright, Virginia Mayo, Cathy O'Donnell, Hoagy Carmichael *cin* Gregg Toland *m* Hugo Friedhofer

One of the best Hollywood films of its era, this recounts the stories of three returning servicemen and their tribulations as they settle back into marriage and work after World War II. It's an epic account of America's transition from war to peace. Robert E. Sherwood's script unsentimentally plays out all the hopes and confusions of the generation, while the starry cast give stirring performances.

Roman Holiday 1953, 135 min, b/w

cast Gregory Peck, Audrey Hepburn, Eddie Albert, Hartley Power, Harcourt Williams *cin* Frank F. Planer, Henri Alekan *m* Georges Auric

Audrey Hepburn's errant European princess goes missing in the Italian capital and ends up in the apartment of opportunistic American correspondent Gregory Peck. Scooting through picturesque post-war Roman locations, the gamine actress became an overnight sensation and won her only best actress Oscar. This romantic confection remains a sheer delight.

Ben-Hur 1959, 217 min

cast Charlton Heston, Jack Hawkins, Haya Harareet, Stephen Boyd, Hugh Griffiths *cin* Robert Surtees *m* Miklós Rózsa

Wyler was not the obvious choice for a three-and-a-half-hour Roman epic with a cast of (literally) thousands, but he acquits himself well with a bit of help from his second unit directors. Charlton Heston is all muscly intensity as Jewish prince Judah Ben-Hur whose friendship with the Roman Messala (Stephen Boyd) turns sour and results in a spell as a galley slave. As with the 1925 version, it's the set pieces that stick in the memory, in particular the thrilling chariot race where Ben-Hur finally gets his revenge.

Edward Yang

China, 1947–2007

In the early 1990s a poll of international film critics nominated Taiwanese director Edward Yang among the five most important filmmakers for the future of the medium, largely on the strength of three movies: *Taipei Story* (1985), *The Terrorizer* (1987) and the unforgettable youth gang epic *A Brighter Summer Day* (1991). Yet these films were barely seen in the English-speaking world, and the subsequent comedies *A Confucian Confusion* (1994) and *Mahjong* (1996) fared even worse. Even after Yang was named best director at Cannes for *Yi yi* (2000) and that film was widely shown, it proved another false dawn. Plans for an animated feature with Jackie Chan never came together, and Yang fought a long and ultimately unsuccessful battle with cancer.

Although their films are very different, Yang's patient, discreet, rational style was as antithetical to prevailing trends in Western cinema as his countryman and sometime collaborator Hou Hsiao-Hsien's. Influenced by modernist European art cinema, Yang made long films with large casts, but eschewed the epic to concentrate on the accretion of behavioural detail (his debut feature, 1983's *The Day On The Beach*, is a typical example). As has been pointed out, his material has more in common with Western soaps than with Western movies. It is the stuff of everyday life.

Which is not to say that his films aren't meticulously designed. Far from it: watching a Yang film it's easy to forget that it's been plotted, yet if you piece it together afterwards the intricacy and depth is truly novelistic. He was profoundly attuned to the flux of modern urban life, the way identities and relationships are buffeted by technology and the pressures of late twentieth-century capitalism. Such concerns were central to Yang's sense of himself: he was born in Shanghai in 1947, brought up in Taiwan, then studied in the US.

"We live three times as long since they invented movies", a youth remarks in *Yi Yi*, shooting the breeze in a downtown café. You might think that's a risky line for a film that clocks in at 173 minutes, but audiences are so immersed in the daily lives of the characters that it can be received as it is meant, without irony, and tacitly endorsed. What the young man is getting at – and it's safe to assume he's speaking for writer-director Yang here – is that by allowing us to see through other people's eyes the movies have incalculably enriched our experience of the world. In Yang's case, it is absolutely true. TC

Yi yi (A One And A Two) 2000, 173 min
cast Wu Nianzhen, Elaine Jin, Issey Ogata, Kelly Lee, Jonathan Chang *cin* Yang Wei-Han *m* Peng Kai-Li

A grandmother falls into a coma, and the doctor suggests that her family speak to her each day. Whether this treatment does the patient any good we cannot say, but over time her kids and grandkids separately discover much about themselves: Min Min finds that she can sum up her day in just two minutes, and that none of it adds up to anything meaningful. Her husband N.J. is in turmoil after a chance encounter with an old flame. Precocious 8-year-old Yang Yang is busily photographing the backs of everyone's heads – to show them the side they cannot see. It's possible to watch *Yi yi* and believe that all human life is here.

Peter Yates

UK, 1929–

Peter Yates is the indisputable king of the car chase. The nine-minute sequence in *Bullitt* (1968) when Steve McQueen hammers his Ford Mustang up and down the hills of San Francisco still occupies pole position in the list of cinema's greatest vehicular face-offs. So it's not surprising that Yates, who also directed episodes of the action TV series *The Saint* (1963–65) and *Danger Man* (1965–66), was once a racing driver. Nor is it a shock to learn that Yates studied acting at RADA, because his best films, like *Breaking Away* (1979), are a careful balancing act, delicately poised between action and reflection.

A motor vehicle of a different kind had been central to Yates's feature debut, *Summer Holiday* (1963), in which Cliff Richard drove a red double-decker

London bus through Europe's most scenic spots while occasionally breaking into song. After the stage adaptation *One Way Pendulum* (1965), Yates drew interest from Hollywood with *Robbery* (1967). When this rubber-burning set piece came to the attention of Steve McQueen, he immediately hired Yates to direct *Bullitt*. The screeching crescendo of the car chase adroitly counterpointed the less spectacular but nonetheless key moments of police procedural. This pattern is repeated in Yates's most successful films, such as *The Hot Rock* (1972), one of the hippest and most taut heist movies, as well as the Hitchcockian thrillers *Eyewitness* (1981) and *The House On Carroll Street* (1988). Other films, such as the low-key, engrossing crime thriller *The Friends Of Eddie Coyle* (1973) and *The Dresser* (1983), a polished adaptation of Ronald Harwood's backstage drama, are fine examples of the muted, reflective side of Yates's personality. LH

Bullitt 1968, 114 min

cast Steve McQueen, Robert Vaughn, Jacqueline Bisset, Don Gordon, Robert Duvall, Simon Oakland, Norman Fell *cin* William A. Fraker *m* Lalo Schifrin

When a Mob witness is murdered on Lt Frank Bullitt's watch, he defiantly hides the facts and the body to give himself time to find the killers, which brings him into direct conflict with an ambitious politician (an oily and sulphurous Robert Vaughn). While the car chase is justly famous, it's easy to forget how still and silent so much of this movie actually is, as if McQueen's fabled laconic cool somehow seeped into the fibres of the film itself. This means that when the action and violence do occur, they jar and shock just like they should.

Breaking Away 1979, 101 min

cast Dennis Christopher, Dennis Quaid, Daniel Stern, Jackie Earle Haley, Barbara Barrie, Paul Dooley *cin* Matthew F. Leonetti *m* Lionel Newman

This is Yates at his best, a vibrant synthesis of action and reflection. Steve Tesich's intelligent script effortlessly changes gears in a quiet survey of the uncertain futures of four friends, investigating themes of class conflict, the end of youth, and the onset of adult responsibility. There's a series of wonderfully choreographed cycling scenes, which climax with a race that's as gripping as you'd expect from an action veteran like Yates.

Terence Young
China, 1915–94

There are directors for hire, and then there's Terence Young. Every filmmaker has to pay the mortgage, but few have had such bizarre employers as Young, the man who gave James Bond his first cinematic outing. The director of *Dr No* (1962) somehow ended up making propaganda for Saddam Hussein and a war movie for the Reverend Sun Myung Moon.

A scriptwriter before and after World War II, Young had his first solo directorial outing with the gothic reincarnation drama *Corridor Of Mirrors* (1948), which critic Bosley Crowther once compared to the work of Jean Cocteau. The comparison may be misleading, because Young was a resolutely no-nonsense director who was openly contemptuous of tricksy cinema. A craftsman first and foremost, he worked across various genres in films such as the musical comedy *One Night With You* (1948), the gangster picture *Too Hot To Handle* (1959), the action movie *Safari* (1956) and the ballet picture *Black Tights* (1960), which he once declared was better than *The Red Shoes* (1948).

Young drew on his experience fighting in World War II for *They Were Not Divided* (1950), *The Red Beret* (1956) and *No Time To Die* (1958). The latter two were produced by Albert R. Broccoli, who was sufficiently impressed to call upon Young's services for the first James Bond movies, *Dr No* and *From Russia With Love* (1963). Retiring from 007 duty after *Thunderball* (1965), his post-Bond career of mediocre, obscure and often politically controversial international co-productions was only notable for three films: edge-of-the-seat thriller *Wait Until Dark* (1967), *The Long Days* (1980), a six-hour movie written by Saddam Hussein, and *Inchon* (1981), a box-office bomb of legendary proportions that was bankrolled by Reverend Moon's Unification Church. LH

Cut to the chase: the bad guys' black Dodge Charger roars through San Francisco's hilly streets in *Bullitt*'s spectacular car chase.

Dr No 1962, 110 min

cast Sean Connery, Ursula Andress, Joseph Wiseman, Jack Lord, Bernard Lee, Anthony Dawson *cin* Ted Moore *m* Monty Norman, John Barry

James Bond's gadget-free debut is by far the most realistic of the money-spinning series. There's a bruising naturalism in *Dr No* that was later replaced with a flippant sheen, Sean Connery's Bond appears all too human at times and there's a discernible lack of memorable set pieces. Young marshals the proceedings with precision if not pace.

From Russia With Love 1963, 115 min

cast Sean Connery, Daniela Bianchi, Pedro Armendáriz, Lotte Lenya, Robert Shaw, Bernard Lee, Eunice Gayson *cin* Ted Moore *m* John Barry

While the spectacular *Goldfinger* remains the *echt* Bond movie of the Connery period, *From Russia With Love* showed the series was developing its own style, boasting one of the great set pieces – the life-or-death fight with Robert Shaw aboard the Orient Express – and the first appearance of Blofeld as 007's dastardly nemesis. It also contains the first truly memorable henchman – or rather henchwoman: Rosa Klebb (Lotte Lenya) who likes to make her point with the aid of a deadly blade secreted at the end of her shoe.

Wait Until Dark 1967, 107 min

cast Audrey Hepburn, Alan Arkin, Richard Crenna, Efrem Zimbalist Jr, Jack Weston, Samantha Jones, Julie Herrod *cin* Charles Lang *m* Henry Mancini

A blind woman (Audrey Hepburn) is terrorized by three bad guys when she comes into possession of a doll stuffed with heroin. Young does not, or cannot, disguise the plot's creaky contrivances with cinematic smoke and mirrors. But while his decision not to open out Frederick Knott's stage play retains its flaws, it also heightens its claustrophobia.

Ronny Yu
Hong Kong, 1950–

Hong Kong director Ronny Yu has enjoyed his fair share of commercial success, and a brief recent stint in Hollywood to boot. Throughout the 1980s he made a string of fairly undistinguished movies, perhaps the best of which was his early film *The Postman Fights Back* (1981), a martial arts flick set in the early days of the 1949 Chinese republic, which benefited from an early appearance by Chow Yun-Fat. He established his international credentials with the 1989 co-production *China White*, which he followed with his biggest home-grown success to date, *The Bride With White Hair* (1993). Following this film's obligatory sequel, he reunited with its star Leslie Cheung for *The Phantom Lover* (1995), a Cantonese spin on the *Phantom Of The Opera* story. A second career in Hollywood yielded a certain level of commercial success with the horrors *Bride Of Chucky* (1998) and *Freddie vs Jason* (2003), although the UK-set *51st State* (2001) was greeted with critical disdain. His return to Hong Kong could not have worked out better, as he subsequently directed the hit film marketed as Jet Li's final martial arts movie, *Fearless* (2006). NN

The Bride With White Hair (Bai fa mo nu zhuan) 1993, 89 min

cast Brigitte Lin, Leslie Cheung, Francis Ng, Elaine Lui, Kit Ying Lam *cin* Peter Pau *m* Richard Yuen

In this Hong Kong fantasy adventure Brigitte Lin stars as a woman raised by wolves who enters the service of a sinister cult as an ace assassin, while swordsman Leslie Cheung is the reluctant heir to the leadership of an enemy clan. A Romeo and Juliet-style romance develops between the two, to the mutual chagrin of their rival groups. Heavy on visual spectacle, it's easy to see why *Bride* remains Ronny Yu's best-loved film.

Brian Yuzna
US, 1951–

If you like your horror spiced with satire, necrophilia and sexual dysfunction, Brian Yuzna is your man. As a producer, he teamed up with director Stuart Gordon for a trio of inventive, witty and blood-soaked movies: *Re-Animator* (1985), *From Beyond* (1986) and *Dolls* (1987). After which he settled comfortably into the director's chair with his debut, *Society* (1989). While it's not exactly the *Citizen Kane* of splatter, Yuzna certainly peaked too early. With the exception of *Bride Of Re-Animator* (1990), he hasn't been able to escape the straight-to-video ghetto. And he isn't afraid of making sequels to other people's movies, taking on the needless additions *Silent Night, Deadly Night 4* (1990) and *Return Of The Living Dead III* (1993). At least the themes, if not the quality, have been constant. *Rottweiler* (2004) demonstrated the same political edge as *Society*, while most of Yuzna's films exhibit a fascination with body horror, particularly a horror of female bodies. As critic Xavier Mendik has noted, Yuzna "repeatedly connects the female body to sexuality, death and disgust". And there's plenty of evidence of that in *The Dentist* (1996), or among the many male heroes who fall for reanimated cadavers, as in *Bride* and *Living Dead* – not forgetting the husband who suspects his pregnant wife is carrying an alien in her womb in *Progeny* (1998). LH

Society 1989, 99 min

cast Billy Warlock, Connie Danese, Ben Slack, Evan Richards, Patrice Jennings, Tim Bartell *cin* Rick Fichter *m* Phil Davies, Mark Ryder

In this grisly flip side to *Beverly Hills 90210* our mullet-haired hero, Billy Warlock, thinks he's different from the rest of his family and their upper-class coterie. He soon discovers that something is very wrong with all his nearest and dearest as the conspiracy thriller abruptly morphs into a protracted orgy of slime, body horror and bad taste that would make even David Cronenberg blanch.

Krzysztof Zanussi

Poland, 1939–

For those who like their cinema on the cerebral side, Krzysztof Zanussi's films are like a shot of ice-cold vodka – sharp but with a lingering afterglow.

He studied physics and philosophy (subjects that would inform his work) before enrolling in the renowned film school at Łódź in the 1960s. His debut, *Death Of A Provincial* (1966), drew international attention, and critical success followed with *Family Life* (1970) and *Illumination* (1972). From the mid-1970s until the early 1980s Zanussi was, like Krzysztof Kieślowski, associated with the so-called "cinema of moral anxiety" in Poland, which challenged the Communist system in its own astute way.

Zanussi's characters tend to have personal or philosophical problems rather than overt political dilemmas. *Camouflage* (1977) was seen as a social and political satire even though it dealt with the psychological struggle between two academics. His films also make innovative use of language, performance and cinematic technique to explore attempts to escape the constraints of social and biological determinism. Pictures like *Behind The Wall* (1971), *A Woman's Decision* (1975) and *Spiral* (1978) all tackle these themes, as well as the question of whether it is our intellect or our intuition that governs our behaviour.

After the Cannes success of *The Constant Factor* and *Contract* (both 1980), Zanussi was forced into exile. He returned to Poland for the acclaimed *The Year Of The Quiet Sun* (1985), which tells of the doomed relationship between a Polish war widow and an American soldier, and continued his fascination with personal dilemmas. He has maintained his vivid, thought-provoking style in films such as *At Full Gallop* (1996) and *Life As A Fatal Sexually Transmitted Disease* (2000). ED

Family Life (Zycie rodzinne) 1970, 93 min
cast Daniel Olbrychski, Maja Komorowska, Jan Nowicki, Jan Kreczmar, Halina Mikolajska *cin* Witold Sobocinski *m* Wojciech Kilar

Wit, a successful engineer, is summoned home to his family's dilapidated mansion and his estranged alcoholic father. His impoverished relations attempt to persuade Wit to remain, but without success. Zanussi's psychological drama uncomfortably invites us to glimpse the life of a family in decline. We are compelled to join Wit's moral struggle amongst the physical and emotional debris he encounters to choose between family loyalty and his own career.

Illumination (Iluminacja) 1972, 91 min
cast Stanislaw Latallo, Monika Denisiewicz-Olbrzychska, Malgorzata Pritulak, Edward Zebrowski *cin* Edward Klosinski *m* Wojciech Kilar

Young physicist Franciszek seeks enlightenment through experience; the film charts his progress as a student, his first sexual encounter, the death of a friend, his hasty marriage and subsequent security via his diploma. Zanussi draws on his own academic career to provide the backdrop for the fictional narrative, while using documentary footage and interviews with scientists.

At Full Gallop (Cwal) 1996, 103 min
cast Maja Komorowska, Bartosz Obuchowicz, Karolina Wajda, Piotr Adamczyk, Piotr Szwedes *cin* Jaroslaw Zamojda *m* Wojciech Kilar

In Poland, during the Stalin era, a young boy is sent from the country to continue his education in the city. He lives with his eccentric aunt who introduces him to horse-riding, a pastime labelled bourgeois by the authorities. Zanussi's visually evocative autobiographical work contrasts stubborn state repression with the sense of liberty gained through riding.

Franco Zeffirelli

Italy, 1923–

As famous as much for his theatre and opera productions as he is for his films, Franco Zeffirelli has – along with Laurence Olivier and Orson Welles – done more than most to inject Shakespeare with widescreen appeal. Many critics would dismiss his whole cinematic career in one line: much ado about nothing. But the public seem to disagree – Zeffirelli has an uncanny knack for transforming apparently uncommercial material (Shakespeare, opera, the life of a saint) into popular hits.

The product of a tempestuous affair between two married Florentines, Zeffirelli lost his mother to tuberculosis at the age of 6, and was finally placed in his father's reluctant custody at the age of 9. There, he was tutored by his father's English secretary, giving him an entrée into the expat world that inspired his 1999 drama *Tea With Mussolini*. After studying at the Academy of Fine Arts in Florence, he worked for Luchino Visconti as a set designer on his production of Shakespeare's *Troilus And Cressida* which in turn led to him being hired as an assistant director on Visconti's neo-realist look at the trials and tribulations of Sicilian fishermen, *La terra trema* (1948).

Zeffirelli's cinematic reputation is primarily due to his Shakespeare films. In *The Taming Of The Shrew* (1967), *Romeo And Juliet* (1968) and *Hamlet* (1990), he cut the text to the bone and demonstrated a vivacious flair and a pacy accessibility. However, too often his non-Shakespearean films suffer badly from flamboyant excess and emotional flatulence. *Brother Sun, Sister Moon* (1972) recast St Francis of Assisi as a flower child accompanied on his spiritual journey by songs from Donovan. *The Champ* (1979) was a syrupy remake of a rather better 1931 boxing movie, while *Endless Love* (1981) was a tragic teen romance which replaced the grit of Scott Spencer's original novel with saccharine and sex.

At least Zeffirelli's visual grandiosity perfectly suited his filmed operas *La traviata* (1982) and *Otello* (1986), and gave people a rare opportunity to see outstanding tenor Placido Domingo up close and personal. His awkward adaptation of Giuseppe Verga's Sicilian melodrama *Sparrow* (*Storia di una capinera*, 1993) bombed at the box office, but the director managed to rein in the gloss on his atmospheric and understated adaptation of *Jane Eyre* (1996) with Charlotte Gainsbourg. The director remained in subtle mode (in Zeffirellian terms, at least) with the militantly old-fashioned *Tea With Mussolini*, starring theatrical dames Joan Plowright, Maggie Smith and Judi Dench as a formidable trio of expats who remain in Tuscany despite the onset of war. He then lost much of his critical goodwill with *Callas Forever* (2002), a valentine to the great opera singer with whom he had worked. This fictionalization of the last tragic days of Maria Callas was dismissed by one reviewer as cheesy, ghastly and "a camp extravaganza of such exquisite awfulness, such unembarrassable silliness that you watch it hypnotized." It seems that many critics are still immune to Zeffirelli's idiosyncratic charms. LH

The Taming Of The Shrew 1967, 122 min

cast Elizabeth Taylor, Richard Burton, Cyril Cusack, Michael Hordern, Alfred Lynch, Alan Webb, Giancarlo Cobelli *cin* Oswald Morris *m* Nino Rota

No opportunities for slapstick or actorly mugging are missed in this rambunctious adaptation. Richard Burton cackles nonstop as Petruchio, the tamer of crude, angry and violent Kate (Elizabeth Taylor). It all proceeds at a

Kiss me Kate: Richard Burton silences a protesting Elizabeth Taylor in *The Taming Of The Shrew*.

cracking pace, even if it is conducted on one hysterical note. It resonates chiefly because of Hollywood's own mad match, the battling Burton and Taylor, playing a version of what many imagined their home life to be.

Romeo And Juliet 1968, 138 min
cast Leonard Whiting, Olivia Hussey, John McEnery, Milo O'Shea, Pat Heywood, Robert Stephens *cin* Pasqualino De Santis *m* Nino Rota

The director follows through the implication of his 1960 Old Vic stage production by casting real-life teenagers in the leading roles. Olivia Hussey and Leonard Whiting are suitably callow and awkward as the star-crossed lovers, but are both overshadowed by John McEnery's energetic and charismatic Mercutio. The director occasionally displays a similar chutzpah, especially in the testosterone-fuelled outdoor fight scenes which have real visual flair.

Hamlet 1990, 130 min
cast Mel Gibson, Glenn Close, Alan Bates, Paul Scofield, Ian Holm, Helena Bonham Carter, Stephen Dillane *cin* David Watkin *m* Ennio Morricone

From *Mad Max* (1979) to *Lethal Weapon* (1987), Mel Gibson has always specialized in heroes who teeter on the brink of madness. As you'd expect, Gibson's is a muscular version of Hamlet in every sense – defiant, angry and troubled. Zeffirelli cuts and pastes his way through Shakespeare's text to arrive at an urgent, earthy and contemporary reading of the play.

Robert Zemeckis
US, 1952–

Robert Zemeckis's films – including *Back To The Future* (1985), *Who Framed Roger Rabbit* (1988) and *Forrest Gump* (1994) – are a curious synthesis of old-fashioned sentiment and cutting-edge technology. But recently, as his fascination with the reality-altering properties of CGI has grown, Zemeckis increasingly resembles the cliché of the obsessive scientist defying nature at his peril.

Following his graduation from the University of Southern California's film school, Zemeckis's talent was spotted by Steven Spielberg. He repaid his debt of gratitude by co-writing the boy wonder's biggest flop, *1941* (1979). Ironically for a director whose movies have made more money than almost every other filmmaker in the history of cinema, Zemeckis was once considered box-office poison after his opening gambits *I Wanna Hold Your Hand* (1978) and *Used Cars* (1980) died inglorious commercial deaths. His career was saved by *Romancing The Stone* (1984), a rollicking adventure yarn of the old school, delicately laced with postmodern cynicism. His next offering, *Back To The Future*, a rousing masterpiece of modern entertainment, finally acquired Zemeckis blue-chip credentials. The first follow-up, made in 1989, was a self-reflexive sequel about sequels, a little too cold in its logic for many, while part three, made in 1990, saw the wacky professor and his sidekick battling Wild West outlaws.

Meanwhile, he made staggering cinematic technological advances with *Who Framed Roger Rabbit*, but an airlessness started to creep into Zemeckis's work with *Death Becomes Her* (1992), which basically remade Aldrich's gothic tale of sibling rivalry, *What Ever Happened To Baby Jane?*, with latex, bad taste and special effects. *Forrest Gump* was an axiomatic blend of chocolate-box soppiness and digital *trompe l'oeil*, while *Contact* (1997) and *Cast Away* (2000) featured an unwelcome New Age element. *What Lies Beneath* (2000) was a technically efficient but unsatisfying exercise in the supernatural with a Hitchcockian edge.

Zemeckis likes to refer to himself as an illusionist, and he seems to have been seduced by the possibilities of CGI, dedicating his time and money to the Robert Zemeckis Center For Digital Arts at USC. The logical and sad conclusion of this obsession was *The Polar Express* (2004), which was nothing but technology and sentiment. Here, human beings were removed entirely from the frame, as the use of motion capture technology spookily transformed actors into animation. The result was both ghoulish and mawkish, but it looked sensational in 3-D – which may be the most important thing for Zemeckis these days. **LH**

Back To The Future 1985, 111 min
cast Michael J. Fox, Christopher Lloyd, Lea Thompson, Crispin Glover, Thomas F. Wilson, Claudia Wells *cin* Dean Cundey *m* Alan Silvestri

In a career-making turn, Michael J. Fox plays teen hero Marty McFly, who is sent back to the moment in the 1950s when his dysfunctional parents first got together. Unfortunately, his marriage counselling plans go awry when his mum fancies the son rather than the father, and McFly has to nimbly fend off his mother's advances and prevent his own (pre-)demise. Breathtakingly adding screwball quantum physics to Capraesque family drama, this smart, funny crowd pleaser is a model blockbuster: popcorn at its most delicious and satisfying.

Who Framed Roger Rabbit 1988, 103 min
cast Bob Hoskins, Christopher Lloyd, Joanna Cassidy, Stubby Kaye, Alan Tilvern *(voices)* Charles Fleischer *cin* Dean Cundey *m* Alan Silvestri

Hapless animated bunny Roger Rabbit, who makes a living acting in slapstick cartoons, is forced to go on the run, wanted for a suspected crime of passion. Private eye Bob Hoskins takes on Roger's case, his investigations leading him into the cartoons' universe. With cameos from Dumbo, Betty Boop and Bugs Bunny, this seamless blend of live action, animation, screwball comedy and *Chinatown* is ingenious, sexy and inventive, combining state-of-the-art special effects with a reassuringly old-fashioned script.

Forrest Gump 1994, 142 min
cast Tom Hanks, Robin Wright Penn, Gary Sinise, Mykelti Williamson, Sally Field, Rebecca Williams *cin* Don Burgess *m* Alan Silvestri

An idiot becomes a national celebrity thanks to his ability to run fast, and manages to witness – and even affect – some of the major events in modern American history. He teaches Elvis how to gyrate his pelvis and unwittingly uncovers the

Watergate conspiracy. It's *Gump*'s greetings-card philosophies that have forever lodged in critics' minds. When faced with accusations of reactionary mawkishness, Zemeckis countered that "it's a story about an idiot who influences the most important events in mankind".

Zhang Yang
China, 1967–

Zhang Yang represents a new breed of film director in China, distinctly different from the preceding generation. Unlike Zhang Yuan, director of *Beijing Bastards* (1993), or Jia Zhang-Ke, director of *Platform* (2000), he hasn't had to make his films underground or had them subsequently banned. Censor-friendly, his movies enjoy state support, while he has a profitable relationship with American producer Peter Loehr and his independent Beijing production company, Imar.

The ex-theatre director's debut, *Spicy Love Soup* (1997), was an amiable ensemble piece about modern love in Beijing. Second only to *Titanic* at the local box office, it swept the boards in Chinese award ceremonies. His three films since have centred on father-son relationships and a generation gap that has grown exponentially since the seismic changes that have occurred in China in recent years. *Shower* (1999) crossed national borders to near universal acclaim, and Zhang switched to a more experimental mode with *Quitting* (2001), in which actor Jia Hongsheng and his family and friends played themselves in a reconstruction of his life-and-death battle with heroin addiction. *Sunflower* (2005) sprawled over three decades in a personal and panoramic account of the Cultural Revolution, viewed from the perspective of a father whose own thwarted aspirations are foisted upon his reluctant son. LH

Shower (Xizao) 1999, 93 min
cast Wu Jiang, Quanxin Pu, He Zeng, Xu Zhu *cin* Jian Zhang *m* Xiaogang Ye

Da Ming is a businessman, a prodigal son and a representative of China's new economic model. He visits his father's bathhouse which is the focus for a dying community increasingly threatened by the forces of modernity. Against his better judgement, he begins to help his father keep the business afloat. Possessing equal measures of charm and melancholy, this sly social allegory flits between genres, styles and rhythms in its opening half, the narrative only coming into sharp focus with the death of the patriarch.

Zhang Yimou
China, 1951–

By any measure one of the great colourists of modern cinema, Zhang Yimou discovered and largely forged the careers of both Gong Li and Zhang Ziyi in a string of emotionally direct, humanist films, often set in rural China.

Sixteen years old when the Cultural Revolution disrupted his own education, Zhang was sent to work in the countryside, first as a farmer, later in a mill. In 1978 he took a national examination held by the Beijing Film Academy, but despite passing with flying colours he was rejected for being too old. Twice he travelled to Beijing to appeal; twice he was rebuffed. Finally he wrote directly to the director of the Ministry of Culture, and within two months was admitted to the Academy, where he was to become the leading cinematographer of the so-called "Fifth Generation" of Chinese filmmakers, shooting both *Yellow Earth* (1984) and *The Big Parade* (1986) for Chen Kaige.

He turned director with *Red Sorghum* in 1987, imbuing with ravishing visuals a folkloric tale about the beautiful young bride (Gong Li) of a wealthy leper. The intensely passionate love story *Ju Dou* (1990), again starring Gong Li, was even better. The two films earned Zhang the nickname "the peasants' director" in China. A third film set in the 1920s, *Raise The Red Lantern* (1991) once more concerned a young woman (Gong again) married to a much older man, but this was a more controlled film about the domestic power struggle between the new wife and her three predecessors.

This loose trilogy won great acclaim abroad, and Zhang and Gong became the most famous celebrity couple in China – where there was also a degree of official suspicion due to Zhang being married to someone else. Western critics' insistence on reading his work as political allegory didn't make things any easier for him. The director routinely denied any ideological agenda, though there is clearly an emancipatory, feminist thrust to the work overall. Perhaps reacting against the stylized impasse he seemed to have constructed for himself, Zhang went on to rifle through different filmmaking styles, veering between hand-held neo-realism (*The Story Of Qiu Ju*, 1992) and glossy melodrama (*Shanghai Triad*, 1995). Generally speaking these middle-period films offer a gentler, more forgiving humanism, which sometimes peters into sentimental populism, as in *Not One Less* (*Yi ge duo bu neg shao*, 1999) the touching tale of a determined 13-year-old given the task of running the village school.

By 1999 Gong had been replaced as Zhang's muse by the younger Zhang Ziyi, who would become an international star the following year in Ang Lee's martial arts export, *Crouching Tiger, Hidden Dragon*. *Hero* (2002) and *House Of Flying Daggers* (2004), both of which starred the young actress, were blatant attempts to reproduce the *Crouching Tiger* formula, giving the traditional Hong Kong heroic swordsman genre a digital makeover. Visually stunning, the films lacked the

N

Gong Li: Zhang Yimou's heroine

More than any of their contemporaries, Zhang Yimou and Gong Li have been crucial to the world's perception of China's "Fifth Generation" of filmmakers and actors. And while each has achieved success separately, their best work has always been together. Zhang's movies offer exquisite visual pleasures, heightened emotions, and, it has been suggested, political allegory. Gong, meanwhile, has brought a compelling mix of *femme fatale* and melodrama heroine to her roles, with a cool beauty and sexual power reminiscent of Greta Garbo. However, while the director's camera adores her to the point of fetishization, there is something tough and defiant about her. In Zhang's films she invariably portrays women who are never subservient, who are angry rather than compliant, and her presence contributes immensely to the subversive power of his work.

Zhang and Gong's first three films together were tragic melodramas, focusing on arranged marriages, adultery and doomed passion in the feudal era. The ravishing *Red Sorghum* (1987), made while Gong was still a drama student, presented a young, passionate and resourceful woman who embodies the exalted, and romantic, values that Zhang attributed to Chinese peasantry. Portraying her as a force of nature, the film broke taboos with its images of female sexual desire and in particular orgasm. In *Ju Dou* (1990), set in a rural dyeing workshop, she played another headstrong woman driven by forbidden sexual longing and righteous anger whilst *Raise The Red Lantern* (1991) moved the setting from the peasantry to the aristocracy. That both were censored in China owed as much to their overt sexuality as to their political subtext. Zhang and Gong had a publicized relationship offscreen which continued into the mid-1990s.

Zhang's films appealed hugely to Western arthouse audiences, who also waxed lyrical about his beautiful star. *Ju Dou* and *Raise The Red Lantern* received Academy Award nominations for best foreign film. Zhang was criticized, however, for presenting an exotic, Orientalist version of China – and, in Gong, of sexualized Chinese womanhood – and for pandering to Western stereotypes. Perhaps in response, the two shifted gear with the more naturalistic *The Story Of Qiu Ju* (1992), set in contemporary rural China. Gong's visceral performance as a pregnant peasant woman fighting for justice for her husband, won her the best actress award at the Venice Film Festival, where the movie also won best film. The powerfully humanistic family saga *To Live* (1994), set during China's first three decades of Communist rule, saw another subtle performance from Gong as a struggling mother. *Shanghai Triad* (1995) was a rather different creature. Playing a hard-bitten showgirl and gangster's moll, Gong was as charismatic as ever, but the film didn't quite work. The director-and-actress partnership was severed soon afterwards.

Zhang achieved limited mainstream success with swordplay spectaculars *Hero* (2002) and *House Of Flying Daggers* (2004). Their star, the fresh-faced Zhang Ziyi, was labelled Zhang's new muse, but she had none of the depth of Gong, and Zhang's camera was in no way as transfixed by her as it was by his old leading lady. Gong, meanwhile, made a decent stab at a Hollywood breakthrough with *femme fatale* performances in disappointing films such as *Memoirs Of A Geisha* (2005), *Miami Vice* (2006), and *Hannibal Rising* (2007).

Zhang and Gong reunited in 2006 with *Curse Of The Golden Flower*. Exquisitely overblown and profoundly tragic, it reaffirmed Zhang's consummate skill as a maker of melodrama, and allowed the 40-year-old Gong to give her most mature performance yet. Her murderous fury as a woman whose marriage is literally killing her is nothing short of terrifying. Though it received mixed critical reviews, the film was a triumph for the pair. Later, however, Gong expressed a wish that she might have had more screen time. An insight, perhaps, into the tensions that have fuelled this complex, richly rewarding relationship. sc

heart of his earlier work, and in an ironic twist, *Hero* was in some places read as an apologia for authoritarianism. *Riding Alone For Thousands Of Miles* (2005) was another sentimental slab of pseudo-neo-realism, leavened with copious comedy, in which a Japanese father, Ken Takakura, takes on a quest to find a Chinese opera singer in honour of his estranged son. *Curse Of The Golden Flower* (2006), a melodrama of epic proportions – and the most expensive Chinese film made to date – showed a return to form for Zhang, and a welcome reunion with Gong Li after a gap of ten years. TC

Red Sorghum (Hong gaoliang) 1987, 92 min
cast Gong Li, Jiang Wen, Teng Rujun, Liu Ji, Qian Ming, Ji Chunhua *cin* Gu Changwei *m* Zhao Jiping

Zhang's directorial debut – a stunning celebration of Chinese peasantry, melding folk tale, melodrama and vibrant expressionism – marked him immediately as a filmmaker of genius. A story told in flashback about the narrator's grandparents, it's a heartbreaking romance that harks back to an era forever lost; its vivid, almost overwhelming palette, dazzling use of light and haunting music combine to potent emotional effect. Gong Li is superb as the young woman at the heart of the story, giving a complex and powerfully erotic performance.

N

Raise The Red Lantern (Dahong dengiong gaogao gua) 1991, 125 min

cast Gong Li, Ma Jingwu, He Caifeng, Cao Chifeng, Jin Shuyuan, Kong Lin *cin* Zhao Fei *m* Zhao Jiping

Although she is educated and independent-minded, 19-year-old Songlian (Gong, in one of her best performances), with little idea of what she is getting herself into, agrees to become the fourth wife of an elderly clan leader. The wives live in separate houses within the man's complex, and vie for their husband's attention, a competition that becomes increasingly intense. Visually sumptuous, more rigorous than Zhang's earlier films (for example, we never get a close-up of the patriarch) and with a finely honed script, *Raise The Red Lantern* is a penetrating study of how subjugation operates. It is probably the director's masterpiece.

House Of Flying Daggers (Shi mian mai fu) 2004, 119 min

cast Zhang Ziyi, Takeshi Kaneshiro, Andy Lau, Song Dangdan *cin* Zhao Xiaoding *m* Shigeru Umebayashi

After the lugubriously convoluted *Hero*, this lighter and more playful attempt to capitalize on the *Crouching Tiger* effect is designed as a showcase for Zhang Ziyi, who recreates her gravity-defying antics as blind dancer/guerilla soldier Mei. Captured by the police, she is rescued by a charming playboy who calls himself "Wind", a double agent who hopes she will lead him to the guerillas' hideout.

Curse Of The Golden Flower (Man cheng jin dai huang jin jia) 2006, 114 min

cast Chow Yun-Fat, Gong Li, Chou Jay, Liu Ye, Ni Dahong, Qin Junjie, Li Man, Chen Jin *cin* Zhao Xiaoding *m* Shigeru Umebayashi

Zhang returns to full-blown melodrama with this breathtaking film, where the music, *mise en scène*, costumes and performance – along with some staggering battle scenes – combine to tell a story of terrible pain and ugly secrets embedded deep within the imperial family of the Tang dynasty. Visually opulent to the point of excess, it recalls the 1950s melodramas of Douglas Sirk and Vincente Minnelli – while hysteria is never far from the glossy surface, the direction is a model of elegant control.

Fred Zinnemann

Austria (formerly Austro-Hungarian Empire), 1907–97

Advocates of the auteur school of filmmaking have found it difficult to accommodate industry veteran Fred Zinnemann. But at his best, Zinnemann represents the genius of the system. He was a collaborator from the beginning. Inspired when he viewed Erich von Stroheim and King Vidor's films in Vienna, he abandoned law studies to break into the movies, taking up assistant cameraman duties in Berlin and Paris. In 1929 he assisted cinematographer Eugen Schüfftan on that collaborative classic *Menschen am Sonntag* (*People On Sunday*) which was co-directed by Robert Siodmak and Edgar G. Ulmer, and scripted by Billy Wilder.

Zinnemann then emigrated to Hollywood and was an extra in Lewis Milestone's *All Quiet On The Western Front* (1930). During the 1930s he became a negative cutter and assistant to director Berthold Viertel. He also worked with Robert Flaherty on a documentary, and with Busby Berkeley on some dance numbers. Zinnemann co-directed the 1935 documentary *The Wave*, written and filmed by Paul Strand, and by 1937 was directing shorts at MGM for the *Crime Does Not Pay* series. In 1938 Zinnemann won his first Oscar for the documentary short *That Mothers Might Live*.

The veracity of documentaries and brevity of shorts fed into the punchy problem pictures and thrillers that remain Zinnemann's best work. Elevated to features, he directed two films in 1942, *Eyes In The Night* and *Kid Glove Killer*, the latter a forensics procedural anticipating post-war releases such as Elia Kazan's *Boomerang* (1947) and Jules Dassin's *The Naked City* (1948). Zinnemann chronicled the rehabilitation of a young Czech boy traumatized by the war in *The Search* (1948), which featured a young Montgomery Clift and won two Oscars (for screenplay and a special juvenile award for Ivan Jandl). The film resembles the Italian neorealism of its day, and also shows signs of being influenced by the German *Trümmerfilme*, or "rubble films", produced immediately after the war.

Zinnemann continued to explore traumatic post-war fallout in *Act Of Violence* (1948), a gripping *film noir* in which Robert Ryan's embittered war veteran threatens the suburban tranquillity of Van Heflin's prison camp informer, while 1950's *The Men* unflinchingly tackled paraplegic rehabilitation. In *Teresa* (1951) Pier Angeli's Italian bride comes to small-town America with her GI husband to face a dark wartime secret.

The precise and engrossing Western *High Noon* (1952) – written by Carl Foreman and produced by Stanley Kramer – was the culmination of Zinnemann's workmanlike phase and probably his definitive film. It was also a big hit, as was *From Here To Eternity* (1953), which won Zinnemann his second Oscar. But this all-star war melodrama also marked his decline into blowsy liberal mush. The Rodgers and Hammerstein songs in *Oklahoma!* (1955) remain rousing but the film seems like widescreen apologia now, and *The Nun's Story* (1959), *The Sundowners* (1960) and *Behold A Pale Horse* (1964) were all worthy but dull.

The Academy dutifully awarded Zinnemann with another Oscar for shepherding Paul Scofield, Orson Welles, Robert Shaw and Susannah York through Robert Bolt's historical play *A Man For All Seasons* (1966). Based on Frederick Forsyth's account of an assassination attempt on Charles de Gaulle, *The Day Of The Jackal* (1973) owed most to Edward Fox's cool screen presence as the assassin, and the thriller seemed closer to Jean-Pierre Melville than to the tense brinkmanship of Zinnemann's crisp and committed heyday. That heyday was long gone by the time he made his final films, the female friendship drama *Julia* (1977) and the tepid Swiss Alps excursion, *Five Days One Summer* (1982). RA

The Men 1950, 86 min, b/w

cast Marlon Brando, Teresa Wright, Everett Sloane, Jack Webb, Richard Erdman, Arthur Jurado *cin* Robert De Grasse *m* Dimitri Tiomkin

Counting the cost of victory at a time of Cold War standoff, this story of a paraplegic war veteran coming to terms with his experience courageously trades in the anguish of its subject. In his first starring role, Marlon Brando brings all his primal energy and inarticulate rage to the brutal emotional confrontations with his devoted fiancée Teresa Wright.

High Noon 1952, 85 min, b/w

cast Gary Cooper, Thomas Mitchell, Lloyd Bridges, Katy Jurado, Grace Kelly, Otto Kruger, Lon Chaney Jr *cin* Floyd Crosby *m* Dimitri Tiomkin

Few films of its day interrogated the conformism of the McCarthy era as astutely as *High Noon*, one of cinema's greatest allegories. As lean and taut as the ageing Gary Cooper, this is the tale of a marshal standing up to a convicted killer arriving on the noon train while the whole town goes to ground. Its compelling narrative roots stand in contrast to the onslaught of wide screens and big budgets.

From Here To Eternity 1953, 118 min, b/w

cast Burt Lancaster, Deborah Kerr, Montgomery Clift, Frank Sinatra, Philip Ober, Donna Reed *cin* Burnett Guffey *m* George Duning

An engrossing adaptation of James Jones's World War II novel, *From Here To Eternity* depicts a varied tapestry of life at Pearl Harbor in the days before the Japanese attack of December 1941. The film benefits from a fine portrait of sexual repression from Deborah Kerr as an officer's neglected wife and from the nuanced performances of GIs Montgomery Clift and Frank Sinatra. The infamous steamy shoreline tryst between Kerr and her sergeant lover Burt Lancaster remains a stock Hollywood metaphor for sex.

Oklahoma! 1955, 145 min

cast Gordon Macrae, Shirley Jones, Gloria Grahame, Gene Nelson, Charlotte Greenwood, Rod Steiger *cin* Robert Surtees *m* Richard Rodgers

Twelve years after *Oklahoma!* had revolutionized the Broadway musical, Hollywood got round to filming it and gave the task to a slightly over-respectful Zinnemann. The widescreen format posed a few directorial problems – when to go for the epic sweep and when to be intimate – but the performances are strong, although the acting of Gordon Macrae as cowboy Curly McLain and Shirley Jones as Laurey seems a bit undercharged next to Rod Steiger's villainous farmhand Jud and Gloria Grahame's sparkling turn as Ado Annie.

Rob Zombie

US, 1965–

A comic-book writer, filmmaker, composer and rock star, Rob Zombie (born Robert Cummings) is best known as the front man for the heavy metal band White Zombie and the man behind the song "Dragula" on the soundtrack to *The Matrix* (1999).

Famous for his love of exploitation horror B-movies, he made his directorial debut with the controversial *House Of 1000 Corpses* (2003), inspired by *The Texas Chain Saw Massacre* (1974). Its even more shocking sequel, *The Devil's Rejects* (2005), made him a member of the "Splat Pack" group of hard-core horror filmmakers that emerged in the early years of the twenty-first century, and in 2007, he wrote and directed *Halloween*, a re-imagining of John Carpenter's classic 1978 horror film. AJ

The Devil's Rejects 2005, 90 min

cast Sid Haig, Bill Moseley, Sheri Moon Zombie, Ken Foree, Matthew McGrory, Leslie Easterbrook *cin* Phil Parmet *m* Rob Zombie, Tyler Bates

The surviving members of the murderous Firefly family go on the run, cutting a grisly path of torture and slaughter across the country. This semi-sequel to *House Of 1000 Corpses* is a sick, nasty road movie that gleefully juggles edgy gore and sex with a sleazy audacity.

Erick Zonca

France, 1956–

Filmmaker Erick Zonca dramatizes the economic and psychological consequences of globalism. Moving from the south to Paris at 16, the Franco-Italian Zonca enrolled in acting classes. Four years later he went to New York to study acting further, and the Method bent of this training can be seen in the immersed performances of his protagonists. Regular attendance at Manhattan's Bleeker Street Cinema extended his knowledge of European film.

Returning to Paris, Zonca studied philosophy and won a television traineeship at 30, becoming an assistant director before graduating to directing sitcoms and documentaries. His shorts of the period included *Seule* (*Alone*, 1997), in which a young woman is driven to crime by unemployment and homelessness. Zonca has no preconceived ideas about his central character – she is simply defined through her actions – and his film was compared at the time to the naturalism of the Dogme group.

Zonca's shorts played the festival circuit, won awards and led to his first feature, the powerful *The Dream Life Of Angels* (1998). Similar themes colour the fast-moving crime drama *Le petit voleur* (*The Little Thief*, 1999), which charts the grim trajectory of a taciturn young baker's assistant who loses his job and gravitates to the Marseilles underworld. Zonca's stories of youth at the sharp end have been compared to early François Truffaut. RA

The Dream Life Of Angels (La vie rêvée des anges) 1998, 113 min

cast Elodie Bouchez, Natacha Régnier, Grégoire Colin, Patrick Mercado, Jo Prestia, Francine Massenhave *cin* Agnès Godard *m* Yann Thiersen

Elodie Bouchez and Natacha Régnier become friends when the almost destitute Bouchez arrives in Lille. Their friendship is forged in the assembly line of exploitation and casual social cruelty, and the two stars – tough-minded and true – evoke a gritty modern passion in the tradition of Robert Bresson.

The Zucker Brothers
David Zucker: US, 1947–
Jerry Zucker: US, 1950–

It's unclear as to whether we should thank or loathe the Zucker brothers. If it wasn't for *Airplane!* (1980) we may have never had *Shriek If You Know What I Did Last Friday The Thirteenth* (2000), or any of the numerous spoofs that are somehow worse than the bad movies they're sending up. But they can't be held entirely responsible. When *Airplane!* was released, it seemed insanely fresh, inventive and iconoclastic. And although there had been a long tradition of film parody, including the work of Bob Hope and Mel Brooks, what the Zuckers did was somehow more relentless, anarchic and scattershot. Sacrificing a coherent plot on the altar of cheap laughs, *Airplane!* played out like a particularly breakneck series of satirical sketches. Which may have something to do with their sketch-show roots as creators of The Kentucky Fried Theatre.

Formed with high-school pal Jim Abrahams after they graduated from the University of Wisconsin, the trio's wildly irreverent revue soon acquired cult status in Los Angeles and successfully transferred its taste-free, pitch-black humour to *The Kentucky*

Fried Movie (1977). Directed by John Landis, the film gleefully took politically incorrect pot shots at various genres, such as blaxploitation, chop-socky and spy movies, and climaxed with a spoof trailer for a skin flick named *Catholic High School Girls In Trouble*. By adding plot (although not much) to parody, *Airplane!* became one of the most influential comedies of the last few decades. But the trio didn't immediately profit from the spoof's phenomenal success (with 1982's *Airplane II: The Sequel* being directed by Ken Finkleman). Their 1982 TV series *Police Squad!* was cancelled after six barely watched episodes and the spy skit *Top Secret!* (1984) never took off in the way its predecessor did. After *Ruthless People* (1986), their brave attempt at a more serious comedy, the three men went their separate ways.

Jerry revealed a serious side, hitting pay dirt with the Patrick Swayze–Demi Moore romantic comedy *Ghost* (1990), whose potter's wheel love scene has been mercilessly parodied by others (including his own brother in 1991's *The Naked Gun 2½: The Smell Of Fear*). Trying too hard to be taken seriously, he bathed the Arthurian tale *First Knight* (1995) in a pointless blue light, before returning to comedy with *Rat Race* (2001), an ill-judged attempt to capture the anarchic ensemble spirit of Stanley Kramer's *It's A Mad Mad Mad Mad World* (1963).

However, David Zucker cannot be serious. Against all the odds, he successfully reanimated the *Police Squad!* corpse into the *Naked Gun* trilogy (1988, 1991 and 1994). But after a few duds, he returned to his spoof roots, attaching himself to

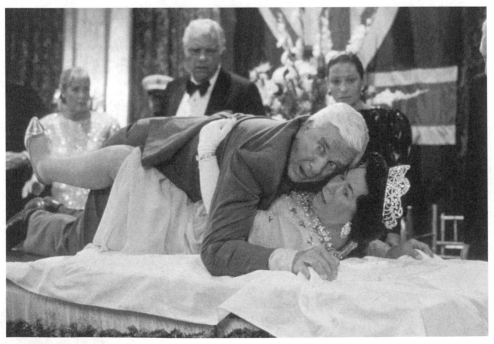

Ace detective Leslie Nielsen gets the royal approval in *The Naked Gun*.

the *Scary Movie* franchise – the most crude, scatological and commercially successful of all *Airplane!*'s bastard children. Clocking on as director for numbers three and four of the series in 2003 and 2006, he's been reduced to making a copy of a copy of his directorial debut. It's almost beyond parody. LH

Airplane! 1980, 88 min

cast Robert Hays, Julie Hagerty, Leslie Nielsen, Lloyd Bridges, Peter Graves, Kareem Abdul-Jabbar *cin* Joseph F. Biroc *m* Elmer Bernstein

Airplane! cleverly integrates dumb gags, smart observations, bad puns and movie references into a coherent narrative. The mid-air disaster movie had already descended into parody with *The Concorde: Airport '79* (1979), but *Airplane!* doesn't just take aim at that franchise: *Saturday Night Fever* (1977) is one of its many targets. Robert Hays boards a plane to rescue his relationship with stewardess Julie Haggerty, but ends up rescuing all the passengers, in a film featuring a gag a second, often of the visual variety, but almost always of the stupid variety ("I am serious… and stop calling me Shirley").

The Naked Gun 1988, 85 min

cast Leslie Nielsen, Priscilla Presley, Ricardo Montalban, George Kennedy, O.J. Simpson, Susan Beaubian *cin* Robert M. Stevens *m* Ira Newborn

Although Leslie Nielsen appeared in *Airplane!*, it was this cop spoof that gave him a whole new career as the deadpan man-child of film parody. Lieutenant Frank Drebin foils an assassination plot against the Queen of England but also destroys priceless works of art, buildings, cars and a fish in the process. While puerile humour is Zucker's stock in trade, it would take a determined curmudgeon not to admit that *The Naked Gun* has a winning combination of insane logic and ceaseless invention.

Terry Zwigoff
US, 1949

Standing out from the crowd – or rather, giving them the widest possible berth – the curmudgeonly Terry Zwigoff is a genuine independent spirit. Like Seymour, the middle-aged vinyl collector in *Ghost World* (2001), Zwigoff is alienated from the modern corporate world. His films find black comedy in the way even misanthropy can be co-opted by consumer capitalism.

Zwigoff moved to San Francisco in the 1970s and became friends with the cult comic-book artist Robert Crumb, who became the subject of his eponymous breakthrough documentary in 1994 – one of the most highly praised nonfiction films of the decade. Earlier, Zwigoff had made *Louie Bluie* (1985), a portrait of blues musician Howard Armstrong.

Zwigoff's fascination with early American folk music and comic-book art came together in his first fiction film, an adaptation of Daniel Clowes' *Ghost World*. The film struck a chord with hipsters everywhere. *Bad Santa* (2003) was a step into the mainstream, but this splenetic Billy Bob Thornton vehicle was still recognizably a Zwigoff film. A second collaboration with Daniel Clowes produced the patchy satire *Art School Confidential* (2006). TC

Crumb 1995, 120 min

with Robert Crumb, Aline Kominsky, Charles Crumb, Robert Hughes *cin* Maryse Alberti

This is Zwigoff's startlingly intimate portrait of his friend Robert Crumb, the comic-book artist who became a countercultural icon with his strip *Fritz The Cat*, but whose taste for lurid caricature alerted the PC police. Zwigoff's analysis of Crumb's controversial life is even-handed, but what really makes the film remarkable is his unprecedented access, over several years, to the artist and his idiosyncratic family.

Ghost World 2001, 112 min

cast Thora Birch, Steve Buscemi, Scarlett Johansson, Brad Renfro, Illeana Douglas, Bob Balaban *cin* Affonso Beato *m* David Kitay

Writer Daniel Clowes adapted his graphic novel for the screen essentially by adding a Terry Zwigoff character into the mix: middle-aged Seymour (Steve Buscemi) collects blues 78s and pines for human companionship – except he doesn't like people very much. He meets his match in Enid (Thora Birch), a determinedly nonconformist teenager who considers herself too cool for school. The movie indulges the characters' elitist snobbery but exposes their kneejerk misanthropy to gentle interrogation.

Picture credits

The Publishers have made every effort to identify correctly the rights holders and/or production companies in respect of the images featured in this book. If despite these efforts any attribution is incorrect, the Publishers will correct this error once it has been brought to their attention on a subsequent reprint.

Index of film reviews

B

C

J

K

M

N

O

P

U

V

W

X

Y

Z

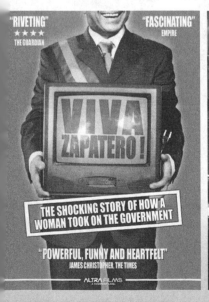

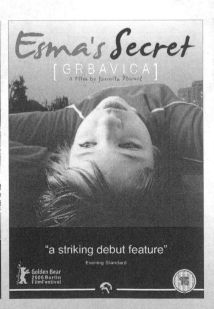

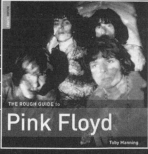